JOHN FIELDER'S BEST OF Colorado

PHOTO CREDIT: RON WILSON

PHOTOGRAPHY AND TEXT

BY JOHN FIELDER

WWW.BIGEARTHPUBLISHING.COM

INTERNATIONAL STANDARD BOOK NUMBER: 978-1-56579-624-9

EDITORS: Jenna Samelson Browning, Martha Ripley Gray, Peggy Morse, David Nuss, Elizabeth Train

DESIGNER: Rebecca Finkel, F + P Graphic Design

PRODUCTION: Craig Keyzer, Carol Pando

PUBLISHED BY: Westcliffe Publishers
a Big Earth Publishing company
1637 Pearl Street, Suite 201
Boulder, Colorado 80302

TO ORDER: 800-258-5830, www.bigearthpublishing.com

PRINTED IN: China by C & C Offset Printing Co., Ltd.

THE LIBRARY OF CONGRESS HAS CATALOGED THE ORIGINAL EDITION AS FOLLOWS:

Fielder, John.
John Fielder's Best of Colorado : photography and text / by John Fielder.
p. cm.
Includes index.
ISBN 1-56579-624-9
1. Colorado—Pictorial works. 2. Colorado—Description and travel. 3. Colorado—History, Local. I. Title.
F777.F52 2002
978.8—dc21 2001052616

For more information about other fine books and calendars from Westcliffe Publishers, a Big Earth Publishing company, please contact your local bookstore, call 1-800-258-5830, write for our color catalog, or visit us on the Web at **BIGEARTHPUBLISHING.COM**.

PHOTO CREDITS: *p. 18,* courtesy Bill Bonebrake (Denver skyline); *p. 19,* courtesy Hotel Boulderado (Hotel Boulderado) and Boulder Convention and Visitors Bureau (Chautauqua Dining Hall); *p. 21,* courtesy Brown Palace Hotel; *pp. 22, 25,* both photos courtesy Denver Public Library Western History Dept.; *pp. 26, 27, 32,* courtesy Bill Bonebrake; *pp. 37, 39, 42–44,* all photos courtesy Boulder CVB; *p. 45* (Dushanbe Teahouse) and *p. 48* (Colorado Shakespeare Festival), courtesy Boulder CVB; *p. 76,* all photos courtesy Colorado Springs Pioneer Museum; *p. 79,* courtesy David Dietemeyer (overlook); *p. 142,* courtesy Colorado Historical Society (John Otto portrait) and Colorado National Monument (Otto on horseback); *p. 160,* Denver Public Library Western History Dept. (Enos Mills); *p. 204,* courtesy Colorado Historical Society, U.S. Geological Survey, and Smithsonian Institution; *p. 225,* both photos courtesy Denver Public Library Western History Dept.; *pp. 344, 379, 440,* all photos courtesy of the Colorado Historical Society.

PLEASE NOTE: Risk is always a factor in backcountry and high-mountain travel. Many of the activities described in this book can be dangerous, especially when weather is adverse or unpredictable, and when unforeseen events or conditions create a hazardous situation. The author has done his best to provide the reader with accurate information about backcountry travel, as well as to point out some of its potential hazards. It is the responsibility of the users of this guide to learn the necessary skills for safe backcountry travel, and to exercise caution in potentially hazardous areas, especially on glaciers, summits, backcountry roads, and avalanche-prone terrain. The author and publisher disclaim any liability for injury or other damage caused by backcountry traveling or performing any other activity described in this book.

Contents

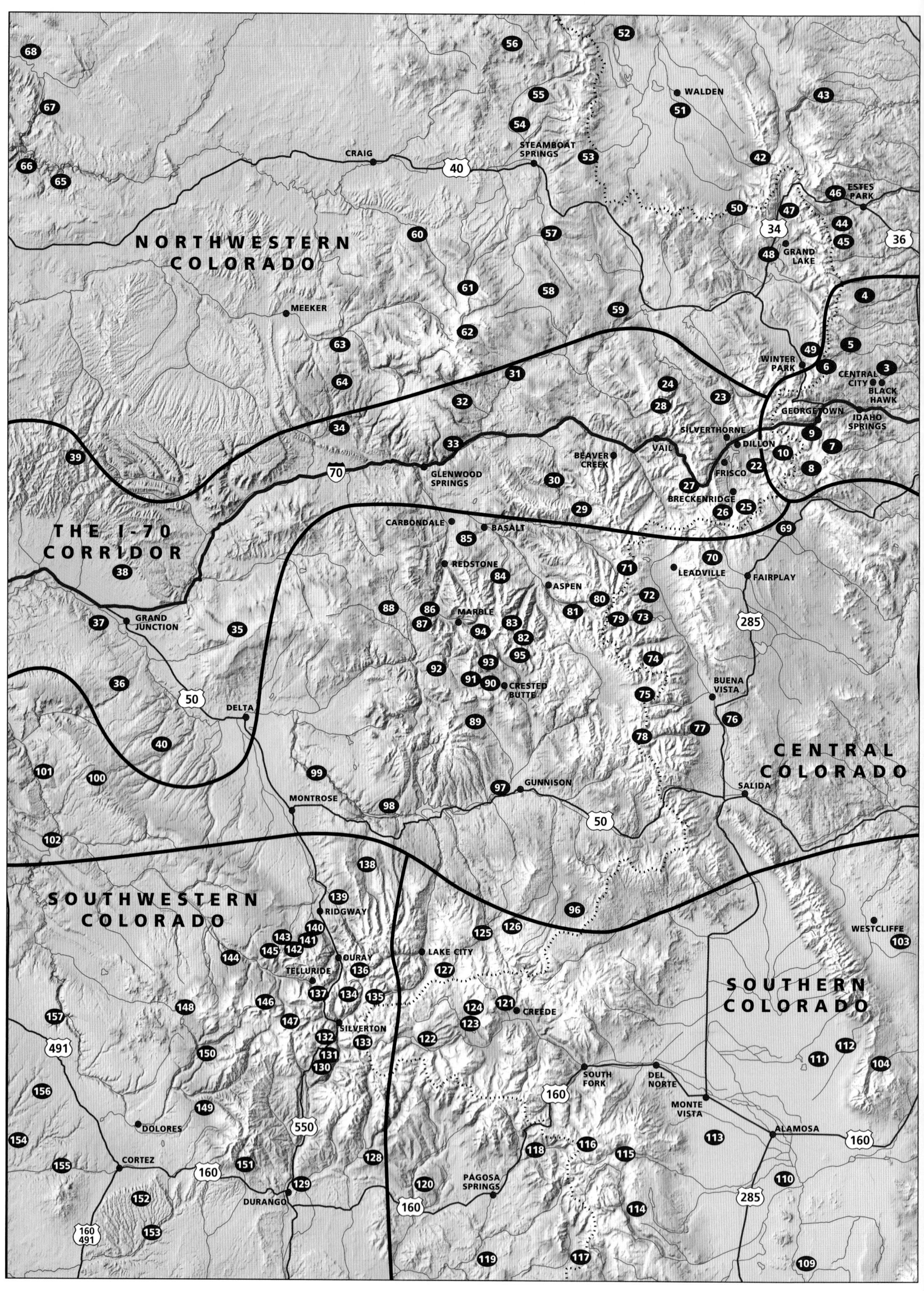
NORTHWESTERN COLORADO
THE I-70 CORRIDOR
CENTRAL COLORADO
SOUTHWESTERN COLORADO
SOUTHERN COLORADO
WALDEN
STEAMBOAT SPRINGS
CRAIG
ESTES PARK
GRAND LAKE
MEEKER
WINTER PARK
CENTRAL CITY
BLACK HAWK
GEORGETOWN
IDAHO SPRINGS
SILVERTHORNE
DILLON
VAIL
BEAVER CREEK
FRISCO
BRECKENRIDGE
GLENWOOD SPRINGS
CARBONDALE
BASALT
REDSTONE
LEADVILLE
FAIRPLAY
ASPEN
MARBLE
GRAND JUNCTION
CRESTED BUTTE
BUENA VISTA
DELTA
GUNNISON
SALIDA
MONTROSE
RIDGWAY
WESTCLIFFE
OURAY
LAKE CITY
TELLURIDE
CREEDE
SILVERTON
SOUTH FORK
DEL NORTE
MONTE VISTA
DOLORES
ALAMOSA
CORTEZ
PAGOSA SPRINGS
DURANGO
40
34
36
70
50
285
491
550
160
160 491

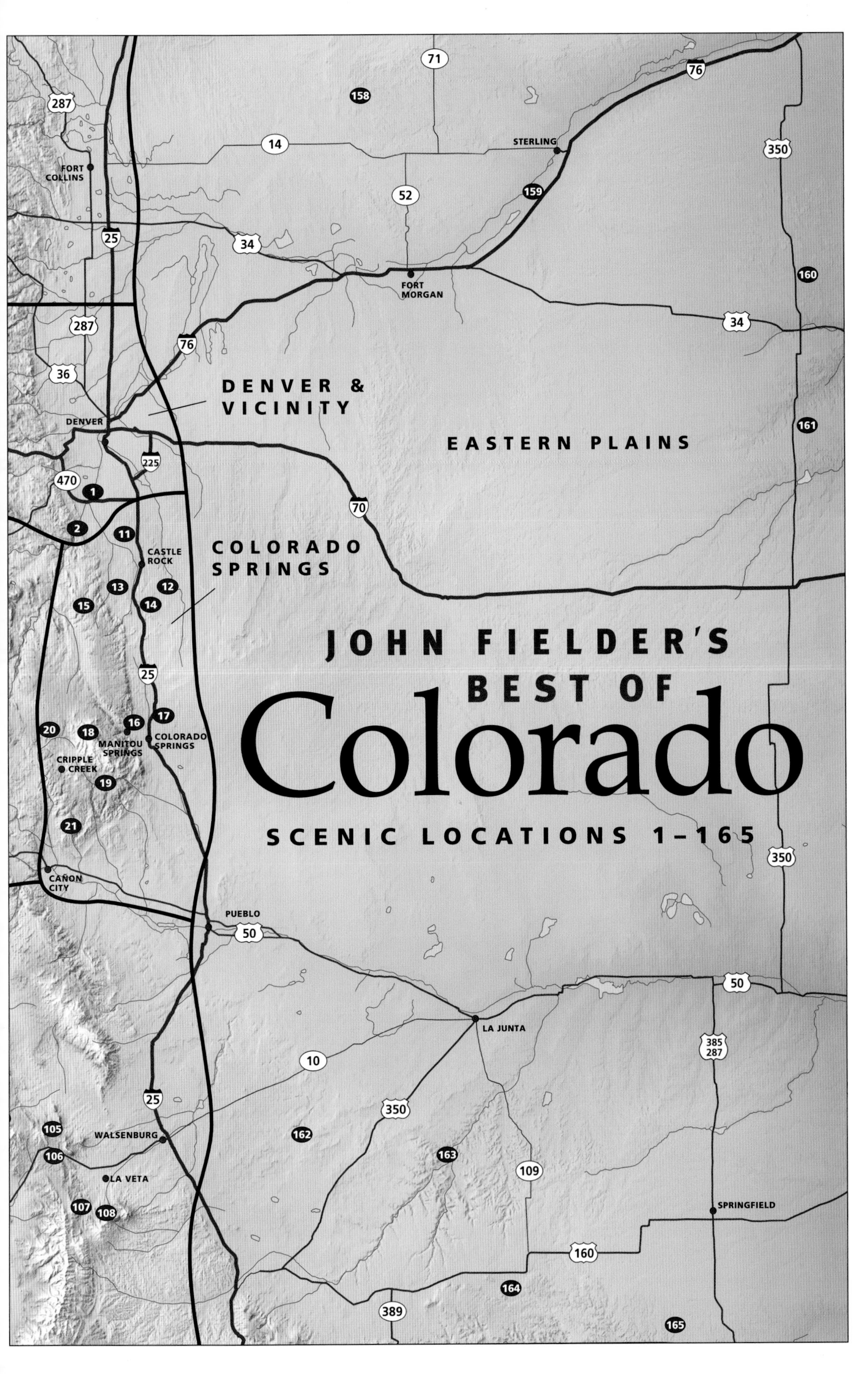

JOHN FIELDER'S
BEST OF
Colorado
SCENIC LOCATIONS 1–165
DENVER & VICINITY
EASTERN PLAINS
COLORADO SPRINGS
FORT COLLINS
STERLING
FORT MORGAN
DENVER
CASTLE ROCK
MANITOU SPRINGS
COLORADO SPRINGS
CRIPPLE CREEK
CAÑON CITY
PUEBLO
LA JUNTA
WALSENBURG
LA VETA
SPRINGFIELD

Welcome to Colorado!

If you like fresh air, cool alpine streams, and wide-open spaces, there's no better place on Earth to be than here in Colorado. From the rolling Eastern Plains to the soaring Rocky Mountains to plateaus and remote river canyons on the Western Slope, Colorado's landscape brims with diversity. Whether out photographing prairie wildflowers, hiking sublime mountain wilderness, rafting whitewater in 2,000-foot-deep sandstone canyons, driving a vast network of Scenic and Historic Byways, making ski turns in deep, dry powder, or just sipping white wine in a hot pool with views of mountains all around—for the lover of the outdoors, nothing tops Colorado. Our 4.3 million ethnically diverse residents stay and relocate here not only for the outdoors, but because boundaries are few for their independent spirits. Views as far as the eye can see cultivate an appreciation for freedom, and the feeling that there are no limits to what a person can accomplish—whether in life or on the trail.

I first saw Colorado's Rocky Mountains while on a five-week school field trip. My exceptional science teacher invited a half-dozen kids to travel with her each summer from our home state of North Carolina. In the summer of 1964 we departed Charlotte for the glaciers of British Columbia, visiting sites along the way that we had read about in our natural history textbooks. I suppose that I experienced nothing less than an epiphany during the drive west across the plains of Colorado. Or was I just hallucinating from the flatland overload of passing through the plains? Epiphanies are usually reserved for events of spiritual enlightenment. But considering Colorado's influence on all aspects of my life—the activities my family and I enjoy together, the things I think about while sitting alone on a mountain ridge, the stories I tell and issues I advocate when speaking in public—I think I had one.

I have never forgotten my first sight of the Rockies rising over the plains as we proceeded west to Rocky Mountain National Park. Having grown up near the tree-shrouded Southern Appalachians, I was simply smitten by this wall of snow-capped peaks above a treeless plain and the long views the mountaintops must afford. And the word *Colorado,* Spanish for "red," was the most poetic place name I had ever heard. My illuminating discovery was that someone or something had guided me to this place, and that I belonged here for the rest of my life.

For the most part, I spent my high school and college summers in the state, working on a ranch, prospecting for gold, and selling real estate in order to finance my visits. Upon college graduation, accounting degree in hand, I returned to establish a career. (Accounting major turned nature photographer? What sense does that make? Read on.) I went into the department store business in Denver, married and began to raise a family, and, after eight years on the corporate fast track, I turned my avocation—nature photography—into a new career.

This is my 32nd book, most of them about Colorado. I've been practically everywhere in the state—driving hundreds of thousands of miles, and hiked and skied thousands more—in search of nature's most sublime places and moments. I have had the pleasure of photographing for and writing picture books showcasing its mountains, rivers, canyon country, wilderness areas, wildflowers and waterfalls, autumn and winter seasons, and its early history in photographs.

It was time to publish a Colorado guidebook that reveals the state's best places and spotlights the reason people treasure Colorado in the first place: the scenery! I have never been particularly tight-lipped about the spectacular Colorado locales I've photographed. Some photographers keep their favorite scenes secret for fear that competitors will copy the shot. For me, the only thing better than the actual moment of making an image—the indelible sights, sounds, tastes, smells, and touch of nature—is the joy of sharing these places and experiences with other people. I simply love to show someone an image and ask, "Can you believe the light?" or "Can you believe this place is real?" I also find it fulfilling to explain to others how I make photographs, as I do in my instructional book, *Photographing the Landscape: The Art of Seeing.* From composition to light, the book encompasses everything I've learned by the seat of my pants while attempting to do justice to nature on film for three decades. You will notice I refer to *Photographing the Landscape* throughout this book when I think a photo tip or two might be useful.

John Fielder's Best of Colorado ***contains my 165 favorite scenic roadside locations where you can simply view our most beautiful of states or, if you choose, make a classic Colorado landscape photograph.*** These are largely places off the beaten path that you could discover only after years of exploring the state by vehicle—and I have left nothing out. The key word here is "roadside." You will not have to hike for miles to get to these sites. These Scenic Locations exist near or next to interstates, two-lane rural highways, improved dirt county roads, and old mining roads that demand a four-wheel-drive vehicle. Sometimes they require a short hike, but for the majority you can stand right next to your car and take the picture. I've included my own photograph of each of these places. You can replicate it or do your own thing. In all cases, I give directions in writing and by map for locating the place.

After a day of taking in the scenery, you need a cozy place to stay and good food to eat. What might surprise those of you who know me only for my wilderness photography, and think I'm strictly a backpacker and camper, is that this book also reveals my favorite "everything-else-to-dos" in the state. My wife, Gigi, and I raised three Colorado children, who were not always amenable to sleeping in a tent. We discovered our favorite hotels, B&Bs, restaurants, hot springs, museums, and historic

Piney Lake near Vail (see Scenic Location No. 28, p. 119)

monuments, as well as campsites—and everything else that we all like to do while touring Colorado by vehicle. As our kids got older and traveled on their own, and as my knees began to protest the 65-pound camera pack on my back, my wife and I rediscovered rural and resort Colorado. With a new desire to experience the good life, we searched for unique places both scenic and comfortable. I share our findings in this book.

The easy part about writing this book was discussing my favorite Scenic Locations—they're always beautiful from one season to the next, year after year. The hard part was picking Colorado's finest amenities and activities, as they change often. Hotels and restaurants go out of business or change hands, and there just isn't enough room in this book to include all of Colorado's premium destinations. To help me reconnect with and select the best of the best, I asked two good friends to travel the state and investigate amenities that I had always enjoyed, as well as new places and those I might have missed during my travels. Carmi McLean and Suzanne Venino drove more than 20,000 miles, visited every region in Colorado, sampled the finest food and service available, and made me pay for it all! I thought nature photography was an enviable occupation until their jobs came along.

If you live in Colorado and think you've already seen and done just about everything in the state, this book is for you. If you are a visitor, this book is also for you. Whether you want to spend the day snowshoeing near home in Denver, or a week exploring old mining towns in the remote San Juan Mountains, here you'll find quintessential Colorado experiences, as well as new places to discover. From Saturday night dining on Boulder's Pearl Street Mall to hiking the trails of the Maroon Bells–Snowmass Wilderness near Aspen, this book tells you where to go for pampering one day and challenge the next.

You might not know that tall buttes, as well as deep river canyons, await the adventurous on Colorado's Eastern Plains. This book takes you there. What's the best B&B to retire to after you photograph the magnificent Pawnee Buttes? I'll tell you. Don't want to hang out with the crowd in Telluride? Try the little town of Ridgway and check into a lodge featuring private hot tubs with distant views. Want a piece of the state's most mouthwatering homemade candy? Visit Pagosa Springs and the store that dubs its chocolate concoctions Elk Poop and Bear Piles. Really. It's all here. You need look no further.

—John Fielder

How to Use This Guide

BOOK ORGANIZATION

This book divides Colorado into eight geographical regions: Denver and Vicinity, Colorado Springs and Vicinity, The I-70 Corridor, Northwestern Colorado, Central Colorado, Southern Colorado, Southwestern Colorado, and Eastern Plains. Each one opens with a regional map and essay, as well as a boxed table of contents showing Scenic Locations (see below) and towns covered in the region.

A map, introduction, and history kick off each town section. Then follow the Main Attractions, the primary reasons you might make a trip to the town. Other great things to do and see are highlighted under the Activities heading. The Restaurants and Accommodations sections offer a variety of establishments, for the most part locally owned. Special Events tell you what's going on at select times throughout the year, and coverage of each town closes with the main contact for general visitor information. Colorado Cameos—historical profiles of notable Coloradans—and Scenic Locations appear throughout.

SCENIC LOCATIONS

At the start of this project, I paged through each of my Colorado photography books to recall the many places I'd photographed since taking the profession seriously in 1973. Ultimately, 165 scenic sites emerged as favorites. Except for some that are only accessible by four-wheel drive or a short hike, you can usually get there in your passenger car. Additional information for many Scenic Locations can be found under the Main Attractions and Activities headings.

Numbered 1 through 165, Scenic Locations are identified by purple ovals on the state, regional, and local maps. A table of contents at the beginning of a region directs you to the page featuring a short essay and color photograph of each Scenic Location. Most of the local maps have enough detail to get you to each place, and written directions appear in the essay. Each essay describes what makes a place unique and how to take specific photographs there.

You'll find out how to compose the scene, what lens focal length might be best, and, in many cases, on which page to find a relevant photography technique in my 1996 instructional book, *Photographing the Landscape: The Art of Seeing*. I discuss seasonal changes, including the prime weeks to photograph spring and autumn colors and to see wildflowers at their peak. I also suggest the optimal times of day and weather conditions during which to photograph a place. Of course, some locations are not single places but entire scenic roads several miles long. If you have trouble finding the exact scene shown in this book, don't waste good light—move on and do your own thing.

MAPS

You'll find three kinds of maps in this book: state, regional, and local. The state map shows the eight regions and all the Scenic Locations and towns featured in this book. The regional maps plot the proximity of Scenic Locations to one another so that you can plan tours to visit any number of them. In general, the local maps contain the necessary road information to get you to a Scenic Location and show important nearby features. However, other map sources will benefit you in your travels around the state (see below).

Please refer to this legend for symbols that appear on the local maps.

- 70 Interstate Highway
- 6 Federal Highway
- 103 State Highway
- Road
- 10 Scenic Location
- City or Town
- Point of Interest
- Forest Boundary
- Lake or Reservoir
- Wetland
- River or Creek
- Continental Divide
- Pass
- Exit

OTHER MAP SOURCES

DeLorme Mapping's *Colorado Atlas & Gazetteer* contains just about every road, improved and unimproved, in the state, as well as major trails and topographic information. I recommend this atlas, and on each local map in this book, I cite the specific DeLorme page numbers for your reference. The gazetteer is available at map and book retailers or by contacting DeLorme. *207-846-7000, www.delorme.com.* (Note that various map sources can differ in matters such as elevation, spelling, and even road numbers, and that our text and maps part ways with DeLorme occasionally in order to reach a consensus among these sources.)

For backcountry travel and visits to remote areas, other map products are also advisable. U.S. Forest Service maps give a good overview of forest roads, land status, and features, if not topographic information. USGS 1:24,000 topographic "quad" maps are indispensable for backpackers and helpful to day hikers and mountain bikers, though some information in them can be outdated. Bureau of Land Management (BLM) 1:100,000-scale maps show land status and are essential for hunters. *USGS, BLM, and Forest Service maps: 888-275-8747, www.usgs.gov.*

Ideal backcountry companions, Trails Illustrated maps—printed on durable, waterproof material—combine and contract adjoining, high-country USGS quads and overlay them with updated trail and other information. *National Geographic Maps: 303-670-3457, 800-962-1643, www.natgeomaps.com.*

ROADS

You'll find several kinds of road delineated on the maps and in Scenic Location essays: interstate highways (I-25, I-70, or I-76), federal highways preceded by "US" (US 285), and state highways preceded by "CO" (CO 91), always paved; county roads preceded by "CR" (CR 25), either improved dirt or paved; and U.S. Forest Service roads preceded by "FR" (FR 625), either improved or primitive dirt. Sometimes one road can take on multiple numbers, shifting from a county road to a forest road as it traverses various land-management jurisdictions (this is a common occurrence on pass roads). I have attempted to indicate where this happens.

Just about all of Colorado's federal and state highways are maintained year-round. A few high-country highways, though, are only open seasonally. Those not plowed for snow in winter are CO 82 over Independence Pass, Trail Ridge Road (part of US 34) in Rocky Mountain National Park, and the Mount Evans Road (CO 5).

Improved dirt roads generally are negotiable by passenger car, but even the smoothest county road might fall victim to wet weather, when some road surfaces, such as fine clay, become soft and muddy. I've seen roads in eastern Colorado become as slick as ice during the May rainy season, requiring a four-wheel drive. Some improved forest roads might otherwise be fine for your car if it weren't for potholes or rocks. I try to warn you about these, but the welfare of your car is always a consideration when you venture onto an unimproved road. I have tried in all cases to indicate where you might need a four-wheel-drive or high-clearance vehicle.

The Activities heading Four-Wheel-Drive Trips merits special attention. The roughest routes in Colorado are "jeep roads," requiring the narrow base of a jeep or similar vehicle. Where jeep tours are listed, I recommend that all but the very experienced take a tour with a professional driver, rather than renting or driving your own jeep. Jeeping in the high country is not for amateurs. Respect the terrain—and the limits of your vehicle.

SYMBOLS, RATINGS, PRICES, AND RESERVATIONS

Several symbols and rating systems will help guide you through this book.

Some activities are rated **EASY**, **MODERATE**, or **DIFFICULT**, depending on the level of fitness or expertise needed, or the amount of difficulty you might encounter. Hiking, Cycling and Mountain Biking, and Rafting sections use these designations. Whitewater rafting trips also include the standard difficulty rating system of Class I–Class VI. Class I whitewater has no rapids and is suitable for families with small children; Class III has constant but relatively safe whitewater; and Classes V–VI can be dangerous and require expert navigation skills.

A "kid-friendly" symbol appears next to activities and amenities that are especially conducive to a family experience. Call ahead when investigating B&Bs or other typically adult-oriented establishments and activities, as well as when you're considering bringing your pet.

You'll see a four-wheel-drive symbol next to certain fishing holes, campgrounds, and other destinations that require a four-wheel drive to access. Note that this symbol does not appear in the Four-Wheel-Drive Trips listings, as the need for such a vehicle is implied, nor does it appear in Scenic Location essays.

Restaurants and Accommodations are rated for affordability on a scale of one to four dollar signs ($). For a single entree at a restaurant: $ = under $10; $$ = $10–$20; $$$ = $20–$30; and $$$$ = $30 and up. For a single-occupancy room: $ = under $80; $$ = $80–$160; $$$ = $160–$200; and $$$$ = $200 and up. Of course, these are generalizations and prices are subject to change. Rates often fluctuate seasonally in Colorado, especially in smaller and mountain communities, and some businesses close during the off-season. Please inquire upon making reservations to check closures, and make sure a destination fits within your budget.

Reservations are also advisable for many campgrounds, as the popular ones tend to fill up between Memorial Day and Labor Day. This book indicates where reservations are either recommended or not accepted for campgrounds, but you can always call ahead for availability.

CONTACT INFORMATION

You'll find addresses, phone numbers, and websites for the amenities and activities discussed in this book. Such things change constantly, so each new printing of this book will incorporate updated contact information. I will also be on the lookout for great new places to go and things to do.

Please feel free to inform me of any mistakes, updates, or suggestions about items that we should consider adding. Write to me at P.O. Box 1261, Englewood, CO 80150.

About Colorado

A BRIEF HISTORY

Evidence of prehistoric humans in Colorado dates back some 18,000 years, when nomadic hunters used stone-tipped spears to bring down woolly mammoths, ancient bison, and other long-extinct mammals. Excavations near the Pawnee Buttes on the Eastern Plains have yielded bones and numerous stone points— artifacts on exhibit at the Denver Museum of Nature and Science.

About 2,000 years ago, small, primitive tribes built pit houses on the desert plateau in what is now Colorado's southwestern corner. Over time their culture evolved, and they constructed complex, multistory dwellings in vertical cliffs. These cliff dwellers, known as the Anasazi or Ancestral Puebloans, seemingly vanished around 1300. Scientists theorize that drought or warfare caused them to abandon their homes, which are now preserved at Mesa Verde National Park.

The first European to enter Colorado is thought to have been Francisco Coronado, who in 1541 passed through in his futile search for the golden Seven Cities of Cibola. Juan Rivera led an expedition here in 1765, searching for gold and silver in the San Juan and Sangre de Cristo Mountains, but he too left empty-handed. In 1682, the French explorer Sieur de La Salle claimed the land east of the Rocky Mountains in the name of France—lands inhabited by the Arapaho, Cheyenne, Kiowa, Comanche, and Pawnee. Utes ranged through the mountains.

In the early to mid-1800s, French fur trappers and American mountain men entered the region, following river corridors. Men such as Kit Carson and Jim Bridger earned their livelihood in the untamed frontier, trapping beaver and trading the pelts, which were used to make hats that were all the rage with high-class gentlemen in London, New York, and Paris.

In 1803, the Louisiana Purchase transferred land east of the Continental Divide and north of the Arkansas River to the United States. The federal government sent exploratory parties to discover and survey what the nation now owned. Lieutenant Zebulon Pike came with a small party of soldiers in 1806; Major Stephen Long's party arrived in 1820; and from 1842 to 1853 Lieutenant John C. Frémont led five expeditions.

The rest of Colorado belonged to Spain, which had granted vast parcels of land in the San Luis and Arkansas Valleys. In 1821, when Mexico won its independence from Spain, the Spanish crown relinquished its land to Mexico—land that was later ceded to the United States at the end of the Mexican-American War in 1848.

Bent's Fort, on the north bank of the Arkansas River, was the first Anglo settlement, serving as a trading post and way station along the Mountain Branch of the Santa Fe Trail from 1833 to 1849. The first permanent town was established in 1851 at San Luis, a small Hispanic village built around a traditional central plaza. Other towns soon sprang up, settled by sheep ranchers and farmers who migrated north from the New Mexico Territory.

As more settlers arrived, conflicts with Indians increased. In 1864 some 150 Arapaho and Cheyenne, mostly women and children, were killed in the infamous Sand Creek Massacre. The last Indian battle, the Meeker Massacre, occurred in 1879, when Utes ambushed U.S. troops and killed Indian agent Nathan Meeker. The Utes were removed to a reservation in the Four Corners region in 1881.

In 1858 the glimmer of gold in Cherry Creek, near its confluence with the South Platte River in what is now Denver, sparked a gold rush to the Colorado Territory. With the slogan "Pikes Peak or Bust," hopefuls from across the country and around the world followed the long, difficult trail to Colorado. Mining camps and towns peppered the Rockies. When placer mining played out, hard-rock mining took its place, first for gold and then for silver. Many of Colorado's mountain towns trace their beginnings to the mining era.

Railroad lines were built to transport ore, equipment, and goods. Coal was mined to run trains, mills, and smelters. The fertile prairies and valleys were plowed and planted to feed the growing population. Newcomers from the East, along with immigrants from Europe and Russia, homesteaded the plains and mined in the mountains. From 1870 to 1880, the population of the Colorado Territory increased fivefold, to nearly 200,000. In 1876 Colorado became the 38th state and was nicknamed the "Centennial State" because it was admitted to the Union during the nation's centennial year.

The mountains buzzed with mining activity and the state prospered. The repeal of the Sherman Silver Purchase Act in 1893, however, sent silver prices plummeting. Many towns and mining camps didn't survive; those that did turned to other precious metals and minerals. By 1900 Cripple Creek was producing $20 million in gold annually. Labor strife marked the mining industry in the early 1900s, with unions and management clashing, martial law enforced, and deadly violence.

By the turn of the 20th century, agriculture dominated the state's economy. The 1910 census counted 46,170 farms, with nearly 3 million acres under irrigation. Wheat production soared during World War I, as did the mining of iron, tungsten, and molybdenum, which is used in making steel. Coal production reached a high of 12.5 million tons in 1918, and in the early 1920s oil was discovered. The advent of the automobile created not only an oil boom but also demand for highways and roads.

Everything changed during the Great Depression. Farmers on the Eastern Plains were hit particularly hard. With the combination of prolonged drought and the dry farming methods they had been using, farmers watched their farms blow away during the Dust Bowl years. It was also during this time that the Civilian Conservation Corps, a federal relief program created to stem massive unemployment, put teams to work building roads, trails, and facilities in Colorado's parks and forests.

World War II brought another economic boom, as once again the mining industry produced materials needed for the war effort. Military bases, arsenals, and training centers established a military presence in Colorado. In 1958 the U.S. Air Force Academy in Colorado Springs matriculated its first class of cadets, and in 1966 the North American Air Defense Command (NORAD), built 1,200 feet beneath Cheyenne Mountain, set to work guarding the country from the threat of foreign missile attack.

The state's spectacular scenery has always been a draw for both tourists and Coloradans. Rocky Mountain National Park was established in 1915, the same year the auto road to the top of Pikes Peak was built. The first commercial ski area opened in Aspen in 1947; today the state has more than 25. The 1973 completion of the Eisenhower Tunnel created a direct route from Denver to the mountains via Interstate 70. Recreation and tourism now rank among the state's leading economic bases, along with agriculture and manufacturing, which now includes high-tech industries such as computers, telecommunications, and biotech.

With a population now topping 4.3 million, Colorado faces the crucial issue of unchecked growth. It's not surprising that people want to live here—the economy is healthy, so is the lifestyle, and there are few places as beautiful as Colorado.

ROCKS, PLANTS, AND CRITTERS

Geographically, Colorado is simple: plains to the east, mountains in the middle—crowned by the Continental Divide—and plateaus to the west. The development of its varied features —its geology—is a bit more complex. Like the segments of a turtle's shell, the crust of the earth consists of various plates about 60 miles thick that are constantly on the move at a rate of about an inch per year. The North American plate has a central weak zone that happens to run through Colorado. Unusually intense movement 300 million years ago caused the formation of long blocks of crust that were lifted to make the ancestral, or first, Rocky Mountains. The process of erosion eventually weathered these peaks down to mountains that looked much like the present-day Appalachians. The almost vertical red sandstone rocks we see at Roxborough State Park near Denver and Garden of the Gods City Park in Colorado Springs are made up of detritus weathered from the ancestral Rockies.

When the ancestral Rockies were eroding, a shallow inland sea covered Colorado and deposited marine shales containing shellfish and other ocean creatures. At the same time, western Colorado was becoming a coastal plain as the seas retreated westward. The sediments deposited by rivers and wind-shaped sand dunes of 200 million years ago are the sandstone strata that define western Colorado and eastern Utah today.

This relatively dry climate was followed by a more humid one during the Jurassic period. Lush vegetation in a marshy environment was a perfect place for dinosaurs. Thick layers of coal were later deposited during the Cretaceous period.

Sixty-five million years ago, a second episode of intense plate movement, the Laramide Orogeny, created the Rockies that we know today. As the mountains rose, tributaries of the Colorado River carved the deep canyons of western Colorado, including Escalante Canyon, the Dolores River canyon, and the canyonlands of Colorado National Monument. During and after this event, mineral-rich solutions percolated upward through cracks and fissures. These solutions and intrusions of igneous rock became the valuable veins and ore bodies that made Colorado the gold and silver mining capital of the country in the late 19th century.

Southern Colorado and the San Juan Mountains underwent great volcanic activity starting 40 million years ago. Exposed walls of igneous rock intrusions, called dikes, manifest this activity around the Spanish Peaks, as does the eroded volcanic Lizard Head formation near Telluride. The movement of the North American plate continued at a lesser rate from about 28 million years ago to as recently as 5 million years ago to uplift an area called the Colorado Plateau, which contains Colorado and parts of Utah, Arizona, and New Mexico. This uplift turned 9,000-foot mountains into "fourteeners." You probably already know that Colorado has the highest average elevation of any state in the continental U.S. Fifty-four of our several thousand peaks top 14,000 feet above sea level. Several glacial periods have occurred during the last 80,000 years, the last of which ended about 10,000 years ago. It carved many of the alpine cirques and U-shaped, subalpine valleys that we see throughout the Colorado Rockies in places like the Slate River valley near Crested Butte.

Because Colorado's landscape varies from plains at 3,800 feet to mountains over 14,000 feet, so, too, do its plants and animals. Ecologists group habitats into vegetative communities defined by dominant species. The Lower Sonoran Zone of western (Great Basin Desert) and eastern (Shortgrass Prairie) Colorado includes sagebrush and scrub oak, prairie dogs and pronghorn, red-tailed hawks and golden eagles. The Upper Sonoran Zone is characterized by piñon pine and juniper, Indian paintbrush and lupine, mule deer, coyotes, and piñon jays.

Stately ponderosa pines define the Transition Zone in the Rocky Mountains from 6,000 to 9,000 feet. Abert's squirrels and Steller's jays inhabit the lodgepole pines and aspens—Colorado's most photogenic trees (which thrive from 7,500 to 10,000 feet in the Transition and Canadian Zones). Aspens propagate via their root systems and are among the first to repopulate open areas swept by fires and avalanches. Mixed with the aspens are wild geraniums and white-and-lavender columbines, the state flower. Beavers and porcupines join elk, mule deer, black bears, and many bird species in the Transition Zone.

Engelmann spruce and subalpine fir trees populate the Canadian and Hudsonian Zones between 9,000 and 11,000 feet. In these thick, dark forests live the "camp robber" or gray jay, and more solitary species like lynx, wolverine, and perhaps a grizzly or two (although the last reported Colorado grizzly was killed in 1978 in a remote part of the South San Juan Mountains near Pagosa Springs). Some of Colorado's bristlecone pines date back to more than 2,000 years ago. The oldest living things in the world, this pine species grows on windswept ridges near treeline. Grouse-like ptarmigans, and marmots and pikas, live in the tundra and talus rocks of the Hudsonian Zone.

The lofty Arctic-Alpine Zone begins at 11,500 feet. Wind-twisted spruce trees called *krummholz* are the last trees you will see before entering the arctic tundra. Here, mountain goats and bighorn sheep live on high. Dwarf wildflowers such as phlox, moss campion, and forget-me-nots color the landscape.

One habitat weaves its way through many life zones. With four dominant cottonwood tree species, the Riparian Forest sheathes rivers and creeks. Alders, box elders, and willows provide the understory, and beavers, muskrats, skunks, foxes, and raccoons make such places home.

Traveling in Colorado

GETTING HERE

BY PLANE: Approximately 25 miles northeast of downtown, Denver International Airport (DIA) is Colorado's main airport. Most major airlines service DIA, as well as many regional ones. DIA is a hub for United Airlines, which offers the most flights. Shuttle vans go from the airport to metro-area destinations and many of the ski resorts. *800-247-2336, www.flydenver.com.*

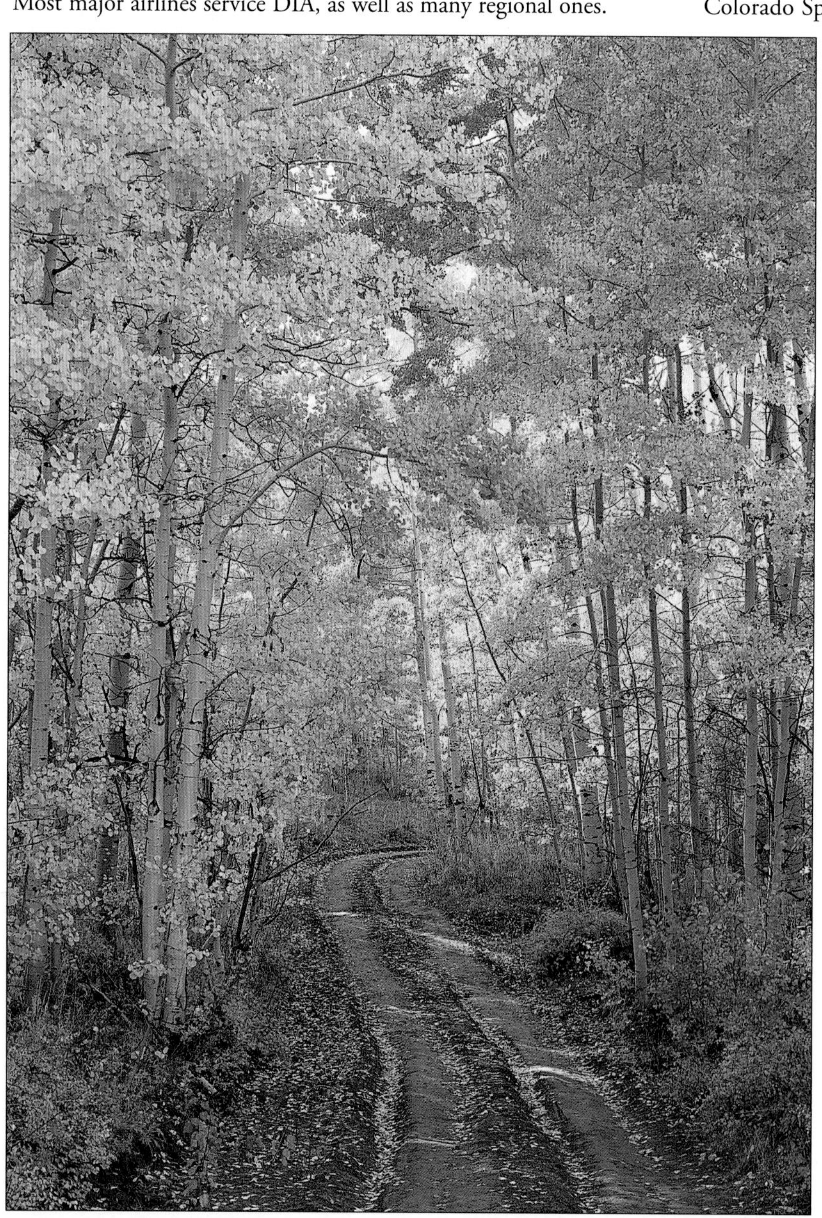

Autumn aspens along Divide Road (see Scenic Location No. 100, p. 289)

Colorado Springs Airport has flights connecting to most major U.S. cities. Served by main airlines, the airport is southeast of Colorado Springs. *719-550-1972, www.flycos.com.*

Walker Field Airport in Grand Junction is a good choice if you are headed to the western part of the state. *970-244-9100, www.walkerfield.com.*

You can also fly (either directly or via connecting flights) to many destination ski towns such as Steamboat Springs, Aspen, Telluride, and Eagle (for Vail and Beaver Creek). These flights are generally on smaller aircraft, but some are on jets.

BY CAR: Two major interstate highways crisscross Colorado. Heading west from Kansas, Interstate 70 crosses the plains, passes through Denver and into the mountains, descends to Grand Junction on the Western Slope, and continues into Utah. Traveling south from Wyoming down to New Mexico, Interstate 25 passes through (or near) most of the major towns and cities along the Front Range: Fort Collins, Denver, Colorado Springs, Pueblo, Walsenburg, and Trinidad.

To elude traffic congestion, don't drive during peak travel times in cities and along the I-70 corridor. "Weekend warriors" head to the mountains on Saturday and Sunday mornings, so westbound I-70 from Denver to Vail sees heavy traffic then—particularly during ski season but increasingly in summer, as well. Avoid Sunday afternoons and evenings on the same stretch of eastbound I-70. Summer weekend traffic on US 285 from Denver to as far as South Park also can be heavy at these times because hikers, kayakers, and mountain bikers heading to and from the Arkansas River Valley often use this route. The stretch of I-25 that runs through Denver's metro area should be avoided during weekday rush hour.

BY TRAIN: Amtrak runs two routes through Colorado. The California Zephyr links Chicago and San Francisco, making stops in Fort Morgan, Denver, Winter Park, Granby, Glenwood Springs, and Grand Junction. Amtrak's Southwest Chief connects Chicago and Los Angeles, crossing the southeastern corner of Colorado via Trinidad, La Junta, and Lamar. *800-872-7245, www.amtrak.com.*

BY BUS: Greyhound has service between many cities in Colorado, including Denver (and DIA), Boulder, Fort Collins, Colorado Springs, Pueblo, Trinidad, Frisco, Glenwood Springs, and Grand Junction. *800-231-2222, www.greyhound.com.*

For general information on travel to and within the state, visit the Colorado Department of Transportation's website at *www.cotrip.org.* This site includes bus and train schedules, a comprehensive list of Colorado's airports, road and weather conditions, and even bike routes throughout the state. *Recorded road conditions: 303-639-1111, 877-315-7623.*

WEATHER

There is an old, and fairly accurate, saying in Colorado: "If you don't like the weather, wait five minutes." The weather here can change drastically throughout the course of a day—even in the span of an hour. It is important to check the forecast and to keep your eye on what's happening in the sky, particularly when you are in the backcountry.

Springtime in Colorado is beautiful. It is characterized by heavy snow in the mountains, spectacular thunderstorms on the Eastern Plains, and warm, sunny days in the Denver area. Summer follows with hot, cloudless mornings and afternoon thunderstorms. Temperatures tend to range from the mid- to high 70s in the mountains to the 80s and 90s at lower elevations. Although days are warm in the high country, evenings are often quite cool, so be sure to take layers to wear after the sun goes down.

Late summer and early autumn are traditionally sunny, warm, and dry—perfect weather for a variety of backcountry trips. Temperatures rest in the 70s during the day and drop into the 40s at night. But once the autumn colors blanket the mountains, expect cool weather and even some snow. Some mountain passes close until spring once the first big snow falls, so be sure to check road conditions before setting out on a scenic drive in late fall.

Winter's cold temperatures sneak up early, allowing many ski resorts to open in mid-November. Although Colorado's winter is snowy and can be quite cold, temperatures at lower elevations rarely dip below 30 degrees for an extended period of time. Colorado's latitude also allows for balmy, sunny days throughout winter and particularly in early spring. Coloradans don summer clothing and head outside whenever there's a warm spell—we love our 300 days per year of sunshine!

HEALTH AND SAFETY SENSE

Colorado has the highest average elevation of any state in the nation. Denver, the "Mile High City," is at 5,280 feet; Leadville, the highest incorporated town in the U.S., is at 10,152 feet; and Colorado's tallest peak is 14,433-foot Mount Elbert, one of the state's 54 "fourteeners." With these soaring elevations come some necessary precautions, particularly if you are visiting from sea level.

High altitudes mean that you are closer to the sun and more susceptible to stronger ultraviolet (UV) rays, which easily penetrate the thinner atmosphere. Wear sunscreen at all times of year—even on cloudy days. If you are enjoying outdoor activities, reapply sunscreen regularly, as snow and water reflect and intensify the sun's rays. Wear sunglasses with good UV protection. A hat with a wide brim, or at least a bill, is also a good idea.

Be alert to the symptoms of altitude sickness (dizziness, drowsiness, headache, nausea, lack of appetite, and shortness of breath) and take care to avoid them by drinking plenty of water, getting lots of rest, and acclimating to the altitude slowly. If you're flying into Denver, for instance, acclimate there for a day or so before heading up into the high country, and then adjust to that altitude before going higher. Don't plan to climb a fourteener on the first day of your vacation! Mild symptoms of altitude sickness can be relieved by drinking water, resting, and taking a pain reliever. If you experience extreme symptoms, go to a lower elevation immediately and seek medical attention.

It is very easy to get dehydrated in semiarid Colorado. Again, drink copious amounts of water, especially if you are exercising (a good rule of thumb is a gallon of water per day). Don't wait until you're thirsty; drink water regularly to keep properly hydrated. And don't drink too much caffeine or alcohol, as they will dehydrate you quickly.

Water from streams and lakes should *always* be treated, regardless of the clarity or source, so take purifying tablets or a water filter when you venture into the backcountry. Drinking untreated water can result in Giardia, an infection of the small intestine caused by a parasite that lives in streams, lakes, and rivers. Symptoms include fatigue, gas, cramps, and diarrhea, and can last up to six weeks.

Colorado's backcountry is nature at its finest—we love it for its wildness and stark, rugged beauty. But it is essential to use good judgment when heading into the mountains and down the rivers. Dress in layers, as the weather is extremely changeable. Synthetics like fleece or polypropylene are great for layering, not only because you can add or remove layers as necessary but also because these fabrics will keep you warm even when they are wet. Wear sturdy shoes or boots when hiking, and always pack rain gear.

Anything can happen in the backcountry (inclement weather, injury, getting lost, encounters with wildlife), so plan ahead. Never hike alone. Let someone know where you are going and when you expect to return. Tell the manager at your hotel or the host at your B&B, or check in at the ranger station if there is one where you are going. Take a backpack with extra clothing, plenty of water (you can't hear that too much!), food, maps, a compass, a signaling mirror, a flashlight, and a first-aid kit. Campers should pack insect repellent to fend off mosquitoes and ticks. And don't forget your camera!

When hiking above treeline, such as a peak climb, be sure to get an early start. Clear skies in the morning can quickly turn to huge thunderheads in the afternoon—the typical weather pattern here in July and August. With thunderstorms comes lightning, a very real threat in the high country. Plan your climb so that you are off the summit or exposed ridges by 1 p.m.

Stay on established trails and routes; don't create your own. Despite the images in auto advertisements, going off-road on four-wheel-drive excursions damages the natural environment and can also get you lost or in trouble. An anecdote illustrates this piece of advice: Some years ago, visitors to the San Juan Mountains embarked on an off-road, four-wheel-drive adventure. Soon the terrain became too steep and the group was in danger of rolling end-over-end into the town of Silverton, thousands of feet below. Abandoning the vehicle, the tourists sought help, but not before they were handed a $600 ticket for driving off-road and damaging public lands. Further, authorities told them to remove the vehicle quickly, as it posed a threat to the town below. Exorbitant solutions included hiring a helicopter to airlift the vehicle or dismantling it and hauling it down piece by piece. In the end, expert jeep guides managed to winch the vehicle back on-road. In short, respect the terrain, know your limits, and consider professionally guided jeep tours.

Note that Wilderness Areas are referred to frequently in this book. Our wildest places, they are legally designated areas that are off limits to any kind of motorized, even mechanized, vehicles, including mountain bikes. You can only hike or ride horseback in designated wilderness.

If you intend to ski or snowshoe in the backcountry, educate yourself on avalanche safety and check on avalanche conditions before you set out. Carry shovels and beacons—and practice using them before you go. Not just for children anymore, helmets on the downhill slopes are becoming more popular—and should be. Be mindful of the regulations at each ski area, and ski or snowboard responsibly. If you're a beginner, consider taking a lesson. Skiing in trees is difficult and dangerous. Snowmobiling off-trail is not only hazardous—it also damages wild areas and harms wildlife.

Even vehicle travel on paved roads requires some smarts and precautions. If you get stranded in a snowstorm, call for assistance on your cell phone, then stay with your vehicle until help arrives. Do *not* leave your vehicle to strike out on your own unless you see inhabited buildings nearby. Don't keep the engine running for warmth as carbon monoxide can build up in your car if the tailpipe is obstructed. In summer on the plains, keep an eye on the horizon for tornadoes. If you see a twister, find a secure shelter fast.

All of the precautions mentioned here might make you fearful about ever venturing out of your hotel room. There are risks, yes, but the payback is well worth it. Just use your head (never, for instance, go exploring in a 100-year-old mine shaft!) and do as the Boy Scouts do—be prepared.

VISITOR INFORMATION

Colorado is in the Mountain time zone, and is two hours behind New York City and one hour ahead of Los Angeles. Metro Denver has two area codes, 720 and 303, and you must dial all 10 digits when making a call. (A "1" is not necessary when calling from within the area.) All phone numbers in this book include an area code.

The following phone numbers and websites provide useful information for the Colorado traveler:

Bed and Breakfast Innkeepers of Colorado: *800-265-7696, www.innsofcolorado.org*

Bureau of Land Management, Colorado: *303-239-3600, www.co.blm.gov*

Colorado Agency of Camping, Cabins, and Lodges: *888-222-4641, www.coloradodirectory.com*

Colorado Hotel and Lodging Association: *303-297-8335, www.coloradolodging.com*

Colorado Ski Country USA: *www.skicolorado.com*

Colorado State Parks: *303-866-3437, www.parks.state.co.us*

Colorado Travel & Tourism Authority: *800-COLORADO*

National Park Service: *www.nps.gov*

State of Colorado: *www.colorado.gov*

U.S. Fish & Wildlife Service: *www.fws.gov*

U.S. Forest Service, Rocky Mountain Region: *303-275-5350, www.fs.fed.us*

Colorado Welcome Centers along major interstates and highways provide maps, information on area tourist attractions, and friendly advice from Coloradans:

Burlington: 719-346-5554
Cortez: 970-565-4048
Dinosaur: 970-374-2205
Fort Collins: 970-491-4775
Fruita: 970-858-9335
Julesburg: 970-474-2054
Lamar: 719-336-3483
Red Rocks: 303-697-2048
Trinidad: 719-846-9512

OTHER RECOMMENDED BOOKS

Camping

Melinda. *Camping Colorado.* Guilford, Conn.: Globe Pequot/Falcon Publishing, Inc., 2001.

Folsom, Gil. *Colorado Campgrounds: The 100 Best and All the Rest.* 2nd ed. Englewood, Colo.: Westcliffe Publishers, Inc., 2008.

Molloy, Johnny. *The Best in Tent Camping: Colorado.* Birmingham, Ala.: Menasha Ridge Press, 2001.

Children's Activities

Keilty, Maureen. *Best Hikes with Children in Colorado.* Seattle: The Mountaineers Books, 1998.

Krudwig, Vickie Leigh. *Hiking Through Colorado History.* Englewood, Colo: Westcliffe Publishers, Inc., 1998.

Liggett, Diane T., and James A. Mack. *Real Cool Colorado Places for Curious Kids.* Englewood, Colo.: Westcliffe Publishers, Inc., 1998.

Children's Activities continued

Perry, Phyllis J. *Colorado Fun: Activities for On the Road and At Home.* Boulder, Colo.: Johnson Books, 2007.

Sutton, Carolyn. *The Family Guide to Colorado's National Parks and Monuments.* Englewood, Colo.: Westcliffe Publishers, Inc., 2006.

Young, Mary Taylor. *On the Trail of Colorado Critters.* Englewood, Colo.: Westcliffe Publishers, Inc., 2000.

Cycling and Mountain Biking

Gong, Linda, and Gregg Bromka. *Mountain Biking Colorado.* Helena, Mont.: Falcon Publishing, Inc., 1998.

Leccese, Michael. *Short Bike Rides in Colorado.* Old Saybrook, Conn.: The Globe Pequot Press, 1995.

Seeberg, Michael. *Road Biking Colorado, The Statewide Guide.* Englewood, Colo: Westcliffe Publishers, Inc., 2008.

Fishing and Hunting

Bartholomew, Marty. *Flyfisher's Guide to Colorado.* Belgrade, Mont.: Wilderness Adventures Press, 1998.

Marlowe, Al. *Fly Fishing the Colorado River: An Angler's Guide.* Boulder, Colo.: Pruett Publishing Co., 1997.

Flora, Fauna, and Geology

Chronic, Halka. *Roadside Geology of Colorado.* Missoula, Mont.: Mountain Press Publishing Co., 1980.

Gray, Mary Taylor. *Colorado Wildlife Viewing Guide.* Guilford, Conn.: Globe Pequot/Falcon Publishing, Inc., 2000.

———. *The Guide to Colorado Birds.* Englewood, Colo: Westcliffe Publishers, Inc., 1999.

Guennel, G.K. *Guide to Colorado Wildflowers. Volume 1: Plains and Foothills. and Volume 2: Mountains.* Englewood, Colo: Westcliffe Publishers, Inc., 2006.

Four-Wheel Driving

Huegel, Tony, and Jerry Painter. *Colorado Byways.* Berkeley, Calif.: Wilderness Press, 1999.

Koch, Don. *The Colorado Pass Book.* Boulder, Colo.: Pruett Publishing Co., 2000.

Massey, Peter, and Jeanne Wilson. *4WD Adventures Colorado.* Castle Rock, Colo.: Swagman Publishing, Inc., 1999.

General

Brown, Roz, and Linda Cornett. *The Insiders' Guide to Boulder and Rocky Mountain National Park.* Helena, Mont.: Insiders' Publishing, Inc., 1999.

Colorado Atlas & Gazetteer, 5th ed. Yarmouth, Maine: DeLorme Mapping Co., 2000.

Harding, Matt, and Freddie Snalam. *Get Out of Town.* Boulder, Colo.: All Points Publishing, Inc., 1994.

Hiking

Colorado Trail Foundation. *The Colorado Trail: The Official Guidebook.* Seattle: The Mountaineers Books, 2001.

Erickson, Bette. *Best Boulder Region Hiking Trails.* Englewood, Colo.: Westcliffe Publishers, Inc., 2005.

Fogelberg, Ben, and Steve Grinstead. *Walking Into Colorado's Past: 50 Front Range History Hikes.* Englewood, Colo.: Westcliffe Publishers, Inc., 2006.

Foster, Lisa. *Rocky Mountain National Park: The Complete Hiking Guide.* Englewood, Colo.: Westcliffe Publishers, Inc., 2006.

Irwin, Pamela, and David Irwin. *100 Best Denver Area & Front Range Day Hikes.* Englewood, Colo.: Westcliffe Publishers, Inc., 2003.

Irwin, Pamela. *Colorado's Best Wildflower Hikes. Volume 1: Front Range. Volume 2: High Country. Volume 3: San Juan Mountains.* Englewood, Colo: Westcliffe Publishers, Inc., 1998.

Irwin, Pamela, and David Irwin. *Colorado's Newest & Best Wildflower Hikes.* Englewood, Colo.: Westcliffe Publishers, Inc., 2008.

Pearson, Mark, and John Fielder. *Colorado's Canyon Country: A Guide to Hiking & Floating BLM Wildlands.* 2nd ed. Englewood, Colo.: Westcliffe Publishers, Inc., 2001.

———. *A Complete Guide to Colorado's Wilderness Areas.* Englewood, Colo.: Westcliffe Publishers, Inc., 1998.

Roach, Gerry. *Colorado's Fourteeners: From Hikes to Climbs.* Golden, Colo.: Fulcrum Publishing, 1999.

History

Bueler, Gladys R. *Colorado's Colorful Characters.* Boulder, Colo.: Pruett Publishing Co., 1991.

Crutchfield, James A. *It Happened in Colorado.* Helena, Mont.: Falcon Publishing, Inc., 1993.

Jackson, William Henry, and John Fielder. *Colorado: 1870–2000.* Englewood, Colo: Westcliffe Publishers, Inc., 1999.

Noel, Thomas J., and John Fielder. *Colorado 1870–2000: The History Behind the Images.* Englewood, Colo: Westcliffe Publishers, Inc., 2001.

Noel, Thomas J. *Guide to Colorado Historic Places: Sites Supported by the Colorado Historical Society's State Historical Fund.* Englewood, Colo.: Westcliffe Publishers, Inc., 2007.

Hot Springs

George, Deborah Frazier. *Colorado's Hot Springs.* Boulder, Colo.: Pruett Publishing Co., 2000.

Wambach, Carl. *Touring Colorado Hot Springs.* Helena, Mont.: Falcon Publishing, Inc., 1999.

Other

Fielder, John. *Photographing the Landscape: The Art of Seeing.* Englewood, Colo: Westcliffe Publishers, Inc., 1996.

Litz, Brian. *Colorado Hut to Hut: Guide to Skiing, Hiking, and Biking Colorado's Backcountry Cabins. Vol. 1: Northern and Central Regions. Vol. 2: Southern Region.* Englewood, Colo: Westcliffe Publishers, Inc., 2000.

Snead, Sherry, and Scott Snead. *Saddle Up, Colorado!* Englewood, Colo.: Westcliffe Publishers, Inc., 2006.

Torkelson, Jean. *Colorado Sanctuaries, Retreats, and Sacred Places.* Englewood, Colo.: Westcliffe Publishers, Inc., 2001.

Scenic Drives

Green, Stewart M. *Scenic Driving Colorado.* Helena, Mont.: Falcon Publishing, Inc., 1994.

Huber, Thomas P. *Colorado Byways: A Guide Through Scenic and Historic Landscapes.* Niwot, Colo.: University Press of Colorado, 1997.

Lampert, Lyndon J. *Lake City Places.* Lake City, Colo.: Golden Stone Press, 1999.

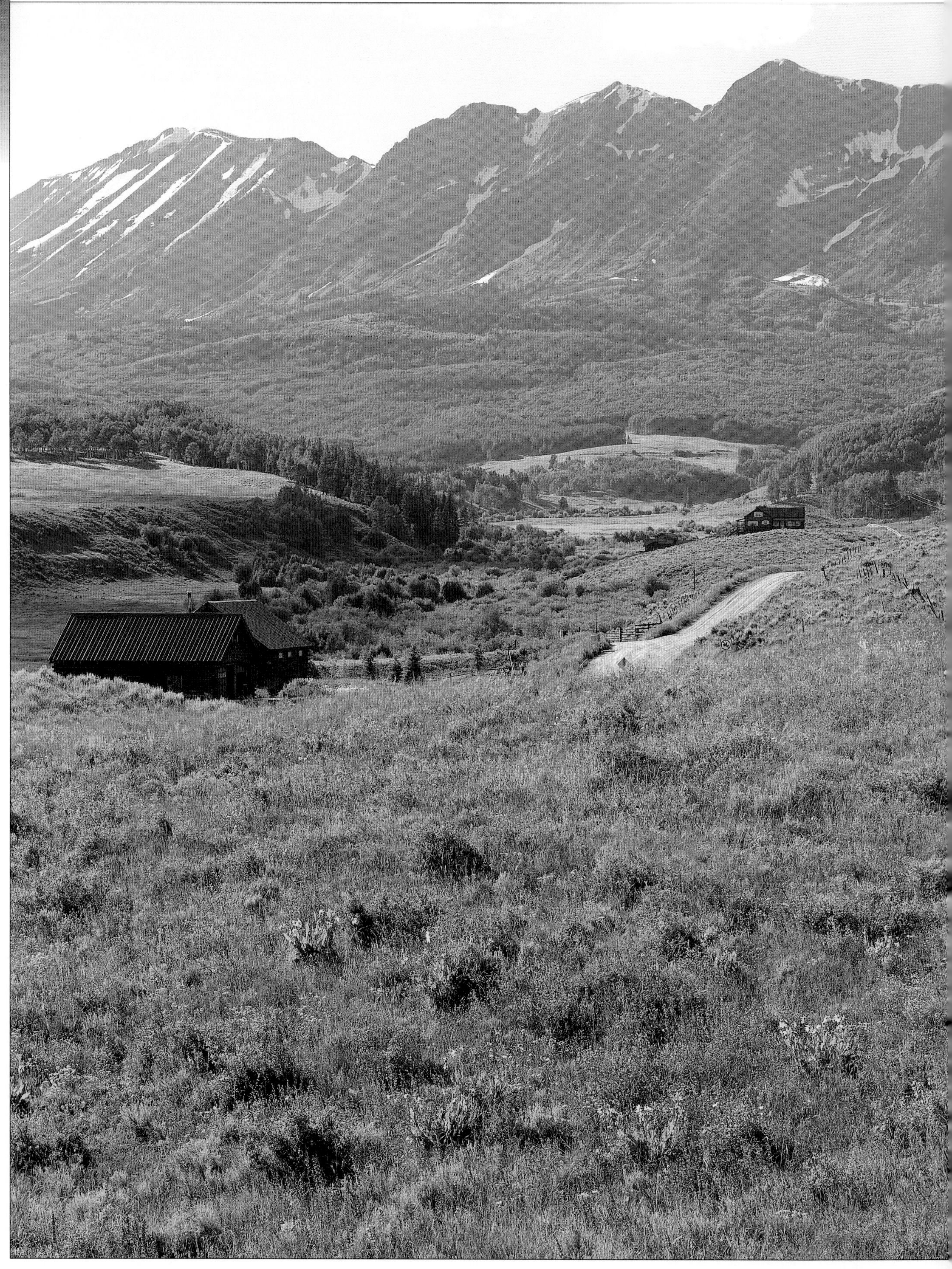

Saving Colorado

Coloradans have done much to safeguard the reasons why so many people, whether residents or visitors, love the state. We've protected more than 3.5 million acres of wilderness. We are the only state in the country whose lottery devotes all its profits to protecting open space and wildlife habitat, and to building parks and trails. Many of our cities and counties tax their residents in order to acquire and protect open space. Nevertheless, Colorado is losing the battle against inadequate planning for future growth.

Colorado is a sought-after place. Our population increased by 1 million during the 1990s alone. As of 2008, we have almost 5 million people, and the head count is expected to increase by another million in the next 10 to 15 years. Though I do not fear change, I have seen much of it since I first visited Colorado in 1964. Some of it has been good, some of it bad.

As a photographer, I employ spatial perspective when composing images of nature. But in daily life, perspective grants me a sense of balance. For instance, a weeklong trek into the wilderness heightens my appreciation for listening to the Colorado Symphony Orchestra play Brahms. Conversely, inching through a traffic jam on I-25 allows me to better value the solitude of nature.

I'm not alone in seeking such a balance between wilderness and civilization, as we all need both. Civilization depends on wilderness. Consider the extent to which art bears the influence of nature. Plenty. Ironically, wilderness also needs civilization: A healthy economy stimulates investment in land protection. But most of all, wilderness needs *wildness.*

Unfortunately, on a global level, wildness is being lost. The web of life—the biodiversity that took 3.5 billion years to develop—is being unraveled in just a few human generations. Thousands of species are going extinct before we have even discovered them because people are not using Earth's resources sustainably. Yet we cannot exist on a lifeless planet. Climate change is accelerating this unraveling.

Locally, Colorado doesn't plan well for its future growth. Sprawl-type development consumes 200,000 acres of open space and ranch- and farmland each year. Cheaply priced land far from town boundaries lures developers into following the path of least resistance. Colorado has yet to see adequate laws that allow communities to implement and legally enforce master plans for growth, or that require protection of open space and wildlife habitat. County commissioners and city councils can ignore their own master plans and, for example, approve development in a place where a park was supposed to go. You and I, citizens of that community, have no legal recourse to challenge such violations. In addition, oil and gas exploration now pervades every corner of the state, affecting both public and private lands in ways from which they will never recover.

Whether you are living in Colorado or just visiting, you have a stake in this issue. If you want your children and theirs to enjoy the activities described in this book—and to delight in and photograph the pristine places featured in these pages —then you must take action. Otherwise, neither Colorado's biodiversity nor its economy will survive the consequences of prolonging the progression of unfortunate changes that have ravaged the landscape in recent decades. If you live here, vote for issues that protect Colorado's natural heritage, and for candidates who have the foresight to propose such laws. Voice your opinions in letters to the editors of Colorado's newspapers. Be an advocate and let our elected leadership know your opinions via e-mail, fax, or phone. They are accessible. Have the courage to vote for your values, not just your pocketbook.

I hope this guide encourages you to spend time exploring Colorado. There is no substitute, not even photographs, for experiencing in the field the sensuousness of nature. The moments you spend outdoors will increase your enthusiasm for advocating the protection of our most beautiful of states.

—John Fielder

Summer wildflowers near Ohio Creek
(see Scenic Location No. 89, p. 267)

Denver skyline

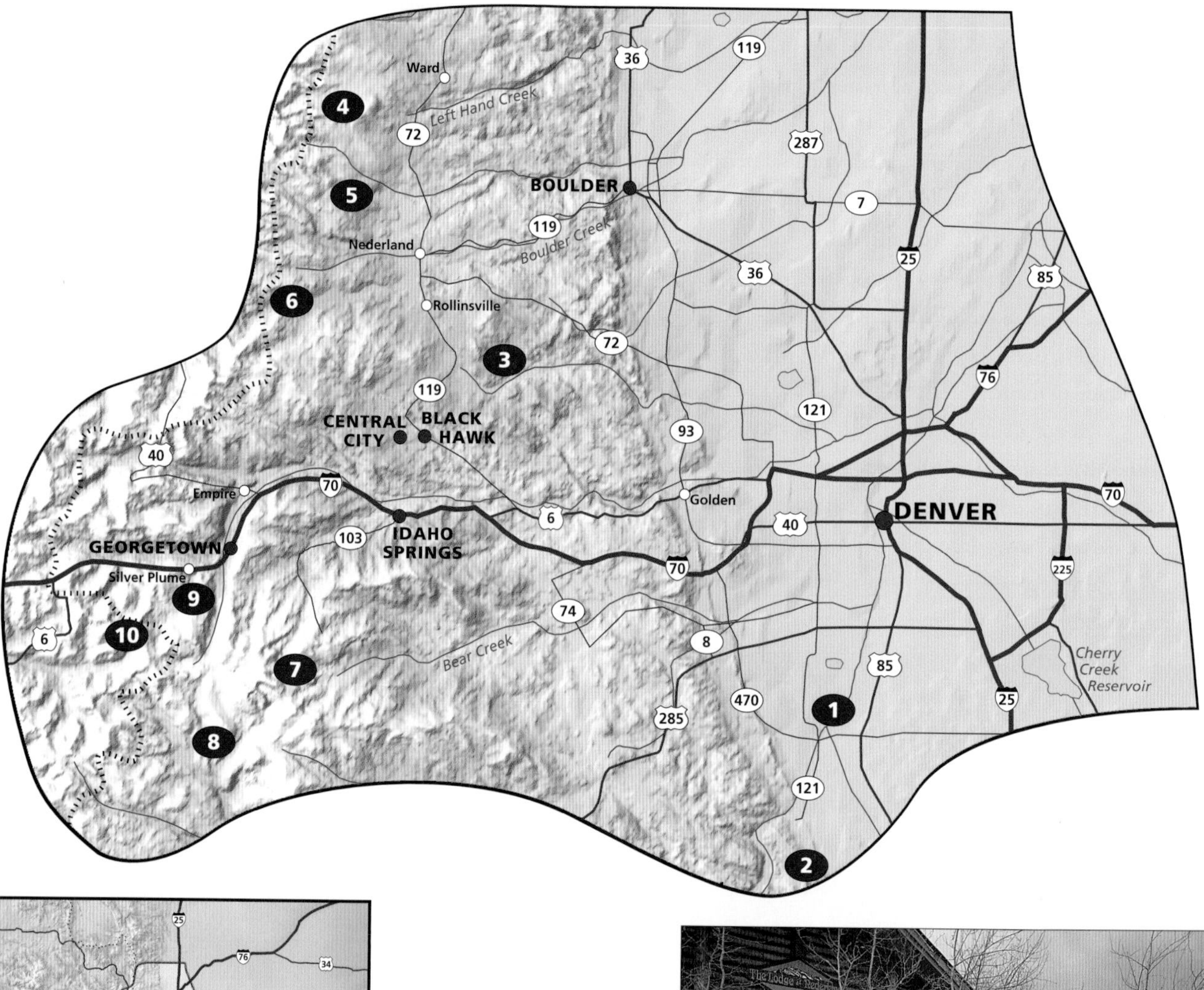

Best Western Lodge at Nederland

Denver & Vicinity

GATEWAY TO THE ROCKIES

Buffalo Herd Overlook, Genesee Park

The well-loved capital of Colorado, Denver is known as the Mile High City or the Queen City of the Plains, because it reigns over thousands of square miles that encircle its diverse neighborhoods. Residents enjoy the blue skies and quality of life in a city that has grown tremendously in the last decade. Denver delivers great museums and parks, historic districts, sports venues, summer events, and world-class dining and shopping. But the city also serves as the gateway to the West, providing visitors entertainment on the plains while they adjust to the mile-high altitude and desert-dry air. Denver and environs remain a fine introduction to the state. You can still glimpse the Old West here and there and appreciate the sometimes tricky negotiations that a recent go-go economy and development have made with a past both opulent and rough-and-tumble.

Hotel Boulderado, Boulder

Mountain visitors often take the well-traveled Interstate 70 out of Denver to the Rockies, ascending through hogbacks and ridges, leaving behind the foothills and the metropolitan area. A favorite stop for the Fielder family is the Buffalo Herd Overlook (Exit 254 at Genesee Park), where you may glimpse the bison and enjoy your first view of the peaks of the Continental Divide. As you proceed west, you will pass the yellow "gob piles" left over from the gold strikes of the 1880s. The town of Idaho Springs still wears a Western style and provides Front Rangers a natural thermal springs close to home. Listen for the shrill whistle of a steam engine along the narrow-gauge rails of the Georgetown Loop Railroad as you pass the quaint Victorian community of Georgetown. If you go no farther west, you still find a bracing historic legacy, scenic grandeur, wildlife, and plenty of recreational options.

Another well-traveled road out of Denver is US 36 to Boulder. Once a charming, quiet university town and bedroom community for Denver, Boulder today is bustling, stylish, and self-consciously progressive, with satellite communities of its own that have mushroomed in the last decade. The University of Colorado gives a cosmopolitan finish to the cultural enclave dubbed "Planet Boulder," where out-of-state students flock to the campus for the rarefied ambiance and proximity to the Rockies as much as the academics. A visit to Nederland, in western Boulder County, returns city dwellers to a slower-paced backcountry. South of Nederland, the historic towns of Central City and Black Hawk have tried their hand at gaming, with mixed results. Lady Luck has at least prevented their extinction. Smaller ski areas, stunning Rollins Pass, and a mining legacy also await nearby, an easy drive from the lights of the big city.

SCENIC LOCATIONS

Chautauqua Dining Hall, Boulder

Denver

Colorado Atlas & Gazetteer p. 40

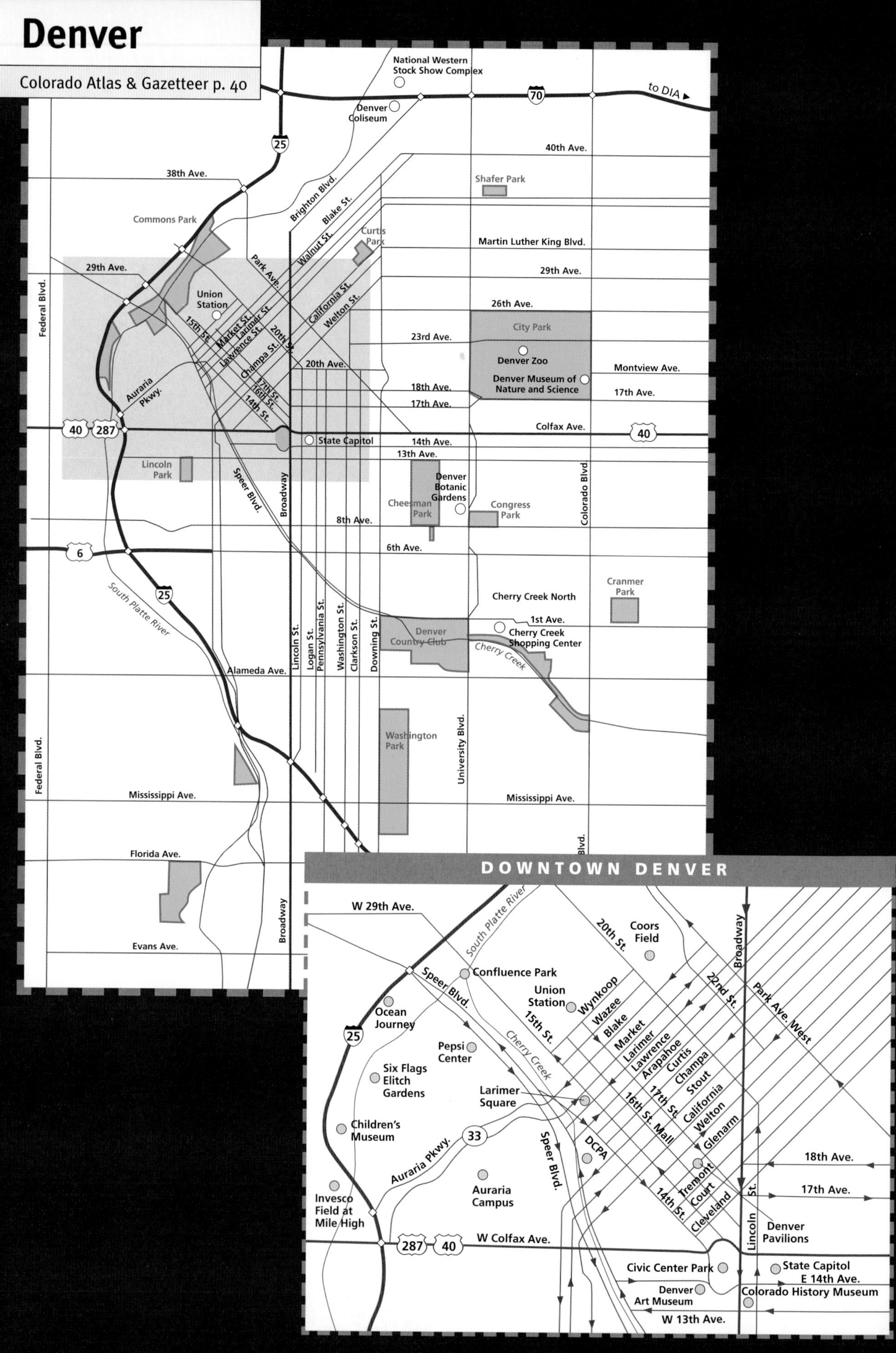
National Western Stock Show Complex
to DIA
70
Denver Coliseum
25
40th Ave.
38th Ave.
Shafer Park
Brighton Blvd.
Blake St.
Commons Park
Curtis Park
Walnut St.
Martin Luther King Blvd.
Park Ave.
29th Ave.
29th Ave.
Federal Blvd.
Union Station
California St.
Welton St.
26th Ave.
City Park
15th St.
Market St.
Larimer St.
Lawrence St.
20th St.
23rd Ave.
Champa St.
Denver Zoo
20th Ave.
Montview Ave.
Auraria Pkwy.
17th St.
16th St.
14th St.
Denver Museum of Nature and Science
18th Ave.
17th Ave.
17th Ave.
Colfax Ave.
40
287
40
State Capitol
14th Ave.
13th Ave.
Lincoln Park
Speer Blvd.
Broadway
Denver Botanic Gardens
Colorado Blvd
Cheesman Park
Congress Park
8th Ave.
6
6th Ave.
Cranmer Park
South Platte River
25
Cherry Creek North
1st Ave.
Denver Country Club
Cherry Creek Shopping Center
Cherry Creek
Lincoln St.
Logan St.
Pennsylvania St.
Washington St.
Clarkson St.
Downing St.
Alameda Ave.
Washington Park
University Blvd.
Federal Blvd.
Mississippi Ave.
Mississippi Ave.
Florida Ave.
Broadway
Evans Ave.
DOWNTOWN DENVER
W 29th Ave.
South Platte River
Coors Field
20th St.
Confluence Park
Speer Blvd.
Union Station
Wynkoop
Wazee
Blake
Market
Larimer
Lawrence
Arapahoe
Curtis
Champa
Stout
California
Welton
Glenarm
Tremont
Court
Cleveland
22nd St.
Broadway
Park Ave. West
Ocean Journey
15th St.
25
Pepsi Center
Cherry Creek
Six Flags Elitch Gardens
Larimer Square
17th St.
16th St. Mall
Children's Museum
33
Speer Blvd.
DCPA
18th Ave.
Auraria Pkwy.
Auraria Campus
14th St.
17th Ave.
Lincoln St.
Invesco Field at Mile High
Denver Pavilions
287
40
W Colfax Ave.
Civic Center Park
State Capitol
E 14th Ave.
Denver Art Museum
Colorado History Museum
W 13th Ave.

Denver

Some people think of me as a wilderness-only kind of guy, but I've always enjoyed the easy transition Colorado allows from the wilds of its backcountry to the amenities of its cities. Whether Denver is your home, your final vacation destination, or a stopover to adjust to the altitude before heading into the mountains, you'll find a vibrant city by turns raucous and urbane. Denver has lively, colorful parks and jazzy late-night venues. It mixes topflight performing arts with funky street fairs. It includes recreation along Cherry Creek and the South Platte River, diverse restaurants and shops, stately historic districts, and distinctive neighborhoods. Sports bars proliferate around town. But you can also find rabid sports fans at fine-art galleries and sophisticated types sipping suds at colorful dives.

Denver has changed a lot in the last few years. It rejuvenated and rebuilt existing neighborhoods and added entirely new neighborhoods at the old Stapleton airport, the former Air Force base at Lowry, and along the South Platte River. It has built three world-class sports stadiums, greatly expanded the central public library, and opened a spanking-new airport. The 1990s population boom transformed Denver forever from a sleepy cattle town where businessmen kicked around in cowboy boots to a major player in the cable, communications, and space industries.

Downtown is the starting point for any appreciation of the city. Look at a map and you can identify it by that weird weave of streets laid at an angle to the rest of town. Here you'll find established and new retail areas, historic buildings alongside modern skyscrapers, a pedestrian mall, a major performing-arts center, and more. But you may also want to spend time in its parks and outer shopping districts, at its museums and neighborhood restaurants, and along the recreational paths at Cherry Creek, the South Platte River, and the Highline Canal.

History

Blame Denver on a few flakes of gold found near the confluence of the South Platte River and Cherry Creek in 1858. Although placer mining—panning for gold in streams—soon played out on the South Platte, rich gold strikes near Central City and Idaho Springs in 1859 funded Denver's first boom. The tough little town that began as two gold camps, Auraria and Denver City, survived a major flood and two fires. When trains arrived in 1870, Denver began to thrive as a supply and transportation center for both the gold towns due west and the cattle ranches and farms to the north, south, and east. Throughout the 1880s, brick, stucco, and sandstone mansions sprang up in Denver's Capitol Hill. The Browns and Tabors of Leadville moved here to conduct business and to join Denver's thickening upper crust. Colorado's mineral riches built parks, fountains, and statues.

As the gold wealth declined, so did Denver's economy. When the government stopped guaranteeing the price of silver in 1893, Denver's first boom sadly greeted its first bust. Luckily, Denver has had no shortage of mayors with vision. Robert Speer in the early years of the 20th century closed down the red-light district and established Denver's outstanding parks system. He built many of the tree-lined avenues we enjoy today, including Speer Boulevard along Cherry Creek. Ben Stapleton established the city's first airport and made innumerable upgrades around town. Federico F. Peña, mayor from 1983 to 1991 and later U.S. Secretary of Transportation and Secretary of Energy, spearheaded the construction of the ambitious Denver International Airport (DIA). Three-term Mayor Wellington E. Webb has overseen the civic improvements of the last decade.

In that time, Denver has become a major trade and tourism center with a real concern for quality of life. Citizens have passed bond issues to improve parks and expand libraries. City planners opened up the Central Platte Valley, long an eyesore, to parks and residential development. Voters underwrote three new major-league arenas: Coors Field for Colorado Rockies baseball, Invesco Field at Mile High (replacing beloved Mile High Stadium) for Denver Broncos football and Colorado Rapids soccer, and the Pepsi Center (a.k.a. "the Can") for Denver Nuggets basketball and Colorado Avalanche hockey. New housing has also transformed landscapes in all directions from Denver.

Despite increasing congestion, great strides have been made to clean up Denver's infamous "brown cloud" of smoggy air. And after long disuse, Denver once again has local trains, the success of its first "light rail" streetcar lines exceeding expectations. The enormous, multiyear "T-Rex" construction project on I-25 and I-225 will blend vehicle lanes with light rail, returning rail to its essential place in this Western town that has come into its own as a great city.

Main Attractions

BROWN PALACE HOTEL

Presidents, movie stars, and the Beatles have stayed at this elegant hotel, constructed in 1892 of sandstone and rare Colorado red granite. A Colorado landmark, it reflects the opulence of times past and present. Gaze up from the lobby into the nine-story atrium to see the wrought-iron railings and Tiffany stained-glass ceiling. Nowadays, such luxury goes hand-in-hand with every high-tech convenience.

Brown Palace Hotel, Denver

Each January, the Champion Steer from the National Western Stock Show (see Special Events, p. 35) makes the Brown the Cow Palace, as the steer parades through the lobby and takes a perch on display—with carpet protection, of course. If beef on the hoof isn't your cup of oolong, stop in for **Tea at The Brown Palace** ($$), held afternoons in the elegant lobby with scones, sandwiches, and pastries. The charming, informal **Ship Tavern** ($$) serves crisp salads and thick sandwiches, seafood, and steaks; **Churchill Bar** is the ultimate Denver cigar bar. **Ellyngton's** ($$-$$$) serves American cuisine for breakfast and lunch and hosts the finest Sunday Champagne Brunch in town. **The Palace Arms** ($$$-$$$$), set in an exceptional, historic dining room, is also one of the finest restaurants in Colorado. Treat yourself with a selection from the celebrated wine list. Jackets are required at dinner. *321 17th St., 303-297-3111, 800-321-2599, www.brownpalace.com.*

DENVER CENTER FOR THE PERFORMING ARTS

On any given night, the DCPA could be hosting a symphony concert, several dramatic and comedy productions, and a Broadway road show. **Denver Performing Arts Complex** is one of the largest arts complexes under one roof anywhere:

COLORADO CAMEO

Molly Brown

If you think the myth of Molly Brown is interesting, you should hear the real story. First of all her nickname wasn't Molly, it was Maggie. And she was generally liked by Denver society, not loathed. And she didn't burn up her husband's nest egg in a stove in Leadville. And when she gave parties at their house on Pennsylvania Street in Denver, people jumped at the chance to visit the home of this multilingual, self-educated, compassionate, lifesaving gentlewoman.

One thing Mrs. Brown did do was board the luxurious *Titanic* in 1912 for its maiden—and final—voyage, and live to tell about it. In fact, it made her a celebrity. Because of the popular 1964 film *The Unsinkable Molly Brown* (based on a Broadway musical), nearly everyone has heard of Denver's rags-to-riches socialite. Though the top-grossing 1997 film, *Titanic,* greatly increased her fame, viewers learned but little about Mrs. Brown. Unfortunately, what most know about her is either dead wrong or so exaggerated as to constitute pure fiction.

She was known as Mrs. Margaret Tobin Brown, "Maggie" to intimates. Her husband, James Joseph "J.J." Brown, was not an ignorant prospector but a clever engineer. His invention of a better method of hard-rock mining so impressed the owners of the Little Jonny Mine—which J.J. supervised—that they gave him a one-eighth share of the proceeds, which made him a millionaire. Further, Mrs. Brown was never so utterly rejected by Denver society as the *Unsinkable* movie and musical portray her to be. But she was never fully accepted either, which probably had as much to do with her religion (Catholicism) and her politics (sympathetic to labor) as it did her background of poverty in newly rich Denver.

Born in Missouri in 1867 to a ditch-digging, Irish-immigrant father, Maggie managed to receive an 8th-grade-level education, rare for a woman of her time. She followed one of her two brothers on a wagon trail west to gold-crazy Leadville, where she worked as a salesclerk. She and J.J. met and married in 1886, struck gold in 1893, and decamped to their Denver manse in 1894. Maggie loved learning and began hiring tutors when she still lived in Leadville to teach her foreign languages as well as literature, art, theater, and music.

Just how aspiring they (at least Maggie) were is apparent as soon as visitors catch sight of the Denver mansion. Like Mrs. Brown herself, the home is a standout: a three-story, stone-walled extravaganza trimmed out in balconies, porches, gables, and highfalutin shingle-work. Bookcases and sumptuous furnishings fill the residence. Maggie and J.J. didn't have a happy marriage, however; while she was outgoing and ambitious, he was reserved and spent most of his time with his work. They separated in 1909 but remained respectful friends. In 1910, she was one of the few women permitted to attend New York's Carnegie Institute; she also began to travel extensively.

Which brings us to the *Titanic.* When she sailed from England on April 12, 1912, Maggie was one of 2,223 people on board. Two days later, at 11:40 p.m., the lookout spotted an iceberg 1,600 feet ahead, but the 882-foot-long ship couldn't steer clear in time. The scene that ensued must have been both terrifying and bizarre: The orchestra playing to calm passengers' nerves; the crew blocking the third-class doors so poorer passengers couldn't escape; staff sending up emergency flares which the nearby *California* took for celebratory fireworks; lifeboats built to save 65 people casting off with only 28 aboard.

While attempting to help some lower-class passengers to escape, Maggie was thrown into Lifeboat No. 6 with 20 other women and three men. She took control immediately—as the steward in charge was, in her words, "a sorry excuse for a man"—and ordered those aboard to row away from the sinking luxury liner. The *Titanic* went down with 1,465 people at 2:20 a.m., but the little lifeboat remained afloat.

She was, indeed, unsinkable. In fact, it was Maggie who gave herself that moniker. Asked how she had survived the great shipwreck, when so many others had perished, she reportedly replied, "Typical Brown luck. We're unsinkable." The Molly Brown House showcases the story of the *Titanic,* including photographs, Maggie's $27,000 insurance claim, and evidence of her charity not seen in any production. On the boat ride to New York, Maggie raised money for the less well-to-do survivors. Perhaps Maggie deserves a bit of Molly's fame.

The eight venues here have a total of more than 10,000 seats. The Bonfils Theatre Complex houses four stages for productions by the resident Denver Center Theatre Co.; Seawell Grand Ballroom hosts single events; Boettcher Concert Hall cradles listeners for the Colorado Symphony and Opera Colorado; the Buell Theatre presents Broadway shows; the historic Auditorium Theatre seats 2,065 for edgier popular acts; and the tiny, 210-seat Garner Galleria Theater presents local productions. The four-block complex is located between Speer Boulevard and 14th at Curtis Street. *303-893-4100, www.denvercenter.org.*

HISTORIC MANSIONS

As the foremost Colorado town and state capital, Denver has long been the address for upscale living in the state. East 8th Avenue and the East 7th Avenue Parkway, among other corridors, afford the chance to admire fine residences from the street. Certain prominent homes, however, are open to the public and afford a taste of the good life of a bygone era.

By far the most famous of these mansions is the **Molly Brown House** at 1340 Pennsylvania St. J.J. and Maggie—who is incorrectly called Molly—Brown bought this stone mansion in 1894. Guides dressed in period costumes tell the story of the Browns and point out interior design features: stone lions, ornate fixtures, leather wallpaper, and an attic ballroom. Clearly, the robust Mrs. Brown enjoyed the high life. The gift shop has excellent *Titanic* and Molly Brown memorabilia. *1340 Pennsylvania St., 303-832-4092, www.mollybrown.org.*

Molly Brown House, Denver

The **Governor's Mansion,** the official residence of Colorado's governor and first family, is more properly known as the Colorado Executive Residence. The red-brick mansion was built by Walter Cheesman and sold to the Boettcher family, which donated it to the state. Short tours are available from May through August, highlighting the grand public rooms. *Corner of 8th Avenue and Logan Street, 303-866-3682.*

Another outstanding residence, the **Byers-Evans House Museum** adjoins the Denver Art Museum and gives a feel for how the neighborhood used to be. This 1883 Victorian structure was once owned by the colorful William N. Byers, founder of the *Rocky Mountain News,* as well as William Gray Evans of the Denver Tramway Co. and subsequent generations of the Evans family. You'll gain a strong sense of what Denver was like for the well-to-do during the World War I era. *1310 Bannock St., 303-620-4933, www.coloradohistory.org.*

LARIMER SQUARE

The first block of downtown to be spared the urban renewal wrecking ball and made a historic district, Larimer Square (the 1400 block of Larimer Street) has become a Denver landmark. Admire the fine old façades that are the pride of the local preservation movement. Dining concepts come and go here, though some are standouts: **Rioja** ($$-$$$) for innovative Mediterranean *(1433 Larimer St., 303-820-2282),* **Red Square Euro Bistro** ($$) for elegant stroganoff and goulash *(1512 Larimer St., 303-595-8600),* and **The Market** ($) for coffee, pastries, deli items, and people watching *(1445 Larimer St., 303-534-5140).* Boutiques, name-brand shops, and live music and comedy nightspots help bring in students, young urban sophisticates, and even Denver's upscale Harley-Davidson riders. Events occur in the area throughout the year, including a summer performance series and Oktoberfest and Winterfest celebrations. *303-534-2367, www.larimersquare.com.*

LOWER DOWNTOWN (LODO)

The heart of Denver is its lower downtown area, called LoDo. This is where Denver began as a mining camp and tent city in 1859. The once boarded-up warehouses, with their fine brickwork, arcaded façades, and decorative details (long since dispensed with on commercial buildings), define the historic district here. One by one the warehouses have been restored, and the area is now a prestigious, mixed residential and commercial neighborhood. Art galleries, live-music nightspots and clubs, taverns from tony to funky to all-sports-all-the-time, upscale shops, coffeehouses, and fine restaurants now occupy what was once essentially Denver's Skid Row. Many buildings have been renovated into stylish lofts and offices. New construction in LoDo now complements the style of the older stock. *www.lodo.org.*

Notice the historical markers on the vintage buildings, then stop at the LoDo branch of the **Tattered Cover Book Store,** housed in another former mercantile warehouse (complete with elevated tram entrance). Purchase a neighborhood walking tour guidebook or drink coffee and read in a wingback chair. *1628 16th St., 303-436-1070, www.tatteredcover.com.*

The **Oxford Hotel** (see Accommodations, p. 35) is as historic as it gets in Colorado. It had the state's first elevator (which has been updated, thankfully), and the piano in the lobby was Baby Doe Tabor's. Stop in the stylish Cruise Room to see an original Art Deco cocktail lounge with playful panels depicting drinking toasts, or dine on seafood at McCormick's.

Oxford Hotel, Denver

Union Station witnessed much history during the heyday of the railroads and is making a comeback as a light-rail hub. On winter Saturday and Sunday mornings, you can board the Ski Train from here to Winter Park Ski Resort (see Winter Park, p. 174). When you return in the evening, LoDo's numerous taverns and restaurants await. *1701 Wynkoop St.; Ski Train, 303-296-4754, www.skitrain.com.*

The first ball was thrown at brick-clad **Coors Field** in April 1995, heralding the arrival of pro baseball in LoDo and the renaissance of the neighborhood. Coors Field's impressive design complements and anchors the LoDo scene, and spending a day at the ballgame is now a favorite Denver pastime.

MUSEUMS

Denver Art Museum is the fortress of fine art in Denver. Built in 1970, this gray-tiled castle-keep designed by architect Gio Ponti houses traveling exhibits, along with more than 30,000 objects and one of the foremost collections of Native American arts and crafts in the country. Also see the fine Asian, Oceanic, pre-Columbian, and Spanish Colonial collections. Ever-popular European painting is well represented, as are photography and local contemporary art. DAM also houses an impressive gathering of late 20th-century furniture, architectural drawings, and high-style everyday objects. Following its tradition of modern design, the museum's new addition, which was finally completed in late 2006, promises to be among the most exhilarating new public buildings in the country. *100 W. 14th Ave., 720-865-5000, www.denverartmuseum.org.*

Denver Art Museum

Colorado History Museum showcases many images by my esteemed predecessor in Colorado outdoor photography, William Henry Jackson. (In my book *Colorado 1870– 2000*, I rephotographed many of Jackson's 19th-century scenes, comparing the Colorado landscape then and now.) In addition, the museum features state history dioramas and artifacts, showcasing native tribes, explorers, pioneers, miners, and cowboys. This is the largest collection of Colorado history in the state. *1300 Broadway, 303-866-3682, www.coloradohistory.org.*

Colorado History Museum, Denver

At **The Children's Museum of Denver,** you don't have to worry about your little ones breaking something; exhibits and displays are meant to be touched and played with, even by the youngest children. Cut the kids loose on the KidSlope ski hill, the CompuLab computer learning center, puppet shows, a child-size grocery store, and other fun displays. *2121 Children's Museum Dr., 303-433-7444, www.cmdenver.org.*

Visit the **Black American West Museum and Heritage Center** to honor the contributions of African-American cowboys to the drama of the American West. In fact, one in every three cowpunchers was black. Intriguing historic photographs tell the story of black Americans on the Western frontier. The museum's location is the former home of Dr. Justina Ford, the first female African-American doctor licensed in Colorado (see Colorado Cameo, opposite). *3055 California St., 303-292-2566, www.blackamericanwestmuseum.com.*

Denver Museum of Nature and Science houses a fine collection of dinosaur and mammal fossils, including that of a very large mammoth. A huge Tyrannosaurus Rex skeleton greets you at the ticket counter. Prehistoric Journey traces Earth's history with do-not-touch genuine fossils and hands-on displays. Famous for its 80 dioramas of animals from all corners of the earth, the museum also has an extensive butterfly and insect collection. The centerpiece of the mineral and gem collection is Tom's Baby—at 14 pounds 10 ounces, the largest gold nugget ever mined in Colorado. The popular **IMAX Theater** here offers larger-than-life nature and adventure films on its four-story screen. Recently added, the all-digital **Gates Planetarium** has semi-reclining seats for an immersive experience. The museum also has traveling and special exhibits. *2001 Colorado Blvd. in City Park, 303-322-7009, www.dmns.org.*

Smaller museums also vie for visitors' attention. At **Four Mile Historic Park,** you can see a pioneer farm complete with animals and crops in the midst of the city. Built in 1859, Four Mile House, a former stage stop, is the oldest building in Denver. *715 S. Forest, 720-865-0800.* **Mizel Museum of Judaica** presents exhibits on the worldwide Jewish experience and tradition. *400 S Kearney, 303-394-9993.* **Golda Meir House** on the Auraria Campus was the Israeli prime minister's Denver childhood home. *1146 9th St. Park, Auraria Campus, 303-556-3220 for appointment.* Doll fanciers must see the **Denver Museum of Miniatures, Dolls and Toys.** *1880 Gaylord St., 303-322-1053, www.dmmdt.org.* Denver's rich Latino heritage is celebrated at **Museo de las Américas** in Denver's Hispanic cultural hub. *861 Santa Fe Dr., 303-571-4401, www.museo.org.*

PARKS AND GARDENS

Denver's public spaces and gardens distinguish it from other burgs its size. The city maintains its own greenhouses, where gardeners cultivate more than 240,000 plants to populate the city's 500 flowerbeds. Fine places to enjoy these annual plantings are at small, quiet **Alamo Placita Park,** at the intersection of Speer Boulevard and Emerson Street, and at popular **Washington Park,** which boasts two lakes and healthy quantities of families, cyclists, dogs, and players of tennis and all manner of field games. **City Park** is a fine spot to relax on the green beneath mature trees, take a paddleboat ride or fish on Ferril Lake, see stately statues, and hear free jazz concerts in the summer. Adjoining the Denver Museum of Nature and Science and the Denver Zoo, City Park also boasts the Laredo Taft–designed Thatcher Fountain, a lakeside Italianate pavilion, and a golf course. Take a stroll on the gravel path around **Cheesman Park** and enjoy the views of both mountains and city from the neoclassical, white-marble pavilion. **Confluence Park** is another civic jewel not to be missed (see Activities, p. 27). A city-sponsored classical concert series is held at various park locations each summer. *Denver Parks & Recreation, 720-913-0696.*

At the southeast end of the 16th Street Mall (just hop on a free shuttle) is **Civic Center Park,** built on the design principles of the City Beautiful Movement of the early 20th century. You can stroll among the pillared curves of the Greek Amphitheater, the location for major annual events (see Special Events, p. 35), and walk beside the geometric flower beds and fountains. The similarly curved Denver City and County Building graces the west end of the park; visit between Thanksgiving and the end of January to see an amazing holiday display of thousands of lights. (Christmas lights were invented in Denver.) To the east is the imposing State Capitol (see p. 27). To the south lie two other remarkable structures: the Denver Art Museum (see Museums, opposite) and the eye-popping, new-with-old Denver Public Library, designed in 1995 by architect Michael Graves.

Denver Botanic Gardens tends a fine variety of themed gardens in an elegant setting. Here, 17,000 plant species, some from as far away as South Africa and Australia, thrive on 23 acres beside Cheesman Park. An Alpine Garden, full of tundra species, blooms in one corner, while the Japanese Tea Garden conveys a sense of serenity in another. The Children's Secret Path Garden, with tunnels and a maze, is also popular. Within the conservatory you can stroll through a dense rainforest. Denver Botanic Gardens offers classes, lectures, guided tours, a café, a popular Kid Camp, and an intimate series of summer concerts. *1005 York St., 720-865-3500, www.botanicgardens.org.*

COLORADO CAMEO "Aunt" Clara Brown and Justina Ford

While black cowboys were making their contribution to the settling of the West, black women were making their own—in Denver, most notably Clara Brown (left) and Justina Ford.

"Aunt" Clara Brown, as she was called, was born into slavery in Virginia, probably between 1800 and 1806. She was never sure of the exact date, but she remembered being a "good-sized girl" during the War of 1812. A Kentucky landowner named Ambrose Smith owned her from 1809 until his death in 1856, after which Brown and her family were sold to different plantations.

Brown bought her freedom in 1856 for $120. She moved to St. Louis, Missouri, and then went on to Leavenworth, Kansas. It was there that she joined up with a party heading to Denver. Because she had no money, she earned her keep cooking for the others in the group.

One of the first black women to settle in gold-crazy Colorado, Brown opened a laundry in Central City, where she was able to save money and perform numerous acts of charity. She nursed the sick, helped to establish St. James Methodist Church in Central City, and provided food and shelter to people in need—becoming known far and wide for her generosity. She even took her ministries on the road, visiting Kansas to help freed slaves become farmers.

At nearly 80, she was asked when she had last seen her husband. She replied, "I can't recollect just when. He was sold nearly 30 years ago. I don't know where they took him. I had four children, too, darlin'. They sold them, too." In 1882, three years before her death, Brown was reunited with Eliza Jane, one of her daughters.

You can see "Aunt" Clara Brown's face in one of the stained-glass windows at the Colorado State Capitol (see State Capitol, p. 27). Her good works were so cherished that the legislature voted her a place of honor there.

Justina L. Ford was the first female African-American doctor licensed to practice in Colorado. She was born in Knoxville, Illinois, in 1871, and grew up in Galesburg, Illinois. According to stories, she was called to be involved in healing from a young age. She graduated from a medical college in Chicago and began her practice in Alabama; four years later, Justina Ford moved to Denver.

Known as "The Lady Doctor," Dr. Ford delivered more than 5,000 babies in her long career. It wasn't easy. She faced uphill battles almost daily as a black woman practicing in a profession dominated by white males.

During much of her career, Dr. Ford was not allowed to practice at Denver General Hospital because of her race, even though she was a member of the Denver Medical Society, the Colorado Medical Society, and the American Medical Society. Even as late as 1950 she was the only female black doctor practicing in Colorado—one of seven black doctors in the state. Dr. Justina Ford passed away in 1952; in 1975 Denver's Ford-Warren Branch Library was renamed to honor her trailblazing achievements.

While the Denver Botanic Gardens are international in scope, **Hudson Gardens** features only plants native to Colorado's arid climate. Sixteen distinct gardens follow in succession on a delightful pathway: cascading streams, conifer groves, wildflower meadows, water gardens, woodlands, wetlands, and even a secret garden. One of my favorite spots is the Fragrance Garden, planted with aromatic flowers. *6115 S. Santa Fe Dr., Littleton, 303-797-8565, www.hudsongardens.org.*

South Platte Park showcases the lovely South Platte River (see Scenic Location No. 1, p. 29). *7301 S. Platte River Pkwy., Littleton, 303-730-1022.*

SHOPPING

A free shuttle bus conveys you along a charming, tree-lined retail corridor that's seen many improvements in recent years: the **16th Street Mall.** The glorious 1910 **D&F Tower** at Arapahoe Street, the highest structure in the city for 50 years, is reason enough to visit. But along 16th Street you'll also find every type of eating, dining, and entertainment option, along with prime retail districts at its northwest and southeast ends (yes, downtown lies at a funny angle to the rest of the city). Start southeast at the Civic Center Station at Broadway. Make your first stop **Denver Pavilions** at Tremont Place. Get your sneakers and gear, CDs and DVDs, fine chocolate and cigars; enjoy deli, Italian, and California cuisine; see a movie at the multiplex; or just gawk at the buskers entertaining crowds on the streetfront. At the next stop, Glenarm Place, check out the 1930, stone-clad **Paramount Theatre,** still one of the top venues in town. Continue northwest on 16th Street to Lawrence Street, where you can stop to visit the **Tabor Center.** This glass-enclosed mini-mall recently underwent an extensive renovation. Thirty stores and restaurants here provide downtown shopping safe from the elements. Your next stop is Larimer Street; two blocks left lies **Larimer Square** (see p. 23), where the downtown scene begins to sizzle. At Market Street, land in **LoDo** (see p. 23), the revitalized old heart of the city.

A survey by the Denver Metro Convention & Visitors Bureau showed that the mall—not pro sports or museums, not Coors or Molly Brown—is Denver's top destination for visitors, specifically the **Cherry Creek Shopping Center,** located at East 1st Avenue and Milwaukee Street. And no wonder: Denver's in-town mall has more than 140 stores, including major department stores, gourmet restaurants, galleries, movie theaters, and every kind of specialty shop you can imagine.

Photo credit: Bill Bonebrake

Larimer Square, Denver

North of the mall is a shopping district as distinctive and elegant as any in town. **Cherry Creek North,** comprising more than 330 businesses from 1st to 3rd avenues and University Boulevard to Steele Street, is a major destination. Art galleries, clothing boutiques, specialty shops, top restaurants, and outdoor cafés cover this high-end district.

For more shopping, drive south to **Park Meadows** at I-25 and County Line Road. The 160 stores here are arrayed along an interior street imagined after a timbered mountain resort; brass and copper fixtures light the stone floors, while a crackling fireplace and overstuffed furniture add to the lodge atmosphere. *8401 Park Meadows Center Dr., Littleton, 303-792-2533.*

In June 2006, Denver's famous flagship **Tattered Cover Book Store** moved from Cherry Creek North to the historic Lowenstein Theater on Colfax at Elizabeth, the store's first move since opening in 1971. "Tattered"—as natives call the stores—is still the definitive Denver book store, including an exemplary children's section (also see LoDo, p. 23). *2526 E. Colfax Ave., 303-322-7727, www.tatteredcover.com.*

The **Art District on Santa Fe** along Santa Fe Drive draws over 2,000 visitors on the first Friday of every month for its Art Walk, a chance to browse the highest concentration of galleries in the nation. *www.artdistrictonsantafe.com.* This artist's hot spot is the new home of my gallery, **John Fielder's Colorado.** *833 S. Santa Fe Dr., 303-744-7979, www.johnfielder.com.*

For dining, entertainment, and discount shopping west of Denver, head to **Colorado Mills.** *14500 W. Colfax Ave., Lakewood, 303-384-3000, www.coloradomills.com.*

Colorado's flagship **REI** store, though, stands out because of its fabulous quarters. This red-brick structure, the city's former tramway powerhouse, perches above Confluence Park. Refitted for retail, the store is the place to upgrade your outdoor equipment and even cut loose on a supervised climbing wall. *1416 Platte St., 303-756-3100, www.rei.com.*

SPORTS EVENTS

Coloradans love their professional sports teams. They watch the Denver Broncos every Sunday during football season. They thrill to see the Colorado Avalanche whack the puck in hockey's Stanley Cup playoffs. They follow the pitching and catching practice when the Colorado Rockies go to Tucson for spring training camp, cheer on the Rapids, and have agonized for years over the Denver Nuggets NBA team. Denver is one of only a few cities to host all five major sports franchises.

In 2001 the **Denver Broncos** moved to more spacious quarters in the new Invesco Field at Mile High, next to the site of the old, beloved Mile High Stadium. Bronco tickets are hard to get; one place to look is in the newspaper classified ads. *720-258-3333, www.denverbroncos.com.* The **Colorado Rapids** soccer team also plays at Invesco Field. The Rapids have won the American Professional Soccer League Championship several times. *303-825-GOAL, www.coloradorapids.com.*

Although hockey came only recently to Denver, Coloradans have taken to the **Colorado Avalanche** in a big way. The Avs have captured hockey's coveted Stanley Cup twice: first in 1996, the year they moved here, and again in 2001, proving the first win was no fluke. *303-830-8497, http://avalanche.nhl.com.* While the **Denver Nuggets** have yet to reward fans with a championship, they often play exciting ball, and the antics of the mascot, Rocky, amaze young and old alike. *303-830-8497; Pepsi Center: 303-405-1111, www.pepsicenter.com.*

Colorado Rockies home games are the place to be on a sunny afternoon. The Rockies play at Coors Field, an elegant brick and ironwork ballpark that epitomizes the LoDo neighborhood. *Coors Field, 800-388-7625, www.coloradorockies.com.*

Colorado State Capitol

STATE CAPITOL

The gold leaf covering the Capitol's dome (47 ounces of 24-karat gold) symbolizes the central role that natural resources have played in Colorado's development. Look for the brass disc marking the exact step where you reach 5,280 feet—one mile—above sea level, explaining Denver's moniker, the Mile-High City. Nearly the world's entire supply of Colorado onyx, a rare stone found near Beulah, Colo., was used for the Capitol's interior paneling. The colorful native marble and stained-glass windows give a history of Colorado and honor outstanding Coloradans. Often there is a special exhibit on display. When the legislature is in session (January through mid-May), visitors may look on at government in action. *200 E. Colfax Ave., 303-866-2604, www.colorado.gov/.*

Activities

AMUSEMENT PARKS

For more than a century in its northwest Denver location, Elitch Gardens provided an amusing mix of heart-pounding thrill rides, carnival fun, lush botanic gardens, summer stock theater, and live musical entertainment. In 1995 it moved onto more spacious acreage in the Central Platte Valley near downtown and became **Six Flags Elitch Gardens.** The thrill rides are better than ever. Beware the XLR8R and its terrifying free-fall. Be warned about the Mind Eraser. Be glad when the kids have had enough and you can merely loop-de-loop around the Twister II, a superlative wooden roller coaster. Elitch's also includes the 10-acre Island Kingdom Water Park, which has water slides, tube rides, and the 28,000-square-foot Commotion Ocean wave pool. Younger kids enjoy the five-story tree house in Hook's Lagoon. *2000 Elitch Cir., 303-595-4386, www.elitchgardens.com.*

One of the best things about summer here are the long, dry days. And one of the best ways to spend a hot afternoon is playing in the liquid at **Water World.** Enjoy two immense wave pools, slides, inner tube rides, and plenty of wet ways to cool off. *1800 W. 89th Ave., Federal Heights, 303-427-SURF, www.waterworldcolorado.com.*

BREWERIES

Coors Brewery in Golden is the largest single brewing facility in the world. Nearly 500,000 people a year take the tour of this pristine, high-tech facility, passing the 15,000-gallon copper kettles, smelling the hops and barley, and feeling the chill required to keep the beer fresh in the packing and shipping areas. After all that anticipation, sample a draft in the tasting room. To get to Coors from Denver, take US 6 west to Golden and follow signs to the brewery. *1221 Ford St., Golden, 303-277-2337, www.coors.com.*

As recently as 1990, Denver had more microbreweries than any other city. (Portland has since overtaken us in the suds department.) **Wynkoop Brewing Company** ($$) is the granddaddy of Denver's microbrewery scene and the nexus of LoDo nightlife, located in one of the more impressive of the historic district's distinctive, converted red-brick warehouses. Try a sampler set of its stouts, ambers, wheats, and ales, all brewed on site. Lighter items and salads supplement the pub fare. *1634 18th St., 303-297-2700, www.wynkoop.com.* If you're on the 16th Street Mall on a warm summer day, plan a sip-stop at **Rock Bottom Brewery.** Sit in the sunshine, sample the brews, and enjoy some fine people-watching near the D&F Tower. *1001 16th St., 303-534-7616, www.rockbottom.com.* After a baseball game, or before, sports fans choose **Breckenridge Brewery,** offering several flavors and a full-service menu. *2220 Blake St., 303-297-3644, www.breckenridgebrewery.com.*

BUTTERFLY PAVILION AND INSECT CENTER

Kids and adults both can get happily buggy at this cultural treasure, but resist the urge to slap anything that lands on you! The Butterfly Pavilion houses 60 species of butterflies and educates visitors about the need to conserve butterfly and invertebrate habitats. One of a just a few butterfly aviaries in the country, walk amongst and enjoy these winged beauties during their twice-daily releases. Kids can also handle hairy tarantulas, see the undulating giant centipede, and recoil from the Madagascar hissing cockroach! *6252 W. 104th Ave., Westminster, 303-469-5441, www.butterflies.org.*

CONFLUENCE PARK AND DENVER'S BICYCLE PATHS

No visit to Denver would be complete without a short trip to Denver's birthplace, **Confluence Park,** where Cherry Creek meets the South Platte River. Prospectors once panned for gold where families now picnic; cyclists, in-line skaters, and joggers share trail space with pedestrians; dogs cool down in the shallows; and kayakers paddle a short whitewater course. Two of Denver's three major paved trails meet here, favorite haunts of active folks and even wildlife watchers.

Continued on page 30

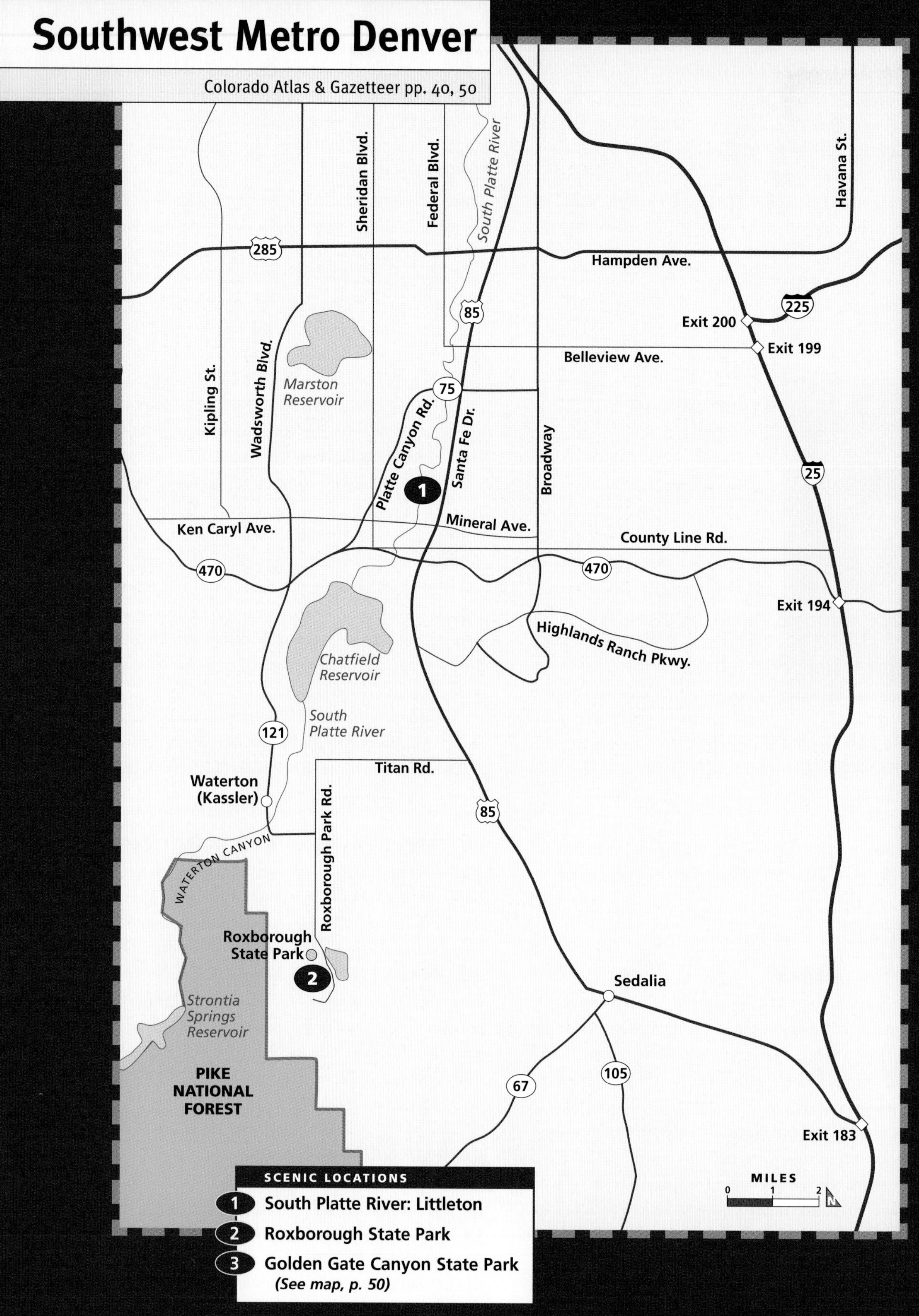
Southwest Metro Denver
Colorado Atlas & Gazetteer pp. 40, 50
Sheridan Blvd.
Federal Blvd.
South Platte River
Havana St.
285
Hampden Ave.
85
225
Exit 200
Exit 199
Belleview Ave.
Marston Reservoir
Kipling St.
Wadsworth Blvd.
75
Platte Canyon Rd.
Santa Fe Dr.
Broadway
25
1
Ken Caryl Ave.
Mineral Ave.
County Line Rd.
470
470
Exit 194
Highlands Ranch Pkwy.
Chatfield Reservoir
South Platte River
121
Titan Rd.
Waterton (Kassler)
85
Roxborough Park Rd.
Waterton Canyon
Roxborough State Park
2
Sedalia
Strontia Springs Reservoir
PIKE NATIONAL FOREST
67
105
Exit 183
MILES
0
1
2
N
SCENIC LOCATIONS
1 South Platte River: Littleton
2 Roxborough State Park
3 Golden Gate Canyon State Park
(See map, p. 50)

1 SCENIC LOCATION

SOUTH PLATTE RIVER: LITTLETON

This urban gem in the Littleton park system, South Platte Park, is nestled between a shopping center, housing developments, C-470, and Santa Fe Drive, yet solitude is still possible. (For contact information, see Parks and Gardens, p. 26.) Its entrance is on the north side of Mineral Avenue just west of Santa Fe Drive, right after the RTD Park-n-Ride lot. A short drive takes you to the Carson Nature Center.

The South Platte River, which runs north and south for a few miles right through the middle of the park, is the main scenic feature. Lining its banks are stately cottonwood trees and many other varieties of deciduous trees and shrubs. Numerous trails, both concrete and dirt, line or start from both sides of the river. The trail that runs south from Carson Nature Center and along the east side of the river passes by a beautiful wetland of cattails and shrubs, as well as a set of cascades in the river. However, my favorite scenic location is on the north end of the park. Take the concrete trail from the nature center north about 0.25 mile until you come to a wooden fence on the left with a pass-through. You will see a conspicuous dirt trail that leads down to the river and into the largest forest of cottonwoods in the park. This trail follows the east bank of the river for about 1 mile.

I've seen owls in the cottonwoods on the east side of the river, and great blue herons and cormorants in the trees across the river on the west side. Ducks and geese always cruise the shallow channels. A five-minute walk from the fence pass-through takes you to an east-west bend in the river, from where you see a lovely view west to the Rocky Mountains. The water runs slowly through the meander and makes for great reflection photographs in the evening. You can use everything from wide-angle to telephoto lenses to record the river in the foreground with mountains and sky in the background. Fall colors are remarkable here in mid- to late October. In winter I photograph the silhouettes of tall, leafless trees against the Colorado blue sky. For microcosmic photographs, check out the bark patterns on the old cottonwoods, and the watercress growing in the side creek near the big meander. Stop in at Carson Nature Center, open year-round, for interpretive information about the ecology of this place.

The **South Platte River Trail** follows the river's course from Littleton, south of Denver, right through town to Thornton on its northern end (of course, the river continues). **Cherry Creek Trail** parallels the creek from the confluence southeast to Cherry Creek Reservoir and State Park. **Highline Canal Trail** zigzags along the historic canal, built in 1883, from a dam at Waterton Canyon (see Day Trips, p. 32) north-northeast to its terminus in far northeast Denver after 68 miles. The Highline Canal is accessible from both the South Platte and Cherry Creek Trails. *To obtain maps for these trails: 720-865-BIKE, www.denvergov.org/Bicycle_Program.* Numerous bike shops near these trails rent bikes by the hour, half day, or full day.

DAY TRIPS

Denver offers easy accessibility to recreation, historical sites, and wildlife viewing along the Front Range and in the foothills just west of Denver. These trips are an hour or less from downtown Denver. *For other day trips convenient to Denver, see Castle Rock, p. 64, and the other towns in this chapter.*

Buffalo Bill Grave and Museum: Wyoming may never forgive Colorado for "stealing" the body of William F. "Buffalo Bill" Cody (1846–1917). The legendary Cody was a Pony Express rider in his youth; after the Civil War, he earned his nickname as a game hunter for workers on the Kansas Pacific Railroad. He later attained the rank of Chief of Scouts for the Fifth U.S. Cavalry. His status as a marksman and soldier caught the attention of Ned Buntline, who published a dime novel about him, which rocketed Cody to fame. From 1872 he worked in show business and for the next decade staged various Western-themed plays. In 1883, Buffalo Bill organized his famous Wild West show, featuring roping moves now seen in rodeos. Buffalo Bill's Wild West was a spectacle that would go on to showcase such Western luminaries as Annie Oakley and Sitting Bull and to perform for European royalty.

Cody returned often to the West. He had a home in North Platte, Neb., and founded the city of Cody, Wyo., hoping to capitalize on the east entrance to Yellowstone National Park. Cody happened to be in Denver, however, at the time of his death. His body lay in state in the Capitol, where 25,000 paid their respects. The folks in Cody thought he should be buried in their town, but his wife granted his wish to be buried on Lookout Mountain. His remains, buried under thousands of tons of concrete, are unlikely to be moved. To see the grave and visit the museum, which houses some of Cody's personal items, take I-70 west from Denver for 15 miles and exit at the Buffalo Bill's Grave sign (Exit 256). *303-526-0747, www.buffalobill.org.*

Buffalo Herd: Denver is one of the only cities in the U.S. that owns bison herds. The Genesee Mountain herd has several dozen head of these noble, shaggy animals; the other herd lives at Daniels Park (see Scenic Location No. 11, p. 66), north of Castle Rock. Take I-70 west from Denver to the Buffalo Herd Overlook sign at Exit 254. If you're

2 SCENIC LOCATION — ROXBOROUGH STATE PARK

This is the most beautiful park in the Colorado State Parks system and one of my favorite places on the planet. Its unique landscape is defined by the intense colors of its rocks and plants. Situated in Colorado's Front Range foothills ecosystem, the park protects more than 3,000 acres of red, white, and yellow sandstone formations, and countless shrub and tree species. Lovely, tree-lined dirt trails crisscross the park, providing access to flowering meadows at lower elevations, while the high ridges here provide views of the entire Denver metropolitan area. To get to the park from Denver, go south on Wadsworth Boulevard (CO 121) past C-470. Pass Chatfield Reservoir to Waterton (Denver Water's Kassler Filtration Plant), where the South Platte River departs the mountains. Follow the signs south to the park. You can also get there by taking Titan Road west from where it intersects with Santa Fe Drive (US 85) 4.5 miles south of C-470.

The dominant features in the park are the tilted sandstone rocks of the Lyons and Fountain geologic formations. You can see similar formations along the foothills of the Front Range, including Garden of the Gods City Park in Colorado Springs (see Scenic Location No. 16, p. 75). These colorful sandstones are interspersed with scrub oak forests and other deciduous trees and shrubs, as well as conifers in the higher reaches of the park. Flowers abound throughout summer but are most numerous during May and June. Deer are ubiquitous, and rattlesnake, bear, and mountain lion sightings are frequent. Raptors patrol the skies above Roxborough.

A most beautiful visitor center divides the park into north and south zones. The south end of the park contains loop trails that take you high into the foothills through oak forests. You leave the rock formations behind, though they are still conspicuous in the distance from the high ridges. South Rim Trail is a 3.5-mile loop that leads to an overlook with fantastic views of the geological formations. For a more challenging hike, take the Carpenter Peak Trail. This 6-mile round-trip hike is accessible from South Rim Trail.

On the north end, a loop trail penetrates the heart of the sandstone. My favorite photograph is made from The Lyons Overlook, reached via a marked side trail 0.5 mile north of the visitor center on the east side of the loop. The overlook reveals views of red and white rocks interspersed with the greens of oaks and aspens. Yes, you'll find hidden pockets of my favorite tree, the quaking aspen!

Springtime provides incredible combinations of light green leaves and red rocks, complementary colors. Purple and yellow flowers decorate the summer landscape, and red rocks are matched by red oaks in the fall. Nevertheless, one of my favorite photographs of the park was made in winter when a foot of fresh snow covered the formations. Roxborough is a morning place. The sun rises slowly over the Eastern Plains, allowing rich red light to bathe an already ruddy landscape. Foothills to the west block the setting sun before it has a chance to color the park.

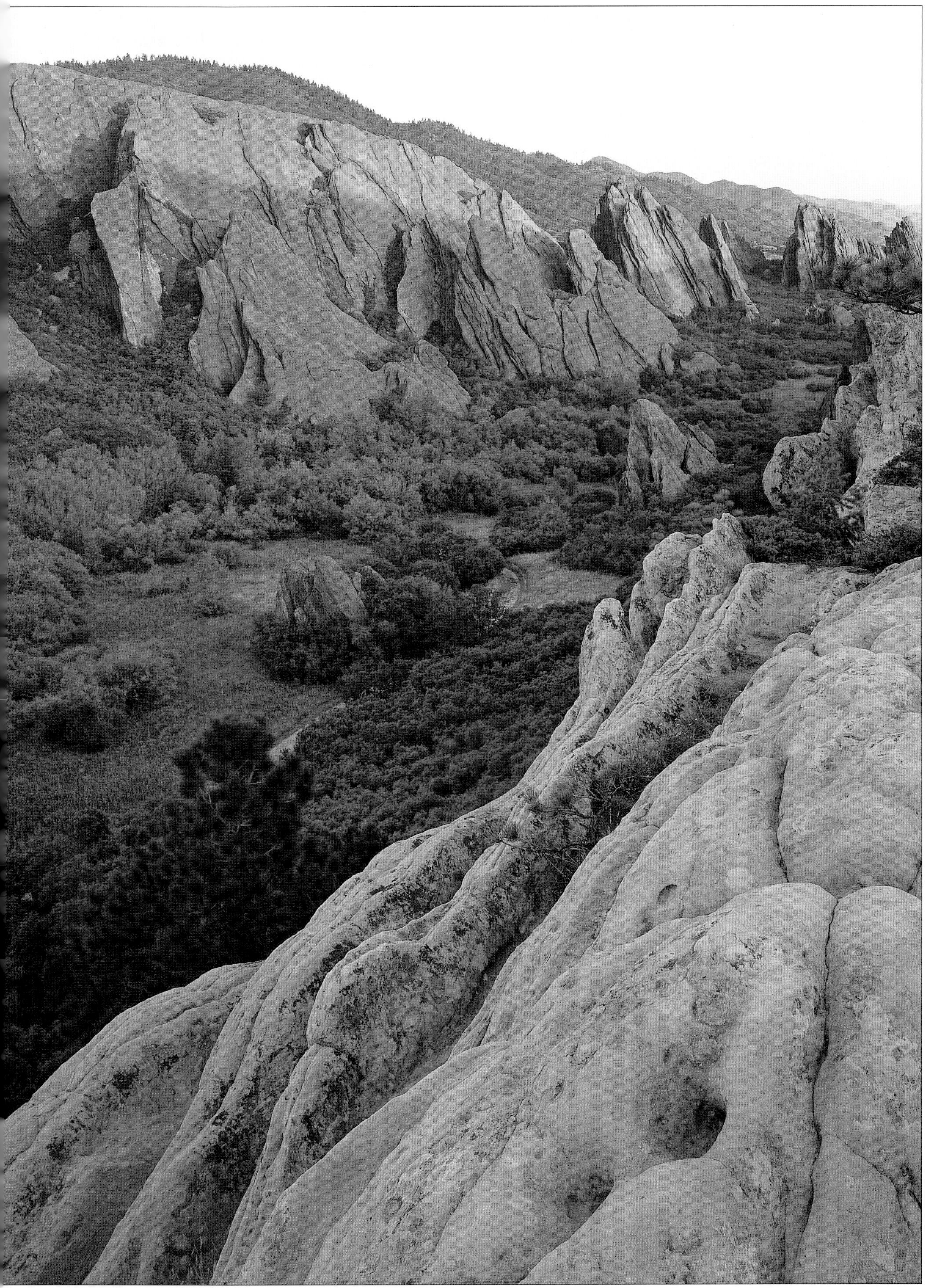

lucky, the bison will be grazing along the fence. Last spring I had the fortune to see the frisky new calves up close. Friendly and curious, the young ones dismayed their mothers, who snorted loudly to urge the calves back to the fold. The bison traverse I-70 by way of a special underpass. Pullouts on either side of I-70 allow you to observe these creatures that once wandered Colorado in great herds.

Red Rocks Park and Amphitheatre and Dinosaur Ridge: West of Denver rises an outcropping of spectacular red sandstone cliffs, forming an amazing natural amphitheater. Fitted with benches and concessions 60 years ago, Red Rocks Amphitheatre does the region proud and has hosted the biggest stars of every generation: Glenn Miller, Elvis, the Beatles, and U2. The 9,000-seat venue also hosts a nondenominational Easter sunrise service. *720-865-2494, www.redrocksonline.com.*

Red Rocks, Morrison

The 2,700-acre **Red Rocks Park** is a favorite for cyclists and hikers. Take the **Trading Post Loop,** MODERATE which starts at the Trading Post Gift Shop below the amphitheater. Stay off the rocks, they can be dangerous when wet or dry and rangers will write tickets. To get to Red Rocks from Denver, take I-70 west to the Morrison exit. Take Morrison Road (CO 8) south to the park entrance.

Dinosaur Ridge is named for the dinosaur fossils and footprints in the Hogback, a sandstone formation just east of Red Rocks Amphitheatre. The Hogback is the site of dinosaur tracks, while the Morrison Formation beside it has been the site of Jurassic discoveries across the West. Stop at 17 interpretive stations on an hour-long self-guided tour to learn the geology and history of the area and to view the tracks. To get to Dinosaur Ridge from Red Rocks Park, take the road through the park to CO 93. Cross the highway and begin your trip at the visitor center. *16831 W. Alameda Pkwy., Morrison, 303-697-3466, www.dinoridge.org.*

Waterton Canyon: The South Platte River has cut a scenic canyon that's a prime destination for mountain bikers and hikers. Follow **Waterton Canyon Trail** EASY through cottonwood groves and into the steep-walled canyon. Hike as far as you like—sharing the road, of course—but a 6.5-mile (one way) path will take you below Strontia Springs Dam. From here, bikers can connect to challenging singletrack options. The canyon also provides access, via **Bear Creek Trail** DIFFICULT, to great trout fishing. Look for bighorn sheep perched on steep canyon walls; raptors such as eagles, hawks, and turkey vultures soar above. To get to Waterton Canyon, follow the directions to Roxborough State Park (see Scenic Location No. 2, p. 30) and continue south on CO 121 to the parking area just south of the Lockheed Martin service road.

GOLF

Winding through mature trees, the **Wellshire Golf Course,** designed by Donald Ross in 1926, maintains its status as one of the nation's best public facilities. *3333 S. Colorado Blvd., 303-692-5636.* Another old, city favorite is the beautiful and challenging **Willis Case,** established in 1928. *4999 Vrain St., 303-455-9801.* Denver's **Foothills Golf Course** has three courses: an 18-hole championship course, a 9-hole executive course, and a 9-hole par 3 course. *3901 S. Carr St., 303-409-2400.* **Mountain View Golf Course** provides family fun with a 9-hole executive course, a miniature golf course, and a driving range. *5091 S. Quebec St., 303-694-3012.*

Arrowhead Golf Club in Littleton is one of the metro area's most picturesque. The course's challenging greens nestle against the same striking red-rock formations as in nearby Roxborough State Park. *10850 S. Sundown Tr., Littleton, 303-973-9614, www.arrowheadcolorado.com.* **Fox Hollow** is a 27-hole facility perfect for the golf enthusiast. *13410 W. Morrison Rd., Lakewood, 303-986-PUTT, www.lakewood.org/CR/Regional/foxhollowpage.cfm.* The championship, prairie links–style course at **The Homestead at Murphy Creek** is considered one of the 10 best municipal courses in Colorado and is steeped in golf's history, with dirt roads, wooden rakes, and old-style flags. *1700 S. Old Tom Morris Rd., Aurora, 303-361-7300.*

DOWNTOWN AQUARIUM

Come within inches of thousands of fish, birds, plants, and mammals in this 106,500-square-foot aquarium and restaurant! More than 500 species are housed in this million-gallon water adventure, which brings 14 habitats to life in re-creations of river-to-ocean journeys. Along the way you'll spot sharks and Sumatran tigers. *700 Water St. (23rd Street exit off I-25), 303-561-4450, www.downtownaquarium.com.*

U.S. MINT

Commemorative coins, medals, and cash are produced at the Denver Mint—one of only two mints to make coins for circulation. See the display on the history of money and, if you're a coin collector, shop for uncirculated commemorative coins. For student, military and veteran group tours, call *303-405-4761. www.usmint.gov/mint_tours.* Tours for smaller groups may be arranged through Congressional sponsorship.

ZOO

Denver Zoo is home to more than 700 species of animals and extraordinary zoological exhibits, all within the verdant confines of City Park. People can watch seals and polar bears romp underwater (though not in the same tank) in the below-ground viewing areas at the Northern Shores exhibit. The zoo has been successful in breeding polar bears and has contributed to populating other zoos with these large mammals.

The most popular exhibit at the zoo is the 1.5-acre Tropical Discovery, which houses rainforest species. Notable inhabitants are the huge Anaconda and Komodo dragons, a fine snake

GOLDEN GATE CANYON STATE PARK

This is another of the more natural state parks in the Colorado inventory—lots of trees and trails for people who prefer hiking over driving a boat on a reservoir. Twelve different trails cover most of the 14,000 acres that comprise the park, allowing you to see and photograph the lush aspen meadows and dark pine forests that define this foothills and montane ecosystem northwest of Golden. The park ranges in elevation from 7,400 to 10,400 feet. From Denver, take 6th Avenue west to Golden, then take CO 93 north from Golden 1 mile to Golden Gate Canyon Road. Turn left and continue 13 miles to the park.

My favorite time of the year at Golden Gate Canyon is autumn. The plentiful aspens reach peak yellow color no later than the third week of September each year. There are many groves here, so plan to explore the network of trails from one end of the park to the other in search of the best. Photograph in the morning and evening, when shadows are long and the translucent leaves are sidelit by the low-lying sun. For the best view in the park, make your way to aptly named Panorama Point on the north end.

From this location you can see up and down the Front Range for a hundred miles. Photograph here in early May when the aspen leaves are just starting to emerge from their buds, producing delicate green color as foreground to the still-snowcapped peaks of the Continental Divide. If you photograph at sunrise, you won't believe how the white peaks contrast against the Colorado blue sky on a clear day. June is the best month for wildflowers in the meadows.

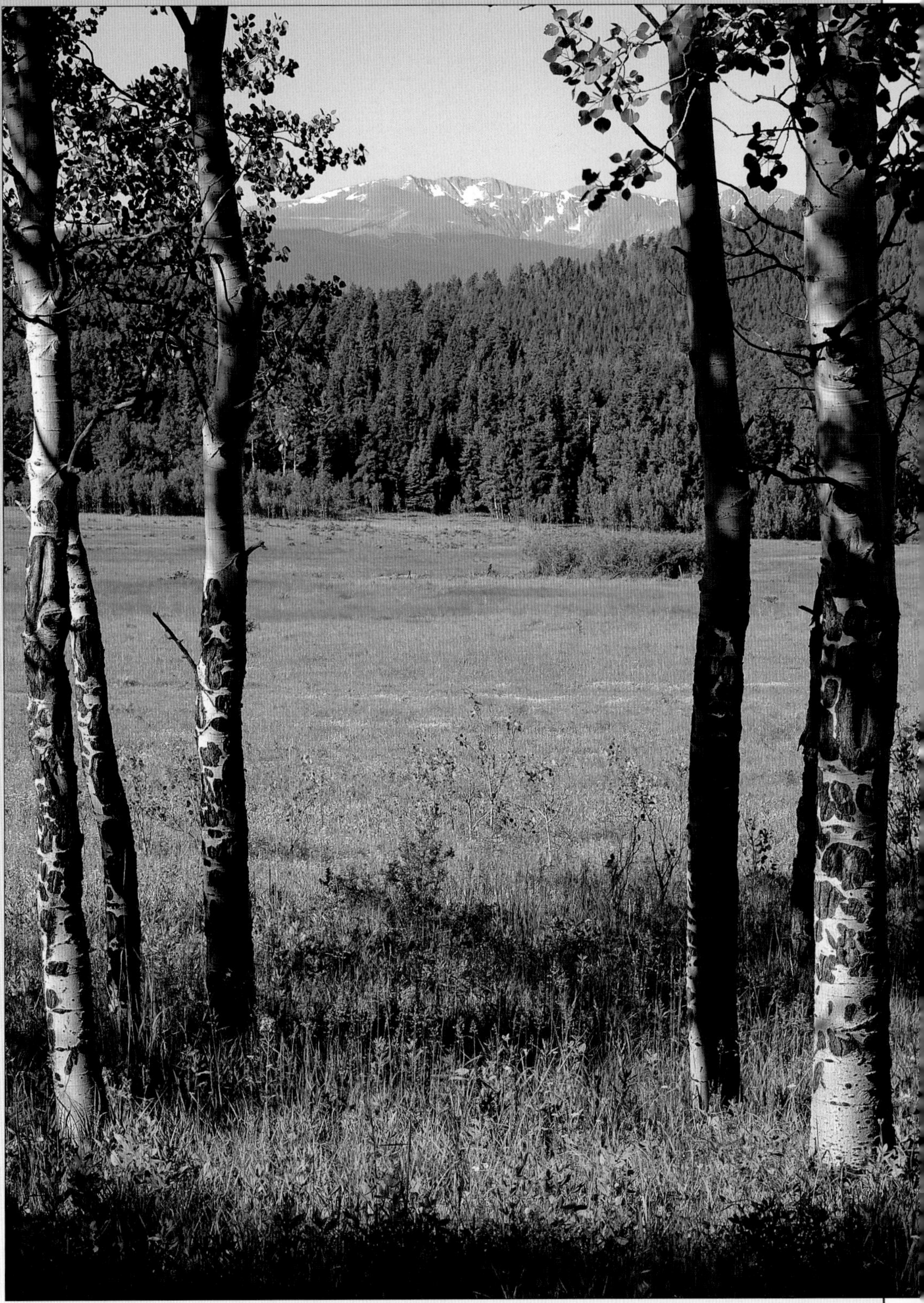

collection, and saltwater aquarium species. See animals native to the Rocky Mountain West, such as the black and grizzly bears at historic Bear Mountain (site of the zoo's origins), the wolf pack at Wolf Pack Woods, and the bighorn sheep on Sheep Mountain. The lowland gorillas and orangutans at the Primate Panorama are also perennial favorites.

For generations, kids have enjoyed the pint-sized train that runs around the perimeter of the **Children's Zoo.** Kids also appreciate the rabbits and peacocks that wander at large on the zoo grounds. The zoo presents concerts in the summer, a Halloween celebration, and a lights display during the holidays. *2300 Steele St. at City Park, 303-376-4800, www.denverzoo.org.*

Restaurants

Not long ago only a handful of great restaurants dished in Denver. But thanks to the city's growth in both population and sophistication, you can now find world-class food here. The following just skim the surface of the culinary delights to be discovered in this town.

In Highland, **Bang!** ($$$) is a casual, cozy spot with flavors from home. There's meatloaf, country-friend chicken, and other classics. *3472 W 32nd Ave, 303-455-1117, www.bangdenver.com.* **El Taco de Mexico** ($$) is a no-frills Mexican place with spectacular carnitas tacos. *714 Santa Fe Dr., 303-623-3926.* With a sleek urban atmosphere, **Vesta Dipping Grill** ($$$) specializes in grilled fare accompanied by a selection of creative sauces such as mango poblano salsa and smoked tomato sage. *1822 Blake St., 303-296-1970, www.vestagrill.com.* **McCormick's Fish House and Bar** ($$-$$$) in the elegant Oxford Hotel is a LoDo favorite. Try the oyster sampler and the award-winning grilled shrimp and portobello mushroom salad. My family and I have been doing Easter brunch here for years. *1659 Wazee St., 303-825-1107.*

McCormick's Fish House and Bar, Denver

For other downtown Denver dining options, see Brown Palace Hotel, p. 21; Larimer Square, p. 23; and Breweries, p. 27.

If you're hankerin' for a taste of the Wild West, try **The Buckhorn Exchange** ($$$-$$$$). Established in 1895, it's Denver's oldest restaurant. Buffalo Bill ate here, and each February 23, people dress in period costume for his birthday bash. The mounted elk, sheep, and buffalo that look down on you while you dine are as legendary as the steaks, game dishes, and bean soup. *1000 Osage St., 303-534-9505, www.buckhorn.com.* **The Fort** ($$-$$$) is fabled both for its menu and its setting. The adobe Fort is patterned after historic Bent's Fort on the Eastern Plains (see La Junta, p. 443), and the cuisine is authentic and at times exotic—rattlesnake, for instance. *19192 CO 8, Morrison, 303-697-4771, www.thefort.com.*

Denver's selection of cuisine has become quite international. **House of Marrakesh** ($$$), right downtown, offers exotic Moroccan fare. Floor seating is available. *1530 Blake St., 303-623-3133, www.houseofmarrakeshdenver.com.* At the trendy and always-hopping **Sushi Den** ($$-$$$), the fish is flown in daily. Don't miss the specials and salads. *1487 S. Pearl St., 303-777-0826.* **Imperial Chinese Seafood Restaurant** ($$-$$$) serves elegantly prepared dishes in a dressed-up room. *431 S. Broadway, 303-698-2800.* **Oshima Ramen** ($$$) makes authentic Japanese ramen noodle soup. The green tea ice cream is fantastic. *7400 E. Hampden Ave., 720-482-0264.* My favorite Vietnamese restaurant has always been **T-Wa Inn** ($-$$). Its clever, sumptuous cuisine has kept the Fielder family coming back for 15 years. *555 S Federal Blvd, 303-922-2378, www.twainn.com.* **India's Restaurant** ($$-$$$) serves up smoky tandoori cooked in a traditional Indian clay oven, as well as curried meats and vegetables. The lunch buffet is a delicious bargain. *7400 E Hampden Ave, 303-755-4284, www.indiasrestaurant.com.*

Parisi Italian Market, Deli and Trattoria ($$-$$$) suits any occasion, *4401 Tennyson St., 303-561-0234, www.parisidenver.com,* as does **Barolo Grill** ($$$-$$$$), whose staff makes an annual pilgrimage to the old country to ensure authenticity. *3030 E. 6th Ave., 303-393-1040, www.barologrilldenver.com.* **The Cherry Tomato** ($$-$$$) is a neighborhood favorite that delivers strong on the pastas, cheeses, and spicy sauce. *4645 E. 23rd Ave., 303-377-1914, www.cherrytomatodenver.com.* **Osteria Marco** ($) is relaxed and affordable with the best thin-crust pizza in town. *1453 Larimer St., 303-534-5855, www.osteriamarco.com.* Make reservations well in advance to dine at **Carmine's on Penn** ($$-$$$) which is famous for its heaping portions. *92 S. Pennsylvania, 303-777-6443, www.carminesonpenn.com.* Don't expect a sit-down meal at **Bubba Chino's** ($), which offers delicious and affordable Mexican favorites in a to-go setting. Try the green chile smothered burritos. *160 Federal Blvd., 303-727-8727.*

In a city bursting with new and innovative restaurants, several Denver standbys always hit the mark. Two delis are Denver dependables. **Zaidy's Deli** ($-$$), just off the beaten path in Cherry Creek, has the best potato latkes in town, not to mention lean corned beef and killer desserts. *121 Adams St., 303-333-5336, www.zaidysdeli.com.* **The New York Deli News** ($-$$) in southeast Denver has a less refined ambiance, but the sandwiches are dangerously thick. The hot pastrami on rye with coleslaw and Russian dressing is as good as you get from Big Apple delis. *7105 E. Hampden Ave., 303-759-4741, www.nydenver.com.* For great hamburgers try **Smashburger** ($). Create your own burger and grab a shake. There's no pretensions to be found here and choices abound! *1120 S. Colorado Blvd., 303-757-4301, www.smashburger.com.* **Rocky Mountain Diner** ($$) serves the ultimate in Colorado comfort food in the historic Ghost Building downtown. *800 18th St., 303-293-8383, www.rockymountaindiner.com.*

For fine dining, the following eateries promise an upscale culinary experience. **Cork House Wine Restaurant** ($$-$$$) is an excellent choice for celebrating that special occasion. The menu is thoughtfully designed to accompany the restaurant's global wine list. *4900 E Colfax Ave, 303-355-4488, www.corkhousedenver.com.* **Highland's Garden Cafe** ($$-$$$) has an amazing patio and ever-changing seasonal dishes. *3927 W. 32nd Ave., 303-458-5920, www.highlandsgardencafe.com.* **Bistro Vendome** ($$$$) whisks you away with French flavors. *1424-H Larimer St., 303-825-3232, www.bistrovendome.com.* **Potager** ($$-$$$) changes much of its menu monthly, which allows the chef to experiment with fresh seasonal ingredients. Luckily she almost always finds the makings for risotto and fresh fish. *1109 Ogden St., 303-832-5788, www.potagerrestaurant.com.* Many Denver food critics consider **Restaurant Kevin Taylor** ($$$$) to be Denver's finest. Here you'll find offerings such as *foie gras* and John Dory well presented in an elegant and historic room. *303-820-2600.* **Prima Ristorante** ($$-$$$) is Taylor's contemporary Italian restaurant at the same posh hotel. Hotel Teatro, *1106 14th St, 303-228-0770.*

Accommodations

The high quality of its architecture, amenities, rooms, and location make the historic **Brown Palace Hotel** ($$$$) the finest place to stay in Denver (see p. 21). *321 17th St., 303-297-3111, 800-321-2599, www.brownpalace.com.* On the opposite end of downtown, the **Oxford Hotel** ($$$-$$$$) has old-Denver charm (see LoDo, p. 23). *1600 17th St., 303-628-5400, 303-628-5421, www.theoxfordhotel.com.* **Hotel Teatro** ($$$-$$$$), a recently restored 1911 tramway building, rivals the Brown Palace with eminently stylish rooms. Drift off on Egyptian cotton sheets while you admire the selections from the owner's art collection that decorate your room. Posters and costumes from the nearby Denver Center for the Performing Arts decorate the lobby. The hotel's two restaurants, Prima Ristorante and Restaurant Kevin Taylor, are among the best in town (see Restaurants, above). *1100 14th St., 303-228-1100, 800-727-1200, www.hotelteatro.com.*

The 1889 **Castle Marne** ($$-$$$) is the B&B of choice for visitors wanting hands-on hospitality, Victorian furnishings, and a full gourmet breakfast. *1572 Race St., 303-331-0621, 800-926-2763, www.castlemarne.com.* The 1891 **Capitol Hill Mansion** ($$-$$$) is another fine Victorian B&B and is listed on both the National and Colorado Historic Registers. *1207 Pennsylvania St., 800-839-9329, www.capitolhillmansion.com.* **Queen Anne Bed & Breakfast Inn** ($$$) is actually two side-by-side Victorians on the east end of downtown. *2147 and 2151 Tremont Pl., 303-296-6666, www.queenannebnb.com.*

Special Events

You'll find fun festivities year-round, especially in summer, in the Mile High City. This list covers a few highlights. For two weeks in mid-January, Coloradans focus on the **National Western Stock Show,** a Denver tradition. The National Western is one of the largest such events in the nation, featuring both rodeos and livestock judging. Roping, racing, riding, and wrestling events draw top-rated professional cowboys. Don't miss the colorful Mexican Extravaganza rodeo, complete with dancing horses, Mariachi music, the traditional hat dance, and more. The whole family can have fun viewing the stock show barns, where the West's top livestock is on display. *National Western Complex, off I-25 and I-70 at 4655 Humboldt St., 303-297-1166, www.nationalwestern.com.*

Held the first weekend in June, **Capitol Hill People's Fair** started as a neighborhood arts and crafts gathering. Thirty years later, it now has hundreds of artisan's booths, food tents, carnival rides, and round-the-weekend musical entertainment. The fair allows booth space for advocates and proponents of every cause imaginable—appropriately close to the gold-domed State Capitol. *Civic Center Park, 303-830-1651, www.peoplesfair.com.*

Top-ranked **Cherry Creek Arts Festival** is on the Fourth of July weekend. A juried event, 200 exhibitors are chosen from over 2,000 applicants. Along the streets of Cherry Creek North, the selected artists set up booths and sell directly to thousands who gather to browse the talent. Youngsters can stop at the Creation Station to get a creative, hands-on perspective of art. *2 Steele St., 303-355-2787, www.cherryarts.org.*

Denverites look forward to great food and entertainment every Labor Day weekend at **A Taste of Colorado.** Take your pick from the delicious fare at the dozens of booths featuring cuisine from local restaurants. Nonstop musical entertainment, craft booths, and carnival rides are all here, too, but the focus is on the food. *Civic Center Park, 303-295-6330, www.atasteofcolorado.com.*

Denver has several major events that celebrate its cultural diversity. The celebration of an 1862 battle heralding Mexican independence, **Cinco de Mayo** (5th of May) brings together the city's Hispanic community for the largest such event in the nation at Civic Center Park. Traditional dress and dances, a parade, strolling Mariachis, and lots of spicy food highlight the festivities. *303-534-8342, ext. 106.* Denver's African-American community celebrates **Juneteenth** in mid-June in one Boulder and two Denver locations. This joyful bash in Denver's historic Five Points neighborhood includes live entertainment, gospel performances, food, and arts and crafts booths. *303-385-3778.*

For More Information

Denver Chamber of Commerce, *1445 Market St., 303-534-8500, www.denverchamber.org;* Denver Metro Convention and Visitors Bureau Information Centers, *1668 Larimer St.* or *DIA Jeppesen Terminal Building, 800-233-6837, www.denver.org.*

Boulder

Colorado Atlas & Gazetteer pp. 29, 39

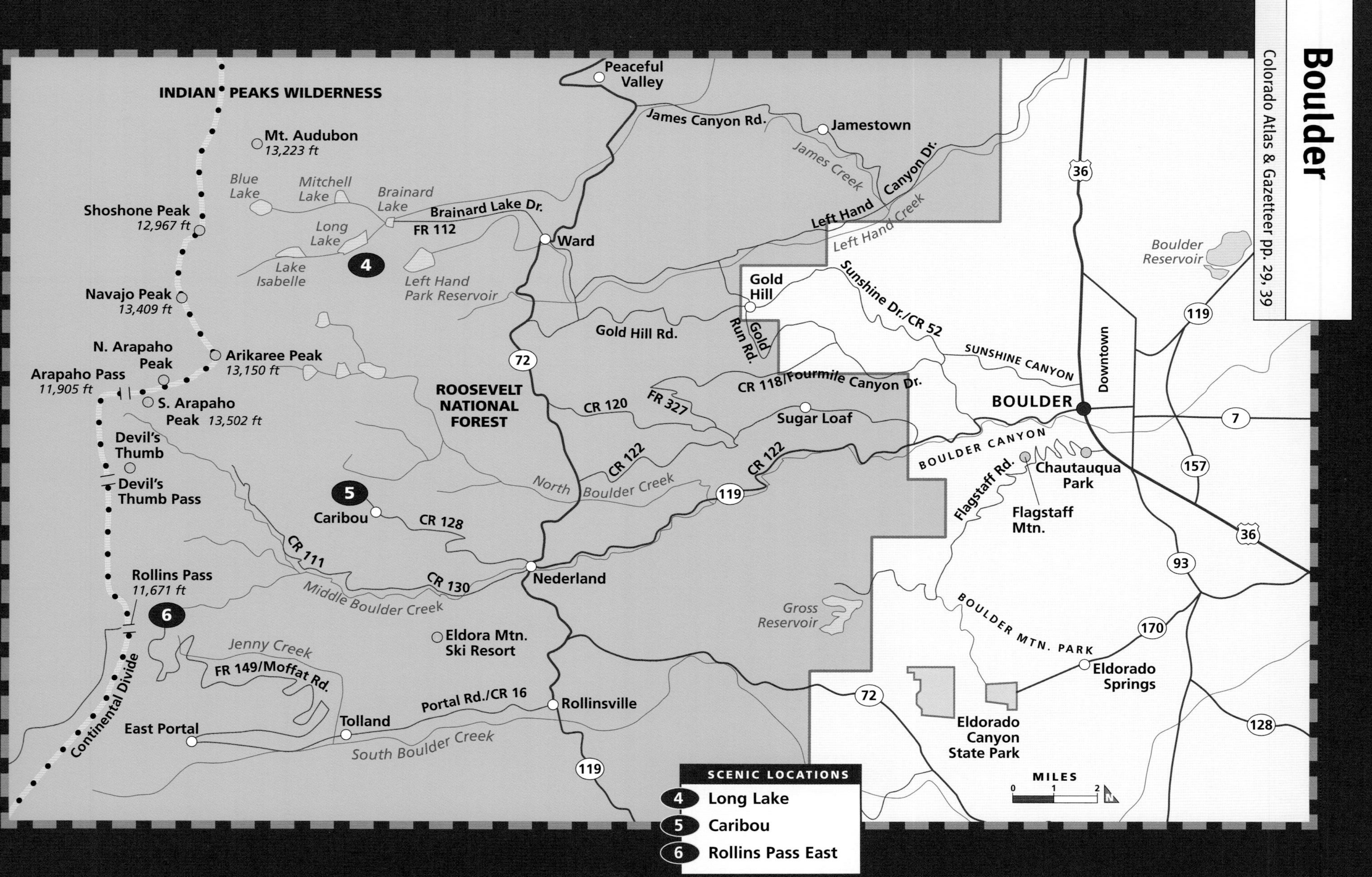

Boulder

The cosmopolitan college town of Boulder sits at the foothills of the Rockies, where the mountains meet the plains. Great tilting slabs of sandstone, known as the Flatirons, angle upward along the western edge of town. Boulder residents enjoy thousands of acres of preserved open space laced with miles upon miles of hiking trails. They consider playing outdoors a priority, whether it be hiking the foothills, climbing the Flatirons, kayaking Boulder Creek, biking the paved pathways that wind through town, or cross-country skiing in the Indian Peaks Wilderness. *Outside Magazine* named Boulder "America's number one sports town."

The heart and soul of Boulder is the Pearl Street Mall, a brick-paved pedestrian mall bustling with outdoor cafés, coffeehouses, shops, and galleries. Musicians and street performers entertain the passersby, and for a few coins thrown into a hat you can hear a bluegrass banjo or watch a busker juggling fire while riding a unicycle. The choice of restaurants in Boulder is mind-boggling, and ethnic eateries abound—from Nepalese to Ethiopian, Korean to Caribbean. The arts scene is equally diverse, and in summer a number of nationally recognized festivals draw audiences to watch Shakespeare plays under the stars or listen to classical music at Chautauqua Auditorium.

Boulder's Flatirons dusted in snow

Counterculture influences of the '60s and '70s still linger here, and New Age thought and practices proliferate. It's also a well-educated place, home to the campus of the University of Colorado; the Naropa University, the only accredited Buddhist college in the country; and many federal scientific research facilities. Boulder remains a perfect locale in which to live, work, and play.

In the mountains west of Boulder lie several small towns that are interesting to visit. Many of them seem like throwbacks to the '60s, and you'll still see hippies as well as rugged mountain-man and Earth-mama types. Nederland, the largest of these mountain towns, is also a gateway to the Indian Peaks Wilderness. Ward is a charming jumble of buildings, the town inhabited by an independent lot. Eldora, Rollinsville, and Jamestown are also intriguing places, and Gold Hill looks like it hasn't changed much at all from the early gold mining days.

History

In 1858, Boulder City, as it was then called, was a ragtag collection of tents and cabins. The fledgling community supplied the mining towns of Gold Hill, Caribou, Sugarloaf, and other camps in the Nederland area. Boulder grew steadily over the years, first supporting the gold and silver mines in the high country, and later the farms and the coal and oil fields on the plains.

Boulder

In 1860 the first school in the Colorado Territory was established in Boulder, and by the time Colorado was admitted to the Union in 1876, the state university was already under construction—after much political wrangling over where to build it. The campus grew, as did enrollment, which increased significantly after World War II when returning soldiers took advantage of the GI bill. Today the University of Colorado at Boulder is the main campus of a four-campus state university system.

In 1950 the National Bureau of Standards located here, later joined by other federal research centers, including the National Center for Atmospheric Research and the National Oceanic and Atmospheric Administration. In 1967 Boulder became the first city in the nation to vote in a sales tax to purchase open space, thus preventing the urban sprawl that has wreaked havoc on other Colorado communities. Some 30,000 acres surrounding Boulder are now set aside, protected from development. The open-space program, along with growth and height limits enacted over the years, have helped Boulder to retain a small-town feel—while also sending real estate prices soaring. Leading businesses include such high-tech industries as computer software, bio-tech, and aerospace.

Main Attractions

BOULDER CREEK PATH

Popular with walkers, runners, cyclists, and in-line skaters, the Boulder Creek Path follows the cottonwood-shaded course of Boulder Creek as it flows 5 miles through the center of Boulder. Many side paths break off from the main corridor, creating a 20-mile network of bike/pedestrian paths throughout the city.

From Eben Fine Park, which sits near the mouth of Boulder Canyon, the paved pathway zips east through town, crossing Boulder Creek on pedestrian bridges and dipping underneath major roads and intersections. Stops along the way include a children's fishing pond, a xeriscape garden, a sculpture garden, the Boulder Public Library, Central Park (with its band shell and

LONG LAKE

Like Piney Lake (see Scenic Location No. 28, p. 119), Trappers Lake (see Scenic Location No. 62, p. 205), and Maroon Lake (see Scenic Location No. 83, p. 250), Long Lake rests just inside a wilderness boundary, in this case the eastern side of Indian Peaks Wilderness. All four lakes lie below spectacular serrated peaks that form a grand background, and are easy pickings for photography in terms of distance from the parking lot! Long Lake requires the longest hike from the car—just under a mile. Take CO 119 west from Boulder to Nederland, then CO 72 north 8 miles to Ward. Turn west on Forest Road 112 and drive 5 miles to Brainard Lake. Follow the road around the north side of the lake to the turnoff to the Long Lake parking area; the trailhead is on the south end.

Long Lake is the largest lake (40.5 acres) inside the Indian Peaks Wilderness. It sits at 10,522 feet and commands unobstructed views of the Front Range to the west. There are plenty of treeless sites along the east side of the lake from which to photograph noble mountains such as Navajo (13,409 feet) and Shoshoni (12,967 feet) Peaks reflecting in the lake. The Indian Peaks catch the full effect of sunrise light, so plan to have your camera on the tripod before sunrise. Coincidentally, that's when the wind is calmest, improving your chances for serene reflections.

Compose your scene to include the green grassy shore of the lake, another layer of landscape that will add more depth to the photograph than if you only included water and mountains. The meadows between Brainard and Long Lakes are filled with wildflowers from late June through July. On your return to the car, photograph these fields as the sun begins to rise, but before it gets too high in the sky and colors begin to wash out (see *Photographing the Landscape,* pp. 93–99).

Better yet, strap on the daypack and head into the wilderness by way of the Pawnee Pass Trail. One of Colorado's most breathtaking hikes, this route gains 2,000 feet on the way to Pawnee Pass (12,541 feet). From the trailhead, it's only 9 miles round-trip to the pass for a perfect alpine hiking day. The views of Navajo and Shoshoni Peaks, as well as Arikaree (13,150 feet), Apache (13,441 feet), and Pawnee (12,943 feet) Peaks on the way up, are sublime. The peek over the pass into the west side of the Indian Peaks Wilderness will take your breath away. On the way down, photograph the deep blue waters of Lake Isabelle far below with your telephoto lens.

a locomotive on display), a stream observatory, Scott Carpenter Park (with a swimming pool and skateboard ramps), prairie-dog towns, and wetland ponds.

Going west from Eben Fine Park, the unpaved route heads up Boulder Canyon, passing through Settlers' Park and on to the Elephant Buttresses and the Dome, where you can watch rock climbers scale the canyon walls. The creek itself is a favorite route during spring runoff; kids of all ages float and tumble down the creek in inner tubes, and kayakers and canoeists tackle the white-water kayak course. Pick up a path map at the chamber of commerce. *2440 Pearl St., 303-442-2911, www.bouldercoloradousa.com.*

BRAINARD LAKE RECREATION AREA

This is a popular spot for hiking, fishing, and picnicking in summer, and cross-country skiing and snowshoeing in winter. Administered by the U.S. Forest Service, Brainard Lake Recreation Area lies just outside the boundary of Indian Peaks Wilderness, and many hikes into the wilderness originate here (see Hiking, p. 42, and Scenic Location No. 4, opposite). *Boulder Ranger District, 2140 Yarmouth Ave., Boulder, 303-541-2500, www.fs.fed.us/arnf.*

CHAUTAUQUA PARK

The Chautauqua Movement first started in 1874 in Lake Chautauqua, N.Y., where Sunday school teachers had gathered for continuing education classes during the summer. The idea of adult education caught on, and by the turn of the century millions of people were enriched and educated through a network of "Chautauquas" that fanned out across the country. People flocked to them to hear concerts and lectures, or to take classes on everything from biology to butterfly collecting. Many permanent Chautauquas were built, while tent Chautauquas traveled to rural areas, bringing education, culture, and entertainment to the masses. An estimated third of the nation had visited a Chautauqua by the 1920s, but the movement died out with the rise of radio and movies.

The Colorado Chautauqua was started by a group of Texas schoolteachers seeking a cooler, less humid summer climate. They decided on Boulder and made an agreement with the town, which donated land at the base of the Flatirons. The auditorium and dining hall were completed in just two months, ready for opening day on July 4, 1898. The Texans settled into a tent community adjoining the site on the near-barren mesa. Over the years the tents were replaced with cottages. Trees were also planted, which today grace the park in profusion.

Now a National Historic Landmark, the Colorado Chautauqua—one of only three permanent Chautauquas still standing—remains a vibrant part of the Boulder community. People gather year-round in the **Community House** for dances, lectures, and poetry readings. **Chautauqua Auditorium** hosts concerts, performances, and silent movies throughout the summer, and is home to the classical Colorado Music Festival (see Special Events, p. 48). Summer evenings find Boulderites picnicking and playing on the lawn before performances. **Chautauqua Dining Hall** serves fine American fare amid unmatched scenery (see Restaurants, p. 45). Many cottages at Chautauqua are available for rent (see Accommodations, p. 47). Quite a number of hiking trails originate at Chautauqua Park; get trail information at the Ranger Cottage. *900 Baseline Rd., 303-441-3408, www.chautauqua.com.*

INDIAN PEAKS WILDERNESS

Many of the mountains in the Indian Peaks Wilderness bear the names of Colorado tribes, such as Pawnee, Navajo, Apache, Shoshoni, and Arapaho Peaks. These sawtoothed summits were shaped by the grinding action of glaciers, and some of the southernmost glaciers in the United States can be seen here. The Continental Divide marches down the center of the wilderness, which counts nearly 50 high lakes and more than 130 miles of hiking trails (see Hiking, p. 42). Because of its close proximity to Boulder and Denver, Indian Peaks receives heavy use, and permits are required for overnight camping June to September. You can get permits at the Indian Peaks Ace Hardware in Nederland, *74 Hwy 119, 303-258-3132*, or the Roosevelt National Forest ranger station in Boulder, *2140 Yarmouth Ave., 303-541-2500, www.fs.fed.us/arnf.*

PEARL STREET MALL

To truly experience Boulder you have to visit the Pearl Street Mall. This four-block-long, pedestrian-only mall lies along a stretch of Pearl Street closed to traffic, paved with brick, and landscaped with shade-trees and flowers. It is the heart of downtown, where people linger in outdoor cafés, children scramble over boulders in designated play areas, and street performers entertain with music, juggling, and feats of magic. More than 80 retail establishments, an eclectic mix of locally owned and national businesses, line the mall, which has been designated a National Historic District. Look up from the street-level action to admire the façades of various turn-of-the-century structures and the Art Deco sandstone of the Boulder County Courthouse at 14th Street.

Pearl Street Mall, Boulder

Named one of the most successful outdoor pedestrian malls in the country by the *Wall Street Journal*, the mall runs from 11th to 15th Streets. But don't limit yourself by street numbers; the sections of Pearl Street directly east and west of the mall also have many interesting shops, restaurants, cafés, and galleries.

UNIVERSITY OF COLORADO

Standing high on a barren hilltop, **Old Main** opened its doors to some 40 students in 1877. Today 30,000 students attend classes at the University of Colorado–Boulder, the tree-shaded main campus of a four-campus state university system. What is most striking about the CU campus is its distinctive architecture, with most of the buildings constructed of native Colorado sandstone in an Italianate style, complete with red-tiled roofs. The CU Buffaloes engender loyalty from students and townspeople who cheer the home team at **Folsom Field** on autumn Saturday afternoons. A stroll on campus is a nice way to spend an hour or two. Stop at the information desk at the **University Memorial Building,** just east of the intersection of Broadway and Euclid Ave., for a map. The CU campus lies between Broadway and 28th Street, and between University Boulevard and Baseline Road. *303-492-1411, www.colorado.edu.*

Activities

CAMPING

The camping options close-in to Boulder are limited, with the nearest campsites available at the **Boulder Mountain Lodge,** a private campground (no reservations) at the mouth of Fourmile Canyon. From Boulder, take Canyon Boulevard (CO 119) west for about 2 miles and turn right onto Fourmile Canyon Drive (CO 118); the lodge/campground is on the left. *303-444-0882, www.bouldermountainlodge.com.*

You'll find the best selection of campgrounds just off the Peak to Peak Highway in Roosevelt National Forest. **Pawnee** campground at Brainard Lake Recreation Area has 55 sites, great views, nearby lakes, and easy access to numerous hiking trails. It is also extremely busy and reservations are recommended for weekend stays. The 16-site **Rainbow Lakes** campground (no reservations) is more remote (with a bumpy access road) but also boasts good fishing. Both **Camp Dick** campground, with 41 fairly open sites, and **Peaceful Valley,** with 17 sites (a number of them wheelchair accessible), sit near the Middle St. Vrain Creek. The **Kelly Dahl** campground has 46 sites and a playground.

To access the campgrounds along the Peak to Peak Highway from Boulder, drive west on Canyon Boulevard/CO 119 for 17 miles to Nederland. For Pawnee campground, drive north on CO 72 for 11.5 miles and turn left onto Forest Road 112 to Brainard Lake. To reach Rainbow Lakes from Nederland, drive north on CO 72 for 6.5 miles, turn left onto FR 298, and go 5 miles farther. For Camp Dick and Peaceful Valley, drive north from Nederland on CO 72 for 17 miles. To reach Kelly Dahl, drive south from Nederland on CO 119 for 3 miles. *Reservations: 877-444-6777, www.reserveusa.com; information: 2140 Yarmouth Ave., Boulder, 303-541-2500, www.fs.fed.us/arnf.*

CYCLING AND MOUNTAIN BIKING

There are many mountain- and road-bike trails in the environmentally conscious Boulder area. *For bike rates, routes, and rentals: University Bikes, 839 Pearl St., Boulder, 303-444-4196.*

Paved **Boulder Creek Path** EASY (see Main Attractions, p. 37) parallels the creek through town and connects with the numerous trails that are part of the Boulder Greenway system, which branches out in all directions. You can ride this for as short or as long a distance as you like.

Taking US 36 to **Lyons** MODERATE is about 16 miles (one way) of rolling hills. From Boulder, head north on either Broadway or 28th Street and continue on US 36 until you reach a "T" intersection at CO 66, just east of the town of Lyons. Take a left to visit Lyons, take a right onto CO 66 to Longmont and CO 119 back to Boulder, or return the way you came.

The road up to **Jamestown** DIFFICULT is a good workout, with a fair amount of climbing on an 8-mile (one way) ride. From the intersection of US 36 and Left Hand Canyon Drive (about 4 miles north of Boulder on US 36), head west on Left Hand Canyon Drive, keeping right at the fork on James Canyon Road. From Jamestown you can turn around or continue 7 miles more to the **Peak to Peak Highway** MODERATE for a longer ride through incredible scenery (see Scenic Drives, p. 44).

For a really tough ride, try **Flagstaff Mountain** DIFFICULT to Sunrise Amphitheater, which is an 8-mile round trip starting from 9th Street and Baseline Road, near Boulder's Chautauqua Park, and heading west up, up, up Flagstaff Mountain. This is a route for serious cyclists, not only because of the prolonged climb, but also because of the vehicle traffic and narrow road.

About one-third of Boulder's open space and mountain park trails are open to mountain bikes. The **East Boulder Trail** EASY is 7 miles (one way), winding along old roads and tracks on the open plains east of town. An old farmstead, this area is also a wildlife and bird preserve. The trail starts from the Teller Farm trailhead on Arapahoe Avenue, 1 mile east of 75th Street.

Community Ditch EASY starts at the Doudy Draw and follows a dirt track that parallels an irrigation ditch. The trail crosses CO 93 and continues to Marshall trailhead for a 4-mile (one way) ride. To reach Doudy Draw trailhead, drive south on Broadway (CO 93) and turn right on CO 170 for Eldorado Springs. Go 1.5 miles and look for the trailhead on the left.

The **Sourdough Trail** MODERATE is a popular singletrack ride, 12 miles out and back in the shade of mixed forests of lodgepole pine. From Boulder, drive west on Canyon Boulevard (CO 119) to Nederland, go north on CO 72 for 7.5 miles, and turn left onto Forest Road 298, at the sign for the University of Colorado Alpine Research Station. The trailhead is 0.5 mile on the right; parking is on the left. Ride north and when you reach Brainard Lake Drive, turn around and head back. Or you can continue north 6 miles to Peaceful Valley.

The **Switzerland Trail** EASY follows an old narrow-gauge railroad grade. The railroad originally served the nearby mining towns, though it also took tourists on scenic excursion rides, which should give you an idea of the natural beauty of the area. There are a number of access points to the Switzerland Trail, and depending on where you pick it up, your

CARIBOU

High above the town of Boulder at almost 10,000 feet in the Front Range is a small valley once known for its rich mineral ores. Before the price of silver crashed during the financial panic of 1893, more than 200 buildings and 600 residents defined the mining town of Caribou. Worse, most of the town burned in 1899. Since then nature has reclaimed her territory. What once was a network of town streets is now a lovely alpine meadow where clear creeks flow from melting snow. Only a few stone foundations and a handful of gravestones remain as evidence of Caribou's first life; the fine views of the Front Range and what is now Indian Peaks Wilderness also endure. From CO 72, 0.5 mile north of Nederland, turn west onto County Road 128 and drive 5 miles to Caribou on a moderately rough road.

The drive to Caribou is lovely but not photogenic until you reach treeline. The meadows around the old townsite are replete with wildflowers beginning when snow melts in mid-June. My favorite view requires climbing the rocky ridge south and east of the road. It looks down on the meadow and captures views of the Front Range to the west. The mountains face east and will catch the rich red light of sunrise on a clear day, so it would be a good investment of your time to arrive early in order to scout for this and other locations prior to first light (see *Photographing the Landscape,* p. 172). I am a big believer in getting to know a place first before you actually begin photographing it. This gives you the opportunity to find interesting subject matter and compositions before optimal light situations demand your full attention.

ride will vary between 9 to 13 miles (one way). The easiest access is from the Sugarloaf Mountain trailhead. From the town of Nederland, drive north on CO 72 for about 3 miles, and turn right onto CR 122. Follow CR 122 for about 5 miles, until the junction with CR 120; turn right and and continue 1 more mile to the trailhead sign at Forest Road 327. Access the trail from Boulder via CO 119 and CR 122 on the south side, or via Fourmile Canyon Drive on the north. Four-wheel-drive enthusiasts also use this route.

FISHING

Ask in a local tackle shop for recommendations on good fishing in the Boulder area, and you'll most likely be pointed farther afield. **South Boulder Creek,** which flows out of Gross Reservoir, yields rainbows and browns. You'll also pull rainbows and browns from the South, Middle, and North branches of **St. Vrain Creek.** Most of the 50 lakes in the **Indian Peaks Wilderness** are stocked with trout, and a good number of lakes are just a short hike from easily accessible trailheads. On the flatlands east of

Boulder, you'll find bass in **Boulder Reservoir, Coot Lake,** and **Sawhill Lakes.** *For information or guide services: Rocky Mountain Anglers, 1904 Arapahoe Ave., Boulder, 303-447-2400, www.rockymtanglers.com.*

FOUR-WHEEL-DRIVE TRIPS

Moffat Road follows an old railroad grade to Rollins Pass (see Scenic Location No. 6, p. 47) on the Continental Divide (see Four-Wheel-Drive Trips, Winter Park, p. 174). The **Switzerland Trail** is a fun, quick, and extremely scenic four-wheel-drive trip (see Cycling and Mountain Biking, p. 40).

GOLF

While there are a number of golf courses in Boulder, the top-rated courses are in neighboring towns. The **Omni Interlocken Resort Golf Club** in Broomfield is open to the public and features a challenging 27-hole course with incredible views of the Rockies. It's about 10 miles south of Boulder off US 36 at the StorageTek Drive/Interlocken Loop exit. *303-438-6600.* An 18-hole, links-style course designed by Robert Trent Jones, Jr., the **Ute Creek Golf Course** has large fairways and lots of sand hazards. It's in Longmont, about 12 miles northeast of Boulder via CO 119. *2000 Ute Creek Dr., 303-774-7662, www.ci.longmont.co.us.* Approximately 10 miles east of Boulder off Baseline Road, **Indian Peaks Golf Course** is an 18-hole Hale Irwin-designed course offering great views of the Indian Peaks and the Continental Divide. *2300 Indian Peaks Trail, Lafayette, 303-666-4706.*

HIKING

A half-dozen trails or so originate from **Chautauqua Park** (see Main Attractions, p. 39); pick up a map at the Ranger Cottage, near the entrance to the park at 900 Baseline Road. The **Mesa Trail** EASY, which starts from Chautauqua, is a favorite among Boulderites. Edging the base of the Flatirons, it goes 6 miles (one way) from Chautauqua to South Mesa trailhead. I like to do this as a shuttle hike, starting at South Mesa trailhead and heading north to finish at Chautauqua, where I then indulge in a late breakfast or early lunch at Chautauqua Dining Hall. To reach the southern trailhead from Boulder, drive south on Broadway (CO 93) and turn right on CO 170 for Eldorado Springs. Go 1.5 miles farther and look for the trailhead on the right. *For information on Boulder Open Space and Mountain Parks trails, go online at www.ci.boulder.co.us/openspace.*

Boulder's Open Space

The hike up **Bear Peak** DIFFICULT will get you huffing and puffing, but the view is incredible. It's only 2.5 miles to the summit, though it gains 2,400 feet in that short distance. There's some rock scrambling at the top, but from there you'll see Pikes Peak and the Denver skyline to the south, the Great Plains to the east, the Continental Divide to the west, and Longs Peak the north. Spectacular! The trail leaves from the parking lot of the National Center for Atmospheric Research (NCAR), first following the Walter Orr Roberts Trail, then joining the Mesa Trail and continuing up the Fern Canyon Trail to the Bear Peak summit . To reach NCAR, go west on Table Mesa Drive, 2 miles from the intersection of Broadway and Table Mesa.

Short and sweet, the trail to **Boulder Falls** EASY is less than 0.25 mile. Stay on the trail, though, and don't be tempted to climb on the rocks, as they are slippery. From Boulder drive west on Canyon Boulevard (CO 119). The parking area is on the left, about 8 miles up Boulder Canyon.

At Brainard Lake, a number of trails branch off to even more trails in the Indian Peaks Wilderness. My favorite hike here is the **Lake Isabelle Trail** MODERATE. It's popular and there will be a good amount of foot traffic on weekends, but the scenery is well worth it. The 2-mile (one way) trail skirts Long Lake and climbs a forested valley through flowered meadows as it ascends to Lake Isabelle, a sparkling gem. From Brainard Lake, take the Long Lake trailhead and then follow the signs to Lake Isabelle. The 4-mile (one way) **Mount Audubon Trail** MODERATE also originates at Brainard Lake. From the Mitchell Lake trailhead, take the Beaver Creek Trail to timberline, where the Mount Audubon Trail then splits off. You'll skirt the edge of Arrowhead Glacier as you hike through tundra and scramble over talus while climbing to the 13,223-foot summit of Mount Audubon. To reach Brainard Lake from Boulder, drive 17 miles west on Canyon Boulevard (CO 119) to Nederland. Head north on CO 72 for about 8 miles. The town of Ward will be on the right and Brainard Lake Drive is just beyond it on the left. Follow it for 2.5 miles to the entrance, where you will need to pay a fee.

A variety of hikes also start from the Hessie and the Fourth of July trailheads in the Indian Peaks Wilderness. The **Devil's Thumb Trail** MODERATE leaves from the Hessie trailhead and climbs 5 miles to Devil's Thumb Lake, traversing both gentle and steep terrain as it winds through forests and across rocky slopes. Starting from the Fourth of July trailhead, **Arapaho Pass Trail** MODERATE goes 3 miles (one way) to the pass. To reach these two trailheads from Boulder, drive west 17 miles on Canyon Boulevard/CO 119 to Nederland. Go three-quarters of the way around the traffic circle, staying on CO 119 and heading south. Go about 1 mile and turn right onto County Road 130, following the signs for Eldora Mountain Resort. Where the road branches to the ski area, keep right on CR 130 and continue through the small town of Eldora. The road then forks to the left for Hessie trailhead, and to the right for the Fourth of July trailhead, which is 4 miles farther up a bumpy unpaved road (suitable for most cars).

The U.S. Forest Service has a ranger station in Boulder, with maps and trail information for **Indian Peaks Wilderness** and **Roosevelt National Forest.** *2140 Yarmouth Ave., 303-541-2500, www.fs.fed.us/arnf.*

HORSEBACK RIDING

Gold Lake Mountain Resort and Spa offers horseback riding year-round, with trail rides into Roosevelt National Forest and Indian Peaks Wilderness. Call in advance to make reservations. *3371 Gold Lake Rd., Ward, 303-459-3544, www.goldlake.com.* In spring and fall **Peaceful Valley Ranch** offers trail rides to the public, with advance reservations; in summer, the ranch schedules two-hour, half- and full-day rides, and overnight pack trips for its guests From Boulder, drive west on Canyon Boulevard/CO 119 for 17 miles to Nederland, then go north on CO 72 for about 20 miles. *475 Peaceful Valley Rd., 303-747-2167, www.peacefulvalley.com.* *(See Accommodations, p. 48).*

MUSEUMS

Boulder Museum of Contemporary Art showcases artwork in a variety of mediums including painting, sculpture, photography, and installation pieces. A small theater upstairs hosts live performances, and on weekends in summer the museum's parking lot becomes an outdoor movie theater, with a screen suspended from the building and bring-your-own-lawnchair seating. *1750 13th St., 303-443-2122, www.bmoca.org.* **Boulder History Museum** traces Boulder's past, including mining, ranching, and everyday life, and features a big vintage clothing collection. *1206 Euclid Ave., 303-449-3464, www.boulderhistorymuseum.org.* **Leanin' Tree Museum of Western Art,** free to the public, has a large collection of paintings and bronze sculptures depicting the history, scenery, and wildlife of the American West. *6055 Longbow Dr., Boulder, 303-530-1442, www.leanintreemuseum.com.*

Leanin' Tree Museum of Western Art

Longmont Museum and Cultural Center, extremely well-curated, has a permanent history collection and changing exhibits ranging from themed artwork to cultural perspectives. The museum, which is free, can be found about 12 miles northeast of Boulder. *400 Quail Rd., Longmont, 303-776-6050, www.ci.longmont.co.us/museum/index.htm.*

NIGHTLIFE

Boulder Theater, a beautiful Art Deco building just off the Pearl Street Mall, presents a wide range of entertainment, from international touring acts to local musicians, offering everything from world beat to bluegrass, salsa to jazz. The Boulder Theater is also home to an arthouse film series and to **E-Town,** a weekly radio show broadcast on National Public Radio that features acoustic music and promotes environmental and recycling issues. *2034 14th St., 303-786-7030, www.bouldertheater.com.*

Regularly winning praise for the quality of its productions, **Boulder Dinner Theater** presents Broadway musicals scaled to a small stage. *5501 Arapahoe Ave., 303-449-6000.* Another small but highly professional venue, **Nomad Theatre** offers a full season of dramatic works. *1410 Quince Ave., 303-443-7510, www.nomadstage.com.* **Dairy Center for the Arts** is both a theatrical and dance venue, as well as an arts exhibition space. *2590 Walnut St., 303-440-7826, www.thedairy.org.*

Fox Theatre on University Hill, presents an eclectic mix of music, mostly for the college crowd. The Fox is located at 1135 13th St. *303-447-0095, www.foxtheatre.com.* Many of the bars in Boulder—too many to list here—have live music. Pick up a copy of the *Boulder Weekly* (free) or check the Friday *Daily Camera* to see the current lineups.

Brewpubs are popular in Boulder, including **Walnut Brewery,** *1123 Walnut St., 303-447-1345;* **Mountain Sun Brewery,** *1535 Pearl St., 303-546-0886;* and **BJ's Brewery,** *1125 Pearl St., 303-402-9294.* There are also a couple of wine bars in town: **The Kitchen [Upstairs],** *1039 Pearl St., 303-544-5973, www.thekitchencafe.com,* and **Bacaro,** *921 Pearl St., 303 444 4888.*

PARKS

It's hard to find a more pleasant spot than **Chautauqua Park,** a Boulder tradition since 1898 (see Main Attractions, p. 39). Other Boulder parks include **Settler's Park, Eben Fine Park, Central Park,** and **Scott Carpenter Park,** which can all be found along the **Boulder Creek Path,** which is essentially a long, skinny park stretched out along a bike/pedestrian pathway (see Main Attractions, p. 37).

Eldorado Canyon State Park, a popular rock-climbing spot, also has hiking, fishing, biking, and kayaking, as well as picnic areas with scenic views (see Rock Climbing, below).

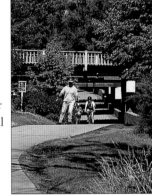

ROCK CLIMBING

The **Flatirons** are an obvious choice for climbing in Boulder, offering a beautiful location, great views, and a variety of routes. The First, Second, and Third Flatirons are the most popular, with both traditional and bolted routes, rated easy to difficult. Check the City of Boulder website for closures: *www.ci.boulder.co.us.* Access to the Flatirons is via Chautauqua Park at 900 Baseline Rd.

Boulder Creek Path

Eldorado Canyon State Park is known for its world-class climbing, with more than 500 routes, classic climbs, and easy access. From downtown Boulder, drive south for about 5 miles on Broadway (CO 93) and turn right onto CO 170. Continue about 3 miles to the end of the road, which becomes unpaved and potholed but remains manageable by car. *303-494-3943, www.parks.state.co.us.*

Boulder Canyon has outcrops attractive to climbers, including the Dome and the Elephant Buttresses (about 0.3 mile up the canyon), Cob Rock (7 miles), and Castle Rock (12 miles). *For information: Neptune Mountaineering,*

633 S. Broadway, 303-499-8866, www.neptunemountaineering.com; or Colorado Mountain Club, 303-554-7688, www.cmc.org.

Outdoor activities, Boulder

The **Boulder Rock Club** has indoor climbing walls suitable for all levels and ages. *2829 Mapleton Ave., 303-447-2804, totalclimbing.com.* **The Spot Bouldering Gym**, widely recognized one of the nation's premier indoor rock climbing facilities, offers a 'natural' indoor climbing experience, as well as complete guiding and instructional services. *3240 Prairie Ave., 303-379-8806, www.thespotgym.com.*

SCENIC DRIVES

Peak to Peak Highway, Colorado's first scenic byway, rolls 55 miles along the Front Range, starting at the gambling towns of Black Hawk and Central City and traveling north to Estes Park. Skirting the Indian Peaks Wilderness, it's a spectacular drive any time of the year, but especially in autumn when aspens burnish the hillsides. The highway was originally planned to extend from Longs Peak, in Rocky Mountain National Park, to Pikes Peak, which is outside Colorado Springs—thus the name Peak to Peak Highway. That ambitious route was never completed, but the section of the paved, two-lane highway that does exist rolls and dips through the mountains west of Boulder, offering expansive views at every curve. Cyclists enjoy this route because of its wide shoulders; motorcyclists revel in the canted, sweeping turns. Small towns along the way provide a glimpse of bucolic mountain living. From Boulder, drive 17 miles west on Canyon Boulevard (CO 119) to Nederland. From there you can pick up the Peak to Peak Highway south by continuing on CO 119, or you can head north on the scenic byway by taking CO 72 to Allenspark, then CO 7 to Estes Park.

A short, scenic drive from Boulder takes you up **Flagstaff Mountain.** It's about 4 miles to the top, with panoramic views of town and the plains below. Head west on Baseline Road and follow the road as it snakes up the mountain in a series of hairpin turns. (Watch out for cyclists.) Pullouts access picnic areas, overlooks, and trailheads. At the top sits sandstone Sunrise Amphitheater, a favorite spot for brides and grooms to take their vows. If you keep going west after reaching the summit, you'll see views of the Continental Divide and Indian Peaks Wilderness. About 3 miles more and you'll come to Walker Ranch, where several hiking trails originate.

SHOPPING

Pearl Street Mall (see Main Attractions, p. 39) is a unique shopping experience, both for its appealing pedestrian-mall setting and its diverse mix of retail shops, restaurants, and galleries. Even if you're not looking to buy, it's fun to browse the myriad shops. **Boulder Arts and Crafts Cooperative** features the original—and often whimsical—works of more than 70 Colorado artists. *1421 Pearl St., 303-443-3683, www.boulderartsandcrafts.com.* **Boulder Book Store** is a great local bookshop, with knowledgeable staff and plenty of nooks and crannies for a quiet read. *1107 Pearl St., 303-447-2074, www.boulderbookstore.com.* **Peppercorn,** an upscale gourmet kitchen and houseware store, boasts the largest selection of cookbooks in the country. *1235 Pearl St., 303-449-5847, www.peppercorn.com.*

Old Town Niwot is just two blocks long but includes a number of antique shops. **Niwot Antique Emporium** has booths from 40 of the top antique dealers in the state. *136 2nd St., 303-652-2587.* From Boulder, drive northeast on the Diagonal Highway (CO 119) for 7 miles, look for the sign for Historic Downtown Niwot, and turn right onto Main Street (which is also 2nd Street).

The **29th Street Mall** is the area's newest upscale mall, where you'll find fine department stores, restaurants, and a cinema. It's in Boulder on 28h Street and Canyon Boulevard. *303-449-1189, www.twentyninthstreet.com.*

TOURS

Celestial Seasonings, the nation's largest manufacturer of herbal teas, offers tours on the hour from 10 a.m. to 3 p.m. Monday–Saturday and 11 a.m. to 4 p.m. on Sunday. The Peppermint Room is a storage facility for some 5,000 bales of mint—a "scent-sation" you won't soon forget. Visit the gift shop, or stop in the cafeteria for a bite to eat. *4600 Sleepytime Dr., 303-581-1202, www.celestialseasonings.com.*

Historic Walking Tours of Boulder conducts summertime guided tours of Boulder's many historic neighborhoods, including Pearl Street, Mapleton Hill, Chautauqua Park, and University Hill. *1123 Spruce St., 303-444-5192, www.historicboulder.org.*

The I. M. Pei-designed **National Center for Atmospheric Research** (NCAR) sits on a high mesa overlooking town. Here scientists study all phenomena related to weather and world climate. Guided and self-guided tours are available, with guided tours offered every day at noon. No reservations necessary. There are also two art galleries, a gift shop (great for budding scientists), and several hiking trails. *1850 Table Mesa Dr., 303-497-1000, www.ncar.ucar.edu/ncar.*

WATER SPORTS

Boulder Reservoir is a popular place on summer weekends. Kids splash and play on the sand swim beach. Windsurfers, sailboats, motorboats, kayakers, and waterskiers also share the "res." Boat rentals and picnic tables with grills are also popular here. From Boulder, drive northeast on the Diagonal Highway (CO 119), turn left onto Jay Road, take an immediate right onto 51st Street, and follow the signs to the reservoir. *5565 51st St., 303-441-3461.*

Boulder Creek is a favorite place for tubing in the spring. There is also a whitewater kayak course near Eben Fine Park. Eldorado Canyon State Park (see Parks, p. 43) has Class III and

IV whitewater kayaking on **South Boulder Creek,** which flows through the park.

Eldorado Springs is an artesian spring pool open during the summer. A popular resort at the turn of the century, Eldorado Springs has seen better days, but it's still a fun, funky place and a pleasant respite. It's located near the entrance to Eldorado Canyon State Park (for directions see Rock Climbing, p. 43). *303-499-1316.* Other outdoor pools managed by the City of Boulder include the **Spruce Street Pool** and the pool at **Scott Carpenter Park.** *303-413-7200.*

WINTER SPORTS

Eldora Mountain Resort is a downhill ski area that is pretty much in Boulder's backyard. Smaller than other Colorado resorts, Eldora is just 30 minutes from Boulder. You can even take a special "Ski-n-Ride" RTD bus from Boulder, Broomfield, or Longmont. It's a locals' ski area, with 1,400 vertical feet and 12 lifts. For snowboarders there are three terrain parks, including a super pipe. The **Nordic Center** has 25 miles of groomed cross-country ski trails, with rentals and instruction available. Two snowmobile terrain parks and evening snowmobile tours are also available. It's often windy at Eldora, so be prepared with layers of clothing. From Boulder, drive west on Canyon Boulevard (CO 119) for 17 miles to Nederland. Go three-quarters of the way around the traffic circle and continue south on CO 119 for about 1 mile. Turn right onto County Road 130 and follow the signs about 3 miles. *303-440-8700, www.eldora.com.*

Many of the hiking trails in the Indian Peaks Wilderness also double as cross-country ski and snowshoe trails. The **Middle St. Vrain Creek Trail** MODERATE is 4.5 miles (one way), following blue blazes along both a trail and a road, which is also used by snowmobilers. From Boulder drive west on Canyon Boulevard (CO 119) for 17 miles to Nederland, then north on CO 72 for 17 miles to Peaceful Valley.

Brainard Lake Recreation Area is also a popular winter playground. **CMC South Trail** EASY is a 2-mile (one way) trail that starts from the Red Rock trailhead. You can return the same way or loop around Brainard Lake and return on Brainard Lake Drive. To reach Brainard Lake from Boulder, drive 17 miles west on Canyon Boulevard (CO 119) to Nederland. Head north on CO 72 for about 8 miles. The town of Ward will be on the right and Brainard Lake Drive is just beyond that on the left. Follow it for 2.5 miles to the trailhead.

Jenny Creek Trail MODERATE is a classic cross-country route, climbing 4.5 miles up to Yankee Doodle Lake, a great picnic spot. The trail starts from Eldora Mountain Resort (see directions above) near the Tenderfoot chairlift, then veers off onto national forest land. Ski up the left side of the chairlift and look for the national forest access sign.

The ranger station in Boulder has lots of information on winter trails in Brainard Lake Recreation Area, Indian Peaks Wilderness, and Roosevelt National Forest. *2140 Yarmouth Ave., 303-541-2500, www.fs.fed.us/arnf.*

Restaurants

Boulder teems with outstanding dining options; here are my very favorites. For a fancy meal with an equally impressive view of Boulder below, try **Flagstaff House** ($$$-$$$$). You'll need to dress up a bit. Drive west on Baseline Road and go about 1 mile up Flagstaff Mountain. *303-442-4640, www. flagstaffhouse.com.* **Chautauqua Dining Hall** ($$), serving creative American cuisine, is another truly Boulder experience (see Main Attractions, p. 39). *900 Baseline Rd., 303-440-3776, www.chatauquadininghall.com.* **Boulder Dushanbe Teahouse** ($-$$) is an exotic, one-of-a-kind structure—a gift to Boulder from its "sister city" of Dushanbe, Tajikistan. Savor international cuisine, or just a slice of gingerbread cake with tea, amid the ornately painted wood, intricately carved columns, and ceramic wall panels—the pride of Tajik artisans. *1770 13th St., 303-442-4993, www.boulderteahouse.com.*

Flagstaff House restaurant, Boulder

Boulder Dushanbe Teahouse

Centro Latin Kitchen and Refreshment Palace ($$) is a hopping place with a heated outdoor bar. They serve memorable Latin food. *950 Pearl St., 303-442-7771.* **Bacaro** ($$-$$$) offers upscale Italian food, and the outdoor deck is a great place on summer evenings. *921 Pearl St., 303-444-4888.* Colorado might not be known as a mecca for good seafood, but in Boulder you're in luck: **Sushi Tora** ($$-$$$) has the freshest sushi in town. *2014 10th St., 303-444-2280, www.sushitora.com.* **The Kitchen** ($$-$$$) offers the quintessential Boulder experience with their simple gourmet dishes, earth-friendly practices, and community atmosphere. *1039 Pearl St., 303-554-5973, www. thekitchencafe.com.* The **14th Street Bar and Grill** ($-$$$) has great pasta, salads, and panini sandwiches. *1400 Pearl St., 303-444-5854, http://14thstreetbarandgrill. com.* In the mood for a high-grade cut of steak? Then try the **Boulder ChopHouse** ($$-$$$$). *921 Walnut St., 303-443-1188, www.chophouse.com.* **Hungry Toad** ($-$$) is the place to go for fantastic British fare and a burger. *2543 N. Broadway St., 303-442-5012.* For a caffeine fix, **The Trident** ($) is a well-loved Boulder institution,

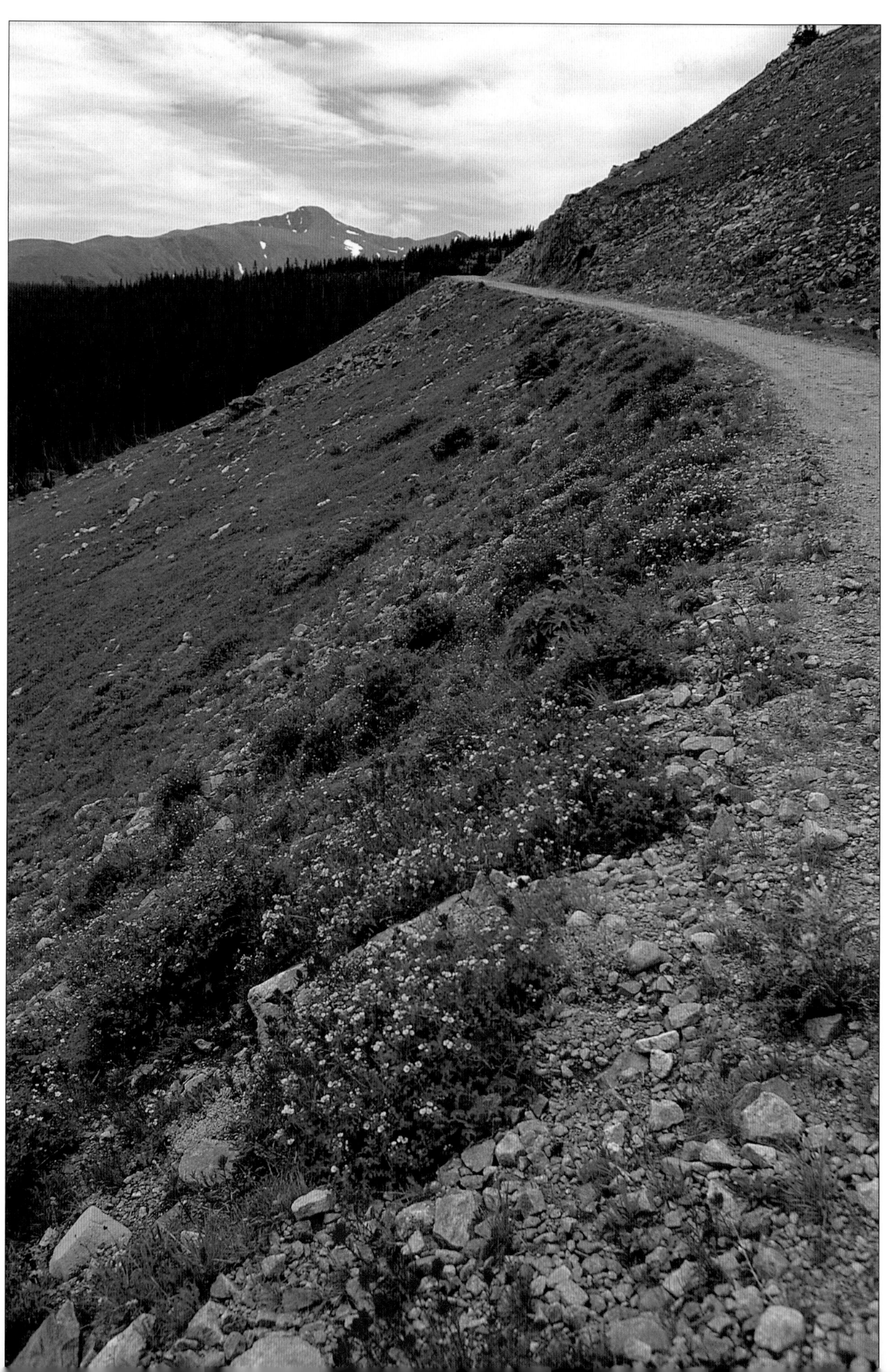

6 SCENIC LOCATION — ROLLINS PASS EAST

Six miles south of Caribou (see Scenic Location No. 5, p. 41) as the crow flies, South Boulder Creek drains down from the east side of the James Peak region of the Front Range. In 1865 a toll road for wagons was constructed along the creek before climbing Rollins Pass (11,671 feet) on its way down to Winter Park. Later, the Denver Northwestern & Pacific Railroad operated along this route—even in winter. The rail route over the pass was ultimately abandoned and replaced by the Moffat Tunnel, which today still allows trains to pass beneath the Continental Divide on the way to the Western Slope. The route over the pass is now a rough four-wheel-drive road. One mile from the top of the pass, the road is blocked by the cave-in of the Needles Eye Tunnel, so you must walk to get to Rollins Pass from this side. Access from Winter Park to the pass is much easier (see Scenic Location No. 49, p. 175). From Boulder, take CO 119 past Nederland south to Rollinsville. Head west on County Road 16 and take Forest Road 149, the Moffat Road, all the way to the tunnel.

This is quite the wild and scenic route. The road bisects the Indian Peaks Wilderness to the north and the James Peak Wilderness to the south. Beginning in July, the route is lined with thick fields of wildflowers, and Yankee Doodle and Jenny Lakes contain beautiful reflections of the surrounding hills and peaks. Compose the road as a lead-in line as it ascends into the alpine tundra. This is a morning place. Sunrise bathes the Front Range in rich red light, all of it reflecting in the two lakes! The trail over the top of the Needles Eye Tunnel passes several old buildings that make an excellent foreground for a composition with peaks behind. Once on top of the pass, hike north down to King Lake, or even Betty and Bob Lakes, all in the Indian Peaks Wilderness, before heading home.

940 Pearl St., 303-443-3133. For breakfast, try **Dot's Diner** ($) *1333 Broadway St, 303-447-9184.* **Bookend Café** ($), attached to the Boulder Book Store, serves fine coffees and teas, bakery items, and prepared dishes all day in a bookish atmosphere. *1115 Pearl St., 303-440-6699.*

Beyond downtown, **Chez Thuy** ($-$$$) features the best Vietnamese dining in Boulder. *2655 28th St., 303-442-1700.* **Ras Kassa's** ($-$$) serves fine Ethiopian cuisine, which you eat sans silverware, instead scooping up the food with spongy *injera* bread. *2111 30th St., 303-447-2919.* If you're hungry in the morning, seek out wonderful **Lucile's Creole Café** ($$). *2124 14th St., 303-442-4743.* **Dolan's** ($$-$$$$) is great for seafood. *2319 Arapahoe Ave., 303-444-8758.* Elegant **Frasca Food and Wine** ($$$$) serves unparalleled Italian fusion cuisine. *1738 Pearl St., 303-442-6966.* **Efrains II** ($) earns their cult following with authentic Mexican fare and bold margaritas. *1630 N 63rd St., 303-440-4045.* **L'Atelier** ($$$) is Boulder's best-kept secret, presenting modern French dishes. *1739 Pearl St., 303-442-7233, www.latelierboulder.com.*

If you're headed up to Nederland, the **Black Forest Restaurant** ($$-$$$) dishes out choice wiener schnitzel, goulash, and stroganoff, as well as American dishes. *24 Big Springs Dr., 303-279-2333.* To feel like a local, stop at the **Pioneer Inn** ($-$$) for a burger, brew, or even a game of pool. *15 1st St., 303-258-7733.* On a Sunday afternoon, you can catch a bluegrass jam on the front porch of the **Acoustic Coffeehouse** ($). *95 E. 1st St., 303-258-3209.*

Also up in the mountains and worth the trip is the **Gold Hill Inn** ($$$), which serves a fixed-price, six-course dinner during the summer season (no credit cards). *401 Main St., Gold Hill, 303-443-6461.* **The Restaurant at Gold Lake** ($$$), at the Gold Lake Mountain Resort and Spa, offers fixed-price, gourmet regional cuisine in a beautiful mountain lodge. *3371 Gold Lake Rd., Ward, 303-459-3544.*

Black Forest Restaurant, Nederland

Accommodations

A national historic landmark, the **Hotel Boulderado** ($$$-$$$$) is just a half-block north of the Pearl Street Mall. It was the classiest place in town when completed in 1909, and, with its Victorian lobby topped by a stained-glass skylight, it retains that distinction today. A modern addition has been added to the original red-brick building, combining modern amenities with turn-of-the-century grandeur. *2115 13th St., 303-442-4344, www.boulderado.com.*

Briar Rose Bed and Breakfast ($$-$$$) features fresh breakfast from the local co-op, complimentary afternoon tea, and private baths and balconies in many of its ten rooms. *2151 Arapahoe Ave., 303-442-3007, www.briarrosebb.com.* **Chautauqua Park** ($-$$) has a range of short-term (four-night minimum in summer, three-night in winter) and long-term lodging, from efficiency apartments to three-bedroom cottages. The cottages all have screened-in porches (though no phones or TVs) and a top cultural and geographical setting (see Main Attractions, p. 39). *900 Baseline Rd., 303-441-3408, www.chautauqua.com.*

Briar Rose Bed and Breakfast, Boulder

Once a stagecoach stop along Boulder Canyon, **The Alps Boulder Canyon Inn** ($$-$$$$) is now a stately, mountain-lodge B&B, with 12 guest rooms, many with fireplaces and private porches. It's located west of Boulder 2 miles on CO 119. *303-444-5445, www.alpsinn.com.* Also in Boulder Canyon,

Foot of the Mountain Motel ($) is reminiscent of a 1930s motor court, complete with rustic charm and lots of knotty pine. *200 Arapahoe Ave., 303-442-5688, www.footofthe mountainmotel.com.*

You'll find two good choices just east of Boulder in the Niwot and Gunbarrel areas. **Niwot Inn** ($$) offers 14 country-contemporary rooms by historic downtown Niwot. *342 2nd Ave., Niwot, 303-652-8452, www.niwotinn.com.* **Boulder Twin Lakes Inn** ($-$$) offers 33 suites, all with mini-kitchens, as well as the use of a local health club. *6485 Twin Lakes Road, Boulder, 303-530-2929, 800-322-2939, www.twinlakesinnboulder.com.*

Staying in the Nederland area will put you closer to the Peak to Peak Highway and Indian Peaks Wilderness. **Best Western Lodge** ($$) is a very impressive log building with spacious rooms featuring handmade furniture and local artwork. *55 Lakeview Dr., 303-258-9463.* **Peaceful Valley Ranch** ($$-$$$$) offers guest-ranch facilities in the summer (for three- or six-night stays, including all meals and activities) and nightly lodging and B&B rooms in fall and winter. Situated near Indian Peaks Wilderness, the ranch specializes in horseback riding in summer and snow sports in winter. From Boulder, drive west on Canyon Boulevard/CO 119 for 17 miles to Nederland, then go north on CO 72 for about 20 miles. *800-955-6343, www.peacefulvalley.com.* **Gold Lake Mountain Resort and Spa** ($$$$) has individual cabins in a mountain setting. Here you can soak in one of four outdoor hot tubs overlooking Gold Lake, or choose from a range of spa treatments and massages, partake in numerous outdoor activities, and dine on organic food at The Restaurant at Gold Lake. *3371 Gold Lake Road, Ward, 303-459-3544, www.goldlake.com.* **Shambhala Mountain Center,** home of the largest Himalayan-style Buddhist Temple in the Western World, offers lodging, retreats, yoga, and organic food in a serene setting. Check out their Japanese Shinto shrine and Alpine Botanic Garden. *4921 County Road 68C, Red Feather Lakes, 970-881-2184, www.shambhalamountain.org.*

Gold Lake Mountain Resort and Spa, Ward

Special Events

Each April the University of Colorado hosts the **Conference on World Affairs,** which brings experts from around the world to discuss an amazing range of topics in panel forums. This week-long event is free and open to the public. *303-492-2525, www.colorado.edu/cwa.*

The **Bolder Boulder** is a 10K race held each Memorial Day weekend. Some 40,000 runners (walkers, too) partake in this event, with both amateur and professional categories. *303-444-7223, www.bolderboulder.com.*

Colorado Music Festival is a seven-week classical music festival presenting orchestral, chamber, ensemble, and guest performances. The festival takes place late June through early August at Chautauqua Auditorium. *900 Baseline Rd., 303-449-1397, www.coloradomusicfest.org.* **Chautauqua Summer Festival** runs from June through September with a wide range of musical, theatrical, and dance performances, as well as a weekly silent movie series with live musical accompaniment. *900 Baseline Rd., 303-440-7666, www.chautauqua.com.*

Since 1958, **Colorado Shakespeare Festival** has been delighting audiences from July through mid-August, performing professional productions of the bard's work in the Mary Rippon Outdoor Theatre on the University of Colorado campus. Four plays are performed in repertoire, with both traditional and contemporary interpretations. Come early and picnic on the green; the bard himself may even visit with you. *303-492-0554, www.coloradoshakes.org.*

For More Information

Boulder Convention and Visitors Bureau, *2440 Pearl St., 303-442-2911, www.bouldercoloradousa.com.*

Colorado Shakespeare Festival

Idaho Springs, Central City, and Black Hawk

(see map on p. 50)

High-country travelers from Denver often stop at Idaho Springs to get a hearty breakfast before continuing west on I-70, or drop by on the return trip from the slopes to devour a pizza. Buses transport visitors from the Front Range up the winding mountain road to the Black Hawk and Central City casinos. But this area is more than bacon, eggs, and one-armed bandits. Rich veins of mining history run through this region, which also provides access to Colorado scenery and wildlife watching.

Visit the quaint shops on Idaho Springs' Miner Street, then take a tour of an old gold mine or soak in the old-time hot springs. After trying your luck at the slots or gaming tables in Black Hawk, walk among the hilly streets of Central City to see the Teller House and Central City Opera House, as you take in the area's romance and history. Idaho Springs is 33 miles west of Denver on I-70, Black Hawk is 29 miles west of Golden on US 6 and CO 119, and Central City is 1 mile west of Black Hawk on CO 279.

History

Idaho Springs, Central City, and Black Hawk started as tumultuous mining camps, populated by Welsh and Cornish laborers who left their cultural mark on the region. In 1859, prospector George A. Jackson found gold at the confluence of Vasquez (now Clear) and Chicago Creeks. With the strike at what was called Jackson's Bar, the Colorado gold rush had begun. Jackson also discovered the hot springs, long known to the Mountain Ute and Arapaho tribes, above present-day Idaho Springs. The thermal springs continued to draw people long after the mines closed. Jackson's Bar is now Idaho Springs, to this day boasting Old West charm, relaxed dining, and the historic Indian Springs Resort.

Also in 1859, Georgia prospector John H. Gregory struck gold near Central City and Black Hawk in what became known as Gregory Diggings. Once known as "The Richest Square Mile on Earth," Central City was founded in 1861 and became a supply center and the main gathering place for miners. Despite a devastating 1874 fire, Central City rebuilt and thrived for many years. The town's opera house bustled with visitors enjoying entertainment and a bit of culture, and the Teller House rivaled Aspen's Hotel Jerome and Leadville's Delaware Hotel.

A New England professor named Nathaniel P. Hill came west to Black Hawk to research smelting techniques in the 1860s. He developed a process, soon to become a model for other Colorado smelting operations, that separated gold from ore. In 1867 he established the Boston & Colorado Smelting Co. in Black Hawk. With the smelter and the arrival of the railroad in 1872, Black Hawk became a major mining center, the "City of Mills."

The fortunes of Central City and Black Hawk, long in decline, were transformed by the introduction of limited-stakes gaming in 1991. Today, Black Hawk's huge casinos command Colorado gaming, though Central City's smaller-scale, historically oriented casinos dominated initially and were in fact the model of mountain-town gaming for those who put it on the ballot in 1990. Love it or loathe it, gaming has funded historic preservation projects around the state.

Main Attractions

CENTRAL CITY OPERA HOUSE

Colorado's most famous opera house opened in 1878 in a manner befitting the affluence of the town. During the heyday of the mining camps, the opera house featured vaudeville, comedy, and circus acts, and hosted such theater greats as Sarah Bernhardt and Edwin Booth. Its early glory was short-lived, however, as the venue went the way of Central City's mining wealth. The University of Denver and the Central City Opera House Association led an aggressive fund-raising effort that succeeded in reopening the 550-seat opera house in 1932 with Lillian Gish in *Camille*. In 1956, Douglas Moore's opera *The Ballad of Baby Doe* premiered here. Henry Mollicone's one-act cabaret-opera, *The Face on the Barroom Floor*, premiered here in 1978. Central City Opera presents three operas each summer season in the National Historic Landmark opera house. *120 Eureka St., 303-292-6700, www.centralcityopera.org.*

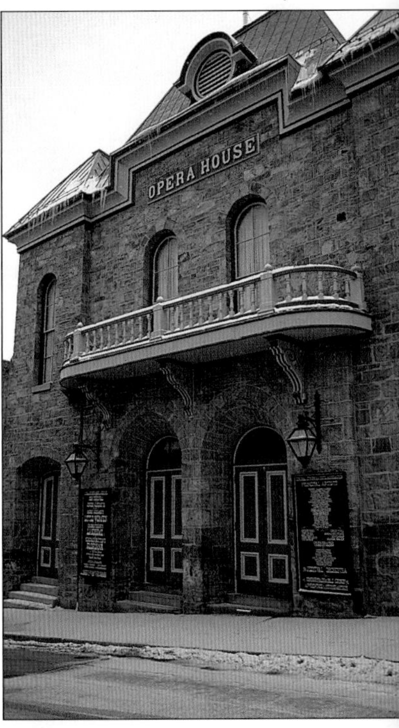

Central City Opera House

Next door to the opera house stands the 1872 **Teller House,** a Central City Opera Historic Property. One of Central City's leading citizens, Henry M. Teller, put up $20,000 to build a fine hotel in Central City. A year later, a silver sidewalk was laid down in front of the hotel for President Ulysses S. Grant, which he reportedly declined to walk on so as not to show favoritism in the silver/gold currency debate. The famous face immortalized on the barroom floor has inspired much controversy and an enduring musical revue, but the young lady was in fact Juanita, the wife of Herndon Davis, who painted her portrait in 1936. A casino operated here for almost a decade but closed its doors in 2000. The venerable structure seems likely to endure, however.

Idaho Springs/Central City/Black Hawk

Colorado Atlas & Gazetteer p. 39

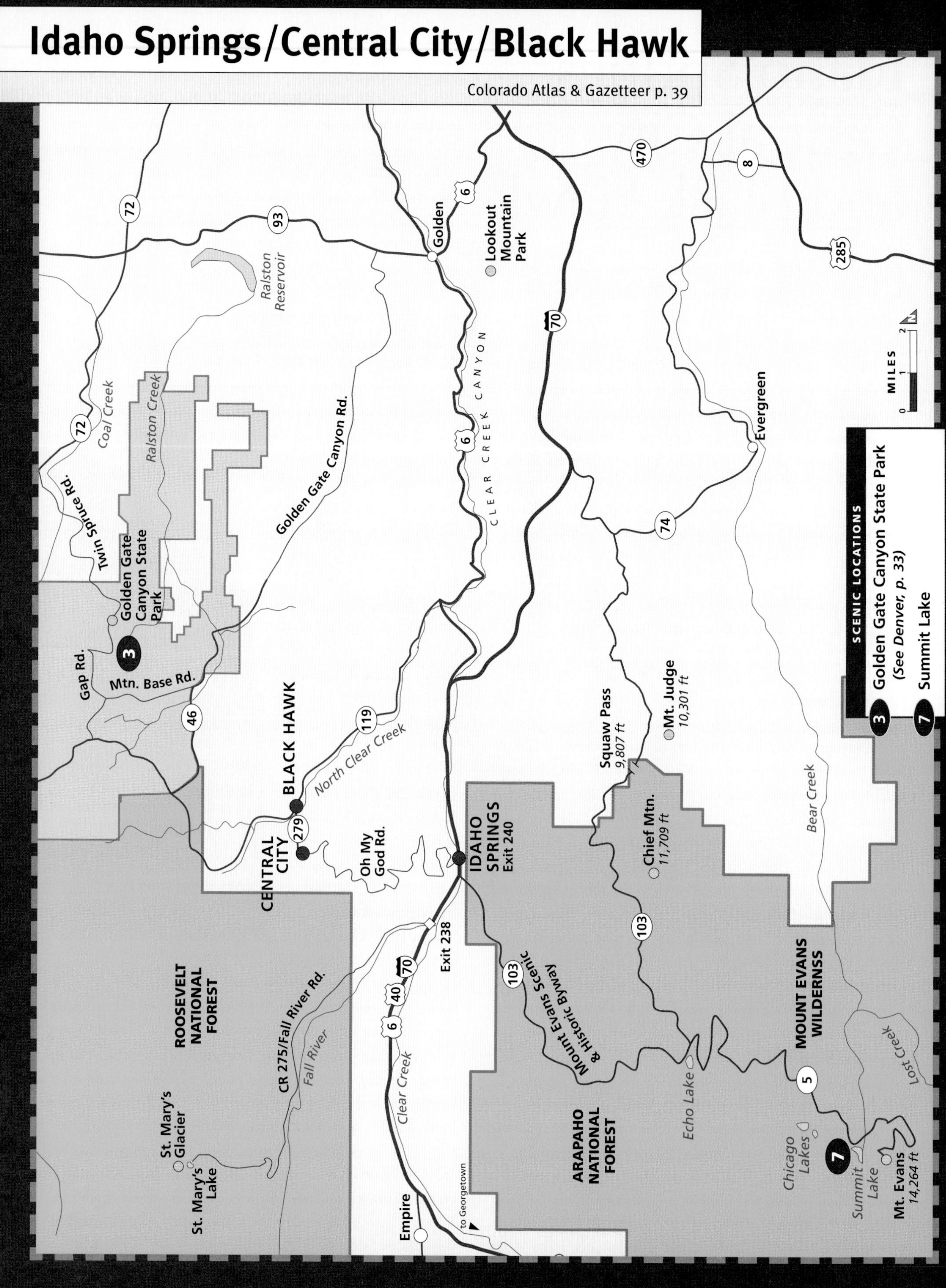

GAMING

The 1990 ballot initiative approving limited-stakes gambling in Cripple Creek, Central City, and Black Hawk remains controversial. Undoubtedly, big casinos have provided an enormous source of revenue, but gaming has also fundamentally changed the character of these historic mountain communities. Central City lost a big gamble that a no-growth measure would please tourists who wanted to play in a charming historic setting. But parking headaches and mom-and-pop halls were not what people wanted, after all, despite the town's considerable appeal. Of 23 casinos operating here in 1991, just a handful remain.

Meanwhile, Black Hawk determined not to be a parking lot for its neighboring town. Instead it seized the opportunity of being first, literally by a mile, on the CO 119 approach from Denver—and welcoming development. Today, enormous Black Hawk casinos have trounced their rivals in Central City and amassed great profits, if at the expense of the town's historical integrity, critics say. Certainly, the formerly humble little town is now the state's gaming engine. Ironically, although Black Hawk's character has been compromised, its gaming wealth has funded $100 million worth of statewide preservation efforts (as of 2001).

If visiting the casinos interests you, I recommend taking a shuttle bus from Denver without worrying about the drive up Clear Creek Canyon. Good, affordable meals abound, and some lodging is also available. *For shuttle information: People's Choice, 303-289-2222.*

INDIAN HOT SPRINGS

The thermal mineral waters at Idaho Springs pay homage to the earliest bathers here. A mural of tribesmen beside "the healing waters" adorns the weathered, historic lobby at Indian Springs. This no-frills resort features men's and women's vapor caves and private hot tubs ranging from 104 to 112 degrees. Baths in a foot-deep pool of mud at "Club Mud" make this resort unique. Tropical gardens grow lushly around the perimeter of the 90-degree swimming pool-with-greenhouse. Massages, a restaurant, and lodging are also available. *302 Soda Creek Rd., 303-989-6666, www.indianhotsprings.com.*

MOUNT EVANS SCENIC AND HISTORIC BYWAY

Colorado boasts many of the highest roads in the nation across its precipitous passes and dodgy shelf roads. Mount Evans Road (CO 5) is the country's highest paved road (Trail Ridge Road near Estes Park being the highest continuous paved road) and climbs to within a few hundred yards of the 14,264-foot summit. Named after John Evans (the second territorial governor of Colorado and a successful physician, educator, financier, and railroad builder), Mount Evans rules Denver's skyline. This amazing, 28-mile road climbs through various altitude zones as it rises more than 7,000 feet.

As your vehicle ascends the road, coniferous forests gradually give way to magnificent views. Stop at Mount Goliath Natural Area and hike through thousand-year-old bristlecone pine and krummholz—trees shaped by the high winds, appearing to grow horizontally. Or climb 3 miles to Summit Lake (see Scenic Location No. 7, p. 53), which is framed by steep mountains. Take the short hike from the south shore to the overlook for the Chicago Lakes, 2,000 feet below. From Summit Lake, the byway becomes a narrow shelf road with a series of switchbacks and hairpin curves. The building near the summit is the University of Denver high-altitude laboratory. Take in panoramic views of both the Front Range and Continental Divide at the top.

The drive allows for up-close viewing of Rocky Mountain bighorn sheep and elusive white mountain goats. Mount Evans is the only place where I have been able to look *down* upon mountain goats. Bighorns are master panhandlers, but resist the temptation to feed them. Human food is disruptive to their diet, and handouts often make these animals dependent on people. Mountain goats prefer meadows and ledges near the summit. Also look for yellow-bellied marmots on the boulders just off the road.

This extraordinary byway can be dangerous. Guard against altitude sickness, and watch the sky in late afternoon for lightning storms. From Idaho Springs, head south on CO 103 to Echo Lake; from there, pick up CO 5 on the south end of the lake to continue up the summit. CO 5 is open usually from Memorial Day through mid-September. *303-567-2138, (Echo Lake Lodge), www.clearcreekcounty.org.*

Activities

CAMPING

Shaded by Engelmann spruce at the intersection of CO 103 and CO 5 on Mount Evans Road, **Echo Lake** campground is managed by Arapaho National Forest. **West Chicago Creek** nestles amid pines and trickling streams. From Idaho Springs, take CO 103 southwest for 6.5 miles to Forest Road 188, turn right, and continue 3 miles to the campground. *877-444-6777, www.reserveusa.com.*

FISHING

Clear Creek parallels I-70 from Idaho Springs to Georgetown and sometimes suffers from its proximity to heavy vehicular traffic. I've had the best luck on the stretch paralleling US 6 from the east end of the canyon near Golden west to CO 119. The water is swift and deep, and you can enjoy solitude on weekdays. Picnic spots line the river on US 6, but keep an eye on your kids around the creek. *www.clearcreekcounty.org.*

HIKING

The 0.5-mile (one way) hike to **St. Mary's Lake and Glacier** EASY is a favorite place for locals and people from Denver to run their dogs (on a leash, of course). St. Mary's Glacier is the southernmost U.S. glacier, and the lake is pristine. Snowshoers frequent the area in winter. This short hike will also take you to the base of 12,136-foot Kingston Peak. From Idaho Springs, take I-70 west 2 miles to Exit 238, Fall River Road (CR 275), and follow signs to the glacier.

SUMMIT LAKE

Just below the top of 14,264-foot Mount Evans, the peak most conspicuous from Denver, lies alpine Summit Lake. A classic tarn, or glacial lake, left behind in a high mountain cirque by glaciers from the Ice Age, breathtaking Summit Lake is literally right off the road. The summit of Mount Evans makes a sublime reflection in the lake, and wildflowers decorate the tundra on all sides. In fact, the entire drive along the Mount Evans Scenic and Historic Byway (see p. 51) is photogenic. Get off I-70 at the Idaho Springs exit (240), then take CO 103, Mount Evans Road, and turn right on CO 5 to ascend the peak. The entire drive is 28 miles (one way).

Both Mount Evans Road and Summit Lake cherry-stem into the Mount Evans Wilderness. Wildlife is everywhere, especially the relatively tame herds of white mountain goats and bighorn sheep. You will also see plenty of marmots and pikas. Have your telephoto lens ready to take photographs of the goats, which you will see more often than not around the peak. Compose them in the foreground with peaks behind, using a larger aperture to keep the goats in focus and the peaks slightly out of focus. This "selected focus" technique draws the eye more quickly to the goats, making them the dominant feature in the scene (see pp. 81, 83, *Photographing the Landscape*).

Now head back down to Summit Lake to try some landscape photography. Look for pools of water in the tundra around the edge of the lake. The wind is less likely to disturb these pools, so you are more apt to catch a good scenic reflection off the water. Using your wide-angle lens, compose the pools in the foreground with Mount Evans behind. If you photograph before sunrise on a clear day, you may chance to see the peak showing deep red. As the sun rises higher, hunt for colorful pockets of wildflowers awash in sunlight.

The 4-mile (one way) **Chicago Lakes Trail** MODERATE leads to the Chicago Lakes Basin and also to the cliffs of Mount Evans. The 6.5-mile (one way) **Resthouse Meadows Trail** MODERATE drops steeply into the remote meadows of Mount Evans Wilderness. You can also access beautiful **Lincoln Lake** if you take a right at the 5-mile point in the hike. Both trails start at Echo Lake campground (see Camping, p. 51).

The 1.5-mile (one way) **Chief Mountain Trail** EASY leads through pine forests and alpine tundra to grand views of Mount Evans, Pikes Peak, and even Longs Peak. The trailhead is 5 miles east of Echo Lake on CO 103.

MINES AND MUSEUMS

At the working **Phoenix Mine,** children can pan for gold, swing a pickax, and listen for Tommyknockers (the elves that supposedly inhabit the mine walls). From Idaho Springs, take the I-70 frontage road 1 mile to Trail Creek Road and go south 0.75 mile. *303-567-0422, www.phoenixgoldmine.com.* You can also take a self-guided tour of the 1885 **Coeur d'Alene Mine** on Academy Hill in Central City. *303-582-5283.*

Miners in the Central City and Black Hawk area used the 22,000-foot Argo Tunnel, built in 1910, to transport ore to the **Argo Gold Mine & Museum** in Idaho Springs. Although the mill shut down during World War II, self-guided tours are available at this landmark building. *2350 Riverside Dr., 303-567-2421, www.historicargotours.com.*

Housed in a former Central City schoolhouse, **Gilpin County Historical Museum** displays Victorian furniture, dolls, carriages, and mining and fire department equipment. *228 E. High St., 303-582-5283, www.gilpinhistory.org.* A tour of the 1874 **Thomas House** gives insight into daily life in turn-of-the-century Central City. *209 Eureka St., 303-582-5283.*

SCENIC DRIVE

The 9-mile **Oh My God Road,** or Virginia Canyon Road, connecting Idaho Springs with Central City, was once a wagon road miners used to haul ore. Today, the road illustrates Colorado's mining history. You will pass hundreds of glory holes, gob piles, and abandoned mines. This is not a place to go hiking, and you certainly want to watch children, as some of these abandoned mine shafts drop hundreds of feet, and side roads lead to private property. Wide, well-maintained, and easily navigated, this road must have earned its exclamatory name for the fine views of Squaw Mountain and Mount Evans. From Idaho Springs, go north at the intersection of Canyon and Placer Streets.

WATER WHEEL

Almost everyone who flies by on I-70 notices the huge **Charlie Tayler Water Wheel** on the south side of the highway across from Idaho Springs. Built in the 1890s, the wheel was restored and moved to Bridal Veil Falls by town citizens. Red, white, and blue lights shine on Bridal Veil Falls on the Fourth of July, when American flags fly from the wheel. During the holiday season you'll see another artful display here.

Without access from I-70, the wheel is somewhat of an enigma to most travelers, but you can actually see the water wheel up close by heading behind the City Hall building.

Restaurants

Owned by the same family since 1948, **Historic El Rancho** ($$) is a roadside landmark serving fine steaks, trout, and game dishes. *12 miles east of Idaho Springs on I-70 at Exit 252, 303-526-0661, www.historicelrancho.com.* In Idaho Springs, the **Buffalo Restaurant and Bar** ($-$$) serves creative breakfasts, great Mexican fare, and of course, almost every buffalo dish imaginable. *1617 Miner St., 303-567-2729, www.buffalo restaurant.com.* Pizza doesn't get much better than the thick-crusted "mountain pies" at **Beau Jo's** ($-$$), a casual Colorado favorite started in Idaho Springs. Satisfy your après-ski appetite here, and though it sounds strange, try drizzling honey on the pizza crust. *1517 Miner St., 303-567-4376, www.beaujos.com.*

In Idaho Springs, **Tommyknocker Brewery and Pub** ($-$$) serves award-winning brews, along with handcrafted soft drinks and pub grub, in a sporty dining room. *1401 Miner St., Idaho Springs, 303-567-2688, www.tommyknocker.com.* Across from Tommyknocker's is the **Two Brothers Deli** ($) a great place for sandwiches, smoothies, soups, salads, and boxed lunches. *1424 Miner St, 303-567-2439, www.twobrothersdeli.com.* If you're looking for great BBQ, try **Smokin' Yards BBQ** ($). *2736 Colorado Blvd, 303-567-9273.* And for Italian in a casual atmosphere, **Mangia** ($$) is the place to be. *1446 Miner St, 303-567-4371, www.mangiamia.com.*

For a hearty breakfast at a reasonable price, eat with friendly locals at **Café Aimee** ($). *1614 Miner St, 303-567-2333,* or at **Marion's of the Rockies** ($), *2805 Colorado Blvd., Idaho Springs, 303-567-2925.* For dining in Central City and Black Hawk, seek out a casino.

Accommodations

I enjoy **Baxter's on the Creek** ($$) because of its remote location, wonderful views, and gracious hosts. *796 Highway 103, Idaho Springs, 303-567-2164, www.baxtersonthecrk.com.* I highly recommend **Chase Creek B&B** ($-$$), a restored Victorian home. *250 Chase St, Black Hawk, 303-582-3550.* In Central City, **Chateau L'Acadienne B&B** ($-$$) offers gourmet breakfast and real Louisiana ambiance. *325 Spring St., 303-582-5209.*

Special Events

On **Lou Bunch Day** in mid-June, Central City and Black Hawk residents dress in period costume to honor one of Central City's notorious madams. The event's highlights include a brass-bed race through Central City streets and an evening ball at the Teller House. *303-582-5251.*

From late June to early August, the Central City Opera House's **Central City Summer Festival** attracts music lovers and history buffs from far and wide. *120 Eureka St., 303-292-6700, www.centralcityopera.org.*

As part of the autumn **Cemetery Crawl,** sponsored by the Gilpin County Historical Society, locals dress as the most intriguing residents of a historic cemetery and relate colorful stories at their respective tombs. The selected cemetery changes each year. Ghoulish fun! *303-582-5283.*

For More Information

Idaho Springs Visitor Center, *2060 Miner St., 303-567-4382; Central City, 303-582-5251; Black Hawk, 303-582-5221.*

Teller House, Central City

Georgetown

(see map on p. 56)

After a day on the slopes, the Fielder family traditionally stops in Georgetown for dinner to let the I-70 bumper-to-bumper ski traffic thin out. Over the years I have become quite taken with this quaint town nestled against the mountains. In many ways Georgetown is a typical Colorado mining town, following the historic pattern of such settlements as Breckenridge and Leadville: Lone prospectors discover gold and silver, mining camp springs up, families follow, town booms, town busts, and, finally, town reinvents itself with recreation and tourism as its base.

Georgetown is unusual, however, in that most of its original wooden buildings are intact. Unlike other mining towns, Georgetown escaped major fires, thanks to the prevention efforts of the renowned Georgetown Fire Department, established in 1868. More than 200 original buildings stand in Georgetown's historic district, centered on 6th Street, and colorful Victorian gingerbread houses abound. Nearby mountains still show the evidence of bygone mining days. Just 46 miles west of Denver on I-70, Georgetown makes a great day trip for visitors from Denver. Empire, just a few miles east of Georgetown off I-70 on US 40, boasts a fine inn, an old-time feel, and antique shops. To reach Empire, take the US 40 exit off I-70 (Exit 233), about 39 miles west of Denver, and continue 2 miles.

History

In 1859, brothers David and George Griffith drifted from the Auraria gold camps in what is now Denver up to the Jackson's Bar gold camps near present-day Idaho Springs. Although David remained at Jackson's Bar, George soon became discouraged and moved west up Clear Creek to just above the present site of Georgetown. After George found a small amount of surface gold, a couple of his brothers and other miners quickly joined him. In 1860, the brothers Griffith claimed the area, called the Griffith Mining District. By 1864, it was George's Town.

Although George Griffith's discovery of gold originally drew miners here, prospectors soon found immense veins of silver near McClellan Mountain and above present-day Silver Plume, 2 miles west of Georgetown. Legend has it that Silver Plume got its name because there was so much silver in the mountains above town that silver flakes broke off like feathers. Between 1860 and 1893—the year of the repeal of the Sherman Silver Purchase Act—more than $2 million in silver and gold was extracted from area mines. Such was the wealth of silver in these parts that Georgetown was dubbed the Silver Queen of the Rockies, and the nearby peaks were called the Seven Silver Mountains.

Following the repeal of the Sherman Silver Purchase Act and the ensuing Silver Panic of 1893, Georgetown suffered the same decline as many other Colorado mining towns. What likely saved Georgetown from becoming a ghost town was the pride of its families and its location on the major road to the Western Slope. Today, Georgetown depends on winter skiers and year-round tourism from the Front Range and beyond.

Main Attractions

GEORGETOWN LOOP RAILROAD

Transporting rich ore from mines high in the mountains down to ore processing mills and assay offices at lower elevations was tricky. Without a dependable route, especially in bad weather, many remote mining camps were doomed to becoming ghost towns. Thanks to railroad visionary and builder General William Palmer (see Colorado Cameo, Colorado Springs, p. 76), narrow-gauge rails solved this dilemma. More than a foot narrower than standard track, narrow-gauge track was ideally suited for the thin rock ridges and steep inclines up to the mines.

By 1877, the Colorado Central Railroad had snaked up Clear Creek Canyon and arrived at Georgetown. The plan was to connect Georgetown with Breckenridge and eventually Leadville. From Georgetown up to Silver Plume, however, the terrain rose more than 600 feet in just 2 miles, creating a 6-percent grade that would challenge even a narrow-gauge track. The engineering solution: the Georgetown Loop, a series of curves and bridges that reduced the grade by half. Two hundred workers toiled seven years to lay the 4 miles of track in the Georgetown Loop, completed in 1884. Most famous of all its engineering feats is the Devil's Gate High Bridge, where the tracks loop over themselves by means of a picturesque bridge. Plans to extend the line, however, were abandoned following the Silver Panic of 1893, and the tracks were finally dismantled in 1939.

Georgetown Loop Railroad

In 1975, the Colorado Historical Society raised funds to rebuild the Georgetown Loop, thereby preserving a unique piece of Colorado history. Now the Loop is under new management. Stop for the guided tour at the Lebanon Silver Mine along the way. To take the railroad tour, exit I-70 at Georgetown, turn right (west) at the stop sign, and head into town. Turn right at the next intersection and continue up the road to the depot. *888-456-6777, www.georgetownlooprr.com.*

Continued on page 58

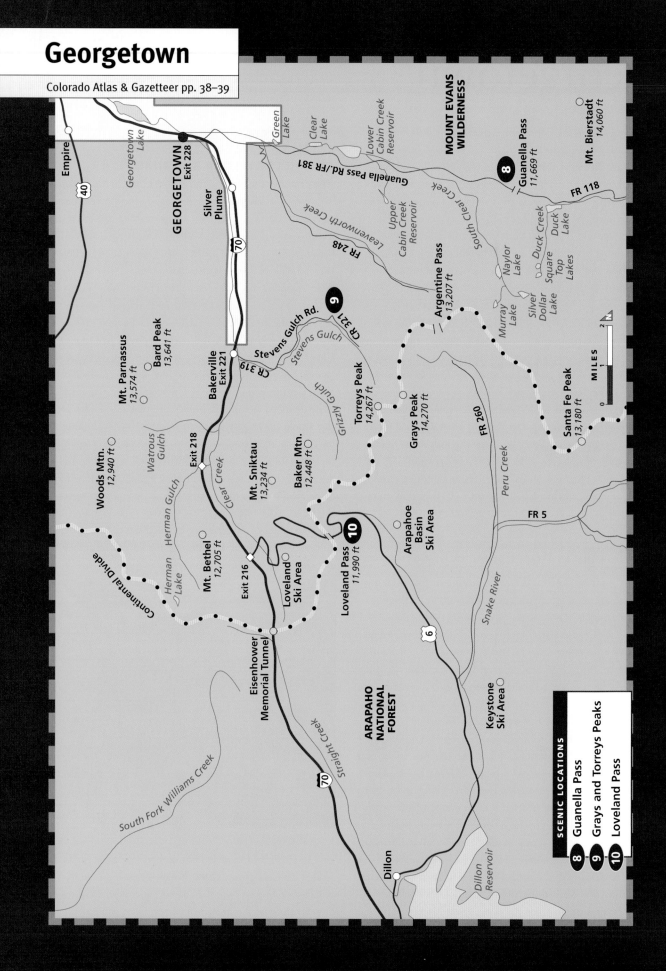

Georgetown

Colorado Atlas & Gazetteer pp. 38–39

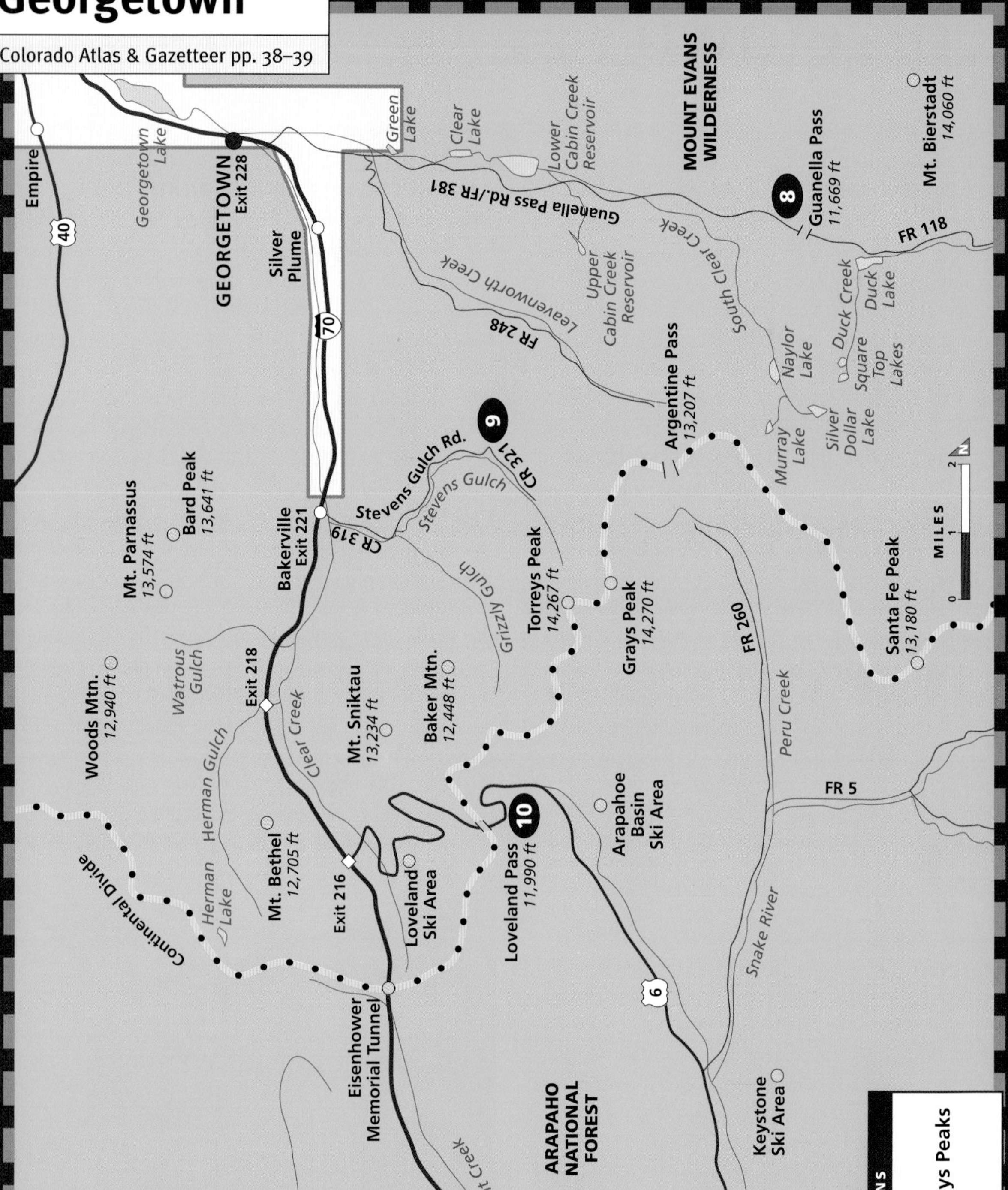

SCENIC LOCATIONS

8 Guanella Pass

9 Grays and Torreys Peaks

10 Loveland Pass

Empire
40
Georgetown Lake
GEORGETOWN
Exit 228
Silver Plume
70
Green Lake
Clear Lake
Lower Cabin Creek Reservoir
MOUNT EVANS WILDERNESS
Mt. Bierstadt
14,060 ft
Guanella Pass
11,669 ft
Guanella Pass Rd./FR 381
FR 118
South Clear Creek
Leavenworth Creek
FR 248
Upper Cabin Creek Reservoir
Duck Creek
Duck Lake
Naylor Lake
Square Top Lakes
Argentine Pass
13,207 ft
Murray Lake
Silver Dollar Lake
Stevens Gulch Rd.
CR 321
Stevens Gulch
Bard Peak
13,641 ft
Mt. Parnassus
13,574 ft
Bakerville
Exit 221
CR 319
Torreys Peak
14,267 ft
Grizzly Gulch
Grays Peak
14,270 ft
FR 260
Santa Fe Peak
13,180 ft
MILES
0 1 2
Woods Mtn.
12,940 ft
Watrous Gulch
Exit 218
Clear Creek
Mt. Sniktau
13,234 ft
Baker Mtn.
12,448 ft
Peru Creek
Herman Gulch
FR 5
Arapahoe Basin Ski Area
Mt. Bethel
12,705 ft
Exit 216
Loveland Ski Area
Loveland Pass
11,990 ft
Herman Lake
Continental Divide
Snake River
6
Eisenhower Memorial Tunnel
ARAPAHO NATIONAL FOREST
Keystone Ski Area
Straight Creek
South Fork Williams Creek
70
Dillon
Dillon Reservoir

8 SCENIC LOCATION

GUANELLA PASS

Guanella Pass Road, like the Mount Evans Road (see Scenic Location No. 7, p. 53), is a federal scenic and historic byway. Topping out at the 11,669-foot pass, the road starts in historic Georgetown and ends 23 miles later at the town of Grant along US 285. Beginning in ponderosa pine and Douglas fir forest, it ascends into aspens and Engelmann spruce before reaching tundra and tree line at about 11,000 feet. Fall color reaches its peak here around the third week of September. Open year-round and less than an hour from Denver, this road provides a great opportunity to make a four-season portfolio of images of the same locale. From the Georgetown exit off I-70 (Exit 228), head south on Argentine Street through town to County Road/ Forest Road 381, Guanella Pass Road.

Be sure to stop at Green Lake, the first lake on the route. When the air is still, dark-green conifers reflect their color into the lake. On the approach to the pass, watch for beaver ponds along the creek to the east of the road. At sunrise and sunset, shadows define the edges of the ponds, while trees and hill-sides reflect on the surface. Park on top of the pass and hike to the small lake immediately to the east. It just might catch a reflection of 14,060-foot Mount Bierstadt. In spite of its elevation, Bierstadt is an easy climb of less than two hours to the top. Be aware, however, of a booby trap: Alpine willows form a barrier to the hike east. Plan on a sloppy, scratchy bushwhack before breaking out into the open. Whatever you do, get to the pass for either sunrise or sunset. Pink clouds often cover the sky, casting their color across the landscape. Imagine winter's white landscape under such conditions.

Hotel de Paris Museum, Georgetown

MUSEUMS

Hotel de Paris Museum, at 6th and Griffith Streets, the foremost historic property in town, was the achievement of the restless Adolphe François Gerard, known in Georgetown as Louis Dupuy. From a prominent Normandy family, Dupuy arrived in the United States without a penny to his name. He joined the U.S. Army, deserted, and even worked the mining-camp beat for the *Rocky Mountain News* before settling on the mining life in 1870. After a serious accident above town in 1873, during which he heroically saved a fellow miner, Georgetown citizens helped him rent the former Delmonico Bakery. Dupuy managed to purchase, greatly expand, and convert the property by 1878 into the Hotel de Paris, where he provided his guests French cuisine, of course, along with luxurious lodging and a center for discussions about art, philosophy, and politics. *409 6th St., 303-569-2311, www.hoteldeparismuseum.org.*

Hamill House Museum at 3rd and Argentine Streets was a modest 1867 cabin turned into an imposing, sumptuous residence by William Hamill in 1879. An expert on mining law, Hamill made a fortune from negotiating ever-present mining disputes and managing the profitable Dives-Pelican and Terrible Mines. Hamill House was the first of five distinctive Georgetown properties to be restored as part of an ongoing project by Historic Georgetown, Inc. Visit its offices for history and tour information. *305 Argentine St., 303-569-2840, www.historicgeorgetown.org.*

In Silver Plume, visit the **George Rowe Museum,** open from Memorial Day to Labor Day, to see photographs and memorabilia from the mining days. *95 Main St., 303-569-2562.*

WILDLIFE WATCHING

Even if you don't stop in Georgetown, you can look for Rocky Mountain bighorn sheep on the slopes above town and north of I-70. Only in Colorado can you have a "ram jam" slowing traffic. With more than 200 head of sheep, Georgetown's is one of the largest of 70 bighorn herds in the state. The Colorado Division of Wildlife often uses members of this herd to help introduce bighorn sheep and strengthen herds in other parts of the state.

For the price of a quarter, you can scan these mountains with strong binoculars at the **Georgetown Wildlife Viewing Area.** The best viewing is in late autumn and winter. From Denver, exit I-70 at the Georgetown exit (228). Take a left (east) at the first stop sign and turn onto the frontage road; continue alongside Georgetown Lake. The viewing station is on the right.

Activities

CAMPING

Small **Clear Lake,** 6 miles up Guanella Pass Road (County Road/Forest Road 381) from Georgetown, boasts panoramic mountain views that are particularly beautiful in fall. Fishing, four-wheeling, mountain biking, and hiking are available nearby. Larger **Guanella Pass** campground is 9 miles up the pass, where you'll find even more lake and stream fishing options. Dust and traffic from the popular road can be a problem at both campgrounds. From the Georgetown exit off I-70 (Exit 228), head south on Argentine Street through town to Guanella Pass Road. *303-567-3000.*

FISHING

Georgetown Lake, just northeast of town off I-70, and **Clear Lake,** on Guanella Pass Road, are both stocked with trout. To get farther from the angling crowds, though, hike 1 mile up to **Naylor Lake** or 2 miles to **Square Top Lakes** from the Guanella Pass campground. For remote fishing for cutthroats, **Silver Dollar Lake** lies a moderate 3 miles from Guanella Pass campground (see Camping, above). *www.clearcreekcounty.org.*

HIKING

Watrous Gulch Trail EASY, 2.5 miles each way, ambles to fine views of Baker Mountain, Mount Sniktau, and Torreys Peak, among others. In early summer the wildflowers are beautiful, and in fall the aspens are spectacular. The hike shares its start with the **Herman Gulch Trail** MODERATE, which passes through 2 miles of wildflower meadows to Herman Lake. From Georgetown, go 9.5 miles west on I-70 to Exit 218 and follow signs to the trailhead.

Thanks to easy accessibility from Denver and I-70, Georgetown is the base for many a climbing trip, especially because three fourteeners are nearby. **Grays Peak** DIFFICULT at 14,270 feet and **Torreys Peak** DIFFICULT at 14,267 feet are relatively steep but popular short climbs, and both are scalable in one day, weather and fitness permitting. After ascending the 4.5-mile trail to the summit of Grays, you can continue 0.5 mile across a saddle to the summit of Torreys Peak (for directions, see Scenic Location No. 9, opposite).

The views from the summit of 14,060-foot **Mount Bierstadt** DIFFICULT are sublime, particularly in autumn. From Georgetown, head 11 miles up Guanella Pass Road (County Road/Forest Road 381) to the top of the pass. The 2.4-mile (one way) trail begins 200 yards north of the pass.

GRAYS AND TORREYS PEAKS

Better known as two of Colorado's easiest and most accessible fourteeners to climb, Grays and Torreys are also very scenic and nearly accessible by car. The cirque, or glaciated mountain valley, at their feet is sublime and contains a beautiful creek flowing down from the peaks and into Stevens Gulch. The peaks face east, making sunrise the time of day to visit for a classic Colorado scenic on film. Exit I-70 at Bakerville (Exit 221) 6 miles west of Georgetown. Drive for five minutes to the end of County Roads 319 and 321 (Stevens Gulch Road) to the parking area. Walk southwest on the trail straight toward the two big mountains in front of you.

The trail initially veers away from the creek off to your left, but meets back up with it a little over a mile later. In July and August, wildflowers fill the basin, so plan on composing flowers in front of the peaks as soon as the sun enters the basin. Given how close you are to these high peaks, you'll need to use your wide-angle lens to contain the entire scene in your viewfinder. Once the creek and trail reconnect, look for compositions that use the creek as a visual lead-in line (see pp. 71, 76–77, *Photographing the Landscape*) with the peaks in the background. Now put your camera in your daypack and continue up the trail to the top of 14,270-foot Grays Peak, then across the easily traversed saddle to the 14,267-foot summit of Torreys. While on top, make photographs to prove you're no couch potato. Remember, however, there's no perspective from a summit when you simply point your camera out into space. The view from one fourteener is not much different than the view from another. Add foreground to these photographs—your climbing friends, a shelter, large rocks—anything to create depth in the scene.

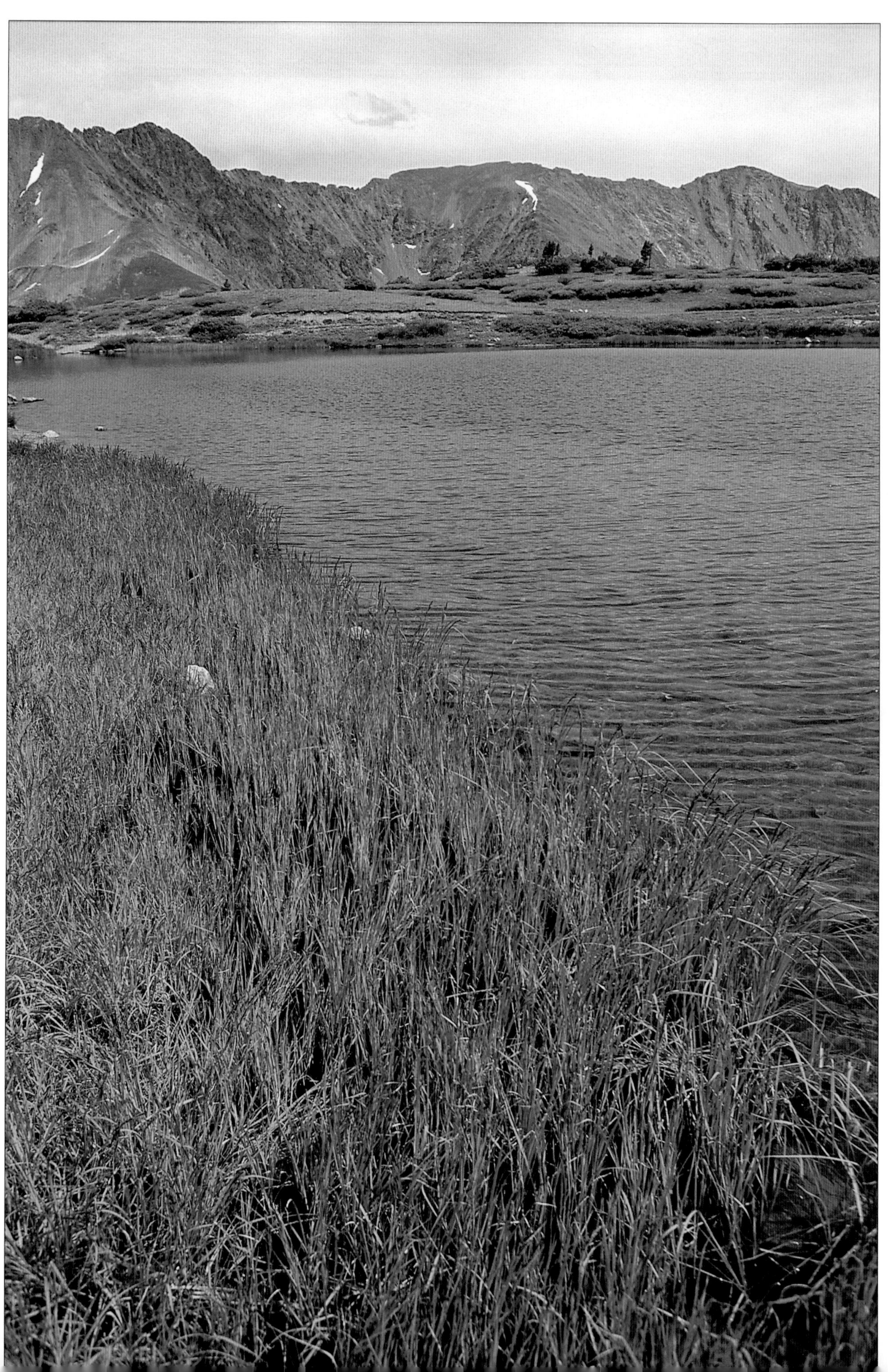

10 SCENIC LOCATION — LOVELAND PASS

Once upon a time, the only way to reach Summit County and beyond was by traversing 11,992-foot Loveland Pass. There was no Eisenhower Tunnel and no four-lane interstate to speed you to the ski slopes. With the bulk of highway traffic now blasting through the I-70 tunnel far below, you gain some privacy making photographs along old US 6 over Loveland Pass. At almost 12,000 feet, there's lots of tundra and wildflowers in the summer, a world of white to photograph in winter, and views year-round to the magnificent peaks of the southern Front Range. Exit I-70 at Loveland Ski Area (Exit 216) just before the tunnel. After crossing over the pass on US 6, you'll end up at Keystone Resort and Silverthorne on I-70.

On your ascent up the pass, stop at the second 180-degree switchback about 3 miles up the road to take in glorious views to the north and east of 12,705-foot Mount Bethel, 12,940-foot Woods Mountain, and 13,574-foot Mount Parnassus on the other side of I-70. Photograph this view at either sunrise or sunset. The shadows are remarkable and the colors rich on a clear day. Drive over the pass and proceed 0.5 mile to Pass Lake off to the right. It's the first dirt side road on the west side of the pass; you can't miss it. Drive up the hill and park next to the lake.

You won't believe what a pristine view you have from the lake to the peaks behind Arapahoe Basin Ski Area in the distance. In fact, this little lake makes one of my favorite reflection photographs in all of Colorado. Again, both sunrise and sunset produce good images on a clear day. As with Guanella Pass, Loveland Pass is open in winter, so plan on photographing here during each of the four seasons.

MOUNTAIN BIKING

Argentine Pass Trail DIFFICULT draws serious mountain bikers (see Mountain Biking, Silverthorne and Dillon, p. 102). This precipitous old wagon trail will amaze you in autumn as you climb over 13,207-foot Argentine Pass and into Summit County. From the west end of Georgetown, take Guanella Pass Road (County Road/Forest Road 381) for 2.5 miles, then turn right (west) onto Waldorf Road (FR 248).

SCENIC DRIVES

Guanella Pass Scenic and Historic Byway (see Scenic Location No. 8, p. 57), a 23-mile former wagon route, extends from Georgetown to Grant, a former silver camp. It's a stunning autumn drive close to Denver, but its real beauty begins past the power plant near Clear Lake and along the dirt section of the road. Watch for bighorn sheep and beavers, whose dams are just off the road, which begins as County Road 381 on the southwest end of town. Guanella Pass Road is also popular with cross-country skiers, snowshoers, and snowmobilers.

Loveland Pass (see Scenic Location No. 10, this page) crosses the Continental Divide and drops into Summit County. From Georgetown, take I-70 west 11 miles to US 6 (Exit 216) just before the Eisenhower Tunnel.

Restaurants

In Georgetown, the friendly staff at **Two Brothers** ($) serves up simple and tasty breakfast and lunch dishes. *406 6th St., 303-569-3320.* **New Prague Restaurant** ($$) provides a welcome taste of middle Europe in the middle of historic old Georgetown. *511 Rose St., 303-569-2861.*

Family-owned, **The Happy Cooker** ($) serves delicious breakfasts and lunches in a homey setting. Try the Belgian waffles and ask to sit on the patio during summer. *416 6th St., 303-569-3166.* **The Red Ram Restaurant & Saloon** ($) is a watering-hole institution in Clear Creek County. This old bar serves great hamburgers and Mexican food, with weekend entertainment. *606 6th St., 303-569-2300, www.redram restaurantandsaloon.com.* **The Peck House** ($$$) restaurant in nearby Empire serves award-winning gourmet Colorado cuisine, with a pronounced French influence, in a superb historic setting. *83 Sunny Ave., 303-569-9870.*

Accommodations

Fine historic inns and guest houses are a specialty of Clear Creek County. **Alpine Hideaway Bed & Breakfast** ($$) sits above Georgetown Lake. Relax beside delightful ponds and fountains and enjoy the valley and mountain views. *2045 Blue Bird Dr., 303-569-2800.*

In Empire, dine and stay at **The Peck House** ($-$$), the oldest hotel in the state, dating from 1860 (with a major expansion in 1873). A fine-dining restaurant, quiet, antique-decorated rooms, and historic charm make The Peck House an unforgettable destination. *83 Sunny Ave., 303-569-9870, www.thepeckhouse.com.* Also in Empire, **Mad Creek Bed and Breakfast** ($) is an updated 1875 structure full of antique appeal. Weather permitting, take your afternoon tea in the gazebo. *167 W. Park Ave., 303-569-2003, 888-266-1498.*

Special Events

During the first two weeks of December, Georgetown holds its annual **Christmas Market,** during which the little Victorian town gets everyone in the holiday spirit. Many people from Denver drive up to see the festive displays, hear the town carolers, sample the home-baked treats, and, of course, do some shopping. *303-569-2840, www.georgetowncolorado.com.*

For More Information

Georgetown Visitor Center, *613 6th St., 303-569-2888, www.georgetowncolorado.com.*

Mueller Ranch State Park

Colorado Grande Casino, Cripple Creek

Holden House B&B, Colorado Springs

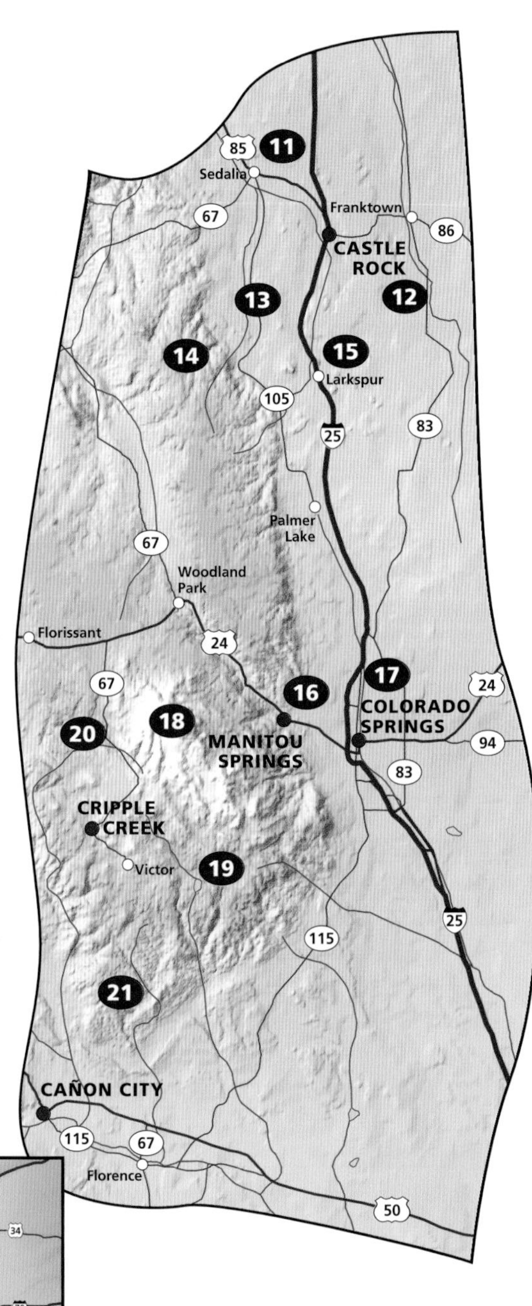

Colorado Springs and Vicinity

PIKES PEAK COUNTRY

Here, you can appreciate what motivated visitor Katharine Lee Bates to write the national hymn, "America the Beautiful." This part of Colorado is where "the fruited plain" meets "purple mountain majesties." From the high plains prairie to Pikes Peak, west to the historic mining district around Victor and Cripple Creek, and south to the magnificent canyon of the Arkansas River, this region abounds with natural splendor, frontier and mining history, unique culture, and activities to enjoy. Even today you can see out-of-state cars with "Pikes Peak or Bust" bumper stickers. At 14,110 feet, Pikes Peak—also known as America's Mountain—towers over the landscape around Colorado Springs and is a magnet for newcomers. The region includes not only this majestic mountain but the aptly named 1,053-foot chasm of the Royal Gorge. Spend enough time in the Pikes Peak region, admiring its heights and depths, and its breadth of history, and you might find yourself whistling the old mining tune, "Sweet Betsy from Pike."

SCENIC LOCATIONS

The Victor Hotel, Victor

Blue Skies Inn, Manitou Springs

Castle Rock

Colorado Atlas & Gazetteer pp. 50–51

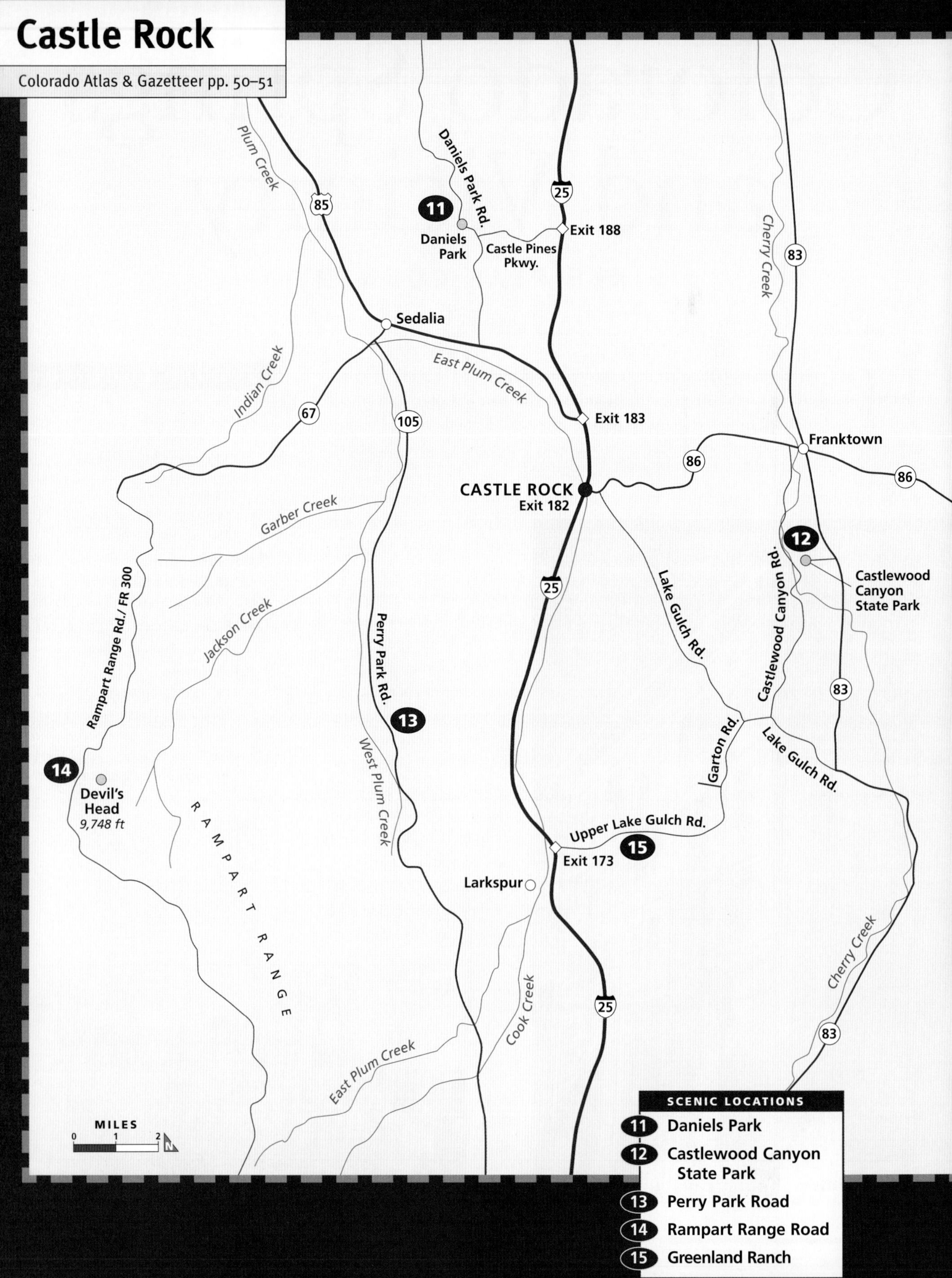

Plum Creek
85
Daniels Park Rd.
11
Daniels Park
25
Exit 188
Castle Pines Pkwy.
Cherry Creek
83
Sedalia
Indian Creek
East Plum Creek
67
105
Exit 183
Franktown
86
CASTLE ROCK
Exit 182
86
Garber Creek
12
Castlewood Canyon State Park
Castlewood Canyon Rd.
Lake Gulch Rd.
25
Rampart Range Rd./ FR 300
Jackson Creek
Perry Park Rd.
83
13
Garton Rd.
Lake Gulch Rd.
West Plum Creek
14
Devil's Head
9,748 ft
RAMPART RANGE
Upper Lake Gulch Rd.
15
Exit 173
Larkspur
Cherry Creek
Cook Creek
25
83
East Plum Creek
MILES
0
1
2
N
SCENIC LOCATIONS
11 Daniels Park
12 Castlewood Canyon State Park
13 Perry Park Road
14 Rampart Range Road
15 Greenland Ranch

Castle Rock

Most motorists just buzz through Castle Rock en route from Denver to Colorado Springs. But the town is a great place to spend at least a day, particularly if you like to catch retail bargains or tune your golf game. The annual PGA International Tournament at Castle Pines has brought the town worldwide recognition, while nearby Larkspur's eclectic Colorado Renaissance Festival is a summer tradition and great family fun. Beyond town limits, the many remarkable rural locations around undeveloped Douglas County, and a wonderful, uncrowded state park, are a nature lover's—and a photographer's—delight. Gently rolling terrain and wide vistas make for easy, enjoyable recreation and exploration not far from either of the two great Front Range cities.

History

Castle Rock was named for the distinctive flattopped rock formation perched above the town just east of I-25. Rumors of gold and the passage of the federal Homestead Act pushed the Arapaho and Cheyenne tribes off these buffalo-rich hunting grounds, and with the discovery of rhyolite around Plum Creek, Castle Rock became a quarry town. In 1875, the arrival of the Denver & Rio Grande Railroad meant that quarry rock could be shipped out and that area ranchers and dairy farmers could get supplies and products to and from market. The railroad's arrival, coupled with the growth of Denver to the north and Colorado Springs to the south, assured Castle Rock's existence. Incorporated in 1881, Castle Rock is the county seat for burgeoning Douglas County, which still contains many singular and pristine landscapes, some preserved by open-space initiatives, others lost to or threatened by unchecked growth. Twenty miles south of Denver on I-25, Castle Rock continues to thrive today as a semirural suburban community with exceptional golf courses and green spaces.

Main Attractions

CASTLEWOOD CANYON STATE PARK

Cherry Creek cuts through a 10-mile sandstone canyon within this off-the-beaten-path state park (see Scenic Location No. 12, p. 67). Castlewood Canyon is an ideal place to see raptors and other bird species; sometimes you can see dozens of turkey vultures riding on the thermals above the canyon. Perhaps the most intriguing inhabitants are the blue herons nesting in the Douglas firs—a "dry rookery" that is a bit unusual for this species. Enjoy the 13 miles of gentle hiking trails, but do watch for rattlesnakes. To get to the park from Castle Rock, go east 6 miles to Franktown on CO 86, then turn right onto CO 83 and drive about 5 miles. Stop at the visitor center for information and maps. *303-688-5242, www.coloradoparks.org.*

SHOPPING

While the golfer in the family is busy, shop at **The Outlets at Castle Rock** for bargains on name-brand merchandise at more than 130 stores. Experiencing this retail paradise demands a full day of serious shopping. (Take a break at the food court and children's playground.) These shops become quite busy around the holidays, of course. Be sure to visit early in the season, ahead of the throngs from both the Denver and Colorado Springs regions who descend on the outlets to purchase their gifts. Take Exit 184 off I-25. *303-688-4494, www.outletsatcastlerock.com.*

Activities

GOLF

Although Colorado has its share of excellent and challenging 18-hole public golf courses, the Castle Rock area is famous for the world-class, PGA tour destination Castle Pines Golf Club (see Special Events, p. 68). But Castle Rock boasts beautiful public golf courses as well. **Red Hawk Ridge** is a newer course with butte and mountain views and is suitable for all levels of the game. *2156 Red Hawk Ridge Dr., 720-733-3500, www.redhawkridge.com.* **The Ridge at Castle Pines North** has been voted one of the top 100 public courses nationally. *1414 Castle Pines Pkwy., 303-688-0100, www.theridgecpn.com.* **The Golf Club at Bear Dance** is the official course of the Colorado PGA and is consistently rated both the best and the most challenging public course in Colorado. *6630 Bear Dance Road, Larkspur, 303-681-4653, www.beardancegolf.com.*

SCENIC DRIVES

The **Rampart Range Road** (see Scenic Location No. 14, p. 70) is among the most picturesque byways in Colorado. This 60-mile gravel road atop the forested range runs from CO 67, 10 miles west of Sedalia, south to Colorado Springs. A Civilian Conservation Corps work project, the road takes you to spectacular views of both prairie and high country. Devil's Head, the 9,748-foot high point of the Rampart Range, dominates the north end of the drive. Its historic fire tower is accessible via a short, moderate National Recreation Trail. Mount Herman Road (Forest Road 320) goes around 9,063-foot Mount Herman to I-25 and the town of Monument. A couple miles north of FR 303 is the turnoff to **Rampart Reservoir**, a popular recreation site. The FR 303 turnoff leads you to 9,727-foot Ormes Peak. Take in a panoramic overlook of Queen's Canyon (named after General William Jackson Palmer's wife, Mary Lincoln "Queen" Mellen) and Glen Eyrie Castle (see Main Attractions, Colorado Springs, p. 75) as you approach Colorado Springs. Although passenger cars should have no trouble negotiating the road in summer, it can become a washboard in places. In bad weather or in winter, use four-wheel-drive vehicles only.

Continued on page 68.

11 SCENIC LOCATION

DANIELS PARK

Have you ever noticed the wide, flat ridge immediately south of the Denver metro area separating the I-25 corridor from the Santa Fe Boulevard/US 85 corridor? This 8-mile-long escarpment also separates Plum and Cherry Creeks, two major tributaries of the South Platte River. Atop this 6,000-foot-high ridge you can catch views in every direction, but my favorite is looking west across the South Platte River drainage toward the Front Range. The ridge's western edge is defined by tall cliffs composed of fragile sediments left from the erosion of the ancestral Rocky Mountains. When the sun sets on a clear day, these gray cliffs are transformed into towers of glowing red.

When I moved to Colorado in the late '60s, this ridge was all open space, but today the developments of Castle Pines and Castle Pines North consume most of the land. The only public place to view the Plum Creek and South Platte drainages is from Daniels Park. To get there from Denver, take I-25 south to the Castle Pines Parkway exit (188) and drive west through Castle Pines North to Daniels Park Road. Turn right (north) and you will see the park on your left. Access is also available from US 85 just south of Sedalia. Daniels Park consists of 1,000 acres owned by the City of Denver. Most of the park is a bison preserve and natural area where visitors can view the animals in their high-plains habitat.

I have taken some of my favorite Denver–Colorado Springs corridor photographs in the evening along this ridge. Not only the cliffs but even the ponderosa pine and scrub oak turn red, especially the warm-toned pine bark. From the Daniels Park shelter house parking lot, climb down to the cliffs and compose a scene looking south or north at right angles to the setting sun. Trees silhouetted against the blue sky with cliffs in the foreground make for a sublime composition, especially with a wide-angle lens. After the sun sets, photograph pink clouds in a composition that contains a lot of sky and a little bit of land, with the camera pointing due west (see *Photographing the Landscape,* pp. 66–67). This is an easily accessible, bountifully photogenic area in any season. In May, the oaks are glorious with their light green leaflets; in fall, they turn ostentatious shades of red and orange; and in winter, the snowswept rocks make a great foreground for any composition.

12 SCENIC LOCATION

CASTLEWOOD CANYON STATE PARK

Like Roxborough State Park, Castlewood Canyon is truly one of the gems of the Colorado State Parks system. As with Roxborough, this park is intended for foot traffic only and protects a valuable, pristine ecosystem. Nestled among stately ponderosa pines in the famous Black Forest, this deep canyon provides scenery usually reserved for the canyon country of western Colorado—yet it's only minutes from Denver. Along its 13 miles of trails, you can photograph from deep in the canyon or from its edges, focusing below or far off to the Front Range. Oaks, cottonwoods, and other deciduous plants provide a new palette of colors from one season to the next, and birds and wildlife keep photographers on their toes. The main entrance to the park is 5 miles south of Franktown on CO 83.

The canyon was carved from the same sedimentary rock found at Daniels Park (see Scenic Location No. 11, p. 66), but because the canyon is oriented north and south, it can be a difficult place to photograph. Neither rising nor setting sun finds its way into the bottom of the canyon, so the canyon walls are never awash with the same reddish light as the west-facing cliffs of Daniels Park. And at the end of the day, the contrast between shadows in the canyon bottom and highlights on the upper edges is too great for film to manage. The shadows appear darker on film than they do to the eye, and the highlights become washed out. So what does a photographer do?

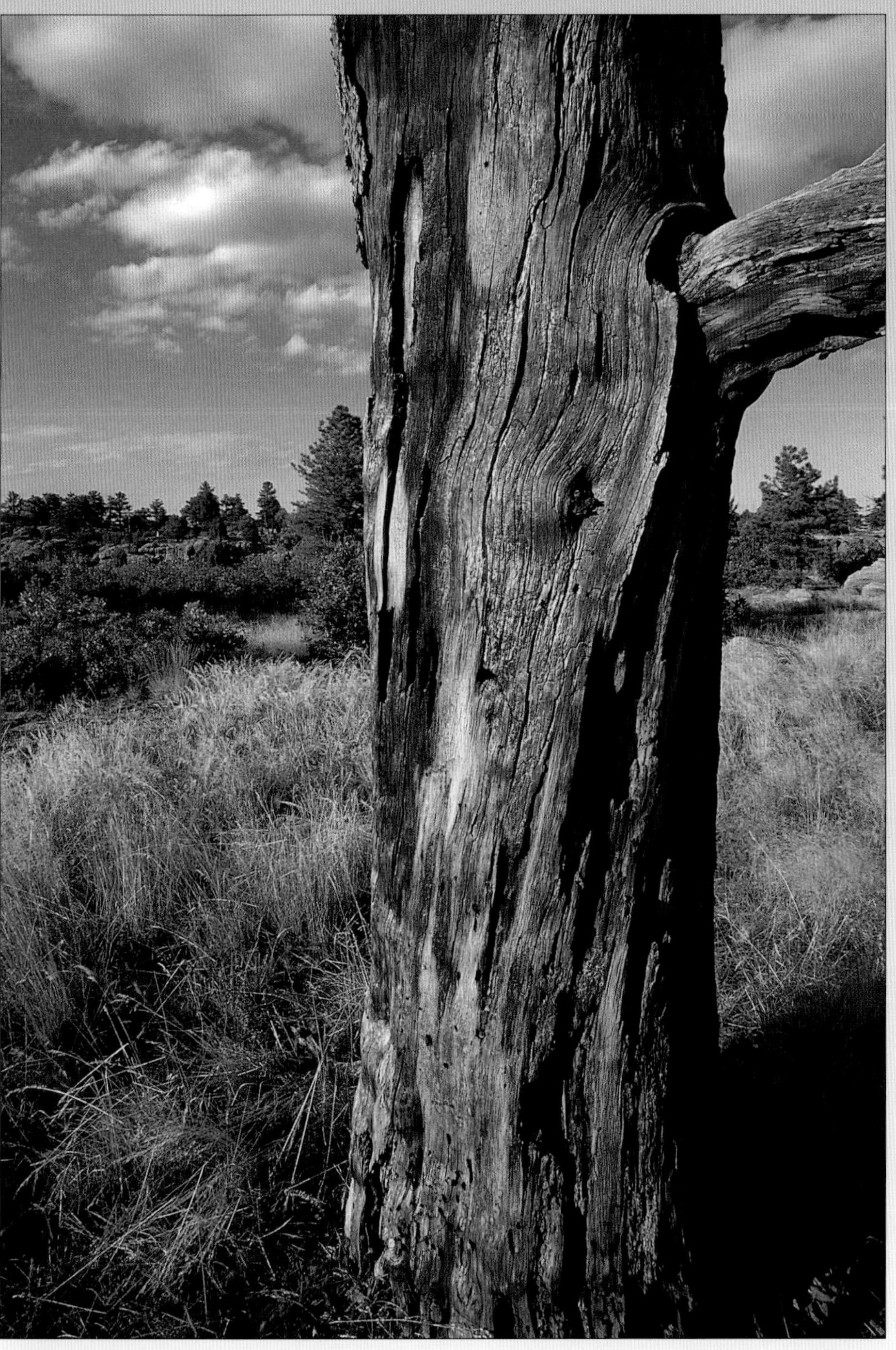

Photograph from within a north-and-south canyon in cloudy light. You can photograph during any part of the day (no need to worry about bright midday light washing out colors) and avoid the high contrasts of morning and evening. Cloudy light is evenly distributed, which allows the subtle details of nature, and its limitless colors, to been seen and recorded on film. The white cascades of Cherry Creek as it flows along the canyon bottom are best photographed in cloudy light, too. A few tips: Look for the isolated pockets of aspens within the canyon. They're a special treat usually reserved for mountain environments. The months of May and June, especially if they're wet ones, bring glorious displays of wildflowers native to the prairie and foothills ecosystems. You won't believe the larkspur! I also love to photograph the area above the canyon. Still-standing dead trees catch the red light of sunset and make a great silhouette of warm color against the cool blue Colorado sky. And don't forget to drive the Castlewood Canyon Road along Cherry Creek through pastoral valleys north and south of the park.

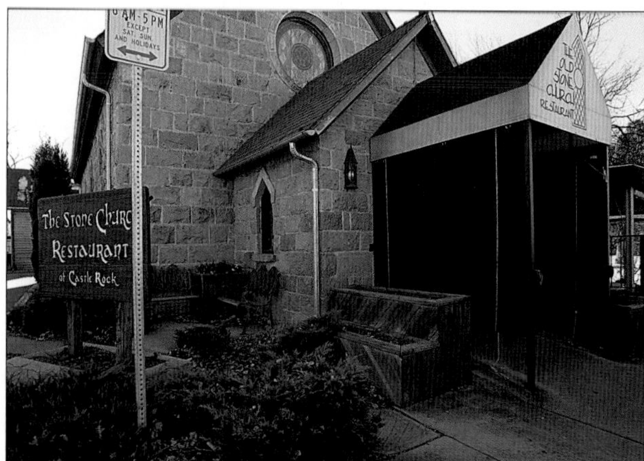

The Old Stone Church Restaurant, Castle Rock

Restaurants

Gabriel's ($$-$$$$) in Sedalia rates highly for its Northern Italian cuisine and extensive wine list. Local and south Denver metro area residents also flock here for the wine-tasting dinner dance. From Castle Rock, take I-25 to Exit 184 and go west on US 85 to its junction with CO 67. Gabriel's is a block west of US 85 on CO 67. *5450 N. CO 67, 303-688-2323.*

In Castle Rock, **The Old Stone Church Restaurant** ($$$), a creative reuse of an 1888 Catholic church, boasts "fine dining beyond belief." A table for two in the old confessional is truly a meal to remember. *210 Third St., 303-688-9000, www.oscrestaurant.com.* **The Augustine Grille** ($$-$$$) features a variety of outstanding American dishes from pasta to poultry. *519 Wilcox St., 303-814-3663.* For a lively menu featuring Mexican and Greek dishes, stop at **Pegasus Restaurant** ($-$$). *313 Jerry St., 303-688-6746.*

Castle Rock has a wide selection of new hot-spots to add to their list of favorites as well. **Union-An American Bistro** ($$) features creative, modern American fare and a nice martini bar as well. *3 Wilcox St, 303-688-8159, www.unionamerican bistro.com.* **Uniscali** ($$), also on Wilcox, is a modern Italian restaurant with a fabulous happy hour selection, if you're looking for something filling earlier in the evening. *611 N Wilcox St, 303-660-2005.* **Siena at the Courtyard** ($$) is a casual restaurant featuring both Italian and American favorites such as pizza, pasta, seafood entrées, and steak. *333 Perry St, 303-688-2622, www.sienacr.com.*

Angie's Restaurant ($) is a local favorite known for its homemade Italian and Mexican dishes. *201 4th St, 303-660-1233, www.angies.us.* **The Castle Café** ($-$$), once a hotel and bar, is now known for its classic home-style favorites, including the famous pan-fried chicken dinner. *403 Wilcox St, 303-814-2233, www.castlecafe.com.* And for a great selection of traditional bar food and locally brewed beers, stop by **The Rockyard American Grill & Brewing Company** ($$). *880 W Castleton Rd, 303-814-9273, www.rockyard.com.*

Accommodations

The **Best Western Inn and Suites of Castle Rock** ($$) *595 Genoa Way, 303-814-8800* and **Quality Inn** ($-$$) *200 Wolfensberger Rd., 303-660-2222* are both centrally located with a variety of amenities and friendly service. **The Wineglass Ranch** ($$) in Parker caters to your horses as well as to you. Set in the heart of Douglas County's famed horse ranching country, The Wineglass provides European-styled apartments complete with fold-out beds, couches, kitchen, and laundry. The stables look just as well-appointed; hay is available for an extra charge. To get to The Wineglass, take Exit 193 off I-25 and drive east on County Road 36 to Parker Road. Make a left, then in 0.5 mile take a right onto Pine. Continue east on Inspiration Road to Piney Lake Road and turn left. At County Line Road (CR 50), turn right and go east 2.8 miles, then turn right. *1765 Michael Gates Dr., 303-840-7772, www.thewineglassranch.com.*

Special Events

The **Colorado Renaissance Festival** is undoubtedly one of the most anticipated events on the Front Range. The festival is pure 16th-century entertainment, complete with jousting knights, swordplay, bards reciting poetry, and King Henry and his queen mingling with the crowds. Vendors dressed in period costume hawk their wares, not least of which are barbecued turkey legs. The Renaissance Festival takes place on weekends in June and July, each weekend distinguished by a slightly different theme. To get to the festival from Denver, take I-25 south to the Larkspur exit. *303-688-6010, www.colorado renaissance.com.*

In August, the **Douglas County Fair, Parade & Rodeo** continues an annual agricultural tradition more than 65 years old. Hear the bands, see the carnival, check out the 4-H contests, and enjoy the barbecue sponsored by the fire department. *For information on these events: 303-688-4597, www. castlerock.org.*

For More Information

Castle Rock Chamber of Commerce, *420 Jerry St., 303-688-4597, www.castlerock.org.* Town of Castle Rock Tourism, *www.visitcastlerock.org*

PERRY PARK ROAD

Now that I know how beautiful the scenery is, I can't believe it took me 30 years to discover Perry Park Road (CO 105). If not for William Henry Jackson, who photographed this area in the 19th century, I would probably still not know about it. During my *Colorado: 1870–2000* "then-and-now" project, I managed to locate several Jackson locations from Palmer Lake to Perry Park. From Denver, take US 85 south to Sedalia and the CO 67 turnoff; at 0.5 mile, turn left (south) onto Perry Park Road (CO 105). Proceed 20 miles south to the town of Palmer Lake. You can also access the road from Castle Rock by taking Wolfensberger Road west.

Perry Park Road sits in the bottom of the West Plum Creek valley, bounded by foothills on the west and the escarpment that separates West Plum Creek from East Plum Creek to the east. Its remarkable pastoral scenes endure, thanks to the preservation of many large horse and cattle ranches. With its rolling hills, beautiful barns, and white picket fences, Perry Park Road looks more like Kentucky than Colorado! Leafing trees in May, peaking fall color in October, and greening hay meadows in summer make this a place to visit year-round. It's extremely easy to make award-winning photographs that feature fences, fields, and trees in the foreground, barns anyplace you want to put them, and forested foothills in the background. The sun rising over the plains makes morning light the best, but the setting sun backlighting the grasses and trees makes evening productive, too.

And that's not all. Perry Park boasts red sandstone spires like those in Roxborough State Park to the north, though not as tall. About halfway from Sedalia to Palmer Lake, Red Rock Road turns west and delivers you into the Perry Park development. Though most of this area is consumed by a golf course, club, and large-lot homes, open space along the way provides vistas that easily can be photographed from the roadside. If not photographing the rock formations at sunrise, wait for cloudy light. Such light enhances the soft red color of the sandstone and eliminates dark shadows between the rocks, which can distract your eye from the composition (see *Photographing the Landscape*, p. 99).

RAMPART RANGE ROAD

The Rampart Range lies just west of the plains between Denver and Colorado Springs. Rampart Range Road runs circuitously for 60 miles along ridge tops and through the heart of the Pike National Forest from CO 67 near Sedalia to Garden of the Gods in Colorado Springs. Nestled among the ponderosa pine, fir, spruce, and aspen trees are various campsites and lookouts that provide spectacular views of the Eastern Plains and the Front Range, and of the South Platte River and Fountain Creek drainages to the west. Your drive south culminates in views of not only Pikes Peak but the Sangre de Cristo Range farther south.

Rampart Range Road is an improved dirt road, bumpy here and there but suitable for the family vehicle in fair weather. From Denver, drive south on US 85 to the town of Sedalia. Make a right at the light and proceed west on CO 67 about 9 miles. Turn left off the pavement onto Rampart Range Road. From Colorado Springs, drive to Garden of the Gods (see Scenic Location No. 16, p. 75), then head south on Garden Drive from Gateway Road. You'll see Rampart Range Road on the right before you get to US 24.

A favorite scenic place of mine along the road is the Devil's Head fire tower. A gorgeous 1.3-mile hike amid large boulders and fir and aspen trees gets you to the top of one of Colorado's last fire observation facilities. Devil's Head, a granite outcrop typical of this region of the South Platte River foothills, was formed during the Pikes Peak uplift millions of years ago. To get there, drive 9 miles south on Rampart Range Road to the turnoff. Drive another 0.5 mile to the trailhead. Wait for cloudy light to reduce the contrast within the forest, and compose the scene using the trail as a lead-in line from the bottom right or left corner of the viewfinder. Though light greens of spring and summer provide a nice contrast, late-September yellows are especially conspicuous against the backdrop of evergreens.

Another area worth seeing is south of the turnoff to Woodland Park. As you descend toward the Garden of the Gods, the north face of Pikes Peak gets "in your face." Take advantage of the numerous composition options here. Remember, however, to find foreground subjects, such as trees, rocks, or the road, to create depth in the scene.

15 SCENIC LOCATION

GREENLAND RANCH

Between I-25 and CO 83 south of Castle Rock stands an escarpment that separates East Plum Creek from Cherry Creek and continues south to Palmer Divide, the divide between the South Platte River and Arkansas River watersheds. The land closest to Castle Rock is under development, but the balance is not, thanks to Douglas County preservation goals. This 100,000-acre domain is unlike any other landscape in Colorado. Buttes and mesas rise above rolling hills, tributaries of the two major boundary creeks wind their way throughout, and Pikes Peak is almost always in view to the southwest. In the heart of this unique ecosystem lies the 22,000-acre Greenland Ranch, the largest intact ranch remaining along the Front Range. One of my favorite Colorado views is on the northern boundary of the ranch. To get there, exit I-25 at Upper Lake Gulch Road (Exit 173), 9 miles south of Castle Rock. At the bottom of the off ramp, turn left, go under the highway, and follow the dirt road east for 1.5 miles until you begin to see views to the south of the buttes and Pikes Peak beyond. Pull over and begin to compose.

Greenland Ranch is private, as is most of the land here, so you won't have the opportunity to do any hiking. Someday, trails will connect Castlewood Canyon to Colorado Springs as Douglas County Open Space purchases land and easements for public use. An individual recently purchased a portion of Greenland Ranch to ensure that it will remain a ranch and never be developed, and some sections will be open to the public in the near future. For now, enjoy the view from the road. After making your image, proceed east on Upper Lake Gulch Road, then north on Garton Road to Lake Gulch Road. From here you can drive northwest to Castle Rock or north-east to the Castlewood Canyon Road. These improved dirt roads take you through beautiful ranching valleys to the tops of ridges with 360-degree views.

The Greenland Ranch view I like most includes meadows and scrub oak in the foreground, Rattlesnake Butte in the midground, and Pikes Peak in the distance. With practically no sign of human impact here, the scene looks much as it must have when John C. Frémont rode through in the 1840s. This south-facing view photographs well at both sunrise and sunset, as well as in colorful May and October, and after a fresh snowfall. However, you can make delightful images here during any season.

Colorado Springs

Colorado Atlas & Gazetteer pp. 62–63

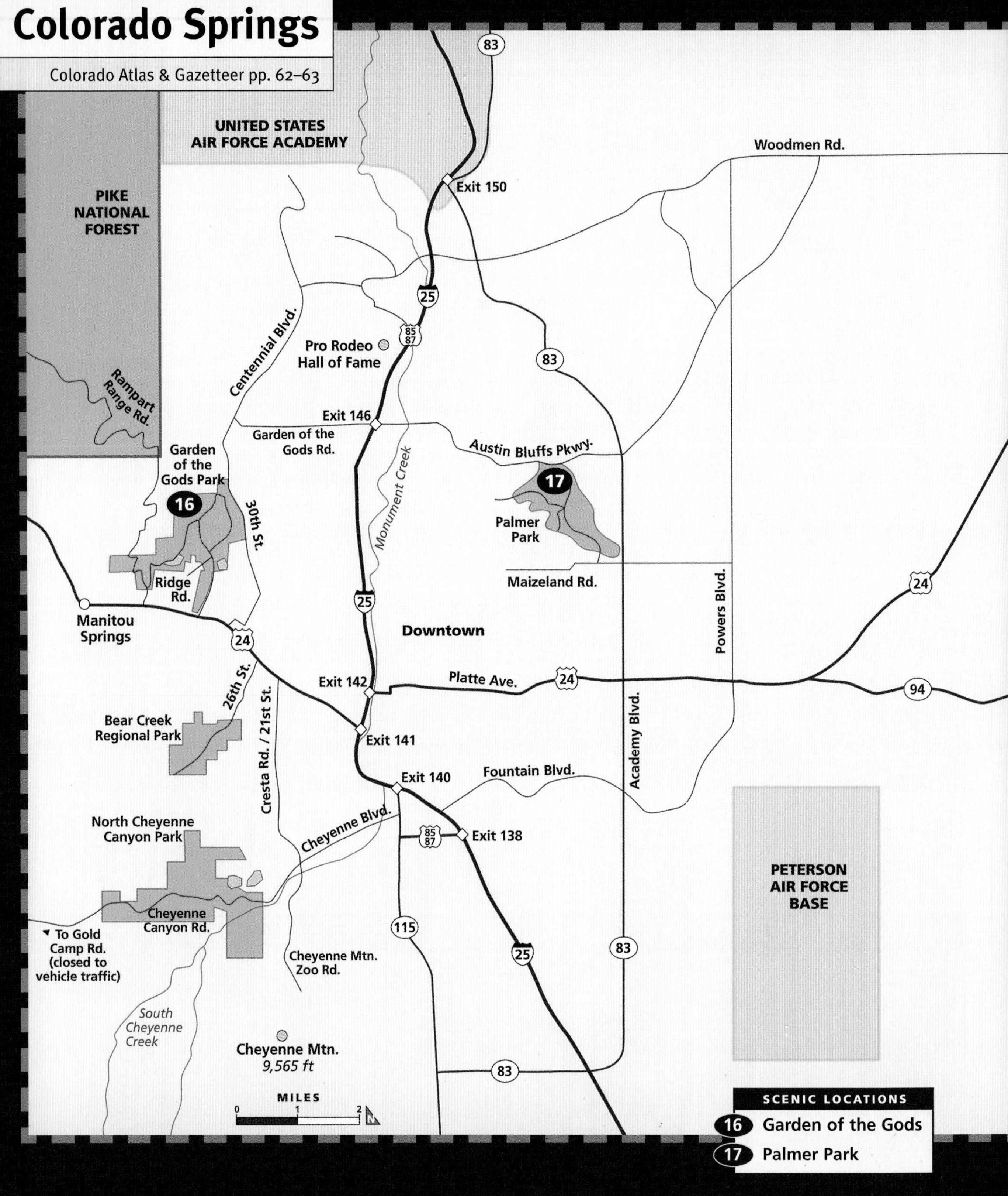

SCENIC LOCATIONS

16 Garden of the Gods

17 Palmer Park

Colorado Springs

Three peaks lord over the Front Range—14,255-foot Longs Peak towers above Rocky Mountain National Park to the north; 14,264-foot Mount Evans rules the Denver skyline; and 14,110-foot Pikes Peak looms over the southern region. Pikes Peak's proximity to the prairie's edge ensured the founding of settlements at its base. Even so, neighboring Colorado Springs and Manitou Springs are dissimilar in history, culture, and even atmosphere. Colorado Springs, of course, is the region's centerpiece.

Because of its magnificent scenery, recreational and tourist attractions, healthy economy, and livability, Colorado Springs (or "The Springs") is one of the fastest-growing communities on Colorado's Front Range. For the many enlisted personnel and officers who have been stationed at the military installations around Colorado Springs over the years, the area is worth remaining in after completion of service. Colorado Springs is an excellent place in which to spend some time and from which to explore the entire Pikes Peak region.

History

Pikes Peak, as it is known today, was a well-recognized landmark to the Utes and Spanish explorers who camped and hunted beneath its massive shadow. Ute legend has it that the Great Spirit took a large stone, gouged a hole in the sky, and poured ice and snow into the hole until he had made a great peak. In 1806 President Thomas Jefferson dispatched army lieutenant Zebulon Pike to find the headwaters of the Red River, one of the southern boundaries of the 1803 Louisiana Purchase. On November 15, 1806, Pike first spied a blue mountain in the distance and named it Grand Peak. When they arrived at its base on November 27, Pike and his expedition attempted to climb the mountain but were turned back by biting winds and deep snow. Discouraged, Pike continued to follow the Arkansas River but never did ascend the famed summit. Slain in the War of 1812, Pike never knew that what he had called Grand Peak would one day bear his name.

Pike's journals describing the Pikes Peak region encouraged other explorers and mountain men to seek out the region, and "Pikes Peak or Bust" became the miners' cry during the Gold Rush of 1858. Prospectors flooded the area, and rich strikes were found just west of present-day Colorado Springs at Cripple Creek and Victor and as far north as Central City and Idaho Springs. The mining camp of Colorado City (long since annexed by Colorado Springs to the east) became for a time the territorial capital of Colorado. Early explorers and prospectors brought enough attention to the region to catch the interest of Civil War general and railroad genius William Jackson Palmer. He would make Colorado Springs not only a major railhead but also a resort. General Palmer advertised extensively throughout the upper-class social circles of America and Britain to recruit people of "good moral character and teetotaling habits." Although elitist in his recruitment efforts, he promoted education and civic projects and encouraged other Gilded Age tycoons to do the same (see Colorado Cameo, p. 76).

The aftermath of World War II brought a strong military presence to the Colorado Springs area, one that remains powerful today. Fort Carson, Peterson Air Force Base, the U.S. Air Force Academy, and the North American Aerospace Defense Command (NORAD, located *in* Cheyenne Mountain) pervade the tone of the town. Along with the tourism and high-tech industries, these military institutions make a generous contribution to the economy and culture of Colorado Springs.

Main Attractions

THE BROADMOOR

Having made a fortune in gold and copper, Spencer Penrose opened this elegant establishment in 1918, intending to attract a cultivated clientele. Today, The Broadmoor still does, a premier hotel in a gorgeous setting, with resort amenities including golf, tennis, a health spa, and boutiques. Many visit The Broadmoor on the strength of its restaurants alone (see below). The Broadmoor's stately grounds have an English country style, with pools and a beautiful lake flocked with waterfowl. You can also rent a paddleboat or take a horseback ride. Staying at The Broadmoor ($$$$) is unforgettable but can be very expensive. Be sure to check for bargain packages. To get to The Broadmoor, take I-25 to Exit 138. Go west on US 85/87 and Lake Avenue to the entrance. *719-577-5775, 866-837-9520, www.broadmoor.com.*

Among The Broadmoor's extensive dining options, three restaurants especially stand out. The posh **Charles Court** ($$$$), *719-577-5774,* showcases a huge wine selection ($12–$1,300 a bottle) and amazing desserts, not to mention Colorado rack of lamb, Copper River salmon, and the Charles Court Game Grill. Jackets are recommended and reservations are required. The **Penrose Room** ($$$$), *719-634-7711* (jackets and reservations required), features French cuisine, live music, and afternoon teas overlooking views of the city and Cheyenne Mountain. My favorite meal here (some even make the trip from Denver for it) is the Sunday buffet brunch. More than 70 exquisite items to enjoy include special-order omelets, Belgian waffles, and champagne. For a 19th-century English pub ambiance, drop in at **The Golden Bee** ($$), *719-577-5776,* behind the International Center. Taste the famous ales with your meal, and save room for the trifle dessert. A ragtime pianist leads a sing-along in the evening, with songbooks provided.

GARDEN OF THE GODS

It still boggles my mind that much of this stunning park once belonged to one family. Charles Elliott Perkins' children donated their parcel of the current 1,367-acre park to the City of

Colorado Springs in 1909 to preserve the land and honor their magnanimous father. This is a favorite place of mine, particularly in the light of early morning or evening. The Garden of the Gods' eroded sandstone cliffs form singular sculptures with imaginative names like "Sleeping Giant," "Weeping Indian," and "Baldheaded Scotchman." Pikes Peak and Cheyenne Mountain are spectacular backdrops for the red and white sandstone cliffs of the Lyons Formation, and structures like the famous Balanced Rock seem to defy the laws of gravity. Eagles and red-tailed hawks soar on the thermals, and small, melodic canyon wrens make their homes on the cliffs. You can often observe Rocky Mountain bighorn sheep grazing in or near the park. Step lightly, as prairie rattlers dwell here also.

The visitor center, along with fine displays on geology, history, and wildlife, provides maps of the 7-mile-loop scenic drive and hikes. If you'd like to stretch your legs, take the 1.3-mile **Perkins Central Garden Trail** EASY, which starts at Signature Rock and meanders around the Twin Spires, Cathedral Spires, and Three Graces. Pulpit Rock stands alone in the meadow, and you have splendid views of the Kissing Camels formation. Another rewarding way to see the park is on horseback. **Academy Riding Stables** (not part of the Air Force Academy) offers 1- and 2-hour guided tours and a 3-hour perimeter ride around the park. *719-633-5667, www.arsriding.com.*

Unless you are a technical climber with a permit, forget about scrambling over the rocks here. If you *are* a technical climber, you already know that the park is an alluring destination, in fact one of the oldest technical climbing sites in the nation. The different rock strata make for tremendous variety among nearly 50 climbs on North Gateway Rock, South Gateway Rock, Gray Rock, Twin Spires, and Montezuma's Tower, a thin 140-foot fin. *For information: Sport Climbing Center of Colorado Springs, 4650 Northpark Dr., 719-260-1050, www.sportclimbcs.com; or Grand West Outfitters, 3250 N. Academy, 719-596-3031.*

Stop at the **Garden of the Gods Trading Post** for Southwestern art and authentic American Indian pottery, weavings, and jewelry, plus patio dining in the summer. Also visit the **Rock Ledge Ranch Historic Site,** a living-history museum with volunteers in costumes. For directions, see Scenic Location No. 16, right. *1805 N. 30th St., 719-634-6666, www.gardenofgods.com.*

16 SCENIC LOCATION

GARDEN OF THE GODS

Garden of the Gods is to Colorado Springs what Roxborough State Park (see Scenic Location No. 2, p. 30) is to Denver. In fact, the same geology exists in both—the red and white sandstone of the Lyons and Fountain Formations, uplifted more than 300 million years ago, are today eroded into spectacular vertical fins. With Pikes Peak looming in the background, the scenic photographic possibilities are limitless. Take the Garden of the Gods Road exit (146) west from I-25 to 30th Street. Make a left and within 2 miles the visitor center will be on your left and Gateway Road into the park on your right.

I've never seen anything quite like the park's vertical sandstone spires anywhere outside of Colorado. Southern Utah certainly contains an infinite number of unique sandstone formations, but none quite like these. The foothills ecosystem in which the formations exist makes this place even more unique. Scrub oak, pine, and fir trees surround the spires, while 14,110-foot Pikes Peak towers above the whole scene.

The classic photograph of the park is the view of Pikes Peak situated between the North and South Gateway Rocks. To get the shot, park in the first parking lot on the left as you go up Gateway Road from the visitor center. Cross the road and hike due east 200 yards until you reach the dirt ridge, which is easy to climb. Walk along the ridge until Pikes Peak is centered between the North and South Gateway Rocks. Because the formations face east, they catch the first light of sunrise, which on a clear day can be pure red. This red-on-red scene makes for an otherworldly composition. In May, the oaks are lime green; in fall, they're orange and red—all decorative additions to an already colorful place. In winter and spring, when Pikes Peak has snow, it's icing on the cake. After taking this photograph, spend the rest of the morning driving the park roads and exploring the trails. You can find numerous hidden compositions here, limited only by the amount of time you are willing to spend searching them out.

GLEN EYRIE CASTLE

Take a trip back to the Gilded Age, when railroad magnate and Colorado Springs philanthropist General William Jackson Palmer built the Glen Eyrie Castle in memory of his wife, Mary Lincoln "Queen" Mellen, who died in 1894. The fortress-like structure attests to Palmer's fascination with European culture, particularly all things English. Many of the furnishings, including the fireplaces, were shipped over from former European estates. Listed on the National Register of Historic Places, Glen Eyrie stands amid 750 acres of towering rock formations, waterfalls, forest, and green. Today, Glen Eyrie is owned and operated by the Navigators, a Christian organization, as a conference center and retreat. It is also open to the public for tours and formal teas; reservations are required. You can also arrange for an audio drive-through tour of the grounds. To get there, follow the directions to the Garden of the Gods (see this page). Glen Eyrie Castle is before the Garden of the Gods entrance. Go about 0.5 mile south on 30th Street to the sign. *719-634-0808, www.gleneyrie.org.*

UNITED STATES AIR FORCE ACADEMY

As you drive south on I-25 and the Air Force Academy comes into view, you can see why Colorado beat out 45 other states when this site was chosen in 1954. Gleaming structures rise gloriously under the blue Colorado sky, while the mountains cut an inspiring backdrop. Stop to take a tour of the United States Air Force Academy, an impressive and exciting family-oriented destination. You'll see both north and south entrances to the academy off I-25; take the more scenic north exit (156B) and go west on North Gate Road, which becomes Academy Drive. Stop at the **Barry Goldwater Visitor Center** and pick up a "Follow the Falcon" map for the 12-mile driving tour of the buildings and grounds. Check out the air exhibits, programs, and a film on cadet life, or take in a show at the planetarium. Aviation enthusiasts can snap up models, posters, and picture books at the gift shop.

From the visitor center you can walk to the famous, architecturally singular **Cadet Chapel** for a tour. Also stop at the **Thunderbird Airmanship Overlook,** named for the Air Force's top pilots, where a Thunderbird jet is on display. You might even see cadets aloft in small planes, gliders, or parachutes.

Falcons are much more than the name of the football team and stadium here. Some of these noble birds, bred and trained at the academy, dazzle audiences at games and other events. Built for speeds of up to 200 mph, the prairie falcon can knock its prey out of the air. These streamlined raptors inhabit the surrounding cliffs and canyons, as do mule and white-tailed deer, pronghorn antelope, elk, and wild turkeys.

The academy's 19,000 acres adjoin the Rampart Range, so it's no secret that you can enjoy some picturesque hikes here. On the right, just before the academy entrance, park for the **New Santa Fe Regional Trail** EASY, a hiking and biking trail. The 12-mile **Falcon Trail** MODERATE and a trail to **Stanley Canyon Reservoir** EASY also take off from the grounds. Maps are available at the academy entrance and at the visitor center. *719-333-1110, www.usafa.af.mil/.*

WATERFALLS

The Pikes Peak watershed has formed many scenic waterfalls that allow for memorable hiking excursions from Colorado Springs. Runoff carved the magnificent **Seven Falls** in South Cheyenne Canyon, where water cascades 181 feet over massive granite cliffs and down seven distinct steps. Next to the falls, a 224-step stairway leads to a trail system that connects to **Midnight Falls.** A remarkable 14-story-high elevator will convey you to the Eagle's Nest platform for gorgeous views. Look for hummingbirds darting about or rare American dippers that sometimes nest near the waterfalls. To get there, take

Cheyenne Boulevard to its west end. For another angle on Seven Falls, take the 1-mile **Mount Cutler Trail** MODERATE, which starts at North Cheyenne Canyon Park. **North Cheyenne Canyon Trail** EASY is a 5-mile loop that passes three springs and overlooks of the city. *719-632-0765, www.sevenfalls.com.*

You can access many trails to waterfalls from Gold Camp Road (see Scenic Location No. 19, p. 86). The 3-mile **St. Mary's Falls Trail** MODERATE connects from the intersection of High Drive and Gold Camp Road. Park and walk about a mile to a closed tunnel and the trailhead. It's another 1.6 miles along the creek to St. Mary's Falls. From Gold Camp Road, turn onto North Cheyenne Road to reach the **Helen Hunt Falls** visitor center. Helen Hunt Jackson was a 19th-century poet and author who focused on the plight of the American Indians in her 1884 novel, *Ramona.* Both challenging and easy trails lead to the sublime Helen Hunt Falls and to **Silver Cascade Falls.** Technical climbers appreciate scaling **Silver Cascade Slab,** nestled above the latter falls. *For information: Sport Climbing Center of Colorado Springs, 4650 Northpark Dr., 719-260-1050, www.sportclimbcs.com.* You can also take an easy hike to Helen Hunt Falls from the interpretive **Starsmore Discovery Center.** *2120 Cheyenne Canyon Rd., 719-385-6086 (limited winter hours).*

COLORADO CAMEO

The Sugar Daddies of Colorado Springs

After the Civil War, General William Jackson Palmer resumed the business of building railroads. While involved with constructing the Kansas-Pacific Railroad west to Denver, General Palmer cherished the idea of creating a railroad from Denver to Pueblo and into the Arkansas Valley. In 1870, the Denver & Rio Grande Railway was incorporated, and in 1871, the southern route construction began. General Palmer decided that Colorado City, a rough mining camp at the base of Pikes Peak, would be an excellent place for a major railroad center. For less than a dollar an acre he bought more than 10,000 acres to build it.

General William Palmer

But General Palmer wanted this settlement to be much more than a rowdy railroad town. He desired to create in the shadow of Pikes Peak a sparkling city, Colorado Springs. His goal was a graceful community of homes on wide, tree-lined streets. A man of strict rectitude, Palmer strongly urged other wealthy people to follow his civic example. He envisioned parks, schools, and even a college, and committed his time and wealth to building this genteel community. In time, the noble city he charted swallowed the rough and dusty mining camp.

Charles Elliott Perkins

General William Palmer convinced his friend Charles Elliott Perkins, a fellow railroad tycoon, to buy 480 acres of what was to become the Garden of the Gods. Perkins expanded but did not develop the parcel, instead leaving it open for public enjoyment during his lifetime. He died in 1907, and in 1909 his family donated his lands as a public park for Colorado Springs. The Garden of the Gods remains a major tourist attraction to this day.

Winfield Scott Stratton may have been short-tempered and impetuous, but he was not heartless. He understood what it meant to be poor. For 17 years he eked out a living as a carpenter in Colorado Springs, spending his free time following the gold strikes around the state. In 1893, he struck it fabulously rich at two mining claims in Cripple Creek. Stratton purchased and developed Colorado Springs' trolley system. Then he spent his considerable wealth on making sure the indigent of Colorado Springs had coal for the winter and could afford transportation on the trolley. He also established the Myron Stratton Home for the elderly and children in need.

Winfield S. Stratton

Spencer Penrose had amassed considerable wealth from copper mining, the Cripple Creek gold mines, and gold-processing mills when he turned his attention to enhancing the Colorado Springs vicinity. He transformed an uneven carriage road into the Pikes Peak Road in 1915 and built The Broadmoor in 1918. In 1926, Penrose founded the Cheyenne Mountain Zoo. He also endowed what was to later be the Colorado Springs Fine Arts Center. His El Pomar Foundation continues to fund community causes. Spencer Penrose is buried on Cheyenne Mountain, close to the Will Rogers Shrine.

Spencer Penrose

Activities

CYCLING AND MOUNTAIN BIKING

Monument Valley Park, notable for its gardens, is a pleasant strip of green for a gentle touring ride; 4.5-mile **Monument Valley Park Loop Trail** EASY follows Monument Creek. From I-25, take the Bijou Street exit (142) and head east. *170 W. Cache La Poudre Blvd.* The 4-mile **Captain Jack's Front Side Loop** DIFFICULT climbs to fabulous, panoramic views but does present some technical difficulties. You can also extend this rigorous mountain ride by adding a 9-mile portion of **Gold Camp Road** DIFFICULT. To get to the trails, take I-25 South to Exit 140 and turn left. Turn right at the first light and right again onto Cheyenne Boulevard (Cheyenne Canyon Road). Continue 1 mile through North Cheyenne Canyon Park, passing Helen Hunt Falls. The street ends at a gate; park and start by riding north on High Drive. Pick up a map to find where to connect with other trails in the area. *For maps, guided bike tours, and information: Challenge Unlimited, 204 S. 24th St., 719-633-6399, 800-798-5954, www.bikithikit.com.*

GOLF

Some of the area's best golf courses—those at The Broadmoor and U.S. Air Force Academy—are, alas, not open to the public (although the academy course welcomes both active and retired military personnel). Even so, you can enjoy peak golfing and views at public courses as well. **Patty Jewett Municipal Golf Course** has for many years been rated the best golf course in town by the *Colorado Springs Independent* newspaper. *900 E. Española St., 719-385-6934.* The 18-hole **Pine Creek Golf Course** is particularly challenging because of strong afternoon winds. Take I-25 to the Briargate exit (151) and drive 3 miles east. *9850 Divot Trail, 719-594-9999, www.pinecreekgc.com.*

HIKING

In addition to the waterfall hikes (see Main Attractions, p. 75) don't miss the popular 4.5-mile **Monument Valley Park Loop Trail** EASY. (For directions, see Cycling and Mountain Biking, above). South of town, the trail at **Fountain Creek Regional Park** EASY ambles by waters where waterfowl such as blue herons and cormorants mingle with other wetland species near glorious cottonwoods. Bring a picnic basket or angle in the fishing ponds. Volunteers from the nature center conduct hikes through the park. Go south on I-25 to Exit 132 and east on CO 16 for 0.5 mile to the junction with US 85/87, then turn right (south). Continue briefly on US 85/87 to Cattail Marsh Road and turn right (west). *719-520-6745.*

Bear Creek Regional Park EASY features short trails, mule deer, and songbirds. Stop by its excellent nature center. Take I-25 to Exit 141 and go west on Cimarron (US 24) 1.8 miles to 26th Street. Turn left (south) and drive 1.4 miles to the Gold Camp Road intersection; it's 0.1 mile to the park entrance. The 15-mile **North Monument Creek Loop** MODERATE winds through the picture-perfect Rampart Range. This is also a four-wheel-drive road, so watch for traffic. To get to the trail from Colorado Springs, take I-25 north to CO 105 (Exit 161) and turn left (west); proceed to Palmer Lake, then take the main road west to the old waterworks and park. Many trails meander and merge in this area; pick up a map of the Pikes Peak area at the U.S. Forest Service Office. *601 S. Weber St., Colorado Springs, 719-636-1602.*

For a wild experience in the Beaver Creek Wilderness Study Area, the 11-mile round-trip **Beaver Creek Loop** MODERATE winds through rugged forests of piñon, juniper, spruce, and pine trees and habitat for mule deer, bighorn sheep, and mountain lions. To reach the trailhead, take I-25 to CO 115 (Exit 140). Go south on CO 115 for 33.6 miles through the town of Penrose to US 50 and turn right (west). Drive 4.2 miles and turn right on Phantom Canyon Road (County Road 67). At 1.7 miles, turn right on CR 123, drive 0.3 mile, and turn left on Beaver Creek Road (CR 132). Continue on this road for 10.8 miles to the trailhead.

MUSEUMS

The **Colorado Springs Fine Arts Center** features an excellent collection of American Indian and Hispanic art, traveling exhibits, and works by such Western painters as Georgia O'Keeffe, Charles M. Russell, and Albert Bierstadt. *30 W. Dale St., 719-634-5581, www.csfineartscenter.org.* You can get buggy at the **May Natural History Museum,** which houses John May's lifetime collection of insects, one of the world's largest and an irreplaceable entomological resource. The May Museum's Space Exploration Wing showcases space photography and documents the history of human flight. You can also continue your natural history tour outside on the museum's trails. The museum is 8 miles south of Colorado Springs on Rock Creek Canyon Road. *719-576-0450, 800-666-3841, www.maymuseum-camp-rvpark.com.* The **Pioneers Museum** displays historic photos of the Pikes Peak region by frontier photographer William Henry Jackson. *215 S. Tejon St., 719-385-5990.*

The **Pro Rodeo Hall of Fame and Museum of the American Cowboy** will please cowboy enthusiasts of all ages. See video presentations on the history of Old West and ranch life, art exhibits, and cowhand memorabilia. The

Pro Rodeo Hall of Fame and Museum of the American Cowboy, Colorado Springs

PALMER PARK

Have you ever noticed the white, rocky bluffs east of I-25 as you drive through the northern half of Colorado Springs? In 1998, I sought the location on these bluffs from which William Henry Jackson had taken a photograph during the 19th century. It was among 300 places he had photographed that I was able to find and rephotograph for a project showing how Colorado's landscape had (or had not) changed in a century. It required two days' worth of hiking in order to discover this particular place, but it was well worth the effort as the accompanying photograph shows.

Thank goodness the 726-acre Palmer Park was protected as a city park many years ago. Since then, housing developments have been allowed among and above this beautiful formation of white sandstones. Among the cliffs and oddly shaped formations are stands of ponderosa pine and scrub oak. Views of the city extend 360 degrees from atop the bluffs. From I-25, take the Garden of the Gods Road exit (146), but instead of driving west to that park, head east on Austin Bluffs Parkway for just over 4 miles to Academy Boulevard (CO 83). Turn right and drive south 1.6 miles to Maizeland Road. Make a right and look for the entrance to the park 200 yards farther on the right.

Paved and improved dirt roads take you to most places in Palmer Park. But don't miss the wonderful network of trails—some hikes extend into roadless places up to 4 miles away. Plan on hiking after you've explored the lay of the land from your vehicle. Trails and roads cover canyon bottoms as well as ridge tops. The canyons, full of oaks and pines, are best photographed against the white rock walls in cloudy light. (Because white is highly reflective, direct sunlight washes out the details on film.)

However, on clear days you can photograph within 30 minutes before sunset or after sunrise. At these times, the direct light is less intense and colors the cliffs yellow and orange without overcoming the detail of the rock. I especially enjoy composing rock ledges or unusual formations in the foreground with ponderosa pines or Pikes Peak in the background. This requires being on the western edge of the park, 1.5 miles up the North Cañon Trail. As in other Front Range locations, the oaks turn bright green in May and orange and red in October. The bluffs are especially pretty with snow draped over the white rocks.

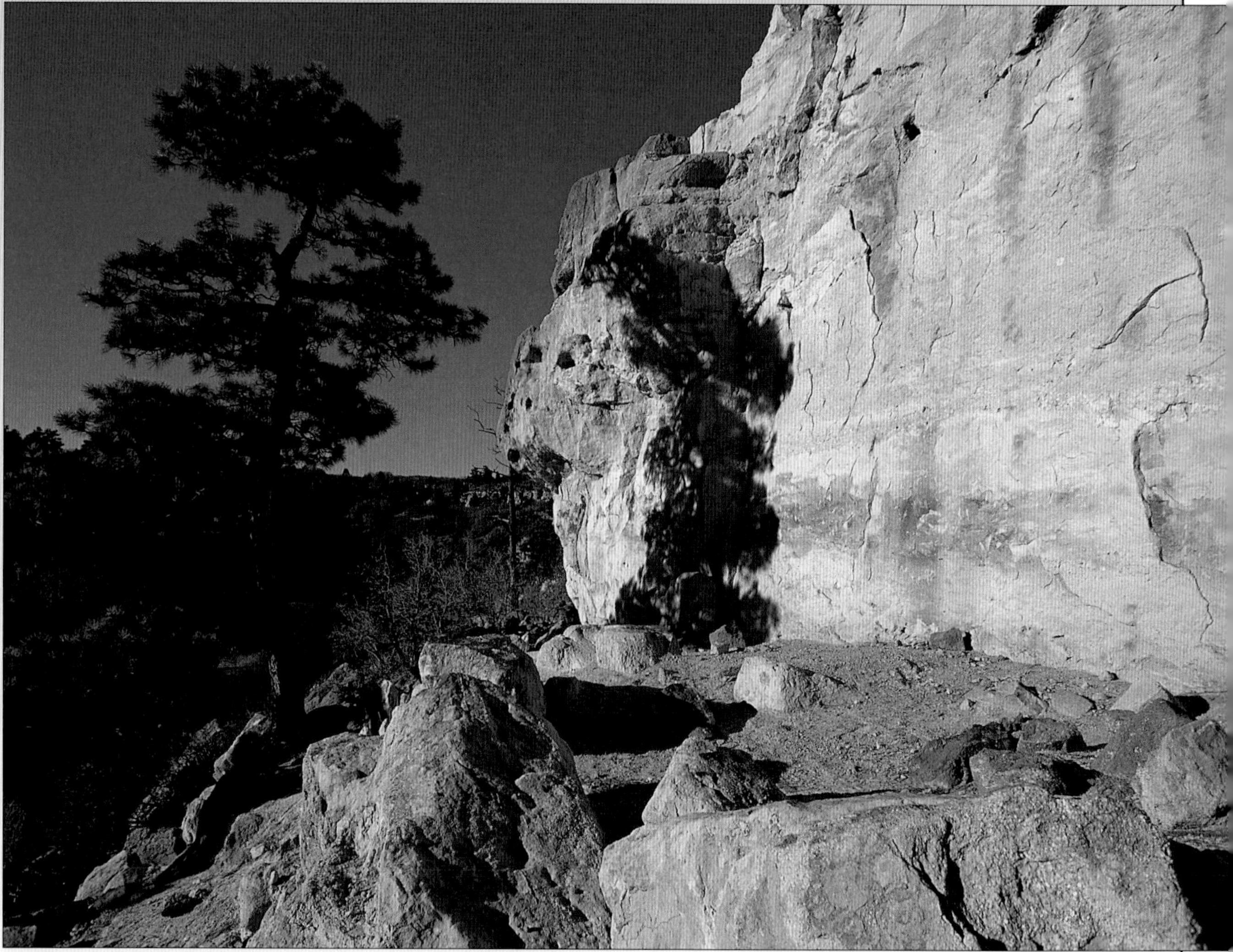

Hall of Champions features incredible belt buckles and trophies. If you're lucky, you might catch a live mini-rodeo at the museum's arena. From I-25, take Exit 147 and go west. *101 Pro Rodeo Dr., 719-528-4764, www.prorodeohalloffame.com.* Another one-of-a-kind museum is the **World Figure Skating Museum and Hall of Fame.** Take in a world-class collection of historical and contemporary ice skates, skating costumes, medals, and trophies, not to mention Olympic history and official skating records. From I-25, take Exit 138 (Lake Avenue) west, then turn right onto 1st Street. *20 1st St., 719-635-5200, www.worldskatingmuseum.org.* The **Ghost Town Museum** re-creates an authentic mining-era town from materials abandoned after the Pikes Peak Region's gold rush, including a saloon, jail, sheriff's office, and blacksmith shop. *US 24 at 21st St., 719-634-0696.*

U.S. OLYMPIC COMPLEX

What Boulder is to training in running and bicycling, Colorado Springs is to almost every other sport in Olympic competition. Thousands of Olympic hopefuls train for the gold at this fabulous facility. Be sure to take the 1-hour tour, on which you can observe athletes in training. To get there, take I-25 to the Uintah exit (143). Follow the signs east. *888-659-8687.*

ZOO

The **Cheyenne Mountain Zoo** is one of the best in the state. The zoo is home to endangered species such as Mexican wolves, Siberian tigers, and great apes. It is also the highest zoo in the nation, and perhaps the safest, atop Cheyenne Mountain and the North American Aerospace Defense Command (NORAD). Near the zoo stands the dramatic stone pinnacle of the **Will Rogers Shrine of the Sun,** which houses memorable murals and celebrates a memorable humorist. To get to the zoo, take I-25 to the Circle Drive exit (138) and head west to The Broadmoor. Turn right at the hotel and follow the signs to the zoo. *719-633-9925, www.cmzoo.org.*

La Petite Maison restaurant, Colorado Springs

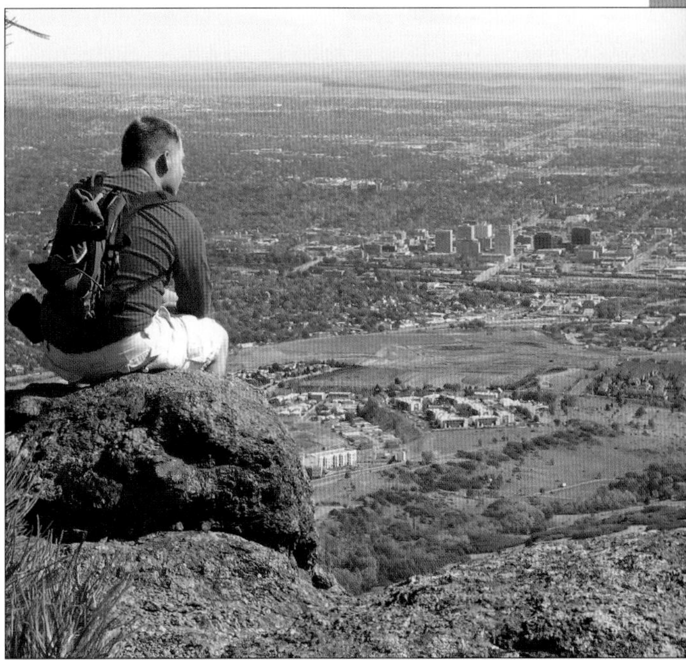

Colorado Springs overlook

Restaurants

If you can't dine at **The Broadmoor** restaurants or miss Sunday brunch at its **Penrose Room** (see The Broadmoor, Main Attractions, p. 73), you can still take your pick of other fine restaurants in town. **La Petite Maison** ($$-$$$) dishes up French and American cuisine in a charming setting for special occasions. Choose the pan-roasted chicken, grilled lamb, or duck, and don't forget dessert. *1015 W. Colorado Ave., 719-632-4887, www.lapetitemaisoncs.com.* One of the best steakhouses in town, **MacKenzie's Chop House** ($$-$$$) serves dry-aged Colorado beef; the Southwestern filet is a treat. *128 S. Tejon St., 719-635-3536.* **Phantom Canyon Brewing Company** ($-$$) pours its own microbrews alongside tasty pub fare and wood-fired pizza. *2 E. Pikes Peak Ave., 719-635-2800.* **Edelweiss Restaurant** ($$) offers authentic German cuisine in a cozy Bavarian setting. It has been a local favorite for 30 years. *34 E. Ramona Ave., 719-633-2220.* At **Walter's Bistro** ($$-$$$), enjoy award-winning chef Ryan Blanchard's dishes, including first-rate seafood. *146 E. Cheyenne Mountain Blvd., 719-630-0201.* The unique dining experiences offered at the following three Colorado Springs eateries make them all excellent choices for families with children. **Giuseppe's Old Depot Restaurant** ($-$$), a converted late-19th-century train station, serves Italian favorites such as pizza and spaghetti. Trains occasionally rumble by, reinforcing the nostalgic theme. *10 S. Sierra Madre, 719-635-3111, www.guiseppes-depot.com.* The **Melting Pot** ($$$) provides an intimate dining experience with its assortments of fondue. *30-A E. Pikes Peak Ave., 719-385-0300.* **Flying W Ranch** ($$), a working cattle ranch, also specializes in Western food including barbecue and Flying W beans. Wander through a reconstructed frontier town here, and see demonstrations of Navajo weaving and blacksmithing. Take Garden of the Gods Road to 30th Street and turn right (north). *3330 Chuckwagon Rd., 719-598-0405, www.flyingw.com.*

Accommodations

The Broadmoor ($$$$) takes the prize as Colorado Springs' premier resort hotel (see Main Attractions, p. 73). The **Cheyenne Mountain Resort** ($$-$$$) attracts both high-tech conferences and active vacationers to its generous grounds. Graceful wooden beams and Oriental furnishings convey a truly restful ambiance. Facilities include an 18-hole golf course; tennis, racquetball, and squash courts; fitness center; a private lake for fishing and sailing; and a spacious outdoor pool. *3225 Broadmoor Valley Rd., 719-538-4000, 800-428-8886, www.cheyennemountain.com.* If you're looking for a small inn with intimate accommodations, **Hughes Hacienda** ($$-$$$) is perfect. The hilltop inn is just a quick drive from downtown and boasts excellent views of the surrounding mountains. *12060 Calle Corvo, 719-576-2060, 800-576-2060, www.hugheshacienda.com.*

The Mission-style **Cheyenne Cañon Inn** ($$) at the foot of Pikes Peak had a colorful history as a casino and bordello. *2030 W. Cheyenne Rd., 719-633-0625, www.cheyennecanoninn.com.* Another highly rated B&B is the centrally located **Holden House Bed & Breakfast** ($$), a restored Victorian complete with carriage house. *1102 W. Pikes Peak Ave., 719-471-3980, www.holdenhouse.com.* You will be greeted in grand style with wine and hors d'oeuvres when you check in at the excellent **Old Town GuestHouse** ($$-$$$) *115 S. 26th St., 719-632-9194, www.oldtown-guesthouse.com.* The rustic log construction and spaciousness of **Black Forest Bed & Breakfast, Lodge and Cabins** ($$), situated on 20 acres of pine forests, match its surroundings. *11170 Black Forest Rd., 719-495-4208, 800-809-9901, www.blackforestbb.com.*

Special Events

Home to the Pro Rodeo Hall of Fame and Museum of the American Cowboy (see Museums, p. 77), Colorado Springs is a fitting host for Colorado's largest outdoor rodeo competition, held in early August. The **Pikes Peak or Bust Rodeo** features the best professional competitors in the nation and is a stop on the Professional Rodeo Cowboys Association circuit. The entire city celebrates with a traditional downtown parade during rodeo week. *Penrose Stadium, 1045 W. Rio Grande Ave., 719-635-1632, www.pikespeakorbustrodeo.org.* The **International Balloon Classic** launches into action in Colorado Springs' Memorial Park, filling the sky with hundreds of colorful balloons and other aerial spectacles each Labor Day weekend. *719-471-4833, www.balloonclassic.com.*

Each Memorial Day weekend, locals celebrate **Territory Days,** an event that began in 1975 as the "Rampart Range Sertoma Territory Days Parade and Buffalo Barbeque." The name was shortened the following year, and the event has been taking place every year since. Today it is a three-day street festival with arts and crafts, food and other vendors, and a ton of family-friendly activities.

Colorado Springs is also known for its annual wine festival. **The Wine Festival of Colorado Springs** has become one of the most well-known in the Front Range and features wine tastings and pairings, food, auctions, and seminars. *For more information on these events: 719-635-7506, 800-888-4748, www.visitcos.com.*

For More Information

Colorado Springs Convention and Visitors Bureau, *515 S. Cascade, 719-635-7506, 800-888-4748, www.visitcos.com.* For details about the entire region: Pikes Peak Country Attractions Association, *354 Manitou Ave., Manitou Springs, 719-685-5894, www.pikes-peak.com.*

Manitou Springs

(see map on p. 82)

Tucked away between the Garden of the Gods and Pikes Peak, Manitou Springs has retained the feel of a small town. I've always liked to stroll along its streets, visit the quaint boutiques, then stop in for a meal at a nearby restaurant. The bubbling springs that gave the town its name have been restored, as have many buildings dating from the Gilded Age, a testament to the efforts of historic preservationists. Just 4 miles west of Colorado Springs, Manitou Springs has its own distinct style and is a federally designated National Historic District. Come sip the mineral waters and enjoy a creative, laid-back community that values its culture and provides easy access to regional attractions.

History

American Indians considered the nine effervescent mineral springs here to be sacred; *manitou* is said to mean "spirit." Tribal conflicts were put aside here when various tribes drank from and soaked in these healing waters, fed by runoff from Pikes Peak. Learning of the area from Zebulon Pike's journals, Major Stephen H. Long's expedition arrived here in 1820 and noted the healing qualities of the springs. Still other explorers followed and spread the word, much to the dismay of the Indians. The later discovery of gold in the area worsened territorial skirmishes between Indians and settlers, conflicts that didn't cease until the tribes were removed to reservations.

In 1868, Civil War General William Jackson Palmer and his friend, Dr. William Bell, arrived and soon made plans to create a palatial health resort around the springs. By the early 1870s, Manitou Springs began to take form, modeled after the finest European resort towns. Alas, the 1873 economic panic dashed their extravagant plans, and a more modest town came into being. The reputation of the bubbling waters continued to grow. Doctors advised "taking the waters" for various ailments, and people suffering from health problems, particularly tuberculosis, steadily arrived here.

By the 1900s, the springs and vicinity began to draw more tourists than patients. Demand surged for first-class hotels and amenities frequented by presidents, moguls, authors, and, not least, photographer William Henry Jackson. The town's elite-resort era ended with the auto age. The aftermath of World War II did bring a military influx and economic boost to the region, but when US 24 bypassed Manitou in the 1960s, many of its remaining tourist spots were stranded. Even the mineral springs were paved over. Fortunately, Manitou Springs was designated a National Historic District in the 1980s. Many historic structures were restored, and the town became home to a growing colony of artists and artisans. Now the pride of the city has returned: Local organizations, the Mineral Springs Foundation, the city, and individuals joined to revive the springs, from which visitors can again drink to their good health.

Main Attractions

CAVE OF THE WINDS

See the underside of the glorious Pikes Peak region in these amazing caverns. First discovered by homesteader Arthur Love in 1869, the network of caverns is the result of millions of years' worth of groundwater and geothermal activity beneath the Manitou Springs area. Of the three tours offered, my choice is the Lantern Tour; exploring by lantern light seems more authentic and mysterious than by electric lights. The serious underground adventurer will want to make reservations for the strenuous, four-hour Explorer's Trip. The flowstone cascades of Canopy Hall and the towering stalactites and stalagmites of the Temple of Silence highlight all of the tours. Experienced cavers can also test their skills at finding new passageways. Cave of the Winds lies just off of US 24 north of Manitou Springs. *719-685-5444, www.caveofthewinds.com.*

MINERAL SPRINGS

Now that many springs have been restored, visitors enjoy taking self-guided "Springsabouts," or walking tours, and filling a jug with the bubbling mineral water that is said to heal body and soul. *Mineral Springs Foundation, 354 Manitou Ave., 719-685-5089, www.manitousprings.org/About/mineralsprings.htm.*

MIRAMONT CASTLE

Father Jean Baptiste Francolon came to Manitou Springs in the 1880s for his health. In 1895 he built the Miramont Castle, an eclectic estate that blends a variety of architectural styles from Byzantine to Tudor. This unique structure was later used as a sanitarium by the Sisters of Mercy and is now a museum. Check out the grand model-train display, which underscores the importance of the railroad in the region's development. The castle is located near the Pikes Peak Cog Railway Depot at 9 Capitol Hill Ave. *719-685-1011, www.miramontcastle.org.*

NORTH POLE/SANTA'S WORKSHOP

This place *is* a bit magical. Children love the rides, reindeer, and magic shows. Pick up decorations to trim both tree and house, and if you really want to get the attention of the folks back home, mail your postcards from the post office at Colorado's North Pole! The workshop lies at the foot of Pikes Peak, 10 miles northwest of Colorado Springs on US 24. *719-684-9432, www.santas-colo.com.*

PIKES PEAK COG RAILWAY

In the late 1880s, inventor Zalmon Simmons made an arduous trip on muleback to the summit of Pikes Peak that he never forgot. He made plans, raised money, and in 1889 founded the Manitou & Pikes Peak Railway Co. On June 30, 1891, the

Manitou Springs/Cripple Creek/Cañon City

Colorado Atlas & Gazetteer pp. 62–63, 72

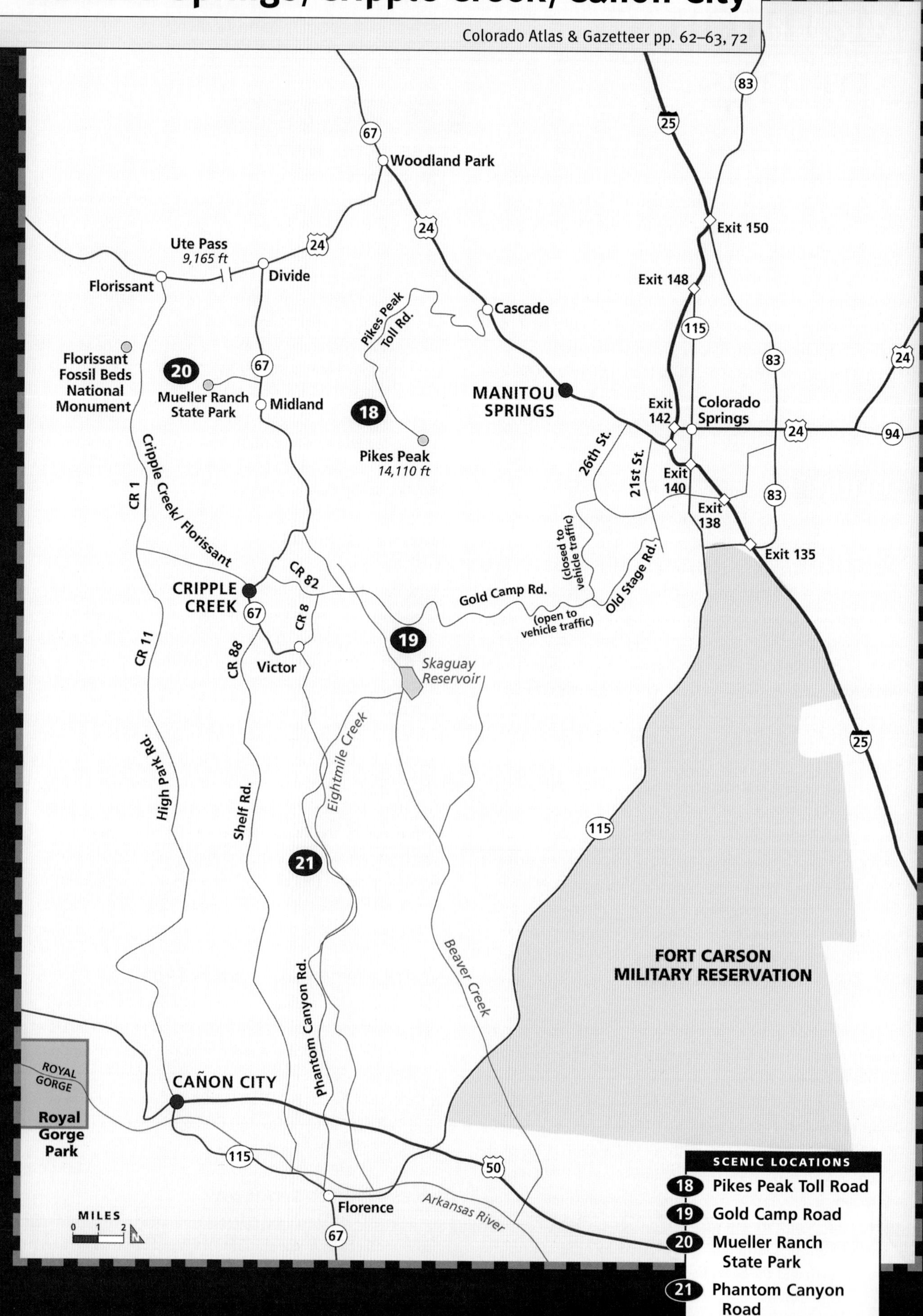

company's first passenger train, carrying a church choir, made it to the summit. The cog railway moves by the meshing of a cog wheel on the locomotive with a special rail mounted between the tracks. Conventional trains can only climb grades up to 6 percent, but the cog system allows trains to tackle grades up to 38 percent. Your 3-hour, 8.9-mile trip on the cog railway is a picturesque journey, and the railway guides provide a running history of the region as you ride.

The climb to the summit starts in spruce-pine forests. Look for deer along the route and, if you're lucky, maybe a mountain lion. The train will eventually pass through Hell Gate, a narrow natural gateway. You will also pass Minnehaha Falls, a name inspired by Longfellow's poem, "Hiawatha." As you ascend toward timberline, notice the gnarled bristlecone pine trees, which can be thousands of years old. Above timberline, listen for the whistles of fat yellow-bellied marmots. And look for bighorn sheep and shaggy mountain goats near the summit. The train stops at the top for about 30 minutes. Standing on the summit of 14,110-foot Pikes Peak, nearly 3 miles past timberline, you will have panoramic views of Colorado's mountain ranges and plains. From this vantage point, you can see the "fruited" Great Plains and the "purple mountain majesties" of the Sangre de Cristos to the south and the great Collegiate Peaks to the southwest that so impressed New Englander Katharine Lee Bates, author of "America the Beautiful." Many passengers welcome a cool drink (or a hot cup of coffee) at the Summit House. The depot is at 515 Ruxton Ave. *719-685-5401, www.cograilway.com.*

Activities

CAMPING

The town of Woodland Park, 12 miles northwest of Manitou Springs on US 24, boasts several beautiful campsites. As the name suggests, **Painted Rocks** campground lies amid sandstone sculptures and formations, and you can fish at nearby Trout Creek. From Woodland Park, go 8 miles north on CO 67 to County Road 78 (Forest Road 340). Turn left (west) and drive 0.5 mile to the campground. **South Meadows** and **Colorado** campgrounds have many sites with shade and privacy. South Meadows is 6 miles north of Woodland Park on CO 67; Colorado is 1 mile farther on CO 67. *For reservations at these campgrounds: 719-636-1602.*

FISHING

Serious anglers drive over to **Elevenmile Reservoir** and **Spinney Mountain Ranch** (see Fishing, Fairplay, p. 219) or the **Arkansas River** (see Fishing, Buena Vista and Salida, p. 231). Because Manitou Lake is being drained and Rampart Reservoir gets so much motorized water traffic, fishing guides recommend trying **Monument Lake, South and North Catamount Lakes,** or **Crystal Lake.** To get to Monument Lake from the Manitou Springs or Colorado Springs areas, take I-25 north to the Monument exit (161). To get to Catamount and Crystal Lakes, take the Pikes Peak Toll Road; be sure to tell the tollgate attendant that you are going fishing. *For information, fishing conditions, and guided trips: The Peak Fly Shop, 5767 Academy Blvd., Woodland Park, 719-260-1415, www.thepeakflyshop.com; Anglers Covey, 295 S. 21st St., Colorado Springs, 719-471-2984, www.anglerscovey.com.*

HIKING

The 7-mile **Waldo Canyon Loop** MODERATE follows Waldo Creek to views of Pikes Peak and is also a popular mountain-biking trip. Bighorn sheep frequent this area. From Manitou Springs or Colorado Springs, take US 24 west; the trail is 2 miles past the sign for Cave of the Winds, on the north side of the parking area. For a real challenge, climb to the summit of Pikes Peak by way of the 13-mile (one way) **Barr Trail** DIFFICULT. This popular route starts on Ruxton Avenue near the railway depot.

MUSEUMS

Although hundreds of miles from the Anasazi cliff dwellings of the Four Corners region (see Main Attractions, Cortez, p. 408), the **Manitou Cliff Dwellings Museum** will whet your appetite for the long trip west to Mesa Verde. You can touch and even venture inside the ruins, built more than 700 years ago under a protective red sandstone overhang. During the summer, be sure to catch the descendants of the Ancient Ones as they perform traditional Native American dances. The museum is on US 24 next to the Cave of the Winds. *719-685-5242, www.cliffdwellingsmuseum.com.*

SCENIC DRIVES

The 18.5-mile **Pikes Peak Toll Road** (see Scenic Location No. 18, p. 84) provides a grand and historical way to ascend Pikes Peak. This mostly dirt road has more than 100 hairpin curves that demand a driver's close attention. Pick up a map at the tollgate and follow the driving tips. The view from the top of this 14,110-foot peak is certainly worth your effort; on clear days, you can see 100 miles in every direction.

After about a mile, you can spy Ute Pass to your left. At a little more than 5 miles, stop at the displays in the Crystal Reservoir Visitor Center. At 9 miles, you begin a steep ascent with a series of tight curves. From here you can see the town of Woodland Park and the Rampart Range. A little farther up the road, you will see what's left of the abandoned Pikes Peak Ski Area. Stop at the Glen Cove Inn for a meal and a visit to the gift shop. At a bit over 14 miles, stop at the Devil's Playground for yet another stunning view. At 18.5 miles, you reach the windy summit of Pikes Peak and one of the most panoramic views in Colorado. Always be aware of the weather, particularly above timberline. On the way down, use low gear and don't ride the brakes. To get to the Pikes Peak Toll Road, take I-25 to the US 24 exit (141). Go west 9 miles. Turn left (south) at the Pikes Peak Highway sign and go 1 mile to the tollgate. *For information and road conditions: 719-684-9383.*

18 SCENIC LOCATION

PIKES PEAK TOLL ROAD

Of the 54 fourteeners in Colorado, there are just two on which you can drive to the top in a vehicle—Mount Evans, west of Denver, and Pikes Peak. The 18.5-mile-long Pikes Peak Toll Road has many pullouts from which it's easy to photograph the different ecosystems you pass. Take I-25 to the US 24 exit (141) and travel west 9 miles to the well-marked Pikes Peak Highway sign. Turn left and proceed to the tollgate.

From the tollgate you'll drive through pine and fir forests, then aspen and spruce. Bristlecone pine sculpted into odd shapes populate the timberline, after which you enter the treeless alpine zone and tundra. In summer, you'll see wildflowers along the entire drive, including dwarf flowers that grow close to the ground in the alpine zone. In fall, the aspen turn golden. The road is open year-round (road conditions permitting) so winter photography is also possible. And many trails depart from the road to provide a less vehicle-impaired view of the ecosystems.

It's always tempting to photograph far-off mountains without providing any perspective. One reason I rarely make good images from the top of high mountains is the lack of foreground subjects to create a sense of depth. Every photograph I've ever made from a mountaintop looks the same—boring views of other mountains too far away to create interest. One of my favorite places to photograph is at mile 14.7, the Devil's Playground. Weathered pink granite rocks of all shapes and sizes dominate this landscape above treeline, creating a great foreground for views to the north and west. The setting sun bathes these rocks in red, while casting long shadows eastward and creating depth in the scene. Snow also provides opportunities for interesting foregrounds. Or bring along a close-up lens and photograph the tundra flowers. Twilight can create beautiful backdrops—skies sometimes replete with pink clouds, other times layered in red at the horizon to deep blue overhead. Compose a little bit of land with a lot of sky when taking photographs of such scenes.

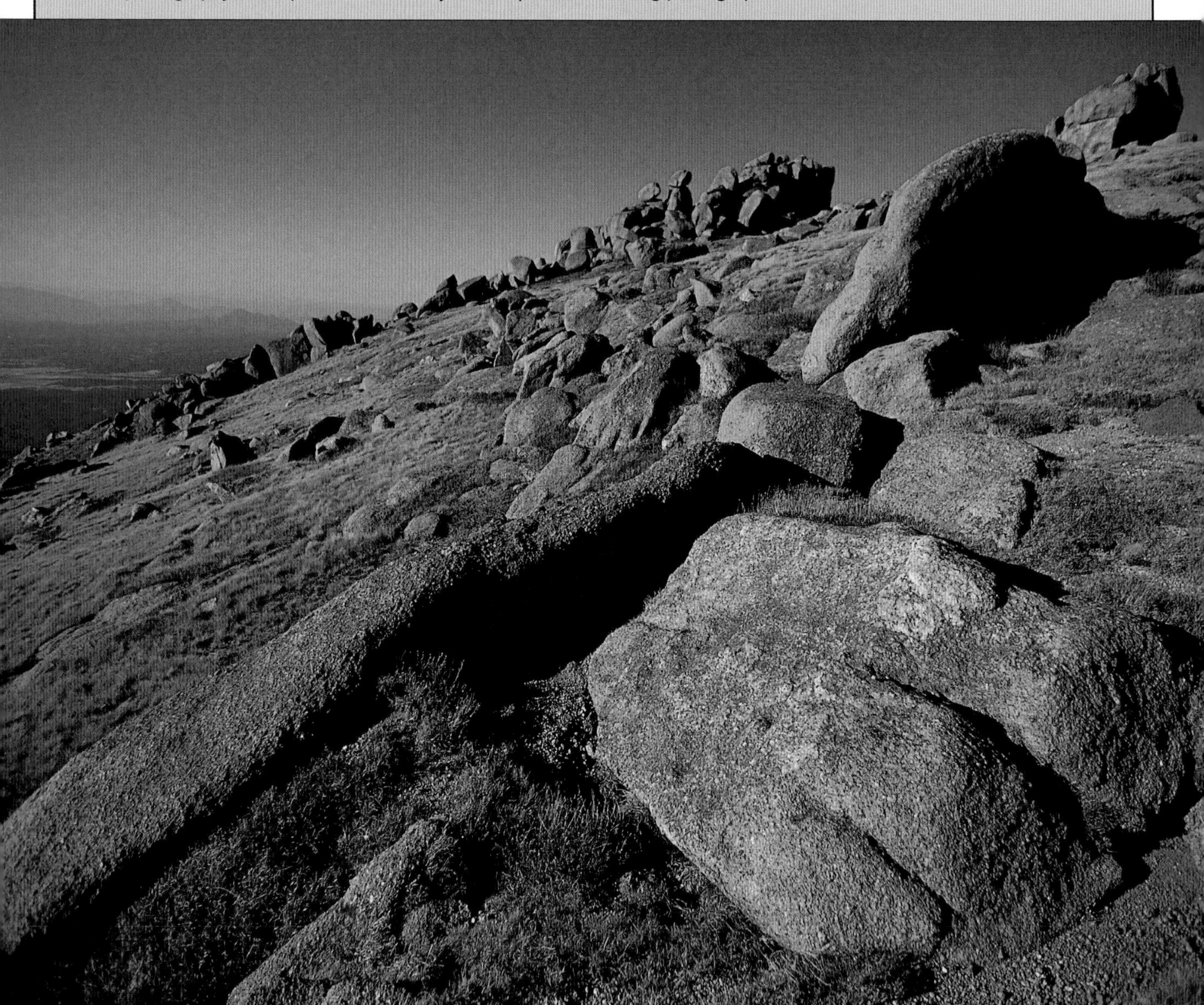

SHOPPING

You would expect a town that has become somewhat of an artist colony to include diverse shops. Manitou Springs does not disappoint; you can find everything from tourist T-shirts to fine art and pottery. The Fountain Creek area has more than 150 shops, galleries, and restaurants, the majority of which are located on Manitou, Cañon, and Colorado Avenues.

THEATER

The **Iron Springs Melodrama Dinner Theater** stages hysterical Western comedy melodramas such as "Honesty Always Wins" and "Danger, Ranger Granger" and serves excellent family-style beef barbecue and fried chicken dinners. *444 Ruxton Ave. across from the cog railway depot, 719-685-5572.*

Restaurants

Visit the eclectic shops, then visit one of Manitou Springs' wonderful restaurants. The beautiful **Briarhurst Manor** ($$-$$$$) serves continental Colorado cuisine, including a great rack of Colorado lamb; the salmon is also a favorite of mine. *404 Manitou Ave., 719-685-1864, www.briarhurst.com.* The **Craftwood Inn** ($$-$$$$) serves excellent buffalo tenderloin and Colorado mountain bass. Try the other Colorado specialties, including elk, quail, and duck. Finish with a great dessert. *404 El Paso Blvd., 719-685-9000.* **Mission Bell Inn** ($$) serves traditional Mexican food. Give the *norteños*, gourmet chile rellenos, a try. *178 Crystal Park Rd., 719-685-9089, www.missionbellinn.com.* **Adam's Mountain Café** ($-$$) has long been a favorite for breakfast. Check out its vegetarian dishes. *110 Cañon Ave., 719-685-1430.*

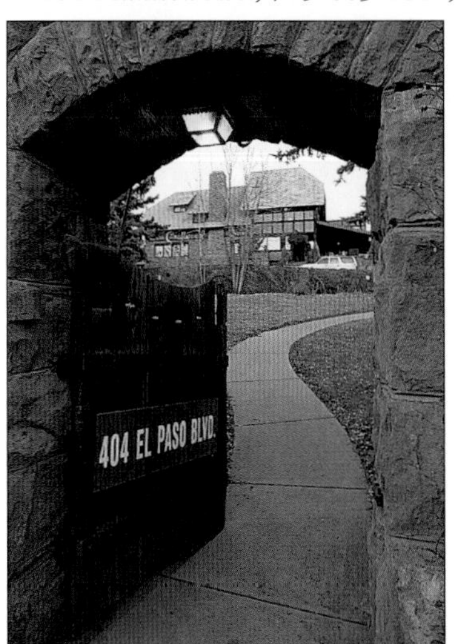

Craftwood Inn, Manitou Springs

Accommodations

The Cliff House ($$-$$$$) is a charming, renovated Victorian inn that was originally a stage stop. Luminaries such as Theodore Roosevelt and Clark Gable have stayed here. The service remains outstanding and includes afternoon tea. *306 Cañon Ave., 719-685-3000, www.thecliffhouse.com.* The **Blue Skies Inn** ($$-$$$) on the estate of Manitou Springs' founder, Dr. William Bell, is another excellent place to stay. Many deer make their home on the land surrounding the inn. *402 Manitou Ave., 719-685-3899, www.blueskiesbb.com.* The **Red Crags Bed & Breakfast Inn** ($$-$$$) provides all the amenities as well as views of Pikes Peak and Garden of the Gods. *302 El Paso Blvd., 719-685-1920, www.redcrags.com.* The award-winning **Two Sisters Inn** ($-$$) is distinctive for its hosts' attention to service. *10 Otoe Pl., 719-685-9684, www.twosisinn.com.*

Red Crags B&B Inn, Manitou Springs

Special Events

In late June, the downtown **Clayfest** puts on wonderful pottery-making competitions for mud-throwers of all skill levels. *719-685-1460.* Over Labor Day weekend, the **Annual Commonwheel Arts and Crafts Fair** ends the summer in style in Memorial Park, with live performers, plenty of food, and, of course, dozens of artists' and artisans' booths. *719-685-1008.*

Traditionally held over the Fourth of July weekend, the **Pikes Peak International Hill Climb,** or the Race to the Clouds, is the second oldest auto race in the United States and draws the best competitive drivers in the world. *719-685-4400, www.ppihc.com.* If you can't afford a competitive racecar, you can always run to the top of Pikes Peak—and Zebulon Pike said his Grand Mountain would never be climbed! The annual **Pikes Peak Ascent** tests runners to try to bag the summit, while the **Pikes Peak Marathon,** perhaps even more grueling, charges runners to make it to the top and back down again. These back-to-back events are held on separate days in mid-August. *719-473-2625, www.pikespeakmarathon.org.*

Two of Manitou Springs's most interesting annual events have been featured in *Ripley's Believe it or Not.* October's **Emma Crawford Coffin Festival,** an all-day event that includes a coffin race and parade is definitely not to be missed. Following the holiday festivities is January's **Great Fruitcake Toss**—bring your own or rent one for $1 and see how far you can toss it! *For more information: 719-685-5089, 800-642-2567, www.manitousprings.org.*

For More Information

Manitou Springs Chamber of Commerce, *354 Manitou Ave., 719-685-5089, 800-642-2567, www.manitousprings.org;* Pikes Peak Country Attractions Association, *354 Manitou Ave., 719-685-5894, www.pikes-peak.com.*

Cripple Creek

(see map on p. 82)

Cripple Creek still calls itself "The World's Greatest Gold Camp." The richest strike of the Pikes Peak gold rush, Cripple Creek continues to produce gold today: The Cresson Mine produces an average 225,000 troy ounces of gold annually and has more than 4,800 patented mining claims. But Cripple Creek is more than mining riches past and present. A visit to the Cripple Creek National Historic District allows you a peek into the past, with the laughter of melodramas and the chance to strike it rich at gaming tables reminiscent of the gold rush days. Now folks "goin' up Cripple Creek to have a little fun," as the old song goes, arrive by car and tour bus rather than mule team and horse.

The small town of Victor lies just 4 miles south of Cripple Creek. Historically, Cripple Creek was the entertainment hub, and Victor the residential quarter for the mining community. The same is true today. Quaint, historic homes and shops line the streets of Victor (the soda fountain makes a great chocolate shake), and remnants of an illustrious mining past dot the outskirts, but you'll find no gaming here. Cripple Creek still entertains, and Victor still relaxes. Take High Park Road, a picturesque route to Cripple Creek and Victor (see Scenic Drives, Cañon City, p. 93), or just drive I-25 to the US 24 exit (141) and go 25 miles west to the town of Divide. Turn left (south) on CO 67 and drive another 20 miles to Cripple Creek.

19 SCENIC LOCATION — GOLD CAMP ROAD

Many of Colorado's most scenic drives are along abandoned railroad beds. Gold Camp Road, which leads to the Cripple Creek and Victor Historic Mining District, is one such route. The Short Line Railroad linked Cripple Creek with Colorado Springs and points beyond. Traversing this route by train in 1901, Vice President Theodore Roosevelt reportedly said, "This is the trip that bankrupts the English language!" I feel the same when I drive Gold Camp Road as it courses along a circuitous route through the spectacular Pike National Forest. An improved dirt road most of the way, it's manageable in most vehicles.

At the time of this printing, a tunnel collapse had closed the 8-mile stretch of Gold Camp Road between North Cheyenne Canyon Park's western edge and Old Stage Road to vehicle traffic, so motorists must start this route on Old Stage Road. From I-25, head west on Circle Drive (Exit 138), which turns into Lake Avenue as it approaches the Broadmoor Hotel. Turn right at the hotel and follow the signs to the Cheyenne Mountain Zoo. At the southwest corner of the Broadmoor Golf Club, just before you reach the zoo, turn west onto Old Stage Road and drive 6.7 miles to the junction with Gold Camp Road. Turn left and continue 26 miles to Cripple Creek.

You will quickly have magnificent views of Colorado Springs as you begin to climb. Remember, however, not to take a picture unless you can find some sort of interesting foreground, perhaps the piñon trees that line the road. Make sure that you have plenty of film for the drive to Cripple Creek.

Some of the most beautiful aspen groves in Colorado are along this route. In late May, they leaf out, adding a delicate light green accent to the dark green conifers. In late September, they turn golden, with a few patches that turn red or orange. The route passes through the Pikes Peak formation, a granite batholith (mass of intruded igneous rock) replete with rock formations that boggle the imagination. Pastoral meadows line creek beds throughout the forest as you ascend, and at 10,000 feet, the conifers give way completely to spectacular aspen forests that cover hillsides once mined for gold.

History

In October 1890, humble rancher Bob Womack struck gold and staked his claim on what he called Poverty Gulch (now Cripple Creek). The gold was so prolific, and the veins were so rich, that he and many others became millionaires overnight (though Womack died a pauper). More than 500 mines in the Cripple Creek and Victor Mining District produced 21 million ounces of gold—more gold than the combined California and Alaska gold rushes. This fortune helped bankroll the development of Colorado Springs.

The region's gold mines never declined to the degree that they did in so many other parts of the state, but many still closed in the wake of economic hard times. Cripple Creek and Victor managed to hold on by attracting tourists who came for the history as well as the scenery. Like the citizens of Leadville, the residents of Cripple Creek and Victor always believed that the mines would one day reopen—and they have. The Cresson Mine, first abandoned in 1929, resumed gold production first in 1946–1949 and again in 1951–1961. The gold mine reopened permanently in 1994 as an open-pit cyanide leaching operation.

The other rich vein being mined today in Cripple Creek is in the pockets and purses of visitors to the slot machines and card tables in the casinos around town. While gaming has its critics, casinos have brought jobs, funded civic improvements, and preserved numerous historic buildings and sites. Time will tell if gaming can ensure a stable economic future.

Main Attractions

FLORISSANT FOSSIL BEDS NATIONAL MONUMENT

Almost 35 million years ago, volcanic eruptions buried a lush valley here, and mudflows captured prehistoric trees, insects, and plants in extraordinary fossil beds beneath long-vanished Florissant Lake. This is a unique site in Colorado, and in 1969, Florissant Fossil Beds were designated a National Monument. Stop by the visitor center to see fossil displays and

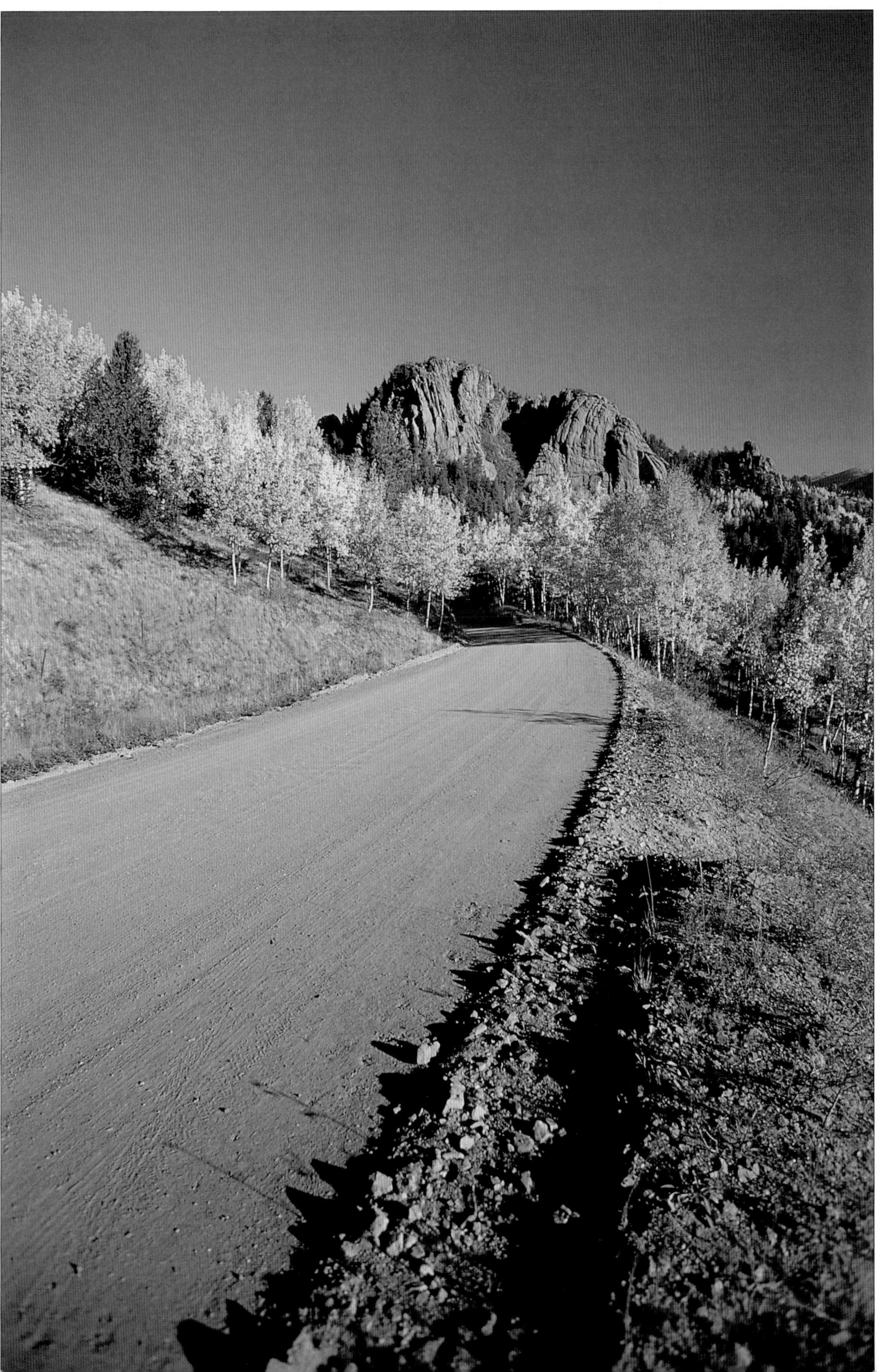

connect to several fascinating, short hikes. The 0.5-mile **Walk Through Time Trail** EASY is a self-guided trail that provides a scenic introduction to the fossil beds and passes giant petrified redwood stumps. The 1-mile **Petrified Forest Loop** EASY features Big Stump, the stone relic of a giant sequoia. The 2.2-mile **Sawmill Trail** MODERATE winds through meadows and streams frequented by elk and leads to views of Pikes Peak. See a rock formation called The Caves on the 3.2-mile **Boulder Creek Trail** MODERATE, which climbs past ponds and wetlands. The 4-mile **Hornbek Wildlife Loop** MODERATE overlooks an ancient lakebed and provides opportunities to view elk or even coyote. The 2.2-mile (one way) **Twin Rock Trail** MODERATE follows a stream and leads to more views of remarkable rock formations and opportunities for observing wildlife. To get to the monument from Cripple Creek, drive 16 miles northwest on County Road 1. *719-748-3253, www.nps.gov/flfo.*

GAMING

In 1990, limited-stakes gaming became legal in three Colorado towns—Central City, Black Hawk, and Cripple Creek. Fifteen casinos operate in Cripple Creek, some with colorful names like Brass Ass, Midnight Rose, and The Virgin Mule. Many are in hotels that offer weekend-getaway packages. Casino revenues bolster the local economy and help support the federally designated National Historic District here, as well as other historic preservation projects around the state. Free live entertainment, excellent restaurants, and charming architecture all contribute to the festive ambiance of the gaming halls. I like to play and stay at the historic **Imperial Casino Hotel.** *123 N. 3rd St., 719-689-7777, 800-235-2922, www.imperialcasinohotel.com.* Because I am also an avid sports fan, I sometimes visit **Bronco Billy's Sports Bar and Casino.** *233 E. Bennett Ave., 719-689-2142.* You're sure to find a casino to your liking here. *For casino shuttle service from Colorado Springs or Woodland Park, call the Ramblin' Express, 719-590-8687, 800-772-6254.*

MUELLER RANCH STATE PARK

Beautiful 5,000-acre **Mueller Ranch State Park** (see Scenic Location No. 20, opposite) is the place for hiking, biking, pond fishing, hunting, horseback riding, cross-country skiing, snowshoeing, and camping. Also called Mueller State Park, it's home to wildlife species such as eagles near Dome Rock and a beaver colony along Four Mile Creek. Ask about interpretive programs and guided hikes at the visitor center. To get to the park from Cripple Creek, go 16 miles north on CO 67. *719-687-2366, www.parks.state.co.us/mueller.*

THEATER

The Imperial Hotel's melodramas were a Colorado institution. People would arrive from all over the state to spend a weekend at Cripple Creek, cheering the heroes and jeering the villains. The Mackin family staged these unique performances from 1946 to 1991. Now the Mackins and the Cripple Creek Players are back at it, producing quality summer melodramas at the newly renovated **Butte Opera House.** These productions will transport you back to the gold rush days. The Butte Opera House is on Main Street over the Fire Station. *719-689-2513, 800-500-2513, www.cripplecreekplayers.com.*

Activities

CAMPING

Although Mueller Ranch State Park (see opposite) is certainly my preference for camping, the park can become very crowded. **The Crags** campground has 17 sites, some of which are shaded and near a stream. This campground also connects to hiking trails (see Hiking, below), including an ascent up Pikes Peak. From Cripple Creek, go north on CO 67 for 14 miles, turn right (east) onto County Road 62 (Forest Road 383), and drive another 3.5 miles. *719-636-1602, www.fs.fed.us/r2/pike.*

HIKING

Given the many abandoned mine sites in the area, be sure to stay on the trails here. The 2-mile loop **Vindicator Valley Trail** EASY winds through remnants of many gold mines from the 1890s. The trail includes signs that explain the history of the mining and the importance of railroads in the region. The trail begins at City Hall in Cripple Creek. **The Crags Trail** EASY takes you 2 miles (one way) past some mysterious pinnacle rock formations that look like castles and connects to the **Devil's Playground** (see Scenic Location No. 18, p. 84) access to Pikes Peak. This route is somewhat easier than the **Barr Trail** (see Hiking, Manitou Springs, p. 83), but because of the altitude, it remains a difficult climb. To link to Pikes Peak, go 200 yards up The Crags Trail and look for a log bridge on the right, which leads to the Devil's Playground Trail. Follow two creeks up a road to the southeast to the junction with the Pikes Peak Toll Road and Devil's Playground turnout. This route can be confusing, so it's a good idea to pick up a map at a sporting goods store. See Camping, above, for directions to The Crags Trail.

MUSEUMS

The **Cripple Creek District Museum,** housed in the historic Midland Terminal Railway Depot and 19th-century assay office, is an artifact in itself. Displays include mining machinery, Victorian clothing, American Indian artifacts, and old photographs. The collection is part of the legacy of the 25 or so towns that made up the mining district. You can even research the ancestry register to see if any of your forebears might have worked the mines and struck it rich. The museum is open on winter weekends and daily in summer. *Bennett Avenue at 5th Street, 719-689-2634, www.cripple-creek.org.*

The Old Homestead House Museum bills itself as "A House with a History!" The Homestead House was originally a brothel in Cripple Creek's red-light district in the 1890s. A guide shares lore about the fabled Parlor House, Myers Avenue, and Cripple Creek. *353 Myers Ave., 719-689-3090.*

The Outlaws and Lawmen Jail Museum is the most authentic jail museum in all of Colorado. Located in the building that once served as Teller County's jail, this popular attraction lets tourists relive the "outlaw days of the Wild West." In addition to the fascinating displays, the original cells of the jail are still intact. Tour the cells themselves, see original police logs from the 1890s, and witness a piece of what life was like for the men who kept the peace and the men who disturbed it in historic Cripple Creek. *136 W Bennett Ave, 719-689-6556.*

RAILROAD

A ride on the **Cripple Creek and Victor Narrow Gauge Railroad** is fun and a great way to get a history lesson on the importance of the railroad to the mining district. Everyone

MUELLER RANCH STATE PARK

Along with Roxborough and Castlewood Canyon State Parks (see Scenic Location Nos. 2 and 12, pp. 30 and 67), Mueller Ranch is a standout in the Colorado State Parks system. Its 5,000 acres are mostly wild and undeveloped, with expansive forests and views of the western face of Pikes Peak to the east and the Sangre de Cristos to the south. Home to elk, deer, black bears, eagles, and hawks, it's also a hiker's paradise, with 55 miles of scenic trails. Take I-25 to the US 24 exit (141) and proceed west 17 miles to the town of Woodland Park. Notice the views of the craggy north face of Pikes Peak. Drive another 8 miles on US 24 to CO 67 at the only stoplight in the town of Divide. Turn left (south) and drive 4 miles to the entrance.

If you could venture only 100 feet from your car, you'd still be able to make a couple of pretty good photographs from the main parking lot next to the visitor center. At sunset, the west side of Pikes Peak catches the full force of the setting sun. On clear days the gray peak turns red for 15 minutes at sunset. There's a grove of aspen adjacent to the lot, which makes a very nice foreground for the peak when colored by the sun. Take care that your shadow doesn't project into the scene, for the sun is directly behind you. To the south are the Sangre de Cristos. The aspen, when lighted by the setting sun, make a nice foreground for these mountains as well. I prefer to use a telephoto lens when photographing this composition, as it makes the far-off mountains appear larger.

The aspen lend a light green to the forest when they leaf out in May. In late September, they burst into an array of yellows. Here's a tip: Do you remember the color wheel? Yellow is essentially the opposite of blue, just as black and white are opposites. Yellow against a blue background will appear more conspicuous than when placed in front of other colors (see *Photographing the Landscape,* p. 24). If you frame yellow aspen against blue skies, they will appear more colorful—as if they needed any help!

can enjoy the 45-minute trip on an old steam engine that billows smoke and gives out periodic shrill whistles. The train trip takes you 4 miles south from Cripple Creek, over a reconstructed trestle, past many historic mines, and terminates near the deserted mining camp of Anaconda. Don't worry, the train returns to Cripple Creek! The train also stops for special points of interest and photo opportunities. Catch it at the Midland Terminal Railway Depot on Bennett Avenue. *719-689-2640, www.cripplecreekrailroad.com*

ROCK CLIMBING

4WD The well-known **Shelf Road** climbing area is a technical climber's dream and features more than 100 one-pitch, mostly bolted routes. These limestone crags are no place for a novice (few climbs rate below 5.9), but it is worth a trip just to watch the agile sport climbers scale faces and cracks with names like "Bambi Meets Godzilla" and "No Tomorrow." Hikers and mountain bikers also use trails in the area. To get to the climbs from Cripple Creek go south on CO 67 and look for signs for rough Shelf Road to the right (west) just outside of town. *For information, maps, and climbing advice: Sport Climbing Center of Colorado Springs, 4650 N. Park Dr., 719-260-1050, www.sportclimbcs.com; Grand West Outfitters, 3250 N. Academy Ave., Colorado Springs, 719-596-3031.*

TOURS

Take a self-guided **Walking Tour of Cripple Creek** by picking up a map from the Cripple Creek Welcome Center on Bennett Avenue and 5th Street.

The **Mollie Kathleen Gold Mine** takes its name from Mollie Kathleen Gortner, who discovered gold here in 1891 and demanded that the claim bear her name, the first woman to do so in the gold camp. The mine was in continuous operation from 1891 to 1961. The journey down the 1,000-foot vertical shaft on the "skip" elevator is a highlight of the tour. The mine is 1 mile north of Cripple Creek on CO 67. *719-689-2466, www.goldminetours.com.*

WINTER SPORTS

The Crags, Florissant Fossil Beds National Monument, and **Mueller Ranch State Park** maintain miles of groomed trails for cross-country skiing and snowshoeing. (For information and directions, see Main Attractions, p. 86, and Mueller Ranch State Park, p. 88.)

Restaurants

Cripple Creek casinos want you to spend money on gaming, so they lure you in with good food—steaks, prime rib, and seafood —at very reasonable prices. Locals rate **Maggie's Place** ($$) in the Colorado Grande Casino as the number-one place to eat in town. *300 E. Bennett Ave., 719-689-3517.* Other good places include **Chef Paul's Steakhouse** ($$) in the Imperial Casino Hotel, *123 N. 3rd St., 719-689-7777,* and **Lombard's Restaurant** ($$-$$$) in the Double Eagle Hotel and Casino, *422 E. Bennett Ave., 719-689-5000.* For the best steak in town, dine at the **Downunder Steakhouse** ($$) in the Midnight Rose Hotel and Casino. *256 E. Bennett Ave., 719-689-0303.* For the best and least-expensive breakfast in town (and good entrees), try **Bronco Billy's Sports Bar and Casino** ($–$$). *233 E. Bennett Ave., 719-689-2142.* Enjoy a drink with the locals at the low-key **Boiler Room Tavern** ($) in the historic Hotel St. Nicholas at 303 N. 3rd St. *719-689-0856.*

Accommodations

Along with well-priced menus, casinos tempt with comfortable and affordable rooms. The historic **Imperial Casino Hotel** ($-$$) is my favorite place to stay in Cripple Creek. *123 N. 3rd St., 719-689-7777, 800-235-2922, www.imperialcasinohotel.com.* The **Double Eagle Hotel and Casino** ($-$$) is relatively new and has nice rooms. *422 E. Bennett Ave., 719-689-5000, www.decasino.com.*

Imperial Casino Hotel, Cripple Creek

For a change of pace, I highly recommend the **Hotel St. Nicholas** ($-$$), a historic mountain inn. Built in 1898 as a hospital run by the Sisters of Mercy, this beautifully restored hotel has won awards for its accomplishments in historic preservation and includes all the amenities of a fine hotel. *303 N. 3rd St., 888-786-4257, www.cripple-creek.co.us/stnick.html.* Staying at a B&B is a fine way to take in the historical heritage of the Cripple Creek and Victor Mining District. The **Cherub House B&B** ($-$$) is a delightful Victorian inn. *415 Main, 719-689-0526, www. cripplecreek.co.us/cher.htm.* The **Last Dollar Inn** ($-$$) is also a highly acclaimed B&B, and the hosts make scrumptious Belgian waffles. *315 E. Carr Ave., 719-689-9113, 888-429-6700.* In Victor, find some peace and quiet at **The Victor Hotel** ($-$$). This historic hotel has been renovated recently; a ride up the original cage elevator, though, may be a little disquieting for some. *4th Street and Victor Avenue, 800-713-4595, www.victorhotelcolorado.com.*

Special Events

Back in the 1930s, for lack of anything better to do, residents decided to round up wild donkeys for a race. Today, **Donkey Derby Days** includes an amateur and professional pack burro race from Cripple Creek to Victor, arts and crafts, a parade, and refreshments. The event is held in late June, and proceeds go to funding resources for the local wild donkey herd. *719-689-3315.*

For More Information

Cripple Creek Welcome Center, *Bennett Avenue and 5th Street, 719-689-3315, 877-858-GOLD, www.cripple-creek.co.us.*

Cañon City

(see map on p. 82)

Cañon City is a place of thrills and comforts, the perfect staging area for a visit to the magnificent Royal Gorge or for an expedition to enjoy world-class rafting and fishing. Nothing is quite like spending a day cruising the Arkansas River; the smell of the water on canyon rock is primal and soothing. Some 1,000 feet above, the world's highest suspension bridge spans the canyon called the Royal Gorge. From atop this awe-inspiring bridge, rafts look like tiny specks spinning and shooting helplessly through the churning rapids. Cañon City still owns the Royal Gorge, which remains a top tourist attraction in Colorado.

With aching muscles, either from carrying heavy camera equipment or taking on adrenaline-packed rafting adventure, I always stop at Merlino's Belvedere for the best Italian food in southern Colorado. These folks serve great dinners even if you arrive damp and unshaven, with your tennis shoes still sloshing from your river trip. To get to Cañon City from I-25 in Colorado Springs, head southwest on CO 115 for 36 miles, turn right (west) on US 50, and drive 11 miles.

History

Cañon City's mild climate and location at the mouth of the spectacular Royal Gorge have for centuries made it a popular stop. Numerous Indian tribes wintered here, and Zebulon Pike himself passed through. The town was established as a supply center in 1860, when a group of men organized the Cañon City Claim Club to serve the upriver coal, iron, gypsum, marble, and granite mines. Residents had voted to call their community the "Town of Canyon City," but a reporter used the Spanish spelling, which stuck.

In the 1870s, Cañon City was the stage for the bloody Royal Gorge Railroad War, which pitted the Atchison, Topeka & Santa Fe Railroad against the Denver & Rio Grande Railroad for right-of-way through the gorge. In the canyon, each side would lay railroad track in the daytime only to see it dynamited each night by the other side. (The courts finally granted access to the Denver & Rio Grande, which made Cañon City a hub.) Cañon City also became a center for paleontologists after the discovery of extensive dinosaur remains in 1878.

Cañon City is also known as a prison town, and its economy is dependent on the jobs that 13 nearby federal and state prisons provide. The first territorial prison was built here in 1871, and Cañon City has since become the center of Colorado's prison system. Cañon City was also a Western filmmaking center, both during the silent screen era and again in the 1950s and 1960s. Buckskin Joe Frontier Town and Railway, a nearby Western theme park, was used as a set for *How the West Was Won, True Grit,* and *Cat Ballou,* one of my favorites. Residents boast that Cañon City is the safest city in the United States.

Main Attractions

BUCKSKIN JOE FRONTIER TOWN AND RAILWAY

Take your children here, and you'll find yourself having a good time as well! Buckskin Joe Frontier Town is a re-creation of an old mining camp, including gambling halls, saloons, stores, hotels, an assay office, banks, and even an undertaker's parlor. Founded in 1859, the original town of Buckskin Joe was located 90 miles northwest of Cañon City near the present town of Alma in South Park. The town was named after Joseph Higgenbottom, who always wore buckskins and eventually sold his claim for a revolver and headed off to the San Juans to seek his fortune there. The mines around the town of Buckskin Joe produced more than $1.6 million from 1859 to 1866, but in 1861 smallpox swept through the community, and most surviving miners moved on to other mining camps.

All the present-day buildings at Buckskin Joe are originals from surrounding ghost towns; the Tabor Building was moved from the original Buckskin Joe townsite. Today, the streets of Buckskin Joe set the stage for medicine and magic shows and for high melodramas complete with gunfights and hangings.

Don't miss the Buckskin Joe Railway, a 15-inch narrow-gauge railway that takes you to the upper rim of the Royal Gorge in open cars. This is the same type of narrow gauge formerly used to haul mining ore. The 30-minute ride takes you to panoramic views of the Royal Gorge and its suspension bridge. Watch for wildlife along the way. Buckskin Joe is 8 miles west of Cañon City on US 50, on the road to the Royal Gorge. *719-275-5149, www.buckskinjoes.com.*

THE ROYAL GORGE

Early explorers called this gorge the Grand Canyon of the Arkansas River. However, the Royal Gorge is an even more fitting name for this 8-mile-long, 1,000-foot-deep chasm. Cross the Royal Gorge by foot or by car over the world's highest suspension bridge, completed in 1929. Even on calm days the canyon creates a wind that makes this 0.25-mile-long bridge creak and sway. If you cross the bridge by foot, you'll enjoy the view down to the Arkansas River flowing below. The roar of this powerful river ascends the canyon walls to the rim. As you look down the canyon, light and shadow lend a unique perspective of depth to the canyon's massive walls. Notice the watchful raptors as they ride the warm thermals within the canyon. To get to the east rim of the Royal Gorge from Cañon City, take US 50 west for 8 miles. My favorite entrance is the west rim, as it is less traveled and more rugged. To get there, pass the first (east) entrance on US 50 and go 3 miles farther to Parkdale. *719-275-7507, www.royalgorgebridge.com.*

Plunge at a 45-degree angle from the rim of the gorge to the floor of the canyon on the Incline Railway. With the exception of rafting the river, this is the best way to get a sense of its power and of the gorge's depth. Another first-rate option is to take the Royal Gorge Scenic Railway, one of the most picturesque train rides in the United States. This 12-mile, 2-hour round-trip journey follows the historic Denver & Rio Grande route from Cañon City to Parkdale along the Arkansas River. Look for rafts navigating the churning white waters. Marvel as the train crosses Hanging Bridge, which clings to the steep walls of the gorge 1,000 feet above the river. The train departs from the Santa Fe Depot at 401 Water St., Cañon City. *719-267-4000, 888-RAILS4U, www.royalgorgeroute.com.*

Although the railroad trip is nothing short of spectacular, rafting the Arkansas River through the Royal Gorge is essential. Rip-roaring Class IV and V rapids course through the gorge, while Brown's Canyon, just upriver, gives you a wonderful chance to see wildlife and enjoy slightly calmer waters. Your guide can give you an excellent history of the area, including the nasty railroad wars of the 1870s, as part of the exciting river experience. *For rafting reservations: Echo Canyon River Expeditions, 45000 US 50 W., 800-755-ECHO, www.raftecho.com; River Runners, 11150 US 50 W., Salida, 800-723-8987, www.riverrunnersltd.com; Whitewater Adventures Outfitters, 50905 US 50 W., 719-275-5344, 800-530-8212, ww.waorafting.com.*

For a bird's-eye view of the Royal Gorge, take a helicopter tour. *Royal Gorge Heli-Tours, 45045 US 50 W., 719-276-9038.*

Activities

CAMPING

Oak Creek campground is fairly primitive but provides abundant shade and solitude. Head 13 miles south of Cañon City on the Oak Creek Grade Road (County Road 143). *719-269-8500.*

FISHING

The **Arkansas River,** the longest river in Colorado, provides some of the best trout fishing in the state. The best stretch is from Buena Vista south to Cañon City along US 24, CO 291, and US 50. Although you find rainbows and cutthroats in the Arkansas, browns are predominant and average 10–14 inches. Fishing the Arkansas can be a bit frustrating because of the heavy rafting traffic during the summer months, but professional river guides do their best to respect anglers. Tributaries of the Arkansas, including **Texas Creek,** produce small browns. To get to Texas Creek, go west on US 50, 26 miles to the namesake town. Turn left (south) on CO 69 and follow the creek. *For information and fly-fishing lessons: Royal Gorge Anglers, 1210 Royal Gorge Blvd., 719-269-3474, www.royalgorgeanglers.com.*

GOLF

The 18-hole **Shadow Hills Golf Club,** south of Cañon City on County Road 143, is a fairly challenging public course with great views. *719-275-0603.*

HIKING

For a relaxing stroll with the opportunity to see wildlife and waterfowl, take the 6-mile **Arkansas Riverwalk** EASY in Cañon City. To get there, take Raynolds Avenue south to the river. **Red Canyon Park** EASY includes several excellent hiking trails and is about 7 miles north on Shelf Canyon Road, which is Field Avenue (County Road 9) in Cañon City. For a solitary 4-mile (one way) hike into the Wet Mountains with both wildflowers and exceptional views of the Sangre de Cristos, take the **Tanner Trail** MODERATE, 12 miles south of Cañon City. Take County Road 143 past the Shadow Hills Golf Course; the trailhead is 1 mile before the Oak Creek campground. Another fun hike is the **Tunnel Drive Trail** (see Mountain Biking, below).

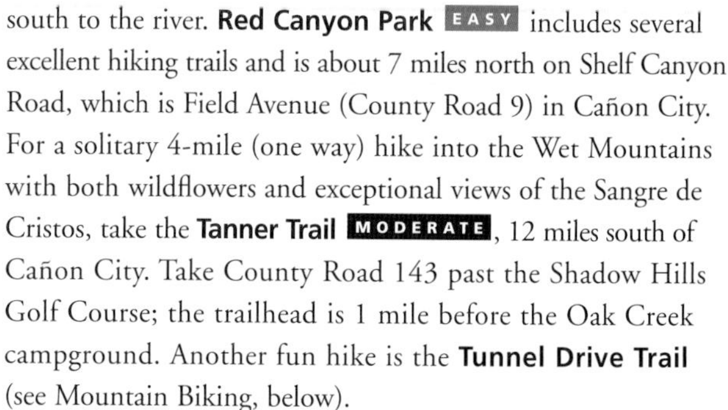

HORSEBACK RIDING

A horseback ride through meadows, gnarled piñon and juniper trees, and pine and spruce forests surrounding the Royal Gorge provides a truly unique Western experience. **Fort Royal Stables** offers guided horseback trips through 3,500 acres of private land that lend the rider a true sense of solitude. Depending on your ability, you can sign up for anything from 1-hour to full-day rides, including a combination Saddle and Paddle (riding and rafting) trip. There's no need to brown-bag it either. These folks provide an incredible lunch that includes roasted chicken, fruit, and cookies. I highly recommend this getaway for the entire family. Fort Royal Stables are one block east of the Royal Gorge turnoff at 44899 US 50 W. *719-275-2962, www.coloradovacation.com/stables/royal.*

MOUNTAIN BIKING

The **Tunnel Drive Trail** EASY takes you 2 miles (one way) through three tunnels on a segment of dirt road that is no longer open to vehicles, and ends at a point overlooking the Arkansas River. To get to the ride, go to the west end of town and pass the prison. Take a left (south) on Tunnel Drive and continue 1 mile to the parking lot. The 64-mile **Shelf Road** and **Phantom Canyon Road** loop DIFFICULT is a favorite of serious mountain bikers. The elevation gain and switchbacks along these old stagecoach roads and railroad beds are challenging but rewarding; the scenery is outstanding. Along the way, use the Gold Belt Tour signs for more information. (For directions from Cañon City, see Scenic Drives, p. 93.)

MUSEUMS

The **Colorado Territorial Prison** opened on June 13, 1871, several years before statehood. The foreboding watchtower exemplifies why this prison was dubbed one of the "Hell Holes of the West." Alferd Packer, one of Colorado's most notorious criminals, was convicted of cannibalism and incarcerated here. Seventy-seven people were executed at the prison, 45 by hanging. In 1988, a museum was established in the old Women's Prison, just outside the deserted main prison building. Displays include 32 cells, a collection of personal effects confiscated from inmates, and even an old noose. *1st St. and Macon Ave., 719-269-3015, www.prisonmuseum.org.*

The **Dinosaur Depot,** which is located in a historic fire station, houses Jurassic fossils, interpretive displays, and a

Colorado Territorial Prison Museum, Cañon City

working laboratory. *330 Royal Gorge Blvd., 719-269-7150, www.dinosaurdepot.com.* Many of the fossils at the museum are from the **Garden Park,** about 5 miles north of Cañon City on the Shelf Road (see Scenic Drives, this page). The Garden Park Fossil Area has been called the world's largest Jurassic graveyard. Today, paleontologists are researching a new type of dinosaur track left on what was once a muddy shore of a great inland sea.

ROCK CLIMBING

Shelf Road Recreation Area is nationally known for its technical climbs (see Cripple Creek, p. 90). From Cañon City, go north on Shelf Road about 10 miles.

SCENIC DRIVES

The **Gold Belt Tour** is a 131-mile loop connecting High Park Road, Shelf Road, and Phantom Canyon Road (see Scenic Location No. 21, p. 94). The landscape is spectacular along every stretch of this federally designated Scenic and Historic Byway. The drive also gives you glimpses of Colorado's mining history, unique rock formations, and fossil beds. Shelf Road and Phantom Canyon Road are old stagecoach roads and railroad beds, and although a passenger car can negotiate them in good weather, it is best to take a high-centered four-wheel-drive vehicle. These two roads form their own, shorter loop that connects Cripple Creek, Victor, Florence, and Cañon City.

High Park Road climbs north from Cañon City to panoramic views of the Sangre de Cristos, Mount Pisgah (just west of Cripple Creek), and Pikes Peak. The northern stretch of road passes through Florissant Fossil Beds National Monument (see Main Attractions, Cripple Creek, p. 86) and terminates in the town of Florissant.

To continue the Gold Belt Tour, head south to Cripple Creek and follow signs to rough **Shelf Road** (County Roads 88 and 9), which is just west of CO 67. Look for a rustic tollbooth cabin below the road. Formerly, a toll collector would scramble up to meet wagons or stagecoaches at this point. A bit farther south, spy technical climbers scaling the renowned limestone crags nearby (see Rock Climbing, Cripple Creek, p. 90). Look to the west for Red Canyon Park and its dramatic red-rock formations. The Garden Park Fossil Area, on the east side of the road, once contained many of the dinosaur bones currently displayed in the Smithsonian and at the Denver Museum of Nature and Science.

Shelf Road ends in Cañon City, but you can proceed to **Phantom Canyon Road** (see Scenic Location No. 21, p. 94) to complete the tour. Head east from Cañon City on CO 115 to the small town of Florence and take CO 67 north, which becomes Phantom Canyon Road. This area is notable for its numerous historic mines and for the Cresson Mine, still in operation. You will also pass the Indian Springs Trace Fossil Site where tracks and fossils have been preserved for more than 400 million years. Phantom Canyon Road ends just outside of the town of Victor at CO 67, which will take you back to Cripple Creek.

SKYDIVING

See Cañon City and the Royal Gorge from a whole new perspective! **Skydive the Rockies,** located at the Fremont County Airport in Cañon City, just minutes from the Royal Gorge Bridge, offers tandem jumps, accelerated freefall training, and a twenty-five jump static line program. Many of the instructors are also full-time parachute instructors for the nearby Air Force Academy. A first-time tandem jump takes about an hour, including training and the plane ride to reach altitude. Skydivers freefall for the first mile before parachute deployment and then enjoy a five-minute canopy ride over the most scenic drop zone in all of Colorado. Gear is provided by Skydive the Rockies. Please note there is a minimum age requirement of 18. *For more information: Skydive the Rockies, 719-528-JUMP, www.skydivetherockies.com.*

WINERIES

Cloistered Benedictine monks established the Holy Cross Abbey in 1924. The Gothic-style abbey, which is on the National Register of Historic Places, was a secondary boarding school until 1985 and housed its own museum until 2006. Today, the Benedictine Brothers are responsible for creating multi-award winning wines at **The Winery at Holy Cross Abbey**. The tasting room and gift shop at the Abbey are open to the public daily. Reserve wines are available to taste for $1.00 while other wines are free to try.

The Winery at Holy Cross Abbey, Cañon City

PHANTOM CANYON ROAD

Like Gold Camp Road (see Scenic Location No. 19, p. 86), here's another abandoned railroad bed turned into a spectacular, if rough, dirt road. The Phantom Canyon Road runs south for about 30 miles from historic Victor to US 50 near the town of Florence. It penetrates Bureau of Land Management (BLM) dry canyon country, although scenic Eightmile Creek follows it for most of the route. It's part of the BLM's Gold Belt Tour that encompasses Phantom Canyon Road, the Shelf Road from Cripple Creek to Cañon City, and the High Park Road from Florissant to Cañon City. The views to the south are incredible, and the higher reaches contain some beautiful aspen groves. The road's a bit rougher than Gold Camp Road, and there's exposure to steep drop-offs, but you can traverse it in a vehicle you don't love too much. The 4-percent railroad grade doesn't require much traction, but the higher clearance of a four-wheel-drive vehicle is always better on rutted dirt roads, especially in wet weather when the fine clay soils can get very slippery. Trailers are not recommended, and anything longer than 24 feet is prohibited.

Though the road is best known for its history as part of the most prolific gold-producing region in Colorado, I find its scenic qualities to be sublime. Views of the Sangre de Cristos to the south are magnificent, and the aspen, cottonwood, and other deciduous plants along the way make for great color in the fall (late September is best). The areas of isolated color are especially conspicuous in this rocky, relatively monotone landscape. Still, the canyon is quite scenic, with walls towering above the road and creek. The aspen silhouette nicely against a blue autumn sky, while the creekside foliage makes good subject matter for compositions with no sky or horizon, especially when framed against the yellow-gray canyon walls in cloudy light or shade. Remember, film makes highlights brighter and shadows darker. When photographing here, keep in mind that canyons create deep shadows that film cannot accommodate in a scene including intense highlights.

Merlino's Belvedere restaurant, Cañon City

The Abbey is also host to the annual Harvest Fest. The festival features wine tastings, the Wild Cañon Harvest grape crush, live music, and food. *For more information: The Winery at Holy Cross Abbey, 3011 E HWY 50, 719-276-5191, 877-422-9463, www.abbeywinery.com.*

Restaurants

If you read the introduction of this chapter, you know that my favorite southern Colorado restaurant is **Merlino's Belvedere** ($$-$$$). The same family has owned the Belvedere since 1946, serving delicious Italian and seafood dishes, and mouthwatering steaks. *1330 Elm, 719-275-5558, www.belvedererestaurant.com.* A Cañon City couple who travel to France annually sing the praises of **Le Petit Chablis** ($$$), where you can enjoy fine French cuisine in a grand Royal Gorge setting. *512 Royal Gorge Blvd., 719-269-3333.* **Big Daddy's Diner** ($-$$) is a classic diner, complete with hand-dipped shakes and great burgers. *420 Royal Gorge Blvd., 719-276-8468.* **Pizza Madness** ($) serves the best pizza for miles and will satisfy the most ravenous of après-whitewater appetites. *509 Main St., 719-276-3088.*

Accommodations

The comfy **Jewel of the Canyons** ($$) is an 1890 Queen Anne B&B with spacious private baths and air conditioning. The owners have taken great care to restore the house with authentic touches and antiques. *429 Greenwood Ave., 719-275-0378, 866-875-0378, www.jeweloftheCanyons.com.* The stately **Florence Rose Guesthouse** ($$-$$$), 8 miles east of Cañon City, has five guest rooms with a great Victorian feel. Because you can rent the whole mansion, it's great for a special family trip or reunion. *1305 W. 3rd St., 719-784-4734, www.florencerose.com.*

Special Events

The annual **Music and Blossom Festival,** more than 60 years old, draws people to Cañon City from the entire region during the first weekend in May. The festival runs in conjunction with the **Royal Gorge Rodeo,** which takes place at the Fremont County Fairgrounds, and the **Spring Craft Fair** at Depot Park. **Fiddlers Along the Arkansas** is a highly competitive event that brings some of the best fiddlers in the country here in August. Cowboy poetry readings (a great favorite of mine) and arts and crafts booths round out the festivities. *www.fiddlersalongthearkansas.com. For information on all of the above events: 719-275-2331.*

For More Information

Cañon City Chamber of Commerce, *403 Royal Gorge Blvd., 719-275-2331, www.canoncitychamber.com.*

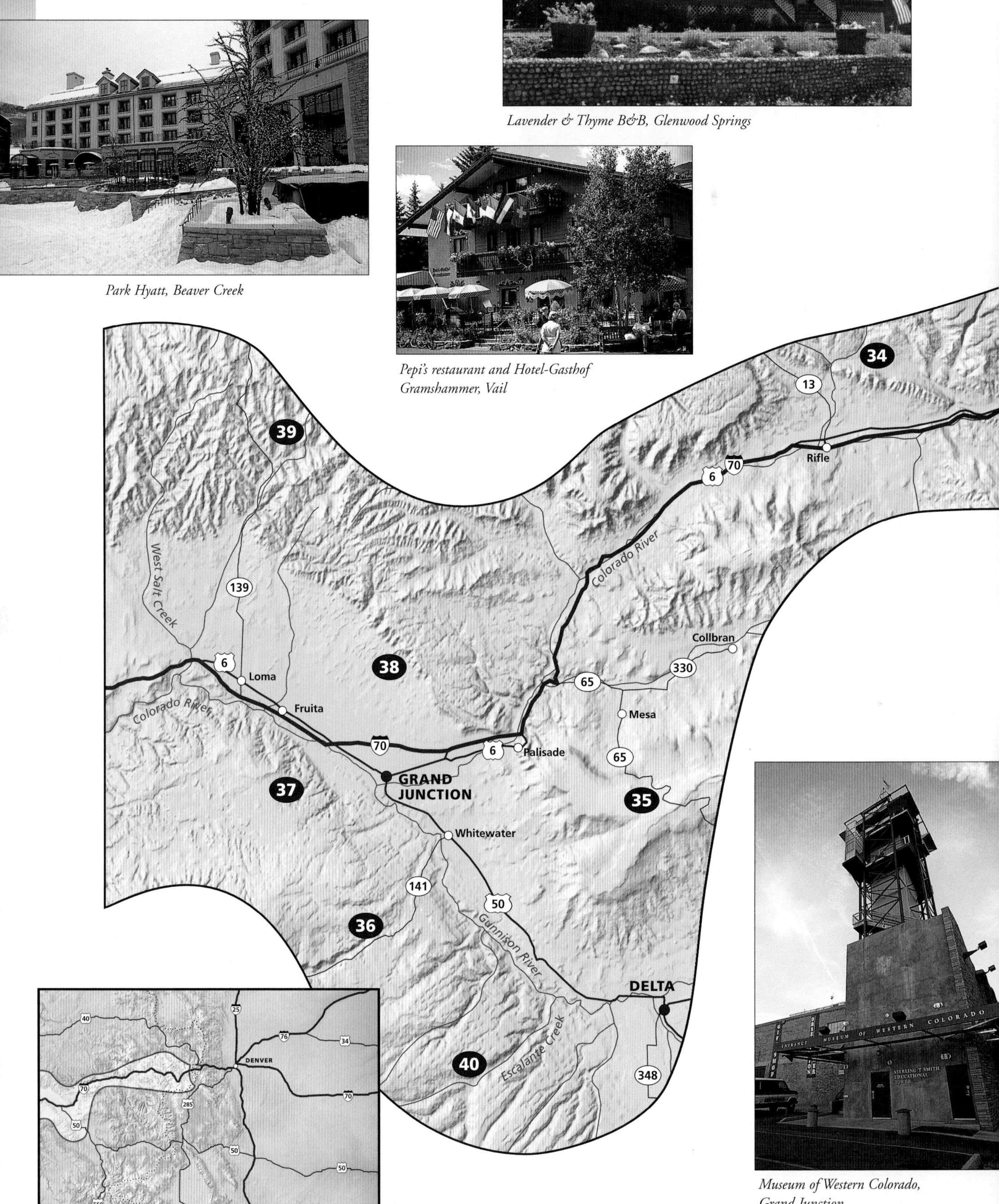

Lavender & Thyme B&B, Glenwood Springs

Park Hyatt, Beaver Creek

Pepi's restaurant and Hotel-Gasthof Gramshammer, Vail

Museum of Western Colorado, Grand Junction

The I-70 Corridor

SKI COUNTRY TO CANYON COUNTRY

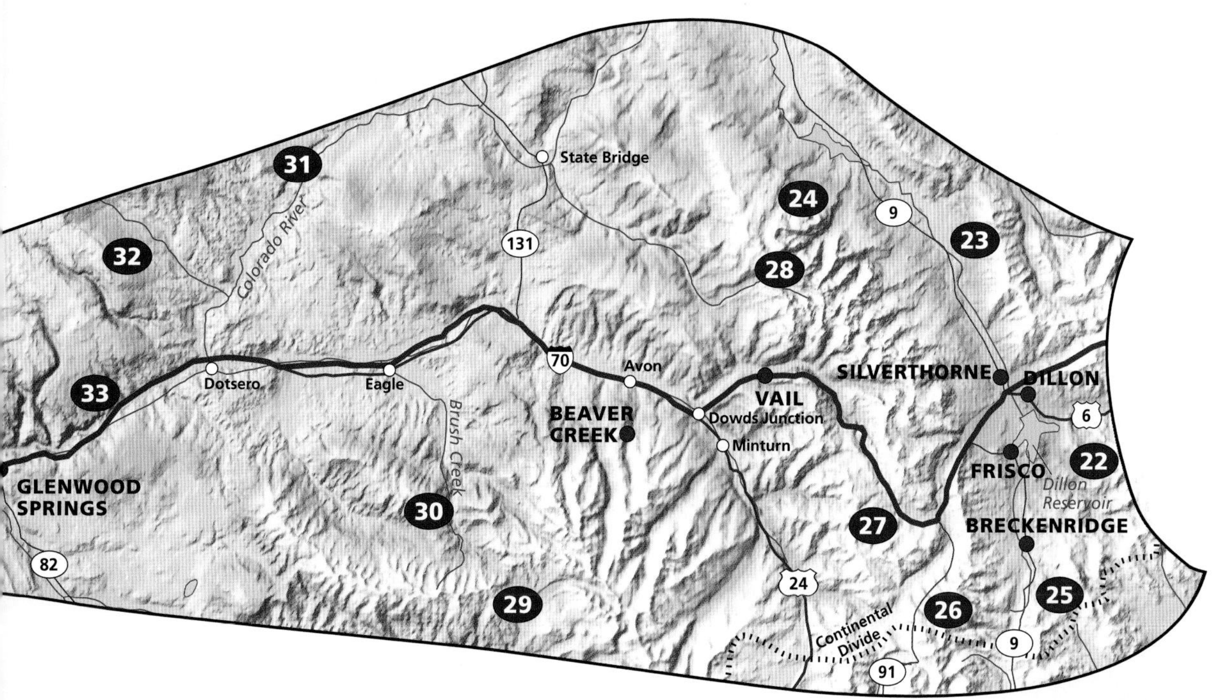

Traveling west on Interstate 70 from Denver to Summit County, you enter Eisenhower Tunnel, an amazing feat of engineering that cuts beneath the Continental Divide. Here, Colorado's fickle weather patterns sometimes result in different climatic extremes that greet you on either side. You can enter the tunnel in a snowstorm and emerge into full sunlight!

As you make the rapid descent from the tunnel into the Silverthorne and Dillon area, a breathtaking scene of snowcapped peaks around Dillon Reservoir comes into view. Vast Dillon Reservoir cradles stunning reflections of the surrounding mountains. Passing the Copper Mountain Ski Area, you begin your ascent of beautiful 10,666-foot Vail Pass. As you descend into the Vail Valley, you can see some of Vail Mountain's famous ski runs to the south.

Minturn Inn, Minturn

Continuing west, I-70 enters 12-mile-long Glenwood Canyon, whose ancient walls of sedimentary rock were carved by the Colorado River and now rise to heights of 1,800 feet. With its tunnels blasted through solid rock and its soaring overpasses, I-70 is an engineering and aesthetic marvel here. It's no surprise that the American Institute of Steel Construction recognized the Glenwood Canyon project, completed in 1990, for the near-seamless way the highway blends with the natural landscape.

West of Glenwood Springs, I-70 follows the meandering Colorado River through the dramatically beautiful canyon country surrounding Grand Junction. More than just the most direct route across the imposing Rocky Mountains, I-70 is an attraction in itself as it passes through the Western Slope of Colorado.

SCENIC LOCATIONS

Silverthorne/Dillon/Breckenridge/Frisco

Colorado Atlas & Gazetteer pp. 37–39, 48

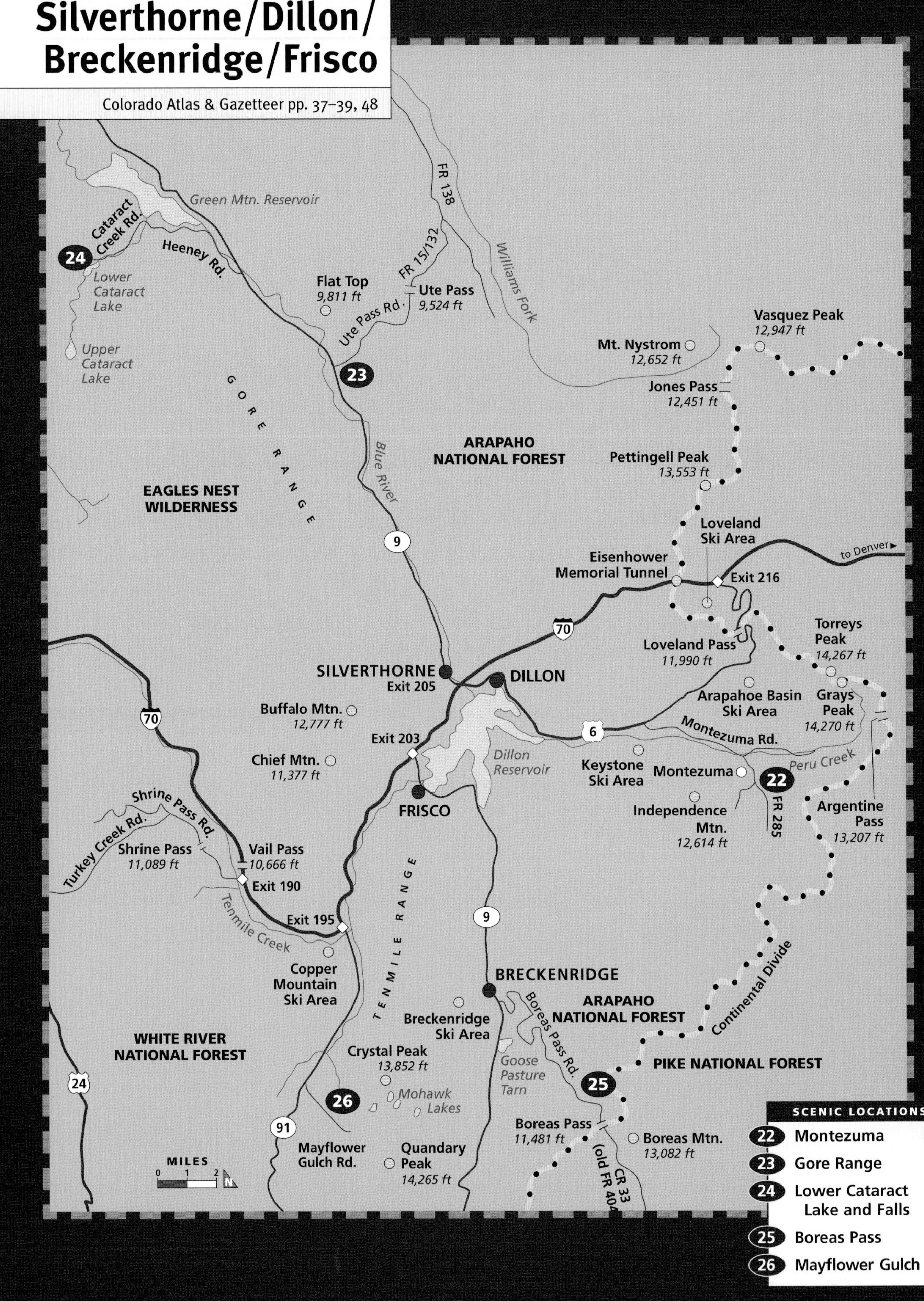

SCENIC LOCATIONS

- 22 Montezuma
- 23 Gore Range
- 24 Lower Cataract Lake and Falls
- 25 Boreas Pass
- 26 Mayflower Gulch

Silverthorne and Dillon

In winter, Silverthorne and Dillon are full-service towns for six nearby ski areas, offering reasonably priced restaurants, lodging, and nightlife. In summer, these towns make great base camps for family biking, camping, hiking, fishing, and shopping excursions. Surrounded by mountains, Silverthorne and Dillon offer spectacular views and recreational opportunities throughout the year. The two towns are almost contiguous, as the Silverthorne area lies to your right (north) and the Dillon area to your left (south) as you drive west on I-70.

History

Although Dillon existed as a town before the explosion of the ski industry, present-day Dillon and the relatively new town of Silverthorne owe their growth primarily to the completion of Dillon Reservoir in the early 1960s and the opening of the Eisenhower Tunnel in 1973. Since then, Dillon Reservoir has become a major recreational destination in the summer. (The old town of Dillon lies under the water of the reservoir.) The Eisenhower Tunnel has made access to skiing and other mountain activities much easier for Front Range residents by providing an alternative to the treacherous climb over Loveland Pass. However, you'll have plenty of company if you drive through the tunnel at peak traffic times—typically Saturday mornings during ski season and Sunday afternoons and evenings all year.

Main Attractions

DILLON RESERVOIR

Dillon Reservoir, which serves as a drinking-water source for the Denver metropolitan area, is fed by the Snake and Blue Rivers and by Tenmile Creek. It also stores runoff from melting mountain snowpack in the spring. The reservoir offers exciting sailing opportunities, as the surrounding mountains make the winds strong and fluky, particularly in the afternoon. The **Dillon Marina** rents sailboats, fishing boats, and touring kayaks by the hour. The marina also offers sailing lessons, which are a good idea for novices on this body of water. *For boat rental and sailing lesson information: 970-468-5100 or www.dillonmarina.com.*

Dillon Reservoir is an excellent place to pitch a tent or park your RV (see Camping, this page). Another way to enjoy the reservoir is to bike the 20-mile **Dillon Lake Loop** EASY, a paved trail that loops around the reservoir. Many people also enjoy hiking this loop. *For information on bike rentals: Christy Sports, 849 Summit Blvd., Frisco, 970-668-5417.*

To reach Dillon Reservoir from Denver, take I-70 west to the Dillon/ Silverthorne exit (205). Make a left at US 6 and turn right on CO 9, the Dillon Dam Road. You can also continue on US 6 to the marina sign and turn right.

SHOPPING

The Silverthorne/Dillon area, the first place in Colorado to have factory outlet stores that offer brand names at discounted prices, is a prime destination for the serious shopper. Many Front Range residents drive over the Continental Divide to do their Christmas shopping at these stores, where items from major-name retailers can be found at bargain prices. This is the only place I know of where you can catch sizable trout on the Blue River as it runs next to the stores and then go shopping! A trail connects the Silverthorne Factory Stores to the Dillon Factory Stores. There are so many options to choose from, it's as if you need a map to shop here! To reach the factory stores, exit I-70 West at the Dillon/Silverthorne exit (205), turn left (south) on US 6, and follow the signs to the Dillon stores on your right. You can also make a right at US 6 and an immediate left to the Silverthorne stores.

WINTER SPORTS

Only a few miles separate Silverthorne and Dillon from six of Colorado's major ski areas: **Loveland Ski Area** (about 12 miles to the east on I-70 through the Eisenhower Tunnel); **Arapahoe Basin** (about 13 miles east on US 6); **Keystone** (6 miles east on US 6); **Breckenridge** (13 miles south on CO 9); **Copper Mountain** (about 11 miles west on I-70); and **Vail** (36 miles west on I-70 over Vail Pass).

All of these ski areas are full-service areas, offering runs for every level of ability, ski schools, day care, restaurants, and ski shops. Lift tickets and season passes are interchangeable among a number of the ski areas, and the Summit Stage provides free bus service between the Summit County ski areas. Breckenridge, Copper Mountain, Keystone, and Vail also have Nordic centers for cross-country skiing and snowshoeing. In summer, these four resorts offer chairlift and/or gondola rides, which provide great scenery and panoramas of Colorado's many mountain ranges. Discount tickets are often available at King Soopers grocery stores along the Front Range. *Loveland Basin and Loveland Valley, 800-736-3754, www.skiloveland.com; Arapahoe Basin, 888-ARAPAHOE, www.arapahoebasin.com; Keystone, 800-222-0188, www.keystoneresort.com; Breckenridge, 800-789-SNOW, www.breckenridge.com; Copper Mountain, 888-219-2441, www.coppercolorado.com; Vail, 888-830-SNOW, www.vail.com.*

Activities

CAMPING

Dillon Reservoir offers excellent camping. With the reservoir's premium lakeside sites, one of the best and most popular campgrounds is **Heaton Bay.** Heaton Bay has more than 70 sites tucked among pine-forested coves. To get to the campground, take the Frisco/Breckenridge exit (203) from I-70 West and go south to the first stoplight. Turn left (northeast) onto Dillon Dam Road (CO 9) and continue 1 mile. Reservations recommended. A popular campground with more than 70 sites, **Peak One** is shaded and sits fairly close to the reservoir. Reservations recommended. To reach Peak One, take Dillon Dam Road south for 2.5 miles. Turn left (north) at the Peak One campground sign and go another mile. With 55 sites, the paved **Pine Cove** campground has good views of the reservoir and mountains. No reservations. To get to Pine Cove, go south on Dillon Dam Road for 2.5 miles. Turn left (north) on Peak One Road and continue 1.5 miles. For **Lowry** campground, with 30 sites and hookups for RVs, take the Dillon/Silverthorne exit (205) from I-70 West, turn left onto US 6, and travel 4.5 miles to Swan Mountain Road. Turn right (west), go 2 miles and turn left at the sign. *970-468-5400.*

Camping along CO 9 offers access to the Blue River, great fishing, and solitude. The **Blue River** campground is 7.5 miles north of Silverthorne on CO 9. No reservations. *970-468-5400.* Located 27 miles northeast of Silverthorne, **South Fork** boasts seven riverside sites. Go north on CO 9 for 13 miles. Turn right (east) on Ute Pass Road (Forest Road 15). Go 10 miles on Ute Pass Road to County Road 30 (FR 138). Turn right (south) on CR 30 and continue 6 miles to the campground. No reservations. *970-887-4100.* With a wheelchair-accessible boardwalk and a trail that spans the river, **Sugarloaf** is 27.5 miles northeast of Silverthorne. Follow the directions to the South Fork campground, but continue an additional 0.5 mile beyond it. No reservations. *970-887-4100.*

22 MONTEZUMA

SCENIC LOCATION

Summit County has grown too big for its own good—development has consumed most of the open spaces within the Blue and Snake River valleys. Thank goodness, then, for the undeveloped public land in the high country that surrounds this large, lovely mountain park. Funky little Montezuma, once a thriving mining town, is a great place for any vehicle and reveals spectacular scenery at the southern end of the Front Range. Driving east on Montezuma Road (Forest Road 5) from the east end of Keystone quickly gets you there. However, the roads beyond Montezuma get a little rough; for those I recommend four-wheel drive.

The Snake River, which parallels FR 5, contains many beautiful cascades that make for wonderful water shots. Remember that anything white is very reflective and is best photographed in cloudy light or when the sun sits below the horizon. Detail in the cascades gets washed out when the sun shines, so wait until a cloud passes over before photographing whitewater. Try using a polarizing filter to further reduce glare and to darken the color of wet river rocks.

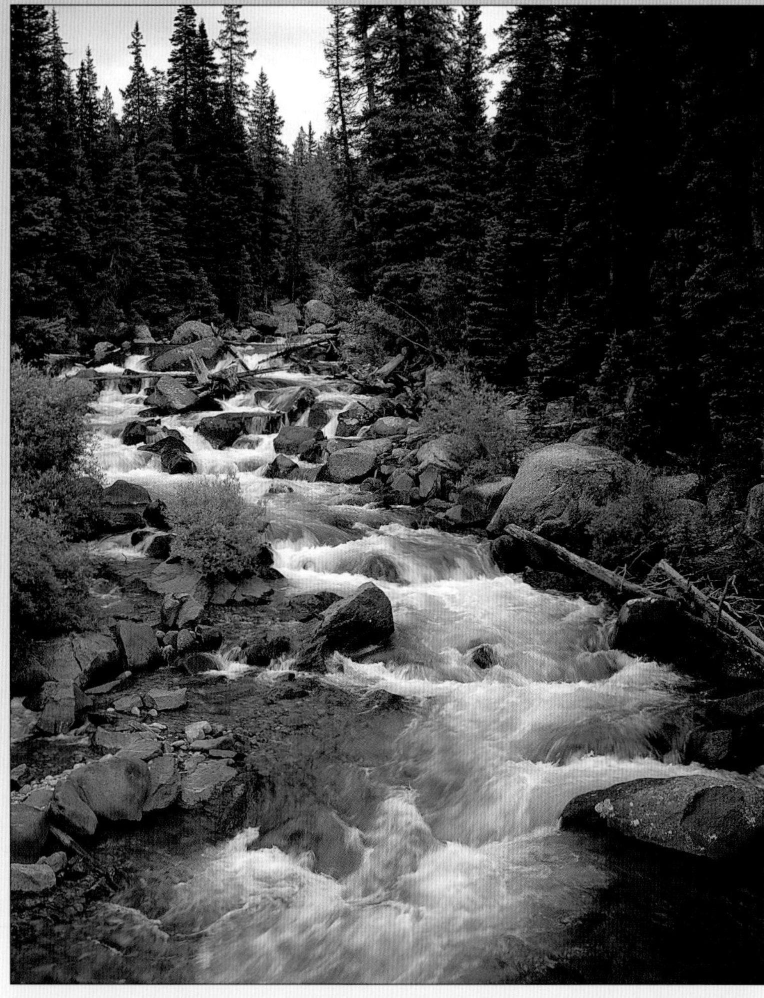

From Montezuma you can take FR 285 south up to Webster Pass. The subalpine valley on the way is glorious with views of high peaks, but beware: Webster Pass is rough and dangerously canted. FR 260 forks to the left before you get to Montezuma and follows lovely Peru Creek. This road, too, crosses a drivable subalpine valley on its way to Argentine Pass, almost as treacherous as Webster Pass. Don't worry if you can't travel high—the scenery around Montezuma is well worth the drive and provides a quick respite from the bustle of Summit County's ubiquitous ski resorts.

My favorite scenes are the ones looking up the creeks toward high peaks. Look for locations along the roads where you can stand creekside and frame the view with spruce and fir trees. A white cascade in the foreground completes the view as the narrowing creek leads your eye through the forest and up to the peaks. Montezuma is a four-season place—the road is plowed in winter.

23 SCENIC LOCATION

GORE RANGE

In my opinion, the two most rugged mountain ranges in Colorado are the Gore Range northwest of Dillon Reservoir and the Needles Range in the remote San Juan Mountains. The Needles are difficult to see up close, but the Gore is easy pickings along CO 9 between Silverthorne and Kremmling. There are many places to pull over along the highway where beautiful ranch meadows visually precede the serrated peaks of the east side of the Gore Range/Eagles Nest Wilderness. The entire 14-mile route from Silverthorne to Green Mountain Reservoir bisects this stretch of the lower Blue River Valley with its large, undeveloped ranches.

From time to time you drive alongside, or cross, the Blue River. At such points you can stop and make photographs looking down and up the river, where stately conifers line the banks. Frame your view without the horizon—a much more intimate portrait of the river without the distraction of peak tops and sky. In May, narrow-leaved cottonwoods brighten the river with light green, in late September with yellow and orange. Ask an angler to pose for you, lending a human touch to the scene.

However, the best photographs to be made here are full scenics, composed with meadows in the foreground, foothills in the midground, and the craggy peaks of the Gore Range in the background—and do include Colorado blue skies this time. Because the Gore Range faces east from this side, the closer to sunrise you photograph, the "warmer" the light. Gray peaks turn red, then orange, then yellow, as the sun rises from behind the Williams Fork Mountains to the east (see pp. 88, 170–171, *Photographing the Landscape*). In May and June, yellow dandelions and purple wild iris decorate the meadows, and freshly leaved aspens on the ridges glow lime green. In September, the fields are golden and the aspen brilliant yellow. The mountains loom close, so wide-angle focal lengths work best. Nevertheless, a telephoto lens allows you to zoom in on trees on the ridges.

Try Ute Pass Road (Forest Road 15/132), too. It ascends the Williams Fork Mountains about 13 miles north of I-70 from CO 9. The views back toward the Gore Range are spectacular, as ever, especially in the morning. You can also drive over the pass and down into the Williams Fork River drainage, a beautiful valley. Continue north on FR 138/County Road 3 to the town of Parshall on US 40. This entire route can be accomplished in a two-wheel-drive vehicle.

FISHING

Fishing in Dillon Reservoir is marginal. However, the trout fishing on the **Blue River** is excellent from Breckenridge to Green Mountain Reservoir toward Kremmling as the river follows CO 9. Below Dillon Reservoir, the Blue River is classified as Gold Medal Water. There are a number of access points and convenient pull-offs along CO 9. *For information, lessons, and guided tours: Cutthroat Anglers, 400 Blue River Pkwy., Silverthorne, 970-262-2878, www.fishcolorado.com.*

HIKING

The Silverthorne/Dillon area has a number of easy hikes that are well suited to families with children. A favorite is the **Lily Pad Trail** EASY. This 2.5-mile, one-way trail takes you through lodgepole pine forests to aptly named Lily Pad Lake in the Eagles Nest Wilderness. To reach the trailhead, take CO 9 south from Silverthorne. Turn right (west) at the 7-Eleven onto Ryan Gulch Road, which takes you through the Wildernest subdivision. Continue 2.4 miles to the end of the road. The trailhead is just beyond the water tower.

The 2-mile **Lower Cataract Loop** MODERATE is a beautiful hike that loops around Lower Cataract Lake (see Scenic Location No. 24, p. 103). Cataract Falls await you just beyond the trailhead. To reach the trailhead, take CO 9 north from Silverthorne for 17.5 miles to Heeney Road (County Road 30). Turn left and go 5.7 miles to Cataract Creek Road (CR 1725). Turn left and go 3 miles to the trailhead.

If you are a birder, the **Rock Creek Trail** EASY is a must. This 1.8-mile one-way trail takes you through the Alfred E. Bailey Bird Nesting Area. You can also reach the Eagles Nest Wilderness from the Rock Creek Trail. Continue on the trail to Rock Creek Falls. To reach the trailhead, go 8.2 miles north from Silverthorne on CO 9 to a dirt road opposite the Blue River campground sign. Go left (west) 1.4 miles to the Rock Creek sign on your left, then another 1.6 miles.

For a longer hike, take the 8.5-mile one-way **Willow Lakes Trail** DIFFICULT. This trail leads to four lakes at an elevation of more than 11,000 feet, as well as to good camping, trout fishing, and wildlife viewing opportunities. From Silverthorne, go left off CO 9 onto Wildernest Road. Go right at the fork and turn left onto Royal Buffalo Drive. Turn right onto Lakeview Drive and continue to the next fork, then turn left onto Aspen Drive. The trailhead is marked as Mesa Cortina.

For panoramic views and a likely encounter with some mountain goats, hike the 2.5-mile **Argentine Pass Trail** DIFFICULT to the top of the pass. The trail is steep and rocky, but certainly worth the effort to walk. To reach the trailhead, take US 6 east past Keystone and turn right (east) on Montezuma Road (Forest Road 5). After about 4.5 miles on Montezuma Road, you will see the Peru Gulch Trailhead on your left. You can either park here and hike the 4.5 miles to the Argentine Pass Trail, or drive on the bumpy dirt road (FR 260) and park at the start of the trail marked by a small sign.

HISTORICAL MARKERS

In 1896, Western railroad expansion was the talk of Junction City, Kansas. Josephine Shane heard from her brother that the railroad planned to extend to the Blue River Valley with a line between Breckenridge and Kremmling. The Shane family left Kansas, and six weeks later (after having to double draft their horses to get over Berthoud Pass) they arrived in Dillon on the Fourth of July. They immediately filed a homestead claim. Because of the fences the homesteaders built, the Shane family and the Kansas immigrants who followed became known as "those Kansas bastards" by area cattlemen.

Although the railroad never came to the Blue River Valley, many homesteading families like the Shanes came and populated towns throughout the area. The Shane family's story is typical of many who sought their fortunes, then settled the land and remained in the West. To visit the **Kansas Gulch Marker and Cemetery,** take CO 9 north from Silverthorne 17.5 miles and turn left on Heeney Road. The dirt road to the marker and cemetery will be on your immediate right.

In the 1940s, when Dillon residents learned that their town was to be submerged under Dillon Reservoir, they couldn't bear to lose the **Wildwood Lodge.** The Wildwood Lodge had become an institutional gathering place for locals and travelers since the late 1930s. So the residents of Dillon carefully disassembled the lodge and reassembled it in Silverthorne, where it now serves as the Elks Lodge. *1321 Blue River Pkwy., 970-468-2561.*

MOUNTAIN BIKING

For adventurers who want more of a challenge than the **Dillon Lake Loop** EASY, select from two outstanding mountain-bike trails in the Silverthorne/Dillon area. The better known of the two, **Argentine Pass Trail** DIFFICULT is steep, narrow, and technical, but the above-timberline views of the surrounding mountain ranges are incredible. The single-track creeps 2.5 miles to the top of 13,207-foot Argentine Pass, and a 7-mile jeep road on the other side leads through the ghost town of Waldorf and down to Georgetown. To reach the Argentine Pass Trail, take US 6 east past Keystone. Turn right (east) onto Montezuma Road (Forest Road 5), continue for 4.5 miles, and park at the Peru Gulch Trailhead on your left in the middle of a big S-curve. If you have a four-wheel drive, you can continue driving to the small Argentine Pass sign. Remember to take lots of water and a good map with you and to set a shuttle in Georgetown if you're biking the entire route.

For another above-timberline mountain-biking experience with spectacular panoramic views of Colorado's mountain ranges, take the 14-mile **Saints John Trail** DIFFICULT. You will pass through the old ghost town of Saints John, the site of Colorado's first major silver strike. To get to the trail, go east on US 6 and pass Keystone. Turn right (east) on Montezuma Road (FR 5) and follow it as it winds for about 5 miles up to the town of Montezuma. Look for the trail to Saints John on the right side of the road. Parking for Saints John Road/Saints John Trail is available at the Peru Gulch Trailhead, about 0.75 miles north of town.

LOWER CATARACT LAKE AND FALLS

Just before you get to Green Mountain Reservoir driving north on CO 9, turn left onto the paved road that goes to the little resort town of Heeney. You'll see the signs. But before you get to Heeney, turn left onto Forest Road 1725 to access the lake and falls. You won't need a four-wheel-drive vehicle for the bumpy road, and I guarantee satisfaction even if you beat up your car a little bit. Lower Cataract Lake is an exceptionally beautiful lake surrounded by meadows and forest in the montane zone. Peaks of the Gore Range (see Scenic Location No. 23, p. 101) and the Eagles Nest Wilderness loom behind, and a short walk reveals Cataract Falls on the back side of the lake.

At some point during the month of May—it varies from year to year—the aspens around the lake leaf and add more light green color to already green meadows. The trail to the lake from the parking area makes a wonderful lead-in line in the composition of a photograph, with trail amid aspens in the foreground, lake and mountains beyond. A vertical composition works best, but the horizontal is no slouch if you put the trail on the left or right of the scene to create an asymmetrical dynamic. A telephoto lens will both shorten the distance from trail to mountains and make the trail more prominent within the composition.

During the summer, find flowers that bloom in the meadows along the east side of the lake. Use your wide-angle lens to compose flowers in the foreground, lake in the midground, and mountains and sky behind: a classic Colorado mountain scene, and almost right off the road! Cataract Falls flows heaviest in May and June but is quite eye-catching the rest of the year, too. It's a good distance behind the lake, so use your longest telephoto lens to make it prominent in your photograph. You can also hike to the falls and photograph it up close.

Lower Cataract Lake is a superb trailhead from which to explore the Eagles Nest Wilderness. Both day-hike and overnight destinations include Upper Cataract Lake and Mirror Lake, and you can connect with the Gore Range Trail, traversing the entire east side of the range and wilderness.

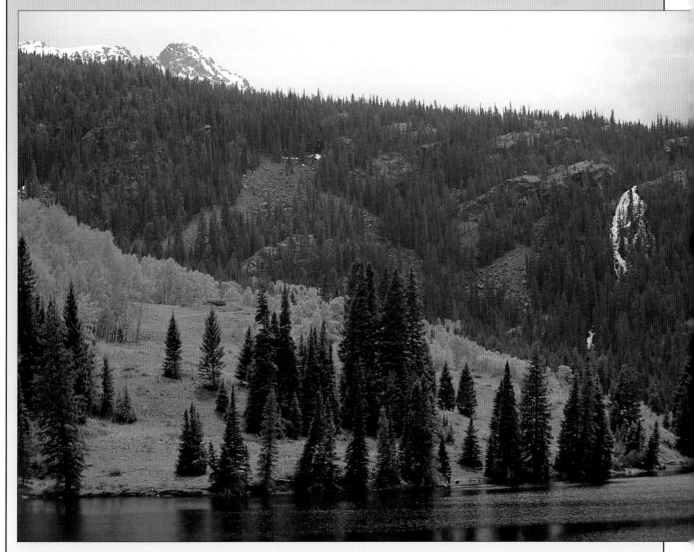

SCENIC DRIVES

Before the Eisenhower Tunnel was built, the only way to get over the Continental Divide on I-70 was over 11,990-foot Loveland Pass (see Scenic Location No. 10, p. 61). Although a beautiful drive, the pass can get extremely icy and windy, with whiteout conditions in winter when wind-driven snow decreases visibility significantly. In pre-tunnel days, homeward-bound skiers were known to be led in caravans by the state patrol, with only the red taillights of the cars in front of them for guidance. Now just about everyone takes the tunnel, winter and summer.

A summertime drive over Loveland Pass offers incredible views from what feels like the top of the world. You may even be able to see people skiing at Arapahoe Basin Ski Area as late as June or July. To make a loop in Summit County, head east on US 6 to Keystone and begin your ascent up the pass. Hairpin curves and switchbacks take you over the pass and down to the Loveland ski areas. Be sure to notice the Seven Sisters avalanche areas on your left just before you reach the Loveland Basin parking lot. To return to the Silverthorne/Dillon area from the Loveland ski areas, take I-70 west through the Eisenhower Tunnel.

Restaurants

For a great Italian dinner, **Marcello's at Town Center** ($$) is a must. *135 Main St, Dillon, 970-468-0551, www.marcellosattowncenter.com.* Stop at the **Dillon Dam Brewery** ($-$$) for beer brewed on site and a variety of brewpub menu choices; enjoy your ale sampler in the summer beer garden. *100 Little Dam Rd., Dillon, 970-262-7777, www.dambrewery.com.* For breakfast, try the **Sunshine Café** ($), also known for its Mexican selections. *250 Summit Place Shopping Center, Silverthorne, 970-468-6663.*

Accommodations

At the corner of Anemone Trail and US 6 is the economical, pleasant, and centrally located **Dillon Inn** ($), *970-262-0801, www.dilloninn.com.* The owners are friendly and helpful. **Western Skies... A Mountain Bed & Breakfast** ($$-$$$) provides easy access to hiking, biking, and skiing from its location at *5040 Montezuma Rd., Dillon. 970-468-9445, www.westernskies-keystone-cabins.com.* The **Mountain Vista Bed & Breakfast** ($-$$) has fine amenities and is centrally located in Silverthorne. *358 Lagoon Lane, 970-468-7700, 800-333-5165, www.colorado-mtnvista.com.*

Special Events

In August, the **Alpenglow Chamber Music Festival** fills the new Silverthorne Pavilion on the Blue River with the melodic strains of classical music performed by internationally recognized musicians. *970-468-4774, www.alpenglowmusic.org.*

For More Information

The visitor center is inside the Summit County Chamber of Commerce building in the Summit Place Shopping Center off US 6 in Silverthorne. *970-262-0817, 800-530-3099, www.summitchamber.org.*

Breckenridge and Frisco

(see map on p. 98)

Over the years, I have become fond of these two mountain towns. In spite of tremendous growth in the area, Breckenridge has maintained its historical roots as a frontier mining town. And even though Vail Resorts recently bought Breckenridge, many still consider it a local ski area, not a corporate ski area. Kids and dogs play in the Blue River as it runs through town, and people stroll on Main Street and along the river, visiting the many shops and restaurants.

Ten miles north of Breckenridge, Frisco possesses an entirely different feeling from its neighbor. In sharp contrast to the often crowded streets of Breckenridge, Frisco is a restful place. One local innkeeper told me, "We roll up the sidewalks at 7 p.m., and we like it that way."

Perhaps I'm so enamored of this area of the state because of all the unforgettable experiences I've enjoyed here. One year on the Fourth of July, for instance, I toured the 13,000-foot Glacier Ridge in a Hummer. As if the scenery wasn't enough excitement on a clear blue-sky Colorado day, we met a very aggressive mountain goat on top of the ridge who was determined to protect his harem and young by challenging our 2-ton Hummer.

The Fourth of July fireworks in most mountain towns are a sight to behold, but in Breckenridge the peaks of the Tenmile Range adjacent to the town make them a spectacle of light and sound. As the professional fireworks explode into color, the sound echoes again and again as the vibrations roll down the canyon in cataclysmic booms.

History

Before the advent of skiing, Breckenridge and Frisco had life as bawdy mining camps and supply towns. Gold was discovered in 1859 at French Gulch several miles above Breckenridge. Soon, other gold and silver strikes were found nearby and the mountains around Breckenridge became dotted with "glory holes" dug with picks and hammers by the hordes of prospectors swarming the area. The mining activity was so frenzied that miners dug holes and erected structures to haul up ore even in avalanche areas, knowing that they would have to rebuild after a heavy winter. A coalition of Methodist ministers attempted to tame the rowdy mining town of Breckenridge by enforcing restrictions on liquor, but to no avail.

Local residents still talk about Tom's Baby—a 13-pound gold nugget that miner Tom Groves carried around in a sack. Today, Tom's Baby graces the Denver Museum of Nature and Science. Legend has it that the nugget weighed much more than 13 pounds but shrank in size when Tom got thirsty. Over the years, the mines in what is now Summit County—including those in French Gulch, Montezuma (see Scenic Location No. 22, p. 100), Saints John, Peru, and elsewhere—produced hundreds of thousands of dollars' worth of gold and silver. By 1882 when the Denver South Park & Pacific Railroad came to Breckenridge from South Park over Boreas Pass, Breckenridge and Frisco had become major supply and transportation centers.

Eventually, however, the familiar tale of boom and bust came to Breckenridge, as its mines played out alongside the economic slumps of the turn of the last century. Good fortune returned to the area with the development of another natural resource: snow. For years the miners had used skis for transportation. Even Methodist minister Father Dyer trekked in on skis to deliver his sermons along with the mail to the far-flung mining camps. By the 1930s, skiing had become a popular sport with the public, and Arapahoe Basin opened shortly after World War II. In 1962, Breckenridge fired up its first tows. The completion of the Eisenhower Tunnel in 1973 assured Front Range skiers easy access not only to the Arapahoe Basin and Breckenridge ski areas, but also to newly opened Keystone and Copper Mountain.

Main Attractions

WINTER SPORTS

Breckenridge Ski Area has expanded from a few tows and chairlifts in the early 1960s to more than 2,000 acres of skiable terrain on Peaks 7, 8, 9, and 10 in the Tenmile Range. One of the first areas to alleviate long waits in lift lines with high-speed quad chairs, Breckenridge is a full-service ski area, offering lessons for all ages, day care, and ski runs and back bowls for skiers of every ability. Breckenridge Ski Area also offers cross-country skiing and telemarking lessons, as well as excellent snowboarding terrain.

Breckenridge lift tickets are interchangeable with those from **Arapahoe Basin** and **Keystone** and can be purchased at a discount at Front Range grocery stores, including King Soopers. The Summit Stage shuttle provides free transportation among the Summit County ski areas. *For information: 800-789-SNOW, 970-453-5000, www.breckenridge.com.*

Because Breckenridge residents have a history of using skis for transportation dating back to the mining days, it's not surprising that its **Nordic Ski Center** is one of the oldest in Colorado. With 35 kilometers of trails for track skiing and snowshoeing, the center also offers rental equipment and lessons. *1200 Ski Hill Rd., 970-453-6855, www.breckenridgenordic.com.*

Cross-country and snowshoe trails lace the area. During the fall, Boreas Pass provides wonderful aspen viewing. In winter, the views of the Tenmile Range make the 3.5-mile **Boreas Pass Trail** EASY a popular cross-country skiing and snowshoeing route. At the old water tank, you can go an additional 3.5 miles to the top of **Boreas Pass** MODERATE. To get there from Breckenridge, go south on CO 9 to Boreas Pass Road. Turn left and proceed 3.5 miles to the end of the plowed road. The 6-mile

BOREAS PASS

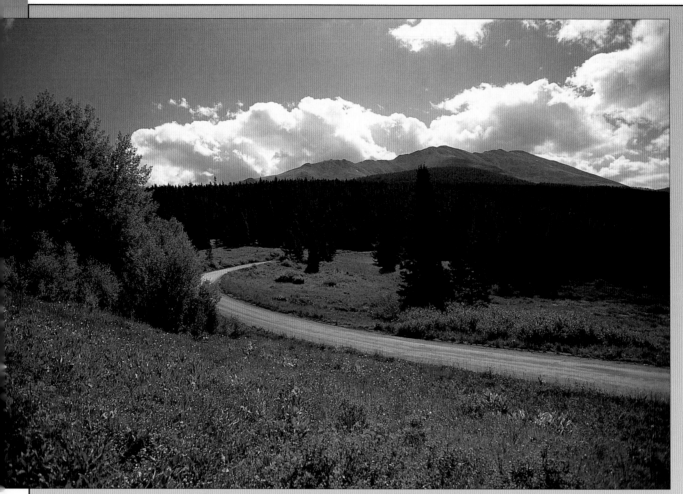

Most of the railroads that once served Colorado's mining communities have been abandoned but often leave us with scenic drives that penetrate otherwise remote mountains. One such route connected the mining towns of Breckenridge and Fairplay by crossing 11,481-foot Boreas Pass. Today this is an improved dirt road over which your vehicle can proceed, if you're not afraid of a few bumps and lots of dust. It's one of the easier alpine-zone dirt roads for a passenger car to travel in Colorado. Take advantage of it. Views of the Tenmile Range to the west and the intermountain basin of South Park to the east are superb, and historic buildings still exist on the route. To get there from Breckenridge, turn east at the southernmost traffic light onto Boreas Pass Road and follow the switchbacks circuitously around various developments until you enter Arapaho National Forest. From South Park, turn north on County Road 15 (10 minutes north of Fairplay off US 285) at the Como town exit and proceed onto CR 33 (old Forest Road 404), Boreas Pass Road.

Aspen trees line the gentle grade on both sides of the pass and make for differing photographic opportunities in color from season to season: light green in spring, dark green in summer, and yellow in fall. Though the road is not plowed in winter, you can easily cross-country ski or snowshoe the route. In fact, some of the old railroad buildings on top of the pass have been restored as ski huts. In winter, aspen trees are not remarkable for their colorful, quaking leaves, but for their white bark and tall trunks. I particularly enjoy photographing winding dirt roads through aspen forests, and Boreas Pass Road has much of this to offer. These scenes are particularly bucolic and seem to make everyone feel good, from serious backcountry types to those who are less active. Use the wide-angle lens to pick up both the tops of trees and the road in front of your feet. Horizontals work as well as verticals. In winter, the low sun makes remarkable shadows of aspen trees across the road. If you have a 35mm SLR camera that allows you to control exposure, add one stop of light to the exposure so that the scene does not end up too dark on film. Remember, white snow reflects light intensely, and the camera will tend to underexpose the scene. If you only use a point-and-shoot, add a little more blue sky to the composition in order to mitigate this effect.

An old red railroad water tower part of the way up from Breckenridge makes a great subject for a photograph, as do the historic buildings atop the pass. In addition, the views of the Tenmile Range are wonderful from the Breckenridge side, especially when you place trees in the foreground of the scene. For the best light, photograph the Breckenridge side in the evening, the South Park side in the morning.

Peru Gulch Trail MODERATE takes you to the Pennsylvania Mine. You can continue up the Peru Gulch Trail through **Horseshoe Basin** DIFFICULT for incredible winter views of the Continental Divide including Argentine Pass. To reach the trailhead from Keystone, take US 6 east and turn right on Montezuma Road. Go 4.5 miles and park at the Peru Gulch Trailhead. Cross-country skiers favor the **Saints John Trail** DIFFICULT for the variety of trails extending off the main route. The trail takes you to the site of the old mining town of Saints John and offers great views of fourteeners Grays and Torreys Peaks. For directions, refer to Mountain Biking, Silverthorne/Dillon, p. 102. Keep in mind that the avalanche danger can be extremely high in these areas. *For trail information: Contact ski shops in Breckenridge that specialize in Nordic sports, or the Keystone Nordic Center, 970-496-4275, 800-354-4FUN.*

Activities

CAMPING

The best camping in the area is around **Dillon Reservoir,** which offers more than 200 campsites with scenery, privacy, and access to all of the area's many recreational opportunities. The Dillon Reservoir campgrounds are situated 13 miles north of Breckenridge and 3 miles north of Frisco via CO 9. See Camping, Silverthorne/Dillon, p. 99.

CHAIRLIFT RIDES

Long after the winter lifts close down and mud season is a distant memory, many ski areas reopen their lifts for summer fun. At Breckenridge, you can take the chairlift up Peak 8 for scenery, mountain biking, or the **Alpine Slide,** a magnet for kids of all ages. Two speeds control the velocity of the slide: scary and super scary. Those who just want to enjoy the scenery can take the longer chairlift ride to the right of Chair 5. From the town of Breckenridge, go west (right) on Ski Hill Road and continue for 1.5 miles. *970-453-5000, www.breckenridge.com.*

CYCLING AND MOUNTAIN BIKING

Summit County boasts more than 40 miles of paved biking trails, which people also enjoy for in-line skating. The most popular are the 35 miles of paved Breckenridge-to-Vail bike paths. The 10-mile **Blue River Bikeway** EASY connects the towns of Breckenridge and Frisco. In Breckenridge, the bike path begins at the junction of Main, Watson, North Park, and French Streets. The 6-mile **Tenmile Canyon Bikeway** EASY connects Frisco to Copper Mountain. Access the bike path in Frisco from the end of 2nd or 7th Street, or from the west end of Mount Royal Avenue. The 13.5-mile **Vail Pass Bikeway** DIFFICULT begins at the Club Med facility at Copper Mountain Ski Area, heads up and over Vail Pass, and continues down to the town of Vail.

For bike touring far from I-70, head south from Breckenridge on CO 9 for the 10-mile ride to the summit of 11,541-foot **Hoosier Pass** DIFFICULT. You will be rewarded with breathtaking views of the fourteener Quandary Peak, especially vivid in full autumn color. Thirteen miles south (and downhill) from the summit is Fairplay, in South Park.

The 10-mile ascent from Breckenridge to the 11,481-foot summit of **Boreas Pass** MODERATE, a classic mountain-bike ride, provides great views of the Tenmile Range. Take CO 9 through Breckenridge, then turn left (south) onto Boreas Pass Road. Once atop the summit, another 13 miles will take you to the old railroad town of Como, in South Park.

Peak 9 at the Breckenridge Ski Area also has several challenging mountain-biking trails that you can reach from the chairlift for the price of an off-season lift ticket. You can also just cruise down the mountains—but check your brakes first! *For information, rentals, and trail maps: Mountain Wave Snowboards, Peak 9 base by ticket office, 800-453-3050, www.mtnwavesnowboards.com.*

For a ride without a lift ticket, try the 17.5-mile **Peaks Loop Trail** MODERATE, which takes you through pine forests, aspen groves, and streams. To reach the trailhead from Breckenridge, begin at the intersection of Main and Ski Hill Road, then head north on Ski Hill Road for 2 miles along the base of Peak 8. Look for the Trails Peak sign on your left. For a more challenging ride, try the 14-mile **Searle Pass Trail** section DIFFICULT of the **Colorado Trail,** which travels past beaver ponds, spruce trees, mining relics, and elk habitat. The panoramic views of the Tenmile, Gore, and Holy Cross Ranges are spectacular. To reach the trail, exit I-70 at Copper Mountain Ski Area. Take Copper Road through the ski resort and follow it to the Union Creek base lodge.

In Summit County, many popular mountain-bike trails are also hiking trails, cross-country ski trails, and four-wheel-drive roads. For information and directions to the **Argentine Pass Trail** and the **Saints John Trail,** refer to Mountain Biking, Silverthorne/Dillon, p. 102. For the **Webster Pass Loop** DIFFICULT and **Georgia Pass** DIFFICULT, see Four-Wheel-Drive Trips, p. 108. Some of the ski and snowboarding shops in Breckenridge also convert to bike shops in the spring and summer. *For information, trail maps, and rentals: Christy Sports, 849 Summit Blvd., Frisco, 970-668-5417; and Peak 9, 645 S. Park, Breckenridge, 970-453-0987.*

FISHING

Just south of Breckenridge are the headwaters of the **Blue River,** which follows CO 9 for 45 miles north to Green Mountain Reservoir. Although the Lower Blue River below Dillon Reservoir is classified as Gold Medal Water, trout fishing can produce rainbows, browns, and brookies a bit upstream from Breckenridge and particularly downstream along the dredged gravel area. Breckenridge has two excellent fishing shops that provide customized lessons and guided trips on public and private waters. *Mountain Angler, 311 S. Main, Breckenridge, 970-453-4665, www.mountainangler.com; and Blue River Anglers, 281 Main St., Frisco, 970-668-2583, www.blueriveranglers.com.*

FOUR-WHEEL-DRIVE TRIPS

Old mining roads make for excellent four-wheel-drive trails, not to mention hiking and mountain-biking routes. Glorious when cloaked in fall color, **Georgia Pass** connects Breckenridge with South Park and presents great views of the Tenmile Range and of the impressive fourteeners Grays and Torreys Peaks. You will also see evidence of the mining activities of more than a century ago. From Breckenridge, go 4 miles north on CO 9 to Tiger Road and turn right. Keep bearing right and follow the Swan River. After reaching the pass, you descend into the town of Jefferson in South Park just off US 285.

Webster Pass Road is another wagon road that connects the old mining area above Breckenridge with the Continental Divide. Again, the views above timberline are spectacular on a clear day. From Breckenridge, take CO 9 north to US 6 and go east to Keystone. Take a right on Montezuma Road (Forest Road 5), proceed about 5 miles to **Montezuma,** and continue through town; after 2.5 miles, it becomes Webster Pass Road (FR 285). The pass is another 4 miles above the town.

GOLF

Breckenridge Golf Club is one of the most highly rated 18-hole public golf courses in the state. Designed by Jack Nicklaus, it features aspen and pine meadows, as well as streams replete with beaver ponds. Head north 3 miles from Breckenridge on CO 9, then turn right on Tiger Road. *970-453-9104, www.breckenridgegolfclub.com.*

HIKING

Masontown Trail EASY is a favorite repeat-hike for Frisco residents. The hike passes historical mining sites and shows you a great view of Dillon Reservoir. This 1.4-mile (one way) hike begins at the Mount Royal/Masontown trailhead and ends at the old mining camp of Masontown, which was destroyed by an avalanche.

If you want more of a challenge, take the **Mount Royal Trail** DIFFICULT from abandoned Masontown up the south face of Mount Royal, the first peak in the Tenmile Range. You will be rewarded with views of the Dillon Valley, Quandary Peak, and the Gore Range. To get there, park at the west end of Main Street in Frisco and cross the bridge over Tenmile Creek. Make a left onto the bikeway and walk 0.5 mile to the trailhead.

Also in the Frisco area is the paved **Tenmile Canyon Recreation Trail** EASY with access to sheer, craggy canyon walls and waterfalls. Four miles long, this trail also serves as a well-traveled bike path. Take the Frisco exit (201) from I-70 West. Go left under the freeway just 0.1 mile to the parking lot and trailhead on the right.

Spruce Creek Trail, EASY 3 miles one way, provides access to waterfalls, wildflowers, and structures left over from the area's mining days. This trail leads you to Continental Falls and the falls above Lower Mohawk Lake. Farther up the trail is Upper Mohawk Lake, where camping is permitted and good fishing luck can produce good-sized cutthroats. From Breckenridge, take CO 9 south for 2.4 miles. Turn right (east) onto County Road 800 (Spruce Creek Road) at The Crown subdivision. Stay on CR 800 for 1.2 miles and go right at the first fork. Turn left at the next fork and continue to the trailhead parking area on the left.

Monte Cristo Gulch Trail MODERATE gives you a scenic snapshot of Colorado's mining history as you pass large, abandoned mine structures and hike amid wildflowers. The Monte Cristo Gulch trailhead enjoys a picturesque setting at Upper and Lower Blue Lakes. This hike also takes you alongside fourteener Quandary Peak. From the Bell Tower Mall in Breckenridge, go south 7.9 miles on CO 9. Turn right on Blue Lakes Road. The Blue Lakes are 2 miles up the road.

A number of Breckenridge residents I talked with take pride in the fact that they have climbed 14,265-foot **Quandary Peak** not once, but several times. The climb up one of the most accessible fourteeners in Colorado affords views of sister fourteeners Grays and Torreys Peaks and of the Blue River Valley. You can see the evidence of the intensive mining that took place throughout the area nearly to the summit. The 2.5-mile trail along the east ridge DIFFICULT is the easiest route to the summit. Follow the directions to Monte Cristo Gulch, previously described, but instead of driving the 2 miles to Blue Lakes, go 0.3 mile and turn right on a dirt road into the parking lot. It's another 0.5 mile to the trailhead.

MUSEUM

The Frisco Historical Society has restored 10 century-old buildings, which you can explore in the **Frisco Historic Park.** One of the most intriguing is the old Frisco Jail, still a very grim place. The park exhibits tell the history of mining in the area, showcase Ute artifacts, and provide information on the construction of Dillon Reservoir. The historic park is on Main Street. *970-668-3428.*

RAFTING

Treat yourself to a raft trip down the **Blue River** EASY. This half-day trip provides Class III whitewater rapids early in the season and great scenery along and above the riverbanks all summer long. For a full-day excursion, take a **Colorado River Trip** EASY, which winds down the lower Gore Canyon through gentle rapids. *Performance Tours Rafting, Breckenridge, 970-453-0661, 800-328-7238, www.performancetours.com.*

SCENIC DRIVES

Boreas Pass Road (see Scenic Location No. 25, p. 106), a 23-mile, graded dirt road, takes you to wonderful views of the Tenmile Range. This winding route dazzles the eye in the fall when the aspens change colors. After ascending to Boreas Pass at 11,481 feet, you drop down into the old railroad town of Como in South Park, just off US 285. Be sure to stop at the **Como Railroad Depot** ($) for a good lunch and a piece of homemade pie.

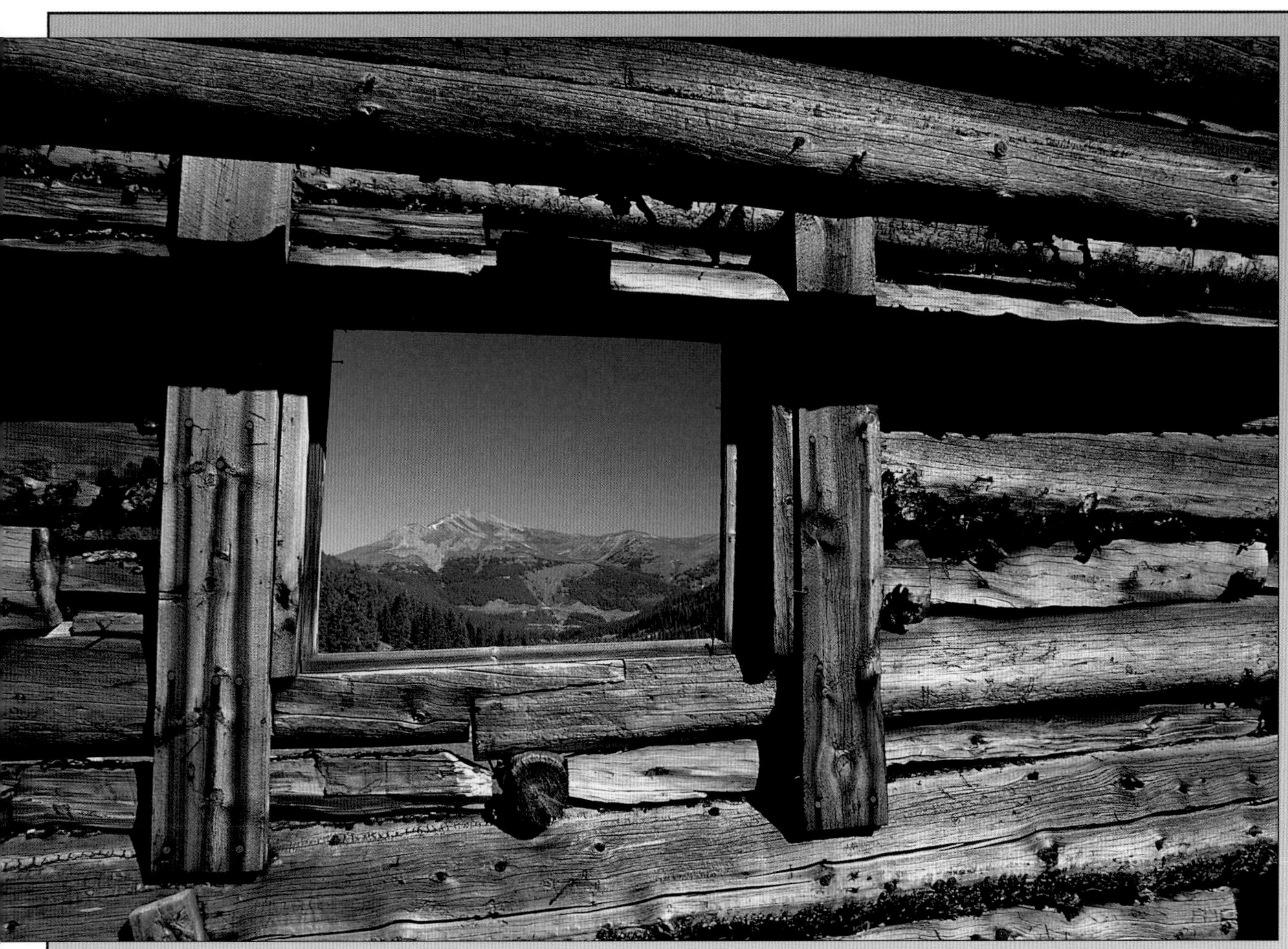

26 SCENIC LOCATION MAYFLOWER GULCH

The Climax Molybdenum Mine has essentially trashed the neck of the woods around Fremont Pass. Open-pit mining has adversely affected most of the drainages on the west side of the Tenmile Range. However, a gem of a high valley still remains available to photograph, and you can drive right to it. It's not pristine by any measure—mining has been conducted off and on here, too, over the years—but the flowers are awesome, and the old mining structures are quite photogenic. From I-70, Exit 195, head south at Copper Mountain on CO 91 for about 4 miles. You can see the glaciated cirques of the range on your left; Mayflower Gulch is the second one. There's a large pullout next to the highway and a dirt road that disappears east into the trees. Drive the road for about 2 miles until the big meadow with a few old buildings opens up in front of you. The road is bumpy with some potholes, but a car can make it without much trouble.

In July and August, Indian paintbrush, both red and pink, carpet the valley floor. The cirque is bounded by sheer granite cliffs that make a fine, primal backdrop for such a fertile field. Though you are quite close to the mountains, a 28mm lens will compose flowers and mountains together, at least in vertical format; you need a 24mm lens to capture it all in horizontal (see pp. 48–50, *Photographing the Landscape*). Bluebell, yellow paintbrush, and columbine grow in patches around the antiquated structures. Your standard, a 50mm lens, photographs these flowers beautifully against the worn log walls.

The windows on both the east and west walls of the westernmost building perfectly frame views up and down the valley. The weathered logs, colored brown to gray, look like a frame around a scenic photograph. But beware, you'll need to expose the film as if you were shooting the scenic outside the building—the dark walls will fool your light meter, and you'll end up with a washed-out scene through the window. If you have a point-and-shoot camera, go outside, point the camera in the same direction, then push your shutter button halfway down and hold it there. This will freeze the correct exposure. Still holding the button halfway down, go back inside, frame the composition, and push the shutter button all the way to make the photograph.

I recommend walking up the rough road that continues up the hill to the right. You will be rewarded with more fields of flowers as you ascend this southern bench in the drainage. White bittercress flowers line the banks of a pretty creek that drains down the hill, and yellow arnica dot the landscape. Mayflower Gulch is best photographed in the morning, but evening light can be productive, too.

For a quicker return to Breckenridge on another scenic byway, go a few miles south of Como on US 285 to Fairplay. Turn right (north) onto CO 9 and start the 23-mile drive over **Hoosier Pass,** also glorious in autumn. At 11,541 feet, Hoosier Pass commands an excellent view of Quandary Peak. To get to Hoosier Pass from Breckenridge, continue south through town on Main Street, which becomes CO 9.

TOURS

Take a ride with Tiger Run Tours to see the incredible, and not easily accessible, backcountry above Breckenridge. Enjoy a jeep trip to **Dry Gulch,** including an excellent historical tour of this mining site. Explore the somewhat restored mining camp and go into an original, dark and damp mining shaft. The Hummer tour takes you over the top of 13,000-foot Glacier Ridge and to panoramic views of the Tenmile Range, Gore Range, and other alps. You are likely to see mountain goats and their young grazing on the high-alpine tundra. ATV and snowmobiling tours are also available. Tiger Run Tours is at the junction of CO 9 and County Road 450 north of Breckenridge. *970-453-2231, 800-318-1386, www.tigerruntours.com.*

The whole family will enjoy the historical **Country Boy Gold Mine Tour,** which takes you down a 1,000-foot mine shaft. The Country Boy Mine and French Gulch area were among the most productive gold sources in Colorado. "Glory holes" still dot the mountains here, and ore "gob piles" still protrude from abandoned mine shafts. Kids will delight in panning for gold (keeping what they find), sliding down a 55-foot ore chute, and petting the descendents of the burros that worked in the mine. The tour takes 45 minutes, and there is a small admission fee. Hayrides are also available. From Breckenridge, take Main Street (CO 9) north to County Road 450. Turn right and continue on CR 450, which becomes French Gulch Road. Drive past the houses; the mine will be to your left. *970-453-4405, www.countryboymine.com.*

Restaurants

Breckenridge has many standouts when it comes to good food. Locals like the **Hearthstone** ($$-$$$) for that special occasion. *130 S. Ridge, 970-453-1148, www.hearthstonerestaurant.biz.* With traditional Mexican food and relaxing views of the Blue River and the ski area, **Mi Casa Mexican Restaurant** ($$$) makes for a favorite après-ski destination. *600 S. Park on the Riverfront, 970-453-2071, www.micasamexicanrestaurant.com.* For a microbrew and a sandwich, try the **Breckenridge Brewery** ($). The fine beers are a hit on the Front Range as well. *600 S. Main, 970-453-1550, www.breckbrew.com.* For breakfast served all day, I recommend the **Columbine Café** ($). Try the creative Eggs Benedict. *109 S. Main, 970-547-4474.*

In Frisco, locals like **Boatyard Pizzeria and Grill** ($$), *970-668-4728.* You can enjoy great Italian food on the patio at **Tuscato** ($$), *970-668-3644.* Both restaurants are on Main Street in Frisco.

Accommodations

The Breck Inn ($$), just north of Breckenridge on CO 9, is a year-round bargain with a Victorian-style coziness. *970-547-9876, 800-661-7614, or www.breckinn.net.*

Breckenridge has outstanding B&Bs at good prices in the summer months. A favorite is **Barn on the River Bed and Breakfast** ($$) *303 North Main St., 970-453-2975, www.breckenridge-inn.com.* The **Allaire Timbers Inn** ($$$), south of Breckenridge, offers a sense of solitude in the pines. *9511 S. Main, 970-453-7530, www.allairetimbers.com.* In town, the **Colorado Coyote Bed & Breakfast** ($$-$$$) is within walking distance of Breckenridge's many restaurants and festivities on the Riverfront. *407 S. Ridge, 970-547-0408, 800-484-9533.*

Frisco River House, Frisco

Adjacent to Tenmile Creek and in the shadow of Mount Royal in Frisco, **The Frisco River House** ($$-$$$) provides a sense of complete solitude and relaxation. *51 W. Main, 877-677-1458, www.thefriscoriverhouse.com. For more information on Summit County's Bed & Breakfasts: www.breckenridgebnbs.com.*

Hearthstone restaurant, Breckenridge

Special Events

The **Breckenridge Music Festival** features diverse concerts and events from mid-June to mid-August at the Riverwalk Center, a showcase for the Breckenridge Music Institute Orchestra and the National Repertory Orchestra. Unique concerts that draw musicians from across the country take place here, and many concerts are free. *Riverwalk Center Box Office, 970-547-3100.* I happened to catch a jazz performance during the weekend **Genuine Jazz & Wine Festival,** with nighttime jams and daytime concerts on a floating outdoor stage. *888-355-6235, www.genuinejazz.com.*

Held in January, the **International Snow Sculpture Championships** attract artisans from all over the world to compete in this truly amazing event. Most sculptures are quite large, and some bear intricate details. The wild and woolly **Ullr Fest** follows. This town party celebrates Ullr, the Nordic god of winter and snow. Many libations are poured to ensure that Ullr will bless Breckenridge with copious amounts of snow for a good ski season. *970-453-5579, www.breckenridge.snow.com.*

For More Information

The visitor center is within the Breckenridge Resort Chamber of Commerce, *311 Ridge St., 970-453-6018, www.gobreck.com or www.breckenridge.com.* In Frisco, contact the Summit County Chamber of Commerce, *916 N. Summit Blvd., 970-668-2051, 800-530-3099, www.summitchamber.org.*

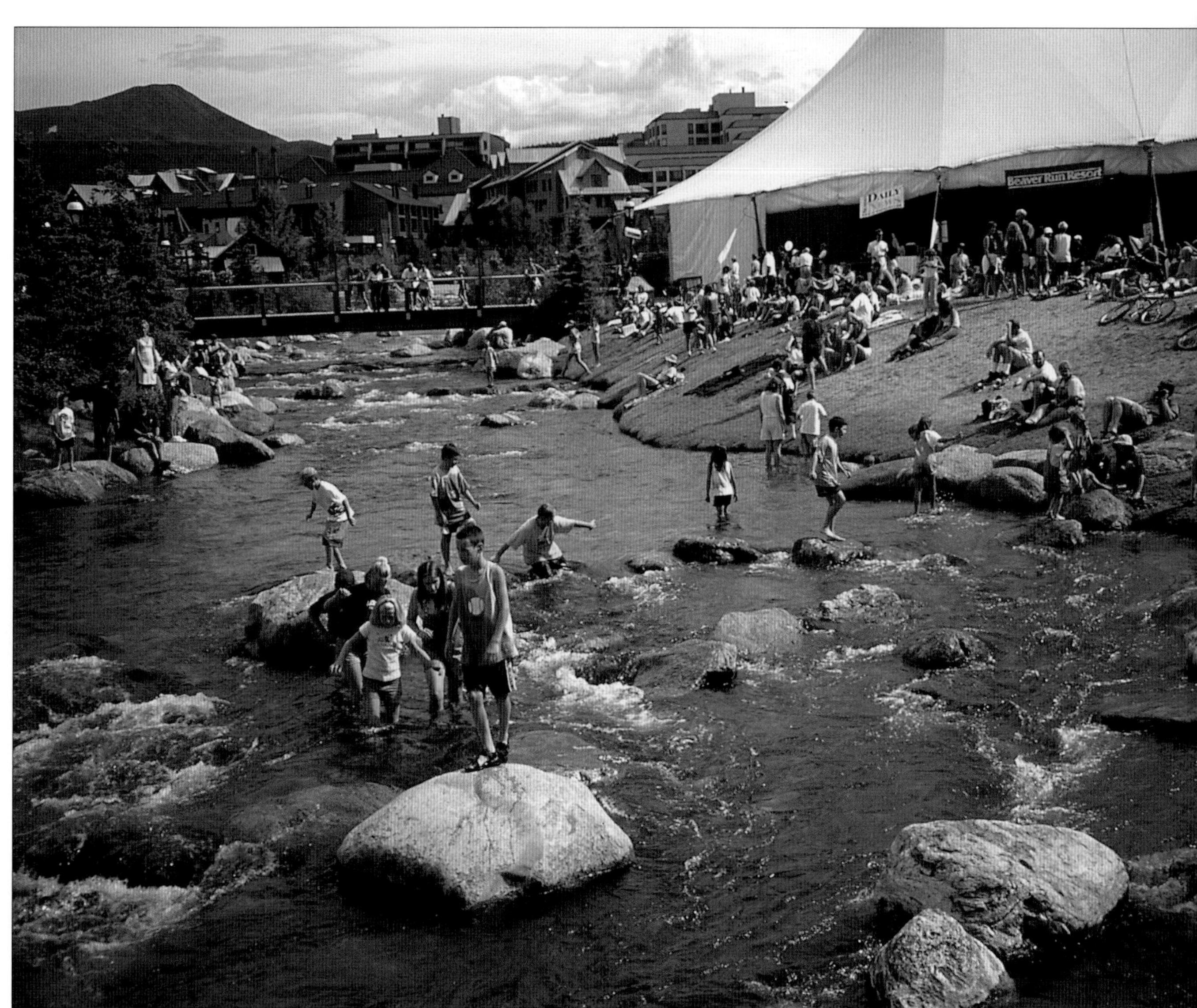

Jazz concert, Breckenridge

Vail/Beaver Creek

Colorado Atlas & Gazetteer pp. 36–38, 47

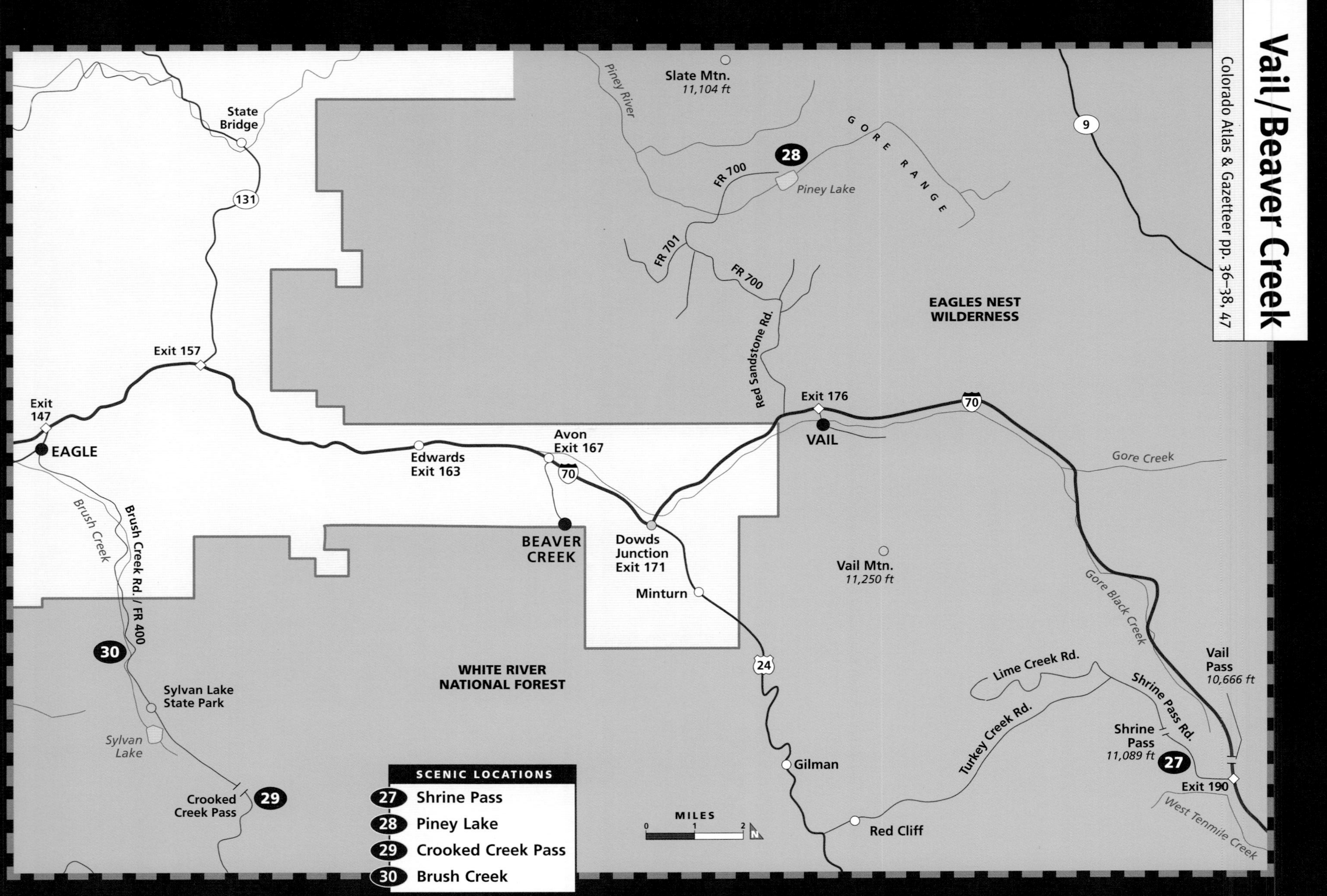

Slate Mtn.
11,104 ft
Piney River
State Bridge
9
28
GORE RANGE
FR 700
Piney Lake
131
FR 701
FR 700
EAGLES NEST WILDERNESS
Red Sandstone Rd.
Exit 157
Exit 176
70
Exit 147
EAGLE
VAIL
Avon Exit 167
Edwards Exit 163
Gore Creek
70
Brush Creek
Brush Creek Rd. / FR 400
BEAVER CREEK
Dowds Junction Exit 171
Vail Mtn.
11,250 ft
Minturn
Gore Black Creek
30
WHITE RIVER NATIONAL FOREST
24
Lime Creek Rd.
Vail Pass
10,666 ft
Shrine Pass Rd.
Sylvan Lake State Park
Turkey Creek Rd.
Shrine Pass
11,089 ft
27
Sylvan Lake
Gilman
Exit 190
Crooked Creek Pass
29
MILES
0
1
2
Red Cliff
West Tenmile Creek
SCENIC LOCATIONS
27 Shrine Pass
28 Piney Lake
29 Crooked Creek Pass
30 Brush Creek

Vail

When I drive west from Vail Pass on I-70 in summertime and make the winding descent into the Vail Valley, I am amazed at how lush and green it is. Although internationally known for its world-class skiing and ski competitions, the Vail Valley is abuzz with summer visitors enjoying a variety of festivals and events, boundless outdoor activities, and the villages' irresistible charm. Set against the nearby Gore Range (see Scenic Location No. 23, p. 101), which evokes visions of the Alps, Vail exudes a European atmosphere famous among Colorado mountain resorts. Colorful blossoms fill flower boxes on the Tyrolean-style buildings in Vail Village; locals jokingly call the area's adaptation of Bavarian architecture "Ba-*Vail*-ian." I first visited Vail in 1973 and have been skiing and photographing the area ever since. In fact, I've been teaching the John Fielder Photography Workshops in Vail every summer since 1994. For more information visit my website at *www.johnfielder.com* or call 303-935-0900. To get to Vail Village, travel west on I-70 from Denver to Exit 176.

History

Although home to the Utes and well known to gold miners, the Vail Valley didn't receive national attention until William Henry Jackson photographed 14,005-foot Mount of the Holy Cross in 1873. Thomas Moran further popularized the peak in a painting, and Henry Wadsworth Longfellow celebrated it in a poem. The Mount of the Holy Cross so impressed the public that it was declared a National Monument in 1929, a designation that lasted until 1951. The cross is formed by a deep vertical couloir that intersects a horizontal bench. Time and erosion have not been kind to the arms of the cross. However, the Mount of the Holy Cross is still awe-inspiring, particularly when snow highlights its features in winter.

In many ways, Vail owes its existence to the ski troops of the 10th Mountain Division. Some of the men who trained at Camp Hale in World War II for mountain warfare became key players in developing Vail as a premier ski area and bringing the sport of downhill skiing to Colorado. Following a Ute "snow" prayer, Vail opened its slopes to the public in 1962.

Main Attractions

BETTY FORD ALPINE GARDENS

Set against a mountain backdrop, the breathtaking Betty Ford Alpine Gardens comprise the highest public alpine gardens in the world. The Alpine Display Garden features nearly 500 species of alpine and subalpine plants in four separate microclimates, and the Perennial Garden displays another 1,500 plant varieties. The gardens are in Ford Park off the South Frontage Road on Gore Creek Drive. *970-476-0103, www.bettyfordalpinegardens.org.*

SHOPPING

As the town of Vail extends west down the valley along I-70, it is divided into six sections—East Vail, Golden Peak, Vail Village, Lionshead Village, Cascade Village, and West Vail. Vail Village, the oldest part of Vail, is a delightful pedestrian community with the atmosphere of a small town in the Alps. From Exit 176 off I-70, head left (east) on the Frontage Road, park in the public garage, cross Gore Creek on the covered bridge, and refuse to be intimidated by Vail's reputation for high prices. Vail merchants offer a variety of quality items at discounted prices in the summer, and meals are reasonable at the many restaurants in Vail Village. The free Vail Shuttle—also a welcome amenity for skiers and snowboarders at the end of a powder day—services Vail's pedestrian shopping areas.

VAIL MOUNTAIN

With the untracked champagne powder of its back bowls and terrain that accommodates every skill level, Vail Mountain provides some of the best skiing in the world. Vail's challenging runs and favorable conditions make it the perfect host for international competitions such as the World Alpine Ski Championships. Vail Mountain also offers excellent snowshoeing at the Golden Peak Center at the bottom of Chair 6. *For information: 970-476-9090, www.vail.com.*

In summer, a trip up Vail Mountain on the gondola or chairlift is a must. (Only the Vista Bahn Express Lift in Vail Village and the Eagle Bahn Gondola in Lionshead are open in the summer.) From the top of Vail Mountain, you can catch spectacular views of the Mount of the Holy Cross and the Gore Range. Hiking and biking trail maps are available at ski lifts and the gondola (see Cycling and Mountain Biking, p. 114, and Hiking, p. 115). Thrill sleds and bikes can be rented by the hour or day at the top or base of Vail Mountain. For a more mellow descent of the mountain, ride the gondola or chairlift back down. *For more information: Top of the Gondola, 970-479-4380; Lionshead, 970-476-3600; Vail Village, 970-479-0600.*

Activities

CAMPING

The campgrounds in the Vail Valley offer wilderness access, great fishing, and panoramic views. I like **Camp Hale Memorial** campground because of its historical significance as the training area for the 10th Mountain Division troops during World War II. The Colorado Trail south of the campground leads to Tennessee Pass, and the paved roads in Camp Hale make for easy walking paths and short biking trails. To get to Camp Hale from Denver, go west on I-70 to the US 24 exit (171), then south on US 24 for 16 miles. The **Blodgett** and **Gold Park** campgrounds offer access to the Holy Cross Wilderness and good fishing at Whitney Lake, Missouri Lakes, and Homestake Reservoir. To reach the campgrounds from Denver, take I-70 west to the US 24 exit (171), then go south on US 24 for 12.5 miles to Homestake Road (Forest Road 703). Turn right (southwest) and go 0.5 mile for Blodgett, 7 miles for Gold Park. Near the boundary of the Eagles Nest Wilderness, **Gore Creek** campground boasts views of the Vail Valley and the ski area's back bowls. Because Gore Creek campground is nearest to Vail, it fills up quickly. To get to the campground, take I-70 west to Exit 180, then go east for 2.3 miles on South Frontage Road. None of these campgrounds take reservations. *970-827-5715.*

If the other campgrounds are full, try **Sylvan Lake State Park,** one of western Colorado's best-kept secrets. Surrounded by the White River National Forest, Sylvan Lake has 50 campsites as well as private cabins. The park is 16 miles south of the town of Eagle on Brush Creek Road. Reservations accepted. *970-328-2021.*

Mountain biking, Vail Mountain

CYCLING AND MOUNTAIN BIKING

Mountain biking in the Vail area can be strenuous, but plenty of opportunities exist for riders of all abilities. The **Lost Lake Loop** MODERATE has spectacular views, and the route shares its access with a network of area trails including Son of Middle Creek and Davos Hill. The 20-mile loop can be easily broken into segments or ridden in its entirety. From the North Frontage Road in Vail, take Red Sandstone Road (Forest Road 700) north, and bear left onto FR 786, which leads to the Lost Lake trailheads. Take Lost Lake Trail for 3.5 miles as it runs between Lost and Piney Lakes to where it reconnects with Red Sandstone Road and turn left. Turn right after roughly 0.5 mile onto Red and White Mountain Road (FR 734) and continue for several miles to the Buffehr Creek Trail, which leads you back to Vail.

The **Meadow Mountain Loop** MODERATE begins at the U.S. Forest Service Station right off of US 24 in Minturn (I-70 Exit 171). Ride uphill for about 3 miles on a dirt road, and bear right at the fork onto FR 738. Stop for a break at the Forest Service cabin and enjoy the views before your westward descent on the single-track trail. Look for a wooden fence line and turn right (even though another trail goes straight down). Enjoy this rolling section of the ride until you hit a jeep road, which will bring you back to US 24 near the Forest Service Station.

A ridable segment of the Colorado Trail on top of **Tennessee Pass** MODERATE winds through lodgepole pine, spruce, and aspen forests and ends (for bikers) after 5.5 miles at the border of the Holy Cross Wilderness. Take US 24 (I-70 Exit 171) to Tennessee Pass; park on the west side of the road.

Many load their mountain bikes onto the gondola or chairlift, or rent bikes on top, and ride down Vail Mountain. The 7-mile **Village Trail** EASY winds down a wide trail from Eagles Nest to Vail Village or Lionshead and provides panoramic views of the Gore Range and Vail Valley. The **Grand Traverse** MODERATE, which begins at the top of the Eagle Bahn Gondola, is a 4-mile single-track trail with stunning views of Vail's back bowls, Mount of the Holy Cross, and the Gore and Tenmile Ranges.

Cyclists can take the 13.5-mile **Vail Pass Bikeway** DIFFICULT, which runs between Vail and the Copper Mountain Ski Area (Exit 195 from I-70), with a steep climb over Vail Pass. This bikeway connects to Summit County's **Tenmile Canyon** and **Blue River Bikeways** (see Cycling and Mountain Biking in the Breckenridge/Frisco section, p. 107). *For information on trails, bike rentals, and repairs: Wheel Base, 610 W. Lionshead Cir., 970-476-5799; open seasonally.*

FISHING

The chance to catch rainbow, brown, cutthroat, and brook trout awaits you in the Vail Valley. The Gold Medal Water of **Gore Creek** runs right through the town of Vail, south of the interstate. Good fishing also exists at **Homestake Reservoir** and **Homestake Creek,** 11 miles from the Blodgett campground on Homestake Road (Forest Road 703). *For directions, see Camping on p. 113. For information, equipment, lessons, or guided trips: Gorsuch Outfitters, 877-926-0900, www.gorsuchoutfitters.com.*

FOUR-WHEEL-DRIVE TRIPS

Vail's jeep trails require a professional driver and vehicles built for steep, rocky terrain. The guides are knowledgeable about the region's history, wildlife, and plants. Tours include the Castle Peak backcountry bordering the Flattops Wilderness, as well as the Holy Cross area, with remote views of the Gore and Sawatch Ranges, Red and White Mountain, the Continental Divide, and Mount of the Holy Cross. *For information and reservations: Nova Guides, 719-486-2656, 888-949-NOVA, www.novaguides.com; Timberline Tours, 970-476-1414, 800-831-1414, www.timberlinetours.com.* You might also like to try a Hummer tour. *Lakota River Guides, 970-845-7238, www.lakotariver.com.*

GOLF

The Vail Valley's mountainous terrain demands elongated courses, which makes for challenging golf. As you drop down into the

Vail Valley from Vail Pass, you'll see Vail's oldest golf course, the **Vail Golf Club,** a picturesque course set against the mountain's dark pines. *970-479-2260, www.vailrec.com.*

HIKING

Vail Valley hikes reveal abundant wildflowers, wildlife, and panoramic scenery. Some of the best trails for novice hikers are right on Vail Mountain.

After taking the gondola or chairlift up Vail Mountain, you can descend along **Eagles View** EASY, a 1-mile paved path with views of Mount of the Holy Cross and the Gore Range. The 4.6-mile **Berrypicker** MODERATE boasts colorful wildflowers and chances to view wildlife. The trail winds from mid-Vail or Eagles Nest (both on Vail Mountain) to Vail Village or Lionshead at the bottom of the ski area.

Enjoy waterfalls, wildflowers, and nearly a dozen alpine lakes on the 3-mile **Missouri Lakes Trail** MODERATE. To get to the trail, take I-70 West to the US 24 exit (171), then go south 12.5 miles to Homestake Road (Forest Road 703). Turn right and continue 8 miles to FR 704. Turn right. Go 2.3 miles to the aqueduct water pipes, and turn right. The trailhead is on the left.

Two favorite hikes among locals are the 5-mile **Pitkin Lake** MODERATE and 6-mile **Booth Creek Trail** MODERATE. Both one-way hikes start in Vail and end in the Eagles Nest Wilderness, and provide views of waterfalls, wildflowers, and the lakes tucked beneath the summits of the Gore Range. To get to Pitkin Lake, take I-70 west to the East Vail exit (180), then head east along the North Frontage Road for 0.2 mile. The parking lot and trailhead are to the left (north) of the road immediately after you have crossed Pitkin Creek. To get to Booth Creek, take I-70 west to the East Vail exit (180) and proceed 0.8 mile west along the North Frontage Road toward Vail Village. Turn right (north) on Booth Falls Road and go 0.25 mile, past the tennis courts, to the trailhead.

Pilgrimages to the Mount of the Holy Cross still take place on the 5-mile **Notch Mountain Trail** DIFFICULT, which commands a sublime view of the Holy Cross. To get to Notch Mountain Trail, take I-70 west to the US 24 exit (171), turn right on US 24, and drive 4 miles to rough and steep Tigiwon Road. Turn right, continue 8 miles and park at the end of the road. Take the Fall Creek Trail and look for the right fork to Notch Mountain.

HISTORICAL MARKERS

As you cross the covered bridge and enter Vail Village, take a moment to stop at the statue of a World War II 10th Mountain Division ski trooper to your right. Fourteen thousand troopers served in the 10th Mountain Division after training at Camp Hale just a few miles from Vail. The division fought in the Aleutian Islands and the Italian Alps, suffering 992 casualties. Another monument honoring the division stands at Ski Cooper on the summit of Tennessee Pass.

MUSEUM

A visit to Vail would not be complete without visiting the **Colorado Ski Museum,** which traces Colorado's 130-year ski history from the miners of the late 1800s to the international competitors of today. Check out the skis and bindings of the past, and take a walk through the Colorado Ski Hall of Fame. The museum, located on the Frontage Road behind the Vail Village parking structure, also screens films and hosts events. *970-476-1876, www.skimuseum.net.*

NATURE CENTERS

The **Vail Nature Center** on Vail Valley Drive offers wildflower walks, early morning bird-watching walks, fly-fishing, stream ecology, a beaver pond tour, stargazing, nature hikes, and eco-tour hut trips. The eco-tour trips include a seasonal mountain wildflowers tour, a peaks and ponds tour, and an autumn colors tour. *For more information: 970-479-2291, www.vailrec.com.* Kids will enjoy the **Dino-Dig** activity at the top of Vail Mountain. The Colorado Division of Wildlife has an excellent tent display of native wildlife and plants. Also see the Betty Ford Alpine Gardens, Main Attractions, p. 113.

SCENIC DRIVES

The **10th Mountain Division Memorial Highway** (US 24) from Minturn to Leadville is part of the Top of the Rockies Scenic and Historic Byway. This 32-mile paved road presents excellent views of the Mount of the Holy Cross and 10 other fourteeners, including the two highest mountains in Colorado —Mount Elbert (14,433 feet) and Mount Massive (14,421 feet). The road parallels the Holy Cross Wilderness. You will pass Camp Hale and the memorial to the ski troopers of the 10th Mountain Division on the summit of Tennessee Pass. You will also see the mining ghost town of Gilman and drop down into the historic mining district of Leadville. From Denver, take I-70 west to US 24 (Exit 171), then go south on US 24.

A particularly gorgeous drive in the fall, **Shrine Pass** (see Scenic Location No. 27, p. 116) provides tremendous vistas of the Mount of the Holy Cross, and the Gore, Sawatch, and Tenmile Ranges. Take I-70 west toward the Vail Pass summit at Exit 190. Just east of the summit, take the Shrine Pass Road west of the parking lot. Though the road is dirt, you can drive it in a passenger car. From the summit of Shrine Pass, the road drops down to US 24 in Red Cliff.

TENNIS

The Vail Tennis Center in Ford Park on the South Frontage Road has eight clay courts and two hard courts, with the Gore Range as a dramatic backdrop. *970-479-2294.*

TENTH MOUNTAIN DIVISION HUT SYSTEM

A group of backcountry enthusiasts, some of whom served in the 10th Mountain Division, formed the 10th Mountain Division Hut Association and built shelters for backcountry skiers. Today, winter sports enthusiasts, hikers, and mountain bikers use

27 SCENIC LOCATION SHRINE PASS

Instead of heading to the restrooms at the Vail Pass exit (190) on I-70, bear right onto Shrine Pass Road. About 10 miles later you'll end up at the old mining community of Red Cliff just east of US 24. But instead of heading to Red Cliff right away, slow down and smell the wildflowers, literally. The best field of Indian paintbrush in the state of Colorado grows on the south side of the road between Vail Pass and Shrine Pass, 3 miles to the west. From about the second week in July until August, the red and pink paintbrush grow profusely among the old stumps from century-old logging ventures. The road is bumpy in places but easily negotiable with a car all the way to Red Cliff.

You can employ all of those flowers in lots of compositions. Put on the macro lens and photograph close up the red bracts of the paintbrush. Wait for the sun to disappear behind clouds so the bright light doesn't wash out the rich color and details. Try photographing clumps of flowers that grow next to the gray stumps, without including any sky. Then put on the wide-angle lens, set up the tripod, and compose flowers in the foreground and Jacques Peak, to the southeast, in the background. Don't forget to stop your aperture down to f22, get within a couple of feet of the closest flower, focus double the distance away (hyperfocal distance), and proceed to make a classic Colorado scenic of which you will be proud.

After you are done here, head west to the Shrine Pass parking area. Park your vehicle and take the only trail west (it splits to the left from the road to the Shrine Mountain Inn) up to the top of Shrine Ridge. You'll recognize the ridge, capped with red sandstone and a line of snow left from last winter's snow cornices. The trail skirts a few beaver ponds in the valley below—a great place to make reflections images of clouds at sunset—then heads up through the forest to the top of Shrine Ridge. Along the way flowers abound: asters and daisies, yellow arnica, larkspur, and the ubiquitous paintbrush. Closer to the top of the ridge, you'll discover clumps of Colorado columbine in the rocks and purple lupine on top of the ridge. Sunrise and sunset are equally sublime here.

In winter, make a reservation at the Shrine Mountain Inn and ski or snowshoe 1.5 miles to this 10th Mountain Division Hut System hut. And before you do that, attend one of my winter photography workshops based in Vail each season. I guarantee you'll make better photographs if you do. *For more information visit my website at www.johnfielder.com or call 303-935-0900.*

these 15 huts adjacent to the Holy Cross, Mount Massive, and Hunter-Fryingpan Wilderness Areas. With more than 500 miles of singletrack trails, this is a coveted area for mountain bikers. The hut system is situated between Aspen, Vail, and Leadville, and the average distance from the trailheads to the huts measures about 6 miles. *For information and maps: 970-925-5775, www.huts.org.*

WALKING TOUR OF MINTURN

"Men-turn," as it was pronounced by its original residents—railroad men and miners—has retained some of its rough, small-town character. But for the most part, quaint shops, art galleries, and a variety of restaurants have replaced the bawdy saloons of the mining days. Minturn also makes a great starting point for hiking and biking trips. From Denver, take I-70 west to the US 24 exit (171).

Restaurants

Although there is no shortage of good places to eat in Vail, I prefer establishments with character and history. One of my favorites is **Pepi's Restaurant** ($$), *970-476-4671, 800-610-7374,* inside the Hotel-Gasthof Gramshammer in the heart of Vail Village. Owned by longtime locals Pepi and Sheika Gramshammer, Pepi's specializes in Austrian food. The Wiener schnitzel is a favorite. Take time to ogle the autographed pictures in the bar, including several from Vail-area residents Gerald and Betty Ford. Another Vail institution, the **Red Lion Inn** ($$), *970-476-7676,* has made its name from its sandwiches, brews, and lively après-ski scene. I've been enjoying great Mexican food at **Los Amigos** ($$) for more than 25 years. It's fun to watch the skiers fly down the expert run across from the restaurant's outdoor deck, which faces the Vista Bahn chairlift. *970-476-5847.* **Lancelot** ($$-$$$), in Vail Village by the Children's Fountain, has a large choice of appetizers and entrees. *970-476-5828, www.lancelotinn.com.* For haute cuisine, plant yourself at **Sweet Basil** ($$$-$$$$), prized for its creative menu and upscale atmosphere. *193 Gore Creek Dr., 970-476-0125, www.sweetbasil-vail.com.* **Terra Bistro** ($$$) boasts a chic atmosphere, innovative cuisine, and one of the finest wine lists in the Vail Valley. *Vail Mountain Lodge, 352 E. Meadow Dr., 970-476-6836.* Cosmopolitan elegance and ski-town charm blend perfectly at Golden Peak's **Larkspur** ($$-$$$). Stop in for a slopeside lunch or a delectable dinner. *458 Vail Valley Dr., 970-479-8050, www.larkspurvail.com.*

Red Lion Inn restaurant, Vail

On Vail Mountain, try **Bistro 14** ($$), *970-479-4530.* For lunch, try the **Talon's Deck** ($) at the top of the mountain. **Game Creek** ($$$-$$$$), *970-479-4275,* is famous for its Sunday brunch and gourmet dinners. Ride the Eagle Bahn Gondola to Eagles Nest, then take the shuttle to the restaurant.

For a change of pace, pay a visit to the **Minturn Country Club** ($$-$$$), *970-827-4114,* on Main Street in Minturn. At this "country club," *you* put the steak on the grill. **The Turntable** ($) at the west end of Main Street in Minturn won the Summit and Eagle County Award for the best green chile. *160 Railroad Ave., 970-827-4164.*

Minturn Country Club, Minturn

Accommodations

For a luxury experience in Vail Village during any season, you can't beat the intimate suites of the **Austria Haus Club & Hotel** ($$$$), *242 E. Meadow Dr., 970-477-5800, www.austriahaushotel.com,* or the **Sonnenalp** ($$$$). The Sonnenalp boasts two restaurants, a spa, a golf course down-valley, and such high-end touches as heated marble floors. *20 Vail Rd., 800-654-8312, www.sonnenalp.com.* You can get great deals on Vail lodging in the "off-season." One of the best deals is the elegant Tyrolean **Hotel-Gasthof Gramshammer** ($$-$$$$) in Vail Village. (The locals call it Pepi's.) *970-476-5626, 800-610-7374, www.pepis.com.* The **Evergreen Lodge** ($$-$$$$) offers good year-round rates, easy access to all of Vail's activities, and exquisite accommodations. To get to the Evergreen Lodge from Denver, take I-70 west to the Vail Village exit (176). Take a right on the South Frontage Road to Lionshead. The lodge will be to your left just before Lionshead. *For information and reservations: 970-476-7810, www.evergreenvail.com.*

Sonnenalp Resort, Vail

Located in West Vail, the **Park Meadows Lodge** ($-$$) ranks as the best bargain for quality lodge accommodations. The lodge has kitchen facilities and offers a handbook of things to do in Vail, especially for children. To get to Park Meadows Lodge from Denver, take I-70 west to the West Vail exit (173) and turn left (south) on the South Frontage Road. Turn right on Matterhorn Circle and continue until the road dead-ends at the lodge. *970-476-5598, www.parkmeadowslodge.com.* The **Vail Cascade Resort and Spa** ($$$$) in West Vail has

28 SCENIC LOCATION — PINEY LAKE

Piney Lake must be one of the most beautiful mountain lakes in Colorado to which you can drive (another is Maroon Lake near Aspen). The backdrop is nothing less than the Gore Range's highest peaks, all of which reflect in the lake. A subalpine lake surrounded by aspen, spruce, and fir trees, and meadows filled with wildflowers in the summer, half of it is actually within the Eagles Nest Wilderness. A trail connects Piney Lake with Upper and Lower Cataract Lakes (see Scenic Location No. 24, p. 103), though you must traverse the range to reach them on the east side. To get there, take the frontage road north of I-70 west from the main Vail exit (176) to Red Sandstone Road, then turn left onto Forest Road 700 and proceed to its end at Piney Lake. The road is rough at the end but negotiable by car. The drive takes about 40 minutes.

At the lake you will find a dude ranch, where food service and horseback riding are available but no overnight accommodations. Though I've used the facility for many years with my photography workshop participants, I would prefer that it was not so close to the wilderness. Loud bands have played there for weddings, antithetical to the quality of solitude we expect from wild places. Still, it's a great opportunity for people to see wilderness up close.

The photographic possibilities are unlimited. One of Colorado's great reflection scenes is available from the west end of the lake at sunset when, on a clear day, the peaks of the Gore Range turn blood red. Rainbows after summer evening thunderstorms are not uncommon here. Aspen trees bound the north side of the lake, and wildflowers carpet the meadows in the vicinity. Red cliffs of sandstone form a marvelous backdrop. The Piney River descends the canyon from the lake and provides not only good fishing but beautiful photographs. I suppose wide-angle lenses work best here. The lake reflection image certainly requires one, and so do images of wildflowers beneath the aspen trees. Telephoto lenses are good for silhouetting aspen against the red cliffs, as well as for shooting the rental canoes against the blue-green water of Piney Lake. Evening is by far the best time to photograph here, as it takes quite a while in the morning for the sun to enter the valley. I prefer cloudy light in the afternoons in order to photograph details of flowers and lichens on rocks without the handicap of glare from a bright sun.

An easy trail goes several miles up the drainage through meadows, aspen, and conifer forests all the way to Upper Piney Lake. This is a place for the less experienced backcountry traveler to see wilderness at its most sublime.

its own ski lift for quick mountain access in winter, and you'll never see a lift line! *1300 Westhaven Dr., 800-282-4183, www.vailcascade.com.*

For plush accommodations, **The Minturn Inn** ($-$$$) on Main Street in Minturn is a bargain in the summer and makes an excellent laid-back base camp for all the hiking and biking activities in the area. From I-70 West, take the Minturn exit (171), go right, and drive 2 miles to the inn. *970-827-9647, 800-MINTURN, www.minturninn.com.*

Special Events

In keeping with the Vail Valley's pseudo-Austrian atmosphere, the hills in summer truly are alive with the sound of music. The **Bravo! Vail Valley Music Festival** brings classical music to the valley from late June through early August. Concerts are held at the Gerald R. Ford Amphitheater's Vilar Pavilion in Vail and the Vilar Center for the Arts in Beaver Creek. The Colorado Symphony Orchestra and many internationally recognized musicians also come to the Vail Valley each summer. *For schedules and ticket information: 877-827-5700, www.vailmusicfestival.org.* The annual **Vail Valley Jazz Festival** is held on Labor Day weekend. *For information and tickets: 1-888-824-5526, www.vailjazz.org. For other concert information: 970-479-1385, 800-525-3875, www.visitvailvalley.com.*

In mid-June, the annual **Chili Cook-Off** fires up in Vail Village. The competition is heated, but, fortunately, the beer is cold. In mid-July, Vail hosts its annual **Vail Block Party,** which features free food, beer, and live music throughout the village. In September, the village's annual **Oktoberfest** brings out German brats, beer, and music. *For information on these and other events: 970-479-1385, 800-525-3875, www.visitvailvalley.com.*

I've been teaching the **John Fielder Photography Workshops** in Vail since 1994. For three days and two nights, 16 participants and I hike and photograph the most scenic places in the Vail Valley. Sunrise and sunset photography, overnight film processing, daily critiques, and slide lectures ensure that each participant reaches a new skill level by the end of the long weekend. It's intended for beginning to advanced photographers with a desire to capture the natural environment on film. *For information: 303-368-5208, www.johnfielder.com.*

For More Information

Vail Valley Partnership, *101 Fawcett Rd., Suite 240, Avon, 970-476-1000,www.visitvailvalley.com.*

Beaver Creek

(see map on p. 112)

Tucked at the head of a high mountain valley, through which one of the state's most challenging golf courses meanders, the elegant resort village of Beaver Creek offers fabulous shopping, art galleries, restaurants, and accommodations. Add that to the wide array of summer and winter outdoor activities available in the area and you'll have a getaway you'll treasure for a lifetime. Just 12 miles west of Vail, Beaver Creek is home to some of my favorite ski runs and often sees less skier traffic than its neighbor. As in Vail, summertime visitors ride the chairlift to exciting hiking and biking opportunities. Beaver Creek and the nearby one-lift Arrowhead and Bachelor Gulch ski areas recall the pseudo-Tyrolean architecture of Vail and Lionshead. To get to Beaver Creek, take I-70 West to the Avon exit (167) and turn left. Drive south through the town of Avon past US 6, proceed past the guard stand, and wind up the hill to the village.

The small town of Eagle anchors the western edge of the Vail Valley. Though Eagle is only 27 miles west of Vail, it's rural atmosphere makes it seem like a century away. Eagle is a laid-back community known for outstanding fishing and recreation. So get off the I-70 fast track and try fishing on the Eagle River. Eagle's airport services flights from across the country, a convenient option for vacationers wishing to circumvent Denver International Airport and the long haul up I-70 in order to maximize their time in the high country. To get to Eagle, take I-70 west to the Eagle exit (147).

History

Opened in 1980, the Beaver Creek Ski Area has added more than 1,600 acres of skiable terrain to the Vail Valley. In recent years, it has also added mass quantities of prime real estate and luxurious amenities such as escalators that whisk skiers and riders up the steep hillside to the lifts at the base of the mountain (no joke!). Gerald and Betty Ford have called Beaver Creek home for some time now, and to enjoy world-class art exhibits and performances, all they (and you) have to do is stop by the Vilar Center for the Arts, a prestigious enhancement to the village's cultural scene.

Beaver Creek

Main Attractions

GOLF

There are four outstanding golf courses in the Beaver Creek area. The challenging **Beaver Creek Resort Golf Club** winds down the valley from the foot of the ski area. *For more information and tee times: 970-845-5775.* The beautiful **Eagle-Vail Golf Course** presents a number of hazards, including the Eagle River. Located off I-70 west of the Minturn exit (171), just off US 6, Eagle-Vail Golf Course is one of the most reasonably priced courses in the Vail Valley. *970-949-5267, www.eaglevail.org.* Patterned on a Scottish design, the **Sonnenalp Golf Course** is 7 miles west of Beaver Creek near Edwards. *970-477-5370, www.sonnenalp.com.* The most beautiful golf course in the area is the challenging **Eagle Ranch Golf Course** in Eagle. Designed by Arnold Palmer, these links embody mountain golf at its best. To get there, take I-70 West to the Eagle exit (147), then go south on the connecting road. Turn right (west) on US 6 and go about 1 mile. Turn left on Sylvan Lake Road at the Eagle Ranch entrance. *970-328-2882, 866-328-3232, www.eagleranch.com.*

WINTER SPORTS

Beaver Creek offers runs suited to all skill levels. The beginner runs aren't stuck at the bottom of the ski area, and such double-black-diamond runs as the Birds of Prey series challenge international competitors. Many skiers prefer Beaver Creek to **Vail** because of the shorter lift lines. (My personal favorite is high-speed Chair 12, which accesses terrain for advanced skiers, so you'll rarely wait in line.) Try Royal Elk run for some of the best glade skiing in Colorado. Beaver Creek is a full-service ski area, offering snowboarding as well as skiing, with lessons for all skill levels. Lift tickets are interchangeable with those for Vail. *888-830-7669, www.beavercreek.com.*

Cross-country skiers and snowshoers can ride the Strawberry Park lift (Chair 12) to the top of Beaver Creek Mountain, where 20 miles of trails await you at **McCoy Park.** Lessons are also available. *970-845-5313, www.beavercreek.com.* More mountaintop cross-country experiences can be had at the **Cordillera Nordic Center,** with 12 miles of groomed cross-country track adjacent to the Lodge and Spa at Cordillera, a superb luxury accommodation in Edwards. To get to the Nordic center, take I-70 to the Edwards exit (163) and go left (south). Follow the signs to Cordillera. *970-926-5100, www.cordillera-vail.com.*

Activities

AVON RECREATION CENTER

A great place to take the family, the Avon Recreation Center has public tennis courts, an outdoor swimming pool, a

Pass on its way east to Leadville. FR 400 is unique for its views of the west side of the Holy Cross Wilderness and its snowcapped peaks, as well as for its pockets of aspen trees that stand isolated on distant ridges. The road is relatively rough and parts of it get extremely slick when wet, mandating four-wheel drive. In dry conditions, however, a passenger car will work (if you don't love it that much).

May and September are my favorite months to drive and photograph along this road, when the aspen don their seasonal light green or yellow attire. There are a number of places along the road between the pass and the Fryingpan where you can compose aspen groves in the foreground with snowcapped peaks of the Holy Cross Wilderness behind. The aspen are wonderful anomalies of color against open, grassy ridges. Add Colorado's deep blue skies to the scene, and it all becomes a photographer's delight. Just past Crooked Creek Reservoir, take a detour along FR 507 to Woods Lake. From here you may take a lovely day hike into the Holy Cross Wilderness and up to Eagle Lake.

The descent to the Fryingpan River provides views of the Hunter-Fryingpan Wilderness and its high peaks to the south. Once down to the river, head west to Ruedi Reservoir or east toward Hagerman Pass. The Fryingpan is famous for its trout fishing, but the views aren't half-bad either. Meadows and wetlands along the river make for great photographs. FR 400 is closed in winter, so slap on a pair of backcountry skis and head up to any number of huts in the vicinity that are part of the 10th Mountain Division Hut System, including the Gates, the Peter Estin, and the Polar Star Inn.

29 SCENIC LOCATION — CROOKED CREEK PASS

Brush Creek Road becomes Forest Road 400 several miles before you reach Sylvan Lake State Park heading south. Four miles past the lake you ascend Crooked Creek Pass and then descend a circuitous dirt road to the Fryingpan River and Fryingpan Road. The Fryingpan Road originates to the west at the town of Basalt and eventually ascends Hagerman giant waterslide, an aquatic play area for kids, and a leisure pool with fountains and bubblers. To get to the center, take I-70 west to the Avon exit (167). Turn right onto Avon Road, then right on West Beaver Creek Boulevard. *970-748-4060, www.avon.org/reccenter.cfm.*

FISHING

The **Eagle River** has excellent fishing for rainbow, brown, brook, and cutthroat trout. Access the confluence of Gore Creek and the Eagle River at Dowds Junction (I-70 Exit 171), or fish Squaw Creek, 3 miles west of Edwards on US 6. Three excellent fly-fishing shops in the Beaver Creek area provide lessons, guided fishing trips, and access to private waters. *For more information: Fly-Fishing Outfitters, Beaver Creek, 970-476-3474, 800-595-8090, www.flyfishingoutfitters.net; Gorsuch Outfitters, on the Riverwalk at Edwards, 0097 Main St., Unit E102, 970-926-0900, 877-926-0900, www.gorsuch-outfitters.com.*

GALLERIES

As a world-class resort, Beaver Creek offers many fine art galleries. The **C. Anthony Gallery** has contemporary works on display by such internationally known artists as Anton Arkhipov, Earl Biss, Frederick Hart, and Rabby Max. The C. Anthony Gallery features exhibits by Rembrandt, Dürer, Dalí, Chagall, and others. *970-845-8645.* The **McClure Gallery,** *970-748-0600,* features the paintings and sculptures of established and emerging international artists, including one of my favorites, Edward Aldrich. Ned (as he likes to be called) does incredibly detailed oil paintings of wildlife. The **Pismo Gallery at Beaver Creek** offers the finest in contemporary art glass, including works by Dale Chihuly. *970-949-0908.* You'll find these three galleries on Market Square in Beaver Creek. The **Philinda Gallery,** located at the Riverwalk in Edwards, displays unique sculptures and paintings from local and national artists. *970-926-9265, www.philinda-gallery.com.*

Because I treasure Southwestern art, one of my favorite galleries is the **Mudhead Gallery,** *970-949-1333,* located at the Promenade–Park Hyatt in Beaver Creek. Mudhead features Hopi kachinas, Pueblo pottery, Navajo weavings, American Indian bronzes, and an extensive collection of traditional and contemporary American Indian jewelry.

HORSEBACK RIDING

At **Bearcat Stables,** you can saddle up for a reasonably priced, one-hour to full-day horseback ride. As you mosey along, guides share stories about the history of the area. Elk, deer, and birds of prey are common sights in the pine stands and aspen groves. Bearcat Stables also offers carriage rides, wagon rides, and, in winter, sleigh rides. Because the carriage rides are offered at various restaurants in Cordillera, you can combine your riding experience with fine dining. The wagon ride (and winter sleigh ride) takes place at sunset and is followed by dinner at the Timber Hearth Grille. To get to Bearcat Stables, take I-70 west to the Edwards exit (163). Go left (south) and turn right at the light (US 6). Turn left on Squaw Creek Road and drive 2.7 miles. The stables are on the right. *970-926-1578, www.bearcatstables.com.*

The **4 Eagle Ranch,** 10 miles east of Eagle, was home-steaded in the late 1800s and remains a working ranch. Operated by Triple G Outfitters, the ranch offers horseback riding options ranging from daily rides for beginners to Western Performance Rides, which provide experienced riders with the best performance horses for a custom experience. Triple G Outfitters also has a half-day cattle roundup and a combination Saddle and Paddle (riding and rafting) trip. Kids will love exploring the working ranch, trying their hands at roping, and meeting the buffalo and farm animals. From I-70, take the Wolcott exit (157) and go 4 miles north on CO 131. *970-926-1234, www.tripleg.net.*

Restaurants

The world-class restaurants at Beaver Creek have attracted the talents of award-winning chefs who pride themselves on creative dishes featuring steak, trout, lamb, seafood, and wild game. Situated at the base of the Larkspur Lift, **Beano's Cabin** ($$$$), *970-949-9090,* is certainly an experience. Guests meet their horse-drawn wagon or sleigh at a designated pickup point for a moonlit ride to the restaurant. You can start with a variety of appetizers, then choose from roasted young duckling, rainbow trout, grilled venison, or Colorado rack of lamb. Reservations are a must. On the Plaza in Beaver Creek, the **Golden Eagle** ($$-$$$$), *970-949-1940,* provides a contemporary American menu. Try the unusual "dinner starters," such as the red deer–scallion empanada or the freshwater eel and avocado roll. **Splendido** ($$$-$$$$) has some of the most creative appetizers and desserts in Beaver Creek; it's located at The Château. *17 Château Ln., 970-845-8808.* For down-home prices, try the **Dusty Boot Steakhouse & Saloon** ($-$$$), *970-748-1146,* at St. James Place in Beaver Creek. You can start off with the gigantic Dusty Boot nachos or the Wild West chipotle wings guaranteed to be "hot as hell." If you have room, build your own burger (beef or buffalo), order chops or a Colorado BLT, and finish up with Kentucky bourbon pecan pie.

I have a great affection for Italian food, and my favorite Italian restaurant in Beaver Creek is **TraMonti** ($$$), located in the Charter at Beaver Creek. TraMonti offers superb veal dishes and creative pizzas, but my favorite is the pasta puttanesca. *120 Offerson Rd., 970-949-5552.* On Market Square in Beaver Creek, **Toscanini** ($$$), *970-845-5590,* provides an incredible antipasti menu.

Mirabelle ($$$), *970-949-7728,* offers cuisine with a French flair. The restaurant sits at the base of Beaver Creek Mountain, before you make the winding drive up to the village. At the Country Club of the Rockies in Arrowhead, the **Vista at Arrowhead** ($$$$), *970-926-2111,* serves up "creative American" appetizers, entrees, and seafood dishes with Pacific Rim accents.

BRUSH CREEK

As of the writing of this book in 2002, the last undeveloped tributary of the Eagle River was Brush Creek. I am not confident that it will remain that way. If it does, take advantage of it. Brush Creek originates high in the New York Mountains of the Holy Cross Wilderness before descending to irrigate a beautiful, wide valley of hay meadows that runs for 10 miles. This area is slated to become suburban Eagle. Even if it does, more scenery to the south and east will not be developed (see Scenic Location No. 29, p. 121). To get to Brush Creek, head west on I-70 from Vail to the town of Eagle (Exit 147). Drive south through town and look for the Brush Creek Road signs. Head south.

Brush Creek is bounded by ranch meadows to the north and cottonwood and aspen trees farther to the south. It's especially pretty here in May and September, when leaves are light green and yellow, respectively. In about 15 minutes you'll arrive at the East Brush Creek turnoff on the left, Forest Road 415, which takes you up to the old town of Fulford. This side valley is spectacular with amazing wetlands now protected by Sylvan Lake State Park. Go back to Brush Creek Road and continue south to Sylvan Lake. Though you find quite a few campsites and structures, the view looking down at the lake from FR 400 is superb.

Because Brush Creek drains to the north, the sun is always at right angles to the scenery in the valley. Called side lighting, sunrise and sunset illuminate leaves on trees and grasses in the fields in a way that makes them glow. In cloudy light, East Brush Creek contrasts beautifully with the willows along its banks (see pp. 100–102, *Photographing the Landscape*). Red sandstone cliffs create a red road as you rise above Sylvan Lake, great to photograph as a color complement (or opposite) to the green aspen all around.

At **Pazzo's** ($), you can create your own pizza or order from a variety of calzones. *82 E. Beaver Creek Blvd., Avon, 970-949-9900.*

Owned by sisters Debbie and Susan Marquez, **Fiesta's! Café & Cantina** ($$), *970-926-2121,* brings the traditional recipes of their New Mexican great-grandparents to the Vail Valley. The restaurant, in the Edwards Plaza, also prides itself in stocking more than 20 kinds of tequila. A longtime stand-by in Edwards, **The Gashouse** ($$) serves up seafood, steaks, and wild game in a renovated 1940s log cabin filling station. *34185 US 6, 970-926-3613.* Set high above the Vail Valley in Cordillera Resort, **Mirador** lives up to its artful name with acclaimed gourmet French cuisine, live piano music, and an art-filled decor. *2205 Cordillera Way, Edwards, 970-926-2200.*

The happening place in Eagle is the authentically Western **Brush Creek Saloon** ($) on the main drag. *241 Broadway, 970-328-5279.*

Accommodations

Accommodations in the Beaver Creek area are expensive, but they are elegant. As in most ski towns, you're more likely to get bargains on rates in late spring, summer, and fall. My favorite place to stay for the past 15 years has been the **Park Hyatt Beaver Creek** ($$$$). The service here is as good as it gets—valets will even release your bindings when you ski down for lunch! *970-949-1234, 800-233-1234.* Colorado's newest luxury mountain resort—and the most expensive hotel ever built here—is the slopeside **Ritz-Carlton Bachelor Gulch** ($$$$). Whether you're relaxing in the grotto-like spa, dining in the fine restaurant, or just kicking back by the three-story stone fireplace, you'll find that the staff caters to your every need. *0130 Daybreak Ridge, Avon, 970-748-6200, www.ritzcarlton.com.* Perched high above the valley, the **Lodge and Spa at Cordillera** ($$$$), adjacent to the Cordillera Nordic Center, is built in the tradition of a European mountain château. Most rooms have fireplaces, balconies, and extraordinary mountain views. The lodge also offers a full-service spa with hot tubs and a pool providing great views of the surrounding peaks. To get there, take I-70 west to the Edwards exit (163) and follow the signs to the Cordillera Nordic Center. *970-569-6480, 800-877-3529, www.cordillera-vail.com.* The **Charter at Beaver Creek** ($$$$) is an elegant ski-in/ski-out European lodge with a full-service spa and spectacular views. *120 Offerson Rd., 970-949-6660, www.thecharter.com.* The **Beaver Creek Lodge** ($$$-$$$$) in the heart of Beaver Creek describes itself as "a quaint, small hotel surrounded by world-class skiing." *26 Avondale Ln., 970-845-9800, 800-525-7280, www.beavercreeklodge.net.* Located on Village Road, the **Inn at Beaver Creek** ($$$-$$$$) is less than 4 yards from the Strawberry Park Lift and offers all the amenities of resort lodging. *970-845-7800, 800-859-8242.* The **Pines Lodge** ($$$-$$$$) is another ski-in/ski-out accommodation with all the amenities and spectacular views of the valley. There is even a ski shop on the premises. *141 Scott Hill Rd., 970-745-7200.*

You can get much better rates, particularly in the summer, if you stay in nearby Avon or Edwards. In Avon, the **Christie Lodge** ($-$$) offers all the amenities of a more expensive resort for less money. *47 E. Beaver Creek Blvd., 970-949-7700, www.christielodge.com.* At 27 Main St. in the heart of Edwards, **The Inn and Suites at Riverwalk** ($$-$$$$) sits adjacent to the Eagle River. *970-926-0606, www.innandsuitesatriverwalk.com.*

Special Events

In summer, the **Bravo! Vail Valley Music Festival** brings classical music to the Vilar Center for the Arts in Beaver Creek and the Gerald R. Ford Amphitheater in Vail. See Special Events in the Vail section, p. 119, for details.

One of the valley's most anticipated events is the annual **Eagle County Fair and Rodeo,** held the first week in August at the Eagle County Fairgrounds in Eagle. This event, more than 60 years old, draws some of the top cowhands in the country as they make their way through the Mountain States Circuit and shoot for a spot in the National Finals Rodeo. As exciting as the rodeo is, the competition is just as hot among the local pie bakers and 4-H competitors. To get to the fairgrounds, take I-70 west to the Eagle exit (147). Turn right at the stoplight after the overpass. *For more information and tickets: 970-328-8600, www.eagle-county.com/fair_rodeo.cfm.*

For More Information

Vail Valley Partnership, *101 Fawcett Rd., Suite 240, Avon, 970-476-1000, www.visitvailvalley.com.* Eagle Visitor Center, off I-70 at the Eagle exit (147) in Chambers Park, *970-328-5220, www.eaglecounty.us.*

Glenwood Springs

(see map on p. 126)

Departing the Vail Valley, I-70 West enters one of the most gorgeous and accessible canyons in Colorado, Glenwood Canyon. Mother Nature is responsible for the steep, limestone canyon walls cut by the Colorado River millions of years ago, and human genius for the road engineering that made this natural wonder available to all. I still marvel at it every time I drive through. (And, oh yes, one piece of advice from personal experience: The Colorado State Patrol is serious about enforcing the speed limit.)

As beautiful as the canyon is, I'm always grateful to "take the waters," as early visitors used to say, in the Glenwood Hot Springs Pool. Whether suffering from sore ski muscles or from hauling 60 pounds of camera equipment around the mountains, I find the warmth of the waters just the right therapy for relaxing. After a good soak in the springs, it's a Fielder family tradition to enjoy an Italian meal in town. If you go, you'll also find this a congenial combination.

History

The town of Glenwood Springs owes its existence to those wonderful waters. The Utes had long used the hot springs and their vapors for healing. But in 1883 Walter Devereux, who made a fortune from Aspen's silver mines, put the town on the map when he decided to develop the hot springs area as a resort town. Originally named Defiance, it became a rowdy place with the likes of Doc Holliday frequenting the barrooms and card tables. The raucous behavior upset proper citizens of the community and led a pioneer's wife to change the town's name from Defiance to Glenwood (after her Iowa hometown). The arrival of the railroad in 1887 and the completion of the luxurious Hotel Colorado in 1893 ensured access to and accommodations for the hot springs, and the rich and famous from throughout the world began to come to Glenwood Springs. Today, the springs are more approachable than ever, via the amazing I-70 corridor through Glenwood Canyon.

Main Attractions

GLENWOOD CANYON

If the sheer 1,800-foot cliffs cut by the Colorado River are a feat of nature, then the 12.5 miles of canyon road—including tunnels through solid rock and stacked fly-bys—are a feat of human ingenuity. You can choose from several ways to see this splendid canyon, and each offers its own perspective: by car, by rail, by bike,

or by foot. The **Glenwood Canyon Recreation Trail** EASY follows the Colorado River and I-70 for 16 miles, from the Vapor Caves at the east end of Glenwood Springs to Dotsero. Residents and visitors regularly hike, bike, and in-line skate this path year-round, though heavy snowmelts in spring can flood it in sections. Four rest areas in the canyon offer riverside picnicking sites from which you can watch rafters and kayakers floating downstream. *For bike rentals, and bike shuttle service: Canyon Bikes, 970-945-8904, 800-439-3043, www.canyonbikes.com.*

For a taste of Colorado's transportation heritage and an entirely different perspective of Glenwood Canyon, take the railroad from Denver to Glenwood Springs aboard Amtrak. *800-872-7245.*

A must-hike is **Hanging Lake** MODERATE, but beware: The 1.2-mile one-way trail climbs steeply. Also expect a lot of company, as it is one of the area's most popular hikes, with good reason (see Scenic Location No. 33, p. 130). Take the Hanging Lake exit (125) off either I-70 East or West.

GLENWOOD CAVERNS

An unforgettable destination for the whole family is the **Glenwood Caverns Adventure Park.** These limestone caves originally opened to the public in 1886. Locals called them the Eighth Wonder of the World, and a wonder they are. The tour winds through caverns, grottos, and labyrinths of stone. Among the features are Exclamation Point, a cliffside balcony with panoramic views of Glenwood Canyon; The Barn, a five-story cave room; and King's Row, a cavern filled with glittering stalagmites and stalactites. Don a lighted helmet and follow a guide to rarely visited and newly discovered areas deep within the caves on the Wild Tour. The cave office is next to the Hotel Colorado, the caves a shuttle ride away. In addition to the cave tours, the park has recently added five new attractions, including a 4-D theater (the only one in Colorado), a new laser tag arena, The Speleobox Cave Simulator, a ride called The Giddy Up!, and the Mine Shaft Shootin' Gallery, an electronic shooting gallery with animation. The more adventurous can't miss one of the park's older favorites, the Swing Shot, a ride that shoots guests out over the canyon for breathtaking views at speeds up to fifty miles an hour. *970-945-4228, 800-530-1635, www.glenwoodcaverns.com.*

Glenwood Hot Springs

Glenwood Springs

Colorado Atlas & Gazetteer pp. 35–36, 46

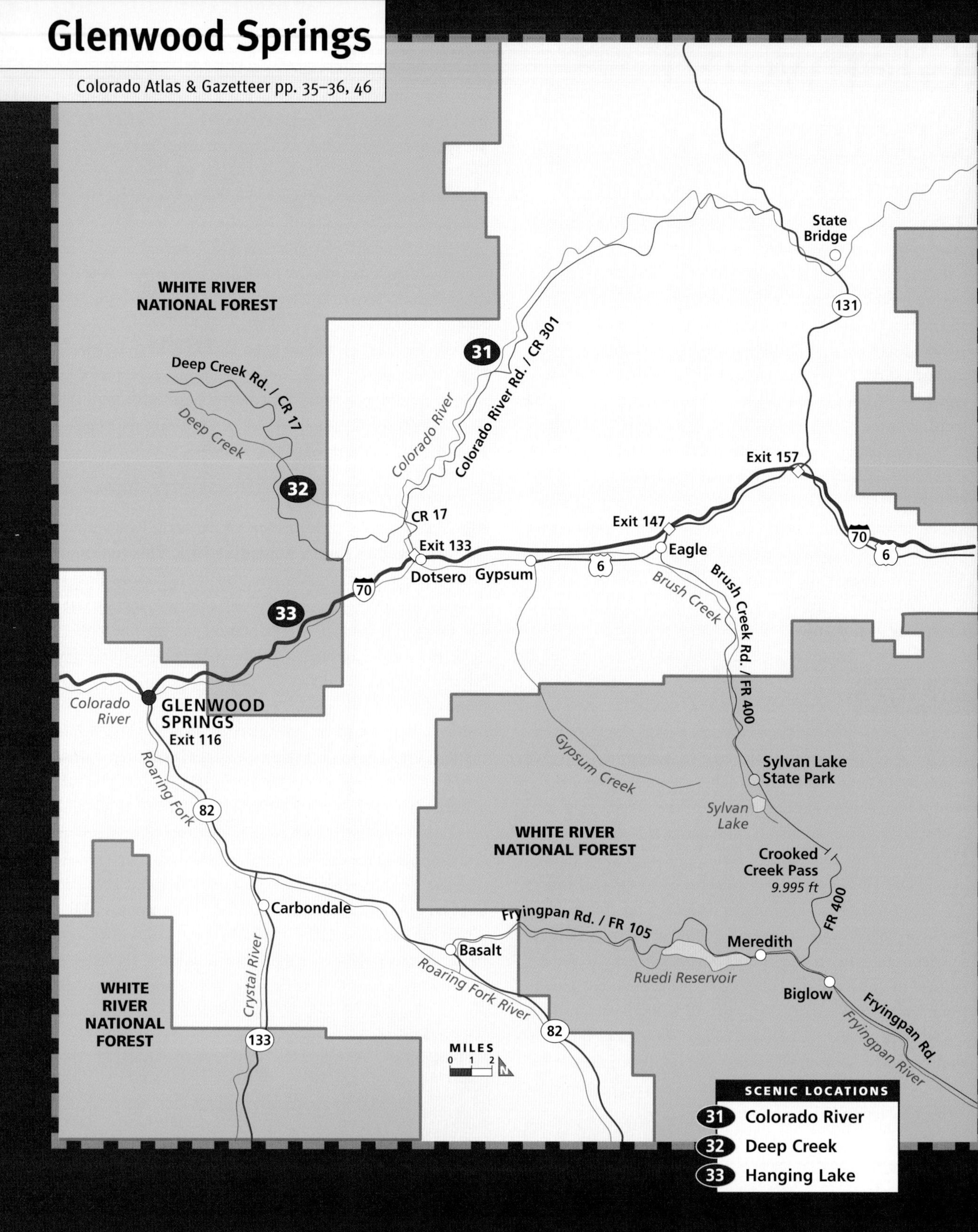

State Bridge
131
WHITE RIVER NATIONAL FOREST
31
Colorado River Rd. / CR 301
Colorado River
Deep Creek Rd. / CR 17
Deep Creek
32
CR 17
Exit 157
Exit 147
Exit 133
Eagle
70
6
Dotsero
Gypsum
Brush Creek
Brush Creek Rd. / FR 400
33
Colorado River
GLENWOOD SPRINGS
Exit 116
Roaring Fork
82
Gypsum Creek
Sylvan Lake State Park
Sylvan Lake
WHITE RIVER NATIONAL FOREST
Crooked Creek Pass
9.995 ft
FR 400
Carbondale
Fryingpan Rd. / FR 105
Meredith
Basalt
Ruedi Reservoir
Biglow
Roaring Fork River
Crystal River
Fryingpan Rd.
Fryingpan River
WHITE RIVER NATIONAL FOREST
133
82
MILES
0 1 2
N
SCENIC LOCATIONS
31 Colorado River
32 Deep Creek
33 Hanging Lake

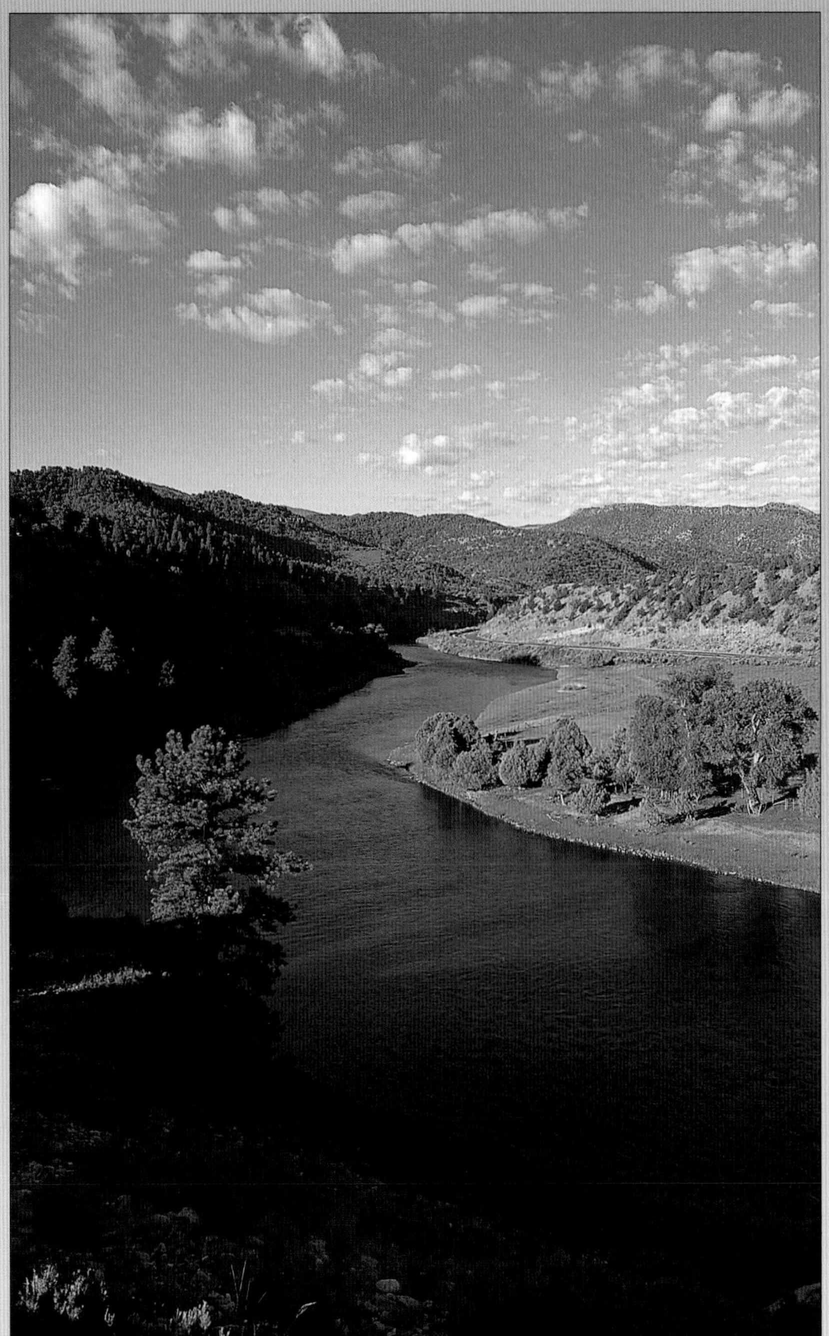

However, the river is not alone. The Union Pacific Railroad and the Colorado River Road (County Road 301) also occupy this route west. Nevertheless, the scenery, fishing, camping, photography, and floating are superb. In fact, the 46-mile river trip from CO 131 to I-70 is one of my favorites. I know this stretch better from my raft than I do from my car.

To begin the drive at the east end, exit I-70 at Wolcott (Exit 157) and drive north 10 miles on CO 131 to the recreational community of State Bridge along the river. Continue north on CO 131; 6 miles later, make a left onto Colorado River Road at the town of McCoy. This dirt road follows the Colorado River all the way to Dotsero on I-70, a few miles east of Glenwood Canyon.

I can make a favorite composition along the river when I find a hill or bluff elevated above the road that allows me to look up or down the river. Twenty feet of elevation above the river is enough to see it narrow in the distance down to nothing. This parallax distortion allows the river to lead your eye into the infiniteness of the scene, thereby creating a great sense of depth and distance. A two-dimensional photograph often lacks the depth that we see with two eyes; this use of perspective is a fine way to restore it. The river not only runs through canyons but also bisects lovely hay fields, so you have the chance to make images of relative wildness, as well as of bucolic ranching scenes, each defined by the bold line of the river.

The river runs northeast to southwest, so the sun never really projects light in parallel with the river. Nevertheless, shooting toward or away from the sun at the end of the day will create different effects on film. The river reflects more glare off its surface when the sun is in front of you, less when the sun is behind you. When you photograph into the sun, the river appears silvery and more prominent as a shape against the greenery along its banks. With the sun behind you, the river appears darker, in shades of blue and green, and less conspicuous within the whole landscape.

Shooting in cloudy light, or waiting until the sun descends behind canyon walls, allows more detail in white cascades to be recorded on film. Direct sunlight on the color white usually washes out detail, so don't be shy about photographing in the middle of the day when afternoon clouds cover the blue sky. Come to photograph in this place year-round. Make it a point to drive this route in all four seasons, as so much deciduous plant life colors the riverbanks.

31 SCENIC LOCATION — COLORADO RIVER

When I think of the Colorado River, I visualize three different rivers—and that's only in the state of Colorado. Its personality changes a few more times as it proceeds into Utah, Arizona, and California. In Rocky Mountain National Park (see Scenic Location No. 47, p. 169) it's only a creek draining from the park's high country. From Glenwood Springs to the Utah border, it's mostly an irrigation canal. But from State Bridge to Dotsero, it's a real mountain river. Spruce, fir, ponderosa pines, cottonwoods—these native trees line the river as it sometimes dawdles, sometimes plunges, westward through deep canyons.

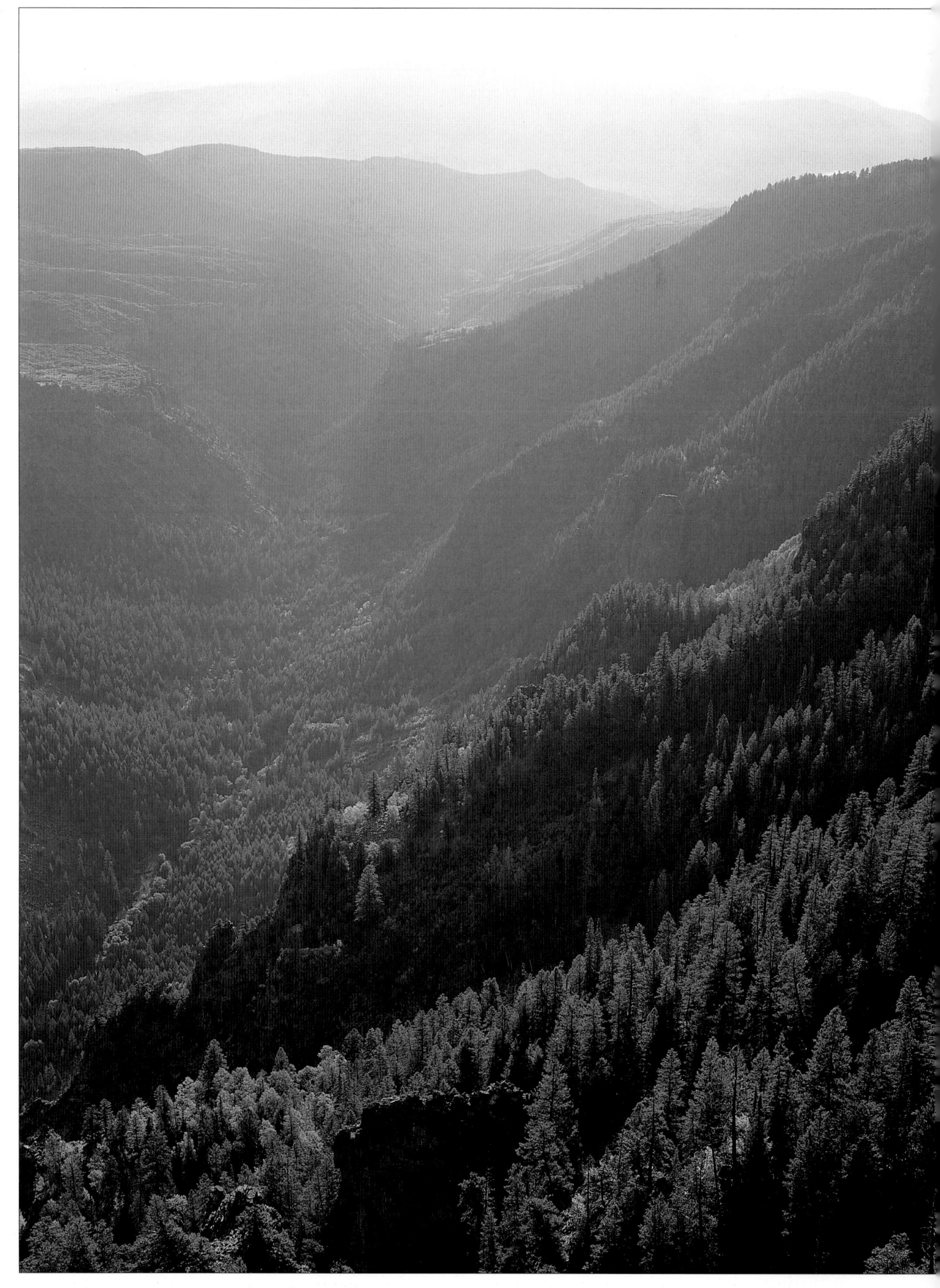

32 SCENIC LOCATION — DEEP CREEK

The Eagle and Colorado rivers meet at the town of Dotsero along I-70 just a few miles before entering Glenwood Canyon from the east. Deep Creek enters the Colorado only 2 miles north of Dotsero. A beautiful road parallels Deep Creek on its south side to Heart Lake in the White River National Forest and comes very close to the Flat Tops Wilderness to the north. The road begins as County Road 17 and becomes Forest Road 600. It's a pretty good road for passenger cars all the way to Heart Lake.

Deep Creek is aptly named—most of it lies deep within a forested canyon made of limestone, the stuff of ancient ocean floors. In fact, from Deep Lake to the Colorado River, Deep Creek plunges 4,500 feet in a span of only 15 miles. Limestone is ideal for cave formation, so it's no surprise that more than 40 exist in the canyon.

Aspen, spruce, and fir cover the highest reaches of Deep Creek. The road runs close to the south rim of the canyon, with many beautiful overlooks along the way. Because the canyon runs east-west, sunrise and sunset make for great photographs: As the sun casts shadows from ridges extending into the canyon, it enhances the canyon's depth. Gray limestone outcrops catch the yellow light of the end of the day to create color contrast against the green forested walls. A wide-angle lens will capture on film the entire canyon with sky and horizon; a telephoto is useful for zooming in on limestone outcrops. Primitive roads and trails emanate from the Heart Lake area into and around the Flat Tops Wilderness. These make for great day hikes as well as overnight backpacks into this 12,000-foot, "flattopped" wilderness.

In some ways, Deep Creek Canyon is like the next limestone canyon to the south, Glenwood Canyon. Deep Creek isn't the Colorado River, but the limestone walls are the same; better yet, it doesn't have a highway and a railroad running right through it!

GLENWOOD SPRINGS WHITEWATER PARK

Newly opened in 2008, the **Glenwood Springs Whitewater Park** has been gaining recognition worldwide and was even selected to host the 2009 Freestyle Kayaking U.S. Team Trials. The park is the first man-made whitewater rafting feature built along the Colorado River and uses the naturally occurring river flow and artificial boulders to create "standing waves." There are also learning pools and areas for beginner kayakers to practice ferrying and rolling before entering the waves. *www.glenwoodwhitewaterpark.org*

HOT SPRINGS

As the Utes were drawn to these waters, so are we. The great pool at **Glenwood Hot Springs** is so vast that you can catch a whiff of sulphur vapors from the highway. In fact, at nearly two blocks long, Glenwood Hot Springs is the largest outdoor hot springs pool in the world. A consistent 90–93 degrees, the main pool can hold a million gallons, and 3.5 million gallons flow through it daily. The adjacent soaking pool, complete with bubbling jets, is an intense 104 degrees. After a day of physical activity, have a restorative soak here: It's open year-round.

Glenwood Hot Springs even has its own ghost, Agnes. Locals report that Agnes goes bump in the night and things disappear, so watch your towel. To get to the hot springs, go west on I-70, take Exit 116, turn right, and drive a block to the stoplight (Village Inn is on your left). Turn right onto 6th Street. Go past the Hotel Colorado and turn right at the edge of the pool grounds. (If you don't feel crowded in the large pool, you may still feel crowded in the parking lot.) *970-945-6571, 800-537-SWIM, www.hotspringspool.com.*

Glenwood Hot Springs has now added the **Spa of the Rockies** to its growing list of attractions. Glenwood Springs's newest spa draws its inspiration from the thermal mineral waters of the Hot Springs Pool and features mineral based treatments to promote health and vitality. *For more information: 970-947-3331, www.spaoftherockies.com.*

Yampah Spa Vapor Caves are the only known natural vapor caves in the country. Vapor caves occur where hot springs coat caves with water, steam, and heat. The Utes used the caves for healing purposes and religious ceremonies. Today the Yampah Spa offers salon services such as massage, facials, and body treatments. A novel experience, but note: The smell can be very pungent. Follow directions to the Glenwood Hot Springs Pool. Drive past the pool and left into the parking lot. *970-945-0667, www.yampahspa.com.*

RIO GRANDE RECREATIONAL TRAIL

One of the area's newest attractions for outdoor enthusiasts is the **Rio Grande Recreational Trail.** This 44-mile trail stretches from Glenwood Springs to Aspen, passing through Carbondale, Basalt, and Woody Creek. The route is relatively flat with some light hills and a two percent grade. Thirty-three miles of the trail are paved and the remaining eleven miles are soft-surface dirt. *For more information and a map of the trail: www.rfta.com/trailmap.pdf*

Activities

FISHING

You have several good options for fishing here, including the **Eagle River** between the Eagle County Fairgrounds in Eagle and the BLM campground west of Gypsum. **Sylvan Lake,** 16 miles south of the town of Eagle on West Brush Creek Road, is also stocked with brookies and rainbows. *For equipment, lessons, or guided fishing trips: Roaring Fork Anglers, 970-945-0180, www.roaringforkanglers.com.*

The **Colorado River** through Glenwood Canyon also boasts good trout fishing. Sizable trout have been caught at the Grizzly Creek Rest Area and at the bridge at New Castle, 12 miles west of Glenwood Springs. The **Roaring Fork River** flows

HANGING LAKE

About 6 miles west of Dotsero on I-70, and well inside Glenwood Canyon, are the Hanging Lake exits (125). From the parking lot, a 1.2-mile hike and a 1,000-foot vertical gain separate you from the "lake," actually a pond. You can reach it in under an hour. A geologic fault created the bench that holds Hanging Lake, fed by a series of cascades and waterfalls in Dead Horse Creek. Two hundred yards above the lake is Spouting Rock, where the creek shoots out of a hole in the limestone cliff. As is the case with Deep Creek Canyon, the walls of Glenwood Canyon and its side canyons are riddled with caves and other features unique to the water-reactive limestone.

Hanging Lake is unique for its blue-green water and for the abundant plant life that clings to the limestone cliffs around the lake. The water from the creek seeps, drips, and pours into the lake along a wide wall of rock and gives the entire setting a paradisiacal atmosphere. The deciduous plants are light green in May, darker green during the summer, and take on fall colors in late September and October (see pp. 42–43, *Photographing the Landscape*).

I suggest waiting for clouds to block the sun before photographing the pond and waterfalls. Direct light in the canyon creates deep shadows and intense highlights at the same time —impossible for the film to record. Film has about one-third the contrast range capability of our eyes, so the highlights get brighter and the shadows darker. The result is a loss of detail in the image. You can also wait for the sun to descend below the canyon walls; however, the light tends to be bluer, which dulls the brilliant colors of the pond. White clouds covering the entire sky in the afternoon make for ideal light.

For a longer hike, try White River National Forest Trail 1850, which proceeds north from Hanging Lake to Deep Creek Road (see Scenic Location No. 32, p. 129). Hanging Lake is accessible in the winter, but beware: The trail can get very icy, especially along the last and steepest stretch to the lake. A winter trek is well worth the trouble, however, to catch the waterfalls and cascades that freeze into white sculptures.

northwest from its headwaters on Independence Pass to its confluence with the Colorado River in Glenwood Springs. You can follow the Roaring Fork along CO 82 and find good trout-fishing spots from a number of access points. *Roaring Fork Outfitters, 970-945-5800, www.rfoutfitters.com.*

FOUR-WHEEL-DRIVE TRIPS

A half- or full-day jeep tour is an excellent way to get a bird's-eye view of the spectacular canyons and alpine lakes around Glenwood Springs. Knowledgeable tour guides tell of the area's history and wildlife. You will see views of the **Flat Tops Wilderness,** including Deep Creek Overlook (see Scenic Location No. 32, this page), Heart Lake, and Deep Lake. Rock Gardens Rafting offers great packages, including jeep excursions combined variously with rafting, cave, and hot springs tours. *Rock Gardens Rafting, 970-945-6737, 800-958-6737, www.rockgardens.com.*

GOLF

Kids love to visit **Johnson Park Crazy Creeks** for its two 18-hole putt-putt courses, waterfalls, and Skee-ball. *970-945-9608.* Johnson Park is in West Glenwood Springs on US 6. For the more serious golfer, tee off at the scenic and challenging 18-hole **Rifle Creek Golf Course.** Take I-70 to Rifle (Exit 90). Drive north on CO 113, turn right on CO 325, and go 4 miles. *970-625-1093, www.riflecreekgolf.com.* In town, check out the nine-hole municipal golf course at **Glenwood Springs Golf Club.** *193 Sunny Acres Rd, 970-945-7086, www.glenwoodgolf.com.*

HISTORICAL MARKERS

Stop at Two Rivers Park, at US 6 and Two Rivers Park Road, to see the **Fallen Firefighters Memorial** of the 1994 Storm King Mountain wildfire. Started by lightning, this huge wildfire killed 14 firefighters, destroyed 2,100 acres, and threatened the town of Glenwood Springs. We Coloradans owe much to these courageous men and women who put their lives on the line to protect families and homes. To witness the devastation wrought by the fire, drive 2 miles west on I-70 from Glenwood Springs to the Storm King marker and make a 1.5-mile hike **MODERATE** up the mountain.

Fallen Firefighters Memorial, Glenwood Springs

Legendary gunslinger and card shark Doc Holliday died in Glenwood Springs in 1887. A dentist by trade, Holliday came to the West to ease his tuberculosis. He took his last sip of whiskey near the vapor caves in 1887. To visit his grave in the **Pioneer** (formerly **Linwood**) **Cemetery,** park at 12th Street and Palmer Avenue and hike up the hill.

MUSEUM

The **Frontier Historical Museum** traces the growth of Glenwood Springs and the hot springs as a resort. You can also learn about famous residents and visitors like Theodore Roosevelt. *1001 Colorado Ave., 970-945-4448, www.glenwoodhistory.com.*

Colorado River rafting, Glenwood Springs

RAFTING

There is no better way to experience a canyon than on the water. As it flows through Glenwood Canyon, the **Colorado River** makes for great rafting, from the Shoshone Falls power plant through Glenwood Springs to New Castle. The **South Canyon** **EASY**, recommended for families, and the **Little Gore/Red Rock Canyon** **EASY** rafting trips offer great scenery, and even some hot springs, in these remote canyons of the river. For a more challenging rafting trip, float the **Shoshone Falls** **MODERATE**. *For information and reservations: Whitewater Rafting, 970-945-8477, 800-993-RAFT, www.coloradowhitewaterrafting.com, Rock Gardens Rafting, 1308 CR 129, 970-945-6737, www.rockgardens.com, or Blue Sky Adventures, 319 6th St, 970-945-6605, www.blueskyadventure.com.*

No question about it, the Colorado River is *the* place to raft when in the Glenwood Springs area. Still, the **Roaring Fork River** also offers exciting rafting possibilities. Take the full-day Roaring Fork raft trip, which includes the heart-pounding **Entrance Exam** and **Slaughterhouse Falls** **DIFFICULT**.

For less-challenging rafting, float the **Eagle River.** Outfitters offer half- to full-day trips for every age and ability level. First-timers can try the **Lower Eagle** **EASY** trip. **Dowd Chute** **MODERATE**, with its continuous rapids, provides more thrills and chills. *For more information and reservations: Lakota River Guides, 970-845-7238, 800-274-0636, www.lakotariver.com or Nova Guides, 970-827-4232, 888-949-NOVA, or www.novaguides.com.*

THEATRE

The new **Glenwood Vaudeville Revue** held at the Masonic Lodge is great for those seeking a bit of culture and a good laugh. This weekly pub-style dinner theater features a two-hour show complete with song, dance, comedy, skits, and jokes. Shows run weekend evenings, seasonally. *901 Colorado Ave, 970-945-9699, www.GlenwoodVaudevilleRevue.com.*

WINTER SPORTS

Unlike its bigger neighbors, Vail and Aspen, **Sunlight Mountain Resort** is a local, laid-back, family-oriented ski resort with runs ideally suited to beginners and intermediate skiers. Ten miles south of Glenwood Springs on Four Mile Road (County Road 117), the ski area also boasts excellent cross-country trails at the Sunlight Nordic Center. *970-945-7491, 800-445-7931, www.sunlightmtn.com.*

Restaurants

Glenwood Springs' restaurants are noted for their fine food, variety, service, and remarkable locations. Dining on Italian food after a soak in the hot springs is a Fielder family tradition, and you just can't go wrong with any Italian restaurant under the CO 82 bridge. **Florindo's Italian Cuisine** ($$) always fits the bill. *721 Grand Ave., 970-945-1245.* A few doors down, local favorite **Italian Underground Ristorante** ($-$$) has been serving good, down-home Italian cuisine since 1983. *715 Grand Ave., 970-945-6422.* The **Riviera Restaurant** ($$) is a great choice for dinner. Entrées include an eclectic selection of beef, lamb, and seafood dishes. *702 Grand Avenue, 970-945-7692.* For good local dishes, try the **Rivers Restaurant** ($$-$$$) for dinner. Rivers is on the Roaring Fork River next to the Sunlight Bridge off Grand Avenue. *970-928-8813, www.theriversrestaurant.com.*

Florindo's Italian Cuisine, Glenwood Springs

Accommodations

The **Hotel Colorado** ($$-$$$), a remodeled National Historic Landmark, is reasonably priced for the grandeur you can enjoy there. Built in 1893, this stately structure became the first Western White House when Theodore Roosevelt was president. During World War II, the Navy converted the hotel (because of its proximity to the hot springs) into a hospital. Not only presidents but notables from all over the world have stayed here, just across the street from the hot springs pool on Pine Street. *970-945-6511, 800-544-3998, www.hotelcolorado.com.* The **Hotel Denver** ($-$$) is less expensive, well-appointed, and just across from the Denver & Rio Grande Railroad depot. President William Taft refused to enter Glenwood from the depot on account of its proximity to saloons and the red-light district. (The neighborhood has since been cleaned up.) *402 7th St., 970-945-6565, 800-826-8820, www.thehoteldenver.com.* You can also look into the award-winning **Lavender & Thyme** ($-$$) at 802 Palmer Ave. *970-945-8289, www.lavenderthyme.com.*

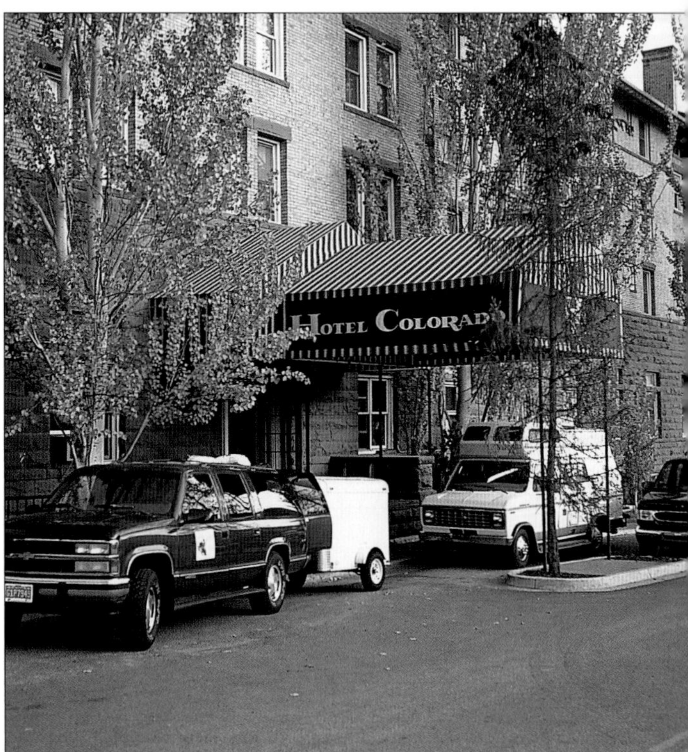

Hotel Colorado, Glenwood Springs

Kids will love staying at the **Red Mountain Inn** ($-$$) adjacent to Johnson Park Crazy Creeks. The rooms are spacious, and some even have fireplaces. *970-945-6353, 800-748-2565, www.redmountaininn.com.*

In Rifle, rest and recreate at the family-owned **Coulter Lake Guest Ranch** ($$) within the White River National Forest. Various ranch activities include horseback riding, fishing, swimming, hiking, jeep trips, snowmobiling, and cross-country skiing. *970-625-1473, 800-858-3046, www.coulterlake.com.*

Special Events

During the summer months, nationally known jazz musicians strut their stuff every Wednesday evening at the **Summer of Jazz,** held at the Two Rivers Park band shell. Glenwood Springs has been celebrating its **Strawberry Days Festival** for more than 100 years with rides, live music, and races—did I forget to mention free strawberries and ice cream? The event is usually held the third weekend in June. *970-945-6589, www.glenwoodchamber.com.*

Held in August in Rifle, the **Garfield County Fair** includes the Cheatin' Woodchuck Chase, Little Miss Fair Days Contest, the Fair Days Parade, and the Fair Barbecue. *970-625-2085.*

For More Information

Glenwood Springs Chamber Resort Association, *1102 Grand Ave., 970-945-6589, www.glenwoodchamber.com.*

Grand Junction

(see map on p. 134)

The Grand Valley is a region of dramatic contrasts. As you descend into Grand Junction on I-70 West, the massive, gray, and stark Book Cliffs (see Scenic Location No. 38, p. 141) loom to your right. To your left grow the lush orchards and vineyards that have made this area famous. Compare the dry and rugged canyonlands of Colorado National Monument against the lakes and subalpine forests of the Grand Mesa to the east. The growing city of Grand Junction exudes a modern feeling in contrast with the ancient aura of nearby dinosaur fossil sites. While some think of the Grand Valley as just an overnight stay or departure point for places farther west, mountain-biking enthusiasts, among others, know and love the special nature of this region. Come enjoy the diversity here and discover why the Grand Valley makes a great destination in its own right.

History

Grand Junction takes its name from the confluence of the Gunnison and Colorado rivers. (Western settlers originally called the Colorado the Grand River.) In spite of some economic boom-and-bust times with the oil industry, Grand Junction has produced a healthy and clean economic base in tourism and agriculture. The town's prosperity and milder climate have lured many Coloradans to retire here. The Grand Valley surrounding Grand Junction is prime ranching and agricultural land, producing award-winning wines and succulent fruit crops. Bagging at least a box or two of Palisade peaches at the end of August is a Fielder family tradition. There's no sweeter, more delicious fruit on the planet!

Main Attractions

COLORADO NATIONAL MONUMENT

Colorado National Monument (see Scenic Location No. 37, p. 140) is one of the state's best-kept secrets. Its 32 miles of deep sandstone canyons recall the massive rock formations and monoliths of Utah's Zion and Arches National Parks. But the Colorado National Monument differs in one important aspect—many fewer people. The monument, inhabited by a variety of wildlife, still imparts a strong sense of solitude. Go west on I-70 past Grand Junction to the Fruita exit (19) and follow CO 340 to the entrance. Rim Rock Drive will take you back into Grand Junction.

Camping: Near the Colorado National Monument Visitor Center, **Saddlehorn** campground accommodates most monument campers. Campsites are on a first-come, first-served basis for a small daily fee. Backcountry camping is free, but a permit is required. No reservations. *970-858-3617.*

Hiking: The overlooks off Rim Rock Drive provide excellent views of the natural red-rock sculptures as well as access to hikes that should take anyone less than an hour. For the more adventurous hiker, I recommend the **Black Ridge** and **Monument Canyon** DIFFICULT hikes. The highest trail in the monument, Black Ridge is a 12-mile round-trip hike with views of the Utah canyonlands and the San Juan Mountains. The Black Ridge area is so rugged that it's been designated as wilderness. Monument Canyon, another 12-mile hike, descends steeply from the plateau into Monument Canyon, where you can see up close such features as Independence Monument and the Kissing Couple.

Scenic Drives: The 23-mile **Rim Rock Drive** affords spectacular views and overlooks of the sandstone canyon country. This road is also a favorite of touring cyclists. Be sure to stop at all the overlooks, as each provides a unique, dramatic view of the monument. For the most spectacular scenery, start your tour at the west Fruita entrance.

THE GRAND MESA

In sharp contrast to Grand Valley's arid canyon country, the Grand Mesa (see Scenic Location No. 35, p. 137) extends for 50 miles with aspen and coniferous forests at 11,000 feet. It is the largest flattop mountain mesa in the world. The mesa is a favorite place for Valley residents to escape the summer heat and enjoy recreational activities, as well as to marvel at fall colors. To get to the Grand Mesa from Grand Junction, take I-70 east 17 miles to Exit 49, turn right onto CO 65, and follow the signs.

Camping: Although the Grand Mesa has around 250 campsites, you cannot make reservations, and campgrounds here fill up early. **Jumbo,** situated between Jumbo Reservoir and Sunset Lake, is an ideal site for fishing enthusiasts. Take I-70 to CO 65 (Exit 49), turn right (east), and go 26 miles to Forest Road 252. Turn right and proceed roughly 100 yards to the campground. **Ward Lake** is a lovely area, and recreational opportunities abound. Follow the directions to Jumbo, but drive east on CO 65 for 35 miles, then turn left on FR 121. *970-242-8211.*

Fishing: The Grand Mesa is an angler's paradise. The Division of Wildlife heavily stocks with trout the mesa's more than 200 lakes. The Jumbo campground is convenient to the eight **Mesa Lakes,** including Jumbo Reservoir, Sunset Lake, Mesa Lake, Beaver Lake, Glacier Springs Lake, and Water Dog Reservoir. Nearby Ward Lake also has excellent fishing.

Hiking: The scenic **West Bench Trail** MODERATE, 5 miles one way, starts near the ranger station at the Jumbo campground (see Camping, above) and is also a favorite with mountain bikers. The **Mesa Shore Hike** EASY makes a 1-mile loop around Mesa Lake. From Grand Junction, take I-70 east for 48 miles to CO 65 and the town of Mesa. Continue 14 miles south and

Continued on page 136

Grand Junction / Delta

Colorado Atlas & Gazetteer pp. 32, 34, 42–44, 54–55

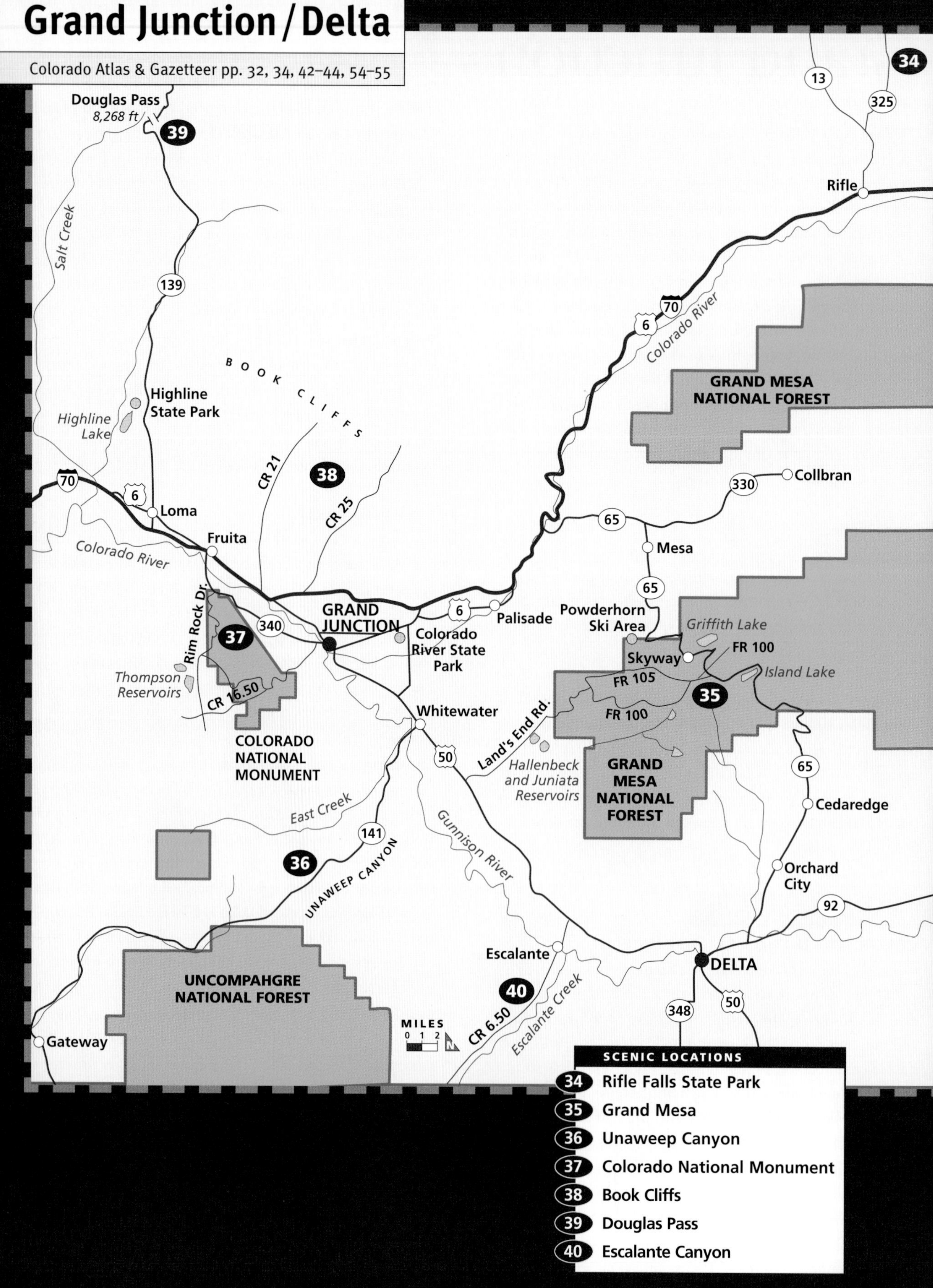

SCENIC LOCATIONS

- 34 Rifle Falls State Park
- 35 Grand Mesa
- 36 Unaweep Canyon
- 37 Colorado National Monument
- 38 Book Cliffs
- 39 Douglas Pass
- 40 Escalante Canyon

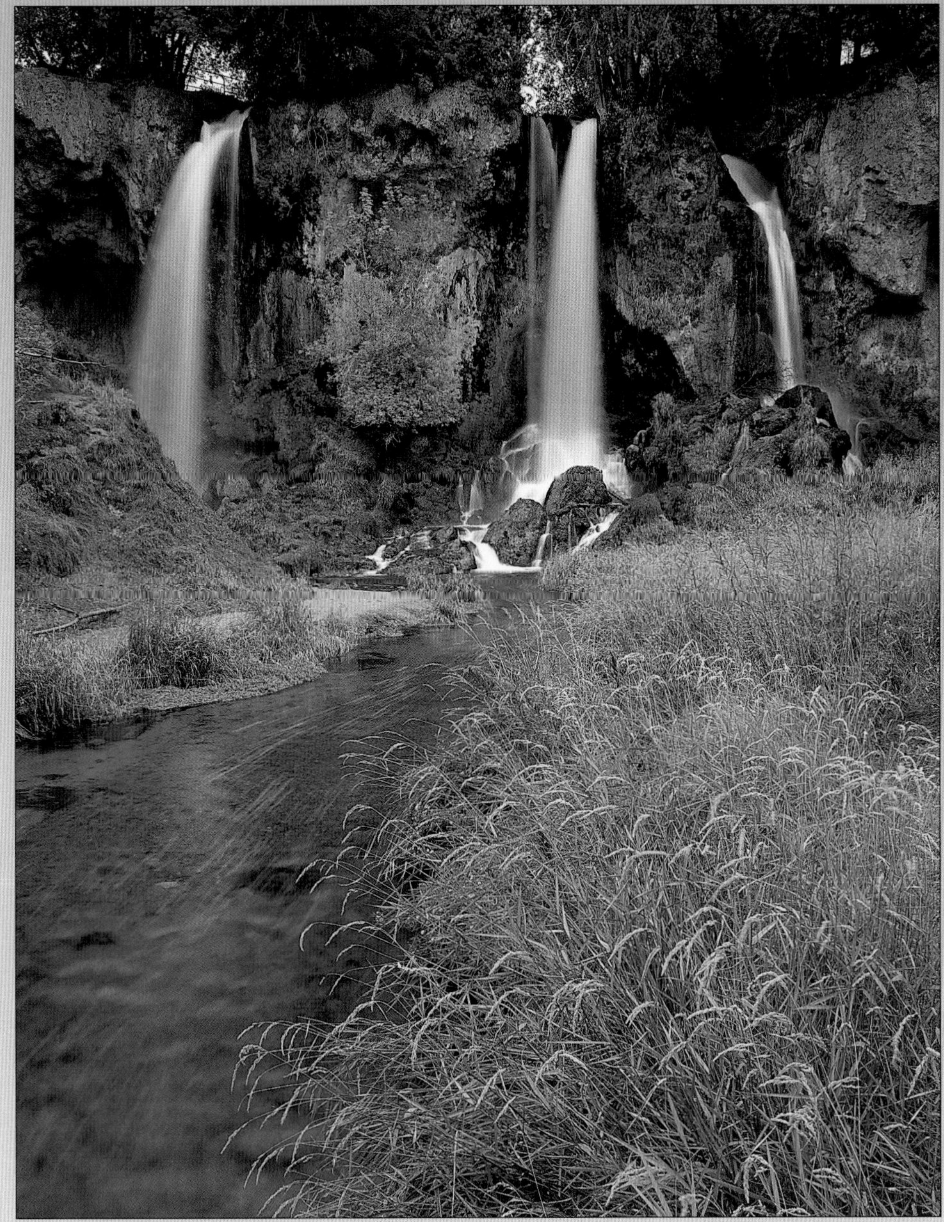

take a circuitous route. In this case, East Rifle Creek plunges over a natural travertine dam into what was probably once a limestone cavern. The spray from the falls keeps everything in the vicinity incredibly green. The lush vegetation and falls remind me more of Kauai than Colorado.

Photographing the falls and plant life meets with the most success when the sun does not directly shine on the scene. Ideal light occurs on an overcast day, when the contrast is low and clouds reflect white light onto the landscape. Colors in the foliage are ample and detail can be seen in the white cascades. The next-best light occurs on a clear day at sunset after sunlight departs or at sunrise before sunlight enters the canyon. These conditions aren't optimal only because the blue sky reflects blue light onto the landscape, which dulls foliage colors and makes the water appear blue.

You can photograph Rifle Falls any number of ways. Compose the creek in the foreground and falls in the background with a wide-angle lens. Use that same lens from off to the side of the falls for a more oblique composition. Put on a telephoto lens and photograph just a portion of the falls, such as the lower part that splashes over the rocks in the creek. Use a tripod and cable release (or the 10-second shutter release) in order to keep the camera perfectly still when making a slow exposure. Exposures of a quarter-second or slower will create the "cotton candy" effect by blurring the motion of the water. In order to achieve this, however, you must be able to "stop" your aperture down to a small diameter—say, f22—in order to force a longer shutter speed. Add a polarizing filter to reduce the amount of light entering the camera by 2 stops, allowing even slower speeds. Slower shutter speeds mean less detail in the water, resulting in a more ethereal-looking scene (see pp. 81–83, *Photographing the Landscape*).

Visit this remarkable place throughout the year. Ice forms all around the falls in winter; deciduous trees turn bright orange during autumn. And check out the canyon to the north while you're at the park. It's well worth the drive.

34 SCENIC LOCATION
RIFLE FALLS STATE PARK

Rifle Falls is one of the most scenic waterfalls in Colorado and the only triple waterfall that I've seen. Though not entirely "natural"— its flow has been manipulated over the years—it's incredibly scenic. In fact, the entire route along East Rifle Creek from the park north into the White River National Forest stands uniquely apart from everything else I've seen in Colorado. Shrubs grow profusely along the creek, adding glorious year-round hues to the limestone cliffs that color the canyon. Take the town of Rifle exit (90) from I-70 north onto CO 13. Three miles north of town, bear right onto CO 325 all the way to the park. Then continue north through Rifle Falls State Park and into the national forest as far as your particular vehicle will allow.

Like Hanging Lake (see Scenic Location No. 33, p. 130), limestone defines the area and causes free-flowing water to turn right (east) at the Forest Service sign for Mesa Lake. Turn left (southwest) at the bottom of the hill; in 0.5 mile, you will arrive at Glacier Springs picnic grounds, the start of the loop. The **Crag Crest National Recreation Trail** MODERATE is a 10-mile hike through alpine forests along sheer cliffsides with panoramic views of Grand Junction's Book Cliffs and even Utah's La Sal Mountains near Arches National Park. Go to the Ward Lake Recreation Area (see Camping, p. 133), turn left (east) on Forest Road 121, and travel 2.4 miles to the junction of FR 123 and CO 65. Turn left and drive 1.8 miles, passing the Eggleston Lake campground, and continue on to the Crag Crest campground.

Scenic Drives: Take the time to drive the 63-mile one-way **Grand Mesa Scenic and Historic Byway** (CO 65). You will ascend from deep canyons to subalpine forests and reach 11,000 feet. The byway drops down to the town of Cedaredge; from there you can return to Grand Junction via Delta on US 50. You can also turn off to the west atop the mesa to see the overlook at **Land's End Road.** From there, continue down the winding gravel road to where it meets US 50 south of Grand Junction. (Note: Land's End Road is closed in winter.)

KOKOPELLI BIKE TRAIL

A premier slickrock biking destination, the Kokopelli Trail DIFFICULT extends for 142 miles from just above Fruita to Moab, Utah. Mountain bikers gather in Fruita from near and far to test their mettle on this grueling, five- to seven-day, singletrack/backroad ride through astounding, rugged canyon landscapes of sandstone and shale. Kokopelli also features several loops, including Mary's Loop, Horsethief Bench Loop, Lion's Loop, Steve's Loop, and Troy Built Loop. To reach the Kokopelli trailhead from Grand Junction, take I-70 west to the Loma exit (15). Head south back over the interstate to a "T" intersection and turn right toward a truck weigh station. Then turn left onto the frontage road and travel 0.75 mile to the trailhead. Before attempting Kokopelli, contact the BLM Grand Junction Field Office, *970-244-3000*, the Colorado Plateau Mountain Bike Trail Association, *www.copmoba.org*, or any of the excellent bike shops in Grand Junction or Fruita for details, maintenance, and rentals.

THE VALLEY OF THE DINOSAURS

The Grand Valley, particularly the area from Fruita to the Utah border, has been prolific in yielding the fossils and bones of dinosaurs of the Jurassic Period. More than 30 species of dinosaur bones have been unearthed in this dried-up floodplain, including the massive plant-eating Brachiosaurus and the dreaded Utahraptor, a meat-eating hunter two times larger than the Velociraptor of *Jurassic Park* movie fame. The Grand Valley continues to be active with dinosaur quarries and digs. The Grand Junction Visitor Center (see p. 143) provides maps and information about some of the best fossil areas.

Dinosaur Journey: The whole family can enjoy a fun, educational, and hands-on experience at the Museum of Western Colorado's Dinosaur Journey museum and research lab. The kids will be amazed by the lifelike, robotically moving dinosaurs here: Apatosaurus, the Utahraptor, and the spitting Dilophosaurus (although the quarry master will be the first to tell you that the spitting ability of the Dilophosaurus was something out of *Jurassic Park* director Steven Spielberg's imagination). The museum is also a working paleontology lab, where paleontologists and volunteers continue to catalog the finds unearthed from neighboring quarries and digs. You can even arrange through the museum an expedition to the quarry field sites, where you can work on actual digs. To get to the museum, take I-70 to the Fruita exit (19). There is a small entrance fee. *888-488-DINO, www.dinosaurjourney.org.*

The Trail Through Time: Many dinosaur fossils, including the remains of Stegosaurus, Colorado's state dinosaur, have been discovered and excavated in Rabbit Valley, 30 miles west of Grand Junction. Rabbit Valley has been an active dinosaur quarry since 1982. The interpretive Trail Through Time EASY, a 1-mile loop, allows you to see dinosaur bones in their natural state. Note: Do not remove anything from the area, and stay on the trail. From Grand Junction, drive west on I-70 for 25 miles to the Rabbit Valley exit (just 2 miles from the Utah border), turn right, and park near the frontage road.

THE WILD HORSES OF LITTLE BOOKCLIFFS

The 1971 Wild Free-Roaming Horse and Burro Act provides for the management, protection, and control of all unbranded horses on public lands. Though wild-horse herds live in many parts of the West, the Little Bookcliffs Wild Horse Area is one of only three ranges in the United States set aside specifically to protect wild and free-roaming horses. The area's more than 36,000 acres of rugged canyons and plateaus provide range among the sagebrush and piñons for from 80 to 120 horses. Although ranchers and farmers turned most of these horses loose, some of them are descendants of Indian ponies introduced by the Spanish.

The wild horses, or mustangs, are most frequently spotted in sagebrush and under piñon trees, traveling in small bands made up of a stud and his harem of mares, or in bachelor bands of young stallions. During summer, some of the best opportunities for catching a glimpse of the wild horses exist near the Indian Park entrance to the horse range and in the North Soda area. During the winter and spring, Coal Canyon and Main Canyon make for excellent viewing areas.

To get to the summer ranges, exit I-70 at DeBeque (62), east of Grand Junction. Drive into the town of DeBeque and stay on the main road (4th Street) until you come to a gas station; turn left onto Minter Avenue and travel two blocks to where you must turn right onto 2nd Street. Follow it to the Winter Flats Road sign. Turn right and travel 20

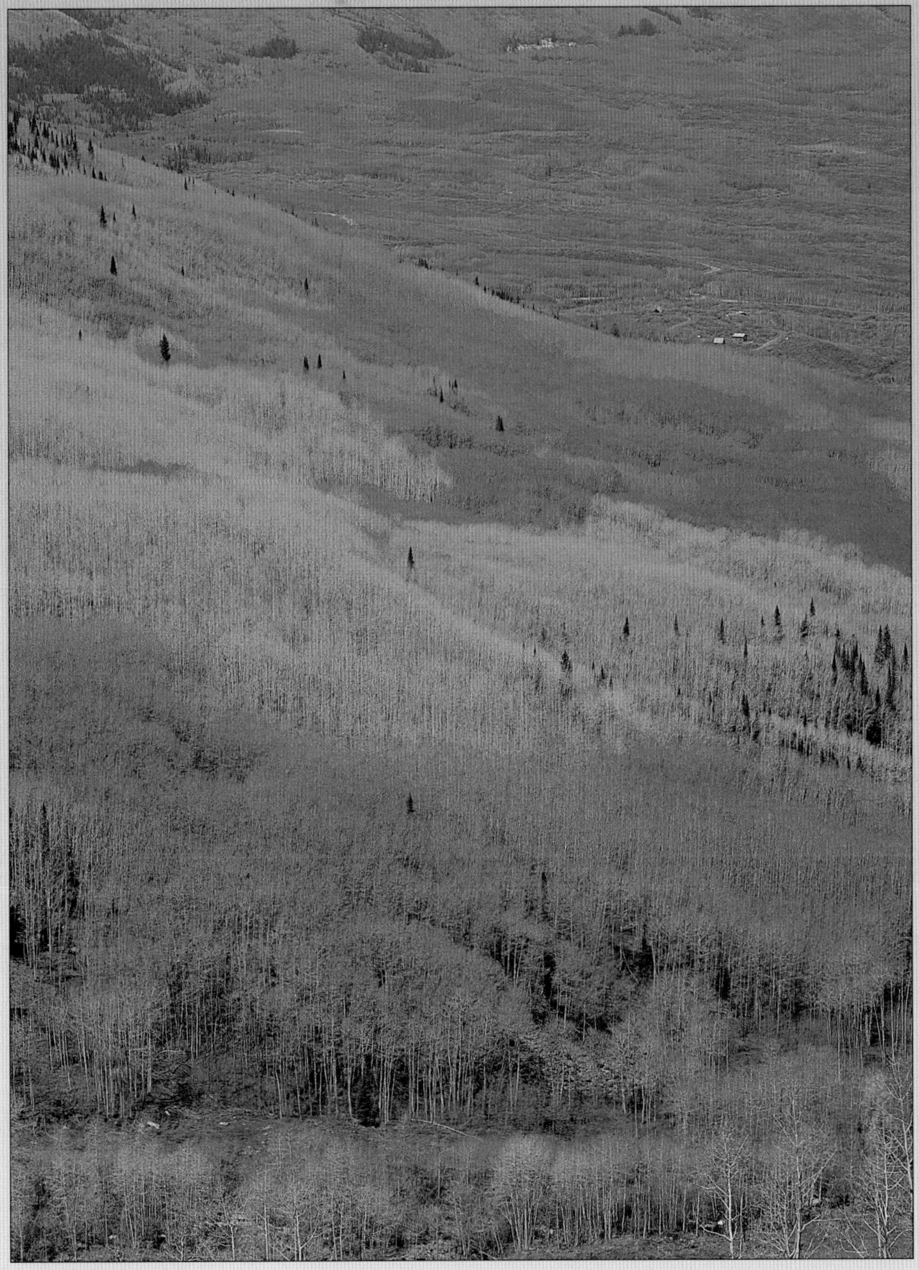

of Palisade. The highway turns south and circuitously climbs the mesa, then winds its way along the top before descending to the towns of Cedaredge and Delta.

The rocky cliffs around the edge of the mesa harbor extremely beautiful stands of aspen in a unique Colorado setting. The month of May provides the lime green color of freshly leaved trees, while late September boasts yellow, orange, and red hues. You can see aspens for miles from many places along the highway, and both in spring and fall you witness the genetic singularity of this plant. Aspens propagate both from seeds and by way of their roots—in fact, thousands of single trees can be connected by root as one single organism. These colonies gain and lose their leaves at the same time. Some of the Grand Mesa views reveal many colonies at once, each manifested as a particular shade of green in the spring, or yellow in the fall. The variegated tones within this sea of trees resembles a Van Gogh painting when seen from high on the mesa.

Do you think you want to take a picture now? I enjoy composing these forests with and without the sky. If I include any sky at all, it's only enough to show the flatness of the mesa top and add a sense of infiniteness to the scene.

The Land's End Road is a must to see and to drive. It departs to the west once you are on top of the mesa, leads you to its western edge, and descends down to US 50. The views across the Gunnison River toward the Uncompahgre Plateau are spectacular on a clear day. But photographers, beware: Just like taking pictures on top of fourteeners, trying to get a great photograph here with any sense of perspective is difficult when you are on the edge of something so high up. Look for something to put in your foreground, an interesting tree or rock, in order to create depth in your composition.

And don't forget that there are more than 200 lakes to photograph. You won't have any high mountains with which to photograph a reflection, just lots of trees and meadows around the shores. The best reflection photographs can occur at sunrise and sunset, when clouds turn orange, red, and pink.

35 SCENIC LOCATION — GRAND MESA

East and a little ways south of Grand Junction is a unique geologic escarpment called the Grand Mesa. It's essentially a flattopped mesa, though elevations reach more than 11,000 feet. Aspen trees decorate its steep sides; spruce and fir cover the top in between acres of mountain meadows. However, its most conspicuous feature is the more than 200 stream-fed lakes and reservoirs that cover this subalpine plateau. Miles and miles of Grand Mesa National Forest roads await exploration, as well as extremely scenic hiking trails. The views to valleys below from the edge of the precipitous mesa are wondrous. Grand Mesa is usually reached by turning east on CO 65 from I-70 after entering DeBeque Canyon from the east. From the west, CO 65 is about 6 miles from the orchard town

UNAWEEP CANYON

The northern terminus of the Uncompahgre Plateau is the broad, U-shaped Unaweep Canyon, carved deep into the plateau by the ancient Gunnison and Colorado Rivers. The Uncompahgre Uplift diverted the rivers to their current locations to the west and north. The walls of the canyon, composed of stark black and gray schist, gneiss, and granite, tower to heights of 4,000 feet above the canyon floor. Proceed south from Grand Junction on US 50, 10 miles to CO 141. Turn west to go through Unaweep Canyon. West of the canyon, CO 141 continues down to the town of Gateway and follows the Dolores River (see Scenic Location No. 101, p. 290) south to US 491.

No other place in Colorado matches the kind of scenery in Unaweep Canyon. Canyon walls are made of gray rock, the relatively narrow valley floor is ranching country, and forests of oak and aspen ascend side canyons up to the top of the contiguous plateaus. The ranch meadows are particularly beautiful, turning bright green in May and golden brown in September and October. The aspens and oaks in the side canyons grow in alluvial patterns, narrow at the top and wide at the base. It's as if the trees are flowing into the valley from the tops of the canyons. Like the grasses, they are brilliant green in spring and are colored yellow, orange, and red in the fall. From the highway I photograph scenics to include meadows, trees, and deep blue sky, and more intimate scenes without the horizon. The canyon lies east to west, so sunrise and sunset both sidelight the foliage.

On the descent to Gateway, you pass a marked and signed Colorado Natural Area called the Unaweep Seep. Spring-fed water floods the area to the north of the highway, providing sustenance to a cornucopia of plant life. From this vantage, the irregular rim of the canyon's north side makes parts of the cliffs appear to be sharp peaks and spires—a great backdrop to the fecundity of the seep. Sunrise on a clear day colors these false peaks with orange light.

miles; this takes you to a fork in the road. The right branch leads to North Soda, the left branch to Indian Park. For directions to the Coal Canyon and Main Canyon trails, see Scenic Location No. 38, p. 141. Pick up a trail map of Little Bookcliffs at the BLM Grand Junction Field Office, 2815 H Rd. *For horse locations or road conditions: 970-244-3000.*

WINE COUNTRY

The Grand Valley's reputation as a producer of fine wines continues to grow. Wine tastings and winery tours are always popular in Palisade. For a safe and comprehensive wine tasting experience, take the four-hour shuttle tour from, and back to, hotel locations. Participating wineries include Canyon Wind Cellars, Carlson Vineyards, Colorado Cellars, Grande River Vineyards, Plum Creek Cellars, Rocky Mountain Meadery, St. Kathryn Cellars, and Two Rivers Winery. The advantages of the shuttle tour are twofold: You will get a more behind-the-scenes look at winemaking, and you will not have to do any explaining to the Colorado Highway Patrol.

A couple of companies offer guided tours of the wine country. For the Prestige Tour, call Absolute Prestige Limousines, *970-858-8500.* Tours start at $30. For a great wine tasting tour, call American Spirit Shuttle, *970-835-5067, www.gisdho.com.*

If you decide to take a self-guided tour, I recommend Grande River Vineyards just off I-70 in Palisade. Not only are their wines excellent (try the Meritage, the Syrah, and the 1999 Viognier), but the tasting room is very appealing. Those wine servers really know their products and will take time with you. *800-COGROWN.* Be sure to stop at a roadside stand and purchase a box of peaches and/or other fruit to take with you.

Activities

CAMPING

On your way west from Glenwood Springs to Grand Junction, you can enjoy a picturesque experience at the campground at

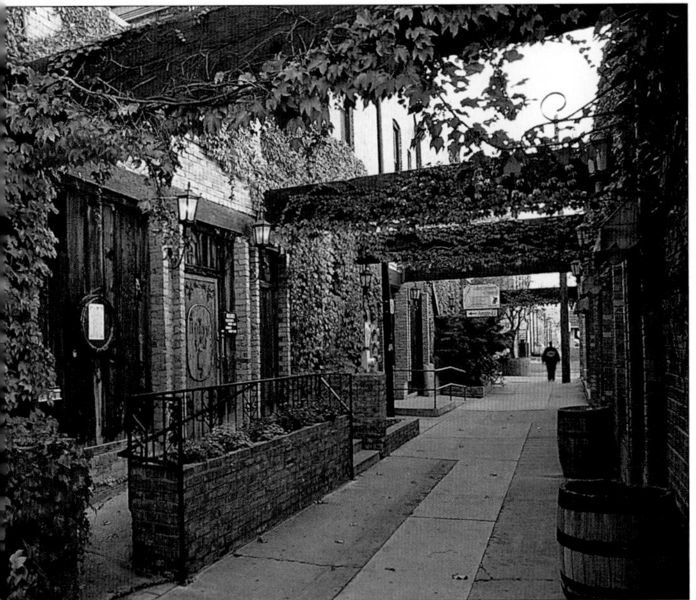

The Winery restaurant, Grand Junction

Rifle Falls State Park. The park's wildflowers, cliffs, caves, and 50-foot falls are stunning (see Scenic Location No. 34, p. 135). You can also camp at nearby **Rifle Gap State Park,** where anglers can find trout as well as walleyes and bass in the reservoir. Take I-70 from Glenwood Springs 26 miles west to the Rifle exit (90). Turn right onto CO 13 and drive 5 miles to the CO 325 junction. Turn right again and go 6 miles, then turn left onto the dirt road to Rifle Gap State Park. For Rifle Falls State Park, drive 10 miles from CO 13 on CO 325. Reservations recommended. *970-625-1607, www.coloradoparks.org.*

GOLF

For golfing with views, try the 18-hole **Tiara Rado Golf Course** at the foot of Colorado National Monument. You can sometimes spot wildlife from the fairway. *970-254-3830.* Suitable for both novices and experts, the 18-hole **Chipeta Golf Course** provides views of the Grand Mesa, Book Cliffs, Uncompahgre Plateau, and Colorado National Monument. *970-245-7177, www.chipetagolf.com.* The nationally recognized **Golf Club at Redlands Mesa** is an amazing course with breathtaking views. *2325 W Ridges Blvd, 866-863-9270, www.redlandsmesa.com.*

HIKING, CYCLING AND MOUNTAIN BIKING

The Grand Valley offers hiking and biking experiences from leisurely to demanding—and plenty of options beyond the famed and sometimes fearsome Kokopelli Trail (see Main Attractions, p. 136). **The Colorado River Trails System** along the Gunnison and Colorado Rivers extends from Clifton through Grand Junction and west to Fruita. You'll also find walkers, runners, in-line skaters, and equestrians on the paved and unpaved stretches of this trail system. The Audubon, Blue Heron, Connected Lakes, Watson Island, and Corn Lakes Trails provide excellent rides and wildlife viewing. For a map of the system, contact the Colorado River State Park on County Road 32 (CO 141) at Corn Lake, beside the Colorado River. *970-434-3388, www.parks.state.co.us.*

For the serious hiker or mountain biker who wants to explore arches and canyonlands that few see, visit the canyons. I particularly recommend **Rattlesnake Canyon** in the recently designated National Conservation Area of the Black Ridge Canyon. To get there, take I-70 to the Fruita exit (19). Travel south on CO 340 to the west entrance of Colorado National Monument and drive 11 miles through the monument. Turn right at the Glade Park sign. From this point on, you will need a high-center four-wheel drive—or start biking or hiking. After 0.2 mile, turn right at the sign for Black Ridge Hunter Access Road, and follow signs 10 miles to the Rattlesnake Canyon trailhead.

From the Glade Park sign, you can also take the trail to the left and hike or ride the Upper Bench Road to the **Mee Canyon** trailhead. If you want to explore even more spectacular canyons, take the **Knowles Canyon** or **Jones Canyon Trails.** To get to these trailheads, follow the directions to Rattlesnake Canyon but turn west on Road BS. Travel 12 miles to the Knowles Canyon

Continued on page 142

COLORADO NATIONAL MONUMENT

Anybody who thinks that you must travel to Utah to see red rock country should make a stop at the Colorado National Monument. The monument was designated in 1911; the rocks were created 65 to 225 million years ago. This place is a photographer's paradise, with lots of trails to hike and a paved road, Rim Rock Drive, that you have to see to believe. The steep canyon walls are visible from just about anywhere in Grand Junction, so getting there is just a matter of pointing your vehicle in the right direction—southwest. Take CO 340, the Redlands Highway, out of town and follow signs to the south entrance. You may also enter the monument from the town of Fruita, west of Grand Junction on I-70. Take CO 340 to reach the monument's north entrance.

Rim Rock Drive is the only major road in Colorado National Monument. From both sides it ascends steep canyons, then loops around and above the monument's three primary canyons. The Monument Canyon View and Independence Monument View are breathtaking, especially if you have a fear of heights! You look straight across toward monolithic spires of sandstone rising several hundred feet from the canyon floor. There are pullouts all along the way at the most scenic spots. The views down Ute and Red Canyons, with their massive vertical walls, are exceptional.

Sunrise is best for photography here. The monument angles slightly to the northeast, allowing the major spires and walls to catch the early light. The sun sits so low in the sky when it rises that the color of light on a clear day is brilliant red. This bathes the already red sandstone, rendering it an indescribable color to which not even film can do justice. Evening light is good, too, but the escarpment behind the monument prevents light from penetrating the canyons late in the evening. Therefore, the colors are not nearly as intense as they are during sunrise.

This is a four-season place. White snow beautifully decorates the red rocks and green piñon and juniper trees that grow around the cliffs. And many great trails in the monument allow access to the bottom of the canyons. Photographs taken upward to spires silhouetted against a Colorado blue sky complement images made looking down canyon. My favorite hike is an easy one: The Monument Canyon Trail takes you right to the base of Independence Monument.

BOOK CLIFFS

A 2,000-foot vertical face of cliffs that frame the Grand Valley and the city of Grand Junction, the Book Cliffs form the edge of a plateau that actually extends west to Green River, Utah. County Roads 21 and 25, which head north off of US 6 between Grand Junction and Fruita, provide quick access by passenger car to the edge of the cliffs. For a great day hike and some solitude, the heart of the Colorado Book Cliffs and the Little Bookcliffs Roadless Area are accessible via Coal Canyon east of Grand Junction. Take the Cameo exit (46) from I-70, head west across the Colorado River, and drive directly past the power plant. Follow the only legal road 1.5 miles beyond the power plant (the others have "No Trespassing" signs) up the mouth of Coal Canyon. Park in the cleared area where the road takes a turn to the west. From here you can hike over to Main Canyon, access to the Little Bookcliffs Wild Horse Area and wilderness solitude.

These white shale cliffs shine against the Colorado blue sky. However, their paleness makes them highly reflective of bright afternoon light. The result is washed-out colors in your images. Therefore, I recommend photographing at sunrise and sunset, or on a cloudy day. Because the cliffs face west, sunset can be glorious, especially when orange light washes the cliffs on a clear evening (see pp. 86–88, *Photographing the Landscape*). Drive to the end of CR 21 and CR 25 and hike onto the nearby ridges. You'll be able to photograph many ridges stacked one behind the other as you point your camera northwest. The sidelighting of the setting sun and resulting shadows will add great depth to your composition.

Mount Garfield is not actually a mountain but a high point along the cliffs northeast of Grand Junction; it also catches the last light of the day, so look for ways to photograph it from this same area. I love to photograph in this vicinity after sunset, too. If the atmosphere provides the pinks of twilight, these subtle hues reflect on the neutral colors of the landscape, turning gray rock into pink. The Book Cliffs are very conspicuous in the evening from some of the view points on Rim Rock Drive in the Colorado National Monument (see Scenic Location No. 37, opposite). A telephoto lens brings the cliffs close to the monument canyons in the foreground of your composition.

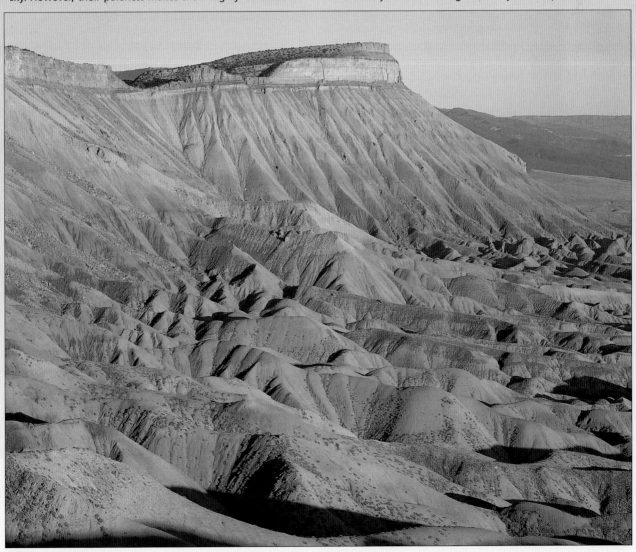

trailhead or continue for several more miles to the Jones Canyon trailhead. *For road and trail conditions and maps: BLM Grand Junction Field Office, 2815 H Rd., 970-244-3000.*

HORSEBACK RIDING

For a great family experience, I recommend a horseback ride. What a relaxing way to enjoy this magnificent canyon country! **Rimrock Adventures** in Fruita offers a number of horseback riding trips to fit your family's interests and abilities. Red Rock, Colorado Canyons, and Devil's Canyon are easy one- to two-hour rides. My favorites are the three-hour Devil's Canyon ride and the Wildhorse Sanctuary ride into the Little Bookcliffs. For the more seasoned rider, take the 25-mile, full-day Ruby and Horsethief Canyons ride, a local favorite.

Another popular event in Fruita is Rimrock's weekly Tuesday Night Rodeo, which features bull riding and bronc-busting by local ranch hands and aspiring cowboys. To get to Rimrock Adventures, take I-70 to the Fruita exit (19), head south on CO 340, and turn left at the sign. *970-858-9555, 888-712-9555, www.rradventures.com.*

COLORADO CAMEO

John Otto

It took a hermit with persistence and a dream of preserving his beloved canyon country to help create what is now the Colorado National Monument southwest of Grand Junction."I came here last year and found these canyons, and they felt like the heart of the world to me," John Otto wrote in 1907. "I'm going to stay and promote this place, because it should be a national park." Thus began Otto's letter writing campaign, which deluged politicians in Washington with letters from Grand Junction residents in support of receiving federal protection for this pristine and remote area.

Living alone in the desolate backcountry, Otto built miles of trails through the proposed park so that others could appreciate its beauty and understand the need for its preservation. Many of these trails are in use today, including Serpents Trail, whose more than 50 switchbacks have earned it the title of "crookedest road in the world."

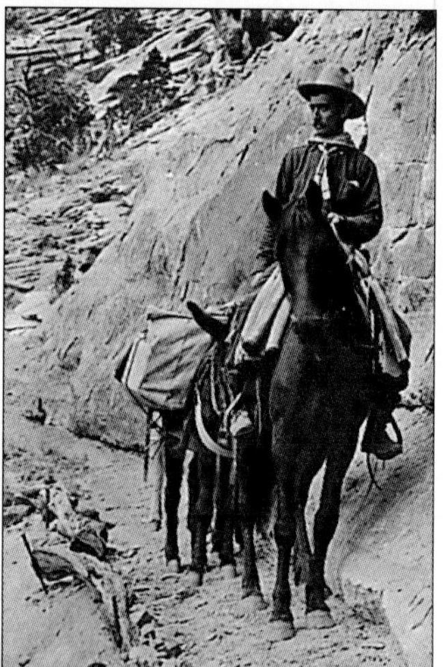

In 1911, John Otto's dream came true: The Colorado National Monument was established. Otto was named the park's caretaker, for which he received a $1 monthly salary until his retirement in 1927. For that meager compensation, as well as for his tireless efforts, we remain in his debt.

MUSEUM OF WESTERN COLORADO

The Museum of Western Colorado operates several cultural facilities in the Grand Valley, including the popular **Dinosaur Journey** in Fruita (see p. 136). You'll also want to see the **History Museum/Sterling T. Smith Educational Tower** in Grand Junction, which shows the Grand Valley from woolly-mammoth days to the present. You can check out extensive fossil and Indian artifact displays, and an impressive firearms collection, as well as an exhibit on Colorado's infamous cannibal, Alferd Packer. There is a small admittance fee. *462 Ute, 970-242-0971, www.wcmuseum.org.*

From 1896 to 1923, what is now **Cross Orchards Historic Farm** was a 243-acre apple orchard, with more than 22,000 trees at its peak of production. Listed on the National Register of Historic Places, a portion of the former grounds is now a living-history museum, with guides dressed in early-20th-century garb. *For information on events, harvest festivals, and holiday programs: 970-434-9814.*

RAFTING

Novices should consider taking a gentle raft trip to learn what seasoned floaters know: There's no better or more unforgettable way to experience the canyon country. Take the **Colorado River Experience** or **Blue Heron Run** EASY float trips available through Rimrock Adventures. Or check out the more strenuous, multi-day float trips down the Colorado, Dolores, and Gunnison Rivers. You can also look into Rimrock's popular packages of saddles-and-paddles: combination horseback riding and floating trips. *970-858-9555, 888-712-9555, www.rradventures.com.*

Restaurants

The **Rockslide Restaurant and Brewery** ($) on Main in downtown Grand Junction is a great brewpub. Try the Widow-maker Wheat beer—my favorite! *401 Main St., 970-245-2111.* **The Winery** ($$-$$$) in downtown Grand Junction is a special treat. My favorite is the slab of spiced prime rib. If you're feeling particularly decadent, get The Palisade for dessert—a three-layer chocolate mousse torte with raspberry sauce. Reservations are a good idea. *642 Main St., 970-242-4100.*

Rockslide Restaurant & Brewery, Grand Junction

WW Peppers ($-$$) offers more choices for the palate and the budget. Try a dish from the Southwestern menu. Peppers gets the prize for creativity with a truly unique combination of Southwestern flavors and traditional Mexican dishes. Peppers is just off the I-70 Horizon exit (31) and does not take reservations. *759 Horizon Court, 970-245-9251.*

Though not a restaurant, **Enstrom Candies,** *200 S. 7th St., 970-242-1655,* is worth a visit for a taste of the almond toffee.

Accommodations

Although hard to find, the **Los Altos Bed & Breakfast** ($$) has awesome views from its hillside perch. *375 Hillview Dr., 970-256-0964, 888-774-0982.* The spacious **Chateau at Two Rivers** ($$) offers breathtaking views of the entire Grand Valley. Situated on the grounds of an award-winning winery, its architecture and decor create the feel of a French chateau. *2087 Broadway, 866-312-9463.* In Fruita, the clear choice of kids is the **Stonehaven Bed and Breakfast** ($$). The main attraction here is an acre of playground equipment and farm animals. *798 N. Mesa St., 970-858-0898, 800-303-0898, www.stonehavenbed.com.*

Special Events

Area bike shops host annual bike festivals with food, live entertainment, and prizes. Fruita's **Fat Tire Festival,** held in late April, is perhaps the most popular. *For a schedule of bike festivals, check with a local bike shop or contact Over The Edge Cycles, 970-858-7220, www.fruitamountainbike.com.*

Held in September, the **Colorado Mountain Winefest** features wine tasting, winery tours, food, and entertainment. *800-962-2547, 970-244-1480, www.visitgrandjunction.com.*

The annual **Downtown Arts & Jazz Festival** is held each May and features live jazz performances, art vendors, and the changing of the city's sculpture display. *970-245-9697, www.dowtowngj.org.*

For More Information

Grand Junction Visitor Center, off I-70 at Horizon exit (31), *740 Horizon Dr., 970-256-4060, www.visitgrandjunction.com.* Grand Junction Chamber of Commerce, *360 Grand Ave., 970-242-3214, www.gjchamber.org.*

39 DOUGLAS PASS

SCENIC LOCATION

From the town of Loma west of Grand Junction, CO 139 proceeds north to the town of Rangely. It leaves the Grand Valley and quickly rises to 8,268 feet at Douglas Pass before descending into White River country (see Scenic Location No. 63, p. 207). The highway follows East Salt Creek on the way up, Douglas Creek on the way down. The ascent takes you through several ecosystems, from forests of piñon and juniper to cottonwood and aspen in the montane zone, as you arrive at the pass. It's a great way to get away from the people and traffic of the Grand Valley, to enjoy nothing but solitude and infinite views.

The abundance of deciduous trees and shrubs along the creeks is an anomaly in an otherwise barren landscape. Spring and fall provide the best opportunities for photography. Because this is drier, hotter country, the trees tend to leaf earlier in May and do not turn their fall color until mid-October. If you hit it just right, these pockets of color will brightly illuminate this stark western Colorado landscape. Continue the drive north to Rangely, then east on CO 64, which follows the White River to Meeker. The cottonwoods along the way are sure to delight.

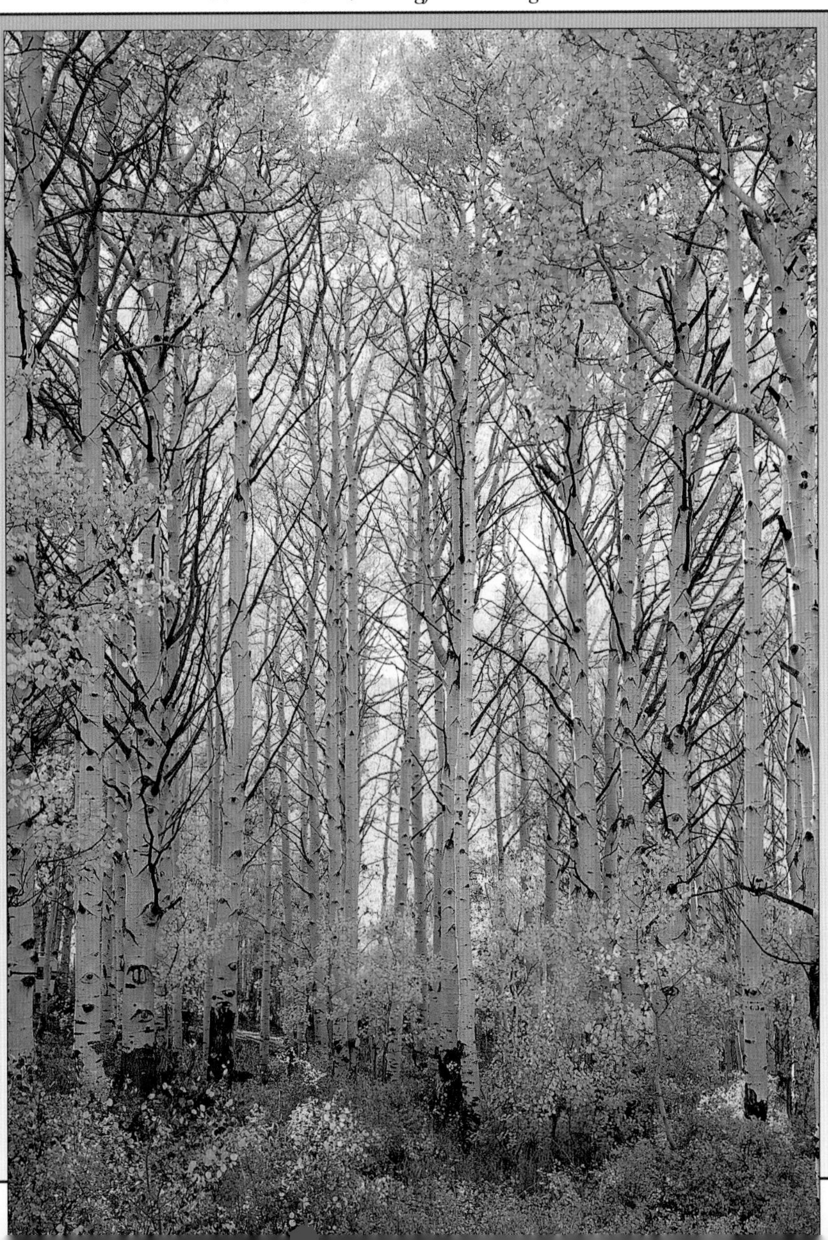

Delta

(see map on p. 134)

Delta brings you near natural wonders and attractions, and world-class recreation, for a modest price. It is also a city where Ute traditions still have a presence, and where rivers and ranchland speak to the bounty of the Grand Valley. Delta adjoins such treasures as the Black Canyon of the Gunnison National Park (only 29 miles east on US 50 to the South Rim, 72 miles east on CO 92 to the North Rim) and three national forests. Only 19 miles from great camping and fishing on the Grand Mesa, Delta is even closer to orchards, state parks, wildlife areas, and the magnificent Gunnison River.

History

Western settlers founded Delta and Grand Junction in 1881. Named for its site on the delta of the Uncompahgre River, Delta is the county seat for some of Colorado's best ranchland. Fruit orchards have long been the mainstay of the economy. The site is also the headquarters for the Grand Mesa, Uncompahgre, and Gunnison National Forests. From the south rim of the Gunnison Gorge, you can follow the Ute Trail down the Gunnison—a path followed for centuries before the arrival of Western settlers.

Main Attractions

COUNCIL TREE POW WOW

Named for a nearly 200-year-old cottonwood where tribal elders met, the Council Tree Pow Wow is an annual gathering where Ute tribes get together and participate or compete in a variety of cultural ceremonies. Held in mid-September, this must-see event is sponsored by the Northern, Southern, and Mountain Ute tribes. You can observe the drum contest, hoop dancing, dance competitions, and the Miss Indian Colorado Pageant. There is a large Indian market, and kids will love the basket- and bead-making classes. Indian foods such as fry bread, Indian tacos, and roasted corn tempt the taste buds. You can even rent a tepee during the event. To get to the Pow Wow grounds from US 50 in Delta, turn west at the McDonald's and proceed 0.25 mile. *800-874-1741.*

ESCALANTE CANYON

Spanish Franciscan missionary Silvestre Velez de Escalante traveled through this region in 1776 in search of an easy route from Santa Fe to California, and several places in Utah and Colorado bear his name. Escalante Canyon (see Scenic Location No. 40, opposite) is a beautiful place with a long history. Two of the largest dinosaur bones ever discovered were found in the canyon. Paleontologists believe that these bones belonged to dinosaurs weighing nearly 80 tons and standing more than five stories tall. The canyon is home to a dinosaur dig, or quarry (visitors are welcome), petroglyphs, and many remarkable original homesteads. Nestled between the lower Gunnison River and the Uncompahgre Plateau, this canyon is not to be confused with the Grand Staircase–Escalante National Monument in Utah. From Delta, go north on US 50 toward Grand Junction and turn left (southwest) on County Road 6.50.

Activities

CAMPING

With its great fishing, **Crawford State Park** makes up for what it lacks in shade. You can also enjoy boating and water-skiing here. Choose from two campgrounds, **Iron Creek** and **Clear Fork,** both with good facilities. *970-921-5721, www.parks.state.co.us.*

FISHING

Crawford Reservoir is well known as a producer of quality perch and catfish. It also has Northern pike, crappie, and trout. To get there from Delta, take CO 92 east 20 miles to Hotchkiss. From Hotchkiss, continue on CO 92 for 11 miles to Crawford, then follow the signs to Crawford State Park.

Sweitzer Lake is an excellent place to teach kids to fish. The lake contains large channel catfish, bluegill, perch, and carp that are fairly easy to catch. But beware: The lake contains selenium, so its fish are not edible. Sweitzer Lake is 4 miles east of Delta on CO 92.

HIKING AND MOUNTAIN BIKING

Explore Colorado's canyonlands and Uncompahgre Plateau by foot or mountain bike. See Hiking, p. 287, and Mountain Biking, p. 288, in the Montrose section.

MUSEUM

Return to frontier times at the **Fort Uncompahgre Living History Museum.** Built around 1826 by fur trapper and trader Antoine Robidoux, Fort Uncompahgre was a center for trade with the Utes. Robidoux is said to have traded in Ute children, selling them as laborers to farmers in the San Luis Valley. Utes and fort settlers at some point had a serious falling-out, and settlers were massacred in a Ute attack in 1844. Staff and volunteers at this living-history museum wear period clothing. You can see the Hide Room, where deer hides and beaver pelts were stored, and visit the living quarters and kitchen. A highlight of the tour is the Churro sheep, the rarest breed of domestic sheep in North America. *530 Gunnison River Dr., just west of US 50 at Confluence Park, 970-874-8349.*

WINTER SPORTS

Powderhorn Ski Area, 43 miles to the north on the Grand Mesa, is particularly suited to families and beginners. Powderhorn also boasts some good intermediate runs, and it's the only ski area in Colorado with views of the canyon country below! From Delta, take CO 92 east for 4 miles to CO 65. Go north on CO 65, 39 miles to the ski area. *970-268-5700, www.powderhorn.com.*

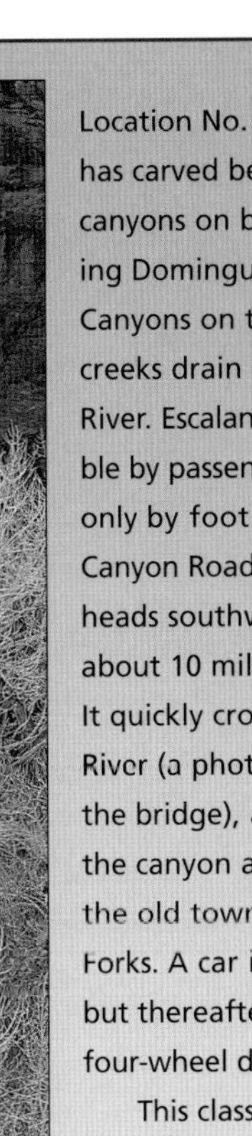

ESCALANTE CANYON

The Uncompahgre Plateau (not to be confused with Uncompahgre Peak and related mountains of the San Juan group near Lake City) runs northwest to southeast, west of the Gunnison and Uncompahgre Rivers between CO 141 and CO 62. It reaches elevations above 10,000 feet (see Scenic Location No. 100, p. 289). Water has carved beautiful sandstone canyons on both sides, including Dominguez and Escalante Canyons on the east side. Both creeks drain into the Gunnison River. Escalante Canyon is accessible by passenger car, Dominguez only by foot. The Escalante Canyon Road, County Road 6.50, heads southwest from US 50 about 10 miles west of Delta. It quickly crosses the Gunnison River (a photo opportunity from the bridge), and proceeds up the canyon about 14 miles to the old town site of Escalante Forks. A car is fine to that point, but thereafter I recommend a four-wheel drive.

This classic western Colorado red-sandstone canyon is highly photogenic. Escalante Creek has cut a canyon 1,300 feet deep. It photographs equally well at sunrise and sunset. The already warm red rocks turn blood red with the color of first light on a clear day. Nevertheless, cloudy light isn't so bad either—this is very colorful sandstone! Parts of the canyon are a Colorado Natural Area, so designated for its unique and rare plants and hanging gardens, fed by water seeps, that grow high on the cliffs. The area has not been heavily grazed, allowing the native vegetation to dominate the landscape. Cacti bloom in the spring and cottonwoods turn in the fall, adding immense color to this already kaleidoscopic place. You can enjoy a visit here in all seasons.

Restaurants

Two restaurants stand out from the pack in Delta. **The Stockyard** ($-$$) is a popular place for breakfast and steak dinners. *1205 Main St., 970-874-4222.* **Miller's Deitch Haus** ($) is a great choice if you're looking for a home-cooked, hometown buffet lunch or dinner. *820 E. CO 92, 970-901-9616.*

Accommodations

With its proximity to a number of tourist attractions and recreational opportunities, Delta has its share of motels and hotels. **The Fairlamb House B&B** ($$) is an historic bed and breakfast that was originally built in 1906. Members of the Fairlamb family, the family the house is named for, were the sole owners for seventy-two years. The house has been completely renovated and updated in the years since and now includes three uniquely designed guest rooms. *700 Leon St., 970-874-5158, www.fairlambbb.com.*

Special Events

The annual **Deltarado Days** take place in late July. Deltarado Days features a parade and a Professional Rodeo Cowboys Association rodeo. The annual **Delta County Fair** also includes a professional rodeo as well as live entertainment. *970-874-8616, www.deltacolorado.org.* See Special Events, Montrose, p. 293, for other regional events.

For More Information

The Delta Area Visitor Center is in the Chamber of Commerce and is closed on weekends. *301 Main St., 970-874-8616, www.deltacolorado.org, www.deltaco.org, www.westerncolorado.org.*

Below: *Moot House restaurant, Fort Collins*
Right: *Grand Lake Lodge, Grand Lake*

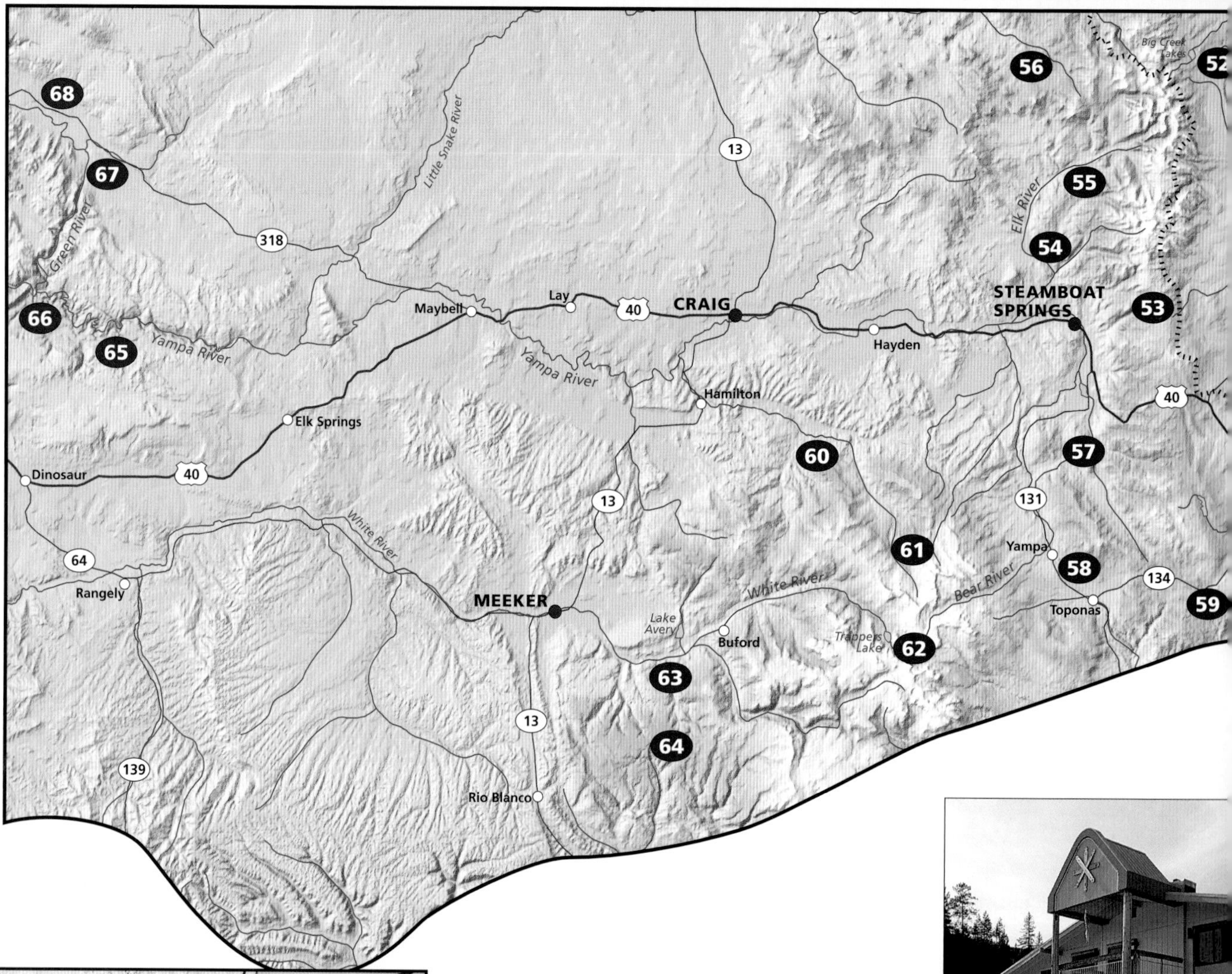

The Sod Buster Inn, Greeley

Hot Sulphur Springs Resort, Hot Sulphur Springs

Northwestern Colorado

NORTHERN FRONT RANGE TO DINOSAUR NATIONAL MONUMENT

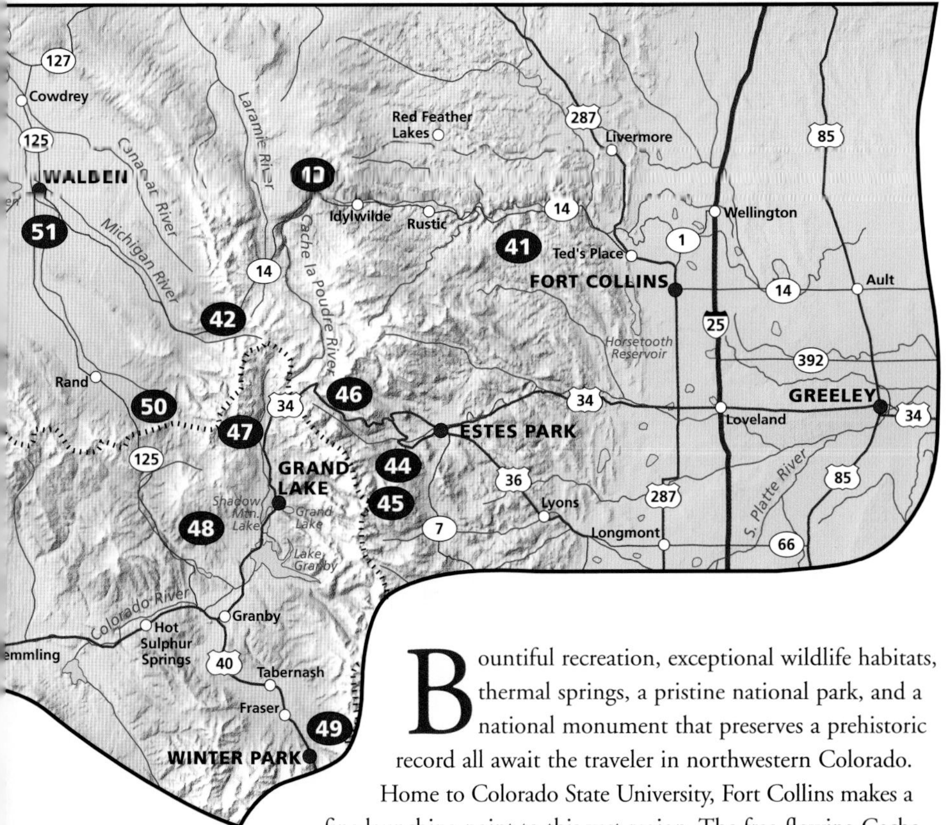

SCENIC LOCATIONS

Bountiful recreation, exceptional wildlife habitats, thermal springs, a pristine national park, and a national monument that preserves a prehistoric record all await the traveler in northwestern Colorado.

Home to Colorado State University, Fort Collins makes a fine launching point to this vast region. The free-flowing Cache la Poudre River, just west of the college town, has carved a magnificent canyon and is Colorado's only federally designated Wild and Scenic River.

A different kind of wild and scenic awaits visitors to Rocky Mountain National Park, a place of headwaters for many rivers, and of alpine lakes, glacially cut peaks, dazzling valleys, and the awe-inspiring Trail Ridge Road. Elk wander at will in the community of Estes Park, and adjacent Rocky Mountain National Park is home to large herds of elk, deer, and bighorn sheep. Grand Lake anchors the west side of the park.

The moguls of Winter Park/Mary Jane, the extensive Middle Park–area ski trails, and the champagne powder of Steamboat Ski Resort attract winter sports enthusiasts from the Front Range and beyond. In summer, river runners, hikers, anglers, and mountain bikers congregate here. The lands around the towns of Meeker and Craig draw hunters from all over the country, and the little town of Walden and its environs are known as the Moose Viewing Capital of Colorado. Dinosaur National Monument, which reaches into eastern Utah, is a bonanza of prehistoric fossils amid layered and colorful canyons that illuminate geological epochs. Experience northwestern Colorado and you'll find exciting recreation, wildlife watching, and remarkable, diverse landscapes—often without the big crowds of the central mountains.

Fort Collins/Greeley

Colorado Atlas & Gazetteer pp. 18–20

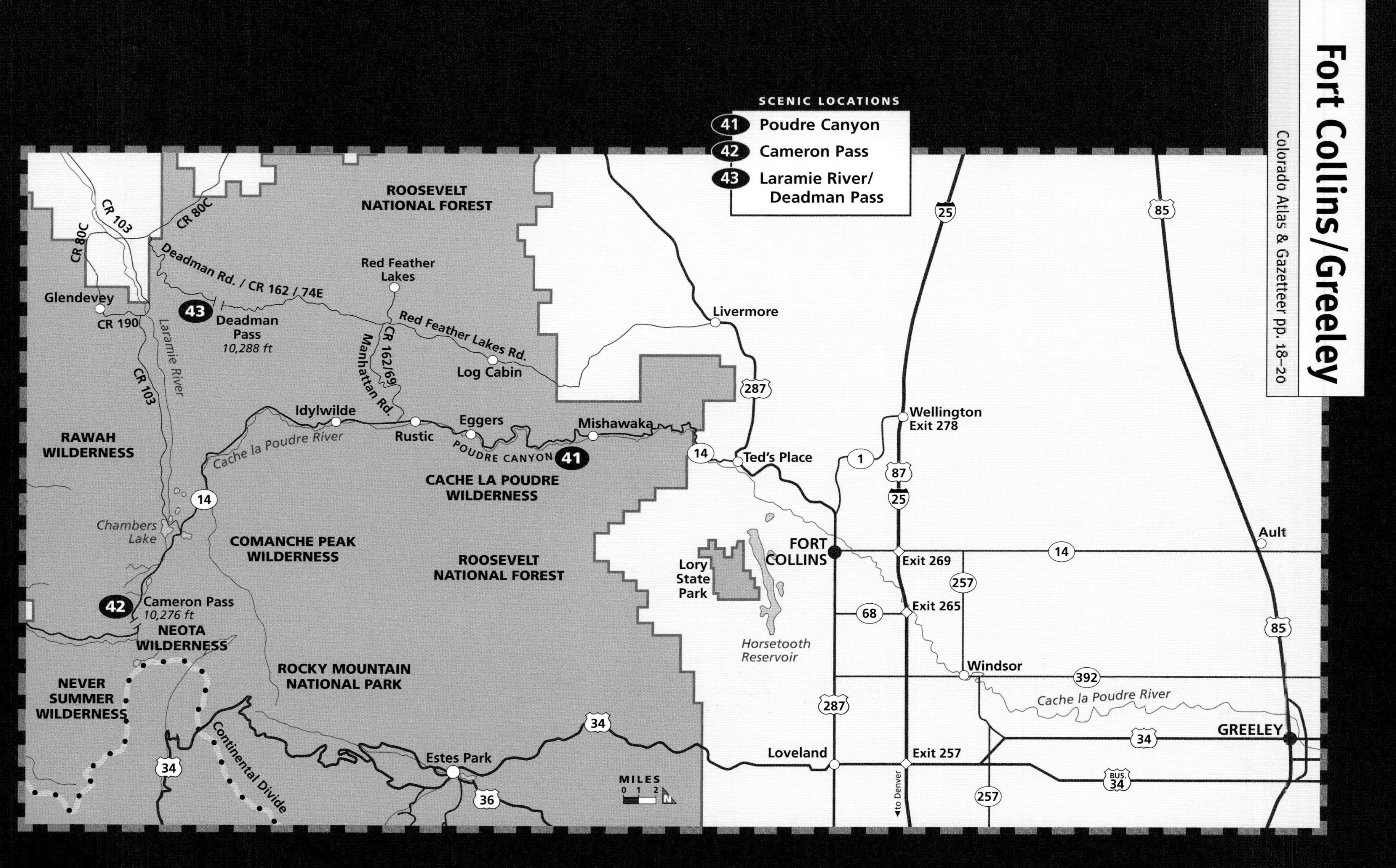

Fort Collins and Greeley

Residents of Fort Collins might believe their town is one of Colorado's best-kept secrets, but the secret is getting out. A&E Television has rated Fort Collins one of the nation's most livable cities. A visit to Old Town, just north of the Colorado State University (CSU) campus, shows why. Clapboard houses and venerable brick structures grace the vicinity of tree-lined Mulberry Street and College Avenue.

The heart of Fort Collins' historic district, Old Town thrives as a quaint pedestrian shopping mall and maintains the feel of a small town, despite significant citywide growth and the expansion of CSU.

Fine-art productions at the Lincoln Center and all manner of CSU-sponsored events, not to mention the lively rivalry between the CSU and University of Colorado football teams, combine for a buzzing cultural life in town. East of Roosevelt National Forest and northeast of Rocky Mountain National Park, Fort Collins also allows hikers, bikers, river rats, and others easy access to their outdoor pursuits. Come see why this vibrant city, the largest on the northern Front Range, is no longer a secret. From Denver, take I-25 north 60 miles.

Fort Collins' neighbor to the southeast, Greeley is another college town known for its quality of life, though its beginnings were extraordinary. Founded as the utopian, agricultural Union Colony, Greeley started with an idealized frontier ethic that locals still hold dear.

The University of Northern Colorado (UNC) contributes to the culture and vitality of the town. The school is known for its fine teaching program as well as its music department. The Union Colony Civic Center sets the stage for various UNC performances, while the Greeley Philharmonic Orchestra is the oldest symphony west of the Mississippi. Author James A. Michener, who taught at the former Colorado State College of Education (now UNC) from 1936 to 1941, based his novel *Centennial* on Greeley and vicinity; the university library is named for him today. Aside from UNC, agriculture and ranching are still the backbone of Greeley's economy, but a stroll through Old Town Square will reveal that this little city on the plains is much more than a cow town. From Denver, take I-25 north to US 34 (Exit 257) and go east for 15 miles.

History

As early as the 1820s, trappers visited the mountains west of present-day Fort Collins. By 1864, the U.S. Army had established Camp Collins as a fort to protect wagon trains coming west on the Overland Trail. Eight years later, speculators bought and subdivided land on the site of the then-abandoned military post, then sold these membership plots to prospective farmers and ranchers. When the Agricultural College of Colorado was established in 1870, this land-grant school put the tiny town of Fort Collins on the map. Like all such colleges, its purpose was to equip future generations of farmers and ranchers with the latest and most productive agricultural techniques. Although modern-day Colorado State University retains its agricultural studies programs, the school has greatly diversified its academic disciplines. Its veterinary school is one of the finest in the country. CSU has greatly enriched the way of life in this northern town.

Barely 35 miles from Fort Collins, Greeley had a very different origin. The Union Colony was established here in 1869, led by idealistic journalist Nathan C. Meeker, to be a cooperative community based on farming, education, and religion. Renamed for Meeker's editor at the *New York Tribune*, Horace Greeley, the town strove to be an exalted example to those who heeded Greeley's exhortation to go west. By 1871, Greeley was a bustling town with beautiful homes, thriving agriculture and businesses, and prosperous families. The town continues to cultivate its founding values. Some of the original Union Colony buildings remain in Centennial Village, a living-history museum that reflects Northern Colorado's growth and culture from the 1860s to the 1930s. Meeker himself moved farther west in 1878, with less happy consequences (see History, Craig, Meeker, and Dinosaur National Monument, p. 203).

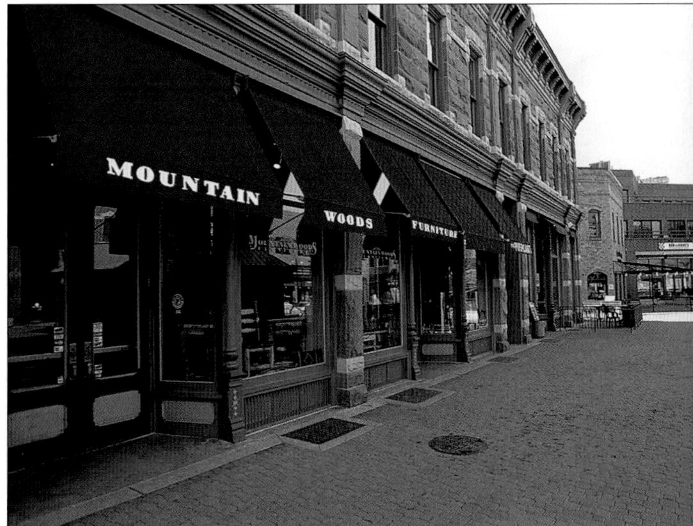

Old Town, Fort Collins

Main Attractions

CACHE LA POUDRE RIVER

The Cache la Poudre River was named, improbably enough, by French trappers in the 1820s who stashed their gunpowder in the canyon's crevices and caves to lighten their loads in the deep snow. The headwaters of the Poudre start at a glacial lake high up in Rocky Mountain National Park and flow north through the Neota Wilderness. From Fort Collins, take US 287 to Ted's Place, then head west on CO 14. As CO 14 follows the river northeast through Fort Collins, you'll find

POUDRE CANYON

The Cache la Poudre River is Colorado's only Wild and Scenic River, a federal designation that protects the river, its canyon, and its waters from further development. While not completely wild—some development along the highway exists in the canyon—the Poudre is incredibly scenic from Fort Collins to where it parts ways with the highway at Big South Trail. Poudre Canyon provides some of Colorado's most spectacular river canyon views, a few of which rival those accessible only by raft in other Colorado canyons. Stately ponderosa pines mix with deciduous trees along the way, and ancient rock walls provide a constant backdrop. The river changes from lazy and deliberate near Fort Collins to Class IV whitewater in the higher reaches, allowing different kinds of water photography from one end of the canyon to the other. From downtown Fort Collins, take CO 14 northwest. Look for the split in the highway at Ted's Place, where US 287 heads north to Wyoming and CO 14 goes west up Poudre Canyon and eventually over Cameron Pass (see Scenic Location No. 42, p. 152) on its way into North Park.

Just as you enter the canyon, look for places where water accumulates and allows reflection photography of the canyon walls and deciduous trees along the banks. You'll be on the north side of the river, so pull over and photograph up the canyon either from the highway above the river or from the small trail down along it. Take care as you scramble down the steep embankment. A wide-angle lens allows you to compose the right-hand bank emerging from the bottom right corner of a horizontal scene, as well as the river and the canyon walls on the other side. Include cottonwood trees in the scene in May and September to add color to the gray/brown canyon. All of this will reflect nicely in the water. Since the canyon is oriented east to west, sunrise photography will add shadows to the scene. On the other hand, soft, cloudy light will reduce the contrast and enhance the detail in the rock walls.

As the highway begins to wind circuitously above the river, look for vantages that allow you to photograph down into the canyon at places where it is long and straight. At such spots the river seems to disappear into merging canyon walls. A telephoto lens will compress distance from these viewpoints and enhance the precipitous nature of the canyon walls.

picnic spots with grills along the highway. The Poudre meanders east to Greeley and eventually joins the South Platte on the Eastern Plains.

Camping: Poudre Canyon's camping areas are a great launching point for fishing, hiking, and enjoying the views. **Ansel Watrous** campground offers access to fishing as well as the popular Greyrock Trail (see Hiking, p. 153). **Mountain Park** campground is the plushest campground in the canyon, with a volleyball court, playground, and Mount McConnel trailhead (see Hiking, p. 153). **Kelly Flats** is a beautiful, private spot with riverside sites and four-wheeling access (see Four-Wheel-Drive Trips, p. 152). From Fort Collins, go north 10 miles on US 287 to Ted's Place, then west on CO 14 for 13 miles to Ansel Watrous, 23 miles to Mountain Park, and 25 miles to Kelly Flats.

Several fine, smaller campgrounds just off CO 14 have great river access, including **Stove Prairie, Narrows, Big Bend,** and **Sleeping Elephant.** Farther down the canyon, just above Chambers Lake, the **Chambers Lake** campground suits anglers and accesses Lost Lake, Joe Wright Reservoir, and trails into Rawah Wilderness. From Fort Collins, go north on CO 287, head west on CO 14 at Ted's Place, and drive 53 miles to the Chambers Lake turnoff (County Road 103). Turn right (northwest) and continue 1 mile. *For more information: 970-498-2770, www.fs.fed.us/arnf.*

Fishing: The **Poudre** is a fly-fishing paradise with rainbows, browns, cutthroats, and brookies. Two sections are designated Wild Trout Water, which can be fished with artificial flies and lures only. River access is good along CO 14. *For information, lessons, and guided trips: St. Peter's Fly Shop, 202 Remington St., 970-498-8968, www.stpetes.com; Angler's Roost, 925 E. Harmony Rd. Suite 200, 970-377-3785, www.anglers-roost.com.*

Rafting: River runners of varying levels of experience come to the Poudre to enjoy its Class II–IV whitewater. Poudre Canyon is among the wildest and most picturesque rafting canyons in Colorado. *For information: A Wanderlust Adventure, 3500 Bingham Hill Rd., 970-484-1219, 800-745-7238, www.awanderlustadventure.com; A-1 Wildwater, 2801 N. Shields St., 970-224-3379, www.A1wildwater.com.*

Scenic Drives: Cache la Poudre Scenic and Historic Byway runs through Poudre Canyon on CO 14 from Fort Collins west to Walden. The 100-mile byway is well maintained, with several pullouts for wildlife viewing, picnicking, and photographing the canyon and valley landscapes.

LORY STATE PARK

With more than 2,500 acres of prairie grassland and pine forests, and 20 miles of easy-to-moderate trails, Lory State Park beckons hikers, mountain bikers, and horseback riders. **Arthur's Rock Trail** MODERATE is a popular, 1.7-mile route that winds through forests and meadows on its way to Arthur's Rock, a summit commanding an expansive view of Horsetooth Reservoir and the Front Range. Six-mile **Lory State Park Loop** EASY takes mountain bikers to great views of Horsetooth Reservoir, Fort Collins, and the Eastern Plains. On-site Double Diamond Stables offer one- and two-hour horseback rides through the park. *970-493-1623.*

From Fort Collins, take US 287 north toward Laporte. Turn left (west) at the Bellvue exit onto County Road 23N. Turn left (south), go 1.4 miles, and turn right on CR 25G. Follow the signs 1.6 miles. *970-493-1623, www.coloradoparks.org.*

Activities

BREWERY TOURS

Fort Collins has its share of fine breweries, complete with tours and samples. **New Belgium Brewing Co.,** producer of the legendary Fat Tire Amber Ale, is a big part of local microbrewing pride. *Self-guided tour information: 500 Linden St., 970-221-0524, www.newbelgium.com.* **CooperSmith's Pub & Brewing Co.** is another purveyor of handcrafted brews and a favorite with the university crowd (see Restaurants, p. 153), with tours conducted on Saturdays. *Old Town Square, 970-498-0483, www.coopersmithspub.com.* A high point of the **Anheuser-Busch Brewery Tour** is the chance to see the magnificent 2,000-pound Clydesdale horses whose ancestors pulled the beer wagons of yesteryear. *2351 Busch Dr., just off I-25 and CR 50, 970-490-4691. Other area breweries offering tours include: Odell Brewery, 800 E Lincoln Ave, 970-498-9070, 888-887-2797, www.odells.com; Fort Collins Brewery, 1900 E Lincoln Ave #B, 970-472-1499, www.fortcollinsbrewery.com*

CAMPING

Shoreline/Horsetooth Reservoir campground has a small number of sites with great access to water activities. From the south end of Fort Collins, go west on Harmony Road (County Road 38E), wind around the reservoir to Shoreline Drive (CR 25G), and turn right. *970-679-4570.* North of Fort Collins near Red Feather Lakes, **West Lake** offers privacy, great scenery, and good trout fishing. From Fort Collins, go north on US 287 for 21 miles to Livermore. Turn left (west) on Red Feather Lakes Road (CR 74E) and continue 23 miles. **Dowdy Lake** promises excellent trout fishing in beautiful surroundings. From Red Feather Lakes Road (CR 74E), turn right (northeast) onto Dowdy Lake Road (Forest Road 218) and continue 2 miles. *For both campgrounds: 970-498-2770.*

FAMILY FUN

Swetsville Zoo is the most unusual zoo in Colorado, or anywhere else for that matter. The 150 zoo "inhabitants" are sculptures built from farm machinery, car parts, and other metal scraps. Some of the creatures are

Swetsville Zoo, Fort Collins

CAMERON PASS

South of Poudre Canyon, CO 14 levels off in the high country and gradually affords views of the surrounding mountain ranges up to 10,276-foot Cameron Pass. To the north rise the Medicine Bow Mountains in the Rawah Wilderness, to the south the Mummy and Never Summer Ranges of Rocky Mountain National Park. The pass barely squeezes in between precipitous peaks, just misses the Continental Divide, and reveals glorious vistas on all sides. From this point, CO 14 is a wonderful drive through North Park to its terminus at US 40 near Rabbit Ears Pass.

After exiting Poudre Canyon, look immediately for County Road 103 to the north and signs to Chambers Lake. This is also the way to the Laramie River (see Scenic Location No. 43, p. 155). "Bathtub" rings caused by low water levels can detract from its beauty, but, nestled as it is in Roosevelt National Forest, Chambers Lake just might make a nice photograph at sunrise when peaks in the background catch early light. Otherwise, continue south to Cameron Pass, looking for views of the beautiful highway snaking through the forest and leading up to peaks in the distance. It's an exceptional highway photograph, especially at sunrise. Use your telephoto lens to compress the distance and make the peaks appear closer and larger.

As you descend the pass, you enter the Michigan River drainage. To the south you will gain views of the spectacular Nokhu Crags on the north end of the Never Summer Range. Rocky Mountain National Park is not far away. Pull over and frame a view of the crags with your telephoto lens. One mile after CO 14 turns west, look for CR 62 on your left. This road connects with hiking trails that can take you quickly up to the crags, as well as to Lake Agnes and the Michigan Lakes, which are set in spectacular cirques.

more bizarre than others, but all are products of the very active imagination of creator Bill Swets. Swetsville Zoo is 0.25 mile east off I-25's Harmony Road exit (265), and admission is free. *4801 E. Harmony Rd., 970-484-9509.*

FISHING

At **Red Feather Lakes** you can find trout as well as seclusion (no wonder it's the site of a major Buddhist shrine). From Fort Collins, take US 287 northwest 22 miles to Livermore. Turn left (west) onto Red Feather Lakes Road (County Road 74E). **Horsetooth Reservoir,** recently drained for repairs, may take time to get its trout, walleye, and bass back to catching weight. The reservoir also draws a legion of recreational boaters. Check with a local fishing shop for the reservoir's current fishing status. From Fort Collins, take Harmony Road west and follow signs to the reservoir. *For information: St. Peter's Fly Shop, 202 Remington St., 970-498-8968.*

FOUR-WHEEL-DRIVE TRIPS

Twelve-mile **Kelly Flats Road** commands spectacular views of Poudre Canyon and Rocky Mountain National Park. Because of stream crossings and several rough sections, you will need a high-clearance vehicle and should not attempt this road during spring runoff or without previous off-road experience. From just past Kelly Flats campground (see Camping, Main Attractions, p. 151), head north. Take County Road 69 to return to the canyon near Rustic.

GOLF

Fort Collins has two good 18-hole public golf courses. Locals favor **Collindale Golf Course.** *1441 E. Horsetooth Rd., 970-221-6651.* **SouthRidge Golf Course,** is also popular. *5750 S. Lemay Ave., 970-416-2828.* Take advantage of the off-peak rates.

HIKING

Convenient and easy trails are sprinkled throughout Fort Collins. One favorite is the paved, 1.5-mile (one way) **Fossil Creek Trail** EASY, which travels from South Shields Street, 0.75 mile south of Harmony Road, across Cathy Fromme Prairie to Taft Hill Road. There is a raptor observation building west of the parking lot on South Shields. Another paved jewel, 8-mile (one way) **Poudre River Trail** EASY follows the Cache la Poudre River through Fort Collins. The trail is lined with cottonwoods, benches for bird-watching, and ponds frequented by waterfowl, including the resident night heron. The trail extends from Taft Hill Road to CSU's Environmental Learning Center near East Drake Road.

Popular 3.5-mile (one way) **Greyrock National Recreation Trail** MODERATE leads from the floor of Poudre Canyon to the 7,513-foot summit of Greyrock Mountain, which commands spectacular views of Fort Collins to the southeast and the Medicine Bow Mountains and Rawah Wilderness to the west. From Fort Collins, take CO 14 west for 17 miles. Trailhead parking is on the left (south) side of the road.

Interpretive signs mark the 2-mile (one way) **Kreutzer Nature Trail** EASY, where fishing access and equipment are available for children. The trail to **Mount McConnel** DIFFICULT ascends the 8,000-foot summit and intersects Kreutzer Nature Trail. From the summit, hikers are rewarded with lovely views of the Mummy Range and Rocky Mountain National Park. From Fort Collins, take CO 14 west for 40 miles to Mountain Park Recreation Area, parking lot, and trailhead.

Five-mile (one way) **Browns Lake Trail** MODERATE heads above timberline and then down to Browns Lake through the Comanche Peak Wilderness. Go west from Ted's Place on CO 14 for 26 miles to Pingree Park Road, turn left (south), and continue 4 miles. Keep right at Crown Point Road (FR 139) and continue another 12 miles to the trailhead on the left. Three-mile (round-trip) **Montgomery Pass Trail** EASY carves through the dense forest of the Neota Wilderness. Wildflowers in the subalpine meadows are lovely throughout the spring and summer. From Fort Collins, take CO 14 west 65 miles to Joe Wright Reservoir. Park at the Zimmerman Lake parking lot, west of the reservoir.

One of my favorite hikes is the 6-mile (one way) trip to **Mirror Lake** MODERATE through remote sections of Rocky Mountain National Park and Comanche Peak Wilderness. Fish the streams and take in views of Hagues Peak, Rowe Mountain and Rowe Peak, and the Desolation Peaks. Mirror Lake is the final reward, an aptly named jewel of a high mountain lake. From Fort Collins, take CO 14 west 52 miles to Long Draw Road, turn left, and follow it to the Corral Creek trailhead. Take the **Mummy Pass Trail** MODERATE 5 miles to where it joins the Mirror Lake Trail. Many of these hiking trails see cross-country ski and snowshoe traffic in winter.

MUSEUMS

In Greeley, **Centennial Village** is a living-history museum that gives a sense of frontier life on the High Plains from the 1860s to the 1930s. Enjoy a tour of the village and its fully furnished, period homes, and check out the gardens and quilt and carriage collections. *1475 A St., 970-350-9220.* The **Meeker Home** became Greeley's first museum in 1929 and has been renovated and restored several times. It is filled with Meeker family memorabilia and traditional 19th-century decor. *1324 9th Ave., 970-350-9221.* **Plumb Farm Museum** hosts numerous events throughout the year including Baby Animal Days, Pets 'n' Popsicles, and Harvest Days, to promote education and appreciation of Greeley's farming life, past and present. Tours of the farm, at 10th Street and 39th Avenue, are available in the summer. *970-350-9275.* Greeley's newest museum, **The Greeley Freight Station Museum,** displays railroad artifacts from across the country. Open Saturdays and the first Friday of each month. *680 1st St, 970-392-2934, www.gfsm.org.*

Meeker Home, Greeley

Restaurants

In Fort Collins, **Moot House** ($$-$$$) is a delightful English pub with chops, steaks, prime rib, and seafood. *2626 S. College Ave., 970-226-2121.* **Austin's American Grill** ($$) is a Fort Collins favorite, with prime rib, grilled salmon, and a great patio. Try the smoked chicken. Two locations *100 W Mountain Ave, 970-224-9691 and 2815 E Harmony Rd, 970-267-6532.* For steaks, get into the popular **Charco Broiler** ($$) at *1716 E. Mulberry. 970-226-5211.* Fort Collins residents mosey down to **Rio Grande** ($$) for margaritas with a kick. No reservations. *143 W. Mountain Ave., 970-224-5428.*

CooperSmith's Pub & Brewing Co

Residents consider **Bisetti's** ($-$$) one of the best Italian restaurants in town. Follow a fine entree with a slice of Bisetti's own cheesecake. *120 S. College Ave., 970-493-0086.*

43 SCENIC LOCATION — LARAMIE RIVER/ DEADMAN PASS

The Laramie River essentially begins at Chambers Lake and merges with the North Platte River in Wyoming. Before it gets there, however, it traverses some of the loveliest valleys and canyons in the West, including a meandering 30-mile (as the crow flies) stretch in Colorado. A road follows the entire route, part of which courses through forest and mountain meadows, the rest through vast hayfields. The access to the river from the east crosses a drainage divide in the Laramie Mountains—Deadman Pass—which affords great views of the Medicine Bow Mountains and Rawah Wilderness.

Exit CO 14 along the Cache la Poudre River at the enclave of Glen Echo by turning north on County Road 69. Follow the signs north to Red Feather Lakes. Turn west onto Deadman Road (CR 162) and follow its circuitous route through Roosevelt National Forest to the Laramie River. You can make the drive in a car, but I recommend a four-wheel drive. Alternatively, you can get to the river via the Chambers Lake exit (CR 103) from CO 14 on the way south to Cameron Pass.

Deadman Road is lost in the forest most of its way, but you reach an incredibly scenic view near Deadman Creek about halfway to the river. You'll know it when you see it: The creek makes a classic Colorado scene, nestled among pristine meadows and below the glaciated peaks of Rawah Wilderness to the southwest. To locate the correct creek crossing and photographic vantage point, find Forest Road 319 on your left just past the creek. Now drive back east on Deadman Road 0.5 mile to the first primitive road heading south. Drive or walk this road a little way until you see Deadman Creek winding through the meadows. From this spot you can make the composition.

At the end of Deadman Road, make a left on CR 80C and proceed 2 miles to CR 103. From here you can drive south along the Laramie River or take a detour west and south along McIntyre Creek to Glendevey, then head back to CR 103. Both drives provide intimate landscape compositions with river or creek snaking through forests of pine, fir, and cottonwood. CR 103 also provides access to the main hiking trails of the Rawah Wilderness.

CooperSmith's Pub & Brewing Co. ($-$$) in Old Town Square, *970-498-0483,* and **New Belgium Brewing Co.** ($-$$) brews Fat Tire, which is served with great pub grub. *500 Linden St., 970-221-0524.* **Walrus Ice Cream** ($) has frozen desserts that will delight kids of all ages. *125 W. Mountain Ave., 970-482-5919.*

In Greeley, **Coyote's Southwestern Grill** ($$) pleases with fresh, innovative Mexican cuisine. *5250 W. 9th St. Dr., 970-336-1725.* **Echo** ($$) serves great Japanese food. *1702 8th Ave., Greeley, 970-351-8548.* **Fat Albert's** ($$) is a town favorite for lunch and has a broad and tasty menu. *1717 23rd Ave., Greeley, 970-356-1999.*

Accommodations

Skip the chain motels and hotels and really enjoy your stay at one of Fort Collins' fine B&Bs. Built in 1904, the elegant, neo-classical-style **Edwards House Bed & Breakfast** ($$) deserves a high rating for its service, as well as its convenient location in a quiet residential neighborhood. *402 Mountain Ave., 800-281-9190, www.edwardshouse.com.* **Sheldon House B&B** ($$), formerly West Mulberry Street B&B, continues the same tradition of cozy lodging and good service. *616 W. Mulberry St., 970-221-1917, www.bbonline.com/co/sheldonhouse.*

Beaver Meadows Resort Ranch ($-$$) near Red Feather Lakes is a year-round resort and ultimate family destination, with fishing, horseback riding, mountain biking, and cross-country skiing. *100 Marmot Dr. #1, 970-881-2450, 800-462-5870, www.beavermeadows.com.*

Sod Buster Inn ($-$$) is a remarkable, octagonal B&B that blends well into Greeley's historic district but has up-to-the-minute amenities. *1221 9th Ave., 970-392-1221.*

Edwards House Bed & Breakfast, Fort Collins

Special Events

In mid-August, **New West Fest** brings great food, entertainment, and artisan booths to downtown Fort Collins, in one of the largest celebrations in northern Colorado. *970-232-3840, www.ftcollins.com.*

The **Greeley Independence Stampede** bills itself as the "World's Largest Fourth of July Rodeo and Western Celebration," and I can't argue with that. The festivities span two weeks, and include a carnival, concerts, demolition derbies, fireworks displays, Western dinner theater productions, and, of course, plenty of bull and bronc riding. *600 N. 14th Ave., 970-356-BULL, www.greeleystampede.org.*

For More Information

Fort Collins Convention & Visitors Bureau, *19 Old Town Square, Suite 137, 970-232-3840, www.ftcollins.com,*Greeley Convention & Visitors Bureau, *902 7th Ave., 970-352-3567, www.greeleycvb.com.*

Estes Park

Colorado Atlas & Gazetteer p. 29

SCENIC LOCATIONS

- 44 Rocky Mountain National Park: Moraine Park
- 45 Rocky Mountain National Park: Bear Lake
- 46 Rocky Mountain National Park: Trail Ridge Road

Estes Park

The captivating beauty of the town of Estes Park, the eastern gateway to Rocky Mountain National Park nestled beneath fourteener Longs Peak, enchants thousands of visitors annually. Summer tourists throng so thickly that Estes Park's cadet officers must regulate pedestrian traffic. Despite the crowds, you just have to love a place where elk graze on lawns and present the biggest hazard on the golf course. Elk bugling each autumn draws sightseers just to see and hear this amazing mating rite.

Most Estes Park residents understand the importance of the elk to the town's economy and admire these wild creatures. Today a bronze statue of Samson, an impressive, 1,000-pound male elk, stands at the junction of US 36 and CO 7. Good-natured Samson had often wandered into Estes Park and was a town favorite. Alas, a poacher killed him in November 1995, both saddening and infuriating the community. In the wake of this tragedy, Samson's Law was passed in the state legislature; the law protects big game by significantly increasing fines for illegal hunting.

Take a leisurely stroll down the town's main street, Elkhorn Avenue, and enjoy the quaint and bustling atmosphere of a true mountain town. Taste the taffy and fudge, and shop for rocks, jewelry, art, and books at the various specialty shops. To get to Estes Park from Denver, take I-25 north 35 miles to Longmont (Exit 243). Go west on CO 66, 16 miles to Lyons. From Lyons, go 20 miles northwest on US 36 to Estes Park.

History

Estes Park lies in the valley below 14,255-foot Longs Peak (named after Army Major Stephen H. Long, who explored the region in 1820) and 13,911-foot Mount Meeker (named for Nathan C. Meeker, a reporter who founded the Union Colony cooperative agricultural settlement in Greeley). In 1864, Longs Peak caught the attention of William N. Byers, founding publisher of the *Rocky Mountain News* in Denver. Byers visited early homesteaders Joel Estes and his family, scaled Longs Peak, and through his newspaper encouraged settlement in the valley.

In 1872, the Irish Earl of Dunraven came to Estes Park to hunt. Dunraven soon fancied making Estes Park his private hunting preserve (see Hiking, p. 161) and attempted to acquire all the valley lands by whatever means necessary, often illegal. His designs were thwarted, however, by the successful efforts of ranchers and homesteaders; Dunraven had to settle for being the proprietor of the "English Hotel" he built in 1877 (destroyed by fire in 1911), where luminaries like "Buffalo Bill" Cody and Kit Carson stayed. Albert Bierstadt also visited Dunraven and made dramatic landscape paintings that further popularized the valley.

Meanwhile, increasing numbers of tourists arrived each year, accommodated in guest ranches and inns both in town and west of Estes Park. The only hotel to rival Dunraven's, however, was the one built by the co-inventor of the Stanley Steamer motor car, Freelan Oscar Stanley, who had come to Colorado in 1903 in hopes of relieving his tuberculosis. On land acquired from Lord Dunraven, he opened the grand Stanley Hotel in 1909 (see Main Attractions, p. 160), a structure that still graces the town. Stanley's health was restored and his reputation assured: After all, who remembers the Steamer today?

The completion of a road (US 34) up Big Thompson Canyon in 1910 enabled even more people to come to Estes Park and visit the stunning wilderness to the west, at that time dotted with guest houses and ranches. By the efforts of Enos Mills (see Colorado Cameo, p. 160) and other park promoters, President Woodrow Wilson signed federal legislation creating Rocky Mountain National Park in 1915, preserving a pristine expanse of glacially cut valleys, peaks, and lakes and ensuring the future of Estes Park as a tourist destination. Today, Rocky Mountain National Park hosts millions of visitors every year; Estes Park continues to cater to and depend on these tourists.

Main Attractions

ROCKY MOUNTAIN NATIONAL PARK

To me, Rocky Mountain National Park is really two very different parks—west of the Continental Divide, it is green with meadows, wetlands, and dense forests (see Grand Lake, p. 167); east of the Continental Divide, the park is more dry, the vegetation more sparse, and craggy rock formations stand out above glaciated valleys. Both areas are equally attractive to me. I can't think of a better place than Rocky Mountain National Park for the entire family to hike and see high alpine lakes, cascading waterfalls, breathtaking vistas, and wildlife. Bring a camera!

At the park's visitor centers you can study displays about the park, talk to rangers who can answer your questions, and pick up maps and information about hiking, fishing, camping, and winter activities. Beaver Meadows Visitor Center is at the park's eastern boundary on US 36; Lily Lake Visitor Center is about 8 miles south of Estes Park on CO 7. There is an admittance fee to enter the park. *800-365-2267, www.nps.gov/romo.*

Camping: At these popular campgrounds, you can often expect to see deer or elk near your campsite at dusk! With more than 200 sites, **Moraine Park** is the largest campground in the park and accesses the Fern Lake Trail. To get to Moraine Park, take the first left past the Beaver Meadows entrance station and go 1.5 miles, then take the first road on the right and follow the signs to the campground. **Aspenglen** offers privacy, mountain views, and access to fishing on the Fall River and hiking on the Lawn Lake Trail, just 1 mile west. To get to the campground from CO 34 west, turn left just beyond the Fall River entrance station. **Glacier Basin,** 5 miles south of the Beaver Meadows entrance station on Bear Lake Road, has great amenities for campers. If you're planning to climb Longs Peak, you might want to stay with the other early risers at the small **Longs Peak** campground on CO 7. *For information and reservations: 800-365-2267.*

Fishing: Fishing for small rainbows, browns, cutthroats, and brookies can be quite good in the park, although you might have to do some hiking. Colorado's state fish, the greenback cutthroat trout, is the dominant species on the eastern side of the park and is managed under a recovery program. These fish are catch-and-release only; handle them with care and return them to the water immediately.

The headwaters of the **Big Thompson River** start on the eastern side of the Continental Divide at Forest Canyon Pass near the top of Trail Ridge Road. The river becomes fishable at Moraine Park about 6 miles downstream, where it splits into several channels and streams. Brookies, browns, and cutthroats here can get as large as 12 inches. Moraine Park is 1 mile south on Bear Lake Road from US 36 (see Scenic Location No. 45, p. 163).

Fall River has deep pockets full of trout. You can fish the Fall River from the Aspenglen campground, just west of the park's Fall River entrance on US 34, or upstream as it meanders through Horseshoe Park. The **Roaring River** also has nice pocket water and is full of catch-and-release greenback cutthroats. Take the Lawn Lake Trail 1.5 miles to the best section of the river. It's a steep climb but it's worth it. **Thunder Lake, Ouzel Lake, Fern Lake, Sprague Lake,** and **Chasm Lake** are fine fishing holes for native greenback cutthroat trout and are well worth the hike (for directions, see below). *For information on fishing, lessons, equipment, and guided tours, contact: Estes Anglers, 338 W. Riverside Dr., 970-586-2110, www.estesangler.com.*

Hiking: The Emerald Lake Trail EASY is the park's most popular hiking trail. This gentle, 1.8-mile (one way) path accesses three stunning mountain lakes—Nymph, Dream, and Emerald—and is also popular with snowshoers. The 0.5-mile **Sprague Lake Nature Trail Loop** EASY leads through pine stands to an alpine lake and is wheelchair accessible. Connect to the trail 0.5 mile south of the Bear Lake shuttle bus parking lot.

Fern Lake Trail MODERATE climbs 8.5 miles (one way) to Fern Falls—actually two spectacular 40-foot falls—and to The Pool, a deep basin carved by the Big Thompson River. The **Flattop Mountain** and **Hallett Peak Trails** DIFFICULT provide fine views, including that of Emerald Lake. It is 4.4 miles to Flattop Mountain and another 1 mile to Hallett Peak. Reach the trailheads for Emerald Lake, Fern Lake, and Flattop Mountain from the Bear Lake parking lot. Take US 36 west 0.2 mile from the Beaver Meadows entrance station, then head south 9.2 miles along Bear Lake Road. These trails are popular and the lot is often full; another option is to take a shuttle from the parking area 5 miles south of US 36 on Bear Lake Road.

The 4.7-mile (one way) **Black Lake Trail** MODERATE goes up Glacier Gorge below the sheer wall of Longs Peak. Alberta Falls, a 25-foot cascade of water, is only 0.6 mile from the trailhead, and beautiful Mills Lake lies 2.5 miles into the hike. The trail is also a popular cross-country skiing and snowshoeing route. The 4.6-mile (one way) **Sky Pond Trail** MODERATE takes you by Alberta Falls, Timberline Falls, and Lake of Glass, and ends at Sky Pond. The Black Lake and Sky Pond trailheads begin at the Glacier Gorge Junction trailhead across from the parking area on Bear Lake Road.

The 6.3-mile (one way) **Bluebird Lake Trail** DIFFICULT goes through forests and meadows to Copeland Falls, Calypso Cascades, Ouzel Falls, Ouzel Lake, and Bluebird Lake. To get to **Thunder Lake** DIFFICULT, take a right off the Bluebird Lake trail 3.6 miles from the trailhead. It's another 2.7 miles to the lake. The trailhead for Bluebird and Thunder Lakes is in the Wild Basin Area, 12.7 miles past the Lily Lake Visitor Center south on CO 7.

The 3.3-mile (one way) **Estes Cone Trail** MODERATE takes you past the remains of the Eugenia Mine and to views of Longs Peak, Lumpy Ridge, the Mummy Range, and the Continental Divide. The 4.2-mile (one way) hike through the tundra up to **Chasm Lake** DIFFICULT commands fine views. Chasm Lake rests 2,000 feet below the sheer east face of Longs Peak. Look for elk, marmots, and pikas.

The easiest way to the summit of 14,255-foot **Longs Peak** DIFFICULT is via the "Keyhole Route," but that is not to say the hike is easy! The 8-mile (one way) trail gains a hefty 5,000 feet in elevation before reaching the summit's spectacular views. It's crucial to get a very early start in order to summit the peak before the afternoon thunderstorms roll in, for Longs is known for its electrifying experiences. Anyone who has climbed this mountain has a special memory of it: the krummholz (dwarfed, gnarled trees shaped by the high winds), the glaciers, the hanging lakes, or The Diamond. For me, it is the memory of the wind howling through the Keyhole.

The Estes Cone, Chasm Lake, and Longs Peak Trails are accessed from the Longs Peak trailhead, 8.9 miles south of the Lily Lake Visitor Center on CO 7. Turn right (west) at the Longs Peak area sign and follow the road a mile to the Longs Peak Ranger Station.

Rock Climbing: Even if you're anything but a technical climber, just watching climbers work these granite walls and spires is a breathtaking experience. **The Diamond,** on the eastern face of Longs Peak, ranks among the most famous—and fearsome—climbs in the nation. Longs' unpredictable and severe weather can often pose real problems. Reach The Diamond from the Longs Peak Trail (see directions, above).

Among Colorado's best-known rock climbs, the **Petit Grepon** is one of the spires on the Cathedral Wall. Park at the Glacier Gorge Junction trailhead and hike to Sky Pond for views of the Petit Grepon. *For information and guided climbing trips: Colorado Mountain School, 341 Moraine Ave., 800-836-4008, www.cmschool.com.*

Trail Ridge Road: This astounding route is not for the faint of heart (see Scenic Location No. 46, p. 165); driving along the narrow shelf above timberline, you will appreciate that it's the highest continuous paved road in the nation. Forty-eight-mile Trail Ridge Road connects Estes Park on

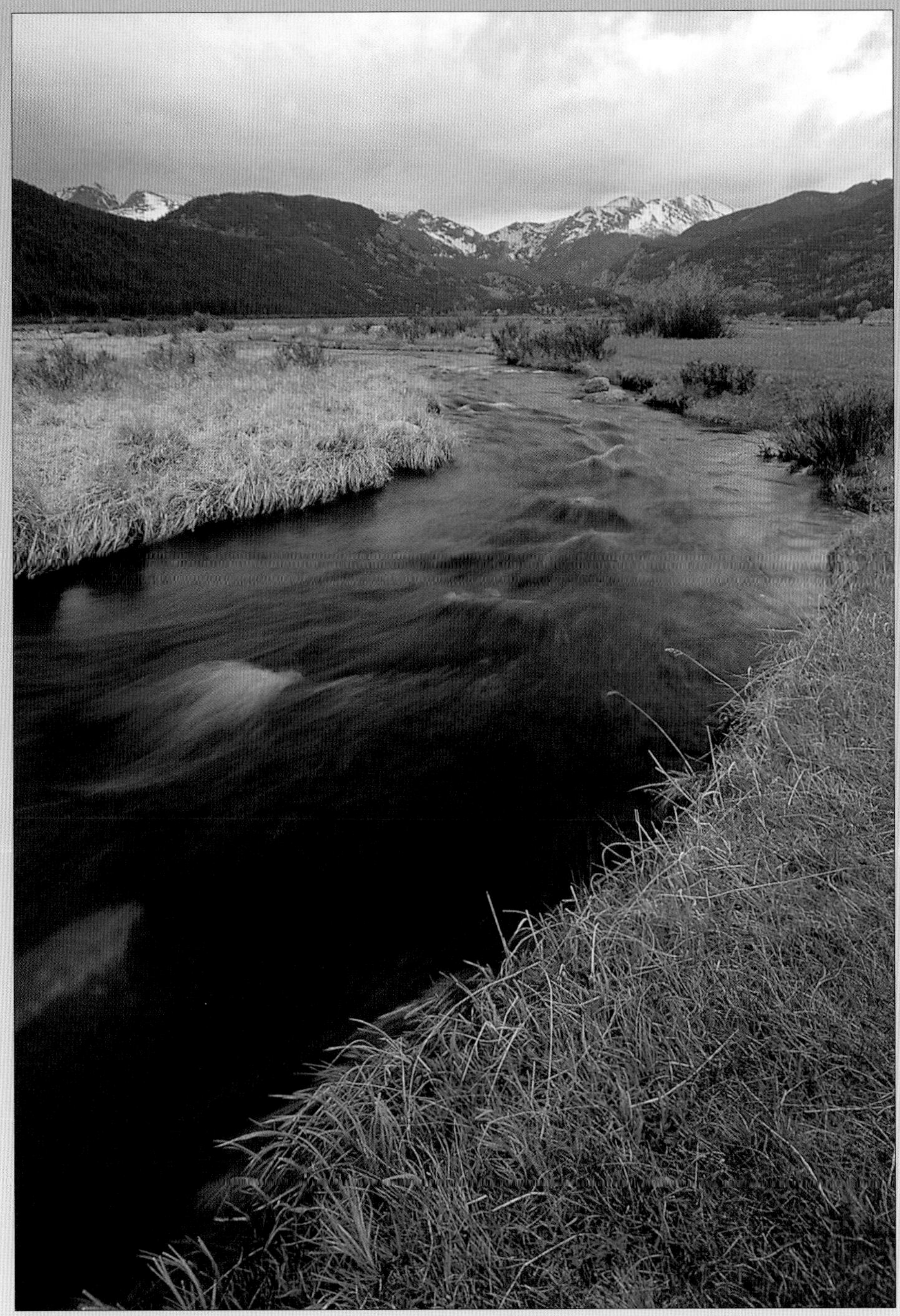

44 SCENIC LOCATION ROCKY MOUNTAIN NATIONAL PARK: MORAINE PARK

This is the first of four great places from which to photograph right off the road in Colorado's largest and most popular national park. In 1995, I published *Rocky Mountain National Park: A 100 Year Perspective,* a large book with color photographs that I made over the course of two summers exploring the park. During those summers, I spent 50 nights camping in the park, photographing each and every lake and hiking nearly every square inch of its 400-square-mile area. The four places I describe in this book are among the most beautiful and accessible. Moraine Park is a classic montane valley on the east side of the park, with views up the Big Thompson River toward the peaks of the Continental Divide. From Estes Park, take US 36 past park headquarters and through the Beaver Meadows entrance station. Make the next left onto the paved Bear Lake Road and follow the signs south to Moraine Park and ultimately Bear Lake (see Scenic Location No. 45, p. 163).

This place defines Rocky Mountain National Park's lower-altitude ecosystems. The Big Thompson River runs right through the middle of the valley on its way to Lake Estes and eventually the South Platte River. Grassy meadows, colorful willows, stately ponderosa pines, quaking aspens, spruce, and fir decorate the river valley.

Drive past the Moraine Park campground and the Moraine Park Museum until the road meets the river. There is a turnoff and parking lot on the right from which you can take a short hike to the edge of the river. Make a photograph looking west up Spruce Canyon to the Continental Divide, with the river in the foreground. Attempt to compose the banks of the river leading from the bottom left- and/or right-hand corners of the frame. Such lead-in lines add depth to the scene, and the parallax distortion made by the riverbanks as they merge in the distance enhances the effect. A wide-angle lens works best here, but remember that the shorter the focal length, the smaller the mountains will appear in the background. Walk north through the meadow and notice the long row of aspens to the north. When they are light green in late May and yellow in late September, they form a conspicuous band that makes an interesting foreground for the Mummy Range in the distance. You can drive to Moraine Park year-round, so go back every season and record each location's personality from one season to the next. Bring your telephoto lens—you never know when a herd of elk might appear. And don't forget to visit the museum to see fascinating artifacts and displays about the park that will further your appreciation for this public resource.

the east with Grand Lake on the west through unforgettable mountain scenery. Stop at the pullouts and walk to the overlooks, but stay on paths to protect the alpine tundra. You might spy elk, bighorn sheep, marmots, and other creatures. From the Alpine Visitor Center you can scan the scenery with binoculars, see exhibits, shop, and get a warm beverage. Even on the hottest day in Estes Park, bring a jacket for Trail Ridge Road overlooks. Be aware of weather changes and lightning. Suitable for a car, Trail Ridge Road is closed in winter. Take the 4-mile (one way) **Ute Trail** MODERATE from the visitor center parking lot, formerly taken by Ute Indians across the Great Divide. Wonder at the landscape and admire the delicate tundra flowers. The thin air at 11,796 feet causes many people to turn around after a half mile; however, you can continue another 3.5 miles to the Milner Pass parking area.

THE STANLEY HOTEL

Freelan Oscar Stanley, co-inventor with his brother of the Stanley Steamer motor car, suffered from tuberculosis and had been given six months to live by his doctors. In hopes of regaining his health, Stanley and his wife, Flora, came to Denver in 1903. A month later, they traveled to Estes Park and stayed in a cabin for the summer. The couple fell in love with the land, and Stanley's health improved dramatically. Stanley began construction of the hotel in 1906, selecting the neoclassical, white-pillared Georgian style of architecture so popular in his native state of Maine. The hotel opened in 1909, and offered luxuries such as electricity, running water, and telephone service (though, as a summer resort, it was heated by fireplaces until 1979). These services required a hydroelectric plant and pipe system that brought electricity and running water to all Estes Park residents.

Overlooking Estes Park, The Stanley Hotel is much the same as it was in 1909. Although the upstairs is reserved for guests, take the tour of the first floor and basement. In the Music Room, you will find Flora Stanley's Steinway grand piano, still played by visiting musicians. The Piñon Room was once reserved for cigar smoking, brandy, and men only. Women were allowed to watch games in the Billiard Room only if they sat on a bench along the wall and remained silent! Ladies and gentlemen dined and danced in the MacGregor Room.

Stanley Hotel, Estes Park

The hotel is one of four buildings on the property. The Manor House, next door, opened in 1910 as bachelors' quarters. Built in 1915 as the hotel's entertainment center, Stanley Hall featured plays and musicals. The Carriage House once stored a fleet of Stanley Steamers. Molly Brown, President Theodore Roosevelt, and, more recently, the Emperor and Empress of Japan have all been guests at The Stanley Hotel. The Stanley was also the inspiration for Stephen King's legendary novel *The Shining*, much of which King wrote in Room 217. *The intersection of US 34 and US 36 at 333 Wonderview Ave., 970-586-3371, 800-976-1377, www.stanleyhotel.com.*

COLORADO CAMEO

Enos Mills

No one today disputes that Rocky Mountain National Park should be a federally designated national park, but at the beginning of the 20th century some thought that national forest protection was adequate. Many who were opposed to establishing a national park feared that the government would seize their property. Those fears were unfounded, though the early lodges and resorts have left little trace today on the landscape west of Estes Park.

Nature guide, conservationist, author, photographer, and innkeeper Enos A. Mills homesteaded near and studied what is now Rocky Mountain National Park from the time of his arrival in 1885, when he was just 14. Having worked as part of a road survey team, Mills had seen the wonders of America's first national park, Yellowstone. He was also deeply influenced by a meeting with naturalist and conservationist John Muir and began to work for national park protection.

Mills joined with other concerned citizens in the Estes Park area and in 1909 initiated a campaign to get Congress to designate the much-visited wilderness a federally protected national park. Mills campaigned tirelessly and gained the support of the Estes Park Protective and Improvement Association, the Colorado Mountain Club, *The Denver Post,* the Colorado Chamber of Commerce, and the state legislature and congressional delegation.

His six-year crusade was finally crowned with success when President Woodrow Wilson signed legislation on January 26, 1915, establishing Rocky Mountain National Park. Ironically, Mills was dissatisfied in the end that the park did not encompass more area to the south, but then he was not a legislator accustomed to compromise. Even so, we owe a large debt of gratitude to Enos Mills for his leadership in protecting what is today one of Colorado's wildest and most pristine places.

Activities

AERIAL TRAMWAY

The aerial tramway will take you to the summit of 8,896-foot Prospect Mountain for views of Estes Park and magnificent Longs Peak. *420 E. Riverside Dr., 970-586-3675, www.estestram.com.*

FISHING

Big Thompson Canyon still shows vestiges of one of the worst flash floods in Colorado history. In July 1976, after heavy rains, a 20-foot wall of water rushed down the canyon, destroying all in its path and taking more than 100 lives. Many could not climb up the canyon to safety, and some residents and campers tragically tried to outrun the deluge.

The **Big Thompson River** below Estes Park is stocked with rainbows and browns that can grow as long as 13 inches. From the river's headwaters in Rocky Mountain National Park and through the park, brook and the catch-and-release greenback cutthroat trout are the predominant species (see Fishing, Rocky Mountain National Park, p. 158). US 34 follows the Big Thompson River from Estes Park to Loveland.

Although **Lake Estes,** just east of Estes Park, is a popular fishing hole, I prefer **Lily Lake,** which has hefty greenback cutthroats and awesome views to Longs Peak. Lily Lake is 6 miles south of Estes Park on CO 7. *For fishing information, lessons, equipment, and guided tours: Estes Angler, 338 W. Riverside Dr., 970-586-2110.*

FOUR-WHEEL-DRIVE TRIPS

An observation platform on the moderate **Pole Hill Road** commands an excellent view of the Mummy Range to the north and Hallett Peak and Flattop Mountain to the west. From Estes Park, go 3 miles southeast on US 36 to the top of Park Hill, then turn left onto Pole Hill Road (Forest Road 122) at the Ravencrest Chalet. Go 1 mile and enter Roosevelt National Forest, then take the first left to the observation platform. **Johnny Park Road,** an easy drive, offers wonderful views of Mount Meeker and Longs Peak. To get to Johnny Park Road, go 10 miles south from Estes Park on CO 7 and turn left (east) onto Big Owl Road (County Road 82), which intersects Johnny Park Road (FR 118). You can loop back to Estes Park on US 36. *For information and tours: American Wilderness Tours, 875 Moraine Ave., 970-586-1626, www.estesparkco.com.*

GOLF

Estes Park has two gorgeous and challenging golf courses—the 18-hole **Estes Park Golf Course** and the **Lake Estes 9 Hole Executive Golf Course.** On these courses you'll have an unusual hazard—elk, which you should never play through. Estes Park Golf Course is 2 miles south of town on CO 7. *970-586-8146, www.estesvalleyrecreation.com/18holegolf.html.* The Lake Estes course is just off US 34 at 690 Big Thompson Ave. *970-586-8176, www.estesvalleyrecreation.com/9holegolf.html.*

HIKING

Many hikes in the Estes Park area are easy and family friendly. The 2.5-mile (one way) **Lion Gulch Trail** EASY has great mountain views and leads into Homestead Meadows, where the ruins of an 1880s homesteaders' village still stand. From Estes Park, go 8 miles southeast on US 36; the trailhead is on the south side of the road.The 3-mile round-trip **Lily Mountain Trail** MODERATE affords a great view of the Mummy Range, Longs Peak, and the Continental Divide from the summit of 9,786-foot Lily Mountain. From Estes Park, go south 5.8 miles on CO 7 and park on the shoulder; the trail begins on the west side of the road.

The 4.5-mile (one way) **North Fork Trail** EASY follows the North Fork of the Big Thompson River in the Comanche Peak Wilderness. The trail enters Dunraven Meadows, where you can see the remnants of Lord Dunraven's hunting lodge. To get there from Estes Park, take MacGregor Avenue north across the US 34 bypass and go 0.8 mile to the MacGregor Ranch gate. Here the road takes a sharp right and becomes Devils Gulch Road. Go northeast another 6 miles to Glen Haven, then continue 2 miles and turn left on Dunraven Glade Road. The trailhead is 2.4 miles down the road.

The 2-mile (one way) **Gem Lake Trail** EASY winds through the Lumpy Ridge rock formations to Gem Lake, a sparkling lake beside vertical granite slabs. A 1.8-mile spur to the left of Gem Lake leads to Balanced Rock, a huge boulder perched on a narrow neck. Take Devils Gulch Road through the entrance to MacGregor Ranch and stay on the road for 0.8 mile to the Twin Owls trailhead. The Gem Lake Trail starts at the eastern end of the parking lot. (For other great hikes, see Rocky Mountain National Park, p. 158.)

HORSEBACK RIDING

Get to one of the fine stables in Estes Park to arrange a horseback excursion. I recommend **Sombrero Ranch Stables,** whose knowledgeable staff will tailor a ride to your ability and interest, with hourly trail rides; a Breakfast Ride; a Steak Fry Ride; cattle roundups; and fishing, hunting, and overnight pack trips. *2 miles east of Estes Park on US 34, 970-586-4577, www.sombrero.com.*

MOUNTAIN BIKING

Mountain biking is not permitted on the park trails, but **Old Fall River Road** DIFFICULT, 4 miles beyond the Fall River entrance station, provides a 9-mile challenge. Turning into a gravel road (one-way for automobiles) as it climbs up 11,796-foot Fall River Pass, Old Fall River Road joins Trail Ridge Road for a loop back to Estes Park. The 11-mile **House Rock Trail** MODERATE affords a great view of Longs Peak. The last part of the ride is steep and strenuous. From Estes Park, go south 8 miles on CO 7 to the Meeker Park picnic area. *Information and guided tours: Colorado Bicycling Adventures, 184 E. Elkhorn Ave., 970-586-4241, www.coloradobicycling.com.*

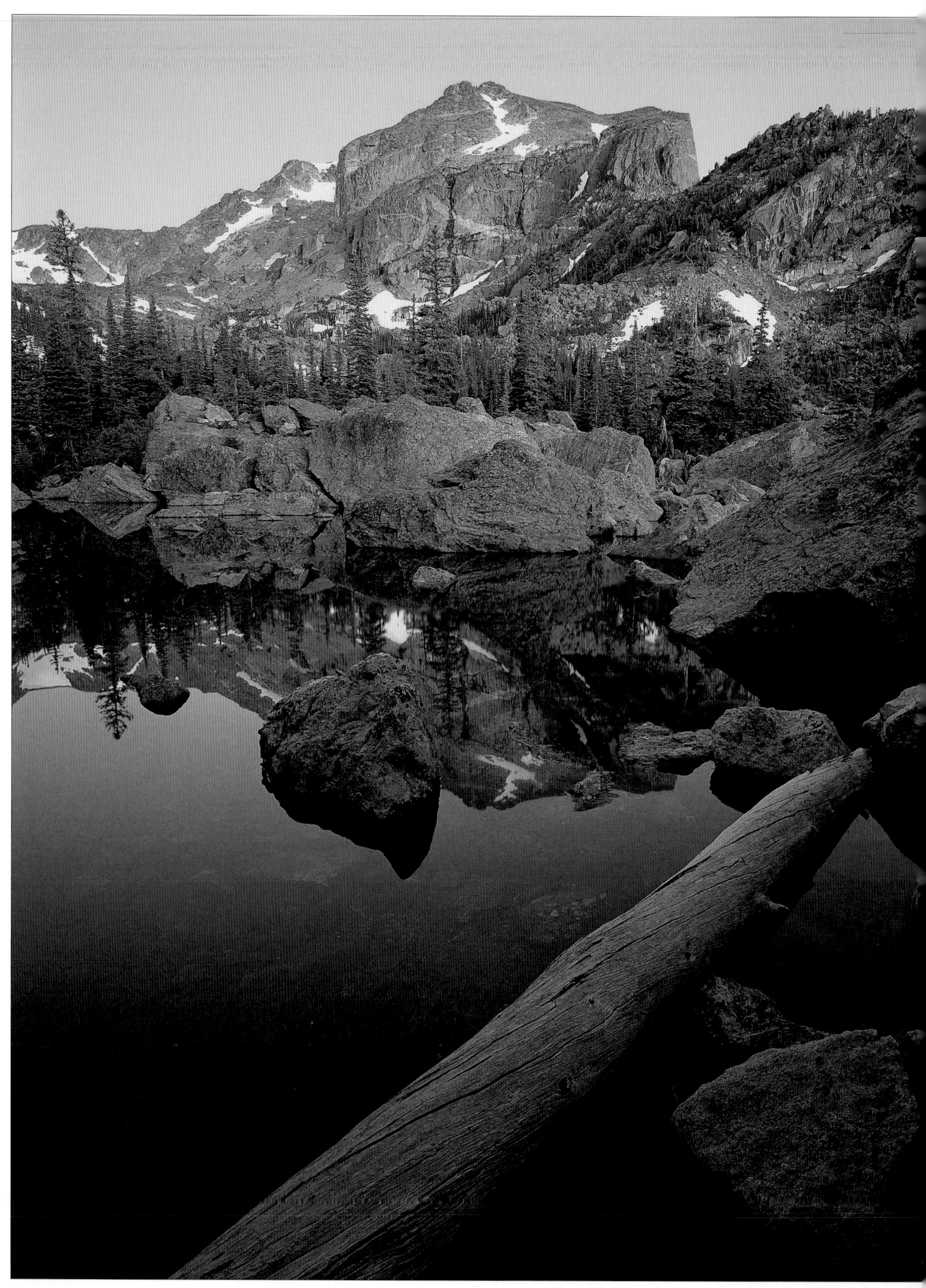

ROCKY MOUNTAIN NATIONAL PARK: BEAR LAKE

Continue on Bear Lake Road from Moraine Park to Bear Lake. (During the busy summer season, you might be required to take the shuttle bus from the Glacier Basin campground to Bear Lake.) No matter how you get here, it's well worth the drive. Bear Lake is in a subalpine cirque nestled below spectacular 12,713-foot Hallett Peak. Several trails start from Bear Lake and provide access to some of the park's most sublime alpine scenery. (For directions to Bear Lake Road from Estes Park, see Scenic Location No. 44, p. 159.)

If you wish to go home with great images of Bear Lake, photograph it in the morning. Hallett Peak and the cirque face due east, catching the warm light of sunrise. Imagine a gray mountain turned red or yellow and reflected in the lake—that's two mountains for the price of one (see pp. 129–133, *Photographing the Landscape*). Because the light is less intense at sunrise, you'll need to use slow shutter speeds (and even slower ones if you "stop down" your aperture to increase depth of field). A tripod and cable release are necessary in order to avoid a blurry image.

An even better place to photograph the Hallett Peak reflection is at one of three nearby lakes—Dream, Emerald, or my favorite, Lake Haiyaha (at left). Each is within 2 miles of Bear Lake. The rocks and logs at Lake Haiyaha can be composed as foreground for the reflection, but you will need to use small apertures in order to keep everything in focus (see pp. 109–117, *Photographing the Landscape*). If you're up for a greater hiking challenge, take the Flattop Mountain Trail 5 miles from Bear Lake to the Continental Divide at just over 12,000 feet. From here you can see the western side of the park as well as the spectacular peaks along the divide. Don't be surprised if you spy wildlife such as elk or bighorn sheep along the way.

MUSEUMS

MacGregor Ranch Museum has a gallery of Western paintings and household items from the homesteading era. Open summers only. *180 MacGregor Ln., just off Devils Gulch Rd., 970-586-3749.* Don't miss the "Light-Hearted History of Tourism" and historic photographs at the **Estes Park Museum,** housed in the original park headquarters. *200 4th St. at US 36, 970-586-6256, www.estesnet.com/museum.*

RAFTING

The **Colorado** and **Cache la Poudre Rivers** have some of the state's best whitewater. Trip outfitters can match your interest and experience (also see Cache la Poudre River, Fort Collins, p. 149). *Rapid Transit Rafting, 161 Virginia Dr., 970-586-8852, 800-367-8523, www.rapidtransitrafting.com.*

ROCK CLIMBING

Lumpy Ridge has more than 50 climbs averaging 2–5 pitches long. Although there are some solid routes for beginners, most of the climbs are in the 5.9–5.11 range. From Estes Park, go 2 miles north on MacGregor Avenue, then take a sharp right onto Devils Gulch Road and park at the Twin Owls trailhead. *For information and guided climbing trips: Colorado Mountain School, 351 Moraine Ave., 970-586-5758, www.cmschool.com.*

WINTER SPORTS

Snowshoeing in Rocky Mountain National Park and in the Estes Park Valley has become very popular (for routes, see Hiking, Rocky Mountain National Park, p. 158). Ask about the guided snowshoe trips in the park that begin in January. *Information, rentals, and guided tours: The Warming House, 790 Moraine Ave., 970-586-2995, www.warminghouse.com.*

Restaurants

The Stanley Hotel ($$-$$$) exemplifies fine dining in Estes Park, and the superb Sunday Champagne Brunch is extraordinary. *Intersection of US 34 and US 36 at 333 Wonderview Ave., 970-586-3371.* **The Dunraven Inn** ($$) serves Italian dishes, steaks, and seafood. *2470 CO 66, 970-586-6409.* Have a pre-hike breakfast at the **Big Horn Restaurant.** *401 W. Elkhorn Ave., 970-586-2792.* The **Grubsteak Restaurant** ($-$$) features elk or buffalo burgers, steaks, and chili. *134 W. Elkhorn Ave., 970-586-8838.* **Mama Rose's Restaurant** ($$) is a local favorite for Italian food. *338 Elkhorn Ave., 970-586-3330.* **Ed's Cantina and Grill** ($) is a popular watering hole and gathering place with good Mexican food. *362 E. Elkhorn Ave., 970-586-2919.* For a fresh brew and some very good pub grub, stop at **Estes Park Brewery** ($). *470 Prospect Village Dr., 970-586-5421.*

For fine dining, visit the **Inn of Glen Haven** ($$-$$$). The restaurant features a seasonal selection of gourmet entrées, a great selection of fine wines, and an intimate atmosphere. *7468 CR 43, 970-586-3897, www.innofglenhaven.com.* If you like German food, you'll love **The Fawn Brook Inn** in Allenspark. Try the lamb or duck dishes. *15 miles south of Estes Park on CO 7, 303-747-2556.*

Big Horn Restaurant, Estes Park

Accommodations

A premier tourist destination for well over a century, Estes Park maintains a comprehensive selection of lodging for all kinds of visitors. No surprise that the historic **Stanley Hotel** ($$-$$$$) is my favorite lodging in town (see Main Attractions, p. 160). *Intersection of US 34 and US 36 at 333 Wonderview Ave., 970-586-3371, 800-976-1377, www.stanleyhotel.com.*

Founded in 1910, the **YMCA of the Rockies Estes Park Center** ($-$$$) is today a popular place for conferences and group meetings and also a wonderful vacation spot for families. With more than 200 cabins and 500 lodge rooms, this huge facility presents programs in every summer activity imaginable and has a great Nordic center. Many celebrities have visited or stayed at the Estes Park facility, including John D. Rockefeller, Mother Theresa, Pat Boone, and Jane Fonda. *2515 Tunnel Rd., 970-586-3341, www.ymcarockies.org.*

The **Aspen Lodge at Estes Park** ($$-$$$) has fantastic views and offers plenty of activities and children's programs. *6120 CO 7, 970-586-8133, www.aspenlodge.net.* **McGregor Mountain Lodge** ($-$$$$) commands panoramic views of the Continental Divide and is ideal for wildlife watching. Cabins have fireplaces, fully equipped kitchens, barbecues, and Jacuzzis. *2815 Fall River Rd., 970-586-3457, www.mcgregormountainlodge.com.* Try the secluded **Timber Creek Chalets** ($$-$$$), located on 11 wooded acres near the park. The cabins and suites are fitted with fireplaces and barbecue patios and complemented by a heated swimming pool and a hot tub. *2115 Fall River Rd., 970-586-8803, www.timbercreekchalets.com.*

I also recommend reserving a cabin or cottage along Fall or Big Thompson River. You'll be close to all the activities in and around Estes Park, and the seasonal rates fit well into a family budget. The **Castle Mountain Lodge on Fall River** ($-$$$$) lies on 35 acres bordering the park and adjoining fine fishing on the Fall River. *1520 Fall River Rd., 970-586-3664, www.castlemountainlodge.com.* **Evergreens on Fall River** ($$-$$$$) rents riverfront cabins with fireplaces, kitchens, outdoor hot tubs, and fishing access. *1500 Fish Hatchery Rd., 970-577-9786, www.estes-park.com/evergreens.* **Ponderosa Lodge** ($-$$$$), *1820 Fall River Rd., 970-586-4233, www.estes-park.com/ponderosa,* and **Streamside Cabins** ($-$$$$), *1260 Fall River Rd., 970-586-6464, www.streamsidecabins.com,* are also located along the beautiful Fall River with amenities including kitchens.

Situated on the Big Thompson River and owned by the same family since 1979, **Brynwood Cabins on the River** ($$-$$$$) has comfortable riverside cabins with hot tubs. *710 Moraine Ave., 970-586-4488, www.brynwood.com.* **Swiftcurrent Lodge** ($-$$) rents economical, rustic cottages and motel-like rooms on the banks of the Big Thompson River. *2512 CO 66, 970-586-3720, www.swiftcurrentlodge.com.* Another lodging bargain is **Whispering Pines Cottages on the River** ($-$$). The cozy cottages have furnished kitchenettes, barbecues, a playground, and some great fishing off of the deck or patio.

46 SCENIC LOCATION

ROCKY MOUNTAIN NATIONAL PARK: TRAIL RIDGE ROAD

If I couldn't do anything else in the park, I'd drive from Estes Park to Grand Lake on Trail Ridge Road. It is the highest continuous paved road in North America, peaking at 12,183 feet! Every year, millions of park visitors get their first dose of the windy alpine zone, views of 14,255-foot Longs Peak and many other mountains, small but profuse wildflowers, and lingering snow here. They also relish encounters with some of the thousands of elk that inhabit the high country during the summer. Unfortunately, the road is closed in winter, but it's generally open from Memorial Day until November. From Estes Park, take either US 34 or 36 (they meet west of the park headquarters), then travel along Trail Ridge Road (US 34).

Old Fall River Road is a shortcut up to Fall River Pass and the Alpine Visitor Center on Trail Ridge Road. This one-way improved dirt road up to the top is manageable by car. The scenery is spectacular, but not as much as along the part of Trail Ridge Road you'll miss, so do Old Fall River Road on another day.

Stop at the Forest Canyon Overlook, which allows you to see into the Big Thompson River Canyon, some 2,000 feet below, as well as across to the peaks of the Continental Divide. One of my favorite Colorado views is south from this overlook into the Gorge Lakes drainage. You look straight across the canyon toward an awesome stair-stepped collection of alpine lakes tucked between steep granite walls. As the road continues to ascend, look back for views to Longs Peak, the highest mountain and only fourteener in the park. Pull over and compose the road snaking along the ridge with the peak looming behind it. Use a telephoto lens, which compresses the distance in front of you, making the peak appear larger than it does to the naked eye. Stop at Farview Curve west of Milner Pass to photograph views of the Never Summer Mountains at the western park boundary. Their rugged peaks make a great background for the tundra in the foreground.

2646 Big Thompson Canyon Rd. (US 34), 970-586-5258, www.estes-park.com/whisperingpines. **Solitude Cabins** ($$) are close to downtown, but secluded in a wooded area. *Fish Creek Rd. & Brodie Ave., 877-704-7777, www.solitudecabins.com.* For a ranch-like experience alongside the Big Thompson River, stay at the **Glacier Lodge** ($$), where you can enjoy fishing, horseback riding, and Western campfire meals. *2166 CO 66, 970-586-4401, www.glacierlodge.com.*

Estes Park also has its share of fine B&Bs that reflect the town's historic status; check for seasonal pricing. Highly rated **Romantic RiverSong Inn** ($-$$$$) lies on 27 acres with streams, ponds, hiking trails, and mountain views. Your hosts can assist in an elegant elopement—or just a renewal of nuptial vows. *1716 Lower Broadview at Mary's Lake Rd., 970-577-1336, www.romanticriversong.com.* Another romantic destination is **Anniversary Inn Bed & Breakfast** ($$); enjoy breakfast with a view from the glassed-in porch. *1060 Mary's Lake Rd., 970-586-6200, www.estesinn.com.* The hosts of historic **Black Dog Inn** ($$) prepare a fabulous breakfast and provide what you need to enjoy your stay, including binoculars for viewing wildlife. *650 S. Saint Vrain Ave., 970-586-0374, www.blackdoginn.com.* **Mountain Shadows Resort** ($$$) is romantic and luxurious, with amenities including a private hot tub and deck in each cabin. *871 Riverside Dr., 970-577-0397, www.mountainshadowsresort.net.*

Special Events

Attend **Longs Peak Scottish/Irish Highland Festival,** held in early September, to see some of the best pipe bands in the United States and Canada. Started by families of Scottish-Irish heritage, this festival has grown to be one of the largest Celtic festivals in the country. Celtic heritage is celebrated with some unusual competitions that call for incredible skill and strength, including hammer and caber (tree trunk) throws. See a clan row and dancing, and stay for the Tattoo, a music and light performance in honor of Celtic-American tradition. This is one of my favorite Colorado events. *970-577-9900, www.scotfest.com.*

An organized event of a different kind takes place in Estes Park each fall: mating season for the venerable elk. The long, high-pitched tones of elk bugling resound far and wide in the valley, especially Moraine Park, Horseshoe Park, and Upper Beaver Meadows. Some visit town just to experience this noisy spectacle at dawn or dusk. The Rocky Mountain National Park Elk and Bugle Corps volunteers can answer your questions and will keep you at a safe distance from the animals. *970-586-6104.*

The official annual **Elk Festival** is held each year on the weekend before Columbus Day. The festival features elk tours—bus tours where festival-goers will learn more about the elk—and educational seminars. The festival also includes live music, food, competitions, and the raptor display. *970-586-6104.*

For More Information

Estes Park Convention and Visitors Bureau, *500 Big Thompson Ave., 970-577-9900, www.estesparkcvb.com.*

Grand Lake

Colorado Atlas & Gazetteer p. 28

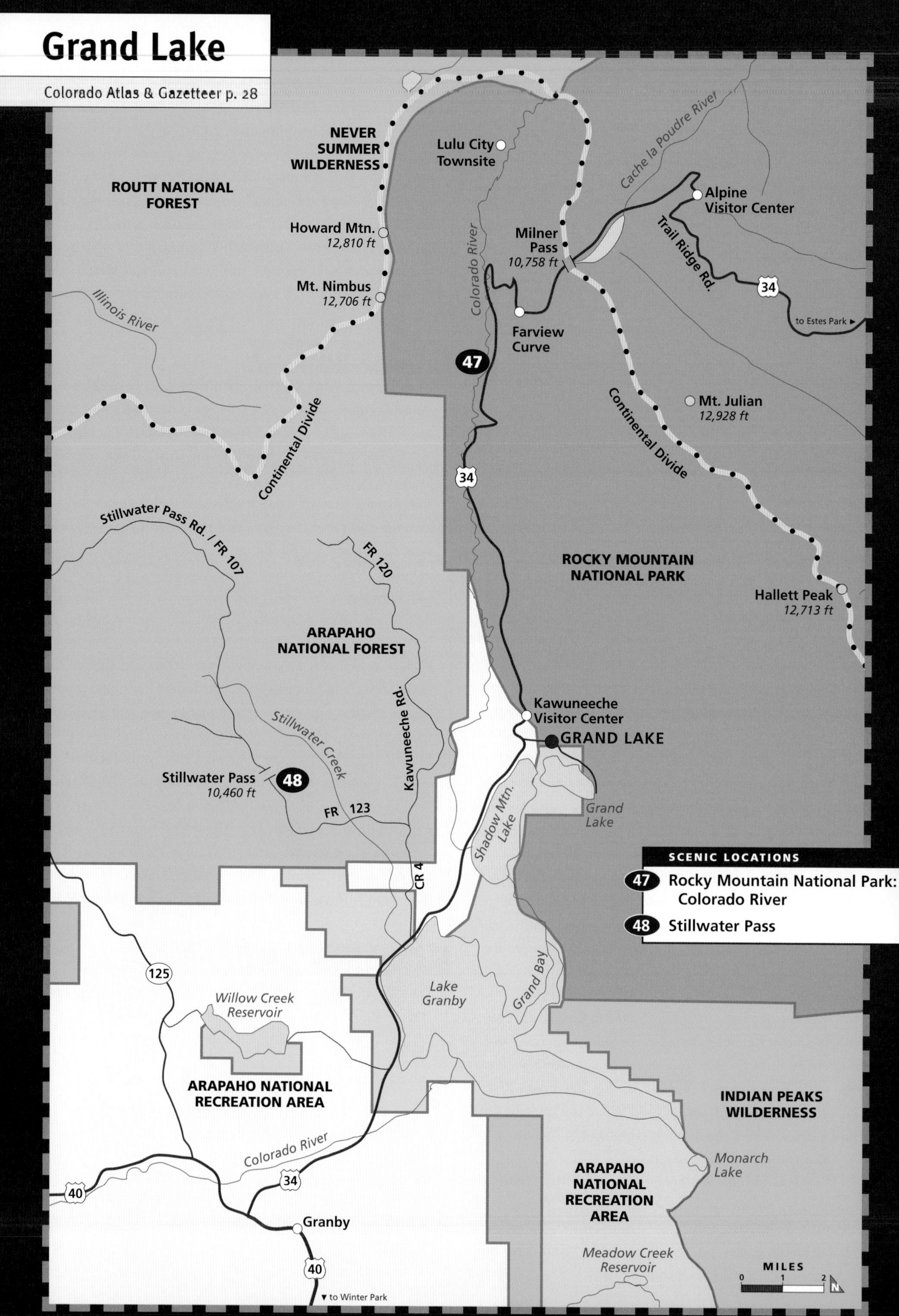

NEVER SUMMER WILDERNESS
ROUTT NATIONAL FOREST
Lulu City Townsite
Alpine Visitor Center
Cache la Poudre River
Trail Ridge Rd.
Howard Mtn. 12,810 ft
Milner Pass 10,758 ft
Colorado River
Mt. Nimbus 12,706 ft
Illinois River
Farview Curve
34
to Estes Park
47
Mt. Julian 12,928 ft
Continental Divide
Continental Divide
34
Stillwater Pass Rd. / FR 107
FR 120
ROCKY MOUNTAIN NATIONAL PARK
Hallett Peak 12,713 ft
ARAPAHO NATIONAL FOREST
Kawuneeche Rd.
Kawuneeche Visitor Center
GRAND LAKE
Stillwater Creek
Stillwater Pass 10,460 ft
48
FR 123
Shadow Mtn. Lake
Grand Lake
CR 4
SCENIC LOCATIONS
47 Rocky Mountain National Park: Colorado River
48 Stillwater Pass
125
Willow Creek Reservoir
Lake Granby
Grand Bay
ARAPAHO NATIONAL RECREATION AREA
INDIAN PEAKS WILDERNESS
Colorado River
Monarch Lake
ARAPAHO NATIONAL RECREATION AREA
40
34
Granby
Meadow Creek Reservoir
MILES
0 1 2
N
40
to Winter Park

Grand Lake

This charming town marks the watery, western entry point to Rocky Mountain National Park. Farther from the populous Front Range, Grand Lake is less crowded and a bit more laid-back than Estes Park on the eastern side. The namesake natural lake, two vast reservoirs—Shadow Mountain Lake and Lake Granby—plus three smaller reservoirs and numerous alpine lakes explain why this area is sometimes called the Great Lakes of Colorado. The serene waters of Grand Lake mirror the surrounding peaks, and many of the lakes afford fine water recreation. Dock the boat and enjoy the shops, restaurants, and beautiful Town Park in this resort enveloped by the dense pines of Arapaho National Forest and Rocky Mountain National Park. From Denver, take I-70 west to US 40, then take US 40 northwest over Berthoud Pass to Granby. Just past Granby, go north on US 34 to Grand Lake. Grand Lake is about 100 miles from Denver.

History

Called "Spirit Lake" by the Ute tribes, the prime hunting ground now known as Grand Lake was once much disputed. Legend has it that during one battle, vast numbers of Arapaho descended upon the Utes. The Ute men put their women and children on a raft and told the women to paddle to safety in the middle of the lake. Alas, a storm capsized the raft and all were lost. The Utes believed they could see the spirits of their loved ones rising from the lake on the early morning mists.

The discovery of gold near Grand Lake in 1879 put the town on the map as a mining camp supply center. When the gold and silver played out in the early 1880s, Grand Lake's demise seemed imminent, but instead, well-to-do gentlemen hunters took notice of the area. By the 1890s, summer homes dotted the shoreline of Grand Lake and the town developed the aura of a resort. Legislation establishing Rocky Mountain National Park in 1915 alone would have made Grand Lake a full-fledged vacation destination. But the completion of the Colorado–Big Thompson water-diversion project in 1957—which filled Shadow Mountain Lake, Lake Granby, and three other reservoirs—also created the popular Arapaho National Recreation Area, where fishing, boating, and camping regularly draw families on holiday. Today, Grand Lake remains a resort town, a haven for visitors who enjoy the natural scenery, wildlife, and lake recreation on the quieter side of Rocky Mountain National Park.

Main Attractions

ARAPAHO NATIONAL RECREATION AREA

Several sizable bodies of water define this region, the Great Lakes of Colorado. The Colorado–Big Thompson Project (C–BT) created five new bodies of water south of Grand Lake, the largest natural lake in Colorado. Completed in 1957, C–BT diverts Western Slope water across the Continental Divide to numerous Eastern Plains communities. The lakes also make up the Arapaho National Recreation Area, a haven for water-lovers. Driving north from Granby on US 34, you can't miss Lake Granby to your right; Shadow Mountain Lake is the second one you will see before reaching the town of Grand Lake. Smaller Willow Creek Reservoir, an excellent fishing hole, lies a few miles west of Lake Granby; Monarch Lake and Meadow Creek Reservoir lie south of Lake Granby's eastern end.

First-rate fishing for rainbows, browns, and gigantic Mackinaws (lake trout) draws visitors to these picturesque lakes year-round, and ice fishing attracts hardy winter anglers. Where the shoreline falls on private property, consider renting a boat; you can also stay at several campgrounds with boat ramps. Watch out for gusts of wind in the late afternoon. Of course, these breezes are perfect for sailors and windsurfers. *For fishing, pleasure boat rentals, and equipment: Beacon Landing Marina, 970-627-3671; Highland Marina, 970-887-3541; or Trail Ridge Marina, 970-627-3586, on Shadow Mountain Lake.*

Camping: The popular **Sunset Point** and **Arapaho Bay** campgrounds adjoin fishing and boating on Lake Granby. The views aren't bad, either. From US 34 at Grand Lake, go about 8.5 miles south to Arapaho Bay Road, and head left (east) along the lake 1.25 miles to Sunset Point; Arapaho Bay campground and boat ramp are about 7 miles farther on Arapaho Bay Road. (From Granby, take US 34 north 5 miles to Arapaho Bay Road.) **Stillwater** campground overlooks Lake Granby and has amenities including showers and a boat ramp. From Grand Lake, go about 5 miles south on US 34; from Granby, it's about 8.5 miles north on US 34. **Green Ridge** campground skirts Shadow Mountain Lake and features a boat ramp. From Grand Lake, take US 34 south about 3 miles, then turn left (east) on County Road 66 and continue 1.5 miles. (From Granby, go 11.5 miles north on US 34 and turn right on CR 66.) Reservations recommended. *For these and other area campgrounds: 970-887-4100, www.fs.fed.us/arnf.*

ROCKY MOUNTAIN NATIONAL PARK

Rocky Mountain National Park has a dual nature, depending on which side of the Continental Divide you see. The more precipitous land east of the Divide brims with waterfalls and lakes (see Estes Park, p. 157); the terrain west of the Divide near Grand Lake is lush with forests, verdant valleys, wetlands, and meadows. Elk roam throughout the park's vicinity, but moose favor the wetter west side. Stop in at the Kawuneeche Visitor Center on US 34 near the Grand Lake entrance station for maps and information about hiking, fishing, camping, and winter activities. *970-586-1206, www.nps.gov/romo.*

Camping: Shaded by pines and often crowded, **Timber Creek** campground, with 100 sites, is the only one on the western side of the park. No reservations. *970-586-1206.* Backcountry permits are required for any off-site camping.

Fishing: The mighty **Colorado River** meanders, tumbles, and rushes 1,440 miles through Colorado, Utah, Arizona, Nevada, California, and Mexico (not quite reaching the Gulf of California anymore). Gaining volume from its tributaries—the Green, San Juan, Gunnison, Escalante, Dolores, and Little Colorado Rivers—the Colorado has carved out much of the West's canyon country, including the Grand Canyon. Its precious water has enabled the incredible growth of the Southwest, whose future still depends largely upon the river. This essential watercourse starts as a small stream fed by melting snows near La Poudre Pass just north of Lulu City (see Scenic Location No. 47, opposite).

I've had good luck fishing the Colorado River and the gentle streams that feed into it in the Kawuneeche Valley. Small browns, rainbows, and brookies populate these waters, although larger trout, particularly browns, inhabit the deep holes and pools. Don't be surprised to share your fishing hole with an elk or moose early in the morning or at dusk. Reach the valley easily from the Never Summer Ranch turnoff, about 8 miles north of the park's west entrance, or from Timber Creek campground, 2 miles farther north. You can also access it from the Green Mountain, Onahu Creek, or Colorado River trailheads (see Hiking below), or the Bowen/Baker trailhead (see Hiking under Activities, at right).

Hiking: Hikes in the western portion of the park wind through dense pine and spruce forests and across pristine meadows populated by wildlife. Several easy hikes are described here. The guided 0.5-mile (one way) tour of the **Never Summer Ranch** EASY affords a peek into the natural history and rough homesteading life of the Kawuneeche Valley. See the Holzworth family's original cabins, which include an icehouse and a taxidermy shop. That small stream running through the ranch is the birth of the mighty Colorado River. From the park's west entrance, go 7.9 miles north on US 34, then turn left into the parking lot.

The first 3.7 miles of the **Colorado River Trail** EASY lead to the old silver mining townsite of Lulu City. The trail parallels the Colorado River through the Kawuneeche Valley, going past the old Shipler Mine and cabin and terminating at Lulu City. After the discovery of silver here in 1879, Lulu City prospered. In 1881 it had a general store, a barber shop, two fine hotels, a brothel, and even a stage line that connected Lulu City to Grand Lake and Fort Collins. By 1882 the silver had played out; by 1883 the town was abandoned. The trail to Lulu City starts 9.5 miles north of the western entrance to the park at the Colorado River trailhead, just off US 34. This is also a popular cross-country skiing and snowshoeing route in winter.

Green Mountain Trail EASY and **Onahu Creek Trail** EASY are delightful, 1-mile hikes through dense pine forests. You'll intersect with **Tonahutu Creek Trail** MODERATE to make an optional 6.8-mile loop. The Green Mountain and Onahu trailheads are 3.5 miles north of Grand Lake, just off US 34.

The first 0.3 mile of **East Inlet Trail** EASY leads to the tumbling Adams Falls. You can continue 5.2 miles beyond the falls through meadows and past beaver ponds to Lone Pine Lake and a fine view of 12,007-foot Mount Cairns. Keep an eye out for moose early in the morning or at dusk. Continue another 1.4 miles to Lake Verna, although the hike becomes more challenging. Beyond Lake Verna lie Spirit, Fourth, and Fifth Lakes. Small lakes in a series such as this, formed along glacially carved basins, are called paternoster lakes after their likeness to the shape of the rosary. Many campsites lie just off the trail, and don't forget to bring a fishing rod. To get to the East Inlet trailhead, take US 34 through Grand Lake, then turn east on CO 278 and take the left fork bypassing the town. Go 2.1 miles, passing the West Portal, to the East Inlet trailhead.

Activities

GOLF

Grand Lake Golf Course is a challenging 18-hole golf course. If you have a poor game, though, you can always blame the scenery! Take US 34 north 0.25 mile, then turn left (west) on County Road 48 and go 1 mile. *970-627-8008.*

HIKING

Adjoining the national park are numerous fine trails. One is the rarely traveled, 6-mile (one way) **Bowen/Baker Gulch Trail** DIFFICULT that winds through the Never Summer Wilderness, connecting to Parika Lake and climbing to views of Mount Nimbus from Baker Pass. From the western entrance to the park, go north 6.4 miles on US 34 to the Bowen/Baker trailhead.

HORSEBACK RIDING

Take a guided horseback ride from Grand Lake into Rocky Mountain National Park, and the only sounds you'll hear are those of streams, small animals and birds, and your horse's hooves. The folks at **Sombrero Stables** will tailor your ride to your interest and experience. Inquire about the Breakfast Ride and Steak Fry Ride. *West Portal Road as you enter Grand Lake, 970-627-3514 (seasonal), www.sombrero.com.*

HOT SPRINGS

Take a rewarding soak at **Hot Sulphur Springs Resort** (see Winter Park, p. 176). *27 miles southeast of Grand Lake on US 40, 970-725-3306, www.hotsulphursprings.com.*

ROCKY MOUNTAIN NATIONAL PARK: COLORADO RIVER

The Colorado River is many rivers to many people—it's Lakes Mead and Powell, the Grand Canyon, Cataract Canyon through Canyonlands National Park, and a much less conspicuous, yet no less central, river in Colorado. The river's origin in Rocky Mountain National Park is understated to say the least. The magnitude it eventually achieves is the result of thousands of tributaries, not of its starting place at La Poudre Pass, the lowly divide on the Continental Divide separating the headwaters of the Cache La Poudre River from the great Colorado. Nevertheless, it's a beautiful river (or creek as it might appear to you). On your drive over from Estes Park, start watching the river from the last 180-degree switchback on Trail Ridge Road as you descend into the river valley from Milner Pass. The road follows the river south for 7 miles before the river splits off. (For directions to US 34 from Estes Park, see Scenic Location No. 46, p. 165.) From Grand Lake, the river is always on your left as you drive north on US 34.

The river courses through wide meadows as it parallels the road, allowing even better views of the Never Summer Mountains. Stop when you spy places that will allow you to create compositions of the river winding through meadows, with scattered trees along its banks, and peaks framing the scene. It's simply sublime! A little more than a mile south of the big switchback, or 9.5 miles north of the park entrance, look for the Colorado River trailhead on the west side of the road. Try hiking north along the river trail, which winds through forest and meadow, revealing views of the river in its infancy. You'll cross a number of creeks descending from the Never Summer Mountains to the west and the Continental Divide to the east. Keep your fingers crossed for cloudy light, which will reduce glare off the surface of the water and saturate the ubiquitous greens of trees and summer grasses.

Also consider hiking west along the Bowen/Baker Gulch Trail. You'll find some great views along the way and a good photo opportunity when you cross the Colorado River. In the fall, the meadows turn golden brown. Aspen decorate the landscape, adding color from one season to the next.

STILLWATER PASS

The Never Summer Mountains lie along the Continental Divide, and two driving passes provide access to less dramatic mountains in this area. Although only one, Willow Creek Pass (see Scenic Location No. 50, p. 180), crosses the divide, and neither pass reaches timberline, the scenery along the way is beautifully representative of Colorado's abundant montane forests. Stillwater Pass Road provides dramatic views of Middle Park, one of Colorado's four intermountain basins. (The others are North Park, South Park, and the San Luis Valley.) Middle Park is bounded by the Rabbit Ears Range and the Never Summer Mountains to the north, the Front Range to the east, and the Williams Fork Mountains and the Gore Range to the west. It receives the headwaters of the Colorado River from all sides and contains Grand Lake and Lake Granby, as well as other large storage reservoirs serving Front Range communities. Take US 34 south 5 miles from Grand Lake, then turn right (west) on County Road 4, which turns into Stillwater Pass Road (Forest Road 123). After reaching the pass, the road descends to CO 125 south of Willow Creek Pass. Its highest parts are a bit rough (although manageable by a car in good weather), so I recommend taking a four-wheel-drive vehicle.

The best photo opportunity along the route is made from the road looking back southeast toward Lake Granby and the Front Range, so you'll need to keep your neck craned as you ascend the pass. When you reach a place where you gain a clear view of Middle Park, pull over and make the image. At the right spot you'll be able to compose foreground trees, with the lake and valley in the midground, all framed by peaks and a bit of sky. At sunset the peaks light up and shadows flow across the valley floor. The balance of the drive winds through forest, so you'll want to look for "intimate" landscapes (see pp. 54–57, *Photographing the Landscape*) that do not require a horizon. The summer wildflowers are wonderful, and in the fall the meadows and aspens along the descent to CO 125 are colorful and bucolic.

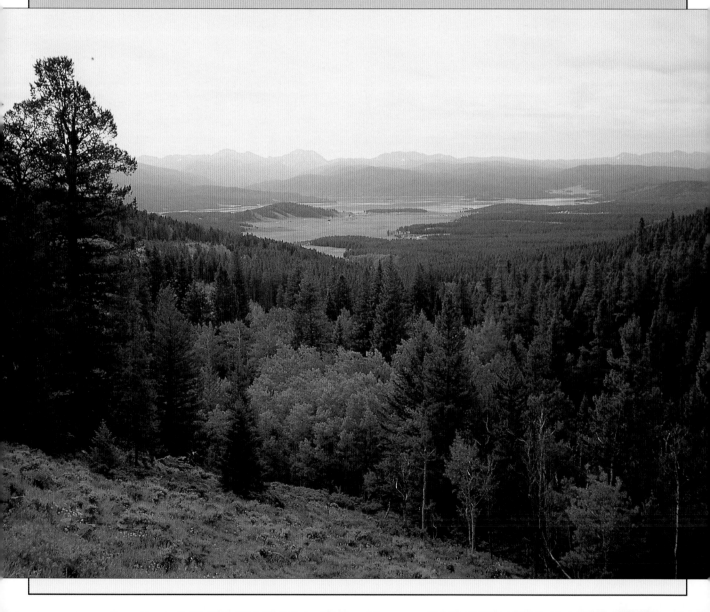

THEATER

Grand Lake Community House in Town Park hosts the **Rocky Mountain Repertory Theatre**, which performs comedies and musicals. Bring a picnic to Town Park before the show, and browse the artisan booths there in the summer. *970-627-5087; www.rockymountainrep.com.*

WINTER SPORTS

Grand Lake Golf Course becomes **Grand Lake Touring Center** in winter, with more than 30 kilometers of groomed cross-country trails, along with rentals and lessons (for directions, see Golf, p. 168). *970-627-8008.* Many of the hiking trails in Rocky Mountain National Park make popular cross-country skiing and snowshoeing routes. (For directions, see Hiking, Rocky Mountain National Park, p. 168.)

More than 130 miles of snowmobile trails make Grand Lake a prime destination for snowmobilers. *For information and rentals: Spirit Lake Polaris & Rentals, 601 Lenter Dr., 970-627-9288, www.spiritlakerentals.com.*

Restaurants

If you're looking for great BBQ, **Sagebrush BBQ & Grill** ($-$$) is the perfect choice. They serve breakfast, lunch, and dinner and have a variety of home-cooked favorites as well as BBQ classics. *1101 Grand Ave, 970-627-1404, www.sagebrushbbq.com.* For upscale dining in a friendly bistro atmosphere, visit **The Terrace Inn** ($$). The menu even features a custom designed wine list to compliment your meal. *813 Grand Ave, 970-627-3000, 888-627-3001, www.grandlaketerraceinn.com.* For great dining with a European flair, stop at **Caroline's Cuisine** ($$-$$$) at Soda Springs Ranch, just south of town. Try a fine seafood entree or the Steak Diane, and I dare you to pass up the chocolate cake sundae! *9921 US 34 #27, 970-627-9404.*

Accommodations

Rapids Lodge ($$) on Tonahutu Creek boasts modern conveniences and a fine restaurant (try the pasta). *209 Rapids Ln., 970-627-3707, www.rapidslodge.com.* **Lemmon Lodge** ($$-$$$$), near the marina at the end of Grand Lake, rents cabins adjoining a playground and volleyball area. *1224 Lake Ave., 970-627-3314 (summer), 970-725-3511 (winter), www.lemmonlodge.com.* **Daven Haven Lodge** ($$-$$$) also rents cabins, and the restaurant sizzles a fine steak. *Next to Grand Lake at the intersection of Marina Dr. and Shadow Mountain Dr., 970-627-8144, www.davenhavenlodge.com.* **The Terrace Inn** ($$-$$$) is a charming Western-style inn with three guest rooms and a suite to choose from. *813 Grand Ave, 970-627-3000, 888-627-3001, www.grandlaketerraceinn.com.* **Western Riviera Motel & Cabins** ($$-$$$) offers a variety of lodging options including rooms at the lakeside motel, small, medium, or large cabins, condos, and apartments. *419 Garfield St, 970-627-3580, www.westernriv.com.*

River Pines Cottages ($$), 12 miles north of Granby on the North Fork of the Colorado River, are close to a Shadow Mountain Lake wildlife sanctuary where you can observe elk, deer, and moose. Although these rustic cabins were built between 1900 and 1940, they include modern conveniences. *12082 US 34, 970-627-3632.* **Spirit Mountain Ranch** ($$), a secluded B&B, sits on 72 acres populated with wildlife. It is 3.9 miles west on County Road 41 off of US 34 north of Granby. *3863 CR 41, 970-887-3551, www.spiritmtnranch.com.*

Special Events

In early August, members of the Grand Lake Yacht Club compete in the **Grand Lake Regatta** and **Lipton Cup Races** for the Lipton Cup, a solid sterling silver cup donated by Sir Thomas Lipton. *970-627-3402, www.grandlakechamber.com.*

For More Information

Grand Lake Area Chamber of Commerce and Visitor Center, *Grand Avenue and US 34, 970-627-3402, www.grandlakecolorado.com, www.grandlakechamber.com.*

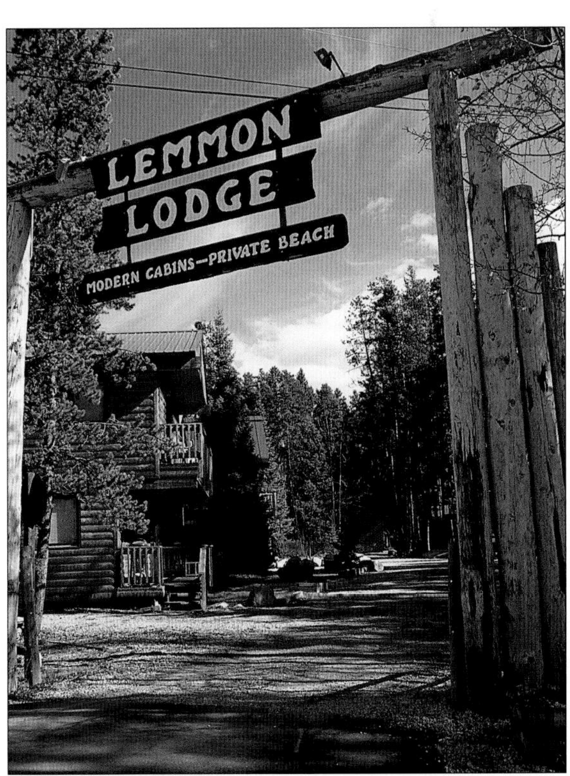

Lemmon Lodge, Grand Lake

Winter Park

Colorado Atlas & Gazetteer p. 39

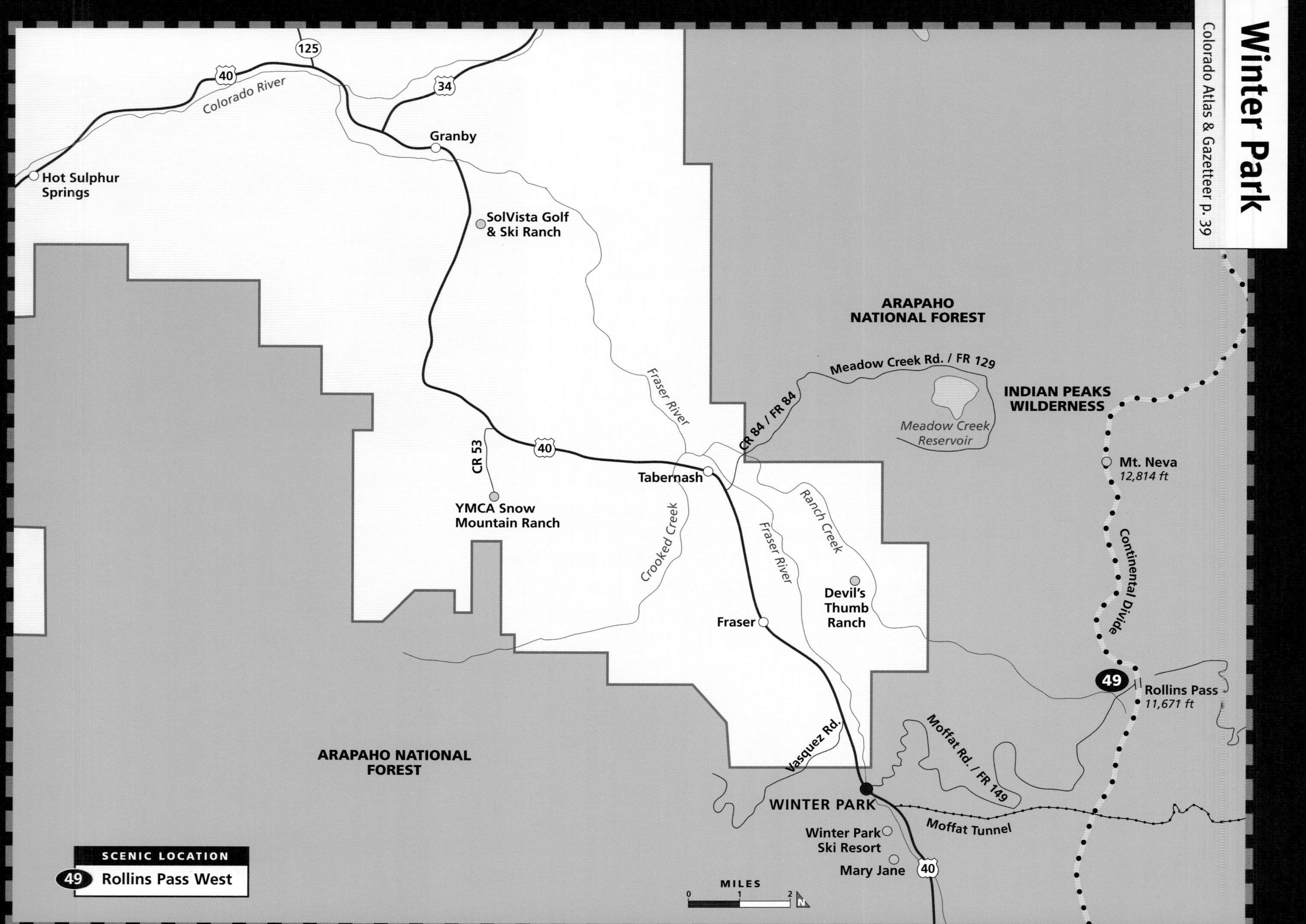

40
125
34
Colorado River
Granby
Hot Sulphur
Springs
SolVista Golf
& Ski Ranch
ARAPAHO
NATIONAL FOREST
Meadow Creek Rd. / FR 129
INDIAN PEAKS
WILDERNESS
Meadow Creek
Reservoir
Mt. Neva
12,814 ft
Continental Divide
Fraser River
CR 84 / FR 84
Tabernash
CR 53
40
YMCA Snow
Mountain Ranch
Crooked Creek
Ranch Creek
Fraser River
Devil's
Thumb
Ranch
Fraser
49
Rollins Pass
11,671 ft
Vasquez Rd.
Moffat Rd. / FR 149
ARAPAHO NATIONAL
FOREST
WINTER PARK
Moffat Tunnel
Winter Park
Ski Resort
Mary Jane
40
MILES
0
1
2
N
SCENIC LOCATION
49
Rollins Pass West

Winter Park

The premier local ski areas for residents of Colorado's Front Range, Winter Park and Mary Jane mountains provide fine skiing at Winter Park Resort. (Owned by the City and County of Denver for 60 years, the resort is now a joint-venture partnership between the city and a private resort development firm.) SolVista Golf & Ski Resort, formerly Silver Creek, and the first-rate cross-country ski trails in the valley also draw powderhounds. However, there is more to the Fraser Valley, also called Middle Park, than winter sports. The valley is a destination for fishing, hiking, horseback riding, or just taking a soak at Hot Sulphur Springs. Like many skiing-rich locales, the valley is also a mountain-biking destination in summer. In short, the Fraser Valley makes for a great family vacation. Winter Park is 67 miles from Denver on US 40. Take I-70 west to US 40 and head north over Berthoud Pass. The towns of Winter Park, Fraser, Tabernash, Granby, and Hot Sulphur Springs follow in succession along US 40.

History

The Fraser Valley provided game for the Utes and pelts for trappers, but it wasn't until the mid-1870s that settlers and ranchers entered the valley in earnest. Loggers worked the forests surrounding the Fraser Valley, and the small town of Tabernash grew up around the lumber mill. Founding *Rocky Mountain News* publisher William N. Byers first saw the thermal waters at Hot Sulphur Springs in 1863 and promoted the area extensively after acquiring the springs in a shady deal. Byers, who died in 1903, wanted to create an elite resort around the springs, but his plans never bore fruit, as the railroad bypassed the area until 1928.

The City of Denver purchased the area to obtain rights to its watershed, and with the completion of the Moffat Tunnel in 1928, people of the Front Range gained railway access to the region. In 1935, Denver parks manager George Cranmer imagined building a winter sports center to rival those in Europe. In 1940, the Winter Park Ski Area, composed of three ski runs, was formally dedicated. Denver's local ski area has grown to include five mountains and a number of high-speed chairlifts, making it a full-fledged tourist destination.

Mary Jane (named after a lady of the night who acquired the land as payment for services) has earned a reputation as one of the best mountains in the nation for long mogul runs. Winter Park Resort also boasts pioneering disabled-skier programs. Retta's Run was named after Retta Stanley, a skier who lost a leg to cancer and was instrumental in developing the area's programs for disabled athletes. Fraser Valley residents have developed more than 600 miles of mountain-biking trails, making the tourist economy a year-round reality.

Main Attractions

CYCLING AND MOUNTAIN BIKING

Summer transforms the mountains of Winter Park and Fraser from a skier's paradise to mountain biker's playground. The Zephyr Express chairlift, equipped with bike racks, takes you to more than 40 trails ranging from beginner to expert. **Upper Roof of the Rockies** MODERATE is a favorite; pick up a trail map at the lift ticket office at the base of Mary Jane or log on to *www.skiwinterpark.com.*

In sharp contrast, the paved, 5-mile (one way) **Fraser River Trail** EASY follows the river from Winter Park to Fraser. The 8-mile **Vasquez Creek Loop** EASY, another fine family ride, begins at the Winter Park visitor center at the intersection of US 40 and Vasquez Road.

The 14.5-mile (one way) **High Lonesome Trail** DIFFICULT is more secluded, with excellent opportunities to see wildlife. Take US 40, 3 miles north of Fraser. Turn right to cross the Fraser River, then left on Devil's Thumb Ranch Road (County Road 84), which curves northeast to Meadow Creek Reservoir, where it becomes Meadow Creek Road (Forest Road 129). Continue 7 miles to the reservoir, then follow the road around the northwest side of the reservoir to a parking area marked by a High Lonesome Trail and Continental Divide Trail sign.

Tipperary Creek DIFFICULT has been called, and may be, the best ride in Colorado. The main event at the Fat Tire Classic (see Special Events, p. 177), this ride is as scenic as it is challenging, with distance and difficulty varying with the route. Pick up a map from the Chamber of Commerce before you hit the trail. *For information and rentals: Christy Sports, 78930 HWY 40, 970-726-8873, www.christysports.com.*

WINTER SPORTS

Winter Park Resort encompasses Winter Park, Mary Jane, Parsenn Bowl, Vasquez Cirque, and Vasquez Ridge, each with its own terrain and appeal. The original ski area, Winter Park, is ideal for families, and Mary Jane, known for its moguls, caters to intermediate and expert skiers. Parsenn Bowl, one of my favorites, is an intermediate area that sports deep powder in its open spaces. Don't even think about diving off of the steep cornices at Vasquez Cirque and Vasquez Ridge unless you are an expert. With an average annual snowfall of 30 feet, Winter Park has plenty of terrain to please any downhill skier or snowboarder, and provides rentals, lessons, shops, and restaurants. *970-726-5514, www.skiwinterpark.com.*

SolVista Golf & Ski Ranch is an intimate ski resort with activities for the whole family. Alpine skiers and snowboarders will enjoy 33 runs, short lift lines, and a wonderful ski school, while cross-country enthusiasts can glide across the 40 kilometers of groomed **SolVista Nordic Trails**. From Winter Park, take US 40 north 15 miles, then turn right (east) at the sign and continue 2 miles to the ski area. *800-757-7669, www.silvercreek-resort.com.*

Devil's Thumb Ranch in Tabernash maintains 100 kilometers of groomed cross-country trails and 20 kilometers of snowshoe trails. The ranch also offers an excellent restaurant (see Restaurants, p. 176) and family lodging (see Accommodations, p. 177). From Fraser, take US 40 north 3 miles, then turn right (east) onto County Road 83 and follow the signs. *970-726-8231, www.devilsthumbranch.com.*

YMCA Snow Mountain Ranch Nordic Center, deemed the best family cross-country ski area by *The Denver Post*, provides 100 kilometers of groomed cross-country trails and access to backcountry skiing and snowshoeing trails. It's also fun to stay at the YMCA (see Accommodations, p. 177). From Winter Park, take US 40 north 12 miles, then turn left (west) on CR 53. *1101 CR 53, Granby, 970-887-2152, www.ymcarockies.org.*

Activities

ALPINE SLIDE

The thrill of navigating Colorado's alpine slide is a must if you have kids—and fun for everyone! Ride the chairlift to the top of the mountain and zip down on this fast, lugelike course. *970-726-5514, www.skiwinterpark.com.*

CAMPING

Idlewild is adjacent to the Fraser River and just 1 mile south of Winter Park on US 40. **Robbers Roost** is a main access point for fishing the Fraser River, 6 miles south of Winter Park on US 40. **St. Louis Creek** campground lies 3 miles southwest of Fraser on County Road 73 (Forest Road 160.2). Offering access to the Byers Peak Trail (see Hiking, p. 176), **Byers Creek** is 7.5 miles southwest of Fraser on CR 73. **Sawmill Gulch** and **Denver Creek** are both situated near streams. From Granby, take US 40 west 2.75 miles, then turn right (north) on CO 125 and continue 10 miles to Sawmill Gulch campground. Denver Creek campground is 2 miles farther down the road. No reservations. *For above campgrounds: 970-887-4100.*

FISHING

The headwaters of the **Fraser River** begin just below the Continental Divide on Berthoud Pass in Arapaho National Forest, and US 40 follows the river through the towns of Fraser, Tabernash, and Granby. Public access to the river is good, and large browns, rainbows, and brookies are common. Just north of Granby, the Fraser flows into the **Colorado River,** but unfortunately the Colorado has little public access from Granby to Kremmling along US 40.

Although **Williams Fork Reservoir** has trout, it also has a well-earned reputation for large Northern pike, which average between 20 and 30 pounds. Try fishing the 2-mile stretch of the **Williams Fork River** that connects the reservoir with the Colorado River. This tailwater contains large rainbows and browns that migrate from the Colorado River. From Winter Park, take US 40 northwest 29 miles to Hot Sulphur Springs. Continue 4 miles, then turn left on Ute Pass Road (County Road 3). Access the reservoir off CR 3 from either CR 33 or CR 341. *For information, lessons, and guided trips: Devil's Thumb Fly Fishing Adventure Center, 3530 CR 83, Tabernash, 970-726-8231, www.devilsthumbranch.com; Mo Henry's Trout Shop, 970-726-9754, HWY 40, Fraser, www.mohenrys.com.*

FOUR-WHEEL-DRIVE TRIPS

Moffat Road, an old railroad bed, once connected Winter Park with Nederland over beautiful Rollins Pass. Since the Needles Eye Tunnel caved in on the east side of the pass near the summit several years ago, the road has been blocked so that you can no longer drive the entire route. Access the west side of the pass from Winter Park (see Scenic Location No. 49, opposite) and the east side (see Scenic Location No. 6, p. 47) from Nederland. Moffat Road (Forest Road 149) remains popular with mountain bikers as well, providing grand views of mountains and the Fraser Valley. Pick up a brochure at the visitor center in Winter Park, and check the weather report before you embark.

GOLF

Rated the best public golf course in the state by *Golf Digest* in 1995, the 27-hole **Pole Creek Golf Club**, 11 miles north of Winter Park on US 40, has challenging hazards and views of the nearby peaks. *6827 CR 5, Fraser, 970-887-9195, 800-511-5076.*

HIKING

The 8-mile (one way) **Mount Nystrom Trail** MODERATE follows the Continental Divide from Mount Nystrom to Mary Jane, with mountain views and abundant wildflowers. Park at the old Berthoud Pass ski lodge on the east side of US 40, cross the highway, then climb the ski slope to the top of the chairlift. From the chairlift, follow the ridge west to its intersection with another broad ridge from the north. The Mount Nystrom trailhead is marked with cairns.

The 3.5-mile (one way) **Byers Peak Trail** DIFFICULT leads to the 12,804-foot summit of Byers Peak and spectacular views. From Byers Creek campground (see Camping, p. 174), go 0.2 mile to the Byers Peak trailhead.

One of my favorite Colorado hikes is the 4.4-mile (one way) **Caribou Pass Trail** DIFFICULT, which commands wonderful views of the Indian Peaks Wilderness. You also have the option to connect to **Columbine Lake Trail** MODERATE, leading to a beautiful alpine lake. I've seen moose grazing in the meadows and wetlands along the trail, and the views are superb. The trailhead for Caribou Pass Trail is above Meadow Creek Reservoir (see directions to High Lonesome Trail, Cycling and Mountain

ROLLINS PASS WEST

The old railroad grade over Rollins Pass (11,671 feet) is now a road. Unfortunately, the road is closed near the top of the pass on the east side, so you must take Berthoud Pass on US 40 to Winter Park if you want to drive the entire route. Both sides of the pass are incredibly photogenic. The Indian Peaks Wilderness lies immediately to the north, and the new James Peak Wilderness is to the south. The drainages along the route east of the divide are less steep and more extensive than those to the west, creating more lakes, creeks, and wildflowers. However, the eastern road is much rougher than its western equivalent, and it doesn't go to the top of the pass. From Winter Park, take Moffat Road (Forest Road 149), northeast from US 40 to Rollins Pass. The road is manageable by car until you reach treeline, at which point it gets bumpy. I recommend using a four-wheel-drive vehicle for this route.

Most of the road winds circuitously through lodgepole pine and a few aspen, and the scenery doesn't get good until you exit the trees and enter the alpine zone. Near the top, you can see a small lake immediately below the road, and a larger one, Corona Lake, a short distance to the north. You can make wonderful reflection photographs at each lake. Park at the top of the pass and enjoy views of James Peak to the south and the Indian Peaks Wilderness to the north. A short hike on the Continental Divide National Scenic Trail reveals a view down to King Lake and the cliffs to the west that protect the cirque. In fact, plan on hiking Roosevelt National Forest Trail 810 down to King Lake. But don't stop there—continue on to Betty and Bob lakes, two of the prettiest alpine lakes you'll see anywhere. If you get there at sunrise, yellow light bathes the Continental Divide and makes a spectacular reflection in these lakes.

Similarly, a hike south along the Continental Divide from Rollins Pass allows views into a half-dozen cirques that drain to the east. Arapahoe Lakes, Iceberg Lakes, and many others can be seen and photographed from this vantage point. Photograph when the sun is high enough in the sky to illuminate the entire basin. Pointing your camera north or south across the cirques will allow you to compose shadows and sidelit tundra grasses, creating more contrast and detail in the scene. Put on the polarizing filter and watch how the surface of the lakes changes from highly reflective to very dark (see p. 145, *Photographing the Landscape*).

Biking, p. 173) at the Junco Lake parking area. To access the Columbine Lake Trail, take Caribou Pass Trail 1.5 miles, then go south at the marked junction.

HORSEBACK RIDING

See the backcountry as few people do—on horseback. **Devil's Thumb Ranch** and **Snow Mountain Ranch** both offer various expeditions to suit your family's interests and skill level. *Devil's Thumb Outfitters, 3530 CR 83, Tabernash, 970-726-8231, www.devilsthumbranch.com; YMCA Snow Mountain Ranch, 1101 CR 53, Granby, 970-887-2152, www.ymcarockies.org.*

HOT SPRINGS

The recently renovated **Hot Sulphur Springs Resort** has a long history and bountiful waters. The spa boasts 21 hot pools that range in temperature from 95 to 112 degrees. The 200,000 gallons that flow into the pools from the Earth's depths every day are rich in minerals and other compounds believed to possess healing properties. In addition to the private vapor caves, a solarium pool, and a swimming pool, there are shallow pools designed especially for children. The resort also provides lodging (see Accommodations, opposite) and light fare. Drink plenty of water! From Winter Park, take US 40 northwest 29 miles. *5609 CR 20, Hot Sulphur Springs, 970-725-3306, www.hotsulphursprings.com.*

MUSEUM

Grand County Historical Museum houses a rather eclectic collection of exhibits that feature tribal artifacts, the contributions of women settlers, historic photographs, and early ski equipment. *110 E. Byers Ave., Hot Sulphur Springs, 970-725-3939, www.grandcountymuseum.com.*

Restaurants

Deno's Mountain Bistro ($-$$) is really two restaurants. Enjoy fine dining, including prime rib, seafood dishes, and pasta, on the main floor, or go upstairs to the pub and enjoy hearty food and a variety of beers. *Downtown Winter Park on US 40, 970-726-5332.* For Cajun food that will warm you up after a day of skiing, try **Fontenot's Cajun Café** ($$). *Downtown Winter Park at the Park Plaza on US 40, 970-726-4021.* **Carvers Bakery Café** ($) is a rustic downtown breakfast and lunch spot with an extensive bakery selection. *983 Vasquez Rd, 970-726-8202.* **Hernando's Pizza & Pasta Pub** ($) located at the north end of HWY 40, offers fresh baked, hand-tossed pizzas, pasta, Italian sandwiches, and stromboli. *970-726-5409, www.hernandospizzapub.com.* **Azteca's** ($-$$) in nearby Fraser is a great choice for Mexican in a great family atmosphere. *5 Grand County Rd, Fraser, 970-726-4145.* **Ranch House Restaurant and Saloon** ($$) occupies the original, cozy homestead at Devil's Thumb Ranch. Try the fresh seafood and check out the impressive wine list. The scenery is also a lovely treat (for directions, see Winter Sports, p. 174). *3530 CR 83, Tabernash, 970-726-5633.*

Accommodations

As far as I'm concerned, there are only two choices for accommodations in the Fraser Valley—guest ranches and B&Bs. I highly recommend **Devil's Thumb Ranch** ($-$$$$), a super destination for families. The ranch has everything —horseback riding, fishing, hiking, rafting, winter activities, a fine restaurant, and friendly staff (for directions, see Winter Sports, p. 174). *3530 CR 83, Tabernash, 970-726-8231, www.devilsthumbranch.com.* **C Lazy U Guest Ranch,** ($$$-$$$$), north of Granby, is a dude ranch with a storybook history and a touch of luxury. The ranch also provides children's programs and supervised activities. *3640 CO 125, Granby,*

Gasthaus Eichler Hotel and Restaurant, Winter Park

970-887-3344, www.clazyu.com. Another great place for the family is the **YMCA Snow Mountain Ranch** ($-$$), where everyone can enjoy horseback riding, swimming, mountain biking, miniature golf, and other activities (for directions, see Winter Sports, p. 174). *1101 CR 53, Granby, 970-887-2152, www.ymcarockies.org.*

The **Gasthaus Eichler Hotel and Restaurant** ($$) provides the cuisine and atmosphere of a European ski haus in downtown Winter Park. *78746 CO 40, 970-726-5133.* **Hot Sulphur Springs Resort** ($$) offers a unique lodging experience. The newly renovated resort and spa is peaceful and comfortable (see Hot Springs, opposite). *5609 CR 20, Hot Sulphur Springs, 970-725-3306, www.hotsulphursprings.com.*

There is no shortage of good B&Bs in Winter Park and the Fraser Valley area. **Bear Paw Inn** ($$$) offers wonderful hospitality, opportunities to see wildlife, and all the amenities of a first-class B&B. Ask your hosts to prepare Eggs Blackstone for breakfast. *871 Bear Paw Dr., Winter Park, 970-887-2772, www.bearpaw-winterpark.com.* **Winter Park Chateau** ($$$-$$$$) is a lovely boutique hotel conveniently located in downtown Winter Park. *405 Lions Gate Dr, 970-726-2884, 970-281-2022, www.winterparkchateau.com.* **Outpost B&B Inn** ($$$), in Fraser, is a beautiful country inn that offers seven cozy guestrooms and breathtaking views of the Continental Divide. *687 County Road 517, Fraser, 970-726-5346; 800-430-4538, www.winterpark-inn.com.*

Special Events

In August, mountain-biking enthusiasts flock to Winter Park for the annual **Fat Tire Classic,** part of the Spirit of the Rockies mountain-bike series. *970-726-4118.* Also in July, the town hosts the **Winter Park Jazz Fest,** which attracts nationally known jazz musicians, and the **Grand County Blues Festival**. *970-726-5514, 800-903-7275, www.winterparkresort.com.*

For More Information

Winter Park and Fraser Valley Chamber of Commerce, *78841 US 40 (at Vasquez), Winter Park, 970-726-4118, www.winterpark-info.com.*

Walden

Colorado Atlas & Gazetteer pp. 17–18, 27–28

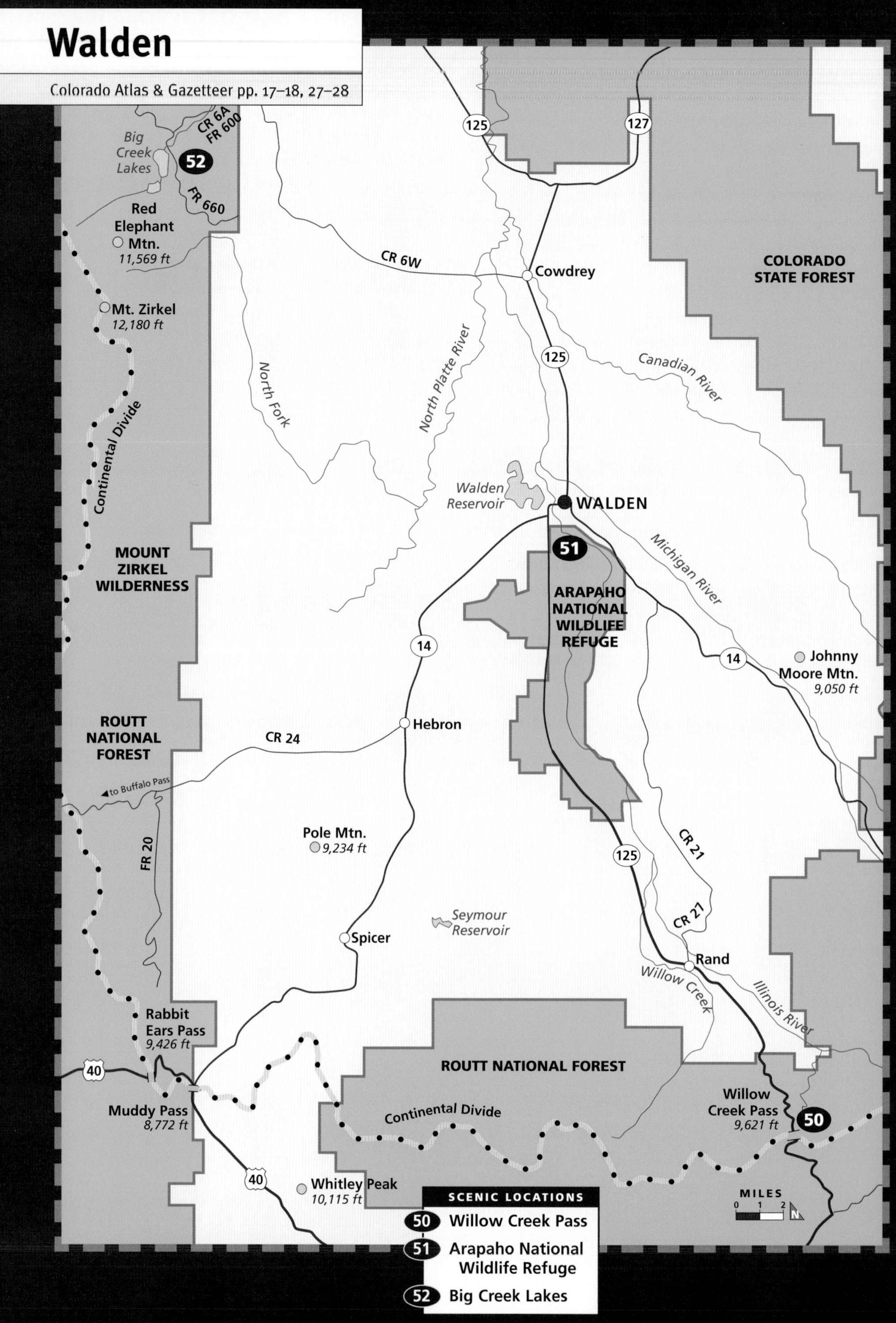

CR 6A
FR 600
Big Creek Lakes
52
FR 660
Red Elephant Mtn.
11,569 ft
Mt. Zirkel
12,180 ft
Continental Divide
MOUNT ZIRKEL WILDERNESS
ROUTT NATIONAL FOREST
to Buffalo Pass
FR 20
Rabbit Ears Pass
9,426 ft
40
Muddy Pass
8,772 ft
125
127
CR 6W
Cowdrey
COLORADO STATE FOREST
North Fork
North Platte River
Canadian River
Walden Reservoir
WALDEN
51
Michigan River
ARAPAHO NATIONAL WILDLIFE REFUGE
14
Johnny Moore Mtn.
9,050 ft
Hebron
CR 24
Pole Mtn.
9,234 ft
CR 21
Seymour Reservoir
CR 27
Spicer
Rand
Willow Creek
Illinois River
ROUTT NATIONAL FOREST
Continental Divide
Willow Creek Pass
9,621 ft
50
Whitley Peak
10,115 ft
MILES
0 1 2
N
SCENIC LOCATIONS
50 Willow Creek Pass
51 Arapaho National Wildlife Refuge
52 Big Creek Lakes

Walden

Visitors to North Park are likely to see more wildlife than humans in this northernmost of Colorado's natural parks. Although the mule deer and antelope play here, as well as elk, Rocky Mountain bighorn sheep, and the occasional bear and mountain lion, North Park is moose country. Reintroduced in 1974 from Utah and Wyoming, the moose population has thrived in this prime wetland habitat and now numbers more than 600 animals. In recognition of this success, the Colorado Senate designated the tiny town of Walden as the "Moose Viewing Capital of Colorado" in 1995.

Roughly defined by the boundaries of Jackson County, North Park is characterized by grassland, brush, and streams hemmed in by mountain ranges and forests. Indeed, the better part of Jackson County is governed by national and state forests, federal and state wildlife refuges, and a national park. These vast public lands are an outdoor dreamland for wildlife watchers and sport hunters. From Denver, take I-25 north 60 miles to Fort Collins. Hop on US 287 north to the junction of CO 14 at Ted's Place. Take CO 14 west over Cameron Pass to Walden. An alternate, scenic route from Denver is to head west on I-70 for 42 miles to US 40. Travel northwest to Granby, then take CO 125 northwest to Walden (see Scenic Location No. 50, p. 180).

History

Lacking the means to transport ore cheaply, the silver town of Teller City, in what is now the Never Summer Range, was abandoned by 1885. However, availability of water, timber, and fertile grassland did not go unnoticed by miners traveling through North Park to the mountains. Ranches began to appear in the mid-1880s, and a town dubbed Point of Rocks soon emerged at a convergence of wagon roads. Renamed Walden in 1889 after a postmaster, the town quickly developed into a regional stagecoach and freight center. Today, traditional ranching continues to be the economic staple of North Park and to sustain the town of Walden, as does the bustling hunting season.

Main Attractions

COLORADO STATE FOREST

The 70,768-acre Colorado State Forest teems with wildlife, beauty, recreational options, and relative solitude. The hiking, mountain biking, four-wheel-drive trips, fishing, and camping can't be beat. Moose and mosquitoes are also abundant.

Ruby Jewel Lake, Kelly Lake, Clear Lake, Lake Agnes, and **American Lakes,** accessed by more than 40 miles of hiking trails, host healthy trout populations. **Bockman, Bull Mountain, Ruby Jewel,** and **Montgomery Roads** offer spectacular views and more than 40 miles of four-wheel-drive roads through remote backcountry. Mountain bikers also share these trails and roads.

Camping within the park is available at **The Crags, Ranger Lakes, North Michigan Reservoir,** and **Bockman** campgrounds, and there are also eleven yurts (round tents on platforms, sleeping six) and two huts for rent. In winter it's possible to cross-country ski from yurt to yurt. *Never Summer Nordic, 970-723-4070.*

Explore the **Moose Visitor Center** to view wildlife displays, pick up a park map, and check the wildlife sightings board. A lifelike moose will greet you. From Walden, take CO 14 southeast 20 miles to the park entrance. *970-723-8366, www.coloradoparks.org.*

Moose Visitor Center, Walden

WILDLIFE WATCHING

With Walden as a base camp, numerous short trips can take you up close to North Park's awe-inspiring, abundant wildlife. The Colorado Division of Wildlife produces an informative brochure, available at the chamber of commerce or Forest Service offices, outlining the best places to view wildlife in North Park. The following are some of my favorites. Note that dawn and dusk—ideal times for an outdoor photographer—are also the times of greatest wildlife activity, so plan accordingly.

For the chance to see large and graceful osprey plunge talons-first into lakes to catch fish for their nesting young, head to **Big Creek Lakes** (see Scenic Location No. 52, p. 183). Enjoy the interpretive nature trail on the west side of the larger lake. From Walden, take CO 125 north 9 miles to Cowdrey. Go west on County Road 6W for 19 miles to Forest Road 600, and go left (southwest) 6 miles to Big Creek Lakes campground.

View raptors such as golden eagles, prairie falcons, and red-tailed hawks swooping down from the 200-foot cliffs of **Sheep Mountain.** From Walden, take CR 12W west 12 miles. Check out **Walden Reservoir,** a vital nesting and brood-rearing habitat, for its large numbers of Canada geese, ducks, cormorants, gulls, avocets, and prairie falcons. From Walden, take CR 12W west 0.5 mile.

One of the more amazing sights nature has to offer is the mating dance of the sage grouse. The males strut their stuff by fanning their tail feathers in a trancelike dance, then inflating their throats as if about to burst, which produces a resonating sound. Catch this phenomenon in early morning from late March through early May at the **Delaney Butte Greater Sage Grouse Viewing Area.** From Walden, head 0.5 mile west on CO 14 to CR 12W. From CR 12W, head west on CR 18 and then north on CR 5 until you come to a two-track road on your left. Parking areas will be marked.

If you want to see some odd ducks or just some beautiful scenery, head to **Teal Lake** and **Hidden Lakes.** You might catch a glimpse of the bufflehead duck (the male is black and white with a large, bonnetlike patch on its head), and you'll have no trouble recognizing the plentiful moose. From Walden,

WILLOW CREEK PASS

If you plan to travel over Stillwater Pass (see Scenic Location No. 48, p. 170) into North Park, don't miss the drive over Willow Creek Pass (CO 125). Though the pass rises only 9,621 feet above sea level, it's still worth the drive. The highway stays in the forest most of the way, but just over the pass on the north side are a number of dirt side roads that enter old clear-cut sites and provide views into North Park. Reach the pass either by turning north onto CO 125 from Stillwater Pass Road, or by turning north onto CO 125 from US 40, 2.5 miles west of Granby.

From US 40 to the pass, be sure to photograph the pretty meadows along Coyote, Willow, and Pass Creeks. The fall color is wonderful around the third and fourth weeks of September. After crossing the pass, look for the first dirt road to the west. It's bumpy, but if you can make it a little way, you'll spy views through the trees of North Park and the mountains around it. Because you are facing north, both sunrise and sunset provide good compositions that include trees in the foreground, shadows, and valley and peaks in the distance. Forest clear-cuts are certainly unsightly, but they do promote wildflower growth. Look for pink fireweed and red Indian paintbrush among the stumps and grasses. Make it a full landscape composition, or photograph the flowers close up with your macro lens (see p. 42, *Photographing the Landscape*).

As you exit the forest on your descent into North Park, look for views of the Illinois River to the north. Better yet, exit the highway at Rand onto County Road 27. Pull over when you cross the river and compose a scene to the southeast to include the river (more of a creek) disappearing into willows and cottonwoods. In late May and late September the spring and fall colors are spectacular. Take pictures along this route all the way to CO 14 and the Michigan River. And always in this country, keep your eyes peeled for moose: In 1974, 12 moose were reintroduced right here. Today, hundreds roam the state.

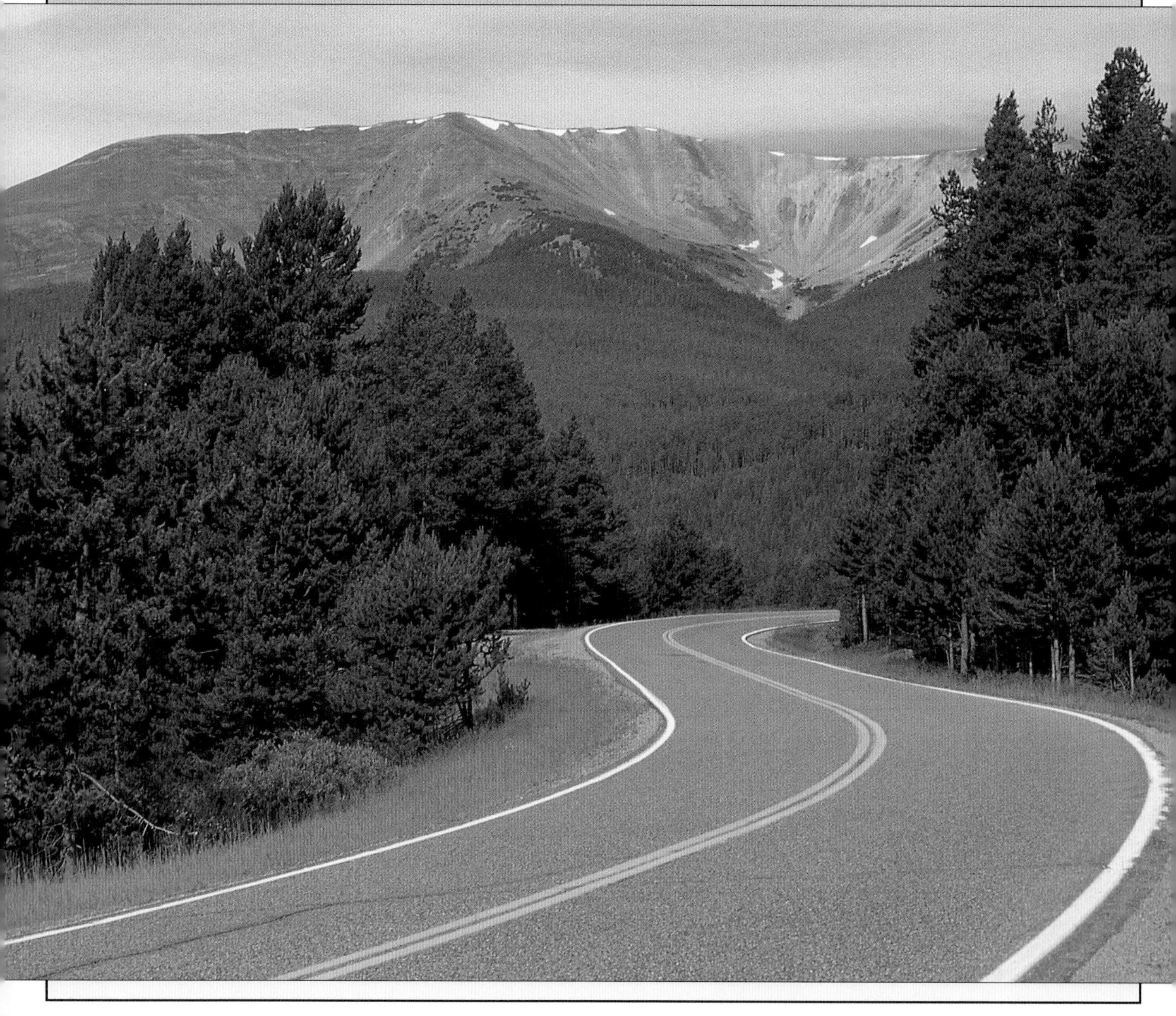

head 12 miles southwest on CO 14 to Hebron. Turn right (west) onto CR 24, and go 11 miles to the Routt National Forest boundary. From here, Teal Lake is 3 miles north on FR 615 and Hidden Lakes are 4 miles south on FR 20.

Hebron Waterfowl Area is another wetland habitat attractive to moose. From Walden, take CO 14 southwest for 16 miles. Turn left (east) on CR 34 and continue 2 miles. Moose also abound along the **Illinois River**. From Walden, take CO 125 south 24 miles to CR 21, 2 miles south of Rand. Turn left (northeast) onto CR 21 and go 0.5 mile, then turn right (east) on FR 740 and go 4 miles. Continue southeast on FR 750 for 2 miles to the river.

Arapaho National Wildlife Refuge (see Scenic Location No. 51, p. 182) is home to waterfowl, raptors, prairie dogs, and pronghorn antelope. Take the 6-mile, self-guided driving tour; at the entrance, grab a pamphlet providing a numbered, site-by-site guide to the route. **Sentinel Mountain** is the place to see large herds of elk in their winter habitat, from December through March. From Walden, take CO 125 north for 12 miles. Sentinel Mountain is just east of the highway. For additional viewing, go east on CO 127 about a mile.

Activities

CAMPING

Small **Hidden Lakes** campground boasts fine scenery and near solitude. From Walden, take CO 14 southwest 13 miles to Hebron. Turn right (west) onto County Road 24 and continue 11 miles to where it becomes Forest Road 20. Go 1 mile on FR 20, then turn left (south), continuing on FR 20 for 5 miles. **Teal Lake** campground provides access to stocked trout fishing. Follow directions to Hidden Lakes, but turn right on FR 615 from CR 24 and continue 3 miles. **Big Creek Lakes** campground accommodates boaters and water-skiers and connects to Mount Zirkel Wilderness. Take CO 125 north from Walden to CR 6W at Cowdrey and turn left (west). Continue 19 miles to FR 600, turn left (south), and go 6 miles. Reservations recommended. *For above campgrounds: 970-723-8204.*

FISHING

Although North Park is known for its excellent fishing on cold-water lakes, one of the area's best-kept secrets is the **North Platte River** as it flows through Colorado from its headwaters at the confluence of Grizzly and Little Grizzly Creeks in North Park. The first public accesses to the North Platte are at the Brownlee and Verner State Wildlife Areas. From CO 14 west of Walden, take County Road 12W west for 5 miles and continue heading west (straight) on CR 18 for 0.5 mile to the Brownlee access, on the right. The Verner access is just down the road. South of the Wyoming border, the North Platte boasts a 5-mile stretch of Gold Medal Water. From Walden, take CO 125 north for 18 miles to Forest Road 896. A sign marks the entrance to Routt National Forest and fishing access.

A major tributary of the North Platte, the **Michigan River** follows CO 125 from Cowdrey to Walden. Although private property can block access, and I've lost many a fly and lure to the brush and willows along the bank, the fishing can be quite good for browns and rainbows. **Lake John** has a reputation for feisty 16- to 20-inch rainbows, browns, and cutthroats. From Walden, go west on CR 12W for 8 miles to where it joins CR 7. Turn right (northwest) and continue to the parking area.

North Delaney Butte Lake is a Gold Medal Water fishery where browns of more than 20 inches are caught regularly. The lake also produces a few hefty rainbows. Although the north lake is the most popular and has the better fishing, **South** and **East Delaney Butte Lakes** have improved now that they are restricted to flies and lures. From Walden, take CR 12W west, continue heading straight (west) when the road joins FR 18, and turn right (north) on CR 20. Follow signs to the lakes. Trout fishing is also very good at secluded **Seymour Lake.** From Walden, take CO 14 southwest 16 miles to CR 11. Turn left (east) onto CR 11 and continue 3 miles to Seymour Lake State Wildlife Area. One note of caution: Most fishing areas in North Park are in moose habitat, so stay alert! *For information and equipment: North Park Anglers, 524 Main St., 970-723-4215.*

HIKING

Lost Ranger Trail DIFFICULT traverses the Mount Zirkel Wilderness along the rugged Red Canyon and up to Red Canyon Saddle, a summer range for elk along the Continental Divide. Lost Ranger Trail intersects **Wyoming Trail** DIFFICULT, which accesses the summit of 11,932-foot Lost Ranger Peak with a panoramic vista of Mount Ethel to the south and Mount Zirkel to the north, as well as a bird's-eye view of the many small lakes in the wilderness area. It's a 3-mile hike to the mouth of Red Canyon and an additional 9 miles (one way) to the summit of Lost Ranger Peak. From Walden, head to Delaney Butte Lakes (see Fishing, above) and continue to the Routt National Forest boundary. Park at Pitchpine trailhead and take Grizzly-Helena Trail to meet Lost Ranger Trail at Red Canyon Reservoir.

The 5-mile (one way) hike to the summit of 12,296-foot **Parkview Mountain** MODERATE climbs to panoramic views with the chance to see wildflowers and wildlife. Parkview Mountain is the high point of the Rabbit Ears Range and separates North and Middle Parks. From Walden, take CO 125 south for about 30 miles to the summit of Willow Creek Pass (see Scenic Location No. 50, opposite). Continue south about 0.6 mile to the second timber road on your right (west). 4WD If you have a four-wheel-drive, high-centered vehicle, you can proceed up the road. If not, park here. (For more North Park hiking options, see Colorado State Forest, p. 179.)

MUSEUM

North Park Pioneer Museum, at 365 Logan St. west of the Jackson County Courthouse, will give you a feel for what life was

Continued on page 184

ARAPAHO NATIONAL WILDLIFE REFUGE

Created to mitigate the loss of wetlands, Arapaho National Wildlife Refuge uses the Illinois River to irrigate meadows that are habitat for 198 bird species, 32 mammal species, nine fish species, and six reptile and amphibian species. Moose were reintroduced in the 1970s, and today you have a very good chance of seeing one or more on any visit.

With its location in the middle of one of Colorado's glacial intermountain basins, scenic North Park, the refuge is a destination for photography as well as wildlife viewing. Wonderful landscapes can be composed of both the Michigan and Illinois Rivers as they meander through the vast meadows of the park. After visiting Poudre Canyon and Cameron Pass along CO 14, continue northwest to the refuge, which sits right beside CO 125 just south of Walden.

Three miles south of town, there's a spectacular overlook from CO 125. You'll see the information kiosk and pull-off, where you can park and set up a camera. From here, compose the meandering Illinois River and vast meadows of North Park in a scene with the Rabbit Ears Range and Continental Divide in the background. Take advantage of the prominence of the river, not the mountains, within this almost infinite landscape. The fields are bright green from late May through August. Blue sky reflects in the river at sunrise on clear days, producing the loveliest combination of blue and green that you'll ever see in a photograph.

Adding a polarizing filter will further intensify the color of the water by reducing glare on its surface (see p. 145, *Photographing the Landscape*). Different focal-length lenses will capture diverse parts of the landscape, but any scene with water and field will make an outstanding image. Similarly, rosy clouds of sunrise or sunset will turn the water pink, also a wonderful contrast to green fields of summer or golden fields of autumn. Numerous county roads in the vicinity cross both the Illinois and Michigan Rivers. At these points you can make pastoral photographs of the rivers winding through meadows and wetlands.

BIG CREEK LAKES

The Park Range, which forms the western boundary of North Park, is part of Colorado's Continental Divide and lies mostly within spectacular Mount Zirkel Wilderness. Many wildlife viewing areas in North Park provide the opportunity for good landscape photography. One in particular stands out from the rest: Big Creek Lakes (two large lakes connected by the South Fork of Big Creek) in the northwestern corner of the park. From Walden, take CO 125 north 9 miles to Cowdrey. Go west 19 miles on County Road 6W to Forest Road 600. Drive southwest 6 miles to Big Creek Lakes. Four-wheel drive is not necessary.

Once at the lake, turn south onto FR 660, which follows along the east side of the largest lake. Beyond the lake loom the peaks of Mount Zirkel Wilderness; look for vantages from which to photograph the Park Range reflecting in the water. You'll want to watch for little bays protected from waves, nature's reflection killer. Look for rocks, logs, or any other interesting features that create foreground and add depth to the scene. Photograph here at sunrise when the peaks are lit with red, orange, and yellow.

Now hike the trail that parallels the south side of the lake on its way to the upper lake. It's less than a 2-mile (one way) trip and well worth the effort, even though views to the peaks are limited by the forest. Practice composing intimate landscapes, which eschew the horizon that most people mistakenly believe is a necessary ingredient in a scenic photograph (see pp. 54–57, *Photographing the Landscape*). Use the edge of the lakes as a lead-in line to draw the viewer into the scene. Photograph both horizontally and vertically, with the lake edge beginning in the bottom left- or right-hand corner of the viewfinder.

If you have time, bushwhack through the lodgepole pines due south from the upper lake. In about 0.5 mile you will begin to encounter hundreds of kettle ponds. These small ponds are glacial remnants that appear out of nowhere as you hike through the trees. They are set in beautiful grassy areas where the forest opens up, and are usually covered with lily pads. Come in early summer and you'll be able to photograph flowers as well. But be sure to tread lightly—these ponds are habitat for an endangered frog species.

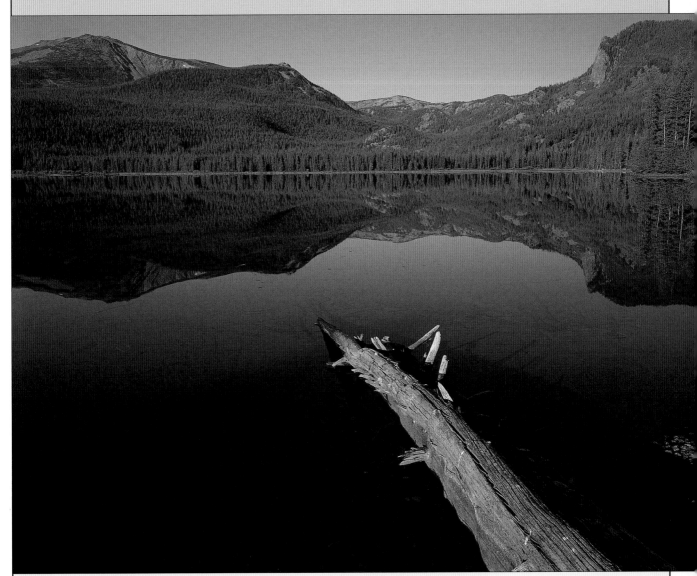

like for North Park's pioneering ranch families. Check out the kitchen with coal range, china room, laundry room, pool hall, and typewriter room. Displays also include period children's toys and dolls, skis and other war memorabilia from Colorado's 10th Mountain Division, a player piano, and Edison and Victrola phonographs. *For information: North Park Pioneer Museum, 365 Logan St., 970-723-3282, www.museumsusa.org/museums/info/1161576.*

SCENIC DRIVES

Upper Jack Creek Road takes you through picturesque backcountry to the silver mining townsite of Teller City in the Never Summer Mountains and along the Never Summer Wilderness boundary. From Walden, take CO 125, 25 miles south. Continue 2 miles past Rand, then turn left (northeast) onto County Road 21. Go 1 mile and bear right. Go 4 miles, bear left (northeast) onto Forest Road 740, and continue 4 miles along Jack Creek.

Poudre Canyon is among the most rugged and scenic canyons in Colorado (see Main Attractions, Fort Collins, p. 149). From Walden, take CO 14 southeast over 10,276-foot Cameron Pass and follow the Cache la Poudre River through Poudre Canyon to Fort Collins.

Restaurants

Moose Creek Café ($) at 508 Main St. features fine sandwiches, barbecue, Mexican, and Southwest favorites. *866-850-6971, www.moosecreekcafe.net.* Have a cup of coffee with a slice of homemade pie at **The River Rock Cafe** ($) at 460 Main St. *970-723-4670.* **The Drifter's Cookhouse** ($$) in Gould is one of the area's best-kept secrets. The full restaurant and bar serves up home-cooked favorites and fine-quality steaks. *55278 CO 14, 970-273-8300, www.drifterscookhouse.com.*

Accommodations

Although Walden has local motels that cater to anglers and hunters, this is an ideal place to camp (see Colorado State Forest and Camping, pp. 179 and 181). For a backcountry resort experience with trout fishing, stay at **Shamrock Ranch** ($$), *4363 CR 11 near Coalmont, 970-723-8413, www.northpark.org,* or **Lake John Resort** ($), *2521 CR 7, 970-723-3226, www.northpark.org.*

Special Events

In late June, the **Never Summer Rodeo** draws people from all over Jackson County and as far away as Fort Collins. The event starts with a parade and ends with a barbecue supper and dancing. *970-723-4600.*

For More Information

North Park Chamber of Commerce, *416 4th St., Walden, 970-723-4600. www.waldenchamber.com.*

Kettle Ponds near Big Creek Lakes

Steamboat Springs

Colorado Atlas & Gazetteer pp. 15–17, 26–27

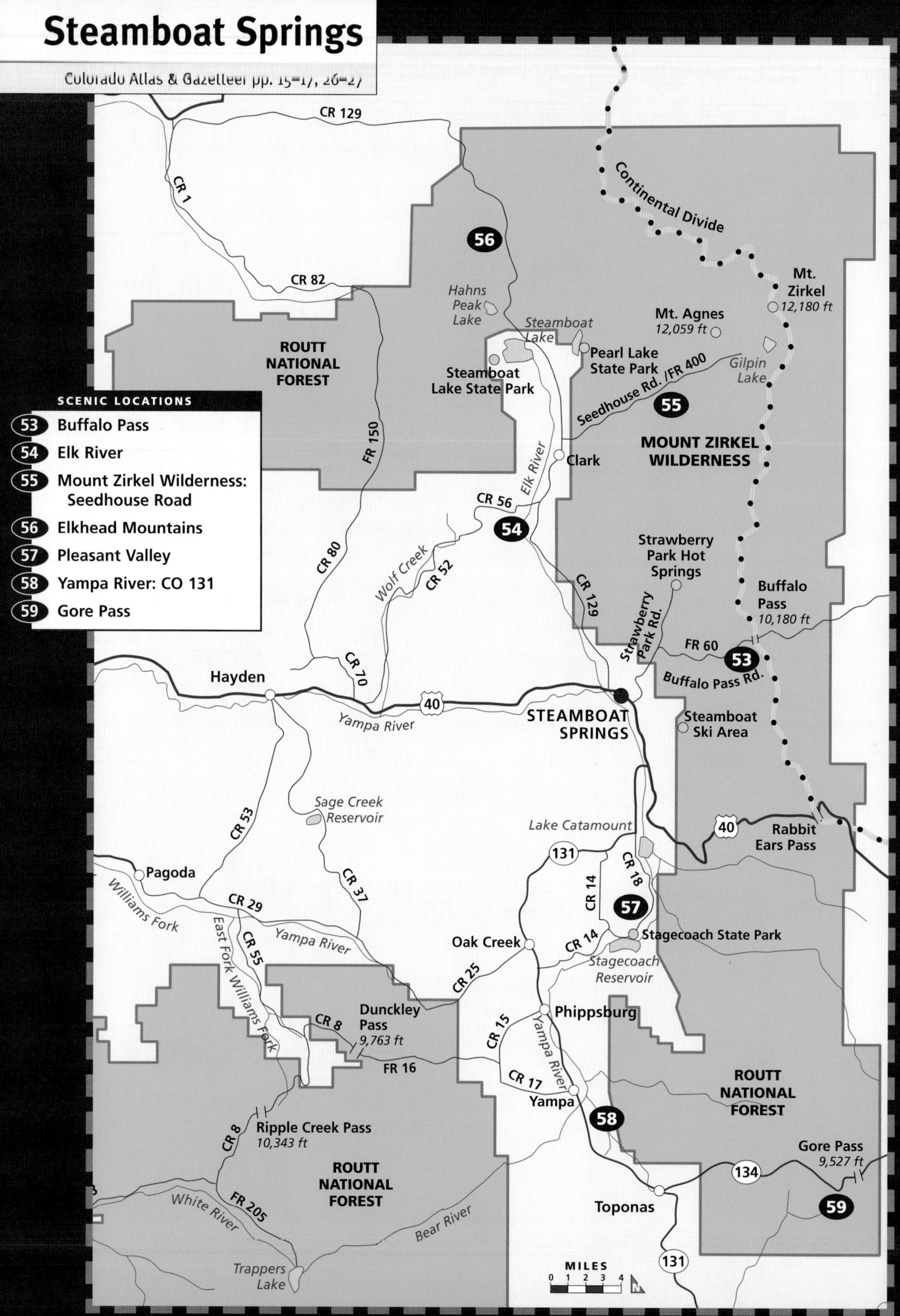
SCENIC LOCATIONS
53 Buffalo Pass
54 Elk River
55 Mount Zirkel Wilderness: Seedhouse Road
56 Elkhead Mountains
57 Pleasant Valley
58 Yampa River: CO 131
59 Gore Pass
CR 129
CR 1
CR 82
56
Continental Divide
Mt. Zirkel
12,180 ft
Mt. Agnes
12,059 ft
Hahns Peak Lake
Steamboat Lake
Pearl Lake State Park
ROUTT NATIONAL FOREST
Steamboat Lake State Park
Gilpin Lake
Seedhouse Rd. /FR 400
55
FR 150
Clark
Elk River
MOUNT ZIRKEL WILDERNESS
CR 56
54
CR 80
Wolf Creek
CR 52
CR 129
Strawberry Park Hot Springs
Buffalo Pass
10,180 ft
Strawberry Park Rd.
FR 60
53
Buffalo Pass Rd.
CR 70
Hayden
40
Yampa River
STEAMBOAT SPRINGS
Steamboat Ski Area
Sage Creek Reservoir
CR 53
Lake Catamount
40
Rabbit Ears Pass
131
Pagoda
CR 37
CR 18
CR 14
57
Williams Fork
CR 29
East Fork Williams Fork
CR 55
Yampa River
Oak Creek
CR 14
Stagecoach State Park
Stagecoach Reservoir
CR 25
Dunckley Pass
9,763 ft
CR 8
Phippsburg
CR 15
Yampa River
FR 16
CR 17
Yampa
58
ROUTT NATIONAL FOREST
Ripple Creek Pass
10,343 ft
CR 8
ROUTT NATIONAL FOREST
Gore Pass
9,527 ft
134
59
Toponas
White River
FR 205
Bear River
Trappers Lake
131
MILES
0 1 2 3 4

Steamboat Springs

In Steamboat Springs, a.k.a. "Ski Town USA," people work hard at play, and its small-town atmosphere makes visitors feel welcome. Steamboat Springs attracts professionals (as well as amateurs) in practically every recreational activity found in Colorado. The town has made a unique contribution to the sport of ski jumping, and has sent many athletes to the world championships and the Olympics. Beyond the champagne powder, you can fish and float the Yampa River, golf at Haymaker, hike up to Fish Creek Falls, soak at Strawberry Park Hot Springs, and top off the day at one of the fine restaurants in town.

One of my favorite memories of Steamboat Springs is landing in a hot-air balloon on a neighborhood street when the wind didn't cooperate. People streamed out of their homes, but instead of being alarmed, they all just cheerfully helped pack up the balloon for transport. You'll love this famous and friendly ski town, a bit off the beaten path, and the seemingly endless recreational options here. From Denver, take I-70 west to the Silverthorne exit (205). Go north on CO 9 to Kremmling, then take US 40 west to Steamboat Springs, for a total of 157 miles.

History

Steamboat Springs gets its name from the more than 150 thermal springs in the vicinity. According to legend, French trappers thought they heard a steamboat chugging up the Yampa River, when what they actually heard was a bubbling spa. (Sadly, dynamite blasting for railroad tracks silenced the rumbles in 1908.) The Yampatika Utes believed the springs had healing properties and soaked in them to rejuvenate. Settlers and ranchers poured into the Yampa Valley during the 1880s, and the valley is still dotted with cattle and sheep ranches. Mining also had a brief history in the Hahn's Peak vicinity, some 25 miles to the north.

But things really took off in Steamboat with the arrival of "The Flying Norseman," Carl Howelsen, an erstwhile stonemason who had performed fabulous ski jumping feats for city circus crowds before retiring to Steamboat Springs. Here he made a lasting contribution to American Alpine skiing by building a ski jump on ideal terrain in 1913 and organizing Steamboat's first Winter Carnival in 1914. Ski jumpers still train on the 30- to 90-meter jumps at Howelsen Hill Ski Area near downtown, the oldest ski area in continuous use in the state. Always a winter mode of transportation, skiing became such an integral part of Steamboat Springs' culture that it was added to the town's school curriculum in 1943. No wonder Steamboat Springs has produced so many Olympians!

In 1963, Storm Mountain opened for downhill skiing. The peak was renamed Mount Werner in 1964 in honor of Steamboat Springs resident and Olympic competitor Buddy Werner, who perished in an avalanche. The same year, Steamboat Springs' own Billy Kidd and Jimmy Heuga won the first U.S. Men's Alpine medals ever, in the slalom, and in 1998, Shannon Dunn was the first U.S. woman to medal (in the halfpipe) in the new Olympic sport of snowboarding. Today, Steamboat Ski Resort comprises more than 2,935 acres of skiable terrain. Nearby Howelsen Hill Ski Area has trained numerous Olympians and World Pro–Circuit competitors in jumping over the years. Olympic Nordic ski teams still regularly train in Steamboat Springs.

Main Attractions

CYCLING AND MOUNTAIN BIKING

The 3-mile paved **Yampa River Core Trail** EASY, part of Steamboat Springs' Town Trail System, follows the Yampa River past several small parks.

If mountain biking is your thing, there is no shortage of trails in the Steamboat area. Take the 5-mile (round-trip) **Mad Creek Trail** MODERATE for a gentle autumn ride. From Steamboat Springs, take US 40 west 1 mile to Elk River Road (County Road 129), turn right (north) and look for the 1100 Trail sign, then cross Mad Creek and turn into the parking area.

The 27.5-mile **Gore Pass Loop** MODERATE (see Scenic Location No. 59, p. 198) passes through forests and meadows along old logging roads. From Steamboat Springs, go south on US 40, then turn right on CO 131, and continue 38 miles. Turn left on CO 134 at Toponas, then go 16 miles up and over Gore Pass to Forest Road 185. Park at the clearing and start your ride on FR 185. You have several options, so consult a good bike outfitter and topo map.

Wyoming Trail MODERATE, a 15-mile loop, is part of the Continental Divide National Scenic Trail and commands outstanding canyon views of Mount Zirkel Wilderness and the deep North Fork of Fish Creek. From downtown Steamboat Springs, turn north on 3rd Street at the sign for Fish Creek Falls, then turn right on Oak Street and left on Amethyst Drive. You will pass a school. Follow the signs for Strawberry Park Hot Springs, then turn right onto Buffalo Pass Road (CR 38/FR 60) and go 10 miles to the parking area at Buffalo Pass (see Scenic Location No. 53, p. 189).

Mountain bikers appreciate the challenge of **Rabbit Ears Pass** to **Fish Creek Falls** DIFFICULT, which can be enjoyed by intermediate riders for the first 10 miles, but the 6-mile Fish Creek section is more difficult. However, your efforts will be rewarded with wonderful views of the Yampa Valley. Connect to the trailhead from Dumont Lake campground (see Camping, p. 189).

Take the Silver Bullet Gondola up Thunderhead Mountain and tackle 50 miles of mountain-bike trails—excellent riding for any ability. *For trail information and rentals: Steamboat Ski & Bike Kare, 442 Lincoln Ave, 970-879-9144, www.steamboatskiandbike.com, Ski Haus, 1450 S Lincoln Ave, 800-932-3019.*

BUFFALO PASS

From Rabbit Ears Pass on US 40 to the Wyoming border, you can cross the Continental Divide at just one place in a vehicle—10,180-foot Buffalo Pass, which connects Walden with Steamboat Springs. Don't plan to use it as a commuter route because its east side is very rough and requires a four-wheel drive. However, you can take a car to the top from the Steamboat Springs side if you don't mind bumps and potholes. At lower elevations, the aspen are glorious, especially on the west side of the pass, and higher up the wildflowers are sublime. From Steamboat Springs, take 7th Street north into Strawberry Park via Strawberry Park Road (County Road 36) and look for the signs for Buffalo Pass Road (CR 38/ Forest Road 60), then head east. From Walden, drive southwest on CO 14 to Hebron, then turn west on CR 24, which becomes Buffalo Pass Road.

Once on Buffalo Pass Road, you quickly ascend into the forest. The lime green aspen are lovely in late May and early June; they turn yellow and red in late September. Some particularly good compositions present the dirt road snaking through the trees, drawing the viewer's eye into the scene. As you near the pass, you leave the aspen and enter the subalpine zone where flowers decorate the meadows between stately spruce and fir.

Compose flowers and trees together, practicing your depth-of-field technique by getting as close to the flowers as you can while keeping the distant trees in focus (see pp. 109–117, *Photographing the Landscape*). Only a short hike to the north along the Continental Divide National Scenic Trail, which crosses Buffalo Pass, will take you into the Mount Zirkel Wilderness, revealing views of the southern Park Range.

WINTER SPORTS

All of Steamboat Springs' and Yampa Valley's outdoor pastimes are the main attractions here, but champagne powder makes the skiing special. Steamboat Ski Resort's Mount Werner receives more than 300 inches of snow annually and offers skiers and snowboarders nearly 3,000 acres of skiable terrain. The area's 142 runs are particularly suited to beginner and intermediate skiers, and Steamboat has an excellent ski school, run by Olympic silver medalist Billy Kidd. The ski area is on Mount Werner Road. *970-879-6111, 877-237-2628, www.steamboat.com.*

Howelsen Hill Ski Area is the largest ski jumping center in the country; it also provides a small section for downhill skiing and snowboarding (including night skiing), as well as 8 kilometers of groomed cross-country trails. Howelsen Hill is across the 5th Street Bridge from downtown. *970-879-8499.*

Steamboat Ski Touring Center has more than 30 kilometers of groomed cross-country trails catering to beginners, intermediates, and experts, near the base of Mount Werner. *970-879-8180, www.nordicski.net.* The trails off **Rabbit Ears Pass** are popular cross-country, snowshoeing, and snowmobiling routes with great views. From Steamboat Springs, take US 40 east 21 miles. *For snowmobile tours: Steamboat Lake Outfitters, 970-879-4404, 800-342-1889, www.steamboatoutfitters.com. Steamboat Snowmobile Tours, 970-879-6500, 877-879-6500, www.steamboatsnowmobile.com.*

Activities

ALPINE SLIDE

Howler Alpine Slide is a summer magnet for kids. Take the chairlift up Howelsen Hill, then turn and hurtle down the slide to the waterfall at the base of the mountain.

CAMPING

Summit Lake campground is nestled at the edge of the Mount Zirkel Wilderness with good fishing for brookies and hiking access to Strawberry Park Hot Springs. From Steamboat Springs, take Strawberry Park Road (County Road 36) north for 2 miles, then go right (east) on Buffalo Pass Road (CR 38) for about 12 miles. You might need a four-wheel-drive vehicle once CR 38 becomes Forest Road 60. **Granite** lies on the shore of Fish Creek Reservoir amid fine scenery. Follow the directions to Summit Lake campground but go 10 miles on CR 38 to FR 310 and turn right (south). Continue 5 miles to the campground. You will need a high-clearance vehicle. **Hahn's Peak Lake** provides seclusion and access to good trout fishing. From Steamboat Springs, take US 40 west 1 mile to Elk River Road (CR 129) and turn right (north). Go 30 miles to the intersection with FR 486, then west for 2.5 miles.

The attractions of **Hinman Park** campground include seclusion, fishing, and wildlife. From Steamboat Springs, take US 40 west 1 mile to Elk River Road (CR 129), then turn right (north) and go 18.5 miles to Seedhouse Road (CR 64/FR 400). Turn right (east) and go 5.5 miles to FR 440, then turn right (south) and continue 0.5 mile. **Seedhouse** has privacy with access to the Elk River and the Three Island Lake Trail (see Hiking, p. 192). Follow the Hinman Park campground directions to Seedhouse Road (CR 64/FR 400), then turn right and go 8 miles. **Dumont Lake,** 2 miles northwest of Rabbit Ears Pass, accesses the trailhead for Rabbit Ears Peak, as well as the trailhead for Rabbit Ears Pass to Fish Creek Falls (see Hiking, p. 192). From Steamboat Springs, take US 40 east for 22 miles. *For above campgrounds: 970-879-1870.* (For more campgrounds, see State Parks, p. 194.)

FISHING

The **Yampa River** is a fly-fishing destination full of large rainbows, brookies, and Snake River cutthroats. From Steamboat Springs south to Yampa, the river is accessible from US 40 and CO 131. West, from Steamboat Springs to the town of Craig, the Yampa is accessible from US 40.

Flowing from the Mount Zirkel Wilderness, the **Elk River** (see Scenic Location No. 54, p. 190) is a main tributary of the

Continued on page 192

ELK RIVER

The Elk River Valley is one of the most beautiful river valleys in Colorado. Cottonwoods line the river's banks, and there's been relatively little development in the valley, which is bordered by rolling, aspen-covered hills. The Elk River carries practically all of the water that drains from the west side of the Mount Zirkel Wilderness before meeting up with the Yampa River west of Steamboat Springs. From Steamboat Springs, take US 40 west 1 mile, then turn right (north) on Elk River Road (County Road 129) and continue 26 miles to Steamboat Lake State Park.

Sometimes the river departs the road, so look for places where the two are contiguous. Generally, the road lies above the river and affords a perspective that makes the river seem to disappear in the distance, creating a wonderful lead-in line. Because cottonwoods line the river, you'll need to pick your spots for a clear view up or down the watercourse. In May, the trees begin to leaf; they lose their leaves by mid-October. At sunrise on a clear day the sun sidelights the leaves, saturating the greens or yellows and providing a colorful contrast to the sky-blue river. (Because blue is the complement, or color opposite, of yellow, the contrast becomes especially dramatic in autumn.) Put on a polarizing filter to reduce the glare off the water and darken the reflected blue.

Where the river departs the road, look to the west for various county roads (CR 52, 54, 56, 58, and 62) that cross the river. You can make dramatic images looking north or south from their bridges above the river. In fact, one of my favorite other drives in this area follows CR 56/52 as it winds away from the Elk River to the west. CR 52's most scenic stretch follows Wolf Creek south until you run into US 40 east of Hayden. Keep an eye out for beautiful ponds backed by aspen on the private Wolf Springs Ranch, which can be photographed from the road. You also might want to explore CR 56 as it winds north into Routt National Forest. The aspen here are exceptional, especially when composed in front of Elk Mountain to the south. Where CR 62 departs Elk River Road, look for the Clark Store, a rustic little general store with lots of goodies, including ice cream and candy!

MOUNT ZIRKEL WILDERNESS: SEEDHOUSE ROAD

At the quaint resort community of Glen Eden, Seedhouse Road (County Road 64/Forest Road 400) departs to the east from Elk River Road (CR 129), following the Elk River into the Routt National Forest on the way to the river's origin in the Mount Zirkel Wilderness. Though it stops short of the wilderness, Seedhouse Road traverses spectacular terrain before dead-ending at a network of wilderness trailheads, including two of my favorite wilderness hikes: Mica Lake and Gilpin Lake. From Steamboat Springs, take US 40 1 mile west to Elk River Road, turn right (north), and go 18.5 miles. At Glen Eden, turn right (east) on Seedhouse Road. You can take your car the entire route, though this is a typical national forest road with plenty of potholes.

The personality of the river changes along this stretch—it's rockier, narrower, and faster than it is along Elk River Road—and it sticks closer to the road. Look for places where you can see the river winding through the meadows and trees for significant distances and compose the river as a lead-in line from the bottom to the top of your view. Don't worry about including sky; this is a place to create intimate landscapes. Although I love the wildflowers that line the road in summer, my favorite times to visit are when the aspens decorate the ridges along the boundary of this narrow valley with their spring and fall shows.

On October 25, 1997, an entirely different landscape was created here when 120-mph winds knocked down 25,000 acres of trees in the national forest and wilderness area. You can view the remains of this amazing blowdown along the last few miles of Seedhouse Road, which also provides views of the Mount Zirkel Wilderness to the east and south.

Yampa; because of private property, access is a problem. The exception is at the Elk's confluence with Mad Creek at Christina State Wildlife Area, about 5 miles north of the junction of US 40 and Elk River Road (CR 129), which roughly parallels the river north of Steamboat Springs. To reach the headwaters of the upper Elk River, turn right (east) onto Seedhouse Road (CR 64/Forest Road 400) from Elk River Road.

Dumont Lake and **Hahn's Peak Lake** are also stocked with trout (for directions, see Camping, p. 189). For guided fishing tours: *Bucking Rainbow Outfitters, 730 Lincoln Ave., 888-810-8747, www.buckingrainbow.com; Blue Sky West, 1724 Mt. Werner Rd., 970-871-4260, www.blueskywest.com; Steamboat Flyfisher, 35 5th St., 970-879-6552, www.steamboatflyfisher.com*

GOLF

Chosen by *Golf Digest* as one of the "Best New Courses," **Haymaker Golf Course** has also achieved Audubon Signature Status for being environmentally friendly. On 230 acres just 3 miles south of Steamboat Springs at US 40 and County Road 131, this is a challenging and scenic golf course. *970-870-1846.*

Kids will enjoy the **Amaze'n Miniature Golf Course,** which, of course, offers a maze and a miniature golf course, behind the Steamboat Springs Visitor Center. *1255 S. Lincoln, 970-870-8682.*

HIKING

Fish Creek Trail MODERATE is 8 miles long (one way) but has several legs of varying difficulty. The first 0.3 mile (paved) leads to Lower Fish Creek Falls, a popular picnic destination. To really appreciate the falls, take the short downhill trail that leads to the rocks and creek below. Continue 2.7 miles to Upper Fish Creek Falls to view the gorge and autumn aspens and enjoy the near-solitude (many are content to enjoy the Lower Falls). The trail continues another 3.3 miles, past lovely Long Lake, and ends at Forest Road 311. Although the Fish Creek Falls and Long Lake hikes are moderate, there are some steep pitches. From the south end of Steamboat Springs, take FR 320 east and follow signs to the trailhead.

The first 1.7 miles of **Mad Creek Trail** EASY climbs above raging Mad Creek and leads to vantage points that allow you to see Mad Creek's waterfalls plunging 200 feet to the canyon below (for directions, see Cycling and Mountain Biking, p. 187). The 3-mile (one way) **Rabbit Ears Peak** EASY hike leads you to remarkable rock formations. Summer wildflowers can be lavish here. Follow the directions to Dumont Lake campground (see Camping, p. 189). Pass the campground and look for the old Rabbit Ears Pass marker. Turn left (north) on FR 311 and travel 0.2 mile.

The 6-mile (one way) **Three Island Lake Trail** MODERATE bears evidence to one of the most violent occurrences in nature—a "blowdown" (see Scenic Location No. 55, p. 191). To get to the trail, follow the directions to the Seedhouse campground (see Camping, p. 189), turn right on FR 443, and go 3 miles.

HORSEBACK RIDING

Steamboat Springs lies in some of Colorado's finest horse country. Working cattle ranches here also cater to "dudes." Real wranglers teach you to ride and rope like a cowboy, bring you on a real cattle drive, and give you a taste of the West with breakfast and dinner rides. *Saddleback Ranch, 37350 CR 179, 970-879-3711; The Home Ranch, 54880 CR 129, Clark, 970-879-1780, www.homeranch.com (see Accommodations, p. 197).*

You can also take a horseback ride or pack trip in the Routt National Forest, through Pearl Lake, Steamboat Lake, or Stagecoach State Parks, or into the Mount Zirkel Wilderness and up to the Continental Divide. *Steamboat Lake Outfitters, 60880 CR 129, Clark, 800-342-1889, www.steamboatoutfitters.com.*

HOT-AIR BALLOONING

Colorful hot-air balloons dot the sky over Steamboat Springs almost every morning in summer and winter. Depending on where the winds take you, you will be able to see hundreds of miles on a clear day. Look for Hahn's Peak to the north, the Flat Tops Wilderness to the southwest, and maybe the Gore Range near Vail and Tenmile Range near Breckenridge to the south. *Pegasus Balloon Tours, 42415 Deerfoot Ln., 970-879-9191.*

HOT SPRINGS

Although railroad construction in 1908 destroyed Steamboat Springs' namesake, seven hot springs continue to flow today. Steamboat Springs Health and Recreation Association distributes "A Walking Tour of the Springs of Steamboat—7 springs, 2 miles, 2 hours," a flyer outlining the history and geology of each spring. *136 Lincoln Ave.*

Strawberry Park Hot Springs is one of the state's most celebrated hot springs. Water escapes the Earth at 147 degrees (early residents once cooked at the springs) on private land within Routt National Forest. The large, rock-rimmed upper pool is usually kept at 104 degrees. The smaller, lower pool is kept at about 102 degrees. Strawberry Park also has a full bathhouse, massage services, and cabin and tent sites. From Steamboat Springs, go north on 3rd Street, then turn right on Oak Street and left on Amethyst Drive. Follow signs to the springs, then continue 8 miles on the winding dirt road. Four-wheel drives are required in winter but advisable year-round: If you're stuck, the county charges $500 to dig you out. *44200 CR 39, 970-879-0342, www.strawberryhotsprings.com.* Arrange a shuttle to this oasis by contacting Sweet Pea Tours. *970-879-5820.*

MUSEUMS

Tread of Pioneers Museum provides insight into the lives of northwestern Colorado's early settlers and traces the rich history of skiing in Steamboat Springs. Take a self-guided historical walking tour of town by picking up the museum's brochure and hitting the street. *970-879-2214.* **Bud Werner Memorial Library** houses an extensive Western heritage and local history collection. *970-879-0240.* Both are at 800 Oak St.

56 SCENIC LOCATION ELKHEAD MOUNTAINS

To the west of the Elk River, a network of county and national forest roads winds through the Elkhead Mountains and some of the most stunning aspen forests and ranch meadows in all of Colorado. Plan to explore the Elkheads in late May, early June, or mid- to late September. Although cars can navigate many of the roads, use a four-wheel-drive vehicle to gain access to the entire area. Begin your journey from Steamboat Lake State Park (for directions, see State Parks, p. 194) and continue north on Elk River Road (County Road 129), which becomes the much rougher Forest Road 129 as it winds its way through aspen forests toward a rendezvous with the Little Snake River.

Landscapes in the Elkhead Mountains are remarkably similar wherever you go: Aspens and cottonwoods line the creeks and rivers, scrub oaks decorate hillsides and turn a brilliant red in the fall, and hilly mountains create the background. Photograph aspens as you go from Steamboat Lake north to the Little Snake River, then cottonwoods in the vast ranch meadows as you drive west along the river. At one point, you'll even briefly cross into Wyoming. Turn south onto CR 1/FR 82 to get back into the Elkheads. Follow Slater Creek to FR 110, heading south through the heart of the Elkheads, or continue east then south on FR 150. Don't worry if you get a little lost—driving west or south eventually will get you to either CO 13 or US 40, then back to Steamboat Springs or Craig.

No matter where you travel, look for compositions that contain meadows in the foreground, aspens and oaks in the midground, and mountains in the background. In addition, you can use the Little Snake River and Slater Creek as lead-in lines within pastoral ranch scenes. Views in this area can involve great distances, so use your telephoto lens to compress the distance between foreground and background.

RAFTING, KAYAKING, AND TUBING

The **Yampa River** is a prime rafting destination for Routt County to its confluence with the Green River near the Utah border. *Rafting and tubing trips and equipment: Blue Sky West, 1724 Mt. Werner Rd., 970-871-4260, www.blueskywest.com. Kayak rentals and lessons: Mountain Sports Kayak School, 800 S. Lincoln Ave., 970-879-8794, mtsportskayak.com; Backdoor Sports, 841 Yampa St., 970-879-6249, http://backdoorsports.com.*

STATE PARKS

Don't forget your fishing pole when you camp at one of these parks. **Pearl Lake State Park** has great fishing for trophy cutthroat trout and graylings. The park accesses beautiful hiking trails that become cross-country skiing and snowshoeing trails in winter. Pearl Lake campground has almost 40 campsites nestled among stands of pine; yurt rentals are also available. From Steamboat Springs, take US 40 west 1 mile to Elk River Road (County Road 129), turn right (north), and go 23 miles to Pearl Lake Road (CR 209). Turn right (east) and continue 2 miles.

Steamboat Lake State Park has nearly 200 campsites at its Dutch Hill, Bridge Island, and Sunrise Vista campgrounds, which connect to hiking and snowshoeing trails in the Mount Zirkel Wilderness. Designated Gold Medal Water in 1996, Steamboat Lake is a superb rainbow fishery and has sizable cutthroats. From Steamboat Springs, take US 40 west to Elk River Road (CR 129), then turn right (north) and continue 26 miles. *970-879-3922, www.parks.state.co.us/steamboat.*

Stagecoach State Park has more than 90 sites at its four campgrounds, but provides little shade or privacy. However, Stagecoach Reservoir boasts northern pike that can reach 40 inches. From Steamboat Springs, go 4 miles south on US 40 and turn right (west) on CO 131. Continue 5 miles to CR 14, then turn left (south) and go 7 miles to the park's entrance. *For park information: 970-736-2436.*

PLEASANT VALLEY

If mountains and forests define the scenery north of Steamboat Springs, the Yampa River and its broad valleys distinguish it to the south. The Yampa is the last major river in the West without a substantial dam, and its banks have avoided the kind of development that has compromised parts of the Eagle, Colorado, and Roaring Fork Rivers in central Colorado. Pleasant Valley is one of my favorite stretches of the river—although it was much more pleasant before the construction of Stagecoach Reservoir. Nevertheless, the brief section of canyon between Lake Catamount and Stagecoach Reservoir is sublime, as are the meadows west of the reservoir. From Steamboat Springs, take US 40 south 4 miles, then turn west (right) on CO 131 and continue 5 miles. When CO 131 angles to the west, turn east onto County Road 18, following this bumpy road through Pleasant Valley all the way to the reservoir before turning south onto CR 14.

The Yampa River meanders through grassy meadows lined with cottonwoods and aspens. In late May, the trees leaf and the grasses emerge after a long winter. Wildflowers such as wild iris and golden banner decorate the meadows in June, followed by arnica and paintbrush as summer progresses. By the end of September, the trees turn yellow and red. Stop at several places along the road to compose the river in the foreground among meadows and trees. As you approach Stagecoach Reservoir, the road rises above the Yampa, providing views of the river winding through the meadows behind you. Photograph this new perspective early or late in the day when shadows spread across the valley at right angles to the river—which runs south to north here—and the sun is high enough to also sidelight the trees.

Once you reach the dam, you get your first view of the reservoir, in what used to be one of the most beautiful valleys in the West. Drive past the reservoir and view the stretch of river from here to CO 131, or explore two other worthwhile trips—a hike along Service (pronounced "Sarvis") Creek Trail in Pleasant Valley, or a drive on CR 16, which cuts south from CR 14 at the west end of the reservoir. This rough but picturesque road eventually meets CO 134 near Gore Pass (see Scenic Location No. 59, p. 198).

WINERY TOUR

Support your local Colorado vintner by touring **Steamboat Springs Cellars,** which prides itself on its Merlot. Also try the Rabbit Ears Red, a Cabernet Franc blended with a Merlot, or Strawberry Park, a mix of fresh strawberries and white wine. *2464 Downhill Dr., 970-879-7501.*

YAMPA RIVER BOTANIC PARK

The Yampa River Botanic Park provides a peaceful way to enjoy the region's vegetation and watch birds and butterflies of the Yampa River Basin. Don't miss the rose and iris gardens, the medicinal herb garden, and the decorative ponds. To reach the park, turn left (west) on Trafalgar Lane off Lincoln Avenue (at the Sinclair gas station), then turn left on Pamela Lane. *970-879-4300, www.steamboat-springs.net.*

Restaurants

Dining establishments here appeal to almost any palate. Ride the Steamboat gondola up to **Hazie's** ($$$), which features a fine Sunday brunch and signature dishes such as wild mushroom lasagna. *970-871-5150.* You can't beat the cuts and prime rib at the **Old West Steak House** ($$$). *1104 Lincoln Ave., 970-879-1441.*

Off the Beaten Path Bookstore & Coffeehouse, Steamboat Springs

Off the Beaten Path Bookstore & Coffeehouse ($$) brews the perfect mountain blend: a deli, bakery, coffeehouse, and bookstore all in one. *56 7th St., 970-879-6830.* For Italian food, two restaurants top my list: **Giovanni's** ($-$$), *127 11th St., 970-879-4141,* and **Riggio's** ($$), *1106 Lincoln Ave., 970-879-9010.* Riggio's has a larger menu. For a family-friendly BBQ spot, **Steamboat Smokehouse** ($$) is definitely the best choice. *912 Lincoln Ave., 970-879-7427, 877-879-7427, www.steamboatsmokehouse.com.*

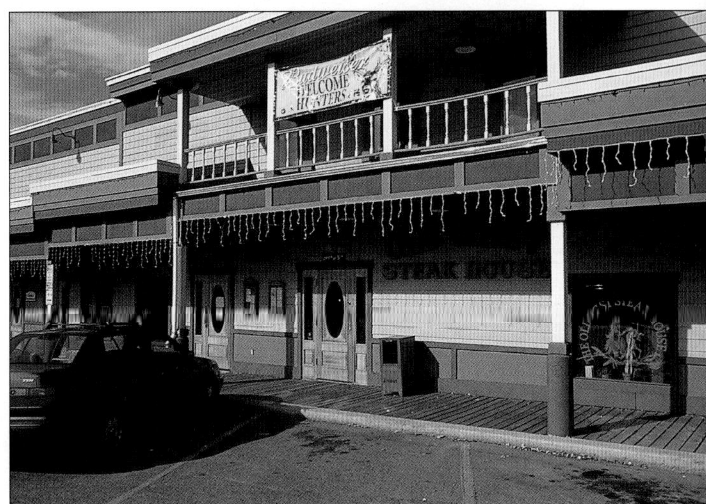

Old West Steak House, Steamboat Springs

58 SCENIC LOCATION YAMPA RIVER: CO 131

The headwaters of the Yampa River originate in the Flat Tops Wilderness to the west of CO 131 and in the Service Creek Wilderness to the east. The river doesn't look like much until various tributaries meet near the town of Yampa on CO 131, where the Yampa becomes a full-fledged river all the way to its confluence with the Green River in Dinosaur National Monument (see Scenic Location No. 66, p. 213). Going from Stagecoach Reservoir south to Yampa, large ranches and hay meadows lend a pastoral air to the river. The landscapes remain lovely along the entire length of CO 131, from Steamboat Springs south to Wolcott on I-70, just west of Edwards.

Hay meadows are best photographed with a wide-angle lens. Park your car safely off the highway, run down to the obligatory barbed-wire fence, and compose a scene of infinite grasses. Add just a little sky for perspective, but if interesting clouds are present, let sky occupy up to one-third of the scene (see pp. 61, 66–67, *Photographing the Landscape*).

My favorite meadows along CO 131 are found just south of Steamboat Springs before you arrive at Lake Catamount, between Phippsburg and Yampa, and from Yampa to Toponas. Along these stretches, fingerlike rock formations make great background for the meadows. You won't believe how thickly the dandelions grow in early June! Several county roads exit west off the highway—CR 25, CR 15, and CR 7 are my favorites—on their way to the edges of the Flat Tops Wilderness, each providing picturesque views of the ranch country above the Yampa Valley and access to the wilderness area's eastern trailheads. Continue exploring CO 131 all the way to I-70. It crosses a number of passes and divides as it travels through glorious groves of aspen and wildflower fields.

Johnny B. Goods Diner ($) is a classic 50's-style diner serving breakfast, lunch, and dinner—from classic comfort foods and blue plate specials to the fantastic milkshakes, Johnny B Goods has just the thing for everyone. *738 Lincoln Ave., 970-870-8400.* **The Boathouse Pub** ($$) features pub house favorites with a great view of the river. *609 Yampa St., 970-879-4797.* Another local favorite is the **Old Town Pub & Restaurant** ($$). Old Town serves lunch and dinner, and guests can choose from the Western-style bar or the dining room. Old Town also features live music in the evenings. *600 Lincoln Ave., 970-879-2101, www.oldtownpub.jimdo.com.*

Hang out at **Harwig's Grill** ($-$$), a laid-back spot with an eclectic menu. *911 Lincoln Ave., 970-879-1980.* **Mahogany Ridge** ($-$$), formerly Steamboat Brewery, boasts a variety of in-house microbrews and great pub food. *435 Lincoln Ave., 970-879-3773.* Try **Winona's** ($) for a large breakfast menu and a great selection of "wicked wraps" for lunch. *617 Lincoln Ave., 970-879-2483.* Try the eclectic eggs Benedict menu at **The Creekside Cafe & Grille** ($-$$). *131 11th St., 970-879-4925.*

Accommodations

Although the highly rated **Inn at Steamboat** ($-$$) is shadowed by condominiums, it is a very economical and friendly B&B. *3070 Columbine Dr., 970-879-2600, www.innatsteamboat.com.* **Mariposa Lodge Bed & Breakfast** ($$), on the banks of Soda Creek, has a Southwestern feel. *855 N. Grand St., 970-879-1467.*

The Home Ranch ($$$$) sits on 1,500 acres bordering the Routt National Forest. Although the first-rate horsemanship program—with trail rides, clinics, lessons, and cattle-working—is the ranch's focus, fly fishing, hiking, cross-country skiing, and snowshoeing are also available. From Steamboat Springs, take US 40 west 1 mile to Elk River Road (CR 129) and go 18 miles north to Clark. The ranch entrance is 0.25 mile past the general store on the right. *970-879-1780, www.homeranch.com.*

Winona's restaurant, Steamboat Springs

Mariposa Lodge Bed & Breakfast

GORE PASS

A short, lovely highway, CO 134, connects US 40 and CO 131. The apex of the drive is Gore Pass, which crosses the north end of the Gore Range at 9,527 feet. Although this doesn't sound like the high country, the views of aspens and mountain meadows are superb. Drive south on CO 131 from Steamboat Springs past Oak Creek, Phippsburg, and Yampa. Nine miles south of Yampa, turn east on CO 134 just past Toponas. From Kremmling to the east, take US 40 north 6 miles to CO 134.

Aspens line the highway for most of the drive, so be ready to pull over and compose a scene. My favorite stretch is just to the west of Gore Pass, where you can photograph the highway winding into the distance through the aspen groves. Early June brings fresh green color, while late September provides the outrageous yellows of autumn.

Special Events

After competing in the National Western Stock Show in Denver in late January, professional cowboys head up to Steamboat Springs, put on skis, and hold onto their Stetson hats in the highly entertaining **Cowboy Downhill.**

One of the most anticipated and delightful events in Colorado, Steamboat's **Winter Carnival** in February features ice-sculpture competitions, fireworks, and the town's pride, ski jumping. Don't miss the Street Events, during which Steamboat's main thoroughfare, Lincoln Avenue, is coated with snow for horsedrawn races, kids' races, and a ski parade. From late June through August, Steamboat Springs hosts the **Pro Rodeo Series** at the Howelsen Hill Rodeo Grounds. Professional wranglers compete every weekend in riding, roping, wrestling, and other events. Young rodeo fans can even participate in a calf scramble for prizes.

One of the region's most inspiring summer events is **Hot Air Balloon Rodeo,** held in mid-July, when the skies above Steamboat become crowded with colorful hot-air balloons. A major artisan display and plenty of good food and entertainment are also on hand. *For event information: 970-879-0880, www.steamboat-chamber.com.*

For More Information

Steamboat Springs Visitor Center, *1255 S. Lincoln Ave., 970-879-0880, www.steamboat-chamber.com.*

Craig/Meeker

Colorado Atlas & Gazetteer pp. 24–26, 34–35

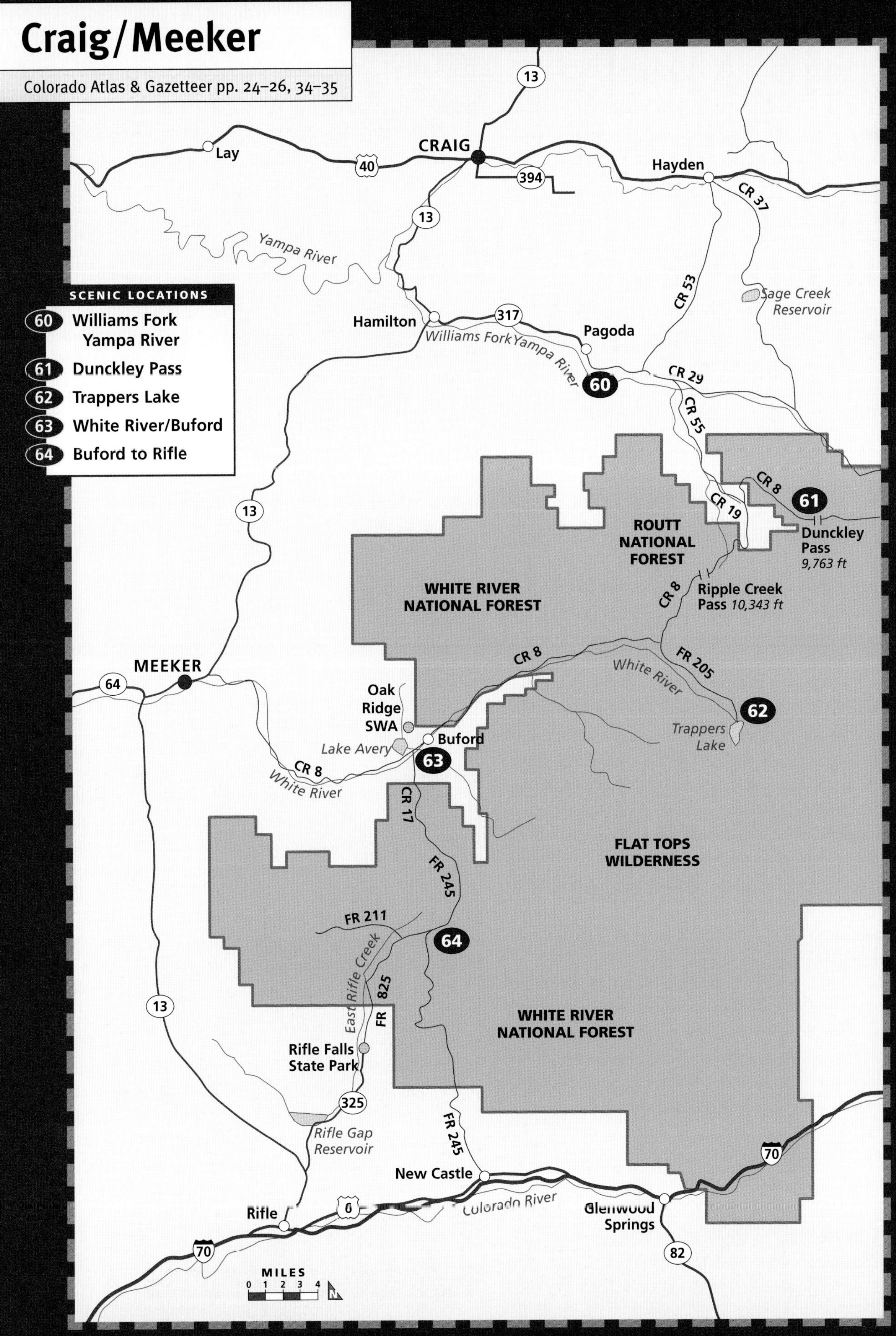
SCENIC LOCATIONS
60 Williams Fork Yampa River
61 Dunckley Pass
62 Trappers Lake
63 White River/Buford
64 Buford to Rifle
CRAIG
Lay
Hayden
Yampa River
Sage Creek Reservoir
Hamilton
Pagoda
Williams Fork
Yampa River
CR 37
CR 53
CR 29
CR 55
CR 8
CR 19
ROUTT NATIONAL FOREST
Dunckley Pass 9,763 ft
Ripple Creek Pass 10,343 ft
WHITE RIVER NATIONAL FOREST
MEEKER
FR 205
White River
Oak Ridge SWA
Buford
Lake Avery
Trappers Lake
CR 17
FLAT TOPS WILDERNESS
FR 245
FR 211
East Rifle Creek
FR 825
WHITE RIVER NATIONAL FOREST
Rifle Falls State Park
Rifle Gap Reservoir
New Castle
Colorado River
Glenwood Springs
Rifle
MILES
0 1 2 3 4

Craig, Meeker, and Dinosaur National Monument

(see Craig/Meeker map on p. 199; Dinosaur map on p. 212)

Whether you approach Dinosaur National Monument from the north through Craig, or from the south through Meeker, your journey will traverse a West little changed since the 1800s. Still sparsely populated, northwestern Colorado is foremost horse, sheep, and cattle country, now joined with coal mining and oil and gas productions. Ranches owned for generations by the same families dot the landscape, and wranglers moving cattle and sheep often block the roads. Moffat and Rio Blanco Counties—home to Craig and Meeker, respectively, and rich with public lands—are magnets for hunting and fishing enthusiasts, while White River National Forest and Flat Tops Wilderness draw campers as well. The land ethic held by the people of northwestern Colorado is straightforward: to protect wide-open spaces and ranching as a way of life. This is the place to go to find old ways, solitude, and prehistoric treasures.

To reach Craig from Denver, go west on I-70 to Silverthorne. Take CO 9 north to Kremmling, then continue north on US 40 to Steamboat Springs. Craig is 42 miles west of Steamboat on US 40. To reach Meeker, take the Rifle exit (90) off I-70. Go north on CO 13 for 42 miles to Meeker. To reach the southern entrance of Dinosaur National Monument from Meeker, take CO 64 northwest 79 miles to the tiny town of Dinosaur. Turn right (east) on US 40 and continue 3 miles to the monument turnoff.

60 SCENIC LOCATION — WILLIAMS FORK YAMPA RIVER

Flat Tops Wilderness sits at the center of a large forested expanse in northwest Colorado. Both Routt and White River National Forests cover this region, with the White River as its primary drainage. There are roads everywhere, so don't be afraid to explore. The Williams Fork, especially its East Fork, drains into the Yampa River south of Craig and is one of the most wet and fertile places in the state. Cottonwood trees line the river, and aspens cover the hillsides that contain the drainage. From the middle of May into early June, the lime greens of newly leafed trees glow; the yellows of autumn peak during the third and fourth weeks of September.

From Meeker, drive north on CO 13 to CO 317 and turn right (east). From here the road parallels the Williams Fork for about 12 miles. At this point, you can either turn south onto County Road 67 to follow the South Fork of the Williams Fork, which dead-ends, or continue east on CR 29 for 6 miles to follow the East Fork. Go east on CR 29, then south onto CR 55 and CR 19, still along the East Fork (10 miles later, this road meets CR 8). Continue south to cross 10,343-foot Ripple Creek Pass before dropping into the White River drainage. This particular route is either paved or highly improved dirt, so don't be afraid to take the car.

Cottonwood trees line most places along the river. When you finally depart the river on the way up to Ripple Creek Pass, aspens begin to fill the landscape at higher elevations. Like the White River to the south, the Williams Fork runs east to west. The rising sun backlights the trees as you drive east, while the setting sun backlights the trees as you head west (see pp. 100–103, *Photographing the Landscape*). Look for places along the road where the river is visible as a lead-in line meandering through the trees.

My favorite vantages are from the road where it rises above the river, allowing you to better compose its course winding through forest and meadows. Two of my best views are from the descent of Ripple Creek Pass. At the westernmost switchback you can see several miles down the White River. One switchback before you reach CR 8 meets with Forest Road 205—the way to Trappers Lake (see Scenic Location No. 62, p. 205). Look east from any point where you can see FR 205 winding through the aspens. The road disappears and reappears in and out of the trees and makes a great compositional lead-in line.

History

In the early 19th century, East Coast demand for beaver hats, muffs, and coats drew trappers and mountain men to the rivers and canyons of northwestern Colorado. Rendezvous were held along the Green River at Brown's Park, just north of what is now Dinosaur National Monument. Word of mouth and the accounts of surveyors such as John Wesley Powell drew homesteaders to the area, who soon established large sheep and cattle ranches. Remote canyons served as hideouts for Butch Cassidy and the Sundance Kid, among other outlaws. The town of Craig, the Moffat County seat, is the ranching center of the region and partakes of this hardscrabble frontier history.

Soon after the turn of the last century, paleontological research was undertaken here. Steel magnate and philanthropist Andrew Carnegie had hired researcher Earl Douglass to dig in the area for dinosaur bones and fossils for Pittsburgh's Carnegie Museum. Douglass hoped to match specimens found in the Morrison formation near Cañon City. He was not disappointed: On August 17, 1909, he discovered eight tailbones of a brontosaurus in a sandstone hogback. During the next 15 years, 350 tons of bone and fossils from 10 dinosaur species were excavated from the site. Worried about losing this precious evidence to homesteading and mining, Carnegie Museum officials lobbied for federal protection of the quarry. In 1915, President Woodrow

DUNCKLEY PASS

Where County Road 19 meets CR 8 along the East Fork of the Williams Fork (see Scenic Location No. 60, p. 200), head north on CR 8 instead of south. CR 8 soon becomes Forest Road 16 and crosses Dunckley Pass, one of several divides between the White and Yampa Rivers in this region. The aspens along this stretch of road are marvelous. FR 16 takes you toward the towns of Yampa and Phippsburg along the Yampa River. In your passenger car, you can negotiate this improved dirt road with ease.

As you ascend the first switchback on FR 16 out of the Williams Fork drainage, look down to the river. Here you gain an incredible view of the cottonwoods that line the river, as well as the aspen trees that cover Egry Mesa to the south. You can make compositions that include river and trees, mesa and sky. Sidelighting at sunset will cause the translucent leaves of spring and fall to glow and the river to shine like silver.

Atop Dunckley Pass you can see Flat Tops Wilderness to the south. From the pass to the wilderness you'll find vast aspen forests, so compose a scene with your telephoto lens to include trees and ridges in the foreground and Flat Tops behind. The east side of the pass reveals beautiful aspens on ridges to the south before the road descends into ranch meadows on its way to the Yampa. Each individual aspen grove, sprinkling the hillsides as far as the eye can see, is a separate and distinct genetic family connected by a common root system. As a result, the groves leaf in spring and turn yellow in fall at varying times, manifesting variegated colors from green to yellow to red.

Wilson declared the 80-acre site a national monument. In 1938, the designation was expanded to include 325 square miles.

Long before the monument gained official protection, however, the nearby town of Meeker came into being, named for the late Nathan C. Meeker, a journalist who in 1869 had founded a cooperative agricultural settlement, the Union Colony, now Greeley (see History, Fort Collins and Greeley, p. 149). Appointed in 1878 as the new Indian agent of the White River Indian Agency near the present-day town, Meeker believed it his duty to Christianize the White River Ute tribe and make them farmers. He sought to build another utopian agricultural community, this time peopled by Indians. Among other acts, Meeker plowed through the Utes' prized horse pastures and racing grounds in an effort to turn their attention to farming.

By September 1879, the long-suffering Utes had had enough: Meeker and 10 agency civilians were killed, five women and children were taken captive, and the agency was torched. Chief Ouray soon secured the release of the women and children, but by then the press had inflamed the incident. The White River Massacre, more commonly known as the Meeker Massacre, was cited as justification for the displacement after 1880 of the Utes onto reservations in barren eastern Utah and the Four Corners region.

Without the threat of Indian raids, mining and homesteading began to thrive on Colorado's Western Slope. In 1883, a fort set up by the U.S. Army to keep peace after the massacre was abandoned, its buildings sold to nearby homesteaders. The town of Meeker was established on the site.

Main Attractions

DINOSAUR NATIONAL MONUMENT

The monument's 325 square miles overlap the border between northwestern Colorado and northeastern Utah, and extend in three directions from the confluence of the Yampa and Green Rivers. These deeply layered and colorful canyons, which make for remarkable river running and birding, have also given insight into geologic time and phenomena. The monument's quarry has produced tons of fossils and bones and given us invaluable information on prehistory, testimony to the life cycle of the "terrible reptiles" that lived and died near ancient rivers. Eventually their bones were carried downstream by currents and deposited, often in piles, then buried by river sand. Over time they became fossilized. Layers of volcanic ash and mud further embedded the fossils and eventually formed rock. Giant upheavals followed by erosion then exposed the fossils, to the delight of paleontologists and other dinosaur fans.

See the bones that made this site famous at the **Dinosaur Quarry.** A large structure shelters the quarry, which is actually an exposed hillside with more than 2,000 fossil bones protruding from the rock surface. It is a bit unnerving to encounter a sharp-faced Camarasaurus skull complete with teeth jutting from the rock. Informative displays take you back in time some 150 million years, and park rangers are on hand to answer questions. From the town of Dinosaur, take US 40 west 20 miles to Jensen, Utah. Turn right (north) on UT 149 and continue 7 miles to the visitor center. Please note that the Quarry Visitors Center is temporarily closed for renovations. All exhibits are currently housed in the Temporary Visitor Center nearby. It is expected that the official visitors center will reopen as early as summer 2011.

At the remote, dramatic northern entrance from CO 318 into the monument, the Green River plunges through the Gates of Lodore—uplifted rock formations—and into 17-mile Lodore Canyon (see Scenic Location No. 67, p. 214). Refer to Scenic Location No. 65, p. 210, for another Colorado-side route into the monument. If you don't relish primitive camping at the monument, the closest lodging is in the Colorado towns of Dinosaur and Rangely, and in Vernal, Utah. *Colorado Welcome Center at Dinosaur, 970-374-2205; monument headquarters, 4545 E. US 40 at Harper's Corner Rd., 970-374-3000, www.nps.gov/dino.*

Camping: Three primitive campgrounds lie within the Colorado portion of Dinosaur National Monument—**Deerlodge Park, Gates of Lodore,** and **Echo Park** (at the confluence of the Green and Yampa Rivers). Only the last two provide drinking water. Developed campgrounds include **Split Mountain** and **Green River,** both on the Utah side. *970-374-3000.*

Fishing: Perhaps the best fishing spot in the monument is on the **Green River** at Jones Hole in Whirlpool Canyon. Here you can catch fairly sizable brookies, rainbows, and cutthroats. Legend has it that Jones Hole was named after Charley Jones, a ranch hand who mistakenly thought he had killed a man, then fled into the canyon. Pick up a map at the ranger station and inquire about backcountry permits.

Rafting: Although dinosaur bones may draw you here, the magnificent canyons and rivers are also exceptional. Unquestionably, the best way to get around is by raft. The **Yampa River** enters the monument from the east, the **Green River** from the north, converging at Steamboat Rock in Echo Park (see Scenic Location No. 66, p. 213). Although their currents are slow as they cross into the monument, both quickly become plunging and raging rivers. Park rules govern river access, and permits are required. *Adrift Adventures, 800-824-0150, www.adrift.com; Don Hatch River Expeditions, 800-342-8243, www.donhatchrivertrips.com. For more information: Dinosaur National Monument river office, 970-374-2468.*

Scenic Drives: The most popular route through the monument is 31-mile **Harper's Corner Scenic Drive** on the Colorado side, which leads to Canyon Overlook, Iron Park Overlook, and Iron Springs Bench Overlook, before ending at Echo Park Overlook where the Green River meets the Yampa River. The views from the 1-mile Harper's Corner Nature Trail, accessed from the overlook, are unbeatable.

Six-mile **Echo Park Road** also has stunning canyon views as well as access to petroglyph sites and Whispering Cave. From the monument headquarters, take Harper's Corner Scenic Drive 28 miles and look for Echo Park Road on the right. The petroglyphs are 4 miles down the road (be sure to look up), the turnoff to Whispering Cave is an additional mile, and the drive ends 0.75 mile from the confluence of the Green and Yampa Rivers. Although a car can navigate Echo Park Road under dry conditions, rain makes it muddy and impassable.

COLORADO CAMEO

John Wesley Powell

Geologist and ethnologist Major John Wesley Powell (1834–1902) is perhaps best remembered today as an adventurer and early conservationist in the vanguard of water issues in the West. A Union volunteer, Powell lost his right forearm at the Battle of Shiloh but returned to serve in other battles. After the war, he studied geology at Illinois Wesleyan College and in summer visited the Rocky Mountains, planning to return to see the unexplored Grand Canyon. In 1869, Powell led a three-month expedition down the Colorado River, starting at the Green River (he wrote with his usual enthusiasm about the Gates of Lodore) and traveling more than 1,000 miles to the southern end of the Grand Canyon.

The rocky trip is now the stuff of legend. Crew members navigated ferocious rapids; some bailed out and were murdered by local tribal warriors. Despite such losses and several hair-raising escapes, Powell named various land features and kept a journal that included maps and notes on geology, plants, wildlife, and native peoples. Many of Powell's feature names have stuck, such as the rapids called Hell's Half Mile and Disaster Falls, where one of Powell's boats was destroyed. Powell's expedition journal, *Report on the Exploration of the Colorado River of the West and Its Tributaries,* appeared in 1875 and was widely published.

Major Powell's independent journey was the last great exploration within the continental United States. An authority on the nature and the native cultures of the West, Powell became director of the nascent U.S. Geological Survey and the Bureau of American Ethnology. Powell believed that the great Western rivers could make the deserts bloom and support an agrarian economy if only their waters could be diverted by dams and impoundments (reservoirs) and used responsibly.

He opposed water monopolies, supporting divided ownership of water rights among small, independent farmers and ranchers. As time passed, however, Powell became suspicious of the interests that grew around Western water policy before the establishment of the U.S. Bureau of Reclamation. His doubts were well founded. Only the fierce self-interest of Western land speculators, whose land grabs were hindered by Powell's deliberative survey work, would force him from public life in the end.

The historic completion of Boulder (now Hoover) Dam on the Colorado River on the Arizona/Nevada border in 1935 was just the start of the thirsty development of the West. In 1950, the Bureau of Reclamation proposed 10 new dams, two of which happened to be at Split Mountain and Echo Park within Dinosaur National Monument. If constructed, these dams would have inundated the canyons. Late Sierra Club Director David Brower led the successful fight to save the monument's canyons. As Powell wrote, "The river had the right of way." (Other gorges, like Glen Canyon—now Lake Powell—were not so lucky.) When you visit the monument, remember river advocates like Brower and Powell.

62 SCENIC LOCATION TRAPPERS LAKE

Trappers Lake ranks with Piney and Maroon Lakes (see Scenic Location Nos. 28, p. 119, and 83, p. 250) as one of the most picturesque and wild lakes in Colorado accessible by car. Trappers Lake Road is actually a cherry stem of private land within the Flat Tops Wilderness that allows access to the lake. While campgrounds and a lodge lie near the lake, once you cast your fly, you are in wilderness surrounded by wilderness.

Forest Road 205 meets County Road 8 at the bottom of Ripple Creek Pass (see Scenic Location No. 60, p. 200) a little way above the White River. From here it's about 8 miles southeast to Trappers Lake, arguably the scenic center of northwest Colorado and the largest natural lake in the area.

FR 205 parallels the White River all the way to the lake, at an elevation high enough to provide views down into the drainage. The valley is a private ranch, bucolic enough to make for great photographs, especially with a telephoto lens to shorten distance. However, the lake is the treasure at the end of the road. Bear right and cross the river as you approach the private lodge, then follow the road above the west side of the lake as far as it goes. Park your car in the lot and hike 0.25 mile down to the edge of the lake.

From the conspicuous finger-shaped inlet, set up your camera to make a reflection photograph of the sheer wall of the Flat Tops that forms the southwestern boundary of the lake. The inlet prevents lake waves from erasing the reflection. Photograph with a wide-angle lens at sunrise or sunset. Either will light up a significant portion of the cliffs that completely surround the lake. Just point your camera in the appropriate direction. Trails ascend the Flat Tops from both the west and east sides of the lake. A slight gain in elevation will provide an entirely different perspective as you look down upon Trappers Lake nestled in this valley surrounded by cliffs of the Flat Tops Wilderness.

Activities

CAMPING

Meadow Lake affords seclusion along with great fishing. From Meeker, take CO 13 east 1 mile to County Road 8. Turn right (east) and go 20 miles to Buford. Turn right (south) onto Buford–New Castle Road (CR 17 and Forest Road 245). Go 13 miles to FR 601 and turn left (east). Go 3 miles, turn right (south) onto FR 823, and continue another 1.5 miles to the campground. *970-625-2371.*

East Marvine is another secluded site alongside East Marvine Creek. From Meeker, take CO 13 east 1 mile to CR 8, turn right (east) and go about 28 miles to CR 12. Turn right (east) and continue 7 miles to the campground. Situated in the pines, **South Fork** provides trail access to Spring Cave, the second largest cave in Colorado. From Meeker, take CO 13 east 1 mile to CR 8. Turn right, go 17.5 miles to CR 10, turn right (east) again, and go 12 miles. For glorious autumn aspens and great fishing access to the White River, head to **Himes Peak** in the Flat Tops Wilderness. Take CR 8 for 41 miles to FR 205, turn right (southeast), and continue 5 miles. *970-878-4039.*

FISHING

Trappers Lake (see Scenic Location No. 62, p. 205) in the Flat Tops Wilderness provides beautiful scenery and outstanding fishing for Colorado cutthroat trout. From Meeker, take CO 13 east for 1 mile to CR 8, turn right (southeast), and continue 41 miles to FR 205. Turn right (southeast) and continue 11 miles to the lake. Twenty miles southeast of Meeker also on CR 8, **Avery Lake** has good trout fishing. **Meadow Lake** is another favorite among local anglers (see Camping, above).

The **North Fork of the White River** is unspoiled and uncrowded, with trout fishing from its headwaters at Trappers Lake down to Meeker. Access is generally good, particularly at Nelson Prather and Sleepy Cat Ponds east of town on CR 8. You can even fish in Meeker's City Park, accessed from Circle Park Bridge at 4th and Water Streets. Past Meeker, whitefish replace trout and the fishing is poor as the White flows west into Utah. Himes Peak campground also has good access to the White River (see Camping, above). *Information and supplies: Wyatt's Sport Center, 223 8th St., Meeker, 970-878-4428.*

FOUR-WHEEL-DRIVE TRIPS

The 12-mile **Long Park Road** combines wonderful views of the Flat Tops Wilderness and North Fork Valley from bumpy Dead Horse Road with a gentle drive beside the White River on CO 8. Dead Horse Road is 35 miles southeast of Meeker, to the left of CR 8. The 25-mile (one way) **Crouse Canyon Road** is a very rough road that crosses the Green River over a swaying bridge and accesses Brown's Park National Wildlife Refuge. The road continues to either the Dinosaur Quarry in Dinosaur National Monument or to Vernal, Utah. From Craig, go west on US 40 to Maybell, and go northwest 62 miles on CO 318 to the turnoff for the wildlife refuge. Turn left and cross the bridge.

HIKING

Hunters descend on this region each fall—also a beautiful time of year for visitors without hunting licenses. When hiking during hunting season, always wear orange or other bright colors, and make your presence known!

Sixteen-mile (one way) **Trappers Lake Trail** MODERATE begins at the Trappers Outlet trailhead, just south of Trappers Lake (see Fishing, at left) and leads to the Flat Tops Plateau. You'll intersect many other trails along the way, so it is a good idea to get a map before your hike. Eleven-and-a-half-mile (one way) **Marvine Trail** MODERATE also climbs to the plateau, with opportunities to fish along the way. From the East Marvine campground (see Camping, at left), continue 1 mile on CR 12 to the trailhead at Marvine campground.

Half-mile (one way) **Spring Cave Trail** EASY leads to the second largest cave in Colorado. Resist the urge to explore deep within the cave! It is dark, dangerous, and extremely easy to get lost. The trailhead is at South Fork campground (see Camping, at left).

The rugged, 8-mile (one way) hike up **Cross Mountain** DIFFICULT climbs to views of Dinosaur National Monument and Cross Canyon, home to Rocky Mountain bighorn sheep, raptors, and mountain lions. Keep your eyes open for petroglyphs and pictographs on the canyon walls. From Craig, head west on CO 40 to Maybell, and continue 16 miles to Deerlodge Park Road, which you will follow along the west side of Cross Mountain to the parking area at the mouth of Cross Canyon.

The 14-mile (one way) hike along **Limestone Ridge** MODERATE winds through the piñon and juniper forests of Colorado's plateau country, with views of colorful geological phenomena in Irish Canyon, Vermillion Creek Basin, and Brown's Park. On a clear day, you can see Wyoming's Wind River Range to the north. Large herds of elk roam the area, and you may see antelope, deer, or even a mountain lion. This is a great route for a short overnight trip. From Craig, take US 40 west 31 miles to Maybell, then head northwest on CO 318 for 41.5 miles to CR 10. Go north 4 miles on CR 10, then turn left (west) on a dirt road and travel 1.5 miles. Park off the main gravel road.

HORSEBACK RIDING

White River National Forest has miles of horseback riding trails that promise great scenery, solitude, and access to fishing holes. The folks at **Sombrero White River Horse Camp** will tailor your horseback trip to fit your skills and interests. You can choose from one- to two-hour guided rides, wilderness trips, and even longhorn roundups. *12900 CR 8, Meeker, 970-878-4382, www.sombrero.com.*

HUNTING

Northwest Colorado is a mecca for hunters each autumn. With 30,000 head of elk, White River National Forest boasts Colorado's second largest elk herd, as well as more than 60,000 deer. The

63 SCENIC LOCATION WHITE RIVER/ BUFORD

The river from Trappers Lake west to the tiny resort town of Buford is technically the North Fork of the White River. This 25-mile stretch of Forest Road 205 and County Road 8 parallels the river and provides spectacular views of the watercourse and the ecosystems through which it runs. Cottonwoods line the river and aspens decorate the hillsides north and south of the drainage. The South Fork meets the North Fork just west of Buford, and the views from here to Meeker are worth the additional drive. By doing so you can complete a circuitous loop of the entire region, with the exception of the Buford-to-Rifle route described in Scenic Location No. 64, p. 208. You can take your car on all of these roads.

Keep your eye out for places where the river almost meets the road in order to compose scenes looking up and down the river. Similarly, watch for pullouts where the road is higher than the river, especially on the upper stretches, from which you can photograph river disappearing into forest. Turn south onto CR 12 to capture a river image from the bridge. CR 12 is also a bypass that runs on the river's south side closer to the riverbank than CR 8. As is the case with the other scenic locations in this area, late May and late September will provide spring and fall color for your photographic delight.

BUFORD TO RIFLE

This 45-mile route from the White River drainage south to the Colorado River drainage is one of my favorite national forest drives in Colorado. It enters the heart of White River National Forest and provides opportunities for aspen tree photography and views of the Flat Tops Wilderness to the east. On the descent into Rifle, you'll be taking the northern route to stunning Rifle Falls State Park (see Scenic Location No. 34, p. 135). Although you'll need a four-wheel-drive vehicle for the high country sections that get a little narrow and bumpy, you won't actually need to engage the four-wheel drive.

From Buford, exit County Road 8 south onto CR 17, which soon becomes Forest Road 245. About 6 miles past the Meadow Creek Lake turnoff, keep an eye out for a series of forks in the road. Make a right onto FR 211, then the next left onto FR 825. The route is well marked, so just watch for the signs to Rifle. FR 825 becomes CO 325, which passes through scenic Rifle Canyon before merging with CO 13, 3 miles north of Rifle. If you stay on FR 245, you'll see some great scenery, but you'll end up in New Castle instead of Rifle.

During the first 4 miles of the ascent out of Buford, you will gain great views to the west of the White River Valley. You'll want to stop at some of these vantages and use your telephoto lens to record the river below winding through ranch meadows. The back- and sidelighting at sunset is marvelous. You will continue to ascend through aspens and conifers, but there won't be any mountains in the background. Therefore, use your skills to compose intimate landscapes (see pp. 54–57, *Photographing the Landscape*) of trees, meadows, and the single pond that you will see on the east side of the road across from the cabin. It provides a great reflection of aspens, especially at sunset.

As you gain the highest elevation along the road, you will pass through spectacular meadows lined with aspens. Notice those snapped off in the middle by high winds, similar to the October 25, 1997, blowdown along Seedhouse Road (see Scenic Location No. 55, p. 191). It's hard to believe such a flexible trunk could break in half without the entire tree being uprooted first. If you have time, I recommend car-camping in this area overnight. Sunset and sunrise color the aspens with rich red light, and you never know what kind of clouds might turn pink and give you one more ingredient for a great photograph. Make the descent through Rifle Canyon at any time when direct light does not enter it, such as early or late in the day, or in the afternoon when clouds block the sun. It's a very narrow canyon, and the contrast of highlight and shadow at other times is too intense for the film to manage.

state also allows hunting of antelope, black bear, and mountain lion. *Information and supplies: Wyatt's Sport Center, 223 8th St., Meeker, 970-878-4428. Guided hunting trips: All-Seasons Ranch, 970-824-4178. For more information: Meeker Chamber of Commerce, 970-878-5510, www.meekerchamber.com.*

MUSEUMS

Craig's **Museum of Northwest Colorado** has an extensive collection of cowboy memorabilia, including guns, spurs, saddles, and chaps. Turn-of-the-century household items, farm implements, coal-mining artifacts, and historic photographs of local cowboys are also on display. Check out the largest known mountain lion killed in the area and the huge canvas depicting the town of Craig in 1895. *590 Yampa, Craig, 970-824-6360, www.museumnwco.org.*

Meeker's **White River Museum** is housed in the original 1880 building constructed as quarters for U.S. Army officers following the Ute conflicts. Historic photographs of early pioneers and cowboys include Nathan C. Meeker and his family. Other 19th-century relics include Chief Colorow's peace pipe and stagecoach driver Rory White's bear-hide coat. *565 Park St., Meeker, 970-878-9982.*

SCENIC DRIVES

Flat Tops Trail Scenic and Historic Byway is a well-maintained, 82-mile paved/gravel road that connects Meeker with Yampa by way of the upper White River Valley, Ripple Creek Pass, and Dunckley Pass (see Scenic Location No. 61, p. 203) on the wild White River Plateau. You may even see wranglers moving cattle and sheep to and from summer pasture along the route, which is glorious in the fall.

Trappers Lake (see Scenic Location No. 62, p. 205) in the Flat Tops Wilderness can also be reached from Flat Tops Trail. Thanks to the efforts of Arthur Carhart to ban development of any kind around the lake in 1919, Trappers Lake is known as the "Cradle of Wilderness." Efforts to protect areas such as Trappers Lake were the first stirrings of the wilderness movement in this country that culminated in the passage of the Wilderness Act of 1964. From Meeker, head 1 mile east on CO 13, then turn east on County Road 8 (Flat Tops Trail). The gravel portions of this road are closed to automobiles in winter, when they become popular snowmobile trails.

Historic **Cañon Pintado** is an excellent place to view native petroglyphs and pictographs on the canyon's sheer walls. Spanish clerical explorers Escalante and Dominguez traveled through the canyon and, no doubt, wondered at this prehistoric artwork. From the town of Dinosaur, go southeast on CO 64 for 18 miles to Rangely, then south on CO 139 into the canyon.

WINTER SPORTS

Hiking trails and four-wheel-drive roads are favorite spots to cross-country ski and snowshoe in the wintertime. Some of the most popular routes include the **Marvine Trail** and **Trappers Lake Trail** (see Hiking, and Fishing, p. 206). The gravel portions of **Flat Tops Trail** (County Road 8) are popular with snowmobilers (see Scenic Drives, at left).

The White River Snowmobile Club maintains 178 miles of snowmobile trails in eastern Rio Blanco County, everything from groomed trails to challenging natural routes. Contact the Meeker Chamber of Commerce for trail maps. *970-878-5510, www.meekerchamber.com/snowmobile.htm.*

Restaurants

You can't beat the aroma of homemade pastries and gourmet coffees at **Serendipity Coffee Shop** ($). *576 Yampa Ave., Craig, 970-824-5846.* If you're looking for great Mexican in Meeker, you'll definitely want to check out **Los Koras** ($-$$). 173 1st St., 970-878-5995. **The Bistro on Park Avenue** ($$) features a great blend of European and American cuisines. Open for dinner Tuesday through Sunday. *364 7th St., Meeker, 970-878-0900, www.meekerbistro.com.*

Meeker Hotel

Accommodations

During hunting season, it can prove difficult to find a place to stay in northwestern Colorado, so make reservations well in advance for an autumn visit. One personal favorite is the historic **Meeker Hotel** ($$-$$$), built in 1896 and now listed on the National Register of Historic Places. Check out the lobby, adorned with mounted game trophies and a painting of the Meeker Massacre. *560 Main St., Meeker, 970-878-5255.* The **Brick House** ($), a delightful 1904 structure in downtown Meeker, was built by the same craftsmen responsible for Redstone Castle in Redstone and the Brown Palace Hotel in Denver. *687 Garfield, 970-878-5055.*

White River Inn ($$) lies on 1.8 quiet acres. *219 E. Market St., Meeker, 970-878-5031.* Meeker's newest hotel, **Blue Spruce Inn** ($$), was completed in January 2009. Located in downtown Meeker, the inn features luxury accommodations and breathtaking views of the surrounding area. *488 Market St., 970-878-0777, www.bluesprucemeeker.com.*

Ute Lodge ($-$$), adjacent to Flat Tops Wilderness, offers comfortable cabins and hosts guided fishing trips, wilderness excursions, horse-pack trips, and hunting

DINOSAUR NATIONAL MONUMENT: YAMPA RIVER

The next four scenic locations are found in or near one of the most amazing places on Planet Earth, Dinosaur National Monument. On the Colorado side, this area is known not so much for its paleontology (go north of Jensen, Utah, to see the dinosaur bones) as it is for sandstone canyons and whitewater rafting. Recounted here are my favorite places accessible by vehicle.

The first is a remarkable drive on a rough dirt road that follows the south rim of the Yampa River canyon and provides views 1,000 feet down sheer cliffs to the river. Take a high-clearance vehicle, but beware—rain will make this route, Yampa Bench Road (called Mantle Ranch Road in DeLorme), impassable. From the tiny town of Maybell, west of Craig, continue west on US 40 for 23 miles. At Elk Springs, turn right (northwest) onto County Road 14. Drive about 14 miles to CR 14N, which heads north for a little way, crosses the well-signed monument entrance, and becomes Yampa Bench Road. Just west of the Harding Hole Overlook on this road is the turnoff for the private Mantle Ranch. About 7 miles west from this turnoff, you meet Echo Park Road (see Scenic Location No. 66, p. 213). A right turn takes you to the park, a left turn to the Dinosaur National Monument Road (Harper's Corner Drive) and back to US 40.

This is sandstone, piñon, and juniper tree country. You may wish to reserve your film for your arrival on the edge of the Yampa River canyon. Consult DeLorme to see how close you are at various points along Yampa Bench Road to the main canyon; don't be fooled by the mini-canyons along the way. A couple of side roads north of Yampa Bench Road will get you to within walking distance of the rim. However, the place to stop and photograph is where the road comes closest to the river, at Wagon Wheel Point. Park your vehicle and walk to the edge of the canyon.

You won't believe the view. Immediately in front of you stands a 1,000-foot cliff. Far below the Yampa River meanders, and great serpentine sandstone canyons and cliffs loom in the distance. Use your wide-angle lens to compose piñon trees in the foreground and the vast expanse of canyons behind. Compose the canyon edge as a lead-in line from the bottom left or right corners of the viewfinder. Or use your standard or telephoto lens to focus only on the river below or to isolate particular features of the canyon. Always be mindful of high-contrast light.

Get here at sunrise and the naturally yellow rocks turn deep yellow. Within 10 minutes of sunrise, the light is saturated and not significantly more intense than the river in shadow below. Try bracketing your exposures in order to find the right one between highlight and shadow (see pp. 126–128, *Photographing the Landscape*). As the sun rises higher, the light becomes more intense, making it impossible to contain both deep shadow and intense highlight in the same scene without loss of detail in the film. This place works well at sunset, too—you'll just point your camera east instead of west.

camps. The folks at this family-oriented lodge do everything they can to make kids feel welcome. *393 CR 75, Meeker, 970-878-4669.*

In Craig, **Taylor Street Bed & Breakfast** ($) is a comfortable and friendly place to stay. *403 Taylor St., Craig, 970-824-5866.*

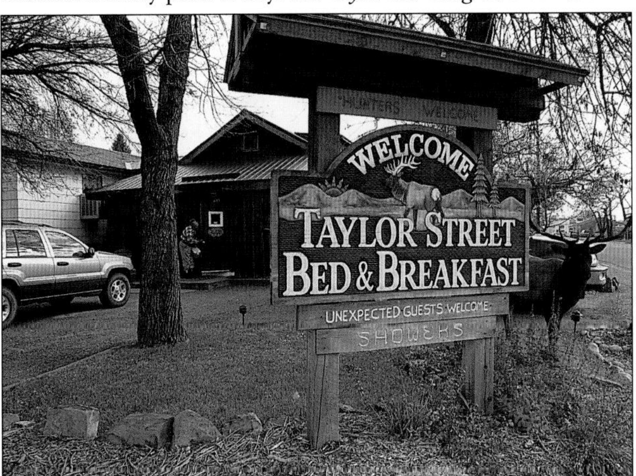

Taylor Street Bed & Breakfast

Special Events

The **Range Call Celebration** is the oldest annual rodeo in Colorado. Since 1885 this celebration has called wranglers, ranch hands, and families from all over northwestern Colorado to Meeker on the Fourth of July weekend. The event always begins with a pancake breakfast, followed by foot races, bike races, and the rodeo. There are games for the kids, a roast pig barbecue, barn dances, and an entertainment headliner. Two of the most anticipated events are the fireworks display and Meeker Massacre reenactment. *970-878-5510.*

In cattle and sheep country, a sheepdog is an important member of the wrangler and horse team. At the **Meeker Classic Sheepdog Championship Trials** in August, which offer the largest purse of any North American dog trials, it's fascinating to see these smart, focused dogs herd and single out their charges. Also on hand are sheep shearing demonstrations, an artisan fair, and plenty of food, including a lamb barbecue. One favorite event is the Border Collie Frisbee Exhibit—these dogs are talented! *970-878-5510, www.meekersheepdog.com.*

For More Information

Moffat County Visitor Center/Craig Chamber of Commerce, *360 E. Victory Way, Craig, 970-824-5689, 800-864-4405, www.craig-chamber.com;* Meeker Chamber of Commerce and Visitor Center, *710 Market St., 970-878-5510, www.meekerchamber.com;* Rangely Area Chamber of Commerce, *209 E. Main St., Rangely, 970-675-8476, www.rangely.com.*

Dinosaur National Monument

Colorado Atlas & Gazetteer pp. 12, 13, 22, 23

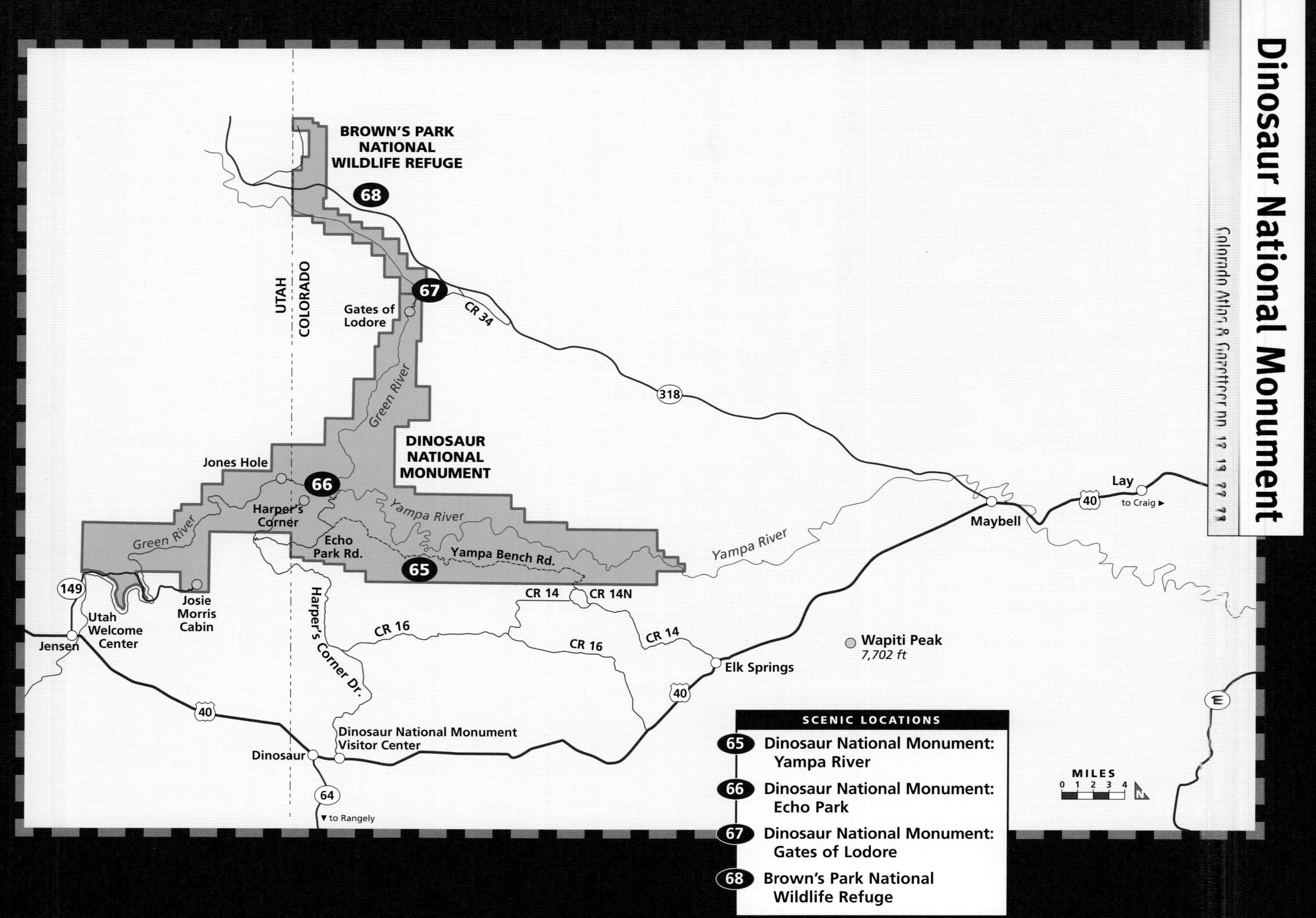

BROWN'S PARK NATIONAL WILDLIFE REFUGE
68
UTAH
COLORADO
67
Gates of Lodore
CR 34
318
Green River
DINOSAUR NATIONAL MONUMENT
Jones Hole
66
Harper's Corner
Yampa River
Green River
Echo Park Rd.
Yampa Bench Rd.
65
Yampa River
Maybell
Lay
40
to Craig
149
Josie Morris Cabin
Utah Welcome Center
Jensen
Harper's Corner Dr.
CR 14
CR 14N
CR 16
CR 16
CR 14
Wapiti Peak
7,702 ft
Elk Springs
40
40
Dinosaur National Monument Visitor Center
Dinosaur
64
to Rangely
SCENIC LOCATIONS
65 Dinosaur National Monument: Yampa River
66 Dinosaur National Monument: Echo Park
67 Dinosaur National Monument: Gates of Lodore
68 Brown's Park National Wildlife Refuge
MILES
0 1 2 3 4
N

DINOSAUR NATIONAL MONUMENT: ECHO PARK

Two great rivers, the Yampa and the Green, meet at the bottom of Dinosaur National Monument. Aptly named Echo Park, here you stand surrounded by 1,000-foot sandstone cliffs watching the two rivers merge—one green, the other silty brown. Cottonwood trees decorate the shores and add life to what otherwise would be a barren, rocky landscape. Though I've rafted past here several times, you can also drive right to this amazing place. From the south rim of the Yampa River Canyon, turn right (north) off Yampa Bench Road onto Echo Park Road (see Scenic Location No. 65, p. 211). Drive 3 miles downhill to the rivers. Or from monument headquarters, take Harper's Corner Scenic Drive 28 miles and look for Echo Park Road on the right.

Spring and fall make Echo Park even more spectacular than it already is. In mid-May, cottonwood trees leaf into shades of delicate lime green. By mid-October, they will have turned yellow. Either way, the trees are wonderful decoration for the rivers before you and the beige cliffs that surround you. Before you begin photographing, explore Echo Park on foot. It's important to avoid instant gratification in beautiful places; it's easy to be tempted to photograph the first thing you see. Instead, look around for the best views and compositional ingredients, making a mental record of all that you find. Then go back and make images of the very best places and the most pleasing views.

For example, with your wide-angle lens, point your camera north up the Green River and make a vertical composition that includes shoreline, cliffs to the right, and plenty of blue sky. Yellow cottonwood trees are the perfect complement to the Colorado blue sky. Now try a horizontal version of the scene. And be sure to photograph the old cabin on the way out of Echo Park. Then turn north (right) at Harper's Corner Drive and drive to the dead end at Harper's Corner. Hike to the edge of the canyon and look back down at Echo Park—an amazing scene. Make images looking east to the sea of canyons as they turn orange at sunset.

DINOSAUR NATIONAL MONUMENT: GATES OF LODORE

While the Yampa River canyon is formed of beige sandstone, the Green River canyon is delightfully red. Its dramatic entrance is a towering pair of cliffs that seem to rise out of nowhere and swallow the Green River whole. They are called the Gates of Lodore, and you can drive very close to them. From Craig, go west on US 40 to Maybell. Head northwest on CO 318 and, about 40 miles later, go west onto County Road 34. Keep an eye out for the conspicuous signs to the Gates of Lodore. CR 34 dead-ends at the river.

Above all, this is a place to be at sunrise. The rising sun colors already ruddy rocks with thick red light, and the gates reflect in the still water of what is at this point a lazy river. (Take a raft trip down the Green and you'll discover a less-than-lazy river at places such as aptly named Disaster Falls, first explored by John Wesley Powell in 1869.) In mid-October, cottonwood trees and shrubs along the shore turn yellow and orange. They, too, catch the sunrise light and add remarkable color to the scene. Colder temperatures in October cause morning fog to form above the relatively warm water of the river. Surreal, misty scenes of the trees and the Gates of Lodore disappearing and reappearing make great photographs as the sun rises and the fog burns off.

Use a wide-angle lens to compose the edge of the river as a lead-in line, extending all the way up to the Gates. Zoom in on the red cliffs with your telephoto lens. Now hike the trail from the campground east and south toward the Gates. A little bit of elevation gain will provide you an entirely new perspective of the river to photograph.

BROWN'S PARK NATIONAL WILDLIFE REFUGE

The Green River doesn't need tall red cliffs to be photogenic. A little way upstream from the spectacular Gates of Lodore, the lazy river meanders through meadows and a couple of low rocky canyons. Although you can make images of waterfowl with long telephoto lenses, the river is also a place to photograph the refuge's unique Colorado landscape. Follow the directions from Craig in Scenic Location No. 67, opposite. Instead of turning west onto County Road 34, continue northwest on CO 318 until you enter the refuge. Or if you are coming from the Gates of Lodore, turn left onto CR 34N, 3 miles from the river.

You'll definitely want the benefit of rich light at sunrise and sunset, accompanied by the long shadows they produce. So plan on car-camping here for a night. After you reenter CO 318, keep an eye out for any dirt roads that head west. There are several before you enter Utah, and all will take you right to the edge of the river. It's from these places that you will be able to compose beautiful photographs of the Green River. It even meanders through a few little canyons, where you can climb to the edge and wait for the rising sun to color them yellow.

Use a wide-angle lens to compose both sides of the river in the viewfinder, with shorelines receding into the distance. Such diagonal lines create tension in a photograph and enhance asymmetrical balance—great ways to avoid a boring image. You can also make compositions of the cottonwood trees lining the curves in the river. On clear days, the light of sunset colors the yellow leaves almost red. In this remote part of Colorado, the foliage leafs into lime green in mid-May and turns yellow in mid-October.

Amicas restaurant (formerly Il Vicino), Salida

Hotel Jerome, Aspen

Donita's Cantina, Crested Butte

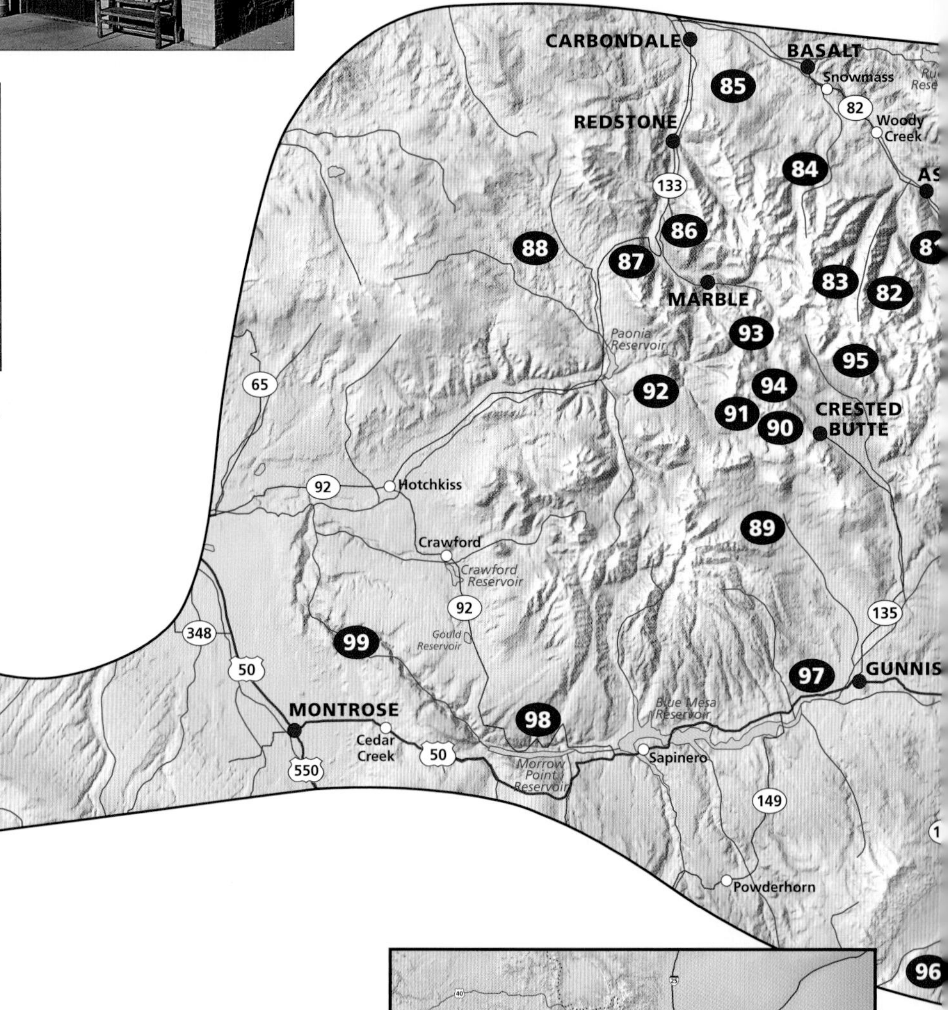

CARBONDALE
BASALT
Snowmass
Woody Creek
REDSTONE
MARBLE
Paonia Reservoir
CRESTED BUTTE
Hotchkiss
Crawford
Crawford Reservoir
Gould Reservoir
Gateway
MONTROSE
Cedar Creek
Morrow Point Reservoir
Sapinero
Blue Mesa Reservoir
GUNNIS
Powderhorn
Bedrock
85 84 88 86 87 83 82 93 95 92 94 91 90 89 99 98 97 101 100 102 96
141 92 65 133 82 348 50 550 135 149 90

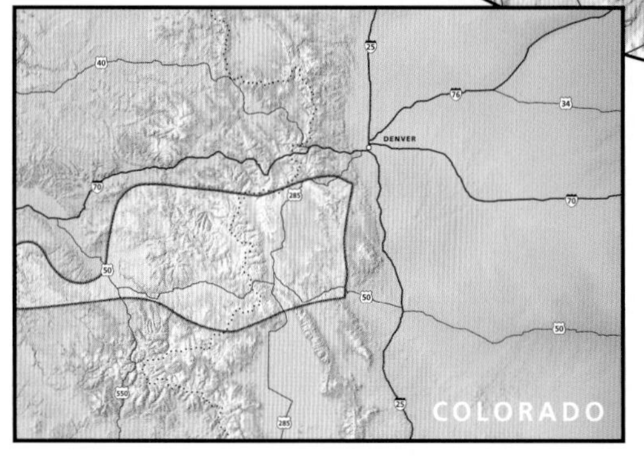

Nordic Inn, Crested Butte

Central Colorado

HEART OF THE ROCKIES

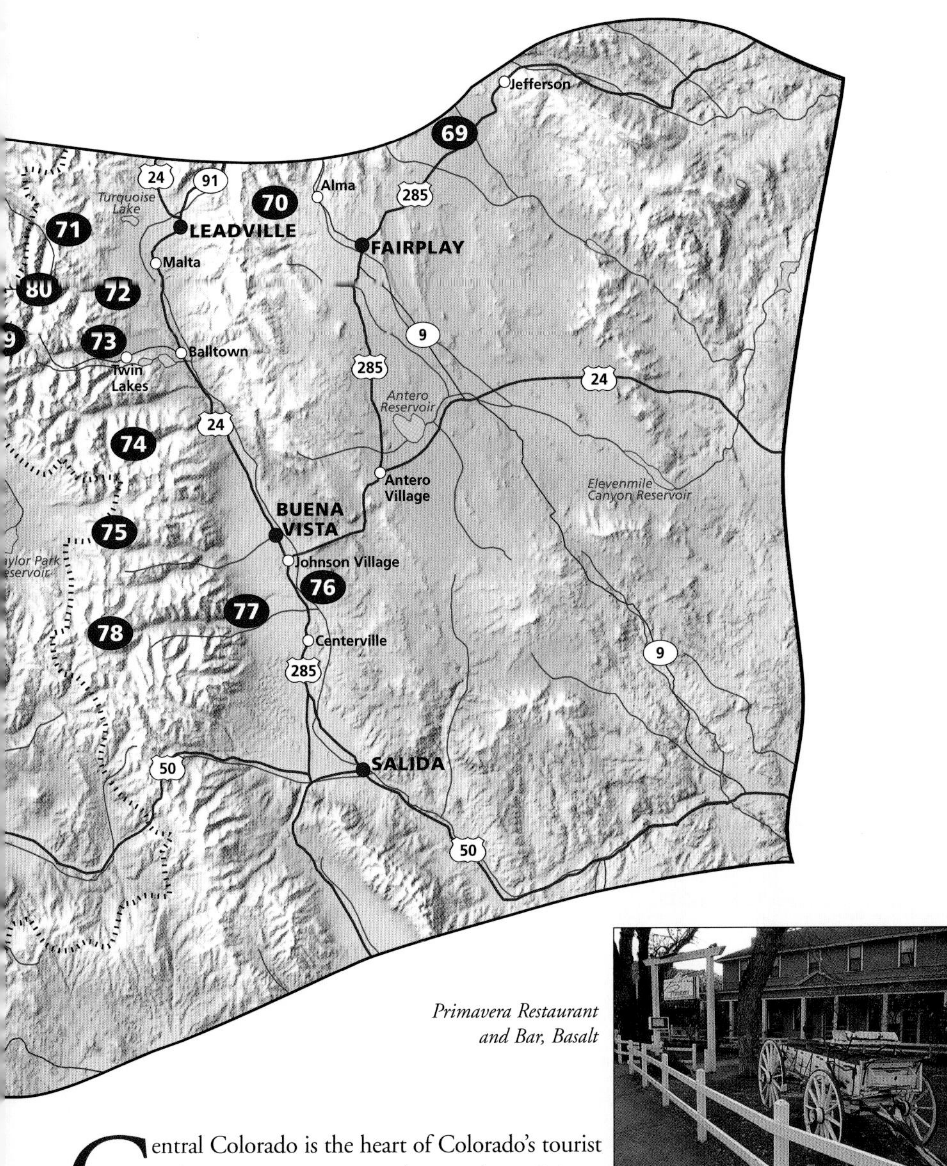

Primavera Restaurant and Bar, Basalt

Central Colorado is the heart of Colorado's tourist and recreation country and correctly so. It is a land of towering mountain ranges and expansive valleys, home to the headwaters of great rivers powerful enough to carve the Black Canyon of the Gunnison, yet tamed enough to provide for irrigation and unbeatable recreation. Central Colorado has produced silver, gold, coal, molybdenum, the marble used in our most famous monuments, and plenty of "white gold"—the snow that fuels the ski economy. It is a region rich in history, mainly stories of mining camps transformed into rafting towns, mountain-bike meccas, historic districts, and especially ski resorts, including such major tourist centers as Aspen and Crested Butte. Farther west from the glorious mountains, the Gunnison Gorge astounds, while the Uncompahgre and lower Dolores River canyon country surrounds the traveler with peaceful and fertile valleys. When visiting the heart of Colorado, you will have a smorgasbord of diversions from which to choose—bon appétit!

SCENIC LOCATIONS

Fairplay/Leadville

Colorado Atlas & Gazetteer pp. 47–48

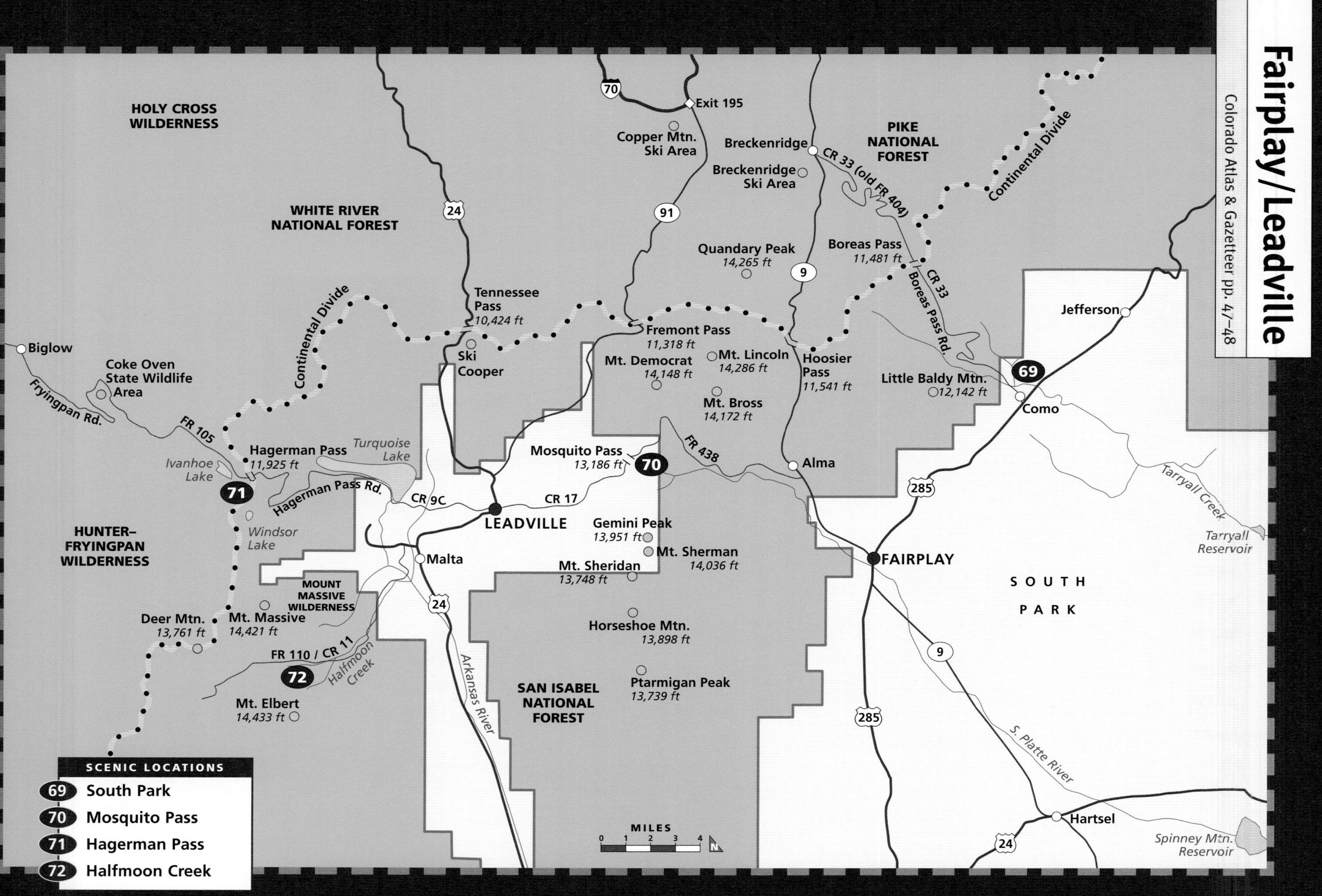

HOLY CROSS WILDERNESS
WHITE RIVER NATIONAL FOREST
70
Exit 195
Copper Mtn. Ski Area
24
91
Breckenridge
Breckenridge Ski Area
PIKE NATIONAL FOREST
CR 33 (old FR 404)
Continental Divide
Quandary Peak 14,265 ft
9
Boreas Pass 11,481 ft
CR 33
Boreas Pass Rd.
Tennessee Pass 10,424 ft
Ski Cooper
Fremont Pass 11,318 ft
Mt. Democrat 14,148 ft
Mt. Lincoln 14,286 ft
Mt. Bross 14,172 ft
Hoosier Pass 11,541 ft
Little Baldy Mtn. 12,142 ft
Jefferson
69
Como
Biglow
Coke Oven State Wildlife Area
Fryingpan Rd.
FR 105
Hagerman Pass 11,925 ft
Turquoise Lake
Ivanhoe Lake
71
Hagerman Pass Rd.
CR 9C
Mosquito Pass 13,186 ft
70
FR 438
Alma
285
Tarryall Creek
Tarryall Reservoir
CR 17
LEADVILLE
Gemini Peak 13,951 ft
Mt. Sherman 14,036 ft
Mt. Sheridan 13,748 ft
FAIRPLAY
HUNTER–FRYINGPAN WILDERNESS
Windsor Lake
Malta
MOUNT MASSIVE WILDERNESS
S O U T H
P A R K
Deer Mtn. 13,761 ft
Mt. Massive 14,421 ft
Horseshoe Mtn. 13,898 ft
FR 110 / CR 11
72
Halfmoon Creek
Arkansas River
SAN ISABEL NATIONAL FOREST
Ptarmigan Peak 13,739 ft
Mt. Elbert 14,433 ft
S. Platte River
Hartsel
Spinney Mtn. Reservoir
MILES
0 1 2 3 4
N
SCENIC LOCATIONS
69 South Park
70 Mosquito Pass
71 Hagerman Pass
72 Halfmoon Creek

Fairplay

I am always struck by South Park's remote wide-open spaces. Here, antelope often graze alongside cattle in the valley's expansive grassland prairie (see Scenic Location No. 69, p. 221). As you drive along US 285, keep an eye out for the painted "cow" rock near Red Hill Pass, a fitting symbol for the region. Those who stop in South Park can fish the bountiful lakes and rivers or explore the backroads and trails leading into the forests and up to the mountains that circle this broad, graceful valley. Unwind in Fairplay, 80 miles southwest of Denver on US 285.

South Park City Museum

History

During the gold rush of 1859, the rich strikes in the mountains to the north of South Park changed the face of this valley. Tent cities and gold camps soon dotted the area, leading to the establishment of Fairplay on the South Platte River. But by 1879, when the Denver South Park & Pacific Railroad finally arrived in South Park, the strikes near Fairplay were no longer important in light of the discoveries at Leadville and other points west. Prospectors moved on, and the railroad here was finally abandoned during the Great Depression. Today, large cattle ranches dominate South Park, while Fairplay provides a stopping point for travelers, scenic cross-country skiing and hiking trails, and prime fishing spots.

Main Attractions

FISHING

South Park's streams and reservoirs lure anglers from Colorado Springs, Denver, Pueblo, and beyond. **Tarryall Reservoir** provides good fishing for northern pike, rainbows, and brown trout. From Fairplay, go north on US 285 and turn right (southeast) on County Road 34. Continue driving 15 miles to the reservoir.

Spinney Mountain Reservoir has been designated Gold Medal Water because of its large rainbows, cutthroats, and even browns. Northern pike and kokanee salmon are also common here. Take CO 9 south from Fairplay 17 miles to Hartsel, turn left (east) onto US 24, and follow the road to the signs for Spinney Mountain and Elevenmile Reservoirs. Turn right (south) on CR 23 and follow it to a split in the road. Turn right on CR 592 and take the next left to the reservoir. The **South Platte River** above and below the reservoir also provides good fishing. **Elevenmile Reservoir** has large trout, northern pike, kokanee salmon, and carp. From Fairplay, follow the directions to Spinney Mountain Reservoir, but go left on CR 592. Both Spinney and Elevenmile require a State Parks pass. Camping is available at Eleven Mile State Park.

For information: ArkAnglers, 5417 N. US 24, Buena Vista, 719-395-1796 (summer only).

SOUTH PARK CITY

Signs along US 285 advertise Fairplay's **South Park City,** but the attraction is not a tourist trap. Seven original buildings, and 28 buildings moved from nearby defunct mining camps, form this re-creation of an 1880s mining town. Some of the most interesting are the livery, blacksmith shop, schoolhouse, doctor's office, and barber shop/dentist's office. Visitors develop a sense of intimacy with the region's past while walking through the "city" and looking over the artifacts. South Park City is at the west end of Fairplay. *719-836-2387, www.southparkcity.org.*

Activities

CAMPING

Aspen campground sits in a large mountain meadow shaded by a grove of its namesake trees. Take US 285 to Jefferson and turn left (northwest) onto CR 35. Continue for about 2 miles to FR 401 (CR 37), then turn right (north) and go about 3 miles to the campground. **Selkirk** nestles in a thick forest. Head north on US 285 to Como, then take Boreas Pass Road (CR 33) for 7 miles. The campground is off the road 1 mile to the left. **Kenosha Pass** campground, an ideal place especially in fall, connects to the Colorado Trail. From Fairplay, take US 285 north 20 miles to the summit of Kenosha Pass. The campground is to your left. *For above campgrounds: 303-275-5610.* Camping is also available at Eleven Mile State Park. *719-836-2031.*

CYCLING AND MOUNTAIN BIKING

Cyclists like to tackle 11,541-foot **Hoosier Pass** DIFFICULT over CO 9, while mountain bikers enjoy scaling 11,481-foot **Boreas Pass** MODERATE via Como over Boreas Pass Road. Both roads lead to Breckenridge (see Cycling and Mountain Biking, p. 107, Breckenridge and Frisco).

Ride through pine forests and aspen and enjoy a great view of the valley on the 6.25-mile **Kenosha Creek Trail** (Forest Road 126) MODERATE, which is also a popular hiking and four-wheel-drive route. From Fairplay, go 20 miles north on US 285 to the parking lot across from the Kenosha Pass campground. The **Kenosha Pass to Georgia Pass Trail** MODERATE, a segment of the Colorado Trail, begins at the 10,001-foot summit of Kenosha Pass and continues 12 miles west to 11,585-foot Georgia Pass. To get to the trailhead, follow the directions to Kenosha Creek Trail.

FOUR-WHEEL-DRIVE TRIPS

Bristlecone Pine Scenic Area, at the foot of fourteener Mount Bross on Windy Ridge, showcases some of the world's oldest trees, tilted and gnarled by wind and age. From Fairplay, go 6 miles northwest on CO 9 through Alma, turn left (west) on Forest Road 315, and continue to Windy Ridge.

HIKING

Bristlecone pine trees, some of the oldest living trees in the world, line the 3-mile round-trip **Limber Grove Trail** EASY. This trail also commands views of South Park and the Mosquito Range. From Fairplay, go 1.5 miles south on US 285. Turn right (west) on County Road 18 and continue 7 miles to the trailhead at the far end of the Horseshoe campground.

Buffalo Meadows Loop MODERATE, an 11.5-mile hike in the Buffalo Peaks Wilderness, takes you through meadows and forests and follows several creeks. From Fairplay, go 5 miles south on US 285 to Weston Pass Road (CR 5). Turn right (west), continue for 7 miles, then bear right at a fork. At 10 miles you will reach the Pike National Forest boundary, marked by a cattle guard. Park beyond the cattle guard and start your hike at the sign marking the South Fork of the South Platte River.

Part of the Colorado Trail, the 12-mile (one way) **Kenosha Pass to Georgia Pass Trail** MODERATE has a great view of South Park. This is also a popular mountain-biking route. (For directions, see Kenosha Creek Trail, Cycling and Mountain Biking, p. 219.) You can extend one of many short hikes, loops, and intersecting trails into a 20-mile overnight backpacking trip in the rugged **Lost Creek Wilderness** MODERATE, known for its box canyons, rock formations, and herds of bighorn sheep. From Fairplay, go north on US 285, pass Jefferson, and continue about 1.5 miles. Turn right on Forest Road 127 (CR 56) and drive 19 miles to Lost Creek campground, where you connect to the **Brookside-McCurdy** and **Wigwam Trails.**

South Park provides serious hikers with four fourteeners that offer panoramic Colorado mountain views. The 2-mile (one way) hike up 14,036-foot **Mount Sherman** MODERATE commands views of the Collegiate Range and of Mount Massive and Mount Elbert, Colorado's highest peaks. The trail also leads to the deserted Dauntless Mine. From Fairplay, go 1.2 miles south on US 285 to Four Mile Creek Road (CR 18), turn right (west) and go 12 miles, then park along the road. There is limited access for four-wheel-drive vehicles farther up the road. The summits of **Mount Democrat**, **Mount Lincoln**, and **Mount Bross** DIFFICULT afford views of the Gore, Elk, and Tenmile Ranges. A peak-bagging enthusiast can do them all in a day. From Fairplay, take CO 9 north 5 miles to Alma. Go left (west) on FR 416 (CR 8) and drive 5.5 miles to Kite Lake and trail access (the last stretch of road is bumpy). *For maps and information: South Park Ranger District, US 285 and CO 9, 719-836-2031.*

WINTER SPORTS

Boreas Pass, **Kenosha Pass**, and the **Bristlecone Pine Scenic Area** provide excellent cross-country skiing and snowshoeing (see Cycling and Mountain Biking, p. 219, and Four-Wheel-Drive Trips, this page). Also, the 5.5-mile **Tie Hack Loop** DIFFICULT traverses meadows and passes by old mining camps. From Fairplay, go 1.2 miles south on US 285 to County Road 18. Turn right (west) and go 3.5 miles to the beginning of the trail.

Restaurants

If you have no luck fishing South Park's waters, stop for a cozy local meal. **Como Depot** ($), *719-836-2594,* 10 miles north of Fairplay on US 285, serves nice meals and a variety of homemade pies. **Millonzi's Restaurant & Delicatessen** ($-$$) serves up classic Italian dishes as well as salads and sandwiches. *501 Front St., 719-836-9501.* For Mexican, check out the **Brown Burro Café** ($-$$). *719-836-2804, 706 Main St.* In nearby Alma, visit **Alma's Only Bistro** ($-$$) for home cooked comfort classics and BBQ. *12 S. Main, Alma, 719-836-1609, www.almasonlybistro.com.*

Accommodations

Frequented by many European travelers, **Hand Hotel Bed and Breakfast** has a distinctive Western flair. The breakfast nook overlooking the South Platte has a wonderful view. *531 Front St., 719-836-3595, www.handhotel.com.* Located on an original homestead in South Park, **American Safari Ranch** offers the ultimate horsemanship program for riders of every ability. Stay at modern log cabins, and enjoy open-fire meals that can include the trout you catch. With barn dances, nightly bonfires, and hayrides, this place is a vacation in itself. From Fairplay, go 6 miles north on 285 to County Road 7; turn right (southeast). *719-836-2700, www.coloradoranchretreat.com.*

Special Events

Burro Days at the end of July celebrates the burro's crucial role in the success of the early mines. The highlight of this 53-year-old event is the World Championship Pack-Burro Race. Starting in Fairplay, race contestants zip to the top of 13,186-foot Mosquito Pass and back. Each burro must carry a 33-pound packsaddle of mining tools; the burro driver may not ride but can push, drag, or even carry the animal! A miner's supper and concert, staged gunfights, gold-panning demonstrations, and arts and crafts displays round out the lively events. **Bayou Salado Old West Gathering,** a traditional mountain-man rendezvous, takes place southeast of town during Burro Days. *719-836-4279.*

For More Information

Park County Tourism Office, 501 Main St., *719-836-4279.*

SOUTH PARK

Colorado contains four intermountain basins—large valleys above 8,000 feet in elevation that are surrounded on all sides by mountains: North Park, Middle Park, the San Luis Valley, and South Park. South Park is surrounded by the Mosquito, Tenmile, and Front Ranges, the Tarryall Mountains, and Pikes Peak. The valley floor averages around 9,000 feet, while the surrounding mountains soar well above 13,000 feet. The headwaters of the South Platte River originate in these mountains. The park comprises vast ranches whose meadows make for bucolic scenes with peaks looming in the background. South Park is accessible via US 285 from Denver or via US 24 from Colorado Springs.

I enjoy driving US 285 from one end of South Park to the other. The view of the park from Kenosha Pass (10,001 feet) with the Mosquito Range in the background is one of Colorado's finest. However, photographing the view is like trying to photograph from the top of a 14,000-foot mountain: With no foreground to compose, very little perspective exists in the scene, making for a boring photograph. So be happy with the candy for your eye and continue driving down into the valley for some better photographs. Beautiful ranch meadows exist at the base of the pass on the north side of the highway. Ample snowmelt in June floods these meadows and produces an assortment of wildflowers. Keep an eye out for Rocky Mountain wild irises and other flowers. Pull over and stand by the fence in order to compose the field in the foreground with the peaks behind. Keep your fingers crossed for cloudy light, which will enhance the green of the meadows and colors of the flowers. Remember, the intensity of midday light mutes colors. Look for flowers throughout the valley.

Autumn is another great time to drive US 285. To the north and west of the highway are aspen groves that look like they've been painted in symmetrical shapes onto the rounded hills below the Mosquito Range. In late September the groves are absolutely glorious against a blue Colorado sky. Though you can make great images with a telephoto lens from the highway, a number of improved county roads get you closer to the action. Boreas Pass Road (see Scenic Location No. 25, p. 106) exits north at the town of Como and will deliver you into aspens quickly. Weston Pass Road (County Road 5) exits 5 miles south of Fairplay to the west and provides wonderful views of aspens blanketing nearby Black Mountain and Round Hill.

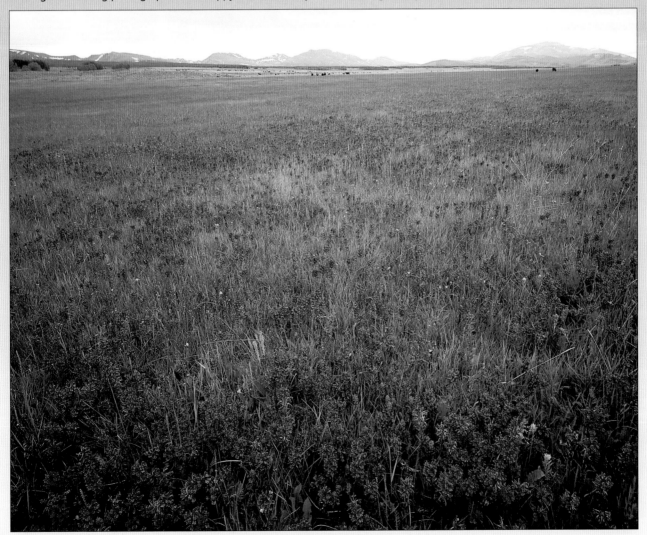

Leadville

(see map on p. 218)

Colorado's consummate mining town, Leadville has it all—a fabled history, Victorian gingerbread houses, a landmark hotel, the obligatory opera house, legendary heroes and heroines who struck it fabulously rich, and, of course, notable mines on the outskirts of town. But Leadville differs from other mining towns in that its mining history was longer lasting and more diverse. That difference has had its costs. You can't help but notice the environmental degradation caused by mining—scooped-out peaks, scarred and deforested mountainsides, and chemical "dead zones" resulting from the use of cyanide and mercury.

Even so, there is still no better place than Leadville to get a sense of the glamour and heartache of Colorado's mining past. Stroll down Harrison Avenue, visit the shops and historical homes, stop at the museums, and tour the Matchless Mine. Look up at the majestic peaks still harboring minerals that made the area one of the country's most productive mining districts. Today, visitors to Leadville can still revel in the town's charm and high-mountain scenery as they glimpse Colorado's Gilded Age history.

MOSQUITO PASS

Higher than the infamous Engineer and Cinnamon Passes of the San Juans, Mosquito Pass crosses the crest of the Mosquito Range at 13,186 feet. Views to west of the Sawatch Range and to the east of the Pikes Peak massif are sublime. Most of the drive courses the alpine zone, and its summer flowers are a photographer's delight. But you'll have to take the four-wheel drive along, for the road is very rough and steep on top, and does not open until the Fourth of July. From Leadville, head east on 7th Street, which becomes Mosquito Pass Road. To get to the pass from the other side of the range, turn west on Forest Road 438 from CO 9, 1 mile south of Alma.

Here you'll find one of the best fields of Colorado columbine wildflowers in the state. From Alma and CO 9, the road heads west for about 7 miles along Mosquito Creek and the valley floor. As you approach timberline, you will notice some fine creek compositions on your left. But where the road makes the first big switchback uphill to the left, look along the hillside immediately below you. If you go between mid-July and mid-August, you will see purple columbine everywhere, interspersed with Indian paintbrush. It's glorious. I prefer just photographing the flowers amid the rocks and stumps, without sky and horizon. But beware, the slightest breeze makes a columbine wave, so be patient. Photograph the highly reflective columbine in cloudy light, or when the sun is behind the mountains, so that the purples are rendered rich on film.

Look for dwarf alpine wildflowers on top of the pass. White phlox and pink moss campion are common, but my favorite is the iridescent blue forget-me-not. They each grow in clumps close to the ground as protection from fierce winds, so use your macro lens if you wish to make these small flowers conspicuous on film. By the way, the views down Mosquito Creek of the green tundra grasses from high up on the pass are quite colorful when backlit by the rising sun (see pp. 100–103, *Photographing the Landscape*).

History

In 1860, the Colorado gold rush began in earnest in an area later dubbed California Gulch. More than $8 million in gold would be taken out of California Gulch, supposedly named after a prospector's remark, "I have all of California in this here pan!" The placer gold eventually played out, but in 1876 prospectors discovered rich silver lodes near town. Leadville incorporated in 1878. Among those made rich in this silver boom were the Guggenheim and Boettcher families, former stonecutter Horace Tabor, David H. Moffat, and J.J. Brown, the husband of "Unsinkable" Molly Brown (see Colorado Cameo, Denver, p. 22).

Almost overnight, Leadville became high-rolling and famous, attracting the likes of Susan B. Anthony, Frank and Jesse James, Walt Whitman, and Buffalo Bill. With around 20,000 residents at its peak, Leadville—high up in elevation at 10,152 feet—was second only to Denver in population in the state. Twin Lakes, a popular summer resort, opened at the foot of Mount Elbert, 23 miles south of Leadville. Tabor Opera House, completed in 1879, hosted Harry Houdini, John Philip Sousa, and Oscar Wilde. In the town's heyday, silver baron Horace Tabor took a much-younger mistress called Baby Doe, an event that unfolded into a saga of infidelity, scandal, and dashed dreams that continues to fascinate tourists and opera-goers to this day (see Colorado Cameo, p. 225).

Following the repeal of the Sherman Silver Purchase Act in 1893, America shifted solidly to the gold standard. The ensuing economic devastation was known regionally as the Bust of the

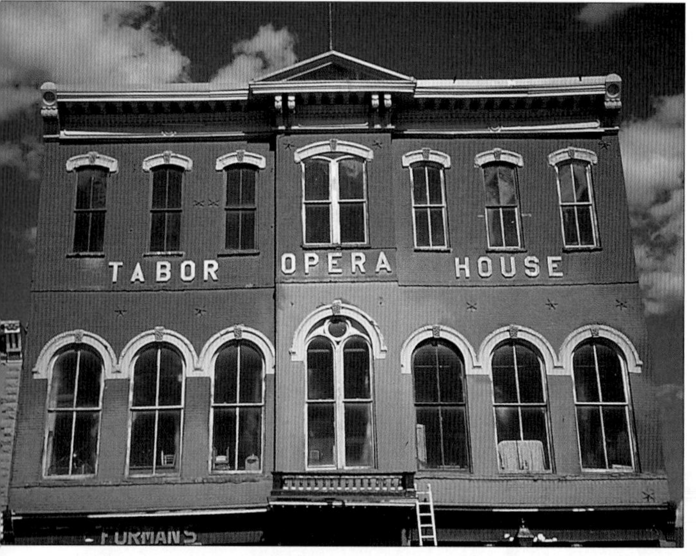

Tabor Opera House, Leadville

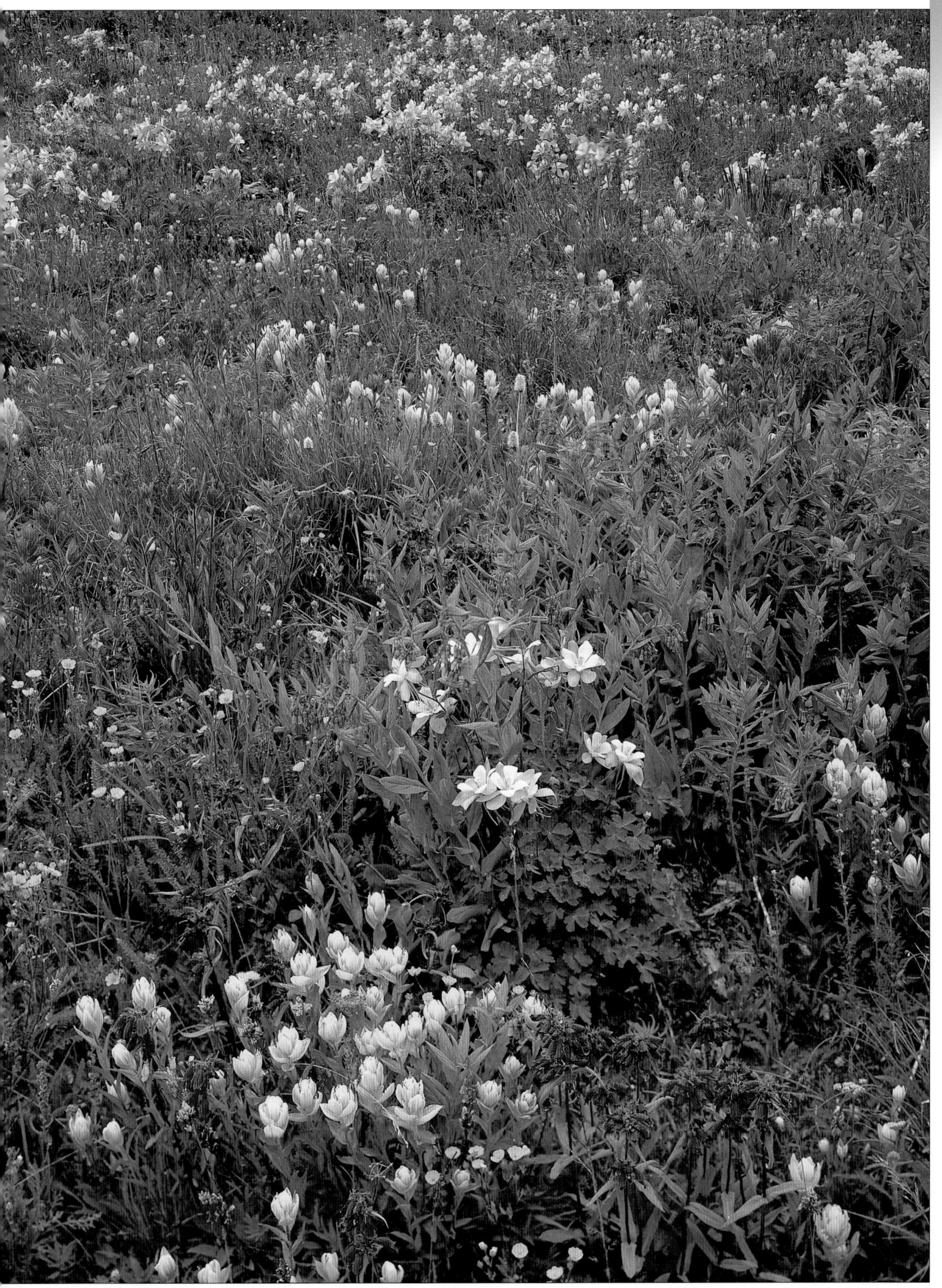

Silver Kings. Nevertheless, the peaks around Leadville also produced zinc, manganese, turquoise, molybdenum, and other minerals, which kept the local economy based in mining. The Climax Mine near Leadville operated one of the largest underground molybdenum mines in the world. Yet the wealth of recreational options and scenic splendor still lying in these famous high mountains continue to draw people here. Today the town's population hovers around 3,000, and Leadville residents understand that while the mining economy is part of their proud past, their future must rely on tourism.

Main Attractions

LEADVILLE HISTORIC WALKING TOUR

Leadville's 70 square blocks comprise one of Colorado's largest and most storied National Historic Districts. Harrison Avenue remains the heart of the town. Notorious gambler Doc Holliday came to Leadville after his adventures in Arizona and shot his last man on the 300 block of Harrison Ave. In 1879, Horace Tabor dedicated his **Tabor Opera House** at 308 Harrison Ave. This handsome venue drew many talented players to Leadville. *719-486-8409.* To make way for the theater, the Tabors moved their home from its original location. At the corner of Harrison and St. Louis Avenues since 1879, the 1877 **Tabor Home** also offers tours (stop by as there is no phone). **Silver Dollar Saloon,** 315 Harrison Ave., opened in 1883 as the Board of Trade Saloon. In 1886, three brothers from Delaware developed the 700 block of Harrison Ave. for $60,000. Today, the **Delaware Hotel** remains one of the best places to stay in Leadville. *719-486-1418, www.delawarehotel.com.* **Leadville City Hall,** on the corner of West 8th and Harrison, was formerly a post office. The Greek Revival **Healy House Museum** and nearby **Dexter Cabin,** two characteristically opulent (yes, that includes the cabin) residences dating from the late 1870s, display fine period furnishings including items once owned by Horace and Augusta Tabor. Ask about the children's tour. *912 Harrison Ave., 719-486-0487.*

Healy House Museum, Leadville

Move off the avenue and go visit the **National Mining Hall of Fame and Museum,** 120 W. 9th St., which includes a walk-through replica of a hard-rock mine and the Gold Rush room. *719-486-1229, www.leadville.com/miningmuseum.* Built as a library in 1902, the **Heritage Museum** at 9th Street and Harrison Ave. has a fine-art gallery depicting Leadville's colorful past. *719-486-1878.*

The Leadville Chamber of Commerce provides maps for your walking tour; take it in summer when the buildings are open and the weather's fine. *809 Harrison Ave., 719-486-3900, www.leadvilleusa.com.*

MATCHLESS MINE TOUR

The riches and misery in its history have made the **Matchless Mine** one of Colorado's most famous. Purchased for $117,000, the Matchless Mine returned $14 million worth of silver to its owner, Horace Tabor. Today, the shaft and headframe remain, as do the original hoist room, blacksmith shop, and cabin where Baby Doe Tabor spent her last, sad days. To get to the Matchless Mine, take 7th Street 1 mile east to the entrance. *719-486-3900.*

Activities

CAMPING

The campgrounds around **Turquoise Lake Recreation Area** offer spectacular scenery, great fishing, and numerous hiking trails. **Baby Doe** campground is only a few feet away from Turquoise Lake. From the north side of Leadville, go south on US 24, turn right (west) just past the Safeway onto Mountain View Drive, and go west 2.7 miles to the intersection. Turn right (north), go 0.6 mile, then turn left (west) and cross the railroad tracks. Continue for about 0.5 mile, turn right (north) onto County Road 9, and go 0.8 mile. **Belle of Colorado** is another beautiful lakeside campground. Follow the directions to Baby Doe, turning right (north) on CR 9 then left (west) to the campground.

Other fine campgrounds include **Molly Brown, Tabor** (no reservations), **Silver Dollar,** and **Father Dyer.** Go west 4 miles on Mountain View Drive and follow the signs to these campgrounds. **Whitestar** campground, near Twin Lakes Reservoir, affords stunning views of the mountains and access to the Colorado and Mount Elbert Trails. From Leadville, go south on US 24 for roughly 15 miles, turn right (west) on CO 82, and go 7 miles. *For camping information: 719-486-0749.*

CYCLING AND MOUNTAIN BIKING

Old wagon roads on **Fryer Hill** EASY east of town are great for mountain biking. The 12.5-mile, paved **Mineral Belt Trail** EASY loops around the city of Leadville and meanders through the historic mining district. Connect to the trail (a cross-country route in winter) from Ice Palace Park and the East 5th Street Bridge. One of the area's most scenic rides is the 6.5-mile **Turquoise Lake Trail** EASY around Turquoise Lake. From Leadville, go west on 6th Street, turn right (northwest) onto Turquoise Lake Road, and continue 3 miles.

Four-wheel-drive roads here are also quite popular with mountain bikers. *For information and maps: Bill's Sport Shop, 225 Harrison Ave., 719-486-0739, www.billsrentals.com.*

FISHING

Heavy-metal contamination from mining has limited the fishing in the Arkansas River Valley. You'll have better luck at the stocked lakes. **Turquoise Lake** is popular, with a number of trout species and kokanee salmon for the taking (for directions, see Cycling and Mountain Biking, opposite). **Twin Lakes Reservoir** is known for its huge Mackinaw trout; it's also stocked with cutthroats and rainbows (for directions, see Whitestar campground, opposite). **Crystal Lakes,** on either side of US 24 about 3.5 miles south of Leadville, is another good option. Sizable cutthroat trout inhabit the high-mountain **Lonesome Lake** (for directions, see Hiking, p. 227). *For information: Buckhorn Sporting Goods, 616 Harrison Ave., 719-486-3944; Bill's Sport Shop, 225 Harrison Ave., 719-486-0739, www.billsrentals.com. For guided fishing trips: Colorado Fly Fishing, 866-908-7547, 800-356-4992, 711 Harrison Ave., www.alpineskiandsports.com/fishing.shtml.*

FOUR-WHEEL-DRIVE TRIPS

Like the peaks of the San Juans, the mountains around Leadville are scored with four-wheel-drive roads providing panoramic glimpses of mining history. Note that hikers and mountain bikers also enjoy these roads. Check in with the chamber of commerce to see if your four-wheel drive can navigate them.

From Turquoise Lake Recreation Area to Basalt, **Hagerman Pass Road** winds for 55 miles and crosses the Continental Divide (see Scenic Location No. 71, p. 226). **Weston Pass** crosses the Mosquito Range and ends 26 miles later at US 285 in South Park. From Leadville, take US 24 south 6 miles to Forest Road 425 and turn left (east). To get to the 4.5-mile (one way) **Bear Lake Road,** take Mountain View Drive west to Leadville Junction. Turn right at the "T" intersection and follow the road to the large parking area. Turn left (west) across the railroad tracks and the Arkansas River. At the next "T"

COLORADO CAMEO

Horace Tabor and Baby Doe

Perhaps the West's most celebrated love triangle happened in Leadville's glittering heyday. In 1860, Augusta and Horace Austin Warner Tabor arrived in the California Gulch area to seek their fortune. After the gold played out in 1862, Horace Tabor became postmaster and the town's first mayor. In 1878, two down-on-their-luck miners begged Tabor to grubstake them for $17 in supplies. In return, he became a partner in their claim at the Little Pittsburg Mine. A year later, the miners struck a rich vein of silver, and Tabor sold his claim for $1 million.

For the next decade, everything Horace Tabor touched turned to silver. He invested in other mines, including the famous Matchless Mine, as well real estate in Leadville and Denver. He began a six-year term as Colorado's lieutenant governor in 1878, and opened two great opera houses, in Leadville and Denver, in the next three years.

In 1880, Elizabeth "Baby Doe" McCourt (right), a 25-year-old divorcee, arrived in Leadville, and Tabor was quickly smitten. The lovers' meetings, through a secret passageway between the Clarendon Hotel and Tabor's office at the opera house, became public knowledge despite their efforts at concealment. Tabor begged Augusta, his wife of 25 years, for a divorce. She refused. Leadville citizens split over the issue, sympathizing with Augusta but not wanting to antagonize the powerful Horace Tabor.

After filing for divorce in Durango, Tabor secretly married Baby Doe in St. Louis in 1882. Augusta had not agreed to the financial terms, though, so the divorce papers were declared illegal. She continued to dispute the divorce and terms. The press made the love triangle a national source of entertainment. Finally Augusta agreed to a substantial settlement and retired to Pasadena, California. With the divorce final, Horace and Baby Doe Tabor wanted the world to know they were indeed husband and wife. They remarried in Washington, D.C., in 1883, in a lavish ceremony attended by Washington's elite, including President Chester A. Arthur.

Still, bad publicity and extravagance had damaged Tabor's career, and his financial and political status declined. Tabor unsuccessfully ran for the Senate in 1886 and for governor in 1888; meanwhile, bad investments depleted his fortune. The 1893 Silver Panic finally broke him. At the age of 65, Horace A.W. Tabor was shoveling slag in Cripple Creek for $3 a day. By 1898, loyal political connections landed him a job as postmaster of Denver, but he died of appendicitis a year later.

Although legend has it that the dying Horace Tabor whispered into Baby Doe's ear, "Hold on to the Matchless, it will pay millions," history shows that the worthless Matchless Mine had been sold long before to pay the Tabors' debts. The new owners allowed Baby Doe to live in the supply shack by the mine after her husband's death, and Leadville residents often brought her food and supplies. On March 7, 1935, worried townspeople found Baby Doe's frozen body on the floor. She had died of a heart attack two weeks earlier.

Leadville residents still hold strong opinions about this piece of Colorado history. Some have warm affection for long-suffering Augusta Tabor, while others feel for Baby Doe, who stood by her husband in sickness and poverty. Perhaps Tennyson's adage applies best: "'Tis better to have loved and lost/Than never to have loved at all."

HAGERMAN PASS

Another fun, rough drive is the road up Hagerman Pass (11,925 feet). Though you can choose among several great ways to get across the great Sawatch Range—Independence Pass (see Scenic Location No. 79, p. 244) and Cottonwood Pass (see Scenic Location No. 75, p. 235) are two—Hagerman is especially historic. This old railroad bed actually reached the other side of the Continental Divide through a tunnel, not over the pass itself. The pass bisects the Holy Cross, Hunter-Fryingpan, and Mount Massive Wildernesses, so the views to the north and south are spectacular. Summer wildflowers are ubiquitous, and the drive along the Fryingpan River is a treat. From Leadville, go west on 6th Street to Turquoise Reservoir Road. Drive around the south side of the lake and watch for the fork to the left onto Forest Road 105 and the signs to Hagerman Pass. On the west side of the pass, you end up on Fryingpan River Road and eventually at the town of Basalt. Take a four-wheel drive.

Hagerman Pass is a summer place, especially after the Fourth of July when things begin to grow again. On the way up, look for signs for the trailhead to Windsor Lake. You can reach the lake in less than a mile, and it's well worth the hike. Back in your vehicle as you approach the pass, you enter the alpine zone, so be on the lookout for tundra flowers. On top of the pass you will have views of the peaks of the surrounding wildernesses. Flowers in the foreground with peaks behind make a great composition. Sunrise and sunset on a clear day slant at right angles to the north and south compositions that you will favor, so the shadows will be long and the light on the peaks dramatic. You see a few pretty groves of aspen on the way down the west side, but I suggest incorporating the Fryingpan River in your photographs as you head to Basalt. The cottonwoods along the way decorate this famous fly-fishing river.

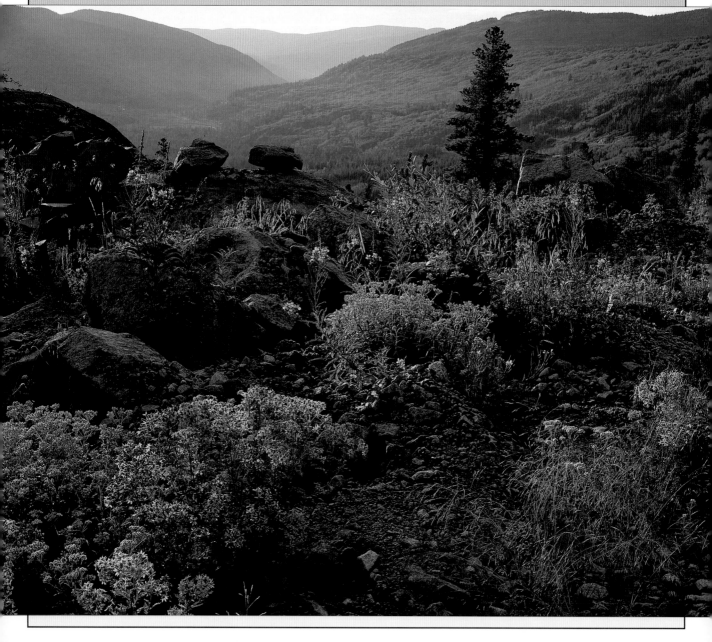

intersection, turn right (north) and go 3 miles to FR 107. All of these trips are relatively easy.

The 2.3-mile (one way) **Chalk Mountain Road** winds to the top of Chalk Mountain to views of the Mount of the Holy Cross, Chicago Ridge, and the Climax Mine. Go north on US 24 to the CO 91 intersection, then go 9 miles on CO 91 toward Climax. Turn onto Chalk Mountain Road (FR 134). **Mining District Road** begins where the pavement on East 7th Street ends, just past the Matchless Mine. This moderate 11.5-mile route is a partial loop past mines and historic buildings, ending on County Road 6, which returns you to Leadville.

At 13,186 feet, **Mosquito Pass** (see Scenic Location No. 70, p. 222) is the highest vehicular pass in North America and may be as famous as the Leadville-area mines to which it owes its existence. This lofty pass is also the midpoint destination of an annual pack-burro race (see Special Events, p. 229). To get to Mosquito Pass Road from Leadville, go east on 7th Street. *For information and maps: Leadville Chamber of Commerce, 809 Harrison Ave., 719-486-3900, www.leadvilleusa.com.*

GOLF

Mount Massive Golf Course, 3.5 miles west of Leadville on Turquoise Lake Road, combines great golfing with views of the Sawatch, Collegiate, and Mosquito Ranges. You can say you played at North America's highest golf course! *719-486-2176.*

HIKING

West Tennessee Lakes Trail EASY takes you through the Holy Cross Wilderness to an unnamed alpine lake at the base of the old Homestake Mine. This trail also connects to several small waterfalls and the West Tennessee Lakes. To reach the trailhead, take US 24 north 10 miles from Leadville to Lily Lake Road (Forest Road 100). Turn left, continue 2 miles, and park. The last section of the road is a bit rough; park low-clearance vehicles at the end of the graded dirt road.

The 4.5-mile (one way) **Lonesome Lake Trail** MODERATE leads to a high alpine lake in the Holy Cross Wilderness with wildflowers, wildlife, and fishing. To reach the trail, go north on US 24, 10 miles past the summit of Tennessee Pass to the junction with Homestake Reservoir Road (FR 703). Turn left (southwest) and go 10 miles, past Gold Park campground, to the junction. Park at the reservoir and look for the trailhead sign next to the East Fork of Homestake Creek.

If you want to "bag" 14,433-foot Mount Elbert, the highest mountain in Colorado, you have several options. The 4.5-mile (one way) **North Mount Elbert Trail** DIFFICULT is shorter, but the 5.5-mile **South Mount Elbert Trail** DIFFICULT is more merciful. To reach the North Trail from Leadville, go 2 miles west on US 24. Head right (west) on CO 300 (US 24 will bear south) for 1 mile, then turn left (south) on Halfmoon Creek Road (FR 110) and go 6 miles to the Halfmoon campground parking area (see Scenic Location No. 72, p. 228). To reach the South Trail from Leadville, go 14 miles south on US 24, turn right (west) on CO 82, and continue 3.5 miles. Turn right (north) onto County Road 24 to the Lakeview campground. Four-wheel-drive vehicles with high clearance can continue to the overlook at the end of the road. Note that you will be sharing some of the trails at lower elevations with mountain bikers and vehicles.

RAILROAD

Ride the rail to see Mount Elbert, Colorado's highest mountain. The 2.5-hour **Colorado & Southern Railroad** route goes round-trip from the Leadville Depot, along the headwaters of the Arkansas River, up to Fremont Pass, and into French Gulch. *326 E. 7th St., 719-486-3936, www.leadville-train.com.*

THEATER

The **Tabor Opera House** presents *The Ballad of Baby Doe* every summer, a fine operatic rendering of the famous love triangle. The storied opera house also presents concert performances throughout the warmer months. *308 Harrison Ave., 719-486-8409.* For those not operatically inclined, **Healy House** offers a live presentation by actress Melva Touchette on the life of Baby Doe. *912 Harrison Ave., 719-486-0487.*

WINTER SPORTS

One of the best-kept secrets in Colorado, **Ski Cooper** is a full-service ski resort complete with a ski school, nursery, cafeteria, and rental shop. Ski Cooper encompasses the area where the 10th Mountain Division trained and offers 26 runs for skiers of all levels. Lift lines are short, ticket prices are reasonable, and the powder is great! Ski Cooper's **Piney Creek Nordic Center** provides 25 kilometers of cross-country trails; you can also take the **Chicago Ridge Snowcat Tour.** To reach Ski Cooper from Leadville, take US 24 north to Tennessee Pass. The ski area is on the right (east). *719-486-2277, www.skicooper.com.*

Many cross-country trails start just west of the **Tennessee Pass** summit, including the 7-mile **Mitchell Creek Loop** EASY and the **Powder Hound** and **Treeline Loops** MODERATE. The **10th Mountain Division Hut Association** has four huts along cross-country trails in the Leadville area. *10th Mountain Division Hut Association, 970-925-5775, www.huts.org.*
For information and maps: Leadville Ranger District Office, 810 Front St., 719-486-0749.

Restaurants

Quincy's Steak & Spirits ($-$$) serves great steaks and prime rib at reasonable prices. *416 Harrison Ave., 719-486-9765.* If you're in the mood for Italian, try the new **Zichittella's** ($$). *422 Harrison Ave., 719-486-1298.* A great place for breakfast or a family dinner, the **Golden Burro Café & Lounge** ($-$$) boasts homemade pies and cinnamon rolls. *710 Harrison Ave., 719-486-1239.* If you like good Mexican food and great margaritas, try the popular **Grill Bar and Café** ($-$$). *715 Elm St., 719-486-9930.* **Provin' Grounds Coffee & Bakery** ($) features organic fair trade coffee and teas as well as fresh baked

HALFMOON CREEK

I found out about Halfmoon Creek a few years ago when exploring the Mount Massive Wilderness for the first time. The creek descends the east side of the Sawatch Range southwest of Leadville and flows between Mount Massive (14,421 feet) and Mount Elbert (14,433 feet), Colorado's highest peak. This drainage is incredibly scenic, not so much for Massive and Elbert, which aren't visible from the best part of the creek, but for the peaks along the Continental Divide to the west. From Leadville, go 2 miles west on US 24. Head right (west) on CO 300 (US 24 will bear south) for 1 mile, then turn left (south) on Halfmoon Creek Road (FR 110).The road is fine for a car just past the Halfmoon campground.

Enjoy the fine views of Massive and Elbert before you enter the forest, but just after the campground the scenery turns sublime. Drive a short distance up the hill until you spy views west up the creek through spectacular meadows. Park your car and walk down to the creek, which meanders through the meadow. Several places allow you to compose an image right in front of the creek. You can also frame trees on either side as the creek disappears into the peaks along the Continental Divide. You are facing due west, so sunrise might project your shadow into the scene—a no-no. On the other hand, sunset produces brilliant backlighting of the tall meadow grasses. In such a case, you'll need to shade the lens with your hand so as to eliminate any lens flares, those multicolored, hexagonal shapes that will ruin a photograph. Be careful not to get your hand into the photograph (see p. 129, *Photographing the Landscape*)! This place boasts lots of wildflowers in summer.

pastries and breads. Stop in for breakfast or for an afternoon treat. *508 Harrison Ave., 719-486-0797.* Another good place for a hearty breakfast is **Doc Holliday's Bar & Grill** ($-$$). *316 Harrison Ave., 719-486-3020.* For great family dining and hearty American classics, check out **Callaway's Restaurant & Bar** ($$) at the historic Delaware Hotel. *700 Harrison Ave., 719-486-1418, www.delawarehotel.com.*

For a unique dining experience, meet at the Piney Creek Nordic Center at Ski Cooper (for directions, see Winter Sports, p. 227) and take the 1-mile route by jeep, mountain bike, snowmobile, or cross-country skis to the **Tennessee Pass Cookhouse** ($$$$). Sit back in this luxurious yurt and enjoy spectacular views and four-course gourmet dinners that include elk tenderloin, rack of lamb, salmon, roast chicken, and vegetarian dishes. Reservations required. *719-486-8114.*

Accommodations

Leadville's historic **Delaware Hotel** ($-$$), 700 Harrison Ave., provides all the modern conveniences, including cable and a Jacuzzi, in the midst of Victorian lace curtains, crystal chandeliers, and oak paneling. *719-486-1418, www.delawarehotel.com.* Leadville has some wonderful Victorian B&Bs where the hosts really go out of their way to make your stay special. Built with lumber salvaged from Leadville's Ice Palace, the elegant **Ice Palace Inn Bed & Breakfast** ($-$$), 813 Spruce St., provides a gourmet breakfast that includes German apple pancakes. *719-486-8272, www.icepalaceinn.com.* For seclusion, scenery, and access to recreation, I highly recommend the **Mount Elbert Lodge** ($), 4.5 miles west of Twin Lakes on CO 82. Encircled by national forest, this B&B connects to the Black Cloud Trail, which ascends Mount Elbert. *719-486-0594, www.mount-elbert.com.*

Special Events

For a flashback to Leadville's mining heyday, attend the annual **Boom Days** celebration on the first weekend in August. Residents in period costumes participate in mining events and competitions. A parade, costume contest, and the famous **International Pack Burro Race** over Mosquito Pass highlight the weekend. *719-486-3900, www.leadville.com/boomdays.*

The annual **Leadville Trail 100 Ultra Marathon** was founded 25 years ago by Ken Chlouber as a way to drive tourism in Leadville. The trail, a fifty-mile out and back outdoor course, takes runners 12,620 feet above sea level in a grueling race of endurance.

The **Leadville Trail 100 Mountain Bike,** added in 1994, has grown to become one of the most popular mountain biking marathon events of all time. Each year, 1,400 cyclists compete for the title of Leadville 100 Winner. Citizen Pictures' 2009 documentary, *Race Across the Sky—The Leadville 100,* follows six-time champion Dave Wiens and seven-time Tour de France winner Lance Armstrong, as well as many other cyclists both professional and amateur, as they race 100 miles to the finish line. *For information: 719-486-3502, www.leadvilletrail100.com*

For More Information

Leadville Chamber of Commerce, *809 Harrison Ave., 719-486-3900, www.leadvilleusa.com.*

Buena Vista/Salida

Colorado Atlas & Gazetteer pp. 47–48, 59–60

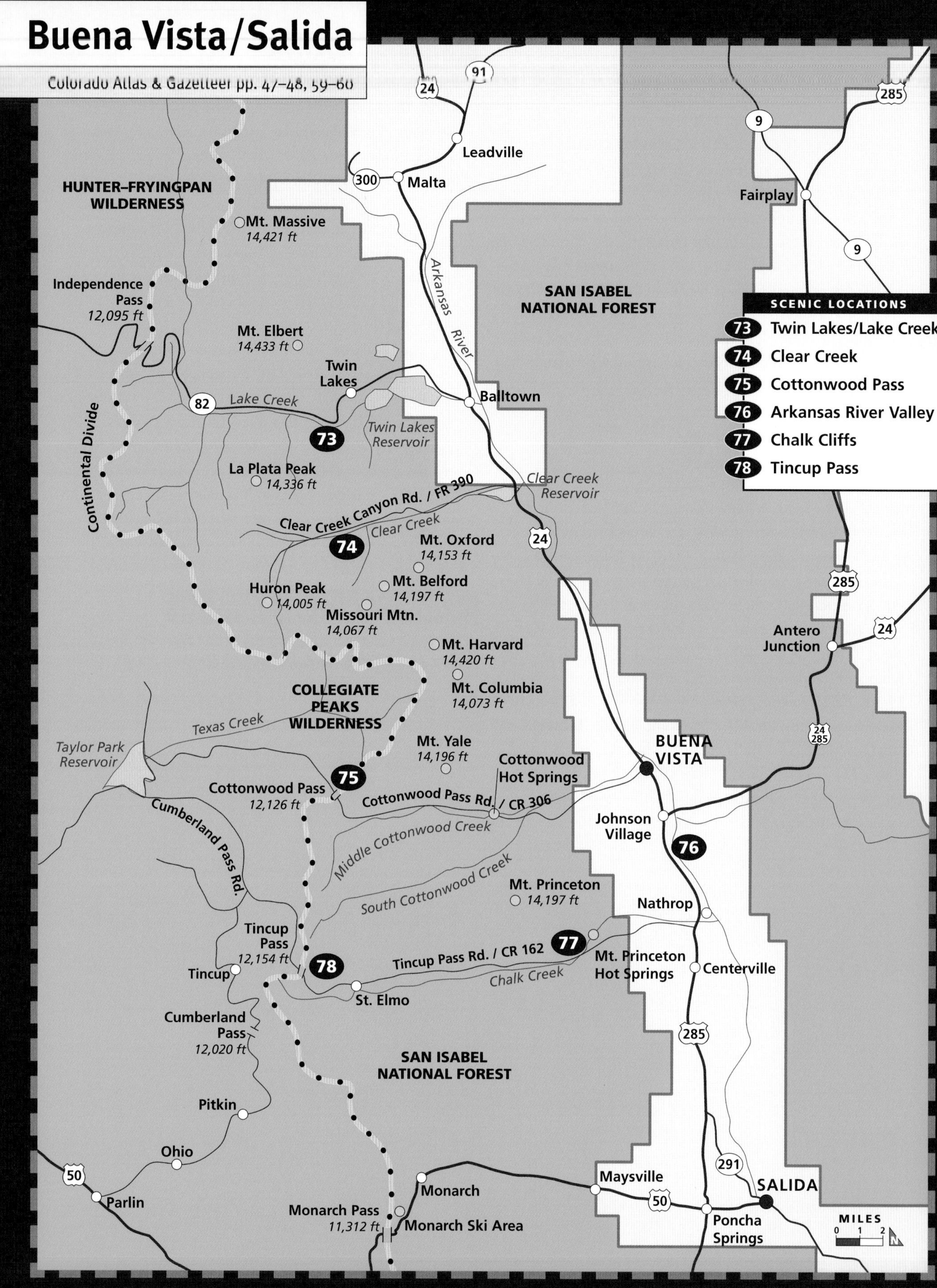

HUNTER–FRYINGPAN WILDERNESS
Mt. Massive 14,421 ft
Independence Pass 12,095 ft
Mt. Elbert 14,433 ft
Twin Lakes
Lake Creek
Twin Lakes Reservoir
La Plata Peak 14,336 ft
Continental Divide
Clear Creek Canyon Rd. / FR 390
Clear Creek
Clear Creek Reservoir
Mt. Oxford 14,153 ft
Mt. Belford 14,197 ft
Huron Peak 14,005 ft
Missouri Mtn. 14,067 ft
Mt. Harvard 14,420 ft
Mt. Columbia 14,073 ft
COLLEGIATE PEAKS WILDERNESS
Texas Creek
Taylor Park Reservoir
Mt. Yale 14,196 ft
Cottonwood Hot Springs
Cottonwood Pass 12,126 ft
Cottonwood Pass Rd. / CR 306
Cumberland Pass Rd.
Middle Cottonwood Creek
South Cottonwood Creek
Mt. Princeton 14,197 ft
Tincup Pass 12,154 ft
Tincup
Tincup Pass Rd. / CR 162
Chalk Creek
St. Elmo
Mt. Princeton Hot Springs
Nathrop
Centerville
Cumberland Pass 12,020 ft
SAN ISABEL NATIONAL FOREST
Pitkin
Ohio
Parlin
Monarch
Monarch Pass 11,312 ft
Monarch Ski Area
Maysville
Poncha Springs
SALIDA
BUENA VISTA
Johnson Village
Antero Junction
Leadville
Malta
Arkansas River
Balltown
SAN ISABEL NATIONAL FOREST
Fairplay
24
91
300
82
285
9
50
291
MILES 0 1 2
SCENIC LOCATIONS
73 Twin Lakes/Lake Creek
74 Clear Creek
75 Cottonwood Pass
76 Arkansas River Valley
77 Chalk Cliffs
78 Tincup Pass

Buena Vista and Salida

From Buena Vista south to Salida, cattle ranches define the Upper Arkansas Valley (see Scenic Location No. 76, p. 236), hemmed in by the headwaters of the Arkansas River to the east and the magnificent 14,000-plus-foot summits of the Collegiate Peaks to the west. This land of flowing water and cloud-piercing mountains is a great place to fish, raft, hike, and explore Colorado's rich mining heritage.

From Denver, take US 285 southwest 104 miles to Antero Junction, where US 285 joins US 24. Continue 13 miles over Trout Creek Pass to a three-way junction just past the small town of Johnson Village. From here, Buena Vista is 2.5 miles to the north on US 24 and Salida is to the south; to reach Salida, follow the Arkansas River south for 14 miles, turning left on CO 291, which leads right into the heart of town.

History

Although linked by a river and a mountain range, the towns of Buena Vista and Salida have distinct histories. In 1864, Buena Vista (Spanish for "good view") was established as a supply town serving the rich mining camps north toward Leadville and south up Chalk Creek Canyon. The Upper Arkansas Valley also drew farmers and ranchers attracted by the availability of water.

In the mid-1880s the Denver & Rio Grande Railroad came to Salida (Spanish for "gateway" or "exit") and left a railroad supply center for farmers and ranchers in its wake. The railroad later laid track as far as Buena Vista and even bored through the solid rock of the Continental Divide to create the historic Alpine Tunnel, which connected the region's remote mining towns to the Gunnison Valley.

During its heyday, Buena Vista was a Saturday-night town, home to dozens of saloons, as well as the Palace of Joy at the Palace Vista Hotel. Owner Elizabeth Spurgen, known as "Cockeyed Liz" because of an eye injury, bought the bordello in 1886. She retired in 1897 to take up respectable married life, but even so, none of the churches in town would hold her funeral when she died at 72. Salida rival Laura Evans turned her bordello, in business until 1950, into something of an institution. Nowadays, other endeavors thrive in Salida, which enjoys new vitality as an artist colony.

The mighty Arkansas River, which first drew settlers here, still provides for the regional economy. After the decline first of mining and then later of the railroads, Buena Vista and Salida now depend on ranching and tourism, including sport fishing as well as a huge whitewater recreation industry. All thanks to this reliable Colorado river.

Main Attractions

ARKANSAS RIVER

The Arkansas River is the longest river in Colorado, from its headwaters at Turquoise Lake near Leadville through the Colorado Rockies and across the Eastern Plains, where it departs Colorado at the Kansas border. The stretch of river from Buena Vista to Cañon City is famous for its world-class whitewater rafting and trout fishing.

Fishing: The best stretch of the Arkansas for browns, rainbows, and cutthroats begins below Buena Vista and flows down to Cañon City. Fisherman's Bridge, between Buena Vista and Nathrop, and Hecla Junction, below Brown's Canyon, have easy access to the river but are also popular rafting put-in and take-out points. Commercial rafting guides make every effort to respect anglers, but rafting traffic in summer can be a problem; guided float trips designed for anglers provide one solution. *For information, lessons, and guided float trips: ArkAnglers, 545 N. US 24, Buena Vista, 719-395-1796 (summer only) or 7500 W. US 50, Salida, 719-539-4223, www.arkanglers.com.*

Rafting: The **Salida** river trip **EASY** is perfect for apprehensive beginners or families with children. This half-day to full-day trip follows the river as it flows near Salida, with views of the Sangre de Cristo Mountain Range and a taste of a few easy rapids. **Bighorn Sheep Canyon** **MODERATE** provides Class III and IV rapids; look for Rocky Mountain bighorn sheep along the red cliffs below Salida. The most popular raft trip along this stretch of river is **Brown's Canyon** **MODERATE**, which passes through a Wilderness Study Area populated with wildlife. Exciting Class III and IV rapids on this stretch include Pinball, Staircase, and the Widow Maker.

For more advanced rafters, **The Numbers** **DIFFICULT** and **Royal Gorge** **DIFFICULT** cross challenging Class IV and V rapids. The Numbers are 10 miles north of Buena Vista just off US 24. (For rafting the Royal Gorge, see Cañon City, p. 91.) Several rafting companies here can guide you safely down the river and educate you about the local history and wildlife. *Wilderness Aware at Johnson Village, 719-395-2112, 800-462-7238, www.inaraft.com; Dvorak's Kayaking and Rafting Expeditions, US 285 at Nathrop, 719-539-6851, 800-824-3795, www.dvorakexpeditions.com; Arkansas River Tours, Cotopaxi, 719-942-4362, www.arkansasrivertours.com.*

Activities

CAMPING

One of the best campgrounds in the area is **Chalk Lake,** with seclusion and views of Mount Antero, Mount Princeton, and the Chalk Cliffs. Because Chalk Lake is stocked, young anglers can find good trout fishing. Mount Princeton

TWIN LAKES/ LAKE CREEK

The Twin Lakes were natural until the lower lake was dammed. Now the inconsistent water level has left a "bathtub ring" around both lakes. Nevertheless, this remains an incredibly lovely place, with Twin Peaks, Mount Hope, and Quail Mountain forming the background for a reservoir/lake that seems to be perpetually blue. And if you want even more, you won't believe the waterfalls a short distance west along Lake Creek. Take CO 82 west from US 24, 14 miles south of Leadville. The lakes will soon appear on your left. CO 82 continues to Aspen over Independence Pass (see Scenic Location No. 79, p. 244).

If the water is calm, you can get great reflection images of the lake and mountains. Look for the turnoff south from CO 82 that takes you right down to the canal connecting the two lakes. From here are some good vantages looking west. Then get back on the highway and drive through the town of Twin Lakes. About 2.5 miles later, find the Parry Peak campground on the south side of the highway and park. Cross the bridge on foot over Lake Creek and proceed either upstream or downstream.

Downstream you'll find beautiful cascades and amazing rocks that form mini canyons along the fast-flowing creek (it really roars in May). Upstream you will discover even more dramatic waterfalls. Remember to photograph the creek in cloudy light, for two reasons: It's difficult for the film to manage the deep shadow and intense highlight of canyons in clear weather, and the highly reflective white water will lose its detail on film. Lake Creek is a good place to practice making "cotton candy" out of the cascades. To do so, you'll need to use shutter speeds slower than 0.5 second (see pp. 81–83, *Photographing the Landscape*). Visit in any season, but the aspens along the creek are especially lovely the third to last week in September.

Hot Springs (see Hot Springs, p. 237) is just down the road. From Buena Vista, go 8 miles south on US 285 just past the town of Nathrop. Turn right (west) on County Road 162 and continue 8 miles to the campground. **Cottonwood Lake** and **Cascade** campgrounds also command views of the rugged peaks. To reach Cottonwood Lake from Buena Vista, take Cottonwood Pass Road (CR 306) west 7 miles to Forest Road 344. Turn left (south) and continue 4 miles. To reach Cascade from Buena Vista, go south on US 285 for 8 miles and turn right (west) on CR 162. Continue 8.5 miles to the campground. *719-539-3591.*

If fishing and rafting the Arkansas are your focus, check out the **Ruby Mountain** and **Hecla Junction** campgrounds. To reach Ruby Mountain from Buena Vista, go south on US 285 for 5.5 miles to CR 301, turn left, then right on CR 300, and go 3 miles. To reach Hecla Junction from Salida, take CO 291 northwest for 7 miles to US 285 and turn right (north). Go 1.75 miles, then turn right (east) onto CR 194 and continue 2.5 miles. *719-539-7289.*

FISHING

In the valley, you can find plenty of fishing spots that are more peaceful than the busy Arkansas River. My favorite fishing in the area is up Chalk Creek Canyon off County Road 162, along **Chalk Creek,** and in the stocked **Chalk Lake** (see Camping, p. 231). **Brown's Creek,** a great area to fly fish for

CLEAR CREEK

Like Halfmoon Creek, Clear Creek traverses the east side of the Sawatch Range and reveals spectacular peaks along the Continental Divide. You'll even find a restored historic mining town at the head of the drainage. Go west on the Clear Creek Canyon Road/Forest Road 390, 1.5 miles south of the town of Granite on US 24, or 15 miles north of Buena Vista. The road is manageable by car to Winfield, after which a four-wheel drive is necessary.

I recommend skipping Clear Creek Reservoir on the left, just one more nondescript, manmade body of water. Proceed through the forest to historic Winfield. Most of the way you'll be driving along the beautiful creek. Before you get to the ghost town, look for beaver ponds, which make for great reflections at both sunrise and sunset. Beaver ponds are small, so the chance of wind erasing the reflection is less than when you try to do the same at a large lake. You are very close to the mountains, so you'll need to use a wide-angle lens to take in the peaks and most of the ponds.

Move on to Winfield and you'll see several restored 19th-century buildings that are lovely to photograph. Cloudy light tends to bring out the texture in the brown, weathered wood, although at sunrise the warm light intensifies these colors. With a four-wheel drive, you can drive to the Lake Ann Trailhead farther up the road from Winfield. Lake Ann is glacial green and one of my favorite alpine lakes in Colorado. You will really enjoy this very scenic hike.

native cutthroat trout, is south of Chalk Creek and descends between Mount White and fourteener Mount Shavano. Its waterfall is quite impressive.

Stocked with trout, **Cottonwood Lake** produces good-sized rainbows. From Buena Vista, take Cottonwood Pass Road (CR 306) west for 12 miles and turn left (south) at the sign for the lake. **South Cottonwood Creek,** just beyond Cottonwood Hot Springs Resort on CR 306, produces 8- to 14-inch rainbows and browns. Trout as large as 24 inches have been caught at **Ptarmigan Lake**. For small brook trout, fish the streams in nearby **Mineral Basin**. Ptarmigan Lake and Mineral Basin are 6 miles west of Cottonwood Lake and require a four-wheel-drive vehicle. Access **Hartenstein Lake** from the Denny Creek trailhead, 12 miles up CR 306 on the right. Take a 3-mile hike to the lake, which feeds into Middle Cottonwood Creek through Denny Creek.

North of Buena Vista, **Clear Creek Reservoir, Lake Ann,** and **Cloyses Lake** all contain native cutthroats. Clear Creek Reservoir—the only one of the four not requiring a four-wheel drive—is 15 miles north of Buena Vista on US 24. Lake Ann is 5 miles south of Winfield on the South Fork of Clear Creek (Forest Road 390, west from US 24). Be sure to stay on the trail that follows the creek or you might end up on top of Huron Peak! Cloyses Lake is 3 miles south of Clear Creek on the Lake Fork. Take FR 388 left (south) across Clear Creek in your four-wheel drive, but watch the water level of the creek, which can rise quickly in a summer storm. *For maps and information: ArkAnglers, 545 N. US 24, Buena Vista, 719-395-1796 (summer only) or 7500 W. US 50, Salida, 719-539-4223, www.arkanglers.com.*

FOUR-WHEEL-DRIVE TRIPS AND GHOST TOWNS

Founded as Forest City in 1880 as a nod to the surrounding terrain, the old mining town of **St. Elmo** served as a stop on the Denver South Park & Pacific Railroad line, supplying the Mary Murphy Mine as well as the mining camps of Tincup and Ashcroft. St. Elmo once had nearly 2,000 residents and was known as a rip-roaring "Saturday-night town." After the mines failed, St. Elmo declined and was deserted for many years. Today, the town has a few residents. From Buena Vista, head south 8 miles on US 285 past the town of Nathrop. Turn right (west) on County Road 162 and continue 15 miles up Chalk Creek Canyon to St. Elmo. Just past Mount Princeton Hot Springs, you will encounter the magnificent, white limestone Chalk Cliffs (see Scenic Location No. 77, p. 239) on your right. The reflection of a full moon on these cliffs is magical.

Heading up to St. Elmo, notice the evidence of beavers by Chalk Creek next to the road. To your left before town, you will see a turnoff for Forest Road 295, which can take your four-wheel drive to the railroad ghost towns of **Romley** and **Hancock** and to the **Mary Murphy Mine.** As you proceed up the road to Hancock, you will pass what little is left of Romley. Past Romley you will see a sign directing you to take a left-hand turn for the Mary Murphy Mine, which is 1 mile up this side road.

Tincup, which still hosts a small community of people, provides a great excuse for taking the four-wheel drive up and over **Tincup Pass** (see Scenic Location No. 78, p. 240). From St. Elmo, cross the bridge and turn west onto Tincup Pass Road, which was once a stagecoach road and supply route to the Gunnison Valley and commands views of the West Elk Mountains and 13,114-foot Fitzpatrick Peak. As you descend northward from the pass, you will see beautiful Mirror Lake just a few miles before town. Vary your return trip by going north to Taylor Park Reservoir and then east over Cottonwood Pass.

Vicksburg, another old mining town, is now maintained as a museum. From Buena Vista, go north on US 24 and turn left (west) at Clear Creek Reservoir on CR 390. Four miles past Vicksburg lies **Winfield,** once a boomtown of 1,500 (see Scenic Location No. 74, p. 233). Consider a commercial jeep tour of these two towns if you don't have a four-wheel drive. *High Country Jeep Tours, 121 N. Gunnison, Buena Vista (summer only), 719-395-6111, www.highcountryjeeptours.com.*

HIKING

Boasting more fourteeners than any other county in Colorado, Chaffee County is a mecca for hikers wanting to bag a fourteener or two. Although **Mount Princeton**, **Mount Harvard,** and **Mount Yale** DIFFICULT are challenging on account of steep slopes and high altitude, each can be summited without technical equipment. To climb Mount Princeton (6 miles one way) from Buena Vista, drive 8 miles south on US 285 to Nathrop. Turn right (west) on County Road 162. Go 4 miles, turn right (north) onto CR 321, and go 1 mile to the entrance of Frontier Ranch (CR 322) on the left. Park in the lot across from the stalls and paddocks. Hike up the road for 3 miles (or drive the 3 miles if you have a high-clearance four-wheel drive) and follow the ridge west to the peak.

The easiest way to the top of Mount Harvard is via **North Cottonwood Trail** through the Horn Fork Basin. Take CR 350, just north of Buena Vista, west 2 miles to paved CR 361 and turn right. In about a mile, turn left onto North Cottonwood Road (CR 365) where CR 361 bends sharply right. Take North Cottonwood Road 8 miles to the trailhead and follow signs to Bear Lake. Leave the trail east of the lake and climb to the top of the boulder-strewn peak.

Access to Mount Yale is 12 miles west of Buena Vista on Cottonwood Pass Road (CR 306) at the Denny Creek trailhead, just to the right of the road. Hike up **Brown's Pass Trail** and, after crossing two streams, watch for a small beaver pond on the left. About 200 yards past this pond, look to your right for a small sign and a path leaving the main trail. Follow this path, cross Delaney Creek, and go 0.5 mile to an open meadow. Continue past a steep section of fallen timber to an open area. Mount Yale will be directly in front of you. Piled rock cairns will lead you to the summit.

North Cottonwood Trail connects to trails leading to Kroenke Lake and Bear Lake, with options to continue up and over Brown's Pass or to the summit of Mount Harvard (above).

COTTONWOOD PASS

Like Hagerman Pass (see Scenic Location No. 71, p. 226), Cottonwood Pass Road crosses the great Sawatch Range and the Continental Divide at a very high elevation, in this case 12,126 feet. Unlike Hagerman, however, this road is manageable by car. In fact, it's paved on the east side and is an improved, if slightly bumpy, dirt road on the west side. For sure it's one of Colorado's most spectacular mountain passes, with amazing views into the contiguous Collegiate Peaks Wilderness and far off to the jagged peaks of the Maroon Bells–Snowmass Wilderness. Take Cottonwood Pass Road (County Road 306) west from US 24 at the stoplight in downtown Buena Vista. You end up in Taylor Park and eventually Gunnison.

The drive up the east side of the pass follows Middle Cottonwood Creek, a pretty route through forest. Look for pullouts where you can compose the creek snaking through the trees as a lead-in line. Remember, cloudy light will reduce the glare off the white cascades of the fast-flowing creek, thereby giving more detail and texture to the water. But the best of the scenery awaits you at timberline. Once you break out of the trees, you won't believe the views to the south of Jones Mountain and Gladstone Ridge! Flowers decorate the landscape beginning in July, which make a great foreground for a composition of the peaks. When you reach the apex of the pass 18 miles west of Buena Vista, you attain views to the north of the Three Apostles in the heart of the Collegiate Peaks Wilderness.

You'll need a telephoto lens to bring these far-off but dramatic spires into view. Or, just below the road on the west side of the pass, compose ponds in the flower-riddled tundra grass as a fine foreground with a wide-angle lens. Find a way to be on top of the pass at sunrise or sunset: The views to the north and south are at right angles to the low-lying sun, which makes for long shadows and dramatic lighting. The drive down to Taylor Park is lovely, but skip Taylor Park Reservoir, at least for photography. The drive along Taylor River, on your way to Gunnison, is more rewarding. Cottonwood Pass has some fine stands of aspen, so try to return during the last two weeks of September.

76 SCENIC LOCATION

ARKANSAS RIVER VALLEY

The Arkansas is Colorado's longest river, so naturally it transforms itself across various ecosystems: a snowmelt-fed creek in alpine zones, a roaring and dangerous river in several precipitous canyons, and a lazy watercourse on the Eastern Plains. Then there is one stretch where the river is the focal point among bucolic fields and meadows lined with stately cottonwood trees, a place that appeases a stressed mind like very few others—if you can block out the noise of the traffic behind you—and great photographs await. From Buena Vista, drive south on US 24 to its junction with US 285. Continue for just under 2 miles until you get the first good view of the Arkansas River meandering south through meadows and cottonwoods—this is the first time that you'll see mountains in the distance to the south.

When you spy this view, pull off the highway and carefully walk to the other side. You are quite a distance above the river, allowing you to see it for a very long stretch. Compose a scene with your standard lens looking south that includes the big cottonwoods in front of you and to the west of the river. This is a sublime photograph in mid- to late May when the leaflets are emerging and the colors of the trees are light green, and in mid-October when the leaves are bright yellow. Because you're pointing your camera south, both sunrise and sunset enhance the colors and create shadows that add depth to the scene.

Right after this view, the Arkansas disappears off to the east and eventually enters Brown's Canyon, Colorado's most famous river-rafting run. At Hecla Junction, 8 miles south of the town of Nathrop on US 285, turn east onto County Road 194, and see the signs to Brown's Canyon. Three miles later on this improved dirt road you meet the Arkansas. This is the place where thousands of rafters take out or put in their boats, but if you climb up the canyon walls, you can get away from people and discover wonderful views of the Arkansas as a rushing canyon river. After your visit, continue south on US 285 for 3 miles, where the river again makes a rendezvous with the highway. Park, cross the highway, and make a photograph looking upriver as the Arkansas exits a particularly beautiful grove of cottonwood trees.

Kroenke Lake Trail MODERATE follows the North Fork of Cottonwood Creek 4 miles to a stunning alpine lake. **Bear Lake Trail** MODERATE heads northwest for 5.25 miles through the Horn Fork Basin to Bear Lake. From Buena Vista, continue 3 blocks north of the stoplight on US 24 to Crossman Avenue (CR 350) and turn left. Drive 2 miles, then turn right onto CR 361. After a mile, turn left onto CR 365 in the middle of a big S-curve, and follow the road (four-wheel drive recommended) 8 miles to the North Cottonwood Trailhead. Take the Horn Fork Trail to the junction for Bear and Kroenke Lakes.

Brown's Creek Trail and **Wagon Loop Trail** EASY form a 3.8-mile loop including a small portion of the Colorado Trail. The loop winds through aspen groves and elk territory to views of fourteener Mount Shavano, the Upper Arkansas Valley, and the Sangre de Cristo Range. Beaver activity is evident along Brown's Creek, where the trout fishing is quite good. From Buena Vista, take US 285 south 12 miles to CR 270. Turn right (west) and follow CR 270 for 1.5 miles, where it becomes CR 272. Continue 2 miles to an intersection, then turn left (south) on Forest Road 255 and go 1.5 miles to the Brown's Creek Trailhead on the right. Hike along the Brown's Creek Trail until it intersects the Colorado Trail, then turn right (north). When the Colorado Trail meets Wagon Loop Trail, take another right, which will bring you back to FR 255. Follow the road back to your car.

To summit 13,114-foot **Fitzpatrick Peak** DIFFICULT, take the 1.5-mile (one way) trail at the top of Tincup Pass. The hike is steep, but the panoramic views are well worth the huffing and puffing it takes to reach the summit. From Buena Vista, head south on US 24 and continue south on US 285 to Nathrop (about 8 miles). Turn right (west) on CR 162 and go 15 miles to St. Elmo. If you have a four-wheel drive you can continue to the top of Tincup Pass (see Scenic Location No. 78, p. 240).

HORSEBACK RIDING

Travel back to the days of the Wild West and explore the magnificent country around Buena Vista and Salida on horseback. **Mount Princeton Riding Stables and Equestrian Center** offers rides along Chalk Creek and on trails overlooking the Chalk Cliffs. *13999 County Road 162 (west of Nathrop), 719-395-3630, www.coloradotrailrides.com.* Seven miles west of Buena Vista on Cottonwood Pass Road (CR 306), **Harvard City Riding Stables** offers scenic rides through pine and aspen forests beneath the Collegiate Peaks as well as ascents to high mountain lakes. *719-207-0976, www.harvardcityridingstable.com.*

HOT SPRINGS

From 1850, Heywood Hot Springs was a stage stop and hotel where weary travelers and prospectors would soak themselves on their way up Chalk Creek. By 1880 the springs, now known as **Mount Princeton Hot Springs,** served as a stop on the Denver South Park & Pacific Railroad. While the cash flow of nearby luxury hotels fluctuated with the fortunes of the mines, visitors continued to enjoy—and do so today—taking the healing waters on Chalk Creek. The soaking pool is kept at 102 degrees and the adjacent swimming pool at 92 degrees. You can reach both by walking through the original 1850 bathhouse, now listed on the Colorado Historic Register.

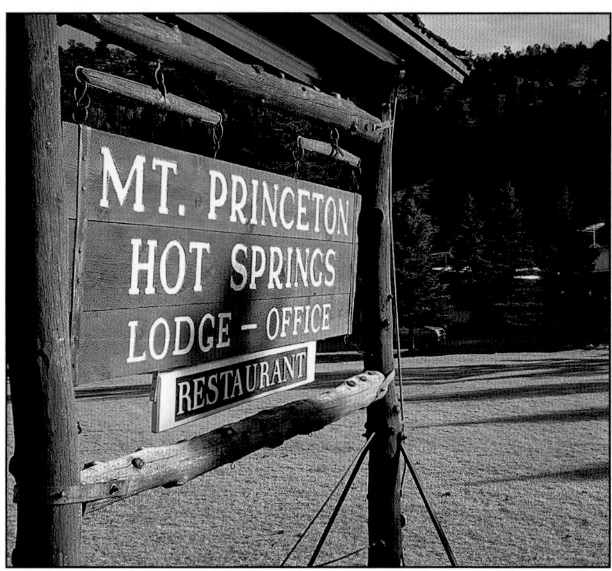

Mt. Princeton Hot Springs Resort, Nathrop

The best and most sought-after springs are sandy pockets in the rock pools along Chalk Creek, which disappear when the creek runs high. Unwind at the restaurant and lodging here, heated by the springs themselves. Reserve a room on the cliffs above and opposite the springs for fantastic peak views. From Buena Vista, go 8 miles south on US 24 and continue south on US 285 to the town of Nathrop. Turn right (west) just beyond Nathrop onto County Road 162, and drive 6 miles. *Mount Princeton Hot Springs Resort, 15870 CR 162, 719-395-2447, 888-395-7799, www.mtprinceton.com.*

Local legend has it that the Utes laid a curse on any white man who tried to make money from the hot springs on Cottonwood Creek, where Indians had gathered for generations. There may be some truth to the curse, as structures around the springs have twice been destroyed by fire. In recent years, however, **Cottonwood Hot Springs Resort** has again revived as an adult-oriented retreat. The largest of five soaking pools, the 104-degree Belly Pool was built from river rocks and is 5 feet deep and 20 feet by 50 feet. The smaller Hand, Elbow, Foot, and Painted Pools are kept at 106 degrees or a bit lower. Lodging, massage, a sauna, and hydrotherapy treatments are available. From Buena Vista, take Cottonwood Pass Road (CR 306) west. Go 5.2 miles to the sign on your right. *719-395-6434, www.cottonwood-hot-springs.com.*

Back in 1937, the town of Salida jumped at the chance to purchase for a mere $40,000 the rights to the hot springs at Poncha Springs 5 miles to the west, having watched that town use its spa income to weather lean economic times. Today, by virtue of a pipeline, **Salida Hot Springs Aquatic Center** is the largest indoor hot springs pool in Colorado. The temperature of the lap pool ranges from 90 to 93 degrees, the children's pool is 96 degrees, and the soaking pool is maintained at about 100 degrees. In a separate building, private European-style hot tubs are available for rent. Salida Hot Springs serves as a community center, with water sports, aerobics, and rehabilitation therapy available. *410 W. Rainbow Blvd., Salida, 719-539-6738.*

MOUNTAIN BIKING

Year-round mild weather and a local passion for the sport have made mountain biking a big draw in Chaffee County in recent years. You can ride trails off the **Midland Railroad Grade** MODERATE as loops or point to point, through piñon and juniper to views of the Collegiate Peaks. Much of the 8-mile (one way) **Midland Trail** follows an old railroad bed for a great introduction to singletrack riding. Most people park one car in Buena Vista and drive another up to the Shields Gulch trailhead. Take US 24 south, follow it left as it merges with US 285, and turn left onto County Road 315, which leads to the parking area and trailhead. Midland Trail dead-ends at a dirt road (turn right); keep your eyes out for the singletrack **Whipple Trail** on your left, which returns to Main Street in Buena Vista.

A singletrack stretch of the **Colorado Trail** DIFFICULT between Buena Vista and Mount Princeton Hot Springs has outstanding views of the Arkansas Valley. Portions of this route are also four-wheel-drive and graded roads. From Buena Vista, head southwest on Main Street, which becomes Cottonwood Pass Road (CR 306). Go 5.5 miles, turn left (south) onto CR 342, then right onto CR 345. Park here and begin your ride. You may continue driving on CR 345 to the Colorado Trail access point, 4WD but you may need a four-wheel-drive vehicle, depending on road conditions. Most people like to set a shuttle for this route; if you park one car at Mount Princeton Hot Springs (see Hot Springs, p. 237), you can enjoy a relaxing soak at the end of your ride!

The 28-mile (one way) **Monarch Crest Trail to the Rainbow Trail** DIFFICULT begins at the top of 11,312-foot Monarch Pass and continues over Marshall Pass along the Continental Divide before ending in Salida. The trail takes you above timberline and along stands of pine and aspen, with views of the valley below. You'll likely notice deer or elk along the trail, as well as signs of a beaver colony. From Salida, head west about 20 miles on US 50 past the ski area to Monarch Pass. Park in the lot on the south (left) side of the highway. Many trails weave along this route, so get a map before you go. *For information and maps: The Trailhead, 707 N. US 24, Buena Vista, 719-395-8001, www.trailheadco.com; Absolute Bikes, 330 W. Sackett, Salida, 719-539-9295, www.absolutebikes.com.*

SCENIC DRIVES

The Highway of the Fourteeners, the 19-mile stretch of US 24 from Trout Creek Pass southwest to Frenchman's Creek north of Buena Vista, takes you to stunning views of 14,000-plus-foot peaks. Nowhere else can you see as many of these giants at once, and at such close range. Enjoy the views as US 24 heads down to the Arkansas River and winds up the valley at the foot of the Collegiate Peaks Range.

At 12,126 feet, **Cottonwood Pass** (see Scenic Location No. 75, p. 235) preceded Independence Pass as the main supply route into the Roaring Fork Valley from Buena Vista and Leadville. As you cross the Continental Divide, you will have a breathtaking view of the Collegiate Peaks Wilderness, access to hiking and fishing trails, and opportunities to view wildlife. From the stoplight on US 24 in Buena Vista, go west on Cottonwood Pass Road (County Road 306) 18 miles to the top of the pass. From there, the dirt Forest Road 209 leads into Gunnison National Forest.

WINERY TOUR

Not all of Colorado's fine wines come from the town of Palisade in the Grand Valley. **Mountain Spirit Winery,** west of Salida, also produces award-winning vintages. Legend has it that a Native American princess gave herself as a sacrifice to end the drought of the lands below Mount Shavano. Apparently her sacrifice worked, for the fertile valley now produces many crops, including wine grapes. Public tours and wine tastings are available at Mountain Spirit Winery, 12 miles west of Salida off US 50 on County Road 220. Wine tastings are also held at Mountain Spirit Gallery, 201 F St. in Salida. *719-539-1175 (winery), 719-539-7848 (gallery), www.mountainspiritwinery.com.*

WINTER SPORTS

Monarch Ski & Snowboard Area has great powder and a diversity of runs from beginner to advanced. Monarch also offers snowcat tours for sightseers and backcountry skiers. From Salida, head 21 miles west on US 50. *719-530-5000, www.skimonarch.com.*

Old Monarch Pass Road, the Avalanche Trail off **Cottonwood Pass Road,** and St. Elmo off **Tincup Pass Road** serve as cross-country skiing and snowshoeing trails ideal for beginners and intermediates. To reach Old Monarch Pass Road from the Monarch resort, go west and look for the pullout and trail on the right side of the road. See Scenic Location No. 75, p. 235, for Cottonwood Pass, and No. 77, opposite, for Tincup Pass directions. *For information and maps: The Trailhead, 707 N. US 24, Buena Vista, 719-395-8001, www.trailheadco.com.*

ZIPLINE TOUR

Experience Colorado in a completely new way! The zipline tour at **Captain Zipline** was built four years ago and offers an adventurous view of the Colorado high desert and mountains that is like no other you've ever experienced. The tour features over 2,000 feet of cables through a series of six different ziplines all styled after the Costa Rican canopy tours. Thanks to Salida's mild climate, the zipline operates almost year-round. *For more information: 877-ZIPLINE. 719-207-4947, www.captainzipline.com*

CHALK CLIFFS

Other than the Sawatch Range to the west, the most conspicuous feature in the Arkansas River Valley between Buena Vista and Salida is the Chalk Cliffs. From the highway near Nathrop, to the west stand spectacular white cliffs at the entrance to a long and deep canyon originating in the Sawatch Range. The cliffs are a highly fractured zone of quartz monzonite whose white hue contrasts sharply against the dark green forest slopes of the mountain range behind. Happily, you can drive right up to the cliffs. Just south of the town of Nathrop on US 285, 8 miles south of Buena Vista, turn west onto County Road 162. You will see the signs pointing to Mount Princeton Hot Springs, just across the road from the cliffs.

A portion of the Colorado Trail runs parallel to the road on its north side and provides hiking access away from the developed areas along the road. From this trail, you can compose the Chalk Cliffs behind meadows and trees. Or you can hike the trails around Wright's Lake State Wildlife Area a short distance west of Mount Princeton Hot Springs. Chalk Creek and the lake provide great foreground for a composition with the cliffs behind. But beware: Just like snow and whitewater cascades, the cliffs are highly reflective of light. If you attempt to photograph the cliffs in the afternoon on a bright day, they will appear washed out. Wait for cloudy light if you want some texture and detail in the scene, or photograph the cliffs just after sunrise. The less intense, warmly colored light will bathe the cliffs in orange and yellow and bring out their texture (see pp. 120–122, *Photographing the Landscape*). Because the cliffs are so close to you from these locations, you'll need a wide-angle lens to contain everything in the viewfinder. Or put on the telephoto lens and zoom in on the cliffs. The many chasms and alcoves in these highly erosive rocks alone make interesting images.

When you are done here, hop into the hot springs or continue west to the old mining town of St. Elmo. Many historic and photo-genic buildings remain. Chalk Creek parallels the road and increases in scenic value as you ascend this old railroad bed to St. Elmo. Your car will get you there just fine; however, if you wish to continue west over Tincup Pass, you'll need a four-wheel drive.

TINCUP PASS

Here's the next way, south of Cottonwood Pass, to get across the Sawatch Range; just as for Hagerman Pass, you'll need a four-wheel drive to do it. A whole network of backroads west of St. Elmo takes you into historic mining country, and Tincup Pass (12,154 feet) traverses some of its best scenery. Along the way you can see 13,000-foot peaks up and down the spine of the Continental Divide, and the alpine wildflowers are easy to photograph from right outside your vehicle. Follow the directions to Chalk Cliffs (see Scenic Location No. 77, p. 239) and continue west to St. Elmo. From St. Elmo, continue west on Forest Road 267 over the pass and eventually down to Taylor Park Reservoir.

The ascent to the pass follows the North Fork of Chalk Creek through trees before breaking out into vast expanses of tundra. Look for flowers galore in July and August. On top of the pass you see Fitzpatrick Peak (13,114 feet) just to the south and Emma Burr Mountain (13,537 feet) off to the north. On a clear day they catch much of the warm light of sunrise and sunset and make for great background to whatever rocks or flowers you can employ as foreground. The descent on the west side of Tincup Pass takes you right by beautiful Mirror Lake. Park and walk around the lake in search of alcoves on the shoreline that protect the water from reflection-erasing wind. From such places you can make reflection photographs of the peaks to the east at sunset. From Mirror Lake the road follows Willow Creek down to Taylor Park. Look for creek shots along the way.

While you're in the area, another route to explore with the four-wheel drive follows Forest Road 295 to the old townsite of Hancock. Before you enter St. Elmo, bear left at the sign to Hancock Pass. At 12,140 feet, it's just as spectacular as Tincup Pass. You can even do a big loop from St. Elmo over Hancock Pass, then north over Cumberland Pass, on to the cute little town of Tincup, and back to St. Elmo over Tincup Pass. It's a wonderful tour reminiscent of the backroads of the San Juan Mountains. Yes, you'll also be treated to much autumn color the last two weeks of September along the lower stretches of these routes.

Grimo's restaurant, Poncha Springs

Restaurants

For beef and buffalo steaks and green chile chicken, dine at the **Buffalo Bar & Grill** ($$). *710 N. US 24, Buena Vista, 719-395-6472.* **Bongo Billy's** ($) is the perfect spot for a relaxing break. Enjoy pastries, soups, and sandwiches along with freshly roasted High Country Coffees. The Buena Vista café is on the south end of town off US 24, *719-395-2634,* and the Salida café is at 300 Sackett St., *719-539-4261.* Sit in a church pew (imported from Walsenburg) at the **First Street Café** ($-$$) in Salida's old red light district. Its breakfasts and Mexican dishes are favorites of mine. *137 E. 1st Ave., Salida, 719-539-4759.* Wood-fired pizzas and local microbrews (with root beer for youngsters) have made **Amicas** ($), formerly Il Vicino, a favorite Salida gathering place. I love sitting on a bench outside this restaurant on a typical blue sky Salida day with the sun in my face munching an Italian sandwich. *136 E. 2nd St., Salida, 719-539-5219.* At **Laughing Ladies** ($$) local artwork adorns the brick walls, and entrees include trout, grilled vegetable polenta, delicious salads, and desserts. *128 W. 1st St., Salida, 719-539-6209.* At the junction of US 285 and US 50 in Poncha Springs, **Grimo's** ($$) creates Italian dishes including chicken, eggplant, and veal parmigiana. Try the wonderful clams and stuffed mushrooms. *719-539-2903.*

Accommodations

The Adobe Inn ($-$$) is a Southwestern hacienda with a solarium, fireplace, and piano. *303 N. US 24, Buena Vista, 719-395-6340.* A reconstructed railroad depot in San Isabel National Forest, the **Trout City Inn** ($) doubles as a breeding and training farm for registered horses. On-site fishing and the Victorian saloon game room keep the entire family entertained. *Trout Creek Pass, 5 miles east of Johnson Village at US 24/285 and McGee Gulch Road, 719-395-8433 (summer only).* Among the pines on Chalk Creek, **Streamside Bed & Breakfast** ($$) is an ideal place to relax. Its location across the road from Sharon's Meadow makes for easy observation of wildlife. *18820 County Road 162, Nathrop, 719-395-2553, www.southwesterninns.com/strmside.htm.*

Centrally located in Salida, **Gazebo Country Inn Bed and Breakfast** ($-$$) is a flashback to yesteryear. Sit and watch the world go by from the quaint porch and savor the egg casseroles and breakfast puddings. *507 E. 3rd St., Salida, 719-539-7806, www.gazebocountryinn.com.* You can't beat the location, price, and porch views at the **River Run Inn** ($), which sits on 5 acres beside the Arkansas River. *8495 CR 160, Salida, 719-539-3818, www.riverruninn.com.* **Tudor Rose Bed & Breakfast** ($-$$), on a hilltop nestled in the piñon pines, commands views of the valley, national forest land, and towering mountain ranges. *1.5 miles southeast of Salida and 0.5 mile south of US 50 on CR 104 at the top of the hill, 719-539-2002, www.bbonline.com/co/tudorose.*

The Adobe Inn, Buena Vista

Special Events

It should come as no surprise that the "Whitewater Capital of the World" hosts an annual rapids celebration—**FibArk (First in Boating on the Arkansas).** In mid-June, FibArk kicks off with food and libations on the Arkansas outside the Salida Steam Plant (a historic powerhouse now a venue for live music and theater). A parade, arts and crafts festival, carnival, and live entertainment, not to mention kayaking and rafting events, draw whitewater enthusiasts from the Upper Arkansas region and surrounding states. *719-539-2068, www.fibark.net.*

The galleries of historic Salida, which display works of local and national artists, open their doors for the annual **Salida Art Walk** in late June. *719-539-2068, www.salidaartwalk.org.* Beginning in July, notable musicians from the Aspen Music Festival head over the mountains to play for residents and visitors in the Upper Arkansas Valley at the **Salida-Aspen Concert Series**. *719-539-2068.* In September, Salida hosts a bicycle race for enthusiasts of all abilities.

For More Information

Buena Vista Area Chamber of Commerce and Visitor Center (in the little red church), *343 S. US 24, 719-395-6612, www.discovercolorado.com/bvcc.* Salida Chamber of Commerce and Visitor Center, *406 W. US 50, 719-539-2068, www.salidachamber.org.*

Aspen

Colorado Atlas & Gazetteer pp. 45–47

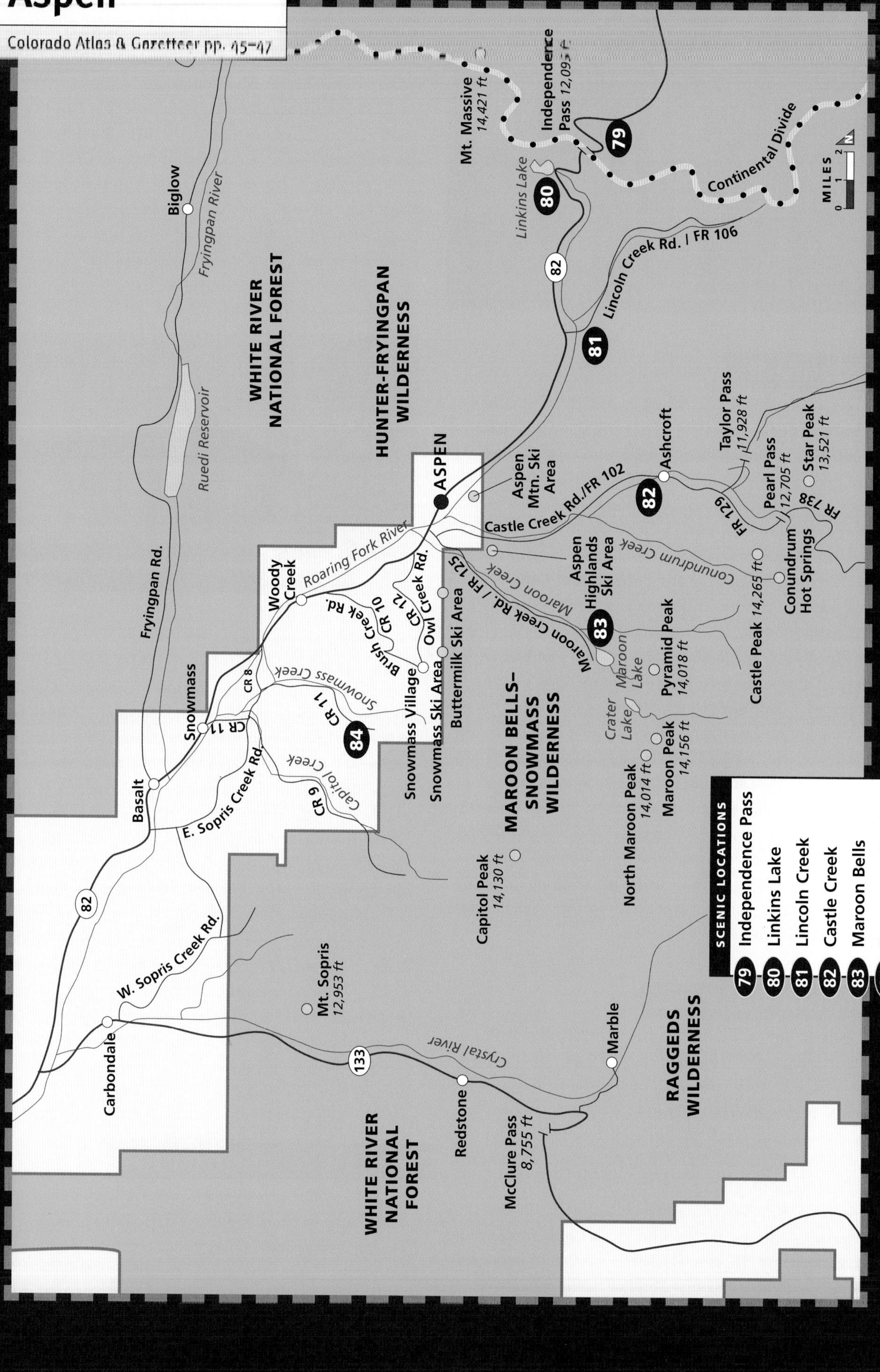

SCENIC LOCATIONS

- 79 Independence Pass
- 80 Linkins Lake
- 81 Lincoln Creek
- 82 Castle Creek
- 83 Maroon Bells
- 84 Snowmass Creek

MILES 0 1 2

WHITE RIVER NATIONAL FOREST

HUNTER-FRYINGPAN WILDERNESS

MAROON BELLS–SNOWMASS WILDERNESS

RAGGEDS WILDERNESS

ASPEN

Continental Divide

Mt. Massive 14,421 ft

Independence Pass 12,095 ft

Linkins Lake

Lincoln Creek Rd. / FR 106

Biglow

Fryingpan River

Ruedi Reservoir

Fryingpan Rd.

Aspen Mtn. Ski Area

Castle Creek Rd./FR 102

Ashcroft

Taylor Pass 11,928 ft

Pearl Pass 12,705 ft

Star Peak 13,521 ft

FR 129

FR 738

Conundrum Creek

Conundrum Hot Springs

Castle Peak 14,265 ft

Aspen Highlands Ski Area

Maroon Creek

Maroon Creek Rd. / FR 125

Maroon Lake

Pyramid Peak 14,018 ft

Crater Lake

Maroon Peak 14,156 ft

North Maroon Peak 14,014 ft

Capitol Peak 14,130 ft

Roaring Fork River

Woody Creek

Brush Creek Rd.

CR 10

CR 12

Owl Creek Rd.

Buttermilk Ski Area

Snowmass Ski Area

Snowmass Village

Snowmass Creek

CR 8

CR 11

Snowmass

Basalt

E. Sopris Creek Rd.

Capitol Creek

CR 9

W. Sopris Creek Rd.

Mt. Sopris 12,953 ft

Carbondale

Crystal River

Redstone

McClure Pass 8,755 ft

Marble

82

133

Aspen

Like many Coloradans who know and love Aspen, I have two different perceptions of the town. The first is of posh restaurants, palatial homes of jet-setters and movie stars, and ankle-length mink coats. The second, and the more compelling, is of the magnificent Maroon Bells; world-class skiing; great fishing, hiking, and rafting; cultural events; and John Denver songs like "Rocky Mountain High." With its distinctive historic buildings, many of which date from the late 19th century, Aspen has managed to preserve the undercurrent of a quaint old mining town, even as it promotes the glamour and resort elegance for which it is now world-famous.

Snowmass Village, Aspen's little sister down the road, shares many of Aspen's cultural events and festivals throughout the year (and hosts some of its own), it also provides more affordable dining and lodging options. From Glenwood Springs, take CO 82 southeast 35 miles to the turnoff for Snowmass Village at Brush Creek Road, or continue another 6 miles to Aspen. To get to Aspen via breathtaking Independence Pass, exit I-70 at CO 91 (Exit 195), go through Leadville heading south on US 24, and after 14 miles take CO 82 west over the pass. Independence Pass is closed in winter.

History

Unlike Vail, the state's other famed resort, which didn't exist prior to World War II, Aspen began as a mining town. Believing that Leadville's silver strikes could be duplicated farther west, prospectors began spilling over Independence Pass into the Roaring Fork Valley in the 1880s. Three mining towns popped up immediately—Independence, Ashcroft, and Ute City (later, Aspen). However, Aspen faced transportation problems in moving the ore to smelters. To the rescue came businessman Jerome B. Wheeler, who built a smelter in the region, which, along with the arrival of the railroad, transformed Aspen into one of Colorado's major cities by 1890. Wheeler also brought culture and class to the community, building Wheeler Opera House and the elegant Hotel Jerome, which remain among Aspen's grandest public buildings.

Wheeler Opera House, Aspen

The town's early prosperity was short-lived, though. The silver mines went bust after the Silver Crash of 1893; generations later, the deprivations of the Great Depression and World War II nearly made the city a ghost town. Another wealthy businessman, Walter Paepeke, saved the town this time. Paepeke was the head of a group of investors who founded what became Aspen Skiing Company. Marketing Aspen's ideal skiing conditions, the group succeeded in bringing not just visitors from all corners of the globe, but international competitions to the region's slopes as well. Champagne-powder runs have proven a major addition to Aspen's heritage.

Main Attractions

THE MAROON BELLS

The sculpted points and serrated, diagonal red rock layers of the Maroon Bells distinguish them from other eminent peaks in the West and have made them famous throughout the world. Known together as the Maroon Bells, **North Maroon Peak** and **Maroon Peak** both tower more than 14,000 feet high (see Scenic Location No. 83, p. 250), anchoring the **Maroon Bells–Snowmass Wilderness.** The lush valleys below these mountains encompass flower-filled meadows, aspen groves, and deep evergreen forests, in contrast with the soaring stone pinnacles above.

Many enjoy hiking the trails at the base of the peaks, particularly in fall when the changing aspens are glorious. The mountains look deceptively easy to climb, but the crumbly rock makes for poor footing; sadly, a number of people have lost their lives by underestimating the difficulty.

These semi-technical climbs require proper equipment and expertise (see Rock Climbing, p. 252). For a mellow hike through forest and wildflowers, take the 3.25-mile **Maroon Creek Trail** EASY, which begins at the Maroon Bells parking lot and leads to the East Maroon Portal, where a bus will return you to your starting point. The more challenging, 28-mile **Four Pass Loop** DIFFICULT winds through magnificent wilderness and over four 12,000-foot passes—West Maroon, Frigid Air, Trail Rider, and Buckskin. The trail begins at Maroon Lake and makes a great multi-day backpacking trip. (For more trails, see Hiking, p. 247.)

Maroon Creek Road is closed to vehicles during the daytime in summer, making it a popular 9-mile hiking and biking trail. Even so, buses run frequently along the road, leaving from the Rubey Park Transit Center in the middle of Aspen. Three small campgrounds lie off of Maroon Creek Road—**Silver Bar, Silver Bell,** and **Silver Queen.** From Aspen, go northwest on CO 82, turn left on Maroon Creek Road, and then go 5 miles to the Silver Bar campground. Silver Bell and Silver Queen are about 0.25 mile farther. *970-925-3445.*

Be sure to check with the Aspen Ranger District for information on backcountry conditions and obtaining maps. *806 Hallam St., 970-925-3445.*

Continued on page 246

INDEPENDENCE PASS

What a way to cross the Sawatch Range over the Continental Divide! The back door to Aspen, CO 82 may be second in magnificence only to US 550, the Million Dollar Highway, in the San Juan Mountains (see Scenic Location No. 137, p. 378). The views along the way are as sensational as those at the top (12,095 feet), which says a lot considering the summit's sublimity. From Aspen, follow Main Street (CO 82) east through town to get to the pass. From Leadville, take US 24 south 14 miles and turn west on CO 82.

I've already described a few of the things you can photograph on the Leadville side near Twin Lakes (see Scenic Location No. 73, p. 232). You remain in the trees west of Twin Lakes, but when you exit the forest, things really start to get good. The meadows along Lake Creek make a great foreground for the peaks that begin to appear as you approach the eastern base of Independence Pass. Once you drive the first big switchback to the left, you gain elevation quickly.

Lake Creek below seems to run eastward forever, so pull over and take a shot of this gorgeous valley flanked by the high mountains back to the east. Soon you begin to see the Sawatch Range peaks that define the edges of the pass. At the top of the pass, numerous tundra pools remain full year-round, while seeming to have no surface source of water. They offer remarkable reflections of the majestic peaks along the Continental Divide, which you'll want to photograph at both sunrise and sunset (see pp. 129–133, *Photographing the Landscape*). In July and August, wait for cloudy light in the afternoon to photograph the wildflowers that abound in the tundra. (Please stay on existing trails to preserve the fragile tundra.)

Descending the pass to Aspen, watch for dazzling views of the headwaters of the Roaring Fork River. From a couple of pullouts within a mile of the pass, you can position the valley in the middle of your scene, with peaks to the south framed by blue sky.

LINKINS LAKE

If you ever wanted to photograph a beautiful alpine lake within a legally designated wilderness without having to hike for miles, Linkins Lake is the one. Only a short, if steep, hike from CO 82, the lake sits on the southern edge of the Hunter-Fryingpan Wilderness and offers up immediate views of the peaks of the Continental Divide. Go 1.5 miles west of Independence Pass and park at the big switchback to the south, where you'll see trailhead signs for Linkins Lake and other destinations. Follow the signs to the lake, which is only 0.5 mile from the parking area.

Linkins Lake reflects the surrounding peaks, and although I enjoy photographing from its banks, I suggest hiking onto the ridge just southwest of the lake, where you will gain a view down to the lake. This perspective also better defines the edges of the lake than if you are right next to it. At sunrise and sunset on a clear day, the low-lying sun lights up the lake basin's green tundra, the lake is a startling sky blue, and the sky makes a perfect background. Remember not to include too much sky in your composition, particularly if it is a cloudless day. Too much sky can distract from the most important part of the scene—the landscape (see p. 61, *Photographing the Landscape*). If clouds linger in the sky at sunrise or sunset, I suggest going down to the edge of the lake and photographing their reflections. Catch the clouds when they are yellow, orange, or pink, and keep your fingers crossed that no wind erases the reflection.

When photographing the fecund wildflowers that grow around the lake, wait for cloudy light, which reduces glare and contrast, rendering richer colors on film. When you are done at Linkins Lake, continue farther into the Hunter-Fryingpan Wilderness. I highly recommend the trail that proceeds north from below the lake and takes you to Independence and Lost Man Lakes. Just go back down the way you came and look for the signs pointing to the left. It's less than 3 miles on foot to the spectacular divide that separates these two drainages from each other. You won't believe the views!

WINTER SPORTS

Aspen/Snowmass really consists of four distinct ski areas, each with a different personality, but all with great snow and diverse terrain. My favorite, **Aspen Mountain,** or Ajax, as locals call it, is home to the World Cup races. The mountain looms above downtown Aspen and is definitely for more experienced skiers and snowboarders. **Aspen Highlands** has thrilled skiers of all abilities since 1958. The view of the Maroon Bells and Pyramid Peak from the Olympic chairlift ranks as one of the most breathtaking sights in Colorado. Although **Buttermilk** has the reputation of being a beginner's "bunny hill," intermediate and advanced skiers flock to ski fresh powder on the challenging Tiehack run. Snowboarders love the Crazy T'rain terrain park. Although I'm partial to cruising Aspen Mountain, my favorite run has to be the Big Burn at **Snowmass,** which opened in 1967 and now includes four mountains, the Super Dragon half pipe, and three terrain parks.

Of course, as a ski resort, Aspen has all the amenities—ski schools, nurseries, and programs for little ones; rentals; spas; boutiques; fine restaurants; and then some. Bus and shuttle services run between the ski areas, and lift tickets are interchangeable. Aspen Highlands and Buttermilk are west of Aspen near CO 82. To reach Snowmass Village, take CO 82 north to the turnoff on your left for Owl Creek Road and drive about 6 miles into the resort. *970-925-1220, www.skiaspen.com.*

Cross-country skiing and snowshoeing have become quite popular along the area's backcountry trails. The **Aspen/Snowmass Nordic Trail System** EASY, suitable for beginners, is 60 kilometers of groomed trails that connect Aspen with Snowmass Village. *www.aspennordic.com. For rentals and information: Aspen Cross-Country Ski Center, 39551 W. CO 82, 970-925-2145.* If you seek fewer crowds, try the groomed trails of the **Ashcroft Ski Touring Center** EASY, just south of Aspen in Ashcroft, 12 miles up Castle Creek Road (see Scenic Location No. 82, p. 249). *970-925-1971.* **Aspen Center for Environmental Studies** offers informative ski and snowshoe tours for all ages and abilities at Hallam Lake Nature Preserve. *100 Puppy Smith St., 970-925-5756, www.aspennature.org.*

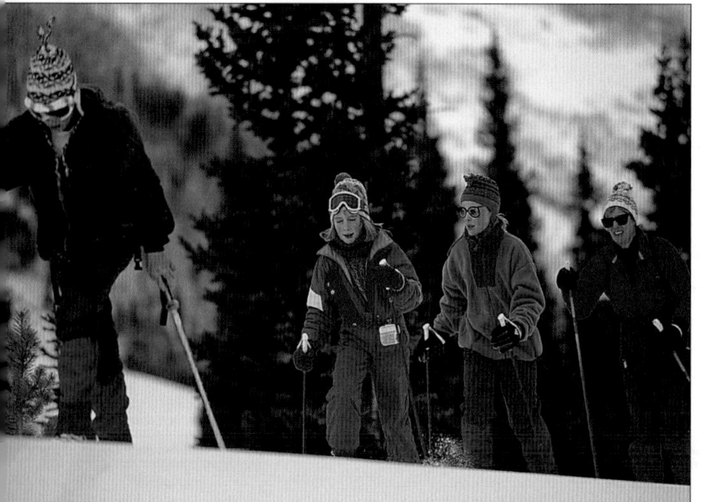

The Fielders skiing the Alfred A. Braun Hut System

For a prime backcountry skiing or snowshoeing adventure, explore the pristine expanse between Aspen and Vail. The trails connecting the **10th Mountain Division Hut System** link Aspen, Leadville, and Vail, and provide great routes for day trips. (Reservations for the huts are taken a full year in advance, so prepare to wait.) The **Alfred A. Braun Hut System,** made up of older, more rustic huts in the backcountry south of Aspen around Ashcroft, also has beautiful trails. In summer, these trails are popular for hiking and biking trips. *For reservations and maps: 1280 Ute Ave., 970-925-5775, www.huts.org.*

Activities

ASPEN CENTER FOR ENVIRONMENTAL STUDIES

A great educational and community concept, Aspen Center for Environmental Studies (ACES) offers public educational programs, including summer nature hikes around Hallam Lake and ski and snowshoe tours focusing on the winter ecology of the area. *100 Puppy Smith St., 970-925-5756, www.aspennature.org.*

CAMPING

Although the campsites on Maroon Creek Road are hard to beat (see The Maroon Bells, p. 243), several campgrounds provide privacy just off CO 82. Despite its name, **Difficult** campground is quite easy to reach, 4.5 miles southeast of Aspen on CO 82. Reservations recommended. **Weller** is 8 miles southeast of Aspen on CO 82, and **Lost Man** is 5.5 miles farther down the highway. No reservations. Although small and remote, **Portal** opens on a great location on Grizzly Reservoir. From Aspen, go south on CO 82 for 9.5 miles to Forest Road 106. Turn right (south) and continue 5.5 miles to the campground. No reservations. *For camping information: 970-925-3445.*

FISHING

The **Roaring Fork River** starts just below Independence Pass and descends 70 miles to Glenwood Springs, where it meets the Colorado River. The Roaring Fork teems with browns and rainbows and is quite accessible, as CO 82 parallels its course. The well-marked North Star access is just 2 miles south of Aspen. North of Aspen, reach the river from the Rio Grande Trail (see Mountain Biking, p. 250) to the upper Woody Creek Bridge. At the lower Woody Creek Bridge, public access extends upstream for 2 miles on the south side of the river. The Old Snowmass Bridge, 5 miles north of Woody Creek, also provides river access. Alpine **American, Grizzly,** and **Snowmass Lakes** are good fishing holes for hardy hikers (for directions, see Hiking, opposite). You might also consider reaching a trout stream or lake by horseback (see Horseback Riding, opposite). *For guided trips and information: Durrance Sports, 516 E. Durant Ave., 970-429-0101, www.durrancesports.com.*

FOUR-WHEEL-DRIVE TRIPS

Smuggler Mountain Road (see Mountain Biking, p. 250) grants views of these noble mountains, as well as a peek into Colorado's mining history. The rugged route over 12,705-foot **Pearl Pass** will take you to Crested Butte via Castle Creek Road. Because these are jeep roads, check with an outdoors shop to see if your vehicle is suitable. If not, go for a guided jeep tour. *Blazing Adventures, 105 Village Sq., Snowmass Village, 970-923-4544, 800-282-7238, www.blazingadventures.com.*

GHOST TOWNS

Ashcroft, about 10 miles south of Aspen on Forest Road 102, was once larger than Aspen. Horace Tabor financed the Tam O'Shanter and Montezuma Mines, and he and his second wife, Baby Doe, often visited Ashcroft. When the railroad came to Aspen, however, Ashcroft rapidly declined. Today, Ashcroft's small population caters to outdoor enthusiasts, particularly cross-country skiers and mountain bikers. Another silver town, **Independence,** 15 miles southeast of Aspen on CO 82, grew up overnight and at its peak had a population of more than 2,000 and no less than 10 saloons. Stop at the overlook and walk down into what's left. It doesn't take much imagination to realize how hard the mining life must have been in this harsh, high-altitude environment.

GOLF

The city-owned **Aspen Golf Course** is the best golf deal in Aspen. This challenging 18-hole course, just off CO 82, has a good driving range and, of course, a superb view of the Maroon Bells. *970-925-2145.* **Snowmass Golf Course,** under renovation until summer 2003, is part of the luxurious Snowmass Club—and priced accordingly—just below the ski area. *239 Snowmass Club Cir., 970-923-5600, www.snowmassclub.com.*

GONDOLA AND CHAIRLIFT RIDES

In summer, take the **Silver Queen Gondola** to the 11,212-foot summit of Aspen Mountain for panoramic views. You can lunch at the Sundeck Restaurant, then hike or bike down. Enjoy twilight barbecue dinners on Tuesday evenings. *970-925-1220.* At Snowmass Village you can take the **Burlingame** or **Sam's Knob** chairlifts. *970-923-2010.*

HIKING

There are several popular family hikes in the Aspen area. **The Grottos** EASY follows an old stage road, and you can still see the marks of wagon wheels on the trail. Farther up the trail, the Roaring Fork River has sculpted the "grottos," a system of river caves. From Aspen, take CO 82 just over 10 miles southeast to the campground sign on the right. Go about 1 mile farther, just beyond the speed limit sign, and turn right (south) onto the gravel road. Another family favorite is the 0.6-mile (one way) **Weller Lake Trail** EASY, which follows a small tributary of the Roaring Fork River along meadows of wildflowers. The trailhead is at the Weller campground (for directions, see Camping, opposite). **Hallam Lake Trail** EASY provides an educational nature hike (see Aspen Center for Environmental Studies, opposite).

The 6-mile round-trip **American Lake Trail** MODERATE takes you through wildflower meadows to a picturesque, high-alpine lake with stunning mountain views. From Aspen, go south on Castle Creek Road (Forest Road 102) and continue for 10 miles to the Elk Mountain Lodge. The parking lot and trailhead are on the right. The **Cathedral Lake and Electric Pass Trail** DIFFICULT is a 9.2-mile hike to a beautiful lake at the foot of Cathedral Peak, with scenic views of the Elk Mountains from Electric Pass farther up the trail. Follow the directions to the American Lake Trail but continue past the Elk Mountain Lodge. Just beyond Ashcroft, take the dirt road for 0.5 mile to the trailhead and park. The 3.5-mile (one way) **Grizzly Lake Trail** MODERATE commands views of the Continental Divide and accesses trout fishing. Follow the directions to Portal campground (see Camping, opposite), but keep your eyes out for a wooden fence and the trailhead sign on the right, with Grizzly Reservoir below, before the campground.

The 6.3-mile (one way) **Capitol Creek Trail** MODERATE leads to beautiful Capitol Lake at the foot of Capitol Peak. This hike will also take you through forests and wildflowers. Go northwest from Aspen on CO 82 and turn left at the turnoff to old Snowmass (County Road 8). Continue about 2 miles, then turn right at the intersection of Snowmass Creek Road (see Scenic Location No. 84, p. 253) and Capitol Creek Road. Follow Capitol Creek Road (CR 9) past the turnoff for St. Benedict Monastery, and head toward a rocky and bare expanse stretching from the distinctive Mount Sopris to Capitol Peak. Parking for the Capitol Creek Trail is 3.5 miles farther up the road; you will need a four-wheel drive to reach it.

The challenging 8.5-mile (one way) **Snowmass Creek Trail** DIFFICULT leads to pristine Snowmass Lake, encircled by stately peaks and home to rainbows and cutthroats. Take Brush Creek Road (Snowmass Village Road/CR 10) and keep to the right when you reach the rodeo grounds. Go under the wooden bridge just beyond the golf course and continue to the Divide Road intersection. Bear right and go about 1 mile on Divide Road until you reach Krabloonik Kennels. From here, follow the dirt road for 1.5 miles to an intersection and continue to the parking lot.

HORSEBACK RIDING

Capitol Peak Outfitters offers scenic half- and full-day rides, and pack trips into Maroon Valley, Capitol Lake, Williams Lake, Thomas Lakes, Hunter Creek, Woody Creek, and the Hunter-Fryingpan Wilderness. This is a nice, peaceful vacation option, and if you like to fish, take a guided horseback fishing trip. You just might have all the fishing to yourself! The stables are located at the base of Snowmass Village. *970-923-4402, www.capitolpeak.com/horseback.htm.*

HOT-AIR BALLOONING AND PARAGLIDING

Get an aerial perspective of Aspen and panoramic views of the fourteeners, valleys, and meadows below from a vantage like nowhere on earth. Look for wildlife and take in the endless vistas as you enjoy the traditional glass of champagne. *Unicorn Balloon Co., 406 B, Aspen Airport Business Center, 970-925-5752.* If you paraglide, soar over the Roaring Fork Valley with an adrenaline rush. A certified tandem pilot will help make your paragliding experience an unforgettable one. *Aspen Paragliding, 426 S. Spring, 970-925-7625.*

LINCOLN CREEK

This remarkable drainage, like Linkins Lake (see Scenic Location No. 80, p. 245), lies west of Independence Pass. Continue from the lake down CO 82 another 8 miles toward Aspen (or 9.5 miles southeast from Aspen). The first major road on your left will be Lincoln Creek Road (Forest Road 106). It "cherry stems" into the Collegiate Peaks Wilderness (i.e., the road is excepted from wilderness designation so individuals can still access private property and water facilities far up the drainage). While this is the wilderness' loss, it is certainly your gain, for the road takes you into a spectacular subalpine valley surrounded by high peaks. The rough route requires a four-wheel drive.

Look for the "grottos" where Lincoln Creek meets the highway. These sculpted granites are best photographed in cloudy light. By the time you reach Grizzly Reservoir, you'll see Grizzly Peak and other summits forming the head of the valley. Although the reservoir is not photogenic, the meadows beyond are carpeted with summer wildflowers. The road continues south past the reservoir for another 4 miles before dead-ending at the old Ruby Mine. The decrepit buildings make an interesting foreground for aptly named Red Mountain to the east. Several short, steep, but rewarding hikes to lovely alpine lakes in the Collegiate Peaks Wilderness take off right from the road. Truro, Petroleum, and Anderson Lakes lie in basins that contain some of the most profuse fields of wildflowers I've seen anywhere.

CASTLE CREEK

The next three Scenic Locations spotlight impressive drainages flowing from the Maroon Bells–Snowmass Wilderness into the Roaring Fork River—Maroon Creek, Snowmass Creek, and Castle Creek—and they're among the most beautiful places in this book. Each has an improved road that follows the creek and either "cherry stems" (provides non-wilderness access) or dead-ends at the wilderness edge. All three have magnificent views of the peaks of the Maroon Bells–Snowmass Wilderness, and each features trails into the heart of the wilderness. As you approach Aspen from the north on CO 82, look for signs to both Castle and Maroon Creeks at the roundabout just before you enter town. Castle Creek Road is suitable for a car as far as the town of Ashcroft.

Castle Creek flows fast and clear. Stop at the places where it runs under the road and compose a photograph of the creek winding south toward the peaks in the wilderness. Remember that cloudy, low-contrast light is best for photographing white-water. Five miles from CO 82, you'll see the Conundrum Creek turnoff on your right. Though the road doesn't go far, it ends at the Conundrum Creek trailhead, with access to the famous Conundrum Hot Springs. This 8-mile hike typically requires camping overnight.

Little Annie Road is 1 mile past Conundrum Creek on the left. The initial section is improved, and the road rises quickly in elevation. The views across the Castle Creek Valley toward Hayden Peak are spectacular. With a four-wheel drive, you can continue up this road until it connects with Forest Road 123 on Richmond Hill. From here, look to the southwest for great views of Conundrum and Castle Peaks. A little south of Little Annie Road down to Ashcroft, Castle Creek Valley opens up into vast meadows. From Ashcroft, you can take FR 122 to Taylor Park over Taylor Pass, or take FR 120/129/738 to Crested Butte over 12,705-foot Pearl Pass.

Both roads are extremely rough, requiring a four-wheel drive, and should not be attempted by novices. This is a land of creeks, peaks, summer wildflowers, and September aspens. Thankfully, Castle Creek Road is plowed in winter all the way to Ashcroft, so you have a great opportunity to photograph frozen landscapes and snowcapped mountains.

HOT SPRINGS

Conundrum Hot Springs has a picture-postcard Colorado setting, with Castle, Cathedral, Hayden, Hunter, and Pyramid Peaks towering above them and spring wildflowers flooding the nearby meadows with color. Three pools with water in the 100-degree range are perfect for soaking after the strenuous jaunt to the springs; note that the springs are clothing optional. Although a backcountry wilderness experience typically involving overnight camping, Conundrum can get very crowded. From Aspen, take CO 82 northwest 0.25 mile, turn left at Maroon Creek Road, then take an immediate left onto Castle Creek Road. Go 5 miles and turn right on Conundrum Road. Go just over 1 mile to the Conundrum Creek trailhead. An 8-mile hike will deliver you to the springs.

MOUNTAIN BIKING

In summer, mountain bikes replace skis and snowboards on the mountains of Aspen and Snowmass, as they do in most Colorado ski towns. The 9-mile (one way) **Maroon Bells Road** EASY is a popular route that rewards riders with incredible views of the Maroon Bells. (Although the road is closed to public traffic during summer days, buses run to and from Maroon Lake.) The 6-mile (one way) **Rio Grande Trail** EASY skirts the gentle valley of the Roaring Fork River along the old Denver & Rio Grande railroad bed. Start at Herron Park on Neal Street and continue 1.5 miles to Cemetery Road or, if you wish, all the way to the upper Woody Creek Bridge.

The area's premier mountain-biking trail is the 8-mile (one way) **Government Trail** MODERATE, which starts at the Buttermilk ski area and goes west to the Snowmass ski area. This ride can be extended to a 20-mile loop DIFFICULT. From CO 82 in Aspen, go northwest to Maroon Creek Road, then pick up the Government Trail to Snowmass ski area. After reaching Snowmass, you will ride another 12 miles, passing Whites Lake and the Buttermilk ski area, for the full loop ride back to Aspen.

The 8-mile **Smuggler Mountain/Hunter Creek Loop** MODERATE follows Hunter Creek through meadows with views of the Williams Mountains. Follow Cooper Street (CO 82) south out of town. Just after crossing the bridge over the Roaring Fork River, turn left (north) onto Park Avenue. Turn right (north) toward the mountain on Park Circle, then right (east) again onto Smuggler Mountain Road, also a four-wheel-drive road. For awe-inspiring scenery, take **Pearl Pass** DIFFICULT to Crested Butte. From Aspen, take Castle Creek Road to Ashcroft and follow the right fork (Forest Roads 120/129/738) over the pass.

Stop at Aspen Mountain's Silver Queen Gondola ticket office or Snowmass ski area's Burlingame and Sam's Knob chairlifts for trail maps. The **Top to the Tavern** ride, from the top of Silver Queen down to Woody Creek Tavern, is a local favorite to a legendary bar. Aspen and Snowmass have an abundance of excellent bike shops, some of which offer tours. *For mountain biking information, rentals, and guided tours: Blazing Adventures, 105 Village Sq., 970-923-4544, www.blazingadventures.com; Aspen Bike Tours & Rentals, 430 S. Spring St., 970-925-9169; Aspen Alpine Guides, 970-925-6618, www.aspenalpine.com.*

MAROON BELLS

Believe it or not, the scenery along Maroon Creek, the next drainage to the north and west, is even better than that along Castle Creek (see Scenic Location No. 82, p. 249). One of the most photographed places on Earth is at the end of Maroon Creek Road—14,014-foot North Maroon Peak and 14,156-foot Maroon Peak (the "Maroon Bells") rise above Maroon Lake in a composition so eye-catching and symmetrical that it defies the imagination of even the most inventive painters. At the roundabout just north of Aspen on CO 82, follow the signs south to Maroon Creek Road. Be aware that during the peak summer season, you will have to take a shuttle bus from Aspen's Rubey Park Transit Center to reach the lake. Also, the road is not plowed in the winter, leaving spring and fall for doing your own thing.

And doing your own thing along this outrageously scenic road is essential. From many points along the way, you can make compositions of the creek as well as the lovely aspen groves in the valley and along the ridges defining the drainage. The third week of September is usually the peak week for autumn color in the Aspen area. Look for the East Maroon Creek trailhead on your left as you ascend the road. I recommend taking a day hike up this side drainage—the wildflowers, including columbines, only 2 miles up the trail are profuse and beautiful. If you don't take the trail, look for the views up East Maroon Creek from the road.

No matter what, save some film for Maroon Lake. On a calm, clear morning, when no wind ripples the lake, you can make a scenic photograph that will amaze your friends. Regardless of the camera, your image will look like a shot for a Sierra Club calendar. Stand at the eastern edge of the lake and compose a wide-angle shot in horizontal format, with the peaks at the top, the drainage ridges on the left and right, and foreground wildflowers in front of the lake. A tranquil lake will reflect the peaks perfectly.

In fall, the aspens to the left and right of the lake turn brilliant yellow, a beautiful accent to the blue sky behind the peaks. Remember to include only enough sky to provide the peaks some clearance from the top of the frame. However, if you are lucky enough to witness pink clouds at sunrise, you might want to add them, too. Before you go home, hike 2 miles up the drainage to secluded Crater Lake.

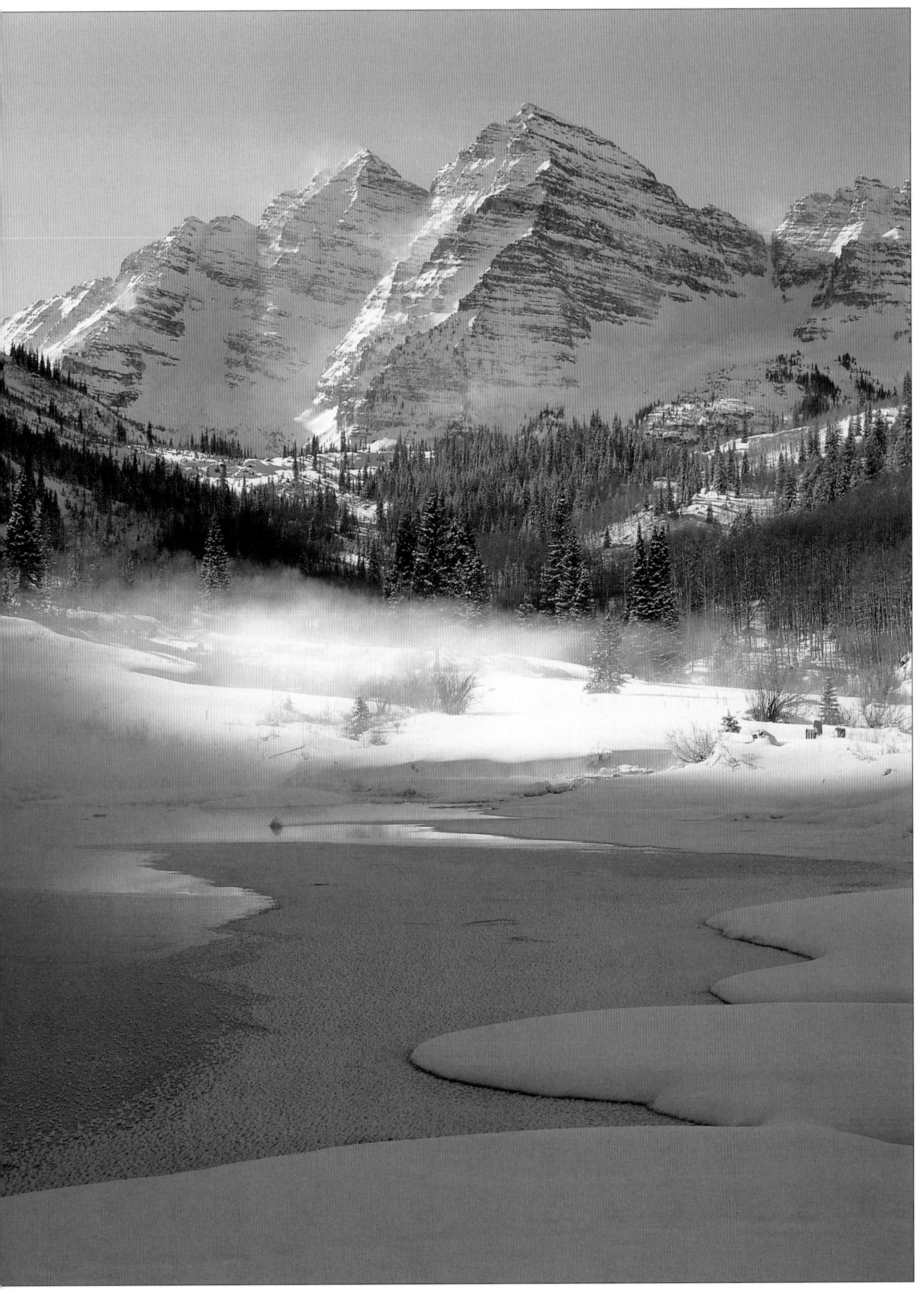

MUSEUMS

In many ways Aspen owes its existence to Jerome B. Wheeler, who financed Aspen's mining-era smelter and established Aspen's cultural identity (see History, p. 243). Visit Wheeler's 1888 home, now the **Wheeler/Stallard House Museum,** on West Bleeker Street. *Aspen Historical Society, 970-925-3721.*

Aspen Art Museum, 590 N. Mill St., showcases contemporary art and visiting exhibits in a historic building beside the Roaring Fork River. *970-925-8050, www.aspenartmuseum.org.*

RAFTING

The **Upper Roaring Fork River** MODERATE offers Class III whitewater, with the creatively dubbed Toothache and Toilet Bowl rapids providing a dash of excitement. More experienced rafters can tackle **Slaughterhouse Falls** DIFFICULT to see if they can pass the Entrance Exam rapids. *For guided trips: Colorado Riff Raft, 555 E. Durant St., Aspen, 970-923-4544, www.riffraft.com; Blazing Adventures, 105 Village Sq., Snowmass Village, 970-925-5405, www.blazingadventures.com.*

ROCK CLIMBING

Independence Pass offers 44 technical climbs on **Weller Slab, Grotto Wall, Olympic Crag,** and **Outrageous Overhangs,** all on the north side of Independence Pass Road. The Weller Slab is just above Weller campground (see Camping, p. 246), with the approach beginning on the north side of the campground loop. The Grotto Wall is about 1.5 miles farther up Independence Pass, across from Lincoln Gulch campground. Olympic Crag and Outrageous Overhangs are about 1 mile beyond the Grotto Wall. If you want to bag one or both of the **Maroon Bells,** contact local mountain-climbing stores. *Aspen Expeditions, Inc., 426 S. Spring St., 970-925-7625; Ute Mountaineer, 308 S. Mill St., Aspen, 970-925-2849.*

THEATER

Aspen's historic **Wheeler Opera House** presents the finest in foreign, independent, and revival films, as well as theatrical productions. Tickets for major events throughout the Roaring Fork Valley are available here. *320 E. Hyman Ave., 970-920-5770.*

TOURS

Take a walking tour 1,200 feet into the famous **Smuggler Mine,** opposite Aspen Mountain on, of course, Smuggler Mountain. The world's largest silver nugget was extracted from this mine, which is listed on the National Historic Register. *970-923-4544.* A tour of **Compromise Mine** on Aspen Mountain allows you to ride an 18-gauge car 2,000 feet underground; above is the Little Nell ski run. The four-wheel-drive shuttle service to the mine provides delightful views of Aspen and its peerless vicinity, while the tour affords a very different mountain view! *970-925-4049.*

Restaurants

For the unusual, try **Krabloonik** ($$$-$$$$), where you can take a dogsled ride and then order wild game and fine wine for dinner. *4250 Divide, Snowmass Village, 970-923-3953, www.krabloonik.com.* Ski, snowshoe, or take a horse-drawn sleigh to the **Pine Creek Cookhouse** ($$$$), and be rewarded with wonderful Colorado cuisine such as stuffed quail or pan-seared venison tenderloin. If you're cross-country skiing near Ashcroft, pick up a gourmet lunch. *Twelve miles up Castle Creek Road, 970-925-1044.* At **Syzygy** ($$$-$$$$), considered one of Aspen's top restaurants, you would think that the Italian, Asian, and French fare would be the star of the show—but just wait until you hear the late-night jazz and see the lengthy wine list. *520 E. Hyman Ave., 970-925-3700.*

Visitors from the coasts are amazed, but fine dining featuring seafood has come a long way in the Rockies. Besides excellent entrees, **Butch's Lobster Bar** ($$-$$$) must have one of the best selections of fresh fish appetizers in all of Colorado. *Timberline Condos, Snowmass Village, 970-923-4004.* Make your oyster bar the **Pacifica Seafood Brasserie** ($$-$$$). The patio is a great place to watch people on Aspen's pedestrian mall. *307 S. Mill St., 970-920-9775.* Nothing's better than hot sake and sushi after a day on the slopes. **Takah Sushi** ($$-$$$) fits the bill with a fine bar and fresh fare. *Hyman Avenue on the pedestrian mall in Aspen, 970-925-8588.*

With several fine seafood dishes and surf-and-turf combinations, **Steak Pit** ($$-$$$) satisfies, but save room for Mom's hot fudge sundae. *305 E. Hopkins Ave., 970-925-3459.* The hearty daily fare at the **Stew Pot** ($) warms you before an afternoon of skiing some Snowmass runs. *62 Snowmass Village Mall, 970-923-2263.*

Brunelleschi's ($-$$) offers a fantastic array of traditional and contemporary pizzas, pastas, calzones, and salads. *205 S Mill St., 970-544-4644, www.zgpizza.com.* For a family-friendly Mexican restaurant, **La Cantina** ($-$$) is a great choice. The menu features classic Mexican fare as well as some twists on the traditional dishes. A wide selection of tequilas and margaritas is also featured. *411 E. Main St., 970-925-3663, www.cantina-aspen.com.* And for the best burger in Aspen, **Little Annie's Eating House** ($-$$) is a must. *517 Hyman Ave., 970-920-1490, www.littleannies.com.*

Three of my favorite watering holes in Aspen are the **Hotel Jerome,** *330 E. Main St., 970-920-1000;* **The Little Nell,** *675 E. Durant Ave., 970-920-6330;* and **Bentley's** at the Wheeler Opera House, *221 S. Mill St., 970-920-2240,* which serves up history and après-ski vitality in this famous local landmark.

SNOWMASS CREEK

Snowmass Creek Road doesn't offer views of majestic peaks right next to the road, but it does wind through some of the most beautiful rural land in Colorado. Not that it wants for snowcapped mountains—they're just a little farther in the distance. About 3 miles south of Basalt on CO 82, keep a sharp eye out for a gas station on your right. This is the town of Snowmass—you'll see the sign—not to be confused with the Snowmass Village ski resort farther up the Roaring Fork Valley. Turn west in front of the gas station onto Snowmass Creek Road (County Road 11). Two miles later, bear left at the first fork in the road, which will take you along Snowmass Creek. The road remains improved for several miles, then becomes a four-wheel-drive route to its end at the Snowmass Lake trailhead.

The first 3 miles of road after the fork wind through ranchland, then the road ascends mesas, passing lovely aspen and cottonwood groves lining meadows along the creek, on its way to the edge of the Maroon Bells–Snowmass Wilderness. Look out for places where you can see 14,130-foot Capitol Peak and 14,092-foot Snowmass Mountain in the distance. Compose images that include the pastoral ranchlands in the foreground with the peaks behind. I especially enjoy photographing here around mid-September when the aspens begin to turn yellow and hay bales dot the fields. Once the road becomes too rough for a car, continue 3 more miles to Snowmass Lake trailhead only if you have a four-wheel drive.

Brilliant aspens line a scenic ridge, and views of the peaks to the west become more dramatic. Try composing with the road as a lead-in line winding through the forest. When you reach the end of the road, hike up the East Snowmass Creek Trail. Within 2 miles you will enter fields of wildflowers along the creek. If you have a 35mm SLR with a wide-angle lens, this would be a great place to practice extreme depth-of-focus photography, the technique that makes flowers in the foreground seem larger than they really are in relation to things in the background. "Stopping down" to your smallest aperture allows you to bring everything into focus, from a couple of feet before you to infinity (see pp. 109–117, *Photographing the Landscape*).

If you'd like to see more of this country to the east of the Maroon Bells–Snowmass Wilderness, check out the Capitol Creek drainage on your way back to CO 82. Just make a left on Capitol Creek Road (CR 9) 2 miles before you reach the town of Snowmass.

Accommodations

As you can imagine, Aspen and Snowmass are very expensive places to stay, particularly in winter. However, if you want to treat yourself, splurge and stay at the **Hotel Jerome** ($$$$). One of the most elegant historic places in Colorado, the Hotel Jerome strives to see that you get your money's worth. *330 E. Main St., Aspen, 800-331-7213, www.hoteljerome.com.* **Molly Gibson Lodge** ($$-$$$) has wonderful amenities, including a swimming pool, hot tubs, and convenient access to all of the activities in Aspen. *101 W. Main St., Aspen, 800-356-6559, www.mollygibson.com.* The **Hotel Aspen** ($$-$$$) is another luxurious place to stay, and depending on the season, you can get a bargain. *110 W. Main St., Aspen, 800-527-7369, www.hotelaspen.com.* You can't beat the location and off-season prices of **Mountain Chalet** ($-$$$), which sports a heated outdoor pool and a hot tub. *333 E. Durant Ave., Aspen, 970-925-7797.* **Redstone Cliffs Lodge** ($$) is cozy and on the river. *433 Redstone Blvd., 970-963-2691, www.redstonecliffs.com.* The same family has owned **Pokolodi Lodge** ($$-$$$) for 20 years, which is unusual in Snowmass Village, where luxury chain hotels are the norm. *25 Daly Ln., Snowmass Village, 800-666-4556, www.pokolodi.com.*

Special Events

The **Aspen Music Festival** is one of the best classical-music festivals in the state. For nine weeks—late June through August—the event features 200-plus musical performances showcasing more than 1,000 classical musicians. Venues include the Wheeler Opera House, Harris Concert Hall, and Benedict Music Tent, as well as churches and auditoriums throughout Aspen. Many events are free, and tickets for the other performances are well worth the price. *970-925-3254, www.aspenmusicfestival.com.*

Jazz enthusiasts flock from all over Colorado and the nation each summer to catch the premier jazz events of the summer at Snowmass Town Park. **Janus Jazz Aspen Snowmass** (JAS) attracts internationally known musicians for its well-regarded jazz series in June. The JAS Labor Day weekend festival brings in top performers of rock, world music, funk, and other popular styles for a dance-oriented, end-of-summer extravaganza. Free concerts and special workshops and programs fill out the rich musical stew. *970-920-4996, www.jazzaspen.com. For tickets: 866-527-8499.*

Snowmass Village Rodeo, Wednesdays only from late June through August, will delight everyone in the family. Beyond the broncos, you can enjoy rodeo parades and live music, pig out at the barbecue, and chime in at the obligatory campfire sing-alongs. Kids can pan for silver and take part in the calf scramble. The rodeo is held at the Snowmass Village Rodeo Grounds on Brush Creek Road (County Road 10) just before the entrance to Snowmass Village. *970-923-2000, www.snowmassrodeo.org.*

Scores of colorful hot-air balloons hang in the mid-June skies over Snowmass and compete in the **Snowmass Balloon Festival,** which includes music and a champagne breakfast, *www.snowmassballoon.com.*

The ever popular **Rocky Mountain Brewers Festival** goes down in mid-August at the Snowmass Village Mall, featuring more than 40 Rocky Mountain breweries. In late August at the mall, the **Chili Shoot-Out** brings out serious competitors to see who can make the meanest, baddest, and spiciest chili in the Roaring Fork Valley. You may wish that Snowmass Village had hosted the Rocky Mountain Brewers Festival at the same time as the fiery cook-off! *For information on the Snowmass Balloon Festival, the Rocky Mountain Brewers Festival, and the Chili Shoot-Out: Snowmass Village, 970-923-2000, www.snowmassvillage.com.*

For More Information

Wheeler Visitor Center (for Aspen tourist information), *320 E. Hyman Ave., Aspen, 970-925-1940, www.aspenchamber.org.* Snowmass Village Resort Association, *Upper Village Mall, 970-923-2000, www.snowmassvillage.com.*

Capitol Peak, as seen from Capitol Creek Road

Basalt/Carbondale Redstone/Marble

Colorado Atlas & Gazetteer pp. 45–46

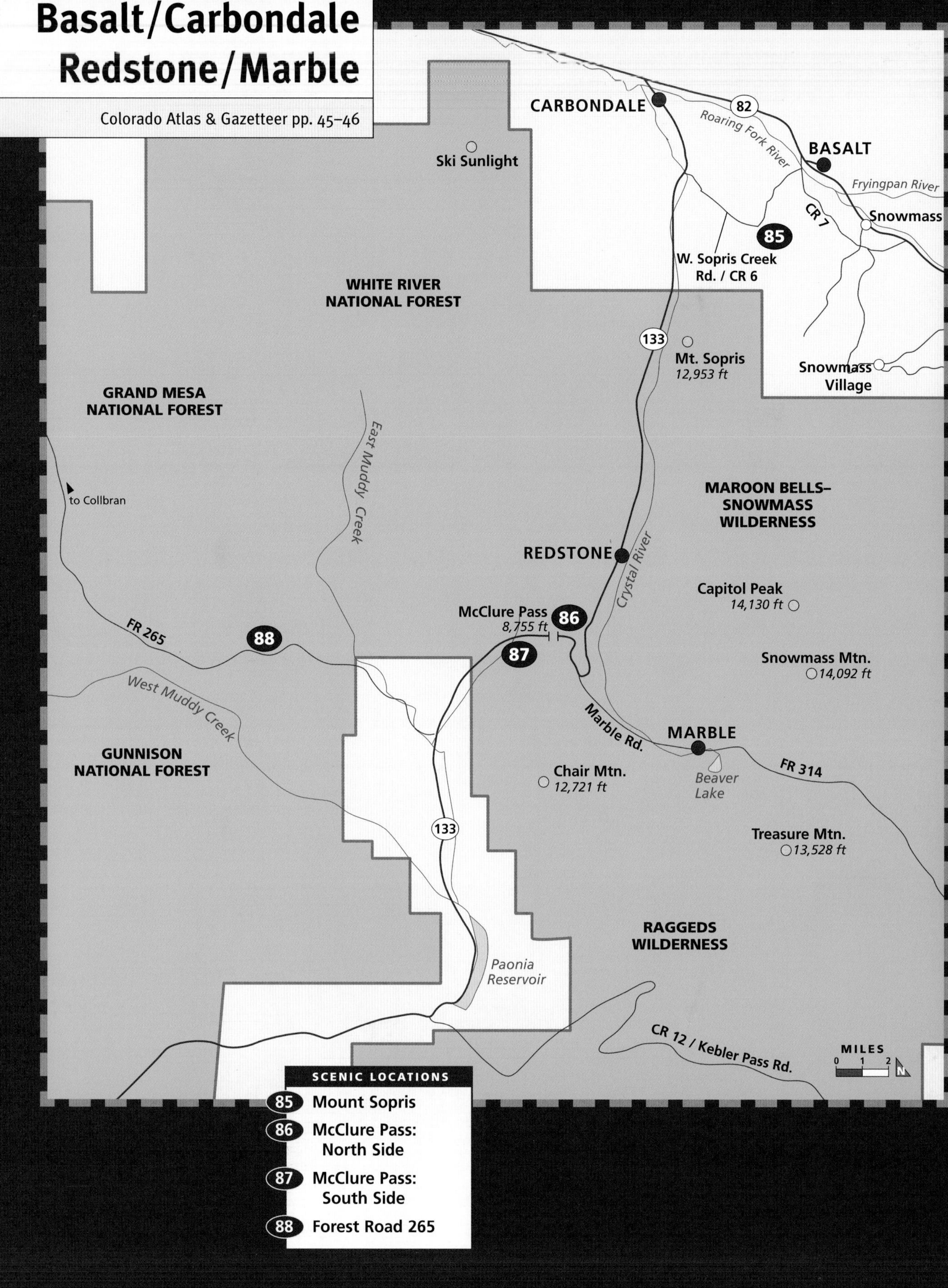

SCENIC LOCATIONS

85 Mount Sopris

86 McClure Pass: North Side

87 McClure Pass: South Side

88 Forest Road 265

Basalt, Carbondale, Redstone, and Marble

Three of Colorado's most pristine rivers run through this classic Colorado valley. The Roaring Fork River defines the region and gives the valley its name. Basalt sits where the Fryingpan River meets the Roaring Fork, an old railroad town close to the heart of sprawling White River National Forest. Carbondale nestles at the confluence of the Roaring Fork and Crystal Rivers, below 12,953-foot Mount Sopris to its south in the Maroon Bells–Snowmass Wilderness. Although the fortunes of their upriver neighbors, Aspen and Snowmass Village, have dictated the destiny of these two towns, Basalt and Carbondale have also come into their own as charming and laid-back outdoor destinations.

Tucked beneath towering mountains farther up the Crystal River, Redstone is one of the best-kept secrets in Colorado. Dubbed the "Ruby of the Rockies," Redstone imparts a fairytale quality, complete with fabulous castle, precipitous cliffs, deep forests, and rushing brooks. Farther down the road, the town of Marble and its historic claim to fame, the Yule Marble Quarry, fill out a charming picture of the past.

Fish, kayak, raft, hike, and generally get away from it all with ease in these little towns. To get to Carbondale from Glenwood Springs, take CO 82 south toward Aspen for about 10 miles. Turn right on CO 133, then go another 2 miles. Don't turn off but continue on CO 82 about 14 more miles to reach Basalt. Redstone is located 17 miles south on CO 133 from its junction with CO 82. The turnoff for the dirt road to Marble (Forest Road 314) is 5 miles south of Redstone to the left off of CO 133, just a few miles shy of McClure Pass.

Marble

History

During the 1879 silver strikes in the Aspen area, miners flooded into the Roaring Fork Valley, prospecting in the mountains to the south and west of present-day Carbondale. Taking notice of the fertile river valleys, some switched their focus to agriculture. By 1881, cattle and sheep ranches dotted the valley, and potatoes had become the staple crop. In 1887, the Colorado Midland Railroad established the town of Frying Pan Junction, which became Basalt in 1901. A transportation center, Basalt brought in immigrants from Switzerland and Northern Italy to work the railroads and mines. Agriculture stabilized the valley's economy as silver mining declined. Carbondale, incorporated in 1888 and named after a town in Pennsylvania, has thrived to this day as a farming and ranching community.

Not until John Cleveland Osgood arrived on a railroad-scouting mission in the early 1880s was there any real interest in the Upper Crystal River Valley. It wasn't gold or silver that issued from these mountains, but coal and marble. Osgood purchased claims in the Coal Basin, west of Redstone, in 1882. A decade later he merged his coal empire with Colorado Fuel & Iron Co. in Pueblo. With the completion of the Crystal River Railroad in the 1890s, Coal Basin coal coked in Redstone ovens was sent by rail to Pueblo. With forward-thinking benevolence, Osgood accommodated his coal workers in chalet-style homes and an inn. He also built a splendid castle for himself.

While Osgood was building his coal empire, marble was being quarried just southeast of Redstone along the Crystal River. When profits from Coal Basin fell, the Yule Marble Quarry became the economic staple of the Upper Crystal River Valley. Because of its high quality, Colorado marble was in demand. This marble adorns several of America's national monuments, including the Lincoln Memorial and the Tomb of the Unknown Soldier. By 1916, the railhead town of Marble had become a major population center. Later deserted for many years, the quarry has since reopened; about 50 full-time residents live in nearby Marble.

Main Attractions

FISHING

The very rivers that enticed miners into agriculture more than a hundred years ago now beckon serious anglers. The **Roaring Fork River** flows 70 miles along CO 82 from Independence Pass above Aspen to the Colorado River in Glenwood Springs, picking up numerous tributaries along the way. From above Aspen to Basalt, you can enjoy trout fishing; from Basalt to its confluence with the Colorado River, the Roaring Fork boasts browns, rainbows, and whitefish.

Classified as Gold Medal Water, the **Fryingpan River** is one of the West's greatest trout streams. Large rainbows, browns, cutthroats, and brookies populate the waters from Ruedi Reservoir to Basalt. The river has yielded rainbows up to 20 pounds and record-breaking brookies. But note, the anglers are as abundant as the fish, and the Fryingpan remains crowded year-round. From Basalt, the river parallels Fryingpan Road (Forest Road 105) 14 miles east to Ruedi Reservoir with good public access.

The secluded **Crystal River** originates in the mountains above Marble and becomes a major tributary of the Roaring Fork 28 miles downstream near Carbondale. Browns and rainbows can reach well over a foot in length and weigh up to 5 pounds. Paralleling CO 133, the river is best accessed along the 15-mile

MOUNT SOPRIS

Mount Sopris looks like a fourteener, but in truth it's just short of a thirteener at 12,953 feet above sea level. It's the most conspicuous mountain in the Roaring Fork Valley, visible from Glenwood Springs to Basalt. A dazzling road takes you as close as you can get by vehicle to its eastern face, which reveals that the peak has two summits, not the single one apparent from the north. This road courses through scrub oaks, cottonwoods, and a vast forest of aspen, as well as ranch meadows similar to those along Snowmass Creek Road, with which it connects. From the town of Snowmass, head south on Snowmass Creek Road 2 miles, bear right onto Capitol Creek Road, then immediately take another right turn west onto County Road 7, East Sopris Creek Road. Continue northwest 6 miles and turn left on CR 6, West Sopris Creek Road, which takes you in front of the peak and toward the town of Carbondale. To do all of this from Carbondale, drive a mile south from town on CO 133, where you will make a left onto CR 111, which becomes CR 5 (west of the divide), Prince Creek Road/West Sopris Creek Road.

The meadows along East and West Sopris Creeks are sublime, but only because Mount Sopris is always looming in the background. However, the best view of the peak exists on the divide that separates West Sopris Creek from Prince Creek. At this point you can almost see the vast forests of oak, aspen, and conifer that pave the way to the peak. Park and hike a short distance up on the hill to the east of the divide—from here you gain enough elevation to look out over the forest to see Sopris shining brightly.

Because it faces east, it might be at its most picturesque at sunrise on a clear day, illuminated by the orange light. Around the end of September, the oaks are red and the aspen yellow, making as colorful a scene as you will ever see in Colorado. Before you head down to Carbondale—if you have a four-wheel drive—turn south from the top of the pass onto CR 6A. In about 2 miles you'll reach Dinkle Lake, a small lake surrounded by aspens. Try out your composition skills on the reflections of the trees on the lake.

stretch in between the towns of Carbondale and Redstone. *For information, lessons, and guided trips: Taylor Creek Fly Shop, 183 Basalt Center Cir., 970-927-4374, www.taylorcreek.com; Frying Pan Anglers, 132 Basalt Center Cir., Basalt, 970-927-3441, www.fryingpananglers.com; Alpine Angling, 981 Cowen Dr., Carbondale, 970-963-9245, www.alpineangling.com.*

REDSTONE CASTLE

Originally known as Cleveholm Manor, Redstone Castle was built between 1898 and 1902 by coal magnate and Redstone founder John Cleveland Osgood. Osgood wanted his estate to impress such tycoons and luminaries as J.P. Morgan, John D. Rockefeller, and Theodore Roosevelt. Osgood brought in stonecutters from Austria and Italy to construct the exterior and the fireplaces. Skilled artisans crafted the mahogany woodwork, inlaid floors, and gilded ceilings. Tiffany chandeliers, Persian rugs, and wall hangings of silk and velvet adorned the castle's 42 rooms.

But this was not all. A successful and wealthy businessman, Osgood was also something of a social reformer. He built a community of 84 well-equipped chalet-style cottages for his workers and their families, plus a 40-room inn—now the Redstone Inn—for his bachelor employees, on the manor grounds. From CO 133, Redstone Castle is just off the main entrance to the town of Redstone. *800-748-2524, www.redstoneinn.com.*

Activities

CAMPING

The popular **Mollie B** campground on the edge of Ruedi Reservoir provides easy access to great fishing and scenery. From Basalt, go 16 miles east on Fryingpan Road (Forest Road 105). **Little Maud, Little Mattie,** and **Dearhamer** campgrounds are also near the reservoir. **Chapman** accesses the Fryingpan River. From Basalt, go 30 miles east on Fryingpan Road (FR 105). The secluded **Elk Wallow** campground also has easy access to the river. From Basalt, take Fryingpan Road (FR 105) 26 miles, then turn left (east) onto FR 501 at Biglow and continue 3.5 miles. **Avalanche** sits on the edge of the Maroon Bells–Snowmass Wilderness near Avalanche Creek. From Carbondale, take CO 133 south for 11 miles to County Road 3D (FR 310). Go left (east) 3 miles to the campground. **Redstone** campground has 37 sites at the north entrance to Redstone in a wooded area just off CO 133. Although near the highway, this renovated campground offers both privacy and amenities. *For the above campgrounds: 970-963-2266.* **McClure** campground sits atop 8,755-foot McClure Pass in a beautiful aspen grove beside CO 133. *970-527-4131.*

FOUR-WHEEL-DRIVE TRIPS

On the 9-mile round-trip **Hubbard Cave Road,** your destination is a 1,400-foot-deep cave with three parallel passages totaling 6,000 feet. Scientists believe scalding groundwater exploding into steam deep beneath the earth created this cave. From Carbondale, go 9 miles north on CO 82 and turn right (east) on Red Canyon Road (County Road 115). Continue 2.5 miles, take a left (north) past the gravel pit, then go 2 miles and turn right (east). Stop at the register 4.5 miles up this road and continue 0.25 mile to the cave. *For guided jeep tours: Crystal River Jeep Tours, 970-963-1991.*

For a beautiful drive with some history, take 4-mile **Marble Road** through Marble and veer to the right (southeast) on the **Crystal River Trail** (Forest Road 314) for 5 miles to the ghost town of Crystal. From here, you have a couple of options: Take **Schofield Pass Road** (FR 317) southeast to Crested Butte Mountain Resort, about 10 miles beyond 10,707-foot Schofield Pass. Or make a loop of it—the **Crystal and Lead King Basin Loop,** to be exact—by continuing north to the Geneva Lake trailhead and going west on **Lead King Basin Trail** (FR 315) back to Marble. The 17-mile trip encircles Sheep Mountain and adjoins the Ragged and Maroon Bells Snowmass Wildernesses en route back to Redstone. Colorado scenery doesn't get any better than this.

GOLF

The Crystal River flows along the 18-hole **River Valley Ranch Golf Course** in Carbondale; note that the stunning views of Mount Sopris might prove distracting to your golf game! *303 River Valley Ranch Dr., 970-963-3625.*

HIKING

Mount Sopris (see Scenic Location No. 85, opposite) towers over the landscape around Carbondale and Basalt. The 6-mile (one way) hike **DIFFICULT** to its twin peaks can be done in a day or as a leisurely backpacking trip, with a stop at the designated campsites at Thomas Lakes. From Carbondale, head 1 mile south on CO 133 until you get to Prince Creek Road (County Road 5). Turn left (east), and follow signs to the trailhead at Dinkle Lake. **Avalanche Creek Trail** **MODERATE** starts at Avalanche campground and leads into the Maroon Bells–Snowmass Wilderness and ultimately to Avalanche and Capitol Lakes. (See Camping, this page, for directions.)

White River National Forest, encompassing 2.25 million undeveloped acres of western Colorado, includes hundreds of hiking trails. *Sopris Ranger District, 620 Main St., Carbondale, 970-963-2266, www.fs.fed.us/r2/whiteriver; www.basalt.com.*

HORSEBACK RIDING

The staff at **Chair Mountain Stables** knows area history by heart and can arrange a ride that fits your abilities and schedule (as if schedules were necessary in Redstone). In winter, arrange a horse-drawn sleigh ride on the grounds of Redstone Castle. Find the stables on CO 133 across from the northern entrance to Redstone. *17843 CO 133, Redstone, 970-963-1232.*

HOT-AIR BALLOONING

For an extraordinary view of the peaks flanking the Roaring Fork Valley, contact **Above It All Balloon Co.,** which provides

86 SCENIC LOCATION — MCCLURE PASS: NORTH SIDE

At only 8,755 feet, McClure Pass may not sound impressive, but it sits on top of one of the most gorgeous stretches of highway in Colorado. From Carbondale to its intersection with CO 92 in Hotchkiss, CO 133 provides some of the state's finest views. The aspen forests on top of the pass alone are worth the trip, not to mention the forests that carpet hillsides in all directions. About 10 miles south of Glenwood Springs, take the Carbondale exit off CO 82 onto CO 133.

CO 133 follows the Crystal River—one of Colorado's most scenic rivers—from Carbondale to the base of the pass. Issuing mostly from the Raggeds and Maroon Bells–Snowmass Wildernesses, the Crystal River runs fast and clear until entering the Roaring Fork. Narrow-leaved cottonwoods line the banks along the way. Late May and late September are the times to photograph colors here: fresh greens in spring and outrageous yellows and oranges in fall. Look for various side roads that cross the river after you leave Carbondale, such as the one to the west that takes you to the Crystal River Inn. From these bridges you can make wonderful compositions with the river disappearing into the distance. If you have the time, scout locations with imposing Mount Sopris in the background.

Unfortunately, development is encroaching upon what remains of ranches and open space south of Carbondale, so go there soon. One spot to look for is the Avalanche Creek turnoff (County Road 3D) east of CO 133. It doesn't go very far and dead-ends at the trailhead, but you find lovely cottonwoods and old mudflows along the way. Hayes Creek Falls are 2 miles south of Redstone on the west side of the highway. They appear quickly, so keep your eyes peeled for the sign and pull over right away. The falls descend a slickrock canyon right next to the road. Photograph them at the beginning or end of the day when no direct light can produce unmanageable contrast or, better yet, photograph in cloudy light (see pp. 81–83, *Photographing the Landscape*).

As you begin to ascend McClure Pass, consider making photographs of the aspens along the highway on your right; they are particularly tall and beautiful. After the first switchback to the right, begin to look back over the Crystal River Valley to the east. You will not believe the massive forests of aspen that cover the hillsides below Mounts Sopris and Daly. Pull over from time to time to make images with your telephoto lens. The third week of September produces a sea of yellow you will not soon forget.

trips from Snowmass Village in bright balloons. *970-963-6148, www.aboveitallballoon.com.*

MOUNTAIN BIKING

The Roaring Fork and Crystal River Valleys have a complex network of four-wheel-drive roads to delight mountain-biking enthusiasts (see Four-Wheel-Drive Trips, p. 259). The secluded **Tall Pines Trail** MODERATE, winding for 17 miles from Carbondale to Redstone, is a nice option if you want a bit more privacy. From Carbondale, go west on Main Street, eventually taking Forest Road 108 across the Crystal River, past Crystal River Ranch and County Road 125. Stay on FR 108 as the road turns south and parallels the South Branch of Edgerton Creek. Turn onto the jeep road (FR 1C) to your left (southeast) and start your ride. FR 1C will eventually dead-end into FR 307, and a left turn will take you east and back to CO 133 in Redstone. If you still have the energy (and haven't set a shuttle), you can make a loop back to Carbondale on CO 133. *For maps and rentals: Ajax Bike & Sports, 0517 Hwy. 133, Carbondale, 970-963-0128, www.ajaxbikeandsport.com.*

SCENIC DRIVES

Carbondale is the terminus of the north spur of the **West Elk Loop Scenic and Historic Byway,** which follows the Crystal River south along CO 133 to Redstone and over 8,755-foot McClure Pass (see Scenic Location Nos. 86 and 87, this page and p. 262). Continue to tiny Somerset, the self-styled "Highest Coal Mine Town in the U.S.," to connect with the main loop. For a full description, see Scenic Drives, Gunnison, p. 284.

WINTER SPORTS

Many skiing enthusiasts lodge in Basalt or Carbondale to avoid steeper resort prices farther up the valley. But you can also stay put and enjoy great cross-country skiing. The Mount Sopris Nordic Council maintains the **Spring Gulch Trail System,** which provides 14 kilometers of groomed trails free to the public. Trails range from the 0.7-kilometer Kid's Trail and Lazy Eight Trail to the more challenging Rodeo and Big Dipper Trails. Holdens Trail (3.2 kilometers) and North Star Trail (1.1 kilometers) provide scenic views of Mount Sopris. The Spring Gulch Trail System is 7 miles west of the traffic light in Carbondale. *Mount Sopris Nordic Council, www.springgulch.org.*

For cross-country skiing off the beaten path, try the 2-mile round-trip Town Trail around Redstone, or tour the many four-wheel-drive roads, covered with snow during winter (see Four-Wheel-Drive Trips, p. 259). *For information and rentals: Redstone Inn, 0082 Redstone Blvd., Redstone, 970-963-2526.*

Restaurants

Primavera Restaurant and Bar ($$-$$$) serves Italian cuisine accompanied by selections from an extensive wine list.

Continued on page 264

McCLURE PASS: SOUTH SIDE

The north side of 8,755-foot McClure Pass drains Crystal River water into the Colorado River, while the south side empties into the Gunnison via Muddy Creek. Once you're over the pass, views quickly open to the peaks of Raggeds Wilderness to the east, ridges lined with aspens and cottonwoods, and ranch meadows along Muddy Creek. Pull over from the highway at several points and frame meadows in the foreground, trees and hills in the midground, and peaks behind it all. From Carbondale, stay on CO 133 to follow this route; from Delta, take CO 92 east to the CO 133 turnoff in Hotchkiss.

At 12,721 feet, Chair Mountain is the first peak you see to the east as you descend McClure Pass southwestward. Like Mount Sopris, another peak under 13,000 feet, Chair Mountain deceives—it's quite prodigious looming above the Muddy Creek Valley. At 12,641 feet, Ragged Peak appears next, creating a dual-peak background. Pull off the highway and compose the cottonwoods and aspens occupying the narrow drainages east of the highway and in front of the peak view. In mid- to late May the trees leaf into lime green hues; during the last week of September they assume shades of yellow and orange.

Farther down the pass in fall, you will see a band of red aspens that also makes a fine foreground. The mid-morning sun backlights the trees to the east, while later in the day the sun setting behind you will saturate tree color. Muddy Creek stays true to its name, yet it can still make a pretty picture. Yellow cottonwoods along the creek complement the brown water.

After passing Paonia Reservoir, you'll follow the North Fork of the Gunnison River all the way to CO 92. Unfortunately, the canyon is narrow, so views are hard to find, especially because you have entered coal-mining country with its ubiquitous conveyor belts and other unsightly structures. Nevertheless, the orchards and vineyards around Paonia are lovely, so explore this fruitful valley by taking County Road 39 as an alternate route from Paonia to CO 92, instead of driving via Hotchkiss.

FOREST ROAD 265

This road is another of my favorite out-of-the-way places. It ascends East Muddy Creek, crosses over to the head of West Muddy Creek, then descends down to the Colorado River, all the while coursing through lovely high meadows with aspens and beaver ponds. In spring and fall it's a delightful drive, not just because of the colorful landscape, but because you won't see anybody else, except perhaps a rancher or two.

To reach Forest Road 265, turn northwest off CO 133 about 7 miles south of McClure Pass. Eventually FR 265 intersects with County Road 330E, which takes you westward and turns into CO 330 at the little town of Collbran. CO 330 intersects to the west with CO 65, which meets I-70 about 7 miles northeast of Palisade. The highest section of the forest road is bumpy and can get very muddy in spring. You can take a car, but I recommend a four-wheel-drive vehicle for the entire route.

The first few miles of road after turning off CO 133 follow East Muddy Creek through pastoral ranchland. In spring the creek is quite brown, a very complementary color when married in a composition with the light greens of May's grasses and trees. From several bridges over the creek, you can compose the river receding as a lead-in line into the distance, with trees on either side. As you begin to climb out of the valley, look back regularly to the east toward the peaks of Raggeds Wilderness, which increase in magnificence as you ascend. You want to find aspens, which by now line the road and nearby ridges, to make a foreground for a composition with the peaks in the background. Eventually you lose sight of them as you enter the high country that separates the Muddy Creek watershed from that of Buzzard and Plateau Creeks.

Now is the time to look for "intimate" landscapes (see pp. 54–57, *Photographing the Landscape*) defined by beaver ponds, meadows, and aspens. Look for the reflection of aspens in ponds, autumn leaves floating on water, meadow wildflowers in summer. Don't even bother including a horizon in the scene! At this point, FR 265 descends Buzzard Creek in the White River National Forest, then enters private rural land where Buzzard meets Plateau Creek. As it flows through the canyon from the junction of CO 330 and CO 65, then west to I-70, Plateau Creek is picturesque as well.

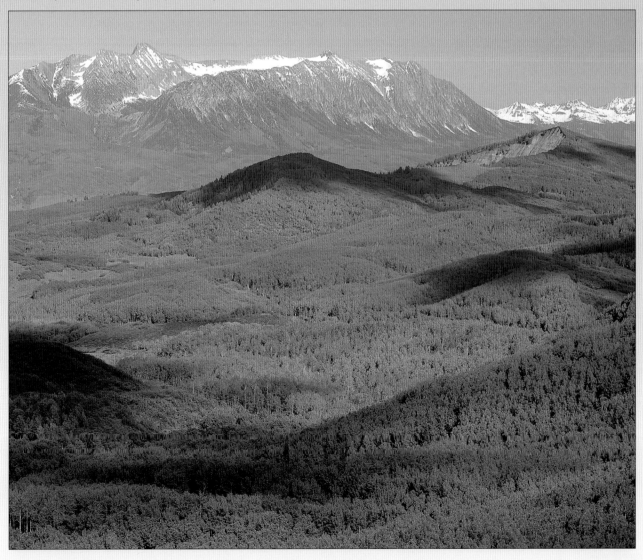

165 Midland Ave., Basalt, 970-927-3342. For Mexican food, stop at **Taqueria El Nopal** ($), *33836 Two Rivers Rd., Basalt, 970-927-1280.* Adventurous diners can try the octopus soup.

In Carbondale, the **Village Smithy Restaurant** ($), at 3rd and Main Streets in Carbondale, serves the best breakfasts in the Roaring Fork Valley. *970-963-9990, www.villagesmithyrestaurant.com.*

Fortunately, the only two restaurants in Redstone serve excellent food! The **Redstone Inn** ($$), not to be confused with Redstone Castle, specializes in Colorado cuisine, including wild game entrees and Southwestern dishes. *0082 Redstone Blvd. at the entrance to Redstone, 970-963-2526.* **Crystal Club Café** ($-$$) is a great family place with a diverse menu. The outdoor patio has nice cliff views. *0467 Redstone Blvd., 970-963-9515.*

Accommodations

The highly recommended **Lodge at River's Edge** ($$) boasts a luxurious hot tub on its riverfront deck. *0600 Fryingpan Rd., Basalt, 970-927-4991.* The hosts at **Ambiance Inn Bed and Breakfast** ($-$$) provide comfortable rooms and will even prepare your picnic lunch. *66 N. 2nd St., Carbondale, 970-963-3597, www.lodgeatriversedgeco.com.*

The following three options are recommended for families. **BRB Crystal River Resort** ($-$$) maintains cabins and campsites along the Crystal River. *7202 CO 133, Carbondale, 970-963-2341, www.cabinscolorado.com.* **Avalanche Ranch** ($$-$$$), on 45 acres situated above the Crystal River in the Elk Mountains, includes 14 cabins and a ranch house. Wildlife is abundant, kids will love the ranch animals (including llamas), and your own pets are welcome. *12863 CO 133, Redstone, 970-963-2846, www.avalancheranch.com.* **Chair Mountain Ranch** ($$), at the Marble turnoff on Forest Road 314, has cabins for rent and is conveniently located for recreation. *970-963-9522, www.chairmountainranch.com.*

Redstone Inn ($-$$) has come a long way from the bachelor quarters John Osgood built for his coal workers. Situated on 22 acres, the inn has a pool, hot tub, tennis courts, and a fine restaurant. Arrange for a sleigh ride or cross-country ski lessons. *0082 Redstone Blvd., 970-963-2526, http://redstoneinn.thegilmorecollection.com.* **Beaver Lake Lodge & Cabins** ($-$$) in Marble is an historic, family-run lodge with cabins located in a quiet woodland setting. *201 E Silver, 970-963-2504, www.beaverlakelodge.com.* **Crystal Dreams Bed & Breakfast** ($$) is a delightful place to stay along the Crystal River. *04[illegible] Redstone Blvd., 970-963-8240, www.crystaldreamsgetaway.com.*

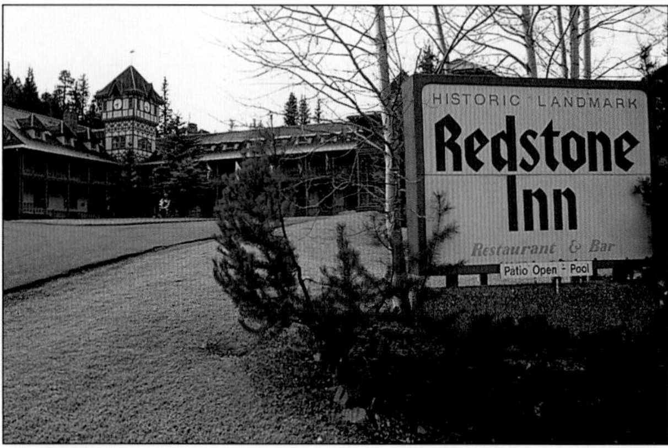

Redstone Inn

Special Events

In July, Carbondale's **Mountain Fair** showcases arts and crafts from more than 140 artisans, with food, live entertainment, and activities for children. *970-963-1680.* Basalt celebrates **River Days** in mid-August at Arbaney Park with fishing, softball, live music, arts and crafts, pie-baking contests, a parade, and lots of family fun. *970-927-4031, www.basaltriverdays.com.*

Celebrate the contribution of farming to the Roaring Fork Valley at Carbondale's **Potato Days.** The late-summer festival features a spud parade, a farmers' market, and barbecue. *970-963-1890, www.carbondale.com.*

Over Labor Day weekend, **Redstone Art Show** shows off Redstone's emergence as an art colony with sculptures, paintings, and more by local and regional artists. *Redstone Art Center, 0173 Redstone Blvd., 970-963-3790, www.redstoneart.com.*

For More Information

Basalt Visitor Center, *train car located off CO 82 at the first Basalt exit, 970-927-4031, www.basalt.com.* Carbondale Visitor Center, *0590 CO 133, 970-963-1890, www.carbondale.com.* Redstone visitor information, *www.redstonecolorado.com.* Marble visitor information, *www.marbletourismassociation.org.*

Crested Butte

(see map on p. 266)

Crested Butte nestles in the shadow of craggy 12,162-foot Mount Crested Butte, surrounded by the West Elk Wilderness to the southwest, Raggeds Wilderness to the northwest, and the Maroon Bells–Snowmass Wilderness to the northeast. It's a haven for not just downhill skiing and snowboarding, but also mountain biking, cross-country skiing, hiking, and fishing. Take a stroll down Elk Avenue, Crested Butte's main street, and soak up the history and character of this little town high in the Rockies. A chrome statue of Saint George slaying the legendary dragon stands at the town entrance on CO 135. Created by local artist Sean Guerrero, this vibrant artwork reflects the character and spunk of this town, a National Historic District.

Crested Butte survived the Silver Panic of 1893, which turned Gunnison County's other mining hamlets into ghost towns. Mining interests have been held back in recent decades, however, by both the prosperity of the ski resort and by the efforts of environmentalists and historic preservationists. Residents today remain joined in their lengthy and successful battle with the huge AMAX molybdenum mine to retain the character and dignity of their town and its surroundings. And the people of Crested Butte haven't allowed their town to be compromised by either the ski industry or water interests, as they continue to fight for their wetlands, their wildflowers, and some of the most gorgeous landscapes in Colorado.

Elk Avenue, Crested Butte

History

Like so many other Colorado mountain communities, Crested Butte was founded as a supply town for gold and silver mines. A year after its incorporation on July 3, 1880, the town was assured a future when the Denver & Rio Grande Railroad arrived from Gunnison. Even the bust of its silver mines after the 1893 crash did not deter Crested Butte, which was buffered by vast stores of coal discovered in 1880. Coal mining sustained the local economy until 1952, when the Colorado Fuel and Iron Co. closed its Big Mine.

Still, the town hung on, as Crested Butte's remote beauty encouraged newcomers to invest in real estate. When Crested Butte Mountain Resort opened in the 1960s, the town's languishing economy began to bounce back. People were drawn to both the historic town and the pristine forests surrounding it, and Crested Butte began to see ski cabins and second homes pop up in its outskirts. New all-year and seasonal residents included not just outdoors enthusiasts but environmental advocates like Linda Powers and Tim and Wren Wirth (the former Colorado senator and his wife, an environmental foundation president).

Crested Butte Mayor Linda Powers, a longtime environmental activist, made her name fighting the AMAX Mining Corp.'s plans to conduct a huge molybdenum mining operation at Red Lady Mine, 2 miles above town, in the late 1970s. She later blocked efforts to divert Taylor River and reservoir water to the Front Range, which would have devastated local agriculture and recreation. Today, Crested Butte has an architectural review board to ensure that new construction and renovation respect the town's unique heritage. Idealistic townsfolk like Powers have made a difference here.

Threats to historic mountain towns and pristine mountain environments do not disappear so easily, though: AMAX maintains its huge molybdenum claim above Crested Butte, and rapid growth on the Front Range continues to put Western Slope water supplies at risk. And Crested Butte Mountain Resort hopes to expand onto the wetlands of Snodgrass Mountain. But now the town economy relies less on mining and development and more on the beauty and historic quality of an environment that its residents have helped to preserve. Development interests here will have to face the plucky and proud citizens of this peerless mountain town.

Main Attractions

CRESTED BUTTE WILDFLOWER FESTIVAL

Crested Butte's high alpine valleys and meadows put on an incomparable wildflower display every summer. Hard-core mountain bikers stop in their tracks at the sight of these lush, blooming carpets, and hikers set out with guidebooks in hand to key and tally their floral findings. Crested Butte celebrates its bountiful blossoms with the annual, weeklong Crested Butte Wildflower Festival in early July. The festivities include guided hikes and botanic lectures, as well as photography, painting, and even a class on cooking with wildflowers. Check the schedule —I could very well be teaching photography! *970-349-2571, www.crestedbuttewildflowerfestival.com.*

MOUNTAIN BIKING

Crested Butte is acknowledged in sports circles as the birthplace of mountain biking. It was here in this Colorado town that old, heavy Schwinn bikes, or "klunkers," were first fitted with low gears and fat, knobby tires suitable for riding the trails on the steep mountains nearby.

First-rate mountain-bike terrain extends in virtually every direction from Crested Butte; it's essential that you get a map and consult one of the town's many bike shops before hitting the

Continued on page 268

Crested Butte

Colorado Atlas & Gazetteer pp. 46, 57, 58

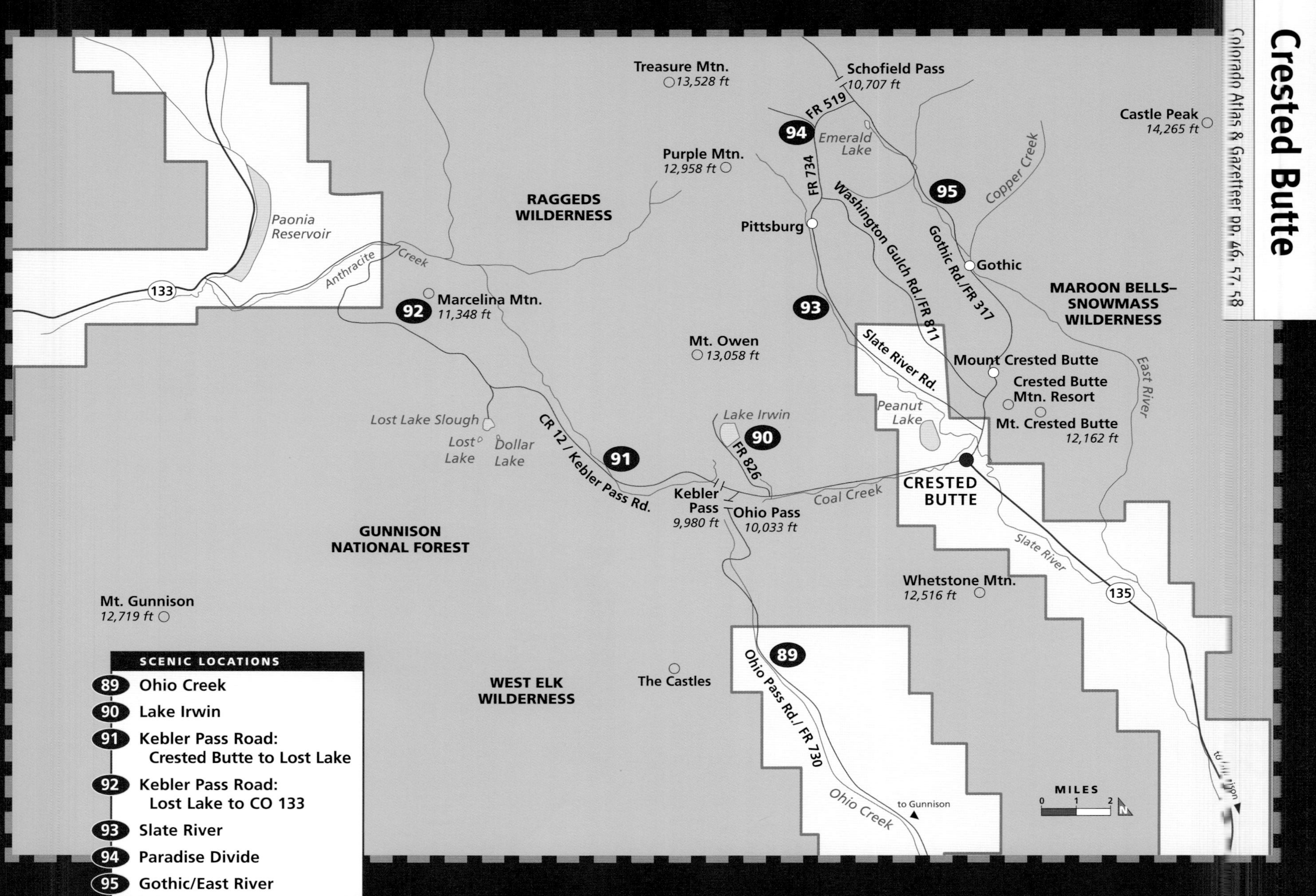

OHIO CREEK

One of my favorite towns, Crested Butte nestles within landscapes as picturesque as any in Colorado. *Favorite* really is an understatement, but then I don't want to give away all of my secrets! Crested Butte is hemmed in by three wilderness areas: Raggeds, Maroon Bells–Snowmass, and West Elk. Backroads leading up to and circling these areas provide amazing vistas to the peaks that define the hearts of these wild places.

Ohio Pass Road, between Gunnison and Kebler Pass Road (see Scenic Location Nos. 91 and 92, pp. 271 and 272), is one such road. It courses through spectacular ranches that line the creek and wide valley, revealing views of the unique mountain called The Castles in West Elk Wilderness. Three miles north of Gunnison, turn left onto Ohio Pass Road. Your car can go most of the way on this improved dirt road, but once you begin ascending to connect with 9,980-foot Kebler Pass via 10,033-foot Ohio Pass, you'll need a four-wheel drive.

The first 16 miles of the road follow the valley floor and get progressively more scenic. To the north you see Anthracite Range, an east-west escarpment that dominates the picture. At about mile 12 you begin to see the peaks of West Elk Wilderness to the west. Until then, watch for views of meadows and cottonwood trees along Ohio Creek to the west. Old fences and ranch buildings make interesting subject matter as well. Some of the meadows beside the road contain fields of flowers so thick they beg to be composed with Anthracite Range in the background. At certain places along the way, you can see north to the road winding through the meadows in the distance, good points from which to compose the road as a lead-in line.

My favorite location is unmistakable: Driving north, all of a sudden to the west appear the eroded spires of The Castles. In front along the road is a meadow, in the midground are hills sprinkled with aspens, and behind are The Castles. If you can climb on foot a little way up the hill to the east, the spires will become more prominent in the composition. At this point you'll need a four-wheel drive if you wish to continue to Kebler Pass Road; the road is bumpy and steep, but it's worth the ride. Views of The Castles get even better, and you enter an aspen forest that in late September rivals any in the San Juan Mountains for its intense autumn color.

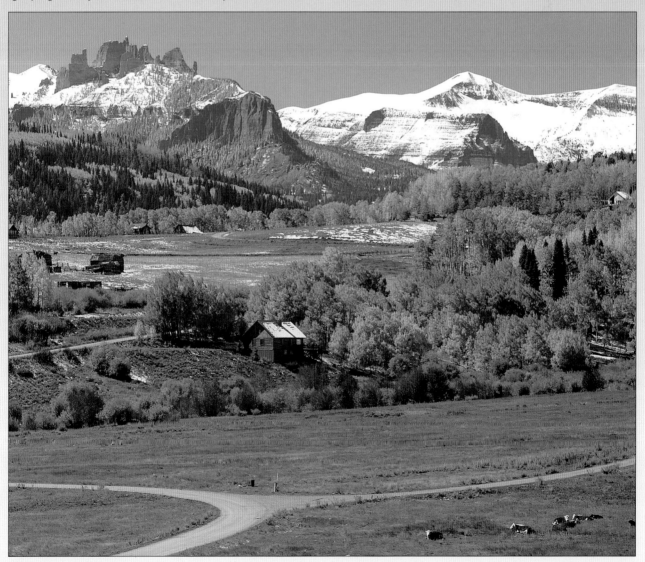

singletrack. The legendary **Trail 401** DIFFICULT is a 9-mile (one way) ride from Schofield Pass to Gothic. It can also be ridden as a rigorous 16-mile loop, beginning in Gothic with a trail that skirts (and crosses) the East River, and returning on Trail 401. From Crested Butte, take Gothic Road to Schofield Pass, or park in Gothic to ride the loop.

The 10-mile **Farris Creek Loop** MODERATE epitomizes Crested Butte scenery, with its wildflower meadows shadowed by Mount Crested Butte. From Crested Butte, take CO 135 south, then turn left (east) onto Brush Creek Road (Forest Road 738) and continue about 4 miles. A gate on the right side of the road marks the trailhead. **Upper Loop Trail** MODERATE is another classic ride to views of Mount Crested Butte. Upper Loop is less than 3 miles long but can be made longer if you start at Crested Butte and/or take the challenging 1.5-mile trail (The *upper* Upper Loop) near the route's end. From Crested Butte, ride north to the ski resort as far as Hunter Hill Road. Turn right (east) and head southeast through the sagebrush.

When you ride over 12,705-foot **Pearl Pass** DIFFICULT to Aspen, you will be repeating mountain-bike history (see Special Events, p. 275). The story goes that a group of motorcyclists traveled from Aspen over Pearl Pass to Crested Butte in the summer of 1976. As these bikers quenched their thirst in the bars of Crested Butte, they became quite obnoxious about their feat. Residents, including a group of Crested Butte firefighters, were not to be outdone, so that September they rode their klunkers over Pearl Pass to Aspen and caroused noisily at the Hotel Jerome. History aside, Pearl Pass is guaranteed to give you that top-of-the-world feeling. Note that the 39-mile road, often impassable because of snow, is also a popular four-wheel-drive route. Check conditions and plan accordingly for this all-day ride.

Another tough but legendary mountain-bike trail is the 22-mile (one way) **Crested Butte to Marble Trail** DIFFICULT over 10,707-foot Schofield Pass to the historic towns of Crystal and Marble. From Crested Butte Mountain Resort, take Gothic Road north along the East River. *For information, maps, service, and rentals: The Alpineer, 419 6th St., 970-349-5210; For guided mountain-bike tours: Pioneer Guide Service, Cement Creek Road, 970-349-5517.*

WINTER SPORTS

Crested Butte Mountain Resort is a prime destination for Colorado skiing and snowboarding, thanks to its uncrowded and wide-open expanses, extreme skiing, and fabulous views of the Elk Mountains. Most of the runs are for beginners and intermediates, which makes the mountain great for family ski outings. The North Face, however, is known for its very difficult, double-black-diamond runs. From Crested Butte, head 3 miles north on Gothic Road. *970-349-2222, www.crestedbutteresort.com.*

Crested Butte Nordic Center, at 2nd Street and Whiterock Avenue in Crested Butte, has more than 20 kilometers of groomed trails. *970-349-1707, www.cbnordic.org.* A favorite cross-country ski trip is the 4-mile trail to Gothic EASY. From Crested Butte Mountain Resort, head north on Forest Road 317 as far as the snow will let you drive. *For rentals and lessons: The Alpineer, 419 6th St., 970-349-5210, www.alpineer.com.*

Originally formed following a visit to Crested Butte by President Jimmy Carter in 1987, the **Adaptive Sports Center** is a non-profit group that facilitates a range of activities for people with disabilities and their families, including ski and snowboard lessons as well as backcountry and snowshoe tours. *For more information: 970-349-2296, 866-349-2296.*

Activities

CAMPING

Lake Irwin campground, which borders the Raggeds Wilderness, adjoins fine fishing and hiking access, along with views of Mount Owen and Ruby and Purple Peaks. From Crested Butte, take Whiterock Avenue, which becomes Kebler Pass Road (County Road 12) 6.5 miles west. Turn right (north) on Forest Road 826 and go 2.3 miles. **Cement Creek** campground sits on the bank of its namesake. From Crested Butte, take CO 135 southeast for 7 miles to FR 740. Take a left (east) and continue 4 miles to the campground. Small **Gothic** campground offers scenery and good fishing access to the East River. The campground is 10 miles north of Crested Butte on Gothic Road (FR 317), about a mile past the town of Gothic. *For the above campgrounds: 970-641-0471.*

Lost Lake campground is close to great fishing and hiking, as well as resplendent wildflowers and views of East Beckwith Mountain. From Crested Butte, take Kebler Pass Road west for 16 miles. Turn left (south) onto FR 706 and continue 2.3 miles to the campground. *970-527-4131.*

Oh Be Joyful is a free campground about three miles northwest of Crested Butte on Slate River Road. There are additional campsites available farther up the road as well. Campers should be aware, however, that forest service roads may be closed due to weather prior to June and after October.

CHAIRLIFT RIDES

In summer, the ride up Mount Crested Butte on the **Silver Queen** and the **Red Lady Express** are a must. I don't know which is more breathtaking: the up-close views of the butte or the more distant views of the Elk Mountains. *970-349-2262.*

FISHING

Although private property restrictions can limit access, the **East River** promises rainbows, cutthroats, brookies, and browns of up to 15 pounds. From its headwaters at Emerald Lake, the East River flows south (along CO 135 for the last 11 miles) to the town of Almont, where it joins with the **Taylor River** to become the **Gunnison River** (see Fishing and Float Trips, Gunnison, p. 281). **Emerald Lake** is known for its rainbow trout and fabulous scenery. From the ski resort, take Gothic Road (FR 317) 7 miles through the town of Gothic, and continue for another 4.5 miles to the lake. **Slate River** is known for browns and rainbows. From

90
SCENIC LOCATION

LAKE IRWIN

Below the peaks of Ruby Range lies splendid, subalpine Lake Irwin. The crest of the Rubies forms the eastern boundary of Raggeds Wilderness, with 12,644-foot Ruby Peak, Mount Owen, and Purple Peak reflecting perfectly on the surface of the lake. The alpine landscape around and above the lake adds to the beauty of this special place. From Irwin Lodge (see Accommodations, p. 275) at treeline, you can enjoy wildflowers galore and 360-degree views of the three major wildernesses that define the Crested Butte area. Follow signs from the west end of Elk Avenue in Crested Butte to Kebler Pass Road (County Road 12). A half-mile before you reach Kebler Pass, turn north on Forest Road 826. You'll see the signs to Lake Irwin, which is on public land. Ask permission to park at the lodge before hiking in the area.

One of my favorite photographs here requires parking at Lake Irwin campground and hiking to the southeast side of the lake. A wonderful reflection of Ruby Range awaits you there—if you arrive at sunrise when the surface of the lake has the best chance of being still. The peaks face east, so the Rubies catch that first red light of dawn. I recommend "bracketing" your exposures when making reflection photographs; that is, making multiple exposures of the same scene in order to ensure a winner. The closer to sunrise you shoot, the lower the contrast in the whole scene, reducing the chance that the directly lighted peaks will be too bright for your film against the unlighted foreground where you and the lake stand. Shooting within a half-hour after sunrise—or a half-hour before sunset—is best (see pp. 129–133, *Photographing the Landscape*).

Beginning the second week of July, wildflowers above the lake and lodge are outrageous. Larkspur, Colorado columbine, and orange sneezeweed are just a few of the varieties that cover the ridges and hills throughout summer. This is a great place to practice extreme depth-of-focus photography: Get as close to the flowers in your foreground as you can, while at the same time keeping them and Ruby Range in focus. This technique creates a sense of depth in the scene that simulates the depth perception we enjoy with two eyes (see pp. 109–117, *Photographing the Landscape*).

One of my favorite hikes here climbs northwest from the lodge to Scarp Ridge. This easy, 3-mile jaunt leads to views as far away as the Maroon Bells. From the ridge, you also peer down into the Oh-Be-Joyful Creek and Peeler Lakes drainages, two of the most exquisite alpine valleys in Colorado.

91 SCENIC LOCATION — KEBLER PASS ROAD: CRESTED BUTTE TO LOST LAKE

Kebler Pass Road (County Road 12) from Crested Butte to CO 133 is so remarkable that I've divided it into two sections: Crested Butte to Lost Lake and Lost Lake to CO 133. Nearly every one of the route's 30 miles has something new to offer the landscape photographer. It's best known for its vast aspen forest and for wildflowers that grow along the way in summer. Several mini-mountain ranges in the vicinity—Anthracite Range, Ruby Range, East and West Beckwith Mountains, and Marcelina Mountain—serve as unbeatable compositional backdrops to the trees and flowers. See Scenic Location No. 90, p. 269, for directions to Kebler Pass Road from Crested Butte. The road is improved dirt, with washboards here and there, but is easily passable by car.

From Crested Butte to 9,980-foot Kebler Pass, the road follows Coal Creek through mostly coniferous forest. Just before the pass, you can head north to Lake Irwin (see Scenic Location No. 90, p. 269), or south to Ohio Creek (see Scenic Location No. 89, p. 267). The really good scenery doesn't begin until you drop down from the pass heading west. By the time the road meets and parallels Anthracite Creek, you begin to see views of 12,432-foot East Beckwith Mountain. As you approach Horse Ranch Park (you'll see the signs), look for a composition with the willow-lined creek in the foreground, aspen-covered rolling hills in the midground, and the mountain in the background. Just after you cross to the south side of the creek, find the short road on your left that takes you 200 yards up to Gunnison National Forest Trail 840. From the end of the road you see an incredible view north to The Dyke, a long rock wall that sits above one of the most beautiful aspen vistas on the planet.

Although an entire aspen forest can be genetically identical, this forest consists of many different aspen families, each of which leafs in spring and loses leaves in fall at different times. In spring some trees are leafless, others fully leaved, and still more newly leaved—all at once. In fall the forest is a mosaic of green, yellow, and leafless trees, with some that even turn red. With a telephoto lens, compose forest, dike, and blue sky beyond, and you'll create one of Colorado's most beautiful photographs. Sunrise backlights the scene; sunset frontlights it. For spring's awakening, arrive in late May or early June. For fall color, come in the third or fourth week of September.

From Horse Ranch Park to Lost Lake, Kebler Pass Road winds through a canopy of aspens. When the leaves are golden, the entire road is bathed in warm light. Many vantage points allow you to situate the road as a compositional lead-in line snaking through the forest. Approaching the side road to Lost Lake (Forest Road 706, bumpy but passable), views open up again to East and West Beckwith Mountains. On a tranquil morning, these peaks make a picture-perfect reflection in the lake.

Crested Butte, take Gothic Road (FR 317) north for 1 mile. Turn left on Slate River Road and continue 4 miles to the public waters. I have also had luck finding some smaller trout at **Cement Creek** and **Roaring Judy Creek,** which both flow into the East River from the southeast below Crested Butte. Locals swear by the **Roaring Judy Ponds** near the Roaring Judy Fish Hatchery, set on 783 acres of waterfowl and wildlife habitat at Roaring Judy State Wildlife Area. Take CO 135 south from Crested Butte for 13 miles and look for the sign. *For information, lessons, and guided trips: Dragonfly Anglers, 307 Elk Ave., 970-349-1228, www.dragonflyanglers.com; CB MacTrout, LLC, 970-349-6727, http://cbmactrout.com.*

FOUR-WHEEL-DRIVE TRIPS

Cement Creek Road is a true backcountry experience that accesses the rugged Collegiate Peaks Wilderness. From Crested Butte, go south 7 miles on CO 135, then turn left (east) onto Cement Creek Road. If you're in the mood for a difficult, even treacherous, route, try **Pearl Pass** from Crested Butte to Aspen (see Mountain Biking, p. 268). Always check road conditions before setting out. **Schofield Pass Road,** connecting Crested Butte and Marble, passes through the gorgeous scenery along the Crystal River and to the old town of Crystal. *For jeep rentals and guided tours: Three Rivers Resort & Outfitting, 130 CR 742, Almont, 970-641-1303, www.3riversresort.com.*

GHOST TOWN

Gothic was once a wild mining town. General Ulysses S. Grant even paid the little town a visit in its heyday, when the population had swelled as high as 8,000. Known as the City of Silver Wires because of the abundant strands of silver found in nearby mines, Gothic met its end as a mining town during the Silver Panic of 1893. A Gothic revival of sorts began in 1928, however, when Dr. John C. Johnson, a biology professor from Western State College in Gunnison, founded the Rocky Mountain Biological Laboratory here, which continues to this day with its scientific research on high-altitude plants and animals. Gothic remains a center for biological research as well as a starting point for recreational adventures. From Crested Butte Mountain Resort, travel 7 miles north on Gothic Road to the town.

GOLF

A backdrop of extraordinary scenery, a challenging 18-hole golf course, spa facilities, tennis courts, and more: What more could a vacationer want? **The Club at Crested Butte** offers it all just south of town off CO 135 at 385 Country Club Dr. This semiprivate club reserves certain tennis and tee times for members, so call ahead. *970-349-6131.*

HIKING

Cliff Creek Trail promises some of the most bountiful wildflower displays in the region. The hike is 5 miles round-trip and climbs to the top of Beckwith Pass, on the edge of the West Elk Wilderness. Go west on County Road 12 over Kebler Pass and look for a bridge and the Cliff Creek trailhead on the left. The 1-mile hike to Judd Falls via the **Copper Creek Trail** EASY follows Copper Creek through wildflowers and aspens to a 100-foot-high overlook of the falls. From the ski area, take Gothic Road (FR 317) north past the town of Gothic, and look for a dirt road in approximately 0.3 mile on your right. Park here and walk up the dirt road. From Judd Falls, you can continue hiking 5 miles on Copper Creek Trail MODERATE into the Maroon Bells–Snowmass Wilderness and connect with **Conundrum Pass Trail** DIFFICULT, which leads to Conundrum Hot Springs and Aspen (see Hot Springs, Aspen, p. 250). *Guided hiking tours: Crested Butte Adventures, 315 6th St., 970-901-5754; Crested Butte Mountain Guides, 218 Maroon Ave., 970-349-5430, www.crestedbutteguides.com*

HORSEBACK RIDING

The accommodating folks at **Fantasy Ranch** will tailor any ride to your interests and abilities. The ranch offers hourly and day rides as well as guided horseback fishing trips and pack trips through wilderness areas. One highlight is the three-day ride over Pearl Pass to Aspen. Fantasy Ranch has stables at Snodgrass Mountain and Brush Creek Ranch. *970-349-5425, www.fantasyranchoutfitters.com.*

MUSEUMS

The **Crested Butte Mountain Heritage Museum** and **Mountain Bike Hall of Fame** are housed together at 329 Elk Ave. Exhibits chronicle Crested Butte's mining days with photographs and memorabilia, and trace the evolution of mountain biking from Schwinn "klunkers" to today. *970-349-6817, www.mtnbikehalloffame.com.* The **Trailhead Discovery Museum & Arts Center** is fun for the whole family. This children's museum was designed "to nourish the imagination and creativity of children by appealing to their senses of curiosity and fun." Built in 2007, this family destination now features interactive art programs, stimulating science projects, music classes, special kid-friendly events, and an indoor jungle gym. The Trailhead is a member of the international Association of Children's Museums. *618 Gothic Ave., 970-349-6525, www.thetrailheadcb.org*

SCENIC DRIVES

Crested Butte is a stop on the magnificent, 207-mile **West Elk Loop Scenic and Historic Byway** (see Scenic Drives, Gunnison, p. 284). Some of the state's most glorious autumn aspens are visible from the 32-mile stretch of County Road 12 known as **Kebler Pass Road** from Crested Butte to just a few miles east of the small coal town of Somerset on CO 133 (see Scenic Location Nos. 91, p. 271, and 92, this page).

KEBLER PASS ROAD: LOST LAKE TO CO 133

The western side of the 30-mile-long Kebler Pass Road from Crested Butte to CO 133 is scenically distinct from the eastern side, but just as impressive. At one point from the road, which is lined by wildflowers in summer, you can gaze over the largest expanse of aspens in the world. Marcelina Mountain or East and West Beckwith Mountains command nearly every vista. Except for ubiquitous washboards, the road is manageable by car, although closed in winter. (See Scenic Location No. 90, p. 269, for directions to Kebler Pass Road.) As you exit Lost Lake Road, notice Marcelina Mountain looming to the northwest. Although only 11,348 feet in elevation, its white rock and fluted south face stand out. Spring and fall are ideal times to compose an image of aspens in the foreground with the peak beyond.

The road continues west on a flat divide with views through the trees of the Ruby Range to the northeast. Marvelous fields of corn lily—large-leaved, tobaccolike plants—carpet meadows amid groves of aspens. In early June when these (poisonous) plant leaves are new and translucent, the rising and setting sun illuminates and renders them a brilliant green. With a wide-angle lens, the plants make a great foreground for the peaks behind. The road then descends through more aspen forests. Look for simple compositions of the aspens' tall, straight, parallel boles. The elegant aspens don't even need leaves to produce a good photograph.

When you break out of the forest, you'll see Marcelina Mountain looming high above you to the north. At this point you'll see the vast aspen forests below and to the west of the Beckwith Mountains. For the next few miles, compose the trees leading up to these peaks from various points along the road. Like the scene near Horse Ranch Park (see Scenic Location No. 91, p. 271), the many aspen families in this forest produce variegated colors in spring and fall. Sunset is the time to photograph here. You won't believe how red the very white Marcelina Mountain turns at the end of a clear day.

From this point down to the road's next rendezvous with Anthracite Creek, the wildflowers are marvelous. In June, lupine line the road. Compose thick clumps of their purple blooms in the foreground with Marcelina Mountain behind. Farther down, meadows of golden banner flowers mix with freshly leaved scrub oak. Once you arrive at Anthracite Creek, now flowing fast and wide after a generous helping of water from Raggeds Wilderness, look for compositions of narrow-leaved cottonwood trees along with the steely gray rocks in the creek.

93 SCENIC LOCATION SLATE RIVER

Three spectacular drainages originate in the mountains northwest of Crested Butte: Slate River, Washington Gulch, and East River. The Slate River drains from the east side of Ruby Range, then follows the bottom of a U-shaped glacial valley before merging with the East River (see Scenic Location No. 95, p. 277) south of Crested Butte. The view looking up this valley is my favorite winter scene in Colorado. One mile north of Crested Butte, turn northwest off Gothic Road (the route to Crested Butte Mountain Resort) onto Slate River Road (Forest Road 734). The road is fine for a passenger car up to the old townsite of Pittsburg.

Immediately at the turnoff are some of Colorado's most valuable wetlands. These vast meadows of willow among beaver ponds, protected from development by the Crested Butte Land Trust, form the scenic entrance to the Slate River Valley. In summer and fall, the best photograph in the valley may very well be from Nicholson Lake, 3 miles north of Crested Butte. When still, the lake reflects the surrounding peaks and aspens that line the nearby ridges. Keep an eye out for places from which to photograph the river (more of a creek) snaking into the distance. The glare of afternoon clouds reflecting on the surface of the water makes the river most distinct as it winds among the spruce and fir trees. To make the colorful rocks beneath the water more of a focal point, attach a polarizing filter and rotate it until the glare is eliminated from the surface of the water.

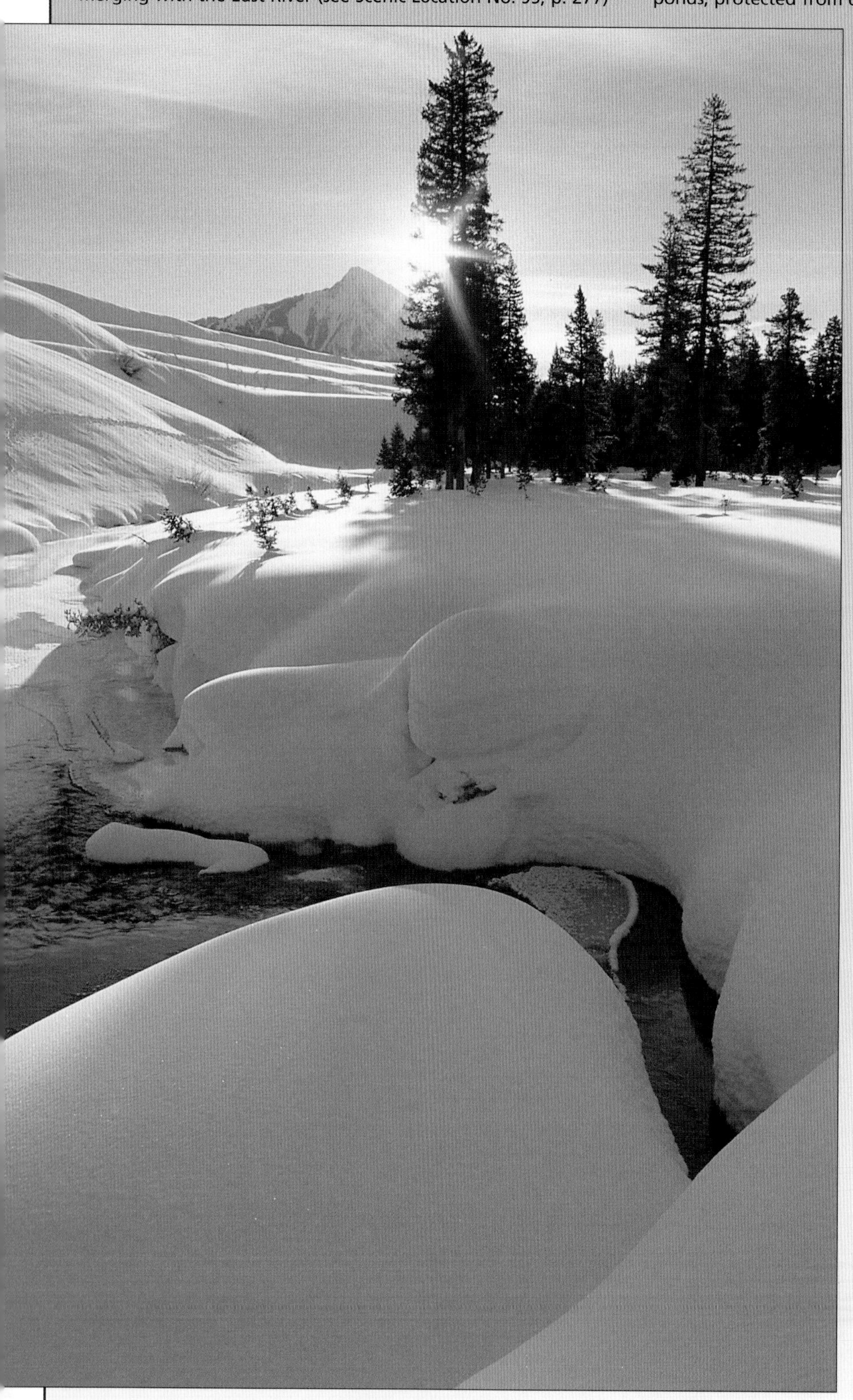

The best photographs in this valley come in winter. About 10 miles north of Gunnison on CO 135, as you make your way toward Crested Butte, you first see the peaks of Ruby Range far in the distance. Although fabulous in summer and fall, they are incomparable in winter for one reason: No other mountains in Colorado hold snow as they do. In a year of normal snowpack, you cannot see a single square inch of mountain that isn't blanketed in white. High winds leave any other Colorado mountains at least partially uncovered, exposing gray beneath the white. Not the Rubies! Drive to where the road is no longer plowed in winter and put on a pair of snowshoes. Hike a little way up valley until you can see the shape of Slate River beneath the snowpack. Notice the snow sculptures created by rocks beneath the surface. These shapes in the foreground, composed with the white peaks of the Ruby Range in the background, make for an incredible image, especially at sunrise.

Restaurants

Crested Butte boasts the fine dining for which ski resort towns are known. **Le Bosquet** ($$-$$$) and **Bacchanale** ($$-$$$) have been Crested Butte dining traditions since the 1970s. Le Bosquet's French sauces and glazes make the chicken, lamb, and game dishes special. *6th and Belleview in the Majestic Plaza, 970-349-5808.* Bacchanale creates scrumptious Italian cuisine. *209 Elk Ave., 970-349-5257.* **Soupçon Bistro** ($$$-$$$$), just down the street, is a romantic, upscale French/American bistro with truly exceptional entrées. Reservations accepted. *127 Elk Ave., 970-349-5448, www.soupconcrestedbutte.com.*

Before you hit the slopes, grab breakfast at **Izzy's** ($-$$), specializing in homemade breads, bagels, muffins, and their signature potato pancakes. *218 Maroon Ave., 970-349-5630.* **Camp 4 Coffee** ($-$$) opens at 6:30 a.m., and you can get a tasty pastry, biscuit, or breakfast burrito to go. *402 Elk Ave., 970-349-2500.*

The **Wooden Nickel** ($-$$$) is a favorite burger place and watering hole at 222 Elk Ave. *970-349-6350.* Next to the Wooden Nickel, **Maxwells** ($$) serves quality steaks, pasta, lamb, and even buffalo burgers, as well as much more. *226 Elk Ave., 970-349-5345, www.maxwellscb.com.*

Donita's Cantina ($), another great town tradition, has excellent Mexican food, homemade salsa, and margaritas. *332 Elk Ave., 970-349-6674.* For excellent sushi, the locals recommend **Lobar** ($$). *303 Elk Ave., 970-349-0480.*

Accommodations

Centrally located **Elk Mountain Lodge** ($$) is affordable and elegant, with modern-day amenities such as a hot tub. *2nd Street and Gothic Avenue, 970-349-7533, www.elkmountainlodge.net.* The **Purple Mountain B&B** ($$) was once a miners' house. Now it's a comfy B&B with fine views and gourmet breakfasts. *714 Gothic Ave., 970-349-5888, www.purplemountainlodge.com.* **Cristiana Guesthaus** ($-$$) is a Crested Butte tradition thanks to the delicious, healthy food and views of Mount Crested Butte from the hot tub. *621 Maroon Ave., 800-824-7899, www.cristianaguesthaus.com.* The **Old Town Inn** ($-$$) offers comfortable rooms at bargain prices. *708 6th St., 970-349-6184.*

The Nordic Inn ($$) is a friendly, slope-side B&B in the town of Mount Crested Butte. Cozy rooms and chalets will make you feel right at home, and hearty breakfasts provide a good start to a day of hiking, biking, or skiing. *14 Treasury Rd., Mount Crested Butte, 800-542-7669, www.nordicinncb.com.*

The recently renovated **Grand Lodge** ($$-$$$$) offers as many resort amenities as you could imagine, as well as a great proximity to the lifts. Most of the rooms are spacious and many have kitchenettes. The on-site Wildflower Spa is a great way to recover from the bumps and bruises you might acquire going down the mountain. Take advantage of the free town shuttle service and explore the local shops. *6 Emmons Loop, 888-823-4446, www.grandlodgecrestedbutte.com.* For luxury accommodations in downtown Crested Butte, **The Inn at Crested Butte Boutique Hotel & Spa** ($$$) is perfect. *1510 Whiterock Ave., 970-349-2111, 877-343-2111, www.innatcrestedbutte.net.* Stay at the **Pioneer Guest Cabins** ($$) on Cement Creek, where rustic but well-equipped cabins provide a sense of seclusion after snowshoeing or biking. In summer, Pioneer offers guided mountain-bike tours. *2094 County Road 740, 970-349-5517, www.thepioneer.net.*

Special Events

See Main Attractions, p. 265, for information about the week-long **Crested Butte Wildflower Festival** held each July. The **Crested Butte Music Festival** presents popular concerts throughout the summer; you can hear everything from orchestral works to bluegrass. The festival focuses on promoting performing arts throughout the Western Slope and hosts poetry readings and dance concerts as well as classes and speakers on the arts. *970-349-0619, www.crestedbuttemusicfestival.com.* **Crested Butte Arts Festival** in early August fills Elk Avenue with booths displaying fine-art outdoor photography, paintings, pottery, jewelry, glassware, and more. *970-349-1184, www.crestedbutteartfestival.com.*

In late June, Crested Butte's famous **Fat Tire Bike Week** draws professional mountain bikers and amateurs alike for serious fun and competition. You can also take rides with local guides, attend informative clinics, and chow down on barbecue. *970-349-6438.* The mid-September **Pearl Pass Tour** is a rowdy reenactment of the first mountain-bike ride to Aspen over Pearl Pass by bold Crested Butte residents in 1976 (see Mountain Biking, p. 268). *970-349-6438.*

Vinotok, a Slavic harvest festival, regenerates hope each September in Crested Butte. A huge Grump figure is built for residents to feed with negative thoughts they have written down on paper. The Grump is then burned in an enormous bonfire, to the celebratory toasts of onlookers. *970-349-6438.*

For More Information

Crested Butte Chamber of Commerce, *CO 135 and Elk Avenue, 970-349-6438, www.visitcrestedbutte.com*

PARADISE DIVIDE

What better name could there be for a place that provides one of the most beautiful reflection photographs in Colorado? At 11,300 feet, this flat divide between the Slate and East Rivers northwest of Crested Butte harbors little ponds that reflect the peaks of the Ruby Range. One mile north of Crested Butte, turn northwest off Gothic Road onto Slate River Road (see Scenic Location No. 93, p. 274). You'll need a four-wheel drive to proceed past the old townsite of Pittsburg on Forest Road 734. The ponds are at the intersection of FR 734 and FR 519.

On a clear day, Paradise Divide is really a morning place. Augusta Mountain and 12,958-foot Purple Mountain in the Ruby Range face due east and catch the warm, direct light of sunrise. The ponds, small and serene, reflect an image of the peaks so perfect that you might not be able to discern which way is up and which way is down if you flop the resulting photograph! Catch the best image from the pond right next to the road. In the foreground compose the front edge of the pond if you want more depth in the scene; for a very graphic, two-dimensional image, compose only mountains and their reflection. Remember that the worst time to photograph a reflection is when direct sunlight shines on the water. Just like ripples on the water, direct light erases the reflection. A polarizing filter can also erase reflections.

Stay on FR 519 for great views of Cinnamon Mountain, named for its brilliant red color. It's very photogenic in the morning and makes a great background for the alpine wildflowers that grow along the road. Continue north on FR 519 to Schofield Pass and Schofield Park, and ultimately south on FR 317 to the headwaters of the East River near Emerald Lake (see Scenic Location No. 95, opposite). Or head back down FR 734 to its intersection with FR 811, which delivers you into Washington Gulch and eventually back to Gothic Road. Washington Gulch is home to some of the best wildflower fields in the region, especially near the old townsite of Elkton.

GOTHIC/EAST RIVER

There's a good reason why Crested Butte is the official Wildflower Capital of Colorado—plants grow in its subalpine valleys, especially Gothic Valley, like no place else in the state. Perhaps it's a combination of so much water and fertile soil, but plants and flowers grow taller and thicker here. This drainage also boasts magnificent 12,625-foot Gothic Mountain and as beautiful a stretch of water as you'll ever see—the East River. From Crested Butte, take Gothic Road north through Crested Butte Mountain Resort. When the road turns to dirt, continue on to the town of Gothic. A car is fine past Gothic on Forest Road 317, but once it begins to ascend Schofield Pass, I recommend a four-wheel drive.

Soon after leaving the ski resort, watch for overlooks far down to the East River. This splendid section of river is as circuitous as any in Colorado. At mid-morning you will not believe how its silvery water shines, reflecting the rising sun's glare against the green meadows along the valley floor. Use a telephoto lens to zoom in on the river, and don't bother including a horizon. Soon you will enter aspen groves that make marvelous autumn images at the end of September. When you reach historic Gothic, you enter the best of wildflower country, where growth peaks in mid- to late July.

Just past town, many little creeks, draining from Gothic Mountain to the west and Avery Peak to the east, provide sustenance to the thick floral growth in the valley. Larkspur, cow parsnip, and corn lily grow tall and make a great foreground for Gothic Mountain. Before you reach the ascent to Emerald Lake (beautiful, but take the four-wheel drive) and Schofield Pass, look for places where the road crosses East River (merely a creek this high up). Compose the creek as a lead-in line with Mount Bellview and Avery Peak in the background. This part of the valley gets as green as green can get and, with a little blue sky, makes a colorful summer scene. Put on the polarizing filter and rotate it until the glare is removed from the water, which will render it deep blue, too.

Gunnison

Colorado Atlas & Gazetteer pp. 58, 67–69

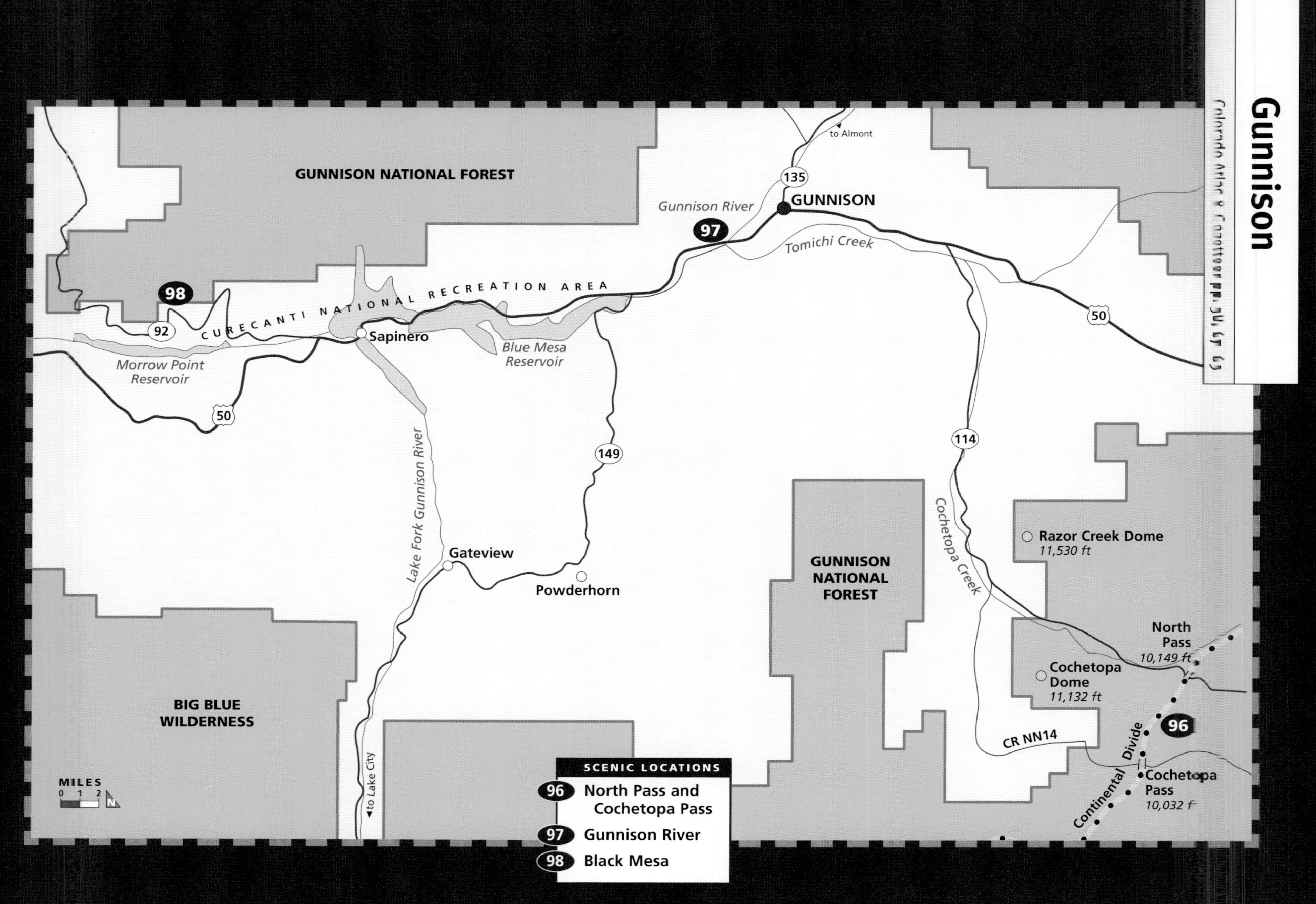
GUNNISON NATIONAL FOREST
GUNNISON
to Almont
135
Gunnison River
97
Tomichi Creek
50
98
92
CURECANTI NATIONAL RECREATION AREA
Sapinero
Blue Mesa Reservoir
Morrow Point Reservoir
50
114
149
Lake Fork Gunnison River
Gateview
Powderhorn
Cochetopa Creek
GUNNISON NATIONAL FOREST
Razor Creek Dome 11,530 ft
North Pass 10,149 ft
Cochetopa Dome 11,132 ft
96
CR NN14
Continental Divide
Cochetopa Pass 10,032 ft
BIG BLUE WILDERNESS
to Lake City
MILES 0 1 2
N
SCENIC LOCATIONS
96 North Pass and Cochetopa Pass
97 Gunnison River
98 Black Mesa

Gunnison

The Gunnison area boasts some of Colorado's best hiking, mountain biking, fishing, wildlife watching, and skiing, with breathtaking scenery around every bend in the river or turn on the trail. Perhaps this is because the Gunnison National Forest, Fossil Ridge Wilderness Study Area, and West Elk, Raggeds, and Collegiate Peaks Wilderness areas are all right in the town's backyard. The variety and quality of outdoor activities, as well as the charm and history of the town, ensure that there is always something for everyone in Gunnison. From Denver, take US 285 southwest 138 miles to Poncha Springs, turn right (west) on US 50, and drive 66 miles to Gunnison.

History

President Franklin Pierce commissioned Army Captain John W. Gunnison, one of the most experienced government surveyors, to find a route for a transcontinental railroad. Gunnison and his party followed the Tomichi (now Gunnison) River, and on September 6, 1853, camped near the present-day town. Within a couple decades, the arrival of the Denver & Rio Grande and Denver South Park & Pacific Railroads transformed Gunnison into a significant transportation center for mining as well as agriculture. Although the area suffered after the Silver Panic of 1893, farming and ranching buttressed the valley's economy, and Gunnison rebounded. In 1901 the Colorado State Normal School, now Western State College, was established here. Today, tourism and education revenues surpass those from agriculture.

Main Attractions

CAMPING

The Gunnison region rivals any in Colorado for camping experiences. **North Bank** campground above the Taylor River provides access both to fishing and to the Colorado Trail. From Gunnison, take CO 135 north 11 miles to Almont. Turn right (northeast) onto Taylor Canyon Road (Forest Road 742) and go about 8 miles to the entrance. **Granite** campground, about 0.5 mile before North Bank campground, is another solid option with views of Taylor Canyon. Enclosed by steep canyon walls along the Taylor River, **Rosy Lane** is a lovely campground popular with anglers. It is about 1 mile past North Bank on Taylor Canyon Road (FR 742).

Mosca campground beside Spring Creek Reservoir pleases enthusiasts of fishing and wildlife watching. From Almont, take Taylor Canyon Road (FR 742) just over 7 miles to FR 744. Turn left (north) onto FR 744 and drive 12 miles. **Lakeview,** as its name suggests, opens upon fabulous fishing at the adjacent Taylor Park Reservoir, with views up to the sublime Collegiate Peaks. From Almont, take Taylor Canyon Road (FR 742) for 23 miles. The campsites at **Mirror Lake** access both fishing and hiking—and again, you can't beat the scenery. From Almont, take Taylor Canyon Road (FR 742) 24 miles to FR 765, just beyond Taylor Park Reservoir, and turn right. After 8 miles you'll reach the old mining town of Tincup. Turn left (east) on FR 267 and continue 3 miles.

Once a stagecoach stop on the road from Tincup to Aspen, **Dinner Station** still serves as a pleasant spot on the Taylor River. From Almont, take Taylor Canyon Road (FR 742) for 33 miles. Secluded **Pitkin** campground accesses top backcountry fishing and hiking. From Gunnison, go east on US 50 for 12 miles to Parlin. Turn left onto County Road 76, go 15 miles to the town of Pitkin, then head east for 1 mile on FR 765. *For campground information: 970-641-0471.*

CURECANTI NATIONAL RECREATION AREA

Named after a Ute Chief, Curecanti National Recreation Area (NRA) encompasses three reservoirs, separated by dams along the Gunnison, extending west nearly from Gunnison to the eastern edge of Black Canyon of the Gunnison National Park (see Main Attractions, Montrose, p. 285). Blue Mesa Reservoir, the largest of the lakes, also ranks as the largest body of water in the state and is a major recreational destination for angling and other water activities. The other two, successively smaller reservoirs lie in the Black Canyon as it winds to the west. The NRA begins about 9 miles west of Gunnison on US 50 and follows the former watercourse for more than 30 miles to the East Portal of the national park. *Curecanti National Recreation Area, 102 Elk Creek, Gunnison, 970-641-2337.*

Camping: Curecanti NRA has campsites all along US 50. **Stevens Creek, Elk Creek, Dry Gulch,** and **Lake Fork** campgrounds all hug Blue Mesa Reservoir as you drive west. The **Red Creek** group campsite, 19 miles west of Gunnison off US 50, provides shade and views of the Dillon Pinnacles. *970-641-2337, ext. 205.*

Fishing: A sprawling lake that contains numerous inlets and three massive basins, **Blue Mesa Reservoir** is also the most accessible at Curecanti. Blue Mesa holds rainbows, browns, and brookies, as well as the state record for the largest Mackinaw, or lake trout, at 38.66 pounds. The best access to Blue Mesa is from US 50, just west of Gunnison. Slender **Morrow Point Reservoir** is just west of Blue Mesa and holds the state record for the biggest brown trout, at 18 pounds. From Gunnison, take US 50 west 28 miles and turn right onto CO 92, following the road north along the reservoir. Continue on CO 92 to reach the thinner **Crystal Reservoir,** flanked by stately canyon walls, where you can find seclusion with trout fishing. *For boating and tour information: Elk Creek Marina, 15 miles west of Gunnison, 24830 W. US 50, 970-641-0707.*

Hiking: Enjoy the diversity of animals, summer flowers, rock formations, and altitude shifts in this special "canyon country." The 2-mile (one way) **Dillon Pinnacles Trail** MODERATE from Blue Mesa Reservoir traverses stands of sagebrush en route to the cathedral-like spires of the volcanic Dillon Pinnacles. This trail climbs to a dramatic

NORTH PASS AND COCHETOPA PASS

Two of the lowest points along Colorado's Continental Divide are North (10,149 feet) and Cochetopa (10,032) Passes, which parallel each other just 4 miles apart as the crow flies. Each crosses the rolling, forested Cochetopa Hills linking the south end of the great Sawatch Range with the east end—and high peaks—of La Garita Wilderness. The landscapes around these passes are some of the most idyllic in Colorado. Exit US 50 south on CO 114 about 9 miles east of Gunnison. Continue over North Pass to Saguache in the San Luis Valley. To drive over Cochetopa Pass, exit CO 114 about 2 miles south of Cochetopa State Wildlife Area on County Road NN14, Cochetopa Pass Road. After crossing the pass, NN14 rejoins CO 114. A portion of NN14 is paved and the road is improved dirt the rest of the way. Cars are suitable.

Consider driving a loop over both passes from US 50. (The west side of the divide is at least as photogenic as the San Luis Valley side, so plan to drive from Saguache to the passes on another trip.) CO 114 follows beautiful Cochetopa Creek to the Cochetopa Pass turnoff, then ascends North Pass. The highway winds through a long, lovely canyon replete with ranch meadows, cottonwood trees, and sheer cliffs. In late September and early October, the colors are breathtaking. North Pass itself snakes across coniferous forests, but panoramic views are few.

Cochetopa Pass Road follows Cochetopa Creek to the scenic Dome Lakes State Wildlife Area, then continues through Cochetopa Park on its way over the pass. If you photograph closer to sunrise and sunset, you'll have the chance to make these settings dramatic without the benefit of stately peaks in the background.

overlook of Blue Mesa Reservoir; keep your eyes peeled for birds such as raptors, ravens, and magpies. The trailhead is just off US 50 at the north end of the bridge crossing Blue Mesa Reservoir.

The 2.5-mile (one way) **Crystal Creek Trail** MODERATE overlooks Crystal Reservoir within the Black Canyon of the Gunnison. The trail leads through sagebrush and summer wildflowers to fabulous views of the West Elk Mountains to the north. Take CO 92 west from Blue Mesa Reservoir about 24 miles to the parking area and trailhead.

Curecanti Creek Trail DIFFICULT descends 2 miles from the rim of the Black Canyon of the Gunnison to Morrow Point Reservoir. The swift Curecanti Creek and views of the Curecanti Needle formation, a 700-foot-tall granite spire, make this steep hike worthwhile, but it is not for everyone. Take US 50 west from Gunnison 28 miles, turn right onto CO 92, and continue 10 miles to the trailhead.

Activities

FISHING AND FLOAT TRIPS

The **Upper Gunnison River** offers some of the best fly-fishing in Colorado (see Scenic Location No. 97, below). CO 135 follows the river from Almont, at the confluence of the Taylor and East Rivers, before veering left at Gunnison; from there, US 50 follows it west to Blue Mesa Reservoir (see Curecanti National Recreation Area, p. 279). Brown trout prevail, but kokanee salmon and large rainbows also live here.

Taylor Park Reservoir is home to northern pike, browns, and Mackinaws. To get to **Taylor River**, a fine trout stream, and Taylor Park Reservoir from Gunnison, take CO 135 north 11 miles to Almont, then bear right onto Taylor Canyon Road (Forest Road 742). **Texas Creek** flows into Taylor Park Reservoir from the east, with good fishing. Follow Taylor Canyon Road (FR 742) to its intersection with Texas Creek Road (FR 755).

The Class I–III whitewater on many of the rivers in the Gunnison area is also perfect for family rafting float trips. *For lessons and guided fishing and float trips: High Mountain Outdoors/ Drifters, 115 S. Wisconsin, Gunnison, 970-641-4243; Three Rivers Resort, Almont, 970-641-1303, www.3riversresort.com.*

GUNNISON RIVER

The Gunnison River flows through much of west-central Colorado, with a particularly beautiful stretch following US 50 from the base of Monarch Pass west to Blue Mesa Reservoir. The section of river east of Gunnison is actually a tributary, Tomichi Creek, which courses through the same type of ranch meadows you find west of Gunnison. The entire valley is bounded by rocky, sage-covered hills, a landscape as pastoral as any in Colorado and perhaps most reminiscent of North Park. In winter the valley is one of the coldest in Colorado.

The highway meets the river 5 miles west of Gunnison. Notice how the barren winter cottonwood trees silhouette against the frozen river and snow-covered terrain. Photograph here at dawn and dusk, when pink clouds might lend their color to the white landscape. In May, the cottonwoods exhibit lime green hues, meadows begin to turn green, and the river runs full. Look for vantage points along the river that allow you to combine all three elements. The sun rises and sets at right angles to the river, so shooting to the south across the river allows sidelighting that creates long shadows and rich color. Photograph during autumn when hay bales linger in the meadows from the last cut, usually from late August to late September. At sunset, the bales cast sharp shadows, and brown grasses turn gold. Catch the cottonwoods west of Gunnison when they change colors. If cattle wander into the scene, so be it—they define the way of life in Gunnison country.

BLACK MESA

One of my favorite autumn aspen haunts is a remote place called Black Mesa, which backs up to the south side of the West Elk Wilderness, defined by large aspen forests and creeks that plunge through steep canyons into Black Canyon of the Gunnison National Park. Black Canyon (see Scenic Location No. 99, p. 288) is the historical name for the entire length of canyon from Sapinero (now beneath Blue Mesa Reservoir) to Montrose. Three reservoirs now occupy much of the canyon. Nevertheless, except for CO 92, Black Mesa looks much like it did 100 years ago—scenic and wild. Exit US 50 to the north on CO 92 at the Blue Mesa Reservoir dam on the west end of the reservoir. CO 92 ends in Delta.

After crossinq the dam, CO 92 ascends Soap Mesa, then Black Mesa, winding in and out of the canyons that drain into Black Canyon until finally crossing Crystal Creek. The hillsides and canyons are filled with aspen and scrub oak trees. Watch for places along the highway where a short hike allows you to see into the Black Canyon and down to either the river or the reservoirs. From some points you can look up or down the canyon, which creates more depth in the scene than viewing across it. To photograph these views, wait for cloudy light, which eliminates the high contrast of direct lighting so difficult for film to manage.

Do take advantage of direct light at sunrise and sunset on Black Mesa late in September. The oaks turn brilliant shades of orange and red, the aspens turn yellow, and both are stunning when sidelit in the mornings and evenings. It's a glorious palette that works especially well on Fujichrome Velvia film, a relatively "slow" slide film rated at 50 ASA that requires more light than most to be exposed properly. You'll be thrilled with the colors (see pp. 151–152, *Photographing the Landscape*).

FOUR-WHEEL-DRIVE TRIPS AND GHOST TOWNS

The 73-mile **Gunnison Scenic Loop** goes to the silver and gold mining towns of **Ohio, Pitkin,** and **Tincup** (see Buena Vista and Salida, p. 234), encircling the mountains of Fossil Ridge and following the Taylor River down to Almont. From Gunnison, take US 50 east 12 miles, then turn left (east) on County Road 76 and continue 9 miles to Ohio, where a few old mining cabins remain. Continue 6 miles on CR 76 to Pitkin, still very much alive with shops and lodging.

A couple miles north of Pitkin, a 6-mile (one way) detour to the right on Forest Road 839 takes you to the Alpine Tunnel. This railroad tunnel was bored through the Continental Divide in 1880 to connect the Gunnison Valley with mining camps near Buena Vista. Now closed to all traffic, the tunnel is still considered one of the great engineering feats of its time. On your way to the tunnel, look for the remains of **Woodstock** and **Sherrod**, two old silver camps.

Once back on CR 76 (now FR 765), continue 15 miles north to Tincup. Then follow FR 765 as it winds 9 miles northwest to Taylor Park Reservoir, where you can take paved Taylor Canyon Road (FR 742) southwest 22 miles to Almont, pick up CO 135, and return to Gunnison. Check in with the Gunnison visitor center for maps and road conditions before heading out. *Town Park, 500 E. Tomichi, 970-641-1501, www.gunnison-co.com.*

HIKING

A diversity of ecosystems and wildlife, wildflowers, and stunningly carved rock awaits the hardy hiker in Gunnison country. Five miles west of Gunnison, just off US 50, the 1.5-mile (one way) **Neversink Trail** EASY follows the north shore of the Gunnison River near a great blue heron rookery. See waterfowl and wildlife, especially active at dusk, on this nature hike. The 8.5-mile (one way) **Timberline Trail** EASY follows streams and ponds to views of Taylor Park Reservoir and the Sawatch Range. Access the trail just north of Mirror Lake campground (see Camping, Main Attractions, p. 279).

The 7-mile (one way) **Henry Lake Trail** MODERATE climbs to an alpine lake at the base of 13,254-foot Mount Henry, in the Fossil Ridge Wilderness Study Area. The trail crosses many small streams to a great view of 12,459-foot Cross Mountain. From Gunnison, take CO 135 north 11 miles to Almont. Turn right (northeast) onto Taylor Canyon Road (Forest Road 742) and go 15 miles to Lottis Creek campground. Turn right at the second campground entrance and follow the road through the camping area to the trailhead.

Mill/Castle Trail MODERATE climbs 9 miles (one way) into the West Elk Wilderness with views of The Castles—a group of volcanic spires—and the Elk Range from the top of Storm Pass. From Gunnison, go north 3 miles on CO 135, turn left onto Ohio Creek Road, and go 9 miles to Mill Creek Road, which bears left and continues for another 4 miles; I recommend a four-wheel drive. The gate marks the boundary of the wilderness area.

HORSEBACK RIDING

Take in Gunnison country by means of its most venerable mode of transportation. Horseback guides can give you a history of this remote backcountry and lead you to the best places to see wildlife. **Gunnison Country Guide Service** can tailor a trip to your family's interest and ability. *970-641-2830,* [illegible]

MOUNTAIN BIKING

The 10-mile **Rage in the Sage Loop** DIFFICULT follows one of the routes of the annual spring Fat Tire Bike Week competition (see Special Events, Crested Butte, p. 275). This exciting ride climbs and plunges through the sage and scrub brush with views of the San Juans, West Elk Mountains, and Fossil Ridge. The route is fairly well marked, but you'd be wise to pick up a map as this trail is rerouted from year to year.

From Gunnison, take US 50 west to Gold Basin Road, then turn left (south) and follow the airport landing strip. After crossing Tomichi Creek, go another mile and turn right (west) onto the dirt road with a sign for Hartmans Rock. Park here and begin your ride. *For information and maps: The Tuneup Bike Shop, 222 N. Main, 970-641-0285.*

MUSEUM

Gunnison Pioneer Museum showcases Victorian furniture, old photographs, American Indian arrowheads, and a narrow-gauge railroad train. The museum also provides summer jeep tours of historic Aberdeen Quarry, which supplied the granite for Colorado's Capitol Building in Denver. *803 E. Tomichi Ave., 970-641-4530.*

SCENIC DRIVES

US 50 west from Gunnison to CO 92 at the Morrow Point Reservoir in Curecanti National Recreation Area forms a stretch of the stunning, 207-mile **West Elk Loop Scenic and Historic Byway.** To continue on the West Elk Loop, take CO 92 north past Crawford Reservoir to Hotchkiss. Turn onto CO 133 and drive northeast 9 miles to Paonia and 8 miles farther to the old coal town of Somerset. About 5 miles east of Somerset, the West Elk Loop forks; turn off CO 133 to continue east on County Road 12 over 9,980-foot Kebler Pass en route to Crested Butte. From Crested Butte back to Gunnison, the West Elk Loop follows CO 135 along the West Elk Wilderness. The other fork near Somerset spurs north on CO 133, away from the main loop, over McClure Pass to Redstone all the way to Carbondale.

The 30-mile **Ohio Pass Road** (see Scenic Location No. 89, p. 267) connects Gunnison with Crested Butte by a more rustic route than CO 135.

Restaurants

Catering to residents and visitors for more than 20 years, **The Trough Restaurant** ($$), 1.5 miles west of Gunnison on US 50, serves ribs, seafood, trout, and wild game. *970-641-3724.* **Mario's Pizza and Ristorante** ($) has been serving delicious Italian specialties for nearly thirty years. *213 W. Tomichi Ave., 970-641-1374.* Though a relative newcomer, **Garlic Mike's** ($$), 2 miles north of Gunnison on CO 135, has found a niche with its piquant Italian entrees. *970-641-2493.*

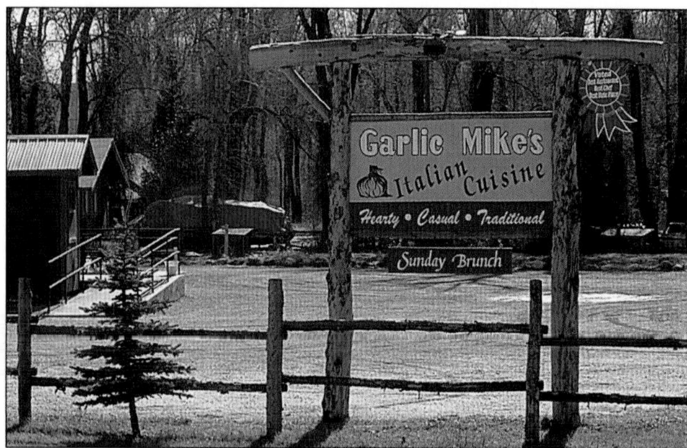

Garlic Mike's restaurant, Gunnison

Accommodations

Nestled in the trees by the Gunnison River, the **Water Wheel Inn** ($$) is a fun family destination complete with a playground, tennis courts, and proximity to outdoor activities. From Gunnison, go 1.5 miles west on US 50. *970-641-1650.* **The Wanderlust Hostel** ($) offers a great alternative to the traditional hotel experience. The hostel offers two dorm rooms that can each accommodate up to six people and two private rooms. *221 N. Blvd., 970-901-1599, www.thewanderlusthostel.com*

Journeying to the **Inn at Arrowhead** ($$-$$$) is half the pleasure of staying there. From Gunnison, take US 50 west 35 miles to the Blue Creek Canyon turnoff to your left (look for the inn's sign). The road follows the Little Blue Creek 5 miles through Blue Creek Canyon, abounding with wildlife including beavers, bears, deer, elk, and moose. At this remote rustic inn you'll find coziness and excellent dinners. Your hosts can also arrange fishing and horseback riding trips. *21401 Alpine Plateau Rd., Cimarron, 970-862-8206, www.innatarrowhead.com.*

Special Events

Known as "The Grandaddy of Colorado Rodeos," the century-old **Cattlemen's Days Rodeo** is held annually during July. Although a Professional Rodeo Cowboys Association–sanctioned event attracting top competitors from across the nation, Cattlemen's Days is also a local event drawing cowhands from the neighboring ranches. See the horse, hog, goat, sheep, and—you guessed it—cattle competitions. There's even a dog and rabbit show! Cowboy poetry, dancing, a barbecue, and a parade add to the festivities. *970-641-1501.*

For More Information

Gunnison Chamber of Commerce, *Town Park, 500 E. Tomichi, 970-641-1501, www.gunnison-co.com.*

Montrose

(see map on p. 286)

Montrose lies in the heart of the beautiful Uncompahgre Valley between Delta and Ridgway, 25 miles north of the jagged San Juan Mountains. The city lies amid lush farm- and ranchland and towns like Paonia, Cedaredge, and Olathe, known more for produce than cattle. Stop at local orchards or produce stands to take some of this heavenly harvest with you. With its proximity to the region's natural attractions, Montrose is a great base camp for enjoying recreation in the valley. Take scenic day trips from Montrose in almost any direction—the Black Canyon of the Gunnison to the east, the Grand Mesa to the north, or Owl Creek Pass and Ridgway to the south.

History

The Uncompahgre Valley was once home to the Ute Indians, who hunted the deer and then-plentiful bison roaming the open rangeland. By the 1880s, however, Western settlers had pushed the Utes out of the valley, eventually displacing most of them to the Four Corners area. Ranchers used the rich valley lands for raising cattle; farmers introduced fruit trees near the turn of the last century. Today, tourism and recreation, along with the long-standing ranches and orchards, define the Uncompahgre Valley.

Main Attractions

BLACK CANYON OF THE GUNNISON NATIONAL PARK

One summer, as we drove along the rim of the canyon with bright sunlight illuminating the green piñon and juniper trees, my traveling companion asked me why it was called the Black Canyon. I was tempted to make something up, but all I said was, "You'll see." Peering over the rim at the visitor center and seeing the sheer, pitch-black walls descending into the shadows of the canyon, my friend said, "Now I understand."

Declaring the region a national park in 1999, Congress also designated the rugged and pristine area below the rim as wilderness to ensure its preservation. The park at the Black Canyon of the Gunnison protects an unparalleled natural wonder and provides areas for camping, hiking, rock climbing, and fishing. You can drive two scenic byways along the canyon's north and south rims. The north rim is closed in winter and, in my opinion, doesn't put forth as impressive views of the canyon as the south rim—but it does have more solitude for contemplative souls.

In 1853, while looking for a transcontinental railroad route, Army Captain John W. Gunnison and his survey party encountered the gorge. In 1870, surveyor Ferdinand Hayden, also in search of a railroad river crossing, declared the Black Canyon "inaccessible and foreboding." Other railroad survey parties tried to cross the canyon by lowering wagons down to the Gunnison River. After their wagons shattered into splinters, they, too, declared a railroad crossing impossible. Finally, under the leadership of railroad genius General William Jackson Palmer, a Denver & Rio Grande narrow-gauge railroad line was built through the canyon from Chipeta Falls past the Curecanti Needle to Cimarron. Today you can see Locomotive 278 displayed on a high trestle within the spectacular high-walled Cimarron River Canyon. (Visit it from Montrose by taking US 50 east 20 miles and turning left at Cimarron onto Road Q83.)

The 53-mile-long canyon ranges from 1,730 to 2,700 feet in depth. At one point the canyon is 1,300 feet wide at the top and as little as 40 feet wide at the bottom. The deepest and most impressive 14 miles of the gorge now lie within Black Canyon of the Gunnison National Park (the canyon begins east of the park boundary by many miles, in what is now Curecanti National Recreation Area). The Gunnison River roars through the canyon at 3,000 to 12,000 cubic feet per second, continually sculpting the canyon. The depth of the canyon mutes the sound of this torrent of water to a small roar.

To get to the canyon's south rim from Montrose, take US 50 east for 7 miles, turn left (north) onto CO 347, and go 6 miles to the park. To reach the north rim from Montrose, take US 50 northwest 21 miles to Delta. From Delta, take CO 92 east 31 miles to Crawford, then follow signs to Rim Drive North (North Rim Road) and the park entrance. You can also access the north rim from Gunnison on US 50 turning right on CO 92 just west of Sapinero, and the south rim 63 miles west of Gunnison via US 50 and CO 347. *970-641-2337, www.nps.gov/blca.*

Camping: With just 13 sites in a dense piñon forest, **North Rim** campground offers seclusion and access to hiking trails. To get there, drive west on Rim Drive North (North Rim Road) and go about 0.75 mile. With 103 small sites spaced together in loops, **South Rim** campground provides a less remote camping experience. The campground is on your right as you enter the park on Rim Drive South (South Rim Road).

The **East Portal** area on the floor of the canyon is the site of the Gunnison Diversion Project, an amazing engineering feat of water reclamation of the early 1900s. Now East Portal provides campsites with shade and easy fishing access. Brave kayakers also like to launch from East Portal into the Class IV–V rapids; note that such expert kayakers must register with the National Park Service. East Portal Road is just to the right (south) of Rim Drive South and the park entrance. The paved, 5.5-mile road has a 16-percent grade, many steep curves and switchbacks, and is closed in winter. You pass private property and wind back into the park en route to the diversion dam at the west end of Curecanti National Recreation Area (see Main Attractions, Gunnison, p. 279).

All campgrounds are on a first-come, first-served basis. *970-641-2337.*

Canyon Overlooks: Although Ellsworth Kolb successfully ran the river in 1916, and Layton Kor scaled the canyon's walls in the early 1960s, this statement in the visitor center offers a cautionary summation of people's relationship with the Black Canyon: "The National Park Service has recorded a number

Montrose

Colorado Atlas & Gazetteer pp. 34–37, 64–67

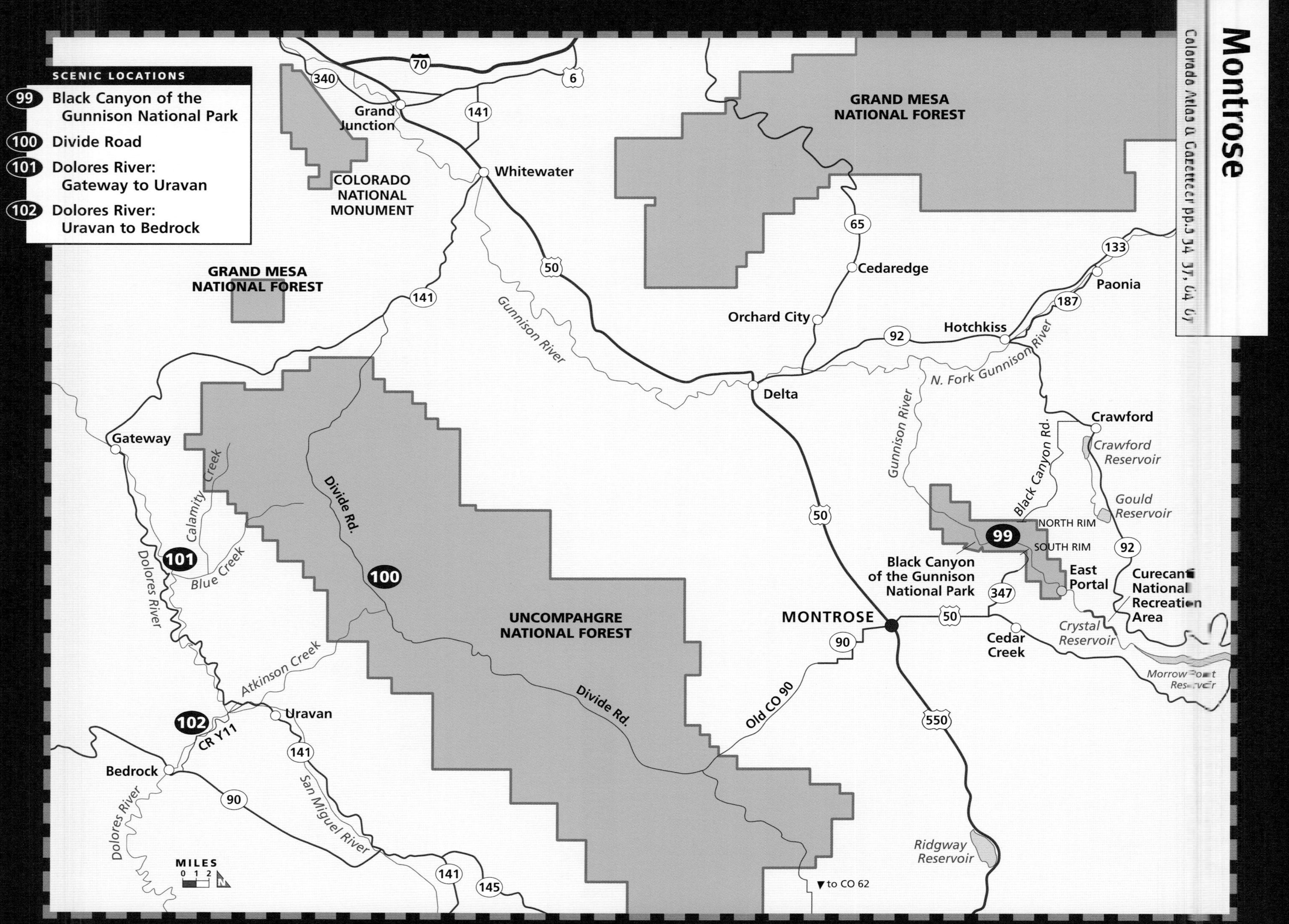

SCENIC LOCATIONS
99 Black Canyon of the Gunnison National Park
100 Divide Road
101 Dolores River: Gateway to Uravan
102 Dolores River: Uravan to Bedrock
GRAND MESA NATIONAL FOREST
GRAND MESA NATIONAL FOREST
UNCOMPAHGRE NATIONAL FOREST
COLORADO NATIONAL MONUMENT
Grand Junction
Whitewater
Gunnison River
Cedaredge
Orchard City
Delta
Hotchkiss
Paonia
N. Fork Gunnison River
Gunnison River
Crawford
Crawford Reservoir
Gould Reservoir
Black Canyon Rd.
NORTH RIM
SOUTH RIM
Black Canyon of the Gunnison National Park
East Portal
Curecanti National Recreation Area
Crystal Reservoir
Morrow Point Reservoir
MONTROSE
Cedar Creek
Old CO 90
Ridgway Reservoir
to CO 62
Gateway
Calamity Creek
Blue Creek
Dolores River
Divide Rd.
Divide Rd.
Atkinson Creek
Uravan
CR Y11
Bedrock
San Miguel River
Dolores River
MILES
0 1 2
70
6
340
141
141
141
141
145
50
50
50
65
92
92
133
187
347
90
90
550
99
100
101
102

of successful rescues of even the most prepared adventurer, but warns that a number of individuals have been impossible to rescue or recover."

Fortunately, visitors to the canyon—if less than ready for precipitous canyon exploration—can simply gawk from the many overlooks along the south and north rims. Each overlook affords a different perspective of the canyon in the changing light (see Scenic Location No. 99, p. 288).

The first overlook on the south rim, **Tomichi Point,** leaves you speechless; **Gunnison Point** near the visitor center is also breathtaking. The visitor center provides resource materials and hosts summer nature walks and campfire programs, and don't miss its geological, ecological, and historical displays. Move on to check out the view at the **Pulpit Rock** overlook. Other south rim overlooks—**Rock Point, Devil's Lookout, Cedar Point,** and **Dragon Point,** to name a few—require only a short hike EASY, and **Sunset View** and **High Point** overlooks provide picnic tables for a sensational natural backdrop to your lunch. While viewing the canyon, watch for darting canyon wrens and birds of prey. At dusk or dawn, you might be fortunate enough to see a great horned owl flying low in search of prey.

The overlooks on the less-populous north rim, including **Chasm View, The Narrows, Balanced Rock,** and **Kneeling Camel,** are more difficult to reach, but the solitude and vistas are well worth the effort.

Hiking: I believe the best way to see and enjoy a canyon is from its depths rather than its rim. However, hiking into the Black Canyon of the Gunnison can be an arduous and even hazardous undertaking. The descent is extremely steep, and footing on ledges is tricky. **Chukar Trail, Bobcat Trail, Duncan Trail,** and **Ute Trail** vary in steepness and difficulty, and all drop down into the canyon. For your own safety, and because the area below the rim is designated as wilderness, you must register for a permit with the National Park Service at the visitor center. *970-249-1914.*

The rim trails are a safer, pleasant alternative. Along the south rim, take the **Rim Rock Trail** EASY to Gunnison Point and the visitor center (the trail follows South Rim Road). From the visitor center, take the meandering 1-mile (one way) **Oak Flats Trail** MODERATE, which commands fine views of the Gunnison River below. Oak Flats Trail connects to the more remote **Uplands Trail** EASY. Access Rim Rock and Uplands Trails from the north loop of South Rim campground. **Warner Point Nature Trail** EASY is a 0.7-mile (one way) stroll with grand views of the canyon, and benches and signposts along the way. The trailhead is at the parking area at the High Point Overlook on South Rim Road. The short and secluded **Chasm View Nature Trail** EASY begins at the end of North Rim campground loop.

The north rim also features two beautiful and more remote hiking trails. The 1.5-mile (one way) **North Vista Trail** MODERATE accesses Exclamation Point just above Painted Wall. To get to the trailhead, take North Rim Road and turn right at the fork to the north rim ranger station. The 2.5-mile (one way) **Deadhorse Trail** MODERATE, with views of Deadhorse Gulch and the East Portal, starts at the Kneeling Camel overlook, just off North Rim Road. Both trails go into newly designated wilderness, so you will need to check in at a ranger station. *970-249-1914.*

Rock Climbing: Rock climbing in the Black Canyon of the Gunnison is only for experts. Spires, crags, and inconsistent rock (not to mention poison ivy) make all of the routes complex and somewhat dicey. The **North Chasm View Wall** on the north rim has the most routes; experienced climbers consider it to be the canyon's best rock. The buttress on **Checkerboard Wall** is also popular. Access to these climbs is from the North Rim campground. The **South Chasm View Wall** and other south rim routes can be accessed from South Rim Road. Permits are required for bouldering and climbing in the canyon; register at the south rim visitor center or at the Forest Service office at the north rim entrance. *For information, climbing lessons, and guide services: San Juan Mountain Guides, 474 Main St., Ouray, 970-325-4925, www.ouray climbing.com.*

Activities

HIKING

The 6-mile (one way) **Transfer Trail** MODERATE follows the Uncompahgre Plateau and accesses beautiful Roubideau Canyon. To reach the trailhead, take Jay Jay Road, off US 50 between Delta and Montrose, west. (Jay Jay Road becomes Deadman's Drive.) Turn right onto Coal Creek Drive, left onto Jasmine Road, then right on Hillside, which becomes Holly. Turn left at Transfer Road and go 7 miles to the national forest boundary, then go 4 miles to Oak Hill. The Transfer trailhead sign is on the right (west) side of the road.

To hike in the heart of the **West Elk Wilderness**, take the 15-mile (one way) **Soap Creek Trail** MODERATE to Sheep Lake. Take County Road 721 north from CO 92 near Blue Mesa Reservoir. Another popular hike is the 5-mile round-trip **Beckwith Pass Trail** EASY, which takes you to Lost Lake, Lost Lake Slough, and Dollar Lake. To get to the trailhead from Paonia, take CO 133 east to CR 12 below Paonia Reservoir. Continue on CR 12 to the Lost Lake campground sign. The trail begins at the end of the campground road.

HORSEBACK RIDING

For remote backcountry rides into the pristine West Elk Wilderness, saddle up with the **Whistling Acres Guest Ranch,** a working cattle ranch near Paonia. Take US 50 north to Delta, then drive 25 miles east on CO 92 and CO 133. Ask about joining a cattle drive. *800-346-1420, www.whistlingacres.com.* For other scenic rides in the Black Canyon area, consider **Elk Ridge Trail Rides.** *12500 Bostwick Park Rd., Montrose, 970-240-6007, www.elkridgetrailrides.com.*

MOUNTAIN BIKING

The 30-mile (one-way) **Roubideau Trail** MODERATE is the southern part of the **Tabeguache Trail** that connects Montrose and Grand Junction. The 140-mile Tabeguache system is the second leg of the Colorado Plateau Mountain Bike Trail System. The first leg is the famous **Kokopelli Bike Trail,** which connects Grand Junction to Moab, Utah (see Main Attractions, Grand Junction, p. 136). Riding Colorado's Uncompahgre Plateau, you will experience cool, rolling hills, and then drop down into hot, dry mesas. Wear orange during hunting season in the fall. Intersecting side roads are popular jeep trails, so be prepared for vehicular traffic.

Take CO 90, then Old CO 90, southwest from Montrose to Divide Road (see Scenic Location No. 100, p. 289) and follow it another 7.5 miles to its intersection with East Bull Road and the trail access. Your ride will end in Delta, so set a shuttle unless you feel very energetic! From Delta, take County Road 348 until it intersects with the Delta-Nucla Road, then follow

BLACK CANYON OF THE GUNNISON NATIONAL PARK

A unique and astounding place, the Black Canyon spectacularly combines a narrow opening, sheer walls, and a 2,000-foot average depth. The south rim is more developed (with paved roads and a visitor center) than the north rim, but both sides have drives that follow the canyon's edge. You can photograph across or down into the canyon from various vantage points and see all the way to the Gunnison River. If you are fit, you also can hike down to the river. Photograph the canyon either in cloudy light or before sunrise or after sunset. Direct light makes deep shadows and intense highlights that create too much contrast for film to manage. (On film, highlights are lighter and shadows darker than they appear to the eye.) White clouds reflect a warm light onto the landscape, rendering colors more brilliant. Blue sky just before sunrise and just after sunset will cast cool light onto the landscape and dull its colors.

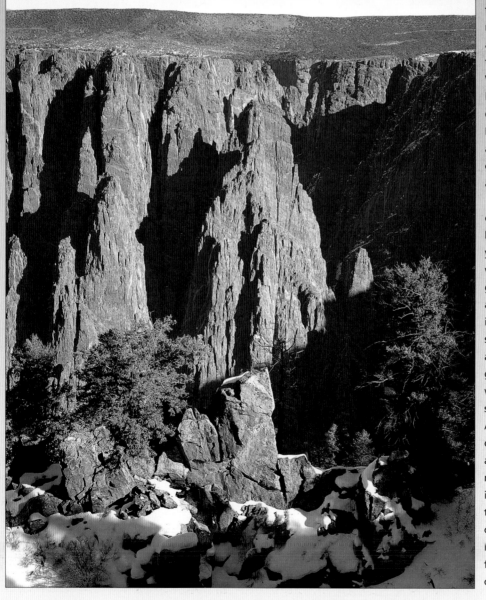

In order to create a sense of depth, employ perspective by including foreground in your scene when composing views into the canyon. Foreground objects could include a piñon pine, juniper tree, interesting rocks, or a friend standing on the edge of the abyss! If you wish to photograph in direct light, find vantages that allow you to see up or down the canyon. Although the canyon runs on a northwest/southeast axis, find places where the rising and setting sun shines into, not across, the canyon, thus reducing the amount of shadow that can ruin the image. Visit in winter when fresh snow creates highlights on the rock walls.

100 SCENIC LOCATION DIVIDE ROAD

Here's another of my secrets I never thought I'd give away! The Uncompahgre Plateau runs on a northwest/southeast axis from Unaweep Canyon (see Scenic Location No. 36, p. 138) south to Dallas Divide (see Scenic Location No. 143, p. 391), about 60 miles as the crow flies. It barely rises above 9,000 feet, but it's one of my favorite scenic places, especially in spring and fall. Divide Road follows the crest of the plateau for its entire length, at times lost in trees, at others providing incredible views over Dolores River country (see Scenic Location Nos. 101, p. 290, and 102, p. 292). The aspens bring me back year after year.

From the Whitewater junction south of Grand Junction on US 50, go west 14 miles on CO 141, then turn south on Divide Road. If you're coming from the south, from Ridgway drive 3.5 miles west of Dallas Divide on CO 62, then turn north on County Road 60X. You have to make four short jogs to the west as you continue heading north to Sanborne Park Road (Forest Road 510). Turn right (north) on FR 510 and proceed 2 miles to an intersection where you bear left on Divide Road (FR 402). From here to CO 141 you encounter many side roads, but if you follow the well-marked Divide Road and continue heading northwest, you'll be fine. The road is improved dirt all the way and can be managed by car—if there's been no rain, recent frost, or thaw. I recommend a four-wheel-drive vehicle for this long, remote drive.

The south end of the road commands views of the Sneffels Range that you can photograph successfully with a telephoto lens, but I especially like the first 30 miles after exiting CO 141 from the north. Aspen forests intermittently line the road on the west slope of the plateau, catching the full intensity of the setting sun, which here at the edge of the Rockies has nothing to set behind save the deserts of eastern Utah. The rays of such a low-lying sun bathe the aspen in vermilion light (see pp. 86–89, *Photographing the Landscape*). Look for places where the road bisects aspen groves, creating a sinuous lead-in line as it winds through the trees. Also be sure to explore side roads here to find scenic gems of your own!

this road to the intersection with Cottonwood Road. Take the left fork and continue another 1.25 miles to the Mesa Station; park just past the cattle guard. *For more information and maps: Cascade Bicycles, 21 N. Cascade, Montrose, 970-249-7375; Ridgway Outdoor Experience, 153 N. Hwy. 550, Ridgway, 970-626-3608.*

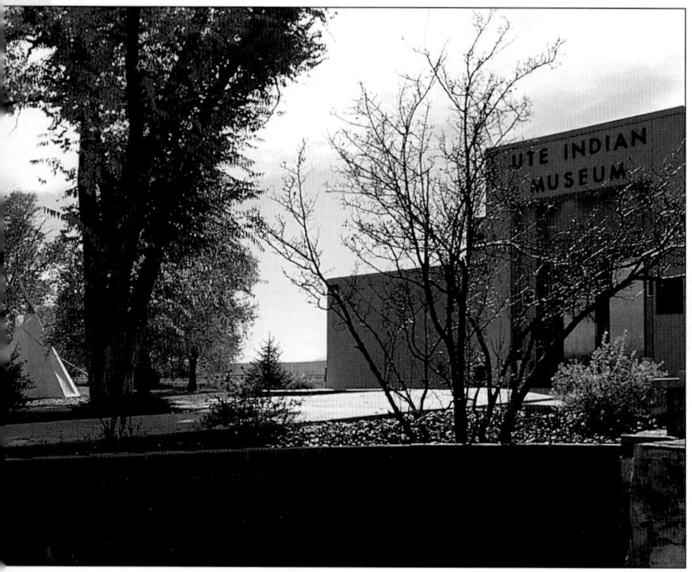

Ute Indian Museum, Montrose

MUSEUMS

Ute Indian Museum and **Ouray Memorial Park,** located on a farm once owned by Chief Ouray and his wife, Chipeta (see Colorado Cameo, Ouray, p. 379), provide a comprehensive collection of Ute artifacts, photos, exhibits, and screenings about the history of the Ute tribes. The museum also hosts tribal festivals, and Chipeta's remains are buried here. Note that the visitor center provides general information on the Uncompahgre Valley area. *3 miles south of Montrose on US 550 at 17253 Chipeta Dr., 970-249-3098, www.coloradohistory.org.*

Montrose County Historical Museum displays everything from mining equipment to dolls to rare Native American artifacts. The large photo collection and Montrose newspapers dating from 1896 to 1940 are fascinating. *21 N. Rio Grande, Montrose, 970-249-2085.*

Stop in Cedaredge, 14 miles north of Delta on CO 65, to take in more valley heritage. **Pioneer Town** is an authentic replica of a turn-of-the-century Western town, with log cabins, schoolhouse, general store, saloon, jail, and blacksmith shop. **Charles States Museum** provides eclectic displays ranging from the art of needlepoint to one of the largest dinosaur footprints ever found. **Sutherland Indian Museum** has one of the most extensive collections of arrowheads in the West. *970-856-7554, www.cedaredgecolorado.com.*

RAFTING

Serious rafters and kayakers know and love this region of rapids and gentler runs beneath storied canyons. The **Gunnison Gorge** MODERATE section of the Gunnison River features spectacular Class II–IV whitewater interspersed with lovely, deep pools.

DOLORES RIVER: GATEWAY TO URAVAN

The Dolores River runs through a sandstone canyon that exemplifies Utah more than Colorado. I know it well from several rafting experiences through the entire length of this desert canyon—173 miles from Bradfield Bridge, near Cahone, to the Dolores' confluence with the Colorado River in Utah. Some of the river route follows roads and highways from which you can photograph the watercourse. From Grand Junction, take CO 141 from US 50 southwest to Gateway. From here the highway parallels the river nearly to Uravan, an abandoned uranium mining community.

Before you head south on the highway, drive north on County Road 4.2 from Gateway. You can take a car part of the way, and a four-wheel-drive vehicle even farther. In either case, you'll be treated to views of The Palisade, a long, high sandstone fin that photographs well at sunset. Just south of Gateway the Dolores winds through a narrowing canyon. Find vantage points along the highway that allow you to compose the river in the foreground with the canyon walls rising to the left and right. Eventually the river enters a narrow, deep chasm, and the highway climbs to the rim, providing incredible views down the canyon. Look for pull-outs where you can see the river and canyon snaking into the distance (and keep your fingers crossed for cloudy light to avoid high contrast). Keep an eye out for a hanging flume still suspended from the vertical canyon walls and the accompanying interpretive sign next to the highway.

For gentler whitewater, raft the Gunnison River between Delta and Grand Junction. Designated wilderness once home to many unsavory outlaws, the **Escalante** and **Dominguez Canyons** EASY can only be visited by boat, and their Class I–II water, along with awesome canyon scenery, makes the route a perfect family float trip.

The **San Miguel River** EASY affords spectacular views of the 14,000-foot San Juans and the canyons of the Colorado Plateau. Its Class II–III water makes for superb rafting and float-fishing. The **Dolores River** DIFFICULT, with Class II–IV water, is famous for its narrow canyons, Indian petroglyphs, and mysterious Anasazi cliff dwellings. *For more information and reservations: Dream West Expeditions, 113 Rose Lane #E, Montrose, 307-250-7389, www.dreamwestexpeditions.com; Gunnison River Expeditions, 970-249-0408, www.cimarroncreek.com.*

TOURS

Although most consider Grand Junction and Palisade the heart of Colorado's wine industry, other valley areas produce delicious grapes for fine wines. Take a tasting tour of **Rocky Hill Winery.**

102 SCENIC LOCATION
DOLORES RIVER: URAVAN TO BEDROCK

At Uravan, the San Miguel River joins the Dolores River from the east (see Scenic Location No. 144, p. 393). CO 141 continues south, but now follows the San Miguel, making this a worthwhile drive. See more of the Dolores by turning off CO 141 onto County Road Y11. Cross the San Miguel River before Uravan and head west. Improved dirt and manageable by car, Road Y11 follows the San Miguel River for about 5 miles, after which the river converges with the Dolores in a canyon that leads to Paradox Valley and Bedrock. This canyon is incredibly scenic but so deep and dark that you should try to photograph it in cloudy light or at least when no direct light falls inside or on the canyon rim. The contrast created by shadow and direct light is too great for film to manage.

Watch for the whitewater rapids along the way. Compose a scene that includes whitewater and canyon walls, not bothering to include any sky. Use slow shutter speeds to render the water soft and conspicuous (see pp. 81–83, *Photographing the Landscape*). The road soon exits the canyon and enters the open Paradox Valley. Look for cottonwoods to photograph along the river, which soon branches away from the road. Turn west (right) from Road Y11 onto CO 90 to get to Bedrock. In front of the Bedrock Store (visited by the heroines of *Thelma and Louise*), turn south on Road Y9 to get to the raft take-out. From here you can take photographs of the river as it exits the next canyon to the south.

1 mile south of the Ute Indian Museum at 1230 S. Towsend Ave., 970-249-3765.

WINTER SPORTS

Cerro Summit Recreation Area, just 10 miles from downtown Montrose, is the place for cross-country skiing, snowshoeing, sledding, and ice skating. *For rentals: Jeans Westerner, 147 N. Townsend Ave., 970-249-8757.*

For a real Western experience complete with cattle drives, horseback riding, and campfire meals, stay at **Whistling Acres Guest Ranch** ($$$) near Paonia. The ranch also arranges for fishing excursions and private tours of the Black Canyon. *3.5 miles from Paonia on 2nd Avenue, 970-527-4560, 800-346-1420, www.whistlingacresranch.com.* Try **West Elk Ranch** in Crawford, a lodge with activities in the West Elk Wilderness. *4444 E. 50 Dr., 866-937-8355, www.westelkranch.com.*

Restaurants

The **Camp Robber Café** ($-$$) serves a great variety of New Mexican and seafood, as well as great sandwiches and vegetarian fare. *228 E. Main St., 970-240-1590.* For a special night out in Montrose, enjoy a select cut of beef at **The Red Barn Restaurant** ($$). *1413 E. Main St., 970-249-9202.* Enjoy the Mexican menu at **Amelia's Hacienda** ($-$$). *44 S. Grand, 970-249-1881.* **Silver Jack Mining Co.** ($-$$) boasts a hearty lunch menu as well as tender steaks and tasty seafood for dinner. For a little post-dinner entertainment, try the attached night club. *10 Hillcrest Plaza Way, 970-240-9101.* **Belly Restaurant & Bar** ($$) features a contemporary American menu with comfort classics all in a great atmosphere. *309 E. Main, 970-252-1488.* For fresh seafood and great steaks, try **The Stone House** ($$$). This fine-dining restaurant welcomes children, but does recommend reservations for dinner. *1415 Hawk Pkwy., 970-240-8899.*

Accommodations

Given Montrose's proximity to Black Canyon of the Gunnison National Park and the San Juan Mountains, much lodging is available here—at a reasonable price. Try the **Country Lodge** ($), *1624 E. Main St., 970-249-4567, www.countryldg.com;* the **Canyon Trails Inn** ($), *1225 E. Main St., 970-249-3426;* or the **Black Canyon Motel** ($), *1605 E. Main St., 970-249-3495.*

The Montrose area also has several fine B&Bs, including the **Uncompahgre Lodge** ($-$$), a converted schoolhouse with easy access to the Uncompahgre River, the lodge has scenery, a convenient central location, and delicious breakfasts. As a bonus, pets are also welcome. *7 miles south of Montrose on US 550 at Uncompahgre Road, 970-240-4000, 800-318-8127, www.uncbb.com.*

You might have overlooked this particular amenity, but a llama herd really does make your stay at **Cedars' Edge Llamas Bed & Breakfast** ($-$$) special. You can also enjoy panoramic views, including the north rim of the Black Canyon. *5 miles north of Cedaredge on CO 65, 970-856-6836, www.llamabandb.com.* Also in Cedaredge, near the base of the Grand Mesa, the charming **Lovett House Bed & Breakfast** ($) is a converted pioneer log home built in 1891. *210 N. Grand Mesa Dr., 970-856-4375, www.lovetthousebandb.com.*

Special Events

Welcome to the land of harvest festivals! In July, Paonia holds its **Paonia Cherry Days** festival with a parade, arts and crafts, fruit, and an impressive array of jams and jellies. *970-527-3886, www.paoniachamber.com.* In August, the **Olathe Sweet Corn Festival** brings out a pancake breakfast, a festive parade with folks actually dressed up as ears of corn, competitions, and live entertainment. *970-323-6006, www.olathesweetcornfest.com.* In October, **Cedaredge Apple Days** features bake-offs, artisan booths, and mouthwatering apple cider. *970-874-8616.*

For More Information

Montrose Visitors and Convention Bureau, *1519 E. Main St., 970-252-0505, www.visitmontrose.net.* Montrose Chamber of Commerce, *1519 E. Main St., 970-249-5000, 800-923-5515, www.montrosechamber.com.*

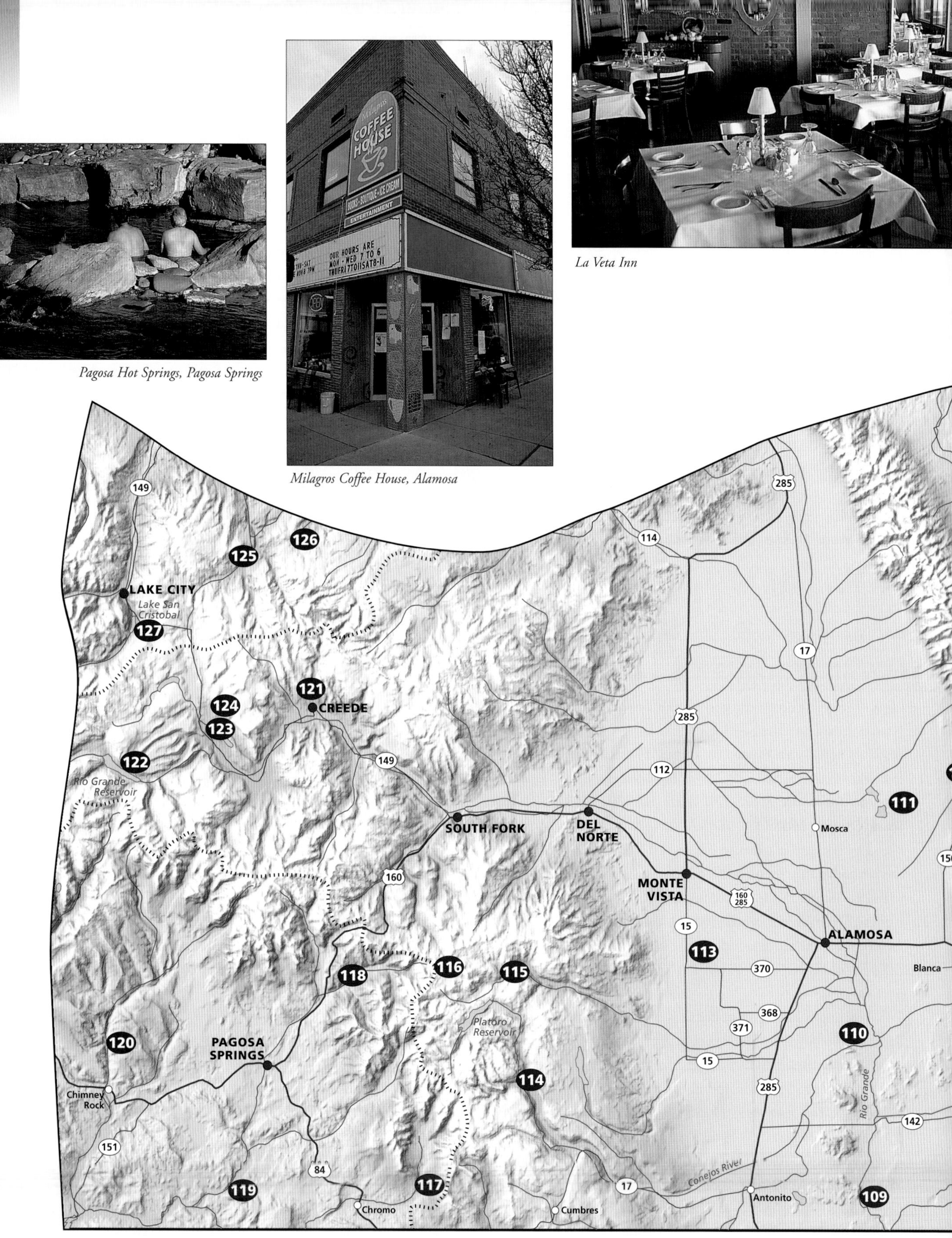

Pagosa Hot Springs, Pagosa Springs

Milagros Coffee House, Alamosa

La Veta Inn

Southern Colorado

I-25 TO THE EASTERN SAN JUAN MOUNTAINS

If I had to describe southern Colorado in just one word, that word would be "diverse." The tallest and largest sand dunes in the country rise in startling splendor beneath snow-capped mountains. The San Luis Valley, a high desert the size of Connecticut, sits atop a vast aquifer that has transformed sagebrush flats into a highly productive agricultural region. Hot springs bubble to the surface, snowmelt tumbles down mountainsides. Soaring in dramatic relief above the surrounding landscape, the San Juan and Sangre de Cristo Mountains are considered the most scenic in a state famous for its mountain scenery.

The human history here is equally diverse, embracing Native Americans, early explorers, Spanish settlers, and immigrant miners who came to Colorado from around the world in search of silver and gold. This is a living history, easily accessible. You can tour ancient Puebloan kivas outside of Pagosa Springs, celebrate Spanish heritage at the Plaza de Leones festival in Walsenburg, or explore ghost towns near Lake City and Creede on backcountry roads. There is so much to do in southern Colorado that I can't begin to summarize it. Look into the many opportunities for exploration, edification, and recreation here—which, in a word, are diverse.

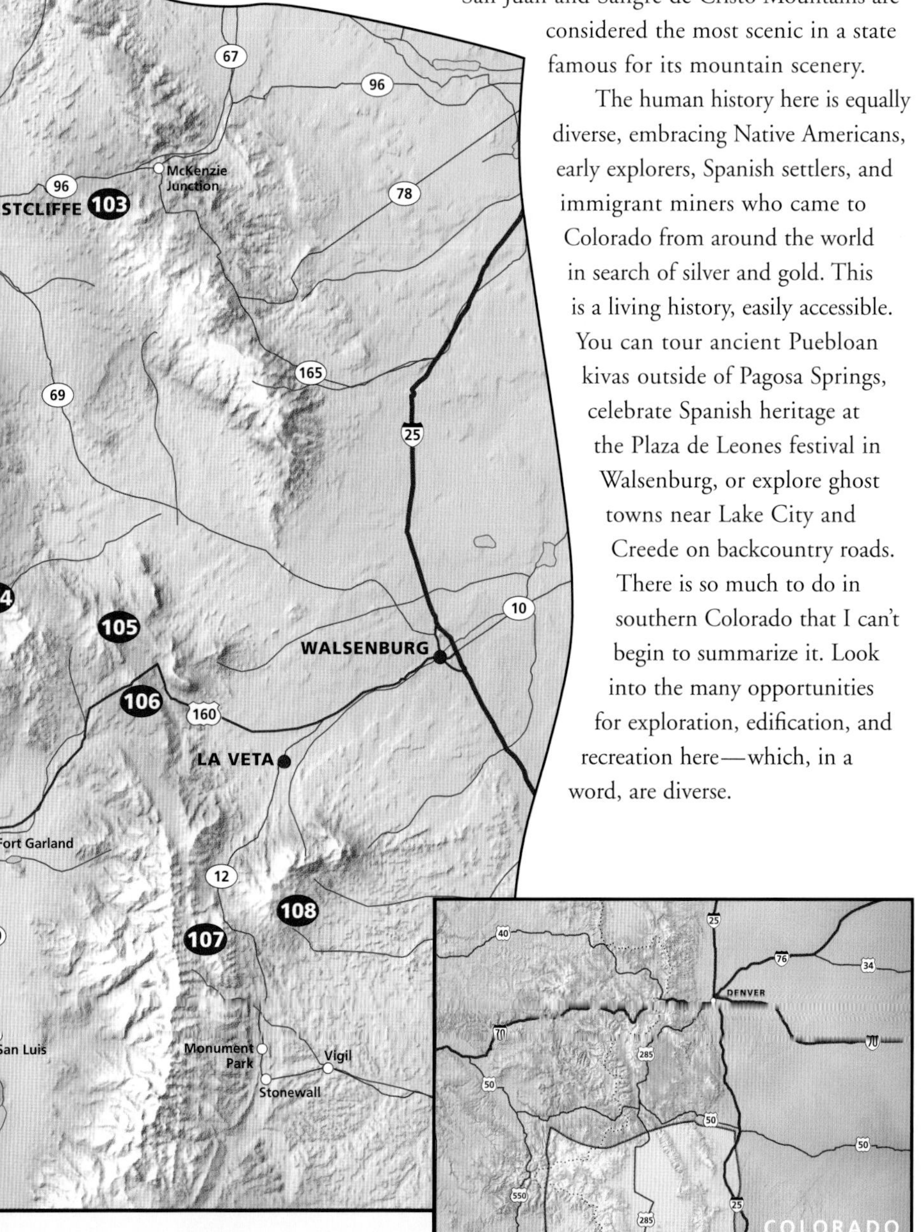

SCENIC LOCATIONS

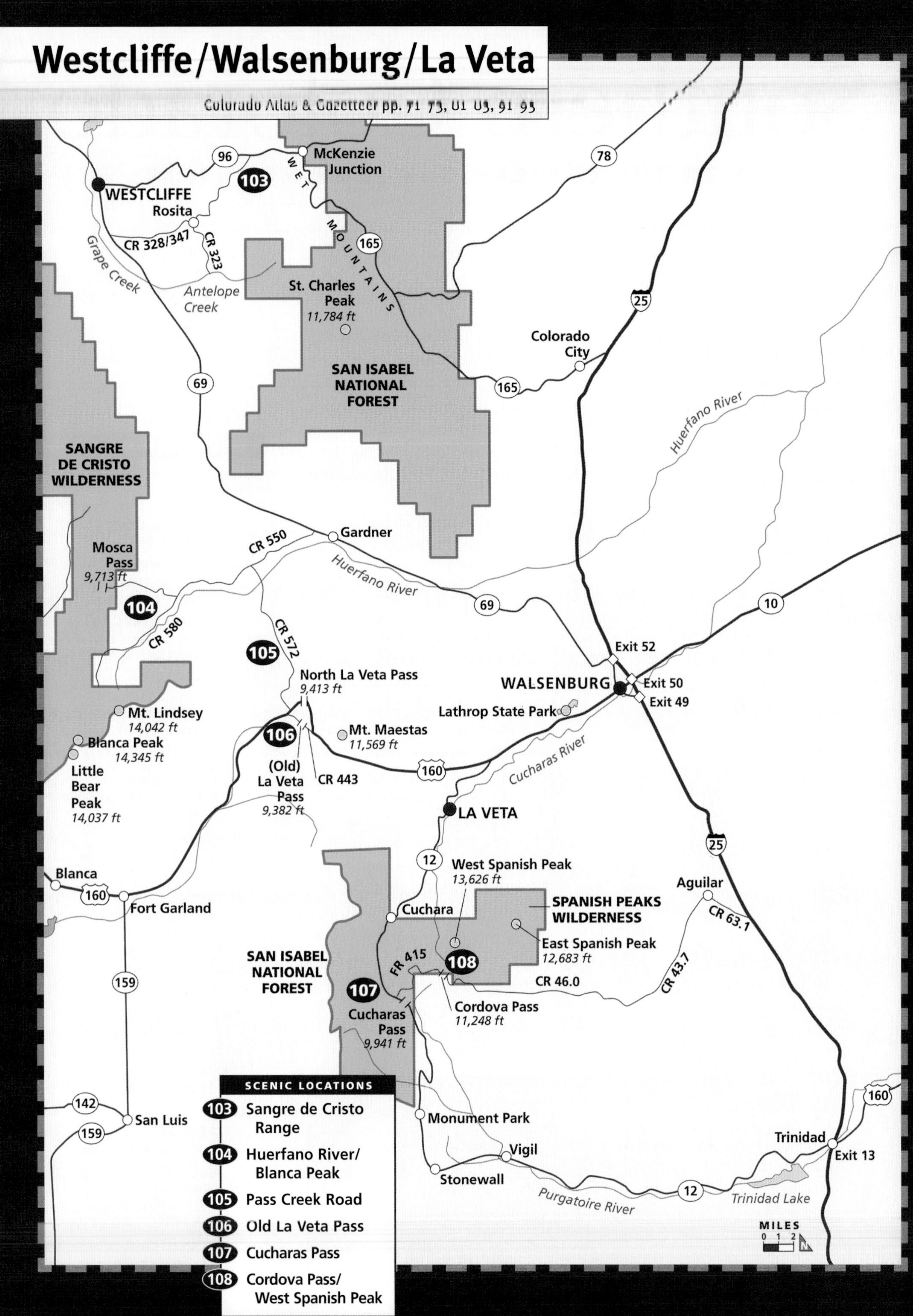

Westcliffe/Walsenburg/La Veta
Colorado Atlas & Gazetteer pp. 71–73, 81–83, 91–93
96
McKenzie Junction
103
WESTCLIFFE
Rosita
WET MOUNTAINS
78
CR 328/347
CR 323
165
Grape Creek
Antelope Creek
St. Charles Peak
11,784 ft
25
Colorado City
SAN ISABEL NATIONAL FOREST
69
165
Huerfano River
SANGRE DE CRISTO WILDERNESS
Gardner
CR 550
Mosca Pass
9,713 ft
Huerfano River
104
69
10
CR 580
CR 572
105
Exit 52
North La Veta Pass
9,413 ft
WALSENBURG
Exit 50
Exit 49
Lathrop State Park
Mt. Lindsey
14,042 ft
106
Mt. Maestas
11,569 ft
Blanca Peak
14,345 ft
Little Bear Peak
14,037 ft
(Old) La Veta Pass
9,382 ft
CR 443
160
Cucharas River
LA VETA
25
12
West Spanish Peak
13,626 ft
Blanca
160
Fort Garland
Aguilar
Cuchara
SPANISH PEAKS WILDERNESS
CR 63.1
East Spanish Peak
12,683 ft
SAN ISABEL NATIONAL FOREST
FR 415
108
159
107
CR 46.0
CR 43.7
Cucharas Pass
9,941 ft
Cordova Pass
11,248 ft
SCENIC LOCATIONS
103 Sangre de Cristo Range
104 Huerfano River/ Blanca Peak
105 Pass Creek Road
106 Old La Veta Pass
107 Cucharas Pass
108 Cordova Pass/ West Spanish Peak
142
San Luis
159
Monument Park
160
Vigil
Trinidad
Exit 13
Stonewall
12
Purgatoire River
Trinidad Lake
MILES
0 1 2

Westcliffe

Westcliffe is where I fell in love with Colorado. I first visited the state many years ago as a high school student, working the summer of 1967 on a cattle ranch near Westcliffe. To the east the Wet Mountains gently roll to the horizon, to the west the sawtoothed peaks of the Sangre de Cristo Range (see Scenic Location No. 103, p. 298) pierce the sky, towering 6,500 feet above the valley floor. The scenic beauty of the Wet Mountain Valley made an indelible impression on me, and I decided to make Colorado my home. I have since traveled to every corner of the state to photograph its many wonders, yet tiny Westcliffe, with its sweeping valley and mountain views, has always held a special meaning for me. Relatively few tourists visit this part of Colorado, but if you do, I guarantee that you'll fall in love with it, too.

History

In the early 1870s, ranching drew a small number of settlers to the Wet Mountain Valley, where the prairie grasses provided natural pastureland. It was the discovery of silver, however, that sparked a population boom. When high-grade ore yielding 75 percent silver was unearthed here, thousands of people streamed into the valley, establishing the town of Silver Cliff. The Denver & Rio Grande arrived in 1881, stopping just short of Silver Cliff to build its own town a mile away in Westcliffe. Silver went bust, but cattle ranching and hay farming held on in this rural valley. Today agriculture and a developing tourist industry are the economic mainstays of Westcliffe—where mercantiles and feed stores share the small downtown with gift shops and galleries.

Main Attractions

BISHOP CASTLE

"Castle Under Construction," says the sign at Bishop Castle. With turrets, spires, winding staircases, flying buttresses, and even a dragon, it is truly a storybook castle—right in the middle of Colorado. In 1969 Jim Bishop started building a simple stone cottage. When someone commented that it looked like a castle, his imagination took off and hasn't stopped since. He works without blueprints and continually changes the design as ideas come to him. Every summer he hauls in tons of rock and hand-sets each stone, calling his endeavor the world's largest one-man construction project. You have to see it to believe it. From Westcliffe, drive 16.5 miles east on CO 96, turn right on CO 165, and drive 12.5 miles.

SANGRE DE CRISTO WILDERNESS

Spanning 70 miles north to south, the quarter-million-acre Sangre de Cristo Wilderness encompasses the Sangre de Cristo Range from Salida to North La Veta Pass (see Scenic Location No. 103, p. 298). The massive profiles of four fourteeners (Crestone Peak, Crestone Needle, Kit Carson Mountain, and Humboldt Peak) can be seen just southwest of Westcliffe. The narrowness of the fault-block range—only 10 to 20 miles wide—makes for an abrupt topography, resulting in numerous creeks and waterfalls cascading down steep-sided valleys. Anglers have lakes galore to choose from, while hikers and campers have hundreds of miles of trails to explore.

Most of the lakes have good fishing July through September, with native cutthroats the predominant fish. Because these high lakes, most over 10,000 feet, are in the wilderness area, you can only access them on foot or by horseback. **Hermit** and **Horseshoe Lakes** have brookies, browns, and cutthroat, and can be reached with a four-wheel-drive vehicle on the Hermit Pass Road (see Four-Wheel-Drive Trips, p. 299). If bagging a fourteener is what you're after, the best choice is **Humboldt Peak** DIFFICULT, a full-day, 14-mile round trip (the other fourteeners are difficult and dangerous, whereas this one is considered moderate for a fourteener). Mountain bikes and vehicles are prohibited in wilderness areas, but the boundary configuration of the Sangre de Cristo Wilderness allows them across Medano and Hayden Passes, and up to the top of Hermit Pass. Wilderness affords countless opportunities for backcountry camping, and the many high lakes make good destinations; just be sure to camp at least 200 feet or farther from any water sources.

Activities

CAMPING

With a lake in the foreground and the Sangres in the distance, camping at **DeWeese Reservoir State Wildlife Area** can't be beat. From Westcliffe, go north on CO 69 for 0.25 mile, turn right onto County Road 241, and continue 4 miles. *719-561-5300.* **Alvarado** campground, with 47 campsites, and **Lake Creek,** with 12, are both on national forest land near the base of the Sangres with easy access to the Rainbow Trail (see Hiking, p. 299). To reach Alvarado from Westcliffe, drive south on CO 69 for 3.5 miles, turn right onto Schoolfield Road (CR 140), and go 6.5 miles more. To reach Lake Creek, drive north on CO 69 for 12.5 miles, turn left onto CR 198, and go 3 miles.

Of the three campgrounds in the Wet Mountains at Lake Isabel Recreation Area, **St. Charles** is the best, with 15 well-spaced sites along the forested banks of the St. Charles River (a stream really). From Westcliffe, drive east on CO 96 for 16.5 miles, turn right on CO 165, and drive 18.5 miles to Lake Isabel. *719-269-8500.*

FISHING

Two easily accessible lakes are also good family choices. **DeWeese Reservoir** is close to town and makes for a fun place to fish while float-tubing. **Lake Isabel,** 35 miles from Westcliffe, is heavily stocked and the kids are pretty likely to get a bite. (See directions to both in Camping, above.)

Grape Creek flows just west of town and yields rainbow, brown, and brook trout in early spring. The **Arkansas River,**

103 SANGRE DE CRISTO RANGE

SCENIC LOCATION

My spiritual center in the universe is the Sangre de Cristo Range. Perhaps that says best how I feel about these mountains. They were the first I ever photographed in Colorado, and since then have been the ones I retreat to first when I need to get away from city life. The Sangres are the longest linear block-faulted range in the world, beginning near Salida and ending near Santa Fe, N.M., more than 200 miles later. The Colorado portion includes 14,000-foot peaks, glaciers, long drainages with creeks and waterfalls, wildlife, and flowers galore. And my favorite Colorado town and valley sit at the base of their east side, Westcliffe and the Wet Mountain Valley.

You have many places from which to photograph the range, including its west side in the San Luis Valley, but my favorite is from the Wet Mountains looking west at sunrise to the range's rugged eastern face. The views are best from Rosita Road (County Roads 347 and 328) as it descends from the crest of the Wet Mountains. Turn southwest on it 4 miles west of McKenzie Junction off CO 96 between Florence and Westcliffe.

The land along the way is private, but you'll find plenty of places from which to photograph along the road. Houses are sprinkled on the ridge tops, so you'll have to do a little maneuvering to get a clear shot, but several spots afford a view of aspens in the foreground with the Sangres behind. This is a morning-only photograph. Find a location before sunrise, and you won't believe how red the mountains turn on a clear day. (Sangre de Cristo is Spanish for "Blood of Christ.") I suggest using your telephoto lens in order the distance between trees and mountains and make the Sangres larger than they appear to the eye.

For another good sunrise view, head out to DeWeese Reservoir north of Westcliffe. You'll see the signs as you drive north on CO 69 just outside of town. On a windless day, you can make nice reflection photos of the mountains. The entire drive north from Westcliffe on CO 69 to US 50 parallels the range and provides excellent views, as does the drive south on 69 to Gardner. Look for the bison herds west of the highway with the rugged Sangres in the background—a view out of the early 19th century.

24 miles north of Westcliffe on CO 69, is a good bet for brown trout in spring (especially during the May caddis hatch) and early August. *For local information: Arkansas River Tours, 10 miles north in Cotopaxi, 719-942-4362.*

FOUR-WHEEL-DRIVE TRIPS

The 21-mile **Medano Pass Primitive Road** takes you up and over the Sangres to the Great Sand Dunes (see Four-Wheel-Drive Trips, Alamosa, p. 315). To approach it from the Westcliffe side, drive south on CO 69 for 24 miles to the intersection with County Road 559 and turn right. After about 8 miles, it becomes a four-wheel-drive road. **Hayden Pass** also goes up and over the Sangres. The 16.5-mile route is easy in places and challenging in others, with steep, rocky spots and a narrow ledge that requires an experienced driver. Along with great views, there are two campgrounds and hiking trails along the route. Because of underground springs, it's best to travel this route in summer when conditions are dry; if you encounter ice, do not continue. From Westcliffe, drive north on CO 69 for 24 miles to the town of Texas Creek, turn left onto US 50, and drive west to Coaldale. Turn left onto CR 6, which becomes Forest Road 6 as it climbs to 11,184-foot Hayden Pass. The road descends to the town of Villa Grove.

Hermit Pass is the highest of the four-wheel-drive routes listed here. The 15-mile (one way) trip follows a creek past beaver dams and Hermit and Horseshoe Lakes as it climbs to 13,020 feet. Once at the pass, you can take a short hike to the summit of Hermit Peak (just 330 feet higher) or hike down the west slope about 1 mile to Rito Alto Lake. From Westcliffe, go west on Hermit Road (CR 160) and veer onto FR 301, which goes to the pass. Return the same way.

GOLF

Keeping your eye on the ball may be difficult amid awesome scenery at **St. Andrews at Westcliffe.** This nine-hole golf course has walkable, rolling terrain crossed by three streams. *800 Copper Gulch Rd., 800-258-9410.*

HIKING

Perhaps it is the proliferation of summer wildflowers or autumn's golden aspens that give this trail its name. Nearly 100 miles long, the mostly wide, multi-use **Rainbow Trail** MODERATE parallels the eastern slope of the Sangres, just below the wilderness boundary. It has 10 different access points, and, once on the trail, you can access all the trails leading up into the wilderness (north of Coaldale, mountain bikers enjoy singletrack riding). Access the Rainbow Trail from Alvarado and Lake Creek campgrounds (see directions in Camping, p. 297) or from Hermit Road (see Four-Wheel-Drive Trips, above). A family-friendly hike is the **Rainbow Trail to Crystal Falls** EASY, starting from the Music Pass Road access and hiking north for about 2 miles. To reach the Music Pass access, drive south from Westcliffe on CO 69 for 4.5 miles and turn right onto Colfax Lane (County Road 119); drive 5.5 miles. At the "T," turn left onto South Colony Road (CR 120), and then right onto Music Pass Road (CR 119). Park your car near the trail intersection. *San Isabel National Forest, 719-269-8500.*

For a more challenging hike, take **Sand Creek Trail** MODERATE, which goes over Music Pass to Lower and Upper Sand Creek Lakes. Starting from the Music Pass Road intersection with Rainbow Trail (see directions this page), it's about a 12-mile round trip. (With a four-wheel-drive vehicle, you can drive 2.5 miles farther up Music Pass Road, shortening the hike by 5 miles.) For other hikes, pick up a copy of Michael O'Hanlon's book, *Sangre de Cristo: A Complete Trail Guide.*

In the Wet Mountains, the **St. Charles Peak Trail** EASY climbs 4.5 miles (one way) through dense evergreen forests of the Wet Mountains, reaching timberline and alpine tundra just before summiting 11,784-foot St. Charles Peak. From here you can see the Sangres and the Wet Mountain Valley to the west and the Great Plains to the east. From the junction of CO 96 and CO 165, drive south on CO 165 about 13.5 miles to the trailhead.

HORSEBACK RIDING AND LLAMA TREKKING

Horseback is a popular way of reaching the high lakes in the Sangres, such as Macy Lakes and Lakes of the Clouds. **Adventure Specialists at Bear Basin Ranch** can guide you along these and other Sangre trails. *719-783-2076 or 719-630-7687, www.adventurespecialists.org.* I have a fondness for llamas, as I often rely on them for long backcountry trips. They carry heavy loads, their grazing is easy on the environment, and they always seem to be smiling. My friend Paul Brown owns some of the best. *Wet Mountain Llamas, 608 County Road 295, Wetmore, 719-784-3220.*

SCENIC DRIVES

Frontier Pathways Scenic Byway winds 53 miles from the valley floor, through rolling foothills, and into the Wet Mountains as it heads east from Westcliffe on CO 96 and then south on CO 165. Bishop Castle (see Main Attractions, p. 297) is 12.5 miles south on CO 165. This marvel of imagination and architecture is just off the road, so be sure to stop. Six miles farther, at Lake Isabel Recreation Area, there's a well-stocked lake and three campgrounds. The road skirts the boundary of Greenhorn Mountain Wilderness and ends in Colorado City at I-25.

The **Sangre de Cristo Drive** is an 86-mile route that follows CO 69 from Texas Creek to Walsenburg, enjoying spectacular views of the Sangres along the way. South of Westcliffe, the views of the Crestone Group (four massive fourteeners) are truly breathtaking. Entering the dry, sagebrush-covered hills of the Huerfano River valley (see Scenic Location No. 104, p. 301), the road blinks through Gardner, whose adobe buildings reflect the town's Hispanic heritage. To the north are the forested slopes of the Wet Mountains and to the southwest the sharp profile of the Blanca Group, a cluster of fourteeners at the southern end of the Sangres. The road winds through sandstone canyons before opening onto the shortgrass prairie of the Great Plains, ending in Walsenburg at I-25.

Restaurants

Considering its small size, Westcliffe has a fair number of good restaurants; however, some may close or have limited hours during the off-season (October to May), so call ahead. **Chile Bears Restaurant** ($) serves up great Mexican fare, burgers, and steaks. *108 S. 2nd St., 719-783-3336.* For barbeque try **Cel Dor Asado** ($$). Entrées are cooked up on their famous wood-fire grill. *213 Main St., 719-783-2650.*

A rustic lodge snug up against the mountains, the **Alpine Lodge** ($-$$$) has a little bit of everything, all of it good. From Westcliffe, drive 3 miles south on CO 69, then 7 miles west on Schoolfield Road. *719-783-2660.* **Letter Drop Inn** ($-$$$) is a cozy restaurant specializing in wild game. From Westcliffe, drive 3 miles south on CO 69, turn left at Rosita Road (County Road 328), and go 6 miles to Rosita. *719-783-9430.*

Oak Creek Grade Steakhouse ($-$$) presents a rollicking dinner show of old-timey Western entertainment on Friday and Saturday nights. From CO 96 in Silver Cliff, turn north onto Oak Creek Grade (CR 255) and go 13 miles. Reservations required. *719-783-2245.*

Accommodations

Again, call ahead to check off-season closures. **Main Street Inn Bed and Breakfast** ($$) is a Victorian home, complete with gingerbread details, a wrap-around porch, and five guest

Main Street Inn Bed and Breakfast, Westcliffe

104 SCENIC LOCATION — HUERFANO RIVER/ BLANCA PEAK

Colorado's 4th highest summit is Blanca Peak at 14,345 feet. Its north face makes it also one of Colorado's most precipitous and spectacular mountains; in fact, the southernmost glacier in North America is at its base. You can drive close to the north side of the peak on a road that penetrates beautiful aspen and cottonwood groves while following the Huerfano River. The road is manageable by car up to the Huerfano State Wildlife Area (SWA), after which a very rocky base requires a high-clearance four-wheel drive. From CO 69, turn west on County Road 550 just north of Gardner. You'll see the sign to Redwing and US 160. The road heads due west past the US 160 turnoff and Red Wing, then southwest as you begin to catch glimpses of Blanca Peak.

Beautiful ranches along the lower Huerfano will tempt you to compose a photograph with meadows and mountains. Go for it, especially at sunrise and sunset as you point the camera to the south at right angles to the sun. Just before the road turns southwest, you ascend a bare hillside just high enough to get a great vantage of the upper Huerfano valley with the Sangre de Cristo Range and Blanca Peak in the background. It's a must-take picture. Then you descend into aspen and conifer forests and pass through several ranches that span the river and the road. Here you'll want to stop your vehicle, get out, and compose an image using the road as a lead-in line through the aspens. Both vertical and horizontal versions work well, especially if you use a wide-angle lens to take it all in. At the SWA, photograph the narrow-leaved cottonwoods along the river. I can't tell you how beautiful it is along the Huerfano in the fall, especially during peak color (usually the last week of September). If you have a four-wheel drive, continue on the rocky road until you reach a clear turn to the right. At this point you will see the Huerfano far below as it exits the great horseshoe-shaped cirque on the north side of Blanca Peak. It is incredibly glacial-looking and makes for a true wilderness photograph. The road gets unbearably rough after this; stop and return the way you came.

rooms. *501 Main St., 877-783-4006, www.mainstreetbnb.com.* The rooms at **The Courtyard Inn** ($) have feather beds with down comforters and are charmingly decorated in a style best described as "second-hand chic." The garden is a pleasant place to enjoy the complimentary continental breakfast and coffee. *410 Main St., 719-783-9616, www.courtyardcountryinn.com.*

In addition to a good restaurant, the **Alpine Lodge** ($) has rustic two-bedroom cabins with kitchenettes available year-round. Go 3 miles south on CO 69, then 7 miles west on Schoolfield Road. *719-783-2660.* The **Historic Pines Ranch** ($$) offers horseback riding and a long list of summer activities,

Historic Pines Ranch, Westcliffe

along with lodge rooms or cabins (minimum two-night stay). Meals (included) are served family style in the dining hall. From Westcliffe, go north on CO 69 for 0.75 mile, turn left onto Pines Road, and drive 7 miles, following the signs. *800-446-9462, 719-783-9261, www.historicpines.com.*

Special Events

On Labor Day weekend, **Wet Mountain Western Days** celebrates the region's ranching and cowboy heritage with an equestrian parade, cowboy poetry, fiddle music, and a chuck-wagon dinner. *877-793-3170.* The Crystal Mountain Center for the Performing Arts, a combined professional and amateur effort, presents a full summer season of plays and concerts at the **Jones Theater**, in downtown Westcliffe. *719-783-3004, www.jonestheater.com.* **The High Mountain Hay Fever Bluegrass Festival** is a must for anyone visiting Westcliffe. Held each July, the festival features an excellent lineup of bluegrass bands. *For more information: 719-783-0883, www.highmountainhayfever.com.*

For More Information

Custer County Chamber of Commerce has a visitor center at the corner of Main and Third in Westcliffe. *877-793-3170, www.custercountyco.com.*

Walsenburg and La Veta

(see map on p. 296)

Walsenburg is a natural stopping place for people traveling through southern Colorado. At the edge of the Great Plains and the junction of three major highways (I-25, US 160, and CO 10), it is on the main route leading into the San Luis Valley from the east. Walsenburg is also the starting point for the Highway of Legends Scenic and Historic Byway.

La Veta, a small, rural town amid farms and ranches, is a friendly place where people stop and visit with each other on Main Street and say hello to strangers passing by. The Spanish Peaks dominate the southern horizon and the Culebra Range (part of the Sangre de Cristo Range) rises to the southwest. Nestled between the two is the tiny resort community of Cuchara, just down the road from La Veta in the Cuchara Valley. Recreational options abound within the San Isabel National Forest and the splendid Spanish Peaks Wilderness.

History

Walsenburg was originally founded in 1859 as Plaza de los Leones (Plaza of the Lions) and was renamed in the 1870s after a local civic leader. The railroad arrived in 1876, and soon the Denver & Rio Grande was carrying away carloads of coal. By the early 1900s, Walsenburg and Huerfano County ranked among the largest coal producers in Colorado, with more than 50 mines working 24 hours a day. The coal mines have since closed, the last in 1959, and Walsenburg is now the center of commerce for the surrounding farms and ranches, as well as a wayside for tourists passing through.

The town of La Veta began as Fort Francisco, established in 1862 as a trading post. Renamed La Veta (the vein), the community prospered from coal mining and came into its own when the railroad arrived in 1876, making it the railhead for the Cuchara Valley. When the trains eventually stopped running, the sleepy little town served the area's farmers and ranchers. Today La Veta is home to a growing arts community and has become a budding tourist destination for travelers discovering the history, scenic beauty, and outdoor recreation of the Cuchara Valley.

Main Attractions

GRANDOTE PEAKS GOLF CLUB

The 18-hole, public Grandote Peaks Golf Club in La Veta is ranked as one of the top 10 courses in the state, a "four-star award winner" according to *Golf Digest.* This Tom Weiskopf/Jay Morrish–designed championship course affords stunning views of the Spanish Peaks and the Culebra Range as it plays through both open and forested terrain and crosses the Cucharas River. This course is very picturesque when the scrub oaks turn red and aspens are yellow at the end of September. Open from May to October, it's just south of La Veta on CO 12. *800-457-9986, www.grandotepeaks.com.*

HIGHWAY OF LEGENDS SCENIC AND HISTORIC BYWAY

A scenic and historic byway, the Highway of Legends starts in Walsenburg, heads west on US 160, turns south onto CO 12, and loops southeasterly to end in Trinidad. The 82-mile drive encompasses a microcosm of Colorado landscapes—plains, mountains, and desert canyons.

The byway passes through the quaint town of La Veta, then skirts the Spanish Peaks, twin mountains that have spawned many legends throughout the centuries—tales of lost gold, angry gods, and evil spirits. The Devil's Stairsteps, just south of La Veta, is a striking example of vertical rock formations called dikes that radiate out from these ancient volcanoes. The two-lane blacktop roller-coasters through picturesque farm- and ranchland, then past Cuchara, a tiny resort town, its unpaved main street reminiscent of the Old West. After climbing 9,941-foot Cucharas Pass (see Scenic Location No. 107, p. 306), the road descends to Monument Lake, a popular recreation and camping area.

The road curves east to parallel the Purgatoire River through the canyons and mesas of the Picketwire Valley (a bastardization of the river's French name). It passes a number of small towns and ruins of old Hispanic villages, then rolls into the former company town of Cokedale, a National Historic District where you can still see coal miners' homes and the old coke ovens. The byway loops north of Trinidad State Park before ending in Trinidad (see p. 439).

The Highway of Legends is a scenic drive any time of year, but especially in fall when the changing aspens seem to give credence to tales of lost gold.

LATHROP STATE PARK

Set among piñon and juniper– studded hills, this 1,594-acre recreation area opened in 1962 as Colorado's first state park. Lathrop boasts picnic areas, two campgrounds, a golf course, and two lakes. The stocked waters of Martin and Horseshoe Lakes attract anglers year-round. In summer, the lakes are busy with boaters, waterskiers, windsurfers, and swimmers. In winter, the park's roads and walking trails make for gentle cross-country skiing. Among the interpretive exhibits at the visitor center is an aquarium with local fish species. From Walsenburg, drive west on US 160 for 3 miles. *719-738-2376, www.coloradoparks.org.*

Lathrop State Park, Walsenburg

PASS CREEK ROAD

After exploring the Huerfano River (see Scenic Location No. 104, p. 301), head south to US 160 over Pass Creek Pass on the road of the same name. Pass Creek winds through all sorts of trees and bushes and a canyon bed, all with colorful displays in the fall and spring. Atop the relatively minor pass, views open up to the Spanish Peaks and rolling hills of La Veta Pass country to the south. There's nothing else quite like it in Colorado. Five miles west of Gardner on County Road 550, turn south at the sign pointing to US 160 onto CR 570. This improved dirt road to North La Veta Pass has some washboards along the way, but it's easily negotiable in your vehicle.

The first 3 miles course through open ranch landscapes with nice views of the two Sheep Mountains to the east. When the road meets the river, keep a sharp eye out for aspens and cottonwoods that make lovely intimate compositions without sky. As you ascend the pass, notice the aspen groves and scrub oak on the hills to the east; they manifest remarkable fall color the last week of September. Once over the pass, compose the road to lead the viewer's eye toward the meadows along La Veta Pass and Mount Maestas in the background (see pp. 71, 76–77, *Photographing the Landscape*). Also check out the lovely aspen grove just off the road to the west.

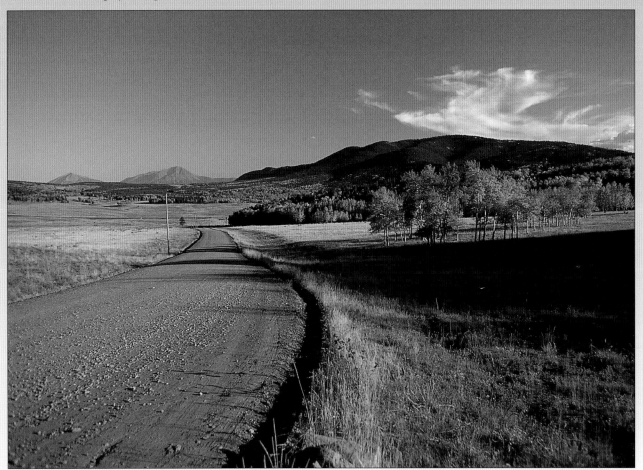

SPANISH PEAKS WILDERNESS

Rising nearly 7,000 feet above the surrounding landscape, the distinctive profiles of East and West Spanish Peaks (12,683 and 13,626 feet, respectively) served as landmarks for Indians, trappers, and early travelers on the eastern prairie. Plains Indians called the twin peaks the "breasts of the earth" and considered them sacred. The mountains are of volcanic origin, and hundreds of rock dikes give a close-up look at the area's unique geology. The dikes were formed as magma squeezed up through fissures and solidified—vertical fins that remained standing long after time and erosion ate away surrounding sedimentary rock. Some dikes are 100 feet high; the longest is 14 miles. This federally designated wilderness area is also a National Natural Landmark (see Scenic Location Nos. 107 and 108, pp. 306–307).

Activities

CAMPING

Lathrop State Park has 100 campsites spread over two campgrounds: **Yucca,** a basic campground with 21 sites, and **Piñon,** with 79 sites plus amenities. Neither campground has shade, so bring your own. Reservations recommended. *303-470-1144 (Denver metro area), www.coloradostateparks.org.*

106 SCENIC LOCATION — OLD LA VETA PASS

There's a historic and scenic alternative to driving over La Veta Pass (to be precise, North La Veta Pass) as you travel from Walsenburg to the San Luis Valley on US 160. Instead, you can crest the original pass, where a 19th-century railroad and driving route preceded the modern highway. At 9,382 feet, Old La Veta Pass is about 30 feet lower than North La Veta Pass. The views are sublime, and the old railroad buildings at the top are interesting and photogenic. If you are heading west on US 160, turn left onto County Road 443, 2.5 miles before the summit of North La Veta Pass. West over the old pass and the Costilla County line, CR 443 becomes Road SS. Partly dirt and partly pavement, it's easily traversed by vehicle.

The views down toward Walsenburg from the east side are nice, but I prefer the aspens and ponderosa pines on the west side. Mount Maestas makes a good backdrop for the trees and meadows. Or compose the old buildings on the top of the pass in the foreground with the mountain looming above. Once back on the highway, keep an eye out for compositions along Sangre de Cristo Creek, which you follow into the San Luis Valley. The willows and cottonwoods here are especially pretty in late fall.

South of La Veta are three campgrounds on national forest land. **Blue Lake** and **Bear Lake**, with a total of 30 sites between them, are on the flank of the Culebra Range, with good shade, mountain views, and their namesake lakes nearby. From La Veta, go 14.5 miles south on CO 12 and turn right onto Forest Road 422. You'll reach Blue Lake first, with Bear Lake 1 mile farther. To reach **Purgatoire** campground (23 sites) from La Veta, drive south on CO 12 for 27 miles, over Cuchara Pass, and turn right onto County Road 34, which becomes FR 34 (North Fork Road), and drive 4.5 miles farther. The surrounding aspens make this a nice place to pitch a tent in autumn. No reservations. *719-742-3681.*

Surrounded by towering pines and rock formations, the 100-site **Monument Lake** campground is a popular spot, with cabins, a restaurant, and many amenities. From La Veta, it's about 30 miles south on CO 12. Reservations recommended. *719-868-2226.*

The Spanish Peaks Wilderness has many opportunities for backcountry camping. Check in with the Forest Service office in La Veta at Field and Main Streets. *719-742-3681.*

FISHING

Martin and **Horseshoe Lakes** in Lathrop State Park are both stocked with rainbow trout, bass, walleye, bluegill, crappie, and the infamous tiger muskie—a large, aggressive fish reputed to eat small boats. Ice fishing is popular here in winter. Lathrop also has a children's pond stocked with small, easy-to-catch fish. From Walsenburg, drive west on US 160 for 3 miles.

The best trout fishing in the La Veta area is at nearby lakes, all of which are stocked. **Blue** and **Bear Lakes** are considered the hot spots (for directions, see Camping, p. 304). **North Lake,** a state wildlife area and reservoir, is 24 miles south of La Veta on CO 12. About 3 miles farther is **Monument Lake,** a popular park and camping area. *For local information: Elk Valley Fly Shop in La Veta, across from the entrance to Grandote Peaks Golf Club, 719-742-5533.*

FOUR-WHEEL-DRIVE TRIPS

The drive to the top of 13,517-foot **Trinchera Peak** in the Culebra Range is rocky and steep, climbing 3,000 feet in just 3 miles. From the top you can look out onto the San Luis Valley and the Spanish Peaks. The four-wheel-drive road starts from Blue Lake campground. From La Veta, go 14.5 miles south on CO 12 and turn right onto Forest Road 422. At the campground, take FR 436 to the summit; return the same way.

GOLF

La Veta's **Grandote Peaks Golf Club** is one of the highest rated courses in the state (see Main Attractions, p. 302). The 9-hole **Walsenburg Golf Club** at Lathrop State Park doesn't have sand traps or water hazards, but the rolling terrain makes for some challenging golf, with the majestic Spanish Peaks in the distance. From Walsenburg, drive west 3 miles on US 160. *719-738-2730.*

HIKING

Many of the roads and trails in San Isabel National Forest are multipurpose, allowing dirt bikes and ATVs (see Mountain Biking, this page, for two nonmotorized trails). Once a narrow-gauge railroad route, **Old La Veta Pass Road** EASY (see Scenic Location No. 106, opposite) is a fun family hike. It follows a gentle railroad grade and passes several old structures, including a historic train depot. From Walsenburg, drive west about 25 miles on US 160 and turn left onto County Road 443, 2.5 miles before the summit of North La Veta Pass. You'll have to look for the turn; it's not well marked.

The multipurpose **Indian Trail** MODERATE starts from Bear Lake campground and heads north along the eastern slope of the Culebra Range—through forest, open meadows, over creeks, and up switchbacks—and ends 15 miles later at Forest Road 421 (see trailhead directions under Camping, p. 304). **Dodgeton Trail** MODERATE is a 4.5-mile (one way) hike up through ponderosa pine and past red-rock formations. From La Veta, drive 12 miles south on CO 12 and park at the Spring Creek picnic area, on the right side of the road just past the town of Cuchara; start from the Spring Creek trailhead.

In the Spanish Peaks Wilderness, the 3.5-mile (one way) **West Spanish Peak Trail** DIFFICULT leads to the 13,626-foot summit of West Spanish Peak (see Scenic Location No. 108, p. 307). It's an easy hike for the first 2.5 miles to timberline, at which point there is no trail, and you must find your own route on a steep, 1-mile scramble over scree. From La Veta, drive south for 16 miles on CO 12 to Cucharas Pass, turn left onto Cordova Pass Road (CR 46/FR 415), and drive 6 miles to Cordova Pass. The trailhead is on the left (north) beside a picnic area.

HORSEBACK RIDING

For two-hour to full-day trail rides in San Isabel National Forest or the Spanish Peaks Wilderness, contact **Echo Canyon Ranch.** From La Veta, drive 4 miles south on CO 12, and look for the sign. *719-742-5524.*

MOUNTAIN BIKING

Many of the roads and trails in the San Isabel National Forest are multipurpose, so be prepared to share them with horses, dirt bikes, and ATVs. For trail information, stop in at the Forest Service office at Field and Main streets, La Veta. 719-742-3681. **North Fork Trail** DIFFICULT is a nonmotorized trail that drops 2,000 feet as it follows the North Fork of the Purgatoire River and opens onto an old burn area where you can see clear to the New Mexico border. It's a 5-mile ride from the trailhead near Blue Lake campground to Purgatoire campground. From La Veta, go 14.5 miles south on CO 12 and turn right onto Forest Road 422. Go 4 miles to the intersection with FR 436, turn left, and continue 1.5 miles to the trailhead. **Dikes Trail** DIFFICULT, also nonmotorized, is a 3.5-mile (one way) trail that parallels a volcanic dike. To reach the trailhead from La Veta, drive 11 miles south on CO 12 and park at the community

center in Cuchara. **Old La Veta Pass Road** MODERATE is a good ride for families (see Hiking, this page).

MUSEUMS

Located in an 1890s jailhouse, the **Walsenburg Mining Museum** tells the history of coal mining in Huerfano County. It's behind the Huerfano County Courthouse. Open Memorial Day through September. *5th and Main Streets, 719-738-1992.* Incorporating the original adobe fort, the **Francisco Fort Museum** complex in La Veta encompasses several historic buildings, displaying Indian and Hispanic artifacts, furniture, and period clothing. An 1876 schoolhouse and 1880s-era blacksmith and saloon buildings were moved onto the grounds alongside replicas of an old general store and doctor's office. Open Memorial Day through September. *314 Main St., La Veta, 719-742-5501.*

SCENIC DRIVES

This area is known for the **Highway of Legends** (see Main Attractions, p. 302). **Cordova Pass Road** (see Scenic Location No. 108, p. 307) gives you ringside seats of the Spanish Peaks. From La Veta, drive 16 miles south to Cucharas Pass and go left onto Cordova Pass Road (County Road 46/ Forest Road 415).

A half-mile down the road, look for the John B. Farley Flower Trail, a short trail abloom with wild iris in summer. The 35-mile drive ends in Aguilar, near I-25.

WINTER SPORTS

The Cuchara Valley is a fun, uncrowded place to bring snowshoes or cross-country skis in winter. **Cordova Pass Road** MODERATE is accessible from Cucharas Pass (see Scenic Drives, p. 305). From [illegible] nect to other, more challenging trails. For cross-country skiing I also recommend the **Indian Trail** and **Old La Veta Pass Road** EASY, the **North Fork** and **Dodgeton Trails** MODERATE, and the **Dikes Trail** DIFFICULT (for directions, see Hiking and Mountain Biking, p. 305).

CUCHARAS PASS

Before heading into the San Luis Valley, check out the lower Sangre de Cristo Range south of the town of La Veta. Also called the Culebra Mountains, this part of the Sangres continues to the New Mexico border. To their east are the conspicuous Spanish Peaks with their volcanic-like walls radiating into the valley. It's heavenly country, with a relatively mild climate and views unique in Colorado. Cucharas Pass (9,941 feet) spans a divide connecting the Sangres and the Spanish Peaks. Ten miles west of Walsenburg, exit US 160 to the south at CO 12. Drive south through La Veta and stay on the highway to the pass.

You have so much to see along the way. Just south of La Veta the highway traverses ranch meadows, then quickly enters vast forests of scrub oak. Both provide a great foreground to views of West Spanish Peak (13,626 feet). You soon pass the first of several dikes that tower as high as 100 feet above you—such symmetrical walls that they seem to be manmade. You are in tight quarters, so wide-angle lenses work best along the highway.

After passing through the town of Cuchara, you enter coniferous forests and a narrow but scenic valley. Photographing to the south allows you to compose the peaks of the Culebra Range in the background. The last 2 miles of the ascent to the pass take you through a beautiful aspen forest. The last week of September, when the oaks and aspens put on a glorious display of color, is the best time to visit. The drive south from Cucharas Pass to the town of Stonewall (it has its own dike) allows you to wander through meadows decorated with majestic ponderosa pines, then into forests that flank the Culebra Range. But don't stop here—continue east on CO 12 down to Trinidad. The views of meadows along the Purgatoire River are wonderful.

108 SCENIC LOCATION

CORDOVA PASS/ WEST SPANISH PEAK

Just east of Cucharas Pass is an equally enthralling drive over Cordova Pass (11,248 feet). This improved dirt road skirts the base of West Spanish Peak on its way to the town of Aguilar, near I-25. The views of the Culebra Range and West Spanish Peak are sublime, and the drive along the Apishapa River makes for a nice contrast. At the top of Cucharas Pass on CO 12, turn east onto County Road 46/Forest Road 415. The road is rough in places, with potholes that will rattle you, but it's traversable if you don't love your vehicle a lot.

The first 4 miles skirt along hillsides replete with lovely aspen groves. Compose aspens in the foreground with the Culebra Range behind. You then enter a spruce-fir forest and quickly ascend the pass. You *must* park your vehicle now and take a short hike north on the West Spanish Peak Trail. Hike through the conifers until the forest opens up into a large meadow. You won't believe the view of West Spanish Peak! Now start scouting around for some of the numerous dead trees, both fallen and standing. They assume beautiful shades of gray and brown as they weather on this windy ridge at tree line. Stick around until sunset to see the red light on a clear day turn these snags into fiery sticks. Compose them in the foreground with the peak behind, now also red as the sun sets behind the Culebra Range. Now pull out the sleeping bag and camp on the pass. Get up early and hike to the top of West Spanish Peak. The climb is worth it, considering the rewarding view at the top.

Restaurants

There were a few good dining options in Walsenburg. A pleasant, family-oriented eatery, the **Iron Horse Restaurant** ($-$$) specializes in steaks and Italian dishes, and also has burgers and sandwiches. If you can't decide, try the Italian Combo—it's delicious and filling. *503 W. 7th St., 719-738-9966.* For Mexican, stop at **Tes'** ($). Not fancy by any means, it's a locally owned fast-food stand with a drive-thru window and a dozen tables inside. I always order the sopapilla burger—seasoned beef and beans piled onto a sopapilla and smothered in green chile. The shakes are a real treat on a hot summer day. *520 Walsen Ave., 719-738-1710.* Locals recommend **George's Drive Inn** ($) as a great lunch option. *564 US 85/87, 719-738-3030.*

In La Veta you're assured of a delicious meal at the **La Veta Inn** ($-$$$). *103 W. Ryus Ave., 719-742-3700.* Just a couple of doors down, you'll find the **Ryus Avenue Bakery** ($), a great breakfast and lunch place, with homemade breads, soups, and sandwiches. *129 W. Ryus Ave., 719-742-3830, www.ryusavebakery.com.* **The Timbers** ($-$$) is an intimate, upscale restaurant with a mountain lodge feel. *23 Cuchara Rd., 719-742-3838.*

The tiny resort town of Cuchara, just 12 miles south on CO 12, also has a number of good restaurants. **Dog Bar & Grill** ($-$$) has the best pizza in the Cuchara Valley. *34 Cuchara Ave., 719-742-6366.*

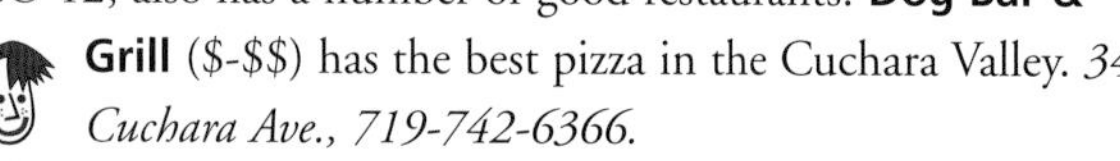

Restaurants in La Veta or Cuchara may be closed or have only limited hours during the off-season (September to May), so call ahead.

Accommodations

The lodging options in Walsenburg are rather limited. My preference is **La Plaza de Leones Bed and Breakfast** ($). Its 16 rooms have high ceilings, private baths, and open onto a common area. Kids are welcome at La Plaza, which is right downtown. *118 W. 6th St., 719-738-5700.* **Rio Cucharas Inn** ($), a two-story, adobe-style motel with a restaurant and indoor pool, is on US 150, 5 miles west of Walsenburg. *719-738-1282.* In La Veta, the delightful and kid-friendly **La Veta Inn** ($) has 18 rooms, eight of them small suites overlooking a courtyard. Rooms are individually decorated and have amenities including computer lines. The bar features local musicians on weekends, with jazz on Thursdays in the summer. *103 W. Ryus Ave., 888-806-4875, www.lavetainn.com.* The **1899 Bed and Breakfast** ($), an old stone house in the center of town, has five guest rooms and a separate cottage. *314 Main St., 719-742-3576.* **The Inn at the Spanish Peaks** ($$) is a Southwestern-style adobe dwelling with three deluxe suites. *310 E. Francisco St., 719-742-5313, www.innatthespanishpeaks.com.*

Rio Cucharas Inn, Walsenburg

La Veta Inn

Cuchara, 12 miles south of La Veta on CO 12, has been a resort town since the early 1900s and remains a fine place to stay. The **Yellow Pine Guest Ranch** ($-$$$) is a popular family getaway with nine rustic cabins in a quiet forest setting, and activities such as horseback riding, fishing, barbecues, and hay-rides. Open June through October, it's 10 miles south of La Veta on CO 12. *719-742-3528, www.yellowpine.us.* The 44-room **Cuchara Inn** ($-$$) is a pleasant, reasonably priced motel in "downtown" Cuchara. *719-742-3685.*

Special Events

In early June, Walsenburg commemorates the days "when coal was king" with the **Black Diamond Jubilee,** complete with a parade, an outdoor arts fair, and historic reenactments. Each September, Walsenburg celebrates the town's Spanish heritage with **Plaza de Leones,** an outdoor street festival. *719-738-1065.*

In La Veta, **Art in the Park** takes place in early July, featuring the work of local and statewide artists. The first weekend in October, La Veta blocks off Main Street and breaks out the lederhosen to celebrate **Oktoberfest** with beer and street dances, art and antiques. *719-742-3676.*

For More Information

In Walsenburg, the Huerfano County Chamber of Commerce visitor center is parallel to the railroad tracks. *400 Main St., 719-738-1065.* The La Veta/Cuchara Chamber of Commerce changes location often, so call or go online. *P.O. Box 32, La Veta, 81055, 719-742-3676, www.lavetacucharachamber.com.*

Alamosa

Colorado Atlas & Gazetteer pp. 80–81, 90–91

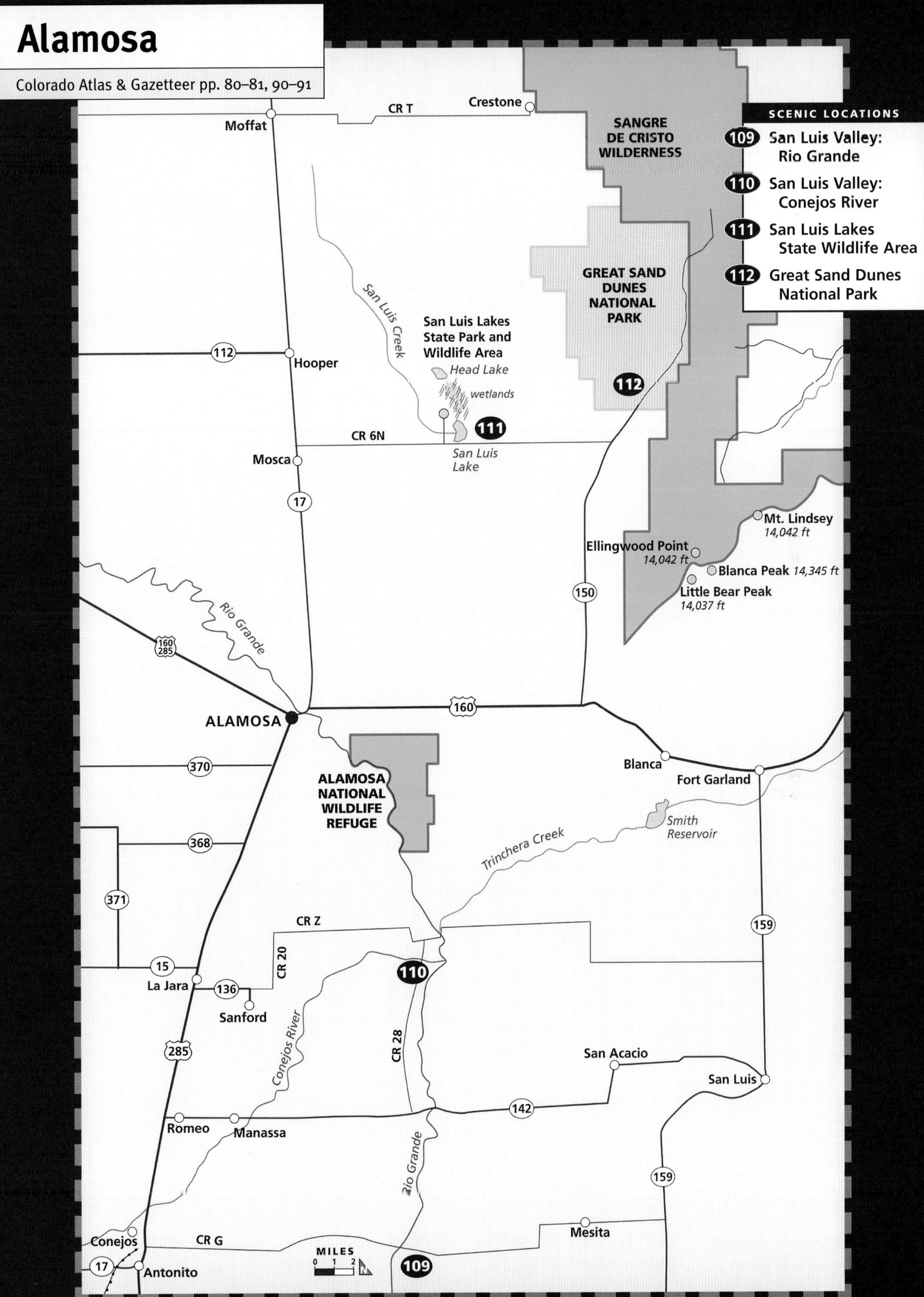

SCENIC LOCATIONS
109 San Luis Valley: Rio Grande
110 San Luis Valley: Conejos River
111 San Luis Lakes State Wildlife Area
112 Great Sand Dunes National Park
Crestone
CR T
Moffat
SANGRE DE CRISTO WILDERNESS
GREAT SAND DUNES NATIONAL PARK
San Luis Creek
San Luis Lakes State Park and Wildlife Area
Head Lake
wetlands
112
Hooper
CR 6N
San Luis Lake
Mosca
17
Mt. Lindsey
14,042 ft
Ellingwood Point
14,042 ft
Blanca Peak 14,345 ft
Little Bear Peak
14,037 ft
150
Rio Grande
160
285
ALAMOSA
160
370
ALAMOSA NATIONAL WILDLIFE REFUGE
Blanca
Fort Garland
Smith Reservoir
Trinchera Creek
368
371
CR Z
159
15
CR 20
La Jara
136
Sanford
Conejos River
285
CR 28
San Acacio
San Luis
142
Romeo
Manassa
Rio Grande
159
Mesita
Conejos
CR G
MILES
0 1 2
17
Antonito

Alamosa

(see map on p. 309)

Alamosa sits at the center of the vast San Luis Valley. Roughly 100 miles north to south and 50 miles wide, it is one of the largest intermountain valleys in the world, bordered on the east by the Sangre de Cristo Mountains and on the west by the San Juans. In between is flat, high desert. For generations, farmers have tapped into deep artesian wells and siphoned water from the Rio Grande to irrigate the valley, transforming it into one of Colorado's highest-producing agricultural regions. The San Luis Valley is a sleepy, workaday place, but not without its scenic wonders—most notably, the Great Sand Dunes.

Even with our children now young adults, the Fielder family still enjoys visiting the dunes because no matter what your age, playing in a big pile of sand makes you feel like a kid. Whether you're slip-sliding down the face of a dune, or hiking up into the Sangres, the terrain offers an incredible amount of variety. Within just a few miles you can climb from piñon and juniper forests, through ponderosa pine, aspen, spruce, and fir, to alpine tundra, sparkling cirque lakes, and 14,000-foot peaks. Tucked away north of the dunes and against the western flank of the Sangres is Crestone, where east of town you'll find a singular holistic community developed over the last 20 years. With great wetlands that attract multitudes of migrating birds, Alamosa and the San Luis Valley hold many surprises.

SAN LUIS VALLEY: RIO GRANDE

The combination of features, both natural and man-made, that define the San Luis Valley make it unique in America, much less Colorado. Sand dunes, 14,000-foot-high peaks, Spanish settlements, historic churches, wetlands, potato farming, and a river canyon are just a few. The latter might be its least-known feature. The last 13 miles of the Rio Grande before it enters New Mexico follow a canyon carved from black volcanic rock. Most of the way is remote wilderness, only within reach by foot or canoe, but the road at the entrance to the canyon accesses great views. From the town of Antonito on US 285, turn east onto County Road G. Drive 14 miles until you cross the Rio Grande at the Lobatos Bridge. The road is improved dirt for cars. Stop on the east side, park, and walk south along the rim.

Colorful lichens decorate the black canyon walls. Rock and lichen make a great foreground for both the river and the San Luis Hills in the distance to the north. Though not particularly deep, the canyon is deep enough so that parallax distortion merges its two walls into one, making it a conspicuous lead-in line. Stand on the canyon edge and point your camera first to the northwest, so that the river cuts diagonally across the composition. Then do the same with the camera pointing to the southwest. Because the river runs north-south, sunrise and sunset create deep shadows in the canyon, rendering the scene unphotographable on film—it just cannot hold the contrast range that the eye can (see pp. 126–128, *Photographing the Landscape*). So photograph just before sunrise or just after sunset. Not only will the lighting be even throughout the scene, but the bright sky will reflect on the still water, rendering it very conspicuous in the canyon. Or photograph the canyon in cloudy light. A wide-angle lens allows you to capture the widest part of the canyon on one side of the scene, in pleasing contrast to the river shrinking into the nothingness of infinity on the other side of your composition. This is a multi-season place to photograph. Spring brings flowers, and winter coats black rocks with white.

History

Alamosa started as a railroad town, literally springing up overnight. In 1878 the Denver & Rio Grande Railroad extended its lines westward from Walsenburg, selecting this site in the middle of the San Luis Valley as its railhead. The railroad loaded nearly 100 buildings from the previous terminus (houses, stores, churches, even a hotel) onto flatbed cars, rolled them to the end of the line, and set up a town. Alamosa became the rail center for the region, and soon tracks were radiating in all directions, serving the silver and gold mines in the mountains, the southern coalfields, and the ranches and farms of the San Luis Valley. The largest town in the valley, it remains the transportation hub for the area's agricultural products (mainly potatoes) and is also a center of commerce for the region and the gateway to the Great Sand Dunes (see Scenic Location No. 112, p. 317).

Main Attractions

ALAMOSA NATIONAL WILDLIFE REFUGE

The wetland and riparian habitats of Alamosa National Wildlife Refuge are an important staging area for birds migrating along the Rocky Mountain flyway. The Alamosa site and nearby Monte Vista National Wildlife Refuge are famous for the arrival of greater sandhill cranes each spring and fall. Alamosa has a visitor center, an auto tour, and a 2.5-mile unpaved trail that parallels the Rio Grande—where songbirds flit among the cottonwoods and willows that line the river. A 3.5-mile road climbs to a bluff overlook with panoramic views of the refuge. From spring to fall, you'll see many species of waterfowl; in winter, look for bald eagles perched in the treetops. Both refuges are open daily from sunrise to sunset. From Alamosa, drive east on US 160 for 4 miles, turn right onto El Rancho Lane, and go 3 miles. *719-589-4021.*

CRESTONE AND THE BACA GRANDE

[illegible] community established at the Baca Grande east of Crestone. Eastern beliefs are well represented alongside Carmelite and even shamanic traditions here, where you'll find an eye-popping and mind-expanding mix of spiritual, interfaith, and environmentally conscious organizations and structures unlike anything you're likely to find in Colorado—or, indeed, the country. This center is for many an ideal place to go to look inward, explore diverse faiths, and heal body and mind. Visitors also come to the Crestone-Moffat area to horseback ride, soak in hot springs, mountain climb, and play golf. From Alamosa, take CO 17 north to Moffat; turn right (east) on Road T to reach Crestone and the Baca Grande. *Crestone-Moffat Business Association, 719-256-5517, www.crestone.org.*

CUMBRES & TOLTEC SCENIC RAILROAD

The Cumbres & Toltec Scenic Railroad is a steam-powered trip back in time. Billowing clouds of black smoke, the train wends its way 64 miles from Antonito, Colo., to Chama, N.M., chugging up mountainsides, through gorges and tunnels, and across high trestles. This mountain route was built by the Denver & Rio Grande in 1880 to haul silver ore and lumber, though even from its inception it was promoted as a way for sightseers to view the spectacular San Juans. The train continued as a workhorse for small mountain towns long past the heyday of narrow-gauge trains, carrying freight up until 1968. Today, using authentic 1925 coal-burning engines, it runs as a tourist attraction from Memorial Day to mid-October. Walking tours of both Antonito and Chama take you past old railway buildings and rail yards, where you can view the country's largest collection of narrow-gauge railroad cars, locomotives, and rolling maintenance-of-way equipment. Plan a full day for this adventure. From Alamosa, drive 28 miles south on US 285 to Antonito. *888-286-2737, www.cumbrestoltec.com.*

GREAT SAND DUNES NATIONAL PARK

The Great Sand Dunes (see Scenic Location No. 112, p. 317) are reason enough to visit the San Luis Valley. The sight of huge piles of sand at the base of snowcapped mountains makes you want to blink and rub your eyes—to make sure you're really seeing what you think you see. What are sand dunes doing in the middle of Colorado? Over millennia, wind and water and melting glaciers eroded the San Juan Mountains, depositing sand and gravel on the valley floor. As the Rio Grande changed its course through the valley, it also left behind sand and silt. Predominant winds picked up debris from the valley floor and carried it eastward, dropping their load at the mountain barrier of the Sangre de Cristo Range. Over time—about 15,000 years—the sand piles grew into the tallest (nearly 750 feet high) and largest (39 square miles) in North America. Today this great big sandbox is a heck of a fun place to play. A hike on the dunes is a must.

It's about a mile to the top. There's no trail to follow in this trackless expanse of sand—just aim for the highest dune and start climbing. At 8,000 feet above sea level, it will get your heart pumping; taking a switchbacking route makes the climb less strenuous. In summer the sand can reach temperatures of 140 degrees, so bare feet are definitely not advisable. Wear sunscreen, take water, and plan on 90 minutes to get to the top. The return trip is faster, especially if you run, jump, or slide down the slipface. You may see people skiing, snowboarding, or sledding—all of which are allowed. Not allowed are hang gliders (because of strong winds) or anything mechanized (because the dunes are a designated wilderness area).

Depending on the time of year you visit, you might have to wade across Medano Creek to reach the dunes. As creeks go, Medano Creek behaves rather oddly. First, waves roll down the creek at 15-second intervals, a phenomenon caused by the buildup of sand on the creek bottom. And then the creek disappears completely, the water gradually being absorbed by an underground aquifer.

Stop at the visitor center for maps and information on park programs and on naturalist-led hikes. To reach the dunes from Alamosa, drive 14 miles east on US 160, turn left onto CO 150, and go 18 miles. *719-378-6300, www.nps.gov/grsa.*

Camping: At the **Great Sand Dunes Oasis Campground and RV Park** on CO 150, 3 miles before the entrance to the dunes, you have amenities including a grocery store, café, and pay showers. Here you can also arrange a guided tour over Medano Pass to amazing dune views. *719-378-2222.* **Piñon Flats** campground within the national park has 88 sites, which fill up quickly in summer (only 44 sites are available in winter). Most have dune and mountain views. No reservations. *719-378-6300.* Backcountry camping, with permit, is permissible in specified areas.

Hiking: Take advantage of the 18 miles of established trails within the park, many less than a mile, some all-day outings. Starting from the Piñon Flats campground, **Sand Ramp Trail** MODERATE is a 12-mile (one way) hike that parallels the Medano Pass Primitive Road for much of the way before branching off to an overlook at Little Medano Creek, then skirting the north side of the dune field. The views are well worth the effort. **Mosca Pass** MODERATE is a 7-mile round trip that follows an old toll road, beginning in piñon-juniper forests and climbing to a subalpine meadow. The trailhead is just past the visitor center on the east side of the road. For other hikes, stop by the visitor center or pick up a copy of Michael O'Hanlon's book, *Sangre de Cristo: A Complete Trail Guide.*

Activities

BIRDING

The San Luis Valley is an ideal place for bird watching, and you'll likely check quite a number of species off your bird-watching life list, including ducks, geese, egrets, herons, and white-faced ibises. The best places to spot birds are the Alamosa National

110 SCENIC LOCATION — SAN LUIS VALLEY: CONEJOS RIVER

The Conejos River originates high in the San Juan Mountains in the South San Juan Wilderness (see Scenic Location No. 114, p. 324). By the time it arrives in the San Luis Valley, the lazy river can barely make it to the Rio Grande. Even so, the Conejos provides sustenance to both farms and valuable wetlands. Lined with cottonwoods and many other varieties of deciduous plants, the river is a scenic anomaly in a place better known for crop production. Most of the river flows through private farms, but here's a way to see it from bridges. From the town of La Jara on US 285, head east on Main Street/ CO 136 to the town of Sanford and follow CO 136 east to CR 20. Go north to Z Road, then east to CR 28 before you get to the Rio Grande. Turn south on CR 28 to the Conejos River.

Late October turns cottonwoods and other deciduous trees a whole spectrum of warm colors along this stretch of the river. Likewise, the lime-green colors of early to mid-May render chromatic magnificence in spring. Stand on the bridges and photograph straight up and down the river, with the river leading the eye inward, and trees forming colorful edges. Then move to the left or right of the middle and photograph obliquely down river to create an asymmetrical balance. You will end up with more trees on the left or right, and the river edge will make a diagonal line across the scene. Photograph at sunrise and sunset to gain shadows as compositional fodder, as well as to intensify the colors of the leaves.

SAN LUIS LAKES STATE WILDLIFE AREA

The San Luis Valley holds several billion acre-feet of water beneath its surface. Water has been draining into the subterranean aquifers of the valley from the mountains that encircle it for millions of years. There is so much groundwater that it leaks to the surface in the form of artesian wells and lakes. These lakes and their accompanying wetlands are valuable ecosystems that sustain much life, including migratory waterfowl. San Luis Lakes State Wildlife Area (SWA) and Monte Vista National Wildlife Refuge (see Scenic Location No. 113, p. 321) are two such places. Both afford wildlife viewing and photographing opportunities, as well as incredible scenic compositions of the valley and the surrounding mountains. Drive 14 miles north from Alamosa on CO 17 to County Road 6N, which is just past the town of Mosca. Turn east and drive 7 miles to the entrance of the SWA on your left. The road provides easy access to the cluster of lakes.

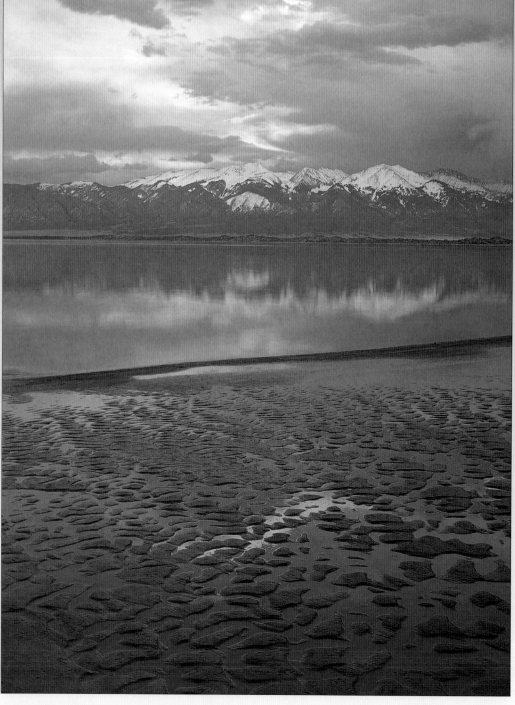

If you have one, be sure to carry a long telephoto lens with which to photograph the birds. Wildlife photographers commonly use lenses 400mm and greater in order to isolate individual birds on film. If you don't have such a lens and don't want to invest in their high cost, consider renting one from a camera shop. Long focal-length lenses are usually "slower" than others, that is, their largest aperture, or f-stop, is relatively small in diameter. Therefore, average shutter speeds tend to be slower than those used with normal lenses. On the other hand, you don't use much depth of field in wildlife photography, so in general, apertures need to be larger and shutter speeds faster. Nevertheless, consider using a tripod and cable release for your wildlife photography, especially when the light is dim at the ends of the day. This will eliminate the chance of camera shake blurring the photograph. As for scenic photography, these lakes provide incredible reflections of the nearby Sangre de Cristo Range. Clouds colored red, pink, and orange reflected in the lakes at sunrise and sunset can make very dramatic images. All you need is still water (see pp. 129–133, *Photographing the Landscape*).

Wildlife Refuge, the Monte Vista National Wildlife Refuge, San Luis Lakes State Wildlife Area—all described elsewhere in this chapter—and Blanca Wetlands, where the rare snowy plover nests. From Alamosa, drive north on CO 17 for 7 miles, turn right on County Road 2S, and go 6 miles to the entrance. *719-274-8971, www.parks.state.co.us.*

CAMPING

San Luis Lakes State Park (see p. 317) has 51 campsites, with views of the Great Sand Dunes and the Sangre de Cristo Mountains. There are no shade trees, but all of the sites have metal canopies, and the campground has modern amenities. The park is just 8 miles west of the Great Sand Dunes on Six Mile Road. No reservations. *719-378-2020.* You can also camp at Great Sand Dunes National Park (see Main Attractions, p. 312).

COLORADO GATORS

Visit one of the most unique and educational alligator and reptile farms in the country at **Colorado Gators Alligator Farm & Reptile Park.** The park features over 400 alligators and dozens of exotic reptiles. Special events at the farm include Eggfest in July, Gatorfest in August, and Sir Chomps O'Lot's birthday in September. The park is family friendly and is open most days at 9 a.m. Located just north of Alamosa, on CO 17. *9162 CR 9 N., Mosca, 719-378-2612, http://gatorfarm.com.*

NATURE CONSERVANCY'S MEDANO–ZAPATA RANCH

The Nature Conservancy's largest preserve in Colorado sprawls over 100,00 acres and includes wetlands, cottonwood groves, meadows, and sand dunes. While there, you can take a tour of their fully-operational historic cattle ranch or explore a prehistoric Native American camp. The resident bison herd and the bordering mountain ranges–the Sangre de Cristos and San Juans—may provide exceptional photo opportunities. The Nature Conservancy chose to preserve this site because of several rare plant and animal species that reside there, some of which are found nowhere else in the world. *303-444-2950, www.nature.org.*

FISHING

The best fishing near Alamosa is about an hour west, where you'll find Gold Medal Water on the **Rio Grande** between Del Norte and South Fork, or an hour south, where the **Conejos River** (see Scenic Location No. 114, p. 324) offers secluded waters just off CO 17 and Forest Road 250. *For information: Colorado Division of Wildlife, 719-587-6900, www.wildlife.state.co.us.*

FOUR-WHEEL-DRIVE TRIPS

Medano Pass Primitive Road is a popular route that starts at the Great Sand Dunes. It plows through sand and splashes through creeks on its way up to 9,940-foot Medano Pass in the Sangre de Cristos, where you have bird's-eye views of the dunes and the San Luis and Wet Mountain Valleys. You can continue down the other side to Westcliffe, or return the same way. The road, which requires a high-clearance vehicle, is open Memorial Day to Labor Day. You can also arrange for a tour over the road in a canopied, 21-passenger vehicle through the Great Sand Dunes Oasis, 3 miles south of the park on CO 150. *719-378-2222.*

GOLF

The 18-hole **Cattails Golf Course,** open March through November, plays through nicely spaced trees along the Rio Grande. *6615 N. River Rd., 719-589-9515.*

HIKING

An old jeep road, the 0.25-mile trail to 60-foot **Zapata Falls** EASY is popular and easily accessible. With views of the Sangres, the San Luis Valley, and the Great Sand Dunes, it's a great place for a picnic. From Alamosa, drive east on US 160 for 14 miles, turn left onto CO 150, and drive 12 miles until you see a sign for Zapata Falls. Turn right onto a dirt road and go 4 miles to the parking lot at the trailhead. From the Great Sand Dunes, drive south on CO 150 for 10.5 miles and turn left. Just before the falls you can pick up **South Zapata Trail** DIFFICULT, which follows South Zapata Creek for 5 miles, through high valleys with views of the Blanca Massif, to South Zapata Lake, which is above timberline and has many good camping spots.

The 5-mile (one way) hike to **Como Lake** MODERATE follows a four-wheel-drive road to a peaceful lake with many camping and fishing options. From Alamosa, drive 14 miles east on US 160, turn left on CO 150, and proceed for 3.3 miles. At Forest Road 975, turn right and drive 1.5 miles to the parking lot, or until the road gets too rough to continue any farther. *For more information: Rio Grande National Forest, 1803 CO 160, Monte Vista, 719-852-5941, www.fs.fed.us/r2/riogrande.* See Main Attractions, p. 312, for hikes in Great Sand Dunes National Park.

MOUNTAIN BIKING

The trails at **Zapata Falls** EASY breeze through piñon-juniper forests, offering views of the Great Sand Dunes and the San Luis Valley (for directions, see Hiking, above). The hard-packed singletracks are a series of stacked loops (4 miles total), which you can just keep riding as much as you'd like. It's a popular place with hikers and horseback riders, so you'll be sharing the trails. Be sure to take the short, 0.25-mile hike up to the 60-foot waterfall. *For rentals, gear, and information: Kristi Mountain Sports, 3217 Main St., 719-589-9759.*

MUSEUM

Fort Garland Museum is a wonderful way to experience history. The garrison was established in 1858, and from 1866 to 1867, famed scout and frontiersman Kit Carson served as its commander. The post was abandoned in 1883 when the Utes were moved to

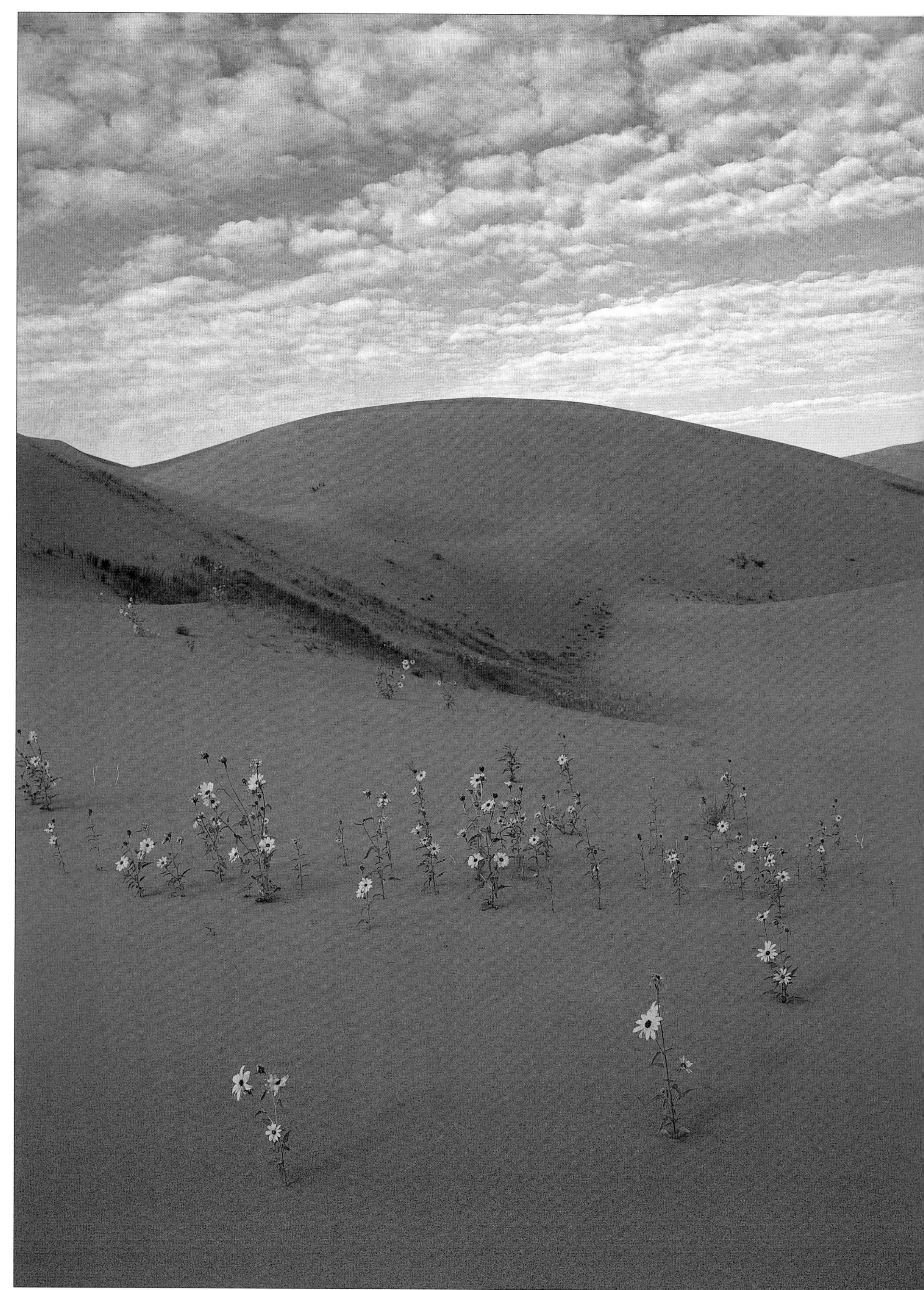

112 SCENIC LOCATION

GREAT SAND DUNES NATIONAL PARK

Colorado's most famous sand dunes are one of the geologic and scenic wonders of the planet—there is nothing quite like them anywhere else. The dunes are both the tallest (up to 750 feet high) and highest (8,000 feet above sea level) in North America. More than 39 square miles of dunes cover the 53-square-mile park. Winds sweeping across the San Luis Valley deposited the sand at the base of the Sangre de Cristo Range on their way through Medano and Mosca Passes. It's taken 15,000 years to create the dunes we see today. With the Sangres in the background, and beautiful Medano Creek beside the dunes, the photographic possibilities are limitless. The park is 35 miles northeast of Alamosa. Take US 160 east from Alamosa to CO 150, which dead-ends to the north at the dunes.

Where do I begin? Sunset is my favorite time to photograph here. The sun gets so low in the sky that on a clear day the dust in the atmosphere above the valley floor colors the light as red as you'll see anywhere (see p. 86, *Photographing the Landscape*). Broad shadows and red light make for some amazing sand dune compositions. The hike to the top of the highest dune doesn't take very long, so try to find yourself there at sunset. Point your camera north or south so as to be at right angles with the sun. The shadows on the east side of the dunes will be intense and manifest the distinct shapes of the dune crests. Photograph the dunes with or without a horizon, and with the Sangre de Cristos in the background while they, too, catch that warm, late light.

Great Sand Dunes National Park is one of my favorite fall places. Medano Creek flows along the eastern edge of the dunes, but it's not a typical mountain creek. It flows across a wide area of sand, and is less than an inch deep in most places. In the second week of October, the cottonwood trees along the creek turn bright orange at sunset and reflect on its surface. It's possible to compose the creek in the middle, cottonwoods on the sides, and mountains behind—one of my favorite Colorado scenics. Even the lowly rabbitbrush and other native plants turn lovely colors during autumn, and all make a great foreground for scenes with the dunes in the background.

If you have a four-wheel drive, try traversing the dunes into the Rio Grande National Forest to the east via the Medano Pass Road. You will need to deflate your tires by about half in order to get through the sand, but the drive through the aspens is glorious. On the way back, pump up your tires at the park.

reservations. Five of the original 22 adobe buildings remain, now restored and housing a collection that depicts life at a military fort during the late 1800s, including infantry barracks and commandant Carson's officer quarters. Historic demonstrations

Fort Garland Museum

and encampments take place on the parade grounds during the summer. From Alamosa, drive east on US 160 for 25 miles, turn right on CO 159, and go 0.25 mile. *719-379-3512, www.loscaminos.com.*

SAN LUIS LAKES STATE PARK

This desert oasis, with the Great Sand Dunes and Sangre de Cristos as a backdrop, is uncrowded even in summer. Nine-tenths of the park (see Scenic Location No. 111, p. 314) are wetlands and lakes, where you can enjoy boating, fishing, and windsurfing. The wetlands attract an incredible number of bird species, making this a prime bird-watching area, but you can also view wildlife such as elk, coyote, and even the tiny kangaroo rat. There are four picnic areas as well as a campground (see Camping, p. 315). The park is just 8 miles west of the Great Sand Dunes on Six Mile Road. *719-378-2020, www.coloradoparks.org.*

SCENIC DRIVES

Los Caminos Antiguos Scenic and Historic Byway ("Road of the Ancients") travels through the very southern portion of the San Luis Valley. Like a capsulized version of the valley's history, the 96-mile route encompasses early Spanish towns, a frontier military post, and a narrow-gauge railroad. It travels through sagebrush flats, agricultural lands, and then crosses the Rio Grande before climbing into the San Juan Mountains. From Fort Garland, drive south on CO 159 to San Luis (the oldest permanent settlement in the state), west on CO 142 to Romeo, south on US 285 to Antonito, and then west on CO 17 to Cumbres Pass and the New Mexico border. *www.loscaminos.com.*

SWIMMING

The sand dunes are one big beach, so why not go swimming? There are a couple of choices, both outdoor pools heated by geothermal waters. With diving boards and kiddie pools, they are a fun break for the whole family. The **Sand Dunes Swimming Pool** is open year-round. From the Great Sand

Dunes, drive west on Six Mile Road and north on CO 17; a [illegible] *719-378-2807.* The **Splashland** pool is only open in summer. From Alamosa, drive north on CO 17 for 1 mile. *719-589-6307.*

Restaurants

If the kids need a fast-food fix, Alamosa is the place. However, a better idea is to pick up some sandwiches and have a picnic in Cole Park, at Chamber Drive and 3rd Street. This pleasant little park on the bank of the Rio Grande is rimmed with cottonwood trees (*alamosa* means "cottonwood" in Spanish). After lunch, you can walk along the levee, pick up brochures at the Alamosa County visitor center (a replica of an 1878 train depot), or tour the free San Luis Valley History Museum, *www.museumtrail.com,* just behind the visitor center.

Milagros Coffee House ($) has sandwiches to go. It's an eclectic kind of place, with ice cream, used books, and live music on weekends. A remarkable thing about Milagros (Spanish for "miracle") is its non-profit status: All proceeds go to helping the homeless. It's in downtown Alamosa at the corner of State and Main. *719-589-9299.*

May-Wa Chinese Restaurant ($-$$) serves delicious Chinese and Vietnamese dishes. *620 Main St., 719-589-9559.* For American and Italian cuisine, try **Hideaway Steakhouse** ($-$$) at the corner of US 285 and 8th Street. *719-589-4444.* Order the chicken Santa Fe burrito at **Cavillo's** ($-$$) and you won't leave hungry. *400 Main St., 719-587-5500.* For great steaks and seafood try **Crocodile Rock** ($-$$) once it reopens in 2007. *2069 First St., 719-589-2747.*

Accommodations

There are plenty of chain motels in Alamosa, spread out all along US 160. For a more local experience, make a reservation at the locally owned **Best Western Alamosa Inn** ($), which has a restaurant and a heated pool. *2005 Main St., 800-459-5123, www.bestwestern.com.* At the entrance to the dunes, **Great** [illegible] pool and full-service restaurant. The attraction is its location and the fact that all of the rooms have private patios looking out onto the dunes. From Alamosa, drive 14 miles east on US 160, turn left onto CO 150, and go 14 miles more. *719-378-2900, www.gsdlodge.com.* For something a little more adventurous, book a stay at the **Zapata Ranch** ($$$$). This working cattle ranch covers more than 100,000 acres and borders the Great Sand Dunes National Park. Multiple night stays are offered and focus on giving guests a true Colorado ranching experience. Zapata offers traditional lodging options as well and is open year round. *5303 CO 150, Mosca, 719-378-2356, 888-592-7282, www.zranch.org.*

Zapata Ranch, Mosca

Special Events

A one-day event, **Castles & Kites** is held in June at the Great Sand Dunes, with kite flying, a sand sculpture competition (individuals and teams), and a free evening concert. **Alamosa Round-up** is the biggest pro rodeo event in the valley, with nationally acclaimed cowboys, a parade, demolition derby, and entertainment; it's held in late June at the Alamosa County Fairgrounds. The **San Luis Valley Fly-In and Airshow,** a one-day event held in July at the Alamosa Airport, features vintage aircraft, World War II fighters, and aerobatic flying. Alamosa's **Early Iron Festival** on Labor Day weekend is a celebration of classic cars and hot rods, with more than 300 antique autos on display in Cole Park. *800-258-7597, www.alamosa.org.*

For More Information

Alamosa County Chamber of Commerce has a visitor center in a restored train depot next to Cole Park, Chamber Drive and 3rd Street, Alamosa. *800-258-7597, www.alamosa.org.*

Monte Vista

(see map on p. 320)

Monte Vista is best known for the flocks of tourists who come each spring and fall, winging in by the thousands to stop over on their yearly migrations through the San Luis Valley. Nearly 25,000 greater sandhill cranes alight here, using the wetlands of Monte Vista National Wildlife Refuge and the surrounding fields as staging areas before continuing south to winter or north to breed. Their arrival is celebrated with the annual Crane Festival in March, when out-of-towners toting binoculars and cameras arrive in droves to see the stately birds.

If you're lucky, you might witness the crane's delicate mating dance, a series of leaps and bows performed to attract a lifetime mate, or to strengthen the bonds between already monogamous pairs. And if you're very, very lucky, you might even spot the endangered whooping crane, a majestic white bird with an 8-foot wingspan. A small number of whoopers migrate with the sandhills each year, the result of introducing whooping crane eggs into sandhill nests in hopes of increasing their population.

History

At first there was just a Denver & Rio Grande water tower and section house, serving the narrow-gauge railroad that extended west from Alamosa. Three years later, in 1884, the town had been platted and incorporated. Unlike other Colorado towns that have experienced boom-and-bust economies, Monte Vista has grown steadily through the years, as it supported the surrounding agricultural interests of the fertile San Luis Valley. Eleven downtown buildings, made from locally quarried rhyolite, have been designated a historic district.

Main Attractions

MONTE VISTA NATIONAL WILDLIFE REFUGE

Nearly 200 species of birds have been counted at Monte Vista National Wildlife Refuge (see Scenic Location No. 113, p. 321), where wetlands provide food and cover during annual migrations through the San Luis Valley. As many as 35,000 ducks—along with other waterfowl, wading birds, songbirds, and raptors—descend during peak fall season at the 14,189-acre refuge and the nearby 11,168-acre Alamosa National Wildlife Refuge (see Alamosa, p. 310). The best times to see the greater sandhill cranes that congregate here are in the morning when they take flight in dramatic V formations to feed in area pastures, and in the evening when they return to roost. A 3-mile self-guided auto tour loops through the refuge, which is open from sunrise to sunset. From Monte Vista, drive south on CO 15 for 6 miles. *719-589-4021.*

Monte Vista National Wildlife Refuge

Activities

CAMPING

Rock Creek and **Comstock** campgrounds (23 and 8 sites, respectively) are situated along the banks of Rock Creek. The scenery is free, and so are the campsites. Both have shade (Comstock has more) but no drinking water. From Monte Vista, drive 2 miles south on CO 15 and turn right onto County Road 2S. After 2.5 miles, turn left onto CR 28 (Rock Creek Road) and go 13 miles to Rock Creek campground. Go 2.5 miles farther to Comstock. No reservations. *719-657-3321.*

Alamosa campground has 10 spacious, well-shaded sites along the Alamosa River (no fishing though, thanks to pollution from mining). No reservations. From Monte Vista, drive south on CO 15 for 12 miles, turn right onto CR 12S (which becomes Forest Road 250), and drive 13.5 miles. If you keep following FR 250 as it parallels the Alamosa River, you'll climb to Stunner Pass, near the Continental Divide (see Scenic Location No. 115, p. 325). Just before reaching the pass, bear right onto FR 380 for 0.5 mile to **Stunner** campground, which has 10 sites and stunning views (pardon the pun). If you stay left and continue on FR 250, you can go over Stunner Pass to **Mix Lake** campground, which has 22 fishing-accessible campsites near Platoro Reservoir. *719-274-8971.*

FISHING

Platoro Reservoir is stocked with rainbow trout and kokanee salmon, and also yields some good-sized browns. (For directions, see Scenic Drives, p. 321.) **Mix Lake** is nearby, and downstream is the **Conejos River** (see Scenic Location No. 114, p. 324), a beautiful and uncrowded river that many consider a well-kept secret. The 8-mile stretch below the reservoir has good public access and several tributary streams.

MOUNTAIN BIKING

Mountain biking is often overlooked in south-central Colorado, which is unfortunate because there are more ridable months here than elsewhere in the state and many great but unknown (and uncrowded) bike trails. **Schillings Spring** EASY is a 7-mile (one way) ride through high mountain meadows and stands of aspen and pine. It follows a twisting forest road before dead-ending. From Monte Vista, drive south on CO 15 for about 12 miles and turn right onto County Road 12S (which turns into Forest Road 250). Drive about 8 miles to the intersection of FR 250 and 251. Park here and start riding west on FR 251. In the same vicinity is the **Cat Creek Trail** DIFFICULT, a 13.5-mile loop with a variety of trail surfaces and a singletrack downhill at the finish. Follow the same directions as to Schillings Spring, but at the intersection of FR 250 and 271, bear right onto FR 271 and drive approximately 7 miles to Cat Creek Trail.

Monte Vista/Del Norte/South Fork

Colorado Atlas & Gazetteer pp. 79–80, 89–90

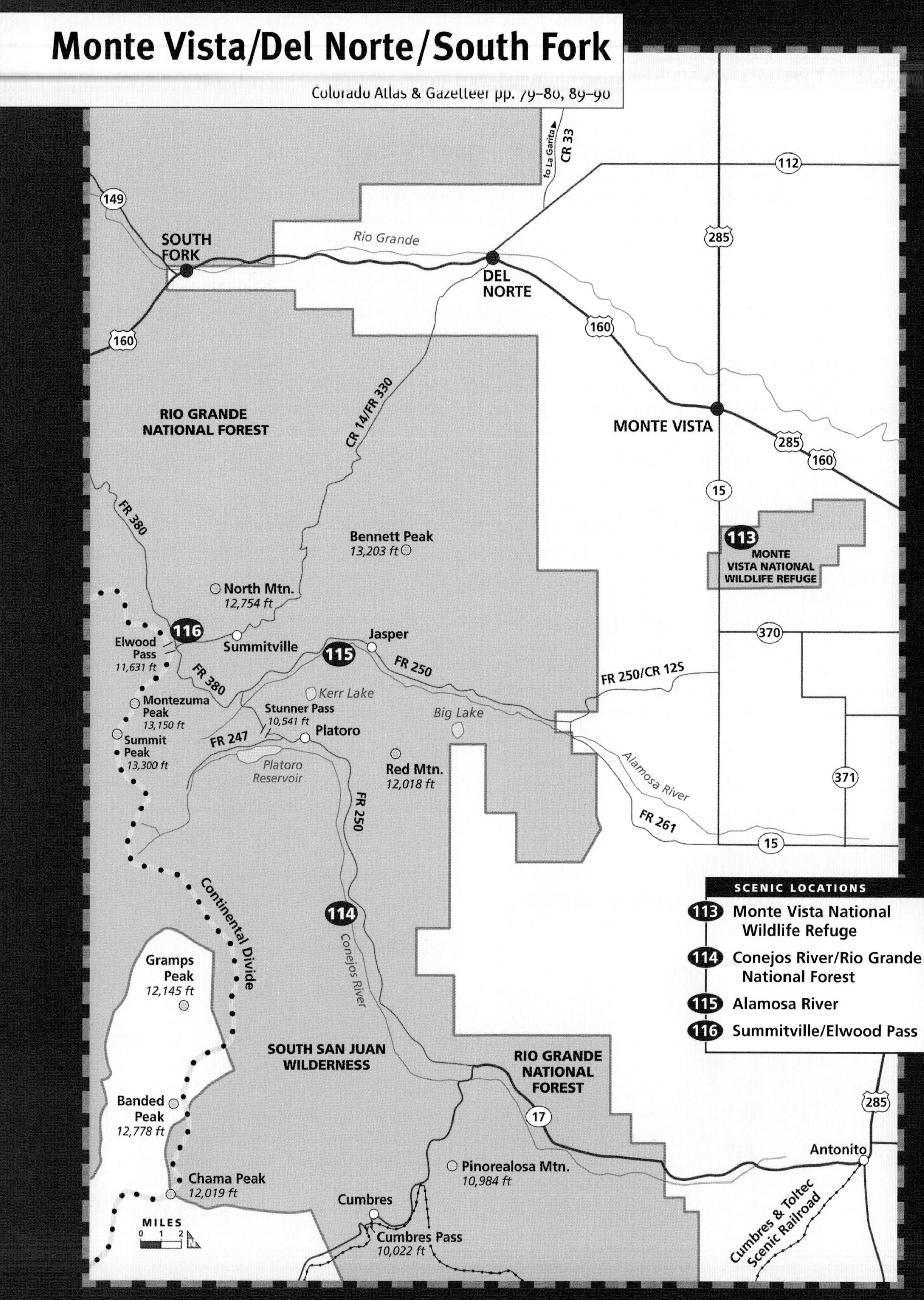

to La Garita
CR 33
112
149
285
SOUTH FORK
Rio Grande
DEL NORTE
160
MONTE VISTA
CR 14/FR 330
RIO GRANDE NATIONAL FOREST
15
FR 380
Bennett Peak
13,203 ft
113
MONTE VISTA NATIONAL WILDLIFE REFUGE
North Mtn.
12,754 ft
116
Summitville
Jasper
115
370
Elwood Pass
11,631 ft
FR 250
FR 250/CR 12S
Kerr Lake
Montezuma Peak
13,150 ft
Stunner Pass
10,541 ft
Big Lake
Summit Peak
13,300 ft
FR 247
Platoro
Platoro Reservoir
Red Mtn.
12,018 ft
Alamosa River
371
FR 261
Continental Divide
114
Conejos River
Gramps Peak
12,145 ft
SOUTH SAN JUAN WILDERNESS
RIO GRANDE NATIONAL FOREST
17
Banded Peak
12,778 ft
Antonito
Chama Peak
12,019 ft
Pinorealosa Mtn.
10,984 ft
Cumbres
Cumbres Pass
10,022 ft
Cumbres & Toltec Scenic Railroad
MILES
0 1 2
SCENIC LOCATIONS
113 Monte Vista National Wildlife Refuge
114 Conejos River/Rio Grande National Forest
115 Alamosa River
116 Summitville/Elwood Pass

SCENIC DRIVES

In summer a high-clearance vehicle can manage the gravel **Alamosa River Road** (Forest Road 250), which parallels the river to its headwaters near the Continental Divide (see Scenic Location No. 115, p. 325). From Monte Vista, drive south on CO 15 for 12 miles and turn right onto County Road 12S (which becomes FR 250). It's about 20 miles to the intersection of FR 250 and FR 380. From there you can continue south on FR 250 to Platoro Reservoir (about 5 miles more) and the tiny town of Platoro. Or you can bear right onto FR 380, which eventually takes you to US 160, between Wolf Creek Pass and South Fork (about another 25 miles). Another option is to take FR 380 west from its intersection with FR 250 to FR 330, then right (east) on FR 330 past the ghost town of Summitville, a former gold-mining operation (see Scenic Location No. 116, p. 329), and up to Del Norte (about 30 miles). Whichever route you choose, the views and the ride are worth the trip; plan a full day.

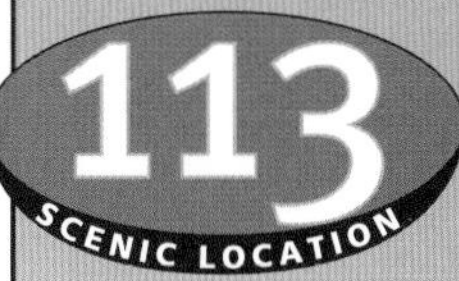

MONTE VISTA NATIONAL WILDLIFE REFUGE

As mentioned with respect to the San Luis Lakes (see Scenic Location No. 111, p. 314), the floor of the San Luis Valley contains numerous wetlands. Both the Monte Vista and Alamosa National Wildlife Refuges (NWR) are crisscrossed with canals and ditches in order to keep them wet. The resulting ecosystem attracts not just waterfowl but all sorts of wildlife, including coyotes and beavers. Monte Vista NWR is famous for the annual visits paid to it between February and April by both the greater sandhill crane and the more rare and endangered whooping crane. Sandhill cranes visit the refuge by the thousands. Monte Vista NWR is 6 miles south of Monte Vista on CO 15.

If you go at the right time, you may not even need a lens longer than 200mm in order to photograph the birds. When the cranes are on the ground or in the air by the hundreds, even standard lenses can make the cloud of birds conspicuous on film. Sunrise and sunset afford the best light in which to photograph, although this darker light requires that the camera be on a tripod. As the birds are in the air at the ends of the day, you will need to handhold the camera and pan with them in the direction of their flight. Panning reduces the chance that the flock will be blurred in using the relatively slow shutter speeds required in darker light. One of my favorite photographs composes the flying birds silhouetted against red clouds of sunrise.

Beautiful scenics can be made here, too. Look for the standing bodies of water in the refuge. Compose ponds in the foreground with the Sangre de Cristo Range in the distance reflecting in the pond. I typically use wide-angle lenses in such cases, which minimize the mountains and render the small ponds as large lakes. The evening blue sky (or pink if you are lucky) casts its color all across the surface of tranquil water.

Restaurants

When traveling in the San Luis Valley, I look for restaurants with pickups parked outside, because if the local farmers and ranchers are eating there, that's where I want to go. That's how I found **Dos Rios** ($-$$). Two miles north of Monte Vista on US 285; it's a family-owned Mexican cantina with an extensive menu. *719-852-0545.* The **Mountain View Restaurant** ($) features authentic Mexican cuisine alongside traditional American fare. Enjoy breakfast, lunch, or dinner. *2099 Sherman Ave., 719-852-9919, www.mountainviewdining.net.* For a real treat, stop at the **Don Tomas Bakery** ($). This establishment serves all sorts of breads and treats. *829 1st Ave., 719-852-0981.*

Accommodations

The **Best Western Movie Manor** ($) gets two thumbs up for the most unique concept in lodging—a combination motel and drive-in movie theater. The drive-in was there first, then owner George Kelloff got the idea to build a motel behind it. The rooms are all wired for sound, so you just jump in bed, open the curtains, and watch a movie. PG-rated current releases are shown nightly during the summer and are included with the price of the room. There's even a concession stand for popcorn and candy, as well as a restaurant (the Academy Award Room), coffee shop, and lounge. The motel is located 2.5 miles west of downtown Monte Vista on US 160. *800-771-9468, www.bestwestern.com, www.coloradovacation.com/motel/movie.*

Offering outdoor programs for grown-ups as well as kids. **The Windmill Bed and Breakfast** ($$) is a large Spanish-style country home with wonderful views. It is centrally located and surrounded by an array of activities. *4340 West U.S. Hwy. 160, 719-852-0438, www.thewindmillbandb.com.* The **Pecosa Inn** ($-$$) features comfy accommodations in a central location. Guests will find a variety of activities nearby. *1519 Grand Ave., 888-732-6724, www.pecosainn.com.*

Special Events

The **Crane Festival** in mid-March celebrates the arrival of sandhill cranes during their annual migration through the valley. The three-day weekend draws birders from all over the country for naturalist-led tours of the wildlife refuge, bird identification and wildlife photography workshops, and wildlife-related crafts and exhibits. *www.cranefest.com.* Colorado's oldest professional rodeo, the **Ski Hi Stampede** takes place in Monte Vista the last weekend in July. *800-214-1240.*

For More Information

Monte Vista Chamber of Commerce, *947 1st Ave., 719-852-2731, www.monte-vista.org.*

Del Norte

(see map on p. 320)

At the western edge of the San Luis Valley and the eastern boundary of the San Juan Mountains, tiny Del Norte provides easy access to both high places and wide-open spaces. The Rio Grande, with its Gold Medal trout fishing, runs just north of town. A little farther north is a network of canyons that have gained renown as a rock climber's paradise.

History

It was the glitter of gold that first drew prospectors to the mountains southwest of here, where gold strikes were recorded in the early 1870s at Summitville, close to the Continental Divide. The town of Del Norte sprang up to supply the mines, and it soon became known as the "gateway to the San Juans." It was here that a miner had to choose: Would he go south to search for gold or northwest to search for silver near Silverton and Lake City?

Many of the late-19th-century buildings—now designated historic landmarks—that line the main street endure as stores and businesses serving the agricultural community of the western San Luis Valley.

Main Attractions

FISHING

The Rio Grande is one of Colorado's top trout rivers, with the section between Del Norte and South Fork rated Gold Medal Water. Here, anglers can expect to catch 16- to 20-inch rainbows and browns (see South Fork, Main Attractions, p. 327). *For information: Rio Grande National Forest office, 13308 W. US 160, Del Norte, 719-657-3321; or Colorado Division of Wildlife, 719-587-6900. For gear: Casa de Madera Sports, 660 Grand Ave., 719-657-2723.*

Kids will enjoy the **Fishing Is Fun Pier** at Centennial Park, which is also wheelchair accessible. *Front St. and Columbia Ave.*

ROCK CLIMBING

Sport rock climbing has gained a foothold in the San Luis Valley relatively recently. Within 15 miles of Del Norte are more than 350 established climbing routes, and the area has garnered international acclaim, particularly **Penitente Canyon.** Since the 1980s, more than 130 named routes have been established in this small, scenic canyon. The texture and stability of its welded volcanic ash walls make for excellent climbing, and the semiarid climate of the high desert allows for year-round use, though spring and fall are considered ideal. The canyon has routes for nearly every level of climber, with all routes less than 80 feet. Most are bolted and have rappel stations.

Other nearby climbing canyons include **Rock Garden, ET Canyon, Witches Canyon, Sidewinder, La Garita Creek Wall, Shaw Springs,** and **Elephant Rocks.** The Bureau of Land Management has improved the area with restrooms, a picnic pavilion, a 17-site campground (no reservations needed), and a network of hiking and mountain biking trails (hike in either direction; bike clockwise). *719-655-2547.* There are also primitive campsites at Witches Canyon and Sidewinder. The nearest resupply is the store in La Garita, where you can buy food, fill up your water jugs, order a sandwich, and swap stories with other climbers.

Penitente Canyon is easily accessible. From Del Norte, drive northeast on CO 112 for 3 miles and turn left onto County Road 33 (which turns into CR 38A). Proceed about 13 miles to the Penitente Canyon sign, turn left, and go about 1 mile more. *For local information or rock climbing gear: Casa de Madera Sports, 660 Grand Ave., 719-657-2723.*

Activities

CAMPING

The closest camping to Del Norte is at **Penitente Canyon** (see Rock Climbing, this page), which has 17 sites. *719-655-2547.* Named for its views of rock cliffs, **Cathedral** campground is a quiet place that rarely fills up. Its 33 heavily shaded sites are spread along Embargo Creek, and you can access a number of trails from here, including Fremont Camp Trail. From Del Norte, drive west on US 160 for 9 miles, turn right onto Embargo Creek Road (County Road 18), and continue on Forest Road 650 and FR 640 as you follow the signs to the campground, about 15 miles more. *719-274-8971.*

HIKING

Easy and moderate hiking trails loop through **Penitente, Witches,** and **Sidewinder Canyons** (see Rock Climbing, this page). The trail to **La Garita Arch** EASY leads to an impressive, 100-foot volcanic dike with a hole eroded from its center. It's a short, steep climb (about 100 yards) to "the window." In summer watch the skies for golden eagles, and scan the hills for deer, antelope, and bighorn sheep. From Del Norte, drive north on CO 112 for 3 miles, turn left on County Road 33 (which turns into CR 38A). Drive about 9.5 miles, turn left onto Forest Road 660, and continue about 6 miles to the base of the arch.

Fremont Camp Trail MODERATE leads to where John C. Frémont camped during the disastrous winter of 1848, when his party became stranded and nearly a third of the 36 men perished. Six-foot-tall tree stumps show how high the snow was when they chopped down trees for fuel and shelter. The 3.5-mile (one way) trail is accessed from Cathedral campground (see Camping, above). Park there and follow a jeep road (FR 640) for about 2.5 miles. For the last mile, you'll climb steeply through forests before reaching an alpine meadow, filled with flowers in July.

You can also access the **Cathedral Trail** MODERATE from Cathedral campground. This 3.25-mile (one way) trail follows a creek, passes Cathedral Rocks, and ends in Groundhog Park.

Continued on page 326

CONEJOS RIVER/ RIO GRANDE NATIONAL FOREST

Scenic Location No. 110 (p. 313) discusses the lazy Conejos River as it winds through the San Luis Valley. This location reveals the Conejos that flows with alacrity from the South San Juan Wilderness west of the valley, the headwaters of a river that eventually meets the Rio Grande. With cottonwoods down low decorating its banks, and aspens up high decorating the ridges, the Conejos is one of the most scenic autumn places in Colorado. Drive west on CO 17 from the sleepy San Luis Valley town of Antonito on US 285. Twenty-two miles past Antonito, turn north onto improved Forest Road 250, manageable by car. Another 22 miles later you will enter the summer resort town of Platoro at the head of the river. The river follows this entire 44-mile route.

The cottonwoods along the river and the aspens on the hillsides are simply amazing when you enter the Rio Grande National Forest west of Antonito. If you visit at the end of September, you will not believe the variegated tones of yellows, oranges, and greens before the fall color reaches its peak. I am actually a pre-peak and post-peak kind of a guy when it comes to autumn. Though I love seas of yellow, I prefer the mix of colors earlier in the season, and the subtle hints of yellow when trees have lost many of their leaves late in the season. Pull over at many places along CO 17 and compose the river as a lead-in line with cottonwoods on either side. Add some blue sky and you've made a very dramatic composition. Remember, blue and yellow are complementary; things yellow appear more conspicuous when set against their complement (see pp. 18–25, *Photographing the Landscape*).

When you turn onto FR 250, you enter first the montane, then the subalpine domains of the river. Ponderosa pines and aspens decorate the hillsides east and west of the river. Rolling hills precede the sometimes visible peaks of the South San Juan Wilderness to the west. It's one of my favorite autumn drives in Colorado, and I promise you won't see a whole lot of people. After passing the town of Platoro, drive west on FR 247 past Platoro Reservoir to the road's end. Park your vehicle at the Middle Fork of the Conejos Trailhead and day-hike up this spectacular wilderness drainage.

ALAMOSA RIVER

Just past the Platoro Reservoir turnoff (see Scenic Location No. 114, opposite), Forest Road 250 climbs over Stunner Pass out of the Conejos River drainage and descends into the head of the Alamosa River drainage. The Alamosa River meanders east to the San Luis Valley, where it meets La Jara Creek before entering the Rio Grande. Like the Conejos, it's very scenic, albeit not nearly as wide and open. Still, the aspen views along the river make this the perfect way to complete the loop back to the San Luis Valley. FR 250 leaves the Conejos drainage and continues east along the Alamosa River to CO 15, about 12 miles south of Monte Vista.

The river will surprise you—it's red! Mineralization washing down from the prominent red mountain (Lookout Mountain) north of the river has rendered the rocks in the river the same color. It's a little disconcerting but actually quite natural. Some folks say that the Summitville Mine and the disastrous overflow of its leaching ponds are the culprit (see Scenic Location No. 116, p. 329), but locals know better. Nevertheless, the aspens along the river make everything look good, and the red river is actually a beautiful complement to the greens of spring's leafing aspens. The first week of June is peak leafing week here. Before heading downriver, compose Lookout Mountain in a scene with aspens in the foreground. Then make intimate landscapes of the bountiful aspen groves along the road back to the valley.

MOUNTAIN BIKING

Both easy and moderate biking trails wind through **Penitente Witches,** and **Sidewinder Canyons** (see Rock Climbing, p. 323). The 6.3-mile **Limekiln Trail** DIFFICULT has a little bit of everything—a variety of surfaces (particularly desert rock), several technically challenging sections, scenery, wildlife, and history. The old kilns along the route were once used to heat limestone to process the lime, which was used for mortar, whitewash, disinfecting, and removing hair from hides. From Del Norte drive east on US 160 for 6 miles and turn right at the stone sculpture onto County Road 5W. Then turn right onto BLM 5120 and drive 4 miles to the stock tank dam and park. Some moderate trails in the area are worth exploring, but note that there is a rifle range to the north.

MUSEUM

For a small town, Del Norte has a big museum. The **Rio Grande County Museum and Cultural Center** highlights the natural and human history of the region, with displays on Hispanic culture, archaeology, Indian rock art, and pioneer life. You can read diary entries from John C. Frémont's winter encampment (see Hiking, p. 323). *580 Oak St., 719-657-2847, www.rgcm.org.*

Restaurants

Boogie's Restaurant ($-$$) serves breakfast, lunch, and dinner, specializing in burgers, sandwiches, and down-home country cooking. Have a slice of coconut cream pie. There are children's and "elder folks" menus. *410 Grand Ave., 719-657-2905.* The **Country Family Inn & Restaurant** ($) is open daily for breakfast, lunch, and dinner. The menu features an eclectic selection that includes classic American favorites as well as southwest specialties. *1050 Grande Ave., 719-657-3581, 800-372-2331, www.countryfamilyinn.com.* The **Tiger Lion** ($) is a great spot for a home-style meal. Open for breakfast, lunch, and dinner. *216 Oak St., 719-657-9135.*

Boogie's Restaurant, Del Norte

Accommodations

Double Spur Lodge & Ranch ($$$-$$$$) is located between Del Norte and South Fork and offers guests multiple accommodation options to choose from. For a more relaxing vacation, you can opt for the lodge itself. If you're looking for a bit more adventure, you can book a Rustic Cabin Overnight, which includes four meals and a horseback riding option. *8501 W. CR 9 N., 719-657-3139, 719-657-2920, www.doublespurlodge.com.* **Country Family Inn & Restaurant** ($) is a family-friendly inn located just minutes from area attractions. *1050 Grande Ave., 719-657-3581, 800-372-2331, www.countryfamilyinn.com*

Special Events

Covered Wagon Days in early August takes you back in time, with displays of covered wagons, buckboards, stagecoaches, chuck wagons, and surreys, as well as logging competitions, mountain man encampments, period costumes, and dancing to old-time music. *888-616-4638.*

For More Information

Del Norte Chamber of Commerce, *505 Grand Ave., 888-616-4638, 719-657-2845, www.delnortechamber.org.*

South Fork

(see map on p. 320)

The sign welcoming travelers to South Fork shows eight different outdoor activities, which pretty much sums up this small town in the foothills of the San Juans. Just about any mountain sport or activity is possible here—from jeeping to snowmobiling, mountain biking to cross-country skiing, snowshoeing, hiking, rafting, hunting, and camping. You name it and you can find it in the vicinity of South Fork, which lies at the center of the vast Rio Grande National Forest. The town's real claim to fame, however, is fishing. The portion of the Rio Grande that flows from South Fork to Del Norte is Gold Medal trout fishing water. The whiz of a fly reel is as predictable here as the sun rising in the morning.

History

At the confluence of the Rio Grande and its south fork, the town of South Fork started out in the 1880s as a logging community. Loggers still harvest spruce and fir trees from the forests surrounding the town, which has one of the largest lumber mills in the area. A 24-foot lumberjack carved from a 450-year-old Douglas fir stands at the intersection of US 160 and CO 149. South Fork grew up at the junction of early toll roads, and it remains a crossroads today. From here you can travel east to the San Luis Valley, southwest to Pagosa Springs, or northwest to Creede and Lake City on CO 149, also known as the Silver Thread Scenic and Historic Byway.

Main Attractions

FISHING

You can expect to reel in trophy-size trout along the 22-mile stretch of the Rio Grande downstream from South Fork. The section of the river between the CO 149 bridge in South Fork to the Farmer's Union outtake canal 1 mile west of Del Norte has earned the designation of Gold Medal Water. June to October is prime time, when the water is warmer and the fish more active. Fly fishing is best in June and July, when stoneflies and mayflies hatch; this is also an ideal time to float the river. It's catch-and-release on rainbows all along the Rio Grande. Other regulations include a limit of two browns 16 inches or larger and artificial flies and lures only. In addition, the section of the Rio Grande between South Fork and Creede has excellent fishing, primarily for brown trout and rainbows. *Rio Grande National Forest office, 13308 W. US 160, Del Norte, 719-657-3321.*

There are 13 lakes within a 20-minute drive of town, the closest being **Beaver Creek Reservoir,** which is stocked with kokanee salmon, rainbows, and browns, and is also a good ice-fishing location. From South Fork, drive west on US 160 for 1.5 miles, turn left on Beaver Creek Road (Forest Road 360), and continue about 5 miles to the reservoir. **Big Meadows Reservoir** has brookies, rainbows, and cutthroats. From South Fork, drive west on US 160 for 11 miles, turn right onto FR 410, and go 2 miles. *For gear and local information: Rainbow Grocery sporting goods section, 30359 W. US 160, Del Norte, 719-873-5545. For lessons or guides: South Fork Anglers, 877-656-3474.*

SILVER THREAD SCENIC AND HISTORIC BYWAY

The 75-mile Silver Thread Scenic and Historic Byway connects the town of South Fork to the old silver-mining towns of Creede and Lake City. Once a toll road and stage route, the byway follows CO 149 up the Upper Rio Grande Valley. The drive takes about two hours, not including stops. From South Fork the route heads northwesterly, paralleling the Rio Grande, and first passes Coller State Wildlife Area, where in autumn huge herds of elk gather; the sheer rock cliffs of the Rio Grande Palisades are prime bighorn sheep habitat. The road slips through Wagon Wheel Gap, once a tollgate for stagecoaches, and rolls into the historic mining town of Creede.

Farther on, the Rio Grande Pyramid, headwaters of the Rio Grande, is visible from Browns Lake Overlook, and dramatic North Clear Creek Falls (see Main Attractions, Creede, p. 341, and Scenic Location No. 124, p. 351) is just a short detour off the highway. The road crests the Continental Divide at Spring Creek Pass, then continues to the Slumgullion Earthflow at mile marker 66. Interpretive signs at the Alferd Packer Massacre Site tell the story of Colorado's infamous cannibal (see Historical Marker, Lake City, p. 349). The byway ends in Lake City. Pick up a guidebook ($1) to the Silver Thread Byway in South Fork, Creede, or Lake City. *800-571-0881, www.southfork.org/silver.*

Activities

CAMPING

With its proximity to Big Meadows Reservoir, **Big Meadows** campground is a popular spot with 54 sites spread among dense spruce trees providing more than adequate privacy. A boat ramp

Welcome sign, South Fork

and fishing pier are on the grounds, and several hiking and horse trails originate here. From South Fork, drive west on US 160 for about 11 miles, turn right onto Big Meadows Road (Forest Road 410), and go 2 miles. **Beaver Creek** (19 sites), **Upper Beaver Creek** (15 sites), and **Cross Creek** (12 sites) are strung along the road to Beaver Creek Reservoir. From South Fork, go about 1.5 miles southwest on US 160, turn left on Beaver Creek Road (FR 360), and continue about 4 miles to the Beaver Creek sites and 2 miles farther for Cross Creek. *719-657-3321.*

The 12 campsites at **Palisade** campground sit on the bank of the Rio Grande with views of the towering Palisades, where you might spot golden eagles or Rocky Mountain bighorn sheep among the rocky cliffs. From South Fork, drive west on CO 149 for 9 miles. No reservations. *719-658-2556.*

FOUR-WHEEL-DRIVE TRIPS

Forest roads wind throughout the wilderness in Rio Grande National Forest. The local snowmobile club publishes a map of these roads, which make good four-wheel-drive routes in summer. You can pick up the map at the South Fork Visitor Center. *For jeep rentals: Cottonwood Cove Guest Ranch, 10 miles west of South Fork on CO 149, 719-658-2242; Twin Pines Motor Sports, 45 Elm St., 719-873-9873.*

GOLF

The 18-hole, 7,200-yard course at the **Rio Grande Club** starts in open meadows, plays through cottonwoods and aspens along the Rio Grande, then rises 500 feet to rolling mountain terrain set against dramatic rock formations—with views of the Continental Divide. In the rarified air at 8,600 feet above sea level, the added distance of the ball's carry will amaze you. This is a semiprivate club, but the course and amenities are open to the public. From the junction of US 160 and CO 149 in South Fork, drive west on CO 149 for 1 mile, and turn right at the sign. *866-873-1995, www.riograndeclub.com.*

HIKING

Big Tree Trail EASY is a 0.3-mile (one way) walk to a Douglas fir 66 inches in diameter, the largest ever found in Rio Grande National Forest. From South Fork, drive west on US 160 for 2 miles, turn left onto Beaver Creek Road (Forest Road 360), then drive 6 miles to the trailhead sign. **Tewksberry Creek Trail** MODERATE is 5 miles one way, making a gentle climb over a scenic pass, through meadows, aspen and fir forests, and past 19th-century log cabins. This is a good fall hike. Take the Beaver Creek Road as described for the Big Tree Trail hike, turn right at the Beaver Creek campground access road, and go 0.5 mile to the corrals; the trail starts south of the corrals. **Hope Creek Trail** MODERATE, considered the most scenic in the area, is a 6-mile (one way) hike along a timbered creek to above timberline in the Weminuche Wilderness. From South Fork, drive west on US 160 for 11 miles, turn right onto Big Meadows Road (FR 410), then turn right onto FR 430 and go 3 miles to the trailhead.

MOUNTAIN BIKING

Trout Creek Trail MODERATE is a [illegible]-mile round trip through ponderosa pine and aspen, past meadows and rock outcrops. It's all singletrack, with some up and down and a number of switchbacks, ending at a private fence, where you turn around and ride back. The creek is a pleasant pit stop. From the intersection of US 160 and CO 149 in South Fork, drive southwest on US 160 for 3 miles to the trailhead parking lot on the right side of the highway. *For more information: South Fork Visitor Center, 800-571-0881, www.southfork.org; or Rio Grande National Forest office, Del Norte, 719-657-3321, www.fs.fed.us/r2/riogrande. For bike rentals: Alpine Cyclery, 28266 W. US 160, 719-873-2495.*

RAFTING

With bouncy Class II and III rapids, the **Rio Grande** between South Fork and Creede EASY is a fun river the whole family can enjoy. *Mountain Man Tours, 719-658-2663.*

SCENIC DRIVES

Beyond the **Silver Thread Scenic and Historic Byway** (see Main Attractions, p. 327) are other remarkable routes. **Lobo Overlook** provides a top-of-the-world view of the Continental Divide. From South Fork, drive west for about 20 miles on US 160, which goes up and over Wolf Creek Pass. Just before the summit, on the right side of the road, you'll see a sign for Scenic Overlook. A gravel road leads 1 mile to the overlook, a great spot for a picnic. For a great day trip, drive up toward the Continental Divide and the old mining town of **Summitville,** now a Superfund site (see Scenic Location No. 116, p. 329). From South Fork, head west on US 160 for 8 miles to Forest Road 380 and turn left. Continue on FR 380 to its junction with FR 330 and turn left again. Summitville is about 3 miles farther on FR 330. If you stay on FR 330, it will take you to Del Norte.

SOUTH FORK SCENIC RAIL EXCURSIONS

Enjoy a scenic train ride through the Upper Rio Grande. The train leaves from the South Fork depot and arrives at Wagon Wheel Gap. You can choose the lunch ride which leaves at 10 a.m. and arrives at 2:15 (includes an hour long lunch stop), or you can choose the evening ride, which leaves at 3 p.m. and returns at 6:15 (includes a 45 minute stop). The train is open-air, so dress appropriately for the weather. The train runs Thursday through Sunday, and all trips are by reservation. *For more information, call 719-873-2003.*

WINTER SPORTS

Wolf Creek Ski Area is just 20 miles west of South Fork on US 160 (see Main Attractions, Pagosa Springs, p. 331). Also, the South Fork Powder Busters Snowmobile Club maintains 165 miles of trails, most of them on Forest Service roads also used for cross-country skiing and snowshoeing. The club publishes a map with route descriptions; pick one up at the visitor center. *Arrange for guided tours through Dilley's Guide Service, 719-657-3554.*

SUMMITVILLE/ ELWOOD PASS

The network of scenic backroads that course the east side of the South San Juan Wilderness does not end with the Conejos and Alamosa River Roads. To the north of these two, Forest Road 380 departs from FR 250 at the Alamosa River. Go right and you end up in the San Luis Valley, go left on FR 380 and you cross Elwood Pass on the way to the old mining town of Summitville. Unfortunately, there's not much left of the town. In the 1980s, the gold mine was reopened as a new mega-mine with aspirations of the owners and their investors to make everyone fabulously rich. Regrettably, the opposite occurred: The company went broke, and the leaching ponds overflowed after a particularly snowy winter. To date the debacle has cost the Environmental Protection Agency and U.S. taxpayers over $120 million to try to repair the damage. Nevertheless, the area around Summitville is particularly scenic. So get to Summitville by heading south either on County Road 14/FR 330 from the west end of Del Norte, or via FR 380 from US 160 about 8 miles south of South Fork. All of these roads are improved but full of potholes in the higher elevations. I recommend taking a high-clearance vehicle.

The scenery from the Alamosa River to Summitville is superb. To the west are the highest peaks of the South San Juan Wilderness, including Summit Peak (13,300 feet) and Montezuma Peak (13,150 feet). The Summitville Mine is not noticeable from the Elwood Pass area, so views of the mountains that surround Summitville are highly photogenic. In the subalpine valley about a mile north of Elwood Pass, find the little cabin surrounded by spruce trees at the end of a short side road. This setting makes wonderful foreground for the peaks to the east. Late afternoon light is best here. The two roads that descend this high plateau toward US 160 are scenic by themselves, especially CR 14/FR 330. It winds along ridge tops through aspen groves and meadows of wildflowers. Drive this area in mid-July and you will not believe the colors.

Restaurants

Chalet Swiss ($$-$$$) specializes in international and Alpine cuisine, including cheese fondue, wiener schnitzel, and black forest cake. There's an impressive wine selection and the aspen-paneled interior creates an inviting ambiance, complete with Tyrolean music. It's on US 160, 1 mile west of the CO 149 intersection. *719-873-1100.* For breakfast, order up some flapjacks at the **Hungry Logger** ($-$$). The lunch and dinner menu features sandwiches, burgers (with three kinds of French fries), steak, seafood, and chicken. *47 W. CO 149, 719-873-5504.* **The Big River Grille** ($$) at the Rio Grande Club is perfect whether you're just finishing a game on the golf course, or looking for a great lunch. The menu features traditional American fare. *285 Rio Grande Club Trail, 719-873-1995.* For great BBQ and a casual atmosphere, check out **The Shaft Restaurant & Bar** ($). *29411 US 160, 719-873-0102.* **Rockaway Café and Steakhouse** ($$) is located in a log cabin nestled in the Rocky Mountains. Entrée choices include steaks, seafood, and pasta dishes. Rockaway also has a varied wine list. *30333 W. US 160, 719-873-5581.*

Accommodations

You'll feel pampered at the **Arbor House Inn Bed and Breakfast** ($$-$$$), which overlooks the South Fork of the Rio Grande. It has five rooms, three of them with private entrances; the honeymoon suite has a whirlpool and a fireplace. Open all year, it's located on US 160 directly across from the Chalet Swiss restaurant. *888-830-4642, www.arborhouseinnco.com.*

Chain and locally owned motels, lodges, and RV parks with cabins abound in South Fork. **Riverbend Resorts** ($$) offers guests rustic and modern riverfront cabins with all the amenities! Full kitchens, fireplaces, and charcoal grills are just a few of the great extras that come with cabin rental. Guests also have access to a private river frontage great for fishing. RV and tent sites are also available. *33846 US 160, 800-621-6512, www.riverbend-resort.com.* **Historic Spruce Lodge** ($-$$) is another great getaway spot in South Fork. Guests can choose from rooms, suites, cabins, or use the RV campsite. *29431 W. US 160, 719-873-5605, 800-228-5605, www.sprucelodges.com*

Special Events

Logger Days Festival & Craft Show in July is a two-day event featuring logging competitions such as log rolling and speed cutting. You and your family can also admire the works of local artisans, grab some food, listen to music, and enjoy activities for the kids. *800-571-0881.*

For More Information

The South Fork Visitor Center is on the north side of US 160, just west of the CO 149 intersection. *800-571-0881, www.southfork.org.*

Pagosa Springs

(see map on p. 332)

Because I complete most of my photography at dawn and dusk, I often have down time in the middle of the day. Whenever I'm near Pagosa Springs, there's no question as to how I will spend that time: relaxing in the luxurious hot springs for which the town is named. A resort town with many fine restaurants and a choice of accommodations, Pagosa Springs is surrounded by San Juan National Forest, with Wolf Creek Ski Area—renowned for receiving the most snow in Colorado—just 25 miles away. There are two wilderness areas nearby: the remote South San Juan Wilderness and the half-million-acre Weminuche Wilderness, the largest in the state. With all this federal land, as well as the San Juan River (see Scenic Location Nos. 118, p. 335, and 119, p. 337) running through the center of town, Pagosa Springs offers itself as an outdoor wonderland—winter, spring, summer, or fall.

Pagosa Hot Springs, Pagosa Springs

History

The mineral-rich hot springs drew American Indian tribes to the area, and both Navajos and Utes used the springs, believing them to have medicinal powers. It is said that "Pagosah" is the Ute word for "healing waters," though some sources suggest that a more accurate translation is "stinking waters," which would not be surprising given the sulphur smell the springs exude.

The town was founded in 1891 after the Utes were moved to reservation lands. With the arrival of the railroad, logging interests took hold, and lumber was shipped out along with ore from the San Juan Mountains. The hot springs had been advertised to tourists since the turn of the century, yet it wasn't until the 1990s, with the development of a multilevel pool complex called The Springs, that it became a major attraction. The town government has even tapped the geothermal springs, which come out of the ground at 153 degrees, to heat municipal buildings.

Main Attractions

CHIMNEY ROCK ARCHAEOLOGICAL AREA

You can see the Great Kiva, the Pit House, and other ancient structures on a high mesa beneath the twin spires of Chimney Rock, where Ancestral Puebloan people lived 1,000 years ago. Archaeologists surmise that it was an outlying settlement of the Chaco Canyon culture. The significance of the location remains a mystery—although it is thought that the structures were built to coincide with astronomical observances. Only guided tours are allowed (four daily, May through September), and during full moons, archaeo-astronomers present special evening programs. From Pagosa Springs, drive west on US 160, turn left on CO 151, go 3 miles more to the sign, and turn left. *970-883-5359 (May-Sept.), 970-264-2287 (Oct.-May), www.chimneyrockco.org.*

LAKE CAPOTE

Open to the general public full-time from May to September, and Thursday-Sunday in October. The area is maintained by the Southern Ute Tribe and is open to fishing, boating, day-use, and overnight camping—both tent and RV sites are available. *For more information contact lake staff, 970-883-2273, or the Southern Ute Division of Wildlife Resource Management, 970-563-0130.*

PAGOSA HOT SPRINGS

For centuries people have come to Pagosa to soak in the mineral hot springs. Native Americans believed the waters had healing properties, a claim that many locals still endorse. A soak in the springs is certainly a great way to soothe the body and relax the mind, and there are two developed sites where you can enjoy the benefits of the naturally occurring hot springs.

On a terraced hillside next to the San Juan River, **The Springs** is a series of 15 pools, all slightly different sizes with varying water temperatures, the hottest being the 112-degree Lobster Pot. (You can always cool down with a dunk in the river.) The complex has a spanking clean, modern bathhouse for changing and showering and a separate building for massages or other spa treatments. If you're staying at The Spring Resort, you can use the pools 24 hours a day; otherwise the pools close to the public at 1 a.m. *970-264-2284, www.pagosaspringsresort.com.*

Across the street, **The Spa at Pagosa Springs** has a geothermally heated outdoor swimming pool, a great place for the kids to splash and play. There are also indoor tubs for adults (gender segregated, clothing optional), as well as changing rooms. *970-264-5910, www.thespaatpagosasprings.com.*

Both The Springs and The Spa are in the middle of town near the visitor center on Hot Springs Blvd. On cold winter nights, you can spot them by the clouds of steam rising from the pools—or just follow your nose, as the smell of sulphur is unmistakable.

Pagosa Springs

Colorado Atlas & Gazetteer pp. 87–89

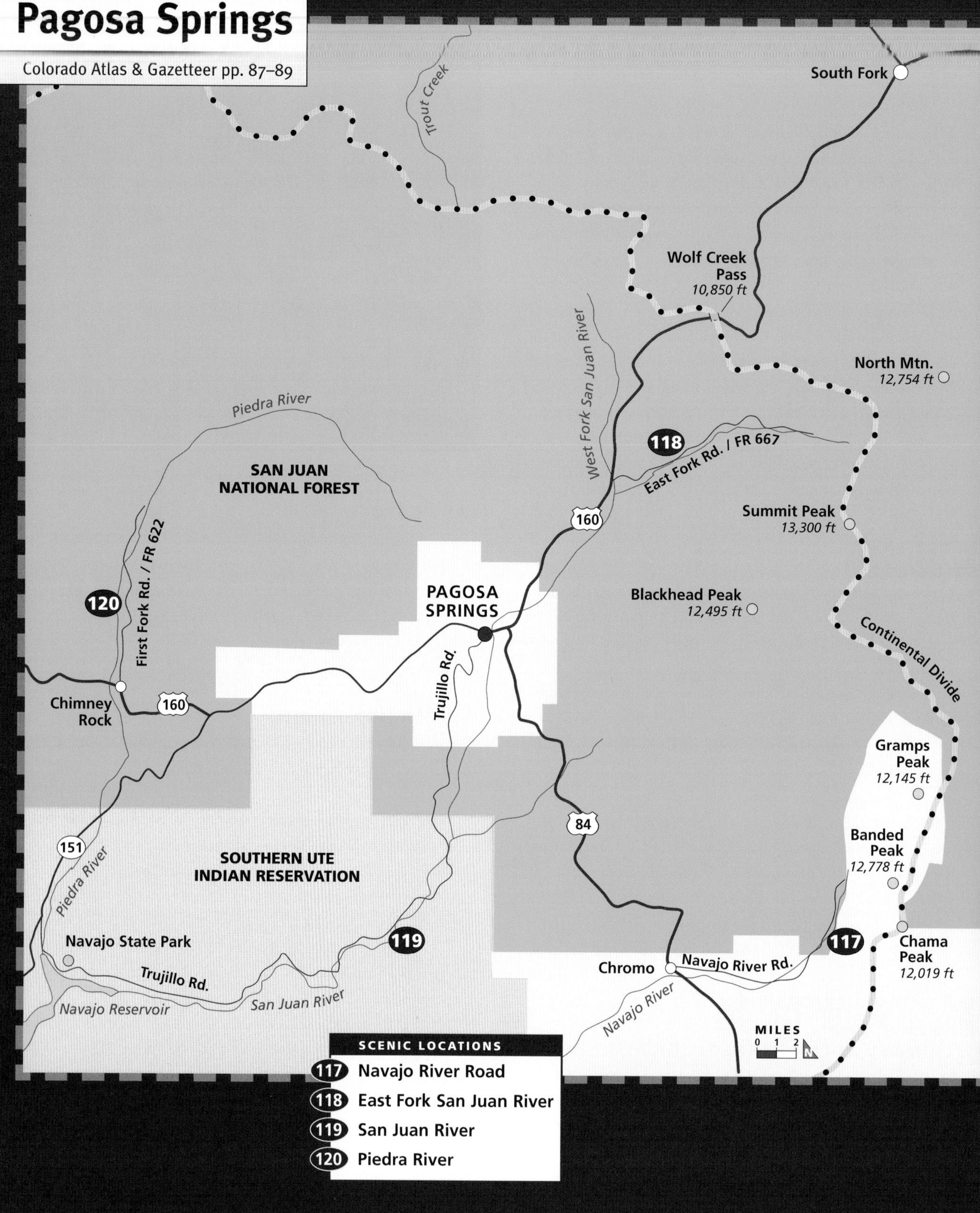
South Fork
Trout Creek
Wolf Creek Pass
10,850 ft
West Fork San Juan River
North Mtn.
12,754 ft
Piedra River
118
East Fork Rd. / FR 667
SAN JUAN NATIONAL FOREST
Summit Peak
13,300 ft
160
First Fork Rd. / FR 622
120
PAGOSA SPRINGS
Blackhead Peak
12,495 ft
Continental Divide
Trujillo Rd.
Chimney Rock
160
Gramps Peak
12,145 ft
84
151
Banded Peak
12,778 ft
SOUTHERN UTE INDIAN RESERVATION
Piedra River
119
117
Navajo State Park
Chama Peak
12,019 ft
Chromo
Navajo River Rd.
Trujillo Rd.
Navajo Reservoir
San Juan River
Navajo River
MILES
0 1 2
SCENIC LOCATIONS
117 Navajo River Road
118 East Fork San Juan River
119 San Juan River
120 Piedra River

117 NAVAJO RIVER ROAD

SCENIC LOCATION

Twenty-five miles southeast of the Summitville area (as the crow flies) you still find yourself on the periphery of the South San Juan Wilderness. A large piece of privately owned land indents this south end of the wilderness and San Juan National Forest. This private ranch, an old Spanish land grant, is shaped in a way that allows it to contain the entire watershed of the Navajo River, a tributary of the San Juan River. (Much of the flow of the Navajo is actually diverted by tunnel into the Rio Grande for the benefit of Albuquerque, N.M.) The Navajo River Road is closed 10 miles up the river where the ranch begins. Nevertheless, these 10 miles are very scenic and provide lots of views along the way to the river and mountains. Take US 84 south from US 160 at the east end of Pagosa Springs. Drive to the one-horse town of Chromo and turn east onto Navajo River Road.

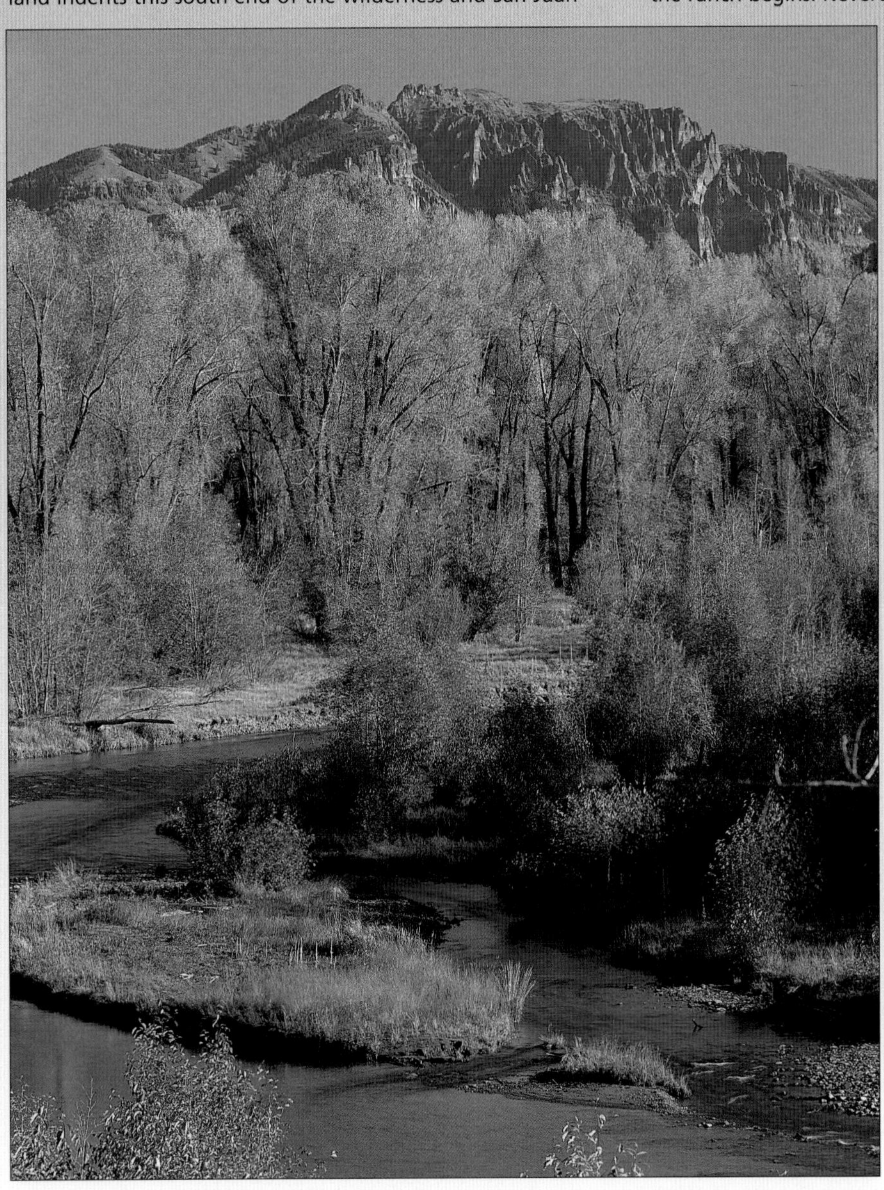

The first 5 miles of the road course through ranch meadows, cottonwoods, and stately ponderosa pines. Chama Peak rises to the east. The second 5 miles enter the forest and look down upon the river. Along this stretch you'll find several places to compose river, trees, and mountains of the South San Juan Wilderness in one lovely vertical composition. Arrive here in late May and you'll photograph spring greens, in early October the yellows of autumn. When you reach the ranch gate, stop your vehicle and imagine what might lie beyond.

I happen to know that it's about as good as it gets. In fact, I photographed the ranch for my book *Along Colorado's Continental Divide Trail.* This book also features images made in the heart of the South San Juan Wilderness.

WOLF CREEK SKI AREA

Sitting on the Continental Divide, Wolf Creek Ski Area consistently receives higher quantities of snow than anywhere else in Colorado—more than 450 inches a year! And that's natural snow, not man-made. Wolf Creek has 1,600 vertical feet open for skiing and snowboarding, and six chairlifts servicing 55 trails, the majority of which are rated intermediate. Black-diamond runs include both bowl and glade skiing. The Magic Carpet conveyor lift makes it easy for beginners and "wolf pups" to get up the hill. Wolf Creek, which opened in 1940, is a friendly, family place 25 miles east of Pagosa Springs on US 160. *Open Thanksgiving to Easter, 800-754-9653, www.wolfcreekski.com.*

Activities

CAMPING

Four of the best campgrounds in the Pagosa Springs area are near Williams Reservoir. **Bridge** campground is along Williams Creek with a meadow on one side and views of the San Juans. Popular **Williams Creek** campground offers 67 nicely shaded sites, mountain views, and access to the Lake Fork of the Gunnison River. The views around **Teal** campground on the reservoir easily make it one of the most scenic campgrounds in Colorado, and also a very popular one. **Cimarrona** campground sits on the edge of the Weminuche Wilderness. All four have hiking trails and fishing nearby. From downtown Pagosa Springs, drive west on US 160 for 2.5 miles, turn right onto Piedra Road (Forest Road 631), and go 19 miles to the Bridge campground; Williams Creek is 4 miles north of Bridge. For Teal, drive about 3 miles farther, turn right onto FR 640, and go 1.75 miles. Cimarrona is about 2 miles past Teal. **Rio Blanco** campground is small (just 6 sites), secluded, and within hiking distance of the South San Juan Wilderness. From Pagosa Springs, drive south on US 84 for 10 miles, turn right onto FR 656, and after the second bridge, keep left and drive 2.5 miles. *970-264-2268, www.fs.fed.us/r2/sanjuan/.*

FAMILY FUN

The activities center at **Wyndham Vacation Resorts** (see Accommodations, p. 339) is open to the public. You can sign up for everything from hot-air ballooning to dog sledding, four-wheeling to fly fishing. The facility offers excursion trips to all the area's attractions and has on-site activities for kids. Wyndham Vacation Resorts is on US 160 about 3 miles west of downtown Pagosa Springs. *970-731-8000.* **Rocky Mountain Wildlife Park** is a small, private zoo exhibiting native wildlife—bears, wolves, coyotes, elk, deer, bobcats, and mountain lions. The gift shop displays a large selection of Western and wildlife art. The park is on US 84, 5 miles south of Pagosa Springs. *970-264-5546.*

FISHING

Williams Creek Reservoir and **Echo Lake** have good trout populations, best fished May through June. In the warmer summer months, lakes 10,000–12,000 feet in elevation are your best bet and can be accessed by foot or on horseback. **Fourmile Lake** (see Hiking, this page) is a favorite destination for anglers.

The **Piedra** and **San Juan Rivers** are good locations during July and August, with the East and West Forks of the San Juan both easily accessible. Smaller streams such as **Wolf Creek, Pass Creek,** and **Plumtaw Creek** generally allow you to have the water to yourself. Check in at local shops for seasonal conditions and hot spots. *For information and gear, contact Let It Fly, 1501 W. Hwy 160 #2, 970-264-3189.*

FOUR-WHEEL-DRIVE TRIPS

The 16-mile (one way) **Mill Creek–Nipple Mountain Road** offers sweeping panoramas of the San Juan Valley. From Pagosa Springs, go south on US 84, drive less than a mile, and turn left onto Mill Creek Road. Bear right onto Nipple Mountain Road (Forest Road 665) and drive to the end. Return the same way. For other four-wheel-drive roads, pick up a flyer for self-guided tours at the Pagosa Springs visitor center.

GOLF

Pagosa Springs Golf Club, open to the public, has 27 holes with three course combinations. The first 18 follow rolling terrain, typical of a mountain course; the back nine are links style—out on the flats with lots of water. All have great views of the San Juans. The club is on US 160 about 3 miles west of Pagosa Springs. *970-731-4755, www.golfpagosa.com.*

HIKING

With the vast Weminuche Wilderness to the north and the South San Juan Wilderness to the east, the Pagosa Springs area has many hiking trails and a variety of terrain. **Ice Cave Ridge Trail** EASY takes you 1.5 miles (one way) to a scenic waterfall at the confluence of the Weminuche and Piedra Rivers. From Pagosa Springs, drive west on US 160 for about 2.5 miles, turn right onto Piedra Road (County Road 631), and go 15 miles to the Piedra River Trailhead. Do not take that trail; instead take the old road to the west.

More waterfalls await you along **Fourmile Falls Trail** MODERATE, a 5-mile (one way) hike through meadows and forests, past sheer cliffs and two thunderous falls, and up to Fourmile Lake. From the center of town, drive north on Fourmile Road, turn left onto Forest Road 645, and drive to the trailhead at the end of the road.

The **West Fork San Juan River Trail** DIFFICULT makes an excellent backpacking trip. This 34-mile loop starts at the West Fork campground at the base of Wolf Creek Pass. It follows the West Fork drainage, joins up with the Continental Divide Trail on Piedra Pass, then switchbacks down the Beaver Creek Trail to meet back up with the West Fork Trail. From Pagosa Springs, drive east on US 160 for about 15 miles, turn left onto FR 648, and go 2 miles. Stop in the San Juan National Forest office for information on the national forest and the Weminuche and South San Juan Wilderness Areas. *180 Pagosa St., 970-264-2268, www.fs.fed.us/r2/sanjuan/.*

HISTORICAL MARKER

Interpretive signs at **Treasure Falls,** a pullout along US 160 on the west side of Wolf Creek Pass, tells the story of gold hidden here by French trappers many years ago, the clues to its location forever lost. What you will find is a dramatic 105-foot cascade and an easy, quarter-mile trail up to an observation deck.

HORSEBACK RIDING

With two nearby wilderness areas and a national forest surrounding the town, Pagosa Springs has many horseback-riding options. *Lobo Outfitters offers one-hour to half-day trail rides as well as pack trips. 4821 US 84, Unit A, 970-264-5546.*

MOUNTAIN BIKING

The San Juan National Forest encircles the town of Pagosa Springs, affording many riding options along trails and access roads. Close to town, **Turkey Springs** MODERATE is a level ride along a combination of old logging roads and singletrack

118 SCENIC LOCATION

EAST FORK SAN JUAN RIVER

Head to the northwest corner of the South San Juan Wilderness and you'll find a spot just as picturesque as any in the wilderness. The East Fork Road follows the river for 8 miles east of US 160. Meadows, old ranch buildings, and views of the wilderness peaks make for absolutely wonderful compositions of a classic Rocky Mountain valley. Drive 10 miles east from Pagosa Springs on US 160 to the East Fork Road on the right.

Four miles up the road, Sand Creek enters the East Fork from the south. Check out the creek composition looking south up this beautiful drainage. Two miles farther, the road enters a beautiful park. On your left are a couple of old ranch buildings that might not be any worse for wear if you walked up the hill and made them foreground for the aspen-covered hillsides to the north. To the south of the road is a gorgeous vantage looking upriver with high peaks in the distance. As of the writing of this book in April 2002, plans to build a golf course–based development in this valley were pulled by the landowner. He was quoted as saying that the valley might just be too lovely to develop. This man should be given an award, and we should keep our fingers crossed!

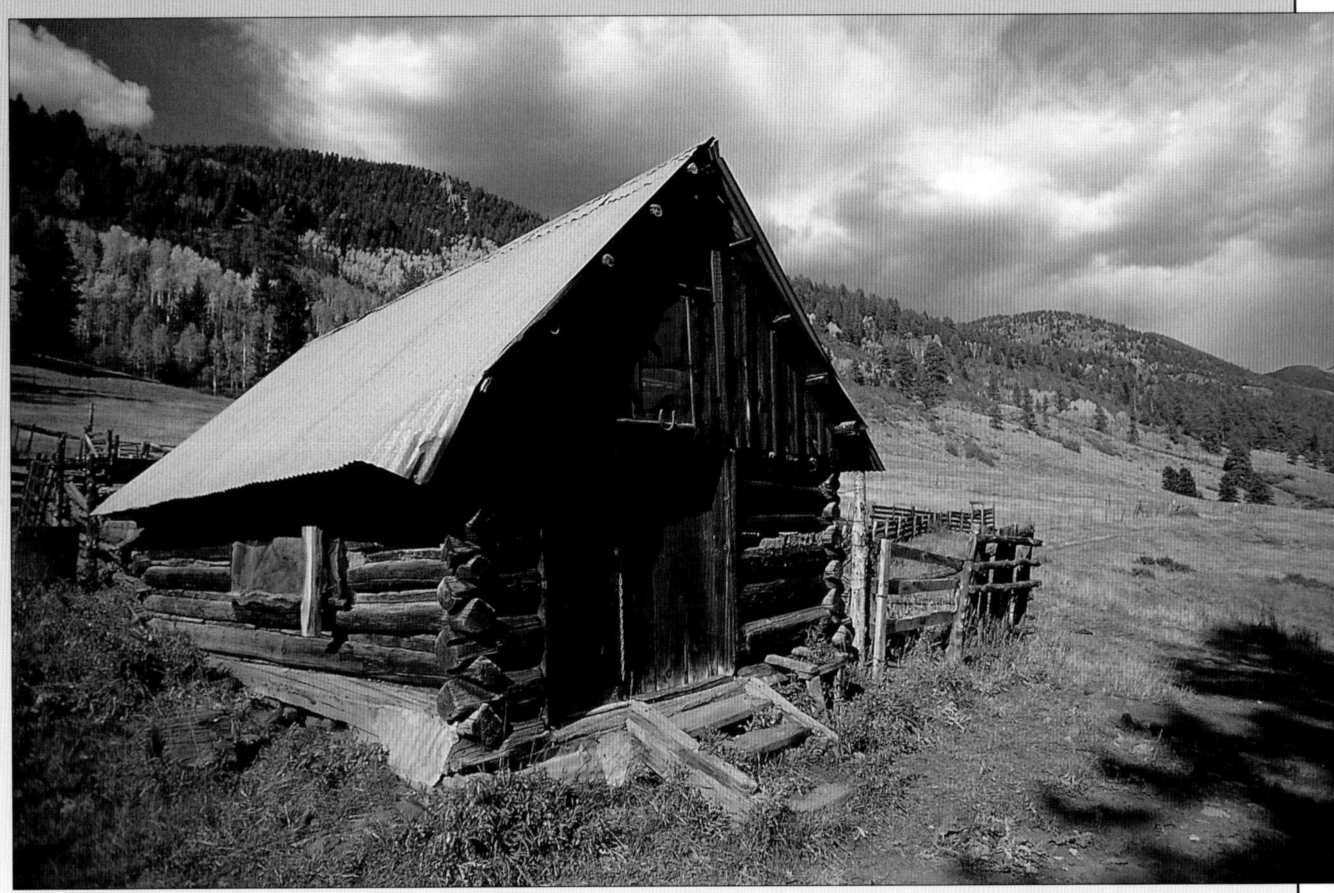

in four loops of about 8 to 10 miles each. From downtown, drive west on US 160 for 2.5 miles and turn right onto Piedra Road. Turn left onto Turkey Springs Road (Forest Road 629) and park your car at the "Y" at New Jack Road. Start riding west on Turkey Springs Road; the trail is marked.

Monument Park Trail MODERATE starts off with a steady 2- to 3-mile climb, then levels out for about 5 to 6 miles before entering Monument Park, a large open area that was once an Indian encampment. The out-and-back trip measures around 18 miles. From downtown, drive west on US 160 for 2.5 miles and turn right onto Piedra Road. Turn left onto Turkey Springs Road and right onto Monument Park Road, then go about 7 miles and park where the road dead-ends. Backtrack 0.25 mile to the trailhead.

Treasure Mountain Trail DIFFICULT is a shuttle trip starting at Wolf Creek Pass and ending at East Fork campground (about 12 miles east of Pagosa Springs on US 160). The 14-mile ride starts at Wolf Creek Ski Area, following a service road from the parking lot to the top of Treasure Lift. You pick up the Continental Divide Trail for a short distance before heading into the East Fork Valley for an 11-mile downhill on a singletrack trail. *For bike rentals and trail information: Pedal and Powder, 100 Country Center Dr., Suite L, 970-731-0338, www.pagosapedalandpowder.com.*

MUSEUMS

The **Fred Harman Art Museum** houses Western memorabilia and the artwork of Fred Harman, whose Red Ryder and Little

119 SAN JUAN RIVER

SCENIC LOCATION

The many forks of the San Juan originate in the South San Juan Wilderness to the east and the Weminuche Wilderness to the north. As one they pass through downtown Pagosa Springs (and by the famous hot springs; see p. 331) before entering the Southern Ute Indian Reservation. The river weaves through bucolic meadows and slips through narrow canyons on its way to Navajo Reservoir at the New Mexico border. It's a unique Colorado landscape that you should see. You do not need permission from the Ute Tribe to drive these roads. From US 160, look for Trujillo Road heading south at the hot springs in Pagosa Springs. Follow it to Carracas Road. Turn west to the reservoir, or watch for Cat Creek Road which will take you back to US 160 west of Pagosa Springs.

I just love this valley. Having been settled by the Spanish several hundred years ago, and visited by the Spanish explorers and missionaries even earlier, the valley remains rich with Hispanic culture. Life moves at a slow place along a river that runs slowly, too. From the roadside atop the mini canyons that briefly consume the river, compose the river as a lead-in line. Notice the lovely, light green junipers that line the river. The most perfectly shaped wild junipers that I've ever seen live in this valley. At twilight before sunrise or after sunset, the river reflects the blue of an almost always blue sky, becoming very conspicuous in the scene. So from one end of this route to the other, take advantage of the bluffs that elevate you high enough to look down on the San Juan. The images you capture on film will not disappoint.

Beaver comic strips were once seen in more than 750 newspapers. The museum has also started a "period park," moving in old homestead cabins, a mercantile, and other historic buildings to re-create life in Pagosa Springs during the early part of the past century. From town, drive west on US 160 for 2.5 miles and turn right on Piedra Road. *970-731-5785, www.harmanartmuseum.com.* The **San Juan Historical Museum** gives a glimpse at life in Pagosa Springs in the late 1800s and early 1900s. *Open Memorial Day through Labor Day, 1st and Pagosa Streets, 970-264-4424.*

RAFTING

Float trips down the **San Juan River** drift through scenic valleys and past canyon walls with bouncy Class I–III rapids that the whole family can enjoy. The **Piedra River** (see Scenic Location No. 120, p. 338) has some adrenaline-pumping Class IV and V rapids. Kayakers can find challenging water in the stretch of the San Juan that flows through downtown Pagosa Springs. *For raft trips or kayak rentals: Pagosa Outside, 350 Pagosa St., 970-264-4202.*

SCENIC DRIVES

Blanco Basin is a spectacular drive any time of the year, but especially in autumn. From Pagosa Springs, drive south on US 84 for 8 miles and turn left onto Blanco Basin Road. Continue to the end of the road, about 13 miles, for stunning views of the Continental Divide. Another spectacular fall drive is the 35-mile **Plumtaw-Piedra Loop,** which starts in town at the corner of Lewis and Pagosa streets. Head north on Four Mile Road (which becomes Plumtaw Road/Forest Road 634) until it intersects with FR 633; turn left. Drive on FR 633 to Piedra Road (FR 631) and turn left; Piedra Road takes you to US 160.

WINTER SPORTS

Alpen Haus Ski Center maintains 6 miles of groomed cross-country ski trails at the Pagosa Springs Golf Course. They also have rental equipment, information, and maps for trails in surrounding national forest lands. It's on US 160, 3 miles west of downtown. *970-731-4755.* For downhill skiing, try **Wolf Creek Ski Area** (see Main Attractions, p. 331), 25 miles east of Pagosa Springs.

The Pagosa Springs area offers many miles of designated snowmobile routes, not all of which are maintained or marked. For signed and groomed trails, try **Turkey Springs** EASY, an 8-mile route that can be combined with **Monument Park** EASY to add 9 more miles. From downtown, drive west on US 160 for 2.5 miles, turn right onto Piedra Road, and then turn left onto Turkey Springs Road, which is the start of the route. Pick up information on snowmobile routes at the visitor center. *For snowmobile rentals and tours: Wolf Creek Outfitters (see Horseback Riding, p. 334, for directions), 970-264-5332, www.subee.com/wco/wcohome.html.*

Restaurants

Farrago Market Café ($-$$) combines Asian influences with eclectic dishes from other aspects of global cuisine. *175 Pagosa St. #1, 970-264-4600, www.farago.tv.* A rustic cabin filled with antiques, **Old Miner's Steakhouse** ($$-$$$$) specializes in, you guessed it, steaks—a dozen different cuts—and also serves barbecue, kabobs, seafood, and poultry. It's on US 160 about 3.5 miles east of town. *970-264-5981.* **Eddie's Uptown Grille** ($$) features Mediterranean fare with an Asian twist. The restaurant offers daily food and drink specials, tapas, and live music. Walk-ins or reservations welcome. *20 Village Dr., 970-731-5448, www.eddiespagosa.com.*

Pagosa Springs Baking Company ($-$$) is a great lunch spot with paninis and baked goods galore. *238 Pagosa St., 970-264-9348, www.pagosabakingcompany.com.* For Mexican, **Ramon's** ($-$$) is a lively place (especially when the fajitas sizzle) with a cantina upstairs. It's west of town in a strip mall, behind McDonald's. *56 Talisman Dr., 970-731-3012.* For delicious ribs and great views, try the **Branding Iron Bar B Que.** *3916 E. Hwy 160, 970-264-4268.*

120 PIEDRA RIVER

SCENIC LOCATION

Like the San Juan River, the Piedra drains out of the great Weminuche Wilderness to the north. At more than 500,000 acres, the Weminuche is Colorado's largest wilderness area. It provides the water that fills most of southwestern Colorado's rivers, including the Rio Grande, San Juan, and Animas. Like the San Juan, the Piedra ends up in Navajo Reservoir. The portion of the Piedra that I enjoy the most penetrates a canyon replete with splendid ponderosa pines. The drive along the river is lovely and wild, and even more so is the ecosystem above the road that is designated wilderness. Drive west from Pagosa Springs on US 160 about 20 miles until you reach the turnoff onto CO 151 that goes to the Chimney Rock Archaeological Area. Continue past CO 151 for 6 miles, then turn north at the river onto the First Fork Road/Forest Road 622. The road dead ends 14 miles later. Your car will work fine, but potholes make for obstacles toward the end.

The Piedra is as lovely a montane river as you'll ever see. As you drive along the canyon bottom, you are treated to a river than runs fast and clear through forests of ponderosa pine and fir. While driving, keep your eye peeled for vantages that allow the river to become a lead-in line through the canyon, places where no trees stand beside the road and the river curves out of sight. Compose river in the foreground and tall trees alongside. Try framing the river banks in the bottom left- and right-hand corners of your viewfinder. This technique will maximize the depth manifest in the scene. Without a lot of deciduous trees in the canyon, this stretch of the Piedra looks about the same from one season to the next. After your drive back to the highway, make a stop at Chimney Rock to visit the Anasazi ruins high on a bluff.

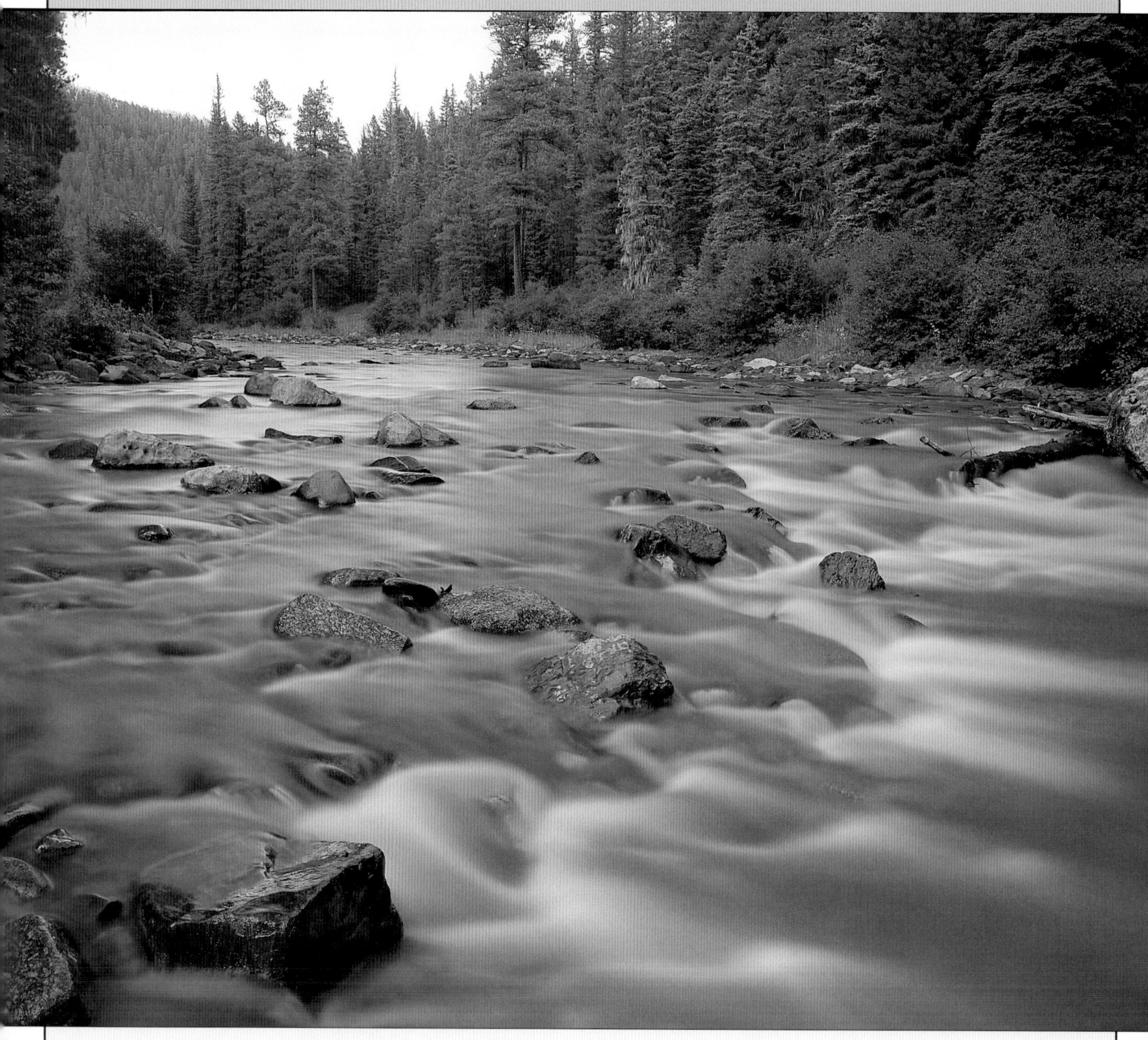

A charming little storefront café, **The Rose** ($) is a good choice for breakfast or lunch. *408 Pagosa St., 970-264-2955.* If you're in a continental mood, try **Victoria's Parlor,** which serves European coffees, teas, and pastries, as well as daily hot entrees and decadent desserts. *274 Pagosa Street, 970-264-0204.*

One place where I always stop is the **Choke Cherry Tree.** It isn't a restaurant but you can buy food—all kinds of locally made jams, syrups, gourmet mustards, and specialty items. Don't miss these chocolates—big, thick chunks of chocolate laden with nuts and caramel—all with clever names that don't really sound like something you would eat. *On US 160 about 2 miles west of downtown, 800-809-0769.*

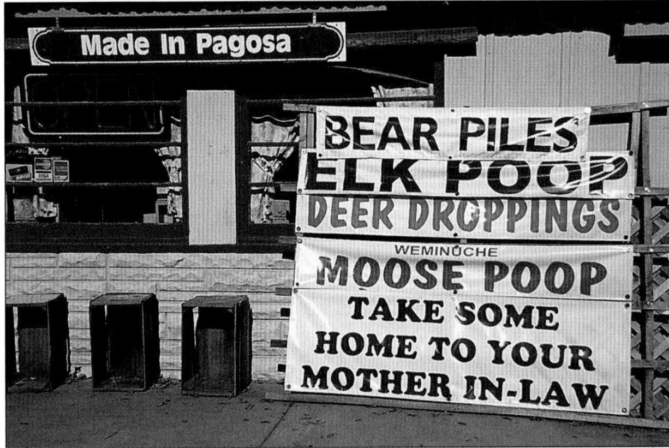

Choke Cherry Tree, Pagosa Springs

Accommodations

Right downtown, **The Springs Resort** ($$-$$$) is connected to The Springs—the multilevel pool complex on the San Juan River (see Main Attractions, p. 331). The inn has a variety of motel rooms, including multi-bedroom suites with kitchenettes, all in a Southwestern theme. Use of the hot springs is included with the price of the room. *800-225-0934, www.pagosaspringsresort.com.* **Wyndham Vacation Resorts** ($$-$$$$), a residential resort complex, rents one- or two-bedroom condominiums. Located at Pagosa Springs Golf Course, it has tennis, swimming, and an incredible activities center (see Family Fun, p. 334). *On US 160 about 3 miles west of downtown Pagosa Springs, 800-731-4123.* Right next door to Wyndham Vacation Resorts sits the **Pagosa Lodge,** a full-service facility with 100 tastefully decorated rooms, an indoor swimming pool, an exercise room, and a restaurant overlooking a lake. *800-523-7704, www.pagosalodge.com.*

High Country Lodge ($-$$) features nice, basic motel rooms and suites and a charming library where you can savor a complimentary breakfast. The lodge also makes available well-appointed log cabins with fireplaces or wood-burning stoves. It's on US 160 about 3.5 miles east of Pagosa Springs, with the Old Miner's Steakhouse just a short walk away. *800-862-3707, highcountrylodge.com.* On US 84, 2 miles south of Pagosa Springs, **Hart's Rocky Mountain Retreat** ($$-$$$) rents two- to four-bedroom luxury log cabins (three-night minimum) secluded among ponderosa pines. *888-441-0023, www.4getaway.com.* **Bruce Spruce Ranch** ($$-$$$) borders the national forest, and consists of several rustic cabins and one large one. *231 West Fork Road, 970-264-5374, www.brucespruceranch.com.*

Special Events

The **Red Ryder Roundup Rodeo** has been a Fourth of July tradition in Pagosa Springs since 1949. This classic rodeo is the real thing, with a parade, fireworks, and a carnival. **Life at Chimney Rock: A Festival of Crafts and Culture,** held in late July at Chimney Rock Archaeological Area, focuses on everyday life in ancient Puebloan culture. The **Four Corners Folk Festival** attracts big-name folk and bluegrass musicians over Labor Day. Celebrating the changing aspens in late September, nearly 100 hot-air balloons make a mass ascent during **Colorfest.** *970-264-2360, www.pagosaspringschamber.com.*

For More Information

Pagosa Springs Area Chamber of Commerce visitor center, on Hot Springs Boulevard in the center of town. *970-264-2360, www.pagosaspringschamber.com.*

Creede/Lake City

Colorado Atlas & Gazetteer pp. 67–69, 77–79

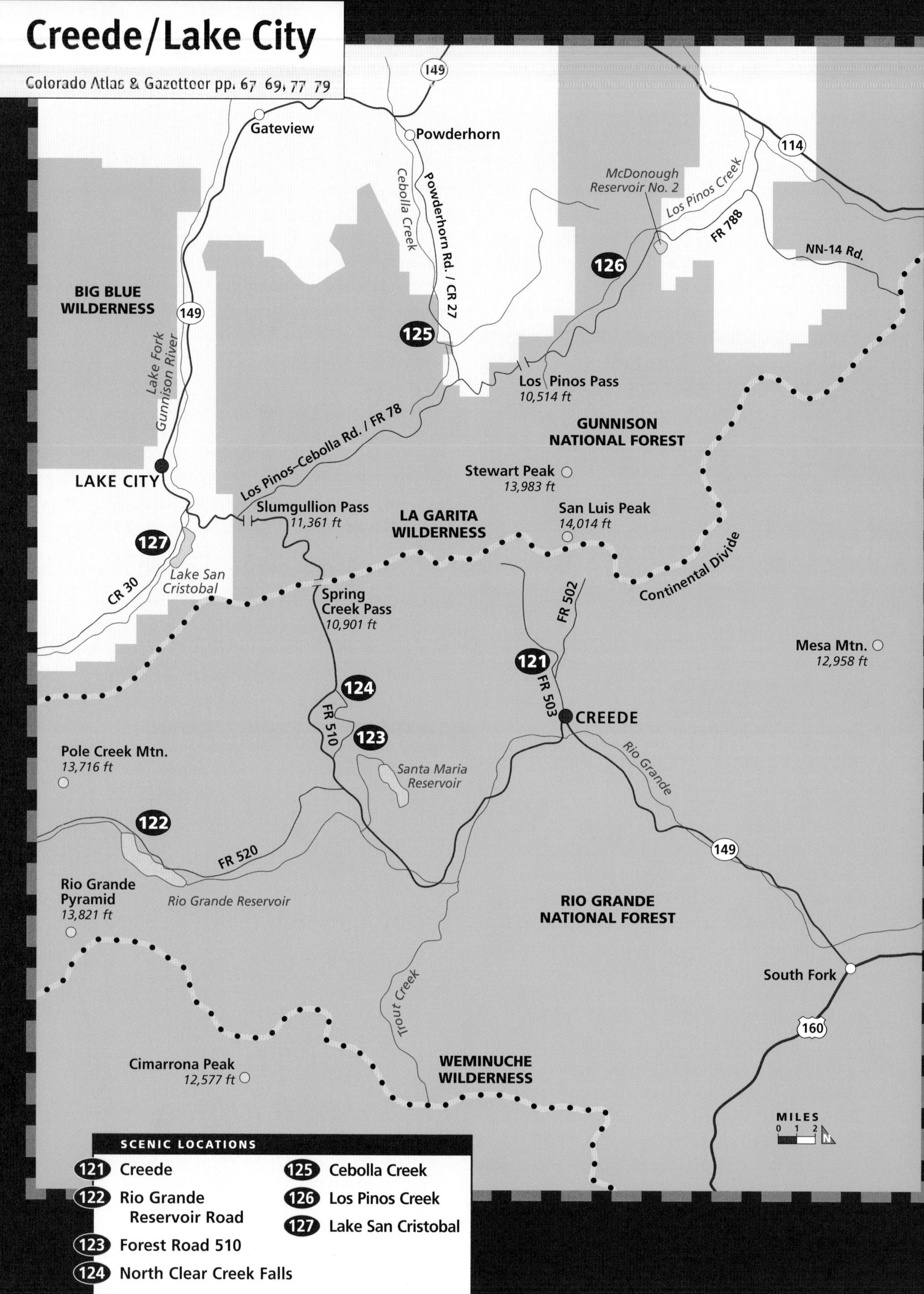

149
Gateview
Powderhorn
114
McDonough Reservoir No. 2
Los Pinos Creek
Cebolla Creek
Powderhorn Rd. / CR 27
FR 788
NN-14 Rd.
126
BIG BLUE WILDERNESS
149
125
Lake Fork Gunnison River
Los Pinos Pass
10,514 ft
Los Pinos–Cebolla Rd. / FR 78
GUNNISON NATIONAL FOREST
Stewart Peak
13,983 ft
LAKE CITY
Slumgullion Pass
11,361 ft
LA GARITA WILDERNESS
San Luis Peak
14,014 ft
127
Lake San Cristobal
CR 30
Spring Creek Pass
10,901 ft
FR 502
Continental Divide
Mesa Mtn.
12,958 ft
121
FR 503
124
CREEDE
FR 510
123
Rio Grande
Pole Creek Mtn.
13,716 ft
Santa Maria Reservoir
122
FR 520
149
Rio Grande Pyramid
13,821 ft
Rio Grande Reservoir
RIO GRANDE NATIONAL FOREST
South Fork
Trout Creek
160
Cimarrona Peak
12,577 ft
WEMINUCHE WILDERNESS
MILES
0 1 2
N
SCENIC LOCATIONS
121 Creede
122 Rio Grande Reservoir Road
123 Forest Road 510
124 North Clear Creek Falls
125 Cebolla Creek
126 Los Pinos Creek
127 Lake San Cristobal

Creede

Centrally located within the vast Rio Grande National Forest, with the La Garita Wilderness to the north and the Weminuche—one of my personal favorites—to the south, Creede (see Scenic Location No. 121, p. 342) is a veritable outdoor playland. The national forest amenities available (backroads, campgrounds, reservoirs, picnic areas) plus the pristine backcountry make it truly the best of both worlds. As icing on the cake, the tiny town of Creede offers up a wealth of history and art. During my college days, I lived in Creede for a summer, prospecting for minerals for my uncle's steel company. The Fielder family loves to take in a play at the Creede Repertory Theatre, one of the best theater experiences in Colorado.

History

It was 1889 when Nicholas Creede discovered silver along the banks of Willow Creek. "Holy Moses" was not only his reaction to the find but also the name of his claim. A string of mining camps quickly sprouted along the creek, and by 1890 it was estimated that the population was increasing by 300 people a day. The following year, the railroad came to town, shipping out a million dollars of ore each month. Some 10,000 people crowded into the valley, mining by day and by night filling the saloons, gambling parlors, dance halls, and brothels. It was a wild and wide-open place, peopled by a colorful cast of characters—lawman Bat Masterson, con man Soapy Smith, card player Poker Alice, and saloon-keep Bob Ford, the man who killed Jesse James. The boom times were short-lived, however, and crashed when the price of silver did in 1893.

But Creede has always been a feisty little town, rebuilding repeatedly after devastating floods and fires, and continuing to mine until 1985. Today the town has re-created itself as an outdoor recreation mecca and arts community. Galleries and studios now occupy the Victorian and false-front buildings along Main Street, where the Creede Repertory Theatre holds center stage. Creede was even included in the 1998 book by John Villani, *100 Best Small Art Towns in America.*

Creede Repertory Theatre and Creede Hotel

Main Attractions

BACHELOR HISTORIC LOOP

This 17-mile drive rings Creede's historic silver mining district, past abandoned mines and ghost towns, and ends at the town cemetery. Starting at the mouth of Willow Creek Canyon, where sheer 1,000-foot walls loom above, the route follows a graded gravel road suitable for cars. Along the way you'll see beaver ponds, aspen forests, and views of the town and the Upper Rio Grande Valley. Stop at the chamber of commerce visitor center to pick up a $1 guidebook with a detailed narrative of the 16 interpretive sites along the way. The road, which may be closed in winter, starts at the north end of town. Take Main Street past the Mineral County Courthouse and keep going.

CREEDE REPERTORY THEATRE

The Creede Repertory Theatre has been entertaining audiences since 1966. Playing to packed houses from mid-June through September, this professional theater company has gained national acclaim for the range and quality of its productions, presenting a rotating series of nine plays each summer—musicals, comedies, classic and contemporary dramas, and children's shows. The theater makes its home in downtown Creede's restored opera house. *719-658-2540, www.creederep.org.*

NORTH CLEAR CREEK FALLS

A tributary of the Rio Grande, North Clear Creek winds peacefully through mountain meadows until it reaches a 100-foot basalt cliff, where it plunges down stair-stepped rocks in a dramatic show of nature (see Scenic Location No. 124, p. 351). Be sure to stop here—not only because this scenic waterfall demands it, but also because it's less than a mile off CO 149, near mile marker 49 on the way to Lake City. Keep an eye out for moose in the vicinity. In the early 1990s the Colorado Department of Wildlife released about 90 moose here, and it is estimated that there are now probably several hundred. Look for them in open meadows or feeding along willow-lined creeks.

UNDERGROUND MINING MUSEUM

In 1990 when the citizens of Creede decided to build a museum to tell the story of hard-rock mining, they blasted and drilled into the side of a mountain to re-create an operating mine. Six-hundred feet of tunnels, shafts, and rooms are the setting for the Underground Mining Museum, which shows the evolution of silver mining from 1892 to 1985, when the last mine closed. Retired miners lead the tours, sharing knowledge and anecdotes. Open all year, the museum is at the north end of town, past the Mineral County Courthouse. *719-658-0811.*

WHEELER GEOLOGIC AREA

Wind and water and time eroded soft volcanic tuff into the steep-cut canyons, spires, and pinnacles of Wheeler Geologic Area. The fantastical formations, which have been compared to Utah's Bryce Canyon, have attracted onlookers for decades. From 1933 to

CREEDE

The old mining town of Creede, at the eastern entrance to the San Juan Mountains, has one of the best combinations of scenic and historic views in Colorado. Surviving mining structures near town are dramatic on their lofty perches; mountains and canyons encompassing Creede are striking. Creede also provides access to the beautiful environment of the Rio Grande headwaters. Drive west on US 160 from Monte Vista in the San Luis Valley, pass through Del Norte, then make a right at South Fork onto CO 149 and take it to Creede.

The drive from South Fork follows the Rio Grande. Views comprise the river, meadows, gorgeous cottonwood trees, and an imposing volcanic-rock canyon near the town of Wagon Wheel Gap. Keep your camera handy all the way to Creede. I love photographing the cottonwoods along the river when they turn yellow in late September. Creede lies at the entrance to a canyon even more imposing than the one at Wagon Wheel Gap. Willow Creek rushes through the narrow gap in the towering rock walls, which also serves as the entrance to Creede's historic mining country.

Drive straight through town and proceed up the canyon. One mile later the road forks into East and West Willow Creek Canyons. Both forks are scenic, historic, and passable by car for at least a couple of miles. Beware, however: The ascent of the West Fork road is steep and precipitous on the left side, so take it slowly. With a four-wheel drive you can actually complete a loop that connects the forks.

More photogenic than the land features are the mine buildings suspended high on hillsides. For these you'll need your telephoto lens. Photography of the narrow canyon will require a wide-angle lens. In both cases remember that canyon photography is a major exposure challenge. Bright sunlight and deep shadows within the same view are impossible for the film to record. Shadows get darker and highlights lighter than they appear to the eye. Either photograph the canyon in cloudy light, or wait until the sun is completely out of the canyon. In this case the light will be muted, so you may need a tripod to accommodate longer exposures. Remember that you should not be handholding a camera at shutter speeds slower than 1/30 second.

1950 it was designated a national monument, but because of its remote location few people visited, and it eventually lost this status. Today it is part of the La Garita Wilderness.

There are two ways to reach Wheeler Geologic Area, both of which require effort. From Creede, drive southeast on CO 149 for 7 miles and turn left onto Pool Table Road (Forest Road 600), a graded gravel road that continues 10 miles to the trailhead at Hanson's Mill. From here it is a 6-mile hike along the East Bellows Trail. Or, you can continue on FR 600 on a slow, bone-jarring, 14-mile, four-wheel-drive road that takes you to within 0.5 mile of the site. Both routes take roughly the same amount of time; however, only attempt the drive in dry weather.

Activities

CAMPING

Tucked into a Rio Grande canyon with 1,500-foot walls, **River Hill** campground has 20 sites. With the Weminuche Wilderness just out the back door, this campground is close to Rio Grande Reservoir. Nearby **Thirty-mile** campground, with 35 sites, is a popular spot near the confluence of the Rio Grande and Squaw Creek. A little farther down the road, **Lost Trail** campground has seven sites set in a meadow with mountain views. From Creede, drive southwest on CO 149 for about 21 miles, turn left onto Rio Grande Reservoir Road (Forest Road 520), and go 10.5 miles to the River Hill campground; continue 1.5 miles to Thirty-mile, and 7 more to Lost Trail. **Silver Thread** campground (11 sites), between Creede and Lake City off CO 149, provides access to several lakes and is just five minutes from South Clear Creek Falls. *719-658-2556.*

FISHING

Trout fishing near the headwaters of the **Rio Grande** offers plenty of public access, where you can cast for rainbows, browns, and cutthroats. **Road Canyon Reservoir** is also a good bet. It's on the way to Rio Grande Reservoir (which is drained occasionally for irrigation, so check locally before planning a fishing trip there). Also inquire about the many great trout streams in the area, where you will find brookies as well; **North Clear Creek** is one good choice. *For local information, gear, or guide services: Rio Grande Angler, 13 S. Main St., 719-658-2955.*

FOUR-WHEEL-DRIVE TRIPS

The 60-mile **Stony Pass Road** goes from Rio Grande Reservoir (see Scenic Location No. 122, p. 345) to Silverton. From Creede, drive about 21 miles southwest on CO 149, turn left onto Rio Grande Reservoir Road (Forest Road 520), then continue west on FR 520 past the reservoir. For a drive with a payback at the end, take the road to **Wheeler Geologic Area** (see Main Attractions, p. 341).

HIKING

Inspiration Point Trail MODERATE switchbacks up Willow Creek Canyon for 2 miles to the top of 1,500-foot cliffs, giving a bird's-eye view of town, East Willow Creek, and the Upper Rio Grande Valley. The trail starts from the Snowshoe Motel on La Garita Avenue (CO 149). **East Willow Creek Road** MODERATE also makes for a nice outing (see Mountain Biking, below). The hike into Wheeler Geologic Area along **East Bellows Trail** MODERATE leads to a wonderland of eroded formations (see Main Attractions, p. 341).

You'll need a four-wheel-drive vehicle to reach the start of the hike for **Bristol Head** MODERATE, a local landmark. You may well see moose, elk, or bighorn sheep along this 6.5-mile (one way) hike that traverses meadows as it leads up to sheer cliffs on the northwest side of Bristol Head. From Creede, drive west on CO 149 for 27 miles. Just past the turnoff for North Clear Creek Falls, turn right on the Bristol Head–Crystal Lake Road, and follow this for about 12 miles. Park and start hiking. Rio Grande National Forest has an office at Third and Main streets, where you can get information on the surrounding national forest lands and wilderness areas. *719-658-2556, www.fs.fed.us/r2/riogrande.*

HORSEBACK RIDING

The Weminuche and La Garita Wilderness Areas offer unlimited horseback riding opportunities, and the Wheeler Geologic Area (see Main Attractions, p. 341) also makes for an incredibly scenic ride. *For guided horseback rides: Cottonwood Cove Guest Ranch, about 10 miles southeast of Creede on CO 149. 719-658-2242.*

MOUNTAIN BIKING

The scenic, 17-mile **Bachelor Historic Loop** MODERATE (see Main Attractions, p. 341), an unpaved road through the old silver mining district, is not technical but it is an arduous climb. During weekends in the summer, there's a good amount of vehicular traffic and you may be eating a lot of dust. The 8-mile **East Willow Creek Road** MODERATE starts at the same place and is also a loop but takes a slightly less-traveled four-wheel-drive road. From downtown, drive 0.7 mile past the Mineral County Courthouse and park in the lot at the intersection of the Bachelor Historic Loop (Forest Road 503) and FR 502. Take FR 502, the dirt road to the right, which is a gradual climb to about the 4-mile point, where the road climbs a series of switchbacks before connecting to FR 503 for a steep descent back to town. For an easy, shorter ride, bike only as far as the first switchback, then turn around, which should take about an hour. Whether the ride is easy or difficult, the expansive valley views are worth the trip.

A classic singletrack, **Deep Creek Trail** MODERATE is a 7-mile (one way) ride with a lot of variety. Most people like to make this a shuttle ride, driving to the top of Snowshoe Mountain and enjoying the downhill ride. Check locally for directions. *For bike rentals and information: San Juan Sports, 102 Main St., 888-658-0851, 719-658-2359.*

MUSEUMS

The **Underground Mining Museum** (see Main Attractions, p. 341) is one of two museums in Creede. The **Creede History Museum** is housed in the old Denver & Rio Grande train depot, built in 1891 during the height of the silver boom. You can see old-time photographs and artifacts such as gaming tables and a horse-drawn hearse. Open June to September. *17 S. Main St., 719-658-2004.*

RAFTING

A 12-mile stretch of the **Rio Grande** upstream from Creede, and a stretch from Creede downstream to South Fork, offers fun, family rafting with Class II and III rapids MODERATE. Arrange trips through Mountain Man Tours. *408 Starlight Cir., 719-658-2663, www.mountainmantours.com.* A 5-mile stretch of the river, starting from River Hill campground, has Class IV and Class V whitewater, but it's not run commercially.

ROCK HOUNDING

The county seat of Mineral County, Creede is a good rock hounding spot, where you can hunt for fossils, jasper, agate, or geodes. Pick up a map at the Chamber of Commerce visitor center at the north end of Main Street.

TOUR

Drilled out of solid rock, the **Creede Underground Firehouse** is a very unique fire station indeed, with fire engines housed in side tunnels branching off the main tunnel. Tours of the firehouse, adjoining the Underground Mining Museum at the north end of town, are given in summer only. *800-327-2102.*

WINTER SPORTS

The Upper Rio Grande Nordic Club maintains nearly 40 miles of groomed cross-country ski trails. Two favorites are the **Deep Creek Trail** MODERATE, a 3-mile loop, and the 3.5-mile **Ivy Creek/Lime Creek Loop** MODERATE. *For ski rentals: San Juan Sports, 102 Main St., 888-658-0851, 719-658-2359; for directions and information: Creede & Mineral County Chamber of Commerce, 800-327-2102.*

San Juan Snow Treks operates two huts near the Weminuche Wilderness. **Fisher Mountain Hut** sleeps six people, and **Lime Creek Yurt** accommodates four; both are fully furnished. Each hut is about 5 miles from the trailhead and from the other hut, so you can ski hut-to-hut. Plenty of intermediate and advanced skiing exists nearby, as well as old logging and mining roads for touring. *888-658-0851, www.creedemountainhuts.com.*

Snow Country Explorers, the local snowmobile club, maintains more than 85 miles of trails, with routes for every level of

COLORADO CAMEO

Soapy Smith

The Western frontier was home to many legendary characters, and in Colorado one of the most colorful was con artist Soapy Smith. He was born Jefferson Randolph Smith in 1860 to an aristocratic Southern family. Financially ruined by the Civil War, the Smiths left the family plantation in Georgia to start anew in Texas, where sixteen-year-old Jefferson got his first job, driving cattle from Austin to Abilene, Kansas. With four months' worth of pay jingling in his pocket, he was suckered out of his wages by a street-corner huckster playing the classic shell game. Jefferson learned quickly that there was a far easier way of making money than sitting in a saddle.

It was a variation on the shell game that earned him the moniker Soapy. Wrapping up small bars of soap in $10, $20, and even $100 bills, the dapper and fast-talking con man worked the mining towns, moving from Leadville to Denver and eventually to Creede. In 1892, Creede was booming, with the mines producing $1 million in silver a month. It was even better than Soapy had hoped.

He bankrolled the money he had fleeced from gullible miners and built a gambling parlor, the New Orleans Club, where the miners now lost their money to Soapy at the poker and keno tables. With wealth and growing power, Soapy proclaimed himself the mayor of Creede, with a gang of associates enforcing his rule. If people didn't follow the "laws" of his makeshift government, they were promptly run out of town. Though Soapy has been referred to as the first true gangster in the annals of the American West, he and his henchmen actually instilled a sense of order in the previously lawless town.

Soapy Smith was a personable man and an eloquent speaker, occasionally given to quoting the Scriptures. He dressed fashionably and enjoyed entertaining his guests with champagne toasts and lavish meals. He loved to gamble and lost regularly at the faro tables. What money he didn't spend or lose, he gave away. A kind-hearted scoundrel, Soapy contributed to churches, gave money to the poor, and paid for the burials of the working girls in Creede's red-light district.

When the people of Creede finally became fed up with mob rule, Soapy moved on, first to Denver, then Mexico, always working a scheme wherever he went. He eventually landed in Alaska, where he tried to take over the town of Skagway and was killed in a gunfight at the age of 38—with less than $300 to his name.

122 SCENIC LOCATION RIO GRANDE RESERVOIR ROAD

The scenery on this river route that follows CO 149 is outstanding all along the wide-open divide that separates Rio Grande from Gunnison River country. The route tops out at 11,361 feet at Slumgullion Pass, although it crosses the Continental Divide at a lower elevation at Spring Creek Pass (10,901 feet). Well before these two passes, the Rio Grande departs the highway and heads into the high country. Rio Grande Reservoir Road follows the upper Rio Grande almost to its headwaters. A large, unimpressive reservoir skirts this road, but the river scenery on the way is superb. The valley is replete with grassy meadows that lead up to aspen-covered hillsides. Volcanic cliffs line the valley. Drive about 21 miles west from Creede on CO 149 toward Lake City. Look for the distinct left-hand turn onto Forest Road 520 and the sign for the reservoir. This improved dirt road allows vehicle travel a short distance past the reservoir.

Plan on photographing along the stretch of CO 149 before you get to the turnoff. The Rio Grande is visible along the way, meandering through high-mountain meadows. Volcanic cliffs loom in the background. I love the vantage along the highway near the turnoff to the reservoir: Elevated above the river, you reach a scenic overlook up the drainage in the direction of the lake. Here the river courses though a very pastoral setting, and the San Juan Mountains tower in the distance. The drive along the reservoir road gets you even closer to the action.

Large rocks that have tumbled down the cliffs make a wonderful foreground for aspens and cliffs. The trees peak in fall color around the first week in October. For a really solitary experience, though, visit this valley early in June. If you are driving your four-wheel drive, you may continue past the reservoir and ultimately over Stony Pass to Silverton (see Scenic Location No. 133, p. 371). The approach to the pass takes you into an alpine zone, full of summer wildflowers which will delight your film.

rider. Trails range 8,000–12,000 feet in elevation and even link with the trail system in Lake City (and, in good snow years, with the system in South Fork). *For snowmobile tours: Continental Divide Services, 719-658-2682; for information, chamber of commerce, 800-327-2102, or the snowmobile club, 719-658-2221.*

Restaurants

Restaurants in Creede may be closed or have limited hours in the off-season (October to May), so call ahead. The **Creede Hotel Restaurant** ($$) offers fine dining downtown, with entrees ranging from vegetarian to prime rib, pasta to seafood. Located next to the Creede Repertory Theatre, it's an excellent choice for a pre-show meal. *719-658-2608.* **Café Olé** ($) is a pleasant spot for a breakfast of fresh-baked muffins or a sandwich or salad for lunch or dinner, plus pizza after 5 p.m. on weekends. *112 N. Main St., 719-658-2880.* **Kip's Grill** ($) is a local favorite that features Baja-style tacos, fresh salsas, and fantastic burgers. They're also known for their fresh-squeezed juices, margaritas, and cocktails served in the restaurant or in The San Juan Room, the Grill's full bar. *Corner of 5th and Main, 719-658-0220, www.kipsgrill.com.* Treat yourself to an old-fashioned sundae from the authentic 19th-century soda fountain at the **Old Firehouse Ice Cream Parlor** ($), across the street from the Creede Repertory Theatre. *719-658-0212.* **Mermaid Café** offers great coffee and espresso, has a large selection of teas, and serves numerous baked goods. *115 Main St., 719-658-1112.*

Antlers Riverside Restaurant ($$) serves American and continental cuisine. From Creede, go southwest on CO 149 for 5 miles. Reservations required. *719-658-2423.* **Blue Creek Lodge** ($-$$) makes available 20 different burgers (including elk), along with steak, chicken, and fresh Rocky Mountain trout. It serves breakfast, lunch, and dinner year-round. Be sure to check out the homage to John Wayne in the back room. It's located at Wagon Wheel Gap, 9 miles southeast of Creede on CO 149. *800-326-6408.*

Accommodations

The **Creede Hotel** ($-$$) offers B&B accommodations with four rooms in a restored 1892 hotel. The hotel is on Main Street and is open May through October. *719-658-2608.* Located above a 19th-century firehouse, the **Old Firehouse Bed & Breakfast** ($-$$) has three rooms plus a suite. *123 Main St., 719-658-0212.* The **Blessings Inn Bed and Breakfast** ($-$$) has five guest rooms, all with private baths. *466 Main St., 719-658-0215, www.blessingsinn.com.*

Besides B&Bs in town, plenty of guest ranches offer accommodations on the outskirts. **Bruces' Snowshoe Lodge & B&B** ($-$$) is a family- and pet-friendly lodge and bed and breakfast open year round. There are 18 units in the lodge and a two-bedroom B&B suite. *202 E. 8th St. & CO 149, 719-658-2315, www.snowshoelodge.net.*

Antlers Rio Grande Lodge ($$), a 100-year-old ranch, has modern cabins, lodge rooms, and an RV park along the river, which has been privately stocked. There's even a petting farm for kids. From Creede, drive southwest on CO 149 for 5 miles. *719-658-2423, www.antlerslodge.com.* **4UR Ranch** ($$$$) bills itself as "fly-fishing heaven," but even if you're not an angler, this guest ranch is glorious. The lodge rooms and cabins are upscale, and when the dinner bell rings you can be assured of a gourmet meal. Seven miles of private stream guarantee uncrowded fishing. With horseback riding, hiking, children's activities, and a geothermally heated, spring-fed pool, there's always something to do. 4UR operates June through September, accepting only week-long stays during the busy summer months. Meals and most activities are included. From Creede, go southeast on CO 149 for 9 miles, turn right at the ranch sign, and go 1 mile. *719-658-2202, www.4urranch.com.*

Special Events

Memorial Day weekend has two events: the **Mountain Man Rendezvous** and **A Taste of Creede,** where local artists show their crafts in downtown galleries and studios. Held on the Fourth of July, the **Days of '92** hark back to 1892 and the days of hard-rock miners. The highlight of the three-day event is the Colorado State Mining Championships, which pits teams of miners in drilling and blasting competitions. In August, the **Mushroom Foray** shows how to find, identify, and cook with mushrooms. *800-327-2102, www.creede.com.*

For More Information

The Creede & Mineral County Chamber of Commerce information center, in a log cabin on Main Street, is by the Mineral County Courthouse. *800-327-2102, www.creede.com.*

Lake City

(see map on p. 340)

If I had to plan a perfect Colorado day, it would be in Lake City. I'd start out jeeping along the southern leg of the Alpine Loop, past ghost towns and abandoned mines, to American Basin, where the summer show of wildflowers is one of the most spectacular in the state. Next I'd hike to Sloan Lake to fish for cutthroat trout, and then ascend Handies Peak to bag a fourteener. Yes, all in one day—and with time enough for dinner at a fine restaurant that evening! Granted, this would be quite a long day, but here it's easy to get ambitious about the wealth of possibilities for outdoor adventure.

To truly appreciate Lake City, however, you should spend several days at the very least. The scenic backcountry roads, fourteeners, fishing spots, and hiking and biking trails will keep you plenty occupied. You can sail on Lake San Cristobal, or tour the downtown historic district. In winter there are miles upon miles of groomed snowmobile routes as well as Nordic ski trails and a backcountry hut system. The recreational opportunities here could take years to explore.

History

Gold was discovered near here in 1874, and the following year Lake City was incorporated as a town, one of earliest on the Western Slope. Mining camps dotted the high country, with miners clanging away in search of gold, silver, lead, copper, and zinc. Lake City became the main supply hub, a position solidified with the arrival of the railroad in 1889. The mines are all quiet now, just ghost towns and ruins where thousands of people once worked and lived. Today Lake City's wealth lies in the abundance of recreational activities here.

Silver Street, Lake City

Main Attractions

ALPINE LOOP NATIONAL BACKCOUNTRY BYWAY

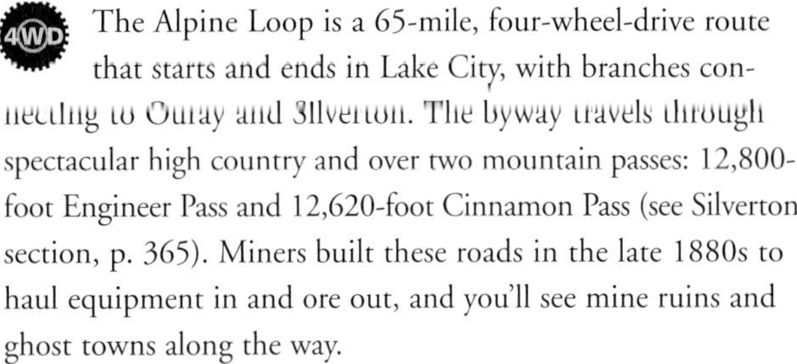

The Alpine Loop is a 65-mile, four-wheel-drive route that starts and ends in Lake City, with branches connecting to Ouray and Silverton. The byway travels through spectacular high country and over two mountain passes: 12,800-foot Engineer Pass and 12,620-foot Cinnamon Pass (see Silverton section, p. 365). Miners built these roads in the late 1880s to haul equipment in and ore out, and you'll see mine ruins and ghost towns along the way.

The Alpine Loop and its many side roads access miles of hiking trails and five fourteeners. Pick up information on the byway at the Lake City visitor center, which has a booklet describing the route, ghost towns, mines, trails, campgrounds, and rest stops. The road is open from May to October, but the best times are in late July or early August when wildflowers are in bloom, or in September when the aspens are turning. The Alpine Loop is a sample of Colorado high country that you do not want to miss! *For jeep rentals, maps, and information: Lake City Auto and Sports Center, 809 N. CO 149, 970-944-2311.*

HISTORIC WALKING TOUR OF LAKE CITY

A National Historic District, Lake City boasts more than 75 buildings dating from the late 19th century, making it the largest historic district in Colorado. Private residences, churches, and business and civic buildings represent a range of architectural styles, from Queen Anne/Victorian homes to chinked log cabins. Built in 1877, the Hinsdale County Courthouse, where the Alferd Packer trial took place (see Historical Marker, p. 349) is believed to be the oldest continuously used courthouse in the state. Two cemeteries also date from the late 1800s. Pick up a map at the visitor center for a self-guided tour.

LAKE SAN CRISTOBAL

The second largest natural lake in Colorado, Lake San Cristobal (see Scenic Location No. 127, p. 354) was created when the Slumgullion Earthflow (see Geologic Site, p. 349) dammed the Lake Fork of the Gunnison River. Its sapphire waters attract anglers, boaters, and kayakers. Facilities include a boat launch, picnic areas with grills, campsites, lakeside lodging, and miles of trails. From Lake City, drive south on CO 149 for 2 miles and turn right at the sign.

SNOWMOBILE TRAIL SYSTEMS

Lake City offers one of the most extensive snowmobile trail systems in the state—178 miles of trails maintained by the Lake City Continental Divide Snowmobile Club. Groomed five times a week, these well-signed trails wind through national forest land, through meadows, forests, bowls, and up and over the divide. The 130-mile **Slumgullion Pass Trail System** and the 48-mile **Alpine Plateau Trail System** are easily accessed from parking areas along CO 149. Restrooms are spaced along the trails, with picnic areas at many of the overlooks. The Lake City

FOREST ROAD 510

Like Lime Creek Road (see Scenic Location No. 130, p. 367), Forest Road 510 is a great shortcut onto a dirt road, bypassing a highway route. The road winds around hillsides covered with aspens and is a must-photograph place in the fall. It's not a long road, but still one of my little secrets that I'd like to share with you. Drive west from Creede on CO 149. Two miles past the well-marked left-hand turnoff to Rio Grande Reservoir, keep a keen eye out for the next road on your right, FR 510. The road is bumpy in places but passable by car.

Plan on savoring this 4-mile drive. Keep your eye open for places where you can use your telephoto lens to photograph the curves of the road in the distance as it winds in and out of the aspen groves. When you enter the groves, park the vehicle and set up your camera in the middle of the road (you might want to have a companion keep an eye out for traffic, though this road is not heavily used). With a wide-angle lens, compose the edges of the road from the bottom corners of your viewfinder along with trees on the sides. The parallax distortion will cause the edges to converge farther into the scene to create a dramatic appearance of depth. Peak autumn color occurs here in early October; greens of spring are delicate and lovely in early June. About halfway along this route, turn east onto FR 509 on the way to Santa Maria Reservoir. You can find a few additional views on this road, but you'll have to turn around before the reservoir: It's on private property and the owners don't seem to like visitors.

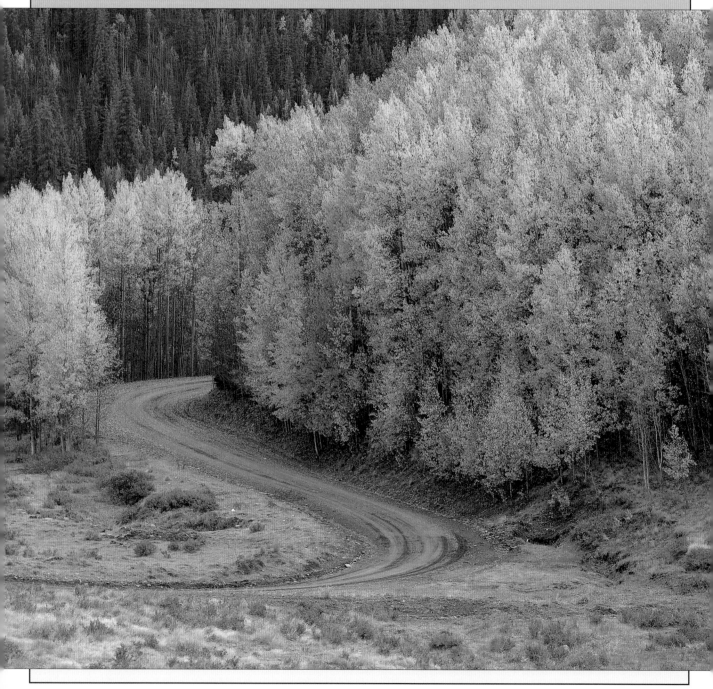

system also links up with groomed trails to Creede and Blue Mesa. *For snowmobile rentals, guided tours, maps, or information: Lake City Auto & Sports Center, 809 N. CO 149, 970-944-2311.*

Activities

CAMPING

Wupperman campground has stunning views of Lake San Cristobal. From Lake City, drive south on CO 149 for 2 miles, turn right for Lake San Cristobal (County Road 30), and loop around the southern end of the lake to its eastern shore. *970-944-2225.* About 6 miles farther on CR 30 is **Williams Creek** campground (see Camping, Pagosa Springs, p. 333). Nestled amid dramatic rock formations, the primitive campsites at **The Gate** stretch out along the Lake Fork of the Gunnison. From Lake City, drive north on CO 149 for 16.5 miles and turn left at the sign. *970-641-0471.*

A wide, forested canyon seems to cradle you at **Cebolla Creek State Wildlife Area,** which is so remote it's like backcountry camping. There are no designated campsites—just pick a spot along the creek. From Lake City, drive south on CO 149 for 9 miles, turn left onto Cebolla Road (Forest Road 788), and go 15 miles. *970-641-0088.*

FISHING

With the **Lake Fork of the Gunnison River, Henson** and **Cebolla Creeks,** high country lakes, and hundreds of backcountry streams, the area around Lake City is an angler's paradise. Brown trout is the predominant fish in the Lake Fork, with a good population of rainbows and cutthroats. **Lake San Cristobal,** while not considered a hot spot, has its share of rainbows and browns, with the best fly fishing at the southern end of the lake. *For maps, guides, or current fishing information: The Sportsman, 238 S. Gunnison Ave., 970-944-2526.*

GEOLOGIC SITE

The **Slumgullion Earthflow** is the dramatic result of a mudslide some 700 years ago, when a high mesa of supersaturated volcanic tuff bulldozed down the mountain in an avalanche of dirt, rock, and mud. Millions of tons of debris dammed the Lake Fork of the Gunnison River, creating Lake San Cristobal. A smaller mudslide occurred 300 years ago, and even today the earth still moves at a rate of up to 20 feet per year. Very little vegetation grows here because continued movement prevents roots from taking hold. Trees along the edges are twisted into strange shapes as they constantly try to grow vertically in a horizontally moving landscape. Designated a National Natural Landmark, the slide can be seen from a pull-off on CO 149, about 6 miles south of Lake City. A half-mile farther is access to an easy hiking trail to the slide site.

GHOST TOWNS

Relics of the silver boom, ghost towns are scattered throughout the high country. **Capitol City, Animas Forks, Sherman,** and **Carson** are all accessible from Lake City, although four-wheel-drive is necessary to reach some of them. Established in 1881, Carson has the most buildings left standing. From Lake City, go south on CO 149 for 2 miles and turn right for Lake San Cristobal (County Road 30). Drive 8.5 miles and turn right onto 4WD Wager Gulch Road. From here you'll need four-wheel drive, or you can hike the 4 miles to the Carson townsite.

HIKING

Carpeted with wildflowers in midsummer, **American Basin** MODERATE is one of the most beautiful valleys in the San Juan Mountains. From Lake City, drive south on CO 149 for 2 miles and turn right for Lake San Cristobal (County Road 30). Follow this road for 12 miles to a fork, bear right, and go 8 miles to another fork. American Basin is to the left. Park your car here; 4WD if you have four-wheel drive, you can go 1 mile into the basin, which sits above timberline beneath craggy peaks.

From American Basin you can hike 1.2 miles to Sloan Lake and 1 mile more to the summit of 14,048-foot **Handies Peak** DIFFICULT. (Seasoned mountaineers consider Handies one of the easier fourteeners in the state.) Return the same way, or hike down Handies Peak on the Grizzly Gulch Trail, which reconnects with CR 30, and turn left to return to your vehicle, making the hike a 10-mile loop. In addition to Handies Peak, there are four other fourteeners near Lake City: Uncompahgre, Wetterhorn, Sunshine, and Redcloud Peaks. All are accessible from the Alpine Loop, with Wetterhorn Peak being the most challenging.

Cataract Gulch Trail MODERATE tracks 4 miles (one way) through dense forest and alpine meadows, past riffling waterfalls and beaver ponds up to Cataract Lake. From Lake City, drive south on CO 149 for 2 miles, turn right to Lake San Cristobal (CR 30). Go about 12 miles, turn left toward the ghost town of Sherman, and watch for the trailhead sign.

An old jeep trail now closed to vehicles, the **Crystal Lake Trail** DIFFICULT climbs 3,000 feet in 4 miles up to Crystal Lake (with good-sized brook trout) and Crystal Lake Campground. From town, drive north on CO 149, and turn left on Balsam, to the Oddfellows Cemetery. The trailhead is above the cemetery. **Alpine Gulch Trail** DIFFICULT is a 12-mile round trip through meadows, past steep cliffs and old mining cabins. From Lake City, take the Henson Creek Road for 2 miles, then look for the trailhead on the left.

Both the **Colorado Trail** and the **Continental Divide Trail,** which connect and run together here, can be accessed from Spring Creek Pass off CO 149, 18 miles south of Lake City. Heading east from the pass leads around Baldy Cinco and eventually into La Garita Wilderness. The first 5 miles tread over gently rolling terrain and through fields of wildflowers.

HISTORICAL MARKER

The **Alferd Packer Massacre Site,** a pull-off along CO 149 about 2.5 miles south of Lake City, tells the story of Colorado's infamous cannibal. In the winter of 1874, Alferd Packer agreed to lead a party of prospectors through the mountains to present-day Gunnison. Having little knowledge of the area, he was ill-equipped

124 NORTH CLEAR CREEK FALLS

SCENIC LOCATION

This is one of the most scenic waterfalls in Colorado, and you can drive right up to it! North Clear Creek innocently winds through the willow brush of a high mountain park, then suddenly plunges over a 60-foot-high vertical cliff of volcanic rock. As you approach the north end of Forest Road 510, take the right-hand fork to the falls instead of returning to CO 149. A sign along the highway also marks the access to the falls (see Main Attractions, Creede, p. 341). You'll need to go around a fence on the cliff's edge in front of the falls to photograph them without obstruction. The creek free-falls before plunging onto large rocks at the base. The scene is very impressive; despite the fence, the entire view looks wild and remote.

I photograph the falls with many different focal lengths of lens. With my longest lenses I zoom in on the cascades at the base of the falls. With others I include the entire waterfall but exclude the horizon. Finally, I compose a scenic to include sky. In each case I make both vertical and horizontal images. In the verticals I center the waterfall. In the horizontals, I place it off-center to create an asymmetrical balance. In the fall, the willow brush and grass next to the waterfall turn a warm brown. In summer and spring the greens make a conspicuous contrast to the pure white water. In winter, snow and ice turn the falls into a sculpture.

You have the choice to stop the motion of the water or let it be blurry and ethereal. Shutter speeds above 0.5 second will freeze the details in the water, whereas slower speeds will render it like white cotton candy. Enhance the latter effect by using a polarizing filter. The filter will not only reduce the amount of light entering the camera by 2 stops, thereby allowing even slower speeds, but will also reduce glare on the peripheral wet rocks, which will appear black in pleasing contrast against the white water (see pp. 81–83, *Photographing the Landscape*).

to lead the party, which became lost in a severe storm with insufficient provisions. Packer was the only one to make it out alive. At first he said he survived by eating roots and pods, but eventually, after their grisly remains were found, he confessed to consuming the flesh of his companions (four of the men had been bludgeoned and one killed by a bullet). Accused of murder and cannibalism, Packer was jailed, but managed to escape. Nine years later he was found and brought to trial in Lake City, where he was sentenced to hang. Because of a legal technicality, he ended up serving prison time instead. Recent forensic evidence seems to have cleared Packer of murder, but he will forever be known as the Colorado cannibal.

HORSEBACK RIDING

There are a number of horse trails around Lake City. All you need is a horse, of course. *For guided trail rides: Vickers' Ranch, 970-944-2249; Cadwell Outfitters, 7208 CR 50, Powderhorn, 970-641-2785, 850-819-9255, www.cadwelloutfitters.vpweb.com.*

MOUNTAIN BIKING

Singletracks in the Lake City area tend to be extreme and grueling, following steep hiking trails. The **Alpine Loop** MODERATE (see Main Attractions, p. 347) and many of its side roads make for invigorating single- and multi-day rides, though you will be sharing the roads with vehicles. The **Cebolla Creek Road** MODERATE is a mostly downhill 25-mile ride, best done as a shuttle with a car at Powderhorn (see Scenic Drives, below). *For bike rentals and information: The Sportsman, 238 S. Gunnison Ave., 970-944-2562, www.lakecitysportsman.com.*

MUSEUM

The **Hinsdale County Museum,** on the corner of 2nd and Silver Streets in Lake City, chronicles the town's silver and gold mining past, including details of its notorious "man eater," Alferd Packer (see Historical Marker, p. 349). Open Memorial Day through September. *970-944-2050, www.lakecitymuseum.com.*

SCENIC DRIVES

The 75-mile **Silver Thread Scenic and Historic Byway** connects Lake City, Creede, and South Fork via CO 149 (see Main Attractions, South Fork, p. 327). You can travel part of the **Alpine Loop National Backcountry Byway** (see p. 347) from Lake City with a high-clearance vehicle, although you'll have to turn back before the high passes. **Cebolla Creek Road** (see Scenic Location No. 125, p. 352), a lovely drive, meanders 25 miles through canyons and valleys, past forested hillsides and mountain meadows, with several campgrounds along the way. From Lake City, drive south on CO 149 for 9 miles and turn left onto Cebolla Road (Forest Road 788). At about 15 miles, stay left at the intersection, toward Powderhorn. You'll end up back at CO 149; turn left and drive 28 miles to Lake City.

WINTER SPORTS

Lake City is a premier snowmobiling destination, with one of the most extensive, groomed trail systems in the state (see Main Attractions, p. 347).

For cross-country skiers, the groomed **Williams Creek Trail System** EASY has gentle grades looping through forests. From Lake City, drive south on CO 149 for 2 miles, turn right to Lake San Cristobal, and go 7.5 miles. The **Slumgullion Pass Trail System** features 3 miles of groomed trails and 3 miles of ungroomed trails. From Lake City, drive south on CO 149 for 12 miles; the parking area is 1.2 miles past the Slumgullion Pass summit sign. From **Spring Creek Pass** on the Continental Divide, you can access backcountry skiing for all levels of ability. Most popular are the existing snowmobile trails on **Snow** and **Hermosa Mesas.** Good telemarking slopes also exist nearby. Avalanche danger is considered moderate, but check locally before striking out. From Lake City, drive 18 miles south on CO 149.

The **Hinsdale Haute Route** makes four fully furnished backcountry huts available to cross-country skiers and snowshoers. The closest is **Wilson Yurt** MODERATE, just 1.5 miles

CEBOLLA CREEK

Amazingly, the drive along CO 149 continues to increase in scenic value as you proceed north and west toward Lake City. For example, the views of the peaks of the La Garita Wilderness north of Spring Creek Pass are sublime. To the north of the highway you can descend into two beautiful drainages of the Gunnison River. They are traveled lightly yet provide scenery unique in Colorado. The first, Cebolla Creek, connects to the second, Los Pinos Creek, and both are accessible by an improved road. Just to the west of Slumgullion Pass, turn north from CO 149 onto Forest Road 788. You'll see signs pointing to the town of Powderhorn. You can also access the drive from CO 149 halfway between Lake City and US 50 near the town of Powderhorn.

Immediately you will drop into the Cebolla Creek drainage. Keep an eye out for views to the east of the peaks of the La Garita Wilderness. However, my favorite scenes to photograph exist where the creek enters a wide valley lined by cliffs of old volcanic rock, and where willow bushes and cottonwood trees define the pastoral valley floor. Farther downstream, hay meadows dominate the river bottom. When the road approaches the narrower parts of the valley, consider hiking up the hillside in order to photograph down on the valley. It only takes a little bit of elevation to achieve such a perspective, so the hike is well worth the effort. Summer wildflowers carpet the hillsides along the way, and autumn renders the willows and cottonwoods variegated tones of yellow and orange. Go as far as the Cebolla State Wildlife Area, then turn back around and head east on the road you would have just passed, County Road 15, Los Pinos Creek Road (which is the continuation of the road you started on, FR 788, described in Scenic Location No. 126, opposite).

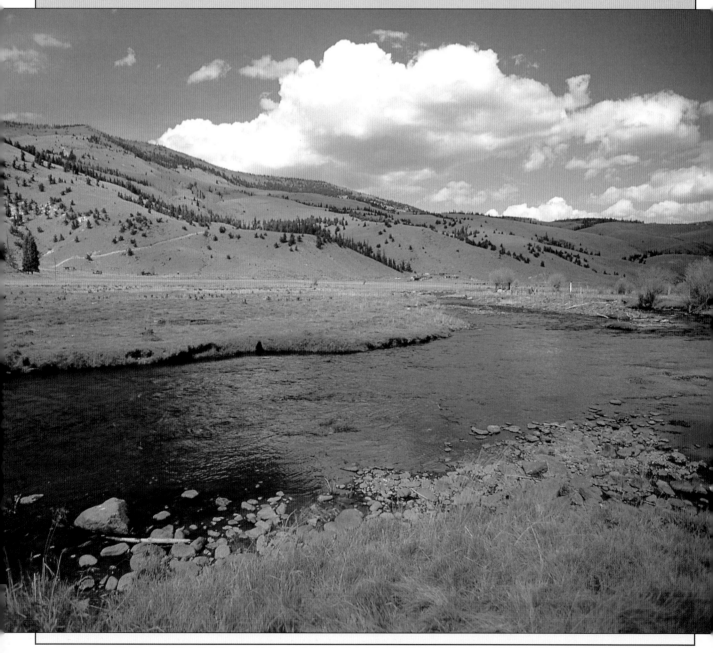

from the trailhead. Access to the trail is 15.5 miles south of Lake City off CO 149. *For hut reservations: 970-944-2269, www.hinsdalehauteroute.org.*

Restaurants

Bruno's Restaurant & Grill ($$) offers Lake City's finest upscale dining. Dinner in the restaurant is by reservation only. Walk-ins are welcome in the grill, which is open for lunch and dinner, serving dine-in or take-out. *1221 N. Hwy. 149, 970-944-2145.* Try **Old Timers Café** ($) for a great home-cooked meal year round. *310 N. Gunnison Ave., 970-944-7007.* **The Tic Toc Diner** ($) takes you back to mom-and-pop diners of the 1930s. Order the blue plate special, an Elvis burger (double everything), meatloaf, or cinnamon toast—yes, like mom used to make. *135 Gunnison Ave., 970-944-0444.* Locals recommend **Luna's** ($$) for great daily specials and Italian entrees. Open seasonally. *808 Gunnison Ave., 970-944-1313.* **Poker Alice** ($) has been voted one of Lake City's best. This friendly and casual diner offers an all-you-can-eat breakfast buffet, a selection of fresh salads, wraps, sandwiches, stone-baked pizza, and pasta. Hours vary seasonally. *188 S. Gunnison Ave., 970-944-4100, www.pokeralice.com.* For breakfast, check out **Lake City Bakery** ($), celebrating 22 years in Lake City. It's also a great place for fresh-baked breads, pastries, and sweets. *922 CO 149, 970-944-2316.*

LOS PINOS CREEK

Like Cebolla Creek, Los Pinos Creek passes through mountain meadows and pastoral ranch scenes on its way to a rendezvous with the Gunnison River. Consult the route described in Scenic Location No. 125 (opposite) to access Los Pinos Creek from the south. You can also reach it from CO 114, which connects US 50 west of Gunnison with the town of Saguache in the San Luis Valley.

From Cebolla Creek, Forest Road 788 heads east and crosses Los Pinos Pass before dropping into the Los Pinos drainage. Keep an eye out for a weathered barn, one of the most beautiful that I've ever seen, on the south side of the road. The road over the pass is bumpy but passable by car. It winds through groves of aspen, which in late September are stunning. The road then enters some of the broadest hay meadows that I've encountered in Colorado. If you have ever wanted a photograph of cattle in a pretty setting, this would be the place. There are a few places where the creek skirts the road, so park the car and compose the creek in the foreground leading up to meadows and the ridges that bound the valley. Spring, summer, and fall each give this place a different visual personality.

LAKE SAN CRISTOBAL

Other large bodies of water in this region of the San Juan Mountains, like Rio Grande Reservoir, are man-made reservoirs. Lake San Cristobal is an exception. Some 700 years ago the first mudslide came down from Slumgullion Pass and blocked the Lake Fork of the Gunnison River, forming the lake. Therefore I'm a little more enthusiastic about making images of this lake. You should be, too! The lake provides marvelous reflections of the peaks along the Continental Divide to the southwest. Two miles south of Lake City on CO 149, turn west onto improved County Road 30. You'll see well-marked signs to the lake. This is also the way to Cinnamon Pass (see Scenic Location No. 135, p. 374), which requires a four-wheel drive.

County roads go around the lake. I enjoy photographing a composition with the lake in the foreground and the peaks behind. At 13,657 feet, Carson Peak is the highest in this range. Try composing images from both the east and west sides of the lake. Look for interesting trees, bushes, or rocks that might serve as foreground subjects. Compose the shoreline of the lake as a diagonal line beginning in the bottom left- or right-hand corner of your viewfinder. This composition creates a lead-in line that will add depth to the scene, drawing the viewer into the photograph. The more tranquil the water, the more beautiful and perfect the reflection (see pp. 129–133, *Photographing the Landscape*). The peaks in the background will catch both sunrise and sunset light, so try photographing at both ends of the day. Deciduous trees and shrubs along the shoreline provide autumn color in the first week in October. Continue past the lake along the Lake Fork of the Gunnison River for more lovely scenes on your way to Cinnamon Pass.

The Tic Toc Diner, Lake City

Accommodations

An 1878 Victorian home, the **Cinnamon Inn Bed & Breakfast** ($$) includes two rooms, two suites, a lovely garden, and great hosts. These folks helped me find a tow truck to retrieve my disabled vehicle high in the San Juan Mountains one summer. *426 Gunnison Ave., 800-337-2335.* Just one block from the historic district, **Matterhorn Mountain Lodge** ($) is a tastefully decorated motel; 6 rooms have kitchenettes. *409 Bluff St., 970-944-2210, www.matterhornmotel.com.* On the Lake Fork of the Gunnison River, **The Texan Resort** ($-$$) is a year-round place with one- to three-bedroom cabins, many with fireplaces. From Lake City, go south on CO 149 about 1 mile and turn right at the Ox Yoke onto County Road 14. *970-944-2246.* **Lakeview Resort** ($-$$) has one- to three-bedroom cabins, lodge rooms, and suites overlooking Lake San Cristobal. It rents paddle and pontoon boats, sea kayaks, and canoes, and also has horses for hourly trail rides or backcountry fishing trips. Open May to October. *800-456-0170, www.lakeview-inc.com.* **Linny's Stay & Play** ($-$$) is one of Lake City's newest lodging options. Guests can choose from lodge bedrooms of the studio apartment and even have the option of booking the entire facility. Linny's also offers a variety of packages with an array of activity choices for guests. *403 Park St., 970-944-2408, www.linnysvacations.com.* For something a little different, check out **Vickers Ranch** ($$) on CO 149. This pet-friendly family-run dude ranch offers cabin rentals, horseback riding, and jeep rentals. The property boasts its own private fishing area and a recreation hall for guest use. *162 S. CO 149, 970-944-2249, www.vickersranch.net.*

Matterhorn Mountain Lodge

Special Events

The **Fourth of July** is a grand tradition in Lake City—true small-town Americana with a parade, street dance, games in Town Park, and fireworks.

Sample wines and listen to music in Town Park during September's **Wine & Music Festival.** *For both events: 800-569-1874, www.lakecityfestival.org.*

For More Information

The Lake City Chamber of Commerce visitor center is on Gunnison Avenue (CO 149) at the north end of town. *800-569-1874, www.lakecity.com.*

Black Bear Manor, Ouray

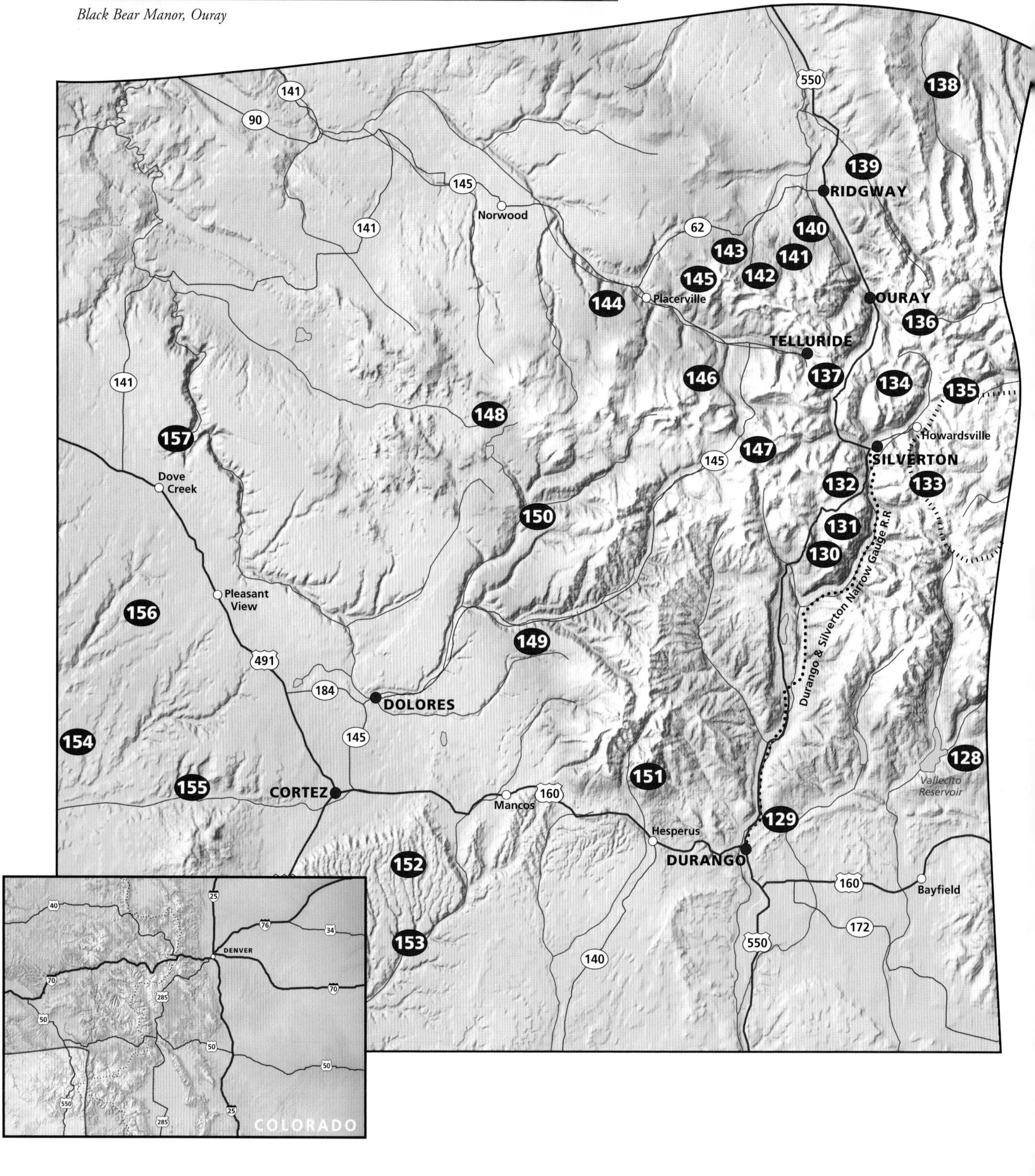

Southwestern Colorado

THE SAN JUAN MOUNTAINS AND ANASAZI COUNTRY

Strater Hotel, Durango

This chapter follows the 236-mile San Juan Skyway, which winds from Durango north to Ridgway and back south to Cortez. This fascinating corner of the state rewards visitors with haunting and magnificent landscapes, historical bounty, and superlative recreational options. All the major towns here, and even several ghost towns and a railroad, are National Historic Districts; Mesa Verde is a World Heritage Site. Come see the vast ranchlands north and south, the towering spires and remote passes of the San Juan Mountains, the meandering river valleys of the Uncompahgre, Animas, Dolores, and San Miguel Rivers, and the strikingly red cliffs of the canyon country. Once in a coffee shop in Ouray I overheard a tourist from Texas comment that there was "just no bad seat in the house." Later, when I bumped into the same family at Mesa Verde, I found them viewing the ancient Cliff House dwelling in astonishment and silence. I couldn't have agreed more.

Above: La Marmotte restaurant, Telluride

Left: Kelly Place, Cortez

SCENIC LOCATIONS

Durango

Colorado Atlas & Gazetteer pp. 86–87

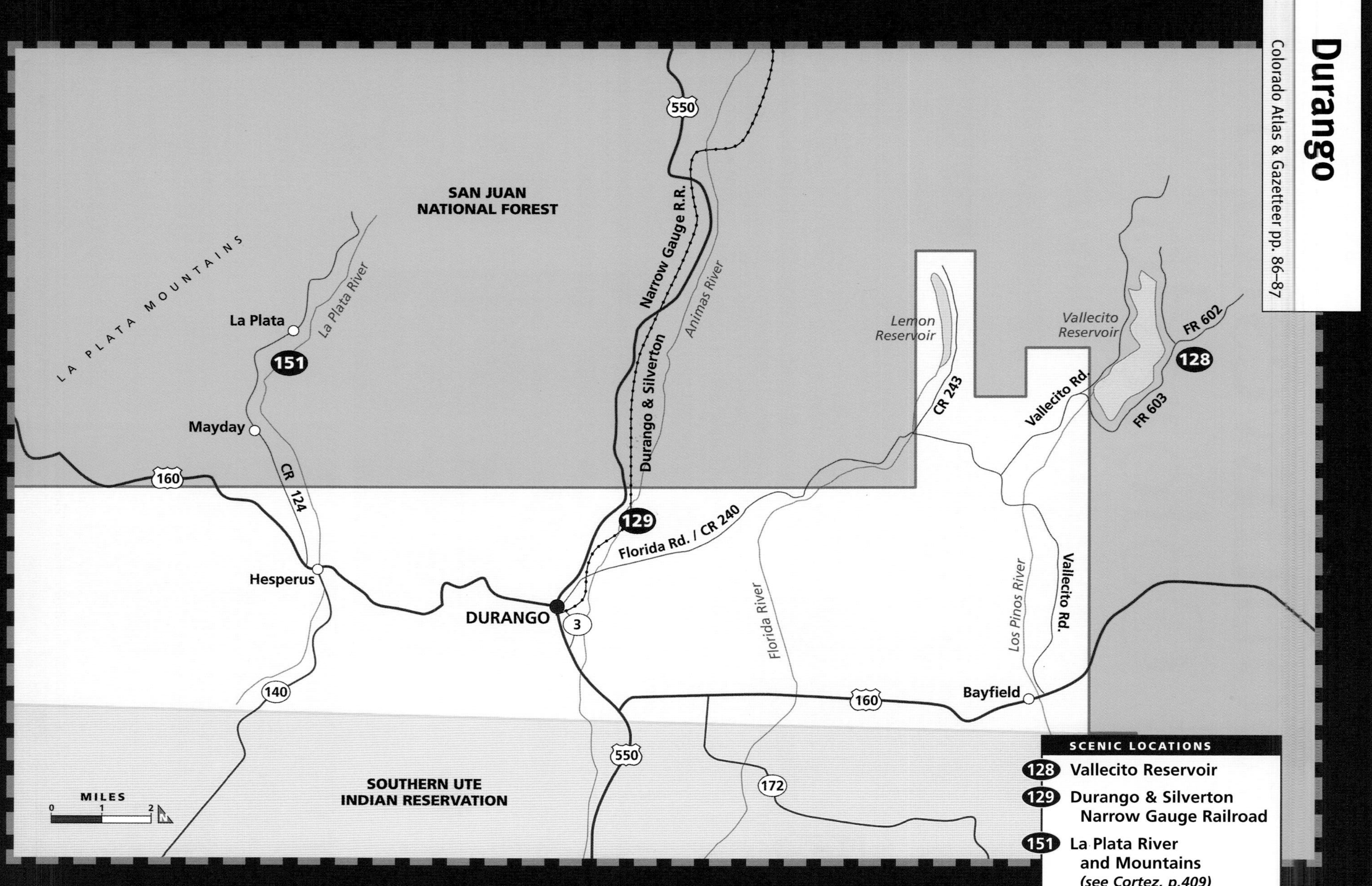

SAN JUAN NATIONAL FOREST
LA PLATA MOUNTAINS
La Plata
La Plata River
151
Mayday
160
CR 124
Hesperus
140
550
Narrow Gauge R.R.
Durango & Silverton
Animas River
129
Florida Rd. / CR 240
DURANGO
3
Florida River
Lemon Reservoir
CR 243
Vallecito Reservoir
FR 602
128
FR 603
Vallecito Rd.
Los Pinos River
Vallecito Rd.
Bayfield
160
550
172
SOUTHERN UTE INDIAN RESERVATION
MILES
0
1
2
SCENIC LOCATIONS
128 Vallecito Reservoir
129 Durango & Silverton Narrow Gauge Railroad
151 La Plata River and Mountains (see Cortez, p.409)

Durango

Durango is the scenic gateway to southwestern Colorado. Leaving the spires of the San Juans and descending into rural ranchlands, I'm always excited to reach Durango and the lands beyond. Here Colorado's railroad history still lives and breathes in the heart of the town. Unlike the restful hot springs of Ouray, the laid-back resort atmosphere of Telluride, and sedate, historic Silverton, Durango hums with activity. It's a hub for train enthusiasts, for people wanting to see new sights and explore new activities, and for those who simply wish to delve back into a fascinating past.

History

One word explains Durango, past and present, and that word is *railroad.* Durango's beginnings, like those of so many late-19th-century Colorado towns, were in mining. Unlike other towns, Durango did not serve primarily as a mining camp or supply point but as an ore processing and transportation center. Tremendous mining activity from the 1870s in the San Juan Mountains to the north created a demand for mining companies to refine ore. Railroad builders came west with coal-fired steam locomotive technology and drove out the former mule-team transportation. In 1880 the Denver & Rio Grande Railway established Durango, which soon became a full-fledged railroad and ore-processing town, complete with a huge smelter that choked the air with black smoke.

As mining suffered, so did Durango; even so, by the time the mines began to play out and the gold standard replaced the silver, Durango had grown into a town that could support itself with just the railroad, tourism, and local industries. Although the cliff dwellings and artifacts at nearby Mesa Verde drew visitors to the area from the 1890s, Durango's destiny as a major tourist center was sealed when Congress declared Mesa Verde a national park in 1906. Hollywood has employed the picturesque and historic Durango-based railroad to good advantage in Westerns over the decades. Designated a historic and civil engineering landmark in 1967, the Durango & Silverton Narrow Gauge Railroad still makes tracks with daily tours.

Main Attractions

DURANGO & SILVERTON NARROW GAUGE RAILROAD

It doesn't take long for newly arrived residents of Durango to become accustomed to the shrill train whistles and sooty black smoke pouring from the locomotives that so delight tourists and children. After all, residents admit, that's the sound and smell of money riding into town on those narrow-gauge rails. It takes a full day to make the 90-mile round trip north to Silverton and back. From your cushioned seat or outside in an open-air car, you will be transported to backcountry locales along the rugged Animas River canyon and within the San Juan Mountains and Weminuche Wilderness that you could never reach in your vehicle (see Scenic Location No. 129, p. 362). First-class passengers can enjoy adult libations in the train's parlor car. You can even reserve an elegant private car for a special occasion.

The train slowly picks up speed through town; children wave and traffic stops to make way for the mighty iron horse and its passengers. The train passes through meadows and pine forests as it climbs the Animas River's sheer canyon walls. The Animas River (originally the "River of Lost Souls" in Spanish) soon drops away until it is thousands of feet below in the canyon bottom. As the train curves around tight switchbacks, you can actually photograph the front of the train from the back.

Before taking on much-needed water at Cascade Station, the train snakes back and forth across the river on unimaginably high trestle bridges. In winter, the train stops at Cascade because the tracks can't be cleared of snow beyond that point, then returns to Durango. In summer, the train continues north along the Animas River, past fourteener Sunlight Peak to your right. You can depart the train at Needleton or Elk Park to hike and fish in the Weminuche Wilderness, then catch a returning train to Durango (see Hiking in this section, p. 363, and in the Silverton section, p. 372). Be sure to tell the conductor that you are getting off and when you expect to return.

Once the train arrives in Silverton, you have two hours to explore, but that gives you time to sample a mere fraction of what this historic town has to offer (see Silverton, p. 365). My recommendation is to purchase a one-way train ticket, spend the night in Silverton, and take the train or bus back to Durango. Be sure also to visit the excellent **Railroad Museum,** including the roundhouse, at the Durango Depot on the south end of town at 479 Main Ave. *Information and reservations (a must): 970-247-2733, 888-TRAIN-07, www.durangotrain.com.*

Durango & Silverton Narrow Gauge Railroad Depot, Durango

Activities

CAMPING

Miller Creek, 18 miles northeast of Durango with 12 campsites, provides both solitude and good fishing at Lemon Reservoir. Lost Lake and Stump Lake Trails start from the campground, and horses are available at Miller Ranch. From Durango, go northeast on Florida Road (County Road 240) for 14 miles. Go left (north) on CR 243 (Forest Road 596) and continue 3.5 miles. With 45 campsites, the very scenic **Haviland Lake,** 17 miles north of Durango, just off CO 550, is a larger campground, with the Hermosa Cliffs as a backdrop and good fishing.

Small **Sig Creek** campground, 25 miles north of Durango, is adjacent to a small creek with nine campsites and easy access to the Hermosa Creek hiking and biking trail (see Cycling and Mountain Biking, below). From Durango, take US 550 north for 24 miles to FR 578. Go left (west) 5.5 miles. **Junction Creek** is a very popular and roomy campground with 34 sites, 5 miles northwest of Durango. From Durango, go northwest on Junction Creek Road (CR 204, also FR 171) for 4.5 miles. Many camping facilities circle the popular Vallecito Reservoir near Bayfield (see Fishing, this page).

For campgrounds with more solitude and access to a river, camp at the **Florida** or **Transfer Park** campgrounds. The Florida campground, 21 miles northeast of Durango, has fishing access to the Florida tributary of the Animas River and to Lemon Reservoir. From Durango, go northeast on Florida Road (CR 240) for 14 miles. Go left (north) on CR 243 and proceed 7 miles to the campground. To reach Transfer Park, follow the directions to the Florida campground, turn left on FR 597, and go 1 mile north. *For all campgrounds: 970-884-2512.*

CYCLING AND MOUNTAIN BIKING

Durango is a mecca for bicyclists—professionals and casual enthusiasts alike. Roads and trails beckon from virtually every corner of Durango's mountain valley. I've included just a few of my favorites. For touring, take the 30-mile **Baker's Bridge** loop **MODERATE** that follows the course of the Animas River. From Durango, go east on 32nd Street. Turn left at the stop sign onto East Animas Road (County Road 250). Cross a narrow bridge and continue until you intersect US 550. Turn left (south) on US 550 to Hermosa, then turn right onto CR 203 and continue back to Durango.

For mountain biking, take the 11-mile one-way **Lime Creek Road** **MODERATE**. This route also crosses the 100-year-old Lime Creek burn and is especially beautiful in autumn (see Scenic Location No. 130, p. 367). The Lime Creek trailhead is 30 miles north of Durango on US 550 just north of the Durango Mountain Resort. Look for the Lime Creek Road (Forest Road 591) sign and a parking area. The 6-mile **Dry Fork Loop** **MODERATE** takes you through pine forests, aspen groves, cottonwood trees, and scrub oak—a great autumn ride. The La Plata Mountains are visible from the trail, which is a segment of the 470-mile Colorado Trail. To get there, drive 3.5 miles west of Durango on US 160, turn right onto Lightner Creek Road, proceed 1 mile to CR 208, and turn right. You'll see the Dry Fork trailhead on your left.

In Spanish, *hermosa* means "beautiful"—an apt name for 20-mile (one way) **Hermosa Creek Trail** **DIFFICULT**, which travels through the dense pine forests and streams of San Juan National Forest. Arrange a shuttle by leaving one car at the town of Hermosa (10 miles north of Durango on US 550). Take a second vehicle 18 miles farther north to Durango Mountain Resort (formerly known as Purgatory Ski Area). Turn left on Hermosa Park Road (FR 578) and go 8 miles to the trailhead.

Kennebec Pass Trail **DIFFICULT** takes you into La Plata Canyon and offers views of the craggy canyon and high mountain meadows covered with wildflowers (see Scenic Location No. 151, p. 409). Arrange a shuttle if possible for this challenging, 26-mile (one way) ride. To reach the trailhead from Durango, go west 11 miles on US 160 to the town of Hesperus. Go north on CR 124 and continue 4 miles to Mayday. The trail begins where the pavement ends and continues for 11 miles on a steep four-wheel-drive road before becoming a technical singletrack for the remaining 15 miles. *For information and rentals: Hassle Free Sports, 2615 Main Ave., 970-259-3874; Southwest Adventures, 12th St. and Camino del Rio, 970-259-0370.*

FISHING

The **Animas River** is one of Colorado's best-kept fishing secrets. This wide and deep-flowing river offers excellent habitat for brown trout of up to 16 inches and rainbows of up to 14 inches. Access is easy, as the best stretch of the river, now designated Gold Medal Water, is right in Durango at its confluence with Lightner Creek, near the intersection of US 550 and US 160. Top-notch fishing continues all the way downstream to the Hermosa Cliffs.

Tributaries of the Animas also provide excellent fishing. **Hermosa Creek** cuts through a steep canyon where brookies and rainbows hiding out in the deep pools can grow up to 12 inches in length. From Durango, go north 10 miles on US 550 to the town of Hermosa. Go left (west) on FR 576 until you reach the creek. The **East Fork of Hermosa Creek** can be reached from the Sig Creek campground (see Camping, this page). The **Florida River** and **Lemon Reservoir** also have excellent off-the-beaten-path trout fishing, which can be reached from the Florida campground (see Camping, this page).

Vallecito Reservoir (Scenic Location No. 128, opposite) is home to trout up to 20 inches long and is also stocked with kokanee salmon. The reservoir holds the state record for pike, at more than 30 pounds. A major recreational site, Vallecito abounds with campgrounds and aquatic activities. *970-247-1573, 970-884-2512.* From Durango, take US 160, 12 miles east to the town of Bayfield. Go north on County Road 501 and follow the signs to the reservoir. *For lessons and guided fishing tours: Duranglers, 923 Main Ave., 970-385-4081, 888-FISHDGO, www.duranglers.com.*

GHOST TOWNS

Once thriving mining camps, **Parrott City** and **La Plata City** are now ghost towns up La Plata Canyon. A few buildings still stand, including a saloon complete with bullet holes. From Durango, go west on US 160 past the town of Hesperus. Head right (north) on County Road 124 to Mayday and follow the dirt road to what's left of the towns and to get great panoramic views of the La Plata Mountains and Animas River Valley (see Scenic Location No. 151, p. 409).

GOLF

Dalton Ranch and Golf Club offers challenges and hazards every step of the way at very reasonable prices. To get there from Durango, go 6 miles north on US 550 and turn right on Trimble Lane. *970-247-8774, www.daltonranch.com.* Guests at **The Cliffs at Tamarron** enjoy an 18-hole course with wonderful views of the nearly 10,000-foot Hermosa Cliffs. From Durango, go 18 miles north on US 550. *970-259-2000, www.lodgeattamarron.com.*

VALLECITO RESERVOIR

Reservoirs are not usually my favorite things to photograph—I prefer natural water bodies such as lakes and creeks. However, I make Vallecito an exception for two reasons. It sits in a gorgeous valley surrounded by peaks and forests, and the road that you have to drive to get there provides splendid scenery. Take the Vallecito Road (County Road 501) north from Bayfield on US 160 to the reservoir. This road eventually follows the more developed west side of the lake, or take a right at the dam on Forest Road 603 to drive along the less developed east side of the reservoir.

The Vallecito Road from US 160 follows the beautiful Los Pinos, or Pine, River. The ranches along the way afford opportunities to photograph hay meadows and cottonwood trees. There's a particularly nice view looking north where the road crosses the river. Compose the river in the middle with meadows and mountains in the distance. This works well both horizontally and vertically. The drive along the east side of Vallecito reveals great views of the reservoir and the Needles Mountains in the distance. Because you are looking west/northwest here, sunrise is the best time to photograph. Continue north on this slightly bumpy improved road until you reach the Los Pinos River where it enters the reservoir. The drive northeast along the river begins in the forest, but eventually opens up into spectacular meadows before dead-ending at a campground.

For hardy souls, the Vallecito Road ends at the Vallecito Creek trailhead into the great Weminuche Wilderness. I have hiked along Vallecito Creek many times to get to the most remote mountains in Colorado, the Needles. A day hike north on this trail will be rewarding for you and your photography.

DURANGO & SILVERTON NARROW GAUGE RAILROAD

This is the only narrow-gauge train ride that I recommend specifically for photography, although the Cumbres & Toltec Scenic Railroad, which runs between Colorado's San Luis Valley and Chama, N.M., and the Georgetown Loop Railroad are also quite picturesque. The Durango & Silverton route, however, is the only one that bisects wilderness and follows one of Colorado's most spectacular river canyons, the Animas. Waterfalls, rapids, cliffs, and the highest and most precipitous of Colorado's peaks line this more than 100-year-old railroad. The train runs most of the year, including a shortened route out of Durango in winter.

The only impediment to the photography is that the train is moving most of the time. This does not mean that you cannot get great photographs, but it does put a premium on the stops that the train makes along the way. (Note that in the third week of September, the railroad hosts an Annual Photographer's Special, during which the train makes more stops than usual to accommodate fall-color photographers.) In either case, you will not have time to use a tripod; you will be handholding the camera from the car. Therefore, it's important to use a very fast shutter speed, no less than 1/250 second, preferably 1/500 second, in order to freeze the landscape without blurs. Higher ASA-rated films such as 200 or 400 will allow your camera, whether SLR or point-and-shoot, to use faster speeds. But be aware that the higher the ASA, the "grainier" the processed film (see p. 151, *Photographing the Landscape*). Because there will not be any subject matter very close to the train, you won't need much depth of field if you are using an SLR; therefore, you won't be using small apertures and the camera will automatically employ faster shutter speeds.

Incredible views abound along the way: down into the river canyon, up to high peaks, or simply straight across to forests of aspen and conifers. If ever the "snapshot" will make a fine photograph, this is the place! However, beware of one potential problem: high contrast. It takes time for a rising sun to project light deep into a canyon. The contrast between shadowy areas and highlights is usually too great for the film to manage—shadows get darker and highlights brighter than they appear to the eye. So don't compose large amounts of shadowy area in your scene if highlights also exist. One way to mitigate the problem is to take midday trains when the sun is directly overhead and shadows are less dominant (see pp. 126–127, *Photographing the Landscape*).

HIKING

The **Animas Overlook Trail** EASY is a 0.6-mile loop with views of the Animas Valley, the Animas River, and the Needles Range. Wildlife is plentiful, especially birds. From Durango, go north on Main and turn left (west) on 25th Street (which becomes Junction Creek Road). Continue 3.5 miles. The road will enter San Juan National Forest and become Forest Road 171. Drive about 8 miles to the parking lot and trailhead on the right. The 1-mile (one way) **Potato Lake Trail** EASY passes near a lily pond as well as beaver ponds on its way to Potato Lake, better known as Spud Lake. From Durango, go 28 miles north on US 550 and turn east onto Lime Creek Road (FR 591). Go 3.5 miles. The trailhead is just to the left past the lily pond.

The **First Fork** and **Red Creek Trails** MODERATE follow Red Creek through a narrow canyon with exceptionally tall aspen and spruce. The best views—especially striking in autumn—are from Missionary Ridge, the only real challenge of the hike. From Durango, go north to the end of East 3rd Avenue and bear right (northeast) onto Florida Road. Continue on Florida Road 9.6 miles until just past an uphill curve. Turn left at the Colvig Silver Camps sign and go 2 miles. From here you will need to start hiking, unless you have a four-wheel drive, in which case proceed to the parking area on the left side of the road.

Goulding Creek Trail DIFFICULT is a 6-mile round-trip that climbs up the Hermosa Cliffs, where you can sometimes see elk and always enjoy bright foliage in autumn. From Durango, head 17 miles north on US 550. The marked trailhead is on the west side of the highway.

Chicago Basin Trail MODERATE is one of the more unusual hiking trails in Colorado because it's only accessible via the Durango & Silverton Narrow Gauge Railroad. This 8-mile (one way) trail offers access to the Animas River to the south. After crossing Needle Creek, take the left trail fork to Chicago Basin and follow along Needle Creek. The panoramic Needle Mountains become visible as you climb through pine forests to timberline. Fourteeners Sunlight and Windom Peaks and Mount Eolus dominate the horizon. Begin your journey at the depot on the south end of Main Avenue in Durango. Be sure to tell the conductor that you will be departing the train at Needleton Station and when you plan to return. You will need to flag down the train for your return trip to Durango (see Durango & Silverton Narrow Gauge Railroad, p. 359).

HOT SPRINGS

Back in the 1870s, Frank Trimble left his work in the mines to become the first white man to settle at these hot springs just north of Durango. Perhaps Trimble believed, as the Utes do, that the springs are "peaceful waters." Today, **Trimble Hot Springs** has grown to include an Olympic-size swimming pool, two therapy pools, spa, massage, body treatments, and an outdoor Jacuzzi. Temperatures range from 85 degrees in the big pool to 108 degrees in one of the therapy pools. From Durango, head 6 miles north on US 550. Go left (west) on Trimble Lane to the springs. *970-247-0111, www.trimblehotsprings.com.*

MUSEUM

Make the drive southeast on CO 172 to the small town of Ignacio to see the **Southern Ute Indian Cultural Center.** The Ute Circle of Life display here chronicles Ute history and culture and imparts a sense of the tribe's worldview. Check out the beadwork collection and exhibit of costumes worn for the powwow, the Southern Utes' annual social gathering and dance competition. Screenings of *The Colorado Ute Legacy* and *The Bear Dance* enlighten viewers on tribal history and tradition. Ignacio is also the final resting place of famed Uncompahgre Ute Chief Ouray (see Colorado Cameo, p. 379). From Durango, go south on US 550 to where US 160 branches off to the left (east). Continue east for 3 miles to CO 172. Go right (south) 16 miles to Ignacio. The cultural center is in the middle of town. *970-563-9583, www.southernutemuseum.com.*

RAFTING

Rafting on the **Lower Animas River** EASY offers views of wildlife and old mining camps, with a few Class II–III rapids thrown in for fun. The **Upper Animas River** DIFFICULT is classified as Class IV–V whitewater. While the views of the San Juans near Silverton are spectacular, I highly recommend paying attention to your river guide on this 28-mile stretch of river. The **Piedra River** MODERATE runs from Durango to Pagosa Springs. Because of its stunning, rugged nature, this portion of the Piedra is under consideration for designation as a federally protected Wild and Scenic River. Keep your eyes open for wildlife, especially the elusive river otter (see Scenic Location No. 120, p. 338). *For information and reservations: Mountain Waters Rafting, 643 Camino del Rio, Durango, 970-259-4191, 800-585-8243, www.durangorafting.com; Mild to Wild, 53 Rio Vista Cir., 970-247-4789, 800-567-6745, www.mild2wildrafting.com.*

ROCK CLIMBING

The **Golf Wall** is a natural formation north of Durango with more than 40 sport routes, nestled just north of The Cliffs at Tamarron golf course. Follow US 550 north and look for a pull-off on the left side of the road just below the cliffs. *For information: Pine Needle Mountaineering, Durango Mall, between 8th and 9th Streets on Main Ave., 970-247-8728, www.pineneedle.com.*

RODEO

The **Durango Pro Rodeo Series** attracts local cowhands as well as professional rodeo riders, so you will see all levels of ability. The rodeo is held from mid-June through mid-August at the La Plata County Fairgrounds on Main Avenue at 25th Street. *970-946-2790, www.durangoprorodeo.com.*

THEATER

Don't miss the opportunity to experience Durango's best professional theater at the **Henry Strater Theatre.** This world-renowned venue, formerly known as the Diamond Circle Theater, has been wowing audiences for forty-seven years and is one of the oldest and longest running theaters in Colorado. The theater has recently been renovated and now operates year round, featuring a variety of community, theater, and live music productions. Located inside the historic Strater Hotel, *7th and Main, 970-375-7160, www.henrystratertheatre.com.*

WINTER SPORTS

The Durango Mountain Resort (formerly Purgatory Ski Area), 28 miles north of Durango on US 550, boasts relatively mild winter temperatures. The resort caters to families with its large number of intermediate trails, as well as beginner and expert runs. The Nordic center maintains 15 kilometers of trails. *970-247-9000, www.durangomountainresort.com.* For cross-country skiing or snowshoeing without a trail pass, head to **Haviland Lake,** an especially good destination for beginners (for directions, see Camping, p. 360).

Restaurants

Ore House restaurant, Durango

Dine at the **Ore House** for prime rib and steaks aged on the premises, as well as good seafood ($$-$$$). *147 E. College Dr., 970-247-5707.* **The Red Snapper** ($$-$$$) specializes in both fine seafood and steaks. Enjoy the oyster bar and award-winning salad bar amid the saltwater aquariums in a historic downtown setting. *144 E. 9th St., 970-259-3417.* For elegant dining and great ambiance, try the **Mahogany Grille** ($$-$$$) in the Strater Hotel at 7th and Main. Features seasonal menus and live music; reservations recommended. *970-247-4433.* Fine northern Italian food, complemented by a good wine selection, is the hallmark of **Ariano's** ($$), *150 E. College Dr., 970-247-8146.* **Francisco's Restaurante y Cantina** ($-$$) at 619 Main Ave. is famous for Enchiladas Durango and margaritas. *970-247-4098.*

Brewpubs are flourishing in Durango, with menus that range from breakfast to burgers to stick-to-the-ribs dinners. For good food and a beer, try the **Steamworks Brewing Co.** ($-$$) at 801 E. 2nd Ave., *970-259-9200,* **Carver Brewing Co.** ($$) at 1022 Main Ave., *970-259-2545,* and **Lady Falconburgh's Barley Exchange** ($-$$) at 640 Main Ave., *970-382-9664.* For barbecue and Western entertainment, check out **Bar D Chuckwagon** ($$). The stage show includes cowboy songs, storytelling, and comedy. The Bar D Ranch is quite a spread, including gift shops of all descriptions, 9 miles north of Durango on County Road 250. *970-247-5753, www.bardchuckwagon.com.*

Accommodations

For a taste of 1880s Durango, stay at the historic **Strater Hotel** ($$-$$$) at 7th and Main Avenue. A friendly staff adds to the elegant Victorian surroundings. Amenities include a fine restaurant, Henry's (see Restaurants, above), the Diamond Circle Melodrama (see Theater in this section, p. 363), and live honky-tonk piano in the Diamond Belle Saloon. *970-247-4431, www.strater.com.* **The General Palmer** ($$-$$$$) is another exquisite Victorian hotel in downtown Durango. *567 Main Ave., 970-247-4747, 800-523-3358, www.generalpalmerhotel.com.*

Durango has an ample selection of excellent B&Bs—some in town and accessible to activities, others in outlying areas that make for a more laid-back getaway. **Aspen Grove Retreat** has a warm country charm in a secluded location. A room includes a private, fully-stocked kitchen, a sunroom, a private patio, and accesss to the large garden area. *3935 County Road 250, 877-972-5433, www.aspengroveb-b.com.* The award-winning **Leland House Bed & Breakfast Suites** and **Rochester Hotel** ($$-$$$) at 726 E. 2nd Ave. in Durango are historic inns. *970-385-1920, www.rochesterhotel.com.* The elegant **Gable House Bed & Breakfast** ($$) is on the National Register of Historic Places and conveys a sense of privacy despite its easy access to town. *805 E. 5th Ave., 970-247-4982, www.creativelinks.com/gablehouse/gable.htm.*

The **Apple Orchard Inn** ($$) and **Blue Lake Ranch** ($-$$$$) are both highly acclaimed and award-winning B&Bs in restful rural settings. To reach the Apple Orchard Inn from Durango, go 6 miles north on US 550 to Trimble Lane and turn left (west), then turn right (north) on County Road 203. Continue 1.4 miles to the inn. *970-247-0751, www.appleorchardinn.com.* To reach Blue Lake Ranch from Durango, go west on US 160 to the town of Hesperus, then south 6.5 miles on CO 140. *970-385-4537, 888-258-3525, www.bluelakeranch.com.* Another superior B&B with a French flair is the **Lightner Creek Inn** ($$-$$$). From Durango, go west on US 160 for 3 miles, turn right at Lightner Creek Road (CR 207), and continue 1 mile. *999 County Road 207, 970-259-1226, www.lightnercreekinn.com.*

Special Events

Watching kayakers race down a quickly moving slalom course right in the heart of Durango is sure to get anyone's adrenaline pumping. **Animas River Days** attracts kayakers from across the region to race this challenging course during the last weekend in June. *970-247-3893, www.riversports.com/events/animasriver.php.*

Every August, the **La Plata County Fair and Fiesta Days** draws participants and spectators from across the region. It is a classic county fair at its best, with entertainment, food and craft competitions, and a traditional Western rodeo. Head to the La Plata County Fairgrounds on Main Avenue at 25th Street. *970-247-0312.*

For More Information

Durango has an excellent visitor center adjoining a park at 111 S. Camino del Rio. *970-247-0312, 800-525-8855, www.durango.org.*

Silverton

(see map on p. 366)

A natural, restful stop after you descend Red Mountain Pass, Silverton envelops the weary traveler in solace and seclusion. This quaint mountain town is also a true snapshot from the past. You can imagine the sounds of laughter and honky-tonk piano rising from the saloons on Greene Street and the commotion of the red-light district on Blair Street. Without fancy resort distractions—no hot springs, no standard ski resort, and certainly no golf games or tennis matches—Silverton instead dazzles with the grandeur of its four surrounding peaks: Kendall, Anvil, Boulder, and Sultan. This summertime destination has plenty of charm; in winter, Silverton hosts training in avalanche safety, a constant concern on treacherous US 550.

One of my fondest memories is of Silverton's local marching brass band warming up for the annual Fourth of July parade. I've heard better brass bands but have never seen one that had as much fun. Store owners, innkeepers, clerks, and waiters came out to cheer and, in some cases, jeer the playing of their neighbors. A great time was had by all, and it struck me that this communal moment reflected the honesty of this Western frontier town. Spend time in Silverton, where the spirit of the Old West still clings; you won't be disappointed.

History

The treaty of 1868 that gave all of San Juan County to the Utes wasn't worth the paper it was written on after the discovery of gold and silver soon thereafter. Chief Ouray, having seen the inevitable, gave up millions of acres of Ute land in hopes of averting bloodshed between his people and the miners and their followers (see Colorado Cameo, p. 379). Chief Ouray understood that there could be no stopping the hordes of prospectors and settlers.

During this treaty-busting, silver-rush era, the mining camp once known as Baker's Park (after a miner) became Silverton, the town of Silver, in 1874. Silverton's prosperity was assured when, in 1882, the railroad arrived (now the Durango & Silverton Narrow Gauge Railroad), a vast improvement over the mule teams that had moved ore and supplies over mountain wagon roads. Silverton was one of the most rowdy mining towns in Colorado. Claims were jumped, and gunfights took place almost daily. Proper citizens even brought in lawman and gunslinger Bat Masterson, of Dodge City fame, to impose some order. (Summer tourists are startled when local actors stage gunfights on Blair Street.)

After the 1893 Silver Panic, mining largely died out in Silverton. But it wasn't until 1991 that Silverton's last mine, the Sunnyside Mine, shut down. Today, what had been "the mining town that never quits" is the backdrop for movies and the final destination of the historic narrow-gauge railroad from Durango. Silverton depends on tourists spending some time in these magnificent mountains.

Main Attractions

DURANGO & SILVERTON NARROW GAUGE RAILROAD

During summer, trains on this historic route make a daily, two-hour stop in Silverton. See Main Attractions, Durango, p. 359.

FOUR-WHEEL-DRIVE TRIPS AND GHOST TOWNS

Of the many sites I have photographed around towns and cities that got their start as mining camps, none have struck me as more hostile to miners than those in the San Juans. A great way to see these amazing, towering mountains and appreciate what it was like to extract silver and gold in the old days is to take a jeep trip. Silverton's history suffuses its present no more vividly than in its precipitous backcountry. You will be rewarded with both unforgettable panoramas and with glimpses into the now-vanished towns and abandoned mines and mining camps of a storied era. But take advantage of the excellent jeep tours rather than endangering your safety: This is hazardous terrain.

The **Alpine Loop National Backcountry Byway** (see Main Attractions, Lake City, p. 347) originally served miners with mule-drawn wagons who carted their ore between Silverton, Ouray, and Lake City. The Alpine Loop road system extends 65 miles, many of them accessible by car, with lofty views and relative seclusion. You can reach seven ghost towns on the loop, not to mention options for mountain biking, hiking, camping, and fishing in alpine lakes. The federally designated loop also 4WD traverses two 12,000-foot passes for which you'll need a four-wheel drive, **Cinnamon Pass** and **Engineer Pass** (see Scenic Locations No. 135, p. 374, and No. 136, p. 375). To reach these roads from Silverton, go east on CO 110 (which becomes County Road 2).

Residents of the town of **Animas Forks** (see Scenic Location No. 134, p. 373), established in 1875, worked in 13 surrounding mines. Winter snow depths often exceeded 20 feet, and avalanches were a constant threat. Today, intriguing elements of the town remain intact, including the old jail. On your way to Animas Forks you pass three ghost towns. **Howardsville** was founded in 1872, served briefly as the county seat of La Plata County, and had the first post office in western Colorado. Not much is left now. Two miles above it is **Middleton.** Although nearly a hundred claims were filed here, and three silver-rich mines were nearby, Middleton never became an established community. All you see now are a few miners' cabins. **Eureka,** founded in the 1870s, had a general store, hotel, and smelter, and even published a monthly newspaper. But its buildings fell victim to rockslides; only the foundations remain.

A 60-foot-thick layer of quartz that led to large veins of silver from Mineral Point Mountain made **Mineral Point** a silver boomtown. The gold standard busted the town, which was gone by 1899. Take CO 110 east for 12 miles toward Animas Forks. As you approach Animas Forks, bear to the right side of the Animas River along the road that passes above the town. Go straight and pass the intersection that leads up to Cinnamon Pass,

Continued on page 369

Silverton/Ouray

Colorado Atlas & Gazetteer pp. 66–67, 76–77

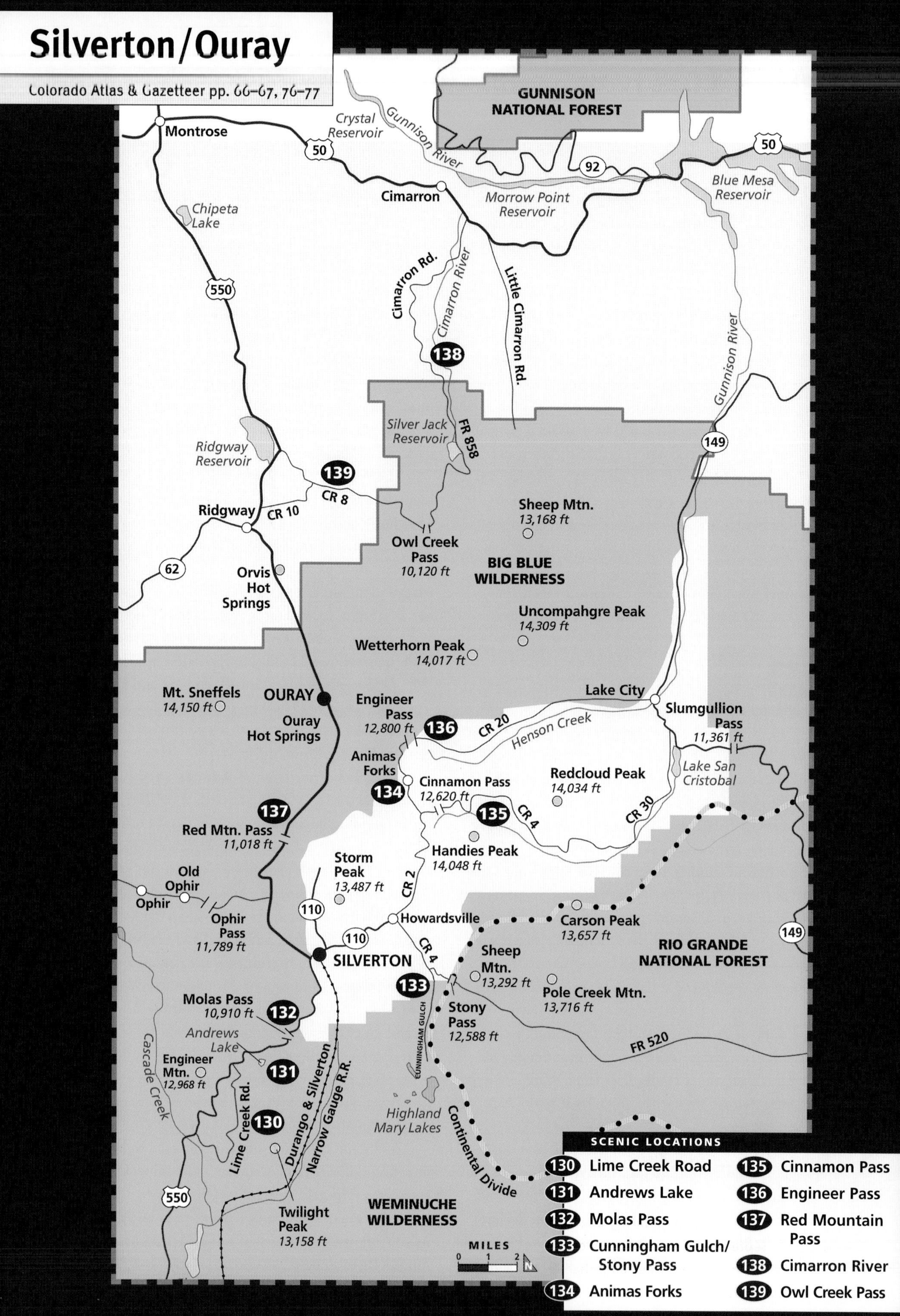

GUNNISON NATIONAL FOREST
Montrose
Crystal Reservoir
Gunnison River
50
92
Blue Mesa Reservoir
Cimarron
Morrow Point Reservoir
Chipeta Lake
550
Cimarron Rd.
Cimarron River
Little Cimarron Rd.
Gunnison River
138
Silver Jack Reservoir
FR 858
149
Ridgway Reservoir
139
CR 8
Ridgway
CR 10
Sheep Mtn.
13,168 ft
62
Orvis Hot Springs
Owl Creek Pass
10,120 ft
BIG BLUE WILDERNESS
Uncompahgre Peak
14,309 ft
Wetterhorn Peak
14,017 ft
Mt. Sneffels
14,150 ft
OURAY
Ouray Hot Springs
Engineer Pass
12,800 ft
136
CR 20
Henson Creek
Lake City
Slumgullion Pass
11,361 ft
Lake San Cristobal
Animas Forks
134
Cinnamon Pass
12,620 ft
135
CR 4
Redcloud Peak
14,034 ft
CR 30
137
Red Mtn. Pass
11,018 ft
Handies Peak
14,048 ft
Storm Peak
13,487 ft
CR 2
Old Ophir
Ophir
Ophir Pass
11,789 ft
110
Howardsville
Carson Peak
13,657 ft
149
RIO GRANDE NATIONAL FOREST
SILVERTON
CR 4
Sheep Mtn.
13,292 ft
Pole Creek Mtn.
13,716 ft
133
Stony Pass
12,588 ft
Molas Pass
10,910 ft
132
Andrews Lake
FR 520
Cunningham Gulch
Engineer Mtn.
12,968 ft
131
Cascade Creek
Lime Creek Rd.
130
Durango & Silverton Narrow Gauge R.R.
Highland Mary Lakes
Continental Divide
550
Twilight Peak
13,158 ft
WEMINUCHE WILDERNESS
MILES
0 1 2
N
SCENIC LOCATIONS
130 Lime Creek Road
131 Andrews Lake
132 Molas Pass
133 Cunningham Gulch/ Stony Pass
134 Animas Forks
135 Cinnamon Pass
136 Engineer Pass
137 Red Mountain Pass
138 Cimarron River
139 Owl Creek Pass

130 SCENIC LOCATION LIME CREEK ROAD

I hate to give this one away, but my mother and father taught me to share. If you love aspen trees and large, craggy mountains, and you would like to see one of the five largest beaver ponds in Colorado, take the 12-mile Lime Creek Road north of Durango. Unfortunately, this unimproved dirt road is very narrow and bumpy, and has a cliff exposure on the way down to the creek. Nevertheless, it is not necessary to engage four-wheel drive if you have it. If you are driving north on US 550 from Durango, Lime Creek Road begins on your right about 3 miles past Purgatory/Durango Mountain Resort and just after the sharp bend in the road where you cross Cascade Creek (marked). From Silverton on US 550, the road starts on your left a little more than 3 miles past Molas Pass.

The southern approach takes you to Scout Lake, which is actually a large beaver pond. In early June, it is covered with blooming lily pads. Aspen trees surround the pond, providing bright green color in late May, dark green in summer, and yellow in late September. Remember, however, that San Juan aspens peak in color at least a week later than Front Range aspens, typically late September to early October. There's even a group that turns red! If you stand on the western edge of the pond, you can see the reflection of the West Needle Mountains. In fact, one of my favorite San Juan Mountain photographs is taken at sunset on a clear day when the sun colors the peaks red. I use a wide-angle lens to include the rocks on the edge of the pond in the foreground all the way up to the sky above the peaks in the background. It's an absolutely outrageous photograph, especially in the fall. When the lilies are in bloom, stand on the southern side of the lake and photograph the reflection of Engineer Mountain (12,968 feet), a conical peak to the north. I prefer a vertical composition for this view—it frames the tall, isolated peak better than a horizontal.

The drive on Lime Creek Road north from the pond takes you down to Lime Creek. Look for the views east across to the flank of Twilight Peak (13,158 feet) as you round the bend with the rock retaining wall. Aspens and cottonwood trees decorate the banks of the creek and make for wonderful views with the creek narrowing into the distance. This is called parallax distortion, which creates depth in a composition by allowing creeks, trails, and roads to serve as "lead-in" lines (see pp. 71, 76–77, *Photographing the Landscape*). On the north end, photograph the road as it winds through aspen groves.

ANDREWS LAKE

Andrews Lake provides spectacular San Juan Mountain reflection photographs. As pretty as is nearby, and better-known, Molas Lake (it can be seen from US 550, Andrews cannot), Andrews provides the better reflection. The reflecting mountain is Snowdon Peak (13,077 feet), which looms behind the lake to the southeast. The Andrews Lake turnoff is well marked and begins on the south side of US 550, 1 mile south of Molas Pass.

Take a short hike to the northwest side of the lake to make the Snowdon Peak reflection photograph. The peak faces west, so sunset is your best bet. The lake is large, enhancing the possibility of wind creating reflection-killing wavelets, so you'll need to be patient (see pp. 129–133, *Photographing the Landscape*). A wide-angle lens works best. Take the Crater Lake Trail from the lake up onto the ridge west of the lake. As you ascend, you will be able to look down on the lake resting in its lovely valley. Compose the lake in the foreground and Twin Sisters, which resemble camel's humps, in the background. These peaks are very green in the summer and complement the blue lake. Note that the lake will only appear blue if blue sky exists overhead; gray clouds will make the lake appear gray.

Now, do yourself a favor. Stay on the same trail and hike the 8 miles to Crater Lake and back. With little elevation change, the hike is relatively easy. Along the way you enjoy views to the west of Engineer Mountain and other spectacular peaks of the San Juans. By the time you get to beautiful Crater Lake, you'll have had a fine view of North Twilight Peak and a couple of hours in Colorado's largest wilderness, the Weminuche.

over a section of slide-rock as you climb up toward Engineer Pass. Where the road forks, go left.

The ghost towns of **Ironton** and **Red Mountain Town** are to the north over Red Mountain Pass. The railroad came to Ironton Park in 1889, and Ironton became a supply center for the rich silver and lead mines. Later gold strikes were fruitless after the Silver Panic of 1893 effectively closed the mines. Ironton is to your left and is marked with a pullout and a historical marker. Red Mountain Town, established in 1879, thrived thanks to four silver-rich mines, including the **National Belle,** which operated until the town was destroyed by fire in 1892. What might have been salvaged was abandoned after the gold standard ended the silver standard during the Panic of 1893. To get there, continue from the top of Red Mountain Pass 0.25 mile; on the north side, take the dirt road that goes east another 0.25 mile to a meadow behind a hill. **Stony Pass** was a supply route connecting Silverton with Creede and Lake City. From Silverton, take CO 110 east to the ghost town of Howardsville, turn right onto CR 4, and go 2 miles to Stony Pass Road on the left (see Scenic Location No. 133, p. 371). *For tour reservations: San Juan Backcountry, 1123 Greene St., 800-494-8687, www.sanjuanbackcountry.com. For jeep rental reservations: Triangle Jeep Rentals, 864 Greene St., 970-387-9990, www.trianglejeeprental.com.* Intrepid mountain bikers enjoy these routes, too (see Mountain Biking, Telluride section, p. 397). *For mountain biking information: Outdoor World, 1234 Greene St., 970-387-5628.*

HISTORIC WALKING TOUR OF SILVERTON

Silverton is a designated National Historic District and retains the feel of an Old West frontier town. Most of the buildings here date from the early 20th century. Wyatt Earp played poker in the saloon that is now the **Backyard Pepper Co.** at 1327 Greene St. The gold-domed **San Juan County Courthouse** has functioned as a county office since 1907. Don't miss the historic **Hillside Cemetery** north of the courthouse. *Maps and detailed descriptions of all the historic buildings are available at the visitor center at the junction of US 550 and CO 110, www.silvertoncolorado.com.*

Activities

CAMPING

Molas Lake Park campground has to be one of the most picturesque campgrounds in Colorado—and the fishing is good! Canoe and horseback rentals are available at the campground; you can even rent a tepee. The Molas Trail (part of the Colorado Trail) is near the south side of the lake. The campground is 5 miles south of Silverton on US 550. *800-752-4494.* **South Mineral** campground, 7 miles west of Silverton, has great views and adjoins a creek and the Ice Lake trailhead. From Silverton, go 2 miles northwest on US 550 and left (west) on Forest Road 585 for 5 miles. No reservations. *970-884-2512.*

CHRIST OF THE MINES SHRINE

The Christ of the Mines Shrine on Anvil Mountain overlooks, and some would say protects, the town of Silverton. This 12-ton statue of Jesus with outstretched arms demonstrates the former centrality of mining here. The statue was carved in Carrara, Italy, of marble from the same quarry that produced the stone for Michelangelo's *David.* In 1959, residents constructed an alcove from the stones of the old Silverton Brewery to protect the newly arrived statue. The shrine was created not just as a tribute to those who worked and died in the mines but in hopes that the mines would once again open and restore prosperity to Silverton.

Miraculously enough, shortly after the shrine was completed the Sunnyside Mine reopened. Soon after, an enormous spring runoff flooded the mine shafts. Had this event occurred on a weekday, hundreds of lives might have been lost. If the miners didn't attend church that Sunday, I bet they did the following Sunday. Even today you will see flowers and notes left at the shrine. The walk up "Shrine Road" starts at 10th Street in town. You can also turn left onto the road as you descend Red Mountain Pass on US 550.

MOLAS PASS

Molas Pass (10,910 feet) is the high point along US 550 between Durango and Silverton. The 3 miles along the highway on either side of the pass afford some of Colorado's greatest roadside views. Peaks abound in all directions: Engineer Mountain (12,968 feet) to the southwest, Twin Sisters (13,432 feet) to the northwest, Sultan Mountain (13,370 feet) to the north, Whitehead Peak (13,259 feet) to the east, and the Needles Mountains of the Weminuche Wilderness to the southeast. Molas Pass is 6 miles south of Silverton on US 550.

Stop at Little Molas Lake 0.5 mile west of the pass. You can drive right to it on an improved, but bumpy, dirt road. Get there after the middle of July and you'll see alpine wildflowers like you've never seen before. Make reflection photographs at sunset of Snowdon Peak (13,077 feet) directly to the southeast. Molas Lake, just north of the pass, is visible from the highway. To the east of Molas Lake are the uniquely shaped peaks of the Needles Mountains, which form a backdrop to the lake and the forested bench on which it sits. Evening light makes this scene one of Colorado's finest. A few old roads and telephone lines in the foreground do affect the integrity of the photograph, but recently some unsightly buildings have been cleared away.

Molas Pass is a great place to pull out the telephoto lens. Instead of composing a scenic with foreground, midground, and background, just zoom in on the mountains around you. These are some of Colorado's most spectacular peaks and make a great photograph all by themselves, especially when colored orange by the rising or setting sun. Or catch them with unique clouds above. Colorful aspens line the way up the pass from either side.

FISHING

The high alpine lakes around Silverton have excellent trout fishing in fairly remote locations. The fishing is superb at **Molas Lake, Little Molas Lake,** and **Andrews Lake** (see Scenic Location No. 131, p. 369). To get to Molas Lake, go 6 miles south on US 550. Molas Lake Road is clearly marked. The road to Little Molas Lake is on the other side of the highway. Andrews Lake is 7 miles south of Silverton on US 550. Four glacial lakes, **Ice Lake, Little Ice Lake, Fuller Lake,** and **Island Lake,** also have excellent fishing, solitude, and wonderful scenery. Connect to these lakes from the trailhead at the west end of South Mineral campground (for directions, see Camping, p. 369). **Clear Lake** has good cutthroat fishing. To get there from Silverton, go to South Mineral campground and take Forest Road 815 for 2 miles. **Crater Lake** and **Highland Mary Lakes** also have good fishing (for directions, see Hiking, p. 372). Unfortunately, because of the pollution from mines, stream fishing in the area is very poor, and you shouldn't eat what you catch. *For information on fishing tours: San Juan Backcountry, 1123 Greene St., 800-494-8687, www.sanjuanbackcountry.com.*

CUNNINGHAM GULCH/ STONY PASS

The area north of Silverton contains some of Colorado's most scenic four-wheel-drive roads, with Engineer, Cinnamon, and Stony Pass roads being the most popular. The Cunningham Gulch road exits the gulch after 2 miles and crosses the Continental Divide at Stony Pass on its way ultimately to Rio Grande Reservoir. Stony Pass is the easiest of the three to drive, and though it does require a sturdy high-clearance vehicle, four-wheel drive does not necessarily need to be engaged. Take CO 110 north to the old town of Howardsville. Turn right on County Road 4 and proceed southeast up the gulch. You can drive your car quite a distance if you don't mind the potholes, but take the four-wheel drive if you want to see it all.

Some views here are remarkable for the old mine buildings, others for just the mountain scenery. I love to photograph old mine buildings; their weathered tones of brown and beige are beautiful on color film. The walls can be photographed close-up, revealing the grain of weathered wood, or the whole building can serve as foreground below towering peaks in a scenic image. One of my favorite compositions is looking through a window from inside to outside. The window can outline a view, making the whole scene look like a framed photograph. When you do this, however, make sure that the inside wall is lit with the same sun as the outside scene so that you do not have high contrast. Even so, you can make the image inside an unlit building. Just make certain that you point your camera first through the window and calculate the exposure of only the outside view. In the photograph, the wall will become darker, almost black, but the scene outside will be just right. See Scenic Location No. 26, Mayflower Gulch (p. 109), for a full explanation of this technique.

You can follow CR 4 all the way up Cunningham Gulch. At its end is a trail for the wonderful day hike to the Highland Mary Lakes. Or you can take a left on CR 3 to get to Stony Pass. Just follow the signs. This road ascends quickly and the views of the surrounding peaks will appear immediately. The higher you go the better it gets. Once on top of the pass, you are above timberline at more than 12,000 feet and can see the Continental Divide winding its way north and south. The tundra flowers peak between mid-July and mid-August. Compose flowers in the foreground and peaks behind. You won't believe how green the grasses get so high up, and how beautiful they are in combination with a Colorado blue sky.

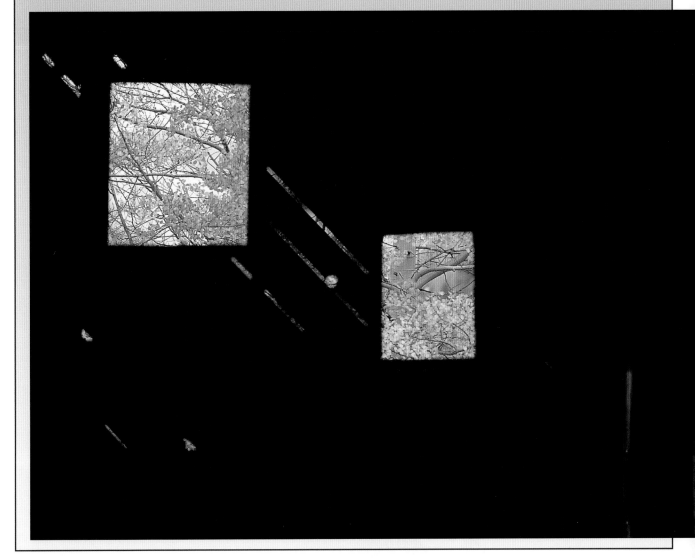

HIKING

Trails here, from gentle to strenuous, all lead to relative solitude and tranquility. For a peaceful walk along the Animas River, take the **Cement Creek Trail** EASY. The trail starts north of Silverton at Memorial Park. The **Kendall Mountain Trail** MODERATE is across the Animas River and past Cement Creek southeast of Silverton. The 6.5-mile (one way) trail veers right and goes around Kendall Mountain. The **Lackawana Mill Trail** EASY starts at the Kendall Mountain Recreation Area southeast of town.

The **Crater Lake Trail** MODERATE takes you through dense pine forests and open, flowered meadows to Crater Lake at the base of Twilight Peak. Twilight and Snowdon Peaks are accessible from the trail. Ascending either peak earns you a fabulous view of the Needles and the Grenadiers. To get there, go to Andrews Lake, 7 miles south of Silverton on US 550. The 5.5-mile trail starts from the southern end of the lake. The 13-mile **Clear Creek Trail** DIFFICULT takes you through forests to the Elk Creek Trail and Animas River. The Elk Creek Gorge is narrow, and the canyon walls are steep. To get there, go to Molas Lake (for directions, see Fishing, p. 370); the trailhead is 0.2 mile south of the parking area. Because of its difficulty and remoteness, the 5-mile **Columbine Lake Trail** DIFFICULT is a favorite of hardy mountain dwellers and ends below Columbine Lake. Pick up the trail 9 miles north of Silverton. Past Burrow Bridge, take the road to the north and look for the signed trailhead.

The **Cunningham Gulch Trail** DIFFICULT climbs above timberline and links to the Continental Divide Trail. The wildflowers and the views of the Grenadier Range are sublime (see Scenic Location No. 133, p. 371). To get there, take CO 110 east from Silverton. Follow signs to the Old Hundred Mine; after 5 miles turn right just past the Howardsville Bridge. Go 2 miles into upper Cunningham Gulch to the trailhead. (If you have a four-wheel-drive vehicle you can go another mile.) Good fishing at Highland Mary Lakes awaits you at the end of this 5-mile hike.

The 8.9-mile **Elk Creek Trail** DIFFICULT leads you into the Weminuche Wilderness with tremendous views of Arrow, Vestal, and Trinity Peaks in the northern Grenadier Range. Start at Molas Lake (see Fishing, p. 370) and hike 5 miles down the Molas Trail to Elk Park. Or take the Durango & Silverton Narrow Gauge Railroad to the Elk Park stop (see Main Attractions, Durango, p. 359). *For information: Outdoor World, 1234 Greene St., 970-387-5628.*

MINE TOURS

The 1-hour **Old Hundred Gold Mine Tour** may be the best mine tour in Colorado. Descend 1,600 feet into Galena Mountain via an electric "mantrip" car that formerly took miners underground for their shift. Your guide explains and demonstrates the machinery used to extract gold and silver from rock. See an actual gold vein and crystal formations in the shafts in which miners labored from 1904 to 1972, when the mine closed. This is as close to the real thing as many of us will ever get—or want to get. Check out the 1904 Cliff Dwellers Boarding House where the miners lived 2,000 feet above on Galena Mountain. Children can pan for gold and probably take a few flakes with them as the sluice is "salted." To get there from Silverton, take CO 110 through town. Pass the courthouse and take the right fork 2 miles past the **Mayflower Mill** entrance. Stop here to see the aerial tram that actor Jimmy Stewart employed in the Western classic, *Night Passage. 970-387-0294.* To continue on to Old Hundred, proceed 2 miles on this gravel road to the ghost town of Howardsville. Cross the creek, turn right onto County Road 4, and drive 1 mile to CR 4A. The way is well-marked with signs. No reservations needed. *970-387-5444, www.minetour.com.*

MUSEUM

San Juan County Historical Society Museum, Silverton

San Juan County Historical Society Museum is at the site of the old town jail and now features a brand new extension, **The Mining Heritage Center.** The museum and heritage center display mining memorabilia, local minerals and handguns, the latter used too often by miners on Saturday nights. Open seasonally. Children under 12 get in free. Ask about the Heritage Pass, which includes tickets to the Museum and Heritage Center, the Mayflower Gold Mill Tour, and the Old Hundred Gold Mine Tour (both mentioned in the Mine Tours section). *15th and Greene St., 970-387-5838, www.silvertonhistoricalsociety.org*

SCENIC DRIVE

Silverton has a central position on the 236-mile **San Juan Skyway,** a federally designated National Scenic and Historic Byway that connects Silverton with Ouray, Ridgway, Telluride, Dolores, Cortez, and Durango. The Skyway's Red Mountain Pass (see Main Attractions, Ouray, p. 379, and Scenic Location No. 137, p. 378) segment from Ouray to Silverton is justifiably renowned for its splendor. Continue to Durango, 48 miles south, on the Skyway (US 550) encircled by the magnificent and craggy San Juans, through forests, over 10,000-foot passes, and along the Animas River. The Animas River Canyon is on the left (east). The rugged peaks of the Weminuche Wilderness make a spectacular backdrop for Molas Lake to the east.

Before you reach Molas Pass, look for Bear Mountain (12,987 feet) and Sultan Mountain (13,368 feet); Snowdon Peak (13,077 feet) is to the south (left). To your right, charred remnants from the 1879 Lime Creek wildfire endure. Ascending Coal Bank Pass, you see 13,158-foot Twilight Peak; Durango Mountain Resort is to the west (right). The mountain with the black rock cap is Engineer Mountain (12,968 feet). The West Needle Mountains loom in the east. Soon you drop into rural ranchlands and valleys, entering Colorado's canyon country.

134 SCENIC LOCATION — ANIMAS FORKS

Animas Forks is a scenic old mining town near timberline at 11,584 feet. It contains several restored structures, including an old house with a bay window, that make for great photographs. The mountain scenery around the town is superb. Take CO 110, which eventually turns into County Road 2, north from Silverton 12 miles past the historic towns of Howardsville, Middleton, and Eureka. You will eventually need a high-clearance vehicle (four-wheel drive doesn't need to be engaged) to get there.

Animas Forks was founded in 1877. The original town had stores, saloons, a hotel, assay offices, and more. The climate was always a challenge, especially in winter when avalanches would roar down the mountainsides and destroy the buildings. Nevertheless, Animas Forks was a booming community until the price of silver crashed in 1893. The house with the bay window was the home of Evelyn Walsh McLean, daughter of Tom Walsh, who discovered Ouray's Camp Bird Mine and who once owned the Hope Diamond.

There are many ways to photograph the town. The bay window house is the most photogenic building. I prefer photographing it obliquely, not directly from the front. This allows the house to appear more dimensional. Drive or hike up the road east of town to gain a vantage point looking down on all the buildings. This photograph portrays the town as a whole, not just a collection of buildings.

THEATER

Silverton's delightful and award-winning theater company, **A Theatre Group,** performs such diverse productions as melodrama, comedy, musicals, and works by major playwrights such as George Bernard Shaw and Neil Simon. See them at the **Grand Imperial Hotel.** *1219 Greene St., 970-387-5337.*

WINTER SPORTS

If you don't want to cross Molas and Coal Bank Passes to ski at Durango Mountain Resort (formerly Purgatory Ski Area; see Durango section, p. 364), you can cross-country ski or snowshoe on top of **Molas Pass** EASY (see Scenic Location No. 132, p. 370). Molas Pass has open runs with deep powder, and also check out the trails around Little Molas Lake, west of the highway just before Molas Pass. From Silverton, go 6 miles south on US 550 to the pass. Although the avalanche danger is usually low in this area, be aware of weather and avalanche conditions. *800-982-6103, www.ski-purg.com.*

Silverton Mountain Extreme Ski Area is perfect for more experienced skiers looking for adventure on the slopes. Open seasonally and featuring both guided and non-guided runs.

Continued on page 376

CINNAMON PASS

Cinnamon and Engineer Passes combine to make the Alpine Loop connecting the towns of Lake City, Silverton, and Ouray. The Cinnamon Pass Road follows the Lake Fork of the Gunnison River from Lake City west over the pass at 12,600 feet, then descends Cinnamon Creek to County Road 2 north of Silverton and near the town of Animas Forks. You can continue north to Engineer Pass (see Scenic Location No. 136, opposite) and down Henson Creek back to Lake City. From the Silverton side, reach the pass by turning east off CR 2 at the well-marked sign. From Lake City, proceed south to the Lake San Cristobal turnoff, CR 30, which eventually turns into CR 4 on its way over the pass. Don't forget to stop at Lake San Cristobal (see Scenic Location No. 127, p. 354) on the way down for a photograph. Four-wheel drive is required above timberline for any of these routes. The Alpine Loop cannot typically be driven in its entirety until the snows have given way and some plowing has occurred, usually not before the Fourth of July.

The scenery is all alpine, or above treeline, on the west side of the pass. Lots of rocks give way to tundra higher up. The less precipitous east side contains vast areas of alpine tundra, replete with wildflowers in peak season, usually early July. The Lake Fork of the Gunnison splits two of Colorado's fourteeners from one another, Handies (14,048 feet) and Redcloud (14,034 feet) Peaks. For some relatively easy "peak-bagging," park your car at the intersection of Grizzly Gulch and Silver Creek and hike the trails to their tops. Do both in one day and I guarantee you'll have a healthy appetite for dinner. Otherwise, take a short hike up each drainage and discover lots of photographic possibilities, including creek shots and beautiful forest scenes with the peaks in the background.

The drive along the lower stretch of the Lake Fork is especially photogenic. There are lots of lakes and beaver ponds between fast-flowing intervals of the creek. The willows and grasses along the Lake Fork make for bucolic photographs without a horizon. Park your car and walk to the edge of the creek, then compose scenes that use the creek as a compositional lead-in line. I enjoy photographing the aspens and cottonwoods here in the fall. Remember, however, that San Juan Mountain aspens peak in color at least a week later than Front Range aspens, typically the first week in October.

ENGINEER PASS

This is the granddaddy of Colorado four-wheel-drive roads and passes. The 360-degree views of the San Juan Mountains are unsurpassed. What else would you expect from a 12,800-foot-high road? Engineer Mountain (13,218 feet, not to be confused with 12,968-foot Engineer Mountain near Coal Bank Pass), colored red, orange, and tan, is a photographic bonus for reaching the top of the pass, and the drive down Henson Creek on the east side is full of great views. From Silverton, just keep driving north on County Road 2, the Animas Forks Road, past the Cinnamon Pass cutoff. The views are prodigious, but so are the drop-offs on the west side. You'll want to be in your lowest four-wheel-drive gear as you approach the pass from the west, both to get up the steep switchbacks and to arrest your speed without brakes as you descend the east side. To access the pass from the east, look for the Alpine Loop signs on the south end of Lake City.

The west side of the pass is too steep and intimidating for much stopping and picture-taking. Just wait until you get to the left-hand turn about 0.5 mile before the pass. If you take this prominent side road, you'll end up on the end of a ridge that sticks out west. It's not as hard as it looks, so go for it. The reward is views in all directions. If you wait until sunset to leave, you won't believe what the setting sun will do to the tundra and mountains. On a clear day, everything will light up all around you. Just pull out the telephoto lens and start snapping shots of the various mountain ranges. The image of Engineer Mountain to the north will amaze you. The red light makes an already red mountain unreal.

The descent of the east side of Engineer Pass reveals views of two of Colorado's most uniquely shaped peaks, Uncompahgre (14,309 feet) and Wetterhorn (14,017). You can make incredible photographs right off the road by composing tundra in the foreground, and the two peaks side by side in the background. Again, evening light catches the peaks best, though sunrise illuminates a part of each peak, too. The best aspens exist below the north side of the pass. Leafing occurs early in June; fall color peaks the first week in October.

970-387-5706, www.silvertonmountain.com. For more family-friendly skiing and other winter activities, check out **Kendall Mountain Recreation Area.** Open weekends or available for private weekday skiing by reservation. *970-387-5228, www.skikendall.com.*

Restaurants

My favorite watering hole is the **Gold King Dining Room,** or Grumpy's, at the **Grand Imperial Hotel** ($-$$) at 12th and Greene Street. The bar and dining room have the feel of a frontier town, with rustic, wooden floors and stuffed trophies on the wall. The piano player, Dan Messinger, is incredible. This guy can play honky-tonk tunes, country, classical, and American favorites in a continuous melody without missing a note. Give him a good tip! *970-387-5834.* **Handlebars Food & Saloon** ($$), also brimming with stuffed game trophies, is known for steaks, ribs, and buffalo burgers. *117 E. 13th St., 970-387-5395.* The **Pickle Barrel** ($$) is a favorite gathering place where you can enjoy sandwiches and beer. *1304 Greene St., 970-387-5713.* **High Noon Hamburgers** ($) is great for the whole family. Lunch is served daily—restaurant open seasonally—and features great burgers, salads, homemade soups, and ice cream. Family owned since 1969. *1205 Blair St., 970-387-5516.* The old red-light district on Blair Street now has several reasonably priced (and now respectable) restaurants, such as the **Bent Elbow Saloon,** at *1114 Blair St., 970-387-5775.*

The Pickle Barrel restaurant, Silverton

Accommodations

I like the **Grand Imperial Hotel** ($$) because of its elegance, history, and central location on the corner of 12th and Greene. *970-387-5527.* The **Teller House** ($), built in 1896 is like the Grand Imperial. It reflects the Victorian era from furnishings to beautiful woodwork. *1250 Greene St., 970-387-5423, www.silvertoncolorado.com.*

Grand Imperial Hotel, Silverton

Wingate House, Silverton

Silverton also has three excellent historic B&Bs. Outfitted with antiques, the **Wyman Hotel & Inn** ($$) is listed in the National Register of Historic Places. Wyman's Go First Class Railroad Package bundles your stay with a ride to Durango in the parlor car of the narrow-gauge railroad. *1371 Greene St., 970-387-5372, www.thewyman.com.* The same family has owned the **Villa Dallavalle Inn** ($$) since 1901. "Home of the people of the valley," this comfortable place exudes a tangible sense of history. *1257 Blair St., 970-387-5965.* The restored, appealing **Wingate House** ($-$$) was built in 1886. *1045 Snowden, 970-387-5520, www.wingatehouse.com.*

Special Events

Imagine festive contests in hard-rock mining activities, Silverton style, and you have **Hardrockers Holidays—A Traditional Mining Celebration.** Check out competitions in singleman drilling (making two holes into solid rock without a machine breakdown), hand mucking (filling a barrel full of gravel the fastest), and other events. Kids participate in their own hand mucking and other competitions. The mountains around Silverton echo with laughter during the event, held in early August. *970-387-5654, www.silvertoncolorado.com.*

You can celebrate other aspects of Silverton's mining history as well as craftsmanship of the turn of the last century at special fall events. In mid-September, the annual **Colorfest Quilt Show** features displays of antique quilts and elegant, handcrafted, traditional quilts for sale. Of course, if the quilt show is too tame for you, you can always join in the lively **Bordello Costume Ball** in October at the Grand Imperial Hotel. *970-387-5654, www.silvertoncolorado.com.*

Not to be outdone by its more famous neighbor to the west, Telluride, Silverton hosts many fine music festivals of its own. The **Silverton Jubilee Folk Festival** brings bluegrass and folk music to town during the first weekend in July. Musicians such as Laura Love, Mollie O'Brien, The Whites, Terri Hendrix, and the Reeltime Travelers have performed here. The always-entertaining **Silverton Barbershop Music Festival** in mid-July attracts top barbershop quartets. Or attend the resounding **Brass Band Festival** in mid-August.

For More Information

Silverton's visitor center is at the junction of US 550 and CO 110. *970-387-5654, 800-752-4494, www.silvertoncolorado.com.*

Ouray

(see map on p. 366)

Nestled at the base of the San Juans is the picturesque town of Ouray, often called the Little Switzerland of America both for its beauty and attractiveness to international visitors. Named after the famous Ute chief (see Colorado Cameo, p. 379), Ouray is an old mining town and a designated National Historic District full of restored and colorful Victorian homes and surrounded by sheer rock walls. The beautiful but perilous Red Mountain Pass Road, or Million Dollar Highway (US 550), begins just south of town (it becomes Main Street in Ouray). On this road you can see glorious scenery and a window onto Colorado's mining past (see Scenic Location No. 137, p. 378). Ouray is well-known for its soothing hot springs: More than 300 hot springs feed the town's swimming pools. A leisurely stroll down Ouray's Main Street also soothes with its old-time tranquility.

History

Ouray owes its founding to the discovery of silver and later gold, and today's town still reflects that legacy. Legend tells that two prospectors discovered a ledge of pure gold at Oak Creek in 1863. They built a hot fire against the ledge, then threw cold water on it, fracturing the ledge and freeing 100 pounds of gold-rich ore. The smoke from the fire alerted the Utes, and although the men escaped with their lives, they lost the ore and the mine. Although this story is the stuff of legend, by the 1870s Ouray was indisputably the heart of the silver mining boom in this area. Ouray owed its mining fortunes first to the cracks, or faults, produced by long-dead volcanoes, faults through which minerals worked their way up from deep inside the earth.

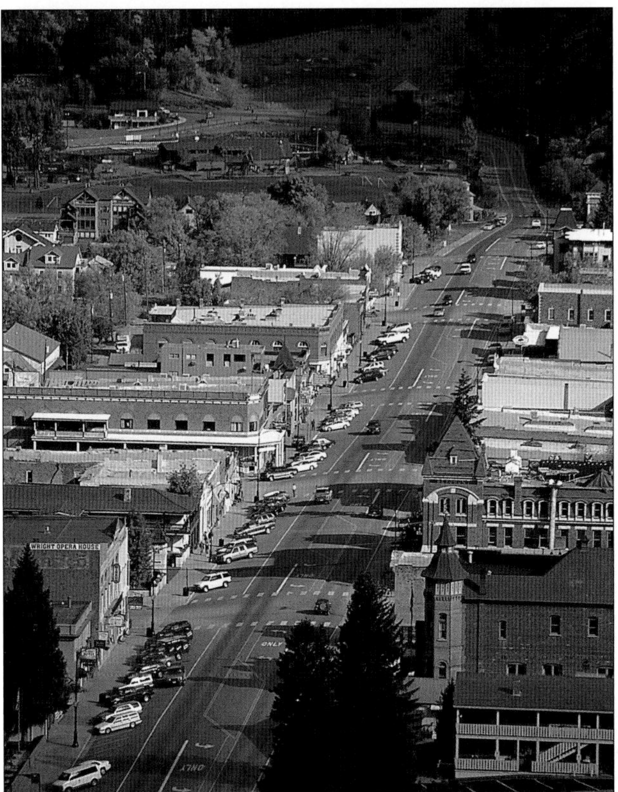

Main Street (US 550), Ouray

Ouray's fortunes were also due to Otto Mears, who built a road over Red Mountain Pass (the Million Dollar Highway, today's US 550) that connected Ouray with nearby mining towns such as Ironton and eventually Silverton. This road was critical in keeping Ouray a viable supply point for the mines. Though the devastating Silver Panic of 1893 closed most of these mines, Ouray got lucky again when a rich gold strike was made in Yankee Boy Basin at the Camp Bird Mine in 1896. The owner, Thomas Walsh, became one of the country's richest men when he sold the mine in 1902 for more than $5 million.

Ouray was and still remains sacred to Ute tribes because of the natural hot springs here. The Utes also valued this portion of the Uncompahgre River for its abundance of game. Today, people continue to be drawn to Ouray for its many riches. These riches include not just the hot springs, but charming historical buildings, magnificent scenery, and a sense of peace.

Main Attractions

HOT SPRINGS

Thanks to its San Juan Mountain setting, Ouray is a source for more than 300 hot springs. We are blessed that several of the major springs are open to the public. **Ouray Hot Springs Pool,** on your right as you enter the town from the north, features a 250- by 150-foot outdoor pool that holds about a million gallons of water. The temperature varies from 76 to 105 degrees. Open year-round, this popular pool welcomes free-form and lap swimmers, as well as soakers. Taking a dip under the stars is a favorite local pastime. In winter, the steam and mist rising from the waters give the pool an otherworldly quality. Fitness amenities are generous; be sure to plan around pool cleaning days. There is a small admission fee. *970-325-7073.*

Ouray Hot Springs Pool

Hot springs pour into the **Wiesbaden Hot Springs Spa and Lodgings** ($$-$$$) at temperatures from 85 to 134 degrees. The Utes considered these miracle waters. Ruins of Chief Ouray's adobe home are on the Wiesbaden property. In addition to the outdoor swimming pool and Lorelei private outdoor spa (both fed by the hot springs), the Wiesbaden is known for its natural vapor cave, where hot springs emanate directly from the mountain into the cave at temperatures of 106–108 degrees. Also available here are therapeutic massages, acupressure, reflexology, facials, and mud and herbal wraps. The Wiesbaden is a wonderful place to stay, within walking distance of Main Street, yet quiet and peaceful. To get there, turn east from Main Street (US 550) at 6th Avenue and go 2 blocks. *625 5th St., 970-325-4347, www.wiesbadenhotsprings.com.*

RED MOUNTAIN PASS

Probably the most famous of Colorado's highway passes is Red Mountain Pass, and for good reason. It is the apex of Otto Mears' historic Million Dollar Highway, today's US 550, and one of our most scenic routes through 19th-century mining country. This highway is at the heart of the world-famous San Juan Skyway Scenic and Historic Byway. Here you proceed with unprotected exposure to the Uncompahgre River canyon into the thick of San Juan jeeping country. This scenic location encompasses not just the 11,018-foot pass but the complete stretch of highway between Ouray and Silverton.

Just south of Ouray, head west in your car on the improved dirt toll road (Forest Road 853) up to Camp Bird, site of Thomas Walsh's fabulously productive mine that yielded valuable ore well into the 20th century. There are a few steep places, and exposure, so keep your eyes peeled straight ahead if you have a fear of heights. It's worth it—along the way you'll pass beautiful aspen groves within a deep mountain canyon, and spectacular mountain views when you reach the mine. If you are four-wheeling, continue over Imogene Pass to Telluride. Back on US 550, you will soon be driving the most precipitous stretch of the route, where the Uncompahgre River flows far below almost vertical cliffs—and there's no guardrail! Stop the car at the Bear Creek Falls overlook and snap a photograph of this massive waterfall. As you continue south, notice some of the old mines precariously perched on the vertical wall across the canyon. If you are jeeping, head east on FR 878 to get to Engineer and Cinnamon Passes the hard way—it's a very rough stretch of unimproved road. Novices should take a jeep tour.

As you approach Red Mountain Pass, you will see its namesake on the left. It's the reddest mountain on the planet, and cloudy afternoon light will make it even more red on film. Notice the inaccessible mine structures to the east, part of the Yankee Girl Mine complex. A telephoto lens will allow you to zoom in on the buildings. On the south side of the pass you drop into the Mineral Creek drainage on the way down to Silverton. Stop at the old townsite of Chattanooga just after the big switchback and make a photograph of the beautiful meadow and mountain canyon to the west.

Box Canyon Lodge and Hot Springs ($-$$) boasts the best scenery while soaking. The 13,000-foot San Juan peaks surround the hot springs, and bird feeders draw colorful birds including hummingbirds and blue jays. The springs feed into four wooden tubs on redwood decks at temperatures of 103–108 degrees; they even heat and provide hot water to the lodge rooms. The Box Canyon Lodge's hot springs are only available to guests. The lodge is on the south end of town just before the Million Dollar Highway. *45 3rd Ave., 970-325-4981, 800-327-5080, www.boxcanyonouray.com.*

RED MOUNTAIN PASS

The road over Red Mountain Pass was built by Russian-born businessman Otto Mears in the 19th century to move ore from the mining towns of Silverton and Ouray. This road is often called the Million Dollar Highway, a reference to the cost of building it or the value of the ore hauled across it. One thing is for sure: The highway provides priceless views, particularly in the early summer when the many falls cascade down steep cliff walls, and in autumn (see Scenic Location No. 137, p. 378). The beauty of Red Mountain Pass Road is matched only by its danger; avalanches make this one of the most treacherous roads in the state. The highway department does its best to keep the pass open with snowplows and uses 105mm howitzers to control the snowpack above the highway. The ascent over Red Mountain Pass starts at the south end of Ouray.

Box Cañon Falls and Backcountry: As you begin your ascent of the pass, stop at Box Cañon Falls and City Park. Rushing water falls 285 feet to the stream below. Climb the short trail to the High Bridge to view the falls from above and peer down into the canyon, or take the stairs (watch your footing) to the bottom of the falls to appreciate them at full force. Amid the deafening roar, look for the rare black swift birds that dwell in the canyon's walls and dart in and out of the falls' mists. In winter, ice climbers try their skills in ascending the frozen falls. There is a small admission fee; you can also picnic, camp, and hike here. *970-325-4464.*

Back on the pass, note the jeeps scaling dirt and rock roads. Make no mistake about it, these are world-class *jeep* roads that require both the right vehicle and technical driving expertise. (See Four-Wheel-Drive Trips and Ghost Towns, Silverton section, p. 365, and Telluride section, p. 395.) *For more information and reservations: Colorado West Jeep Rentals and Tours, 701 Main St., 970-325-4014, 800-648-JEEP, www.coloradowesttours.com; Switzerland of America Jeep Tours, 226 7th Ave., 970-325-4484; Canyon Creek Jeep, 827 Main St., 970-325-4833; or Outlaw Tours, 726 Main St., 970-325-0100.*

Mining Past and Present: Take the Box Cañon Falls turnoff, pay the Forest Service fee, and proceed to Forest Road 853, Camp Bird Road, to enter the richly historical **Yankee Boy Basin** through meadows of wildflowers to the abandoned Camp Bird Mine, the townsite of Sneffels, Wright's Lake, and several abandoned mining sites. From here, the adventurous can try to bag 14,150-foot Mount Sneffels or take the breathtaking 2-mile hike to Blue Lakes.

Continue beyond Box Cañon Falls and past the Twin Peaks that tower over Ouray. Crystal Lake is to your right (west). Soon, notice three bare, deep-red peaks to your left (east), the vibrant red colors a result of high levels of iron oxide in the rock: These are the mountains for which the pass is named. Stop by the ghost town of **Ironton,** at about 8

COLORADO CAMEO

Chief Ouray and Chipeta

The reputation of Chief Ouray ("Arrow") as a peacemaker has grown through the years, but he still remains a controversial historical figure among Indian tribes. Ouray's mother was Ute and his father was half Apache, but he was raised by a Mexican family in New Mexico and even attended Mass. He spoke Ute, Apache, Spanish, and some English. In 1850 he moved to Colorado and soon became a well-respected warrior and leader of the Uncompahgre Utes.

After the discovery of gold in the San Juan Mountains, treaties with the Utes became meaningless. Confrontations became more frequent and more bloody. White settlers demanded that the Utes be moved off any land the settlers considered valuable either for mining or homesteading. During the Mexican-American War (1846–1848) and the Taos Rebellion (1847), Ouray had seen how the seemingly endless numbers of U.S. troopers could decimate populations in revolt. He feared for his people and for 20 years pursued negotiations between Washington and the tribes.

Among the five Ute tribes living in the Southwest there was certainly no consensus on how to deal with these invaders. If Ouray did not represent all the tribes, he did in the minds of the whites —and Ouray did nothing to clear up this misrepresentation. He worked both to negotiate a lasting settlement and to urge the tribes to adapt to the ways of the whites. By the 1880s, however, the Utes had been moved to reservations in the barren Four Corners region. To many Utes, then and now, Ouray was a traitor. But many ancestors of today's Utes had not seen the bloodshed Ouray had seen nor did they understand the inevitability of the movement West by the settlers.

Ouray died shortly before the Uncompahgre Utes were moved to a barren reservation in eastern Utah. Brokenhearted from the loss of her husband and the tribal lands, Chipeta, his beloved wife, moved with the tribe. Chipeta was extremely well-respected and is believed to have been the only woman allowed to sit at the Ute Council Tree near Delta. Her remains were returned home and buried on the property of the Ute Indian Museum in Montrose (see p. 290). Chief Ouray is buried in Ignacio, Colorado.

miles, which had been a mining supply and transportation center (see Silverton, p. 369). Ironton is the site of the Iron Dog Challenge sled dog races each January. At Ironton, turn left for **Corkscrew Gulch Road** to reach the summit of Red Mountain No. 1 and the ghost town of **Gladstone.**

You can also see the **Idarado Mine's** huge, ongoing mining operation just below the pass. (The Environmental Protection Agency has ordered the mine to clean up its toxic mine tailings, which have caused severe environmental problems.) After reaching the 11,018-foot pass, you enter the San Juan National Forest. As you drive down Mineral Valley you will continue to see abandoned mines all the way to Silverton. Look for moose in wetlands areas as you descend. The mining legacy of the San Juans has left picturesque, ghostly ruins that continue to fascinate, but enjoy them with care as the old mining structures remain dangerous. Do not enter mine areas without a guide or expert.

138 CIMARRON RIVER

SCENIC LOCATION

I once saw a Nature Conservancy commercial on TV promoting the protection of our nation's last, great natural places. For a setting they chose one of the Cimarron River forks, with its bucolic meadows and gorgeous aspens below serrated peaks. Rolling hills, cottonwoods and aspens, and four major river forks make this place unlike any other in Colorado. From the north: Two-and-a-half miles east of the tiny town of Cimarron, turn south off US 50 onto Cimarron Road. (Don't mistake it for Little Cimarron Road, which turns south a mile later, though this valley is delightful in autumn.) Or drop into the Cimarron drainages from Owl Creek Pass. For directions from Ridgway or Ouray, see Scenic Location No. 139, p. 382.

The road from US 50 begins along the river but soon ascends the side of a sage-covered ridge, which it follows south for several miles. The views east across the drainage of hillsides of aspen and cottonwood are very special, so use the telephoto lens to zoom in on the groves. As you approach Silver Jack Reservoir, notice the serrated spires of the Big Blue Wilderness ahead. You will see amazing scenic compositions that contain meadows, trees, and peaks. You can't make a mistake here!

One mile south of the reservoir, look for the turnoff to the East and Middle Forks. The East Fork road quickly ends at a trailhead, but the Middle Fork road continues up the drainage for a few miles, though the road gets a little rough for a car. Nevertheless, some great photographs can be made along the creek. The road along the West Fork takes you over Owl Creek Pass and down into equally sublime Ridgway country, all navigable by car. I love this drive in late May/early June when the aspens and cottonwoods are leafing. The delicate greens make a great foreground for still-white peaks, while the smells of melting snow and new growth in the cool air stimulate the senses. Be sure to return in the fall.

Activities

CAMPING

Ouray boasts the panoramic **Amphitheater** campground, 600 feet above the town of Ouray. This gorgeous site connects to the Portland/Upper Cascade Falls Trails and is open in winter for snowshoeing. From Ouray, go south on US 550 for 0.5 mile and turn left (east) onto County Road 16. Call early for reservations. *877-444-6777.*

San Juan Hut Systems is great for visitors to southwestern Colorado who are looking for a little adventure with their camping. The system is a series of backcountry huts that you can hike or bike to in the summer or snowshoe and ski to in the winter. There are six wooden huts, each able to accommodate up to eight people. The huts come equipped with padded bunks, propane cook stove, lights, a woodstove, and "necessary kitchen facilities." *970-626-3033, http://sanjuanhuts.com.*

HIKING

The 4.2-mile (one way) **Bear Creek National Recreation Trail** MODERATE provides views of the Grizzly Bear and Yellow Jacket Mines. Ascend 13,218-foot Engineer Mountain by taking the fork to the right at the Yellow Jacket Mine; the left fork takes you back to Ouray. To reach the trailhead, go south 2 miles on US 550 to a tunnel, and park at its south end. The trailhead is on the west side of the highway.

The 1.75-mile one-way **Portland Trail** MODERATE climbs to tremendous views of Ouray and surrounding peaks, including the Twin Peaks, and connects with the **Upper Cascade Falls Trail** MODERATE, a 2-mile (one way) hike up a series of switchbacks to the falls and the Chief Ouray Mine. Both trails begin at the Amphitheater campground (for directions, see Camping, above). To reach the gentler **Lower Cascade Falls** hike, EASY head south on Main Street (US 550) past the visitor center, turn left onto 8th Avenue, and follow it to its end. Other great trails include **Dallas, Weehawken,** and **Oak Street.** Stop at many local stores for trail maps.

HISTORIC WALKING TOUR AND MUSEUM

Ouray County Museum, Ouray

Ouray, a designated National Historic District, hosts a historic walking tour for visitors. *Ouray Chamber Resort Association, 970-325-4746, 800-228-1876, www.ouraycolorado.com.* The **Ouray**

County Museum, housed in the 1887 miner's hospital, will help you (and youngsters) to discover the town's storied mining history. Exhibits include a re-created hard-rock mine and assayer's office. Call for limited winter hours. *420 6th Ave., 970-325-4576.*

MINE TOUR

In 1884, three bachelors discovered silver near Ouray. Investors from Syracuse, N.Y., soon underwrote the prospecting of the

OWL CREEK PASS

They didn't film the John Wayne movie *True Grit* on 11,120-foot-high Owl Creek Pass for nothing! If there is such a thing as a classic San Juan Mountain setting, this has got to be it. This is a place to see in autumn. Aspen trees line the edges of serene little meadows, eroded peaks such as Courthouse Mountain and Chimney Rock forming the backdrop. The road descends toward Ridgway through extensive scrub oak brush that can turn blood red in a good year. See Scenic Location No. 138, p. 381, for directions from US 50. From the Ridgway side, turn east on County Road 10 from US 550, 2 miles north of Ridgway, or 13.5 miles north of Ouray, and continue east on Road 8. You'll see the Owl Creek Pass sign. Your car will be just fine.

The first 2 miles of road west of Owl Creek Pass provide great aspen photographs. Instead of trying to compose big scenics, be content to make "intimate landscapes" with meadows and trees and a little bit of sky (see p. 54, *Photographing the Landscape*). Farther down the road you exit the aspen forest and enter the oak brush. Now you can look back to the east on the incredible ridge of cliffs that forms the western boundary of the Big Blue Wilderness. From the road you can compose oaks interspersed with aspens (yellows combined with reds in the fall) with the ridge in the background.

In this part of the state, the sun can descend very low before disappearing behind the horizon. Therefore, the red light on a clear day is as intense as it gets in the desert, and colors the landscape in warm shades you just won't believe. It can turn pale yellow aspen into red! Now continue down CR 8 and CR 10 past some of the most beautiful ranches in the West. The Sneffels Range to the southwest looms in the distance, while picket fences, cattle, horses, and hayfields make a strong foreground. Photograph the ranches by pointing the camera south at sunset, when sidelighting makes the cottonwoods and oaks glow.

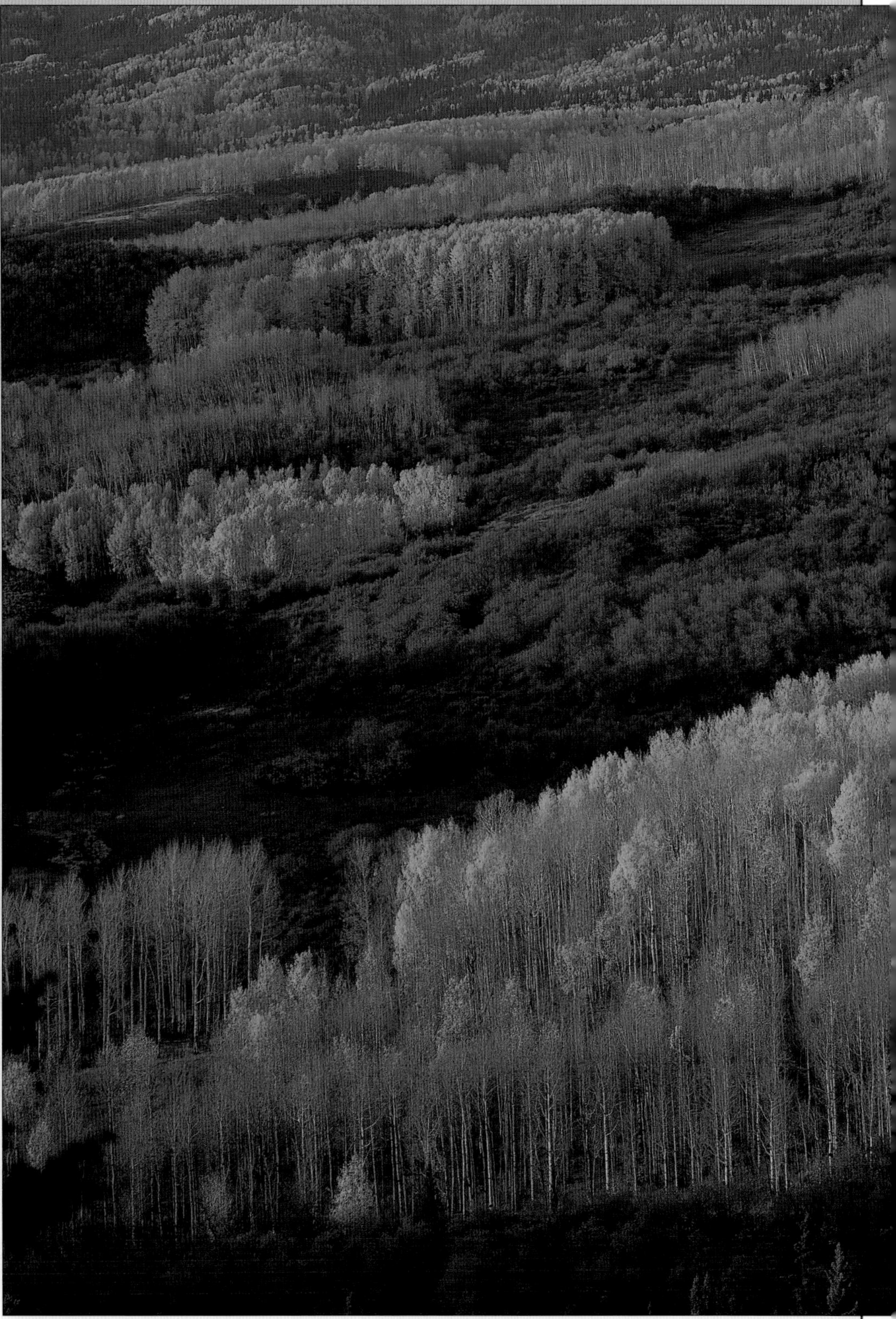

Bachelor shaft. Since that time, the mine has produced $90 million in silver, $8 million in gold, and $5 million in lead, zinc, and copper. A great way to learn firsthand about Colorado's mining history, the **Bachelor-Syracuse Mine** tour takes you inside with real miners as guides. A mine train or "trammer" will take you into "Gold Hill," a 3,350-foot horizontal shaft. Learn how to pan for gold and keep what you find. Dress warmly! From Ouray, go 1 mile north on US 550, turn right (north) on County Road 14, and drive another mile. *970-325-0220.*

THEATER

The **San Juan Odyssey** at the **Main Street Theater** is a new summer event that has everyone talking. This Silver Anniversary edition of the show features the original music from the London Symphony Orchestra and narration from C.W. McCall. Once a 35mm slide that was projected onto five screens to create a fifty-foot panorama, the show has now been completely converted to digital. The feature plays each night during the summer season. *630 Main St., 970-325-4940*

WINTER SPORTS

Cross-country skiers prefer the trails around the summit of Red Mountain Pass. The manmade and sensational **Ouray Ice Park** caters to ice climbers. These ice formations attract climbers from all over the world to nearby Uncompahgre Gorge. *www.ourayicepark.com. For lessons: Above Ouray Ice and Tower Guides, 480 Main St., 888-345-9061, www.towerguides.com.*

Restaurants

The Coachlight ($$-$$$) is a local fine dining favorite, featuring steaks, seafood, and local game. The main restaurant is closed in the winter, but they do deliver pizza on the weekends—and they're known for their great pizza! *118 Seventh Ave., 970- 325-4361.* **Bon Ton** ($$-$$$) in the historic St. Elmo Hotel has been called one of the best restaurants in town. Visit this 100-year-old landmark for beef Wellington, wonderful Italian dishes, and Sunday brunch. *426 Main St., 970-325-4951.* For a great breakfast, visit the new **Ouray Café.** They also serve lunch and dinner and will deliver. *225 7th Ave., 970-325-7989.* **Buen Tiempo** ($) is a popular Mexican spot with outstanding spinach enchiladas. *515 Main St., 970-325-4544.* **The Outlaw** offers excellent steaks and seafood, and their "Outlaw Cookout" takes you and your party to the wilderness for a meal. *610 Main St., 970-325-4366.*

St. Elmo Hotel & Bon Ton restaurant, Ouray

Accommodations

Although you might prefer a place with hot springs on site (see Main Attractions, p. 377), you can select from many fine, historic places to stay in Ouray. (And you can always visit the nearby hot springs.) The 100-year-old, newly renovated **Ouray Hotel** ($-$$) offers charm at a very reasonable price (closed in winter). *303 6th Ave. (at Main), 970-325-0500.* A former boardinghouse for miners, the historic **St. Elmo Hotel** ($$) boasts elegant furnishings and the fabulous Bon Ton restaurant downstairs. *426 Main St., 970-325-4951, www.stelmohotel.com.* The **Hot Springs Inn** ($$) is a family-friendly lodge with forty-two rooms to choose from, each featuring a fun western theme. *1400 Main St., 970-325-7277, 800-706-7790.* **The Secret Garden Bed & Breakfast** ($$) features lovely Victorian accommodations and is a great place for special occasions. *101 6th Ave., 970-325-4226, 970-596-3730, www.secretgardenouray.com.*

The **China Clipper Inn** ($-$$) is a custom-designed B&B with great views. *525 2nd St., 970-325-0565, 800-315-0565, www.chinaclipperinn.com.* Formerly Damn Yankee Country Inn, **Black Bear Manor** ($-$$$) is known for its great breakfasts and access to the Uncompahgre River. *118½ 6th Ave., 970-325-4219, 800-845-7512, www.blackbearmanor.com.* For a truly unique experience, try the **St. Paul Lodge** ($$-$$$), built over the St. Paul Mine at 11,400 feet on Red Mountain Pass. This unique, rustic place is not for everybody, but it rewards the serious cross-country skier or snowshoer. *For directions and reservations: 970-387-5494 (seasonal), 970-387-5367 (year-round).*

The **Beaumont Hotel** ($$$-$$$$), an 1886 landmark, reopened in summer 2003 after an extensive and painstaking renovation (open seasonally). The elegant, slate-roofed structure long beloved of local residents now includes a spa, guest rooms, an outdoor wine and coffee garden, and the excellent **Tundra** restaurant. *505 Main St., 888-447-3255, www.beaumonthotel.com.*

Special Events

Late in January, the **Ouray Ice Festival,** sponsored by the Ouray Ice Park, features ice-climbing and competitions for everyone. You can watch as metal-booted participants with pickaxes make routes over sheer walls of ice, and you can even join in or take a lesson. *www.ourayicepark.com.* Each June, Ouray becomes a foodie paradise with the **Taste of Ouray.** Enjoy delicious samples of local cuisine and beverages. **Grillin', Chillin', & Thrillin'** is an annual music and brewfest held each August in Ouray. The festival features live music, BBQ, and western slope breweries showcasing their favorite brews. And in December, the town holds **Festivus for the Rest of Us,** a holiday street party with bonfires, seasonal food and drinks, and events with a non-traditional holiday theme. *970-325-4746, www.ouraycolorado.com*

For More Information

Ouray Chamber Resort Association, *1230 N. Main., 970-325-4746, 800-228-1876, www.ouraycolorado.com.*

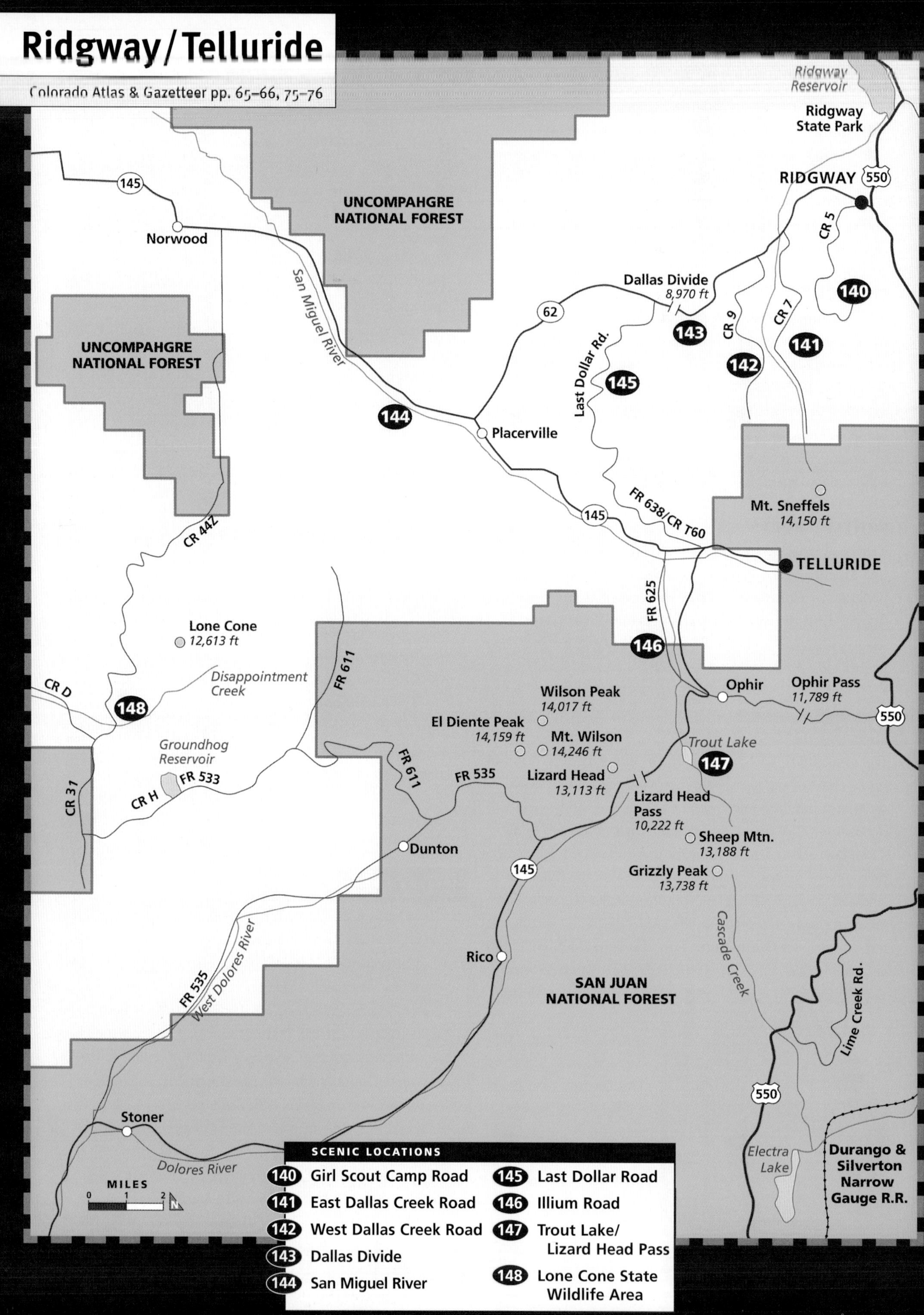

Ridgway/Telluride
Colorado Atlas & Gazetteer pp. 65–66, 75–76
Ridgway Reservoir
Ridgway State Park
RIDGWAY
550
145
Norwood
UNCOMPAHGRE NATIONAL FOREST
San Miguel River
Dallas Divide
8,970 ft
62
CR 5
CR 9
CR 7
140
143
141
142
145
Last Dollar Rd.
UNCOMPAHGRE NATIONAL FOREST
144
Placerville
Mt. Sneffels
14,150 ft
FR 638/CR T60
145
CR 442
TELLURIDE
FR 625
Lone Cone
12,613 ft
146
FR 611
Disappointment Creek
CR D
148
Wilson Peak
14,017 ft
Ophir
Ophir Pass
11,789 ft
550
El Diente Peak
14,159 ft
Mt. Wilson
14,246 ft
Groundhog Reservoir
Trout Lake
147
FR 611
CR 31
CR H
FR 533
FR 535
Lizard Head
13,113 ft
Lizard Head Pass
10,222 ft
Sheep Mtn.
13,188 ft
Dunton
145
Grizzly Peak
13,738 ft
West Dolores River
Cascade Creek
Rico
SAN JUAN NATIONAL FOREST
FR 535
Lime Creek Rd.
550
Stoner
Electra Lake
Durango & Silverton Narrow Gauge R.R.
Dolores River
MILES
0
1
2
N
SCENIC LOCATIONS
140 Girl Scout Camp Road
141 East Dallas Creek Road
142 West Dallas Creek Road
143 Dallas Divide
144 San Miguel River
145 Last Dollar Road
146 Illium Road
147 Trout Lake/ Lizard Head Pass
148 Lone Cone State Wildlife Area

Ridgway

The historic railroad town of Ridgway heralds the entrance to the San Juan Skyway, the picturesque route through the southwestern mountains. Just a short drive from Ouray, Telluride, and Silverton, but far enough away to avoid tourist crowds, Ridgway is a gem all its own. Nearby Ridgway State Park draws people from all over the nation to begin their journey into Colorado's fabled southwest.

History

Nestled in the lush Uncompahgre Valley, the Ridgway area was once prized by the Utes for its plentiful game. Ridgway's pastoral setting and tiny population belie its origins as a lively railroad hub. Named for a rail superintendent, the town was founded in 1891 when the Rio Grande Southern Railroad established a railhead here to serve Ouray and Telluride. Though Ridgway's economy today is based in farming and ranching, it continues to benefit from its proximity to the larger San Juan towns to the south.

Main Attractions

RIDGWAY STATE PARK

Spectacular scenery in every direction is the hallmark of Ridgway State Park. Rising to the south are the rugged pinnacles of the Sneffels Range, while to the east loom Chimney Rock, Courthouse Mountain, and Turret Ridge in the Cimarron Range. To the west, the Uncompahgre Plateau stretches 70 miles toward Grand Junction. Visit Ridgway State Park to camp, picnic, fish, swim, boat, hike, and bike. Then enjoy its easy access to the mountain towns to the south. The park is home to deer, elk, black bears, marmots, eagles, skunks, and myriad waterfowl. Bring your dog to the park, and she'll find plenty of canine company. Fourteen miles of hiking, biking, and nature trails EASY offer good vantage points for wildlife watching. In winter the park is open for cross-country skiing, snowshoeing, and sledding. *970-626-5822, www.coloradoparks.org.*

Camping: With nearly 300 campsites, Ridgway State Park is a great place to spend the night. The **Dutch Charlie Recreation Site** is the largest campground in the park and includes the **Elk Ridge** and **Dakota Terraces** campgrounds, with a combined 187 sites, nature trails, and boat and beach access to Ridgway Reservoir. The **Pa-Co-Chu-Puk** campground (Ute for "Cow Creek"), a few miles north of Dutch Charlie, has hiking and biking trails—including access to the Enchanted Mesa Trail—stocked trout ponds, and trout fishing on the Uncompahgre River. **Dallas Creek Recreation Area** at the south end of the park has fishing and boating access to Ridgway Reservoir. Yurts (circular canvas tents) with electricity, propane heaters, and wood floors are also available. *800-536-5308, www.coloradoparks.org.*

Water Sports: The **Dutch Charlie Recreation Site** provides a good beach and facilities for swimming. Boating and sailing are also popular at the reservoir. **Ridgway Marina** offers boat rentals for all interests, ranging from kayaks and paddleboats to fishing and pontoon boats. *970-626-5094.* **RIGS Fly Shop & Guide Service** offers multi-day trips, guided fly fishing, and white water rafting or kayaking for all levels of experience. *888-626-4460, http://fishrigs.com.*

Activities

CAMPING

Decked with wildflowers in summer, the 60 campsites at secluded **Silver Jack** campground rank right up there with those at Ridgway State Park (see Main Attractions, at left). Take an easy 0.5-mile hike to the Silver Jack Reservoir Overlook. From Ridgway, take US 550 about 1.75 miles north to County Road 10 and turn right. Go about 3.75 miles to CR 8 (Forest Road 858), turn right, and drive roughly 20 miles up this gravel road, over Owl Creek Pass and down to Silver Jack. *970-240-5300.*

FISHING

Some of the best trout fly fishing in the state is in Ridgway State Park as the river parallels US 550 from Ridgway to Ouray, as well as on the **Uncompahgre River** at or below Ridgway Reservoir. Rainbows of 20–24 inches are common in this area. **Beaver Lake** and **Silver Jack Reservoir** are scenic fishing spots favored by locals. Beaver Lake is a short distance up Owl Creek Pass, while Silver Jack Reservoir is about 15 miles on the other side of the pass. (See Camping, above, for directions to Owl Creek Pass.) *For information and guided fishing tours: Gunnison River Expeditions, 195000 S. CO 550, 970-249-0408, www.cimarroncreek.com.*

GOLF

Surrounded by the San Juan and Cimarron Mountains, 18-hole **Divide Golf Course** is exceptionally picturesque. *Golf Digest* named Divide the best new public golf course in 1996. From Ridgway, head west on CO 62 and follow the signs. *970-626-5284.*

HIKING

With great views of Uncompahgre and Wetterhorn Peaks, the 22-mile **Cimarron River Loop** DIFFICULT traverses the Big Blue Wilderness past abandoned mines. Take Owl Creek Pass Road (see Camping, above, for directions). Go south past Silver Jack Reservoir until the road turns west. Continue 0.25 mile past the junction with West Fork Road (Forest Road 860), turn left onto Middle Fork Road (still FR 860), and follow the road 6.4 miles to the parking area.

HORSEBACK RIDING

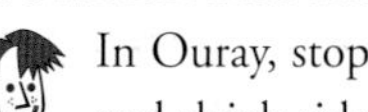

In Ouray, stop by the **Ouray Livery Barn** for trail and sleigh rides. *834 Main St., 970-325-4606 (summer), 970-626-5695 (winter).*

Continued on page 388

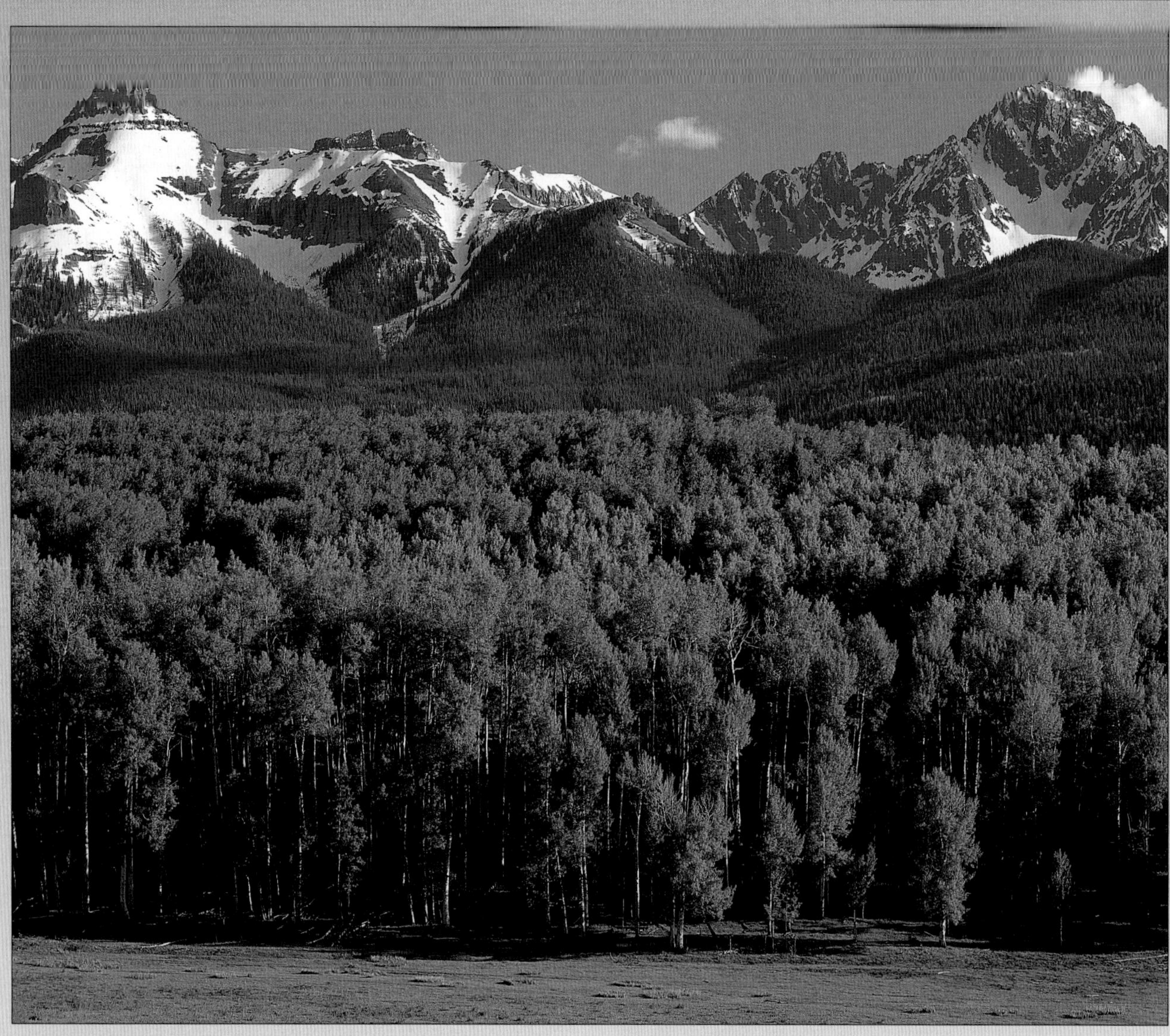

140 SCENIC LOCATION

GIRL SCOUT CAMP ROAD

I hate to give this one away, but sharing's a good thing, right? Three improved dirt roads head south from CO 62 west of Ridgway. All three end close to perhaps the most scenic mountains in Colorado, the Sneffels Range, and the Mount Sneffels Wilderness. All three wind through hillsides and valleys of aspen and scrub oak, enjoy unsurpassed views of the range, and provide public access to the Uncompahgre National Forest. The least known of the three is County Road 5, which leads to a Girl Scout camp, yet it may be the best. Turn south on Amelia Street off of CO 62 on the western edge of Ridgway and make your next right onto CR 5. It's a little bumpy but fine by car.

The road quickly ascends Miller Mesa and places you in the middle of aspen groves and meadows outlined by classic aspen bole fences. Most of the mesa is privately owned, so photography must be done roadside—no impediment at all to making great images here. The road then winds around the mesa for several miles, with 14,150-foot Mount Sneffels always towering in the background. Make various compositions with meadows in the foreground, aspens in the middle, and the Sneffels Range behind. Where the road enters aspen groves, try composing the road as a lead-in line with aspens left and right. It makes an inviting image.

Early June provides the light green of leafing trees, while the first week in October is usually the peak of fall color here. The road is plowed only halfway in winter, so put on a pair of snowshoes or cross-country skis to enter this remarkable world of white. The road is usually packed as a trail leading up to a backcountry ski hut, so you should enjoy easy movement on whatever gear you prefer. Remember that the color white is very reflective. Most photographs of snow-filled scenes look very dark. The camera's light meter sees white and wants to render the scene a medium tone of gray, so it underexposes your photograph. If you use a point-and-shoot, there's not much you can do unless it has a "backlighting" compensation mode, which you should employ in order to add more light to the scene. If you use an SLR, "open up" your exposure 1–1.5 stops with your exposure compensation mode or dial (see pp. 120–122, *Photographing the Landscape*). With some blue sky in the scene, you need less compensation. Bracket your exposures to be safe (shoot both 0.5 stop over and under your first exposure).

141 SCENIC LOCATION EAST DALLAS CREEK ROAD

The most glorious part of this route is toward its end near the Mount Sneffels Wilderness boundary. About 4 miles west of Ridgway, turn south off of CO 62 onto the East Dallas Creek Road (County Road 7) and proceed 6 miles (over a few bumps). The first mile passes by beautiful cottonwood trees growing along the creek. Ralph Lauren's spectacular Double RL Ranch lies just to the west. The cottonwoods make for a scenic foreground with the ranch in the distance, especially in late May and around the second week of October. The road then ascends switchbacks before traversing a long ridge high above the creek. Here you begin to see the Sneffels Range in all its glory. Groves of aspen on the far ridge are a nice foreground for the peaks, so zoom in with a telephoto lens.

After the long traverse, the road winds to the left around the head of the ridge and reveals the best view of Mount Sneffels in the entire Ridgway area. In front of you is one of the most beautiful montane valleys anywhere. Willow bushes, scrub oaks, cottonwoods, and aspens line the creek as it winds through a huge, grassy meadow up to the base of Sneffels. Pull over just after rounding the bend, hop out, and point your camera directly at the mountain. With a wide-angle lens you will be able to compose the entire valley in the scene with Sneffels presiding over all of it. It is simply sublime.

I prefer that the valley be in the light, so I make this image in mid-morning or early evening. The path of the sun cuts obliquely across the meadow, sidelighting all in its path and intensifying the yellows of fall and greens of spring. Tree shadows add depth to the scene. A few white clouds hovering around the top of Sneffels are icing on the cake! Continue photographing details in the valley as the road follows the left-hand edge of the meadow into the coniferous forest on the edge of the wilderness. Then park at the Blue Lakes trailhead and take a marvelous, 3-mile hike to Lower Blue Lake. You won't believe its glacial blue/green color.

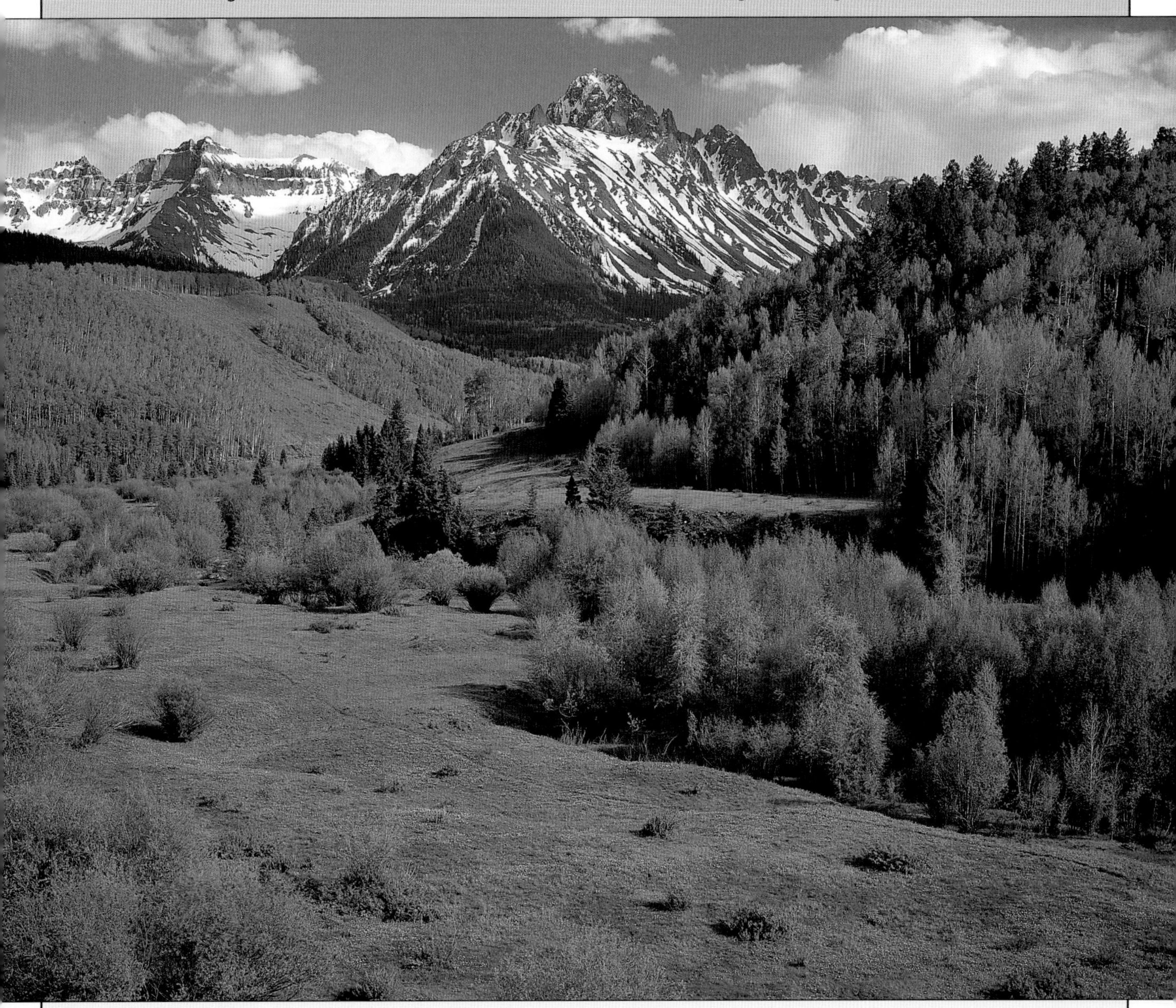

HOT AIR BALLOONING

San Juan Balloon Adventures offers one of the most unique and spectacular site seeing tours you will ever experience. Daily flights are offered May through September, weather permitting. Flights can be arranged by appointment during the off-season. The flight will take you over the Ridgway valley and lasts about 1 hour. Afterwards, you will enjoy champagne and a continental breakfast. *976-626-5495, www.sanjuanballoon.com.*

HOT SPRINGS

Named "Red Water Standing" by the Ute Indians, today's **Orvis Hot Springs** has a special history and a gorgeous setting. Centuries ago, the Utes dug canals to create small bathing pools that would cool the 127-degree water that rushes from below ground. In the 1860s the pools were renamed for a homesteading family. Orvis' main, gravel-bottomed pool is 5 feet deep and 30 feet wide with temperatures of 102–106 degrees. A smaller soaking pool maintains temperatures of 108–114 degrees. Less rustic indoor pools, lodging, and camping are also available. Some areas of the resort are clothing-optional. From Ridgway, go 1.3 miles south on US 550. Turn west at the sign onto County Road 3. *970-626-5324, www.orvishotsprings.com.*

MUSEUM

Known as the birthplace and headquarters of the famed Rio Grande Southern Railroad, Ridgway sits on the northern edge of the rugged San Juan Mountains, where railroads played a key role in mining and transportation. The **Ridgway Railroad Museum** is dedicated to preserving the history of railroading in the San Juans. The museum, at the intersection of US 550 and CO 62, also operates a vintage Galloping Goose rail bus. *970-626-5181.*

SCENIC DRIVES

Owl Creek Pass Road (see Scenic Location No. 139, p. 382) follows the route of an 1885 cattle drive through national forests of aspen groves and river basins filled with wildflowers. Chimney Rock and Courthouse Mountain are visible from the road. Scenes from *How the West Was Won* and John Wayne's *True Grit* were filmed here. Debbie's Park, which stretches for 7 miles along Cow Creek, is named for Debbie Reynolds, who appeared in *How the West Was Won*. From Ridgway, go 2 miles north on US 550, then turn right (east) at the Owl Creek sign.

Dallas Divide Road (see Scenic Location No. 143, p. 391) takes you to stunning views—especially in autumn—of the Sneffels Range and Mount Sneffels. From Ridgway, go west on CO 62. The summit is 10 miles up the road, which continues on to Placerville and forms a 25-mile portion of the 236-mile San Juan Skyway.

WINTER SPORTS

Cross-country skiing and snowshoeing are available without a trail fee at the **Miller Mesa Trail** EASY, which winds to the top of the mesa and fantastic views of the Uncompahgre Valley and Mount Sneffels. Take CO 62 west and turn left onto County Road 5 at the Girl Scout Camp sign (see Scenic Location No. 140, p. 386). Go 0.25 mile, turn right, and drive 5 miles to Elk Meadows. The 7-mile (one way) **East Dallas Creek Trail** MODERATE leads into the Mount Sneffels Wilderness to awesome views of 14,150-foot Mount Sneffels (see Scenic Location No. 141, p. 387). From Ridgway, turn left (west) on CO 62 and continue 5 miles. Turn left onto CR 7 and follow the signs into Uncompahgre National Forest.

WEST DALLAS CREEK ROAD

Just over a mile west of the East Dallas Creek Road, turn south onto West Dallas Creek Road (County Road 9). Don't mind either the large Double RL Ranch log entrance gate, or the ranch managers farther down the road. Despite ongoing litigation, public access to the Uncompahgre National Forest is still available right through the heart of this trophy ranch. I've had the managers admonish me about stepping off the right-of-way while photographing scenes from the edge of the road. Don't worry, it's your right as a taxpayer.

This is one of the great places to drive a car in Colorado. The road heads south before ending at the national forest boundary. Mount Sneffels is to the south, so photographs here catch only its west façade. Nevertheless, the scrub oaks are very prominent along the road, and in combination with aspen groves clinging to nearby ridges, the colorful compositions are stupendous. Get here in early June to witness the lime green shades of the aspens and oaks, and around the second week in October to see red oaks and yellow aspens make powerful visual music together.

Restaurants

Try the Duke's Cut at the **True Grit Restaurant** ($-$$$), where dining room walls display movie posters, photographs of John Wayne, a mural, and a gun and vest he wore while shooting the

Adobe Inn restaurant, Ridgway

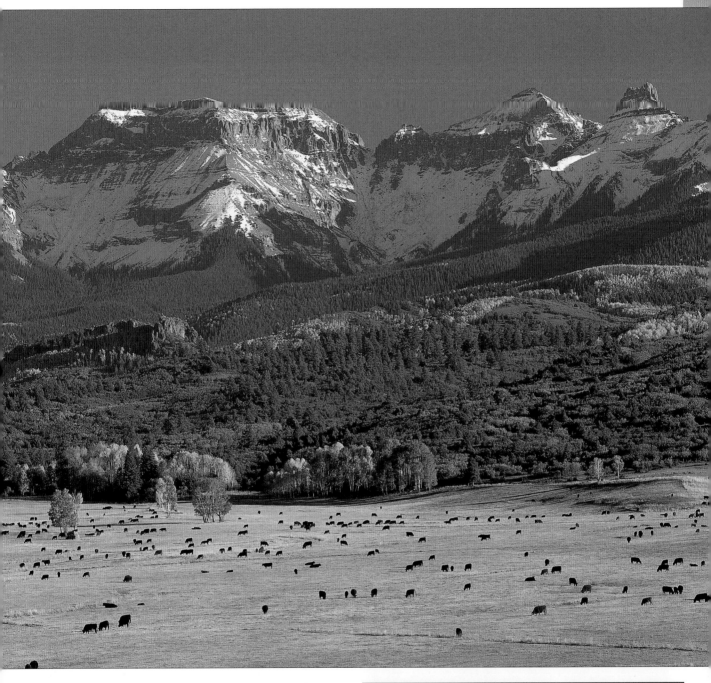

namesake 1969 movie. *123 N. Lena St., 970-626-5739.* The **Adobe Inn** ($$) at 251 Liddell Dr. is known for its enchiladas, margaritas, and Mexican beers. It's one of my favorite Mexican restaurants anywhere! *970-626-5939.* **Galloping Goose Bakery & Café** ($) serves breakfast and lunch and has a variety of fresh bakery items to choose from daily. *153 US 550, 970-626-5531.* **Kate's Place** ($) is a charming café that specializes in local ingredients and organic foods. They are open Tuesday through Sunday for breakfast and lunch. *615 W. Clinton St., 970-626-9800.*

Accommodations

Chipeta Sun Lodge and Spa ($$-$$$) is a full-service fitness center and spa, with hot tubs in many rooms, plus swimming pool, sauna, and steam rooms. Professional massage therapists and

Chipeta Sun Lodge and Spa, Ridgway

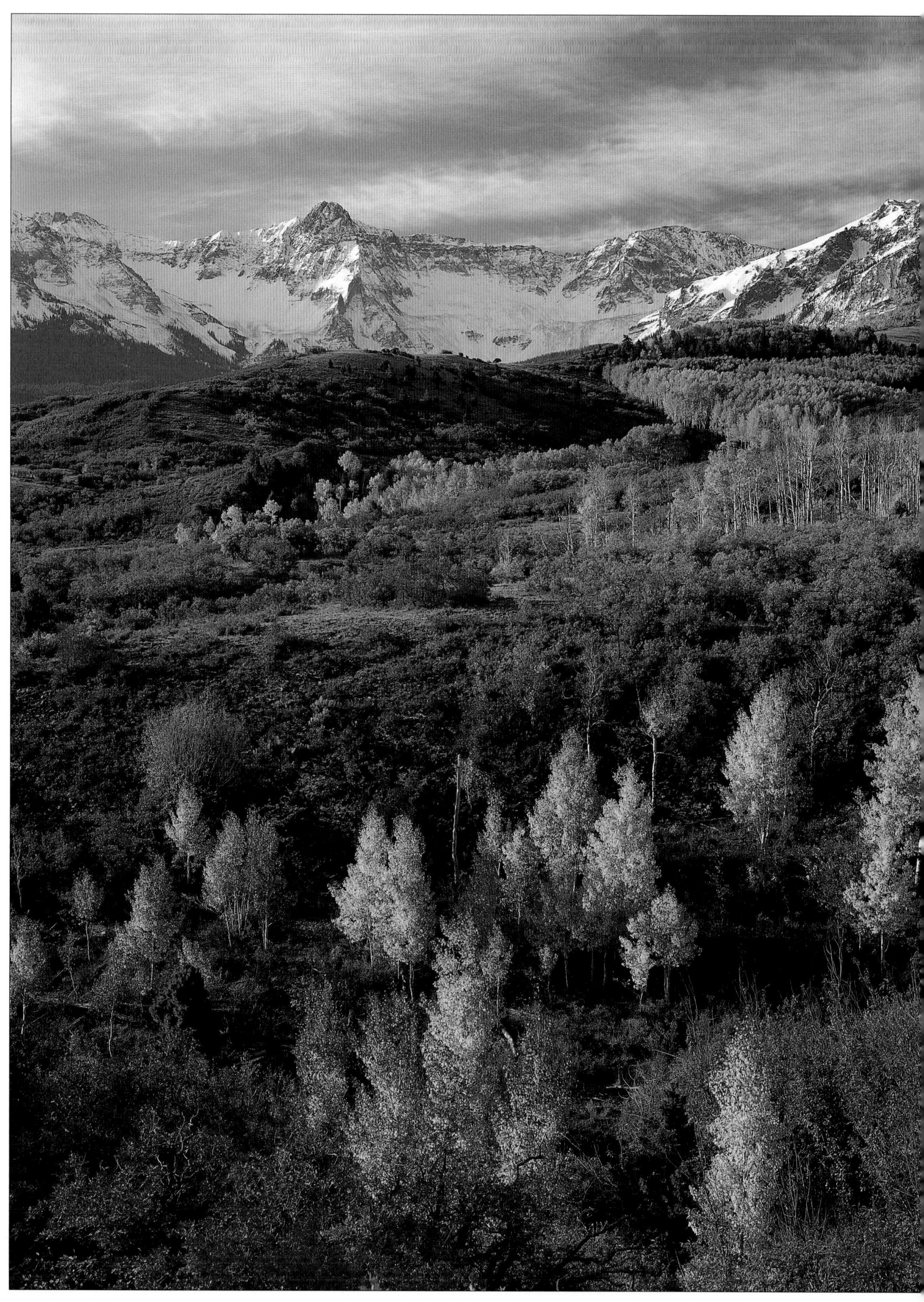

143 SCENIC LOCATION — DALLAS DIVIDE

Four miles west of the West Dallas Creek Road (see Scenic Location No. 142, p. 388) is the world-famous Dallas Divide (8,970 feet). The drive along CO 62 up to and down from the divide affords many unique scenes of the Sneffels Range. Here, that well-known zigzagging fence made of aspen boles provides a great foreground to the view of Mount Sneffels. You need only drive onto the very large pullout at the top of the pass, get out, point, and shoot to make a fine photograph. Actually, you need not even hop out—just shoot from the car. The fence ascends the nearby hillside in such a way that a vertical composition with Mount Sneffels behind works best. The scene is beautiful at any time of year in almost any kind of light or weather. Deep snows cover this landscape from November to April.

Before you start climbing the pass from the east, notice the views of the Double RL Ranch's cottonwood meadows to the south of the highway. In the fall, the grasses stay green while the cottonwoods turn yellow, which, when added to snow-dusted mountains and a Colorado blue sky, makes for an amazing, bucolic scene. Closer to the pass, you find wonderful combinations of scrub oak and aspen, whose alternating red with yellow make for one of the most colorful scenes in the state. And what's best about this place is that the mountain range runs on an east-west axis, very unusual for Rocky Mountain ranges. Therefore, the rising and setting sun is always side-lighting the translucent foliage, allowing the colors to glow dramatically. So don't be lazy—rise early for sunrise light and stay late for sunset at this place!

personal trainers are available, as well as aerobics, yoga, and tai chi courses. This is a cozy getaway any time of year, and it's a great place to beat the Telluride rush. *304 S. Lena, 970-626-3737, 800-633-5868, www.chipeta.com.* **Ridgway-Ouray Lodge & Suites** ($$) offers guests spacious rooms, spa areas, and even an indoor heated pool. Guests can also choose the whirlpool suites for something a little more special. *373 Palomino Trail, 970-626-5444, www.ridgwaylodgeandsuites.com.*

Special Events

The Ridgway Hot Air Balloon & Classic Car Festival, aka Balloons-N-Varooms, is held each May. The festival began in 2004 and has become an annual event that combines hot air balloons with classic cars and trucks from the region. *970-626-5181, www.ridgwaycolorado.com.* The **Annual Ridgway Arts & Crafts Rendezvous** is a popular juried show that takes place each August in Ridgway Town Park. *970-626-5181, www.ridgwaycolorado.com.*

For More Information

Ridgway Area Chamber of Commerce. *150 Racecourse Rd., 970-626-5181, www.ridgwaycolorado.com.*

Telluride

(see map on p. 384)

Telluride is the most famous of San Juan Mountain towns, nestled in a gorgeous box canyon that backs up to sheer canyon walls from which Colorado's highest waterfall, Bridal Veil Falls, cascades down 365 feet. The main street is a National Historic District, and many restored Victorian homes adorn the east end of town. Historic Telluride reflects its mining past and commonality with those other gems of the San Juans, Ouray and Silverton. Telluride is also home to some of the best skiing in the nation and to several outstanding summer festivals. With the famous ski runs have come the promotion of the area abroad and the inevitable local development. Telluride's incredible charms have also brought the beautiful people here; several big celebrities are now part-time residents. Telluride enjoys both a rich heritage and a glamorous present; maybe you can have the best of both worlds here.

History

This stunning box canyon was sacred to the Utes, who called it the "valley of hanging waterfalls." Fur trappers traded here as early as the 1830s. Prospectors arrived in the mid-1870s to find rich veins of silver, and mines popped up. Battered by avalanches, covered by great depths of snow, and set in utter isolation, Telluride was a particularly perilous mining site. (Mineralogical meaning aside, legend has it that Telluride's name refers to its remoteness—To-Hell-You-Ride!) Even so, the town soon became a rowdy mining camp. Butch Cassidy robbed his first bank here in 1889. Nearby Smuggler Union Mine was said to be involved in claim jumping. In its heyday, Telluride's population was about twice what it is today.

In 1890 the nearly inaccessible town welcomed the arrival of the railroad, which at last connected it with the rest of the world (even now there is only one road into town). But like all Colorado mining towns, Telluride's fortunes rose and fell. By World War II, mining appeared to be in steep decline, and Telluride with it. In the early 1950s, though, giant Idarado Mining Co. came to Telluride's back door, bought up all the nearby mines, and put people back to work extracting zinc, lead, and copper. Yet still greater fortunes lay in store for Telluride.

Given the deep winter snows, Telluride's residents had always used skis for transportation. Eventually, on a ridge off Gold Hill, citizens created a recreational ski area, which started to draw visitors. Very soon, the nascent ski industry began to boost Telluride's economy. The Telluride Ski Area was established in 1971 and grew exponentially after the 1987 unveiling of the ski-in/ski-out Mountain Village. A major expansion of Prospect Bowl opened in the 2001–2002 ski season. The resort today is a world-class destination with first-rate amenities, services, lodging, dining, and retail establishments.

Main Attractions

TELLURIDE BLUEGRASS FESTIVAL

This is among the best Americana music jams in the nation. Coloradans put the annual mid-June celebration on their calendars and take the picturesque journey southwest from all over the state. Telluride's biggest event, the festival transforms the town into a musical party. Major stars such as Emmylou Harris, Sam Bush, Tim O'Brien, and James Taylor join musicians from the region for the four-day extravaganza. *800-624-2422, www.bluegrass.com.*

WINTER SPORTS

The celebrated resort at **Telluride** encompasses 1,700 acres of skiable terrain. The free gondola from Station St. Sophia connects the historic town with slopeside **Mountain Village.** From the ski runs you can take in spectacular views of the 13,000-foot San Juans and even the La Sal Range in Utah. Because of Telluride's inaccessibility, particularly in winter, lift lines are shorter than elsewhere.

The Spiral Stairs and The Plunge descend from the summit of the mountain directly behind Telluride and end right at the edge of town. Watching advanced and expert skiers negotiate these steep and mogul-filled runs can confound beginner and intermediate skiers. However, Gorrono Basin above Mountain Village has intermediate runs, and The Meadows below Gorrono has excellent runs for beginners. Telluride is also popular with snowboarders. The 13-acre Surge Air Garden Terrain Park includes banks, tabletops, and a competition-size half pipe. *970-728-6900, 800-778-8581, www.tellurideskiresort.com.*

Telluride's Nordic center rewards adventurous cross-country skiers and snowshoers. Enjoy 50 kilometers of groomed trails that connect with **Town Park** and the **River Corridor Trail,** which follows the San Miguel. Nordic skiing lessons are also available at Town Park. The **San Juan Hut System** comprises five huts between Telluride and Ouray that traverse the Uncompahgre National Forest across the north side of the sublime Sneffels Range. *970-626-3033, www.sanjuanhuts.com.*

Activities

CAMPING

Sunshine campground, 7 miles southwest of Telluride, is notable for its privacy, shade, and wildflowers. Newly renovated, Sunshine is a great base camp for mountain bikers. From Telluride, go west on CO 145 for 3 miles, then south on CO 145 for 5 miles. The 11,000-foot **Alta Lakes** campground has panoramic views, access to the ghost town of Alta, and good fishing. From Telluride, follow directions to Sunshine campground, 4WD then turn left (southeast) onto Forest Road 632, and continue for 4.5 miles up a four-wheel-drive road. The paved **Matterhorn** campground has luxury amenities, wildflowers, and proximity to hiking trails and to fishing at Priest and Trout Lakes. From Telluride, follow directions to Sunshine campground but go 4 miles farther on CO 145. **Woods Lake**

and one of its most beautiful, Mystic. As these forks combine into one river, the San Miguel roars westward down the valley parallel to CO 145, picking up even more water from the San Miguel Mountains to the south. Eventually, it flows into the Dolores River near the old uranium mining town of Uravan.

This drive along CO 145 is remarkable for not only the river but for the red sandstone hillsides and the lush cottonwood forests that line it. In spring, the light green color of leafing cottonwoods is the perfect complement to the red walls. Red and green are opposites on the color wheel, making each color more conspicuous on film than it would otherwise be (see pp. 20–25, *Photographing the Landscape*). In fall, the yellow cottonwoods make an almost equally dramatic marriage with the red rocks. Many vantages and pullouts along the highway reveal the river snaking through the trees, my favorite composition. In cloudy light, or when the sun is not high enough to enter the canyon, the white cascades of the fast-moving river allow it to contrast starkly with all of the color.

SAN MIGUEL RIVER

Once CO 62 makes its way down from Dallas Divide to meet CO 145, it also meets the San Miguel River. The river originates high in the mountains that ring the Telluride basin, its many forks contributing massive amounts of snowmelt throughout the year. Its upper stretches contain some of Colorado's highest and most scenic waterfalls, such as the state's tallest, Bridal Veil,

Vertical compositions here work just as well as horizontal ones. I tend to use telephoto more often than wide-angle lenses to make tight compositions with trees to the sides, river in the middle, and red rocks in the background. I rarely include sky in the scene. Follow the San Miguel River to the intersection of CO 145 and CO 141, then follow CO 141 until the river meets the Dolores near Uravan. You have just made the transition from mountain to desert canyon. The Dolores flows through steeply cliffed walls of sandstone that you might only expect to see in southern Utah!

LAST DOLLAR ROAD

Here goes another coveted Fielder secret out the window. I've made some of my favorite aspen tree photographs during the past 30 years along Last Dollar Road. Skirting the west end of the Sneffels Range, this rough dirt road winds through the most beautiful aspen groves and forests in the San Juan Mountains. Views of the Sneffels Range and San Miguel Mountains are breathtaking. This is the shortcut to Telluride, and one that requires a high-clearance vehicle, though it's not necessary to engage four-wheel drive unless the road is wet on the south side of Last Dollar Pass. A little over a mile west of the Dallas Divide, turn south off CO 62 onto the well-marked Last Dollar Road and immediately get the film loaded into the camera.

The first few miles of road wind along ridges and descend into valleys full of large ranches. With buildings hidden by the trees, though, the views to the Sneffels Range are pure. Pockets of aspen decorate the hillsides. Within these groves you can make intimate compositions of the trees—yes, spring and autumn are the seasons to visit. The first week in June and the first or second week in October are best in this mild microclimate. I just love wandering into a grove, setting up the camera on a tripod, and pointing straight toward a setting sun blocked by a tree trunk. The backlit leaves turn golden, and the white boles reflect blue of the Colorado sky, making for wonderful color contrast (see pp. 100–103, *Photographing the Landscape*).

The road next ascends Last Dollar Pass through spruce and fir, then rounds a bend to reveal grand southern views of the San Miguel Mountains, including oft-photographed Mount Wilson (14,246 feet). You then descend toward Telluride, the road winding through large forests of aspen and intermittently revealing views out to the peaks. Along this stretch I enjoy composing the road as a lead-in line, to draw the viewer's eye into the scene. Both vertical and horizontal compositions work well. Find places where the road winds through the trees, and create an asymmetrical balance by placing more trees on one side than the other. The lower stretch of road then exits the trees to provide views of ranches blanketing vast mesas. Unfortunately, development and an airport have severely compromised the integrity of these views in the past 20 years.

campground, 22 miles southwest of Telluride, adjoins good fishing at the lake. From Telluride, go 13 miles west on CO 145, turn left (south) on County Road 57.P (FR 618 or Fall Creek Road), and drive 9 miles. *For above campgrounds: 970-327-4261.* Telluride's **Town Park,** at the east end of town, has 40 or so campsites and is open to RVs under 30 feet, but can get extremely crowded, particularly during the festivals. No reservations are accepted. *970-728-2174.*

FISHING

The picturesque **San Miguel River** (see Scenic Location No. 144, p. 393) has been heavily degraded by the mining activities of the last century, though the river is making a comeback. The best fishing is along the stretch that parallels CO 145 from Telluride to Placerville and down the **South Fork** to Ophir. Browns are predominant here, averaging 10–14 inches. Rainbows also average 10–14 inches here; you can catch brookies and cutthroats as well. Rainbows, browns, and brookies of 6–10 inches thrive in the tributaries, including **Big Bear Creek** and **Fall Creek,** which afford a sense of seclusion and more of a wilderness experience. To get to the South Fork, take CO 145 to Forest Road 625 south. To find Big Bear Creek, go another 4 miles west on CO 145 and take County Road 60M south. Fall Creek's confluence with the San Miguel is 4 miles downstream from Big Bear Creek, where CR 57.P heads south to Woods Lake.

Reliable fishing holes abound in the stocked mountain lakes in the area. Get to **Silver Lake** via the Bridal Veil Falls Trail. (For directions, see Hiking, p. 397) Reach **Priest Lake** and **Trout Lake** from the Matterhorn Campground (see Camping, p. 392). The road to **Alta Lakes** is about 12 miles south of Telluride. From Telluride, drive 8 miles south on CO 145 and turn left on FR 632. Drive 4 miles to the ghost town of Alta, turn right at the town, and follow signs to Alta Lakes. Reach **Wood Lake** from Telluride by going 10 miles northwest on CO 145, just beyond the town of Sawpit. Turn left (south) onto Fall Creek Road (FR 618/CR 57.P) and drive 9 miles to the lake. Local outfitters also offer guided fishing trips on the nearby Dolores River. *For information, lessons, or guided fishing trips: The Telluride Angler, 121 W. Colorado Ave., 970-728-3895, www.tellurideoutside.com; or RIGS Fly Shop, 565 Sherman St., Ridgeway, 888-626-4460, www.fishrigs.com.* When all else fails, cast into the well-stocked **Kid's Fishing Pond** at the east end of Telluride (if you're 12 years of age or under).

FOUR-WHEEL-DRIVE TRIPS AND GHOST TOWNS

For those not content with topflight winter sports and summer festivals, Telluride's backroads beckon. Consider guided tours for the more remote areas over rocky ridges and high passes. The region's history haunts its steep backcountry, but San Juan jeep roads are not for amateurs. Take a jeep tour with professionals who are great storytellers (and who often have access to roads on private property). Enjoy these awe-inspiring mountains, but bring your common sense.

From Telluride's box valley the noble Ingram Peak rises to the southeast. It is carved dramatically by the switchbacks of lower **Black Bear Pass Road,** a 10-mile one-way road that accesses numerous old mining sites and ascends to nearly 13,000 feet as it makes its way to Red Mountain Pass. This hair-raising route may be the most difficult and dangerous pass in the country. Rental jeeps are forbidden on this road, on which many lives have been lost. You can, however, drive up as

146 SCENIC LOCATION ILLIUM ROAD

After driving southwest from Ridgway on CO 62 and making a left onto CO 145 to get to Telluride, you ascend the canyon of the San Miguel River. Just before arriving in the Telluride basin, take the road to the right that follows the South Fork of the San Miguel for about 7 miles. It's a short drive but one I've enjoyed returning to throughout the past 30 years. Aspens and cottonwoods fill the landscape, and views to Sunshine Mountain (12,930 feet) complete the recipe for a great scenic photograph. Look for Forest Road 625, Illium (South Fork) Road, heading south just before the last uphill stretch of CO 145 to Telluride. You can also descend the road by heading south on CO 145 and looping north onto Illium Road just across from the old town of Ophir. I prefer the ascent with its accompanying views of Sunshine Mountain. The Nature Conservancy maintains a preserve along this lovely upper stretch of the San Miguel River.

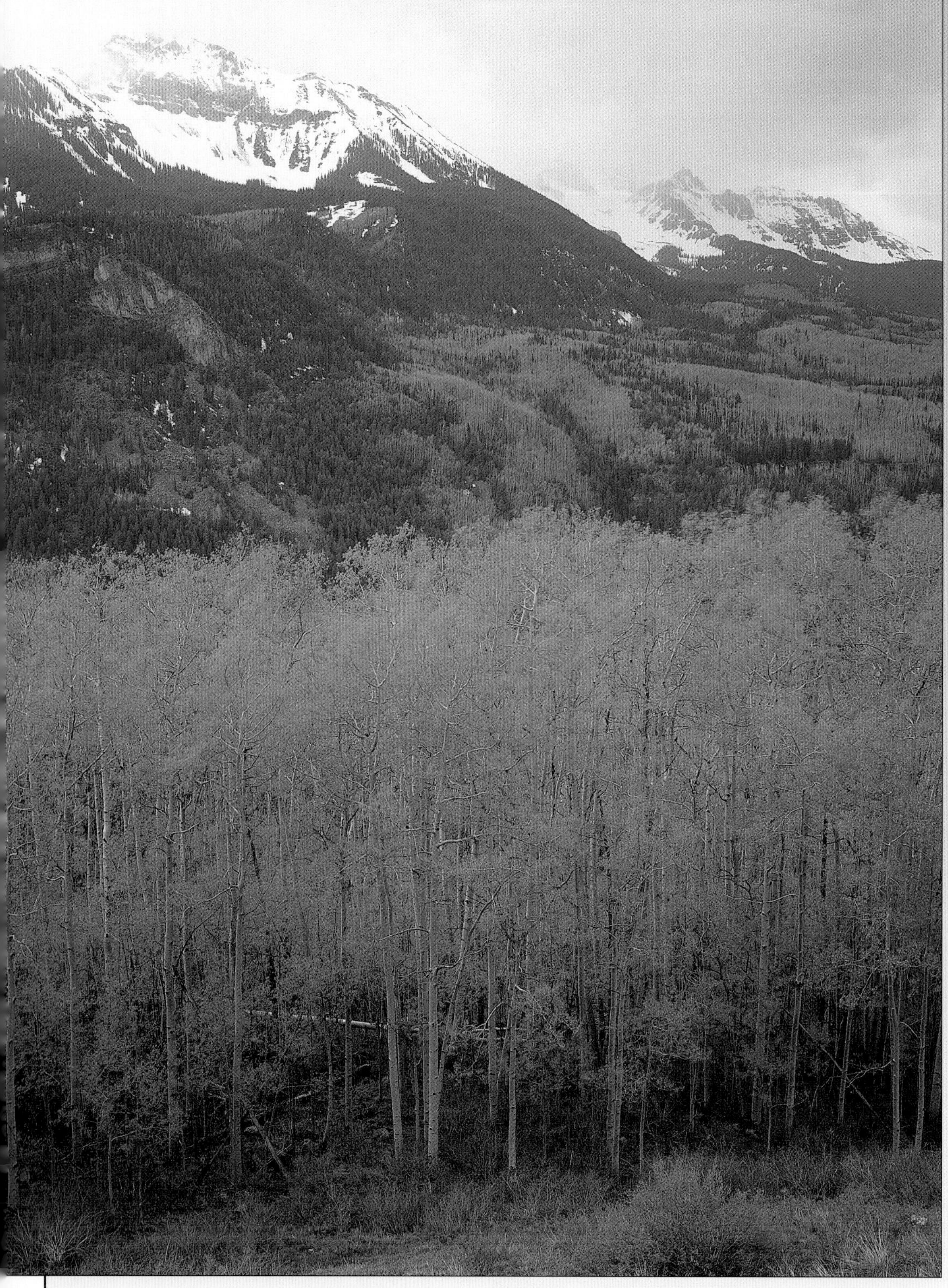

I make one of my favorite photographs by climbing above the road not long after exiting the highway and composing the road as a lead-in line. Aspen stands are left and right, and Sunshine Mountain occupies the top of the scene. It's a classic Colorado scenic that's especially glorious in the fall. Farther up the road you enter the aspen forest. Along this stretch, the tall, parallel aspen boles are particularly white and conspicuous against darker spruce and fir. Aspen trunks can range in color from gray to green to white. I ignore the sky and mountains here—even the colorful leaves—to focus the camera on the sublime shapes of the trunks (see pp. 28, 37, *Photographing the Landscape*). The longer the lens' focal length, the more compressed the space between the trees, rendering the grove thicker and more striking on film than to the eye.

far as the stunning Bridal Veil Falls (for directions, see Hiking, below). Thereafter, this is a one-way route down from Red Mountain Pass.

The old town of **Pandora** was known for aerial trams that carried miners and ore from peak to peak and also for frequent, thundering snowslides. Pandora is just 2 miles east of Telluride; the old townsite is 0.5 mile down the San Miguel River from the mill. The town of **Ophir** was first founded in 1870, and people still live at the newer site today. The 6-mile **Ophir Pass Road** takes you to views above timberline from the 11,789-foot summit and connects Telluride with Silverton. The steep, narrow road is cut entirely from slide-rock. From Telluride, go south on CO 145 for 8 miles. Turn left onto a dirt road and through the abandoned town of **Old Ophir.** (The living Ophir is 2.5 miles farther.) You encounter waterfalls, pass through a tunnel, and ascend to amazing vistas over formidable **Imogene Pass Road**, a pass that gives Black Bear competition as the most dangerous. Imogene Pass connected Telluride to the famous **Tomboy** and **Camp Bird Mines** (see History, Ouray, p. 377) and to Ouray. Head 5 miles up Tomboy Road to reach the mining site from the end of Oak Street in Telluride. The 13,114-foot, historic **Imogene Pass** is another 7 miles up the steep grade. The pass is also accessible from US 550 south of Ouray. **Alta Lakes Road** takes you to the 1870s mining camp of **Alta,** now listed on the National Register of Historic Places. Another mile or so beyond Alta are the pristine Alta Lakes, created by miners. Both are easy to reach from Telluride. (For directions, see Camping, p. 392). *For information and reservations: Telluride Outside, 121 W. Colorado Ave., 970-728-3895, 800-831-6230, www.tellurideoutside.com; or Dave's Mountain Tours, Inc., 970-728-9749.*

GLIDER AND GONDOLA RIDES

I can't imagine a more exciting way to see the craggy, towering San Juans than from a glider. *For information: Telluride Soaring, Telluride Airport, 970-728-5424.* Or fly up the slopes on the free gondola that runs between the town of Telluride and Mountain Village. Catch it from the base of the mountain (either side), check out the magnificent scenery going up, and connect to hiking and mountain-biking trails at the top, Station St. Sophia.

GOLF

You can take a swing at the 18-hole, public **Telluride Golf Club** at Mountain Village. If your high-altitude golf game is way over par, you can still enjoy the majestic setting; watch out for elk on the course. *970-728-2608, www.telluride.com, www.tellurideskiresort.com.*

HIKING

Hikers should be prepared to share the trails here with runners, mountain bikers, and Jeeps. The 1.8-mile (one way) hike to **Bridal Veil Falls** DIFFICULT takes you to the tallest waterfall in Colorado, at 365 feet. The trail also provides access to **Blue Lake** and **Silver Lake,** the latter stocked with trout. The trailhead is at the east end of Telluride on CO 145 (Colorado Avenue). Take the dirt road 1.2 miles and park. You can take the popular **Bear Creek Trail** MODERATE (2 miles one way) to Bear Creek Falls. This trail takes you through pine and fir forests, aspen groves, and wildflowers to the bottom of the falls. Before you get to the bottom of Bear Creek Falls, look for a three tiered waterfall on the left in the distance.

Get to Telluride's creative and popular playground, **Imagination Station,** via a side trail leading downhill to **Bear Creek Preserve**. The Bear Creek Trail also accesses the 15-mile **Wasatch Trail** DIFFICULT. To get to the Bear Creek Trail, go to the end of Pine Street in Telluride and follow Bear Creek up the canyon to the waterfall. The Wasatch Trailhead is 0.25 mile up the Bear Creek Trail.

For a less demanding but equally gorgeous hike, take the 2.7-mile **Jud Wiebe Trail** EASY, which makes a loop from Aspen to Oak streets. This loop ambles to views of waterfalls, the steepest ski runs, and mountain ranges as far away as the La Sals in Utah. After 0.5 mile on the Jud Wiebe, the hardy can connect to the 13-mile **Sneffels Highline Loop** DIFFICULT, which rises above timberline. Take the path to the left and cross Butcher Creek. Reach the Jud Wiebe Trailhead from the north end of Aspen Street in Telluride.

Another peaceful hike is the **San Miguel River Trail** EASY, which follows the river for 2.5 miles one way. From the southwest bridge into Town Park in Telluride, follow the trail along the river. The 13-mile (one way) **Wilson Mesa Trail** MODERATE will take you from Woods Lake to Sunshine Mesa and wildflowers, views, and colors in fall. To get there, go 14 miles west from Telluride on CO 145. Turn left on Fall Creek Road and drive 7.75 miles to the trailhead. Hiking trails here often intersect; be sure to carry a map. *For information and maps: Telluride Outside, 121 W. Colorado Ave., 970-728-3895, 800-831-6230, www.tellurideoutside.com; or Further Adventures/Boot Doctor in The Inn at Lost Creek, Mountain Village, 970-728-8954.*

HORSEBACK RIDING

Horseback riding remains an ideal way to see this rugged and historic country. **Telluride Horseback Adventures** promises to suit the horse to the ability of the rider. Roudy, who runs the outfit, offers daily and multi-day pack trips, depending on the toughness of your posterior. Try the breakfast and dinner rides, too. *970-728-9611, www.ridewithroudy.com.*

MOUNTAIN BIKING

Telluride is naturally a rigorous and rewarding destination for mountain bikers in summer. The 70-mile **Sneffels Range Loop** DIFFICULT connects Telluride with Ouray and Ridgway. The views of the San Juans are inspiring as you traverse dense pine forests, meadows, and streams. From Telluride, follow Oak Street to Tomboy Road. And don't miss the **Illium Valley/Local's Loop** MODERATE. Illium Valley is a 6.5-mile round-trip, narrow singletrack that winds through boulders and pine forests to great views of Mount Wilson. The trail starts on Colorado Avenue

TROUT LAKE/ LIZARD HEAD PASS

As you continue your drive away from Telluride to the southwest along CO 145, you eventually ascend Lizard Head Pass (10,222 feet). The highway winds along the ridge above the South Fork of the San Miguel River, revealing incredible views of Sunshine Mountain to the south and the old Rio Grande Southern rail route that descended to the town of Dolores. This stretch of the San Juan Skyway is one of America's most scenic roads. Though the ascent to the pass is glorious, so, too, is the descent along the main fork of the Dolores River (see Scenic Location No. 149, p. 404).

Trout Lake comes into view on the left just before you arrive at the top of Lizard Head Pass. This natural lake makes a great compositional foreground for the peaks of the West Silverton mountain group that divides this basin from the Animas River Basin near Silverton. In fact, as the crow flies, Silverton is only about 11 miles from where you stand. You can make my favorite composition of Trout Lake along the highway. Pull over where the lake is centered below the ridge of mountains to the south. A standard focal-length lens will take it all in. Or you can drive down to the lake and photograph reflections of mountains, if the wind is not strong.

The pass is 2 miles west of the lake. However, continue down the highway until Lizard Head Peak (13,113 feet) looms in the background to the north. You can't miss it—a singular, 800-foot-high finger of volcanic rock. Though surrounded by the peaks and ridges of the Lizard Head Wilderness and the San Miguel Mountains, Lizard Head still dominates this view. The meadows along the north side of the highway make for good foreground with the mountains behind. Try climbing up the embankment a bit on the south side of the highway to make the best composition of these meadows.

(CO 145 west of town), parallels the San Miguel River, and terminates at Illium (South Fork) Road (see Scenic Location No. 146, p. 396). Turn left at Society Junction and look for the unmarked trail just to your left. To extend this thrilling ride, connect here to the Local's Loop, which takes you along dirt and paved roads to panoramic, four-wheel-drive Deep Creek and Last Dollar Roads (see Scenic Location No. 145, p. 395). The entire Illium Valley/Local's Loop is a 19-mile ride.

The ski area's gondola provides access to great mountain-biking trails. Catch it at the mountain base (either side) up to Station St. Sophia. *For more information: 970-728-7538.* The **San Juan Hut System Trail** MODERATE is popular with mountain bikers for its scenic splendor and diverse ecosystems. The 215-mile San Juan Hut Trail starts in Telluride and works its way down to the canyon country, ending in Moab, Utah. *For information and directions: 970-626-3033, www.sanjuanhuts.com.*

LONE CONE STATE WILDLIFE AREA

Aptly named Lone Cone (12,613 feet) towers over the middle of nowhere. You can see it for miles when you are high up in the neighboring San Juan Mountains. The scrub oaks, aspens, mountain meadows, and ranchlands around the peak will reward you with a unique Colorado landscape. Elk and deer here attract hunters in the fall. Rather than trying to explain the access, I suggest that you consult your *Colorado Atlas & Gazetteer.* The roads that run closest to Lone Cone and actually enclose it in a big triangle, County Roads 31 and H and Forest Road 611, are improved dirt roads manageable by car. Nevertheless, the San Juan and Uncompahgre National Forest roads that surround Lone Cone are so numerous that I highly recommend a four-wheel drive if you want some flexibility to explore this remote country.

Along each of these roads you often spy views through the forest of Lone Cone in the distance. It has the shape of an old volcano and rises gracefully above the rest of the landscape. Watch for pullouts where you can compose aspens and oaks in the foreground with Lone Cone looming behind. It's a subtle mountain, yet its shape can complete a unique scenic composition. Between views of Lone Cone, look for bucolic meadow scenes with trees behind. Spring and fall will lend wonderful color to it all, and I guarantee that you will be alone most of the time. You might consider exiting the area via Disappointment Creek on Road D west to CO 141 and Dolores River Canyon country, a big, open valley that I've not seen the likes of elsewhere in Colorado.

Many hiking trails and four-wheel-drive roads also make for excellent mountain biking. These routes include Bear Creek Canyon, Bridal Veil Falls, Jud Wiebe Trail, Tomboy Road, San Miguel River Trail, Alta Lakes Road, Black Bear Pass, Ophir Pass, and Wilson Mesa Trail. (For directions, see Hiking, p. 397, and Four-Wheel-Drive Trips and Ghost Towns, p. 395). *For mountain-bike tours, information, and rentals: Back Country Biking, 970-728-8954; Telluride Sports, 150 W. Colorado Ave., 970-728-4477, 800-828-7547, www.telluridesports.com.*

MUSEUM

The **Telluride Historical Museum** showcases artifacts from the Ute era, photos and memorabilia from early mining days, and skiing history exhibits. Of particular interest is the story of Telluride resident and engineer L. L. Nunn and the inventor Nikola Tesla. These two men brought the use of alternating-current technology to the world. Telluride was the first Colorado town to have AC power, which lit the streets of Telluride in 1891 and even crossed 13,114-foot Imogene Pass. Nunn would go on to install the hydraulic water plant at Niagara Falls. Originally a hospital, the museum also sheds light on stomach-turning stories of frontier medical practice. *Corner of Fir and Gregory Streets, 970-728-3344, www.telluridemuseum.com.*

RAFTING

The **San Miguel River** EASY is one of the few rivers in Colorado that remains un-dammed and flows naturally. A raft trip down the San Miguel, with Class II–III rapids, provides unmatched scenery of both the San Juans and sandstone canyons (see Scenic Location No. 144, p. 393). Native peoples left petroglyphs still visible on the canyon walls. The **Norwood Canyon** EASY trip will take you below the towering sandstone walls at the confluence of the San Miguel and Dolores Rivers. The full-day **Hanging Flume Float** EASY gives an unparalleled view of a mining structure that pays tribute to the courage and ingenuity of the early miners. *For information and reservations: Further Adventures/Boot Doctor in The Inn at Lost Creek, Mountain Village, 970-728-5678; or RIGS Fly Shop, 565 Sherman St., Ridgeway, 970-626-4460, www.fishrigs.com.*

ROCK CLIMBING

The **Ophir Wall**, 8 miles west of Telluride on CO 145, is very popular with climbers for its steep pitches and magnificent cracks. Multi-pitch climbs here are rated from 5.3 to 5.14—not to be scaled casually. Just east of Ophir Wall, **Mirror Wall** is composed of smooth cliff towers and has great sport climbs. Another popular and easily accessible climbing area, **Cracked Canyon** offers traditional and sport climbs for all abilities. *For information, maps, and lessons: Telluride Mountain Guides, 970-728-6481.*

SCENIC DRIVES

The 33-mile stretch of the San Juan Skyway from Telluride to Ridgway includes 8,970-foot **Dallas Divide** (see Scenic Location No. 143, p. 391), gorgeous in the fall when the aspens change color. From Telluride, take CO 145 west to Placerville, then head northeast on CO 62 to Ridgway. The 60-mile **Lizard Head Pass Road** (see Scenic Location No. 147, p. 398) section of the San Juan Skyway takes you south from Telluride to Dolores, past views of 14,017-foot Wilson Peak, 12,930-foot Sunshine Mountain, and the incredible stone pinnacles of the Ophir Needles. The highway passes Old Ophir (see Four-Wheel-Drive Trips and Ghost Towns, p. 397), then goes above the South Fork Valley to ascend meadows and pine forests to the summit of 10,222-foot Lizard Head Pass.

Descending from the summit, 13,188-foot Sheep Mountain looms before you. The highway follows the beautiful Dolores River. You enter tiny **Rico** (Spanish for "rich"), an old mining town named for its ore strikes. Soon you see the sandstone formations so common in the Southwest's canyon country as you follow the river into the town of Dolores.

Restaurants

A consistent dining favorite here is **La Marmotte** ($$-$$$), known for its French cuisine, wonderful appetizers, and extensive list of domestic and French wines. Try the salmon or sea bass. *150 W. San Juan, 970-728-6232.* For Telluride's most unique fine dining experience **Allred's** ($$$) at 10,551' accessible only by the gondola and open for dinner only. *970-728-7474.* American cuisine is in fashion at the **Cosmopolitan** ($$-$$$). The Cosmo (as it's called locally) has breakfast and lunch fare, and creative beef, lamb, fish, and duck entrees. The Cosmo also houses **The Tasting Cellar,** featuring a five-course menu complemented with four wines. *In the Hotel Columbia, 300 W. San Juan Ave., 970-728-1292.* **Appaloosa** ($$-$$$) is well known for its wild game selection. Enjoy a sunset dinner with great views of the fouteeners at this classic Colorado steakhouse. *136 Country Club Dr., 970-728-6800.*

For Mexican food at reasonable prices try **Sofio's** ($-$$). *100 W. Colorado Ave., 970-728-5114.* **Fat Alley** ($-$$) has great barbecued ribs and sandwiches. *122 S. Oak St., 970-728-3985.* An exceptional tavern is the **Sheridan Bar** in the historic New Sheridan Hotel. Now serving lunch and dinner from the Sheridan Chophouse kitchen. *231 W. Colorado Ave., 970-728-3911.* And for the early morning crowd, try **Telluride Coffee Company,** featuring locally roasted coffee, a variety of teas, and fresh pastries. Open at 7 a.m. every day. *Mountain Village Heritage Plaza, 970-369-4400.* **Baked in Telluride** ($) is a complete bakery that also serves soups, salads, and a variety of sandwiches and dinner entrées. They deliver. *127 S. Fir St., 970-728-7445.* Another great breakfast spot, the **New Sheridan Hotel Chop House Restaurant** ($-$$) offers a variety of omelettes, light options, and even take out. *231 W. Colorado Ave., 970-728-9100.*

The Aspen Street Inn, Telluride (previously the San Sophia Inn)

Accommodations

Although you have many posh lodging options in Telluride, I prefer the historic hotels and B&Bs. For sheer elegance, make reservations at the **Hotel Columbia** ($$$-$$$$) along the San Miguel River at the Oak Street ski lift and gondola, just 2 blocks from downtown Telluride. Room balconies look out to waterfalls and the San Juan peaks. The wonderful Cosmopolitan and The Tasting Cellar restaurants are here, too. *300 W. San Juan Ave., 970-728-0660, 800-201-9505, www.columbiatelluride.com.* For a real sense of what Telluride was like in its mining heyday, stay at the renovated **New Sheridan Hotel** ($$-$$$), the finest hotel in town at the turn of the 20th century. William Jennings Bryan gave a speech here during the presidential campaign of 1902. Enjoy the historic bar, and look into the schedule of theatrical and musical entertainment at the Sheridan's Opera House. *231 W. Colorado Ave., 970-728-4351, 800-200-1891, www.newsheridan.com.* **The Victorian Inn** ($-$$) is the best bargain in town. Although built in the 1970s, the inn has a 19th-century ambiance. *401 W. Pacific Ave, 970-728-6601, 800-611-9893.*

Telluride also has terrific B&Bs near downtown at reasonable rates. Formerly Franklin Manor, the **Wildwood Canyon Inn** ($$$-$$$$) is upscale and cozy, with private baths and balconies and a rooftop hot tub. *627 E. Colorado Ave., 877-332-1275, www.wildwoodcanyoninn.com.* The well-appointed **Aspen Street Inn** ($$-$$$$) is just a half-block from the Oak Street ski lift. *970-728-3388, 800-376-9769, www.alpinelodging.com/aspen-street-inn.*

New Sheridan Hotel, Telluride

Hotel Columbia, Telluride

Special Events

Telluride is known for its topflight summer festivals. The most famous is the **Telluride Bluegrass Festival** (see Main Attractions, p. 392). For classical music enthusiasts, the annual **Telluride Chamber Music Festival,** held the second week in August, is the one to catch. Hear internationally known musicians, attend a free concert in Town Park, take in the open rehearsals and Children's Concert at the Sheridan Opera House, and, of course, be there for the big Opening Night Gala. The Dessert Concert features an evening of musical favorites paired with a buffet of gourmet desserts. The **Telluride Jazz Celebration** in early August gathers the jazz faithful to hear both locally and nationally revered jazz musicians. Past performers have included the Ray Brown Trio, Kenny Walker, and Terence Blanchard.

Join fellow fungi fanciers during the mid-August **Mushroom Fest,** which includes a unique parade and mushroom-tasting events. In late August, you will be amazed by the aerial acrobatics of participants in the **Telluride Hang Gliding Festival.** Rounding out the summer is the **Telluride Film Festival,** which has attracted national and international attention from film buffs and critics alike. Held over Labor Day weekend, the festival has screened the premieres of various independent and foreign films and continues to grow in stature in the industry. *510-665-9494, www.telluridefilmfestival.com.* Outdoor adventure, environmental, and cultural films are the focus of the annual **Mountainfilm in Telluride,** held Memorial Day Weekend. *970-728-4123, www.mountainfilm.org/. For other festival information: 970-728-4431, www.visittelluride.com.*

For More Information

Telluride Visitor Center, *700 W. Colorado Ave., 970-728-4431, www.visittelluride.com.*

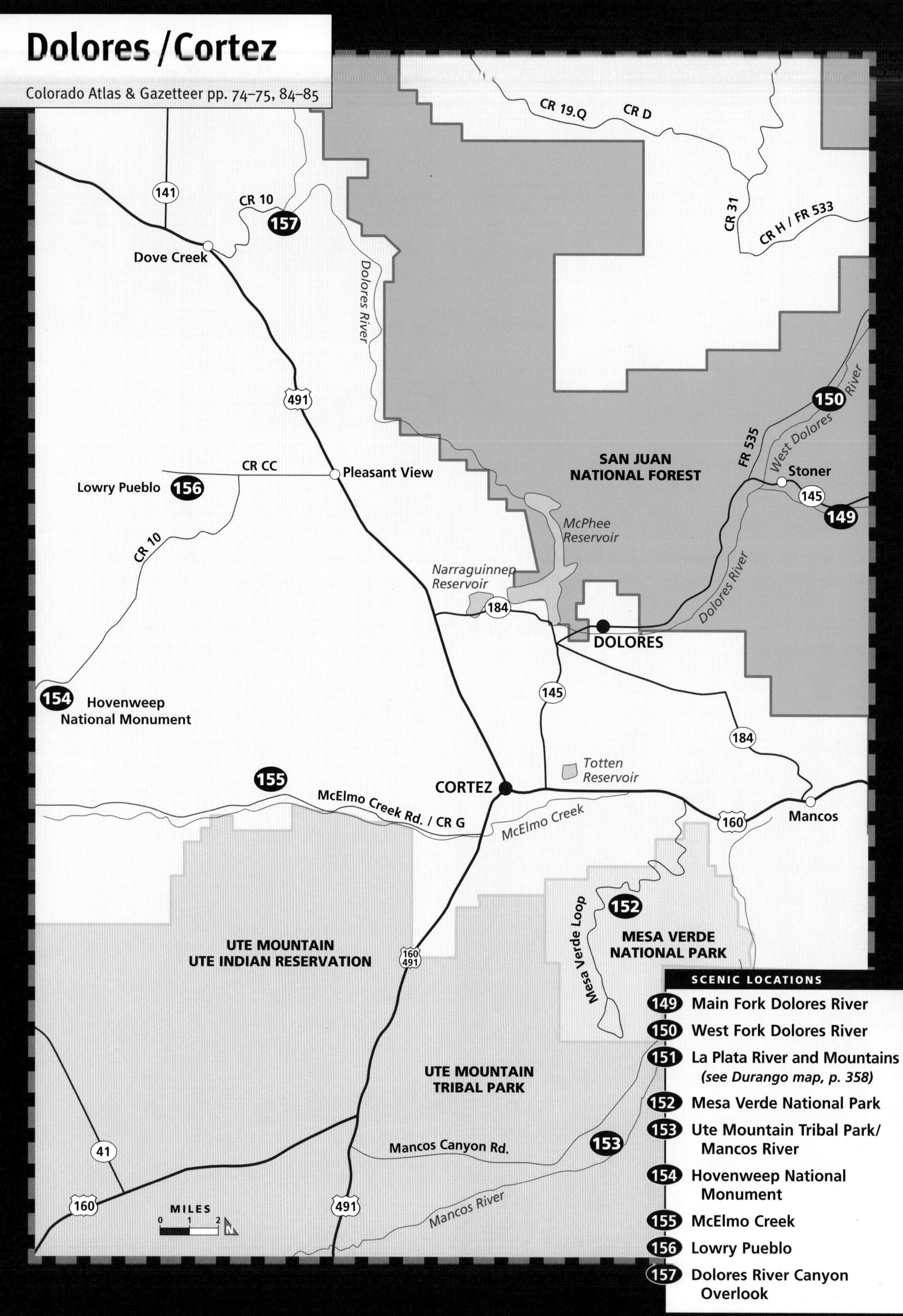

Dolores / Cortez
Colorado Atlas & Gazetteer pp. 74–75, 84–85
CR 19.Q
CR D
CR 31
CR H / FR 533
141
CR 10
157
Dove Creek
Dolores River
491
SAN JUAN NATIONAL FOREST
150
West Dolores River
FR 535
Stoner
145
149
CR CC
Pleasant View
Lowry Pueblo
156
CR 10
McPhee Reservoir
Narraguinnep Reservoir
184
Dolores River
DOLORES
154
Hovenweep National Monument
145
184
Totten Reservoir
155
CORTEZ
McElmo Creek Rd. / CR G
McElmo Creek
160
Mancos
152
Mesa Verde Loop
MESA VERDE NATIONAL PARK
UTE MOUNTAIN UTE INDIAN RESERVATION
160 491
UTE MOUNTAIN TRIBAL PARK
Mancos Canyon Rd.
153
41
160
MILES
0 1 2
N
491
Mancos River
SCENIC LOCATIONS
149 Main Fork Dolores River
150 West Fork Dolores River
151 La Plata River and Mountains (see Durango map, p. 358)
152 Mesa Verde National Park
153 Ute Mountain Tribal Park/ Mancos River
154 Hovenweep National Monument
155 McElmo Creek
156 Lowry Pueblo
157 Dolores River Canyon Overlook

Dolores

With easy access to Colorado's canyon country, Anasazi ruins, and recreation, tiny Dolores is named for the great river that runs beside it. The sublime Dolores River (see Scenic Location Nos. 149, 150, and 157, this chapter, as well as 101 and 102 on pages 290 and 292) and vicinity attract people who want to recreate and relax in a rural setting. Nowhere else in Colorado do autumn's narrow-leaved cottonwood trees display a more vibrant yellow than they do along the Dolores. This long canyon-country river makes for the most secluded and stunning rafting experience you'll find anywhere.

History

Franciscan friars Silvestre Velez de Escalante and Francisco Atanasio Dominguez traveled through this country in 1776 and recorded the river's name, *Rio de Nuestra Señora de los Dolores* ("River of Our Lady of Sorrows"). Credit the railroad industry, though, for putting Dolores on the map. Founded in 1900 with the arrival of the railroad, Dolores became a major stop on the Rio Grande Southern rail line through the San Juans. The people of Big Bend, the original river settlement just to the south, moved everything lock, stock, and barrel to the new town. Dolores served the mining operations to the northeast and the agricultural communities of the Montezuma Valley. When the rail line was abandoned in the early 1950s, though, Dolores hit an economic downturn, but then evolved into a sleepy little town on a beautiful river. In recent years, Dolores has begun promoting itself as a recreational destination with easy access to Mesa Verde National Park and other Anasazi ruins.

Main Attractions

THE DOLORES RIVER

This remote, remarkable river runs for 250 miles from the San Juans to its confluence with the Colorado north of Moab, Utah. Adjacent to the glorious San Juan Skyway (CO 145) from Lizard Head Pass southwest to the town of Dolores, the river then turns north-northwest for more than 150 miles to the Utah border. From its alpine beginnings the river travels through several ecosystems before entering the Colorado-Utah slickrock canyon country. Along the river are abundant opportunities for rafting, hiking, mountain biking, and, of course, fishing. The Dolores was recently named one of the 50 best trout streams in America by *Trout Magazine.*

Fishing: The Colorado Division of Wildlife stocks the Dolores every year, and you can find good access points to the river along CO 145. The Dolores River is dammed at **McPhee Reservoir** just west and north of Dolores. McPhee is a popular watering hole stocked with cold- and warm-water species, trout, crappies, and catfish. The reservoir has more than 50 miles of shoreline, good access points, and a full-service marina. Land a small-mouth bass from its more shallow waters. At **Narraguinnep Reservoir,** due west of McPhee on CO 184, you can enjoy warmwater fishing for catfish, bass, pike, and walleye.

The **Lower Dolores** is an 11-mile stretch of Gold Medal Water from McPhee Reservoir to Bradfield Bridge. This section of the river contains rainbows, cutthroats, and browns. To reach it, turn right (east) off US 666 onto County Road DD 1 mile north of Pleasant View, then turn left and go 3 miles north on CR 16 and follow the signs to Bradfield Bridge. Turn on Lone Dome Road, which follows the river.

The tributaries to the Dolores River are also worthwhile angling spots. The biggest tributary is the **West Fork** (see Scenic Location No. 150, p. 406). Forest Road 535, or West Dolores Road, runs along the West Fork and connects to CO 145, 12.5 miles north of the town of Dolores. **Barlow Creek,** which enters the Dolores River about 5 miles north of the town of Rico, is known for its wild trout. **Taylor Creek** and **Bear Creek,** which enter the river several miles east of Stoner along CO 145, are home to cutthroats and rainbows as well as wild trout. For excellent fishing accessible only by foot, try **Stoner Creek** (see Hiking, p. 405). *For information and reservations, including guided backcountry fishing and horseback trips: Circle K Ranch, 27758 CO 145, 970-562-3826, www.ckranch.com; or West Fork Outfitters, 11471 CR 26, 888-777-0403.*

Groundhog Reservoir is stocked with rainbows and cutthroats. Perched on the western edge of the San Juans, this reservoir offers wonderful scenery along with camping spots, a boat ramp, and a marina. From Dolores, take CR 31 (FR 526) north about 23 miles to the turnoff on your right. *Division of Wildlife, Durango, 970-247-0855.*

Rafting: Although the rafting season is short on the Dolores River, it affords the rare chance to run a river through the sandstone canyons and nearby Anasazi ruins of the desert Southwest. It can be a challenging river to run, particularly when the flows are low, but you should try to visit in the high-water season to have this unforgettable experience on a long and beautiful backcountry river. *For information and reservations: Dvorak's Kayak and Rafting Expeditions, 800-824-3795, www.dvorakexpeditions.com.*

Activities

CAMPING

The **McPhee** campground makes an excellent base camp for visiting the archaeological sites and ruins in the area, including Mesa Verde National Park, Hovenweep National Monument, and Ute Mountain Tribal Park. McPhee Reservoir, below the campground, is known for its great cold- and warmwater fishing (see Fishing, at left). From Dolores, go southwest on CO 145 for 2 miles, turn right (north) on CO 184, and go 7 miles. Turn right (north) onto County Road 25, then immediately turn

149 SCENIC LOCATION

MAIN FORK DOLORES RIVER

The drive down from Lizard Head Pass on CO 145 follows the main fork of the Dolores all the way to the town of Dolores. It begins in the subalpine domain of spruce and fir forests at the pass, then enters vast forests of aspen in the montane zone, and ends up in oak brush and ponderosa pine country where narrow-leaved cottonwoods line the riverbanks. The extraordinary size of the aspen forests that cover the hills on either side of the highway makes this one of my favorite spring and autumn drives in the state. Don't forget to stop in the old mining town of Rico for a bite to eat at the Rico Theatre and Café, a one-of-a-kind town and restaurant.

I make my favorite compositions in the upper stretch of this route by parking along the highway and discovering views that incorporate meadows in the foreground, cottonwoods along meadow edges, and aspens rising high onto the hillsides. You can include sky behind the ridge if you wish, but I find that it distracts from the marriage of just fields and trees. As you get closer to Dolores, the highway follows the river and the cottonwoods along it. These views are intensified at sunset when side- and backlighting make the leaves glow. Notice in the fall how the aspens grow as families. Within a vast purview of trees will be leaves in many different stages of change—some green at the same time that others are already yellow. In the spring, some groups of trees have leafed while at the same time others have not. Aspens propagate via their roots as well as by seed, therefore whole groups are genetically connected and reflect this in both their leafing and de-leafing cycles. The main fork of the Dolores is one of the best places in Colorado to witness and photograph this phenomenon. Pull out the telephoto lens and zoom in on these variegated displays of color. Fill the viewfinder from edge to edge with nothing but aspens. Armed with this type of composition, you won't believe the number of variations you will find along this stretch of highway.

right again onto Forest Road 271 and go 2 miles. The **House Creek** campground, 13 miles north of Dolores, borders McPhee Reservoir to the east. From Dolores, go northeast on CR 31 (FR 526) for 7.25 miles to FR 528. Turn left (southwest) on FR 528 and continue for 6 miles. **Dolores River RV Park and Cabins** offers a traditional campsite along the river, a number of RV spaces, and full service and sleeper cabins. Pets are allowed, but a pet fee may be required in for cabin rental. The grounds also have a 24-hour laundry facility and a recreation hall for camp use. The **West Dolores** and **Mavreeso** campgrounds provide pleasant sites by the river. To reach West Dolores campground, take CO 145 northeast from Dolores for 12.5 miles to FR 535. Turn left (north) on FR 535 and drive 8 miles to reach Mavreeso. *For above campgrounds: 970-882-7296.*

HIKING

One hike not to be missed is the 1.25-mile (one way) **Geyser Spring Trail** EASY. This hike takes you through meadows and aspen groves to the only geyser in Colorado. You'll smell the sulfur before you come to the geyser, which erupts every 30 to 40 minutes and then boils for about 10 minutes. From Dolores, head northeast on CO 145 for 12.5 miles and turn left onto Forest Road 535 (West Dolores Road). Go another 20 miles to the trail, which is on your right, 2 miles past the Jonny Bull trailhead. Another wonderful hike is the 8-mile (one way) **Bear Creek Trail** MODERATE, which travels through aspen groves and forests of pine and scrub oak before reaching the waterfalls and pools of Bear Creek. From Dolores, head northeast for 22 miles on CO 145 to the Bear Creek Trail sign. Turn right onto the dirt road and cross the bridge to the parking area. Go through a gate and continue 0.1 mile to the well-marked trail on the north side of the road.

The 17.5-mile (one way) **Stoner Mesa Trail** DIFFICULT takes you to Twin Springs and Stoner Creek and provides an excellent, remote backcountry fishing experience. From Dolores, go northeast 12.5 miles on CO 145 to West Dolores Road (FR 535). Go 3 miles to the Emerson campground and park. **Calico Trail,** MODERATE created in the 1930s by the Civilian Conservation Corps, runs for 13.5 miles through alpine meadows to great views of fourteeners Mount Wilson and El Diente in the Lizard Head Wilderness. From Dolores, go northeast on CO 145 for 12.5 miles. Turn left onto West Dolores Road (FR 535). Continue 25 miles, then turn right onto FR 471 to reach the trailhead. If you want to do this 17-mile hike in one day, you can set a shuttle at the far end of the Calico Trail where it meets CO 145, just east of the Bear Creek Trail (see above). **Navajo Lake Trail** MODERATE takes you into Lizard Head Wilderness to great views of nearby fourteeners Wilson Peak, Mount Wilson, and El Diente. From Dolores, take CO 145 northeast 12.5 miles and bear left on FR 535. Continue 22 miles to the town of Dunton, then go another 2.5 miles to the turnoff for Navajo Lake Trail on your left.

HORSEBACK RIDING

Enjoy hourly, half-day, full-day, and overnight trips along the Dolores River through **Sun Canyon Ranch.**

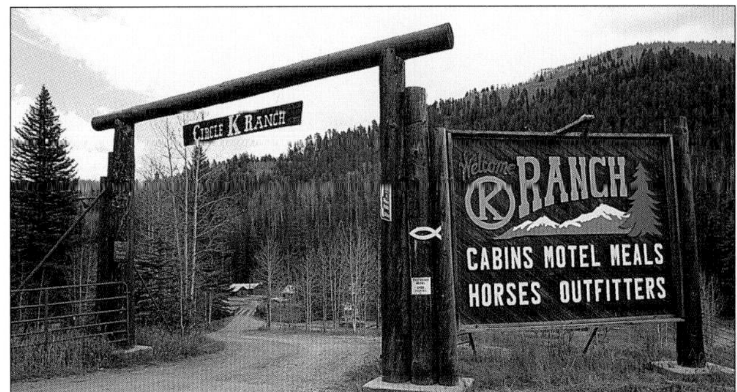

Circle K Guest Ranch, Dolores

It's also a bed and breakfast. From Dolores, head 9 miles northeast on CO 145. *866-737-3377, www.suncanyonranch.com.* **Circle K Guest Ranch** also specializes in horseback tours. Ask about the Horseback Native Trout Adventure. From Dolores, head 25 miles northeast on CO 145. *970-562-3826, 800-477-6381, www.ckranch.com.*

HOT SPRINGS

Dunton Hot Springs are returning to their former glory under new ownership. Much-needed renovations are infusing energy into the small, historic town of Dunton as well. Back in its rowdy gold-mining days, Dunton served as a hideout for Butch Cassidy after he robbed the Telluride bank in 1889. Cassidy's initials are still carved in the restored town saloon. Today the hot springs, a consistent 105 degrees, are covered by a tepee. From Dolores, take CO 145 northeast 12.5 miles to the turnoff for West Dolores Road (Forest Road 535) on the left (north) and continue 22 miles to the town. *970-882-4800.*

MOUNTAIN BIKING

The **McPhee/House Creek Trails** run for 8 to 16 miles, depending on your time and route. From Dolores, follow the McPhee Reservoir and House Creek Recreation Area signs north onto Forest Road 526. Continue 7 miles, then turn left onto FR 528. Go another 5.5 miles to the reservoir and recreation area. Another good route for mountain bikers is the **Stoner Mesa Trail** (see Hiking, at left), but you'll want to explore the great slickrock trails around Cortez as well (see Mountain Biking, Cortez, p. 415).

MUSEUMS

Canyons of the Ancients National Monument contains more than 6000 archaeological sites, the highest density of these sites in the nation. Dispersed camping is allowed in most areas, but there

Anasazi Heritage Center, Dolores

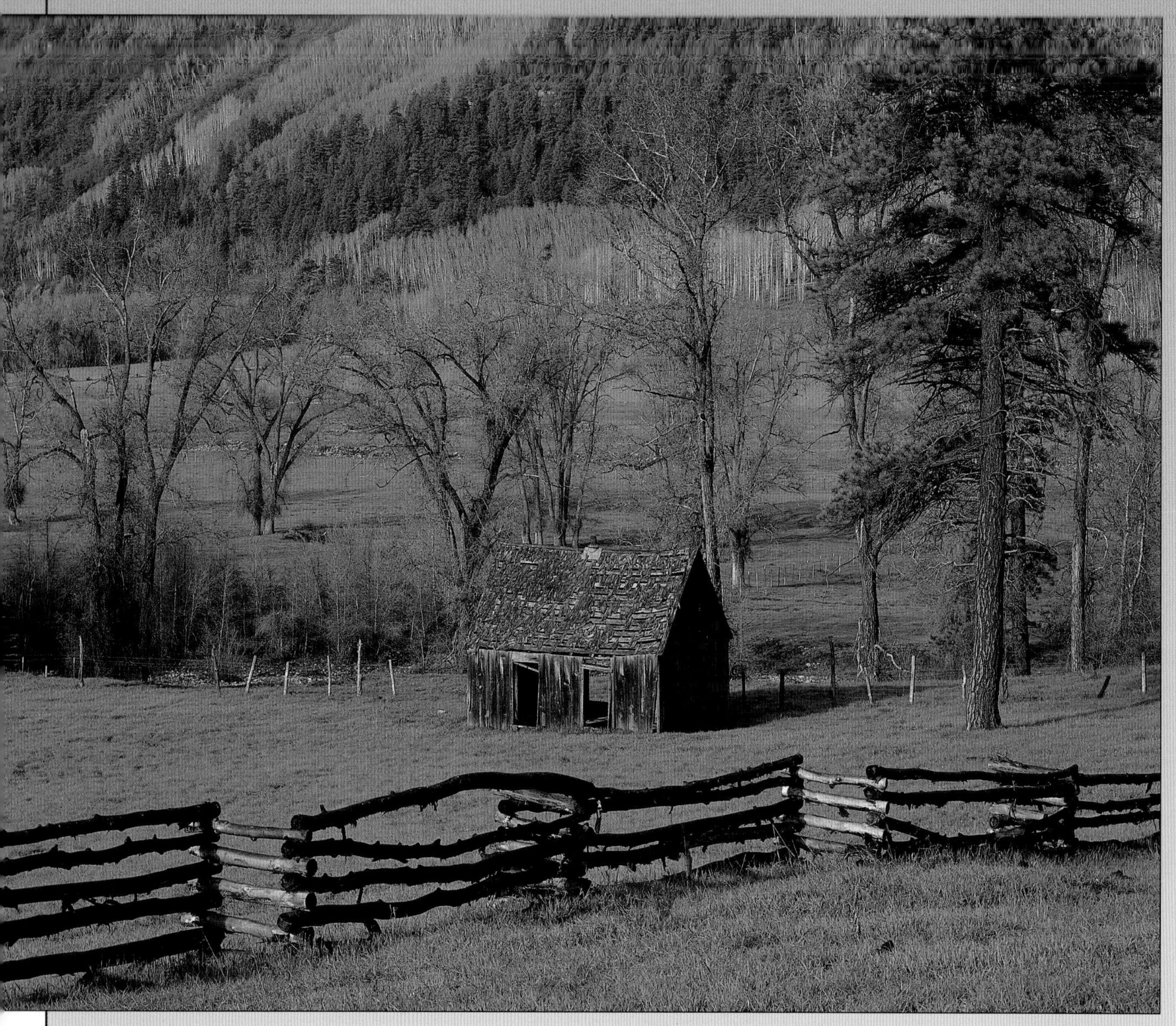

150 SCENIC LOCATION WEST FORK DOLORES RIVER

What I described along the main fork of the Dolores River gets even better along the West Fork, and you don't have to contend with a highway. The dirt road from Lizard Head Pass that takes you to the West Fork, however, is narrow and bumpy in places, but passable by (long-suffering) car. The upper stretch of road traverses subalpine meadows that afford incredible views to the north of the San Miguel Mountains. This road also takes you through the old town of Dunton and its hot springs. The descent from Dunton down the valley of the West Fork of the Dolores starts to resemble the views along the main fork, with aspens and cottonwoods galore! Twelve-and-a-half miles north of the town of Dolores, turn north off CO 145 onto Forest Road 535 to get to the West Fork. Or drive about 5 miles west on CO 145 from Lizard Head Pass until you see FR 535 on your right. It's the very first road on your right after the pass, and the sign mentions Dunton. Eventually you will end up right back at CO 145 just below the old town of Stoner where the main and west forks of the river meet.

On the upper stretch, compose the meadows north of the road with the San Miguel Mountains behind. This landscape lies on an east-west axis, therefore both sunrise and sunset provide great sidelighting. Before you actually arrive in Dunton, make a stop at the well-marked trail to Navajo Lake. You probably won't be able to make it to Navajo Lake and back on a day hike, but the hike partway up the creek is still worth it. A few miles west of Dunton you descend into a valley that looks much like the main fork. Aspens completely cover the hillsides, providing the same kinds of telephoto compositions of variegated autumn and spring aspen colors that I described along the main fork. The lower reaches of the valley open up into large ranch meadows that make for as pastoral a composition as I've seen in Colorado. About halfway to the highway you'll see FR 686 on the left, an old logging road that ascends the south hillside and takes you into the aspen forest. These intimate scenes of the trees form an appropriate photographic complement to images made from afar.

Rio Grande Southern Railroad Museum, Dolores

are no developed campsites. Remember, it is illegal to remove artifacts or disturb dig sites. *27501 Hwy 184, 970-882-4811, www.co.blm.gov/canm.* Many of the artifacts at the **Anasazi Heritage Center** arrived under a cloud of controversy. In 1987, despite attempts by historic preservationists to protect Anasazi cultural sites, agricultural interests succeeded in flooding the area to create nearby McPhee Reservoir. Farmers and ranchers gained a reliable water supply and a recreational jewel—and many artifacts were recovered from what is now the bottom of the reservoir—but much Anasazi history was lost. Even so, this is simply one of the finest museums in Colorado. The center hosts lectures, films, and special events. You can actually touch real artifacts, grind corn, and weave on a loom. Be sure to check out the replica of a pit house and take the 0.5-mile nature trail to the Escalante Pueblo for views of Mesa Verde, McPhee Reservoir, and the Four Corners area. The center is just south of Dolores at 27501 CO 184. *970-882-5600, www.co.blm.gov/ahc/.* Railroad enthusiasts flock to the **Rio Grande Southern Railroad Museum** in Dolores to catch a glimpse of the newly refurbished engine, Galloping Goose #5. The museum is housed in the Dolores Depot, a re-creation of the original Rio Grande Southern Railroad Depot, and recounts the town's railroad history through dioramas, photographs, and other memorabilia. *421 Railroad Ave., 970-882-7082.*

Restaurants

Ponderosa Restaurant ($-$$) is a family restaurant serving breakfast, lunch, and dinner daily. Enjoy a great steak in a casual and friendly atmosphere. *8th St. and CO 145, 970-882-7910.* Another great spot is **The Southern Restaurant & Eating House** ($-$$), located in the Rio Grande Southern Hotel. The restaurant is open for breakfast and lunch every day except Tuesday. Sundays they serve brunch, and Wednesday through Saturdays they are open for dinner. Don't miss Fish Fry Friday! *101 S. 5th St., 970-882-2125.* If you're looking for something a bit lighter for breakfast or lunch, check out the **Bears Den Café** ($). They're open through lunch every day except Tuesday. *1319 Railroad Ave., 970-882-3001.*

Accommodations

Dolores Mountain Inn

The **Dolores Mountain Inn** ($), at 701 Railroad Ave., is a wonderful place to stay at a very reasonable price. *970-882-7203, 800-842-8113, www.dminn.com.* For a great vacation, try the **Circle K Guest Ranch** ($-$$). The Circle K has riverside cabins, motel units, lodge rooms, numerous activities, and, of course, storytelling around the camp-fire. The ranch is 25 miles northeast of Dolores on CO 145. *970-562-3826, 800-477-6381, www.ckranch.com.* The **Rio Grande Southern Hotel B&B** ($-$$) features Victorian-style lodging in Dolores's oldest building. *101 S. 5th St., 970-882-2125, 866-882-3026, www.rgshotel.com.* **Outpost Motel Cabins & RV Park** ($) has something for every sort of traveler —they offer rooms with kitchens, cozy cabins, and access to full RV hook-ups. *1800 Central Ave., 970-882-7271, 800-382-4892, www.doloreslodgings.com.*

Special Events

The annual **Dolores River Festival,** held each June, is a fantastic community get-together that celebrates the Dolores River and its connection to the town and the environment. Features music, food, and entertainment and the annual Fun-Run. *www.doloresriverfestival.com.* Every year in early August, Dolores throws itself a party. **Escalante Days** includes bike races, water fights, arm wrestling, softball, an egg toss, a coin hunt, a parade, and even a chainsaw competition. The festivities are topped off with a barbecue and street dance. *970-882-4018.*

For More Information

Dolores Chamber of Commerce/Visitor Center, *201 Railroad Ave., 970-882-4018, www.doloreschamber.com.*

Cortez

(see map on p. 402)

Drop down into Cortez, a rural ranching town touched by tourism, archaeology, and ancient spirits. Every minute spent in this area is special. Although many stay in Durango when visiting Mesa Verde, I prefer to save the drive time and stay either right in the national park or in Cortez. But Cortez isn't merely a convenient town to the national park; Cortez is the heart of the ancestral lands of Colorado's native peoples, past and present. The Pueblo Indians of the Four Corners region are the descendants of the cliff dwellers whose ruins haunt these lands. This is the home of the Anasazi (the ancestral Puebloans, "ancient ones"), who mysteriously disappeared centuries ago. Cortez is encircled by their kivas, pit houses, and cliff dwellings at not just Mesa Verde, but at Hovenweep National Monument, Lowry Pueblo, and the Ute Mountain Tribal Park. In Cortez, the spirit of the mythical Kokopelli comes to life (see Colorado Cameo, p. 413). The lands of Mesa Verde ("green table") and environs remain sacred to native peoples—and attract thousands of tourists each year.

History

Founded in 1886 on the edge of the Ute Mountain Ute Indian Reservation, Cortez was a new town in a place with a much longer history. As many as 100,000 Anasazi may have dwelled in the sprawling lands radiating from what is now called the Four Corners as early as the 9th century, in places like Canyon de Chelly, Ariz., Chaco Canyon, N.M., and Mesa Verde. Spanish Catholic priests later crossed these lands, seeking a route to California and proselytizing within the tribes. Too far from the high country to benefit from the spoils of mining, Cortez has long been the center of the surrounding farming and ranching country and is the seat of Montezuma County. Intermittently engaged in lumber extraction, coal mining, and gas exploration, the town today relies strongly, as it did at its beginnings, on nearby Mesa Verde for its vitality. Awestruck visitors, diligent scholars, and spiritual seekers all keep Cortez a unique corner of the state.

Main Attractions

HOVENWEEP NATIONAL MONUMENT AND LOWRY PUEBLO

Be sure to take time to see the archaeological sites and ruins beyond Mesa Verde in the Cortez area. You can escape the crowds and enjoy a unique experience at the Hovenweep National Monument (see Scenic Location No. 154, p. 414), which straddles the Utah border. More than 700 years old, Hovenweep's ruins are remarkable for their variously shaped stone towers. The Square Tower Group is the best preserved and includes the remains of nearly 30 kivas. Battle Rock, now known as Castle Rock, on McElmo Canyon Road, was the site of a conflict between Ute and Navajo warriors (see Scenic Location No. 155, p. 416). It is said that from this rock many Navajos jumped to their deaths rather than surrender to the victorious Utes. Hovenweep is 45 miles west of Cortez; drive 3 miles south on US 666, turn right onto McElmo Canyon Road, and follow signs to the monument. You can also camp at the Hovenweep campground. No reservations.

A wonderful side-trip on the return to Cortez is **Lowry Pueblo** (see Scenic Location No. 156, p. 417), notable for its large ceremonial kiva and painted wall. Northwest of Cortez, the Lowry ruins are just 9 miles west of the town of Pleasant View and US 666 on Road CC. These dirt roads can be very treacherous after heavy rains. *970-562-4282, www.nps.gov/hove.*

MESA VERDE NATIONAL PARK

In 2000 the Bircher and Pony Fires burned more than 28,000 acres of federal, Ute Mountain Ute, and Mesa Verde National Park lands here, yet the celebrated cliff dwellings survived. Perhaps this is a testament to the enduring mystery of these national treasures. I've often wondered what the Wetherill brothers and their brother-in-law Charles Mason said when they first saw Cliff Palace in 1888 while herding cattle. In the years that followed, the brothers and other nearby settlers explored what are now known as Balcony House, Spruce Tree House, and other cliff dwellings. Unfortunately, many of the ancient artifacts disappeared. Even so, Mesa Verde became world famous, attracting such early enthusiasts as author Frederick Chapin and Swedish archaeologist Gustaf Nordenskiold, who collaborated on book projects. (Visit the **Chapin Mesa Archaeological Museum** near Spruce Tree House to gain insight into what everyday life might have been like for the cliff dwellers.) Encompassing more than 52,000 acres and 4,000 archaeological sites today, Mesa Verde National Park (see Scenic Location No. 152, p. 410) is 10 miles east of Cortez on US 160 and 35 miles west of Durango. *970-529-4465, www.nps.gov/meve.*

Artifact Plunder and Site Preservation: It was one thing to have ancient artifacts disappear into the homes of local people, or be exhibited in Denver, but it was quite another to have them boxed and shipped off to Europe. A local judge issued an injunction to stop the exodus of these irreplaceable items, an action that brought attention to the need to protect the ruins from further vandalism and destruction. The Colorado Cliff Dwellings Association formed in 1900 and began lobbying in earnest to protect this extraordinary place. By its efforts, Mesa Verde was designated a federally protected national park in 1906. The concurrent Antiquities Act of 1906, a watershed of the historic-preservation movement in America, made the disturbance of historic and prehistoric sites on federal lands a crime. Mesa Verde National Park is unique among our national parks in that it achieved its status based not on scenery but on its singularity as an archaeological site. Mesa Verde is also a United Nations Educational, Scientific, and Cultural Organization (UNESCO) World Heritage Site. Visitors make the pilgrimage to these ruins from all over the nation and the world.

151 SCENIC LOCATION — LA PLATA RIVER AND MOUNTAINS

Between Durango and Cortez, and south of the Dolores River forks described in Scenic Location Nos. 149 and 150, pages 404 and 406, lies the last major range of mountains in the southwestern Colorado Rockies, the La Platas. Incredibly scenic, they are visible from high places around the San Juan Mountains and penetrable via an old mining road. The river along the way is lovely and reveals a few waterfalls in its upper stretches. The road gets quite rough up high, but nothing that a four-wheel drive can't handle. Head west on US 160 from Durango (see Durango map, p. 358). Less than a mile after the turnoff to CO 140, look for La Plata River Road (County Road 124) on your right. Fine for the first 8 miles, the road turns rough as it enters Cumberland Basin. Take a four-wheel drive if you can.

You meet many nice views along the river during the first part of the drive. Open meadows give way to coniferous forests and smatterings of aspen. When the road turns rough, you ascend into the subalpine zone and some of the most beautiful wildflower fields in Colorado. But you have to make it to Cumberland Basin to see the best of the best. Flowers flourish along the road, and if you make it to the end, hike the Colorado Trail 2 miles west up to Indian Trail Ridge. Between mid-July and mid-August, you won't believe just how lush the flowers are.

Cumberland Basin is a fine place in which to practice extreme depth of focus. With an SLR you can "stop down" to your smallest aperture, thereby maximizing depth of field to make your flowers prominent in the foreground of your composition (see pp. 109–117, *Photographing the Landscape*). It's easy to get flowers and mountains together in the scene. On the way back down the road, look for the waterfalls along the river. If the light is cloudy, or the sun sits behind the ridges, make images of the falls using slow shutter speeds to create the "cotton candy" appearance of the whitewater (see pp. 81–83, *Photographing the Landscape*).

152 SCENIC LOCATION

MESA VERDE NATIONAL PARK

Situated in the heart of Anasazi cliff-dwelling country, Mesa Verde National Park protects these special ruins. Yes, access is all too controlled, but you still have freedom and time enough to make wonderful photographs, if you follow a few tips. The beige color of the dwellings and the sandstone cliffs is highly reflective of direct sunlight, so details in the dwelling walls become difficult to see and record on film. Therefore, always try to photograph in cloudy light or when the sun is so low in the sky that *every* part of your view is within shade. I emphasize "every" because the worst thing that you can do is try to include both shadow and light within the same scene. The film simply cannot handle such extreme contrast. The shadows in your photograph will appear even darker on film than to your eye, and the highlights will be completely washed out. I prefer cloudy light to the kind of light you get in the shade. When clouds cover the sky, a "warmer" light results, very complementary to the subtle colors of the ruins. In shade, the blue sky mixes with colors in the landscape, turning subtle shades of beige into less appealing shades of green.

When you are not photographing ruins, the ubiquitous canyons of Mesa Verde provide plenty of wonderful subject matter. Watch for prominent vistas as you drive around the park. From various pullouts you can compose the parallax distortion of wide canyon mouths in the foreground shrinking into narrow canyons in the distance. It's another variation of the lead-in line that creates depth in the scene. In autumn the oak brush turns fiery orange and red. Visit the park in mid- to late October to photograph these colors without the summer crowds.

Campground and Lodge: The largest public campground in Colorado, **Morefield** is complete with an amphitheater, grocery store, gas station, and laundry. Morefield is about 4 miles into the park, to the left. No reservations. *800-449-2288.* One of my favorite overnight spots in Colorado is the **Far View Lodge** ($$), about 12 miles from the park entrance, to your right just before the Far View Visitor Center. The rooms, arranged in a terrace fashion, provide spectacular park views. The lodge's Southwestern-style restaurant looks out to panoramic views from the bar on the top of the roof. To your left (north) you can see the snowcapped peaks of the La Plata Mountains near Durango; to your right you can see as far as Shiprock, N.M., and even to the canyons of Arizona. In the late evening, mule deer often graze nearby. *970-529-4421, www.visitmesaverde.com.*

Far View Lodge, Mesa Verde National Park

Cliff Dwelling Tours: Having provided protection to the Anasazi from both the elements and enemies, cliff dwellings still endure in mystery and majesty throughout the park. The most famous of these is **Cliff Palace,** a labyrinth of more than 200 rooms and 23 kivas. To tour the ruins, purchase a ticket at the Far View Visitor Center; shuttles will take you to various sites. The National Park Service also provides a map as you enter the park. The excellent ranger-guided tours leave on the hour from the Cliff Palace overlook. Although the climb up on a ladder between rock walls can be rather strenuous, the tour is rewarding. Or get tickets for a ranger-guided **Balcony House** tour, but be sure to note the restrictions on how many major ruins you can visit per day. Enjoy a self-guided tour of **Spruce Tree House** without tickets. From the museum, it is an easy 15-minute walk to this cliff dwelling, and rangers are available to answer questions. If you see the park by car, stop at the overlooks and view the smaller cliff dwellings and grain-storage structures across the canyon. Take the binoculars.

For a less-populated experience, exit from the visitor center onto the 12-mile, hairpin Wetherill Mesa Road. Along this road you can visit **Step House, Long House,** and the **Badger House Community.** Long House is Mesa Verde's second largest ruin, and tickets are required. If you are pressed for time, Aramark Tours provides excellent half-day and full-day tours. *970-533-1944, 800-449-2288.* To arrange for a tour, stop at the tour desk at Far View Visitor Center. Tours depart from Morefield campground and the Far View Lodge. *www.visitmesaverde.com.*

Mesa Verde Tours are "The Four Corners Tour Specialists," providing site-seeing tours throughout the Chaco Canyon, Telluride, Ouray, and Monument Valley areas, including historic mining towns and other scenic tours. They provide round-trip transportation from your lodging, beverages throughout the tour, and a picnic lunch. Each of the Mesa Verde Tours guides has been chosen for their knowledge of the region, and many have socio- or anthropological backgrounds focusing on the area. Group tours are limited so that your experience will be more one-on-one, so call at least one day ahead to book a spot for you and your family. *970-565-1278, www.mesaverdetours.net.*

Cycling: Mesa Verde's 32 miles of roads are becoming more popular with cyclists, particularly off-season. The ruins and overlooks make good rest stops, and you can often view wildlife in these austere canyons. The hairpin curves as you enter the park can be challenging, though, so use caution around vehicles, especially when passing through the tunnel near the park entrance. Note that no designated bike lanes exist on park roads.

Hiking: Because of the many archaeological sites in the park, you won't find many hiking trails, but the handful here do show you the ruins and canyons from a different angle. **Point Lookout Trail** EASY affords views of the Mancos and Montezuma valleys and may have been used by the U.S. Cavalry as a signal station. **Knife Edge Trail** EASY leads you across sandstone cliffs. **Prater Ridge Trail** EASY is a 7-mile loop that provides solitude and a good chance to see wildlife. Mesa Verde is home to mule deer, bears, mountain lions, wild turkeys, and raptors—especially hawks and turkey vultures—not to mention wild horses and Indian ponies. All the above trails start from the Morefield campground.

If you hike just one trail, make it the **Petroglyph Point Trail** EASY, a popular, 2.8-mile loop that brings you to ancient Anasazi rock art. The petroglyphs give us a glimpse into Anasazi spiritual beliefs and worldviews. Petroglyph Point Trail and the shorter **Spruce Canyon Trail** EASY start from the Spruce Tree Ruin. Short trails that provide great views of the cliff dwellings and other ruins include the **Soda Canyon Overlook Trail** and the **Balcony House Overlook Trail** EASY.

Historical Driving Tour: With the help of a park map, you can trace thousands of years of human history by taking a self-guided driving tour of the park. You'll see the evolution of the cliff dwellings from the earliest pit houses of the basketmakers, which provided shelter for the Anasazi from about A.D. 550 to 750, to the glorious Cliff Palace of about 1200. Some of these early remains have indications of rudimentary kivas, or religious ceremonial rooms. Notice that the pit houses on the south end of the park are bigger, with more rooms, and that the ceremonial kivas seem more prominent. The next evolution in Anasazi culture is evident in the large farming communities at the top of the mesa. Thousands of people lived in

153 UTE MOUNTAIN TRIBAL PARK/ MANCOS RIVER

SCENIC LOCATION

Mesa Verde is actually the name of the entire geologic escarpment that is so conspicuous south from Cortez and US 160. Some two dozen canyons drain down its south side into the Mancos River. Within these canyons stand hundreds of cliff dwellings and related structures. Some of the ruins lie within the national park, the rest within Ute Mountain Tribal Park. These tribal lands are off-limits to non-Indians, but access is available from the tribe on a guided basis. I have made several trips into the tribal park to explore Anasazi ruins visited by relatively few people—not only since they were discovered in modern times, but since they were actually vacated by their residents around A.D. 1250. It's an amazing experience to walk on trails littered with potsherds a thousand years old. (See Ute Mountain Tribal Park, below, for information about making reservations to tour the ruins.)

Should you wish to drive the Mancos River Road without an escort, be sure to ask permission at the tribal headquarters in the town of Towaoc, 11 miles south of Cortez off US 160/666. The picturesque Mancos River Road south of Towaoc provides access to many dramatic ruins suspended high on cliff walls. Cottonwoods and other deciduous plants line the riverbanks, making a wonderful foreground for the beige cliffs to the north. In late October the yellow cottonwoods are especially scenic. The Mancos River can also be accessed from the north through Bureau of Land Management public lands not restricted to travel. Four miles west of the town of Mancos on US 160, drive south on County Road 38. The road is improved at first, then turns rough. Nevertheless, the scenery is sublime, so consider taking the four-wheel drive. You can bushwhack by foot up the canyon walls, which reveal great views of the La Plata Mountains to the northeast.

these communities from about 800 to the mid-1200s. Rooms were simply added on when families increased in size.

Although these farming communities continued to thrive up until the late 1200s, some began to build and move into the cliff dwellings for which Mesa Verde is famous. The cliff dwellings are quite sophisticated, with separate rooms and grand ceremonial kivas. Be sure to walk the **Far View Trail** that links the mesa-top farming villages of Far View House, Pipe Shrine House, Coyote Village, Megalithic House, and Far View Tower. The Far View Ruins are the first you see south of the Far View Visitor Center; a sign marks the pull-off.
Shopping: Mesa Verde National Park merchants offer Southwestern wares including Navajo and Hopi jewelry, Zuni fetishes, and pottery. Handcrafted items are for sale at the Far View Lodge, the Far View Terrace, and the Spruce Tree House gift shops. An elderly Navajo woman in traditional dress has set up her loom in the gift shop at the Far View Terrace; you can actually see how the Navajo weave their splendid rugs. One of the most unusual but best spots for native jewelry and other items is a trailer on the one-way loop to Cliff Palace and Balcony House, on the Ute Mountain Ute Indian Reservation just a few feet from the park boundary.

UTE MOUNTAIN TRIBAL PARK

Ute Mountain Tribal Park is a unique experience not only because of its setting on the Ute Mountain Ute Reservation but because of the requirement that a tribal guide accompany you (see Scenic Location No. 153, this page). Guides provide both a historical and spiritual understanding of this exceptional region. This

COLORADO CAMEO

Kokopelli

"Kokopelli! Kokopelli!" Commonly portrayed as a humpbacked figure wearing a spiked, feather headdress and playing a long flute, he is everywhere in the Southwest, particularly in the Four Corners region. He appears more frequently than any other figure on the petroglyphs and pictographs of the Anasazi dwellings. He also adorns artwork, T-shirts, and all matter of merchandise. Children recognize him and call out his name in regional boutiques and tourist gift shops.

The variety of Kokopelli images has led to much speculation among scholars about his identity, powers, and ceremonial role in religious and cultural life. Kokopelli (his Hopi name) is sometimes portrayed lifting his flute toward the heavens or carrying a bow. Some versions hobble on a clubfoot or carry a stick. In northern New Mexico and Arizona, Kokopelli is sometimes shown with both flute and a bow or arrows. Did he lure game with his music? When portrayed lying on his back, Kokopelli looks like an insect. Insects, particularly locusts, were also associated with music and healing.

Local tribes interpret him in various intriguing ways. The Hopis believe that Kokopelli was a trader, carrying a large sack of goods on his back. Indeed, trading was vigorous among the tribes of the Southwest, Mexico, and Central America. (Notice the seashells and coral used in native jewelry, now on display in area museums, obtained by this trade.) The Pueblo people believe that Kokopelli was a traveling musician; the hump on his back is a sack of songs. Of course, the haunting sounds of the flute remain as central to the music of the Southwest today as they were in Anasazi culture. The Zuni believe that Kokopelli was a rain priest who brought precious water to the arid Southwest. This would be consistent with the belief that Kokopelli made crops grow and women fertile and explains the emphasis on sexual virility in some pictographs. To me, Kokopelli is a delightful, whimsical character who brought healing and happiness to native peoples and continues to bring joy to all today.

154 SCENIC LOCATION

HOVENWEEP NATIONAL MONUMENT

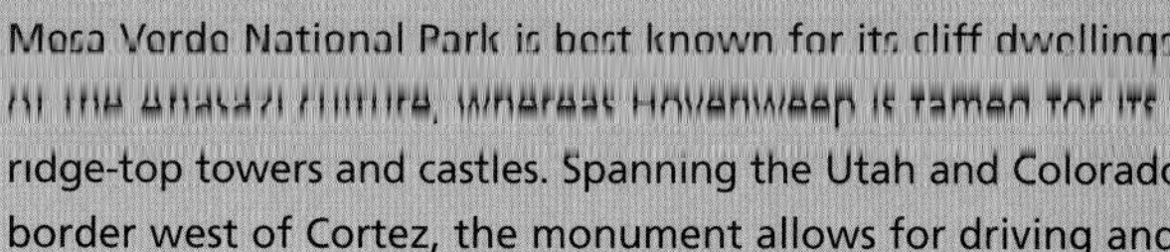

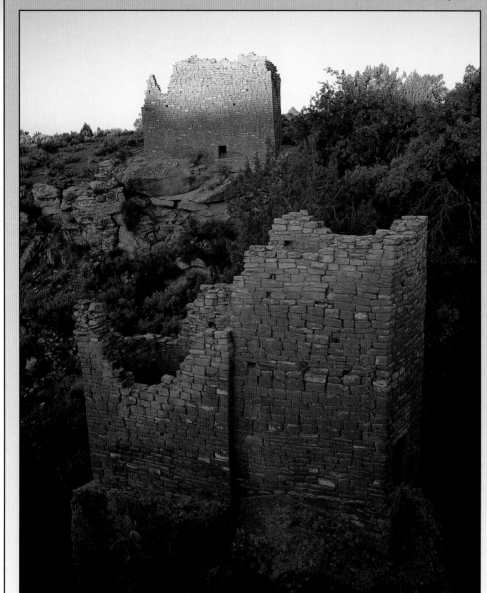

Mesa Verde National Park is best known for its cliff dwellings of the Anasazi culture, whereas Hovenweep is famed for its ridge-top towers and castles. Spanning the Utah and Colorado border west of Cortez, the monument allows for driving and hiking access to some of the most intact ruins in the Four Corners region. Three miles south of Cortez, turn to the west off US 160/666 onto McElmo Canyon Road (County Road G) and drive past the Ismay Trading Post at the border. Follow the signs north to the monument. These are dirty, dusty roads but otherwise should be no problem for a passenger car.

Unlike the cliff dwellings, which are too hidden to catch sunrise or sunset light, the Hovenweep towers light up like fire at the end of the day. Especially at sunset, orange light turns already beige/orange ruins into red. It's a property of physics that the more particulate matter that exists in the atmosphere, such as dust stirred up during a day in the desert, the redder the light will be when the sun is just above the horizon (see pp. 86–88, *Photographing the Landscape*). The ruins are high enough on the ridges to catch the very last of the setting sunlight. Long shadows off the ruins add depth to the scene, so compose your image using sidelighting. Cutthroat Castle and Square Tower ruins stand especially large above the horizon.

125,000-acre park, which follows the Mancos River, was set aside by the tribe to preserve the history and culture of the prehistoric civilization and its ruins. Hundreds of surface ruins and cliff dwellings remain here, along with wall paintings and ancient petroglyphs. Because the goal of the park is to protect the natural setting of the ruins, you'll find few amenities. Be prepared to hike. *970-565-3751 ext. 330, 800-847-5485, www.utemountainute.com.*

Activities

CAMPING

Transfer campground gives you a grand prospect of the West Mancos River Canyon and La Plata Mountains; solitude beyond the Mesa Verde multitudes; and access to the West Mancos River and other hikes and to the Transfer Park/Windy Gap mountain-bike trail (see Mountain Biking, p. 415). From Cortez, go 18 miles east on US 160 to the town of Mancos, head north 0.5 mile on CO 184, turn right (east) onto County Road 42 (Forest Road 561), and drive 10 miles. No reservations. *970-882-7296.* **Mancos State Park** has shade and privacy adjacent to Mancos (Jackson Gulch) Reservoir. From Mancos, take CO 184 north 0.5 mile to CR 42, turn right, drive 4 miles to Road N, turn left, and go 0.5 mile. *970-883-2208.*

DUDE RANCHING

If you're looking for a great Colorado vacation idea, check out

Echo Basin Ranch ($-$$$) in Mancos. The ranch sits at 7,800 feet above sea level and the grounds are covered with ponds, streams, and aspen and pine forests. Breathtaking views surround the area. The ranch offers a variety of lodging options, including a-frame and deluxe cabins and RV campgrounds. Ranch facilities also include horseback riding—book hourly and/or with breakfast, lunch, or dinner—an outdoor pool and hot tub, basketball, horseshoes, billiards, volleyball, and a driving range. Fishing and hiking areas can also be found nearby. The grounds even include the Echo Basin Amphitheater, where concerts are held throughout the year. And Echo Basin has its very own restaurant and saloon featuring a full-service bar, southwest dinners, dancing, and facilities for private parties and events. *43747 CR M, 970-533-7000, www.echobasin.com.*

FISHING

Trout, perch, crappie, blue gills, and large-mouth bass fill the reservoirs in the Mancos area. To get to **Mancos (Jackson Gulch) Reservoir** from Mancos, see Camping, above. To get to **Joe Moore Reservoir** State Wildlife Area (SWA), take CO 184 to County Road 40 and go north. A bit farther west on CO 184 are the **Puett** and **Summit Reservoirs,** both SWAs. **McPhee Reservoir** is a favorite local fishing spot (see Main Attractions, Dolores, p. 403). *Division of Wildlife, Durango, 970-247-0855.*

GAMING

Ute Mountain Casino, owned and operated by the Ute Mountain Ute Tribe, draws tourists and tribe members alike. It is not uncommon to see older women in traditional dress at the casino. Gaming on reservations is controversial, but the Ute Mountain Casino provides jobs for tribal members and good fun for tourists. Weekly entertainment takes place in the Indian village adjoining the casino. An RV park and a campground with full facilities are also available here. Shuttles run on a regular basis from Cortez to the casino, 15 miles south on US 160/666. *For information and shuttle schedules: 970-565-8800, 800-258-8007, www.utemountaincasino.com.*

GOLF

The public **Conquistador Golf Course's** 18-hole, par-72 course has views of Sleeping Ute Mountain and the La Plata Mountains. Conquistador is northeast of Cortez off CO 145. *210 E. Main St., 970-565-3402.*

HIKING

Trails around Cortez all lead to distinctive sandstone landscapes dotted with ruins and desert wildflowers in early spring. You'll be well-served by picking up maps and information on these remote trails at any sporting goods store in Cortez. **Box Canyon Trail** EASY follows the West Mancos River, so take your fly rod. This 2.75-mile trail (one way) starts near the Transfer campground on the east side of the road and heads south (see Camping, at left).

Sand Canyon Trail MODERATE affords views of remote Anasazi cliff dwellings across sandstone canyons and slickrock. This hike is 1 to 5 miles one way, depending on the route. To get to the trail from Cortez, go 2.5 miles south on US 666 until you reach McElmo Canyon Road (Road G) and turn right (west). Drive about 12 miles on McElmo Canyon Road and cross McElmo Creek (see Scenic Location No. 155, p. 416). The trailhead is 0.2 mile past the creek to the right of the parking lot.

HORSEBACK RIDING

One of the best ways to see the scenery in southwestern Colorado, is by horse. **Rimrock Outfitters,** in Mancos, features horseback trail and dinner rides, as well as romantic carriage rides and holiday sleigh rides. Trail rides can be booked by the hour, or you can book for the day. There is also a Breakfast Ride, where you'll enjoy a scenic horseback ride and an authentic cowboy cooked breakfast with eggs and pancakes. For a little more adventure, you can take advantage of Rimrock's four day Ute Mountain Tribal Park backpack trip, where you'll explore cliff dwellings in the park and enjoy breathtaking scenery. The trip does include strenuous hiking and horseback riding, and reservations need to be made three months in advance, but it's a great way to experience the area. Shorter camp trips are also available. *12175 CR 44, 970-533-788, www.rimrockoutfitters.com.*

MOUNTAIN BIKING

Biking in the Four Corners region combines slickrock canyon country riding with both prehistoric and historic sites. The 13-mile **Railroad Loop** EASY follows an old narrow-gauge railroad easement. You can see the remnants of railroad tracks and trestle along Forest Road 568. The trail starts at the Madden Peak Road, 5.6 miles east of the town of Mancos (18 miles east of Cortez on US 160) at the top of Mancos Hill. Go north on Madden Peak Road (FR 316) for 1 mile, then turn right onto FR 568. You then connect with FR 320, which runs into US 160. The **Transfer Park/Windy Gap Trail** MODERATE is a 22-mile loop to spectacular views through aspen groves and pine stands. You also see an abandoned fire-watch tower. From Mancos, go 0.25 mile north on CO 184 and turn right onto County Road 42, which becomes West Mancos Road (FR 561). Go 10 miles and park near the Transfer campground entrance. The bike route follows FR 565 out and FR 561 back.

One of the most popular mountain-bike trails here is the **Cannonball Mesa Trail** MODERATE. This 10-mile round-trip ride over an old wagon trail is very well marked and takes you through piñon and juniper trees, passing remote Anasazi ruins and the famous Navajo/Hopi war site of Battle Rock, now called Castle Rock. To get to the trail from Cortez, go south 2 miles on US 160/666 and turn right at the M&M Café onto McElmo Canyon Road. Drive 20.4 miles to an unmarked country road on the right with a cattleguard and park. Take time to visit the ruins and enjoy the view from the overlook at the trail's turnaround.

continued page 416

McELMO CREEK

County Road G heads west from US 160/666, 3 miles south of Cortez, and follows McElmo Creek all the way into Utah. Not only does it provide access to Hovenweep National Monument but it's also home to Anasazi ruins and lovely scenery. The sandstone cliffs that begin to appear to the north of the road a few miles from Cortez are dramatic, and Sleeping Ute Mountain to the south looms high overhead to make a great backdrop for the cliffs in the foreground.

Twelve miles west off US 160/666, look for the Castle Rock Anasazi historic site on the north side of the road. There are signs in front of this conspicuous sandstone outcrop. My book *Colorado: 1870–2000* (see p. 209) includes a William Henry Jackson photograph of Castle Rock, actually called Battle Rock when he made the photograph in 1875, which shows a prominent ruin against its northeast wall. My repeat photograph reveals that the ruin had disappeared in the ensuing 125 years. Archaeological excavations suggest that Battle Rock was the scene of a violent skirmish around the year 1270. The remains of 41 people were found here. Though the ruin that was built against the wall is gone, there is a free-standing pueblo nearby to the east. See if you can find it! Then explore north of Castle Rock for more ruins. But whether you find the ruins or not, there are many fine scenics along this route. Take advantage of sunrise and sunset light and its ability on a clear day to turn already red rocks into shades you won't believe.

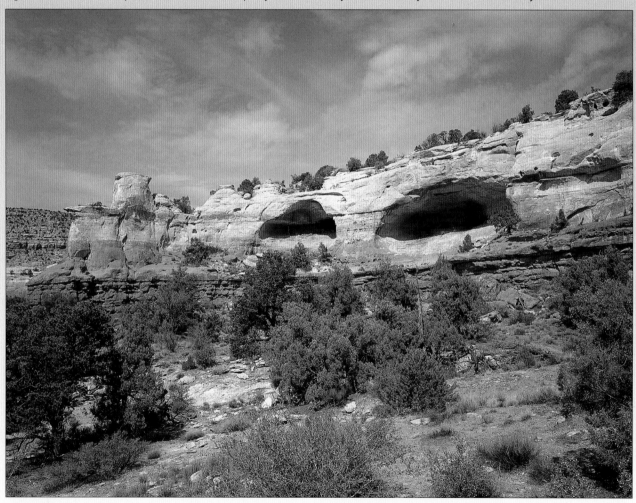

The 16.2-mile (one way) trail up **McElmo Canyon** MODERATE has tremendous views plus access to archaeological sites. From Cortez, go north on US 666 for 5.3 miles and turn left onto Road P, drive 4.5 miles, and turn left onto Road 18. At 5 miles, turn right onto Road P. At 6.4 miles (before the red house), turn left onto Road N, bear to the right and continue to mile 9.5, then look for the BLM sign on the left that marks the Sand Canyon Pueblo excavation.

The 17-mile **Cutthroat Castle Trail & Negro Canyon Loop** MODERATE reaches the more remote ruins in Hovenweep National Monument and through Hovenweep and Negro canyons. To get to the trail and loop from Cortez, go north on US 666 and turn left after 17.5 miles at the Hovenweep National Monument sign (Road BB). Look for a smaller Hovenweep sign and dirt road where you can park. Return by continuing 2 miles from the last hill to the Pleasant View Road and turning right. *For bike maps and rentals: Kokopelli Bikes, 30 W. Main St., 970-565-4408.*

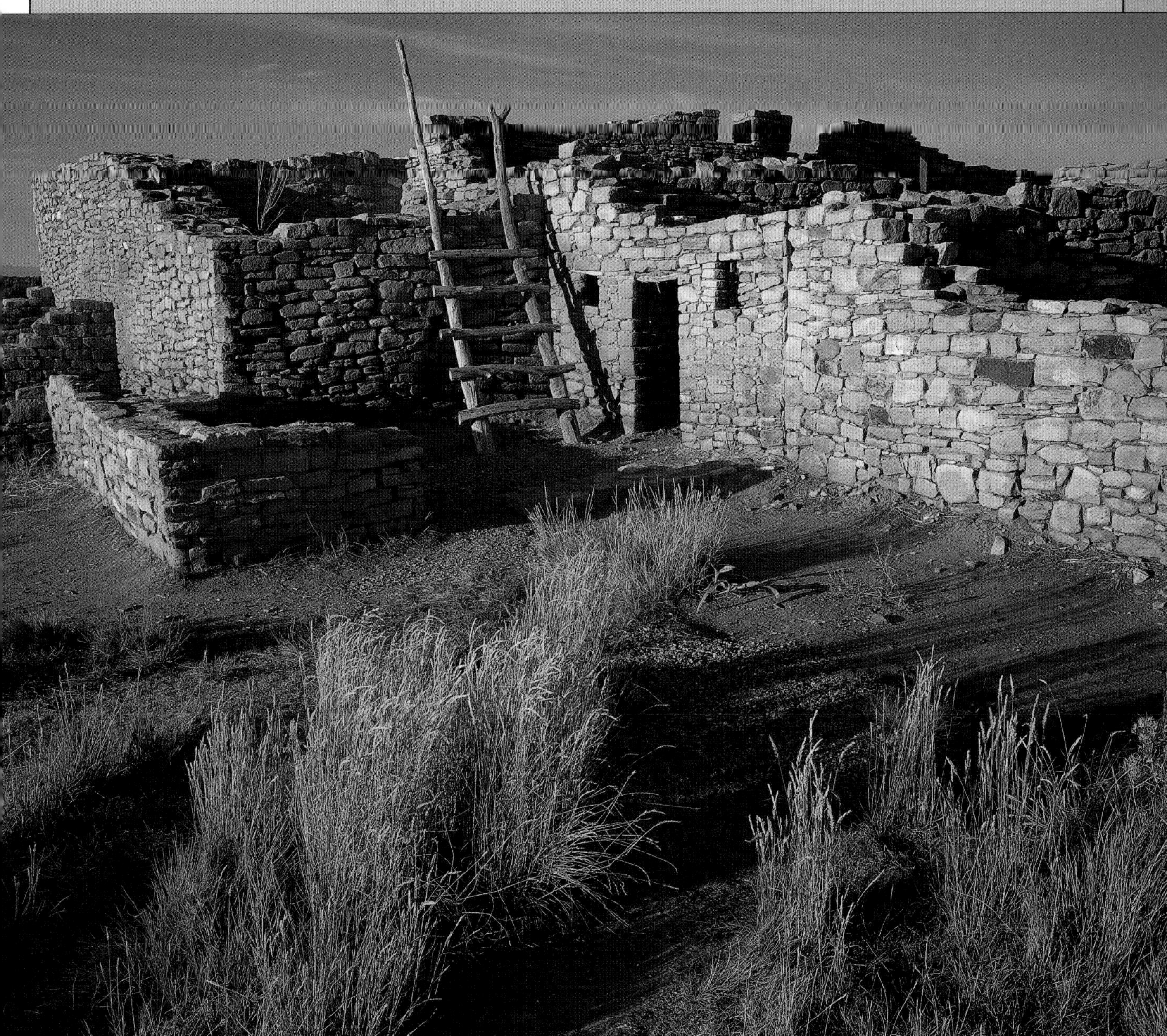

156 SCENIC LOCATION LOWRY PUEBLO

This Anasazi ruin is a highly excavated and restored pueblo well worth visiting and photographing. Named for homesteader George Lowry, this site is typical of the medium-sized pueblos that once dotted the Montezuma Valley around present-day Cortez. The pueblo had a total of almost 40 rooms and eight kivas at its peak around the year 1000 and was home to about 100 people. A great kiva of nearly 50 feet in diameter stands on the periphery of the ruins. Turn to the west from US 666 onto County Road CC at the town of Pleasant View, 19 miles north of Cortez, and drive to the end of the road.

Lowry ruin lies high on the mesa so, like the Hovenweep structures, it catches warm sunset light until the very end of the day. In addition, Sleeping Ute Mountain, sacred to the Ute Mountain Ute tribe, is very conspicuous to the south. Because the ruin has been fortified, there are places where you may climb on top of the walls if you are fit. From this vantage point you can compose scenes that contain much of the ruin in the immediate foreground and Sleeping Ute Mountain in the background. At sunset on a clear day, this can be a spectacular composition. From the ground, the ruins silhouette nicely against the Colorado blue sky. Photographing the ruins obliquely, that is, from angles that focus on the corners of the walls, adds depth to their structure. Stand behind the great kiva and compose it in the foreground with the pueblo behind. The circular shape of the kiva is a wonderful contrast to the right angles of the pueblo.

MUSEUMS AND MONUMENTS

Cortez's museums don't just display artifacts but also host many Native American cultural events, programs, and hands-on activities. I was fortunate enough to see a Navajo and Lakota Sioux family perform Native American dances, including the Prairie Chicken Dance, at the **Cortez Cultural Center.** You should see this if you can. A sand painting demonstration and class were scheduled for that evening. The center includes a museum, art gallery, and gift shop; also be sure to visit the Farmers Market here on Saturdays in the summer. *25 N. Market St., 970-565-1151, www.cortezculturalcenter.org.*

If hands-on archaeology is your thing, then you must visit the **Crow Canyon Archaeological Center.** The center provides classroom instruction and opportunities to go on real "digs," led by scholars in Puebloan archaeology and related fields. Tour one of Crow Canyon's current working archaeological sites such as Sand Canyon. You can also weave baskets and throw pottery alongside Native American artisans. Reservations required. *23390 County Road K, 970-565-8975, www.crowcanyon.org.* The **Anasazi Heritage Center** has a collection of more than 3 million artifacts and is just west of the town of Dolores. (See Museums, Dolores, p. 405).

The Four Corners is the only place in the United States where the boundaries of four states (Colorado, Utah, New Mexico, and Arizona) come together. You can literally be in four states at once (if you're limber) by straddling your feet on two states and bending over to place your hands on the other two states. The flags of the Navajo and Ute nations fly beside that of the United States over the **Four Corners Monument.** Browse the arts and crafts booths here that sell Native American pottery and jewelry, and try the Navajo fry bread and tacos. The monument is 38 miles southwest of Cortez on US 160. *928-871-6647.*

SLEEPING UTE POTTERY FACTORY OUTLET

You should see this unusual outlet store even if you're not a pottery collector. Owned and operated by the Ute Mountain Ute Tribe, the outlet takes 25% off of the remarkable inventory. Native American artists paint on the premises. Visit it 8 miles south of Cortez on US 160/666 near the Ute Mountain Casino. *970-565-8800.*

Restaurants

Francisca's ($$) at 125 E. Main is one of my favorite restaurants for Mexican food. The stacked enchiladas and sopapillas, served with the meal like bread, are outstanding. Tortillas are made on-site. It's a drop-in place. *125 E. Main, 970-565-4033.* For Italian food, locals will tell you that **Nero's** ($$) is the best. My favorite is the seafood. Without the patio in the winter, there can be a wait, so call ahead for reservations. *303 W. Main, 970-565-7366.* A popular gathering place is the **Main Street Brewery** ($-$$). *21 E. Main, 970-564-9112.* **Blondies Pub & Grub** ($-$$) is a "biker-friendly" bar with a friendly atmosphere and an extensive lunch and dinner menu. Features three large TVs for sports fans and regular live music events. *45 E. Main St., 970-565-4015, www.blondiespubandgrub.com.*

Francisca's restaurant, Cortez

Accommodations

Because Cortez caters to Mesa Verde tourists, you find no lack of chain hotels. The **Tomahawk Lodge** ($), though, is downright cheap, clean, comfortable, and has a swimming pool. *728 S. Broadway, 970-565-8521.* Check out the **Cortez Mesa Verde Inn** ($) for relaxing accommodations just minutes from Four Corners and the Cortez Municipal Airport. *640 S. Broadway, 970-565-3773.* The highly acclaimed **Kelly Place** ($-$$) is a unique B&B that includes archaeological sites and ruins on the property and offers horseback riding trips to get to them. The Kelly Place is just over 10 miles west of US 160 on the Hovenweep National Monument Road (Road G). *970-565-3125, www.kellyplace.com.*

Special Events

A legacy of ranching and agriculture, as well as the Native American heart of the culture, infuses the summer attractions here. The **Ute Mountain Roundup Rodeo** has been held every June in Cortez for more than 70 years, at the American Legion Post 75 Arena. *970-565-8151.* In August at the Montezuma County Fairgrounds east of Cortez, the **Montezuma County Fair** showcases the best of the community's agricultural bounty. *970-565-1000.* Summer-long **Indian Dances** and cultural programs take place six nights a week at Cortez Cultural Center. *25 N. Market, 970-565-1151.* Though Navajo and Ute arts and crafts abound at trading posts all over Cortez, the June **Arts & Crafts Fiesta** and September **Colorfest** are summer events that bring all kinds of Southwestern styles together in Cortez City Park. *970-565-3414.* In October, the **Indian Summer Run** half-marathon/run/walk and celebration sees participants make their way from Mesa Verde to Cortez. *970-565-3414.*

For More Information

Colorado Welcome Center at Cortez, *928 E. Main St., 970-565-4048, www.cortezchamber.org.*

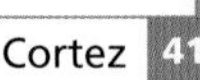

DOLORES RIVER CANYON OVERLOOK

In the Central Colorado chapter I discuss rafting the Dolores River into Utah and two places along roads from which you can make great photographs of the river from its banks (see Scenic Location Nos. 101 and 102, pp. 290 and 292). This overlook, high above the Dolores, adds a completely different perspective to your collection of Dolores River photographs. From Bedrock, in Dolores River country, head east on CO 90 to CO 141. Go south through the town of Slick Rock (you cross the Dolores here) to US 666. Turn left (south) onto US 666 and immediately proceed through the town of Dove Creek, then turn east on County Road J just east of the town. Make an immediate turn north onto CR 9, then east onto Road H. One mile later turn north onto CR 10, which takes you to the Dolores River Canyon Overlook. You can also get here by driving north from Cortez on US 666.

The overlook reveals a view of the Dolores River 1,000 feet below, winding through the upper stretch of the most commonly rafted part of the river. This 50-mile course penetrates a mountain ecosystem full of ponderosa pines and scrub oak trees, whereas the lower stretch, also about 50 miles long, is a desert ecosystem dominated by piñon and juniper trees. Still, both share the same red sandstone rock walls that complement the greens along the river. Because the canyon lies on a north/south axis at the overlook, shadows and high contrast at sunrise and sunset can be a problem for your photography. Cloudy light is best for two reasons: Your film's contrast limits won't be challenged by having to accommodate both shadow and highlights in the same scene, and the greens of the trees and shrubs will be more intense against the background of red walls. Or photograph the canyon before sunrise and after sunset. High contrast will not be a problem, and the river will be more evident in the scene. At this time of the day, the canyon gets dark, but the surface of the water reflects the bright sky, making it prominent within the canyon. You may need to use slower shutter speeds to make the exposure, so break out the tripod and cable release.

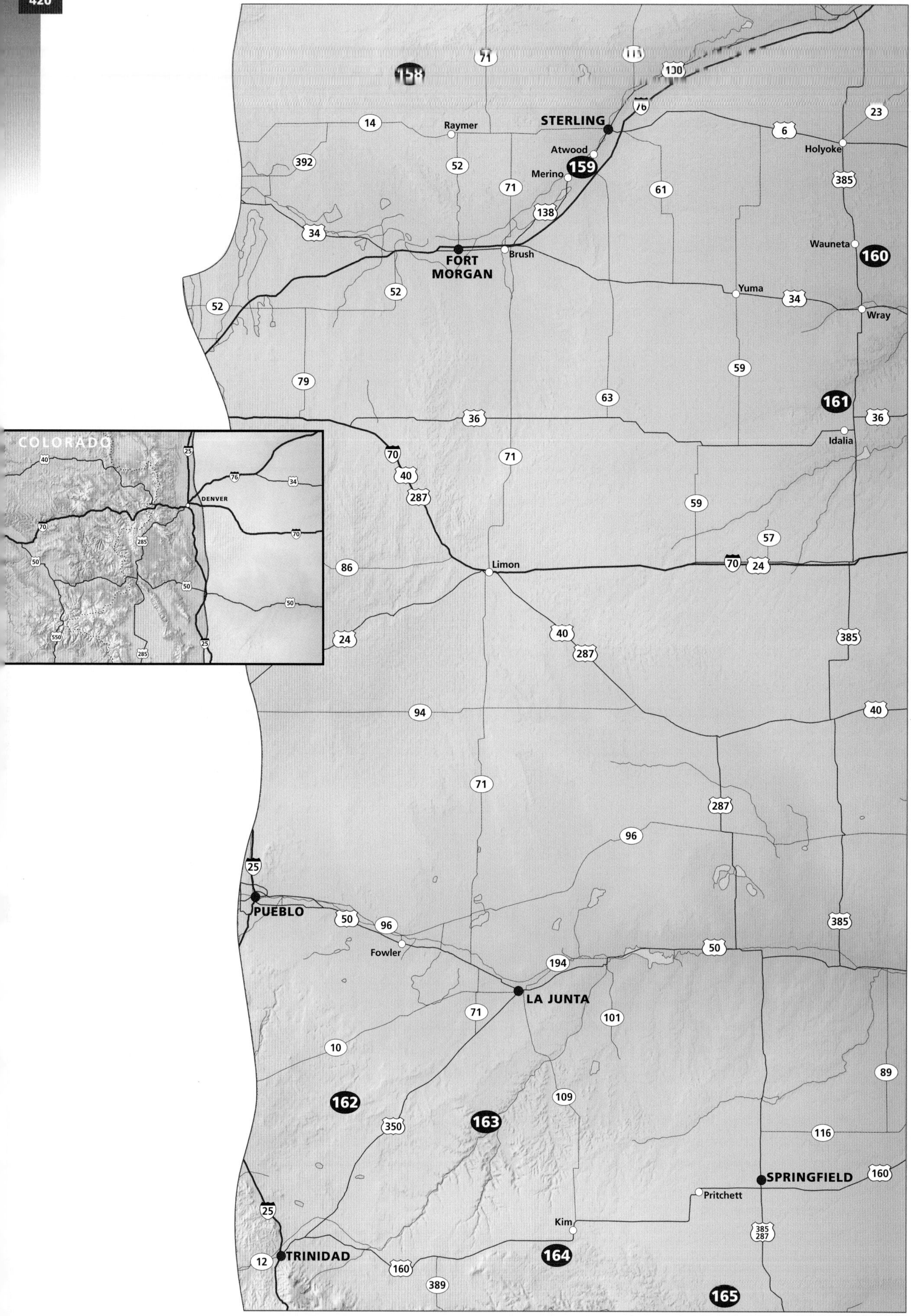

STERLING
Raymer
Atwood
Merino
159
Holyoke
Wauneta
160
FORT MORGAN
Brush
Yuma
Wray
161
Idalia
COLORADO
DENVER
Limon
PUEBLO
Fowler
LA JUNTA
162
163
SPRINGFIELD
Pritchett
Kim
TRINIDAD
164
165

Eastern Plains

THE PRAIRIE GRASSLANDS

Bloom Mansion, Trinidad

Most people think of the mountains when they think of Colorado, yet the Great Plains account for nearly 40 percent of the state. Often called "the other Colorado" or even "Colorado's outback," the Eastern Plains are a part of the state unfamiliar to many. This is unfortunate, for a wealth of history exists here, as well as state parks, small towns, burgeoning cities, and, of course, incredible scenery!

On the northeastern plains, you can look out over Pawnee National Grassland and see miles upon miles of prairie, much as homesteaders saw it when they immigrated west in the mid-1800s. On the southeastern plains, you can travel back in time to the 1830s at Bent's Old Fort, a restored trading post, or follow the route of the Santa Fe Trail. Go even farther back in time to see rock art drawn by Native Americans thousands of years ago, or walk beside dinosaur tracks some 150 million years old!

Old Library Inn, Sterling

Fort Morgan Museum

SCENIC LOCATIONS

Fort Morgan

Colorado Atlas & Gazetteer pp. 34–35

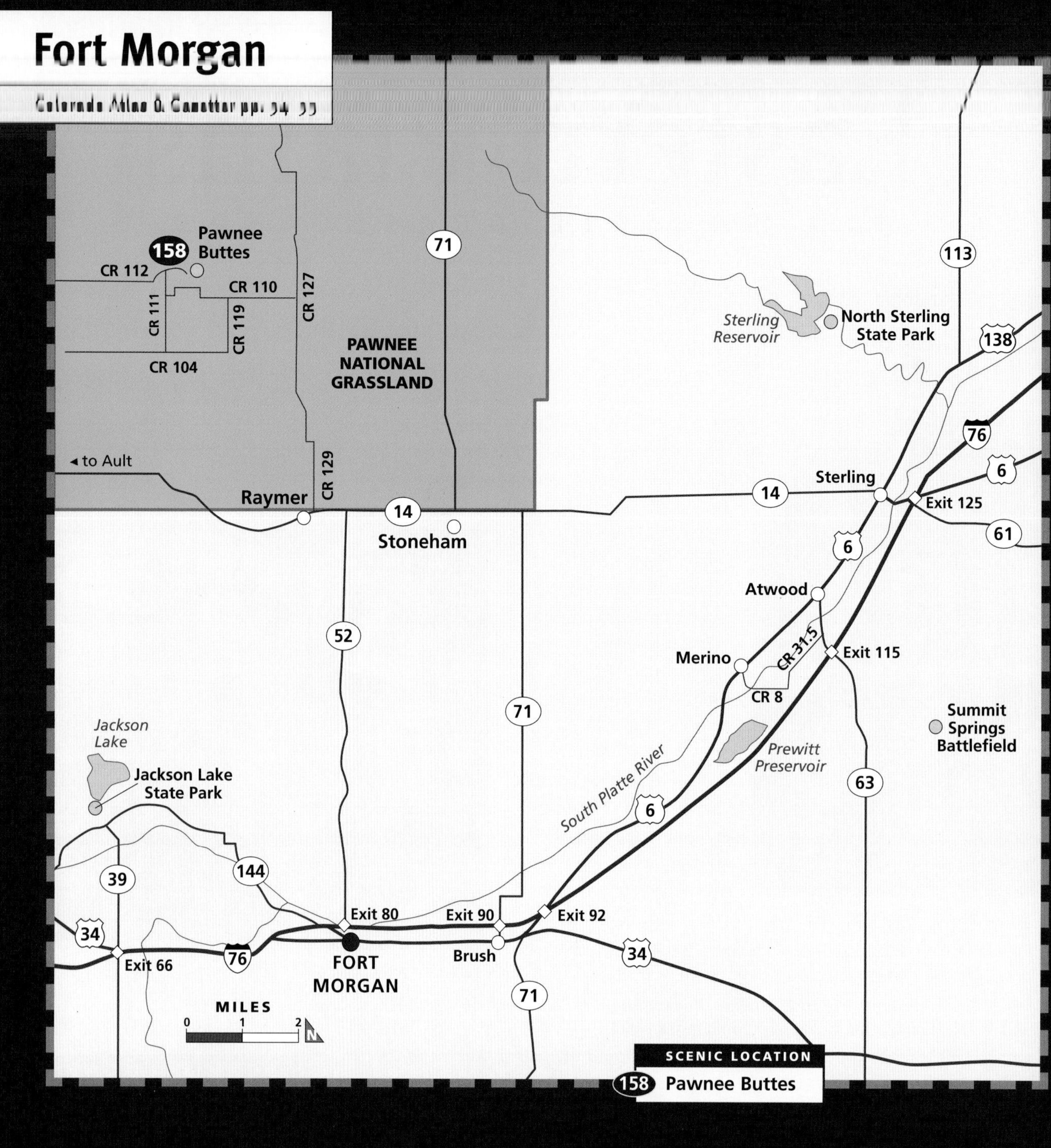
158
Pawnee Buttes
CR 112
CR 110
CR 111
CR 119
CR 127
CR 104
PAWNEE NATIONAL GRASSLAND
71
113
Sterling Reservoir
North Sterling State Park
138
76
6
Sterling
Exit 125
61
◂ to Ault
CR 129
Raymer
14
Stoneham
Atwood
52
Merino
CR 31.5
Exit 115
CR 8
Summit Springs Battlefield
Jackson Lake
Jackson Lake State Park
Prewitt Preservoir
South Platte River
63
39
144
34
Exit 80
Exit 90
Exit 92
Exit 66
FORT MORGAN
Brush
MILES
0
1
2
N
SCENIC LOCATION
158 Pawnee Buttes

Fort Morgan

Fort Morgan is one of the gateway towns to Pawnee National Grassland, an ideal location for watching birds and wildlife. History buffs will also enjoy visiting the grassland, much of it reminiscent of the landscape homesteaders saw as their covered wagons creaked across the prairie in the 1800s. Even more history awaits in Fort Morgan, from the architecture to the annual celebration in honor of the town's most famous native son, big-band leader Glenn Miller. From Denver, travel east on I-76 for about 80 miles.

History

Fort Morgan was founded in 1884 and grew slowly, settled by immigrant families who came to farm and ranch. Irrigation ditches flowed from the South Platte River, watering semiarid plains planted with corn, beans, and grains. It was sugar beets, however, that spurred the local economy when the Great Western Sugar Co. built a refinery in 1906. The original building is now part of the "sugar factory" that still processes beets. Fort Morgan experienced a small oil boom in the 1950s, but agriculture remains the chief economic force in this family-oriented community.

Main Attractions

BIRDING

More than 300 bird species have been counted at **Pawnee National Grassland**. Harvested fields and open range provide staging areas for both migratory birds and resident species such as burrowing owls, mountain plovers, and lark buntings (the Colorado state bird). May and June are the best months. The 36-mile **Pawnee Self-Guided Birding Tour** starts from Crow Valley Recreation Area and travels over paved and unpaved roads. Pick up a map and a bird checklist at the grassland's headquarters. *660 O St. East, Greeley, 970-353-5004, www.fs.fed.us/grasslands.*

Another prime birding spot is **Jackson Lake State Park,** a wintering area for bald eagles and a stopover for migratory waterfowl and shore birds (see Parks, p. 426).

PAWNEE NATIONAL GRASSLAND

Native prairie once covered the entire Midwest, from Canada to Mexico. Shortgrass prairie characterized the thirsty, semiarid plains of Colorado, where blue grama and buffalo grass swayed in the ever-present wind. These grasses provided a nutrient-rich diet for vast herds of buffalo, which in turn provided meat, clothing, shelter, and tools for the Plains Indians who hunted them. With the arrival of homesteaders in the mid-1800s, settlers plowed up the sod and planted crops, the buffalo reached near extinction and were replaced with domestic cattle, and the native prairie was turned into agricultural land. Drought and dryland farming methods took their toll, and the topsoil blew away.

During the Dust Bowl days of the 1930s, many families packed up and left. The federal government stepped in, buying up foreclosed farms for cents on the dollar and replanting the land with native grasses in hopes of restoring the natural ecosystem. Today, Pawnee National Grassland covers 193,060 acres in two separate units, both of which are checkerboards of public and private lands. Farms and ranches dot the landscape, as do windmills and the occasional oil pump.

The Pawnee Pioneer Trails Scenic and Historic Byway (see below) bisects both parcels, leading to an overlook at the Pawnee Buttes (see Scenic Location No. 158, p. 425), twin sentinels that served as landmarks for early travelers. A hiking trail leads to the buttes, where the bones of long-extinct mammals have been excavated, along with projectile points of prehistoric big-game hunters. Unpaved county and national grassland roads make for good mountain biking, and camping is available at Crow Valley Recreation Area.

Springtime is an ideal time to visit—the wildflowers are in bloom and the searing heat of summer has yet to set in. Take your binoculars, for the prairie ecosystem supports an incredible array of flora and fauna, especially birds. Pick up information and maps at the ranger station. *660 O St. East, Greeley, 970-353-5004, www.fs.fed.us/grasslands.*

PAWNEE PIONEER TRAILS SCENIC AND HISTORIC BYWAY

Three starting (or ending) points frame this 125-mile scenic byway: Fort Morgan, Sterling, and Ault. From Ault the route heads east on CO 14, north on County Road 77, then stairsteps along county roads as it leads to the overlook near the Pawnee Buttes, where you can take a hiking trail to the West Butte. The byway continues on county roads to Raymer. From there you can continue on CO 14 to Sterling, or head south on CO 52 to Fort Morgan.

You can get a cold drink or bite to eat in several of the small towns along the way, but be sure to fill up with gas before you go, and check the weather: Some of the unpaved roads become impassable when wet.

Activities

CAMPING

The campgrounds at Jackson Lake State Park total 262 sites, most on the lakeshore. You'll find amenities, food, and supplies at the Shoreline Marina. **Lakeside, Pelican,** and **Fox Hills** are the larger campgrounds, and **Dunes, Cove, Sandpiper,** and **Northview** are more intimate. *303-470-1144, www.parks.state.co.us.*

Crow Valley is the only developed campground in Pawnee National Grassland, with 10 sites and three group sites shaded by cottonwoods and elms. It's 24 miles east of Ault on CO 14. *Information: 970-353-5004; reservations (group sites only): 877-444-6777, www.reserveusa.com.* **Riverside Park** in Fort Morgan has free RV camping (see Parks, p. 426).

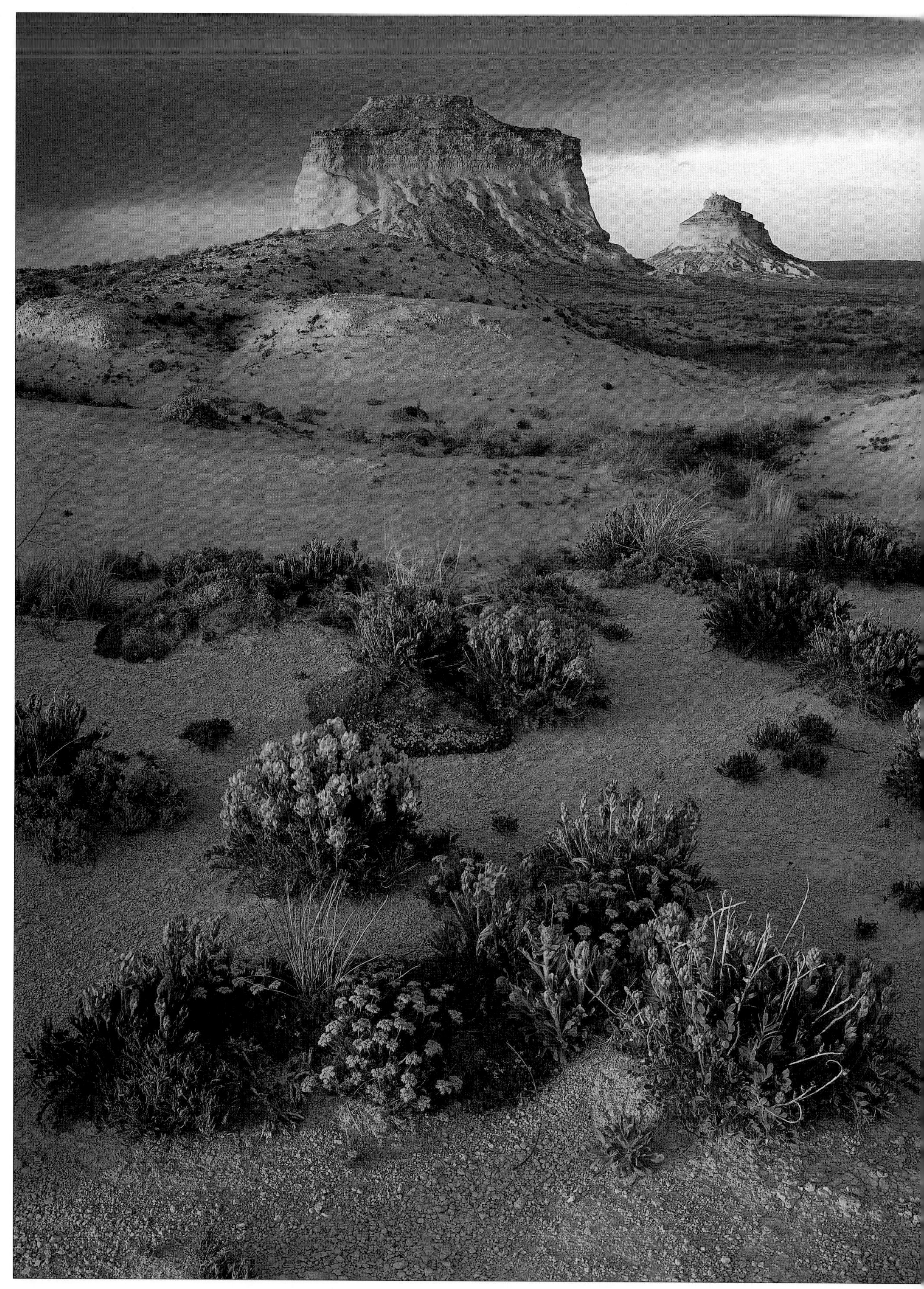

CYCLING AND MOUNTAIN BIKING

The **Pawnee Self-Guided Birding Tour** in Pawnee National Grassland includes a 12-mile mountain-bike loop EASY. You can also bike unpaved roads near Pawnee Buttes (though bikes are not allowed on the butte hiking trail). *970-353-5004, www.fs.fed.us/grasslands.*

158 SCENIC LOCATION PAWNEE BUTTES

Whenever someone remarks to me that the Eastern Plains of Colorado are flat and boring, the first thing I think of in their defense are the Pawnee Buttes. Though these two sandstone buttes rise only 250 feet above the plains, they are visible for many miles around. The buttes are made of Upper Cretaceous Period sandstones laid down by a shallow sea well before the rise of the ancestral Rockies. This is a place where sky, landscape, and weather combine in an infinite number of scenes. Moreover, the federally protected buttes are the focal point of what little remains of the native prairie in northeastern Colorado, Pawnee National Grassland.

The approach to the buttes recalls the scene in the movie *Close Encounters of the Third Kind,* when Richard Dreyfus' character sees Devil's Tower for the first time. As you drive and ascend that last bluff, the buttes suddenly appear out of nowhere. Drive north from Fort Morgan on CO 52 to CO 14. Go west 1 mile and turn north at the town of Raymer onto County Road 129 (which becomes CR 127). Six miles later, turn west onto CR 110 and follow the signs to the Pawnee Buttes.

It's hard to take a bad picture of the buttes. The only such circumstance would occur in the middle of a clear day when the overhead sun washes out color and contrast in the landscape. Nevertheless, a few wonderful vantage points, and certain felicitous times to be here, can improve your composition. Wildflowers abound in the grasslands during May when it begins to rain again in Colorado. Find a location southwest of the buttes that allows you to compose both the east and west buttes together with space between. Look for purples, yellows, and reds to compose in the foreground with the buttes behind. Try both vertical and horizontal formats. At any time other than spring when falcons and hawks are nesting here (you'll see signs warning you about this, so please pay attention), climb the bluffs immediately southwest of the buttes. The slight elevation gain is enough to significantly change the perspective, especially if you compose these bluffs as foreground to the buttes in the background.

Photograph at sunrise and sunset: Pink clouds often fill the prairie sky, and the first yellow rays of the sun color both the white bluffs and the buttes. In summer the weather is unpredictable, often dangerous—this is tornado country. Still, rainbows and mammatus clouds make great compositional decoration of this unique Colorado landscape, so watch the forecasts and head for the buttes!

GOLF

The 18-hole **Fort Morgan Golf Course** has a dual personality: the front nine plays through tree-lined fairways, and the links-style back nine through native vegetation. From Fort Morgan, drive north on CO 52 for about 2 miles and turn left on County Road T5. *970-867-5990, www.fortmorgangolfcourse.com.*

HIKING

Pawnee Buttes Trail EASY in Pawnee National Grassland wends 1.5 miles (one way) from Butte Overlook to the West Butte (the East Butte is on private property). Part of the trail is closed from March to June to protect nesting hawks.

A house in the Sherman Street National Historic District, Fort Morgan

HISTORIC WALKING TOUR

Fort Morgan's historic areas include parts of downtown, the **Sherman Street National Historic District,** and **Rainbow Bridge,** which is both a National Historic Landmark and a Colorado Historic Engineering Landmark. Pick up information and walking tour maps at the Fort Morgan Chamber of Commerce, housed in a stunning 1930s Art Deco bank building. *300 Main St., 800-354-8660.*

HUNTING

The Walk-In Access Program is an effort by the Colorado Department of Wildlife to provide hunters easy access to private lands by leasing hunting rights from local farmers. Hunters who purchase a special stamp can hunt in signed fields without seeking individual permission. The program is currently open to pheasant hunting only (with more than 113,000 acres of quality pheasant cover leased) but will include other small game in the future. *303-297-1192, www.wildlife.state.co.us.*

I-76 SPEEDWAY

Locals know that the best way to spend a Saturday evening is at the races! Between 4 and 6 divisions compete on the quarter-mile, high-banked dirt race track each week. Divisions include Late Models, Midgets, Modified, Street Stocks, Econos, 1200 Outlaws, Dwarfs, Mini Stocks, Mini Sprints, and Trucks. Race start times vary according to season, and children under 5 get free admittance. For a little extra, look into purchasing pit pass tickets for you and the family. *16359 CR S, 970-867-2101, www.i-76speedway.com.*

MUSEUM

Fort Morgan Museum has a small but well-curated collection detailing area history, including an exhibit on big-band leader Glenn Miller, who spent his boyhood years here. Admission is free. *414 Main St., 970-542-4010, www.ftmorganmus.org.* The **U.S. Military Historical Museum** honors the men and women who have served our country. The museum features items from every American war. Call ahead; visitation is by appointment only. *404 State St., 970-867-5520.*

PARKS

The 2,700-acre reservoir at **Jackson Lake State Park** has boating, fishing for both cold- and warmwater species, and camping. During summer, enjoy a full-service marina, a sand swim beach, picnic sites, and ranger-led nature programs. Wildlife watching and hunting are popular in winter, along with ice skating and ice fishing. From Fort Morgan, drive 14 miles west on I-76 to Exit 66A. Go north on CO 39 for 7 miles, turn left onto County Road Y5, and continue 2.5 miles. *970-645-2551, www.parks.state.co.us.*

At Exit 80 off I-76 in Fort Morgan, **Riverside Park** is a pleasant place for a picnic or a stroll along nature trails that skirt the South Platte River. The park has tennis courts, ball fields, fishing ponds, a swimming pool, and free overnight camping for RVs.

Restaurants

Cable's Italian Grille ($-$$) has a casual ambiance and great Italian food. Order the minestrone, a meaty version with Italian sausage. *431 Main St., 970-867-6144.* **Rocco's Grotto** ($-$$) is a casual family restaurant that describes itself as an "Italian Chophouse." The restaurant is open all week, serving lunch and dinner. *20359 US 34, 970-542-3076.* **Memories** ($-$$) is a delightful, antique-filled restaurant connected to the Best Western Park Terrace Inn. *725 Main St., 970-867-8205.* **Maverick's Country Grill** ($-$$), located at the Rodeway Inn, is a great place to get good burgers and pizza. *1409 Barlow Rd., 970-542-9482.* Formerly In the Mood Coffeehouse, **Café Lotus** ($) combines influences from the East and West, and offers an all-day lunch with unique sandwiches. *307 E. Kiowa Ave., 970-542-0800, www.cafe-lotus.com.*

Accommodations

The Best Western Park Terrace Inn ($-$$) is conveniently located at *725 Main St., 970-867-8256.* **The Comfort Inn** ($-$$) is another great option that puts you close to downtown. *1417 Barlow Rd., 1-877-477-5817.* They both include quality restaurants and comfortable lounges. **Rodeway Inn** ($) is conveniently located in the heart of town, just north of I-76. The inn is family- and pet-friendly. *1409 Barlow Rd., 970-867-9481.*

Special Events

The Windmill Century Classic, held every June, features an open route with very little traffic and beautiful scenery. Participants can ride the 40-mile half-century, the 60-mile metric century, or the 100-mile century trails. Entrants are treated to a spaghetti dinner the night before and breakfast the day of the ride. *800-354-8660, www.fortmorganchamber.org.* Fort Morgan's annual **Glenn Miller Festival** takes place in late June, with dances, big-band music (including the Glenn Miller Orchestra), vintage fashions, a swing dance contest, and cars and aircraft from the World War II era.

For More Information

Fort Morgan Area Chamber of Commerce, *300 Main St., 800-354-8660, www.fortmorganchamber.org.*

Sunrise at the Pawnee Buttes

Sterling

Colorado Atlas & Gazetteer pp. 95, 97, 102

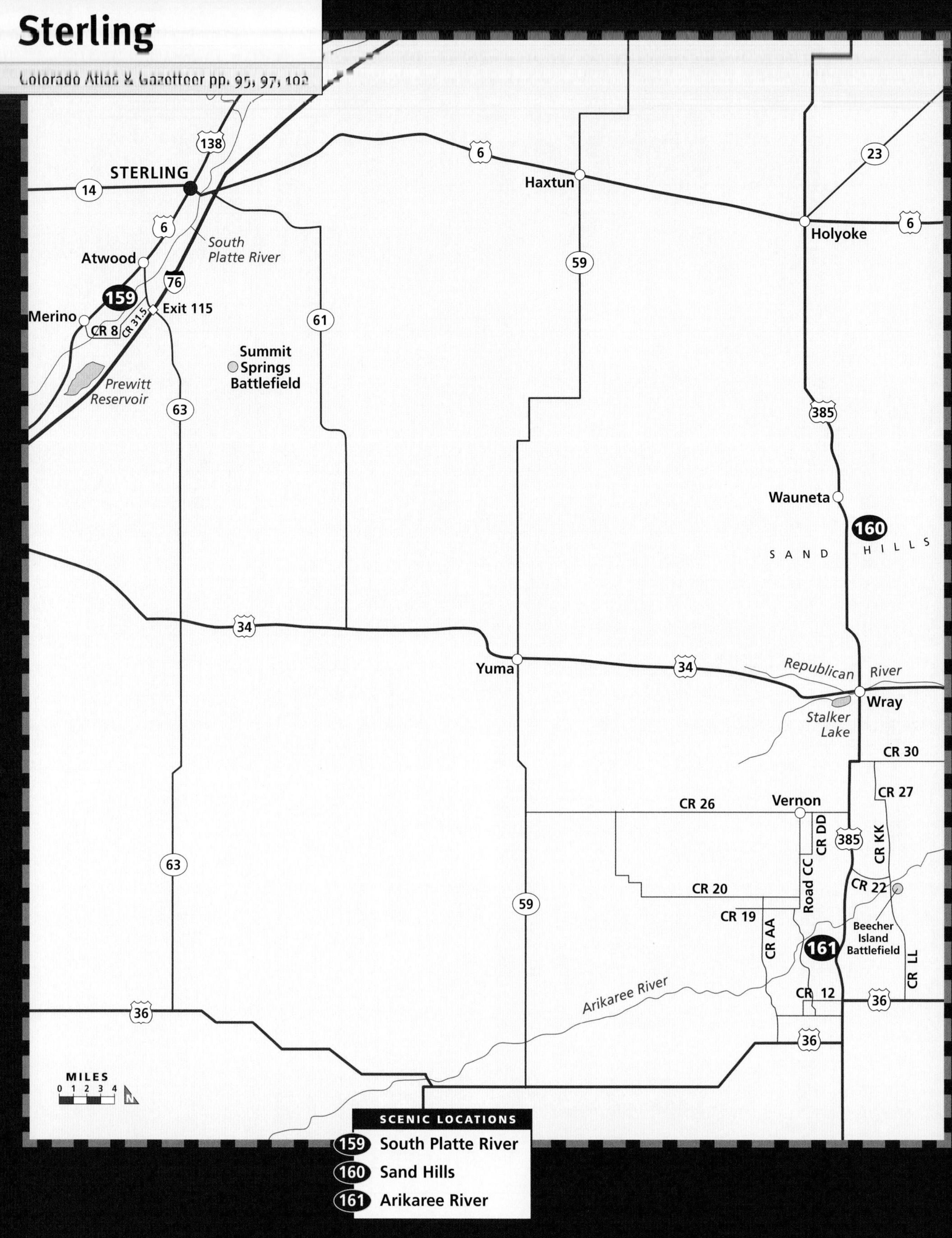

SCENIC LOCATIONS

159 South Platte River

160 Sand Hills

161 Arikaree River

Sterling

Between 1862 and 1868 the Overland Trail was one of the most heavily traveled wagon routes in the country. Early pioneers, miners, and homesteaders followed the South Platte River along a branch of the trail that angled southwesterly into the Colorado Territory. You can relive the history of the pioneer era at Pawnee National Grassland and at the Overland Trail Museum in Sterling. Much of the South Platte has now been dammed or diverted, and the resulting reservoirs provide a wealth of water recreation. From Denver, Take I-76 east for about 80 miles to Fort Morgan, and continue roughly 50 miles to Sterling.

History

Sterling started out in the early 1870s as a few sod houses along the South Platte. In 1881, a local landowner and businessman gave 80 acres to the Union Pacific Railroad, in hopes that free land would motivate the railroad to locate a division station here. It did. The Union Pacific built a depot, a roundhouse, and a hotel; the town was platted and became the junction of the Union Pacific and Burlington railroads. Sterling grew steadily over the years. Today it is an important transportation hub and commercial center for surrounding farms and ranches, as well as the fastest-growing city in northeastern Colorado.

Main Attractions

BIRDING

One of the draws of the northeastern plains is the variety of birdlife. Pawnee National Grassland (see Birding, Fort Morgan, p. 423) counts more than 300 species. Other good birding locations include North Sterling State Park (see below); the South Platte River (see Scenic Location No. 159, p. 430); Tamarack Ranch State Wildlife Area, where you might spot the greater prairie chicken, a Colorado endangered species; and Prewitt Reservoir State Wildlife Area, a wintering area for bald eagles and a stopover for migratory waterfowl and shore birds. *Division of Wildlife, 122 E. Edison St., Brush, 970-842-6300.*

CITY OF LIVING TREES

Sterling is known as the "City of Living Trees" because of a city-wide collection of sculptures carved out of tree trunks by local artist Brad Rhea. Eighteen of these sculptures are displayed around town, the most popular being a giraffe herd that seems to be feeding on the treetops in Columbine Park. Pick up a map at area businesses or the chamber of commerce for a self-guided tour of these awesome artworks.

NORTH STERLING STATE PARK

North Sterling State Park is *the* local destination for recreation. The 3,000-acre lake is busy with boaters, waterskiers, windsurfers, and anglers. Enjoy a sand beach for swimming, picnic areas, three campgrounds, a visitor center, and ranger-led nature programs. The views are impressive, too, with high bluffs and endless prairie. The park is 12 miles northwest of Sterling. To get there, drive north on 7th Avenue and follow the signs. *970-522-3657, www.parks.state.co.us.* (See map on p. 422.)

City of Trees sculpture, Sterling

PAWNEE NATIONAL GRASSLAND

This 193,060-acre preserve gives visitors a sense of the landscape that greeted early settlers (see Main Attractions and Activities, Fort Morgan, p. 423).

Activities

CAMPING

At North Sterling State Park, **Elks, Chimney View,** and **Inlet** campgrounds have many amenities and a total of 141 campsites. The lack of nearby city lights makes it a great place to sleep under the stars. Reservations are recommended. *303-470-1144.* For directions, see North Sterling State Park, above.

FISHING

Warmwater fish species lure anglers to the lakes, inlets, and finger coves at **North Sterling State Park,** where you can cast for walleye, catfish, bass, crappie, perch, and tiger muskie. As for trout, in spring you can easily catch three times your limit (releasing them, of course). Mid-summer and fall are best for catfish. The bluegills are easy-catching for kids. For directions, see above.

Prewitt Reservoir State Wildlife Area, 17 miles southwest of Sterling off US 6, and **Jumbo Reservoir State Wildlife Area,** 30 miles northeast of Sterling off US 138, are also choice fishing spots. *970-842-6300.*

GOLF

Riverview Golf Course in Sterling has rolling terrain and is an incredible value—18 holes for just $18! And there's seldom a wait. *13064 CR 370, 970-522-3035.* **Pawnee Pines Golf Club** (formerly Sterling Country Club), a semi-private golf course with a restaurant and banquet facilities for weddings and parties, has been recently opened their facilities to the public. *17408 CO 14, 970-522-3776.*

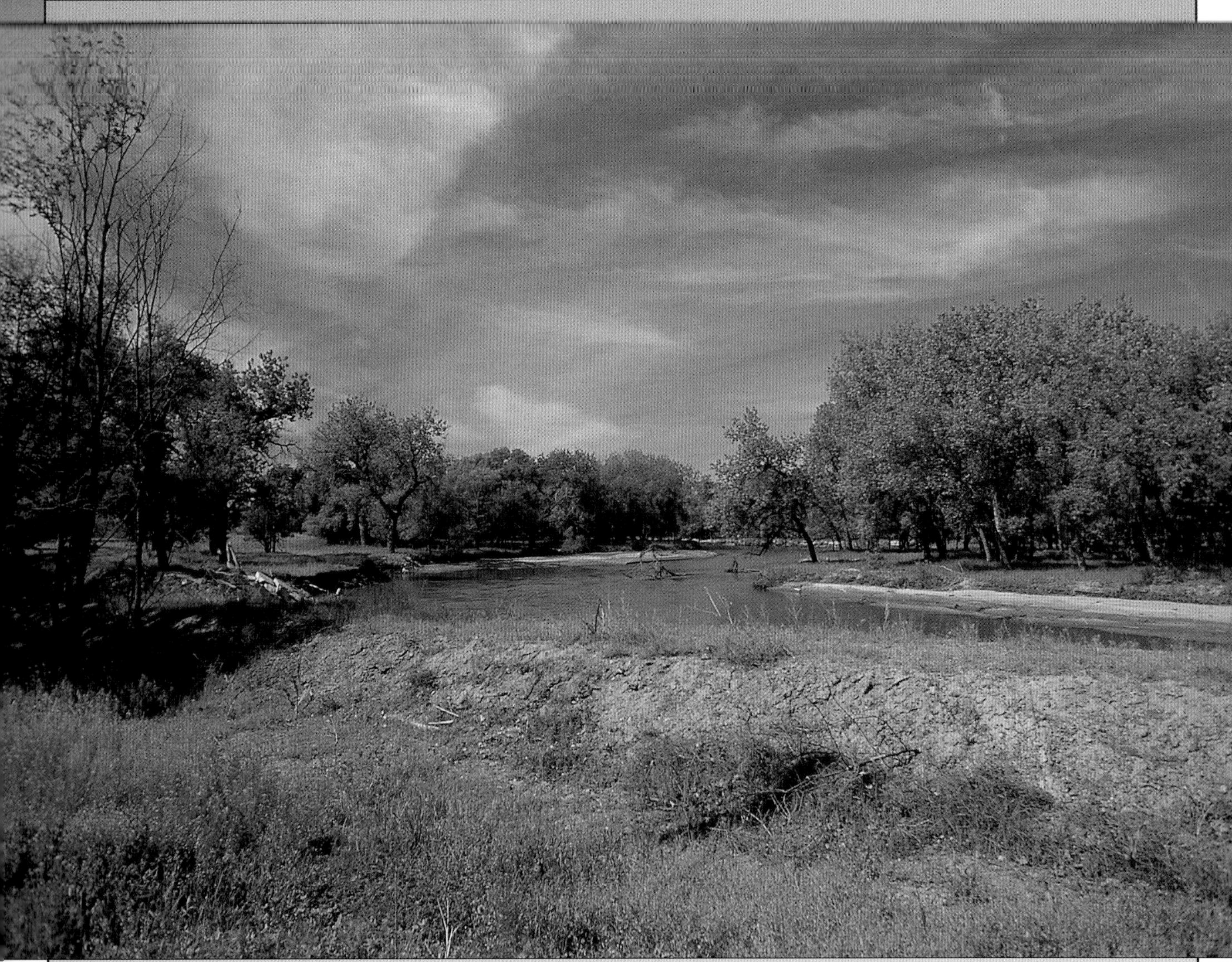

159 SCENIC LOCATION SOUTH PLATTE RIVER: STERLING

The entire South Platte from Denver to the Nebraska border varies from environmentally trashed to pristine. It's hard to find photographic locations that don't include power lines, buildings, railroad tracks, highways and bridges, or fences and farm animals. But when you do find places where meadows and cottonwood trees define the landscape, you can imagine how beautiful the prairie riverine landscape once was. Yet even these places don't represent what the South Platte used to be. Before damming and irrigation, this river was an inch deep and a mile wide; today it's a much narrower channel. US 34 east of Greeley and US 76 northeast of Denver follow most of the South Platte; here are a couple of places that will save you some time searching for photographic-quality scenery.

From downtown Sterling, head east on CO 61, cross the Platte, and turn south onto County Road 37, also called Riverview Drive. Along the way are lovely views of meadows and cottonwood trees. If you stay next to the river, you will connect with CO 63, where you should turn north to cross the river. Park your car before the bridge, and walk across it until you find a good view of the river lazily meandering through the cottonwoods. At sunrise and sunset the sidelighting intensifies the colors of the cottonwood leaves. Be here in the beginning to the middle of May in order to enjoy light greens of freshly leaved trees, or at the end of October to witness radiant yellows.

Back in your car, drive across the bridge to US 6, turn south, then drive 6 miles to CR 25. Head south and look for the next bridge from which to photograph a similar scene. If you arrive before sunrise, or remain until just after sunset, you may be able to photograph pink clouds reflecting in the South Platte. Turn east onto CR 4 for more tree and river views. You can apply this "South Platte River jog" from Greeley to the Nebraska border, exploring side roads that get you next to or across the river. And this is a four-season opportunity. Even defoliated cottonwoods, with their complex pattern of trunks and branches, make great images when silhouetted against the twilight sky (see pp. 28–37, *Photographing the Landscape*).

160 SCENIC LOCATION SAND HILLS

Parts of eastern Colorado are covered with ancient sand dunes now stabilized with vegetation. Some are quite high and, when standing atop them, you can imagine that these places might have once looked much like the Great Sand Dunes (see Scenic Location 112, p. 317) in the San Luis Valley. They are thought to have been formed during the Ice Age, when glacier-fed streams overflowed their banks, depositing sand that was later carried off by strong winds whipping down from the glaciers. On a certain stretch of highway between the towns of Holyoke and Wray, you can make fine photographs of these dunes. Take US 6 east from Sterling to US 385. Head south, and in a few miles you will be in the middle of this particular expanse of dunes.

Most of the land along the way is fenced and private. Never-the-less, you can attain good vantage points along the highway if you merely walk to the fence. Several county roads cross the highway along the route, so plan on exploring them, too. Sunrise and sunset make the dunes most conspicuous on film. The low-lying sun makes shadows in the troughs and creates warm highlights on the dune crests, so compose scenes at right angles to the sun.

With a telephoto lens you can compress distance, thereby making the individual dunes more conspicuous. With a wide-angle lens you can focus on the grasses and cacti that grow in the sand. Look for sections of dunes that have no vegetation, where the beige sand is most manifest. A wide-angle lens enlarges the section of sand by increasing its proportion. Arrive in May and you'll see a vibrant green landscape. If thunderstorms continue through the summer, the green will last longer.

ARIKAREE RIVER

A few small tributaries of the South Platte and Arkansas rivers originate in the High Plains of eastern Colorado. One of them, the Arikaree River (it's more of a creek, except when it floods during summer thunderstorms), is particularly lovely, and in some of its sections grazing has been limited, allowing the land to remain in a relatively natural state. Native grasses and cottonwood trees, wetlands, and lots of wildlife define this ecosystem. You won't believe all the turkeys that hang out here!

Two places along the Arikaree are especially beautiful. The first, Beecher Island, is also a historic site. In September 1869, a battle was waged between Plains Indians and frontiersmen. Twenty settlers and 100 Indians were killed over a 9-day period in what General George Custer—who was not there—described as the fiercest of all the plains battles. From the town of Wray, drive 12 miles south on US 385. Turn east on County Road 22 and proceed to Road KK. Here you can continue east on CR 22 to cross the Arikaree, and ultimately to get to Road RR. Or drive south on Road KK to cross the Arikaree. Beecher Island historic site is just north of the river on Road KK. Both of these routes follow scenic drainages with gorgeous meadows and cottonwoods. You'll know what to do with the camera when you get there! (But don't forget to photograph up and down the river at the crossings.)

To arrive at the other fine location, continue south on US 385 to its intersection with US 36. Turn west onto CR 12 and proceed to Road DD. Drive north across the river. Again, the crossing is a wonderful place from which to photograph the river (creek). Arrive here in early- to mid-May for greenery, or late October for outrageous yellows and oranges in the cottonwood trees.

HUNTING

The plains of northeastern Colorado make for ideal hunting habitat, and more than 20,000 acres near Sterling are set aside as state wildlife areas (SWAs). Many local hunters consider **Tamarack SWA,** 20 miles northeast of Sterling near Crook on US 138, as their own well-kept secret. **North Sterling State Park** (bow and arrow or shotgun only) and **Prewitt Reservoir SWA** are prime duck and waterfowl hunting spots. Check with the Colorado Department of Wildlife for information on hunting seasons. *970-842-6300, www.wildlife.state.co.us.* Also inquire with the DOW about the Walk-In Access Program, which has designated 113,000 acres of private and public land for pheasant hunting.

MUSEUM

Overland Trail Museum and Village tells the story of the homesteaders who settled the Sterling area. Built in the 1930s as a replica of an old fort, the museum has a down-home appeal, with many of the items donated by locals, from cattle brands to turn-of-the-century wedding dresses to pump organs that made their way west in the back of a covered wagon. Behind the museum is a small village with a country store, a blacksmith shop, and a one-room schoolhouse. The museum offers free admission and is just west of the South Platte River bridge, at the I-76 and US 6 junction. *970-522-3895.*

Overland Trail Museum, Sterling

WATER SPORTS

With a 3,000-acre reservoir, a full-service marina, and three boat ramps, **North Sterling State Park** is a prime place for water sports such as boating, sailing, waterskiing, windsurfing, fishing, and swimming. For directions, see Main Attractions, p 429.

Restaurants

Why bother with the fast-food outlets in Sterling when you can enjoy fine hometown restaurants? For homemade soup and creative sandwiches, stop at the **Hot Java Café** ($). *118 N. 2nd St., 970-522-1120.* **Delgado's Dugout** ($) is the best place in town for Mexican food. There's no sign, but look for an old church at the corner of 2nd and Beech Streets. *970-522-0175.* Light and airy, **Gallagher's River City Grill** ($-$$) is a cheery restaurant and sports bar with an extensive menu. *1116 W. Main St., 970-521-7648.* **TJ Bummer's Family Restaurant** ($) features "everything from sandwiches to prime rib" in a friendly and casual atmosphere. Breakfast is served all day, and the restaurant is open all week. *203 Broadway St., 970-522-8397.*

Accommodations

The Best Western Sundowner ($) has a great location and many amenities. *125 Overland Trail, 970-522-6265.* The **Fountain Lodge** is a pleasant little place that is quaint and quiet. *619 North 3rd St., 970-522-1821.* **The Old Library Inn** ($$) is an historic bed and breakfast housed in what was once an Andrew Carnegie Library. The library has been beautifully restored and now includes 3 guest rooms you can choose from. Children welcome. *210 S. 4th St., 970-522-3800, http://lodging4vacations.com/old-library-inn.*

Special Events

The calendar of events for northeastern plains towns reflects life in a rural community, with tractor pulls, farm shows, rodeos, county fairs, and harvest festivals. The **Logan County Fair and Rodeo** takes place over two weeks in August, with nationally known musicians and a demolition derby. **Sugar Beet Days** in mid-September celebrates the area's sugar beet harvest with a craft fair and entertainment on the courthouse square. *866-522-5070.*

For More Information

Logan County Chamber of Commerce, located in an old train depot, *109 N. Front St., Sterling, 866-522-5070, www.sterlingcolo.com.* Colorado Welcome Center, *US 6 just west of I-76, 800-544-8609.*

Pueblo/Trinidad

Colorado Atlas & Gazetteer pp. 73, 83, 100

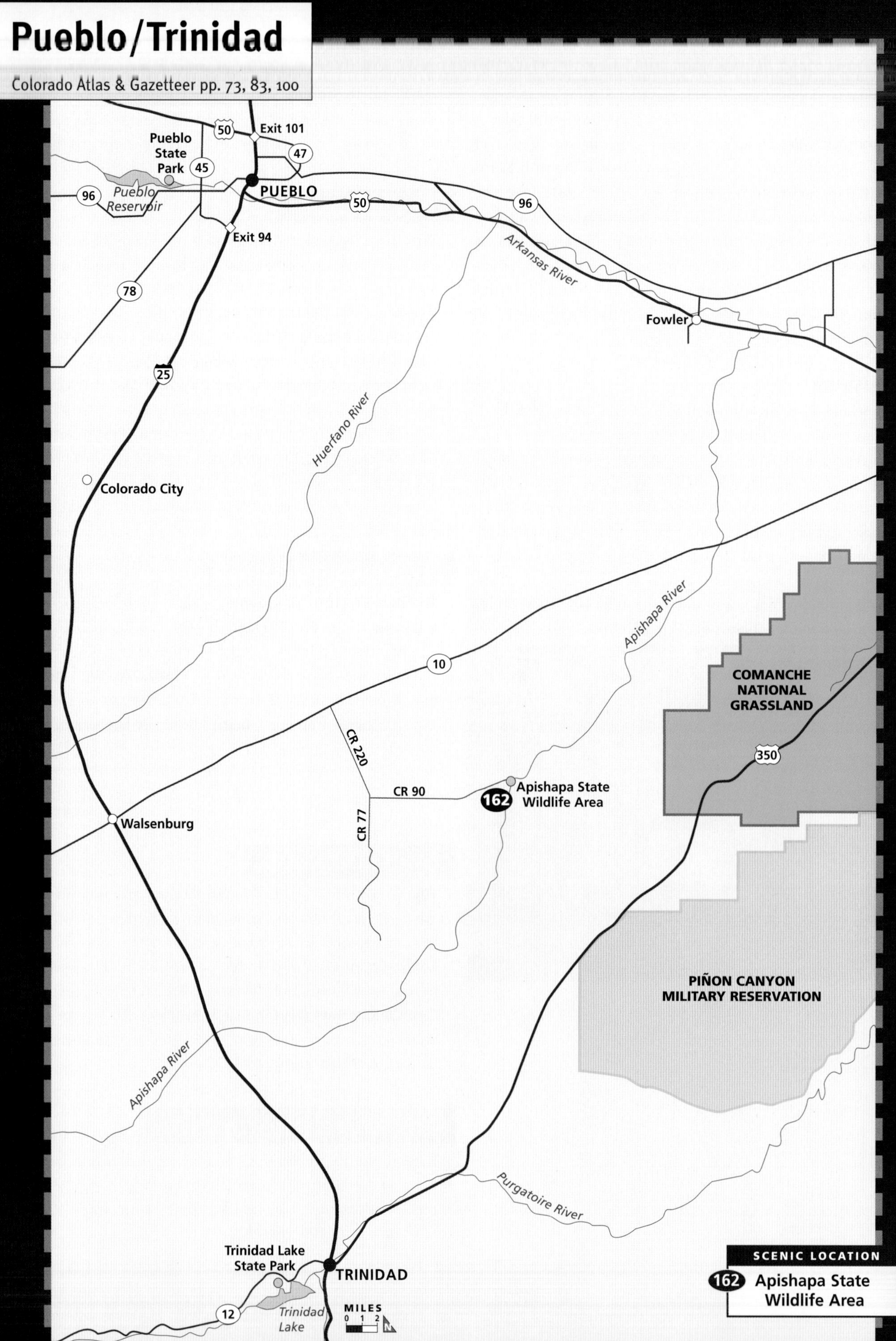

Pueblo

If you drive past Pueblo on Interstate 25, you might not think much of it, as it looks like one long commercial strip. But get off the highway and you'll discover a town with historic charm, tree-lined neighborhoods, parks, good restaurants, and numerous museums. This is a city on the move, with the new Riverwalk poised to revitalize the downtown area near the Union Avenue Historic District. Just west of the city, Lake Pueblo State Park provides rewarding recreational opportunities. You'll find more to do in Pueblo than you'd imagine. So put on your blinker and pull off the interstate. You won't be disappointed. From Denver, take I-25 south for 112 miles to Pueblo.

History

Situated on the Arkansas River at the edge of the Great Plains, the site that would become the city of Pueblo was a natural stopping place for early travelers. Zebulon Pike camped here in 1806 during his exploratory expedition through Colorado. A trading post was established in 1842, but it wasn't until the Gold Rush of the 1850s that a town started to take hold. The railroad came through in the 1870s and in 1881 the Colorado Coal and Iron Co. started manufacturing steel here. Bankers and company executives built grand houses, and ethnic neighborhoods sprouted up as immigrants from Mexico and Europe settled here to work the steel mills, which mostly closed down in the 1980s. High-tech, manufacturing, and service industries are moving to Pueblo, ranked one of the most livable cities in the United States by Partners for Livable Communities.

Main Attractions

HISTORIC WALKING TOURS

Along five blocks of Union Avenue, from the Arkansas River north to 1st Street, more than 40 buildings stand that are listed on the National Register of Historic Places. Pick up a brochure for a self-guided walking tour of the **Union Avenue Historic District** at the chamber of commerce or businesses along the avenue, where you can find treasures in dusty old antique shops, or browse upscale designer stores and gift shops. Be sure to visit the Union Depot on B Street, one of the most impressive surviving train stations in the country.

Union Avenue Historic District, Pueblo

In the heart of downtown, the new **Historic Arkansas Riverwalk of Pueblo** waterfront park encompasses a 32-acre section of the Arkansas River that remained after the river was diverted for flood control in the 1920s. Gardens, fountains, sculptures, and food carts line the pedestrian walkway that snakes around the canal. You can stroll, rent a pedal boat, or take a narrated tour in a flat-bottomed riverboat as it cruises the waterway. The city's goal is to eventually develop the banks of the riverwalk with restaurants and retail stores. Phase three of the riverwalk is to be finished in November and includes Veterans Bridge at Gateway Park. *200 W. 1st St., 719-595-0242, www.puebloharp.com.*

LAKE PUEBLO STATE PARK

Activities at Lake Pueblo State Park center on the 11-mile reservoir rimmed by buttes and limestone cliffs. Motorboats and waterskiers zip across the lake, anglers cast for bass and other warmwater species, and sailors and windsurfers take full advantage of the steady winds. Swimming is restricted to the Rock Canyon area south of the dam, where you'll find a sandy swim beach, bumper boats, a pool with a three-flume waterslide, and concessions. Seven campgrounds serve park visitors. Hiking and biking trails and two marinas with slips and boat rentals are also available. From Pueblo, drive west on Thatcher Avenue, which turns into CO 96, then continue about 3 miles. *719-561-9320, www.parks.state.co.us.*

Activities

CAMPING

More than 400 campsites exist at Lake Pueblo State Park, in five separate campgrounds: **Arkansas Point, Prairie Ridge, Yucca Flats, Juniper Breaks,** and **Kettle Creek.** Even with so many campsites, the park tends to fill up on summer weekends. Most sites have good views but little shade. *303-470-1144.* For directions, see above.

CYCLING AND MOUNTAIN BIKING

Thirty-six miles of hard-surface biking trails wind through Pueblo—16 miles in **Lake Pueblo State Park** and another 20 through the city on the tree-shaded **River Trails System**. Starting at Runyon Lake, you can ride north along Fountain Creek to the University of Southern Colorado, or start pedaling west, following the Arkansas River to the state park. Bike rentals and a trail map are available at the Greenway and Nature Center of Pueblo. *5200 Nature Center Rd., 719-549-2414, www.gncp.org.*

FISHING

The fishing at **Lake Pueblo State Park** is exceptional, with high catches of largemouth and smallmouth bass, as well as walleye, wipers, channel catfish, rainbows, and browns. Enjoy

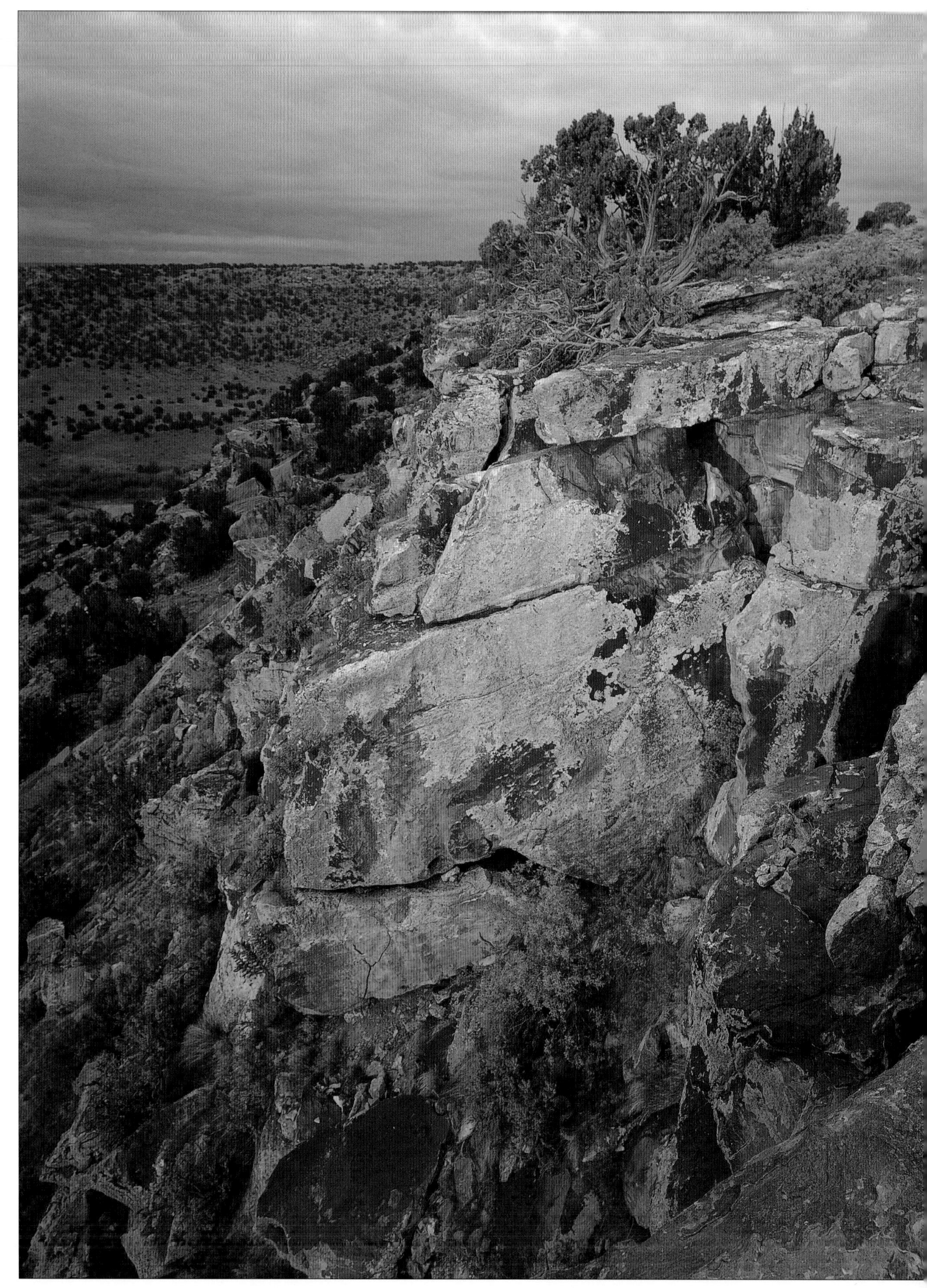

APISHAPA STATE WILDLIFE AREA

This remote wildlife area covers a vast expanse of weathered landscape on the High Plains southeast of Pueblo and east of Walsenburg. Here the Apishapa River and its tributaries have carved a dramatic red-rock canyon out of an otherwise level landscape—another eastern Colorado location that proves that the plains are not always flat. From Pueblo, take I-25 south to Walsenburg, then go 18 miles east on CO 10 to County Road 220. Turn south. This road becomes CR 77, then heads east as CR 90, which dead-ends in the middle of the area. A car will get you most of the way, though the road becomes bumpy at the end.

I enjoy climbing among the rocks that define this canyon. The views from the top looking into the canyon are sublime. The canyon runs on a southwest/northeast axis, so certain walls catch sunrise light, and others the light at sunset. The sun descends low in the sky on the plains, allowing the light on a clear day to become quite red. This color bathes the rocks at dawn or dusk, a great time to compose rock walls on the left or right of your scene, with the canyon disappearing into the distance on the other side.

A hike into the canyon produces an entirely different image. Compose the river as a lead-in line, with rock walls rising up on either side and framing your view. On top of the canyon stand many dead piñon and juniper trees, which make for shapely silhouettes against twilight skies before sunrise and after sunset. In May and early June, or as long as spring rains last, wildflowers abound in this prairie landscape. In the absence of a high background—the peaks of the Sangre de Cristo Mountains (see Scenic Location No. 103, p. 298) are quite a distance to the west—make intimate landscape and microcosmic compositions of these flowers without any horizon (see pp. 52–57, *Photographing the Landscape*). You should also bring your telephoto lens to zoom in on the wildlife area's multitude of game, including bighorn sheep.

4,500 surface acres of water, 60 miles of shoreline, and plenty of coves. For directions, see Activities, Main Attractions, p. 435.

Another good spot is the Arkansas River between the reservoir and the Greenway and Nature Center of Pueblo (see Nature Center, this page).

GOLF

Ranked the fifth top public course in the state, the 18-hole links-style **Walking Stick** is the newest golf course in Pueblo. *4301 Walking Stick Blvd., 719-584-3400.*

Hollydot is 22 miles south in Colorado City. With the Wet Mountains as a backdrop and 27 holes that play through meadows, links, and tree-lined fairways, many Puebloans prize this golf getaway. *55 N. Parkway, Colorado City, 719-676-3341.*

HISTORICAL MARKERS & PLACES

The **Union Avenue Historic District** is a must (see Main Attractions, p. 435), but don't overlook **Pitkin Place Historic District**. The 300 block of Pitkin Avenue features seven historic mansions from the 1890s, when coal and steel dominated Pueblo, and company chiefs, lawyers, and bankers lived in a grand style. But don't stop there. Drive around the neighborhoods; the diversity of architectural styles in Pueblo is impressive, with Victorian, Arts and Crafts, Spanish Mission, Art Deco, Gothic, and Greek Revival—sometimes all on one block!

MUSEUMS

I have limited this list to the must-sees. If you have time for more exploring, stop by the chamber of commerce to pick up information on other fine museums in town.

Rosemount Museum gives you a look into the elegant life at the turn of the century. Built by a wealthy banker, this 37-room Victorian mansion is clad in pink granite. Handcrafted woodwork, Tiffany chandeliers, and a 9- by 13-foot stained-glass window adorn the interior, and most of the furnishings are original. Take an hour-long tour. The carriage house has been turned into a restaurant, a lovely place for lunch. *419 W. 14th St., 719-545-5290, www.rosemount.org.*

Buell Children's Museum has lively interactive exhibits that focus on art, science, history, and technology, including a functioning robot and a human kaleidoscope. The museum is located at the **Sangre de Cristo Arts and Conference Center,** which has six art galleries and a theater for performing arts. *210 N. Santa Fe Ave., 719-295-7200, www.sdc-arts.org.*

At the Pueblo Airport, **Pueblo Weisbrod Aircraft Museum** displays two dozen vintage military aircraft. *31001 Magnuson Ave., 719-948-9219.*

El Pueblo History Museum features exhibits highlighting the mix of cultures that converged in Pueblo (American Indian, Mexican, and European) as well as the region's economy, from early trading post to 20th-century steel mills. *301 N. Union, 719-583-0453, www.coloradohistory.org.*

NATURE CENTER

The **Nature & Raptor Center of Pueblo** is a hands-on environmental center that educates children and adults on the area's flora, fauna, and ecosystems. This facility on the Arkansas River also includes a fishing pier, picnic areas, bike paths and bike rentals, and a raptor rehabilitation center. The Raptor Center cares for more than 250 injured birds of prey each year, releasing about half back into the wild and housing those unable to survive on their own. Participate in one of the naturalist-led programs on Sunday afternoons or just pay a visit to the caged birds. *5200 Nature Center Rd., 719-549-2414, www.natureandraptor.org.*

PARKS

Most outdoor recreation in Pueblo centers on **Lake Pueblo State Park** (see Main Attractions, p. 435). Pueblo's **City Park** has ball fields, tennis courts, a swimming pool, duck ponds, hiking trails, a 27-hole golf course, the Pueblo Zoo, and old-time kiddie rides. On evenings and Sunday afternoons in summer, children can ride an antique miniature train or enjoy a restored 1911 carousel, with hand-carved horses and a Wurlitzer band organ. *800 Goodnight Ave., 719-553-2790.*

ZOO

Pueblo Zoo began in the 1930s with the help of the Works Progress Administration (later renamed the Work Projects Administration). See more than 100 different kinds of animals, from lions to camels, penguins to monkeys. At the Pioneer Ranch, kids can hand-feed goats, sheep, geese, and other farm animals. *800 Goodnight Ave., 719-561-1452, www.pueblozoo.org.*

Restaurants

Located in a beautiful old church, **La Renaissance** ($-$$$) offers continental cuisine, with a fixed-price, three-course lunch and a five-course dinner—fine dining and a good value. *217 E. Routt Ave., 719-543-6367.* **Shamrock Brewing Company** ($-$$), features traditional-style beers with big flavor and a combination of pub fare and American cuisine. Menu offerings include daily pot pies, traditional fish and chips, fresh salads, and sandwiches. They're open all week and also offer Sunday brunch. *108 W. 3rd St., 719-542-9974.*

With a large ethnic population in Pueblo, you'll find many good Italian and Mexican restaurants. **Cactus Flower** ($) specializes in Mexican and American fare. *4610 Elizabeth St., 719-545-8218.* **Pass Key Restaurant** ($) is a Pueblo fixture. Try a sausage sandwich. *518 E Abriendo Ave., 719-542-0827.*

Jorge's Sombrero ($) serves authentic Mexican food (even homemade chorizo sausage), as well as sandwiches, burgers, and steaks. *1319 E. Evans, 719-564-6486.* **Mexi-Deli** ($) is a short-order place that's long on taste. It's a good family place because you can specify large or small portions. *215 E. Abriendo Ave., 719-583-1275.*

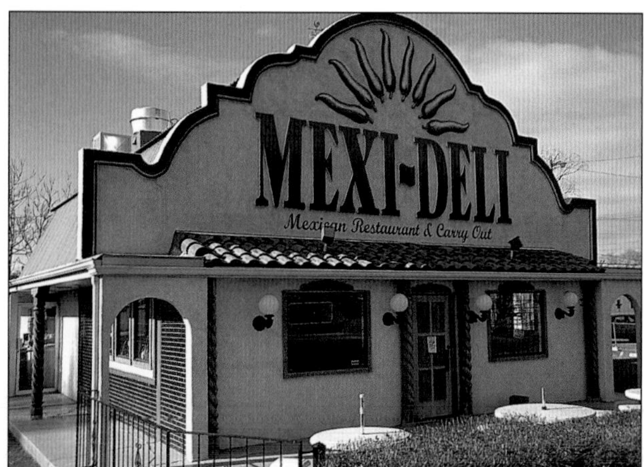

Mexi-Deli, Pueblo

The **Do Drop Inn** ($) has a unique, sweet-crust pizza as well as family specials. *1301 Santa Fe Ave., 719-543-0818.* For pizza, search out **Angelo's Pizza Parlour** ($), which also has traditional Italian dishes. *223 S. Union Ave., 719-544-8588.*

Accommodations

The usual hotel chains are the rule in Pueblo, but for accommodations with local flavor, book a room at the elegant **Abriendo Inn** ($-$$). This turn-of-the-century, four-square house sits just blocks from the downtown historic district. The 10 comfortable guest rooms and common areas are decorated with antiques and period furnishings. You will find comprehensive amenities, including in-room data ports, and enjoy a full gourmet breakfast in the sunny breakfast room or garden patio. *300 W. Abriendo Ave., 719-544-2703, www.abriendoinn.com.*

Abriendo Inn, Pueblo

Special Events

The **Rocky Mountain Street Rod Nationals** in late June display more than 2,000 cars and motorcycles at the State Fairgrounds, at the corner of Prairie and Arroyo Avenues. A tradition since 1872, the **Colorado State Fair** takes place in August—17 days of rodeo, livestock contests, carnival rides, crafts and food booths, and concerts with big-name rock and country-and-western singers. The aroma of roasting chiles fills the air in late September during the **Chile and Frijoles Festival,** celebrating the chile and pinto bean *(frijole)* harvest with mariachi music, Hispanic and Native American dancing, traditional foods, bands, and a fiery chile competition. *800-233-3446, www.pueblo.org.*

For More Information

Pueblo Chamber of Commerce, *302 N. Santa Fe Ave., 800-233-3446, www.pueblo.org.*

Trinidad

(see map on p. 434)

Hemmed in by hills and mesas, Trinidad sits at the foothills of the Rockies, just 13 miles from the New Mexico border. History abounds here; the names of people who lived in or passed through Trinidad read like a history lesson on the Old West: Kit Carson, Bat Masterson, Wyatt Earp, Billy the Kid, Carrie Nation, and Mother Jones. The brick and sandstone buildings in the heart of downtown—Corazón de Trinidad National Historic District—offer a glimpse of 19th-century Colorado. The Santa Fe Trail lives on as a scenic byway, and the Trinidad History Museum tells the town's fascinating story. From Pueblo, head south on I-25 for 85 miles to Trinidad.

Baca House, Trinidad

History

Trinidad was an important stop along the Mountain Branch of the Santa Fe Trail in the 1800s. Here, by the banks of the Purgatoire River, wagon trains rested and resupplied before attempting Raton Pass. Settlers moved north from the New Mexico Territory to ranch sheep and cattle, bringing with them a rich Hispanic heritage. The Atchison, Topeka and Santa Fe Railroad came through in 1878, and soon fancy hotels and a Harvey House (see p. 443) were also here. It was an era of cattle barons and cowboys, entrepreneurs and immigrants. With the discovery of underground seams of coal in southern Colorado, Trinidad became a melting pot, with Slavs and Italians working the mines alongside Germans and Irishmen. Labor strife erupted in 1914 in a deadly episode known as the Ludlow Massacre. The coal mines closed in the 1980s; the Coal Miner's Memorial, dedicated in 1997, honors those who worked the area's mines. Today, Trinidad is home to a variety of industries including manufacturing, construction, and even filmmaking.

Coal Miner's Memorial, Trinidad

Main Attractions

CORAZÓN DE TRINIDAD NATIONAL HISTORIC DISTRICT

In the "heart of Trinidad," at the intersection of Main and Commercial, stand numerous late-18th- and early-19th-century buildings. You can stroll through the Corazón de Trinidad National Historic District, reading the interpretive markers, or pick up a walking-tour map at the Trinidad History Museum (this page). But your best bet is to hop on the Trinidad Trolley. This free, narrated tour takes about 45 minutes and runs daily in summer, leaving on the hour from the Colorado Visitor Center. *719-846-9512.*

TRINIDAD HISTORY MUSEUM

The town's main tourist attraction, Trinidad History Museum encompasses one square block in the downtown historic district, including two landmark residences, a converted adobe servants' quarters, and historic gardens. Built in the 1870s, **Baca House** is a two-story Territorial-style adobe, an unusual combination that melds East Coast architectural styles with Southwestern construction materials. See the period furnishings, Hispanic folk art, and some of the Baca family's personal items. Completed in 1882 during the heyday of Trinidad's growth, the restored **Bloom Mansion** has an opulent French style. The adobe **Santa Fe Trail Museum** exhibits photographs and artifacts (such as Kit Carson's buckskin coat) dating from the 1820s to the 1920s. Open May to September, the three buildings are linked by brick paths amid gardens of native plants and century-old trees. *300 E. Main St., 719-846-7217, www.coloradohistory.org.* The **Louden-Henritze Archaeology Museum**—located at the Trinidad State Junior College—offers free admission and a great place for families to learn more about Colorado's fascinating archaeological history. *Frudenthal Memorial Library, 719-846-5508.*

TRINIDAD LAKE STATE PARK

High mesas rise above the 800-acre reservoir in Trinidad Lake State Park, where miles of trails lace the piñon and juniper forests of the Purgatoire River Valley. This is an ideal place for fishing, boating, and waterskiing; swimming is prohibited. Camp at **Carpios Ridge,** with 62 sites situated above the lake. *Reservations: 303-470-1144.* You can cast for rainbow and brown trout, as well as largemouth and smallmouth bass, channel catfish, and walleye. Keep an eye open for water hazards during low-water periods.

Four of the park's six hiking trails are 1 mile or shorter. **Levsa Canyon Trail** EASY is a 1-mile loop through piñon and juniper with interpretive signs describing the plant and animal life. **Reilly Canyon Trail** MODERATE is a 4-mile (one way) path along the lake's northern shore. Connect to both trails from Carpios Ridge campground. **South Shore Trail** MODERATE tracks 2.5 miles (one way) and has views of the Culebra Range and Fisher's Peak. Access it from the South Shore picnic area. **Long's Canyon Watchable Wildlife Area** consists of a 0.75-mile (one way) nature trail to two observation blinds overlooking a wetland and pond. You'll likely see migratory birds and waterfowl, as well as mule deer, elk, and even an occasional black bear. The best viewing is at early morning and dusk.

Open year-round, the park is 3 miles west of Trinidad on CO 12. *719-846-6951, www.parks.state.co.us.*

Activities

CAMPING

Monument Lake, a popular recreation area with 100 campsites and many amenities, also has cabins and a restaurant. It's about 36 miles west of Trinidad on CO 12. Reservations are a good idea. *719-868-2226.* For camping at **Carpios Ridge,** see Trinidad Lake State Park, this page.

HISTORIC DISTRICTS

A stroll or a trolley ride through the **Corazón de Trinidad National Historic District** is a must (see Main Attractions, p. 439). **Cokedale** was established as a company town by the American Smelting and Refining Co. in 1906. It's now a National Historic District where you can see old coke ovens. Retired miners still live here, having purchased their homes from the coal company after it shut the mines down in the late 1940s. Cokedale is 7 miles west of Trinidad on CO 12.

MUSEUMS

Besides **Trinidad History Museum** (see Main Attractions, p. 439), visit the **A.R. Mitchell Museum of Western Art and Gallery** to see works by Arthur Roy Mitchell and other Western artists. Here you'll also find Hispanic folk art and

COLORADO CAMEO Felipe Baca

A well-known historic landmark in Trinidad, the two-story Baca House on Main Street was once the home of Felipe Baca—a poor Hispanic orphan who grew up to become a prominent citizen, a wealthy rancher, and a representative in the Colorado Territorial Legislature.

Born in Mexico in 1828, Felipe Baca was raised by an uncle. He started work at the age of six, herding goats for $1 a month, with sometimes only a daily bowl of mush to eat. At 21 he married Maria de los Dolores Gonzales, and they settled in Mora County, New Mexico Territory, to raise a family, along with crops and herds of sheep and cattle.

In his early 30s, Baca journeyed north to deliver four wagonloads of flour to the mining camps along Cherry Creek, near present-day Denver. On the way Baca was impressed by the rich bottomland he saw along the Purgatoire River. He returned the following year to stake a claim.

Baca cleared a portion of the land, planted crops, and dug a ditch to irrigate his fields. With a bumper harvest he took wagonloads of wheat and melons back to Mora County—incentive, he hoped, to convince other families to join him in settling in the Purgatoire Valley. In 1862, Felipe, Dolores, and their six children (three more would be born in Colorado) moved north with twelve other Mexican families.

Baca's 400 acres of land sat along the Mountain Branch of the Santa Fe Trail, at the heart of what would become the town of Trinidad. He farmed and ranched, raising large herds of sheep. As protection against Indian attacks, he befriended the Utes and the Arapahos, offering them flour and corn meal when they needed food. Baca built a sawmill and a granary and opened a grocery store with a business partner. He also donated land and money to build a Catholic church, a convent, and a school.

Chosen as a delegate to the Colorado constitutional convention, he lobbied against statehood, fearing that the southern, Hispanic part of the state would be ignored by Anglo-dominated Denver. In 1870 he was elected as a representative to the Colorado Territorial Legislature. It was during this time that Baca purchased the distinctive two-story house on Main Street for $7,500 worth of wool. When he died in 1874 at the age of 46, he was one of the wealthiest men in the valley.

Today the Baca House is part of Trinidad History Museum, the main tourist attraction in the town that Felipe Baca helped build. Baca County in southeastern Colorado was named in his honor, and he is included in the list of Colorado's 100 Top Citizens—lasting honors to a poor boy who saw the realm of possibilities and grew up to fulfill them.

a photographic survey of Trinidad from its early days to the present, including old-time cameras and studio props. *150 E. Main St., 719-846-4224.*

SCENIC DRIVES

The **Santa Fe Trail Scenic Byway** follows US 350 from La Junta to Trinidad, an 80-mile drive that traces the old wagon route (see Scenic Drives, La Junta, p. 445). The **Highway of Legends Scenic and Historic Byway** loops northwesterly from Trinidad, following CO 12 through the Cuchara Valley, then taking US 160 east to Walsenburg. This 82-mile route encompasses a variety of scenery and historic sites (see Main Attractions, Walsenburg, p. 302). *www.highwayoflegends.org.*

Restaurants

Black Jack's Saloon Steakhouse & Inn ($-$$) has a Western feel—you almost expect to see Bat Masterson, illustrious sheriff here in the 1880s, standing at the bar. You can also stay overnight at the inn (see Accommodations, below). *225 W. Main St., 719-846-9501.* **The Trinidad Brewing Company** ($-$$) has now opened a pizzeria in addition to its brewpub. Enjoy a selection of finely crafted brews and wood-fired pizza, paninis, and daily specials. There is also live music throughout the month. *516 Elm St., 719-846-7069.* **Mission at the Bell Restaurant** ($) is a cool retreat on a hot summer day, but beware, the *enchiladas rojas* at this Mexican eatery can heat things up. *134 W. Main St., 719-845-1513.*

Wonderful House ($) serves up large portions of Chinese food in a friendly atmosphere. *415 University, 719-845-1888.* **Nano & Nana Monteleone's Deli and Pasta House** ($) specializes in Italian food and deli items. Lunch is your best bet, as the hours are rather unusual (closing at 5:30 on weekdays and 7:30 on weekends). *418 E. Main St., 719-846-2696.* **Rino's Italian Restaurant & Steakhouse** ($$), is probably one of Trinidad's most original dining options. The restaurant serves up gourmet Italian fare Wednesday through Sunday evenings. You'll also enjoy the famous singing waiters! Reservations recommended. *400 E. Main St., 719-845-0949.* **Chef Liu's Chinese Restaurant & Lounge** ($-$$) features a menu of authentic Chinese dishes and is a great place for the whole family. Closed Mondays. *1423 Santa Fe Trail, 719-846-3333.*

Accommodations

For something different, stay at **Black Jack's Saloon Steakhouse & Inn** ($$). This B&B is actually a former brothel, with the five antique-decorated rooms named after ladies of the evening (Daisy, Lily, Brandy, Opal, and Rose). *225 W. Main St., 719-846-9501.* **Stone Mansion Bed and Breakfast** ($-$$) is a restored Victorian house just blocks from historic downtown. Visit with the resident cat and take afternoon tea on the front porch. *212 E. 2nd St., 877-264-4279, www.stonemansionbb.com.* **Tarabino Inn** ($$) is an historic bed and breakfast and a great alternative to a typical hotel. Children age 8 and older welcome. Call ahead for reservations. *310 E. 2nd St., 719-846-2115, www.tarabinoinn.com.* **Riverside Spa B&B** ($$) is perfect for couples, or singles, looking for a place to unwind and be pampered. *453 N. Commercial St., 719-846-1408, www.riversidespabandb.com.*

Special Events

Santa Fe Trail Days takes place on the second weekend in June, featuring music, dancing, craft booths, and food. *719-846-9285.* **Trinidaddio Blues Fest** is an annual, all-day Blues festival that includes live music, food, and craft vendors. Tickets can be bought in advance or at the gate. *719-859-8031*

For More Information

Colorado Welcome Center, off I-25 Exit 14A, *309 Nevada, Trinidad, 719-846-9512.* The Trinidad Chamber of Commerce is upstairs in the same building. *719-846-9285, www.trinidadco.com.*

Colorado Welcome Center, Trinidad

La Junta

Colorado Atlas & Gazetteer pp. 100–101

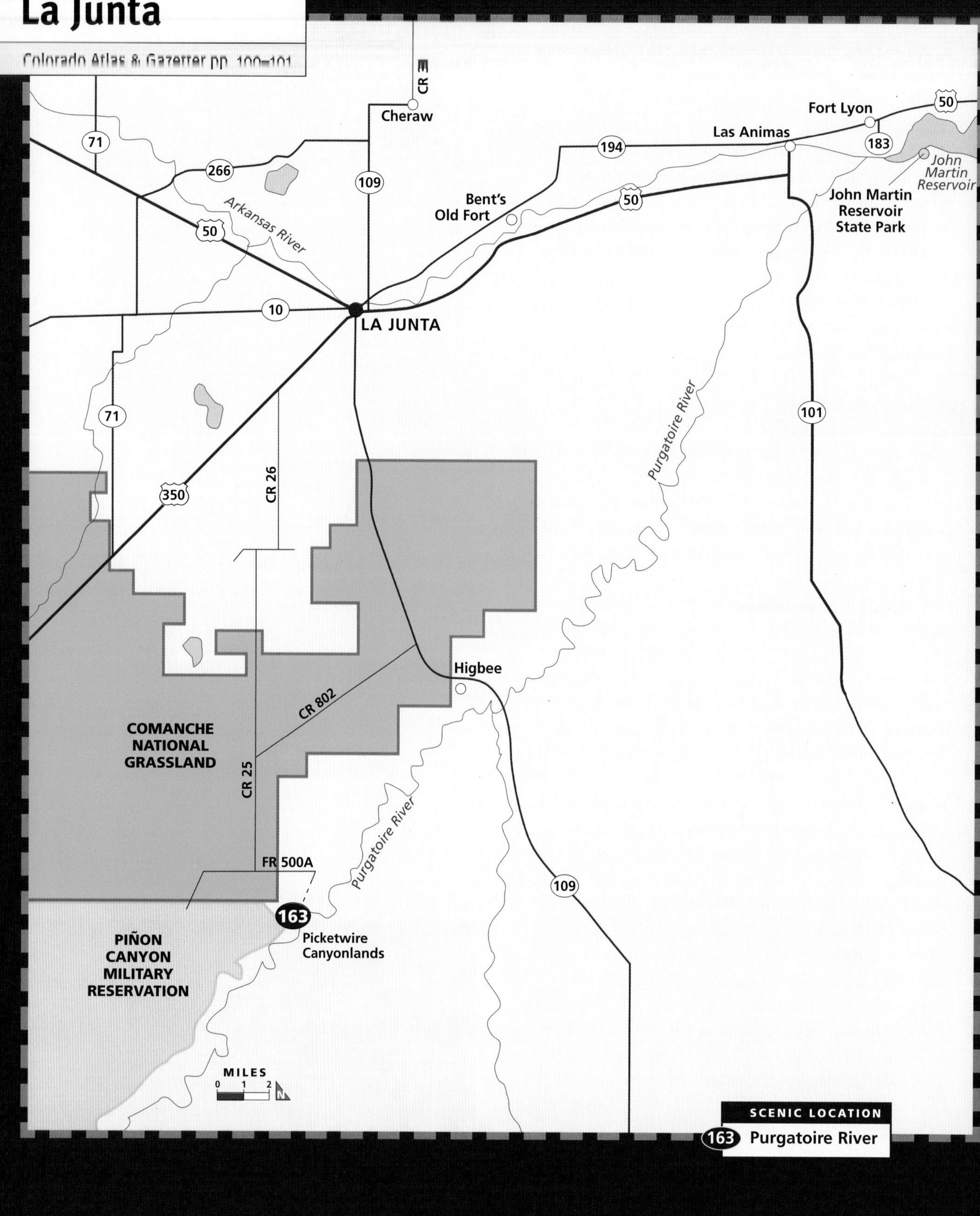

SCENIC LOCATION

163 Purgatoire River

La Junta

I like visiting La Junta in late summer, when the roadside stands are piled high with fresh fruits and vegetables. Rocky Ford cantaloupes, honeydews, and watermelons are some of the best you'll ever taste. But you can do more here than slice into a juicy melon. Delve into local history—lots of it—such as Indian rock art, Bent's Old Fort, the Santa Fe Trail, Comanche National Grassland, even 150-million-year-old dinosaur tracks. From Pueblo, take CO 50 east for about 65 miles.

History

In 1875 the Santa Fe Railroad selected this site along the Arkansas River as a stop on its line. The railroad built a depot and a roundhouse, and four years later La Junta became the railroad's Colorado headquarters. It was also the location of the state's first Harvey House, where "Harvey girls" in starched uniforms served meals to passengers passing through. La Junta remains an important regional transportation hub and agricultural center.

Main Attractions

BENT'S OLD FORT

During the 1830s and 1840s, Bent's Old Fort was a vital trading post along the Santa Fe Trail, where Native Americans, French trappers, Mexican frontiersmen, U.S. military, and early pioneers stopped for supplies, repairs, and respite. In 1975 the National Park Service rebuilt the adobe fort according to drawings of the original structure, and today it is a National Historic Site. Guides in period dress lead living-history tours daily, bartering in the trading room or fixing wagon wheels in the blacksmith shop. It's easy to imagine you have stepped back in time to the early settlement of the American West. From La Junta, drive northeast on CO 194 for 8 miles. *719-383-5010, www.nps.gov/beol.*

COMANCHE NATIONAL GRASSLAND

Comanche National Grassland covers nearly 440,000 acres in two separate parcels, with one unit south of La Junta and the other south of Springfield. Like Pawnee National Grassland in northeastern Colorado (see Main Attractions, Fort Morgan, p. 423), Comanche comprises federal land interspersed with private property. Amid the rolling plains and sandstone canyons lie dinosaur tracks, Indian rock art, and the Santa Fe Trail, plus prime birding and wildlife watching. Stop at the four major sites to see rock art in the grassland: Picketwire Canyonlands and Vogel Canyon near La Junta, and Picture Canyon and Carrizo Creek near Springfield. *1420 E. 3rd St., La Junta, 719-384-2181.*

Bent's Old Fort, La Junta

During the Jurassic period 150 million years ago, dinosaurs left tracks in the mud on the shore of an ancient lake. See some 1,300 dinosaur tracks at **Picketwire Canyonlands Dinosaur Tracksite** (see Scenic Location No. 163, p. 444), a Forest Service–administered site on the Purgatoire River and below the southeastern corner of the La Junta–area grassland. A quarter mile in length, it is one of the longest dinosaur trackways in the world. Guided four-wheel-drive tours take place each spring and fall.

Hiking: The images pecked and painted onto the walls of **Picketwire Canyonlands** were created anywhere from 375 to 4,500 years ago. Hikers, mountain bikers, and horseback riders can view the art and access the Dinosaur Tracksite on a 5-mile (one way) trail; the trailhead is about an hour from La Junta. See Scenic Location No. 163, p. 444, for directions.

Indian drawings in **Vogel Canyon** are estimated to be about 1,000 years old. The four trails here, 1–3 miles in length (round-trip), can be combined as you go from mesa top to canyon floor. **Canyon Trail** EASY passes old homestead ruins and Indian rock art. **Prairie Trail** MODERATE leads to old stagecoach tracks. From La Junta, drive south on CO 109 for 13 miles, turn right (west) onto CR 802, go 1.5 miles, then turn left onto FR 505A and proceed for 1.5 miles.

Mountain Biking: An 18-mile, out-and-back mountain-bike ride, **Picketwire Canyonlands** MODERATE traverses desert and canyon country to the old Rourke Ranch, 4 miles past the Dinosaur Tracksite. The 250-foot-drop into the canyon is steep, but then the ride levels out on an old jeep road. The best riding is in spring and fall.

Activities

BIRDING AND WILDLIFE WATCHING

The grassy plains and juniper canyonlands of the **Comanche National Grassland** are prime birding habitats, where you might see golden eagles perched in the treetops, hawks riding the air thermals, or burrowing owls poking their heads out of prairie dog burrows. More than 275 bird species have been spotted here; get a checklist at grassland headquarters. Also, bring the binoculars to see pronghorn antelope, foxes, badgers, and even the elusive roadrunner. Wile E. Coyote lives here, too. *1420 E. 3rd St., 719-384-2181, www.fs.fed.us/grasslands.*

John Martin Reservoir State Park is also good for birding, with a permanent blind at the Santa Fe Slough. *719-829-1801.*

163 SCENIC LOCATION

PURGATOIRE RIVER

Also called the Purgatory or "Picketwire," this is the last of my really big secrets that I feel obliged to reveal in this book! I mentioned the upper Purgatoire in my discussion of Cucharas Pass (see Scenic Location No. 107, p. 306). It originates high in the Sangre de Cristo Mountains, passes through the town of Trinidad, then carves its way through the southeastern Colorado plains to rendezvous with the Arkansas River near the town of Las Animas. "Carve" is the appropriate word, because over time it has made a spectacular sandstone canyon 75 miles long and at one point more than 1,000 feet deep. So, I hope by now you see my point that eastern Colorado is not *all* flat.

Most of the Purgatoire is inaccessible—the restricted Piñon Canyon Military Reservation sits to its north, and the south side is lined with several large, private ranches. However, the U.S. Forest Service manages a portion of the land on the north side of the river that contains the largest documented dinosaur tracksite in North America. It extends more than 0.25 mile and contains more than 1,300 visible tracks on 100 different trackways. From La Junta, drive south on CO 109 for 13 miles to County Road 802. Turn right and drive 8 miles to Road 25. Turn left and drive 6 miles, then turn left on Forest Road 500A. Look for the interpretive sign here. Up to this point, a car works fine. It's another 3 miles to the trailhead, but the road is rough and you'll need a four-wheel drive to get there. From here you are on foot. It's 1 mile to the river and 5 miles to the dinosaur tracks from the trailhead, each way. Or you can park the car at the start of FR 500A and walk the extra 3 miles each way.

If you are in reasonably good physical condition, you can make this hike to the dinosaur tracks at a rate of at least 2 miles per hour. A 10-mile round-trip, therefore, would take you 5 hours plus an hour for lunch and exploring the site. It's well worth the time and effort. Along the way you can photograph the beautiful Purgatoire. At one point the river departs the trail to the south: Point your camera upriver to make a wonderful composition of it disappearing into the valley with lovely trees and shrubs on its banks. In mid-May colors are light green, and in late October they glow bright yellow.

Look for the ancient rock art on large boulders right next to the trail. Photograph them in cloudy light or when the sun does not create both shadow and highlight in the same scene. The Dolores Mission and Cemetery was built sometime between 1871 and 1889. Its old gravestones make a remarkable photograph, especially when you compose the old building in the background. And, of course, the dinosaur tracks make an outrageous photograph. Carry an empty container with you so that you can fill the tracks with water from the adjacent river. That will make them more conspicuous on film.

CAMPING

Take your pick from 100 campsites each at **Lake Hasty** and **The Point** in John Martin Reservoir State Park. Take an awning for shade. From La Junta, drive east on US 50 for 37 miles to the town of Hasty, turn right onto County Road 24, and go 2 miles. *Reservations: 800-678-2267, 303-470-1144; park information: 719-829-1801, www.parks.state.co.us.*

HIKING

Be prepared for desert hiking in this region: Bring a good hat, sunscreen, and plenty of water. Don't miss the hikes into **Picketwire Canyonlands** and **Vogel Canyon** in Comanche National Grassland (see Main Attractions, p. 443).

Strike out along the **Santa Fe National Historic Trail** EASY following old wagon ruts. From the Timpas picnic area it's 3 miles (one way) to Sierra Vista Overlook. A 0.5-mile nature trail at the picnic area loops to Timpas Creek. From La Junta, drive southwest on US 350 for 13 miles, turn right (north) onto County Road 71, continue 0.5 mile, then turn left (west) into the parking lot. **Red Shin Hiking Trail** MODERATE at John Martin Reservoir State Park tracks 4.5 miles (one way) along the Arkansas River, through wetlands and grasslands (see Parks, below).

MUSEUMS

Koshare Indian Museum has an impressive collection of Native American art and artifacts, especially early-20th-century beaded clothing. The museum also houses a kiva-shaped stage where the local Boy Scout troop performs authentic Native American dances, a program started in 1933 as a way to learn about the traditional dances, songs, and crafts of the Plains and Pueblo Indians. Known as the Koshare Indian Dancers, they perform on weekend nights during June and July, and a winter show in December. *115 W. 18th St., 719-384-4411, www.koshare.org.*

Otero Museum reflects La Junta's growth from the 1870s to the 1940s with a little bit of everything, all of it interesting. It's open in summer and is free. *218 Anderson Ave., 719-384-7500.*

PARKS

John Martin Reservoir State Park became one of Colorado's newest state parks in October 2001. The 2.6-mile-long dam on the Arkansas River was completed in 1948, and since then the reservoir and shoreline have been popular spots for fishing, water sports, camping, hiking, and birding. Anglers cast for walleye, saugeye, wiper, bream, channel catfish, and largemouth and smallmouth bass here and at nearby **Lake Hasty,** which is also stocked with rainbow and cutthroat trout (but where gas-powered boats are prohibited). From La Junta, drive east on US 50 for 37 miles to the town of Hasty, turn right onto County Road 24, and go 2 miles. *719-829-1801, www.parks.state.co.us.*

Sand Creek National Park, in Eads, is a new attraction open to the public in the area. This historic site was once privately owned but is now open seasonally. The park entrance is located along CR W, a mile east of CR 54. *For more information: 719-729-3003, www.nps.gov/sand/.* **La Junta City Park,** at Colorado Avenue and 10th Street, is a pleasant place for a picnic lunch.

SCENIC DRIVES

Across 80 miles of US 350 from La Junta to Trinidad, the **Santa Fe Trail Scenic Byway** reveals a portion of the old trade route, which originally spanned 900 miles between Missouri and Mexico. After stopping at Bent's Fort northeast of present-day La Junta, wagon trains angled along the Mountain Branch of the Santa Fe Trail. Today you can still see old wagon ruts and the ruins of stage stops. At Sierra Vista Overlook you can view the distant Spanish Peaks. Spring and fall are the best travel times. For a brochure, contact Comanche National Grassland. *1420 E. 3rd St., 719-384-2181, www.fs.fed.us/grasslands.*

Restaurants

If it's caffeine time, drop by **The Barista** ($), a pleasant storefront cyber-cafe where you can grab a bagel and check your e-mail. They also cater. *204 Santa Fe Ave., 719-384-2133.* **Thyme Square** ($) features an all-you-can-eat soup and salad buffet and fast, diner-style food. They're open from 11–2 p.m. Closed on Sundays. *302 Colorado Ave., 719-383-0808.*

A La Junta mainstay, the **Copper Kitchen** ($) is a great greasy spoon with a tradition of hospitality. Give it a try instead of the typical roadside chain restaurants; you won't be disappointed. Serves breakfast and lunch only. *116 Colorado Ave., 719-384-7216.* When it comes to Mexican food, I'm partial to **Felisa's Mexico Food & Lounge** ($-$$), which has authentic south-of-the-border food and atmosphere. *27948 Frontage Rd., 719-384-4806.* **Mexico City Café** ($) is a great place to take the whole family. Enjoy fresh, homemade salsa while you peruse a menu of traditional favorites. *1617 Raton Ave., 719-384-9818.*

Accommodations

The **Stagecoach Motel** ($) is a mom-and-pop place, clean and conveniently located. *905 W. 3rd St., 719-384-5476.* **Midtown Motel** ($), winner of La Junta's Best of the Best Hotel/Motel in 2008, is conveniently located right on the Historic Santa Fe Trail. *215 E. 3rd St., 719-384-7741.* For those in campers and RVs, the **La Junta KOA** ($) provides a convenient location, swimming pool, and a rec room. *26680 W. US 50, 719-384-9580.*

Special Events

Each August, the **Arkansas Valley Fair,** held since 1878, fills Rocky Ford Fairgrounds with fun for all—and free watermelon! *719-254-7483.* In September, **Early Settlers' Day** celebrates frontier life in La Junta and draws thousands. *719-384-7411.*

For More Information

La Junta Chamber of Commerce, *110 Santa Fe Ave., 719-384-7411, www.lajuntachamber.com.*

Springfield

In the southeastern corner of Colorado, Springfield is the base for venturing out onto the southern unit of Comanche National Grassland. Here you'll find a number of intriguing sites: Indian rock art at Carrizo Creek and Picture Canyon; Crack Cave, also in Picture Canyon; and the mating grounds of the lesser prairie chicken.

History

The town of Springfield was incorporated in 1887, founded by settlers from Springfield, Missouri, who came to ranch and farm. The few stores that set up shop in the early years often went a week or more without serving any customers. Today, about a hundred businesses operate here, a rural community in the heart of cattle and wheat country.

Main Attractions

BIRDING

Each spring birders from around the world come to watch the mating dance of the lesser prairie chicken. Males establish their territories on leks, or mating grounds, stomping and bowing to attract a mate. Their "booming" can be heard up to a mile away. A special viewing area near the town of Campo allows you to watch from your car or from a photo blind. Both require advance reservations through Comanche National Grassland. *719-523-6591.*

COMANCHE NATIONAL GRASSLAND

South of Springfield lies the larger of the two units of Comanche National Grassland, a remote quarter of Colorado characterized by undulating plains dotted with farms, ranches, and abandoned homesteads. Juniper- and cottonwood-fringed creeks accent the plains at places like Picture Canyon (see below) and Carrizo Creek, where Native Americans etched pictures of elk, deer, and sheep onto the canyon walls. Lunch at the Carrizo Creek picnic area (where primitive camping is allowed) and take the short loop trail. From Springfield, drive south on US 287 for 17 miles, turn right onto County Road M, and continue for 22 miles. Turn left onto Forest Road 539 and drive 2 miles to the parking area. *719-523-6591.*

PICTURE CANYON

Picture Canyon (see Scenic Location No. 165, p. 449) is the site of prehistoric petroglyphs, unusual rock formations, and Crack Cave, where during each vernal and autumnal equinox the rising sun illuminates ancient writing on the cave wall. Comanche National Grassland allows people to observe this phenomenon

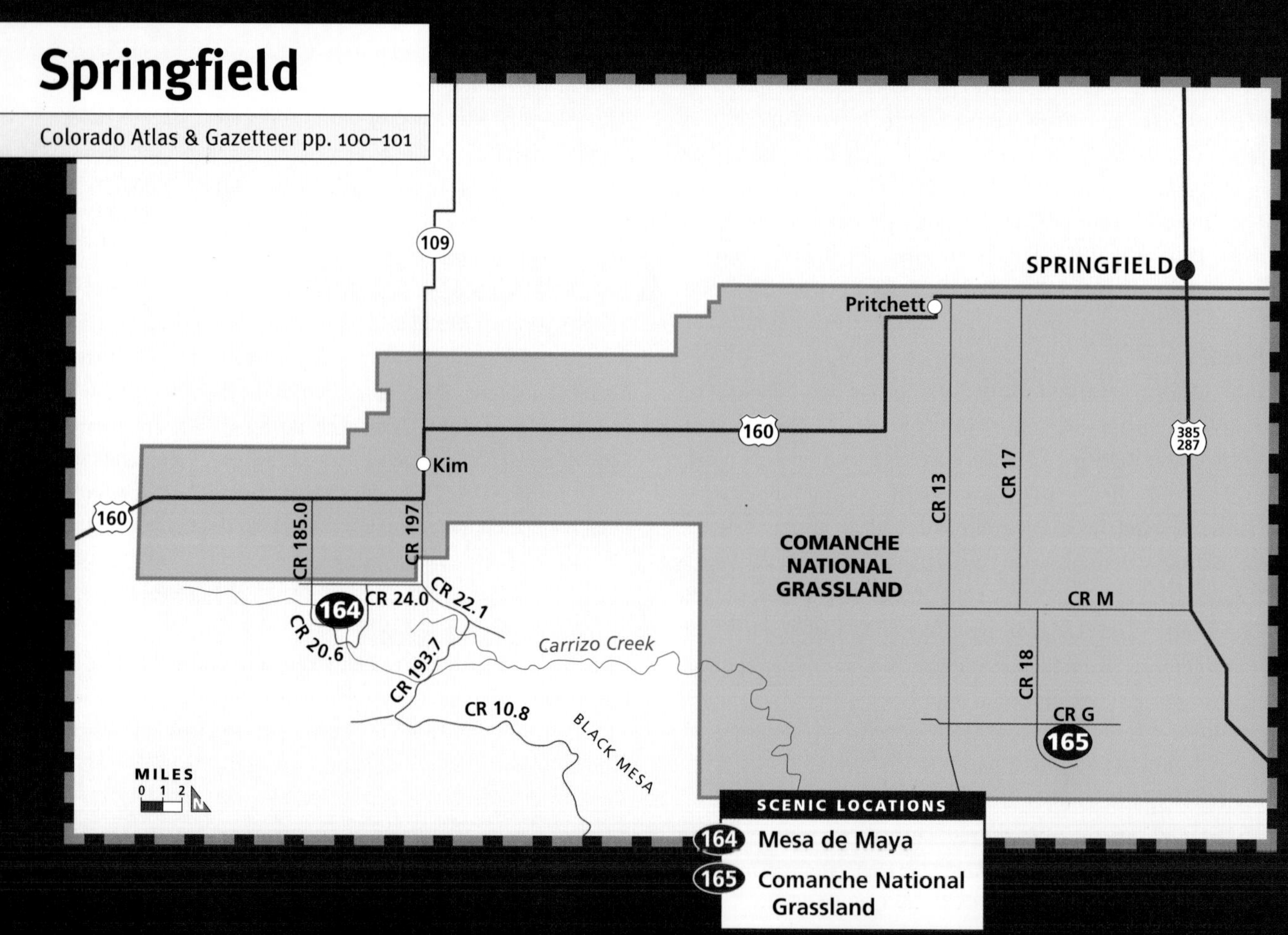

164 SCENIC LOCATION — MESA DE MAYA

On the Colorado–New Mexico border lies a large plateau called Mesa de Maya. The mesa is on private property, but you can drive around it through beautiful ranches, where meadows back up to rolling hills and bluffs, and cottonwood trees dot the broad landscape. There is no other topography quite like this in Colorado. The closest thing to it might be Greenland Ranch near Castle Rock (see Scenic Location No. 15, p. 71). From the intersection of CO 109 and US 160 near the town of Kim, drive south on County Road 197 for 3.5 miles. From here you can either continue south on CR 22.1 and explore Middle and Black Mesas, or turn west on CR 24. If you do the latter, after 3 miles, turn south on CR 189. This road winds around to the west and connects with CR 20.6, which turns into CR 185 and heads north to meet with US 160. If you don't want to follow my route, consult pages 100–101 of your *Colorado Atlas and Gazetteer* and just explore any road you wish north of Mesa de Maya. Exploring is how I discover new places! Your passenger vehicle is suitable on most of these roads.

In May this place is extremely green: Grasses grow in the meadows, and cottonwoods are beginning to leaf. Where cattle don't graze, wildflowers abound. The intriguing old ranch buildings that stand all over this area—including a few built with native sandstone—make for wonderful images. This is a place to compose classic scenics of two-thirds landscape and one-third sky. Place buildings, meadows, or juniper bushes in the foreground, hills and mesas in the midground, and blue sky behind. At sunset and sunrise, long shadows add depth to the scene. Experiment with your polarizing filter on a clear day, which will work best when the sun is low in the sky and to your left or right. Rotate the filter to eliminate glare on the landscape and enhance the brilliant greens. But beware, polarizing filters will make an already deep blue Colorado sky unnaturally blue, so use them judiciously (see p. 145, *Photographing the Landscape*).

COMANCHE NATIONAL GRASSLAND

Both managed by the U.S. Forest Service, Colorado's two grasslands—Pawnee National Grassland in northeastern Colorado (see Scenic Location No. 158, p. 425) and Comanche National Grassland in southeastern Colorado—are actually easy to distinguish. The Pawnee is flat with buttes and bluffs rising up from the plains, whereas the Comanche is flat with canyons descending below the plains. Two sites in the southernmost unit of the Comanche grassland have particular compositional interest; the first is the more obscure.

From the town of Pritchett 13 miles west of Springfield on US 160, turn south onto County Road 13. Drive 22 miles to Road G and continue south through Gallinas Canyon. Keep your eyes peeled for the sandstone hoodoos—tall, eroded formations—to the west. It's only a short hike to them from the road. Compose a photograph from far enough away to include them all, or closer in to include just a few. Create an asymmetrical balance by composing one hoodoo large and to the left or right, and the rest smaller, in the distance, and on the other side of the scene (see pp. 64–65, *Photographing the Landscape*). Continue south on Road 13 all the way to Oklahoma. That's right, Oklahoma borders Colorado for a short distance.

Return to Road G and turn east. Go 5 miles, turn south on Road 18, and follow the signs to Picture Canyon. Leave your car in the parking lot at the mouth of the sandstone canyon and hike less than a mile south to the wetland and the extensive rock wall on the east side of the canyon. Before approaching the wall, study the composition that includes wall on the left, cottonwood trees in the middle, and the canyon on the right. The wall makes a great lead-in line from the bottom left corner of the frame. Now approach the wall and discover the ancient rock art. Unfortunately, it is mixed with contemporary graffiti. Photograph the art in the shade, as direct light on the lightly colored walls is too intense for your film. Take the time to explore other trails in the area. With rock art everywhere, the scenic possibilities are endless.

Prairie wildflowers abound in May, when three-day-long intervals of rain drench the otherwise arid landscape. Get there a few days later and you won't believe the colors!

(the cave is usually locked to keep vandals out), and in the fall offers a bus tour. A hiking trail loops through the canyon (for directions see Hiking, below). *For information: 719-523-6591.*

Activities

HIKING

The 4-mile loop trail in **Picture Canyon** EASY takes you to Balanced Rock, Natural Arch, and Indian rock art. These relatively level trails are also open to mountain bikers. From Springfield, drive south on US 287 for 17 miles, turn right onto County Road M, and go 8 miles. Turn left onto CR 18, continue 8 miles, turn right onto Forest Road 533, and drive 1 mile to the parking and picnic area.

HUNTING

Springfield calls itself the Goose Hunting Capital of the U.S.A. In winter it is home to 50,000 ducks and 30,000 Canada geese. **Two Buttes Reservoir** is a prime location. Ask at the chamber of commerce for information and directions. *719-523-4062.*

Restaurants

Trails End ($-$$) satisfies downtown diners with a wide array of dishes from steaks to sandwiches, and is closed Sundays and Mondays. *964 Main St., 719-523-4460.* **Beep's Burgers** is a great place to grab a quick burger before heading out to Picture Canyon. *381 Main St., 719-523-6788.* The **Bar 4 Corral** ($-$$) restaurant opens early and features daily specials, burgers, and sandwiches. *27080 US 287, 719-523-4065.*

Accommodations

Lodging options are limited in Springfield. The **Starlite Motel** ($) is a good choice. *681 Main St., 719-523-6236.* Another is the **Crawford Motel.** *288 Colorado St., 719-523-6276.*

Special Events

The annual **Baca County Fair & Rodeo** takes place each summer in Springfield and features junior competitions, a parade, and booths and exhibits, including 4-H projects and events, food, and crafts. Each October, Springfield also holds its **Pumpkin Shine,** an evening of pumpkin carving and scarecrow stuffing with awards for originality and creativity. For more information: *www.springfieldcolorado.com/events.html.*

For More Information

Springfield Chamber of Commerce, *948 Main St. in the Treasure Chest Mall, 719-523-4061.*

Index of Scenic Locations

NOTE: Citations followed by the letter "p" denote photos and citations followed by the letter "m" denote maps.

General Index

NOTE: Citations followed by the letter "p" denote photos, citations followed by the letter "m" denote maps, and bold citations denote Scenic Locations entries.

A

B

D

M

Q

R

T

U

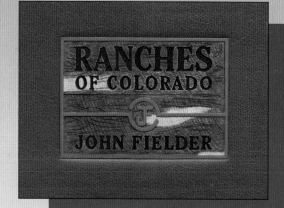

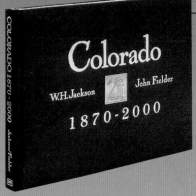